THE TIMES

COMPLETE HISTORY OF THE WORLD

Ninth Edition

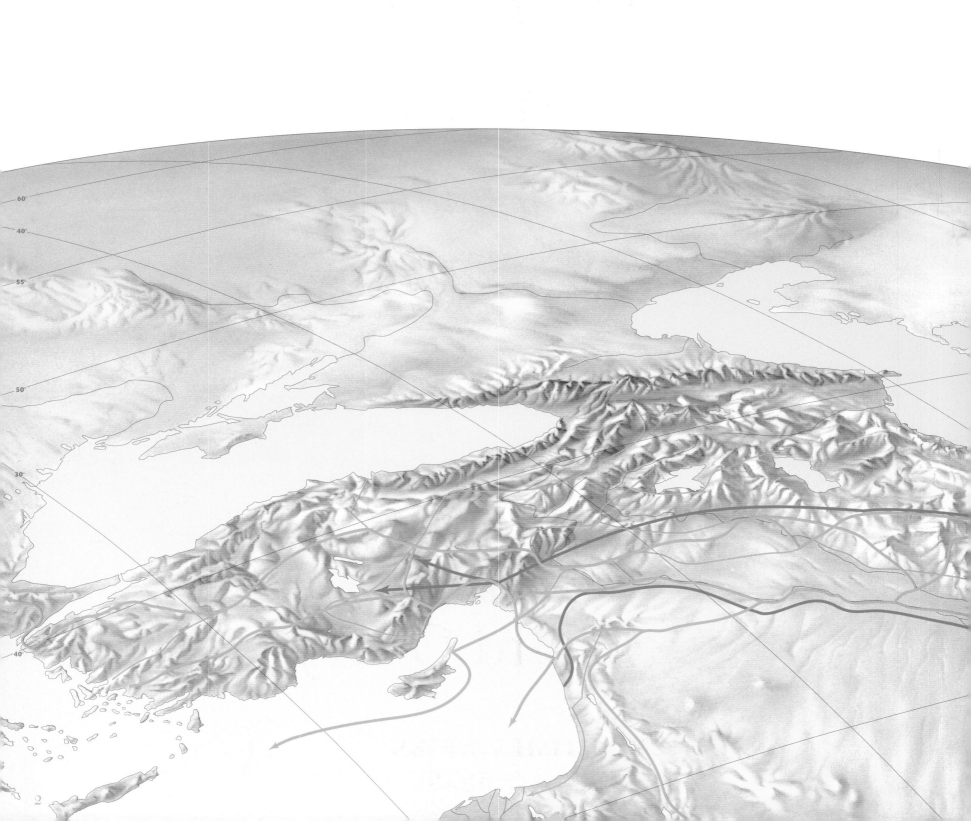

THE TIMES

COMPLETE HISTORY OF THE WORLD

Ninth Edition

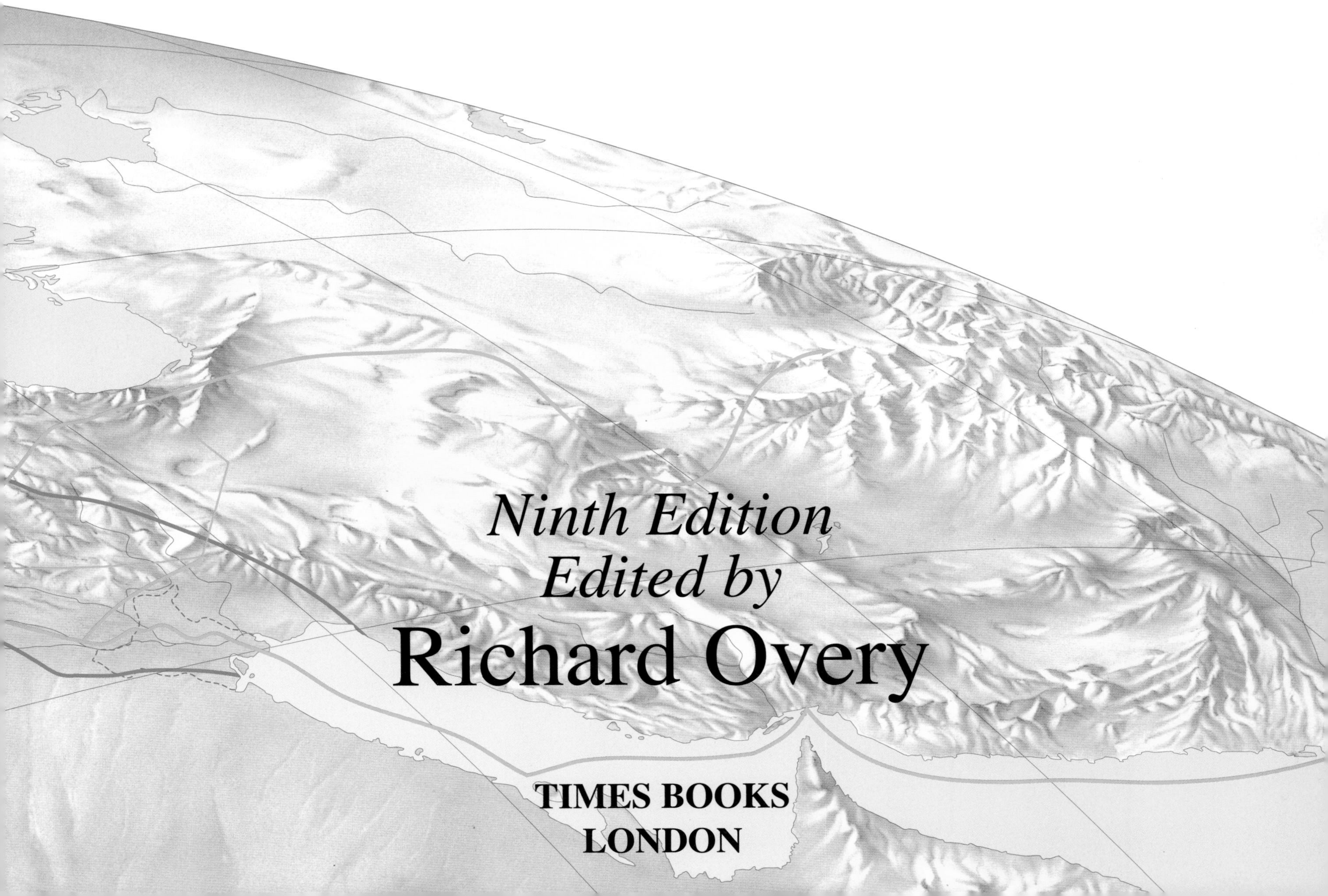

Ninth Edition
Edited by

Richard Overy

TIMES BOOKS
LONDON

Ninth Edition
First published in 2015 by
TIMES BOOKS

An imprint of
HarperCollins*Publishers*
1 London Bridge Street
London SE1 9GF

www.harpercollins.co.uk

First edition published 1978
Reprinted with revisions 1979
Reprinted 1979, 1980, 1981, 1983
Second edition published 1984
Reprinted 1985
Reprinted with revisions 1986
Reprinted 1988
Third edition published 1989
Reprinted 1992
Fourth edition published 1993
Reprinted 1994, 1996, 1997
Fifth edition published 1999
Reprinted 1999, 2000, 2001, 2002, 2003
Sixth edition published 2004
Reprinted 2005, 2006
Seventh edition published 2007
Reprinted 2007, 2008
Eighth edition published 2010

**British library Cataloguing in
Publication Data**
A catalogue record for this book is available
from the British Library

ISBN 978-0-00-795956-3

HARPERCOLLINS*PUBLISHERS*

FOR NINTH EDITION
EDITORIAL DIRECTION
Martin Redfern

Essie Cousins

Kate Tolley

Philip Parker

Kathy Dyke

PRODUCTION
Paul Harding

Chris Wright

DESIGN/CARTOGRAPHIC REVISIONS
Martin Brown

INDEX
Mark Bolland

ORIGINAL CONCEPTION
Barry Winkleman

Malcolm Swanston

**ORIGINAL INDEX, INDEX CONCEPTION
AND PLACE-NAME CONSULTANT**
P. J. M. Geelan

COLOR ORIGINATION
BORN Group

Printed and Bound by
Graficas Estella, Spain

CONTRIBUTORS

EDITOR:

Richard Overy
Professor of History
University of Exeter

CONSULTANTS:

Stacey Hynd
Senior Lecturer in African History
University of Exeter

Tehyun Ma
Lecturer in Chinese History
University of Exeter

Claire McCallum
Lecturer in Modern
European History
University of Exeter

Philip Nigst
Lecturer in Palaeolithic
Archaeology
University of Cambridge
Max-Planck-Institute for Evolutionary
Anthropology, Leipzig, Germany

Catriona Pennell
Senior Lecturer in History
University of Exeter

Matthias Reiss
Senior Lecturer in Modern History
University of Exeter

CONTRIBUTORS TO PREVIOUS EDITIONS

David Abulafia
Daud Ali
F R Allchin
R W Van Alstyne
David Arnold
John Barber
Geoffrey Barraclough
James R Barrett
Iris Barry
Peter Bauer
Christopher Bayly
W G Beasley
Ralph Bennett
Amira K Bennison
A D H Bivar
Brian Bond
Hugh Borton
Hugh Bowden
David Brading
Warwick Bray
John Breen
Carl Bridge
F R Bridge
Michael G Broers
Hugh Brogan
Tom Brooking
Ian Brown
Anthony Bryer
Muriel E Chamberlain
David G Chandler
John Cannon
Eric Christiansen
Colin Coates
Peter Coates
Frank Cogliano
Irene Collins
Michael Crawford
James Cronin
Douglas Dakin
John Darwin
Ralph Davis
Kent Deng

Robin Dunbar
I E S Edwards
Robert Evans
John Ferguson
Felipe Fernándo-Armesto
Stefan Fisch
David H Fischer
John R Fisher
Kate Fleet
Michael Flinn
Timothy Fox
Alan Frost
Robert I Frost
Clive Gamble
W J Gardner
Carol Geldart
John Gillingham
Ian Glover
Martin Goodman
Graham Gould
D G E Hall
Norman Hammond
John D Hargreaves
Tim Harper
David R Harris
Jonathan Haslam
Ragnhild Hatton
M Havinden
Harry Hearder
W O Henderson
Colin J Heywood
Sinclair Hood
Albert Hourani
Henry Hurst
Jonathan Israel
Edward James
Nicholas James
Richard H Jones
Ulrich Kemper
Hugh Kennedy
David Killingray
George Lane

Mark H Leff
Colin Lewis
James B Lewis
Karl Leyser
Wolfgang Liebeschuetz
D Anthony Low
David Luscombe
John Lynch
Rosamond McKitterick
James M McPherson
Isabel de Madriaga
J P Mallory
P J Marshall
A R Michell
Christopher D Morris
A E Musson
Thomas Nelson
Linda A Newson
F S Northedge
Joan Oates
David Ormrod
Caroline Orwin
Geoffrey Parker
J H Parry
Thomas M Perry
David Phillipson
Sidney Pollard
Andrew Porter
Avril Powell
T G E Powell
John Poynter
Benjamin Ravid
Tapan Raychaudhuri
B H Reid
Michael Roaf
Francis Robinson
A N Ryan
Gören Rystad
H W F Saggs
S B Saul
Peter Sawyer
Chris Scarre

Roger Schofield
D J Schove
H M Scott
H H Scullard
Andrew Sharf
Stephen Shennan
Andrew Sherratt
Peter Sluglett
R B Smith
Frank C Spooner
Jocelyn Statler
L S Stavrianos
Zara Steiner
Sarah Stockwell
Melvyn Stokes
Norman Stone
W C Sturtevant
Julian Swann
Alan Sykes
Martin Thomas
E A Thompson
Hugh Tinker
Malcolm Todd
R C Trebilcock
Hugh R Trevor-Roper
Denis C Twitchett
Frans von der Dunk
F R von der Mehden
Ernst Wangermann
Geoffrey Warner
Anne Waswo
D Cameron Watt
Bodo Wiethoff
D S M Williams
Glyn Williams
H P Willmott
David M Wilson
Jon E Wilson
Peter Wilson
George D Winius

CONTENTS

1

HUMAN ORIGINS AND EARLY CULTURES   28

2

THE FIRST CIVILIZATIONS   52

Contents

Contents

7

THE AGE OF GLOBAL CIVILIZATION 280

Contents

INTRODUCTION

FOR THE PAST 35 years, *The Times Atlas of World History*, now in its new form as *The Times Complete History of the World*, has established itself as the undisputed leader in its field. Its reputation owes a great deal to the conception of its founding editor, Geoffrey Barraclough, who set out in the early 1970s to create a work that would provide an authoritative history of the world in maps, pictures and text. His priorities were to avoid too Eurocentric a treatment and too great an emphasis on the modern age. The result was a history that did indeed cover the whole globe, and which devoted more space to the pre-modern age than was usual in world histories. Barraclough was also determined that the atlas should reflect history as a process, not simply as a series of unconnected stories. Many of the maps from the original edition show change through time, often a long period of time, and try to demonstrate the forces that shaped such changes. These traditions have been maintained in subsequent editions, and feature extensively in this ninth edition.

One significant innovation has been introduced since the fourth edition. The original maps were hand-drawn. This process was repeated for the second edition, edited again by Barraclough, and in the third and fourth editions, edited respectively by Norman Stone and Geoffrey Parker following Barraclough's death in 1984. For subsequent editions the old method was discarded in favour of digitized map-making. For the first time, all the maps in these editions have been generated by computer. The technical change allowed a comprehensive overhaul and revision of the entire atlas in 1998, and has been applied generally to the changes in all subsequent editions. The traditional format of the atlas has been replaced with a new design, incorporating a chronology, a quotation significant to the text, more pictures and the redrawing and recolouring of the maps. The texts have also been revised and in many cases rewritten entirely to take into account the vast amount of new historical and archaeological research from the last decade and a half.

The sixth edition was expanded beyond the four additional spreads introduced into the fifth. The geographical range was extended yet again with new spreads on New Zealand and Polynesia, Korea, Canada and Mexico. In addition thematic spreads were added to the modern section of the atlas on warfare since 1945, terrorism, racism and deportation, and the violent crisis of the last 15 years in the Balkans, the Caucasus and the Middle East. In the eighth edition the atlas built on these developments by adding more spreads on conflicts in the Middle East and Africa, which have dominated the past 20 years, and on the modern United States. The major events of the past five years have now made it necessary to add spreads on contemporary China, Russia and the Arab world. The new spreads on the modern age are intended to reflect the lengthening period since the end of the Second World War, which for much of the last century, and for those who edited the first editions, was the dominant event of the last hundred years. Though its shadow still lingers, the nature of the world system and the issues that confront the world have changed very substantially since 1945. It is to take account of these dynamic changes that the ninth edition has been produced. The latest spreads in the history have been thoroughly revised and brought up-to-date.

The fifth edition coincided with the end of the millennium and a sense of summing up or ending was perhaps unavoidable at the time. In the 15 years since the fifth edition was published an extraordinary amount has happened, not all of it predictable. The twenty-first century has already shown that any optimistic expectations of a new age of peace and stability after the end of the Cold War and the spread of "globalization" have been misplaced. The big issues that shape the development of modern history – population growth, food supply and the condition of the environment – though they have been the object of intense debate and action over the past 40 years are still major concerns. The effect of environmental damage has been reversed in some areas, but greatly enlarged in others. Concern for ecological development has become a major aspect of policy and a growing source of political argument. The materialism of Cold War Marxism has given way to new movements against global capitalism and the damage that unrestricted economic development can inflict on the physical environment and the human populations which are often its victims.

Over the past ten years the shape of world politics has changed a great deal. This is in large part a result of the revival of popular religion worldwide, an outcome that seemed unlikely when the first edition of the atlas was put together in the 1970s. Then, religion was widely regarded in the liberal West as a force that was waning in world history. A glance at the atlas might have suggested that this belief was misplaced, for conflicts between and within the different religious faiths play a large part throughout its pages. Since the late 1970s religion has revived and in many cases helped to generate a more radical, religiously-based politics. The signal was given by the Islamic revolution in Iran in 1979 which overthrew the secularist monarchy, and radical Islam has continued to play an important part in shaping modern politics from Morocco to Indonesia. In the former communist bloc, religious faiths have returned and play an important part in people's lives. In the West fundamentalist Christianity has revived. It is a central question in the insurgent struggles and civil wars going on still in Afghanistan, Iraq, Syria and Pakistan, symbolized by the rise of the "Islamic State" movement. In the end, neither communism nor fascism, for all their extraordinary impact on the last century, has survived, but religious faith and religious ideologies have demonstrated a remarkable resilience.

All of these new perspectives on current world history are explored in the later spreads of the book, but it is important to remember that the headline events are not all the history of the recent age. Over the past 40 years the spread of political emancipation has been continuous, though uneven. South Africa, Eastern Europe, the Soviet Union, Spain, Greece, Portugal and the Philippines have all developed into parliamentary democracies. The costs of economic globalization have often been adverse (no more so than during the recent world financial crisis) but growth will continue and its fruits, if unevenly distributed, are more broadly available than they were 50 years ago. More people are able to influence the course of their own lives through the ballot-box or in the marketplace than would have been thinkable a century ago, and impossible for much of recorded history. That process of emancipation, so often distorted, interrupted, paradoxical or unjust, has not ended. Its development, and survival, remains the chief challenge for the new century.

The new edition has been made possible with the help of the team at HarperCollins – and through the work of the many contributors and consultants who have supplied the core material for past editions and for the changes incorporated into this one. This new edition celebrates more than 35 years in the life of an indispensable work of reference, which continues to build on the inherited strengths first established by the atlas in the 1970s. It is a work designed for a global audience, which captures global history in ways that we hope continue to be visually arresting and intellectually stimulating.

RICHARD OVERY
JULY 2015

ASIA EXCLUDING THE NEAR EAST	EUROPE	NEAR EAST AND NORTH AFRICA	OTHER REGIONS	CULTURE AND TECHNOLOGY
		9000–8000 Evidence of domesticated cereals and pulses in the Levant – the "Neolithic revolution" in the Near East; first permanent settlements	*c.* **9000** Southern tip of South America colonized	
c. **7000** Evidence of rice cultivation in China	*c.* **7000** First farming in Greece and Aegean; reaches Iberia and Low Countries *c.* 5000; Britain and southern Scandinavia *c.* 4000	**8350–7350** Jericho founded: first walled town in the world (4ha/10 acres) *c.* **7000** Early experiments with copper ores in Anatolia **6250–5400** Çatal Höyük (Anatolia) flourishes: largest city of its day (13ha/32 acres)		
		c. **6000** Earliest cereal cultivation in north Africa *c.* **5000** Colonization of Mesopotamian alluvial plain by groups practising irrigation. Agricultural settlements in Egypt *c.* **4000–3000** Desiccation of Sahara begins; north African populations expand south and east *c.* **4000** Bronze casting begins in Near East; first use of plough *c.* **3500** Eanna in Uruk and other ceremonial complexes built as centres of the earliest cities in Mespotamia		*c.* **6000** First known pottery and woolen textiles (Çatal Höyük) *c.* **3500** Construction of Megalithic tombs and circles in Brittany, Iberian peninsula and British Isles (Stonehenge *c.* 2000). Invention of wheel and plough (Mesopotamia) and sail (Egypt)
	3200–2000 Early Cycladic civilization	*c.* **3100** Traditional date of unification of Egypt under Menes		*c.* **3200** Earliest readable documents from Mesopotamia *c.* **3100** Pictographic writing invented in Sumer
c. **3000** First agricultural settlements in southeast Asia	*c.* **3000** Spread of copper-working. Beginning of Greek Early Bronze Age	*c.* **3000** Development of major cities in Sumer *c.* **2686** The "Old Kingdom" (pyramid age) of Egypt begins (to 2181 BC)	*c.* **3000** Maize first cultivated in Mesoamerica. First pottery in Americas (Ecuador and Colombia)	
c. **2500** Beginnings of Harappan culture in the Indus valley		**2296** Sargon I of Agade founds first empire in world history		*c.* **2590** Cheops builds great pyramid at Giza *c.* **2500** Domestication of horse (central Asia)
	c. **2000** Indo-European speakers (early Greeks) invade and settle Peloponnese; beginnings of "Minoan" civilization in Crete	*c.* **2000** Hittites invade Anatolia and found empire (1650) *c.* **1990** Egyptian conquests of Nubia begin	*c.* **2000** First metal-working in Peru. Settlement of Melanesia by immigrants from Indonesia begins	*c.* **2000** Use of sail on sea-going vessels (Aegean)
c. **1750** Abandonment of major Indus valley cities		*c.* **1749** Shamshi-Adad founds Assyrian state *c.* **1728** Hammurabi founds Babylonian empire	*c.* **1750** Northernmost Greenland settled	
c. **1650** Indo-Aryans begin to arrive in China	*c.* **1628** Massive volcanic eruption on Aegean island of Thera	*c.* **1648** Hyksos control Egypt		
c. **1600** Start of Bronze Age in China *c.* **1550** Aryans destroy Indus valley civilization and settle in N India *c.* **1520** Beginnings of Shang dynasty in China *c.* **1500** Bronze Age in northeast Thailand and north Vietnam	*c.* **1600** Beginnings of Mycenaean civilization in Greece	*c.* **1540** Kamose and Amose expel Hyksos invaders and inaugurate Egyptian "New Kingdom" (to 1069 BC)		*c.* **1500** Ideographic script in use in China; "Linear B" script in Crete and Greece; Hittite cuneiform in Anatolia *c.* **1450** Development of Brahma worship; composition of *Vedas* (earliest Indian literature) begins *c.* **1360** Akhenaten enforces mono-theistic sun worship in Egypt; builds new capital, Akhetaten
	c. **1300** Start of Urnfield culture	*c.* **1420** Tudhaliya I begins expansion of Hittite power	*c.* **1300** Settlers of Melanesia reach Fiji, later spreading to Western Polynesia	
		1275 Battle of Kadesh between Ramses II of Egypt and Hittites *c.* **1200** Collapse of Hittite empire. Jewish exodus from Egypt and settlement in Palestine **1152** Death of Ramses III, last great pharaoh of Egypt		*c.* **1200** Beginning of Jewish religion (worship of Yahweh). Teachings of Zoroaster
c. **1030** Shang dynasty in China overthrown by Chou; Aryans in India expand eastwards down Ganges valley *c.* **1000** Indo-Aryan settlements established in the Upper Ganges plains	*c.* **1100** Earliest fortified hilltop sites in western Europe *c.* **1000** Etruscans arrive in Italy	*c.* **1100** Spread of Phoenicians in Mediterranean region (to 700 BC) *c.* **1025** Emergence of Israelite kingdom	*c.* **1150** Beginning of Olmec civilization in Mex	*c.* **1100** Phoenicians develop alphabetic script (basis of all modern European script)
		c. **900** Kingdom of Meroe established *c.* **840** Rise of Urartu **814** Traditional date for foundation of Phoenician colony at Carthage		
c. **800** Aryans expand southwards in India **771** Collapse of Chou feudal order in China				**800–400** Composition of *Upanishads*, Sanskrit religious treatises **776** Traditional date for first Olympic Games, in Greece
	753 Traditional date for foundation of Rome *c.* **750** Greek city-states begin to found settlements throughout Mediterranean *c.* **750–450** Hallstatt culture in central and western Europe: mixed farming, iron tools			*c.* **750** Amos, first great prophet in Israel. Homer's *Iliad* and Hesiod's poetry first written down
	c. **700** Scythians spread from central Asia to eastern Europe	**721–705** Assyria at height of military power		

ASIA EXCLUDING THE NEAR EAST	EUROPE	NEAR EAST AND NORTH AFRICA	OTHER REGIONS	CULTURE AND TECHNOLOGY
c. 660 Jimmu, legendary first emperor of Japan **c. 650** Introduction of iron technology in China **c. 600** Kausambi and Ujjayini develop as earliest post-Harappan cities	**c. 650** Rise of "Tyrants" in Corinth and other Greek cities	**671** Assyrian conquest of Egypt; introduction of iron-working **612** Sack of Nineveh by Medes and Scythians; collapse of Assyrian power **586** Babylonian captivity of the Jews		**c. 650** First coins: Lydia (Asia Minor) and Greece (c. 600). Rise of Greek lyric poetry (Sappho born c. 612) **585** Thales of Miletus predicts an eclipse: beginnings of Greek rationalist philosophy
		c. 550 Iron use begins in sub-Saharan Africa; Bantu speakers expand southwards **539** Cyrus the Great of Persia captures Babylon **521** Persia under Darius I (the Great) rules from the Nile to the Indus **c. 520** Darius I completes canal connecting Nile with Red Sea		**c. 551** Birth of Confucius **550** Zoroastrianism becomes official religion of Persia **c. 550** Chinese silks known in Athens **540** Deutero-Isaiah, Hebrew prophet, at work during exile in Babylon **c. 530** Pythagoras, mathematician and mystic, active **528** Traditional date for death of Mahavira, founder of Jain sect **520** Death of Lao-tzu (born 605), traditional founder of Daoism
c. 500 Sinhalese, an Aryan people, reach Ceylon. Iron introduced to southeast Asia; development of political elites	**511** Expulsion of Tarquinius Superbus, last of Rome's kings **c. 505** Cleisthenes establishes democracy in Athens **490** Battle of Marathon: Persian attack on Athens defeated **480** Battles of Salamis and Plataea (479): Persian invasion of Greece defeated	**494** Persians suppress Ionian revolt	**c. 500** Foundation of Zapotec capital, Monte Albán, in Mexico. Iron-making techniques spead to sub-Saharan Africa **c. 500–AD 200** Period of Nok culture in northern Nigeria	**c. 500** Achaemenid Persians transmit food plants (rice, peach, apricot, etc.) to western Asia. Caste system established in India. First hieroglyphic writing in Mexico (Monte Albán) **c. 486** Birth of Buddha **479–338** Period of Greek classical culture: poetry, Pindar (518–438); drama, Aeschylus (525–456), Sophocles (496–406), Euripides (480–406), Aristophanes (c. 440–385); history, Herodotus (c. 486–429), Thucydides (c. 460–400); medicine, Hippocrates (c. 470–406); philosophy, Socrates (469–399), Plato (c. 437–347), Aristotle (384–322); sculpture, Phidias (c. 490–417), Praxiteles (c. 364); architecture, Parthenon (447–431) **479** Death of Confucius
475–221 "Warring States" period in China	**478** Foundation of Confederacy of Delos, later transformed into Athenian empire **c. 450** Celtic (La Tène) culture emerges in central and western Europe **431–404** Peloponnesian War between Sparta and Athens **390** Sack of Rome by Gauls **356** Philip II, king of Macedon (to 336) **338** Battle of Chaeronea gives Macedon control of Greece	**334** Alexander the Great (of Macedon) invades Asia Minor; conquers Egypt (332), Persia (330) reaches India (327) **323** Death of Alexander: empire divided between Macedon, Egypt, Syria and Pergamum **304** Ptolemy I, Macedonian governor of Egypt, founds independent dynasty (to 30 BC)		**447** Parthenon begun in Athens **350–200** Great period of Chinese thought: formation of Daoist, Legalist and Confucian schools; early scientific discoveries
322 Chandragupta founds Mauryan empire at Magadha, India				**312/311** Start of Seleucid era; first continuous historical dating-system
	290 Rome completes conquest of central Italy		**c. 300** Rise of Hopewell chiefdoms in North America	**c. 290** Foundation of Alexandrian library
265 Ashoka, Mauryan emperor, converted to Buddhism	**241** First Punic War (264–241) with Carthage gives Rome control of Sicily			**277** Death of Ch'ü Yüan (b. 343), earliest major Chinese poet
221 Shih Huang-ti, of Ch'in dynasty, unites China (to 207)	**218** Second Punic War (218–201): Hannibal of Carthage invades Italy **206** Rome gains control of Spain	**238** Arsaces I seizes Parthia from the Seleucids		
202 Former Han dynasty (to AD 9) reunites China; capital at Chang-an				
185 Demetrius and Menander, kings of Bactria, conquer northwest India	**168** Rome defeats and partitions Macedonia **146** Rome sacks Carthage and Corinth; Greece under Roman domination	**149** Third Punic War (149–146): Rome destroys Carthage and founds province of Africa	**c. 150** Settlement of Marquesas Islands	

ASIA EXCLUDING THE NEAR EAST	EUROPE	NEAR EAST AND NORTH AFRICA	OTHER REGIONS	CULTURE AND TECHNOLOGY
141 Wu-ti, Chinese emperor, expands Han power in eastern Asia **c.138** Chang Chien explores central Asia **130** Yüeh-chih tribe (Tocharians) establish kingdom in Transoxania **c.112** Opening of "Silk Road" across central Asia linking China to West **88 BC** Bactria and Indus valley overrun by the Shakas	**133–122** Failure of reform movement in Rome, led by Tiberius and Gaius Gracchus **89** All Italy receives Roman citizenship **58–51** Julius Caesar conquers Gaul **49** Julius Caesar crosses Rubicon; begins march on Rome **47–45** Civil war in Rome; Julius Caesar becomes sole ruler (45) **31** Battle of Actium: Octavian (later Emperor Augustus) establishes domination over Rome **27 BC** Collapse of Roman republic and beginning of empire	**64** Pompey the Great conquers Syria; end of Seleucid empire **53** Battle of Carrhae; Parthia defeats Roman invasion **30 BC** Death of Antony and Cleopatra: Egypt a Roman province	**100 BC** Camel introduced into Saharan Africa	**142** Completion of first stone bridge over river Tiber **79** Death of Ssu-ma Ch'ien, Chinese historian **46** Julius Caesar reforms calendar; Julian calendar in use until AD 1582 (England 1752, Russia 1917) **31 BC–AD 14** The Augustan Age at Rome: Virgil (70–19 BC), Horace (65–27 BC), Ovid (43 BC–AD 17), Livy (59 BC–AD 17) **c. 5 BC** Birth of Jesus Christ
AD 9–23 Hsin dynasty in China **25** Later Han dynasty (to AD 220); capital at Lo-yang **c.60** Rise of Kushana empire **78–102** Kanishka, Kushana emperor, controls north India **91** Chinese defeat Hsiungnu in Mongolia	**AD 43** Roman invasion of Britain	**AD 44** Mauretania (Morocco) annexed by Rome **70** Romans destroy the Jewish Temple in Jerusalem **97** Chinese ambassador Kan Ying visits Persia	**c. AD 50** Expansion of kingdom of Aksum (Ethiopia) begins **c. 100** Rise of Teotihuacán in Mesoamerica	**c. AD 33** Jesus of Nazareth, founder of Christianity, crucified in Jerusalem **46–57** Missionary journeys of St Paul **65** First Buddhist missionaries arrive in China **c. 90–120** Great Silver period of Latin: Tacitus (c. 55–120), Juvenal (c. 55–c. 140), Martial (c. 38–102) **105** First use of paper in China
166 Roman merchants at the Chinese imperial court **184** "Yellow Turbans" rebellions disrupt Han China	**117** Roman empire at its greatest extent **165** Smallpox epidemic ravages Roman empire	**116** Roman Emperor Trajan completes conquest of Mesopotamia **132** Jewish rebellion against Rome leads to "diaspora" (dispersal of Jews)	**c. 150** Berber and Mandingo tribes begin domination of the Sudan	**c. 125** Third Buddhist conference: widespread acceptance of the sculptural Buddha image **150** Earliest surviving Sanskrit inscription (India). Buddhism reaches China **c. 200** Completion of *Mishnah* (codification of Jewish Law). Indian epic poems *Mahabharata*, *Ramayana* and *Bhagavad Gita*. Earliest Sanskrit writing in southeast Asia **c. 200–250** Development of Christian theology: Tertullian (c. 160–220), Clement (c. 150–c. 215), Origen (185–254)
220 Last Han emperor Hsien-ti abdicates **245** Chinese envoys visit Funan (modern Cambodia), first major southeast Asian state	**212** Roman citizenship conferred on all free inhabitants of empire **238** Gothic incursions into Roman empire begin	**224** Foundation of Sasanid dynasty in Persia	**c. 250** Kingdom of Aksum gains control of Red Sea trade	
280 China unified under Western Chin **304** Hsiungnu invade China; China fragmented to 589 **320** Chandragupta I founds Gupta empire in northern India **c. 350** Hunnish invasions of Persia and India	**293** Emperor Diocletian reorganizes Roman empire **312** Conversion of Constantine **313** Edict of Milan: toleration proclaimed for all religions in the Roman empire **330** Capital of Roman empire transferred to Constantinople **361–3** Emperor Julian attempts to restore pagan religion **370** First appearance of Huns in Europe **378** Visigoths defeat and kill Roman emperor at Adrianople **395** Division between east and west Roman empire permanent		**c. 300** Rise of Maya civilization in Mesoamerica; large civilized states in Mexico (Teotihuacán, Monte Albán, El Tajín). Settlement of eastern Polynesia	**271** Magnetic compass in use (China) **274** Unconquered Sun proclaimed god of Roman empire **276** Crucifixion of Mani (b. 215), founder of Manichaean sect **285** Confucianism introduced into Japan **c. 300** Foot-stirrup invented in Asia **350** Buddhist cave temples, painting, sculpture (to 800)
420 Overthrow of Eastern Chin dynasty	**406** Vandals invade and ravage Gaul and Spain (409) **410** Visigoths invade Italy, sack Rome and overrun Spain	**429** Vandal kingdom in North Africa	**c. 400** Aksum destroys kingdom of Meroe (Kush). Settlement of Hawaiian islands	**404** Latin version of Bible completed **413** Kumaragupta; great literary era in India **426** Augustine of Hippo completes *City of God*

Asia Excluding the Near East	Europe	Near East and North Africa	Other Regions	Culture and Technology
	449 Angles, Saxons and Jutes begin conquest of Britain			
480 Gupta empire overthrown	**476** Deposition of last Roman emperor in west			
	481 Clovis becomes king of the Franks			
	493 Ostrogoths take power in Italy			**497** Franks converted to Christianity
511 Huns rule northern India				**c. 520** Rise of mathematics in India: Aryabhata and Varamihara invent decimal system
				529 Rule of St Benedict regulates Western monasticism
534 Northern Wei dynasty fragments	**533** Justinian restores Roman power in north Africa and Italy (552)			**534** Justinian promulgates Legal Code
				538 Hagia Sophia, Constantinople, consecrated
		540 Chosroes I sacks Antioch		**c. 540** Silkworms brought into Byzantine empire from China
	c. 542 Bubonic plague ravages Europe			**c. 550** Buddhism introduced into Japan from Korea
				563 St Colomba founds monastery of Iona: beginning of Irish mission to Anglo-Saxons
589 China reunified by Sui dynasty	**568** Lombard conquest of north Italy			**597** Mission of Augustine to England
	590 Gregory the Great extends papal power		**c. 600** Apogee of Maya civilization	**607** Chinese cultural influence in Japan begins
607 Unification of Tibet				
	610 Accession of East Roman Emperor Heraclius; beginning of Hellenization of (East) Roman empire, henceforth known as Byzantine empire	**611** Persian armies capture Antioch and Jerusalem and overrun Asia Minor (to 626)		
617 China in state of anarchy				
618 China united under T'ang dynasty (to 907)		**622** Hegira of Mohammed; beginning of Islamic calendar		
		628 Heraclius defeats Persians at Nineveh		**625** Mohammed begins his prophetic mission
		632 Death of Mohammed: Arab expansion begins		
		636 Arabs overrun Syria		
		637 Arabs overrun Iraq		
c. 640 Empire of Sri Harsha in northern India		**641** Arabs conquer Egypt and begin conquest of north Africa		
645 Fujiwara's "Taika reform" remodels Japan on Chinese lines				**c. 645** Buddhism reaches Tibet (first temple 651)
658 Maximum extension of Chinese power in central Asia; protectorates in Afghanistan, Kashmir, Sogdiana and Oxus valley				
665 Tibetan expansion into Turkestan, Tsinghai				
676 Korea unified under Silla	**680** Bulgars invade Balkans			
	687 Battle of Tertry: Carolingians dominate Frankish state			**c. 690** Arabic replaces Greek and Persian as language of Umayyad administration
				692 Completion of Dome of Rock in Jerusalem; first great monument of Islamic architecture
	711 Muslim invasion of Spain		**c. 700** Rise of empire of Ghana. Decline of kingdom of Aksum. Teotihuacán destroyed	**c. 700** Buddhist temples built at Nara, Japan. Golden age of Chinese poetry: Li Po (701–62), Tu Fu (712–70), Po Chü-i (772–846)
712 Arabs conquer Sind and Samarkand		**717** Arab siege of Constantinople repulsed		**722** St Boniface's mission to Germany
				725 Bede (673–735) introduces dating by Christian era
	733/4 Battle of Tours halts Arab expansion in western Europe			**c. 730** Printing in China
745 Beginning of Uighur empire in Mongolia		**750** Abbasid caliphate established		
751 Battle of Talas River establishes boundary between China and Abbasid caliphate	**751** Lombards overrun Ravenna, last Byzantine foothold in northern Italy			**751** Paper-making spreads from China to Muslim world and Europe (1150)
755 An Lu-shan's rebellion in China				
	774 Charlemagne conquers northern Italy			**760** Arabs adopt Indian numerals and develop algebra and trigonometry
				c. 780–850 Temple at Borobudur (Java) constructed by Shailendra kings
				782 Alcuin of York (735–804) organizes education in Carolingian empire: "Carolingian renaissance"
				788 Great mosque in Córdoba
793 Japanese capital moved to Kyoto from Nara	**793** Viking raids begin			
c. 802 Jayaxarman II establishes Angkorean kingdom (Cambodia)	**800** Charlemagne crowned emperor in Rome; beginning of new Western (later Holy Roman) empire	**809** Death of caliph Harun al-Rashid		**802** Foundation of Angkor, Cambodia
836 Struggle for control of Indian Deccan				
840 Collapse of Uighur empire				
842 Tibetan empire disintegrates				
	843 Treaty of Verdun: partition of Carolingian empire			**849** Pagan (Burma) founded
			c. 850 Collapse of Classic Maya culture in Mesoamerica	**853** First printed book in China

---

Asia Excluding the Near East	Europe	Near East and North Africa	Other Regions	Culture and Technology
	862 Novgorod founded by Rurik the Viking			**863** Creation of Cyrillic alphabet in eastern Europe **864** Mission of Cyril and Methodius to Moravia **865** Bulgars and Serbs accept Christianity
	871 Alfred, king of Wessex, halts Danish advance in England **882** Capital of Russia moved to Kiev			**c. 890** Japanese cultural renaissance: novels, landscape painting and poetry
907 Last T'ang emperor deposed	**906** Destruction of Moravia by Magyars			**910** Abbey of Cluny founded
916 Khitan kingdom in Mongolia founded **918** State of Koryo founded in Korea	**911** Vikings granted duchy of Normandy			
	929 Abd ar-Rahman III establishes caliphate at Córdoba	**936** Caliphs of Baghdad lose effective power		**935** Text of *Koran* finalized
939 Vietnam independent of China **947** Khitans overrun northern China, establish Liao dynasty with capital at Peking	**955** Otto I defeats Magyars at Lechfeld **959** Unification of England under Edgar **960** Mieszko I founds Polish state **962** Otto I of Germany crowned emperor in Rome			
967 Fujiwara domination of Japan begins	**972** Beginning of Hungarian state under Duke Geisa	**969** Fatimids conquer Egypt and found Cairo		
979 Sung dynasty reunites China	**983** Great Slav rebellion against German eastward expansion **987** Accession of Capetians in France			
			c. 990 Expansion of Inca empire (Peru)	**988** Foundation of Russian church
	1001 Stephen recognized as first king of Hungary		**c. 1000** Vikings colonize Greenland and discover America (Vinland). First Iron Age settlement at Zimbabwe	**c. 1000** Great age of Chinese painting and ceramics
1018 Turkic armies sack Kanauj, ending the reign of the Pratiharas. Rajendra Chola conquers Ceylon	**1014** Battle of Clontarf breaks Viking domination of Ireland **1018** Byzantines annex Bulgaria (to 1185) **1019** Cnut the Great rules England, Denmark and Norway (to 1035). Kievan Rus at height of its political influence (to 1054) **1031** Collapse of caliphate of Córdoba			**1020** Completion of *Tale of Genji* by Lady Murasaki. Death of Avicenna, Persian philosopher
c.1022 Cholas invade Bengal **1025** Mahmud of Ghazni destroys Shiva temple at Somnath **1038** Tangut tribes form Hsi-hsia state in northwest China **1044** Establishment of first Burmese national state at Pagan				**c. 1045** Moveable type printing invented in China
	1054 Schism between Greek and Latin Christian churches begins **1066** Norman conquest of England **1071** Fall of Bari completes Norman conquest of Byzantine Italy **1073** Gregory VII elected Pope: beginning of conflict of Empire and Papacy	**1055** Seljuk Turks take Baghdad **1056** Almoravids conquer north Africa and southern Spain **1071** Battle of Manzikert: defeat of Byzantium by Seljuk Turks **1096** First Crusade: Franks invade Anatolia and Syria, and found crusader states	**1076** Almoravids destroy kingdom of Ghana	**1094** Composition of old Javanese *Ramayana* by Yogisvara **c. 1100** First universities in Europe: Salerno (medicine), Bologna (law), Paris (theology and philosophy). Omar Khayyam composes *Rubaiyyat* **1111** Death of al-Ghazali, Muslim theologian
1126 Chin overrun northern China; Sung rule restricted to south	**1125** Renewal of German eastwards expansion	**1135** Almohads dominant in northwest Africa and Muslim Spain	**c. 1100** Toltecs build their capital at Tula (Mexico). Height of Pueblo culture (North America)	
	1154 Accession of Henry II: Angevin empire in England and France		**c. 1150** Beginnings of Yoruba city states (Nigeria)	**c. 1150** Hindu temple of Angkor Wat (Cambodia) built **1154** Chartres Cathedral begun; Gothic architecture spreads through western Europe **c. 1160** Development of European vernacular verse: *Chanson de Roland* (c.1100), *El Cid* (c.1150), *Parzifal, Tristan* (c.1200)
1170 Apogee of Sri Vijaya kingdom in Java under Shailendra dynasty **1175** Muhammad Ghuri invades India and begins the establishment of a Muslim empire **c.1180** Angkor empire (Cambodia) at greatest extent **1185** Battle of Dannoura (Japan): first shogunate founded	**1198** Innocent III elected Pope	**1171** Saladin defeats Fatimids and conquers Egypt **1187** Saladin destroys Frankish crusader kingdoms	**c. 1175** Tula abandoned by Toltecs; political fragmentation in Mesoamerica **c. 1200** Rise of empire of Mali in west Africa	**1193** Zen Buddhist order founded in Japan **1198** Death of Averroës, Arab scientist and philosopher

c. 1200

19

Asia Excluding the Near East	Europe	Near East and North Africa	Other Regions	Culture and Technology
			c. 1200 Emergence of Hausa city states (Nigeria). Aztecs occupy valley of Mexico **1200–1400** Buildings of Great Zimbabwe	
1206 Mongols under Genghis Khan begin conquest of Asia. Sultanate of Delhi founded	**1204** Fourth Crusade: Franks conquer Constantinople and found Latin empire **1212** Battle of Las Navas de Tolosa **1215** Magna Carta: King John makes concessions to English barons			**c. 1215** Islamic architecture spreads to India **1216** Foundation of Dominican and Franciscan orders
c. 1220 Emergence of first Thai kingdom				**1226** Death of St Francis of Assisi
1234 Mongols destroy Chin empire		**1228** Hafsid dynasty established at Tunis		
	1237 Mongols invade and conquer Russia (1238) **1241** Mongols invade Poland, Hungary, Bohemia **1242** Alexander Nevsky defeats Teutonic Order **1250** d. of Emperor Frederick II: collapse of imperial power in Germany and Italy **1260** Expulsion of Jews from England **1261** Greek empire restored in Constantinople	**1258** Mongols sack Baghdad; end of Abbasid caliphate	**c. 1250** Mayapan becomes dominant Maya city of Yucatán	
1264 Kublai Khan founds Yüan dynasty in China **1274** Mongol attack on Japan defeated (and in 1281) **1279** Mongols conquer southern China **1289** Mongol attacks on Pagan defeated	**1291** Beginnings of Swiss Confederation			**1272** Death of St Thomas Aquinas: his *Summa Theologica* defines Christian dogma **1275** Marco Polo (1254–1324) arrives in China **1290** Spectacles invented (Italy)
	1305 Papacy moves from Rome to Avignon (to 1376) **1314** Battle of Bannockburn: Scotland defeats England **1315–17** Great Famine in northern Europe **1325** Ivan I begins recovery of Moscow	**1299** Ottoman Turks begin expansion in Anatolia	**c. 1300** Kanuri empire moves capital from Kanem to Bornu. Emergence of empire of Benin (Nigeria) **1325** Rise of Aztecs in Mexico: Tenochtitlán founded	**c. 1320** Cultural revival in Italy: Dante (1265–1321), Giotto (1276–1337), Petrarch (1304–71)
1333 End of Minamoto shogunate: civil war in Japan **1335** Sultan Muhammad ibn Tughluq rules most of India **c. 1342** "Black Death" starts in Asia **1349** First Chinese settlement at Singapore; beginning of Chinese expansion in southeast Asia **1350** Golden age of Majapahit empire in Java	**1337** Hundred Years' War between France and England begins (to 1453) **1347** Black Death from Asia ravages Europe (to 1351)			**1339** Building of Kremlin (Moscow) **c. 1350** Japanese cultural revival
1368 Ming dynasty founded in China **1370** Hindu state of Vijayanagar dominant in south India	**1354** Ottoman Turks capture Gallipoli, gain first foothold in Europe **1360** Peace of Brétigny ends first phase of Hundred Years' War **1361** Ottomans capture Adrianople		**1375** Chimú conquest of central Andes begins	**1377** Death of Ibn Battuta (b. 1309), Arab geographer and traveller
1380 Tamerlane (Timur) begins conquests	**1378** Great Schism in West (to 1417) **1386** Union of Poland and Lithuania			**1387** Lithuania converted to Christianity **1392** Death of Hafiz, Persian lyric poet
1392 Korea reduced to vassal status **1394** Thais invade Cambodia; Khmer capital moved to Phnom Penh **1398** Tamerlane invades India and sacks Delhi **c. 1400** Establishment of Malacca as a major commercial port of southeast Asia **1405** Chinese voyages in Indian Ocean begin **1427** Chinese expelled from Vietnam	**1389** Battle of Kosovo: Ottomans gain control of Balkans **1394** Expulsion of Jews from France **1397** Union of Kalmar (Scandinavia) **1410** Battle of Tannenberg: Poles defeat Teutonic Knights **1415** Battle of Agincourt: Henry V of England resumes attack on France **1428** Joan of Arc: beginning of French revival	**1402** Battle of Ankara: Tamerlane defeats Ottomans in Anatolia **1415** Portuguese capture Ceuta: beginning of Portugal's African empire	**c. 1400** Songhay breaks away from Mali	**1400** Death of Chaucer, first great poet in English **1406** Death of Ibn Khaldun, Muslim historian
1467–77 Onin Wars: Japan plunged into civil war **1471** Vietnamese southward expansion: Champa annexed	**1453** England loses Continental possessions (except Calais). Ottoman Turks capture Constantinople: end of Byzantine empire **1475** Burgundy at height of power (Charles the Bold, d.1477) **1478** Ivan III, first Russian tsar, subdues Novgorod and throws off Mongol yoke (1480)		**1434** Portuguese explore south of Cape Bojador **c. 1450** Apogee of Songhay empire; university at Timbuktu. Mwenemutapa empire founded **1470** Incas conquer Chimú kingdom **1487** Bartolomeu Dias rounds Cape of Good Hope	**1455** Johannes Gutenberg (1397–1468) prints first book in Europe using moveable type

— first occurrence

ASIA	EUROPE	AFRICA	NEW WORLD	CULTURE AND TECHNOLOGY
	1492 Fall of Granada: end of Muslim rule in Spain; Jews expelled from Spain	**1492** Spaniards begin conquest of north Africa coast	**1492** Columbus reaches America: discovery of New World	
	1494 Italian wars: beginning of Franco-Habsburg struggle for hegemony in Europe	**1493** Askia the Great ruler of Songhay	**1493** First Spanish settlement in New World (Hispaniola). Treaty of Tordesillas divides New World between Portugal and Spain	
1498 Vasco da Gama: first European sea-voyage to India and back	**1499–1552** Jews expelled from many German states		**1497** Cabot reaches Newfoundland	
1500 Shah Ismail founds Safavid dynasty in Persia			**1498** Columbus discovers South America	*c.* **1500** Italian Renaissance: Leonardo da Vinci (1452–1519), Michelangelo (1475–1564), Raphael (1483–1520), Botticelli (1444–1510), Machiavelli (1469–1527), Ficino (1433–99)
		1505 Portuguese establish trading posts in east Africa		**1509** Watch invented by Peter Henle (Nuremberg)
1511 Portuguese take Malacca			*c.* **1510** First African slaves to America	
1516–7 Ottomans overrun Syria, Egypt and Arabia (1517)	**1519** Charles V, ruler of Spain and Netherlands, elected Holy Roman Emperor		**1519** Cortés begins conquest of Aztec empire (to 1520)	
	1521 Martin Luther outlawed: beginning of Protestant Reformation. Suleiman the Magnificent, Ottoman sultan, conquers Belgrade		**1520–1** Magellan crosses Pacific	
	1523 Collapse of Union of Kalmar; Sweden independent			
1526 Battle of Panipat: Babur conquers Delhi sultanate and founds Mughal dynasty	**1526** Battle of Mohács: Ottoman Turks overrun Hungary			
	1529 First Ottoman siege of Vienna		**1531** Pizarro begins conquest of Inca empire for Spain (to 1533)	
	1534 Henry VIII of England breaks with Rome			**1539** Death of Kabir Nanak, founder of Sikh religion
1543 Portuguese traders arrive in Japan	**1541** John Calvin founds reformed church at Geneva			**1543** Copernicus publishes *Of the Revolution of Celestial Bodies*
	1545 Council of Trent: beginning of Catholic Reformation	**1546** Mali empire destroyed by Songhay	**1545** Discovery of silver mines at Potosí (Peru) and Zacatecas (Mexico)	
1550 Mongol Altan-khan invades northern China; Japanese "pirate" raids in China	**1555** Charles V abdicates; divides inheritance			
	1556 Ivan IV of Russia conquers Volga basin			
1557 Portuguese enclave established at Macao (China)			*c.* **1560** Portuguese begin sugar cultivation in Brazil	**1559** Tobacco first introduced into Europe
	1562 Wars of religion in France (to 1598)			
	1563–70 Nordic Seven Years' War			*c.* **1565** Introduction of potato from South America to Europe
1565 Akbar extends Mughal power to Deccan	**1569** Union of Lublin unites Poland and Lithuania			
	1571 Battle of Lepanto: end of Turkish sea power in central Mediterranean	**1571** Portuguese colony established in Angola	**1571** Spanish conquer Philippines	
	1572 Dutch Revolt against Spain			
		1578 Battle of Al-Kasr al-Kebir: Moroccans destroy Portuguese power in northwest Africa		
1581 Yermak begins Russian conquest of Siberia				
1584 Phra Narai creates independent Siam				
1587 Accession of Shah Abbas: apogee of Safavid state	**1588** Spanish Armada defeated by English			
		1591 Battle of Tondibi: Moroccans destroy Songhay kingdom		
	1598 "Time of Troubles" in Russia	*c.* **1600** Oyo empire at height of its power		**1598** Shah Abbas I creates imperial capital at Isfahan
	1600 Foundation of English and Dutch (1602) East India Companies			
1603 Beginning of Tokugawa shogunate in Japan	**1603** Union of Crowns between England and Scotland		**1607** First permanent English settlement in America (Jamestown, Virginia)	**1607** Monteverdi's *La Favola d'Orfeo* establishes opera as art form
			1608 French colonists found Quebec	
	1609 Dutch Republic becomes independent			**1609** Telescope invented (Holland)
				c. **1610** Scientific revolution in Europe begins: Kepler (1571–1610), Bacon (1561–1626), Galileo (1564–1642), Descartes (1596–1650)
	1618 Outbreak of Thirty Years' War			**1616** Death of Shakespeare (b. 1564) and Cervantes (b. 1547)
1619 Foundation of Batavia (Jakarta) by Dutch: start of Dutch colonial empire in East Indies			**1620** Puritans land in New England (Mayflower)	**1620** First weekly newspapers in Europe (Amsterdam)
			1625 Dutch settle New Amsterdam	
		1628 Portuguese destroy Mwenemutapa empire		

ASIA	EUROPE	AFRICA	NEW WORLD	CULTURE AND TECHNOLOGY
	1630 Gustavus Adolphus of Sweden intervenes in Thirty Years' War			**c. 1630** Apogee of Netherlands art: Hals (1580–1666), Rembrandt (1606–69), Vermeer (1632–75), Rubens (1577–1640)
1638 Russians reach Pacific				**1636** Foundation of Harvard College, first university in north America
1641 Dutch capture Malacca from Portuguese	**1642** English Civil War begins			
1644 Ming dynasty toppled; Manchus found new dynasty (Ch'ing)			**1645** Tasman circumnavigates Australia and discovers New Zealand	
	1648 Peace of Westphalia ends Thirty Years' War			
	1649 First Anglo-Dutch War: beginning of Dutch decline	**1652** Foundation of Cape Colony by Dutch		
	1654 Ukraine passes from Polish to Russian rule			**1653** Taj Mahal, Agra, India, completed
	1655–60 Second Northern War; zenith of Swedish power	**1659** French found trading station on Senegal coast		**1656** St Peter's Rome, completed (Bernini)
				c. 1660 Classical period of French culture: drama, Molière (1622–73), Racine (1639–99), Corneille (1606–84); painting, Poussin (1594–1665), Claude (1600–82); music, Lully (1632–87), Couperin (1668–1733)
		1662 Battle of Ambuila: destruction of Kongo kingdom by Portuguese	**1664** New Amsterdam taken by English from Dutch (later renamed New York)	**1662** Royal Society founded in London and (1666) Académie Française in Paris
1674 Sivaji creates Hindu Maratha kingdom	**1667** Beginning of French expansion under Louis XIV			
	1683 Turkish siege of Vienna			
			1684 La Salle explores Mississippi and claims Louisiana for France	**1687** Isaac Newton's *Principia*
	1688 "Glorious Revolution"; constitutional monarchy in England			
1689 Treaty of Nerchinsk between Russia and China	**1689** "Grand Alliance" against Louis XIV			**1690** John Locke's *Essay concerning Human Understanding*
1690 Foundation of Calcutta by English			**1693** Gold discovered in Brazil	
1697 Chinese occupy Outer Mongolia	**1699** Treaty of Carlowitz: Habsburgs recover Hungary from Turks	**c. 1700** Rise of Ashanti power (Gold Coast)		**c. 1700** Great age of German baroque music: Buxtehude (1637–1707), Handel (1685–1759), Bach (1685–1750)
	1700 Great Northern War (to 1721)			
	1702 War of the Spanish Succession (to 1713)			
	1703 Foundation of St Petersburg, capital of Russian empire (1712)			
1707 Death of Aurangzeb: decline of Mughal power in India	**1707** Union of England and Scotland			
	1709 Battle of Poltava: Peter the Great of Russia defeats Swedes			**1709** Abraham Darby discovers coke-smelting technique for producing pig iron (England)
	1713 Treaty of Utrecht ends War of the Spanish Succession			
1722 Last Safavid shah overthrown by Afghan rebels			**1718** New Orleans founded by France	
			1728 Bering begins Russian reconnaissance of Alaska	
		c. 1730 Revival of ancient empire of Bornu (central Sudan)		**1730** Wesley brothers create Methodism
				c. 1735 Wahabite movement to purify Islam begins in Arabia
1739 Nadir Shah invades India and sacks Delhi	**1740** War of the Austrian Succession (to 1748): Prussia annexes Silesia			
1747 Ahmad Khan Abdali founds kingdom of Afghanistan				
1751 China overruns Tibet, Dzungaria and Tarim Basin (1756–9). French gain control of Deccan and Carnatic				
1755 Alaungpaya founds Rangoon and reunites Burma (to 1824)	**1756** Seven Years' War begins		**1754** Renewed war between Britain and France for control of North America	
1757 Battle of Plassey: British defeat French				
			1760 New France conquered by British: Quebec (1759) and Montreal (1760)	**1760** European enlightenment: Voltaire (1694–1778), Diderot (1713–84), Hume (1711–76)
1761 Capture of Pondicherry; British destroy French power in India			**1763** Treaty of Paris transfers most French North American possessions to Britain	**1762** J. J. Rousseau's *Social Contract*
1765 British granted the revenues of Bengal by Mughal emperor			**1768** Cook begins exploration of Pacific	
	1772 First Partition of Poland (Second and Third Partitions 1793, 1795)			**c. 1770** Advance of science and technology in Europe: J. Priestley (1733–1804), A. Lavoisier (1743–94), A. Volta (1745–1827), Harrison's chronometer (1762), Watt's steam engine (1765), Arkwright's water-powered spinning-frame (1769)
	1774 Treaty of Kuchuk Kainarji: beginning of Ottoman decline		**1775** American revolution begins	

ASIA	EUROPE	AFRICA	AMERICAS AND AUSTRALASIA	CULTURE AND TECHNOLOGY
			1776 American Declaration of Independence	**1776** Publication of *The Wealth of Nations* by Adam Smith (1723–90) and *Common Sense* by Tom Paine (1737–1809)
			1778 France enters American War of Independence	
	1783 Russia annexes Crimea		**1783** Treaty of Paris: Britain recognizes American independence	**1781** Immanuel Kant's *Critique of Pure Reason*
			1788 British colony of Australia founded	
	1789 French revolution begins; abolition of feudal system and proclamation of Rights of Man		**1789** George Washington becomes first president of United States of America	**c. 1790** Great age of European orchestral music: Mozart (1756–91), Haydn (1732–1809), Beethoven (1770–1827)
	1791 Russia gains Black Sea steppes from Turks			**1792** Cartwright invents steam-powered weaving loom
	1792 French republic proclaimed; beginning of revolutionary wars			**1793** Decimal system introduced (France). Eli Whitney's "cotton gin" (USA)
1793 British embassy under Macartney to the Chinese court	**1793** Attempts to reform Ottoman empire by Selim III			
1796 British conquer Ceylon		**1798** Napoleon attacks Egypt		**1796** Jenner discovers smallpox vaccine (UK)
	1799 Napoleon becomes First Consul and (1804) emperor of France			**1798** Malthus publishes *Essay on the Principle of Population*
		1804 Usuman dan Fodio begins to establish Fulani empire	**1803** Louisiana Purchase nearly doubles size of USA	
	1805 Battle of Trafalgar: Britain defeats French and Spanish fleets			
	1806 Abdication of Emperor Francis I; end of the Holy Roman Empire	**1806** Cape Colony recaptured by Britain		
	1807 Abolition of serfdom in Prussia	**1807** Slave trade abolished within British empire		
		1811 Mohammed Ali takes control in Egypt	**1808** Independence movements in Spanish and Portuguese America: 13 new states created by 1828	
1813 British defeat the Marathas and become the effective rulers of India	**1812** Napoleon invades Russia; suffers catastrophic defeat. Last major outbreak of bubonic plague in Europe (to 1815)			**1812** Cylinder printing press invented, adopted by *The Times* (London)
	1815 Napoleon defeated at Waterloo, exiled to St Helena. Congress of Vienna	**1818** Shaka forms Zulu kingdom in southeast Africa		**1817** Foundation of Hindu college, Calcutta, first major centre of Western influence in India
1819 British found Singapore as free trade port			**1819** USA purchases Florida from Spain	
			1820 Missouri Compromise bans slavery north of 36 degrees 30 minutes	**c. 1820** Romanticism in European literature and art: Byron (1788–1824), Chateaubriand (1768–1848), Heine (1797–1856), Turner (1775–1851), Delacroix (1798–1863)
	1821 Greek declaration of independence	**1822** Liberia founded as colony for freed slaves		**1821** Electric motor and generator invented by M. Faraday (Britain)
1824 Treaty of London formalizes British control of Malaya and Dutch control of East Indies. British begin conquest of Burma and Assam		**1824** British merchants establish post in Natal; first Anglo-Ashanti war	**1823** Monroe Doctrine asserts that Europe should not interfere in affairs of the Americas	**1822** First photographic image produced, by J.-N. Niepce (France)
1825–30 Java war: revolt of Indonesians against Dutch	**1825** "Decembrist" uprising in Russia suppressed			**1825** First passenger steam railway: Stockton and Darlington (England)
1830 Russia begins conquest of Kazakhstan (to 1854)	**1830** Revolutionary movements in France, Germany, Poland and Italy; Belgium wins independence. Greece independent	**1830** French begin conquest of Algeria		**1828** Foundation of Brahmo-samaj, Hindu revivalist movement
1833 Death of Rammohan Roy (b. 1772), father of modern Indian nationalism	**1833** Slavery abolished in British empire.			**1832** Death of Goethe (born 1749)
	1834 Formation of German customs union, Zollverein			**1833** First regulation of industrial working conditions (Britain)
		1836 "Great Trek" of Boer colonists from Cape, leading to foundation of Republic of Natal (1839), Orange Free State (1848) and Transvaal (1849)		**1834** First mechanical reaper patented (USA)
				1836 Needle-gun invented (Prussia), making breech-loading possible
				1837 Pitman's shorthand invented
1839–42 First Opium War: Britain annexes Hong Kong				**1838** First electric telegraph (Britain)
			1840 Britain annexes New Zealand	**1840** First postage stamp (Britain)
1843 British conquer Sind				
1845–9 British conquest of Punjab and Kashmir	**1845** Irish famine (to 1849) stimulates hostility to Britain and emigration to USA		**1845** Texas annexed by USA	
	1846 Britain repeals Corn Laws and moves towards complete free trade		**1846** Mexican War begins: USA conquers New Mexico and California (1848). Oregon Treaty delimits USA–Canada boundary	
	1846–7 Last major famine in Europe			
	1848 Revolutionary movements in Europe; proclamation of Second Republic in France			**1848** Communist Manifesto issued by Marx (1818–83) and Engels (1820–95)
				1849 Death of Chopin (b. 1810); apogee of Romantic music with Berlioz (1803–69), Liszt (1811–86), Wagner (1813–83), Brahms (1833–97), Verdi (1813–1901)
1850 T'ai-p'ing rebellion in China (to 1846), with immense loss of life			**1850** Australian colonies and (1856) New Zealand granted responsible government	
				1851 Great Exhibition in London
	1852 Fall of French republic; Louis Napoleon (Napoleon III, 1803–73) becomes French emperor	**1852** South African Republic (Transvaal) established by agreement between Britain and Boers		
1853 First railway and telegraph lines in India. Perry arrives in Japan; proposes commercial arrangements between Japan and USA	**1853** Crimean War (to 1855)	**1853** Livingstone's explorations begin		**1853** Haussmann begins rebuilding of Paris
				1855 Bessemer process permits mass-production of steel
1856–60 Second Opium War				

ASIA	EUROPE	AFRICA	AMERICAS AND AUSTRALASIA	CULTURE AND TECHNOLOGY
1857 Indian Mutiny				
1858 Treaty of Tientsin: further Treaty Ports opened to foreign trade in China				
	1859 Sardinian-French war against Austria; Piedmont acquires Lombardy (1860); unification of Italy begins			**1859** Darwin publishes *The Origin of Species*. First oil-well drilled (Pennsylvania, USA)
1860 Treaty of Peking: China cedes Maritime Province to Russia		**1860** French expansion in west Africa from Senegal	**1860** Abraham Lincoln US president; South secedes	**c. 1860** Great age of European novel: Dickens (1812–70), Dumas (1802–70), Flaubert (1821–80), Turgenev (1818–83), Dostoyevsky (1821–81), Tolstoy (1828–1910)
	1861 Emancipation of Russian serfs		**1861** Outbreak of American Civil War	**1861** Pasteur evolves germ theory of disease. Women first given vote (Australia)
1863 France establishes protectorate over Cambodia, Cochin China (1865), Annam (1874), Tonkin (1885) and Laos (1893)	**1864** Prussia defeats Denmark: annexes Schleswig-Holstein (1866). Russia suppresses Polish revolt		**1863** Slavery abolished in USA	**1863** First underground railway (London)
			1864 War of Paraguay against Argentina, Brazil and Uruguay (to 1870)	**1864** Foundation of Red Cross (Switzerland)
	1866 Establishment of North German confederation and of dual monarchy in Austria-Hungary		**1865** End of American Civil War	**1866** First trans-Atlantic telegraph cable laid
			1867 Russia sells Alaska to USA. Dominion of Canada established	**1867** Marx publishes *Das Kapital* (vol. 1)
1868 End of Tokugawa shogunate; Meiji restoration in Japan				
		1869 Suez canal opens	**1869** Prince Rupert's Land, Manitoba (1870) and British Columbia (1871) join Canada	**1869** First trans-continental railroad completed (USA)
	1870 Franco-Prussian war			**1870** Declaration of Papal infallibility
	1871 Proclamation of German empire, beginning of Third French Republic: suppression of Paris commune			
	1875 Growth of labour/socialist parties: Germany (1875), Holland (1877), Belgium (1885), Britain (1893), Russia (1898)	**1875** Disraeli buys Suez Canal Company shares to ensure British control of sea route to India	**1876** Porfirio Diaz (1830–1915) gains control of Mexico (to 1911)	**1874** First electric tram (New York); telephone patented by Bell (USA 1876); first electric steetlighting (London 1878). Emergence of Impressionist school of painting: Monet (1840–1926), Renoir (1841–1919), Degas (1834–1917)
1877 Start of Tanzimat reform era in Ottoman empire. Queen Victoria proclaimed empress of India			**1877** Reconstruction formally ended in Southern states of USA	
	1878 Congress of Berlin held; leads to the Treaty of Berlin: Romania, Montenegro and Serbia become independent and Bulgaria autonomous.			**1878** First oil tanker built (Russia)
1879 Second Afghan War gives Britain control of Afghanistan	**1879** Dual alliance between Germany and Austria-Hungary		**1879** War of the Pacific (Chile, Bolivia, Peru)	**1879** F. W. Woolworth opens first "5 and 10 cent store"
		1881 French establish protectorate over Tunisia		**1880** First consignment of frozen Australian beef arrives in London
		1882 Revolt in Egypt leading to British occupation		**1882** First hydro-electric plant (Wisconsin, USA)
		1884 Berlin Conference on the partition of Africa. Germany acquires SW Africa, Togoland, Cameroons		**1884** Maxim gun perfected
1885 Foundation of Indian National Congress		**1885** King of Belgium acquires Congo	**1885** Completion of Canadian Pacific railway	**c.1885** Daimler and Benz pioneer the automobile (Germany)
1886 British annex Upper Burma		**1886** Germany and Britain partition east Africa		
1887 French establish Indo-Chinese Union		**1889** British South Africa Company formed by Cecil Rhodes; begins colonization of Rhodesia (1890)	**1888** Brazil becomes last Latin American country to abolish slavery	**1888** Dunlop invents pneumatic tyre
	1890 Dismissal of Bismarck; Wilhelm II begins new policy		**1890** US Bureau of Census declares the western frontier closed	**c. 1890** Beginnings of modern literature in Japan on western models. Europe – realistic drama: Ibsen (1828–1906), Strindberg (1849–1912), Chekhov (1860–1904), Shaw (1856–1950)
				1891–1905 Trans-Siberian railway built
1894–5 Russo-Japanese War: Japan occupies Formosa	**1894** Franco-Russian alliance			**1895** Röntgen discovers X-rays (Germany); first public showing of motion picture (France)
		1896 Battle of Adowa: Italians defeated by Ethiopians		**1896** Marconi builds first radio transmitter. Herzl publishes *The Jewish State* calling for Jewish National Home
1898 Abortive "Hundred Days" reform in China	**1898** Germany embarks on naval building programme: beginning of German "world policy"	**1898** Fashoda crisis between Britain and France	**1898** Spanish-American war: USA annexes Guam, Puerto Rico and Philippines	**1898** Pierre and Marie Curie observe radioactivity and isolate radium (France)
		1899 The South African ("Boer War") begins (to 1902): Britain conquers Boer republics, Transvaal and Orange Free State		**1899** Howard's *Garden Cities of Tomorrow* initiates modern city planning
1900 Boxer uprising in China		**1900** Copper mining begins in Katanga		**1900** Planck evolves quantum theory (Germany). Freud's *Interpretation of Dreams*, beginning of psychoanalysis (Austria)
			1901 Commonwealth of Australia created	**1901** First wireless message sent across Atlantic
			1903 Panama Canal Zone ceded to USA	**1903** First successful flight of petrol-powered aircraft (Wright Brothers, USA)
1904 Partition of Bengal: nationalist agitation in India	**1904** Anglo-French entente			
1904–5 Russo-Japanese War; Japanese success stimulates Asian nationalism	**1905** Revolution in Russia, followed by tsarist concessions. Norway independent of Sweden	**1905** First Moroccan crisis		

ASIA	EUROPE	AFRICA	AMERICAS AND AUSTRALASIA	CULTURE AND TECHNOLOGY
1908 Young Turk revolution: Ottoman sultan deposed	**1907** Anglo-Russian entente	**1908** Belgian state takes over Congo from King Leopold	**1907** Peak year for immigration into USA. New Zealand acquires dominion status	**1907** Exhibition of Cubist paintings in Paris: Picasso (1881–1973), Braque (1882–1963)
1910 Japan annexes Korea	**1908** Bulgaria becomes independent; Austria annexes Bosnia and Herzegovina	**1910** Formation of Union of South Africa	**1910** Mexican revolution begins	**1910** Development of abstract painting: Kandinsky (1866–1944), Mondrian (1872–1944). Development of plastics
1911 Chinese revolution; Sun Yat-sen provisional president of new republic; rise to power of Warlords (to 1926)		**1911** Italy conquers Libya		
1914 German concessions in China and colonies in Pacific taken over by Japan, Australia and New Zealand	**1912–13** Balkan wars: Turkey loses bulk of remaining European territory		**1914** Panama canal opens	**1913** Henry Ford develops conveyor belt assembly for production of Model T automobile (Detroit, USA)
1915–16 Armenian massacres in Turkey	**1914** Outbreak of First World War	**1914–15** French and British conquer German colonies except German East Africa		
1917 Balfour Declaration promises Jews a National Home in Palestine	**1915** Italy enters war on the side of the Allies		**1917** USA declares war on Central Powers	**1917** First use of massed tanks (Battle of Cambrai)
1917–18 Arab revolt: Ottoman territories in Middle East lost	**1917** Revolution in Russia: tsar abdicates (February), Bolsheviks take over (October); first socialist state established		**1918** President Wilson announces "Fourteen Points"	
	1918 Treaty of Brest-Litovsk; Russia withdraws from First World War. Germany and Austria-Hungary sue for armistice (November); end of First World War. Civil war and foreign intervention in Russia			
1919 Amritsar incident; upsurge of Indian nationalism	**1919** Paris treaties redraw map of Europe	**1919** Former German colonies distributed as League of Nations mandates. Nationalist revolt in Egypt against British protectorate		**1919** Rutherford (1871–1973) splits atom (UK). Bauhaus school of design at Weimar (Germany). First crossing of Atlantic by air (Alcock and Brown)
1920 Mustafa Kemal (Atatürk) leads resistance to partition of Turkey; Turkey Nationalist Movement	**1920** League of Nations established (headquarters Geneva)		**1920** USA refuses to ratify Paris treaties and withdraws into isolation	**1920** First general radio broadcasts (USA and UK). Emergence of jazz in USA: Louis Armstrong (1900–71), Duke Ellington (1899–1974), Count Basie (1904–84)
1920–2 Gandhi leads Indian non-cooperation movement	**1921** Lenin introduces New Economic Policy	**1921** Battle of Anual: Spanish army routed by Moroccans	**1921** USA restricts immigration	
1921–2 Washington Conference on situation in east Asia	**1922** Mussolini takes power in Italy	**1922** Egypt independent		
1922 Greek army expelled from Turkey; last Ottoman sultan deposed; republic proclaimed (1923)			**1923** General Motors established: world's largest manufacturing company	**1923** Development of tuberculosis vaccine (France)
	1924 Death of Lenin; Stalin eventually emerges as Soviet leader (1929)			**1924** Thomas Mann (1875–1955) publishes The Magic Mountain
	1925 Locarno treaties stabilize frontiers in west			**1925** Franz Kafka (1883–1924), The Trial; Adolf Hitler, Mein Kampf
1926 Chiang Kai-shek begins reunification of China		**1926** Revolt of Abd-el Krim crushed in Morocco		
	1928 First Five-Year Plan and (1929) collectivization of agriculture in USSR			**1927** Emergence of talking pictures. Rise of great film makers: D.W. Griffith (1874–1948), Chaplin (1889–1977), John Ford (1895–1973), Eisenstein (1896–1948), Clair (1898–1981), Hitchcock (1899–1980), Disney (1901–66)
1930–1 Civil disobedience campaign in India (and in 1932–4)			**1929** Wall Street crash precipitates Great Depression	
1931 Japan invades Manchuria	**1931** Collapse of central European banks begins major recession		**1930** Military revolution in Brazil; Vargas becomes president	
1932 Iraq independent. Kingdom of Saudi Arabia formed by Ibn Saud	**1933** Hitler made Chancellor in Germany; beginning of Nazi revolution	**1934** Italians suppress Senussi resistance in Libya	**1933** US President Franklin D. Roosevelt introduces New Deal	
1934 "Long March" of Chinese communists begins		**1935–6** Italy conquers Abyssinia	**1935** Cárdenas president of Mexico: land redistribution and (1938) nationalization of oil	
1935 Government of India Act: Indians gain provincial autonomy				
1936 Japan signs anti-Comintern pact with Germany. Arab revolt in Palestine against Jewish immigration	**1936** German reoccupation of Rhineland. Spanish Civil War begins (to 1939). "Great Terror" launched by Stalin in Russia	**1936** Anglo-Egyptian alliance; British garrison Suez Canal Zone	**1936** Pan-American congress; USA proclaims "good neighbour" policy	**1936** First regular public television transmissions (UK)
1937 Beginning of full-scale war between Japan and China	**1938** Germany occupies Austria. Munich conference: Czechoslovakia dismembered			**1937** Jet engine first tested (UK); invention of nylon (USA)
1939 Russian forces defeat Japan at Khalkin Gol (Manchuria); Russo-Japanese neutrality pact (1941)	**1939** Germany occupies Czechoslovakia; Germany-Soviet non-aggression pact; Germany invades Poland; Britain and France declare war on Germany			**1939** Development of penicillin (UK). Development of DDT (Switzerland)
	1940 Germany overruns Norway, Denmark, Belgium, Netherlands, France; Italy invades Greece but is repulsed; Battle of Britain	**1940–1** Italians expelled from Somalia, Eritrea and Ethiopia		
1941 Japan attacks USA at Pearl Harbor; USA declares war	**1941** Germany invades Russia; declares war on USA. "Final solution" initiated by Nazis	**1941** Germans conquer Cyrenaica and advance into Egypt (1942)	**1941** USA enters war against Germany and Japan	
1942 Japan overruns SE Asia. Battle of Midway; USA halts Japanese expansion. Gandhi and Indian Congress leaders arrested	**1943** German VI army surrenders at Stalingrad; Italian capitulation	**1942** Battle of El-Alamein; German defeat and retreat. Anglo-American landings in Morocco and Algeria. Apartheid programme inaugurated in S Africa		**1942** Fermi builds first nuclear reactor (USA)
	1944 Anglo-American landing in Normandy; Russian advance in E Europe			
1945 USA drops atom bombs on Japan forcing surrender	**1945** Yalta Conference; defeat of Germany and suicide of Hitler		**1945** Death of Roosevelt; Harry Truman US president. United Nations established (headquarters New York)	**1945** Atom bomb first exploded (USA)
1946 Civil war in China (to 1949). Creation of Philippine Republic. Beginning of Vietnamese struggle against France (to 1954)			**1946** Perón comes to power in Argentina	**1946** First electronic computer built (USA)
1947 India and Pakistan partitioned and granted independence	**1947** Development of Cold War; Truman Doctrine enunciated. Marshall Plan for economic reconstruction in Europe			**1947** First supersonic flight (USA)
1948 Burma and Ceylon independent. Establishment of State of Israel; first Arab-Israeli war (to 1949)	**1948** Communist takeover in Czechoslovakia and Hungary; Berlin airlift (to 1949). Split between Yugoslavia under Tito and USSR		**1948** Organization of American States established	**1948** Transistor invented (USA)
1949 Communist victory in China; Chiang Kai-shek retreats to Formosa (Taiwan). Indonesia independent	**1949** USSR tests its first atomic bomb. Formation of NATO alliance and of COMECON			
1950 China invades Tibet. Korean War begins (to 1953)				

ASIA	EUROPE	AFRICA	AMERICAS AND AUSTRALASIA	CULTURE AND TECHNOLOGY
1951 USA ends occupation of Japan	**1952** European Coal and Steel Community founded	**1952** Beginning of Mau Mau rebellion in Kenya. Military revolt in Egypt; proclamation of republic (1953)	**1951** Australia, New Zealand and USA sign ANZUS Pact	**1951** First nuclear power stations
1953 Military coup in Iran	**1953** Death of Stalin; East Berlin revolt crushed	**1954** Beginnings of nationalist revolt in Algeria (to 1962)		**1952** Hydrogen bomb first exploded (USA). Contraceptive pill developed (USA)
1954 Geneva conference: Laos, Cambodia and Vietnam become independent states	**1955** Four-power occupation of Austria ended. Warsaw Pact signed		**1955** Overthrow of Perón regime in Argentina	**1953** Crick and Watson explain structure of DNA (UK)
1956 Second Arab-Israeli war	**1956** Soviet leader Khrushchev denounces Stalin at Party Congress. Polish revolt, Gomulka in power. Hungarian revolt crushed by Russians	**1956** Suez crisis: Anglo-French invasion of Canal Zone	**1956** Civil rights protests in Alabama	**1956** Beginning of rock and roll music (USA): Elvis Presley (1935–77)
	1957 Treaty of Rome: Formation of European Economic Community and (1959) of European Free Trade Association	**1957** Beginning of decolonization in sub-Saharan Africa: Gold Coast (Ghana) becomes independent		**1957** First space satellite launched (USSR)
1958 "Great Leap Forward" in China (to 1961)	**1958** Fifth Republic in France: de Gaulle first president			
1959 War between North and South Vietnam (to 1975)			**1959** Fidel Castro takes power after Cuban insurgency	
1960 Sino-Soviet dispute begins		**1960** "Africa's year"; many states become independent; outbreak of civil war in former Belgian Congo. Sharpeville massacre in South Africa	**1960** John F. Kennedy elected US president	
1961 Increasing US involvement in Vietnam	**1961** East Germans build Berlin Wall	**1961** South Africa becomes independent republic		**1961** First man in space: Gagarin (USSR)
1962 Sino-Indian war		**1962** Algeria becomes independent	**1962** Cuban missile crisis	**1962** Second Vatican Council reforms Catholic liturgy and dogma
		1963 Nationalist uprising against Portuguese rule in Angola	**1963** Kennedy assassinated; Lyndon Johnson succeeds (to 1968)	
1964 China tests first atomic bomb	**1964** Khrushchev ousted as Soviet leader; succeeded by Leonid Brezhnev		**1964** US Civil Rights Act inaugurates President Johnson's "Great Society" programme	**1964** Publication of *Thoughts of Chairman Mao*
1965 Sukarno overthrown in Indonesia. Indo-Pakistan war		**1965** Rhodesia declares independence – UDI		
1966 Cultural Revolution in China (to 1976)		**1966** South African prime minister, Hendrik Verwoerd, assassinated	**1966** Eruption of Black American discontent; growth of Black Power	
1967 Third Arab-Israeli war (Six-Day War)		**1967** Civil war in Nigeria with secessionist Biafra (to 1970)		
1968 Viet Cong launch Tet Offensive in Vietnam	**1968** Liberalization in Czechoslovakia halted by Russian invasion		**1968** Assassinations of Martin Luther King and Robert Kennedy; R.M. Nixon elected US president	**1968** World-wide student protest movement
	1969 Outbreak of violence in N Ireland			**1969** First man lands on moon: Armstrong (USA)
1971 Indo-Pakistan war leads to breakaway of East Pakistan (Bangladesh)			**1970** Allende elected president of Chile (killed 1973)	
			1971 USA initiates policy of detente with China and USSR. USA abandons Gold Standard and depreciates dollar	
			1972 President Nixon visits China	
1973 US forces withdraw from South Vietnam. Fourth Arab-Israeli war; OPEC countries triple oil price	**1973** Oil crisis ends post-war economic boom. Britain, Ireland and Denmark join EEC		**1973** Overthrow of Allende regime in Chile. Major recession in USA triggered by oil crisis	
	1974 Death of Salazar; end of dictatorship in Portugal. Turkish invasion of Cyprus	**1974** Emperor Haile Selassie of Ethiopia deposed by Marxist junta	**1974** President Nixon resigns after Watergate scandal; Gerald Ford succeeds	
1975 Civil war in Lebanon: Syria invades (1976). Communists take over Vietnam, Laos and Cambodia	**1975** Death of Franco; end of dictatorship in Spain	**1975** Portugal grants independence to Mozambique and Angola		
1976 Death of Mao Zedong; paves way for economic re-orientation and modernization under Deng Xiaoping		**1976** Morocco and Mauritania partition Spanish Sahara. Unrest in Soweto, South Africa, suppressed	**1976** Jimmy Carter elected US president	**1976** First supersonic trans-Atlantic passenger service begins with Concorde
1977 Egypt/Israeli peace talks (Camp David Peace Treaty, 1978). Military coup ends democratic rule in Pakistan				
1978 Vietnam invades Cambodia				
1979 Fall of shah of Iran, establishment of Islamic Republic under Ayatollah Khomeini (d.1989). Afghanistan invaded by USSR (to 1989). Sino-Vietnamese War. Vietnam expels Khmer Rouge government from Cambodia		**1979** Tanzanian forces invade Uganda and expel President Amin	**1979** Civil war in Nicaragua (to 1990). Civil war in El Salvador (to 1992)	
1980 Outbreak of Iran/Iraq War (to 1988)	**1980** Death of Marshal Tito. Creation of independent Polish trade union Solidarity; martial law (1981)	**1980** Black majority rule established in Zimbabwe (Rhodesia)	**1980** Ronald Reagan elected US president	**1980s** Computer revolution: spread of computers in offices and homes in Western world
	1981 Greece joins EEC	**1981** President Sadat of Egypt assassinated	**1981** US hostages released after 444 days in US embassy in Iran	**1981** First re-usable shuttle space flight (USA)
1982 Israel invades Lebanon, expulsion of PLO from Beirut. Israel withdraws from Sinai peninsula	**1982** Death of USSR president, Brezhnev, succession of Yuri Andropov (d.1984), then Konstantin Chernenko (d.1985)		**1982** Argentina occupies South Georgia and Falkland Islands; surrenders to UK forces	
			1983 Democracy restored in Argentina. USA invades Grenada	
1984 Indira Gandhi assassinated		**1984** Famine in Sahel and Ethiopia; continuing war against secession		
1985 Israel withdraws from Lebanon	**1985** Mikhail Gorbachev leader of USSR (to 1991)		**1985** Democracy restored in Brazil, Bolivia and Uruguay	
1986 Fall of Marcos in the Phillipines; Cory Aquino succeeds	**1986** Spain and Portugal join EEC	**1986** USA bombs Libya in retaliation for terrorist activities		**1986** Launch of world's first permanently manned space station (USSR). Major nuclear disaster at Chernobyl power reactor (Ukraine). US space shuttle *Challenger* explodes
			1987 INF treaty between USSR and USA: phased elimination of intermediate-range nuclear weapons. US stock market crash	**1987** World population reaches 5 billion
1988 Benazir Bhutto restores civilian rule in Pakistan. Palestine uprising (*intifada*) against Israeli occupied territories. PLO recognizes State of Israel	**1988** Gorbachev introduces *glasnost* and *perestroika* in USSR		**1988** George Bush elected US president (to 1993)	**1988** Global recognition that ozone layer is being depleted; global ban on CFCs (chlorofluorocarbons) (1990)
1989 Death of Ayatollah Khomeini. Student pro-democracy demonstration crushed in Beijing	**1989** Communist bloc in E Europe disintegrates; Berlin Wall demolished		**1989** Democracy restored in Chile	
1990 Iraq invades Kuwait	**1990** Reunification of Germany		**1989–90** US military intervention in Panama; arrest and extradition of Manuel Noriega	

ASIA	EUROPE	AFRICA	AMERICAS AND AUSTRALASIA	CULTURE AND TECHNOLOGY
1991 Gulf War: UN Coalition forces led by USA attack Iraq and liberate Kuwait; Rajiv Gandhi assassinated	**1991** Boris Yeltsin elected president of Russian Federation; USSR disintegrates; Disintegration of Yugoslavia; Slovenia and Croatia declare independence	**1990** Namibia independent; S African government moves towards accommodation with ANC, frees Nelson Mandela, and (1991) announces intention to dismantle apartheid	**1990** Democratic elections in Nicaragua end Sandinista rule	**1990** Voyager space probe mission completed; last planetary encounter (Neptune)
	1992 Civil War in Bosnia-Herzegovina; Czech Republic and Slovakia emerge as separate states	**1992** US forces intervene to end Somalia's famine and civil war; Prolonged terrorism in Algeria after elections are cancelled	**1992** Bill Clinton elected US president	
1993 Israel and PLO sign Palestinian autonomy agreement for limited Palestinian self-rule	**1993** Russian parliament building shelled after its occupation by hardline opponents of Yeltsin			
	1995 Dayton Agreement temporarily halts war in former Yugoslavia	**1994** Nelson Mandela elected as South Africa's first black president; Up to one million Tutsis and moderate Hutus massacred by Hutu extremists in Rwanda	**1994** US military intervention in Haiti	**1994** Cross-Channel rail link between Britain and France inaugurated
			1995 Oklahoma City terrorist bombing	**mid-1990s** Growth of the world-wide web
1997 Hong Kong returned to China; Death of Deng Xiaoping; Jiang Zemin emerges as Chinese leader; Reformist Khatami elected president of Iran		**1997** President Mobutu Sese Soko overthrown by Laurent Kabila as ruler of Congo	**1996** President Clinton re-elected	
			1997 Pope visits Cuba	**1997** Kyoto global warming agreement
1998 India and Pakistan carry out nuclear tests; President Suharto resigns after Indonesian unrest	**1998** Fighting in Albanian-majority province of Kosovo (Serbia)	**1998–2000** War between Eritrea and Ethiopia	**1998** USA bombs Afghanistan and Sudan after terrorist attacks on US embassies in Kenya and Tanzania	
1999 Civil war in East Timor ends in independence from Indonesia	**1999** European single currency (euro) launched; NATO campaign against Serbia over Kosovo	**1999** Thabo Mbeki elected President of South Africa; Seizure of white-owned farms in Zimbabwe		
	1999–2004 Renewed civil war in Chechnya			
	2000 Slobodan Milosevic ousted as President of Serbia		**2000** George W. Bush elected US President	**2000** First successful animal cloning; entire human genome sequenced
2001 Taliban regime overthrown in Afghanistan			**2001** Al Qaeda attacks on World Trade Center and Pentagon	
2002 India and Pakistan near war over Kashmir; Sri Lankan civil war ended; Terrorist bombing in Bali	**2002** NATO enlargement includes states from former communist bloc	**2002** End of Angolan civil war; Sierra Leone civil war ended by UK intervention; Civil war in Côte d'Ivoire	**2002** Luis da Silva elected president of Brazil	
2003 SARS virus outbreak; US-led coalition attacks Iraq and topples Saddam Hussein	**2003** European Constitution drafted	**2003–** continuing civil war in Darfur	**2003** Bush declares global "War on Terror"; USA intervenes in Haiti coup	**2003** Space probe finds water on Mars
				2003 first video-phone
2004 Israel assassinates Hamas spiritual leader	**2004** EU enlargement takes in ten new states; Terrorist bombing in Madrid; Vladimir Putin re-elected Russian president	**2004** ANC wins landslide victory in South Africa; Libya agrees to abandon weapons of mass destruction	**2004** George W. Bush re-elected president	**2004** Olympic Games return to Greece
2004– religious civil war in Iraq				
2004 *tsunami* kills 150,000 in Indian Ocean area				
2005 Iraq granted limited sovereignty	**2005** terrorist bombings in London			**2005** death of Pope John Paul II
				2005 *Harry Potter and the Half-Blood Prince* becomes the world's fastest-selling book – over 9 million copies in 24 hours
2006 Israel attacks Lebanon	**2006** Silvio Berlusconi defeated in Italian general election			
2006 trial and execution of Saddam Hussein	**2006** Race riots in French cities			
2006–7 confrontation with Iran over nuclear programme				
	2007 Bulgaria and Romania join European Union	**2007** refugee crisis in Chad	**2007** Washington Declaration on global environment	**2007** scientists create first image of the 'dark matter' of the universe
		2007 Islamic regime in Mogadishu overthrown		**2007** first artificial sperm cells created
		2007 political crisis in Zimbabwe		
		2007 Johnson-Sirleaf of Liberia becomes Africa's first elected head of state		
		2007 Massacres follow elections in Kenya		
2008 Israel launches invasion of Gaza strip	**2008** Dmitri Medyedev elected president of Russia	**2008** Jacob Zuma becomes president of South Africa	**2008** Barack Obama becomes US president	**2008** Olympic Games held in Beijing
	2008 Kosovo declares its independence		**2008** Emergency Economic Stabilisation Act in US to stem financial crisis	**2008-9** Major international financial crisis
			2008 Raúl Castro replaces his brother Fidel as Cuban president	
2009 Tamil Tigers finally defeated in Sri Lanka	**2009** Lisbon Treaty becomes EU law	**2009** Power-sharing agreement reached in Zimbabwe		**2009** Copenhagen climate summit
2009 Hamid Karzai wins second term as Afghan president				**2009** Barack Obama awarded Nobel Peace Prize
2009 Anti-government riots in Iran				
2009 North Korea detonates a major nuclear device				
2009 Benjamin Netanyahu becomes Israeli prime minister				
	2010 Terror attack on Moscow subway		**2010** Haiti earthquake leaves estimated 100,000 dead	
			2010 Barack Obama's health reforms become law in US	
			2010 First all LatinAmerica Summit	
			2010 Obama signs Strategic Arms Reduction Treaty with Russian President	
2011 Start of Syrian civil war		**2011** Tunisian revolt sparks Arab Spring		
2011 Assassination of Osama bin Laden		**2011** Revolts overthrow Muammar Gaddafi in Libya and Hosni Mubarak in Egypt		
2011 US troops leave Iraq		**2011** New state of Southern Sudan created		
2011 Earthquake and tsunami seriously damage Fukushima nuclear plant in Japan			**2012** Barack Obama elected for second term as president	**2012** Facebook achieves one billion active users worldwide
2013 Islamic State of Iraq and Syria (ISIS) launches religious war	**2013** Croatia becomes 28th state to join EU	**2013** President Morsi deposed by military in Egypt		
		2013 Death of Nelson Mandela		**2013** Francis becomes first non-European Pope for more than 1,000 years
2014 NATO combat forces leave Afghanistan	**2014** Ukrainian "Euromaidan" revolt		**2014** Hugo Chávez dies	**2014** United States and China agree carbon emissions deal
	2014 Russia annexes Crimea			
	2015 Radical left-wing government under Alexis Tsipras elected in Greece			
	2015 Ukrainian civil war ceasefire			

1

HUMAN ORIGINS AND EARLY CULTURES

RECORDED HISTORY is only the tip of an iceberg reaching back to the first appearance on earth of the human species. Anthropologists, prehistorians and archaeologists have extended our vista of the past by hundreds of thousands of years: we cannot understand human history without taking account of their findings. The transformation of humankind (or, more accurately, of certain groups of humans in certain areas) from hunters and fishers to agriculturists, and from a migratory to a sedentary life, constitutes the most decisive revolution in the whole of human history. The climatic and ecological changes which made it possible have left their mark on the historical record down to the present day.

Agriculture made possible not merely a phenomenal growth of human population, which is thought to have increased some 16-fold between 8000 and 4000 BC, but also gave rise to the familiar landscape of village communities which still characterized Europe as late as the middle of the 19th century and which even today prevails in many parts of the world. Nowhere are the continuities of history more visible. The enduring structures of human society, which transcend and outlive political change, carry us back to the end of the Ice Age, to the changes which began when the shrinking ice-cap left a new world to be explored and tamed.

STONEHENGE, WILTSHIRE, UNITED KINGDOM.

Human origins

Global cooling between five and six million years ago saw savannahs replace the tropical forests of sub-Saharan Africa. The appearance of this new environment was in turn matched by an evolutionary pulse that gave rise to new carnivores and omnivores. Among them were the hominins, the ancestors of modern man.

THE EARLIEST HOMININ FOSSILS, discovered in the Afar region of Ethiopia, are the fragmentary 4.5-million-year-old remains of *Ardipithecus ramidus*. Better evidence is available of the later and more widespread Australopithecenes, or "southern apes". Skeletal and fossilized footprints of *Australopithecus afarensis*, dated to between three and four million years ago, indicate a serviceable if not fully bipedal gait, hands still partly adapted for specialized tree climbing and a brain approximately one-third the size of ours. This species is the probable ancestor both of the robustly built *Paranthropus aethiopicus*, *Paranthropus robustus* and *Paranthropus boisei*, all with large teeth and herbivorous diets, and of our genus, *Homo*, meaning "man". Fieldwork since the 1950s has revealed that these closely related but nonetheless distinctive species lived at the same time side by side in the same habitats. Finds of more species are expected.

From between two and three million years ago, there is evidence of important evolutionary trends in *Homo*: brains became much bigger, a process known as encephalization. As larger brains need better diets to sustain them, the increase in brain size could only have occurred as a result of significant evolutionary pressures. The problem was compounded because hominins stayed the same size, with the result that their bigger brains could be achieved only by reducing the size of another organ, the stomach, a trade-off which in turn reduced the efficiency of the digestive tract, which in turn demanded a still better diet.

Early technologies

The most convincing explanation of this development – the expensive tissue hypothesis – holds that a move towards an energy-rich diet, particularly animal proteins, was responsible. And indeed the earliest-known stone tools, found in Gona, Ethiopia, suggest that 2.5 million years ago meat was a central part of hominin diet, with sharp-edged stones used to cut flesh and break marrow-rich bones to get

1 Human origins and colonization of the world

dates of first human occupation

	5 million to 1.8 million years ago
	1.8 million years ago
	1.5 million years ago
	500,000 years ago
	100,000 years ago
	50,000 to 5000 years ago
	5000 years ago to AD 1492

fossil sites

○	more than 4 million years old
●	Australopithecines / Paranthropi
●	early *Homo ergaster / rudolfensis*
●	Asian *Homo erectus*
●	*Homo heidelbergensis* / African archaic *Homo sapiens*
●	Denisovans
○	Neanderthals
●	late *Homo erectus*
●	*Homo sapiens sapiens*

1 Important fossils of human ancestors have been found at sites in Africa, Asia and Australia **(map right)**. East Africa's Great Rift Valley is a crucial area since fossils found here in the stratified deposits can be reliably dated. The location of the remains suggest that these early humans lived away from the more densely populated forests and inhabited the grasslands where a different range of resources could be exploited with less competition. Even here, life was not without its dangers: some early hominin skulls found in southern Africa have leopard teethmarks on them.

2 Hominin evolution

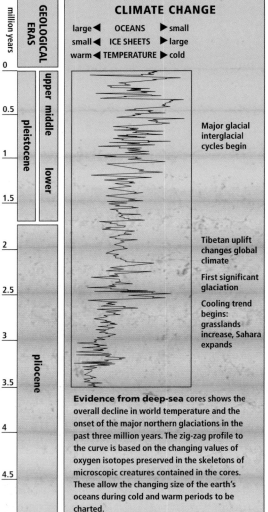

CLIMATE CHANGE

large ◄ OCEANS ► small
small ◄ ICE SHEETS ► large
warm ◄ TEMPERATURE ► cold

Major glacial interglacial cycles begin

Tibetan uplift changes global climate

First significant glaciation

Cooling trend begins: grasslands increase, Sahara expands

Evidence from deep-sea cores shows the overall decline in world temperature and the onset of the major northern glaciations in the past three million years. The zig-zag profile to the curve is based on the changing values of oxygen isotopes preserved in the skeletons of microscopic creatures contained in the cores. These allow the changing size of the earth's oceans during cold and warm periods to be charted.

GEOLOGICAL ERAS		
	upper	pleistocene
	middle	
	lower	
	pliocene	

million years: 0, 0.5, 1, 1.5, 2, 2.5, 3, 3.5, 4, 4.5, 5

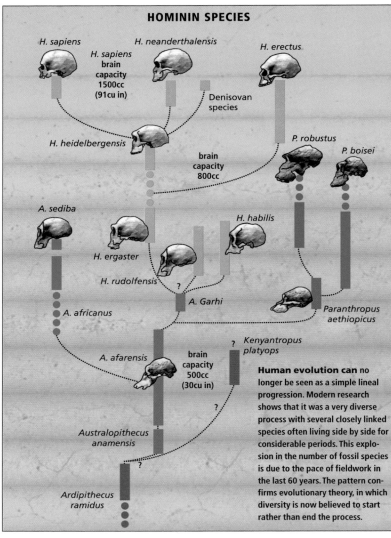

HOMININ SPECIES

H. sapiens
H. neanderthalensis
H. erectus
H. sapiens brain capacity 1500cc (91cu in)
Denisovan species
H. heidelbergensis
brain capacity 800cc
P. robustus
P. boisei
A. sediba
H. habilis
H. ergaster
H. rudolfensis
A. Garhi
A. africanus
Paranthropus aethiopicus
Kenyanthropus platyops
A. afarensis
brain capacity 500cc (30cu in)
Australopithecus anamensis
Ardipithecus ramidus

Human evolution can no longer be seen as a simple lineal progression. Modern research shows that it was a very diverse process with several closely linked species often living side by side for considerable periods. This explosion in the number of fossil species is due to the pace of fieldwork in the last 60 years. The pattern confirms evolutionary theory, in which diversity is now believed to start rather than end the process.

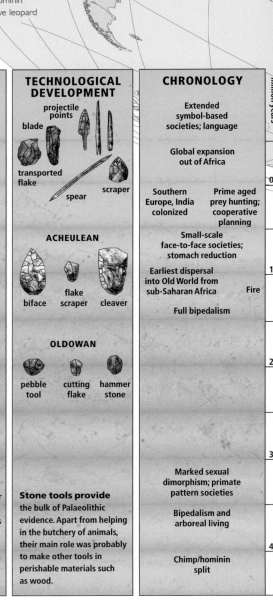

TECHNOLOGICAL DEVELOPMENT

projectile points
blade
transported flake
spear
scraper

ACHEULEAN

biface
flake scraper
cleaver

OLDOWAN

pebble tool
cutting flake
hammer stone

Stone tools provide the bulk of Palaeolithic evidence. Apart from helping in the butchery of animals, their main role was probably to make other tools in perishable materials such as wood.

CHRONOLOGY

Extended symbol-based societies; language

Global expansion out of Africa

Southern Europe, India colonized

Prime aged prey hunting; cooperative planning

Small-scale face-to-face societies; stomach reduction

Earliest dispersal into Old World from sub-Saharan Africa

Fire

Full bipedalism

Marked sexual dimorphism; primate pattern societies

Bipedalism and arboreal living

Chimp/hominin split

million years: 0, 0.5, 1, 1.5, 2, 2.5, 3, 3.5, 4, 4.5, 5

North Pacific Ocean

SOUTH AMERICA

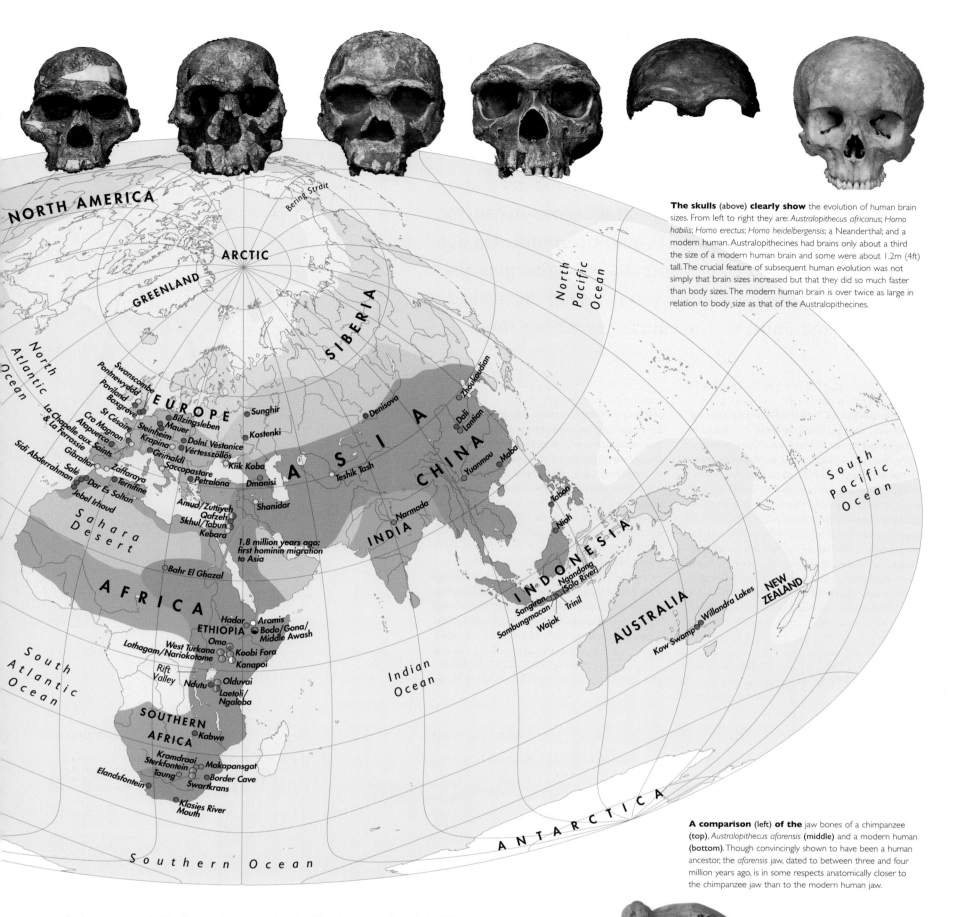

The skulls (above) clearly show the evolution of human brain sizes. From left to right they are: *Australopithecus africanus*; *Homo habilis*; *Homo erectus*; *Homo heidelbergensis*; a Neanderthal; and a modern human. Australopithecines had brains only about a third the size of a modern human brain and some were about 1.2m (4ft) tall. The crucial feature of subsequent human evolution was not simply that brain sizes increased but that they did so much faster than body sizes. The modern human brain is over twice as large in relation to body size as that of the Australopithecines.

A comparison (left) of the jaw bones of a chimpanzee (top), *Australopithecus afarensis* (middle) and a modern human (bottom). Though convincingly shown to have been a human ancestor, the *afarensis* jaw, dated to between three and four million years ago, is in some respects anatomically closer to the chimpanzee jaw than to the modern human jaw.

access to the bone marrow inside. Cut-marks on bones from Dikika, Ethiopia, show that stone tools were used at least 3.4 million years ago. The flesh and bones are from carcasses either scavenged or hunted by hominins. The role of plant food is not well understood, because plant remains hardly survive in the archaeological record. Tiny plant pieces trapped in the dental calculus (silicified dental plaque) of hominins suggest consumption of a wide range of plants including nuts, bark and grasses.

Out of Africa

About 1.8 million years ago hominins first dispersed out of Africa. One of the first sites outside Africa is Dmanisi in Georgia with deposits containing hominin remains, stone tools and animal bones about 1.7 million years old. Around 1.5 million years ago, *Homo erectus* reached southeast Asia. Later, around 800,000 years ago *Homo heidelbergensis* colonized large parts of Europe, including areas as far north as England. *Homo erectus* and *Homo heidelbergensis* are considered to have shared a common ancestor, *Homo ergaster*, and best known from the skeleton

found at Nariokotome in Kenya's Rift Valley. By perhaps 1.5 million years ago, all three had brains of about 1000cc (61 cu in) and an adaptable stone technology: the edges of their distinctive handaxes, whether pointed or oval, made them effective butchery tools.

Stone technology in itself did not play a part in the evolutionary pressures that led to larger brains. The Australopithecines, for example, had stone tools but their brains did not grow as a result, nor did they migrate from Africa. Instead, the importance of *Homo*'s larger brain had less to do with the food quest, more to do with allowing hominins to remember, to manipulate, to support and to organize others in more complex ways.

Modern humans

From about 500,000 years ago, this early burst of colonization came to a halt. Instead, though there were undoubtedly many dispersals of populations and much intermingling of genes, regional groups of separate populations living side by side such as the Neanderthals, modern humans and Denisovans

developed. Neanderthals and Denisovans are extinct species of *Homo* occupying large parts of Eurasia. Currently, it is thought that Neanderthals, Denisovans and modern humans share a common ancestor, *Homo heidelbergensis*. But from 125,000 years ago, another major dispersal began when modern humans – *Homo sapiens* – dispersed from Africa into the Near East and Arabia. By 50,000 years ago, Australia had been reached, by boat; 33,000 years ago, the western Pacific islands were colonized; 15,000 years ago, the Americas were reached. Major expansion into the Arctic began about 4500 years ago as the continental ice sheets retreated. Finally, 2000 years ago, humans began to settle the deep Pacific islands from where they reached New Zealand around 1200 years ago, 1000 years before the island's discovery by Captain Cook.

The spread of modern humans

Fossil and DNA studies have revealed that the first anatomically modern humans – *Homo sapiens* – arose in Africa between 250,000 and 140,000 years ago. Though much has still to be discovered about their origins and dispersal, by almost 28,000 years ago *Homo sapiens* had become not only the sole human species but the first truly global one.

THE EARLIEST MODERN-LOOKING human skulls yet found are about 130,000 years old and come from the Omo basin in Ethiopia, Klasies River Mouth in southern Africa and Jebel Irhoud in Morocco. Perhaps 125,000 years ago, these populations began to disperse, migrating northwards out of Africa. Modern humans went through population bottlenecks when population levels fell and remained small for several thousand years. A possible contributing factor to bottlenecking was the eruption at Toba in northwest Sumatra around 71,000 years ago, an environmental catastrophe on an extraordinary scale: parts of India were covered with ash up to 3m (10ft) deep, global temperatures were lowered for a

millennium. At the same time, the restricted populations generated by bottlenecking had the side effect of encouraging rapid changes in genetic structures thereby increasing the pace of evolutionary change.

Archaeological and genetic evidence then point to a further rapid expansion of modern human populations between 50,000 and 60,000 years ago. The archaeological evidence highlights the different behaviour of these dispersing modern humans compared with the local ancient hominins. In some regions, lighter, multi-component weapons have been found, including spears with skilfully produced stone tips fixed to wooden shafts and handles. There is evidence, too, of textiles and baskets, and dwellings and possibly food storage facilities. Trading and exchange networks also increased dramatically. Raw materials, particularly stone, which

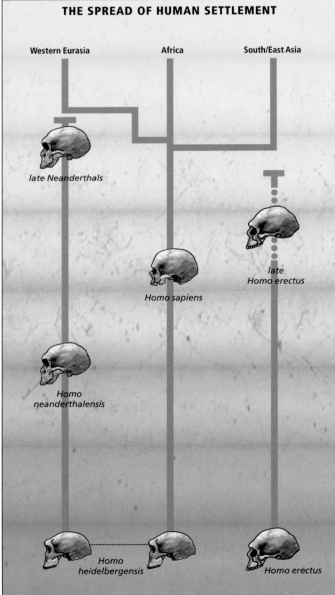

2 The evolution of modern humans

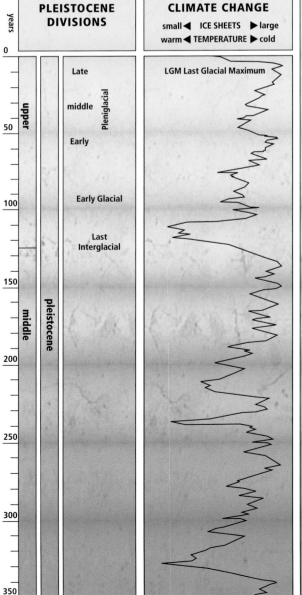

1 & 2 The appearance of anatomically modern humans – *Homo sapiens* – in Africa between 150,000 and 250,000 years ago was followed by the relatively rapid dispersal of these new populations. However, between 100,000 and 50,000 years ago, population movements stopped. About 50,000 years ago, modern human populations began to grow again and migrations to many new areas of the world took place (**map above and chart left**). There was nothing inevitable about the ultimate success of *Homo sapiens* in becoming not only the sole hominin species but the only global one as well. For many thousands of years, *Homo sapiens* shared the world with *Homo erectus* and the Denisovans in Asia and the Neanderthals in Europe and the Near East, groups in many ways as sophisticated and successful in their mastery of their environments as *Homo sapiens*. The similarities between these contemporary hominin species – all with small populations and simple technologies and all vulnerable to climate change or environmental catastrophes such as the Toba eruption 71,000 years ago – are in most respects more striking than the differences. Nonetheless, it was the greater social sophistication of *Homo sapiens* which was decisive in allowing these early peoples to colonize a much wider range of habitats than any previous hominin.

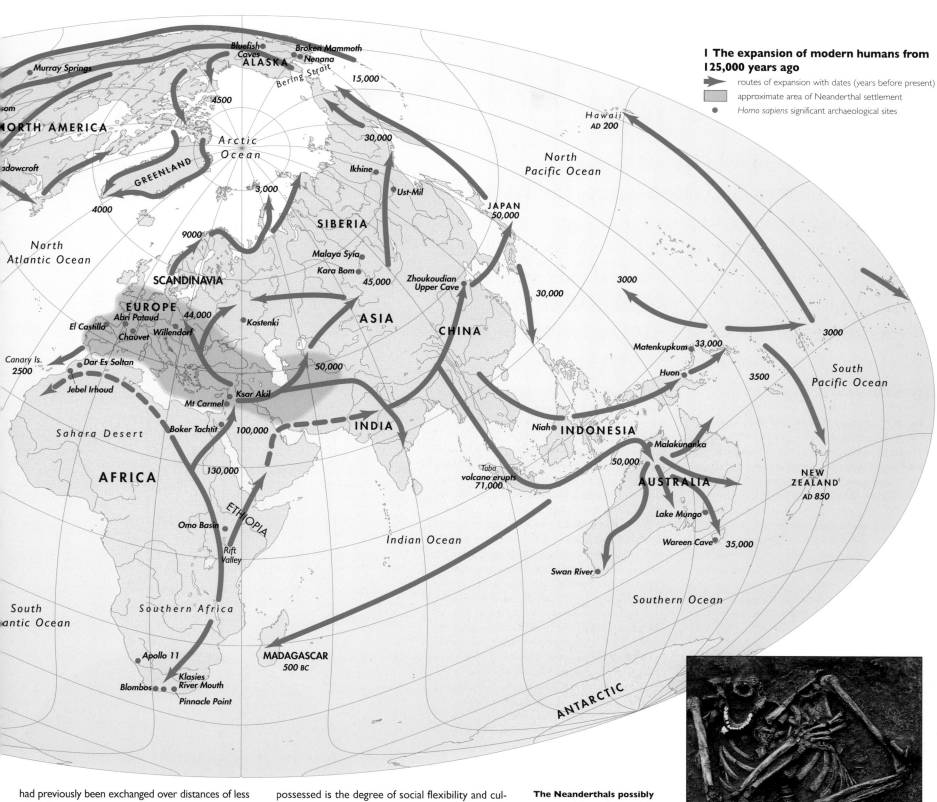

I The expansion of modern humans from 125,000 years ago
→ routes of expansion with dates (years before present)
▨ approximate area of Neanderthal settlement
• *Homo sapiens* significant archaeological sites

had previously been exchanged over distances of less than 60km (40 miles), were now exchanged over hundreds of kilometres. The same is true for shells; Mediterranean shells are found in archaeological sites deep in Eastern and Central Europe.

The Neanderthals

Homo sapiens was by no means the only human species in the world of 50,000 years ago. In East and Southeast Asia lived the descendants of those *Homo erectus* populations who had colonized the region over a million years earlier. Among all extinct hominin populations the best known are the Neanderthals, distinguished from modern humans by their distinctive large and low-crowned heads with prominent brows and big teeth and powerful stocky bodies well adapted to cold. By contrast, the incoming modern people had an African body pattern – slender with long legs and small torsos – that copes better with heat stress. The Neanderthals had brains as large as modern humans and were in many ways highly successful. They adapted well to a wide range of habitats and climates ranging from the relatively arid Middle East to the cold of central Europe; their use of tools was sophisticated; and they were effective hunters of animals in prime condition such as bison, horse and reindeer. Some Neanderthals buried their dead. Neanderthals did not use personal ornaments or produce art, with the exception of some of the very latest Neanderthals after contact with dispersing modern humans. They almost certainly had language, too. But what the Neanderthals seem not to have

possessed is the degree of social flexibility and cultural tradition that more than any other characteristic singles out *Homo sapiens* and explains our ultimate success in becoming the only global hominin.

This social and intellectual sophistication reveals itself in a number of ways but the result of it was almost always the same: the evolution of more complex social relations which allowed early humans to thrive in a much wider range of habitats and societies than previous hominin species had managed before. Whether living in large or small groups, *Homo sapiens* was able to overcome its environment to an unprecedented degree. The most striking evidence is provided by the wide variety of artefacts that have been discovered: engraved stones, ornaments, figurines, exotic shells, amber and ivory and, most famously, cave paintings. That the latter were frequently inaccessible and could have been seen only with ladders and artificial light suggests that a variety of factors motivated their creators. Whatever the explanation, these early works of art are an evocative monument to the humanity of these early hunter-gatherers.

It is significant that the Neanderthals had almost no cultural traditions of this kind. A few incised bones have been found; similarly, the very occasional exotic piece of raw material occurs. By about 30,000 years ago all non-modern hominins, including Neanderthals and Denisovans, were extinct. Modern humans had already colonized Australia 20,000 years before, and were set to colonize the Americas before 12,000 years ago. Henceforth modern humans were the sole surviving hominin in the world.

The Neanderthals possibly represent the earliest hominin species who took care of one another. The 60,000 year-old skeleton of a powerfully built male found at Kebara Cave in Israel **(right)** had been carefully placed in a shallow grave. Elsewhere, at La Chapelle-aux-Saints in France **(below right top)** and at Shanidar in Iraq **(below right bottom)**, individuals have been discovered who suffered from a number of complaints – severe arthritis, broken bones, blindness. Although few are likely to have lived much beyond 40, they would have needed the help of others to obtain food and, in the case of those with broken bones which subsequently healed, while they were recuperating..

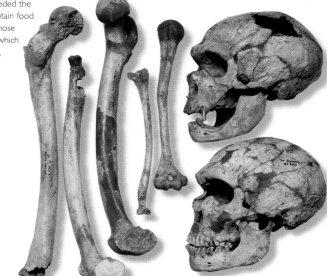

The Ice Age world

By 10,000 years ago, humans had colonized almost the whole of the habitable world. It was an achievement made in the face of the last of a series of Ice Ages, when vast sheets of ice periodically advanced and retreated. The human species today is the product of this long process of adaptation to the varied conditions of the Ice Ages.

THERE HAVE BEEN EIGHT Ice Ages in the last 800,000 years, each interspersed with warmer periods of about 10,000 years known as interglacials, brief and extreme parts of this cycle. The Ice Ages were periods of exceptional cold away from the equator. Ice sheets advanced across the frozen wastes of the northern hemisphere as temperatures fell by up to 15 degrees centigrade. With so much of the earth's water locked into the ice sheets, sea levels fell by up to 150m (500ft). As they did so, land bridges and large coastal plains appeared, linking many major land areas and present-day islands into larger continental land masses.

Equatorial regions were also affected: as rainfall diminished, half the land area between the tropics became became desert and semi-desert. With each advance of the ice, the plants and animals of the northern hemisphere withdrew to warmer latitudes. As the ice retreated, so they moved northwards again. Humans, too, must have migrated with these changing climates. Yet despite the extremes of cold, the human species continued to develop, spreading from its original African homeland to East and southeast Asia and to Europe. Mastery of fire and the invention of clothing were crucial to this achievement, as were new social and communication skills.

Ice Age humans

The height of the last Ice Age or LGM (last glacial maximum) was reached about 20,000 years ago. As the ice expanded, human populations contracted into a small number of more favourable habitats. Across almost the whole of the Eurasian landmass between the ice to the north and the deserts to the south, from the glacial cul-de-sac of Alaska to southern France, productive grasslands and steppes were created. Rich in seasonal grasses, they sustained large herds of mammoth, bison, horse and reindeer, all of them important food sources for Palaeolithic hunters.

Much the same sort of habitat seems to have developed in North America. By the time modern humans migrated there about 15,000 years ago, the rolling grasslands were teeming with animal life: including bison, camels, mastodons and mammoths. So effectively did the new human population hunt them that by about 10,000 years ago almost all of them were extinct, including the horse, re-introduced to the New World only by Europeans following in the wake of Columbus.

South of the Eurasian mammoth steppe lay an extensive zone of drier conditions. Indeed parts of the Sahara, the Near East and India became almost entirely arid, forcing their populations along permanent watercourses such as the Nile. Similar patterns of settlement are found in Australia, where cemeteries discovered along the Murray river bear marked resemblances to those along the Nile.

In Europe modern humans appeared earlier in eastern and central Europe (about 48,000 years ago) than in western Europe (about 43,000 years ago). In southwest France, the Pyrenees and northern Spain, hundreds of caves decorated with paintings of symbols and animals have been discovered, evidence of a rich cultural tradition.

By 12,000 years ago, the last Ice Age was drawing to a close. As temperatures rose, vegetation spread and animals re-colonized the cold northern wastes. With them went hunters and gatherers. By 10,000 BC in Central America and the Near East, people had begun to move beyond their existing resources and to investigate new ways of producing food and manipulating plants and animals in the first experiments in farming.

3 The peopling of the Americas, c. 13,000 years BC

- maximum extent of ice caps
- → routes of colonization
- • sites inhabited 13,000–10,000 years BC

3 It was only about 15,000 years ago that the first humans migrated to the Americas (map above). As the Bering Strait emerged as dry land, so humans colonized the Americas and gradually moved south as the ice melted and sea levels rose again. By 12,000 years ago they had reached the southern tip of South America.

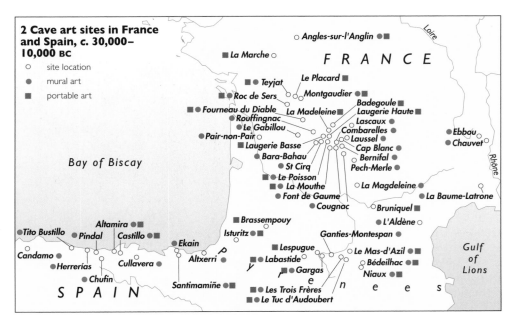

2 Cave art sites in France and Spain, c. 30,000–10,000 BC

- ○ site location
- ● mural art
- ■ portable art

FRANCE

○ Angles-sur-l'Anglin ●■
■ La Marche ○
Loire
■ ● Teyjat
■ Roc de Sers ○ Le Placard ■
○ ● Montgaudier ●
■ ● Fourneau du Diable ■ Badegoule ■
● Rouffignac La Madeleine ■ Laugerie Haute ■
■ ● Le Gabillou Lascaux ●
■ Pair-non-Pair Combarelles ■
● Laussel ● Ebbou
■ Laugerie Basse Cap Blanc ● Chauvet
● Bara-Bahau Bernifal ■
● St Cirq Pech-Merle ■
■ Le Poisson
● La Mouthe ○ La Magdeleine
■ Font de Gaume ■ La Baume-Latrone
● Cougnac ■ Bruniquel ■
■ Brassempouy ● L'Aldène ○
Isturitz ■○ Ganties-Montespan ●
Altamira ■■
○ Tito Bustillo Pindal Castillo ■ ● Le Mas-d'Azil ○
Candamo ● ○ Ekain ■ Lespugue ● Bédeilhac ■
● Herrerias Altxerri ● ● Labastide ○ Niaux ■
● Chufin ● Gargas
Santimamiñe ●■ ■ ● Les Trois Frères
■ Le Tuc d'Audoubert

Bay of Biscay

SPAIN

Rhône

Gulf of Lions

2 Small or "portable" works of art have been found throughout the area inhabited by European hunters between about 30,000 and 10,000 years ago. These include sculptures and engravings of animals on bone and antler and thousands of engravings on small stone plaques. Very occasionally the engravings take the form of abstract patterns of lines and dots, or sequences of notches or grooves. Decorated ornaments were also made, such as fine carved amber swan pendants from Russia or cut beads of ivory and antler from the same region. Venus figurines are particularly striking. These pieces are carved in the round and are representations of a highly striking female form with exaggerated breasts and buttocks. An analogous style is found in cave art where bas-relief engravings of Venuses, perhaps representations of the mother goddess, have been discovered. Portable works of art have been discovered across Europe. The bulk of cave art from the period is, however, in the valleys of the Vézère and Dordogne in southwest France, the Pyrenees and the Cantabrian Mountains of northern Spain, though paintings and engravings have also been found in sites far beyond these areas (map left).

The sophistication of Ice Age artists is amply attested by this delicately carved and elegant female head, found at Brassempouy in southwest France (above). No more than 3.5cm (1¼in) high, it dates from about 20,000 years ago.

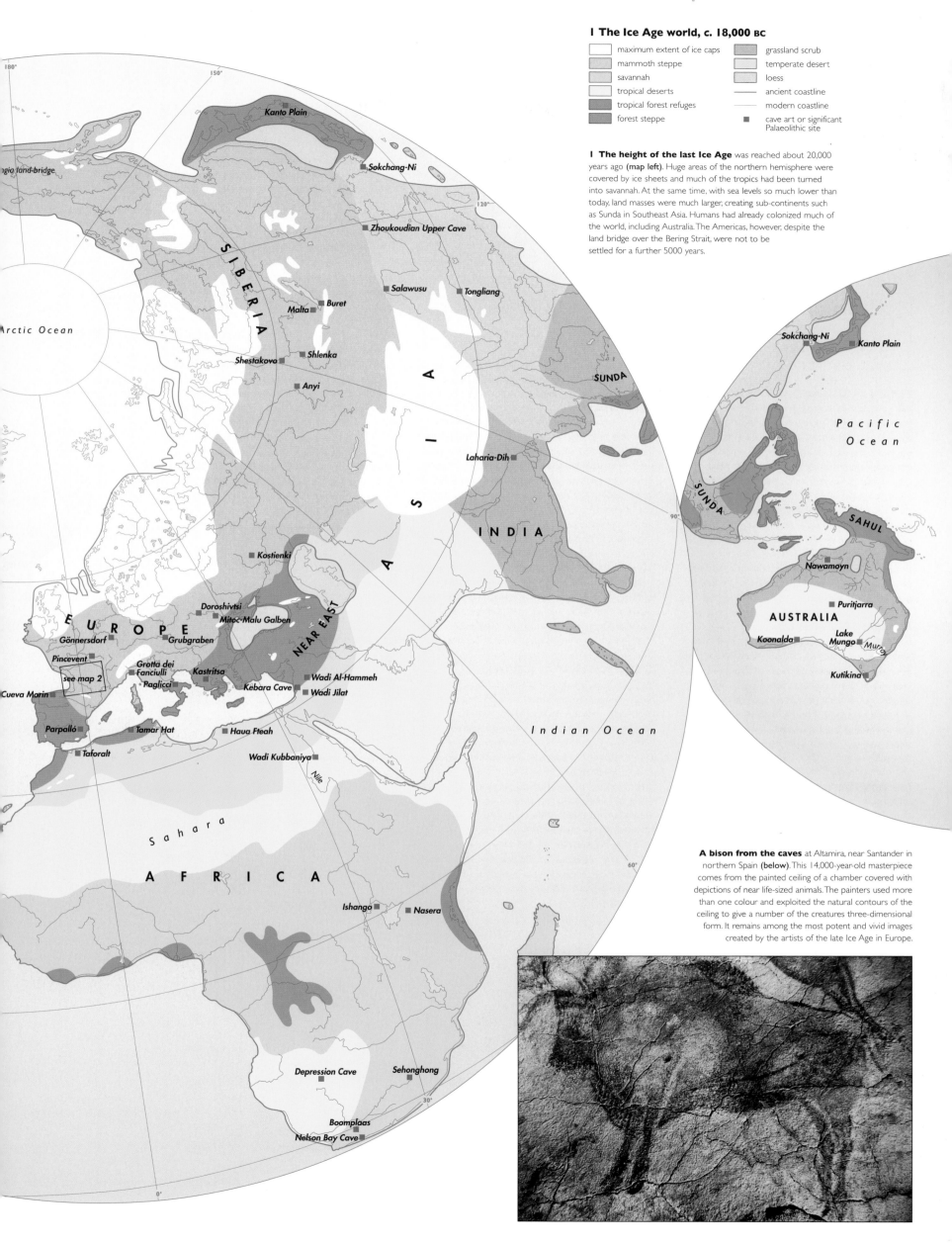

Kanto Plain

1 The Ice Age world, *c.* 18,000 BC

☐ maximum extent of ice caps	grassland scrub
mammoth steppe	temperate desert
savannah	loess
tropical deserts	— ancient coastline
tropical forest refuges	— modern coastline
forest steppe	■ cave art or significant Palaeolithic site

1 The height of the last Ice Age was reached about 20,000 years ago **(map left)**. Huge areas of the northern hemisphere were covered by ice sheets and much of the tropics had been turned into savannah. At the same time, with sea levels so much lower than today, land masses were much larger, creating sub-continents such as Sunda in Southeast Asia. Humans had already colonized much of the world, including Australia. The Americas, however, despite the land bridge over the Bering Strait, were not to be settled for a further 5000 years.

Kanto Plain

Sokchang-Ni

Zhoukoudian Upper Cave

S I B E R I A

Salawusu   Tongliang

Malta ■ Buret

Shestakova   ■ Shlenka

■ Anyi

Arctic Ocean

ngia land-bridge

A S I A

SUNDA

Laharia-Dih

INDIA

■ Kostienki

■ Doroshivtsi
■ Mitoc-Malu Galben

E U R O P E
Gönnersdorf   ■ Grubgraben

NEAR EAST

Pincevent
see map 2   Grotta dei Fanciulli
Paglicci   ■ Kastritsa
Cueva Morin   Kebara Cave   ■ Wadi Al-Hammeh
■ Wadi Jilat

Parpalló   ■ Tamar Hat   ■ Haua Fteah
■ Taforalt

Wadi Kubbaniya

Nile

S a h a r a

A F R I C A

Indian Ocean

Ishango   ■ Nasera

Depression Cave   Sehonghong

Boomplaas
Nelson Bay Cave

Pacific Ocean

Sokchang-Ni   ■ Kanto Plain

SUNDA   SAHUL

Nawamoyn

AUSTRALIA   ■ Puritjarra

Koonalda   Lake Mungo   Murox

Kutikina

A bison from the caves at Altamira, near Santander in northern Spain **(below)**. This 14,000-year-old masterpiece comes from the painted ceiling of a chamber covered with depictions of near life-sized animals. The painters used more than one colour and exploited the natural contours of the ceiling to give a number of the creatures three-dimensional form. It remains among the most potent and vivid images created by the artists of the late Ice Age in Europe.

From foraging to farming: the origins of agriculture

The transition from hunting and gathering to agriculture irreversibly changed human society, but it involved the domestication of relatively few plants and animals and occurred independently in a very few areas. The earliest evidence of agriculture comes from the Levant 10,000 years ago, from where it spread to Europe, northern Africa and central Asia.

TEN THOUSAND YEARS AGO, at the end of the last Ice Age, the entire world population numbered only a few millions and all their food came from wild plants and animals. Then people began to domesticate some species, so that today the vast majority of humans depend for food on a relatively small range of crops and domestic animals. During the 150,000 years that preceded the "agricultural revolution", anatomically modern humans had colonized most of the the globe (see p. 32) and had learned to survive as foragers, subsisting on a great diversity of plant and animal foods. Foragers moved seasonally in small groups to obtain their food supplies and population densities remained low for tens of thousands of years.

Foraging to farming

By 8000 BC, some groups of foragers had settled down and occupied favourable sites year-round. Their populations increased, as restraints on fertility imposed by the seasonally mobile way of life were relaxed, and they ranged less far for their food. This profound change in human behaviour led to the beginnings of agriculture, enabling more people to be supported on a given area of land – although at the cost of the greater effort needed to cultivate crops and raise domestic animals. The effects of settling down, population increase, and growing dependence on agriculture led to increases in the number and size of settlements, to social changes including the development of more complex, less egalitarian societies, and, eventually, to urban life and civilization.

The earliest evidence of agriculture consists of the remains of wild species that have been altered in their morphology or behaviour by human intervention. Foremost among the crops are the cereals and pulses (peas, beans and other herbaceous legumes), the seeds of which provide carbohydrate and some protein and are easily stored. They sustained early civilizations and are still staples today. They were domesticated from wild grasses in subtropical regions, for example wheat, barley, lentil, pea and chickpea in southwestern Asia; rice, soya and mung bean in southern and eastern Asia; sorghum, other millets and cowpea in tropical Africa; and maize and the common bean in Mexico. Root crops have also become staples in many areas, such as the potato, which was domesticated in the Andes and is now a major crop of temperate areas, and manioc (cassava), yams, taro and sweet potato, all of which were native to the tropics.

Domestication of animals

Whereas cereals and root crops were brought into cultivation and domesticated in all the habitable continents except Australia (where agriculture was introduced by European settlers in the 18th century AD), animals were domesticated in relatively few areas, principally in western Asia, where there is evidence for the early domestication of sheep, goats, pigs and cattle, followed later by asses, horses and camels. Some forms of cattle and pigs, as well as chickens, were domesticated in southern and eastern Asia, and cattle

and pigs may also have been domesticated independently in Europe. Very few animals were domesticated in the Americas – turkey in North America and llama, alpaca and guinea pig in South America – and none in tropical Africa or Australia.

The spread of farming

The earliest known transition to agriculture took place in the "Fertile Crescent" of southwestern Asia during the Neolithic period starting about 8000 BC. Sites in the Levant have yielded charred seeds and chaff of barley, wheat and various pulses, as well as the bones of domestic goats and sheep. Grain cultivation began here about 1000 years before goat and sheep pastoralism. Dependence on agriculture increased very gradually, paralleled by the spread of village settlement, the development of techniques of irrigation and terracing, and the cultivation of fruits. By the end of the Neolithic in southwestern Asia, about 6000 years ago, agriculture had spread west and east into Europe, northern Africa and central and southern Asia.

People began to domesticate plants and animals independently in China between 7000 and 6000 BC, in the Americas by about 3000 BC and in tropical Africa by about 2000 BC. By the time of the 16th century AD European expansion in the agricultural and pastoral economies occupied most of Eurasia, Africa and Central and South America.

c. 8000 BC Foragers using sites year-round

c. 8000 BC Evidence of domesticated cereals and pulses in the Levant

c. 7000 BC Evidence of rice cultivation in China

c. 4000 BC Agriculture established across Europe

c. 3000 BC Evidence of maize cultivation in Mesoamerica

c. 3000 BC Evidence of tree crop cultivation in tropical Africa

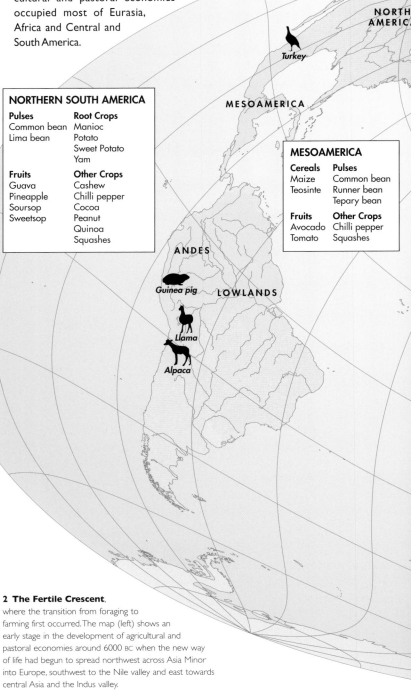

NORTHERN SOUTH AMERICA

Pulses	Root Crops
Common bean	Manioc
Lima bean	Potato
	Sweet Potato
	Yam

Fruits	Other Crops
Guava	Cashew
Pineapple	Chilli pepper
Soursop	Cocoa
Sweetsop	Peanut
	Quinoa
	Squashes

MESOAMERICA

Cereals	Pulses
Maize	Common bean
Teosinte	Runner bean
	Tepary bean

Fruits	Other Crops
Avocado	Chilli pepper
Tomato	Squashes

2 The Fertile Crescent, where the transition from foraging to farming first occurred. The map (left) shows an early stage in the development of agricultural and pastoral economies around 6000 BC when the new way of life had begun to spread northwest across Asia Minor into Europe, southwest to the Nile valley and east towards central Asia and the Indus valley.

2 The Fertile Crescent and the origins of agriculture

- irrigation agriculture
- agriculture and pastoralism
- pastoralism

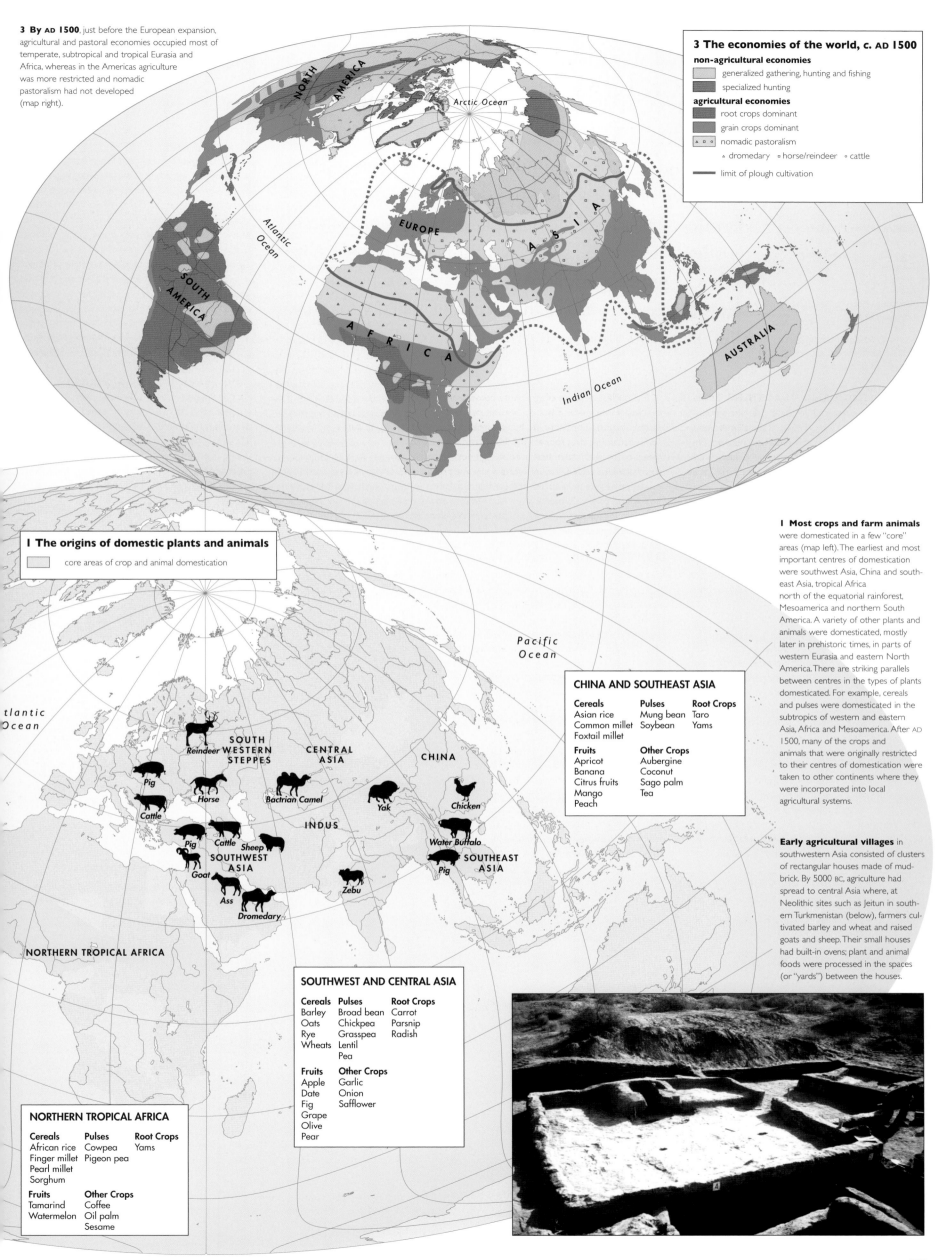

3 By AD 1500, just before the European expansion, agricultural and pastoral economies occupied most of temperate, subtropical and tropical Eurasia and Africa, whereas in the Americas agriculture was more restricted and nomadic pastoralism had not developed (map right).

3 The economies of the world, c. AD 1500

non-agricultural economies
- generalized gathering, hunting and fishing
- specialized hunting

agricultural economies
- root crops dominant
- grain crops dominant
- nomadic pastoralism
  - ▲ dromedary ▫ horse/reindeer ○ cattle
- —— limit of plough cultivation

NORTH AMERICA
Arctic Ocean
EUROPE
ASIA
Atlantic Ocean
SOUTH AMERICA
AFRICA
Indian Ocean
AUSTRALIA

1 The origins of domestic plants and animals
- core areas of crop and animal domestication

Pacific Ocean

Atlantic Ocean

1 Most crops and farm animals were domesticated in a few "core" areas (map left). The earliest and most important centres of domestication were southwest Asia, China and southeast Asia, tropical Africa north of the equatorial rainforest, Mesoamerica and northern South America. A variety of other plants and animals were domesticated, mostly later in prehistoric times, in parts of western Eurasia and eastern North America. There are striking parallels between centres in the types of plants domesticated. For example, cereals and pulses were domesticated in the subtropics of western and eastern Asia, Africa and Mesoamerica. After AD 1500, many of the crops and animals that were originally restricted to their centres of domestication were taken to other continents where they were incorporated into local agricultural systems.

Early agricultural villages in southwestern Asia consisted of clusters of rectangular houses made of mud-brick. By 5000 BC, agriculture had spread to central Asia where, at Neolithic sites such as Jeitun in southern Turkmenistan (below), farmers cultivated barley and wheat and raised goats and sheep. Their small houses had built-in ovens; plant and animal foods were processed in the spaces (or "yards") between the houses.

Reindeer
SOUTH WESTERN STEPPES
CENTRAL ASIA
CHINA
Pig
Horse
Bactrian Camel
Yak
Chicken
Cattle
INDUS
Pig Cattle Sheep
Water Buffalo
SOUTHWEST ASIA
SOUTHEAST ASIA
Goat
Pig
Ass
Zebu
Dromedary

NORTHERN TROPICAL AFRICA

CHINA AND SOUTHEAST ASIA

Cereals	Pulses	Root Crops
Asian rice	Mung bean	Taro
Common millet	Soybean	Yams
Foxtail millet		

Fruits	Other Crops
Apricot	Aubergine
Banana	Coconut
Citrus fruits	Sago palm
Mango	Tea
Peach	

SOUTHWEST AND CENTRAL ASIA

Cereals	Pulses	Root Crops
Barley	Broad bean	Carrot
Oats	Chickpea	Parsnip
Rye	Grasspea	Radish
Wheats	Lentil	
	Pea	

Fruits	Other Crops
Apple	Garlic
Date	Onion
Fig	Safflower
Grape	
Olive	
Pear	

NORTHERN TROPICAL AFRICA

Cereals	Pulses	Root Crops
African rice	Cowpea	Yams
Finger millet	Pigeon pea	
Pearl millet		
Sorghum		

Fruits	Other Crops
Tamarind	Coffee
Watermelon	Oil palm
	Sesame

Before the first cities: southwest Asia

The period 10,000 to 4000 BC witnessed three critical developments: the origins of settled life; the first farming; and the first cities. The origin of agriculture is often referred to as the "Neolithic revolution", but archaeology reveals only gradual changes in techniques of food acquisition over thousands of years, which by 8000 BC led to villages dependent on food production.

THE EARLIEST CHANGES visible in the archaeological record relate not to food production but to social relations, indicated not only in the tendency to reside in one location over longer periods and in the investment of labour in more substantial and more permanent structures, but also in the growth of ritual, an important factor in social cohesion. Indeed it is possible that this "symbolic revolution" was of greater immediate significance than the economic changes we associate with the origins of agriculture.

Lakeshore and riverine sites were important for their rich and varied resources, while the utilitarian date palm flourished in marsh areas in southern Mesopotamia, rich also in fish and waterfowl. The earliest permanent settlements tend to be found at the junctions of discrete environmental zones, with greater access to a variety of resources (for example Abu Hureyra on the boundary of the dry steppe and the Euphrates flood plain, and Ain Mallaha in the Jordan valley). The importance of ritual house fittings and skull cults, perhaps suggestive of the increasing importance of the family and property, is attested at some of the earliest sites (Qermez Dere), while 9th-millennium villages in Anatolia, with early evidence for the cultivation of cereals, contain impressive ritual buildings (Çayönü, Nevali Çori). The carving of stone (Göbekli Tepe, Jerf al Ahmar, Nemrik) and the working of copper (Çayönü) are found well before the appearance of true farming villages. The early use of clay for containers is attested at Mureybet on the Euphrates (9000 BC) and at Ganj Dareh in the Zagros; white lime plaster vessels are characteristic of the latest pre-pottery Neolithic phases, especially at sites in the Levant and Anatolia.

The development of villages

Among the best-known pre-pottery Neolithic sites is Jericho, in the 9th millennium BC already a settlement of some 1.5ha (4 acres) with, uniquely, a rock-cut ditch and stone wall with a huge circular tower ascended by means of an internal circular stair. A millennium later Basta and Ain Ghazal in Jordan are farming settlements of over 9.5ha (24 acres). Human skulls on which faces

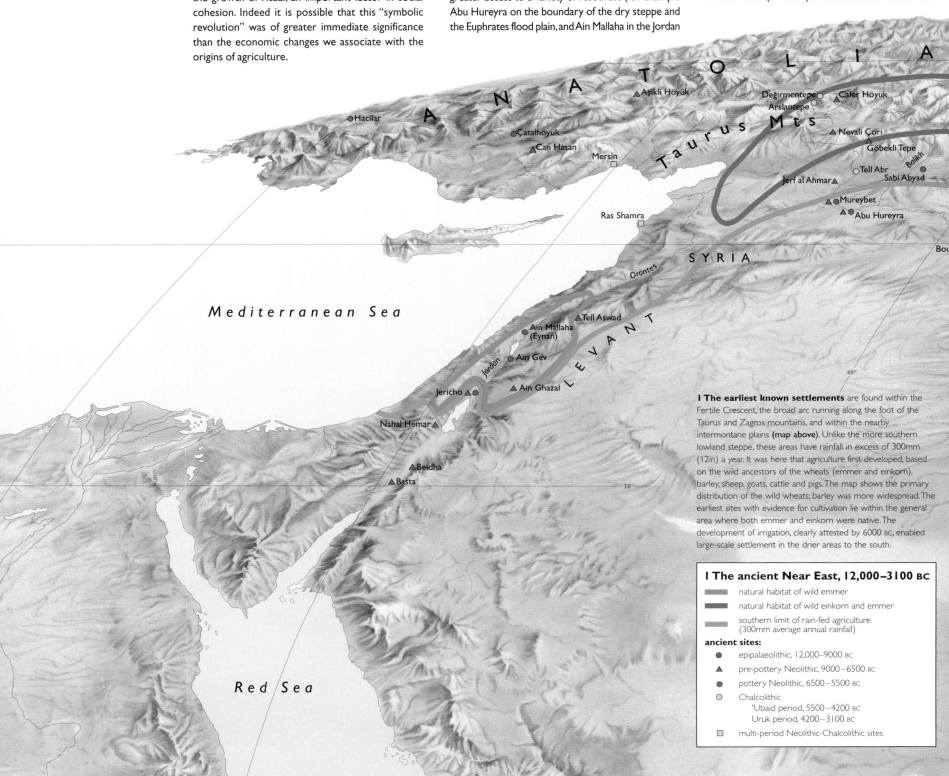

1 **The earliest known settlements** are found within the Fertile Crescent, the broad arc running along the foot of the Taurus and Zagros mountains, and within the nearby intermontane plains **(map above)**. Unlike the more southern lowland steppe, these areas have rainfall in excess of 300mm (12in) a year. It was here that agriculture first developed, based on the wild ancestors of the wheats (emmer and einkorn), barley, sheep, goats, cattle and pigs. The map shows the primary distribution of the wild wheats; barley was more widespread. The earliest sites with evidence for cultivation lie within the general area where both emmer and einkorn were native. The development of irrigation, clearly attested by 6000 BC, enabled large-scale settlement in the drier areas to the south.

1 The ancient Near East, 12,000–3100 BC

- natural habitat of wild emmer
- natural habitat of wild einkorn and emmer
- southern limit of rain-fed agriculture (300mm average annual rainfall)

ancient sites:
- ● epipalaeolithic, 12,000–9000 BC
- ▲ pre-pottery Neolithic, 9000–6500 BC
- ● pottery Neolithic, 6500–5500 BC
- ○ Chalcolithic
    'Ubaid period, 5500–4200 BC
    Uruk period, 4200–3100 BC
- □ multi-period Neolithic-Chalcolithic sites

had been realistically modelled were kept by the inhabitants of these sites, while at Ain Ghazal deposits of cultic statues have been recovered.

In the 7th and 6th millennia BC, developed Neolithic villages appear over much of the landscape. They are characterized by economies dependent on domesticated plants and animals, and on sophisticated technological developments (for example an "industrial" area of two-stage pottery kilns, and the presence of lead and copper at Yarim Tepe around 6000 BC). Well-fired painted pottery characterizes these villages, which are often classified by their ceramic styles. One of the most spectacular early pottery sites is Çatalhöyük, 13ha (32 acres) in area, with extensive evidence for wealth in the form of valuable commodities such as obsidian and semi-precious stones. The house fittings bear elaborate ornaments including wall paintings and the plastered skulls of wild cattle.

Trade and temples

An important development attested in the Neolithic villages of north Mesopotamia and Syria is the earliest record-keeping, effected by the use of combinations of small clay tokens and the stamping of distinctive clay or stone seals onto clay lids and other fastenings (most importantly at Sabi Abyad in the Samarran period and slightly later at Arpachiyah). Such simple methods of validating social contracts and other transactions formed the basis of later literate urban recording systems.

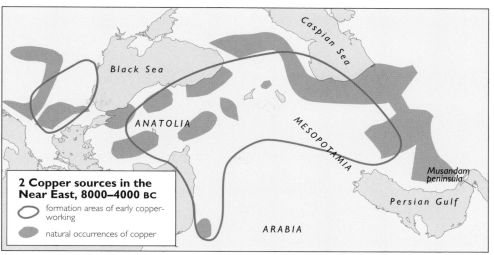

2 Copper sources in the Near East, 8000–4000 BC
- formation areas of early copper-working
- natural occurrences of copper

Mesopotamia had no metals or semi-precious stones, and by the 5th millennium BC demand for such luxury goods led to the establishment of small colonies in Anatolia, even as far as the Malatya plain (Değirmentepe) and the sea-borne exploitation of the resources of the Persian Gulf (Dosariyah, Abu Khamis), even as far as the Musandam peninsula. The first temples were built at this time in southern Mesopotamia, precursors of the institutions around which the earliest urban states were organized. There was a temple on the same site at Eridu for 3500 years, striking evidence of the continuity of tradition which was one remarkable feature of the world's earliest city-states.

Despite their precocious development, sites like Jericho and Çatalhöyük did not form the focus of more complex polities. By 4000 BC the foundations of literate, urban civilization had been laid in Mesopotamia, where it was the organizational and economic potential of the highly productive irrigation economy in the south and the powerful, strategic positions of sites like Nineveh in the north, controlling access to areas rich in raw materials, that saw the growth of the world's first complex states.

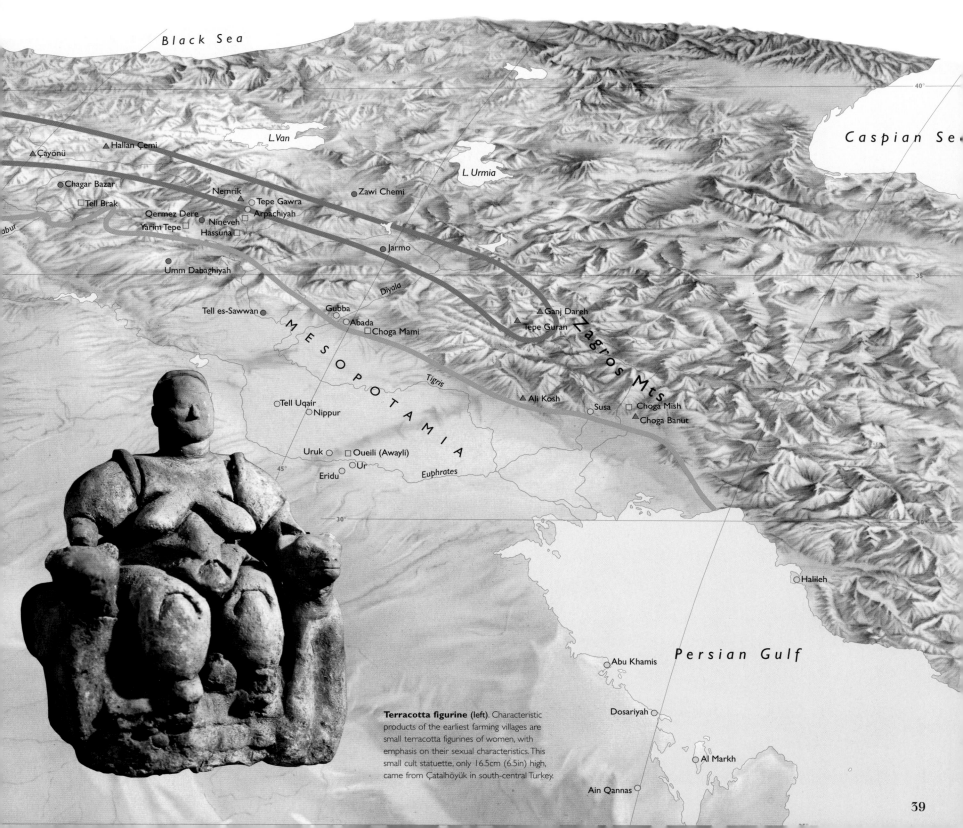

Terracotta figurine (left). Characteristic products of the earliest farming villages are small terracotta figurines of women, with emphasis on their sexual characteristics. This small cult statuette, only 16.5cm (6.5in) high, came from Çatalhöyük in south-central Turkey.

Early Europe:
the colonization of a continent

7000 BC First agricultural settlement of Europe

5000 BC Agriculture reaches Iberian Peninsula and the Low Countries

4500 BC Beginning of significant copper production in the Balkans

4000 BC Agricultural economy in Britain and southern Scandinavia

3500 BC Spread of cart and plough across Europe

3000 BC Megalithic tombs in western Europe

2000 BC Beginning of large-scale tin-bronze production in central Europe

Farming first spread from the Near East to southeast Europe c. 7000 BC and then along the Mediterranean coast and across central Europe, reaching the Low Countries by 5000 BC. After a brief pause it spread to Britain and northern continental Europe by 4000 BC. It was only c. 2000 BC that farming reached the more northerly parts of European Russia and the Baltic.

2 Megalithic monuments (map below). The farmers of the loess lands built their houses and cult-centres of wood. Further west, while houses continued to be built mostly of wood, public monuments were constructed from large undressed boulders or slabs of stone. Such monuments, built to serve many generations, were mainly concerned with mortuary rituals and ancestor-worship. Three or four main areas began independently to build simple structures, but as the monuments grew more elaborate, ideas and techniques were exchanged.

THE EARLIEST FARMING VILLAGES in Europe, dating to immediately after 7000 BC, were on the western side of the Aegean (eg Argissa) and on Crete (eg Knossos), but by 5500 BC such villages were distributed widely across the Balkans. They consisted of clusters of mudbrick buildings, each with a similar layout of hearth and cooking and sleeping areas. Their economy was based on keeping sheep and cultivating wheat and legumes. Such villages were situated in areas of good soil with a plentiful water supply and were often occupied for hundreds of years.

Agricultural villages
Villages of this kind spread inland as far as Hungary but from here northwards a new pattern developed. The mudbrick dwellings were replaced by wooden longhouses whose remains did not build up into settlement mounds. Agricultural settlement spread in a broad band from northeast France to southwest

Russia on soils produced by the weathering of loess – a highly fertile windblown dust laid down during the Ice Age. Over this area the characteristic pottery was decorated with incised lines in spiral or meandering bands, a uniformity which reflects the rapid spread of settlement between 5500 and 5000 BC. Cattle were more important than sheep in the forested interior of Europe but wheat continued as the main cereal crop. The settlers did not clear wide areas of land but practised intensive horticulture in the valleys around their settlements.

At the same time as it was spreading into continental Europe, aspects of an agricultural way of life were also spreading westwards along the northern shore of the Mediterranean, reaching Spain by around 5500 BC; in this zone environmental conditions were much closer to those where agriculture started and fewer adjustments had to be made.

Alongside the early agricultural communities, small groups of foragers pursued their way of life in areas untouched by the new economy. Hunting populations were rather sparse in the areas first selected by agriculturists, and the rapidity with which farming spread across the loess lands may in part reflect a lack of local competition, but elsewhere foragers were more numerous. They were especially well-established in the lake-strewn landscapes left by the retreating ice sheets around the Alps and on the northern edge of the North European Plain.

There has been much debate about whether the spread of agriculture was due to the expansion of colonizing populations from the southeast or to the adoption of the new way of life by existing foragers. Current evidence from archaeology and the analysis of the DNA of modern populations suggests that there was a colonizing element, probably associated with the expansion through the Balkans and the loess lands of central Europe, but that in most of Europe the dominant process was the adoption of agriculture and its material attributes by existing populations, perhaps in part because of the prestige of the new way of life.

Megalithic Europe
In much of western Europe, farming was first adopted around 4000 BC and the clearance of land in rocky terrain provided the opportunity to build large stone (megalithic) monuments as burial places and mortuary shrines for the scattered hamlets of early farmers. Some of the earliest megalithic tombs were built in Brittany and Portugal around 4500 BC, but particularly elaborate forms were made in Ireland and Spain up to 2000 years later. Alongside the tombs, other kinds of megalithic monuments were constructed in some regions, such as the stone circles of the British Isles.

From 4500 to 2500 BC, important developments occurred which were to change the established pattern of life. Early metallurgy of copper and gold developed in the Balkans from 4500 BC, although whether

this was an independent invention or came from the Near East is still in dispute. Fine examples of the products come from the rich Copper Age cemetery of Varna on the Black Sea coast.

From around 3500 BC there is evidence of contact between eastern Europe and the steppe zone north of the Black Sea; some link this to the spread of Indo-European languages to Europe. The time around 3500 BC also saw the rapid spread across Europe of wheeled vehicles and the plough, both associated with the first large-scale use of draught animals. These slowly changed the nature of agricultural production. Widespread

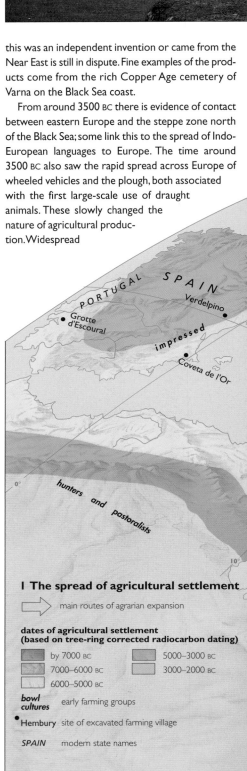

2 Megalithic monuments, 3000 BC
- ● chambered tombs
- ▲ axe factories
- ■ flint mines
- ▨ areas of megalithic chambered tombs

1 The spread of agricultural settlement

⇨ main routes of agrarian expansion

dates of agricultural settlement (based on tree-ring corrected radiocarbon dating)
- by 7000 BC
- 7000–6000 BC
- 6000–5000 BC
- 5000–3000 BC
- 3000–2000 BC

bowl cultures early farming groups

● Hembury site of excavated farming village

SPAIN modern state names

The origins of Stonehenge (below) pre-date those of the "Wessex culture" of rich burials which surround it. But it was a sacred site of such significance that it was maintained for over 1000 years. The work involved in quarrying, transporting and erecting the stones in c. 2500 BC make it one of the most astonishing monuments of prehistoric Europe.

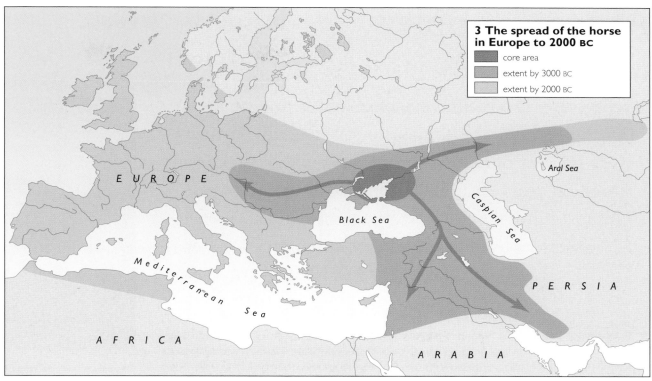

1 Early farmers spread from one side of Europe to the other by two main routes: the Vardar-Danube-Rhine corridor, and the Mediterranean littoral **(map below)**. The former was the more important. Nonetheless, for thousands of years the most densely settled part of Europe was the southeast.

3 Horses seem first to have been domesticated on the steppes of the Ukraine **(map above)** and were initially used for meat or for traction (the pulling of wagons and ploughs). By the end of the 3rd millennium BC they were in widespread use throughout Europe and western Asia, and during the 2nd millennium BC they appear in Egyptian tomb and temple reliefs pulling two-wheeled chariots.

clearance of forests took place and flint mines produced stone for large quantities of axes. It was only after 2000 BC that stone axes were superseded by metal ones in western Europe.

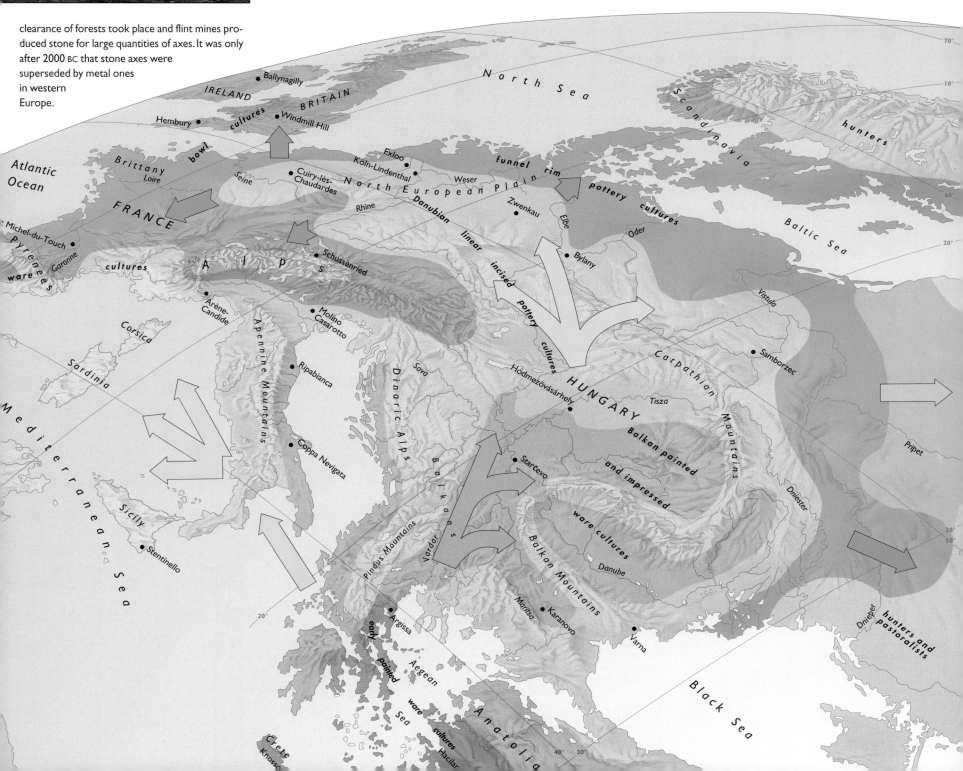

African peoples and cultures

Archaeology is revealing evidence that strongly suggests that the evolution of humans began in Africa. Virtually every stage of our development – stretching back over 5 million years – can be traced in the African record. Almost throughout this vast span of prehistory our ancestors lived in mobile groups engaged in scavenging, gathering and hunting.

FROM ABOUT THE 10TH MILLENNIUM BC onwards, conditions in large parts of Africa were wetter than they are today, and human settlements began to spring up by lakes and rivers, from the Rift valley and Sudanese Nile valley in the east, across what are now the central and southern Saharan regions, to the Senegal River in the west. These earliest African settlements were based on fishing and were characterized by certain shared aspects of material culture, most notably barbed, bone harpoon heads. Such similarities between the disparate settlements have led to the view that

Examples of ancient rock art survive in various parts of Africa and represent an important source of evidence for African prehistory. Dating rock art can be problematic but this example **(above)** from the Messak Plateau in south-western Libya is thought to date from 5000 BC. It belongs to a time when the Sahara, far from being the inhospitable desert it is today, could support nomadic or transhumant cattle-herders and provide grazing and water for their livestock. Cattle are a frequent motif in Saharan rock art, indicating their importance to the prehistoric people who lived here.

c. 6–4 MYA Early hominid evolution in Africa

c. 2.6 MYA Earliest evidence of stone tools

c. 120,000 BP Emergence of *Homo sapiens*

c. 10,000 Beginning of human settlement in Africa

7th millennium BC Earliest evidence of cattle-herding; cereal cultivation in Egypt

4th–3rd millennium BC Dessication of Sahara; domestication of tropical plants; rise of pharaonic Egypt

c. 1720–1550 BC Second Intermediate Period in Egypt; Kerma at the peak of its power

c. 1550–1069 BC New Kingdom Egypt; end of Kerma

c. 900 BC Egypt disunited; rise of Napata

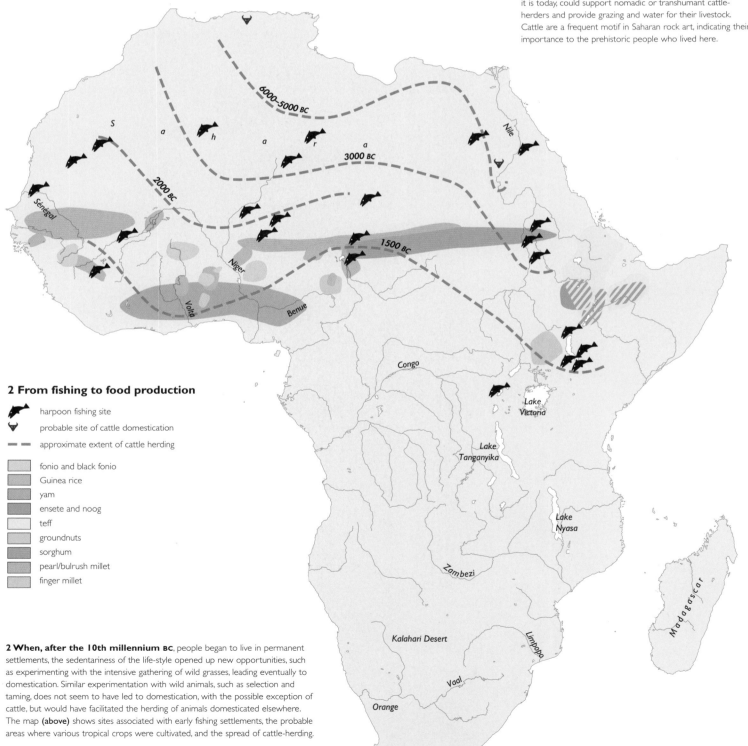

2 From fishing to food production

- harpoon fishing site
- probable site of cattle domestication
- approximate extent of cattle herding
- fonio and black fonio
- Guinea rice
- yam
- ensete and noog
- teff
- groundnuts
- sorghum
- pearl/bulrush millet
- finger millet

2 When, after the 10th millennium BC, people began to live in permanent settlements, the sedentariness of the life-style opened up new opportunities, such as experimenting with the intensive gathering of wild grasses, leading eventually to domestication. Similar experimentation with wild animals, such as selection and taming, does not seem to have led to domestication, with the possible exception of cattle, but would have facilitated the herding of animals domesticated elsewhere. The map **(above)** shows sites associated with early fishing settlements, the probable areas where various tropical crops were cultivated, and the spread of cattle-herding.

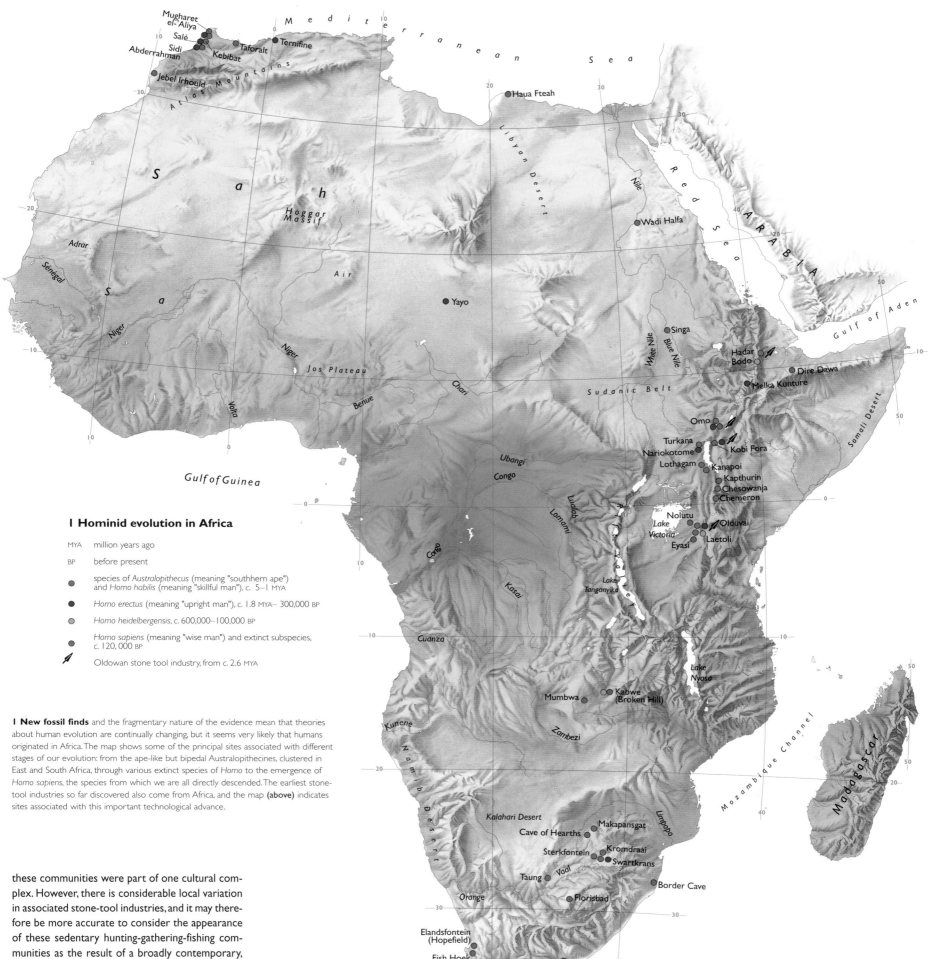

1 Hominid evolution in Africa

MYA   million years ago

BP   before present

●   species of *Australopithecus* (meaning "southhern ape") and *Homo habilis* (meaning "skillful man"), c. 5–1 MYA

●   *Homo erectus* (meaning "upright man"), c. 1.8 MYA– 300,000 BP

◐   *Homo heidelbergensis, c.* 600,000–100,000 BP

●   *Homo sapiens* (meaning "wise man") and extinct subspecies, c. 120,000 BP

➶   Oldowan stone tool industry, from c. 2.6 MYA

1 New fossil finds and the fragmentary nature of the evidence mean that theories about human evolution are continually changing, but it seems very likely that humans originated in Africa. The map shows some of the principal sites associated with different stages of our evolution: from the ape-like but bipedal Australopithecines, clustered in East and South Africa, through various extinct species of *Homo* to the emergence of *Homo sapiens*, the species from which we are all directly descended. The earliest stone-tool industries so far discovered also come from Africa, and the map (**above**) indicates sites associated with this important technological advance.

these communities were part of one cultural complex. However, there is considerable local variation in associated stone-tool industries, and it may therefore be more accurate to consider the appearance of these sedentary hunting-gathering-fishing communities as the result of a broadly contemporary, but independent, adaptation of different groups of people to the changing environment.

It was this ability to adapt to changing circumstances that led to the gradual transition to food production, that is, the cultivation of domesticated plants and herding of domesticated animals. It must be stressed that our current understanding of African food production is far from comprehensive. However, the view that food-producing techniques spread from the Fertile Crescent via the Nile valley to the rest of Africa is no longer tenable as far as plant cultivation (with the exception of wheat and barley) is concerned, and it may not be so for cattle domestication. From the 7th millennium BC onwards there is evidence of cattle-herding in present-day Algeria and the Egyptian Western Desert at Nabta Playa, which may be indicative of local domestication. At about the same time barley, wheat and domestic small stock, such as sheep and goats, were

introduced from the Near East into the Nile delta. In central and southern Sahara early food production involved a move from fishing to livestock herding. The domestication of plants in these regions seems to be associated with progressive dessication after about the 5th millennium BC. As water and grazing land disappeared in the emerging desert, cattle-herding communities dispersed. These climatic and demographic factors initiated, or perhaps accelerated, the independent development of tropical agriculture.

However, it was only in the Nile valley that the advantages of food production led to state formation before about the 1st millennium BC. This is seen most spectacularly in the rise of dynastic Egypt at the end of the 4th millennium; but as early as about

2400 BC there is evidence of a substantial town at Kerma, near the Third Cataract, which includes fortifications, facilities for copper-smelting and eight large mound graves. Because of the many Egyptian artefacts recovered from the site, Kerma was once thought to have been an Egyptian colony. But there is plentiful evidence to support the view that it was a Nubian site and that the indigenous people had a prolonged, primarily commercial, contact with Egypt. Kerma reached a political and cultural peak during Egypt's Second Intermediate Period (c. 1720–1550 BC) but failed to survive the militaristic imperialism of the New Kingdom. The kingdom of Napata, which succeeded Kerma, did not emerge until about 900 BC.

Peoples of the Americas

First colonized by Siberians during the Ice Age, the Americas then developed in complete isolation from the rest of the world. Nonetheless, ways of life and forms of social organization evolved in much the same ways as in the Old World, though languages and customs were distinct as was much of the technology that was developed.

> THE STAPLE FOODS WERE THE INGREDIENTS FOR ... THE HUMAN DESIGN, AND THE WATER WAS FOR THE BLOOD ... OUR FIRST MOTHER-FATHERS ... TALKED AND THEY MADE WORDS ... LOOKED AND LISTENED. THEY WALKED, THEY WORKED.
>
> From the *Popol Vuh*, the sacred book of the Quiché Maya

c. 13,000 BC First human settlement

c. 11,000 BC Mammoth kill near Clovis (North America)

c. 9000 BC Southern tip of South America colonized

c. 3600 BC Mesoamerica: evidence maize cultivated

c. 3000 BC First pottery in America (northern South America)

c. 2000 BC First metal-working in the Central Andes

c. 1750 BC Northernmost Greenland settled

c. 1150 BC Beginnings of Olmec civilization in Mexico

c. 500 BC Foundation of Zapotec capital, Monte Albán, in Mexico

WHEN WERE THE AMERICAS first peopled and by whom? Long controversy is now deepening with the results of new research on genetics. But the general view remains that humans first entered the Americas from Siberia around 15,000 years ago. A second Asiatic immigration in about 8000 BC brought the first speakers of the Na-Dene languages of northern and western North America, and then came the ancestors of the Aleuts and Inuit. From this point on, the Americas remained almost entirely isolated from further human contact until the European discovery of the continent 500 years ago.

Linguistic diversity today shows that these early colonists soon spread. Archaeology confirms that the southernmost tip of South America was inhabited by 9000 BC and northernmost Greenland by 1750 BC (by "Independence" cultures). The way of life – travelling in small bands, gathering, fishing and hunting – encouraged such wide dispersal. Yet in some areas large groups assembled regularly. Buffalo hunts on the Great Plains of North America called for extensive cooperation. Gatherings on this scale would have been annual highlights for the people involved. They continued in remoter areas into the early 1900s, allowing anthropologists to discover something of the organization, knowledge and skills of this largely unchanged way of life.

The first settlements

With the end of the Ice Age, peoples in the temperate and tropical zones of the region came to rely increasingly on both non-migratory prey and migratory wildfowl, on shellfish beds and on seasonal farming, all of which encouraged settled ways of life and population growth. Along the west coast of North America and the southeast coast of South America, fishing was to remain a mainstay but elsewhere – in Mesoamerica, the Central Andes and Amazonia – gathering and hunting gradually declined in favour of farming. Both cause and effect, villages were flourishing in many areas by 1500 BC.

The most widely grown crop was maize, though manioc (cassava) became important in lowland South America and potatoes and cotton in the Andes. Other early crops included gourds, squashes, beans, tomatoes, avocados, chillies and aloes. Turkeys and dogs were kept for food in Mesoamerica, guinea pigs in the Andes. Herding was restricted to the Andes, where llamas were important as pack animals, and both llamas and alpacas were raised for wool.

Settled village life did not preclude long-distance trade. Sea shells and metal tools and ornaments were circulated widely in eastern North America. Pottery provides evidence that sailors ranged along much of the west coast of South America as well as north to Central America. It is not known whether it is diffusion of this kind or a common and older Siberian heritage that explains the cultural similarities widespread among native Americans even today.

Early civilizations

Settled life permitted rising populations. Similarly, the need for farm labour may have encouraged the trend. But how were larger groups to live together? Across the continent, political leaders emerged. They used religious institutions to reflect and mould new forms of organization. Across the eastern half of North America, families gathered around ceremonial earthworks for festivals. Their tombs suggest that funerals were political occasions, too. There is evidence from these burial places of distinctions between rich and poor, governors and governed.

In the Central Andes, temples stood guard over warehouses built to store seasonal surpluses and precious imports. Community assets were the objects not only of local rivalry but of outsiders' jealousy as well. Gruesome sculptures at Cerro Sechín may depict warfare. Later, around 700–400 BC, the Chavín cult transcended local rivalries. Associated with ideas about supernatural spirits, its rites, architecture, sculpture, goldwork and fine textiles were used in many districts, probably partly to justify the privileges of chieftains. These ideas were to last long (see p. 62).

In Mesoamerica during the same period religion was almost certainly used to the same ends by the Olmecs, whose cult was also widespread and also part of a tradition that lived on. Chiefs seem to have claimed pivotal roles in the organization of the cosmos. Earthworks, rock art, sculpture and decorated pottery served the cult and illustrated it. Again probably for the same reasons, the Maya adorned their pyramids with similar religious and political symbols.

All the while, chiefs were supposed not to order their people but to depend on them. The break came in Mexico, in about 500 BC, with the foundation of Monte Albán as a new capital for the Zapotecs. Whether or not this move was prompted by a need for local cooperation in managing water resources or by common interests in defence, it was soon evident – from the site's architecture, its symbolism, and the rulers' effects on the surrounding villages and their conquests further afield – that a more powerful and centralized form of rule had arisen: the state. From the same period at Monte Albán is the earliest evidence for hieroglyphic writing: dated records of conquest.

2 The first millennium BC saw the emergence of a series of increasingly developed societies in Mesoamerica (**map right**). The Gulf of Mexico was the main area of settlement of the Olmecs, though there were major Olmec highland sites, too. The Huastecs to the north seem to have been closely affiliated to the Maya on the Yucatán peninsula. But by 500 BC the Maya had emerged as a distinct group. At the same time, the Zapotecs were also emerging as a distinct culture.

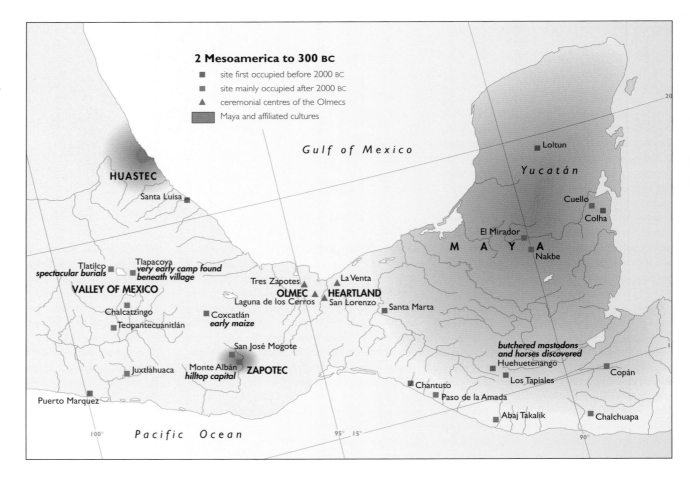

2 Mesoamerica to 300 BC
- ■ site first occupied before 2000 BC
- ■ site mainly occupied after 2000 BC
- ▲ ceremonial centres of the Olmecs
- Maya and affiliated cultures

Gulf of Mexico

HUASTEC
Santa Luisa

Yucatán

Loltun
Cuello
Colha

El Mirador
M A Y A
Nakbe

Tlatilco
spectacular burials
Tlapacoya
very early camp found beneath village
VALLEY OF MEXICO

Tres Zapotes
La Venta
OLMEC ▲ HEARTLAND
Laguna de los Cerros   San Lorenzo
Santa Marta

Chalcatzingo
Coxcatlán
early maize
Teopantecuanitlán

San José Mogote

butchered mastodons and horses discovered
Huehuetenango
Copán
Los Tapiales

Juxtlahuaca
Monte Albán
hilltop capital ZAPOTEC

Chantuto
Paso de la Amada

Puerto Marquez

Abaj Takalik
Chalchuapa

Pacific Ocean

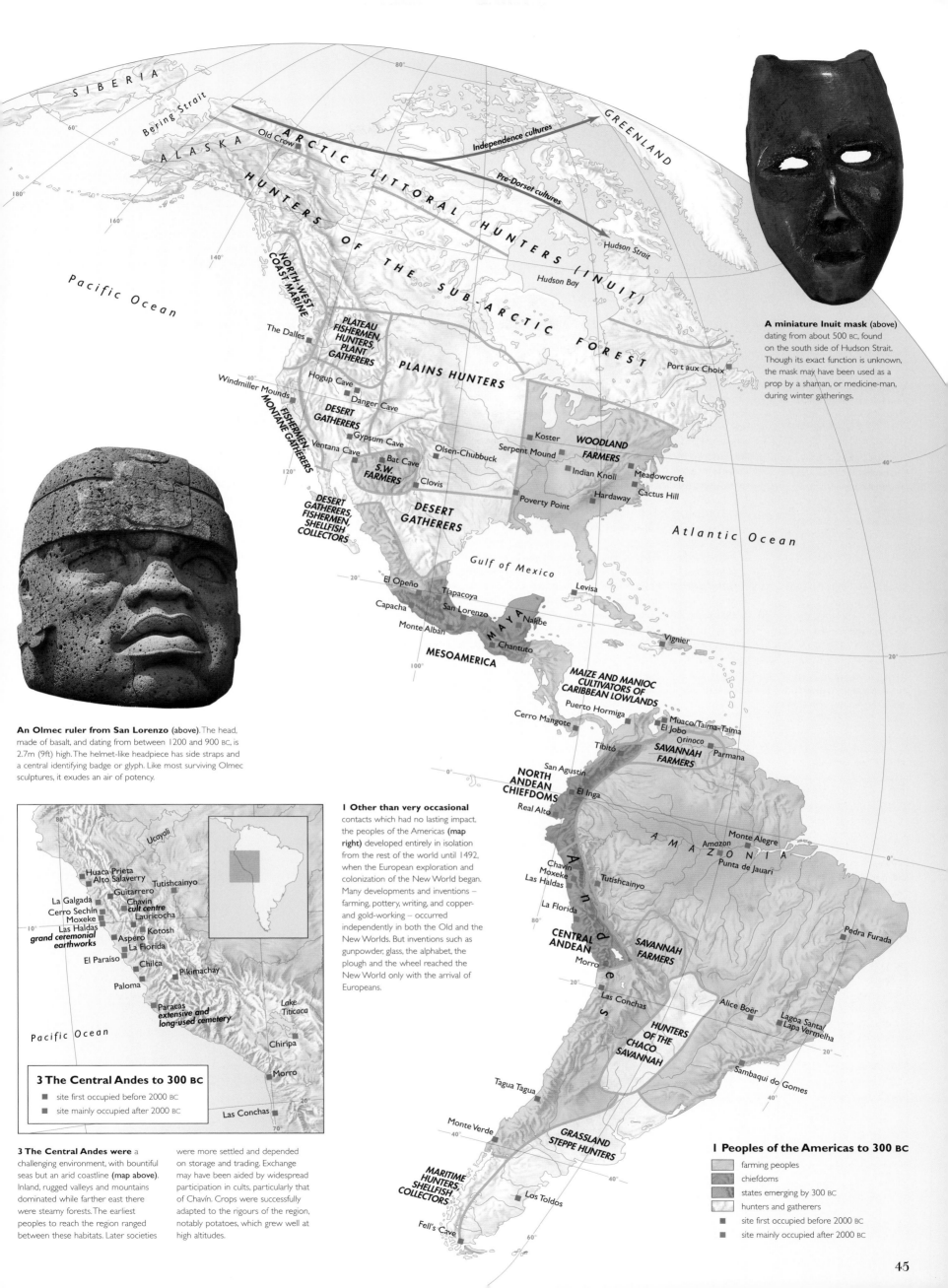

SIBERIA

Bering Strait

GREENLAND

Old Crow

ALASKA

ARCTIC LITTORAL HUNTERS (INUIT)

Independence cultures

HUNTERS OF THE SUB-ARCTIC FOREST

Pre-Dorset cultures

Hudson Strait

Hudson Bay

Pacific Ocean

NORTH WEST COAST MARINE

The Dalles

PLATEAU FISHERMEN, HUNTERS, PLANT GATHERERS

PLAINS HUNTERS

Port aux Choix

Hogup Cave

FISHERMEN MONTANE GATHERERS

Windmiller Mounds

DESERT GATHERERS

Danger Cave

Gypsum Cave

Koster

WOODLAND FARMERS

Ventana Cave

S.W. FARMERS

Bat Cave

Olsen-Chubbock

Serpent Mound

Indian Knoll

Meadowcroft

Clovis

Hardaway

Cactus Hill

DESERT GATHERERS, FISHERMEN, SHELLFISH COLLECTORS

Poverty Point

DESERT GATHERERS

Atlantic Ocean

Gulf of Mexico

El Opeño

Levisa

Capacha

Tlapacoya

San Lorenzo

Nakbe

Monte Alban

MAYA

Vignier

MESOAMERICA

Chantuto

MAIZE AND MANIOC CULTIVATORS OF CARIBBEAN LOWLANDS

Cerro Mangote

Puerto Hormiga

Muaco/Taima-Taima

El Jobo

Orinoco

Tibitó

SAVANNAH FARMERS

Parmana

San Agustín

NORTH ANDEAN CHIEFDOMS

El Inga

Real Alto

AMAZONIA

Monte Alegre

Amazon

Punta de Jauarí

Chavín

Moxeke

Las Haldas

Tutishcainyo

A n d e s

La Florida

Pedra Furada

CENTRAL ANDEAN

Morro

SAVANNAH FARMERS

Las Conchas

Alice Boër

Lagoa Santa
Lapa Vermelha

HUNTERS OF THE CHACO SAVANNAH

Sambaqui do Gomes

Tagua Tagua

Monte Verde

GRASSLAND STEPPE HUNTERS

MARITIME HUNTERS, SHELLFISH COLLECTORS

Los Toldos

Fell's Cave

A miniature Inuit mask (above) dating from about 500 BC, found on the south side of Hudson Strait. Though its exact function is unknown, the mask may have been used as a prop by a shaman, or medicine-man, during winter gatherings.

An Olmec ruler from San Lorenzo (above). The head, made of basalt, and dating from between 1200 and 900 BC, is 2.7m (9ft) high. The helmet-like headpiece has side straps and a central identifying badge or glyph. Like most surviving Olmec sculptures, it exudes an air of potency.

---

1 Other than very occasional contacts which had no lasting impact, the peoples of the Americas (map right) developed entirely in isolation from the rest of the world until 1492, when the European exploration and colonization of the New World began. Many developments and inventions – farming, pottery, writing, and copper- and gold-working – occurred independently in both the Old and the New Worlds. But inventions such as gunpowder, glass, the alphabet, the plough and the wheel reached the New World only with the arrival of Europeans.

Ucayali

Huaca Prieta
Alto Salaverry

Tutishcainyo

Guitarrero

La Galgada

Chavín cult centre

Cerro Sechin

Lauricocha

Moxeke

Las Haldas
grand ceremonial earthworks

Kotosh

Aspero

La Florida

El Paraíso

Chilca

Pikimachay

Paloma

Paracas
extensive and long-used cemetery

Lake Titicaca

Chiripa

Pacific Ocean

Morro

3 The Central Andes to 300 BC

■ site first occupied before 2000 BC
■ site mainly occupied after 2000 BC

Las Conchas

---

3 The Central Andes were a challenging environment, with bountiful seas but an arid coastline (map above). Inland, rugged valleys and mountains dominated while farther east there were steamy forests. The earliest peoples to reach the region ranged between these habitats. Later societies were more settled and depended on storage and trading. Exchange may have been aided by widespread participation in cults, particularly that of Chavín. Crops were successfully adapted to the rigours of the region, notably potatoes, which grew well at high altitudes.

---

1 Peoples of the Americas to 300 BC

    farming peoples
    chiefdoms
    states emerging by 300 BC
    hunters and gatherers
■ site first occupied before 2000 BC
■ site mainly occupied after 2000 BC

Southeast Asia before civilization

With its long coastlines, mountain ranges and great river valleys fed by heavy seasonal rains, both the mainland and islands of southeast Asia provided a wealth of resources for early humankind. The diversity of flora and the abundance of metal ores allowed the growth of agricultural communities from at least the 4th millennium BC.

Before 1,000,000 BC *Homo erectus* enters Asia

c. 60,000 BC *Homo sapiens* spreads through southeast Asia

c. 40,000–10,000 BC Late Pleistocene flake-and-blade-tool tradition

c. 10,000–4000 BC Hoabinhian hunter-gatherer traditions on the mainland

c. 7000–4000 BC Rice agriculture expands through central and south China

c. 3000 BC First agricultural settlements in southeast Asia

c. 1500–500 BC Bronze Age in northeast Thailand and north Vietnam

c. 500 BC Introduction of iron, trade with India and development of political elites

2 The great river systems of southeast Asia together with its extended coastlines encouraged the use of boats which carried natural products and manufactured goods such as iron, glass and ceramics throughout the region, **(map below)** linking the islands and the mainland in a complex network of trade routes which extended north to China and Japan and westwards to India and the Mediterranean world.

3 Mainland southeast Asia is linguistically highly complex **(map right)** with at least eight major language families represented, but most of the languages of the Philippines and Indonesia belong to the Austronesian family which is thought to have expanded from a homeland in south China 6000 years ago. But this pattern hides considerable diversity and in Timor alone over 43 distinct languages are spoken.

THERE SEEMS LITTLE DOUBT that *Homo erectus*, the ancestor of all modern humans, was established in southeast Asia west of the "Wallace Line" more than one million years ago. But only Java, with its favourable geological conditions, has provided the skeletal evidence; elsewhere only discoveries of stone tools along river terraces and in some limestone fissure deposits reveal his passing.

Archaeological evidence
Abundant archaeological evidence for modern human hunter-gatherers comes only in the Late Pleistocene, and mainly from sites in the limestone mountains: among the best known are Tham Khuong and Nguom in northern Vietnam, Lang Rongrien in Thailand, Leang Burung in Celebes, and Tabon Cave in the island of Palawan in the Philippines. From about 40,000 years ago a varied range of flake stone tools have been found in these caves, left by people who exploited a wide range of plants, small and large animals and molluscs.

This way of life persisted until about the 6th millennium BC, with changes in the toolkit from flake tools to pebble choppers – the Hoabinhian tradition, called after the region in north Vietnam where it was first described.

From at least 6000 BC village settlements with evidence for rice growing and pottery making have been found in southern China, but perhaps because there has been relatively little research on early village sites in southeast Asia no settlements of rice farmers older than 3000 BC have been found in northern Vietnam and inland areas of Thailand, although Phung Nguyen in the Red River valley of Vietnam and Ban Chiang and Non Nok Tha in northern Thailand have all been well investigated. But the best evidence for late Neolithic occupation of southeast Asia comes from Khok Phanom Di, a 7m (23ft)-deep village mound occupying about 5ha (12 acres) near the coast southeast of modern-day Bangkok. Here over 150 burials and rich occupation layers dated to between 2000 and 1400 BC provide evidence of intensive exploitation of the sea and adjacent mangrove forests, and the beginnings of social differentiation.

Metal technologies
From early in the 2nd millennium BC bronze tools were added to the existing stone, bone and antler toolkits in central and northeast Thailand and northern Vietnam, where we can refer to a true Bronze Age from about 1500 to 500 BC. The best known Bronze Age locations in Thailand are Ban Chiang and Ban Na Di in the northeast and Nil Kham Haeng near Lopburi in the Chao Phraya valley. In Vietnam more sites of this phase are known including Dong Dau, Viet Khe, Cau Chan, Trang Khen, Lang Vac and Dong Son on the Ma river where a rich burial ground has been excavated since the 1920s and given its name to the late Bronze Age culture of the region, best known for its great bronze drums. These are widely distributed from Yunnan in southwest China to Thailand, Malaya and many parts of Indonesia where they seem to have been traded in antiquity as objects of great prestige and magical power.

Influence from India
In western and peninsular Thailand, Malaysia, Burma (Myanmar), Indonesia and the Philippines bronze metallurgy seems to have arrived only with iron after about 500 BC and to have been introduced from India as maritime trade routes were extended across the Bay of Bengal. In graves of this period are found glass and semi-precious stone jewellery of great aesthetic and technical sophistication together with iron tools and weapons, while in inland areas

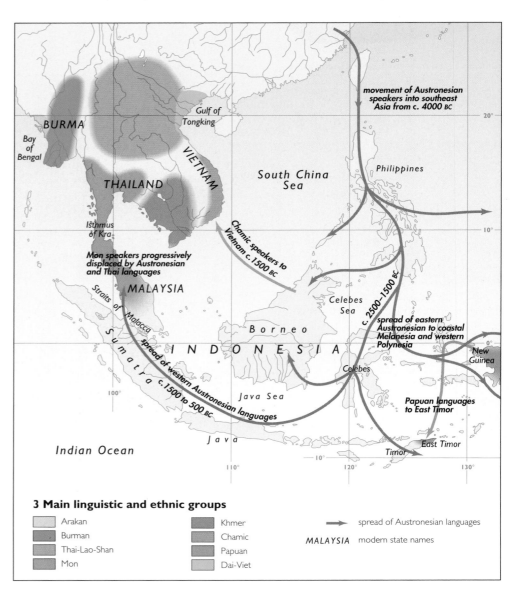

2 Early trade routes

— early trade routes between the Mediterranean and India and southeast Asia and south China, principally iron, beads, glass, spices, ivory, tortoise shell and cotton cloth

— trade routes linking eastern Indonesia via Philippines to south China taking exotic tropical products north

— trade in Dong Son bronze drums from north Vietnam to southeast Asia

3 Main linguistic and ethnic groups

Arakan		Khmer
Burman		Chamic
Thai-Lao-Shan		Papuan
Mon		Dai-Viet

→ spread of Austronesian languages

MALAYSIA modern state names

The map contains the following labels:

Matsu

T'ai-p'eng-k'eng
Yüan-shan
Quemoy
Taiwan
Feng-pi-t'ou
Pei-nan
K'en-ting

Haimenkou
Dabona
Tianzimao
Tajishan
Shizhaishan
Lijiashan
Red River

Taungthaman
Padah Lin
Tham Khuong
Lang Ca
Co Loa
Nguom
Viet Khe
Phung
Nguyen
Dong Dau
Go Mun
Trang Kenh
Plain of Jars
Chau Can
Hoabinh
Mts.
Da But
Hoa Loc
Gulf of Tongking
Lang Vac
Dong Son
Hainan
Quynh Van

Chao Phraya
Phu Lon
Bau Tro
Ban Chiang
Ban na Di
Non Pa Kluay
Non Nok Tha
Ban Chieng Hian
Hau Xa
Binh Chau
Khok Charoen
Ban Lum Khao
Nil Kham Haeng
Ban Prasat
Sa Huynh
Ongbah
Non U-Loke
Sai Yok
Ban Don Ta Phet
Ban Tha Kae
Mlu Prei
Long Thanh
Ban Kao
(Bangkok)
Khao Jamook
Khok Phanom Di
Nong
Samrong Sen
Khok Phlap
Nor
Laang Spean

Doc Chua
Long Giao
Cau Sat
Hang Gon
Rach Nui
Oc Eo
Giong Ca Vo
and Giong Phet

Khuan Lukpad
Isthmus
of
Kra
Lang Rongrien

Bukit Tengku Lembu
Gua Bintong
Pengkalen Bujang
Kota Tampan
Gua Cha
Gua Kepah
Gua Musang
Kuala Selinsing
Gua Baik
Jenderam
Gua Kecil
Hilir
Gua Kintamani
Kampong
Sungei Lang

Nias Is.
Sumatra
Malacca
Straits of
ukajadi Pasar

Lake Kerinci
Bangka
Tianko Panjang
Billiton
Pasemah Plateau
Mentawi Is.

Indian Ocean

Anyar
Plawangan
Leuwiliang
Buni
Ngandong
Gua Lawa
Java
Sangiran
Trinil
Lamongan
Sambungmacan
Gilimanuk
Pacitan
Gunung
Sembiran
Wajak
Kidul
Bali
Lombok

South China
Sea

Rabel
Lal-lo
Andarayan, Arku
and Musang
Cagayan Valley
Dimolit
Luzon
Pintu
Novaliches

Kalanay
Batungan
Bagumbayan
Batu Cave

Palawan
Tabon
Guri
Duyong
Mangunggul

Mindanao

Tingkayu
Madai
Baturong
Leang Tuwo Mane'e
Talaud Is.
Niah
Sanga Sanga
Leang Buidane
Celebes Sea
Sangihe Is.

Halmahera

Gua Sireh
Borneo
Paso
Ternate
Tidore

Celebes
Amboina
Kalumpang
Bada

Java Sea
Ulu Leang
Leang Burung

Sumbawa
Bui Ceri Uato
Aru
Flores
Lie Siri
Uai Bobo
Mengeruda
Sumba
Timor
Nikiniki
Melolo
Sumba

large moated-mound settlements and well laid-out cemeteries mark the emergence of powerful chiefdoms whose rulers, attracted by the rituals and prestige of Indian culture, soon adapted these to enhance their own status and power. Sites such as Ban Don Ta Phet, Khao Jamook, Khuan Lukpad, Ban Prasat, Non U-Loke, Ban Lum Khao and Ban Chieng Hian in Thailand, and Giong Ca Vo, Giong Phet, Doc Chua, Long Giao, Hang Gon and Hau Xa in southern and central Vietnam have all produced rich examples from this last stage of prehistoric culture on the mainland of southeast Asia, as have Plawangan and Lamongan in Java and Gilimanuk and Sembiran in Bali, where glass beads imported from south India and a potsherd with a Brahmi inscription serve to mark the end of prehistory.

Magnificent cast bronze drums (right) were made in southwest China and northern Vietnam from at least 500 BC and served in ceremonies to initiate agricultural work and to summon villagers in times of war. Many were traded south to Indonesia and along the riverine routes into Laos and Thailand.

1 Southeast Asia to c. 500 BC

age of sites:	type of site:	
● Pleistocene/ Mesolithic	▲ cave	● village
● Neolithic	⊟ cemetery	⬓ walled town
● early metal age	⬛ jar burial	◆ other sites
● metal age	▢ open site	‡ port
● Iron age	▲ shell midden	--- "Wallace Line"

1 The past 30 years has seen much new archaeological research including, very recently, in the south of Vietnam, and this is reflected in the distribution of marked sites (map above), of which only the more important or better investigated are shown. Many sites are multi-period and most village settlements include some burials. Symbols are chosen to indicate the most significant aspect of each archaeological site. The "Wallace Line" marks a major biogeographical boundary between the Asian fauna to the west and Australasian fauna to the east. The islands to the west were connected to the Asian mainland as recently as 12,000 years ago, while the islands to the east are separated by deep submarine trenches.

47

Australia

About 40,000 years ago, when lower sea levels linked Tasmania, Australia and New Guinea, man first ventured onto Sahul, the greater Australian continent. That journey from a southeast Asian homeland was a pioneering one, as it involved at least one major sea crossing. The original Australians were therefore among the world's earliest mariners.

1 & 2 Adzes for working hardwoods appeared in Australia 10,000 years ago, followed by spear points and by backed blades used as spear barbs and, eventually, by edge-ground axes **(maps below)**. Fine-grained stones for axes and red ochre were quarried and traded up to 800km (500 miles) from their source. Ornamental shells were exchanged over longer distances. Bone and shell artefacts appeared 2000 years ago, indicating more emphasis on marine resources. Thousands of coastal shell middens are known, especially from the last two millennia. Eel traps provide other evidence for more intensive exploitation of the sea. Thousands of rock art sites are known, but they are difficult to date. The simple pecked outlines of the Panaramittee style may extend back into the Pleistocene. Simple figurative art with engraved or painted outlines may have become common after 5000 years ago. Complex figurative art is found only in the northwest and is the most recent style, continuing to the present.

Pleistocene Australia

The strange new world that greeted these newcomers was of enormous size, and ranged from tropical north to temperate south. Some of the edible plants found in more northerly latitudes were related to those of Asia and were therefore familiar; but this was not so of the animals. In addition to the mammals that have survived until today, there was a bewildering assortment of giant forms: 3m (10ft) tall kangaroos, various enormous ox-like beasts, a large native lion and rangy, ostrich-like birds. This megafauna was a rich and easily available food source but it was reduced and eventually killed off by the advancing human tide.

Consequently, it was on the plentiful supply of fish and shellfish along the coasts and in the rivers that the newcomers focused their attention, and it was in these areas of Australia that the first human settlements were concentrated. Most of the sites are lost to us, for between 40,000 and 5000 years ago the sea level was lower than it is at present, and the sites now lie offshore, on the continental shelf.

The Pleistocene inhabitants of Australia used red ochre to create elaborate rock paintings, thus laying the foundations of a rich and long-lived Aboriginal custom. Their stone core implements and crude scrapers belong to what is known as the Australian Core Tool Tradition. This tradition, which underwent remarkably little change in more than 40,000 years, is pan-Australian, but there are a number of regional elements that have links with New Guinea and southeast Asia. One of these is the

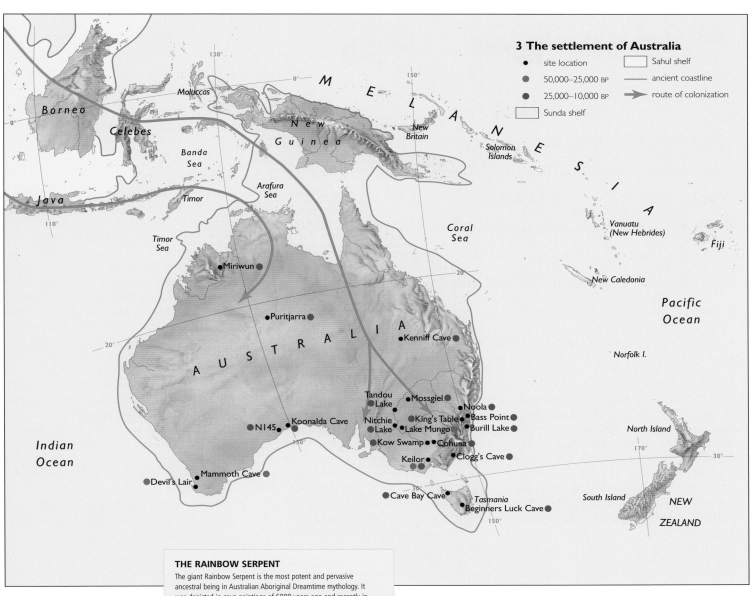

3 The settlement of Australia

● site location   ☐ Sahul shelf
● 50,000–25,000 BP   — ancient coastline
● 25,000–10,000 BP   → route of colonization
☐ Sunda shelf

3 Lowered sea levels created land bridges that joined up the various islands of southeast Asia, and also resulted in the appearance of two major land masses in the tropical regions: Sunda-land and Sahul-land. These land bridges were severed by a rise in sea level 10,000 years ago. There were two possible routes for migration into Australia, although both still required the crossing of large distances of open sea (map left). Populations of fully modern man were certainly established in China and southeast Asia by 40,000 years ago; their fossil remains and stone tools have been recovered from a number of sites throughout the region.

THE RAINBOW SERPENT

The giant Rainbow Serpent is the most potent and pervasive ancestral being in Australian Aboriginal Dreamtime mythology. It was depicted in cave paintings of 6000 years ago and recently in the gigantic Aboriginal mural at suburban Sydney's Redfern railway station. Recent computer analysis of ancient Rainbow Serpent rock art has now linked the advent of the Rainbow Serpent to the flooding of vast tracts of northern Australia by the rising sea after the last ice age. Large numbers of ribboned pipefish, a relative of the seahorse, came with the tide and were associated with the disruption and warfare that arose as hunting sites were inundated and people faced starvation. Consequently, in mythological terms, the humble pipefish grew in stature and became the all-powerful Rainbow Serpent.

40,000 BP Man first reaches Sahul (the ancient Australian megacontinent)

35,000 BP The Australian megafauna are hunted to extinction

12,000 BP Tasmania and mainland Australia separated by rising sea levels

6500 BP The land bridge between New Guinea and Australia cut by rising sea levels

3500 BP The dingo (wild dog) arrives in Australia

AD 1522 A secret Portuguese expedition under Cristovao de Mendonca possibly sails down the east coast as far as Westernport Bay

AD 1606 Dutchman Willem Jansz sails through Torres Strait

AD 1642–4 Dutchman Abel Tasman lands in Tasmania and NW Australia

AD 1688 Englishman William Dampier lands in NW Australia

AD 1770 Englishman James Cook charts the east coast of Australia

edge-ground axe, which has been dated to 22,000 years in Arnhem Land. Similar ground-stone tools found in Japan are up to 30,000 years old. Ground-stone tools were ultimately developed in most other parts of the world also, but only in a much later period.

Aboriginal society

About 5000 years ago, following the end of the last ice age, the sea rose to its present level; and while Aboriginal settlements were still concentrated along the coasts there was a rapid increase in the exploitation of inland resources. At about this time a range of small, finely finished flake implements especially developed for hafting sharp tools, and known as the Australian Small Tool Tradition, appeared across the continent. The dingo was also introduced.

Political, economic and religious development continued and by the time the first European settlement arrived in the 18th century, there were about 750,000 Aborigines living in around 500 tribal territories. Although the Aborigines' way of life was still based on hunting and gathering (they never became full-scale agriculturists) they had developed very intricate and finely balanced relationships with their environment. In desert areas, small nomadic groups ranged over thousands of square kilometres, while in richer parts of the continent there were settled, permanent villages. Fish traps were constructed, grasses and tubers were replanted to assist nature,

Rock art (above) became common in Australia 5000 years ago. This much more recent painting shows the two "Lightning Brothers", ancestral spirits of the Wardaman Aboriginal people from northwestern Australia.

and fire was used systematically to burn old vegetation and encourage the growth of rich new plant cover and the abundant new game it attracted. Rare goods, such as ceremonial axes, shells and ochres, were traded from one side of the vast continent to the other, as were stories down the accompanying "song lines".

FIRE, GRASS AND KANGAROOS, AND THE HUMAN INHABITANTS, SEEM ALL DEPENDENT ON EACH OTHER FOR EXISTENCE IN AUSTRALIA; FOR ANY ONE OF THESE BEING WANTING, THE OTHERS COULD NO LONGER CONTINUE. FIRE IS NECESSARY TO BURN THE GRASS, AND FORM THOSE OPEN FORESTS, IN WHICH WE FIND THE LARGE FOREST KANGAROO; THE NATIVE APPLIES THAT FIRE TO THE GRASS AT CERTAIN SEASONS, IN ORDER THAT A YOUNG GREEN CROP MAY SUBSEQUENTLY SPRING UP, AND SO ATTRACT AND ENABLE HIM TO KILL OR TAKE THE KANGAROO WITH NETS. IN SUMMER THE BURNING OF THE LONG GRASS DISCLOSES VERMIN, BIRD'S NESTS, ETC. ON WHICH THE FEMALES AND CHILDREN, WHO CHIEFLY BURN THE GRASS, FEED. BUT FOR THIS SIMPLE PROCESS, THE AUSTRALIAN WOODS HAD PROBABLY CONTAINED AS THICK A JUNGLE AS THOSE OF NEW ZEALAND OR AMERICA, INSTEAD OF THE OPEN FORESTS IN WHICH THE WHITE MEN NOW FIND GRASS FOR THEIR CATTLE, TO THE EXCLUSION OF THE KANGAROO.

Thomas Mitchell, the explorer, describes the ecological importance of traditional fire-stick farming (T. Mitchell, *Journal of an expedition into the interior of tropical Australia*, London, 1848)

Melanesia and Polynesia

Melanesia and Polynesia were first settled, from around 50,000 years ago, by modern people from southeast Asia. These adventurous people were the world's first great blue-water sailors and seaborne colonists. They moved in waves, initially into New Guinea and its adjacent islands, and over time they gave birth to the Melanesian and then the Polynesian traditions. There were many great migrations, and the furthermost Pacific islands were reached as late as AD 750.

40,000 BP Modern people (*Homo sapiens*) arrived in New Guinea

25,000 BP First evidence of settlements in highland New Guinea

6000 BP Austronesians advance through coastal regions of New Guinea and beyond

5000 BP Evidence of slash-and-burn horticulture in Melanesia

3500 BP Coastal parts of New Guinea, the Solomons, New Hebrides and Fiji settled by Austronesian Lapita-pottery makers who originated in Indonesia

c. AD 400 Settlement of the Hawaiian Islands and Easter Island

c. AD 1500 The southeast Asian coconut reaches Panama, and the sweet potato reaches highland New Guinea

AD 1567 Spaniard Alvaro de Mendana lands on the Solomon Islands

AD 1595 Spaniard Fernandez de Quiros arrives in the Marquesas, Santa Cruz Ndeni

AD 1642 Dutchman Abel Tasman arrives in Tasmania, Tonga, Fiji, northern New Guinea and New Zealand

3 New Zealand's early settlers were basically coastal hunter-gatherers, though the inland resources of South Island were seasonally exploited **(map below)**. Cultivated plants were only grown in sheltered localities in North Island.

First migrants

THE PACIFIC ISLANDERS' ancient ancestors, the early people or *Homo erectus*, lived in southeast Asia two million years ago. During this period, the Pleistocene, sea levels meant that the land mass of southeast Asia included much of the western part of what is now the archipelago. Remains of these people have been found in Java, part of the ancient continent known as the Sunda shelf, which is, for the most part, submerged today.

Around 50,000 years ago, *Homo sapiens*, or modern people, arrived in the region. These people were hunters and gatherers who drifted the short distance to the ancient continent of Sahul (modern-day Melanesia, which at the time was attached to Australia) around 40,000 years ago. Skulls of *Homo sapiens* found in the area date back to this time. These people had settled the New Guinea highlands by 25,000 years ago. Eight thousand years ago rising seas following the end of the last ice age caused the separation of New Guinea from the continent of Australia.

A second wave of southeast Asian immigrants known as the Austronesians, or Lapita people, arrived in New Guinea 6000 years ago. Lapita is their distinct, red-slipped pottery, often intricately decorated with geometric patterns, which can be traced right across the western Pacific. These new migrants were aided by

their revolutionary new technologies, such as the sail and the outrigger canoe, and the development of root crops (taro) and pig and chicken farming. These advances made it possible for the Austronesians to discover and settle the islands across the vast expanse of the Pacific Ocean. Recent archaeology, genetic mapping and linguistic analysis show that this was not a rapid "express-train" migration, as initially thought, but rather a "slow-boat" penetration. Most of the rest of island Melanesia was settled as recently as 4000 years ago, and Fiji (the blurred boundary between Melanesia and Polynesia) was reached as late as 3500 years ago.

In the Tonga (reached 3200 BP) and Samoan (3000 BP) regions, the Melanesian material culture gradually evolved over a thousand years of relative isolation into what we now call Polynesian. Polynesian mariners using sophisticated navigation techniques and large ocean-going canoes reached and settled the Marquesas as late as AD 300, and from there the remaining Polynesian islands were discovered and settled. Early evidence shows settlement of Easter Island by AD 400, there to give birth to an extraordinary culture. The Society, Cook and Hawaiian Islands were settled by AD 600 and New Zealand by AD 750. Coconuts from southeast Asia reached Panama by AD 1500, and the sweet potato, though native to eastern Polynesia, travelled in the other direction, reaching highland New Guinea in the 16th century.

Island resources

Between AD 750 and 1300, a multitude of largely independent cultures evolved on these little "island universes". In the New Guinea highlands, where farming flourished, population density was the greatest in the world and easily sustainable. On most Pacific islands a balance was reached between population and natural resources; in less hospitable places, such as Easter Island and New Zealand, initially abundant resources became very depleted and, by the time of European contact in the 17th and 18th centuries, populations were in conflict and decline. When the Maoris arrived in Aotearoa (New Zealand) from about AD 750, they found large numbers of a flightless bird, the Moa. Some of these were gigantic, up to 3m (10ft) high and weighing up to 250kg (550lb). Unafraid of man, the Moa proved a readily available food source, and over the next 400 years they were hunted to extinction. The first Maoris thus established themselves with a Moa-fed burst in population numbers, while succeeding generations had to battle hard to sustain themselves.

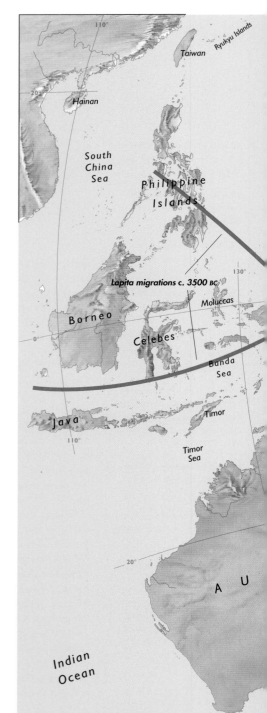

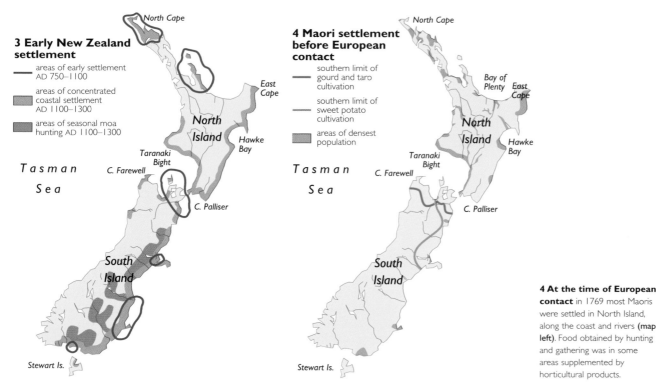

3 Early New Zealand settlement

— areas of early settlement AD 750–1100

areas of concentrated coastal settlement AD 1100–1300

areas of seasonal moa hunting AD 1100–1300

4 Maori settlement before European contact

— southern limit of gourd and taro cultivation

— southern limit of sweet potato cultivation

areas of densest population

4 At the time of European contact in 1769 most Maoris were settled in North Island, along the coast and rivers **(map left)**. Food obtained by hunting and gathering was in some areas supplemented by horticultural products.

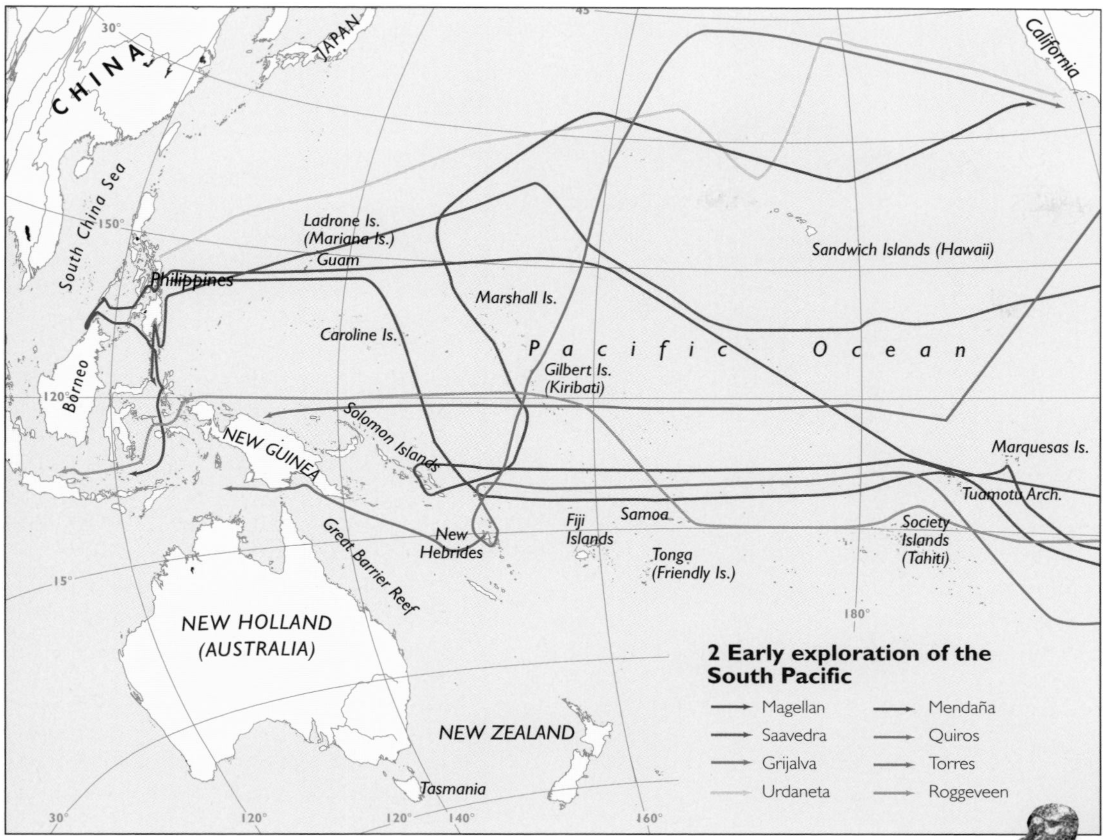

Oh the great fish hook of Maui!
Manai-i-ka-lani "Made fast to the heavens" – its name;
An earth-twisted cord ties the hook.
Engulfed from the lofty Kauiki.
Its bait the red billed Alae,
The bird made sacred to Hina.
It sinks far down to Hawaii,
Struggling and painfully dying.
Caught is the land under the water,
Floated up, up to the surface,
But Hina hid a wing of the bird
And broke the land under the water.
Below, was the bait snatched away
And eaten at once by the fishes,
The Ulua of the deep muddy places.

A translation of the traditional Hawaiian "Chant of Kualii" (c. AD 1700), which describes how the demi-God Maui brought the Hawaiian Islands into existence by drawing them from the ocean floor. The story is common to many parts of Polynesia.

2 Early exploration of the South Pacific

→ Magellan   → Mendaña
→ Saavedra   → Quiros
→ Grijalva   → Torres
→ Urdaneta   → Roggeveen

2 Computer simulations of currents have shown that the islands of the Pacific were not colonized simply by people drifting there by chance (although some of the nearer ones might have been). Rather they were settled by people who purposefully navigated their way to them. Ancient Pacific mariners did this by using guides such as stars and wave patterns. They also relied on natural signs such as scavenging birds returning to land at dusk, driftwood, clouds wreathing high mountains, and the phosphorescence thrown up by atolls at a distance. Some of these tell-tale signs can be picked up at distances up to 160 km (100 miles). Once in the Society Islands it is possible to drift to most of the rest of Polynesia, with the exception of Hawaii, Easter Island and New Zealand. To get to these islands full-scale voyages of exploration were needed, and this is exactly what was done – in large ocean-going canoes whose seaworthiness and manoeuvrability prompted the 18th-century European navigator James Cook to pronounce their qualities superior to those of his own ship *Endeavour*. It is thought that New Zealand was reached by following the flight of millions of birds migrating south **(map above)**.

I Initial settlement of Polynesia and Island Micronesia

the Lapita potters:

→ Lapita migrations
— Lapita pottery area
• sites with Lapita pottery
— other contemporary Melanesian pottery traditions
➡ settlement of Eastern Polynesia 150 BC–AD 1000

Easter Island is one of the most isolated islands in the world, but 1200 years ago a double-hulled canoe filled with seafarers landed upon its shores. Over the centuries that followed, a remarkable society developed in isolation there. For reasons that are still unknown, the islanders (who called themselves the Rapa Nui) began carving giant statues, known as moai, out of volcanic rock **(above)**. These 9m (30ft) high monuments in the shape of stylized human heads are among the most dramatic ancient relics ever discovered. Unfortunately, the island's population outstripped the resources available to sustain it, and by the time Europeans visited in the 18th century it was in catastrophic decline and warfare was endemic. The forests had disappeared, escape was impossible as there were no long-distance, seagoing canoes left, and many of the great statues had been cast down. From a peak of 8000 in the 1600s, numbers had fallen to 2000 by 1722 and, by 1877, to a mere 111.

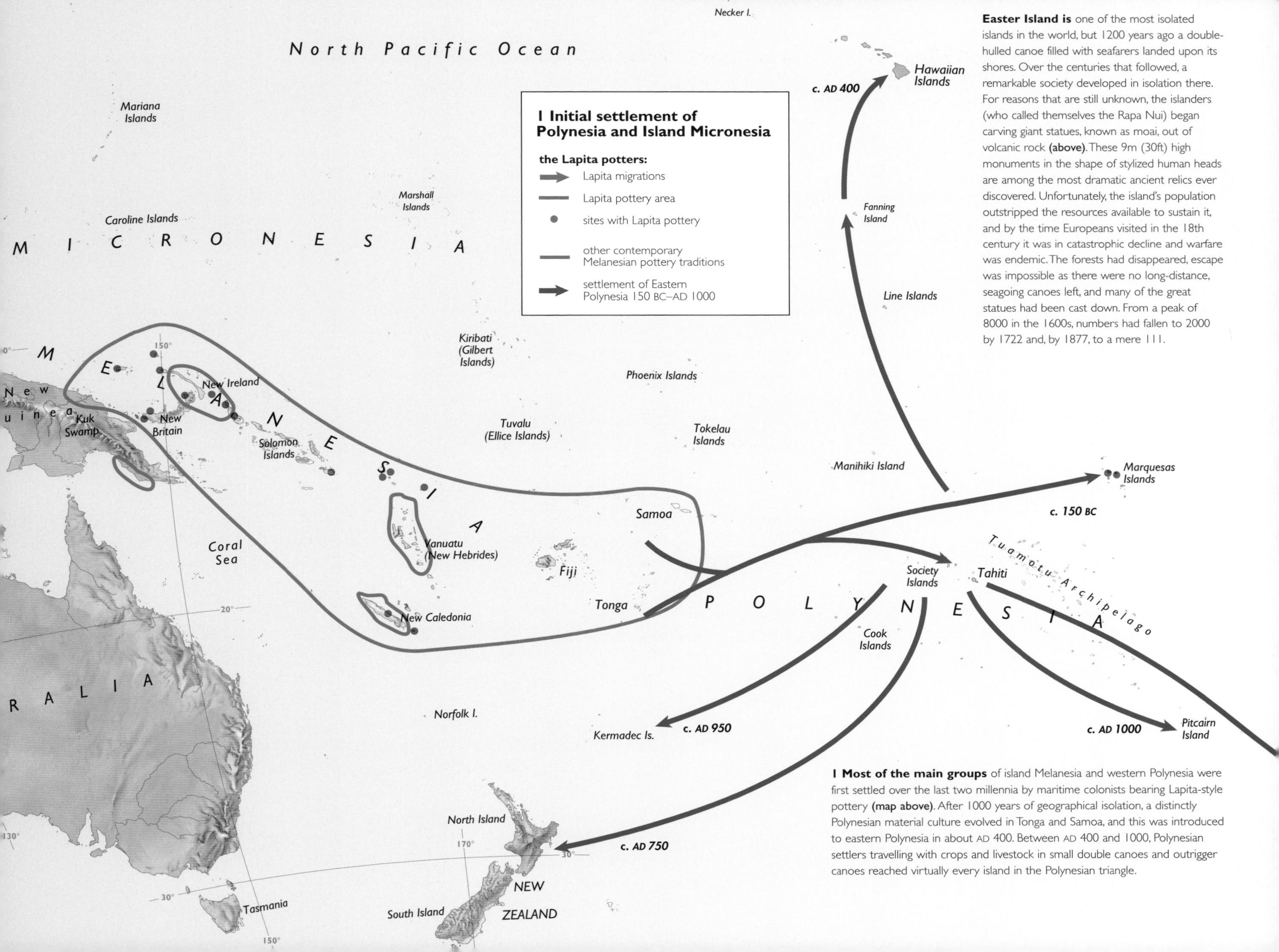

I Most of the main groups of island Melanesia and western Polynesia were first settled over the last two millennia by maritime colonists bearing Lapita-style pottery **(map above)**. After 1000 years of geographical isolation, a distinctly Polynesian material culture evolved in Tonga and Samoa, and this was introduced to eastern Polynesia in about AD 400. Between AD 400 and 1000, Polynesian settlers travelling with crops and livestock in small double canoes and outrigger canoes reached virtually every island in the Polynesian triangle.

2 THE FIRST CIVILIZATIONS

ABOUT 6000 YEARS AGO, in a few areas of particularly intensive agriculture, the dispersed villages of Neolithic peoples gave way to more complex societies. These were the first civilizations, and their emergence marks the start of a new phase of world history. They arose, apparently independently, in four widely dispersed areas (the early civilizations of America emerged considerably later): the lower Tigris and Euphrates valleys; the valley of the Nile; the Indus valley around Harrappa and Mohenjo-Daro; and the Yellow River around An-yang. The characteristic feature of them all was the city, which now became an increasingly dominant social form, gradually encroaching on the surrounding countryside, until today urban civilization has become the criterion of social progress. But the city possessed other important connotations:a complex division of labour; literacy and a literate class (usually the priesthood); monumental public buildings; political and religious hierarchies; a kingship descended from the gods; and ultimately empire, or the claim to universal rule. A dichotomy already existed between the civilized world and the barbarian world outside. The onslaught of nomadic peoples eager to enjoy the fruit of civilization became a recurrent theme of world history until the advent of effective firearms in the 15th century AD tilted the balance in favour of the civilized peoples.

THE SPHINX AND KHAFRE (CHEPHREN) PYRAMID, GIZA, EGYPT.

The beginnings of civilization in the Eurasian world

Urban civilizations developed independently in four different areas of Eurasia, as the exploitation of fertile river valleys allowed complex forms of social organization. The sudden growth of cities was a dramatic development in human history, and was accompanied by the beginnings of literacy. From this period it becomes possible to write true history.

c. 3500 BC Eanna in Uruk and other ceremonial complexes built as the centres of the earliest cities in Mesopotamia

c. 3200 BC Earliest readable documents from Mesopotamia

c. 3100 BC Palatial complexes at Abydus established under First Dynasty of Egypt

c. 2500 BC Growth of urbanism in the Indus valley

c. 2350 BC First ceremonial centre built at Troy in western Anatolia

c. 1800 BC Beginning of Shang dynasty in China

DRAW NEAR TO EANNA, THE DWELLING OF ISHTAR, WHICH NO FUTURE KING, NO MAN, CAN EQUAL. GO UP AND WALK ON THE WALLS OF URUK, INSPECT THE BASE TERRACE, EXAMINE THE BRICKWORK: IS NOT ITS BRICKWORK OF BURNT BRICK? DID NOT THE SEVEN SAGES LAY ITS FOUNDATION?

The Epic of Gilgamesh

T**HE DEVELOPMENT OF URBAN** societies seems to have been triggered by a sudden concentration of population in certain river valleys, which in some cases may have been a result of climate change which made the surrounding areas outside the valleys less attractive for habitation. The need to exploit the fertile land of these valleys and their alluvial plains to feed a growing population then led to the development of irrigation and flood-control mechanisms. In Mesopotamia and China this involved the construction of canals to carry water away to the land around the Tigris-Euphrates and the Yellow River, while in Egypt and India the annual flooding of the Nile and Indus provided fertile silt in which crops were grown.

The first cities

The concentrated populations were able to produce surplus crops which could be exported to areas beyond the rivers in return for raw materials and precious items not locally available, above all bronze. The food surplus also made possible social groups not directly involved in agriculture, whether specialized craftsmen or rulers and military leaders.

It was when ambitious individuals and families succeeded in diverting resources into the construction of monumental ceremonial centres that provided a focus for the populations living near them that the first true cities appeared. This took place in Mesopotamia in c. 3500 BC and in Egypt in c. 3100 BC, while the Indus valley cities appeared in c. 2500 BC, and in China urbanism began in c. 1800 BC.

1 Between c. 3500 and c. 1500 BC, complex societies characterized by urbanism, literacy and specialization of labour grew up independently in the valleys of the Tigris-Euphrates, Nile, Indus and Yellow rivers (**map right**). In the 2nd millennium BC urban societies developed in Anatolia and the Aegean, and these further influenced the communities of the Balkans, south of the Carpathian mountains. Although amber from the Baltic found its way as far south as Mycenae, changes in the Near East had little impact on north and west Europe, where the 3rd and 2nd millennia saw the emergence of a common culture, the Bell-Beaker groups, while villages remained the normal form of community. At the same time the steppes of central Asia saw the domestication of the horse and the rise of nomad pastoralists who were to be a continuing influence on the urban civilizations of west and east.

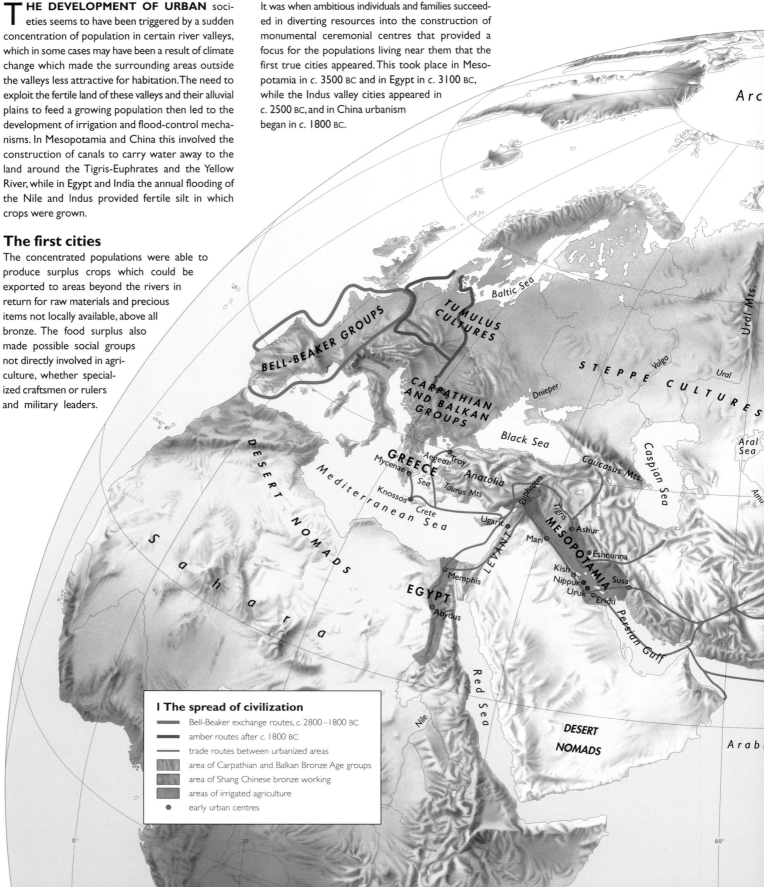

1 The spread of civilization

— Bell-Beaker exchange routes, c. 2800–1800 BC
— amber routes after c. 1800 BC
— trade routes between urbanized areas
▨ area of Carpathian and Balkan Bronze Age groups
▨ area of Shang Chinese bronze working
▨ areas of irrigated agriculture
● early urban centres

Temple at Eridu in Mesopotamia, built c. 3000 BC. The large platform on which it stands is a forerunner of later Mesopotamian ziggurats. The "Sumerian king list" names Eridu as the earliest seat of power in Mesopotamia. All early cities were important as ceremonial centres with large temple-complexes constructed early in their development: works which required both large-scale labour and considerable organization.

The political development of these different regions was not uniform: in Egypt a single unified kingdom emerged almost immediately, extending from the Nile delta south to the first cataract; in China the earliest civilization is associated with the Shang dynasty, although the Shang rulers may have just been leaders of a loose confederacy. In Mesopotamia, by contrast, no one city was able to establish control for any period, and competition for dominance between the leading cities characterized the history of the area for nearly three millennia. The situation in the Indus valley is less clear, but the major cities of Harappa and Mohenjo-Daro appear to have coexisted until the decline of the Indus cities after about 2000 BC. It appears that in all these civilizations, religious, political and military power was concentrated in the hands of a few ruling families.

Trade and exchange were important in the expansion of the

THE EARLIEST FORMS OF WRITING

Methods of writing can use signs in two distinct ways: logographically and phonographically. Logograms are semantic symbols, signs that stand for words and ideas. Some logograms, known as pictograms, are actually pictures of the objects or actions they represent.

Other logograms work indirectly: ancient Egyptian used a picture of a shepherd's crook as the symbol for "ruler". Phonograms represent sounds, often syllables, and can also develop from pictograms. Where known, meanings (in bold) and sounds are shown below.

Mesopotamian pictograms and cuneiform, c. 3000 BC & 2400 BC
The earliest script developed gradually over a wide area of Mesopotamia: it was pictographic, inscribed on damp clay with a stick or reed. Used for record-keeping in economic transactions, the characteristic use of a stylus to make wedge-shaped marks ("cuneus" is Latin for "wedge") led to stylized signs. It developed into a syllabic system for writing Sumerian, and later other Mesopotamian languages.

Egyptian hieroglyphics, c. 3100 BC
The earliest examples are found as labels on small objects. They use a combination of logographic and phonographic signs. Over 6000 are known, but fewer than 1000 are thought to have been in use at any one time, and only a small proportion used frequently. Fully developed from its earliest appearance, it continued in use until the 4th century AD. The ancient Egyptian language was the ancestor of Coptic.

Indus valley script, c. 2500 BC
These signs are found mainly on seal stones, pottery, copper tablets, bone and ivory. About 400 separate signs have been distinguished in about 3500 short inscriptions. The script is not yet deciphered, but this language may be related to the Dravidian group which includes modern Tamil and Malayalam.

Linear A & B, c. 1800 BC & c. 1500 BC
Both have been found on clay tablets used for record-keeping: Linear A only in Crete, Linear B in later contexts in Crete and on mainland Greece. About 90 signs have been found and they suggest that these were syllabic systems, with some logographic elements. Linear A is as yet undeciphered; Linear B was adapted from it by Mycenaeans to write Greek, and a version was used in Cyprus down to the 5th century BC.

Shang "Oracle Bone" script, c. 1400 BC
The earliest examples are found on "oracle bones", pieces of bone and turtle shell used for divination by later rulers of Shang dynasty (c. 1500–1000 BC). About 4500 signs have been distinguished, of which about 1000 have been identified. Some signs are pictographic, but not all. It is a direct ancestor of modern Chinese scripts.

ox / gu	head / sag	day / ud	barley / se	orchard / kiri	water / a
wr	nb	sw	nfr	sm	ndm
				undeciphered	
				undeciphered	
pa	pe	pi	ra	re	ri
woman	mouth	sun	moon	mountain	water

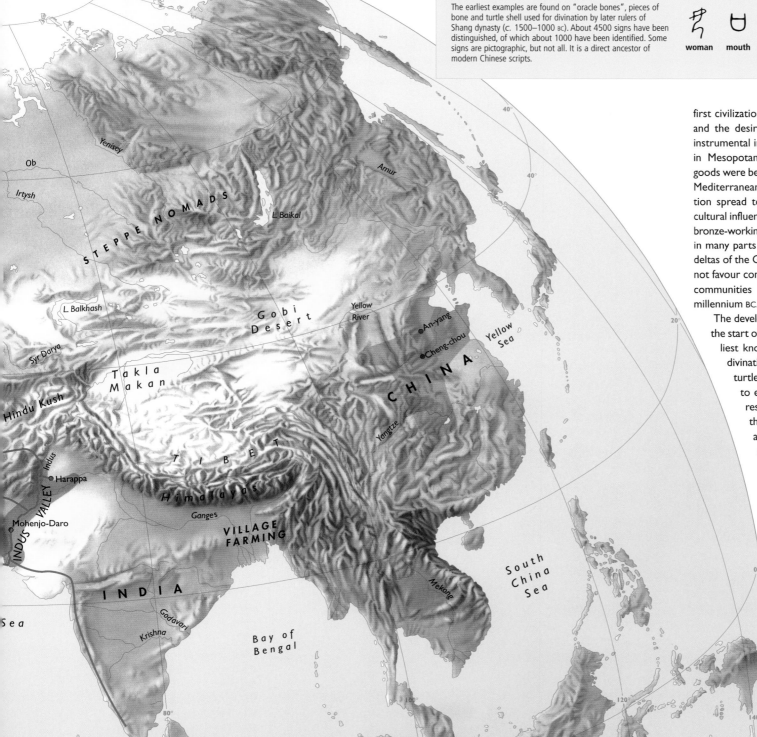

first civilizations. The possession of prestige goods and the desire to acquire more resources were instrumental in the emergence of the first empires in Mesopotamia. During the 3rd millennium BC goods were being traded between the Indus and the Mediterranean. In the 2nd millennium BC urbanization spread to Anatolia and the Aegean, and the cultural influence of the Near East can be seen in the bronze-working of the Balkan communities. However, in many parts of Eurasia, including the fertile river deltas of the Ganges and Mekong, the landscape did not favour concentrations of population, and village communities remained the norm until the 1st millennium BC.

The development of writing occurred almost at the start of each of the four civilizations. The earliest known use of writing in China was for divination: the Shang rulers used prepared turtle shells and ox scapulae heated in a fire to establish the will of the gods, and the result of the enquiry was scratched onto the shell or bone. In Mesopotamia, Egypt and the Indus valley writing was used mainly for administrative activities, with inventories and accounts being inscribed on clay. Early examples of writing have often survived because clay tablets were accidentally baked, fixing the messages permanently. Clay inscriptions spread to Crete and Greece by around 1500 BC. In Egypt and Mesopotamia the use of writing developed rapidly, as large public inscriptions, including law-codes, were erected by the rulers as monuments to their wisdom, justice and power. It is from monuments such as these, celebrating their victories or their public works, that the earliest true history can be reconstructed.

The early empires of Mesopotamia

The broad plain through which the Tigris and Euphrates rivers flow gave birth to the world's first cities. Irrigation systems made it possible to support substantial populations and complex administrative structures. With urbanization came more developed economies and trade, while competition between cities led to warfare and the first empires.

c. 3500–3200 BC Earliest written records from Mesopotamia

c. 2900 BC Beginning of Early Dynastic period

c. 2296 BC Beginning of the reign of Sargon, first ruler of the empire of Agade

c. 2029 BC Beginning of the reign of Shulgi of Ur

c. 1749 BC Amorite Shamshi-Adad I conquers Ashur and takes the Assyrian throne

c. 1728 BC Beginning of the reign of Hammurabi of Babylon

c. 1686 BC Hammurabi publishes his law code shortly before his death

c. 1595 BC Hittite Mursili I sacks Babylon

THE EARLIEST CITIES appeared in Mesopotamia in the second half of the 4th millennium BC: at Uruk, Ur, Tell 'Uqair and Susa vast and elaborately decorated ceremonial complexes were built as the centres of urban settlements, probably under the leadership of families eager to display their power and their respect for the gods. The fertile plains and valleys watered by the Tigris and the Euphrates produced food surpluses sufficient to support these elaborate new centres and their complex social structures.

The cities were the basic political units of Mesopotamia. Religion was fundamental to their social organization: the rulers of cities presented themselves as favoured servants of the gods, while lower down the social scale agricultural workers had a necessary role in producing the materials for sacrifices and offerings to the gods. The cities established diplomatic and trade relationships with each other, although little is known of the mechanisms for this. Finds of goods from Uruk, the predominant city in Mesopotamia from around 3500 BC have come from as far afield as Susa and Syria. The effect of trade and gift-exchange between cities encouraged the development of a common culture from the edges of the Persian Gulf to Mari in the

MAY A CITIZEN WHO HAS BEEN WRONGED AND IS INVOLVED IN A LAWSUIT COME BEFORE MY STATUE NAMED "KING OF JUSTICE", MAY HE READ MY LAW CODE, MAY MY LAW CODE MAKE CLEAR THE LAW FOR HIM, MAY HE SEE HIS JUDGEMENT, MAY HE LET HIS HEART BREATHE EASILY AND SAY "HAMMURABI, THE LORD, WHO EXISTS FOR THE PEOPLE LIKE A TRUE FATHER, HAS CARED AT THE COMMAND OF HIS LORD, MARDUK, PLEASED THE HEART OF HIS LORD MARDUK AND DETERMINED THE WELL-BEING OF HIS PEOPLE FOR EVER, AND HELPED THE LAND OBTAIN JUSTICE."

Hammurabi (1728–1686 BC)
Law Code

1 Mesopotamia occupies a key position (map below) on the lines of communication between central Asia and Europe and between the Persian Gulf and the Mediterranean. Southern Mesopotamia had no sources of metals, and the need to ensure the supply of bronze and other goods including timber was an important stimulus for military campaigns and imperialism. Although the rulers of Agade and Ur gained control over large territories, they did not establish new imperial identities to replace loyalty to individual cities.

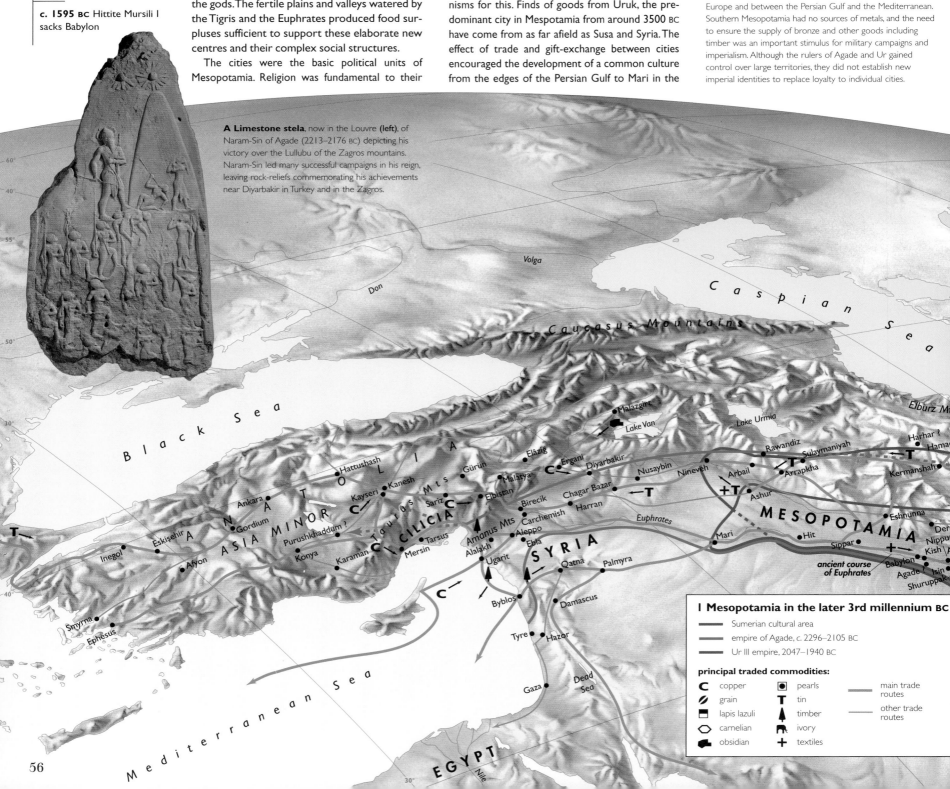

A Limestone stela, now in the Louvre (left), of Naram-Sin of Agade (2213–2176 BC) depicting his victory over the Lullubu of the Zagros mountains. Naram-Sin led many successful campaigns in his reign, leaving rock-reliefs commemorating his achievements near Diyarbakir in Turkey and in the Zagros.

1 Mesopotamia in the later 3rd millennium BC

— Sumerian cultural area
— empire of Agade, c. 2296–2105 BC
— Ur III empire, 2047–1940 BC

principal traded commodities:

C copper
⬤ pearls
main trade routes

grain
T tin
other trade routes

lapis lazuli
timber

carnelian
ivory

obsidian
+ textiles

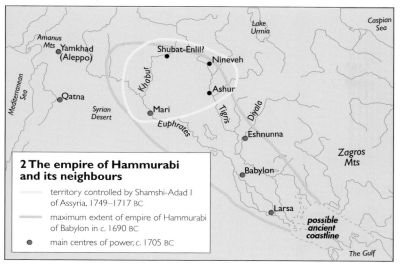

2 The empire of Hammurabi and its neighbours

territory controlled by Shamshi-Adad I of Assyria, 1749–1717 BC

maximum extent of empire of Hammurabi of Babylon in c. 1690 BC

● main centres of power, c. 1705 BC

2 The politics of Mesopotamia in the 18th century BC was characterized by shifting alliances between the rulers of the major cities (**map above**). Shamshi-Adad I seized control of Ashur and carved out an empire in northern Mesopotamia, while establishing good relations with cities to the south. His former ally Hammurabi of Babylon later absorbed Assyria into his own empire.

northwest and Ashur in the north. Although other languages were spoken, the early use of Sumerian as a written language has led to the use of the term "Sumerian" to describe the culture and society of early and middle 3rd millennium.

The empire of Agade

Towards the end of the 3rd millennium powerful leaders attempted to expand their influence over a wider area. The first was Sargon (c. 2296–2240 BC), who created a new political centre at Agade, also known as Akkad, before conquering the cities of southern Mesopotamia and claiming authority over areas as far west as Byblos. The empire of Agade was enlarged by Sargon's grandson Naram-Sin (2213–2176 BC), but within a generation of his death it had disappeared, as its subject cities reasserted their independence. The rise of Agade had long-lasting effects on the region, with Akkadian (whose variants included Babylonian and Assyrian) replacing Sumerian as the main language of Mesopotamia.

A century later the rulers of the Third Dynasty of Ur (Ur III: 2047–1940 BC), beginning with Ur-Nammu, built an empire in southern Mesopotamia, but in common with the other early Mesopotamian empires it was not long-lasting and its decline left a number of important cities competing

for power. The centre of activity moved to northern Mesopotamia, and a new elite emerged – the Amorites – who had previously been excluded from power. The most successful Amorite leader was Shamshi-Adad I, who established a short-lived empire in Assyria in the years after 1750 BC. After his death the region returned to a period of competing rulers, as reflected by the assessment of an advisor to Zimri-Lim of Mari (c. 1714–1700 BC): "There is no king who is strong by himself: 10 or 15 kings follow Hammurabi of Babylon, as many follow Rim-Sin of Larsa,

Ibalpiel of Eshnunna and Amutpiel of Qatna, while 20 kings follow Yarim-Lim of Yamkhad." Soon after this Hammurabi was able to establish an empire of his own, and Babylon became a leading power in the region for the first time.

The law code of Hammurabi

Hammurabi is most famous for his law code, inscribed on a large stone with a carving of the king in the presence of Shamash, the Babylonian sun-god. Although it is presented as a practical collection of laws including the principle of punishment with "an eye for an eye", the primary function of the document was probably to advertise the achievements of Hammurabi's reign. After his death, his successors in the First Dynasty of Babylon ruled for about 90 years before the city was raided by the Hittites, and a new phase in the history of Mesopotamia began (see p. 60).

3 Mesopotamia in the Early Dynastic Period

fertile area

marsh area

irrigation and ancient water courses

● city or other important site

3 Urban populations grew during the Early Dynastic period (**map above**) with 80 per cent of the population living in cities. Shuruppak, for example, had a population by 2600 BC of 15–30,000 and an area of about 100ha (247 acres), with a city wall and a developed military organization.

← ◻ route terminated at Badakhshan in Afghanistan

Ancient Egypt

The history of the ancient Egyptian state is one of successive periods of unification and fragmentation. Counterbalancing this is a pattern of civilization – characterized by such features as the use of writing, an organized system of religion and divine kingship, and dependence on the annual Nile floods for the fertility of the land – which links the different periods together through a span of 3000 years.

HOW MANY ARE YOUR DEEDS
THOUGH UNKNOWN TO US,
O SOLE GOD WHO HAS NO EQUAL!
YOU MADE THE WORLD IN YOUR FASHION,
YOU ALONE,
ALL MEN, HERDS AND WILD BEASTS
ALL THAT IS ON EARTH
AND WALKS ON LEGS,
ALL THAT IS IN THE AIR AND FLIES
WITH WINGS OUTSTRETCHED,
ALL THE FOREIGN LANDS,
FROM SYRIA TO THE SUDAN,
AND THE LAND OF EGYPT.

The Great Hymn to the Sun
Akhenaten (c. 1364–1347 BC)

TRADITION DATES THE UNIFICATION of Upper and Lower Egypt to 3100 BC, but it is more accurate to see the emergence of a unified state around this time as the outcome of formative processes stretching back into prehistory. The 4th-Dynasty pyramids at Giza, the largest of which was built by Khufu (Cheops), are the most famous examples of Egypt's monumental funerary architecture, which expressed the divine status and power of the pharaohs of the Old Kingdom. Construction projects on this scale were possible only because of the enormous wealth of the state, derived mainly from agriculture. The pharaohs controlled this resource through a system of assessment, taxation, collection and redistribution. Central rule broke down at the end of the 6th Dynasty. Although the reasons for this are not entirely clear, it is probable that a series of low Nile floods and consequent famines were one factor in the loss of political and social stability that marks the onset of the First Intermediate Period.

Middle Kingdom reunification

Egypt was reunified under Mentuhotep of Thebes, and a new era, known as the Middle Kingdom, began. Thebes became an important centre, and its god, Amun, was identified with the sun god, Re, who had been closely connected with royalty since Old Kingdom times. During the 12th Dynasty, which represented the high point of the Middle Kingdom,

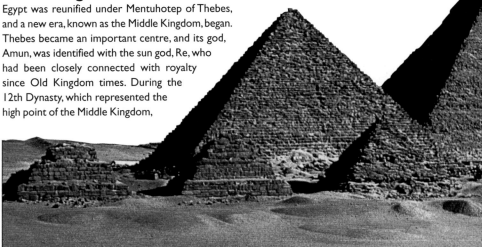

trading expeditions were sent to Palestine, Syria, and south to Nubia, where the Egyptian presence was consolidated by the construction of several forts clustered around the Second Cataract (see map 3). During the Second Intermediate Period power devolved to various local rulers until foreigners from the east, known as the Hyksos, extended their authority over a large part of Egypt. The Hyksos were eventually expelled by the independent rulers of Thebes, who reunified Egypt from the south.

Expansion and disunity

During the New Kingdom, military conquests created an Egyptian empire stretching from the Euphrates in the north to Nubia in the south (see map 2). Within Egypt, imperial expansion was matched by magnificent construction works of tombs and temples.

The cult of the most important god Amun-Re was temporarily set back when Akhenaten (c. 1364–1347 BC) built a new capital at Amarna, where the worship of the Aten or solar disc was promoted.

Under Rameses II Egypt reached a pinnacle of wealth and power, but there are clear indications that from the reign of Rameses III onwards there were growing external and internal problems. Egypt's empire in Syria and Palestine was lost. Its eastern and seaward borders were threatened by the sea peoples. On the western border, despite the victories of Rameses III, the Libyans posed a continuing and destabilizing problem. Internally, royal power was eroded by such factors as weak rulers, administrative inefficiency and the growing authority of the high priests of Amun at Thebes. By the end of the 20th Dynasty (c. 1069 BC) Egypt was once again a disunited land.

Map

ASIA MINOR

HITTITES

Carchemish
Alalakh
Aleppo
Zalkhi
Ugarit (Ras Shamra)
MITANNIANS
Euphrates
Neya
Siyannu
Zinzar
Tunip
Arvad
Qatna
Simyra
Qadesh
Irqata
Ullaza Riblah
Tripolis Ardata
Byblos
Berytus
Sidon
Kumidu
Tyre
Damascus
Hazor
Megiddo 1457
Aruna Taanach
Shechem
Joppa
Jerusalem
Ascalon
Dead Sea
Gaza
Sharuhen

Alashiya (Cyprus)

Mediterranean Sea

Sinai

2 Egyptian campaigns in Syria and Palestine

— northern limit of campaigns of Tuthmosis I (1507–1494 BC) and Tuthmosis III (1490–1436 BC)

— boundary between Egyptian and Mitannian zones of influence at the end of the reign of Amenophis II (c. 1436–1412 BC)

— boundary between Egyptian and Hittite zones of influence at the end of the reign of Akhenaten, 1347 BC

2 The fertile land between the Mediterranean and the Syrian desert became a target for Egyptian imperialism during the early years of the 18th Dynasty. By the reign of Tuthmosis I, Egypt's power reached as far north as the Euphrates. Under his grandson, Tuthmosis III, 17 campaigns were fought in Palestine and Syria. Boundaries were established by treaties, first with the Mitannians, later with the Hittites. During the next 130 years much of this empire crumbled away. It was partly recovered by Seti I and Rameses II, but all these territories were lost after the reign of Rameses VI (c. 1142–1134 BC).

THE DYNASTIES OF ANCIENT EGYPT

Early Dynastic, c. 3100–2686 BC	9th and 10th Dynasties, c. 2160–2040 BC	15th Dynasty, c. 1648–1540 BC	23rd Dynasty, 828–712 BC
1st Dynasty, c. 3100–2890 BC		16th Dynasty, c. 1648–1540 BC	24th Dynasty, 724–712 BC
2nd Dynasty, c. 2890–2686 BC	**Middle Kingdom, c. 2040–1720 BC**	17th Dynasty, c. 1648–1552 BC	25th Dynasty, 770–664 BC
Old Kingdom, c. 2686–2181 BC	11th Dynasty, c. 2040–1991 BC		**Late Period, 664–630 BC**
3rd Dynasty, c. 2686–2613 BC	12th Dynasty, c. 1991–1783 BC	**New Kingdom, c. 1550–1069 BC**	26th Dynasty, 664–525 BC
4th Dynasty, c. 2613–2494 BC	13th Dynasty, c. 1783–1730 BC	18th Dynasty, c. 1550–1295 BC	27th Dynasty, 525–404 BC
5th Dynasty, c. 2494–2345 BC		19th Dynasty, c. 1295–1187 BC	28th Dynasty, 404–399 BC
6th Dynasty, c. 2345–2181 BC	**Second Intermediate Period, c. 1720–1550 BC (various contemporaneous dynasties)**	20th Dynasty, c. 1186–1069 BC	29th Dynasty, 399–379 BC
First Intermediate Period, c. 2181–2040 BC	13th Dynasty, c. 1730–1648 BC	**Beginning of the Third Intermediate Period, c. 1069**	30th Dynasty, 379–341 BC
7th and 8th Dynasties, c. 2181–2160 BC	14th Dynasty, c. 1720–1648 BC	21st Dynasty, c. 1069–945 BC	31st Dynasty, 341–332 BC
		22nd Dynasty, 945–712 BC	32nd Dynasty, 332–330 BC

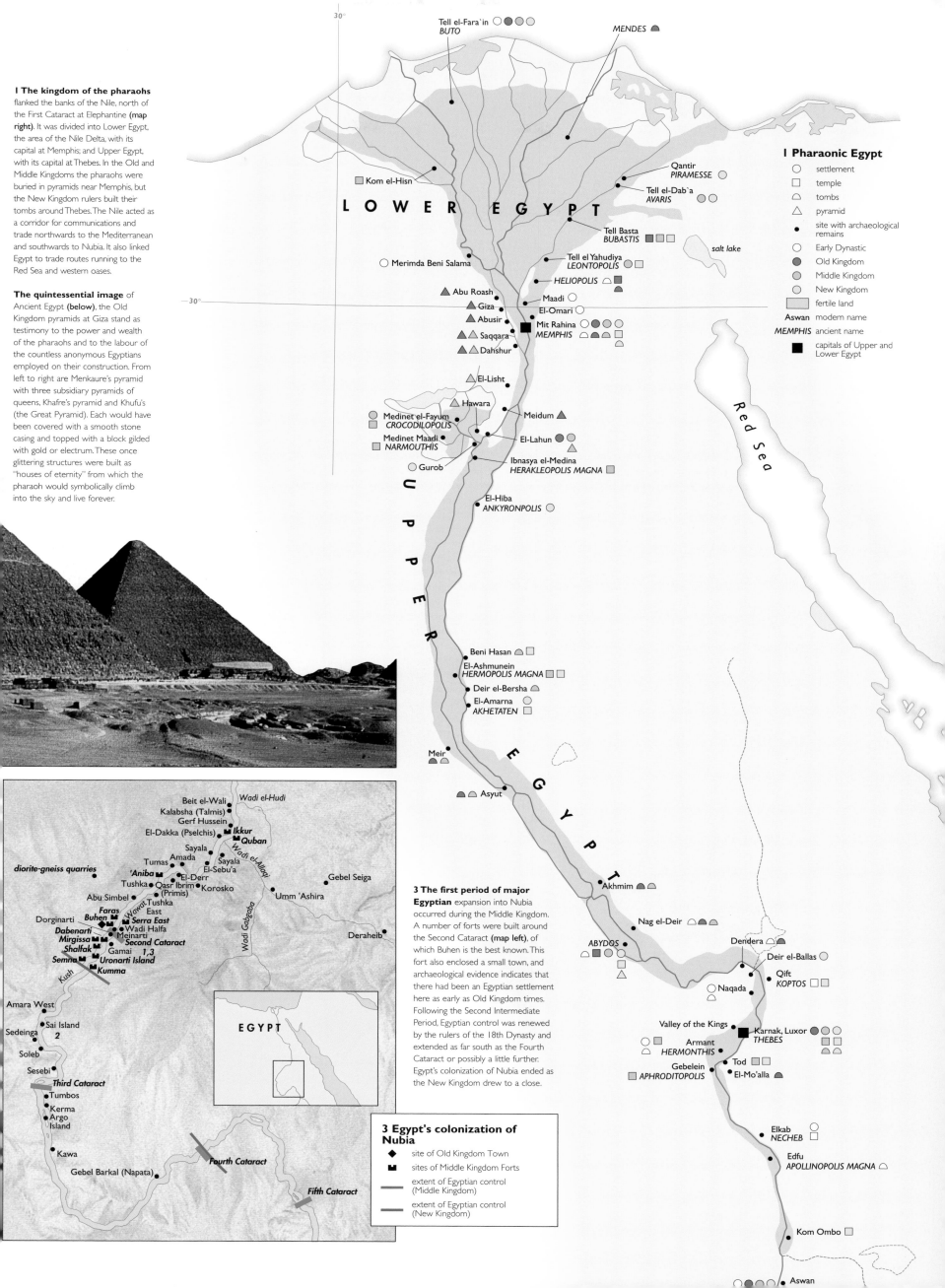

1 The kingdom of the pharaohs flanked the banks of the Nile, north of the First Cataract at Elephantine (**map right**). It was divided into Lower Egypt, the area of the Nile Delta, with its capital at Memphis; and Upper Egypt, with its capital at Thebes. In the Old and Middle Kingdoms the pharaohs were buried in pyramids near Memphis, but the New Kingdom rulers built their tombs around Thebes. The Nile acted as a corridor for communications and trade northwards to the Mediterranean and southwards to Nubia. It also linked Egypt to trade routes running to the Red Sea and western oases.

The quintessential image of Ancient Egypt (**below**), the Old Kingdom pyramids at Giza stand as testimony to the power and wealth of the pharaohs and to the labour of the countless anonymous Egyptians employed on their construction. From left to right are Menkaure's pyramid with three subsidiary pyramids of queens, Khafre's pyramid and Khufu's (the Great Pyramid). Each would have been covered with a smooth stone casing and topped with a block gilded with gold or electrum. These once glittering structures were built as "houses of eternity" from which the pharaoh would symbolically climb into the sky and live forever.

3 The first period of major Egyptian expansion into Nubia occurred during the Middle Kingdom. A number of forts were built around the Second Cataract (**map left**), of which Buhen is the best known. This fort also enclosed a small town, and archaeological evidence indicates that there had been an Egyptian settlement here as early as Old Kingdom times. Following the Second Intermediate Period, Egyptian control was renewed by the rulers of the 18th Dynasty and extended as far south as the Fourth Cataract or possibly a little further. Egypt's colonization of Nubia ended as the New Kingdom drew to a close.

1 Pharaonic Egypt

- ○ settlement
- □ temple
- ◠ tombs
- △ pyramid
- • site with archaeological remains
- ○ Early Dynastic
- ◔ Old Kingdom
- ◑ Middle Kingdom
- ◕ New Kingdom
- fertile land
- **Aswan** modern name
- *MEMPHIS* ancient name
- ■ capitals of Upper and Lower Egypt

3 Egypt's colonization of Nubia

- ◆ site of Old Kingdom Town
- ◼ sites of Middle Kingdom Forts
- — extent of Egyptian control (Middle Kingdom)
- — extent of Egyptian control (New Kingdom)

Map labels (main map)

LOWER EGYPT

UPPER EGYPT

Red Sea

Tell el-Fara`in / BUTO
MENDES
Qantir / PIRAMESSE
Tell el-Dab`a / AVARIS
Kom el-Hisn
salt lake
Tell Basta / BUBASTIS
Tell el Yahudiya / LEONTOPOLIS
HELIOPOLIS
Merimda Beni Salama
Maadi
El-Omari
Abu Roash
Giza
Abusir
Saqqara
Dahshur
Mit Rahina / MEMPHIS
El-Lisht
Hawara
Medinet el-Fayum / CROCODILOPOLIS
Meidum
Medinet Maadi / NARMOUTHIS
El-Lahun
Gurob
Ibnasya el-Medina / HERAKLEOPOLIS MAGNA
El-Hiba / ANKYRONPOLIS
Beni Hasan
El-Ashmunein / HERMOPOLIS MAGNA
Deir el-Bersha
El-Amarna / AKHETATEN
Meir
Asyut
Akhmim
Nag el-Deir
ABYDOS
Dendera
Deir el-Ballas
Qift / KOPTOS
Naqada
Valley of the Kings
Karnak, Luxor / THEBES
Armant / HERMONTHIS
Gebelein / APHRODITOPOLIS
Tod
El-Mo'alla
Elkab / NECHEB
Edfu / APOLLINOPOLIS MAGNA
Kom Ombo
Aswan

Map labels (Nubia inset)

EGYPT
Beit el-Wali
Wadi el-Hudi
Kalabsha (Talmis)
Gerf Hussein
El-Dakka (Pselchis)
Ikkur
Quban
Sayala
Wadi el-Allaqi
diorite-gneiss quarries
Tumas
Amada
Sayala
'Aniba
El-Derr
El-Sebu'a
Gebel Seiga
Tushka
Qasr Ibrim (Primis)
Koroska
Abu Simbel
Umm 'Ashira
Tushka East
Dorginarti
Faras
Buhen
Serra East
Wadi Gabgaba
Dabenarti
Wadi Halfa
Mirgissa
Meinarti
Derahelb
Shalfak
Gamai
Second Cataract
Semna
Uronarti Island
Kush
Kumma
Amara West
Sai Island
Sedeinga
Soleb
Sesebi
Third Cataract
Tumbos
Kerma
Argo Island
Kawa
Gebel Barkal (Napata)
Fourth Cataract
Fifth Cataract

The Near East

c. 1420 BC Tudhaliya I begins expansion of Hittite power

c. 1390 BC Amenophis III of Egypt marries the daughter of Kassite King Kurigalzu I of Babylon

1275 BC Battle of Kadesh between Rameses II of Egypt and the Hittites

c. 1025 BC Emergence of Israelite kingdom

The period after 1600 BC saw the fertile lands of Mesopotamia and the Levant become the battleground between rival empires: Hittites, Mitannians, Assyrians, Babylonians, Elamites and Egyptians. After 1200 BC, however, these powers collapsed in a dramatic sequence of events that is still not fully understood by historians. The resulting two centuries of upheaval marked the end of the Bronze Age in the Near East.

AFTER THAT HATTUSILI RULED AS KING AND HIS SONS, HIS BROTHERS, HIS SONS-IN-LAW, THE PEOPLE OF HIS FAMILY AND HIS SOLDIERS WERE GATHERED AROUND HIM. WHEREVER HE CAMPAIGNED HE HELD THE LANDS OF HIS ENEMIES CONQUERED WITH HIS ARM. HE CONSTANTLY DESTROYED THE LANDS OF HIS ENEMIES AND SUBJECTED THEM ENTIRELY, AND HE MADE THEM INTO THE FRONTIERS OF THE SEA. AS SOON AS HE HAD RETURNED FROM CAMPAIGNING, EACH OF HIS SONS WENT INTO A COUNTRY AND IN HIS HANDS EACH CITY FLOURISHED.

Telepinu (1525–1500)
Edict

MUCH OF THE DETAILED knowledge of the relationships between the warring empires comes from the "Amarna letters". This collection of documents written in Akkadian (the international language of diplomacy in this period), consists of correspondence between the Egyptian pharaohs Amenophis III, Akhenaten and Tutankhamun (1390–1327 BC) and the rulers of the other great powers. The letters reveal the dynastic marriages and gift-giving that typify relations between rulers: the personal and the political were intimately bound together.

The most important new power in the region was the Hittite empire in central Anatolia. The Hittites had been expanding their power from their centre at Hattushash since the reign of Hattusili I (c. 1650–1620 BC). Mursili I (c. 1620–c. 1590 BC) led an expedition that destroyed Aleppo and Babylon, but it was Tudhaliya I (c. 1420–1400 BC) and Suppiluliuma I (1344–1322 BC) who made the Hittites an imperial power. The empire consisted of a large number of small territories governed by client kings who owed

their position entirely to the "Great King" who ruled from the capital, Hattusa. Client rulers were required to raise troops for the king's campaigns, and to provide labour and goods for the central administration. They were often bound to the king by marriage ties.

The Hittites faced frequent pressure on their borders from Arzawa to the west and the Gasga to the north, but their biggest rivals were Egypt and the kingdom of Mitanni to the south. Mitanni first appears in the historical record in c. 1480 BC, when its ruler, Parrattarna, is described as controlling Aleppo. For the next 140 years Mitanni was a major power, controlling Assyria by 1400 BC. Mutual concern about Hittite power saw an alliance between Mitanni and Egypt, and the last independent ruler of Mitanni, Tushratta, married his daughter to Amenophis III and, after the pharaoh's death, to his son Amenophis IV (Akhenaten). Tushratta was assassinated in c.1340 BC, and his son Shattiwaza was installed as a vassal of the Hittites. Hostility continued between the Hittites and the Egyptians, leading to the great but inconclu-

sive battle of Kadesh in 1275 BC between the pharaoh Rameses II (1279–1213 BC) and the Hittite king Muwatalli (1295–1271 BC).

Assyrian expansion began under Ashur-uballit I (1353–1318 BC), as Mitanni began to collapse under Hittite pressure. Adad-nirari I (1295–1264 BC) seized what was left of Mitanni from the Hittites, and Assyrian power grew to its greatest extent in the reign of Tikulti-ninurta I (1233–1197 BC), who conquered Babylon and installed a series of puppet rulers. Up until then Mesopotamia had been through a period of stability, ruled from Babylon, which came under the control of the Kassites in c. 1595 BC. Little is known about their origins, but they were noted for their horses and chariots, and maintained power for four centuries.

The Assyrian attack on Babylon led to counterattacks from Elam to the southeast. The Elamite kings Kiden-Hutran (c. 1235–1210 BC) and Shutruk-

1 The second half of the 2nd millennium saw the growth of a number of competing powers in the Near East. The map (below) indicates the territorial position in c. 1330 BC. To the west, New Kingdom Egypt fought for control of Syria-Palestine first with Mitanni and then with the Hittites, while to the east the Kassite kings of Babylon were increasingly threatened by the emergent powers of Assyria to the north and Elam to the east.

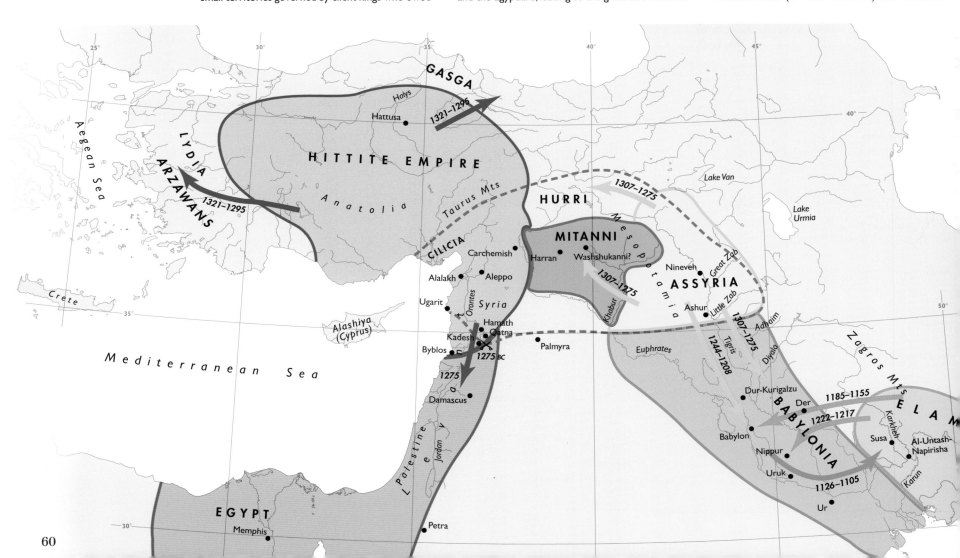

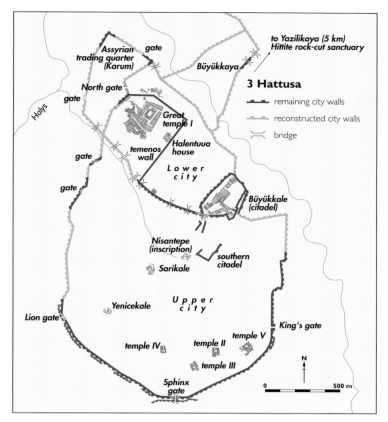

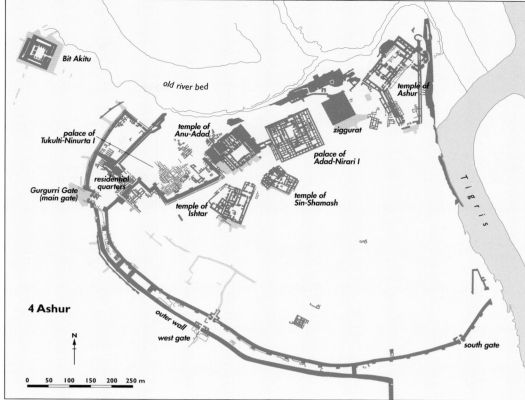

3 Hattusa

- ▬▬ remaining city walls
- ▬▬ reconstructed city walls
- ╫ bridge

to Yazilikaya (5 km)
Hittite rock-cut sanctuary

Assyrian trading quarter (Karum)
Büyükkaya
gate
North gate
gate
Hâlys
Great temple I
Halentuua house
temenos wall
Lower city
Büyükkale (citadel)
gate
gate
Nisantepe (inscription)
southern citadel
Sarikale
Upper city
Yenicekale
Lion gate
temple IV
temple II
temple V
King's gate
temple III
Sphinx gate
N
0 — 500 m

4 Ashur

Bit Akitu
old river bed
temple of Ashur
palace of Tukulti-Ninurta I
temple of Anu-Adad
ziggurat
palace of Adad-Nirari I
residential quarters
Gurgurri Gate (main gate)
temple of Ishtar
temple of Sin-Shamash
Tigris
outer wall
west gate
N
south gate
0 50 100 150 200 250 m

The excavated remains (maps above) of the central cities of the Hittite empire and Assyria can tell us much about the nature of government in the period 1600–1200 BC. Both cities are dominated by symbols of royal authority in the form of the massive city walls, palaces and citadels, and by symbols of divine authority in the form of great temple complexes. Religious and political control were not separated, and the cities were ceremonial centres where rulers could demonstrate their power and that of the gods who protected them.

The Near East, c. 1340 BC

- Hittite Empire established by Suppiluliuma I, 1344–1322 BC
- Mitanni territory at its greatest extent, c. 1480–1340 BC
- Mitanni after c. 1340 BC (under Hittite and Assyrian control)
- Assyrian territory gained by Ashur-uballit I, 1365–1330 BC
- Babylonia under Burnaburiash II, 1359–1333 BC
- Elam under Tepti-ahar, c. 1365–1330 BC
- Egypt under Amenophis IV and Tutankhamun, 1352–1327 BC

Nahunte (1185–1155 BC) led campaigns into Mesopotamia, the latter capturing Babylon. Despite a Babylonian revival under Nebuchadnezzar I (1126–1205 BC), the general upheaval that brought an end to the Bronze Age saw both Babylon and Elam

A letter from Amarna (left) sent by Tushratta of Mitanni to Amenophis IV (Akhenaten) in c. 1348 BC. Tushratta sends greetings to the pharaoh, his mother Tiye and his wife Taduhepa, Tushratta's daughter. He goes on to complain of the treatment of his envoys, who have been detained in Egypt rather than being sent back with gifts. Letters like these, written in cuneiform script on clay tablets, provide invaluable information about relations between the powers in this period.

2 The period after 1200 BC saw a number of dramatic events in the Near East (map below). Cities and palaces were destroyed as the old imperial powers either disappeared or shrank in size. In their place subordinate populations were able to establish their own governments, and these peoples – Phrygians, Aramaeans, Philistines, Chaldaeans and Persians – who were not dependent on the political, social and economic structures of the Bronze Age, enter the historical stage for the first time.

more or less disappear from the historical record within a few years.

Around 1200 BC there was a wave of destruction throughout the eastern Mediterranean from Greece to Syria and Palestine. Fifty years later several cities in Mesopotamia were also destroyed. There are reports from the city of Ugarit of attacks from the sea, and the Egyptian pharaohs Merneptah (1213–1203 BC) and Rameses III (1184–1150 BC) describe battles with "sea peoples". Although this obscure group was once considered the cause of widespread destruction it is now thought that they were merely taking advantage of a widespread breakdown in political organization. Earthquakes, drought, interruption to the supply of metals, and many other things, have been suggested as the cause of the collapse. It is likely that no one explanation will suffice, and that a number of external factors, combined with the fragility of the centralized power structures of the Bronze Age kingdoms, led to the dramatic end of the civilizations of the Bronze Age.

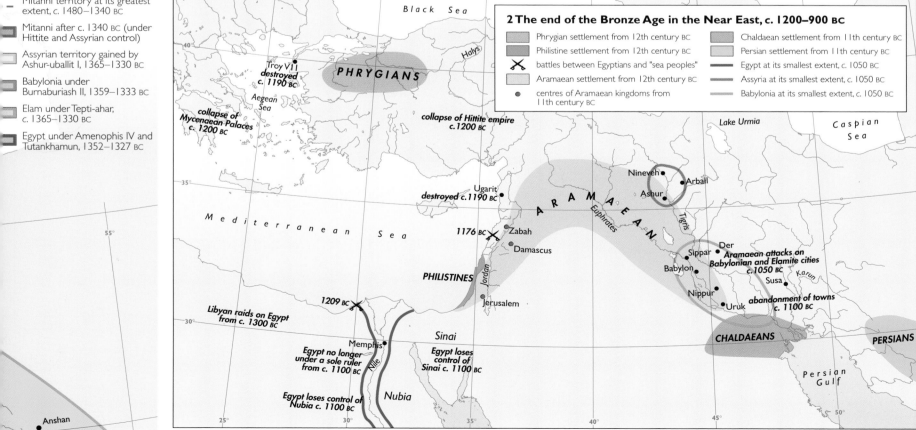

2 The end of the Bronze Age in the Near East, c. 1200–900 BC

- Phrygian settlement from 12th century BC
- Philistine settlement from 12th century BC
- ✕ battles between Egyptians and "sea peoples"
- Aramaean settlement from 12th century BC
- centres of Aramaean kingdoms from 11th century BC
- Chaldaean settlement from 11th century BC
- Persian settlement from 11th century BC
- Egypt at its smallest extent, c. 1050 BC
- Assyria at its smallest extent, c. 1050 BC
- Babylonia at its smallest extent, c. 1050 BC

Black Sea
Hâlys
PHRYGIANS
Troy VII destroyed c. 1190 BC
Aegean Sea
collapse of Mycenaean Palaces c. 1200 BC
collapse of Hittite empire c. 1200 BC
Lake Urmia
Caspian Sea
Nineveh
Arbail
Ashur
ARAMAEAN
Euphrates
Tigris
Mediterranean Sea
Ugarit destroyed c. 1190 BC
1176 BC Zabah
Damascus
PHILISTINES
Jordan
Jerusalem
Der
Sippar
Aramaean attacks on Babylonian and Elamite cities c. 1050 BC
Babylon
Susa
Karun
Nippur
Uruk
abandonment of towns c. 1100 BC
1209 BC
Libyan raids on Egypt from c. 1300 BC
Memphis
Sinai
Egypt loses control of Sinai c. 1100 BC
Egypt no longer under a sole ruler from c. 1100 BC
Nile
Egypt loses control of Nubia c. 1100 BC
Nubia
CHALDAEANS
PERSIANS
Persian Gulf
Anshan

Peoples of South America and the Caribbean

By 300 BC most people in South America had become farmers, although some hunter-gathering persisted in the southern part of the continent where farming was difficult. By 750 BC, complex societies were developing in the Andes. As in Mesoamerica, they went through phases of growth and decline, but in the central Andes there was a degree of cultural unity in that artistic differences between the highlands and lowlands were not as marked.

South America

The coast of the central Andes is best known, archaeologically, for the graphic pottery of the Moche, dating from AD 100 to 600. It reveals much about daily life and religion. The Moche were the first to assert themselves more widely by conquest. Both pottery and tombs show that, like their contemporaries in Mesoamerica, Moche kings exhibited their authority in elaborate rites.

Yet from about AD 600 the coast succumbed to conquest from the Tiahuanaco and the Huari (see map 3). Both these civilizations developed elements of the earlier Chavín cult (see p. 44). The city of Tiahuanaco was centred on the Titicaca Basin in Bolivia where the people grew potatoes and herded llamas and alpacas. Renowned for their stone buildings and sculpture, their expansion seems to have been achieved through the establishment of religious and commercial colonies. The reasons for its collapse about AD 1200 are not fully understood, but may have been related to climate change that affected agricultural production. The Huari are often considered to have been the precursors of the Inca. Among the hallmarks of Huari civilization was a network of roads and logistical, perhaps administrative, bases. Following two centuries of political fragmentation, the Moche tradition was revived among the Chimú, consummate engineers who developed vast irrigation systems. They controlled parts of the Andean coast until their destruction by the Incas (see p. 162).

In the northern Andes and southern Central America, along the Amazon and in the plains southwest of the Amazon, there were other large populations. Much of the most telling evidence for them is in the form of extensive field systems. In northwestern South America chiefdoms had emerged, and in the southernmost parts of Central America superb sculpture, goldwork and pottery indicate powerful patrons (see map 1).

The Caribbean

There is some evidence that peoples exploiting wild food resources occupied Cuba, Haiti and the Dominican Republic about 4000 BC. However, it was

c. 500 BC to 250 BC First movement of Arawak-speaking peoples to the Caribbean

c. 100 BC First Nasca lines constructed

c. AD 100 to AD 700 Moche culture dominates the Pacific coast

c. AD 600 Huari and Tiahuanaco expansion begins

c. AD 1200 Collapse of Tiahuanaco

AD 1275 Chimú conquests begin

2 and 3 By the 6th century AD, each of the major regions of the Andes had its own local art style. This diversity probably reflects a lack of political unity and the existence of many independent and fragmentary states (maps below). With soldiers, battle scenes and severed heads a frequent theme in pottery decoration, relations between these states may have been warlike. In artistic terms, the people of Moche and Nasca were supreme. After AD 600, the balance of power began to shift from the coast to the highlands, where the cities of Tiahuanaco and Huari between them came to dominate the central Andes. Except in the north, regional styles of architecture and pottery decoration fell under the influence of a single new art style whose subject matter was taken from Tiahuanaco-Huari mythology.

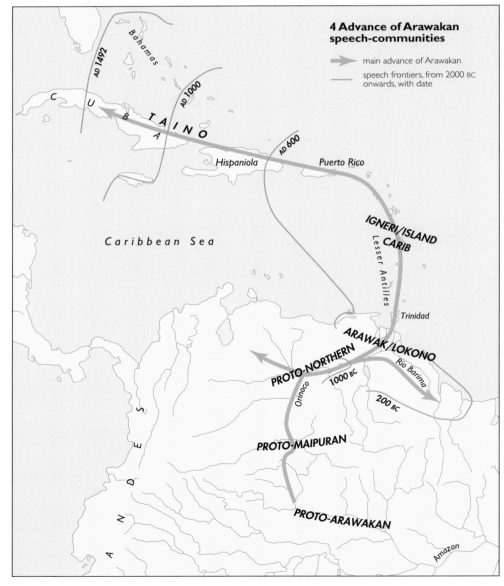

4 Advance of Arawakan speech-communities

→ main advance of Arawakan

— speech frontiers, from 2000 BC onwards, with date

4 Arawak-speaking peoples entered the Caribbean from the Guianan and Venezuelan coasts. Their migrations have been dated by the presence of a distinctive form of red and white pottery and through linguistic analysis. These people introduced the cultivation of manioc (cassava) and they carved stone and shell objects, known as zemis, which were important symbols in their religion.

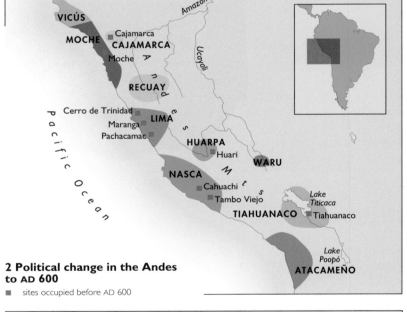

2 Political change in the Andes to AD 600

■ sites occupied before AD 600

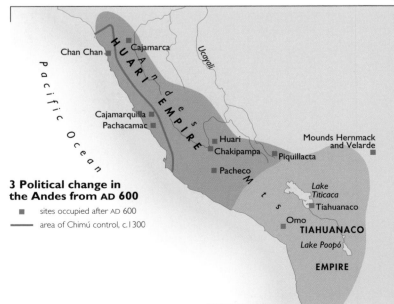

3 Political change in the Andes from AD 600

■ sites occupied after AD 600

— area of Chimú control, c.1300

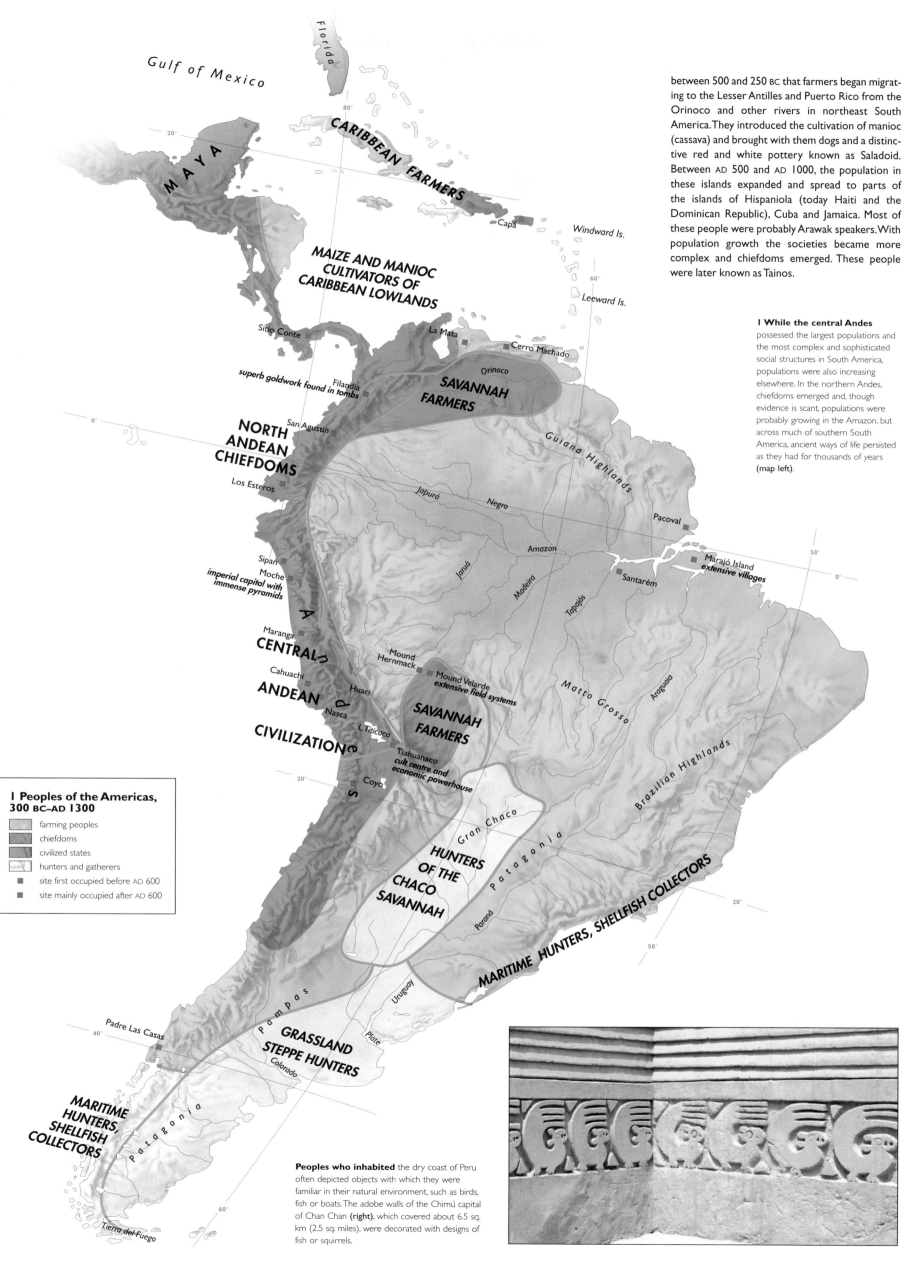

Gulf of Mexico

Florida

80°

20°

CARIBBEAN FARMERS

M A Y A

Capa

Windward Is.

60°

Leeward Is.

between 500 and 250 BC that farmers began migrating to the Lesser Antilles and Puerto Rico from the Orinoco and other rivers in northeast South America. They introduced the cultivation of manioc (cassava) and brought with them dogs and a distinctive red and white pottery known as Saladoid. Between AD 500 and AD 1000, the population in these islands expanded and spread to parts of the islands of Hispaniola (today Haiti and the Dominican Republic), Cuba and Jamaica. Most of these people were probably Arawak speakers. With population growth the societies became more complex and chiefdoms emerged. These people were later known as Tainos.

MAIZE AND MANIOC
CULTIVATORS OF
CARIBBEAN LOWLANDS

Sitio Conte

La Mata

Cerro Machado

1 While the central Andes
possessed the largest populations and the most complex and sophisticated social structures in South America, populations were also increasing elsewhere. In the northern Andes, chiefdoms emerged and, though evidence is scant, populations were probably growing in the Amazon, but across much of southern South America, ancient ways of life persisted as they had for thousands of years **(map left)**.

superb goldwork found in tombs

Filandia

San Agustin

Orinoco

SAVANNAH
FARMERS

0°

NORTH
ANDEAN
CHIEFDOMS

Guiana Highlands

Los Esteros

Japurá

Negro

Pacoval

Sipan

Japurá

Amazon

Marajó Island
extensive villages

50°

Moche

imperial capital with
immense pyramids

Santarém

Madeira

Tapajós

0°

A

Maranga

CENTRAL

Mound
Hernmack

Matto Grosso

Araguaia

Cahuachi

ANDEAN

Huari

Mound Velarde
extensive field systems

Nasca

L. Titicaca

SAVANNAH
FARMERS

Brazilian Highlands

CIVILIZATION

Tiahuanaco
cult centre and
economic powerhouse

20°

Coyo

**1 Peoples of the Americas,
300 BC–AD 1300**

Gran Chaco

farming peoples

chiefdoms

Patagonia

HUNTERS
OF
THE
CHACO
SAVANNAH

MARITIME HUNTERS, SHELLFISH COLLECTORS

civilized states

hunters and gatherers

Paraná

■ site first occupied before AD 600

■ site mainly occupied after AD 600

50°

20°

Uruguay

Padre Las Casas

Pampas

Plate

40°

GRASSLAND
STEPPE
HUNTERS

Colorado

MARITIME
HUNTERS,
SHELLFISH
COLLECTORS

Patagonia

Peoples who inhabited the dry coast of Peru often depicted objects with which they were familiar in their natural environment, such as birds, fish or boats. The adobe walls of the Chimú capital of Chan Chan **(right)**, which covered about 6.5 sq. km (2.5 sq. miles), were decorated with designs of fish or squirrels.

60°

Tierra del Fuego

63

Peoples of Mesoamerica

Many societies in the Americas changed little in the 2000 years before 1300. In Mesoamerica, however, complex societies were developing by the end of the first millennium BC. They then underwent cycles of growth and decline that included periods of outstanding intellectual and artistic achievement.

Zapotec ball court at Monte Alban **(below).** A distinctive feature of Mesoamerican culture was a ball game for which special courts were constructed. The game was played by two teams with a rubber ball; the sloping sides were used in the game, not for spectators. It was not merely a sport, but a complex ritual based on religious beliefs, in which the ball represented the sun, and which normally ended with members of the losing team being sacrificed.

THE LORDS ... COULD NOT HAVE DONE THE WORK OF BUILDING THEIR HOUSES OR THE HOUSES OF THEIR GODS, WERE IT NOT ... THAT THEIR VASSALS HAD BECOME NUMEROUS.

From the *Popol Vuh*, the sacred book of the Quichè Maya

B Y 300 BC, ALMOST EVERY way of life that the Europeans would later encounter had developed in Mesoamerica: while some societies in northern Mexico continued to live by hunting, fishing and gathering, most had adopted farming and some were developing into states that extended their influence by trade or force.

The Rise of Teotihuacán

Earlier developments in Mesoamerica were eclipsed in about AD 100 by the sudden rise of Teotihuacán. The city grew to about 200,000, much larger than cities in the Old World at the time. There are doubts about the nature of the city's economy but the centre – with the Temple of Quetzalcoatl and the Pyramids of the Sun and the Moon – was clearly planned for rites that involved human sacrifices. The city also possessed thousands of artisans who produced many items for foreign trade, including many articles made of obsidian, which they obtained from mines they controlled at Pachuca. Whether or not in association with trade, the Teotihuacános' influence spread widely through present-day Mexico and Guatemala and was apparent in their distinctive pottery, crafts and architecture. In the 7th century AD Teotihuacán was attacked either by insiders or outsiders, or both, and its power destroyed, although it continued to function as a town.

I The Maya, 300 BC–AD 300

- late formative and proto-Classic site (300 BC–AD 300)
- Northern Lowlands
- Southern Lowlands
- Highlands

Yucatán

Dzibilchaltún
Acancéh
Chichén Itzá
Yaxuná
Maní
Kabáh · Loltun Cave
Santa Rosa Xtampak
Cerros
Cuello
El Mirador
Río Azul
San Jose
Uaxactún
Barton Ramie
Holmul
Tikal
Tzimin Kax
Bellote
San Miguel
Altar de Sacrificios
San Felipe
San Augustín · Chiapa del Corzo
Santa Rita
Santa Cruz
Santa Rosa
Copán
Tonalá
Yarumela
Abaj
Takalik · Kaminaljuyú
Izapa
El Baúl
El Jobo · Chocolá
Obrero · Chalchuapa
Salinas
la Blanca · Monte
Finca Arizona · Usulután
Alto

c. AD 100 Rise of Teotihuacán

c. AD 600 Apogee of Maya civilization

c. AD 700 Teotihuacán destroyed

c. AD 850 Collapse of Maya civilization

c. AD 900 First migration of Nahua-speaking peoples to Central America

c. AD 1175 Tula abandoned by Toltecs

I By AD 250, Mesoamerica was dominated by Teotihuacán, the Maya and the Zapotecs **(map left).** Three centuries later, new civilizations – the Totonacs, the Mixtecs and others – were emerging. The extraordinarily diverse Maya area comprised a number of geological zones; the limestone plateau of the Yucatán, the mountains of central Guatemala, the volcanic belt of southern Guatemala, the Pacific lowlands and the Tabasco plain. With vegetation as various as seasonal swamps just above sea level, tropical rain forests and 4000-metre peaks, and with rainfall ranging from 570 to 3000 millimetres a year, the diversity in geological and ecological resources was enormous.

MAYA HIEROGLYPHS

The Maya hieroglyphic script was the most complete script system in the ancient Americas. Hundreds of inscriptions survive, on stelae, lintels and the other stone monuments, although only four Post-Classic codices survive (the rest having been destroyed in the aftermath of the Spanish conquest). At the heart of the writing system lies the Long Count calendar, a complex of five different calendrical systems which could measure cycles of time as long as 4,000 years. The birth and accession dates of rulers were frequently marked on Classic monuments as well as the conquest of their foes. The glyphs for several major Maya cities are given below.

Tikal

Naranjo

Yaxchilán

Palenque

Copán

Quiriguá

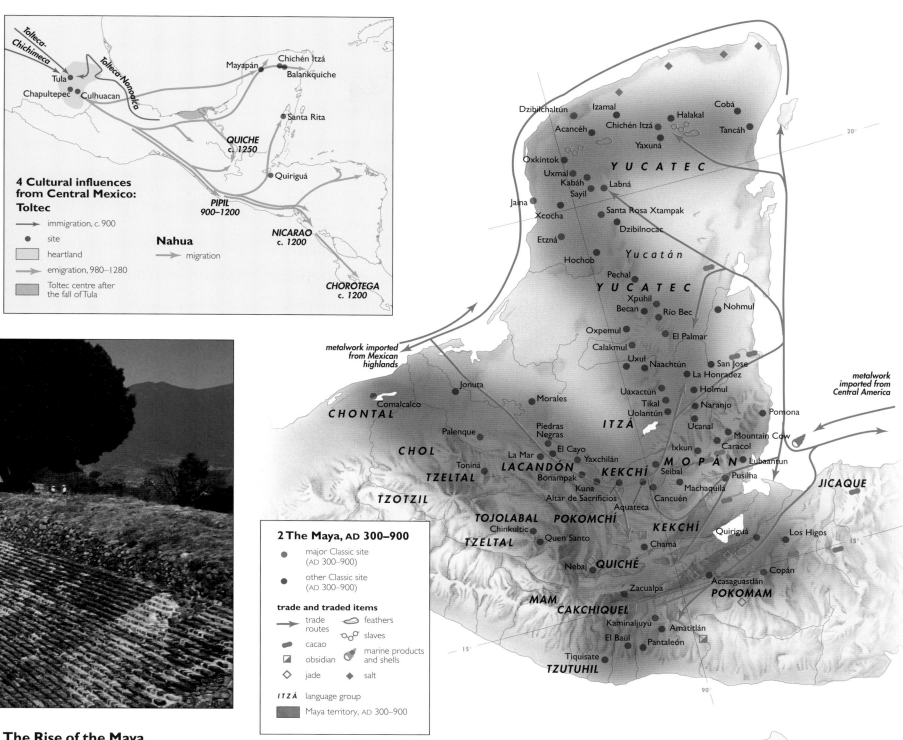

4 Cultural influences from Central Mexico: Toltec

→ immigration, c. 900
• site
▭ heartland
⟶ emigration, 980–1280
▭ Toltec centre after the fall of Tula

Nahua
⟶ migration

Tolteca-Chichimeca
Tolteca-Nonoalca
Tula
Chapultepec
Culhuacan
Mayapán
Chichén Itzá
Balankquiche
Santa Rita
QUICHE c. 1250
Quiriguá
PIPIL 900–1200
NICARAO c. 1200
CHOROTEGA c. 1200

metalwork imported from Mexican highlands

metalwork imported from Central America

Dzibilchaltún
Izamal
Acancéh
Oxkintok
Uxmal
Jaina
Xcocha
Etzná
Hochob
Pechal
Kabáh
Sayil
Labná
Santa Rosa Xtampak
Dzibilnocac
Chichén Itzá
Yaxuná
Halakal
Cobá
Tancáh

YUCATEC
Yucatán
YUCATEC

Xpuhil
Becan
Río Bec
Nohmul
Oxpemul
El Palmar
Calakmul
Uxul
Naachtún
San Jose
La Honradez
Holmul
Uaxactún
Tikal
Naranjo
Uolantún
Pomona
Jonuta
Morales
Comalcalco
CHONTAL
Palenque
Piedras Negras
El Cayo
Ucanal
Mountain Cow
Caracol
ITZÁ
Ixkun
MOPÁN
Lubaantun
CHOL
Toniná
La Mar
Yaxchilán
Seibal
Pusilha
TZELTAL
LACANDÓN
KEKCHÍ
Bonampak
Machaquila
JICAQUE
TZOTZIL
Kuna
Altar de Sacrificios
Aquateca
Cancuén
Chinkultic
Quen Santo
Chamá
Quiriguá
Los Higos
Nebaj
QUICHÉ
Zacualpa
Copán
MAM
CAKCHIQUEL
POKOMAM
Kaminaljuyú
Amatitlán
El Baúl
Pantaleón
Tiquisate
TZUTUHIL

2 The Maya, AD 300–900

• major Classic site (AD 300–900)
• other Classic site (AD 300–900)

trade and traded items
⟶ trade routes
▭ cacao
▭ obsidian
◇ jade
◠ feathers
slaves
marine products and shells
salt

ITZÁ language group
▭ Maya territory, AD 300–900

El Meco
Dzibilchaltún
Cobá
Xelhá
San Gervasio
Tihoo
Aké
Chichén Itzá
Mayapán
Maní
Tulum
Huaymil
Chacmool
Yucatán
Champotón
Cilvituk
Ichpaatun
Santa Rita
Xicalango
Topoxte
Tayasal
El Pajaral
Naco
Quen Santo
Chaculá
Nebaj
Pantzac
Chutixtiox
Zacualpa
Zaculeu
Cahyup
Tajumulco
Utatlán
Mixco Viejo
Sololá

3 The Maya, AD 900–1500

• important post-Classic site (AD 900–1500)
— approximate border of Post-Classic Mayan state

The Rise of the Maya

At the same time the small but brilliant kingdoms of the Maya flourished. Their capitals were pyramid-studded ceremonial centres with densely settled sub-urbs. Voluminous inscriptions reveal a sophisticated but typically Mesoamerican concern with astrology. For a long time it was not understood how these cities in a tropical forest were supplied with food. It now seems they built terraces, drained fields and made extensive use of game and fish. However, whether it was on account of the chronic wars that are recorded, or of popular discontent, or of environmental degradation by excessive population – or of all of these factors – most of the towns were abandoned between AD 790 and the mid-9th century. Many districts revived later in what is known as the Post-Classic period, but the Maya never regained their grandeur.

The Rise of the Toltecs

The Maya "collapse" followed the dissolution of Teotihuacán in about 700. But between these poles of power a new generation of thriving towns had emerged, including some of Teotihuacán's protégés, such as Cholula, which established their independence from the traditional order. They appear to have been eclipsed in turn by the Toltecs, soldiers and probably traders, whose influence subsequently extended throughout Mesoamerica and beyond. In about 1175 their reign, too, ended, possibly on account of refugees from the north driven south by changing climatic conditions. Meanwhile, two Nahua-speaking migrations from central Mexico had extended Mesoamerican influence to societies on the Pacific coastal plain as far south as Costa Rica.

4 The Toltecs ruled much of Mayan central Mexico from their capital at Tula from the 10th to the 12th century AD (map top left). The emergence of the Toltecs marked the rise of militarism in Mesoamerica, and its influence spread through what is now Mexico and Guatemala where the Toltecs conquered lands previously controlled by the Maya. Meanwhile, following the collapse of Teotihuacán, Nahua-speaking peoples known as Pipil, whose language was related to that of the Aztecs, emerged in the highlands and subsequently migrated south along the Pacific coastal plain.

2 The Maya civilization (map above) had its origins in the highlands and Pacific coastal plain of Mesoamerica between 400 BC and AD 250, but when it reached its zenith between AD 300 and 900, power was concentrated in the lowlands. Following the Maya collapse in the southern lowlands about AD 900, the population moved to northern Yucatán where Maya civilization was regenerated.

3 Following the collapse of Classic Maya civilization around AD 900, the cities of the northern lowland such as Uxmal and the great urban centre of Chichén Itzá began to flourish (map right). However, these northern cities also declined after several centuries, and Chichén Itzá was abandoned in about 1200. A new capital, Mayapán in northern Yucatán, was founded in 1328. However, the city was destroyed in the civil wars of the mid-15th century, and by the early-16th century only a few small towns flourished.

Peoples of early North America

The early cultures of North America were predominantly agrarian-based, with small communities developing in and around areas where the natural environment provided rich sources of food. By AD 700 three distinct cultures had developed. These were more urban and culturally diverse, and they were heavily influenced by Mexican civilizations. By the beginning of the 15th century, however, these cultures were in decline.

BY 300 BC, the area stretching from Ohio to West Virginia had already been settled.

Small communities and villages developed in river valleys, where natural food resources (such as mammals, birds, fish and vegetable foods) were both abundant and close at hand. Horticulture also developed around this time: sunflowers, marsh elder and squashes were cultivated.

Archaeological evidence from this period points to the existence of chiefdoms: the elaborate burial sites, such as that at Hopewell in Ohio, are excellent indicators of the social, religious and trade networks through which imported goods, as well as ideas, filtered. By AD 700, three distinct cultural traditions had emerged in southwestern North America: the Hohokam, Mogollon and Anasazi. Their area of influence covered much of the territory that is now Utah, Colorado, Arizona and New Mexico, and also extended south into Sonora and Chihuahua.

The Hohokam, Mogollon and Anasazi cultures all had contact with Mexico, and this contact became a significant influence on their development. Excavations have revealed ball courts and Mesoamerican-style mosaics, bracelets, effigy vessels and figurines. The architectural layout of the towns (which were used as economic, religious and trading centres) also reveals Mexican influence, and the Mexicans may even have established Casas Grandes in Chihuahua as the "capital" of the Mogollon culture.

The first true towns in North America appeared in the Middle Mississippi Valley from AD 700. They were characteristically built on large, flat-topped, rectangular mounds, which supported temples and mortuary houses for the elite society and more modest timber houses for the town's merchants and officials. A town generally consisted of up to 20 mounds grouped together around a plaza and enclosed by a defensive wooden stockade. The towns had substantial populations: it is estimated that some reached 10,000 inhabitants.

The large rural population (about 200 people per square km) was based predominantly in the fertile river valleys surrounding the towns. Again, Mexican influence here is evident: after AD 700, a hardier strain of maize, popular in Mexico, was introduced and cultivated. In addition, the introduction of the bow and arrow to replace the spear-thrower and dart meant more efficient hunting of the abundant game on the uplands.

By the time 16th-century French explorers discovered the area, the population had advanced to a ranked, matrilineal society headed by a chief who ruled four well-defined classes. Archaeological evidence from Mississippi to Minnesota and from Oklahoma to the Atlantic coast also bears witness to the widespread existence of a religion known as the Southern Cult. Reaching its peak in 1250, the cult was strongly influenced by Mexican practice, especially in regard to the importance of the four cardinal points and the significance placed upon death.

Disease, caused by unhealthy overcrowding and poor sanitation, heralded the slow decline of the early North American cultures after AD 1300. However, their demise was a but a pale foreshadowing of the destruction that was to befall these cultures when Europeans arrived in the New World.

1 In both the eastern woodland and the Southwest, abundant wild plant food provided a very significant part of the diet long after the introduction of agricultural crops such as maize, beans and squash **(below)**. The varied environmental zones of California supported over 500 specialized hunting, gathering and fishing cultures, while the desert land of the Great Basin was sparsely populated by small groups of far-ranging foragers.

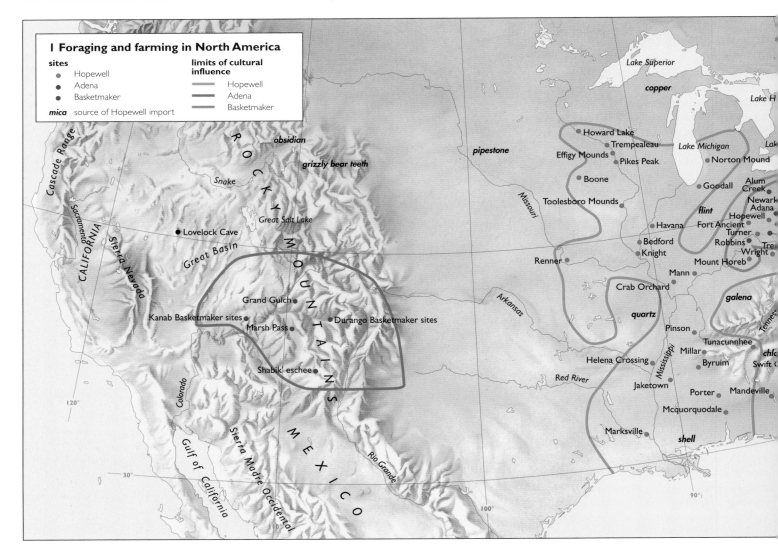

1 Foraging and farming in North America

sites
- Hopewell
- Adena
- Basketmaker

mica source of Hopewell import

limits of cultural influence
- Hopewell
- Adena
- Basketmaker

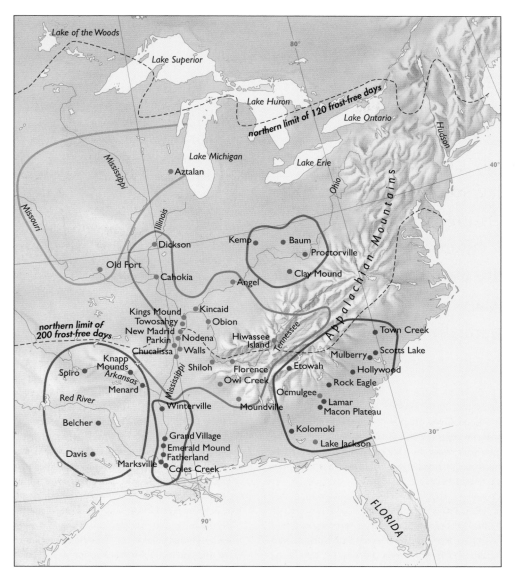

northern limit of 120 frost-free days

Lake of the Woods
Lake Superior
Lake Michigan
Lake Huron
Lake Ontario
Lake Erie
Hudson
Mississippi
Missouri
Ohio
Illinois
Tennessee
Arkansas
Red River
Appalachian Mountains
FLORIDA

Aztalan
Dickson
Old Fort
Cahokia
Kemp
Baum
Proctorville
Clay Mound
Angel
Kings Mound
Kincaid
Towosahgy
Obion
New Madrid
Nodena
Parkin
Walls
Chucalissa
Hiwassee Island
Knapp Mounds
Spiro
Shiloh
Florence
Owl Creek
Etowah
Mulberry
Town Creek
Scotts Lake
Hollywood
Rock Eagle
Menard
Ocmulgee
Winterville
Lamar
Macon Plateau
Moundville
Moundsville
Belcher
Kolomoki
Davis
Grand Village
Lake Jackson
Marksville
Emerald Mound
Fatherland
Coles Creek

northern limit of 200 frost-free days

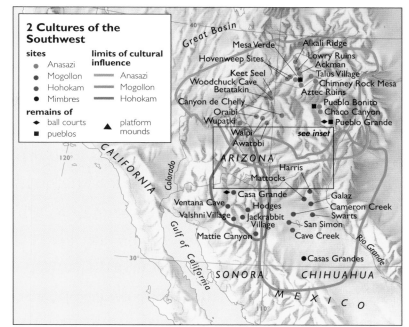

2 Cultures of the Southwest

sites
● Anasazi
● Mogollon
● Hohokam
● Mimbres

remains of
◆ ball courts
■ pueblos

limits of cultural influence
— Anasazi
— Mogollon
— Hohokam

▲ platform mounds

Great Basin
CALIFORNIA
ARIZONA
Colorado
Gulf of California
Rio Grande
SONORA
CHIHUAHUA
MEXICO

Mesa Verde
Alkali Ridge
Hovenweep Sites
Lowry Ruins
Ackman
Keet Seel
Talus Village
Woodchuck Cave
Chimney Rock Mesa
Betatakin
Aztec Ruins
Canyon de Chelly
Pueblo Bonito
Oraibi
Chaco Canyon
Wupatki
Pueblo Grande
Walpi
Awatobi
see inset
Harris
Mattocks
Casa Grande
Galaz
Ventana Cave
Hodges
Cameron Creek
Valshni Village
Swarts
Jackrabbit Village
San Simon
Mattie Canyon
Cave Creek
Casas Grandes

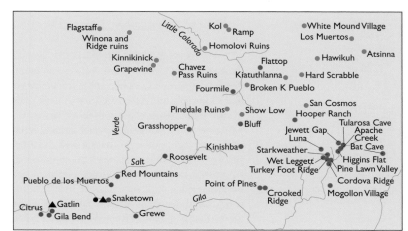

Flagstaff
Little Colorado
Kol
Ramp
White Mound Village
Winona and Ridge ruins
Homolovi Ruins
Los Muertos
Kinnikinick
Flattop
Hawikuh
Atsinna
Grapevine
Chavez Pass Ruins
Kiatuthlanna
Hard Scrabble
Fourmile
Broken K Pueblo
Verde
Pinedale Ruins
Show Low
San Cosmos
Hooper Ranch
Grasshopper
Bluff
Jewett Gap
Tularosa Cave
Luna
Apache Creek
Kinishba
Starkweather
Bat Cave
Salt
Roosevelt
Wet Leggett
Higgins Flat
Turkey Foot Ridge
Pine Lawn Valley
Pueblo de los Muertos
Red Mountains
Point of Pines
Cordova Ridge
Citrus
Gatlin
Snaketown
Gila
Crooked Ridge
Mogollon Village
Gila Bend
Grewe

3 The rugged terrain of the Southwest seems unlikely territory for agricultural settlement (above). Yet the Mogollon, Anasazi and Hohokam agriculturalists succeeded in growing maize, beans, cotton and other crops, although hunting and gathering remained important in their economies. All three cultures had contact with Mexico, and the copper bells, brightly coloured parrot and macaw feathers and rubber balls were all imported from there.

3 The temples of North America
● site — extent of cultural influence

cultures: (colour coded accordingly)
■ Middle Mississippi
■ South Appalachian Mississippian
■ Plaquemine Mississippian
■ Caddoan Mississippian
■ Fort Ancient
■ Onoeta

2 The central area of the Mississippian tradition was the Middle Mississippi Valley (above). Peripheral groups known as the Caddoan, Plaquemine, Southern Appalachian Mississippian, Oneota and Fort Ancient cultures were coeval with the Middle Mississippian culture, developing along the same lines because of similar local conditions and events. There was contact between these different and distant groups by river.

Before 1100, the Anasazi culture had settled near rivers or on uplands where there was fertile, wind-blown soil. Around 1100, the Anasazi left these villages and took refuge in well-defended positions. In the Mesa Verde area, communal apartment houses and storerooms were constructed in rock shelters high in the canyon cliffs, guarded by watchtowers, such as the "Cliff Palace" (below).

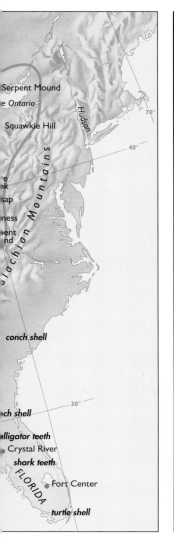

Serpent Mound
e Ontario
Squawkie Hill
Hudson
Appalachian Mountains
FLORIDA
conch shell
ch shell
alligator teeth
Crystal River
shark teeth
Fort Center
turtle shell

The beginnings of Chinese civilization

Geographically and climatically China has a range of favourable conditions for human settlement, which took place 500,000 years ago. A turning point was reached at about 1600 BC when China entered the Bronze Age. It was then that Chinese culture took shape, as written languages, philosophies and stable socio-political and economic structures gradually emerged.

A COUNTRY OF A THOUSAND WAR-CHARIOTS CANNOT BE ADMINISTERED UNLESS THE RULER ATTENDS STRICTLY TO BUSINESS, PUNCTUALLY OBSERVES HIS PROMISES, IS ECONOMICAL IN EXPENDITURE, SHOWS AFFECTION TOWARDS HIS SUBJECTS IN GENERAL, AND USES THE LABOUR OF THE PEASANTRY ONLY AT THE PROPER TIMES OF THE YEAR.

Confucius, 551–479 BC
Analects

CHINA HAS BEEN INHABITED continuously by humans since very early times. Remains of early hominines, which are similar to those from Java, have been found across large areas of southeast China. In about 500,000 BC Peking Man – *Homo erectus* – was living around Pohai and in the southeast and possibly in central and southern China as well. *Homo sapiens* first appeared in Palaeolithic cultures in the Ordos region, in the north and in the southwest in about 30,000 BC (see p. 30). Later Mesolithic cultures flourished in the north, south and southwest and in Taiwan (see p. 32).

Early agriculturalists

Neolithic agricultural communities, the immediate ancestors of Chinese civilization, arose around 7500 BC in what is now southern China and in the loess-covered lands of the north and northeast, where the well-drained soil of the river terraces was ideal for primitive agriculture (see map 1). One of the best early sites is Pan-p'o, with round and rectangular houses, pottery kilns and a cemetery area. In the valley of the Yellow River, early agriculture depended heavily on millet, but in the Yangtze delta area evidence of rice-paddies dates from the 5th millennium BC. By 3000 BC, more sophisticated skills developed, including the carving of jade, and small townships rather than villages began to emerge.

Around 1600 BC China entered the Bronze Age with its first archaeologically proven dynasty, the Shang (c. 1520–1030 BC). Chasing copper mines, the Shang moved their capital at least six times, and three, at

Cheng-chou, Erh-li-t'ou and An-yang, have been excavated. Many smaller Shang sites have been found and some are now known from the Yangtze valley in central China indicating the Shang expansion southward. In addition, the Shang had trade relations with most of the northern and central east Asian mainland.

The Chou dynasty

In the 11th century BC the Shang territory was conquered by the Chou, of different ethnic origin, who inhabited the northwest border of the Shang domain. The Chou gradually extended their sovereignty, including the entire middle and lower reaches of the Yellow River and parts of the middle basin of the Yangtze. At first their capital lay near Hsi-an. The Chou territory was divided into numerous domains among the king and the elites – a system of delegated authority similar to the later European feudal system.

Until the 8th century BC the Chou constantly extended their territory. About 770 BC, however, internal disorders broke the kingdom into numerous units and forced the Chou king to abandon his homeland in the Wei valley and move to the eastern capital at Lo-yang, where his power diminished. Over the next two and a half centuries wars caused more than 100 petty units to be swallowed up by some 20 of the more powerful ones, among whom there emerged a clear pecking order.

The Shang and early Chou periods were differentiated from their predecessors by their political organization and their bronze technology, and also

by the use of writing; their culture was already recognizably "Chinese". Their cities maintained a hierarchy of nobles, royal officers and court servants. They drew support from communities of craftsmen working in bronze, jade, wood, stone, ceramics and textiles. Peasants working the various domains that belonged to the landed classes produced revenues and foodstuffs. Market activities were common and mint currencies were in use.

Bronze was used for ritual objects and a wide range of weapons and tools, with the exception of farming equipment. Farmers working in the fields continued to use stone implements, growing rice, millet, barley and hemp and raising pigs, poultry and silkworms.

Towards the end of the period, the old social order began to collapse. The more powerful units employed bureaucrats rather than the hereditary nobility of older times. A new group of administrators (*shih*) emerged. A leading figure among this group, Confucius, formulated a new ethos, which was to have currency far into the future and far beyond China's territory.

2 The Longshan period, named after its characteristic black pottery, saw the first signs of cultural homogenization spreading from the east coast Shantung Longshan (map below). Increasing social and cultural complexity emerged, as well as walled settlements and more sophisticated technology, including the potter's wheel. These developments formed the prelude to the rise of the first Chinese civilization, named after the Shang dynasty. Extensive walled cities, rich tombs, sophisticated craftsmanship and the earliest Chinese writing all demonstrate the wealth and originality of Shang civilization.

Shang ritual food vessel (below) in Ho or Yu style, in the form of a tiger protecting a man. The vessel is covered with animal motifs related to a fertility cult.

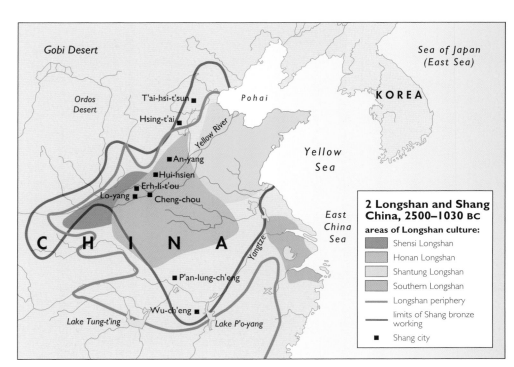

2 Longshan and Shang China, 2500–1030 BC
areas of Longshan culture:
- Shensi Longshan
- Honan Longshan
- Shantung Longshan
- Southern Longshan
- Longshan periphery
- limits of Shang bronze working
- Shang city

Gobi Desert

Ordos Desert

T'ai-hsi-t'sun
Hsing-t'ai
Pohai
Yellow River
Sea of Japan (East Sea)
KOREA
An-yang
Hui-hsien
Erh-li-t'ou
Lo-yang
Cheng-chou
Yellow Sea
Yangtze
C H I N A
East China Sea
P'an-lung-ch'eng
Wu-ch'eng
Lake Tung-t'ing
Lake P'o-yang

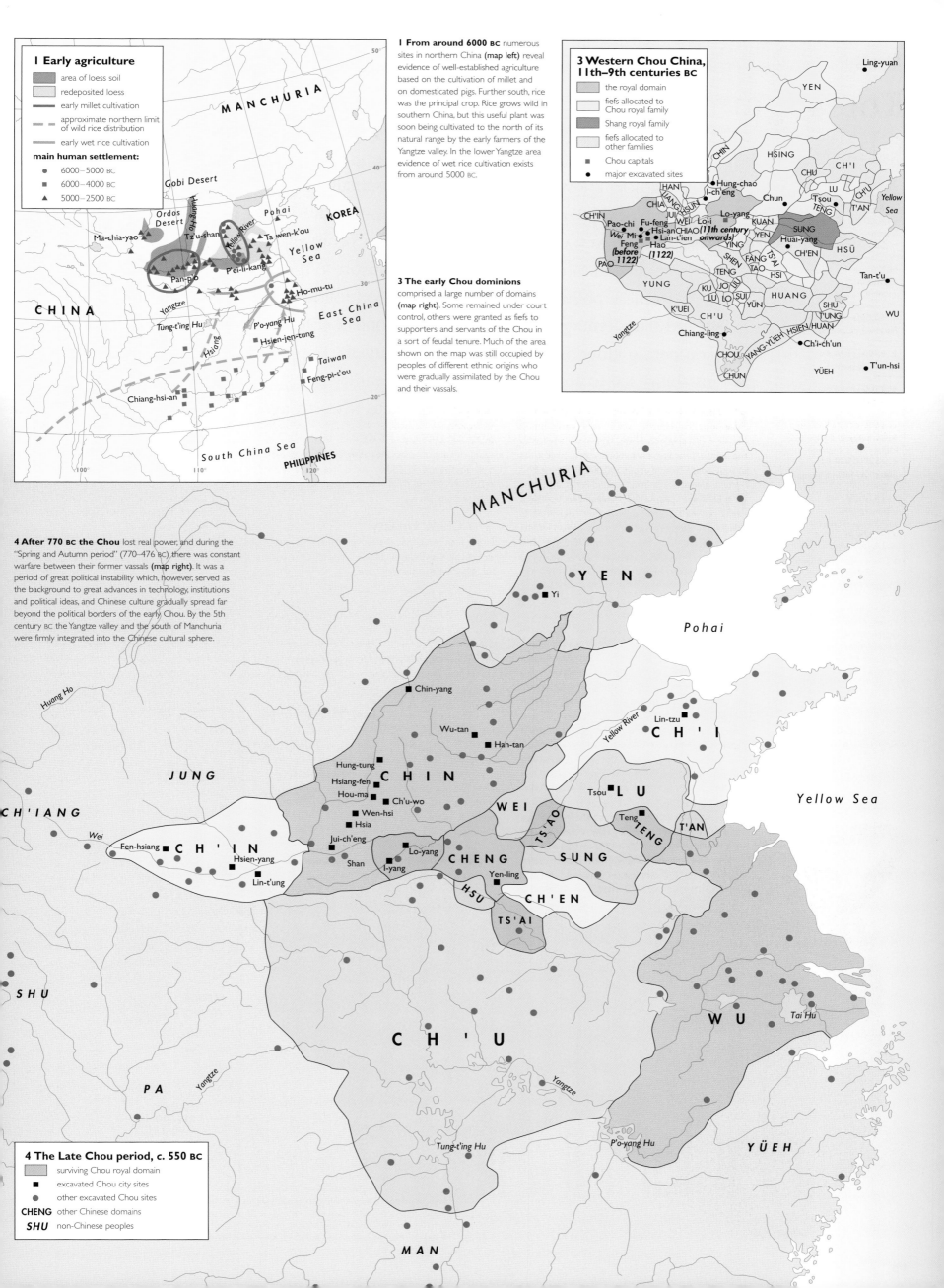

1 Early agriculture

- area of loess soil
- redeposited loess
- early millet cultivation
- approximate northern limit of wild rice distribution
- early wet rice cultivation

main human settlement:
- 6000–5000 BC
- 6000–4000 BC
- 5000–2500 BC

1 From around 6000 BC numerous sites in northern China (map left) reveal evidence of well-established agriculture based on the cultivation of millet and on domesticated pigs. Further south, rice was the principal crop. Rice grows wild in southern China, but this useful plant was soon being cultivated to the north of its natural range by the early farmers of the Yangtze valley. In the lower Yangtze area evidence of wet rice cultivation exists from around 5000 BC.

3 The early Chou dominions comprised a large number of domains (map right). Some remained under court control, others were granted as fiefs to supporters and servants of the Chou in a sort of feudal tenure. Much of the area shown on the map was still occupied by peoples of different ethnic origins who were gradually assimilated by the Chou and their vassals.

Map 1 labels
MANCHURIA • Gobi Desert • Ordos Desert • KOREA • CHINA • Ma-chia-yao • Tz'u-shan • Ta-wen-k'ou • Pan-p'o • Pei-li-kang • Ho-mu-tu • Yellow River • Huang-ho • Pohai • Yellow Sea • Tung-t'ing Hu • P'o-yang Hu • Hsien-jen-tung • Yangtze • Hsiang • East China Sea • Taiwan • Feng-pi-t'ou • Chiang-hsi-an • South China Sea • PHILIPPINES

3 Western Chou China, 11th–9th centuries BC

- the royal domain
- fiefs allocated to Chou royal family
- Shang royal family
- fiefs allocated to other families
- Chou capitals
- major excavated sites

Map 3 labels
Ling-yuan • YEN • HSING • CHU • CH'I • CHIN • LU • CH'U • T'AN • Yellow Sea • HAN • CHIANG-SHUI • JUI • WEI • Hung-chao • I-ch'eng • Lo-i • Lo-yang • Chun • Tsou • TENG • SUNG • Huai-yang • HSÜ • CH'IN • Pao-chi • Fu-feng • Hsi-an • CHIAO • YEN • YING • Wei Mi • Feng • Lan-t'ien • Hao • SHEN • FANG • TSAI • CH'EN • PAO • (before 1122) • (1122) • 11th century onwards • K'UEI • CH'U • KU • JO • LIU • SUI • YÜN • HUANG • SHU • T'UNG • WU • Chiang-ling • YANG-YÜEH • HSIEN/HUAN • Ch'i-ch'un • Tan-t'u • YÜEH • T'un-hsi • CHOU • CHUN • MAN

4 After 770 BC the Chou lost real power, and during the "Spring and Autumn period" (770–476 BC) there was constant warfare between their former vassals (map right). It was a period of great political instability which, however, served as the background to great advances in technology, institutions and political ideas, and Chinese culture gradually spread far beyond the political borders of the early Chou. By the 5th century BC the Yangtze valley and the south of Manchuria were firmly integrated into the Chinese cultural sphere.

4 The Late Chou period, c. 550 BC

- surviving Chou royal domain
- excavated Chou city sites
- other excavated Chou sites
- CHENG other Chinese domains
- *SHU* non-Chinese peoples

Map 4 labels
MANCHURIA • Pohai • Yellow Sea • Huang Ho • YEN • Yi • Chin-yang • Wu-tan • Han-tan • Lin-tzu • CH'I • JUNG • Hung-tung • Hsiang-fen • CHIN • Hou-ma • Ch'u-wo • Tsou • LU • CH'IANG • Wen-hsi • Hsia • WEI • Teng • TENG • T'AN • Wei • Fen-hsiang • CH'IN • Jui-ch'eng • TS'AO • SUNG • Hsien-yang • Shan • Lo-yang • CHENG • Lin-t'ung • I-yang • Yen-ling • CH'EN • HSÜ • TS'AI • Yellow River • SHU • CH'U • Tung-t'ing Hu • P'o-yang Hu • WU • Tai Hu • PA • Yangtze • YÜEH • MAN

Korea

The area now known as Korea was the mountainous eastern edge of the Eurasian continent until the Yellow Sea formed and the west coast emerged to define a peninsula. Peoples migrated into and through the peninsula to the islands. Chinese political culture and Buddhism followed on, and states emerged. With Chinese aid, one of three competing kingdoms conquered the peninsula, but instability led to anarchy by the late 9th century. The successful kingdom created a bureaucratic state with strong aristocratic characteristics and established a Korean identity.

IN SILLA, THERE ARE MANY MOUNTAINS AND GOLD; THE CLIMATE IS GOOD.

Arabic text from 845

I Chinese empires attempted to control Korea, but with limited success **(map below)**. At its height, Koguryŏ claimed territory west to Liaodong, north to modern-day Harbin, and south below the Han River near modern Seoul. South of Koguryŏ were the three Han tribes of Mahan, Pyŏnhan, and Chinhan. Mahan in the southwest straddled maritime trade routes to the continent and to the south. Pyŏnhan and Chinhan produced iron and traded with the Japanese islanders.

DURING THE LAST GLACIAL maximum, "Korea" was high ground across a low plain (Yellow Sea) at the eastern end of Eurasia. Sea levels rose and a peninsula appeared between 14,000 BC and 6000 BC. Humans from 22,000 BC; villages from 10,000 BC; rice between 6000 and 4500 BC. Bronze was worked from 1000 BC and dolmens appeared.

By 108 BC, the Han Empire had established colonies to trade for iron. Only the Lelang colony near Pyŏngyang survived until AD 313, when it was destroyed by a tribe from the middle reaches of the Yalu River, the Koguryŏ, who first revolted against the Chinese in AD 12. Over several centuries, the south politically evolved into Paekche in the southwest, Silla in the southeast, and the iron-rich principalities of Kaya in between.

By the 6th century, the peninsular states were importing Chinese law, bureaucratic government, and land was monopolized by the state to centralize power. Koreans and Japanese fashioned compromises between the Chinese ideal of centralization and the native system of aristocracy, which resulted in semi-centralized political orders based on inheritance. Buddhism permeated every corner of the peninsula by 540 and was exported to Japan.

An alliance between T'ang China and Silla destroyed Paekche in 660 and Koguryŏ in 668. The T'ang had promised to withdraw but betrayed Silla, attempting

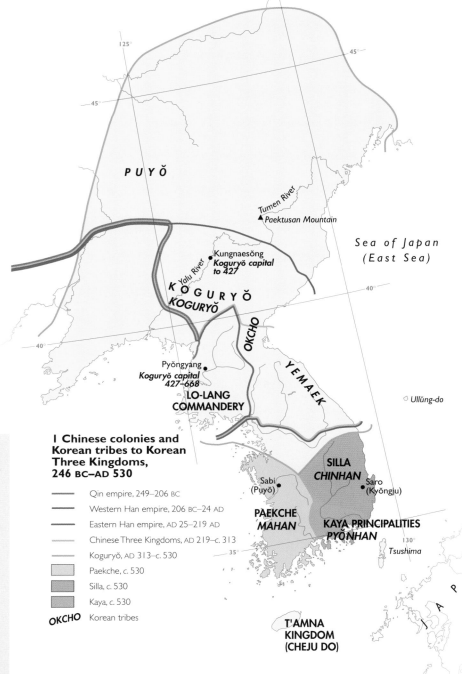

I Chinese colonies and Korean tribes to Korean Three Kingdoms, 246 BC–AD 530

— Qin empire, 249–206 BC
— Western Han empire, 206 BC–24 AD
— Eastern Han empire, AD 25–219 AD
— Chinese Three Kingdoms, AD 219–c. 313
— Koguryŏ, AD 313–c. 530
▮ Paekche, c. 530
▮ Silla, c. 530
▮ Kaya, c. 530
OKCHO Korean tribes

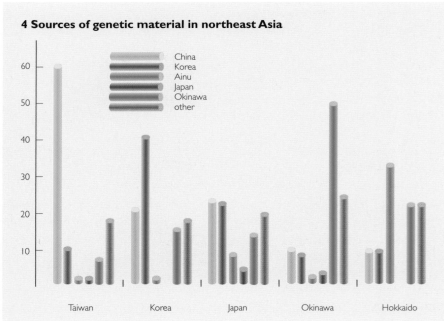

4 Sources of genetic material in northeast Asia

China / Korea / Ainu / Japan / Okinawa / other

Taiwan   Korea   Japan   Okinawa   Hokkaido

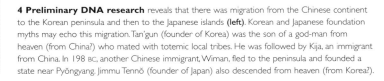

4 Preliminary DNA research reveals that there was migration from the Chinese continent to the Korean peninsula and then to the Japanese islands **(left)**. Korean and Japanese foundation myths may echo this migration. Tan'gun (founder of Korea) was the son of a god-man from heaven (from China?) who mated with totemic local tribes. He was followed by Kija, an immigrant from China. In 198 BC, another Chinese immigrant, Wiman, fled to the peninsula and founded a state near Pyŏngyang. Jimmu Tennō (founder of Japan) also descended from heaven (from Korea?).

East Asian Buddhism came from central Asia, bringing with it an anthropomorphised Buddha, a Messiah of the future, a cult of saints (Bodhisattvas) and an organic world view that emphasized stability, obligations and duty (Vairochana). The Sillan state promoted syncretic Buddhism after the wars of unification and built the Pulguk-sa Temple (above) ("Buddha-nation temple") and the Sokkuram ("stone grotto hermitage") in the 8th century. Most major sects were represented within the Pulguk-sa.

2 Three Korean Kingdoms to Unified Silla (668–918) and Pohai (Parhae) (712–926)

- Koguryŏ, 568–668
- Silla, c. 568–660
- Paekche, c. 568–660
- Unified Silla, 668–918
- Pohai (Parhae), 712–926
- battles and movements in the wars of unification, 598–668

2 Koguryŏ plagued China's northeast with raids (map above). The Sui dynasty attempted to destroy Koguryŏ, but collapsed in the effort. The T'ang inherited claims to the peninsula and allied with Silla from 648. T'ang armies attacked Paekche on the west, while Silla came from the east. In 660, Paekche's capital fell and, in 663 at the mouth of the Paekmagang River, the last Paekche pretender supported by a Japanese navy was defeated. Koguryŏ was destroyed in 668.

3 Koryŏ gives us the name Korea. In 918, Koryŏ arose at the end of Unified Silla, defeated Later Paekche, absorbed Silla and, from 1232, faced invading Mongols (map right). While the Japanese slid into feudalistic militarism, Koryŏ established a bureaucratic elite that held office in aristocratic fashion. They were called *yangban*, meaning officials of the two branches of government, civil and military. The bureaucratic structures laid by Koryŏ carried over into the Chosŏn dynasty.

to seize the whole peninsula. By 676, Silla drove T'ang out, demonstrating that outside powers were unable to succeed on the peninsula without a local ally. T'ang completely retreated, and a new state called Pohai (Korean *Parhae*, 712–926) formed in Manchuria from tribal elements and Koguryŏ refugees.

From the 8th century, northeast Asia saw peace: great cities, long-distance trade, and a cosmopolitan, state-oriented Buddhism. Kyŏngju, Silla's capital, was a world city known to Arab traders. Ch'ang-an may have had nearly two million inhabitants, and Kyŏngju approached 900,000, swollen by slaves from the wars. Monks, merchants and diplomats wandered among Ch'ang-an, Kyŏngju, and Nara in Japan. Thereafter, "Korea" and "Japan" began to form separate identities.

Sillan central control lapsed, and in 918, Wang Kŏn, a general outside the old aristocratic order, emerged to found a new dynasty named Koryŏ. Wang Kŏn peacefully absorbed the Sillan court in 935. His successors inherited the aristocratic pretensions of Silla and the desire to centralize. During the 10th century, a bureaucratic state was created, with examinations, ideology, salary ranks and centralized provincial appointments. Where Silla had conquered, Koryŏ unified. In 1126, the Liao (Jurchen) destroyed the Chinese Song Empire and Koryŏ faced a dilemma of identity:

take the opportunity to expand out of the peninsula or accept its limitations. A rebellious faction argued for continental destiny in Manchuria. Kim Pu-sik, the general who suppressed them, produced an official history (*Samguk sagi*, c. 1145) that defined Koryŏ's heritage as peninsular. After the Mongols invaded in 1232, an unofficial history (*Samguk yusa*, c. 1283) reaffirmed a peninsular identity and recorded foundation myths.

Koryŏ nearly slipped into feudalism when abuse of civil privilege sparked a military coup d'etat in 1170. Military dictators did not create a new government, but ruled through the central government. Perhaps Koryŏ never disintegrated into feudalism because of the threat from northern barbarians, a threat Japan never faced. The Mongols invaded in 1232, but the Korean court resisted until 1270. The Koryŏ kings became sons-in-law to the Mongol Khans, and Koryŏ was press-ganged into supporting Mongol efforts to conquer Japan in 1274 and 1281. Both invasions failed.

From the mid-14th century, Japanese piracy appeared to ravage Korea. In the north, the Mongols weakened and, in 1368, the new Ming dynasty dislodged the Mongols. Indecision at the Koryŏ court over whether to support the Mongols or the Ming resulted in a coup d'etat in 1388 and a new dynasty, the Chosŏn, was founded in 1392.

3 Koryŏ, 918–1392

- Pohai (Parhae), 712–926
- Khitan (Liao), 926–1232
- Mongol (Yuan), 1232–1392
- Koryŏ, 918–935
- Later Paekche, 892–934
- Silla, 892–935
- Koryŏ, 918–1232
- Koryŏ, 1232–1392
- battles of the Mongol/Koryŏ invasion of Japan

The beginnings of Indian civilization

India was the home of one of the oldest civilizations of history, which grew up along the banks of the Indus river. The Indus Valley culture and the Vedic culture, which succeeded and was influenced by it, were the basis for the development of later Indian society, in particular for the major religious systems of Hinduism, Buddhism and Jainism.

> WITH THE BOW LET US WIN COWS, WITH THE BOW LET US WIN THE CONTEST AND VIOLENT BATTLES WITH THE BOW. THE BOW RUINS THE ENEMY'S PLEASURE; WITH THE BOW LET US CONQUER ALL THE CORNERS OF THE WORLD. NEIGHING VIOLENTLY, THE HORSES WITH THEIR SHOWERING HOOFS OUTSTRIP EVERYONE WITH THEIR CHARIOTS. TRAMPLING DOWN THE FOES WITH THE TIPS OF THEIR HOOFS, THEY DESTROY THEIR ENEMIES WITHOUT VEERING AWAY.
>
> *Hymn to Arms, Rig Veda (c. 1200–900 BC)*

c. 3500 BC Beginning of Early Indus period

c. 2500 BC Beginning of Harappan culture in the Indus Valley

c. 1750 BC Abandonment of major Indus Valley cities

c. 1650 BC Indo-Aryans begin to arrive in India

c. 1000 BC Indo-Aryan settlements established in the Upper Ganges plains

c. 600 BC Kausambi and Ujjain develop as earliest post-Harappan cities

THE EARLY HISTORY OF INDIA is very difficult to recover. Archaeology can reveal something about the way of life of its earliest inhabitants, but little can be learned from written evidence. The earliest works of Indian literature, the *Vedas*, were composed in the centuries after 1200 BC, but they were not written down until probably the 5th century.

Harappa and Mohenjo-Daro

Although the subcontinent had substantial human occupation from the Stone Age onwards (*see map 1*), the first great Indian civilization was the Harappan culture which emerged in the Indus Valley in the 3rd millennium BC. Like the slightly older civilizations of Mesopotamia and Egypt it was based on flood-plain agriculture, as the cultivation of the fertile land on either side of the Indus was able to provide enough of a surplus to support a complex urban society. Several substantial cities were built (*see map 2*), of which the best explored are Harappa and Mohenjo-Daro.

The Indus civilization also developed writing, and about 2000 seals with short pictographic inscriptions on them have been discovered. The script has not been deciphered, and until it is, little will be known about the political structure or religious beliefs of the Indus Civilization.

The presence of cylinder seals from Mesopotamia at Mohenjo-Daro and of Indus seals in Mesopotamia is evidence of trade between the two areas via the Persian Gulf, and tin and lapis lazuli from Afghanistan and Central Asia also made their way to the Indus. However around 2000 BC the 'Harappan period' came to an end, as the cities ceased to function and were replaced by a settlement pattern of agricultural villages and pastoral camps.

Post-Indus India

From around 1500 BC a new culture becomes apparent in India, characterized by a new language and rituals, and the use of horses and two-wheeled chariots. The traditional way to explain the changes was to talk of an "Aryan invasion", with mounted bands of warriors riding in from the northwest and conquering the indigenous Indus population before moving eastwards to the Ganges. Support for this picture was claimed from one of the *Vedas*, the *Rig*

Veda, where the Aryans are presented as conquering the cities of the darker skinned indigenous Dasas. Archaeological evidence offers little support for this theory however. The styles of pottery associated with the Indo-Aryans, known as Painted Grey Ware, which appears from c. 1100 BC, is similar to earlier Painted Black and Red Ware, and this may indicate that Indo-Aryan speakers were indigenous to the Indus plain. Whatever their origins, Indo-Aryan languages, from which Sanskrit developed, became widespread through Northern India.

The south

Southern India was left largely untouched by the civilizations of the north. There were probably trading links between the Indus valley and the southern tip of the peninsula, but there was no urbanism in the south, where villages were the normal form of social organization. However, some limited form of common culture in the south is suggested by the distinctive megalithic tombs found over most of the area.

Terracotta figurine (right) from Mohenjo-Daro, probably representing a mother goddess. A large number of such figurines have been found in the Indus Valley. The worship of goddesses was common in this period, and became a feature of Hindu worship. The figurine may, however, be more closely connected with Sumerian deities.

2 The civilization of the Indus Valley (map far right) was centralized to a large degree. The major cities acted as centres of storage and distribution for the agricultural produce of the surrounding area, mainly wheat and barley but also rice. The annual flooding of the river produced fertile silts on which crops could be grown with little need for irrigation works.

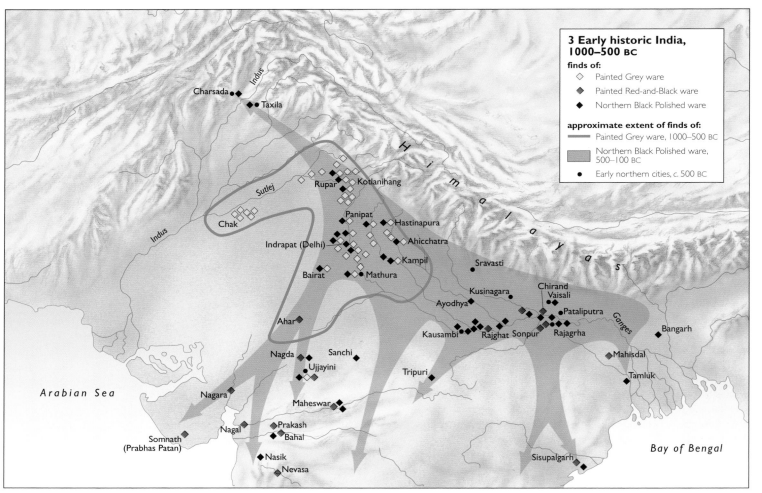

3 Early historic India, 1000–500 BC

finds of:
◇ Painted Grey ware
◆ Painted Red-and-Black ware
◆ Northern Black Polished ware

approximate extent of finds of:
— Painted Grey ware, 1000–500 BC
▨ Northern Black Polished ware, 500–100 BC
● Early northern cities, c. 500 BC

3 The spread of Vedic civilization in the 1st millennium BC can be followed using the evidence of pottery (map left). Painted Grey ware, found in central north India, is associated with the earlier Aryan settlement in the upper and middle Ganges, while the later Red-and-Black ware is found further east and south. The spread of Northern Black Polished ware, which dates from the time of the foundation of the first cities on the Ganges, indicates the growing influence of Vedic culture throughout northern and central India.

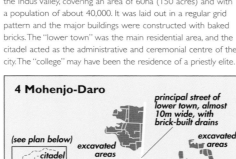

In the north, where, unlike the hilly, fragmented geography of the south, great plains lent themselves to large-scale agriculture and the growth of substantial kingdoms, cultural coherence became more widespread as, in the period after 1000 BC, the new civilization spread gradually east from the Indus to the Ganges. Evidence from finds of pottery characteristic of particular periods suggests that there was also movement southwards (*see map 3*). The late Vedic texts depict the early first millennium BC as a period of frequent warfare between rival tribal territories. During this period the society of Northern India became increasingly stratified, and this culminated, around 600 BC in the emergence of states ruled by hereditary monarchs. Trading networks developed, agricultural activity increased, and this led to a new phase of urbanism in India. Once again cities began to be built, although they were not on the scale of Harappa and Mohenjo-Daro, being constructed largely from mud-bricks. No known public buildings survive from this period. Yet by the 5th century BC there were political entities that might be called states or polities, most significantly Magadha, with its substantial fortified capital at Pataliputra (*see p. 92*).

Vedic religion

Religious practices in India in the first millennium BC were influenced in part by the earlier culture of the Vedas, and animal sacrifice had a central role in it. The religion was polytheistic, and the *Rig Veda* includes hymns to a number of deities, including the warrior god Indra, the fire god Agni, and Soma, identified with a mind-altering drug of some kind, possibly derived from mushrooms. These cults were the forerunner of Hinduism, and the urban societies that developed along the Ganges were the communities among whom appeared in the 5th century Mahavira, the founder of Jainism, and the Buddha himself.

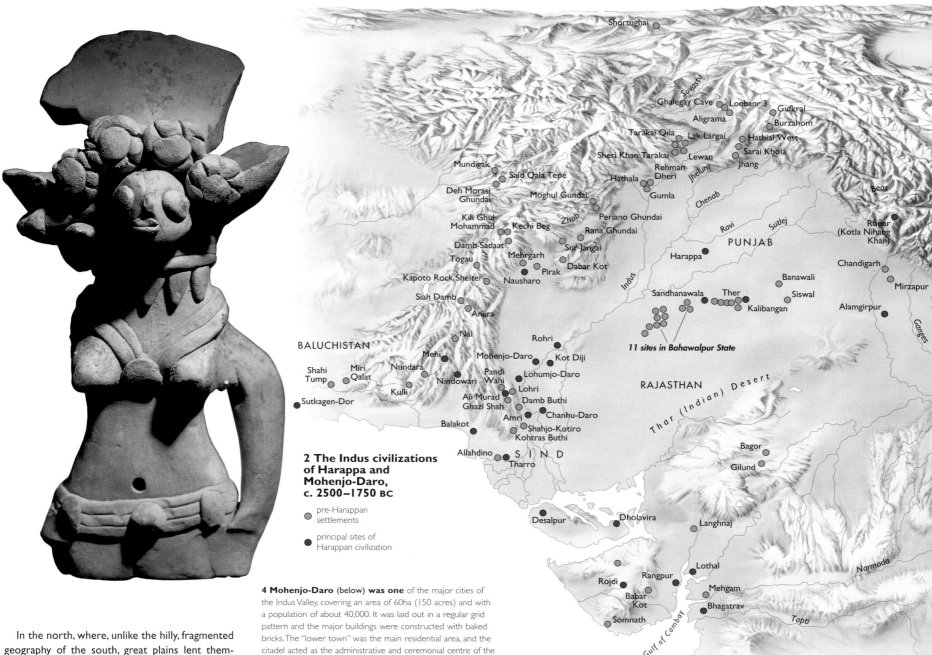

2 The Indus civilizations of Harappa and Mohenjo-Daro, c. 2500–1750 BC

- pre-Harappan settlements
- principal sites of Harappan civilization

4 Mohenjo-Daro (below) was one of the major cities of the Indus Valley, covering an area of 60ha (150 acres) and with a population of about 40,000. It was laid out in a regular grid pattern and the major buildings were constructed with baked bricks. The "lower town" was the main residential area, and the citadel acted as the administrative and ceremonial centre of the city. The "college" may have been the residence of a priestly elite.

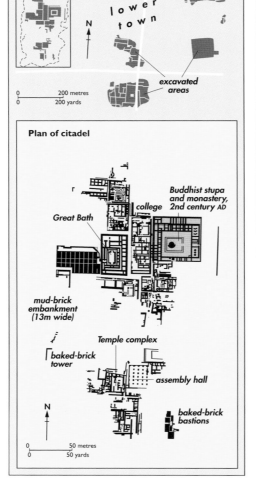

4 Mohenjo-Daro

principal street of lower town, almost 10m wide, with brick-built drains

(see plan below)

citadel

excavated areas

lower town

excavated areas

N

excavated areas

0   200 metres
0   200 yards

Plan of citadel

Buddhist stupa and monastery, 2nd century AD

Great Bath

college

mud-brick embankment (13m wide)

Temple complex

baked-brick tower

assembly hall

baked-brick bastions

N

0   50 metres
0   50 yards

1 Archaeological evidence indicates human occupation throughout the whole Indian peninsula from the Stone Age onwards (**map below**). Intensive agriculture made possible the growth of cities in the Indus Valley and, later, on the Ganges, but village-level societies flourished in the hillier land to the south. The spread of metal-working from the north and the diffusion of Iron Age megalithic burials in the south indicates regular contact between the scattered communities.

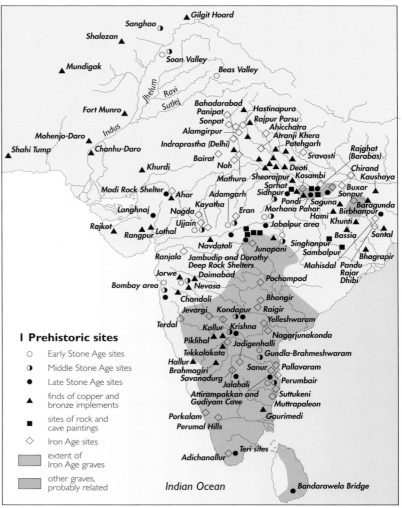

1 Prehistoric sites

- ○ Early Stone Age sites
- ◐ Middle Stone Age sites
- ● Late Stone Age sites
- ▲ finds of copper and bronze implements
- ■ sites of rock and cave paintings
- ◇ Iron Age sites
- extent of Iron Age graves
- other graves, probably related

Minoan and Mycenaean civilizations

In the late 19th century, Heinrich Schliemann and Sir Arthur Evans unearthed the remains of previously unknown civilizations. Although the names of Troy, Mycenae and Knossos were familiar from the poems of Homer, the Bronze Age societies of the Aegean revealed by these excavations had much more in common with contemporary Near Eastern societies than they had with later Greece.

THERE IS A LAND CALLED CRETE, IN THE MIDDLE OF THE WINE-DARK SEA, FAIR AND FERTILE AND SEAGIRT; IT HAS COUNTLESS NUMBERS OF MEN, AND NINETY CITIES, AND LANGUAGES MIX THERE ONE WITH ANOTHER ... AND THERE IS KNOSSOS, THE GREAT CITY, WHERE MINOS RULES, NINE YEARS BY NINE YEARS, WHO HAS THE EAR OF MIGHTY ZEUS.

Homer, *Odyssey*

FATHER ZEUS, LET THE LOT FALL TO AJAX, OR TO THE SON OF TYDEUS, OR TO HIM WHO IS KING OF GOLDEN MYCENAE.

Homer, *Iliad*

c. 3000 BC Beginning of Greek Early Bronze Age

c. 1900 BC Beginning of First Palace Period on Crete

c. 1750 BC Destruction of First Palaces. Beginning of Second Palace Period

1628 BC Massive volcanic eruption on the Aegean island of Thera

c. 1500 BC Mycenaean conquest of Crete

c. 1400 BC Appearance of Palaces on the mainland

c. 1190 BC Abandonment of Mycenaean Palaces

SUBSTANTIAL SETTLEMENTS appeared in mainland Greece and Crete by the end of the 3rd millennium BC. These were subsistence farmers, with households producing goods for their own consumption. The subsequent appearance in Crete of large stone-built complexes marked the emergence of a new form of social organization. There are some parallels between these "First Palaces" and Near Eastern buildings, and they are accompanied by other signs of such influence, including the appearance of a form of hieroglyphic writing in Crete. However, it is likely that local needs as much as outside influence determined the island's overall development.

There is no agreed explanation for the later destruction of the "First Palaces", but in their place the large complexes of the "Second Palace Period" emerged. These were not fortified, but they were

the focus of the economic and religious life of the Minoan communities.

By 1700 BC Knossos had achieved a dominant position within Crete, and the palace there reveals much information about Minoan society. Surviving frescoes depict scenes of communal activity including processions, bull-leaping, dining and dancing. It is clear from Knossos and other palaces that Cretan society depended upon intensive agriculture – the palaces incorporate large storage areas where crops could be gathered for later redistribution to the population. Outside the towns, especially in eastern Crete, large "villas" (see map 2) had a similar role, and acted as processing centres for grape and olive crops.

The two hundred years of the Second Palace Period witnessed considerable destruction and re-building at a number of sites. The eruption of Thera in

1628 BC left its mark on sites in eastern Crete but otherwise appears to have had little long-term impact. More significantly, a little over a century later many Cretan settlements were widely devastated, possibly as a result of invasion from the Greek mainland.

Mycenaean Greece

Mainland Greece did not share in the prosperity of Crete and the Aegean islands until after *c.* 1700 BC, when rich burials, especially in the "shaft-graves" at Mycenae and in *tholos* tombs, point to the emergence of a powerful warlike elite. After 1500 BC mainlanders, called Mycenaeans, appear to have been in control of Knossos, where the palace functioned for another

3 Bronze Age Greece and Crete were part of the wider eastern Mediterranean and Near East (map below). The rulers of these developing civilizations needed raw materials such as copper and tin to make bronze, as well as luxury goods. In return, the Aegean supplied rare materials such as obsidian and fine works of craftsmanship. These goods often circulated as gifts or dowries rather than as items of trade.

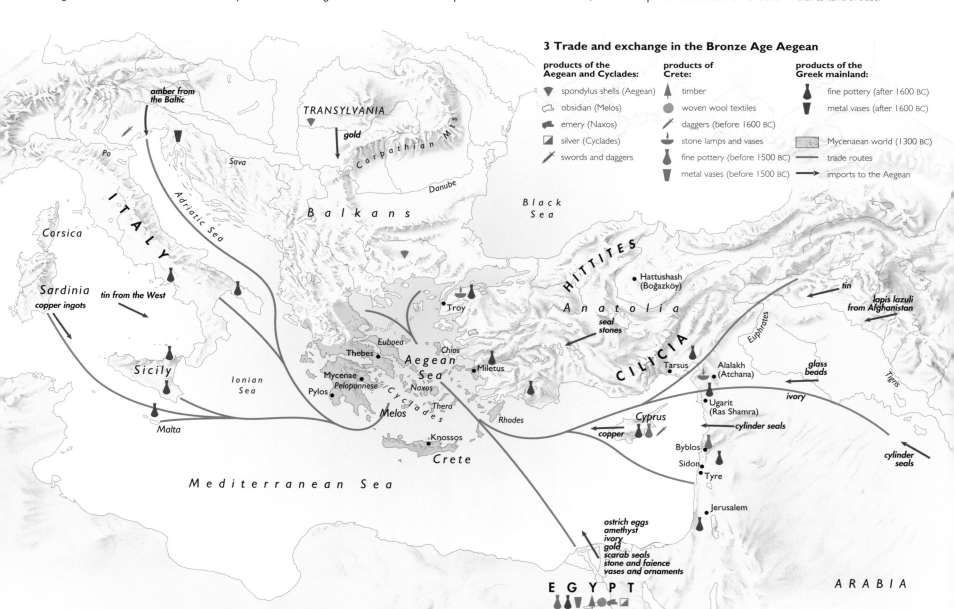

3 Trade and exchange in the Bronze Age Aegean

products of the Aegean and Cyclades:
- spondylus shells (Aegean)
- obsidian (Melos)
- emery (Naxos)
- silver (Cyclades)
- swords and daggers

products of Crete:
- timber
- woven wool textiles
- daggers (before 1600 BC)
- stone lamps and vases
- fine pottery (before 1500 BC)
- metal vases (before 1500 BC)

products of the Greek mainland:
- fine pottery (after 1600 BC)
- metal vases (after 1600 BC)
- Mycenaean world (1300 BC)
- trade routes
- imports to the Aegean

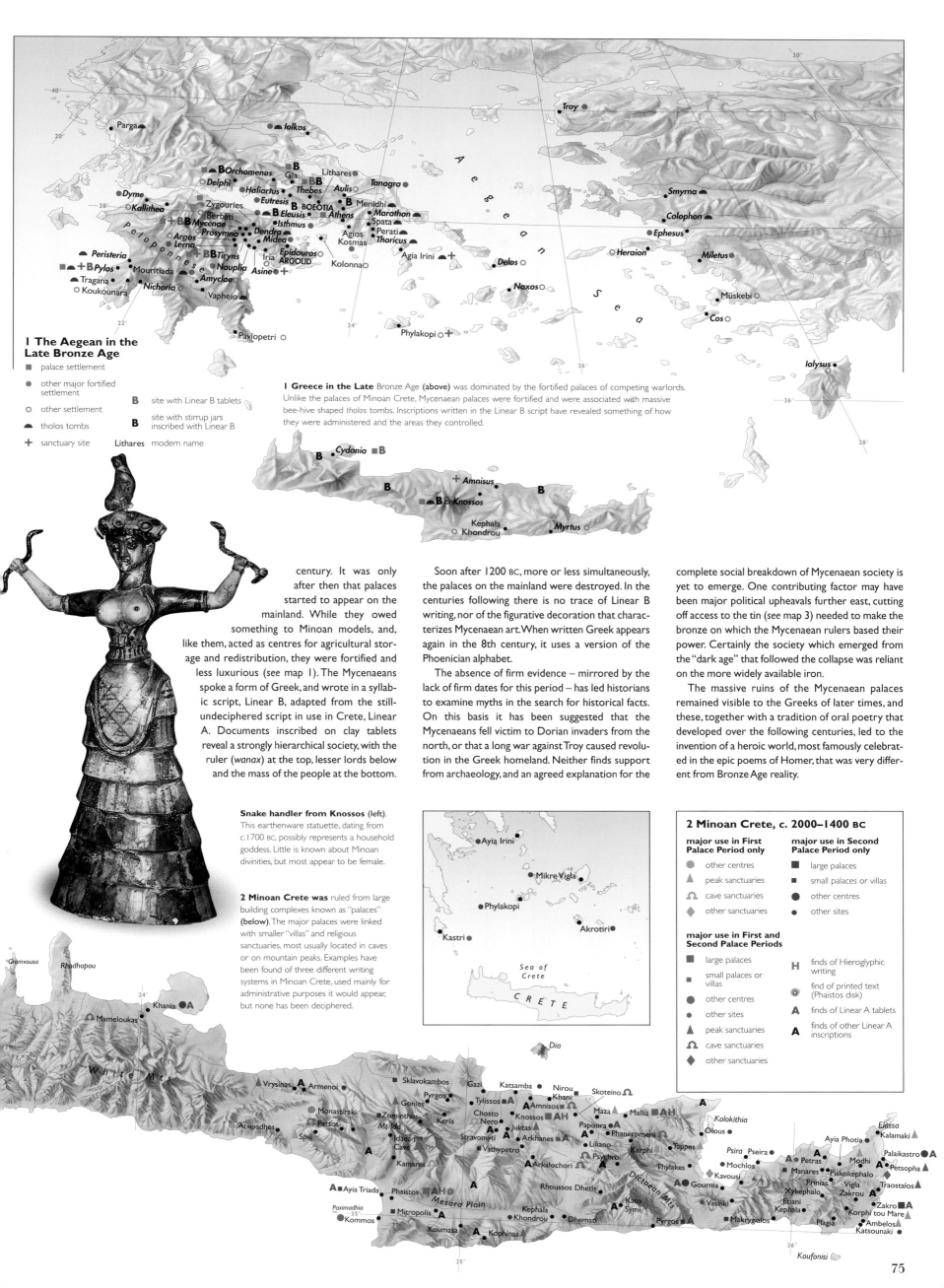

1 The Aegean in the Late Bronze Age

- ■ palace settlement
- ● other major fortified settlement
- ○ other settlement
- ◗ tholos tombs
- ✛ sanctuary site
- **B** site with Linear B tablets
- **B** site with stirrup jars inscribed with Linear B
- *Lithares* modern name

1 Greece in the Late Bronze Age (above) was dominated by the fortified palaces of competing warlords. Unlike the palaces of Minoan Crete, Mycenaean palaces were fortified and were associated with massive bee-hive shaped *tholos* tombs. Inscriptions written in the Linear B script have revealed something of how they were administered and the areas they controlled.

Map 1 labels: Parga, Iolkos, Troy, Orchomenus, Delphi, Gla, Lithares, Tanagra, Smyrna, Haliartus, Thebes, Aulis, Dyme, Eutresis, BOEOTIA, Menidhi, Colophon, Kallithea, Zygouries, Athens, Marathon, Berbati, Eleusis, Spata, Mycenae, Isthmus, Perati, Ephesus, Prosymna, Dendra, Agios Thoricus, Argos, Midea, Kosmos, Heraion, Miletus, Lerna, Peristeria, Tiryns, Iria, Epidauros, Agia Irini, Pylos, Nauplia, ARGOLID, Mouritiada, Asine, Kolonna, Delos, Tragana, Amyclae, Naxos, Koukounara, Nichoria, Müskebi, Vapheio, Cos, Pavlopetri, Phylakopi, Ialysus, Aegean Sea, Peloponnese

Crete map 1 labels: Cydonia, Amnisus, Knossos, Kephala Khondrou, Myrtus

Snake handler from Knossos (left). This earthenware statuette, dating from c.1700 BC, possibly represents a household goddess. Little is known about Minoan divinities, but most appear to be female.

2 Minoan Crete was ruled from large building complexes known as "palaces" (below). The major palaces were linked with smaller "villas" and religious sanctuaries, most usually located in caves or on mountain peaks. Examples have been found of three different writing systems in Minoan Crete, used mainly for administrative purposes it would appear, but none has been deciphered.

century. It was only after then that palaces started to appear on the mainland. While they owed something to Minoan models, and, like them, acted as centres for agricultural storage and redistribution, they were fortified and less luxurious (see map 1). The Mycenaeans spoke a form of Greek, and wrote in a syllabic script, Linear B, adapted from the still-undeciphered script in use in Crete, Linear A. Documents inscribed on clay tablets reveal a strongly hierarchical society, with the ruler (*wanax*) at the top, lesser lords below and the mass of the people at the bottom.

Soon after 1200 BC, more or less simultaneously, the palaces on the mainland were destroyed. In the centuries following there is no trace of Linear B writing, nor of the figurative decoration that characterizes Mycenaean art. When written Greek appears again in the 8th century, it uses a version of the Phoenician alphabet.

The absence of firm evidence – mirrored by the lack of firm dates for this period – has led historians to examine myths in the search for historical facts. On this basis it has been suggested that the Mycenaeans fell victim to Dorian invaders from the north, or that a long war against Troy caused revolution in the Greek homeland. Neither finds support from archaeology, and an agreed explanation for the complete social breakdown of Mycenaean society is yet to emerge. One contributing factor may have been major political upheavals further east, cutting off access to the tin (see map 3) needed to make the bronze on which the Mycenaean rulers based their power. Certainly the society which emerged from the "dark age" that followed the collapse was reliant on the more widely available iron.

The massive ruins of the Mycenaean palaces remained visible to the Greeks of later times, and these, together with a tradition of oral poetry that developed over the following centuries, led to the invention of a heroic world, most famously celebrated in the epic poems of Homer, that was very different from Bronze Age reality.

2 Minoan Crete, c. 2000–1400 BC

major use in First Palace Period only
- ● other centres
- ▲ peak sanctuaries
- ⋒ cave sanctuaries
- ◆ other sanctuaries

major use in First and Second Palace Periods
- ■ large palaces
- ■ small palaces or villas
- ● other centres
- • other sites
- ▲ peak sanctuaries
- ⋒ cave sanctuaries
- ◆ other sanctuaries

major use in Second Palace Period only
- ■ large palaces
- ■ small palaces or villas
- ● other centres

- **H** finds of Hieroglyphic writing
- ◉ find of printed text (Phaistos disk)
- **A** finds of Linear A tablets
- **A** finds of other Linear A inscriptions

Cyclades inset labels: Ayia Irini, Mikre Vigla, Phylakopi, Akrotiri, Kastri, Sea of Crete, CRETE

Crete map 2 labels: Gramvousa, Rhodhopou, Khania, Mameloukas, White Mts, Vrysinas, Armenoi, Sklavokambos, Gazi, Katsamba, Nirou Khani, Skoteino, Dia, Pyrgos, Tylissos, Amnisos, Maza, Mallia, Kolokithia, Elassa, Kalamaki, Gonies, Chosto Nero, Knossos, Papoura, Phaneromeni, Ayia Photia, Palaikastro, Monastiraki, Zominthos, Keria, Juktas, Arkhanes, Liliano, Karphi, Tappes, Psira, Pseira, Petras, Modhi, Petsopha, Patsos, Mt Ida, Stravomyti, Vathypeto, Psychro, Thylakes, Psiro, Mochlos, Manares, Prinias, Piskokephalo, Vigla, Atsipadhes, Idaean Cave, Arkalochori, Dictaean Mts, Kavousi, Xykephalo, Zakrou, Traostalos, Spili, Kamares, Arkalochori, Gournia, Vasiliki, Etiani Kephala, Zakro, Korphi tou Mare, Ayia Triada, Phaistos, Mesara Plain, Rhoussos Dhetis, Kato Symi, Pyrgos, Plagia, Ambelos, Katsounaki, Paximadhia, Mitropolis, Kephala Khondrou, Dheman, Makrygialos, Kommos, Koumasa, Kophinas, Koufonisi

3 THE CLASSICAL CIVILIZATIONS OF EURASIA

THE EARLIEST CIVILIZATIONS AROSE at a few scattered points in the vast and sparsely inhabited Eurasian landmass. Between 1000 BC and AD 500 the pattern began to change. Although America, Australasia and Africa south of the Sahara still stood outside the mainstream of world history, and were to stay so for a further thousand years, the civilizations of Europe and Asia now formed a continuous belt. By AD 100, when the classical era was at its height, a chain of empires extended from Rome via Parthia and the Kushana empire to China, constituting an unbroken zone of civilized life from the Atlantic to the Pacific.

This was a new and important fact in the history of the Eurasian world. The area of civilization remained narrow and exposed to unrelenting barbarian pressures, and developments in the different regions remained largely autonomous. But with the expansion of the major civilizations and the elimination of the geographical gaps between them, the way lay open for inter-regional contacts and cultural exchanges which left a lasting imprint. In the west, the expansion of Hellenism created a single cultural area which extended from the frontiers of India to Britain; in the east, the expansion of the Chinese and Indian civilizations resulted in a kind of cultural symbiosis in Indo-China. These wider cultural areas provided a vehicle not only for trade but for the transmission of ideas, technology and institutions, and above all for the diffusion of the great world religions. Beginning with Buddhism, and continuing with Judaism, Zoroastrianism, Christianity and Islam, religion became a powerful unifying bond in the Eurasian world.

THE ANCIENT CITY OF PALMYRA, SYRIA.

The commercial and cultural bonds of Eurasia

The rulers of the empires of the ancient world had no commercial policies, and were seldom interested in trade. Yet the activities of traders, operating at the margins of society, and rarely mentioned in ancient literature, had a profound effect on the development of the world, transmitting not only goods, but also cultural ideas – and occasionally deadly organisms.

c. 550 BC Chinese silks known in Athens

c. 116 BC Eudoxus of Cyzicus sails from Arabia to India using the monsoons

102 BC Chinese emperor leads an expedition to Ferghana to seize horses

AD 97 Chinese ambassador Kan Ying visits Persia

AD 166 Roman merchants at the Chinese imperial court

c. AD 540 Silkworms brought into the Byzantine empire

A wall painting (below) from Tun-huang shows a Chinese official mounted on a horse from Ferghana. The Han Chinese emperors needed to equip their cavalry to fight against the nomads north of the Great Wall, and the horses of Ferghana were highly prized. Chinese tradition claimed that they were descended from winged heavenly horses. In 102 BC the emperor Wu-ti attempted to purchase a supply from Ferghana, and when he was refused sent two military expeditions into Ferghana to attempt to seize them.

THE QUANTITY OF GOODS passing across the Eurasian landmass varied enormously depending on the political conditions of the time. Between 200 BC and AD 200 stable regimes in the Roman Mediterranean, the Persian Parthian empire, the Kushan empire and China under the Han dynasty, helped to stabilize the routes between Europe, Persia and China. Such favourable conditions for the movement of goods and people did not recur until the 8th century AD. These earlier empires, however, were not directly interested in facilitating trade. Chinese campaigns in the area of the Silk Road in Sinkiang, north of Tibet, such as that of Pan Ch'ao against the Kushans in c. AD 90 confronted a military rather than a commercial threat. The Han emperors certainly wanted valuable commodities like horses from Ferghana, but they expected to receive them as diplomatic gifts, tribute or booty from war.

Since the time of Assyrian merchants in Anatolia in the 2nd millennium BC there are examples of communities of traders who settled in foreign territories to import goods from their homelands. In the 8th century BC Greek and Phoenician trading posts were established across the Mediterranean for the same purpose. These "trade diasporas" made possible effective communication between different cultural groups. The people who made up the diaspora communities were not wealthy merchants, but of much lower status. The "Roman" traders who sailed across the Indian Ocean or visited the Chinese court would not have been Italians, but inhabitants of the eastern provinces, who were probably not even Roman citizens.

Trade was not the only way in which goods travelled across this route. The Han rulers of China maintained peace on their northwest frontier by regular gifts of large quantities of silk and lacquerware to the Hsiungnu tribes outside the Great Wall. Some items would have been passed on in dowries or as gifts, and gradually made their way to the Mediterranean where silken clothing was sought by Roman senators, much to the distaste of more austere emperors.

While silk was the major import from China to the Mediterranean, a variety of goods found their way westwards. The Roman writer Pliny (AD 23–79) complains that the desire for eastern goods was draining the empire of its gold and silver, but this is not supported by the archaeological evidence. Glass was certainly sought after, but slaves were probably also a significant item of trade, and there are references in Chinese sources to "Syrian jugglers" reaching the Chinese court.

Maritime trade

Maritime trade developed at the same time as the overland routes, making increased use of the monsoons for trade between southern Arabia and south India. Vital information about the goods traded between the Roman empire and the east comes from *A Voyage around the Red Sea*, an anonymous handbook for traders written in the 1st century AD, which describes the coastal routes from the Egyptian Red Sea ports of Myos Hormus and Berenice to east Africa and the Ganges delta. The author knows of China as a vast city, but east of India his geographical knowledge is hazy.

The exchange of goods might have profound cultural effects. Begram in Gandhara was the location of the summer palace of the Kushan emperors. A rich hoard from there dating from around AD 100 included lacquer from China and ivory from India, as well as bronzes, glassware and pottery from the Mediterranean. The Kushan interest in Mediterranean artefacts illustrated by the Begram hoard had a profound effect on local practices, acting as a catalyst for the development of Gandharan art which emerged in the 2nd century AD, in part modelled on Greco-Roman styles.

I The carrying of goods along the Silk Road to the Mediterranean began in the 6th century BC (map right), and trade along this route flourished between c. 200 BC and AD 200 when stable empires controlled the territories through which the traders passed. The usual starting point, on the edge of China proper, was Tun-huang, from which the route continued west over the Pamirs, to Samarkand and Merv. At the same time traders began to take advantage of the monsoons for sea-borne trade with India and beyond. Archaeology has done much to reveal the extent of trade over the Eurasian landmass. Chinese silks have been found in Britain, and a Roman coin in Vietnam. The Shoso-in, the treasure-house of the Todaiji temple at Nara in Japan, built by 752, contains glass from the Byzantine empire as well as goods from Sasanid Persia and China.

AFTER THIS, HEADING EAST WITH THE OCEAN ON THE RIGHT, YOU REACH THE GANGES REGION AND NEAR IT THE EASTERNMOST POINT OF THE MAINLAND, CHRYSE. THERE IS A RIVER NEAR IT THAT IS ITSELF CALLED THE GANGES, THE GREATEST OF ALL RIVERS IN INDIA, WHICH RISES AND FALLS LIKE THE NILE. ON IT IS A TRADING POST WITH THE SAME NAME AS THE RIVER, GANGES, WHICH EXPORTS MALABATHRON, GANGETIC NARD, PEARLS AND COTTON GARMENTS OF THE VERY FINEST QUALITY, WHICH IS CALLED "GANGETIC".

Anonymous (1st century AD)
A Voyage around the Red Sea

I The commercial and cultural bonds of Eurasia

● trading centre ——— trade route
——— Silk Road

distribution of:

🪞 Han mirrors

🧵 Chinese silks

◆ treasures of the Shōsō-in

△ Graeco-Roman objects found in southeast Asia, dated as AD 1–300

■ sites known to the author of *A Voyage around the Red Sea*

→ dispersion of Jews to AD 500

→ spread of Christianity

→ spread of Buddhism

--- first area of Buddhist missionary activity

-·-·- area of rise of Mahayana Buddhism

Parthia AD 224

maximum extent of Kushan empire

Roman empire, AD 235

Han empire, c. AD 220

2 Before the spread of Christianity, and later of Islam, the civilizations of Eurasia and North Africa were largely polytheistic **(map left)**. Religious activity consisted largely of sacrifices and festivals in honour of a large number of deities who, it was hoped, would favour their worshippers. Even those societies where religion focused on a single God, such as those in Judaea or Zoroastrian Persia, recognized that other gods might exist. Religious identity was closely linked to political and social identity and this led to the emergence of distinctive regional religious philosophies: Hinduism in India, Daoism and Confucianism in China. In an era of relative stability, some new religious ideas and practices were spread well beyond their places of origin by a combination of missionary work and political enforcement. Thus Buddhism spread over much of the Far East, while Christianity was carried from its birthplace in Palestine, east into Persia and west as far as the Atlantic.

79

The Near East

934 BC Ashur-dan II begins Assyrian recovery

671–656 BC Assyrians gain temporary control of Egypt

612 BC Nabopolassar of Babylon sacks Nineveh

539 BC Cyrus the Great of Persia captures Babylon

As the Near East recovered from the upheavals of the Late Bronze Age, Assyria re-emerged as the great regional power. At its greatest extent Assyrian territory stretched from the Mediterranean to the Persian Gulf, and from southern Egypt to Lake Van. At the height of Assyrian power, internal conflict saw the Babylonians replace the Assyrians as the rulers of the empire, but less than a century later they, in their turn, were overthrown by the Persians.

I BROUGHT BACK THE EXHAUSTED PEOPLE OF ASSYRIA WHO HAD ABANDONED THEIR CITIES AND HOUSES IN THE FACE OF WANT, HUNGER AND FAMINE, AND HAD GONE UP TO OTHER LANDS. I SETTLED THEM IN CITIES AND HOUSES WHICH WERE SUITABLE AND THEY DWELT IN PEACE. I CONSTRUCTED PALACES IN THE DISTRICTS OF MY LAND. I HITCHED UP PLOUGHS IN THE DISTRICTS OF MY LAND AND PILED UP MORE GRAIN THAN EVER BEFORE. I HITCHED UP MANY TEAMS OF HORSES FOR THE FORCES OF ASSYRIA.

Ashur-dan II (934–912 BC)

A polychrome glazed brick relief (right) of a *mushussu* dragon from the Ishtar Gate. The *mushussu* was sacred to the god Marduk, and reliefs like this lined the walls of the gate and the Processional Way that led to his sanctuary.

OUR KNOWLEDGE OF THIS PERIOD is drawn largely from Assyrian, and later Babylonian, documents, but some idea of how neighbouring states saw Assyria can be gained from the Hebrew Bible, which contains historical material from the 8th century BC onwards. Although its narrative was revised several times in later centuries,

3 The evidence of archaeology, combined with information from Babylonian texts, has made it possible to identify the gates and some of the temples of Nebuchadnezzar's city. It was built as a great ceremonial centre, with Esagila, the sanctuary complex of Marduk, at its heart. This contained the ziggurat Etemanaki (the house of the frontier of heaven and earth), a vast tower that gave rise to the legend of the Tower of Babel.

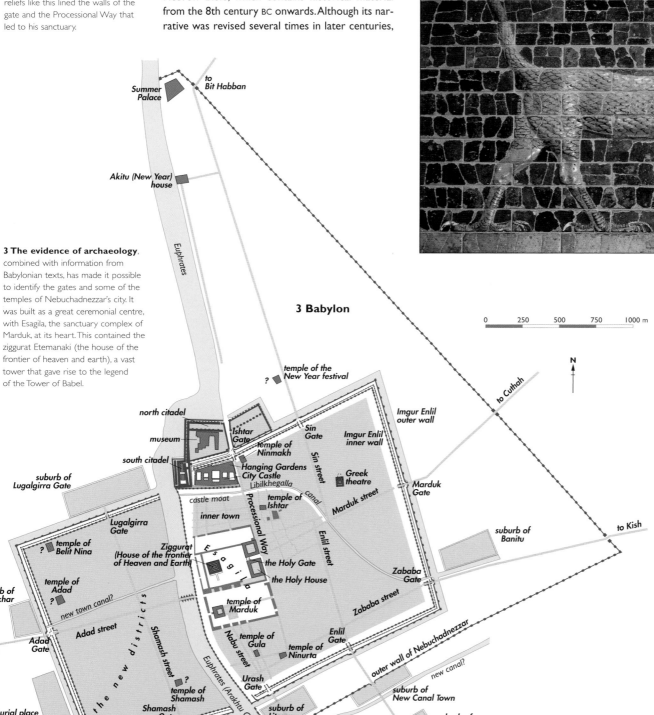

3 Babylon

0   250   500   750   1000 m

the Bible provides information about the kingdoms of Israel and Judah, which emerged in the area of Palestine in around 1000 BC, initially as a single kingdom with its centre at Jerusalem. Over the next 300 years Israel and Judah came increasingly into the Assyrian sphere of influence, with their kings adopting varying attitudes to the neighbouring superpower.

Assyrian expansion started in the reign of Ashurnasirpal II (883–859 BC), who rebuilt and expanded the city and palace of Nimrud to be his capital. His successor Shalmaneser III (858–824 BC) extended the power of the kingdom westwards, partly by conquest and partly by accepting tribute from the local rulers in Syria and the Levant. In the following century Assyrian expansion turned south and east under three powerful rulers, Tiglath-pileser III (744–727 BC), Sargon II (721–705 BC) and Sennacherib (704–681 BC). Repeating the achievements of the 13th-century kings they conquered the city of Babylon and brought Mesopotamia under Assyrian control.

At this time a new power was growing on Assyria's northern border in the shape of Urartu. Little is known about this state, which had its capital at Tushpa on Lake Van. Many Urartian sites were heavily fortified, and the state flourished from the 9th to the 7th centuries BC. If the Assyrians did try to conquer it, they had little success. Along with its western neighbours, Phrygia and Lydia, Urartu had grown up after the collapse of the Hittite empire, but a number of "neo-Hittite" city-states also emerged in the region of northern Syria.

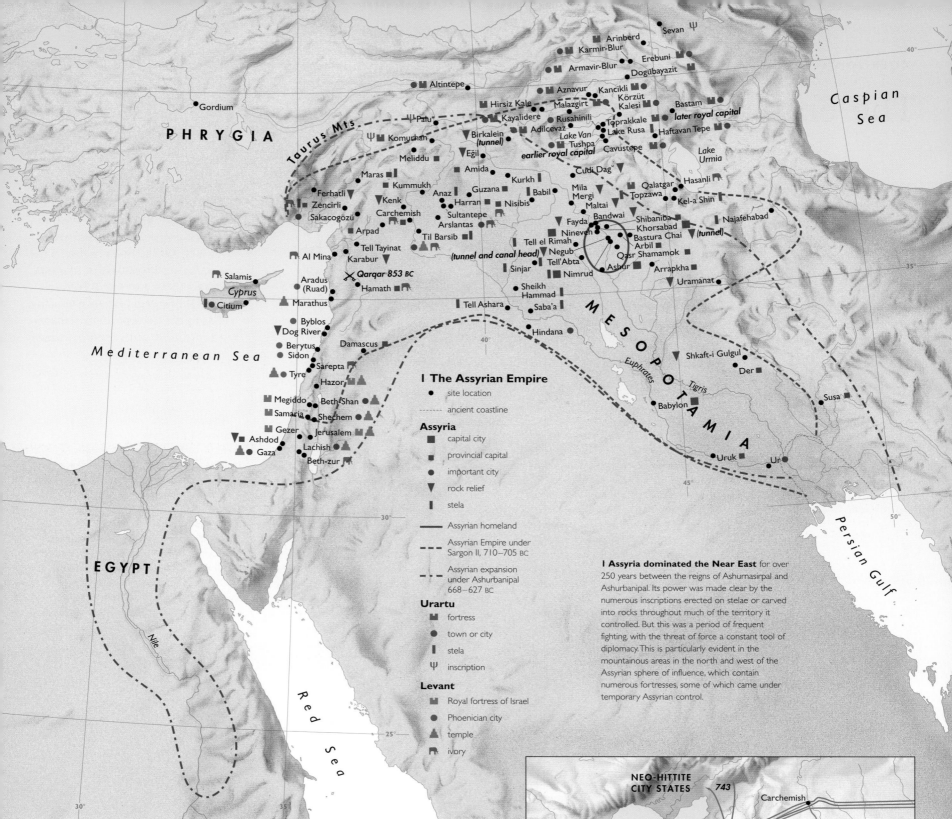

1 The Assyrian Empire

- ● site location
- ┈┈┈ ancient coastline

Assyria
- ■ capital city
- ▪ provincial capital
- ● important city
- ▼ rock relief
- ▮ stela

- ▬▬▬ Assyrian homeland
- ┈┈┈ Assyrian Empire under Sargon II, 710–705 BC
- ─·─·─ Assyrian expansion under Ashurbanipal 668–627 BC

Urartu
- ▪ fortress
- ● town or city
- ▯ stela
- Ψ inscription

Levant
- ▮ Royal fortress of Israel
- ● Phoenician city
- ▲ temple
- ▥ ivory

1 Assyria dominated the Near East for over 250 years between the reigns of Ashurnasirpal and Ashurbanipal. Its power was made clear by the numerous inscriptions erected on stelae or carved into rocks throughout much of the territory it controlled. But this was a period of frequent fighting, with the threat of force a constant tool of diplomacy. This is particularly evident in the mountainous areas in the north and west of the Assyrian sphere of influence, which contain numerous fortresses, some of which came under temporary Assyrian control.

A little before 700 BC Egypt was beginning to recover from the disorganization of the Third Intermediate Period after the end of the New Kingdom, and attempted to influence affairs in the Levant. In response Esarhaddon (680–669 BC) and Ashurbanipal (668–627 BC) led campaigns into Egypt, going as far south as Thebes and more or less installing pro-Assyrian rulers in the country. Ashurbanipal also invaded Elam, extending his empire further than ever before. His death in 627 BC however marked the end of Assyrian power: within 15 years his capital, Nineveh, had been sacked, and his empire had come under the control of Babylon.

It has been suggested that the transformation of the neo-Assyrian empire into the neo-Babylonian empire should be seen as the result more of an internal dynastic conflict than of conquest. With the help of the Medes, who were settled on the northeastern borders of Assyria, the first neo-Babylonian ruler, Nabopolassar (626–605 BC), took advantage of quarrels within the Assyrian ruling house to seize control of the whole empire. In the process, Median and Babylonian armies destroyed Ashur, Nimrud and Nineveh, but, with the exception of Egypt, the empire that these cities controlled held together under its new rulers.

When the Egyptians tried to take advantage of the upheaval, Nabopolassar and his successor

2 In the period after the end of the Bronze Age (map right), small city-states grew up in the area between the Mediterranean and the Syrian and Arabian deserts. By 800 BC the southern part of the area contained the two kingdoms of Israel and Judah, which spent a lot of time at war with each other and their neighbours. From the middle of the 8th century the growing power of Assyria had a major influence on political relations in the area, with the kingdom of Israel being brought under Assyrian control, and the territory of Judah considerably reduced. The rise of Babylon after 626 BC led to the final conquest of Judah in 597 BC and 587 BC.

Nebuchadnezzar (604–562 BC) marched to the Levant, drove the Egyptians away, and at the same time captured Jerusalem and deported its leaders. The wealth of the empire was used to rebuild the cities of Mesopotamia, and above all Babylon. Excavation in the early 20th century revealed the splendour and the sheer size of the city as it was rebuilt by Nebuchadnezzar.

After Nebuchadnezzar's death there was a period of instability, which ended with a palace coup that placed Nabonidus (555–539 BC) on the throne. Although he had a long reign, his religious reforms appear to have made him unpopular with many leading members of the kingdom. This may have critically weakened Babylonian military strength when, in 539 BC the city was taken by the Persians under Cyrus I (752).

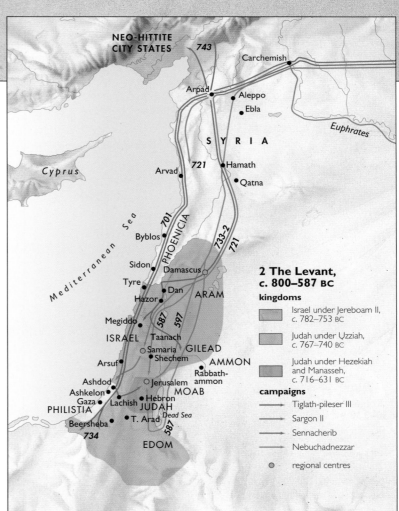

2 The Levant, c. 800–587 BC

kingdoms
- Israel under Jereboam II, c. 782–753 BC
- Judah under Uzziah, c. 767–740 BC
- Judah under Hezekiah and Manasseh, c. 716–631 BC

campaigns
- Tiglath-pileser III
- Sargon II
- Sennacherib
- Nebuchadnezzar
- ● regional centres

The empires of Persia

539 BC Cyrus the Great captures Babylon

525 BC Cambyses conquers Egypt

330 BC Darius III, last Achaemenid King, assassinated

238 BC Arsaces I seizes Parthia from the Seleucids

53 BC Parthians defeat Roman legions under Marcus Crassus at Carrhae

AD 259 Sasanid Shapur I captures the Roman emperor Valerian at Edessa

AD 540 Chosroes I sacks Antioch

AD 637 Arabs capture Sasanid capital Ctesiphon

The Iranian plateau was the heartland of three great empires whose territory stretched from the ancient centres of civilization in Mesopotamia to India. For more than a millennium, the Persian empire was governed successively by the Achaemenid, Arsacid and Sasanid ruling families, and offered a constant challenge to the Mediterranean lands to the west.

DARIUS THE KING SAYS: THESE ARE THE LANDS WHICH CAME TO ME. I BECAME THEIR KING BY THE WILL OF AHURA MAZDA: PERSIA, ELAM, BABYLONIA, ASSYRIA, ARABIA, EGYPT, THOSE BY THE SEA, SARDIS, IONIA, MEDIA, ARMENIA, CAPPADOCIA, PARTHIA, DRANGIANA, ARIA, KHWARAZM, BACTRIA, SOGDIANA, GANDHARA, SHAKALAND, SATTAGYDIA, ARACHOSIA, MAKA, A TOTAL OF TWENTY-THREE LANDS.

Inscription of Darius (522–486 BC) at Behistun

THE DOWNFALL OF THE Assyrian empire around 612 BC (see p. 60) was brought about by the Babylonians and the Medes, a loose confederacy of tribes in western Iran. It was the Persians, however, who proved to be the main beneficiaries. The Persian state emerged in the 7th century BC on the edge of the area dominated by Assyria, and in 550 BC its ruler, Cyrus (559–530 BC), defeated an invading Median army at Pasargadae. The next 11 years saw attempts to stop the growth of Persian power by both Croesus of Lydia and Nabonidus of Babylon. Both were defeated, leaving Cyrus in possession of Anatolia, the Levant and Mesopotamia.

The absorption of Lydian territory into Cyrus's empire brought Persia into contact with the Greeks.

He then turned his attention eastwards, gaining control of much of Afghanistan and south central Asia. Though Cyrus's successor, Cambyses (530–522 BC), added Egypt to the empire in 525 BC, his death was followed by the first of several upheavals within the empire as uncertainty over the succession encouraged widespread revolts.

These were quickly suppressed by Darius (522–486 BC), who also incorporated northwest India into the empire. The northwestern boundary of the empire remained a problem, but after the failure of expeditions into Europe (see p. 84) by Darius and Xerxes (486–465 BC), the Persians protected their interests by a series of peace treaties with the Greek states.

Achaemenid rule was brought to an end by the invasion of Alexander the Great in 334 BC (see p. 86). Dynastic struggles in the 330s may have had an effect, but no entirely satisfactory explanation has been given for the rapidity with which the Achaemenid empire fell.

The Parthian empire

After Alexander's death, Iran and its neighbouring territories became part of the Seleucid kingdom (see p. 86). In the 3rd century BC internal disputes and conflict with other Hellenistic kingdoms weakened Seleucid control of their eastern territories. Bactria broke away to become an independent kingdom, and the provinces of Parthia and Hyrcania

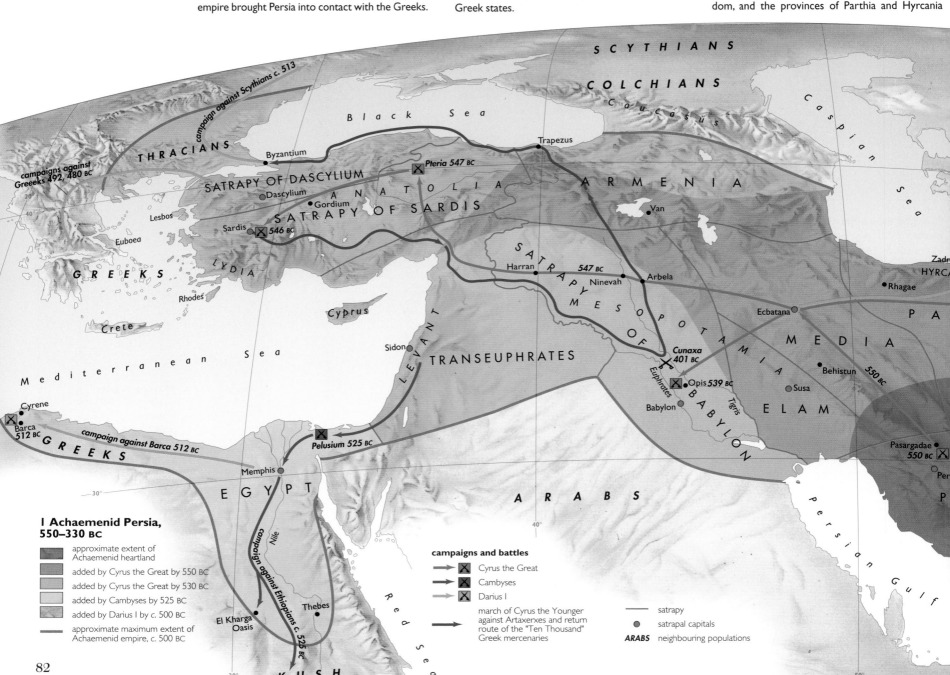

I Achaemenid Persia, 550–330 BC

- approximate extent of Achaemenid heartland
- added by Cyrus the Great by 550 BC
- added by Cyrus the Great by 530 BC
- added by Cambyses by 525 BC
- added by Darius I by c. 500 BC
- approximate maximum extent of Achaemenid empire, c. 500 BC

campaigns and battles

- Cyrus the Great
- Cambyses
- Darius I
- march of Cyrus the Younger against Artaxerxes and return route of the "Ten Thousand" Greek mercenaries
- satrapy
- satrapal capitals
- **ARABS** neighbouring populations

2 The Parthians overran much of the territory of the Seleucid kingdom (map right). Their advance westwards brought them into contact with the expanding power of Rome and in 53 BC their mounted archers surrounded and destroyed the legions of the Roman general Crassus. In the following centuries several Roman campaigns against the Parthians were mounted, including one under Trajan (AD 98–117), who briefly annexed Armenia and Mespotamia, but the Euphrates came to be acknowledged as the uncertain frontier. In the east, the Parthians had to endure raids by a number of nomadic peoples until the rise of the Kushana empire provided some stability.

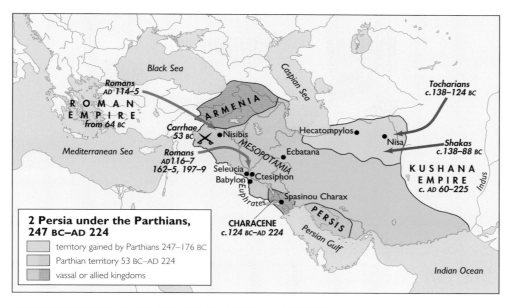

2 Persia under the Parthians, 247 BC–AD 224

	territory gained by Parthians 247–176 BC
	Parthian territory 53 BC–AD 224
	vassal or allied kingdoms

3 The new rulers of Persia rapidly annexed the western parts of the Kushana empire and installed their own governors under the title "king of the Kushans" (map right). Control of this part of their territory was threatened by further nomadic invasions of Hephthalite and Chionite Huns from the 4th century. On the western frontier, the Sasanids were able to withstand further attacks from Roman armies, capturing the Emperor Valerian at Edessa in 259. Their greatest successes came under Shapur II (310–79) and Chosroes I (531–79), under whose rule Arab territory was annexed as far south as Yemen. But conflict to the west continued, draining Sasanid resources and leaving the empire vulnerable to the Arab invasion of the 7th century.

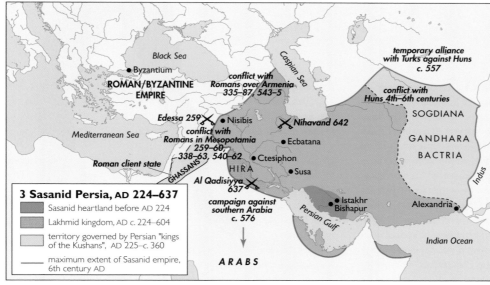

3 Sasanid Persia, AD 224–637

	Sasanid heartland before AD 224
	Lakhmid kingdom, AD c. 224–604
	territory governed by Persian "kings of the Kushans", AD 225–c. 360
	maximum extent of Sasanid empire, 6th century AD

were taken over by Arsaces, leader of the Parni in 238.

The early history of the new kingdom of Parthia is uncertain, but under Mithradates I (171–138 BC) its territory was extended into Mesopotamia and as far east as the mouth of the Indus, its success, like that of Sasanid Persia later, largely the result of the use of mounted archers and armoured cavalry. In the years after Mithradates's death the empire was threatened by the Tocharians and the Shakas in the east, but order was restored by Mithradates II (123–87 BC). From the 1st century BC onwards, in spite of further severe Shaka incursions from the east, the main threat to Parthian security was Rome. But although there were a number of wars between the two empires, they were well matched militarily and Arsacid, or Parthian, rule remained secure until it was challenged from within.

Sasanid Persia

Considerable autonomy was left in the hands of local ruling families, and it was from one of these in Persis that the new rulers of Persia arose. The first Sasanid ruler, Ardashir, defeated his Arsacid overlord Ardavan in AD 224 and rapidly took control of the whole of Parthia's empire and the areas beyond. Roman and Byzantine rule in Mesopotamia, Syria and eastern Anatolia was constantly challenged over the next centuries. The last century of Parthian rule had seen the rise of the Kushana empire in the east (see p. 92). This ended in 225 and Gandhara, Bactria and Sogdiana were brought under Sasanid control. From the 4th century this territory was threatened by Hephthalite and Chionite Huns and in the 6th century by the Turks.

The Arabs were a constant presence to the southwest of Persia's empires. The Achaemenids had established some control over northern Arabia, but in the Parthian period an independent state of Characene emerged at the head of the Persian Gulf, whose rulers styled themselves "kings of the Arabs". The Sasanids ended the independence of Characene, but maintained friendly relations with the Lakhmid Arab kingdom of Hira in western Mesopotamia which supported them against the Romans. Southern Arabia was never brought under Persian control, and in c. 604, after the Sasanid Chosroes II had ended Lakhmid independence, the Persians were defeated in battle by a confederacy of Arabs from the south. Success created confidence and increased Arab unity to such an extent that with further victories at Al Qadisiyya (637) and Nihavand (642) they brought Sasanid power to an end.

1 The Achaemenid empire was the creation of the first three Persian kings – Cyrus, Cambyses and Darius – who in less than 50 years united the very disparate inhabitants of the area from the Mediterranean to the Indus under a single administration (map left). According to the Greek historian Herodotus, there was a Persian saying that "Cyrus was a father, Cambyses a tyrant and Darius a tradesman", and indeed it was under Darius that the empire was organized into satrapies, tribute-paying provinces usually ruled by Persian governors which nonetheless retained a variety of local forms of administration. The sheer size of the empire meant that its kings were sometimes slow to react to problems. The Greek mercenary and historian Xenophon described his involvement in an abortive attempt in 401 BC by the crown prince Cyrus to overthrow his brother Artaxerxes: Cyrus and his "Ten Thousand" Greek mercenaries were able to march nearly half-way across the empire before they were stopped and Cyrus killed. Nonetheless, the empire was strong enough to withstand such shocks and remained a potent and united force until it was invaded by Alexander the Great in 334 BC.

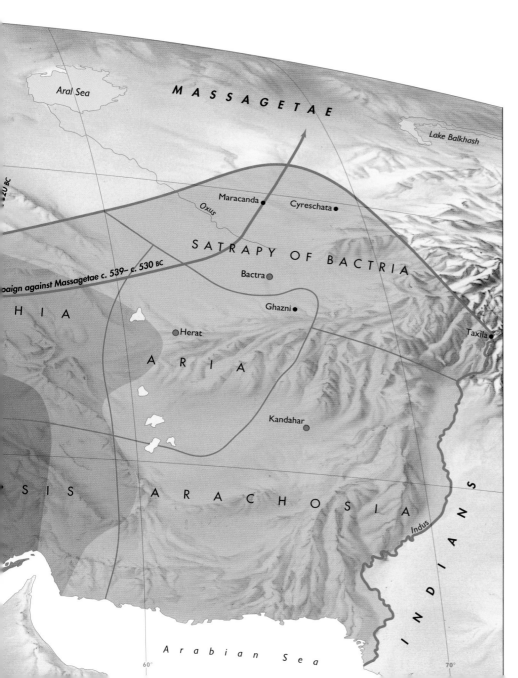

Relief from the royal palace at Persepolis (right). King Darius is shown on his throne, and above him is the flying disk of Ahura Mazda, the chief god of Zoroastrianism, a religion whose origins lie in the second millennium BC. All three Persian regimes adopted versions of Zoroastrianism and the kings claimed a special relationship with Ahura Mazda.

The spread of Greek civilization

The Greek heartland is an area of islands and plains divided by mountains. After the collapse of the Mycenaean palace system, a new form of political and religious community emerged here, the *polis*, or city-state, which became the Mediterranean world's dominant form of political organization.

776 BC Traditional date for first Olympic Games

c. 750 BC First Greek colonizing expeditions

7th–6th centuries BC Emergence of tyrants in many Greek states

508 BC Reforms of Cleisthenes establish Athenian democracy

478–404 BC Athens dominates Aegean through Delian League

447 BC Parthenon begun in Athens

399 BC Socrates tried and executed at Athens

371 BC Thebans defeat Spartans at Leuctra: end of Spartan influence in Greek affairs

338 BC Battle of Chaeronea: Philip II of Macedon gains control of Greece

THE EIGHTH CENTURY BC was a period of great transformation in Greece. It saw the appearance of the first monumental public buildings, and with them other indications of the emergence of new communities, including changes in burial practices and artistic styles. At the same time literacy was reintroduced into Greece, with a new alphabet. Though contact with the wider world had not been totally broken in previous centuries, it now increased dramatically, above all on the island of Euboea. Although it is impossible to be certain what produced this transformation, one important factor was the activities of the Phoenicians, who at this time began to explore and settle throughout the Mediterranean.

The age of expansion

From the middle of the century, following in the wake of the Phoenicians, groups of Greeks began to create settlements around the Mediterranean (see map 1). The earliest were in Italy and Sicily, but by the middle of the 6th century there were numerous Greek communities in north Africa and, to the east, along the Black Sea coast. These colonies were set up for a variety of reasons. Some of the earliest were trading posts, which over time developed into permanent settlements. Others were formally dispatched as a response to land shortage in the mother city. Others may have been founded by bands of discontented young men looking for a new and better life away from old Greece. It is probable

that the experience of the colonists had an effect on the political development of their mother cities.

From its earliest existence, decision-making in the Greek *polis* lay with an assembly of adult male citizens. Leadership, however, would have been in the hands of the wealthy elite. Increasing wealth and overseas contact in the 7th and 6th centuries led to the emergence in many city-states of powerful individuals, known as tyrants, who were able to impose their will on the community, usually with popular support. The "age of the tyrants" was a period of urban development, with new buildings, in particular enormous temples such as those of Hera on Samos, Artemis at Ephesus and Olympian Zeus at Athens. City-states published law-codes on large stone tablets, advertising to the world that they were communities governed by the rule of law. Poetry flourished, with the *Iliad* and *Odyssey* of Homer and the poems of Hesiod appearing in the early 7th century, followed by the great lyric poets, among them Archilochus, Anacreon and Sappho. Certain religious sanctuaries, above all Olympia and Delphi, gained "pan-Hellenic" status, and became meeting places for the leading members of the different Greek communities.

3 The whole Greek world became involved in the prolonged war between Athens and Sparta (**map below**). Sparta was stronger on land, but Athens kept firm control of the sea. After ten years an uneasy peace was made (421 BC), but when Athens lost almost its entire fleet in Sicily, the Spartans pressed home their advantage. Even so, it was only with considerable naval and financial support from the Persians that they were able to overcome the Athenian navy.

3 The Peloponnesian War, 431–404 BC

▨	Athens and members of the Delian League
▨	ally of Athens
▨	Sparta and allies
▨	neutral states
●	allies of Athens in Magna Graecia
●	allies of Sparta in Magna Graecia
→	Athenian campaigns
→	Spartan campaigns
✕	Athenian victory
✕	Spartan victory

Rome • — LATIUM — Cumae • • Neapolis — Tarentum • — *Adriatic Sea* — • Epidamnus — MACEDONIA — THRACE — • Byzantium — Amphipolis ✕ 422 — • Stagira — Thasos — Aegospotami ✕ 405 — Cyzicus ✕ 410 — Lampsacus • — Abydus • — Spartalos ✕ 429 — Lemnos — Cynossema ✕ 411 — PERSIAN EMPIRE — *Gulf of Tarentum* — *Tyrrhenian Sea* — *Aegean Sea* — Lesbos • ✕ Arginusae Islands 406 — • Sardes — IONIA — Decelea taken by Sparta 413 — Delium ✕ 424 — EUBOEA — Chios • — ✕ Notium 407 — • Ephesus — MAGNA GRAECIA — Lipara • — *Ionian Sea* — Chaeronea • — Thebes • Piraeus • ATTICA — Athens • — Samos • — Locri • — Messana • — Rhegium • — Corinth • — Elis • Mantinea ✕ 418 — Argos • — Sparta • — Segesta • — Himera • — *Sicily* — Catana • — Pylos • Sphacteria ✕ 425 — *Melos taken by Athens 416* — Rhodes • — Selinus • — Gela • ✕ Syracuse 413 — Camarina • — Cythera (taken by Athens 424) — CRETE — *Mediterranean Sea*

The Athenian empire

The experience of the Persian invasion of Greece under Xerxes (see map 2) encouraged the Greeks in the Aegean and Asia Minor to join together to defend themselves from future threats. Athens, which had by far the largest fleet, took command, turning this alliance of city-states into an Athenian empire. Member states were required to pay tribute to finance the Athenian fleet, which guaranteed security. The existence of the Athenian empire considerably affected life in Athens. The fleet gave employment and status to the poorer citizens, who served as oarsmen and were able to participate in political activity to an extent unequalled elsewhere in the Greek world. A proportion of the tribute, along with some of the booty from successful naval campaigns, was given to the gods, funding great building programmes in Athens. The last three decades of the 5th century were also the period of Athens' most enduring literary achievements. Following the work of Aeschylus earlier in the century, Sophocles and Euripides wrote tragedies, and Aristophanes his comedies, for performance at the great dramatic festivals, the City Dionysia and the Lenaea. Herodotus, the first historian, lived in Athens for some time, while sophists, philosophers and rhetoricians flocked there to make their names and their fortunes. Athens also produced its own great historian, Thucydides.

At the same time, Athens' growing power was seen as a threat by the states of the Peloponnese, above all Sparta. After some inconclusive conflicts in the mid-century, in 431 BC Sparta declared war on Athens. This, the Peloponnesian War, developed into a conflict which ended 27 years later in the defeat of Athens and the disbanding of its empire (see map 3).

The rise of Macedon

The economies of all Greek city-states were dominated by agriculture, and, except perhaps in Sparta, which relied on the labour of its conquered Messenian subjects (the "helots"), most of the population was made up of small-scale farmers, who were available for military service in the periods of less intense agricultural activity. One effect of this was that even prolonged periods of warfare had little long-term impact on the economies of the city-states involved. Thus within a decade of surrendering to the Peloponnesians, Athens was again at war with Sparta, this time supported by several of her former opponents.

The Spartans had originally defeated the Athenians with Persia's help. In 387 BC the Persian king attempted to impose a peace settlement on Greece, and the next 30 years saw Athens, Sparta and Thebes vying for dominance in Greece, looking always for backing from Persia. In 359 BC Philip II became king of Macedon. He united the country and took advantage of conflicts elsewhere in Greece to gain control of Thrace to the east and Thessaly to the south. This gave him a firm base for involvement in Greek affairs, and, after Philip had brought to an end the "Sacred War" of 356–46, Macedon was left as the major power in Greece. In 338 BC Philip defeated the Athenians and Thebans at Chaeronea, and imposed a settlement on the whole of Greece, the "League of Corinth". His death two years later left his son Alexander a more or less united Greece, from which he was able to launch his invasion of the Persian empire.

Bronze statue of Zeus (left) of around 460 BC. The work, more than life-size, was retrieved from a wreck off Cape Artemisium. Few large bronze sculptures have survived from the period, and this is a superb example of early classical statuary.

2 In 499–494 BC several Greek cities in Asia Minor, with support from Athens, revolted unsuccessfully against the Persian empire. In response the Persian king, Darius, sent two expeditions (map right) against mainland Greece: one was abandoned after storms, the other defeated at Marathon. Darius's successor Xerxes personally led a larger force, including contingents from many Greek cities, and sacked Athens before being defeated by sea at Salamis and on land at Plataea. Despite these defeats, however, Persia continued to be influential in Greek affairs for nearly 150 years.

1 The earliest Greek settlements overseas (map above) were from Chalcis and Eretria in Euboea, while Corinth was the first and most important Peloponnesian mother-city; in contrast Sparta and Athens had little involvement. It became usual to consult an oracle, especially Delphi, before launching an expedition. Miletus, with its own oracle at Didyma, sent out many colonies to the Black Sea.

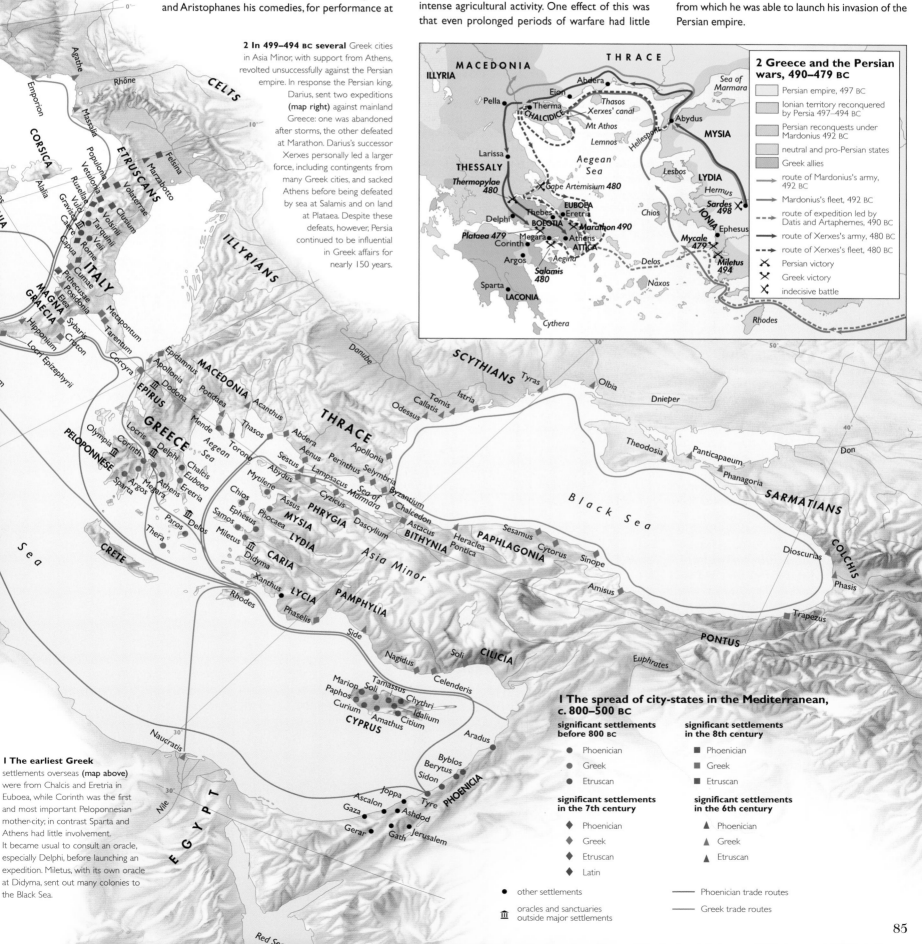

2 Greece and the Persian wars, 490–479 BC

- Persian empire, 497 BC
- Ionian territory reconquered by Persia 497–494 BC
- Persian reconquests under Mardonius 492 BC
- neutral and pro-Persian states
- Greek allies
- route of Mardonius's army, 492 BC
- Mardonius's fleet, 492 BC
- route of expedition led by Datis and Artaphernes, 490 BC
- route of Xerxes's army, 480 BC
- route of Xerxes's fleet, 480 BC
- ✕ Persian victory
- ✕ Greek victory
- ✕ indecisive battle

1 The spread of city-states in the Mediterranean, c. 800–500 BC

significant settlements before 800 BC
- ● Phoenician
- ● Greek
- ● Etruscan

significant settlements in the 7th century
- ◆ Phoenician
- ◆ Greek
- ◆ Etruscan
- ◆ Latin

significant settlements in the 8th century
- ■ Phoenician
- ■ Greek
- ■ Etruscan

significant settlements in the 6th century
- ▲ Phoenician
- ▲ Greek
- ▲ Etruscan

- ● other settlements
- 𝚰𝚰𝚰 oracles and sanctuaries outside major settlements
- —— Phoenician trade routes
- —— Greek trade routes

The Hellenistic world

Alexander the Great's conquest of the Persian empire transformed the eastern Mediterranean and Middle Eastern world. The spread of Greek culture and political organisation which followed in his wake shaped the region for a millennium. Greek became the common language, and the city-state the common form of social organisation.

A LONG WITH THE KINGDOM of Macedon, in 336 BC Alexander inherited from his father the leadership of a league of Greek states that he had intended to use to campaign against the Persian empire. Through his ambition and brilliant generalship, by the time of his death less than 13 years later at the age of 32, he was recognized as legitimate ruler of an empire stretching from Egypt to India (see map 1). From the moment he died there was competition between his closest companions and generals. Until the assassination of Alexander's young son in 307 BC, the contenders, for all that each had ambitions to take over the whole empire, could at least claim to be acting as regents. Thereafter, they were fighting for themselves, rapidly styling themselves as kings, and attempting to carve out areas of personal influence. By 276 BC, a division of the empire into three main kingdoms – Antigonid Macedon, Seleucid Asia and Ptolemaic Egypt – had been established.

Cultural life in the successor states

The basic political units of these new kingdoms was the city-state, some nominally independent, but most owing allegiance to one of the successor kings. The cities of old Greece, such as Athens, retained their prestige, but they were eclipsed by the newly created or reorganized cities of the east, named inevitably after their founders or rulers: Alexandria, Seleucia, Antioch. The new cities had all the elements of their older counterparts, with gymnasia, theatres and temples to the gods, and regular festivals, some including athletics, which might be attended by Greeks from far afield. Citizenship was restricted almost entirely to the Greek and Macedonian minority, and the land was in the hands of citizens or of the kings and their friends. The local populations might farm the land as tenants or as labourers, but they were excluded from administrative positions. The network of cities helped the spread of a common Greek culture and language throughout the region: Clearchus, a pupil of Aristotle, brought a collection of maxims from Delphi in central Greece to the city of Ai Khanoum in eastern Afghanistan. In a number of cities, but above all in Alexandria, with its access to papyrus, and Pergamum, from where parchment got its name, the kings established great libraries, and these became centres for literary work.

Even before Alexander's conquest, some communities within the Persian empire had adopted aspects of Greek culture. This "Hellenization" continued, at least among the elites: conflict between "Hellenizers" and "traditionalists" in the 2nd century led to violence in Jerusalem. However, especially in Seleucid territories, elements of older cultures, including cuneiform writing, remained important, and in those areas which were to become the Parthian empire (see p. 82), Greek culture was never firmly established.

There were advances in geometry and mathematics, especially with Euclid of Alexandria and Archimedes. The great Alexandrian librarian, Eratosthenes of Cyrene, attempted with some success to calculate the circumference of the earth. However, this was not a period of great technological change. The basis of the Hellenistic economy was agriculture, and this changed little. Merchants continued to trade, and writers of the time praise the range of goods available in the great cities, but there is evidence too of an increasing gulf between rich and poor. Only in warfare were there major developments, with the creation of ever more advanced artillery and siege engines, and the introduction by the Seleucids and the Ptolemies of elephants onto the battlefield.

336 Philip of Macedon assassinated

334 Alexander invades the Persian empire

323 Death of Alexander

301 Battle of Ipsus; final break-up of Alexander's empire

146 Following rebellions, Macedonia becomes a Roman province

133 Attalus III of Pergamum dies, leaving his kingdom to Rome

64 Romans annex Syria, ending Seleucid rule

30 Death of Cleopatra; Romans annex Egypt

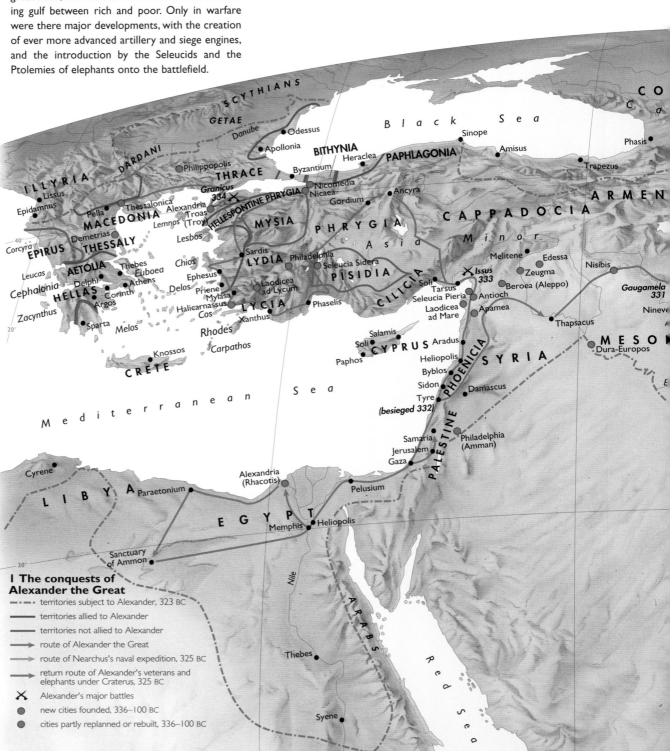

I The conquests of Alexander the Great
- – – – territories subject to Alexander, 323 BC
- ——— territories allied to Alexander
- ——— territories not allied to Alexander
- → route of Alexander the Great
- → route of Nearchus's naval expedition, 325 BC
- → return route of Alexander's veterans and elephants under Craterus, 325 BC
- ✕ Alexander's major battles
- ● new cities founded, 336–100 BC
- ● cities partly replanned or rebuilt, 336–100 BC

From the late 3rd century, a new player entered the game. Threats to Roman operations in the Adriatic, and Macedonian support for the Carthaginian Hannibal, led to a Roman invasion of Greece and Asia Minor. The Macedonian phalanx proved inferior to the Roman legions.

The growth of Roman power

Wars gave Roman commanders an opportunity for booty and glory, and initially they withdrew their forces after each campaign; but as Rome acquired more allies in the east, the reasons for maintaining their presence grew. After the battle of Pydna (168) the kingdom of Macedon was divided into four independent republics. 18 years later it was made a Roman province. The involvement of Cleopatra VII in the civil war between Mark Antony and the future emperor Augustus led after the battle of Actium (see p. 99) to the Roman annexation of Egypt, the last major successor kingdom. A few small client kingdoms, tolerated by the Romans for a while, were all that remained of Alexander's territorial inheritance.

1 Alexander spent almost his whole reign on campaign in the Persian empire **(below)**. Victories over the Persians at Granicus (334), Issus (333) and Gaugamela (331) allowed him to take over the title of Great King. He continued eastwards to end resistance to his rule, and reached the mouth of the Indus. Having sent his older veterans back to Macedonia under the general Craterus, and while his fleet under Nearchus explored the Persian Gulf, he led his army on a gruelling march through the Gedrosian desert back to Babylon, where he died. The legacy of his campaigns was a series of colonies, made up of veteran soldiers, each named Alexandria. His successors continued the founding of new Hellenistic cities throughout the area of his former empire.

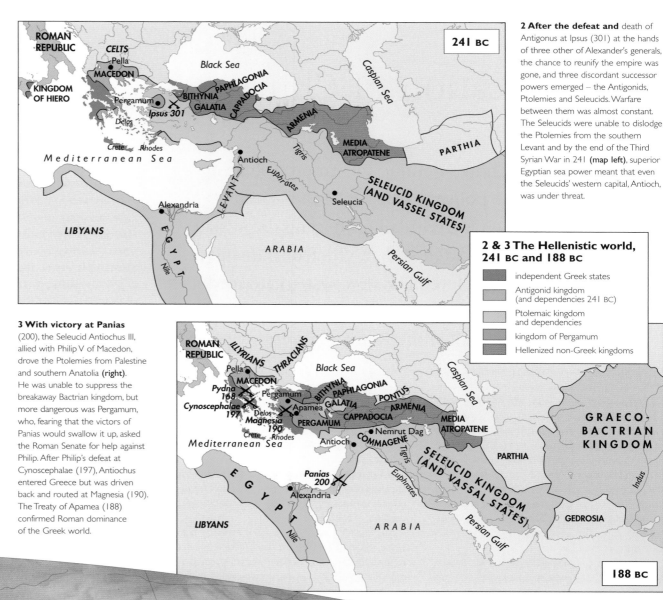

2 After the defeat and death of Antigonus at Ipsus (301) at the hands of three other of Alexander's generals, the chance to reunify the empire was gone, and three discordant successor powers emerged – the Antigonids, Ptolemies and Seleucids. Warfare between them was almost constant. The Seleucids were unable to dislodge the Ptolemies from the southern Levant and by the end of the Third Syrian War in 241 (map left), superior Egyptian sea power meant that even the Seleucids' western capital, Antioch, was under threat.

2 & 3 The Hellenistic world, 241 BC and 188 BC

- independent Greek states
- Antigonid kingdom (and dependencies 241 BC)
- Ptolemaic kingdom and dependencies
- kingdom of Pergamum
- Hellenized non-Greek kingdoms

3 With victory at Panias (200), the Seleucid Antiochus III, allied with Philip V of Macedon, drove the Ptolemies from Palestine and southern Anatolia **(right)**. He was unable to suppress the breakaway Bactrian kingdom, but more dangerous was Pergamum, who, fearing that the victors of Panias would swallow it up, asked the Roman Senate for help against Philip. After Philip's defeat at Cynoscephalae (197), Antiochus entered Greece but was driven back and routed at Magnesia (190). The Treaty of Apamea (188) confirmed Roman dominance of the Greek world.

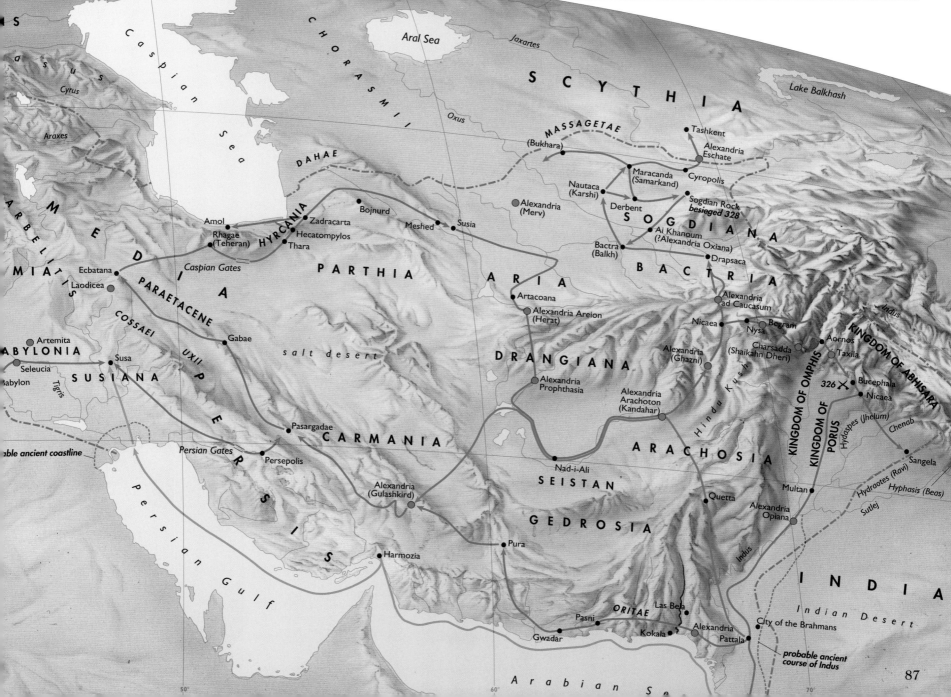

The unification of China

The process of China's nation- and empire-building began with the political anarchy of the Warring States period but ended with a highly centralized state headed by a single monarch and an efficient bureaucracy that reached village level. The new system attained its full glory under the Han, whose wealth and territory matched the Roman empire.

THEY RECALL THE AGE OF DISORDERED CONFUSION WHEN THE LAND WAS DIVIDED AND SEPARATE STATES ESTABLISHED, SO OPENING WIDE THE FISSURES OF STRIFE, WHEN ASSAULTS AND BATTLES EVERY DAY AROSE, AND BLOOD FLOWED ON THE PLAINS, AS IT HAS SINCE EARLIEST ANTIQUITY ... UNTIL NOW, WHEN THIS OUR EMPEROR HAS MADE THE WORLD ONE FAMILY, AND WEAPONS OF WARFARE ARE LIFTED UP NO LONGER.

Imperial edict
Found on Mount Yi, from c. 215 BC

475–221 BC Warring States period

221–207 BC Ch'in dynasty

221 BC Shih Huang-ti crowned the first emperor of China

210 BC Death of Shih Huang-ti; decline of the Ch'in

202 BC–AD 9 Former Han dynasty

87 BC Death of emperor Han Wu-ti; decline of Former Han

AD 9–23 Hsin dynasty

AD 25–220 Later Han dynasty

AD 220 Last Han emperor Hsien-ti abdicates

THROUGHOUT THE WARRING States period (475–221 BC) seven major rivals contended for supremacy. At first, following the decline of the power of the Chou king (see p. 68), the principal contenders were the old-established dukedoms of Ch'i, Ch'u, Han and Wei. But from the beginning of the 3rd century BC the border state of Ch'in established firm control over the northwest and west, adopting the title "king" in 325 BC, and during the latter half of the 3rd century BC it began gradually destroying its rivals (see map 1).

Throughout China, it was a period of constant warfare, waged on a massive scale by powerful and well-organized political units. But at the same time, this Warring States period coincided with major economic and social changes. The introduction of iron tools from about 500 BC and the use of animal power for cultivation greatly increased agricultural productivity. Population multiplied, commerce and industry flourished and large cities emerged. It was also a period of innovation in technology and science, and of philosophical ferment, in which the main schools of thought – Confucianism, Daoism and Legalism – took shape.

That the Ch'in emerged from this period to unify China under their leadership was at least in part due to the success of the "Legalist" system adopted by them in the 4th century, whereby a universal code of rewards and punishments was established that induced a high level of popular obedience and military discipline. Under this system, a centralized bureaucracy took measures to improve the production and distribution of grain, and organized the population to provide manpower for construction works and for the army, enforcing the system through a ruthless penal code.

The first emperor

When the Ch'in king, Shih Huang-ti, was crowned the first emperor of China in 221 BC, the "Legalist" institutions were extended throughout the country. But although the emperor tried to eliminate all hostile factions, under the burdens imposed on the

2 The Former Han Empire in AD 2 (map left) included not only the territory of Ch'in, but extended civil administration over Chinese colonies in the north of Vietnam, Korea and over territories in the northwest. Effective control over much of the south was limited to a few main centres. The southeast and southwest were still occupied by unassimilated aboriginal peoples. Much of the densely populated north was administered by feudal princes.

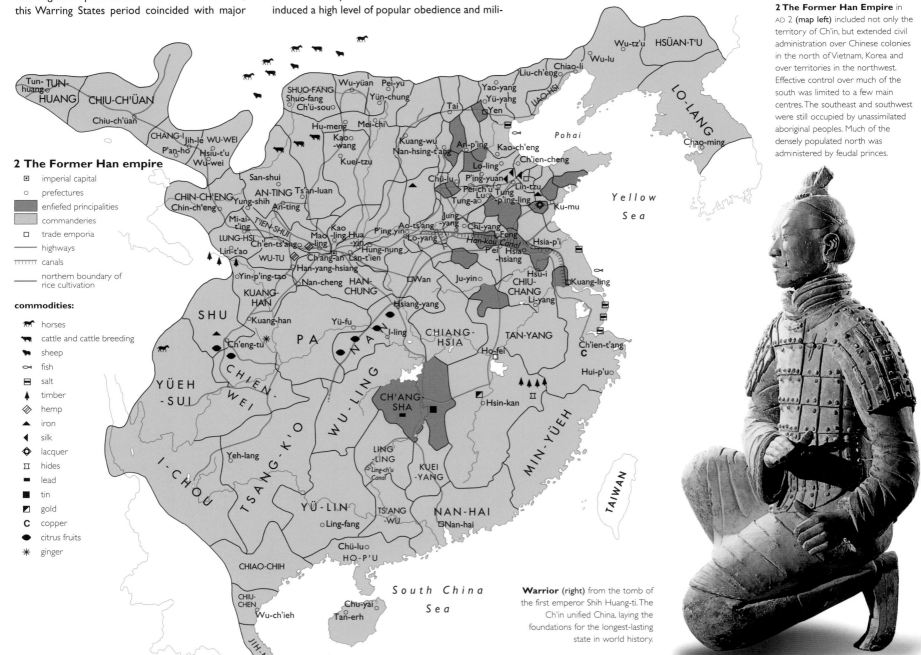

2 The Former Han empire

- ⊡ imperial capital
- ○ prefectures
- ▨ enfiefed principalities
- ▢ commanderies
- ▢ trade emporia
- highways
- canals
- northern boundary of rice cultivation

commodities:

- 🐎 horses
- 🐂 cattle and cattle breeding
- 🐑 sheep
- ∞ fish
- 🧂 salt
- ▲ timber
- ◈ hemp
- ▲ iron
- ◀ silk
- ◆ lacquer
- Ⅱ hides
- ▬ lead
- ■ tin
- ▧ gold
- C copper
- ● citrus fruits
- ✳ ginger

Warrior (right) from the tomb of the first emperor Shih Huang-ti. The Ch'in unified China, laying the foundations for the longest-lasting state in world history.

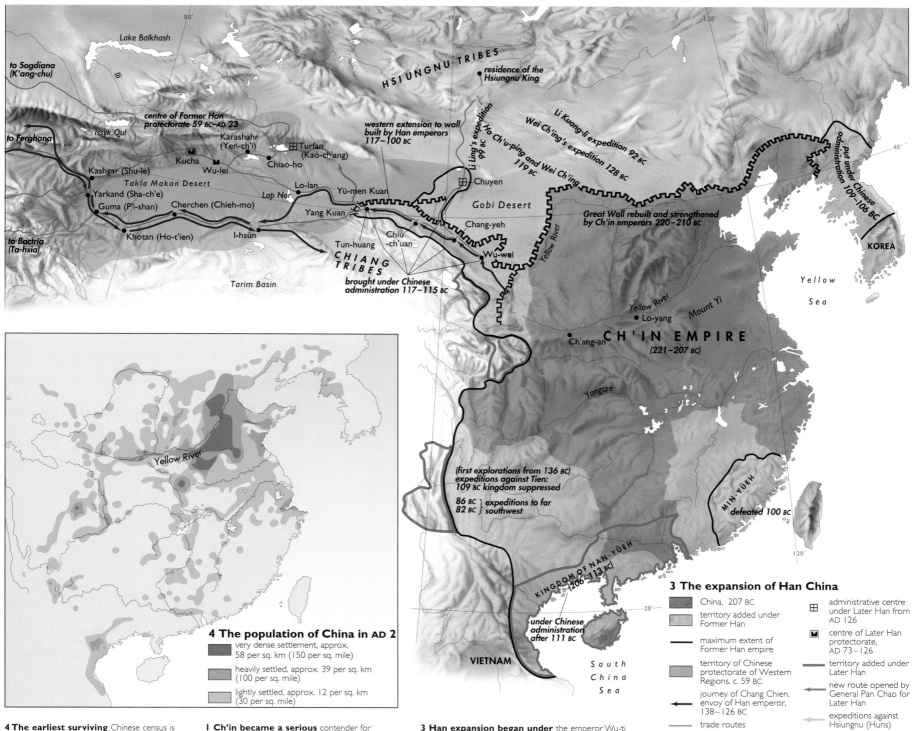

4 The population of China in AD 2

- very dense settlement, approx. 58 per sq. km (150 per sq. mile)
- heavily settled, approx. 39 per sq. km (100 per sq. mile)
- lightly settled, approx. 12 per sq. km (30 per sq. mile)

1 The Warring States and the unification of China

- defensive walls with dates of first construction. Rebuilt by Ch'in after 220 BC.
- original Ch'in territory, 350 BC
- Ch'in expansion before 300 BC
- other major states with dates of annexation by Ch'in
- new areas annexed by Ch'in after unification

3 The expansion of Han China

- China, 207 BC
- territory added under Former Han
- maximum extent of Former Han empire
- territory of Chinese protectorate of Western Regions, c. 59 BC
- journey of Chang Chien, envoy of Han emperor, 138–126 BC
- trade routes
- administrative centre under Later Han from AD 126
- centre of Later Han protectorate, AD 73–126
- territory added under Later Han
- new route opened by General Pan Chao for Later Han
- expeditions against Hsiungnu (Huns)

4 The earliest surviving Chinese census is from AD 2, and shows a population of 57 million, concentrated in the lower Yellow River plain **(map above)**. Before 500 BC, population growth had been limited by the lack of the technology needed to clear new land for cultivation, but after the introduction of iron, and with the emergence of large-scale new states in the 5th century BC, massive drainage and irrigation projects were undertaken. Population growth was further boosted by the wealth and stability of Han China.

1 Ch'in became a serious contender for supremacy after its expansion from 328 BC. The other states were eliminated **(map below)** until in 221 BC Ch'in controlled all China. The Ch'in then expanded its territories to the south and northeast. Earlier, several of the "warring" kingdoms had erected earthworks as a defence against their neighbours or potential invasions from the non-Chinese peoples to the north. Faced with a threat from the Hsiungnu, the first Ch'in emperor unified these into a single coordinated system.

3 Han expansion began under the emperor Wu-ti (140–87 BC), whose generals took the offensive against the Hsiungnu, and extended Han territory in the south and northeast **(map above)**. Thanks to the pioneer exploration of Chang Chien, diplomatic initiatives were started to expand trade and forge alliances with some of the peoples of the northwest, and under his promptings the "Silk Road" was established carrying Chinese trade to central Asia and beyond. To protect these routes, annexations and extensions to the Great Wall in the northwest followed. Chinese power was again briefly extended to the west under the Later Han after AD 94.

people by his military campaigns and vast construction works, his dynasty collapsed in a nationwide rebellion in 206 BC, shortly after his death.

After a period of civil war a new dynasty, the Han, was established by Liu Pang (256–195 BC). Copying the general outlines of the Ch'in system, but softening its harshness and in part restoring a system of feudal principalities, the Han gradually evolved an effective central government and system of local administration. The "Legalist" approach was replaced by Confucianism which emphasized benevolent rule and good statesmanship.

Han expansion

The Ch'in had taken strong defensive measures against the nomad Hsiungnu (Huns) in the north. Under the emperor Wu-ti (140–87 BC), though probably driven by his generals in the north, Han China again took the offensive against the Hsiungnu, and opened up the route to central Asia known as the Silk Road. A large export trade, mainly in silk, reached as far as the Roman empire. The Han also reaffirmed the Ch'in conquests in the southern region, eliminated the Yüeh kingdoms of the southeast coast, and occupied northern Vietnam. Chinese

armies also drove deep into the southwest, seeking to establish Han control. In addition, Wu-ti's armies placed parts of northern Korea under Chinese administration.

The Han empire grew extremely prosperous and China's population reached some 57 million. Many large cities grew up and the largest, the capital Ch'ang-an, housed a population of a quarter of a million and was the centre of a brilliant culture. At the beginning of the Christian era the Han empire rivalled that of Rome in size and wealth.

But under a series of weak emperors during the latter half of the 1st century BC, the authority of the throne was challenged by powerful court families. In AD 9 Wang Mang usurped the throne. His reign (the Hsin dynasty, AD 9–23) ended in a widespread rebellion that restored the Han (Later Han, AD 25–220), and the capital was moved to Lo-yang.

The collapse of the Han empire

After some decades of consolidation, in the late 1st century the Chinese resumed active hostilities to drive the Hsiungnu westward to central Asia. But trouble with the Chiang tribes of the northwest and virulent factionalism at court had seriously weakened the Han state by AD 160. A wave of agrarian distress culminated in 184 in a massive uprising led by the "Yellow Turbans", a religious movement based on popular cults. Although the Han survived in name until 220, power now lay with regional commanders. In 220 the empire was divided into three independent kingdoms, ushering in a long period of territorial fragmentation.

China and east Asia

The period after 220 was one of the most chaotic and bloody in Chinese history. Not only was the north lost for long periods to non-Chinese regimes, but the governments in the south often lost effective control as well. Political instability was the norm across the country, and economic growth was minimal until the advent of the Sui dynasty.

THE HAN EMPIRE BROKE up into three kingdoms in 220: the Wei in the north; the Wu in the south; and the Shu in the west. The militarily strong Wei had conquered the Shu in the southwest by 263, but in 265 a military family, the Ssu-uma, took over the Wei kingdom through a coup d'état. They then proceeded with a series of military campaigns to unify China under the name of the Western Chin dynasty. The target of unification was finally achieved in 280.

The Western Chin

The new authorities granted farmers land-holding rights to re-establish household farming in accordance with the Han model. "Salary land" for officials was granted and cultivated by tenants. Overall, this helped the recovery of the agricultural economy. The adoption of a laissez-faire Daoism by the new rulers as the state philosophy was also precedented in the Han. At the same time Buddhism became increasingly widespread.

Politically, however, the ruling class was deeply divided. In the period from 291 to 306, there were numerous assassinations and violent struggles within the royal family, known as the "Wars between Eight Princes". The unitary empire existed only in name. The weakness of the Western Chin regime created opportunities for the non-Chinese peoples within and on the borders of the empire – the Hsienpei, Hsiungnu, Chieh, Ti and Ch'iang – to move in and establish their own kingdoms, as many as 16 at one time. This was known as the "Five Barbarians' Disruption of China" and practically ended the Western Chin. The Chinese regime survived under the Eastern Chin only in south China. Its territory was much smaller than the area controlled by the non-Chinese regimes in the north and its authority over the population severely weakened. Tax avoidance became endemic.

During the years of the Eastern Chin, north China saw near permanent conflict among the non-Chinese regimes. The unification of the north finally arrived in 382 under the Ch'ien Ch'in and after their failed invasion of the south in the following year an era of co-existence was ushered in between the non-Chinese regime in the north and the Chinese one in the south. Based on this ethnic division, the period is called the "Northern and Southern Dynasties" (see chart 5).

In the south the Eastern Chin dynasty ended with its overthrow in 420 by one of its generals, who established the Sung dynasty. There followed another three short-lived dynasties, each in turn brought down by either a general or another member of the ruling family, although outside the court there was a measure of peace and prosperity.

The Northern Wei

In the north a dynasty of Hsienpei descent, the Northern Wei, managed to conquer all of north China in the early 5th century, but split into two lines in 534, to become, in 550 and 557 respectively, the Northern Ch'i and Northern Chou. Although the latter was smaller and poorer, it had a more efficient military organization, and overcame the Northern Ch'i in 577. Within a few years, however, its ruling family was overthrown by one of its partly-Chinese generals, Yang Chien, who went on to conquer the south and establish the Sui dynasty. Although it was itself short-lived, the Sui had at last reunified China.

205 Ts'ao Ts'ao, founder of the Wei dynasty, in effective control of north China

220 Last Han emperor abdicates

280 China unified under Western Chin

311 Ch'ang-an first attacked by Ti armies

316 Lo-yang sacked by Hsiungnu

420 Overthrow of Eastern Chin dynasty

534 Northern Wei dynasty fragments

611–14 Sui launches unsuccessful and draining invasions of north Korea

618 Last Sui emperor, Yang-ti, assassinated

K'UNG-MING OFFERED HIS PRAYER:
"BORN INTO AN AGE OF TROUBLES,
I WOULD HAVE BEEN CONTENT TO LIVE
OUT MY TIMES AMONG THE GROVES AND
STREAMS, BUT FOR THE LATE KING, WHO
COMMITTED ME TO TOIL IN THE SERVICE
OF OUR CAUSE ..."

Lo Kuan-chung (c. 1330–c. 1400)
Three Kingdoms (Romance based on The Records of the Three Kingdoms by Ch'en Shou, AD 297)

1 After the collapse of the Han dynasty the strongest military forces were commanded by the Wei in the north (map below), who further expanded their fighting strength through a huge programme of public farming projects to support the vast armies. Although the Shu and the Wu forged an alliance for their mutual protection, both were overrun by the Wei between 263 and 280.

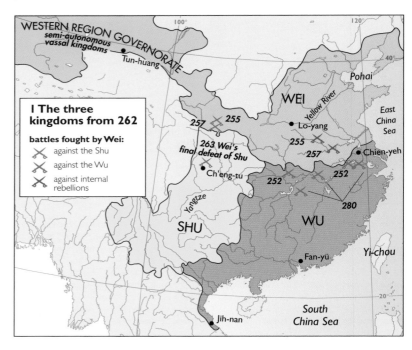

1 The three kingdoms from 262

battles fought by Wei:
✕ against the Shu
✕ against the Wu
✕ against internal rebellions

The lasting turmoil between 218 and 618 left few cultural relics of the period. However, a corridor of Buddhist sculptures (left), 51,000 in all, in the 53 "Yun-gang Caves" built in AD 460–94, have survived to this day. These two clearly show the strong Indian influence of the time. Buddhism and Daoism were to undermine or even replace Confucianism during this period.

3 Having eliminated their rivals in north China, the Northern Wei (map left) proceeded to attempt to balance the claims of their own Hsienpei people and the ethnic Han Chinese. In fact the dynasty became thoroughly Sinicized to the extent that under the emperor Hsiao-wen-ti (471–99) many of the old Hsienpei ways and even the use of the Hsienpei language in court were outlawed. The same emperor undertook a programme of drastic reform, including a reorganization of the civil service and an overhaul of civil laws. He also moved the capital to the ruined site of Lo-yang, which within 20 or 30 years had a population of half a million people, with magnificent buildings. The forced pace of change, however, together with the greed and incompetence of the court, destabilized the ever-fractious border regions, and led to the sacking of the new capital and the end of the dynasty. In the south the Sung, established by the general Liu Yu, provided only 30 years of capable rule before falling into decline.

3 The Northern Wei and the Sung, 449

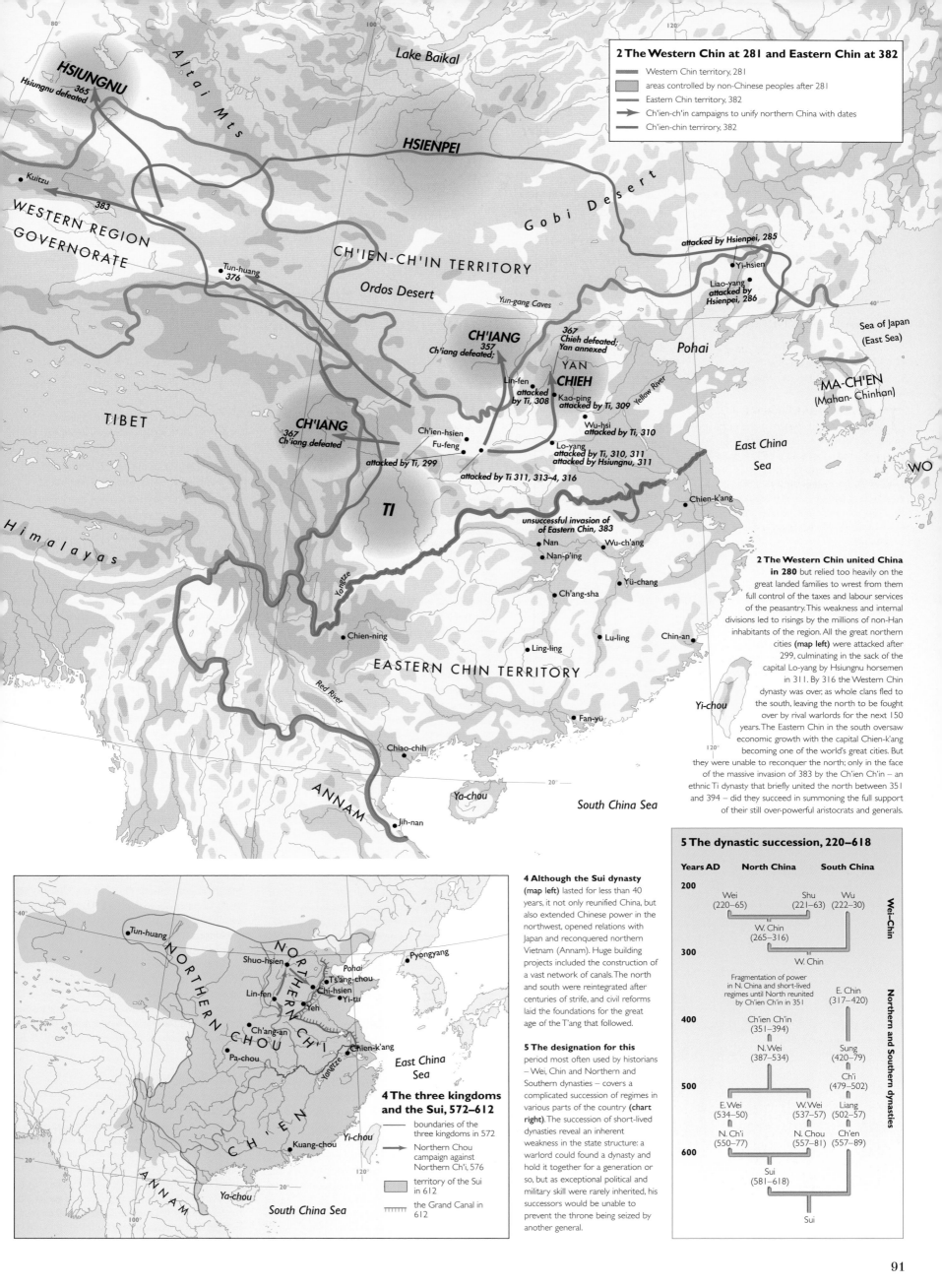

2 The Western Chin at 281 and Eastern Chin at 382
- Western Chin territory, 281
- areas controlled by non-Chinese peoples after 281
- Eastern Chin territory, 382
- Ch'ien-ch'in campaigns to unify northern China with dates
- Ch'ien-chin terrirory, 382

HSIUNGNU
365
Hsiungnu defeated

Altai Mts

Lake Baikal

• Kuitzu

383

HSIENPEI

Gobi Desert

WESTERN REGION GOVERNORATE

CH'IEN-CH'IN TERRITORY

Ordos Desert

Yun-gang Caves

• Tun-huang
376

attacked by Hsienpei, 285

• Yi-hsien

Liao-yang
attacked by Hsienpei, 286

Pohai

Sea of Japan
(East Sea)

CH'IANG
357
Ch'iang defeated;

367
Chieh defeated;
Yan annexed

YAN
CHIEH

MA-CH'EN
(Mahan- Chinhan)

TIBET

CH'IANG
367
Ch'iang defeated

Lin-fen
attacked by Ti, 308

Kao-ping
attacked by Ti, 309

Ch'ien-hsien
Fu-feng

Wu-hsi
attacked by Ti, 310

Lo-yang
attacked by Ti, 310, 311
attacked by Hsiungnu, 311

East China Sea

WO

attacked by Ti, 299

TI

attacked by Ti 311, 313–4, 316

Yangtze

Himalayas

• Chien-k'ang

unsuccessful invasion of Eastern Chin, 383

• Nan
• Nan-p'ing

• Wu-ch'ang

• Yü-chang

• Ch'ang-sha

• Chien-ning

Red River

• Ling-ling

• Lu-ling

Chin-an

EASTERN CHIN TERRITORY

Yi-chou

• Fan-yü

• Chiao-chih

ANNAM

• Ya-chou

• Jih-nan

South China Sea

2 The Western Chin united China
in 280 but relied too heavily on the great landed families to wrest from them full control of the taxes and labour services of the peasantry. This weakness and internal divisions led to risings by the millions of non-Han inhabitants of the region. All the great northern cities (map left) were attacked after 299, culminating in the sack of the capital Lo-yang by Hsiungnu horsemen in 311. By 316 the Western Chin dynasty was over, as whole clans fled to the south, leaving the north to be fought over by rival warlords for the next 150 years. The Eastern Chin in the south oversaw economic growth with the capital Chien-k'ang becoming one of the world's great cities. But they were unable to reconquer the north; only in the face of the massive invasion of 383 by the Ch'ien Ch'in – an ethnic Ti dynasty that briefly united the north between 351 and 394 – did they succeed in summoning the full support of their still over-powerful aristocrats and generals.

4 Although the Sui dynasty
(map left) lasted for less than 40 years, it not only reunified China, but also extended Chinese power in the northwest, opened relations with Japan and reconquered northern Vietnam (Annam). Huge building projects included the construction of a vast network of canals. The north and south were reintegrated after centuries of strife, and civil reforms laid the foundations for the great age of the T'ang that followed.

5 The designation for this
period most often used by historians – Wei, Chin and Northern and Southern dynasties – covers a complicated succession of regimes in various parts of the country (chart right). The succession of short-lived dynasties reveal an inherent weakness in the state structure: a warlord could found a dynasty and hold it together for a generation or so, but as exceptional political and military skill were rarely inherited, his successors would be unable to prevent the throne being seized by another general.

• Tun-huang

NORTHERN CHOU

NORTHERN CH'I

• Shuo-hsien

• Pyongyang

Pohai
• Ts'ang-chou
• Chi-hsien
Lin-fen • • Yi-tu
• Yeh

• Ch'ang-an

CH'IEN

• Pa-chou

• Chien-k'ang

East China Sea

4 The three kingdoms and the Sui, 572–612
- boundaries of the three kingdoms in 572
- Northern Chou campaign against Northern Ch'i, 576
- territory of the Sui in 612
- the Grand Canal in 612

Yangtze

• Kuang-chou

Yi-chou

ANNAM

Ya-chou

South China Sea

5 The dynastic succession, 220–618

Years AD	North China		South China	
200	Wei (220–65)	Shu (221–63)	Wu (222–30)	Wei-Chin
	W. Chin (265–316)			
300	W. Chin			
	Fragmentation of power in N. China and short-lived regimes until North reunited by Ch'ien Ch'in in 351		E. Chin (317–420)	Northern and Southern dynasties
400	Ch'ien Ch'in (351–394)			
	N. Wei (387–534)		Sung (420–79)	
500			Ch'i (479–502)	
	E. Wei (534–50)	W. Wei (537–57)	Liang (502–57)	
	N. Ch'i (550–77)	N. Chou (557–81)	Ch'en (557–89)	
600	Sui (581–618)			
		Sui		

91

India: the first empires

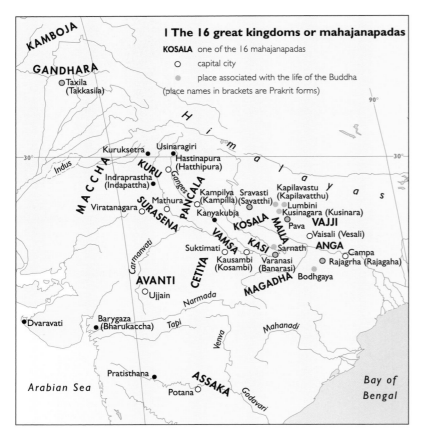

I The 16 great kingdoms or mahajanapadas

KOSALA one of the 16 mahajanapadas
○ capital city
● place associated with the life of the Buddha
(place names in brackets are Prakrit forms)

I In 500 BC, north India (map above) was dominated by small polities, one of which, the eastern kingdom of Magadha, contained the seeds of empire. Eastern India was also the home of Gautama Buddha who, born in around 486 BC in Lumbini near Kapilavastu, renounced the pleasures of royal life and attained spiritual enlightenment at Bodhgaya. He gave his first sermon at Sarnath and died at Kusinagara, from where his remains were carried away by kings and enshrined in burial mounds known as stupas.

3 In the 1st century BC migrations by the Shaka clans had destabilized the northwest. They were followed by new invaders, the Kushanas, who reduced the Shakas settled in western India to provincial governors (Satrapas) and subjugated much of north India, although they failed to dislodge the powerful Satavahanas of central west India (**map below**). By the 3rd century AD, the Kushana empire had ended: its western reaches were tributary to the Persian Sasanids and its eastern provinces fragmented into small polities.

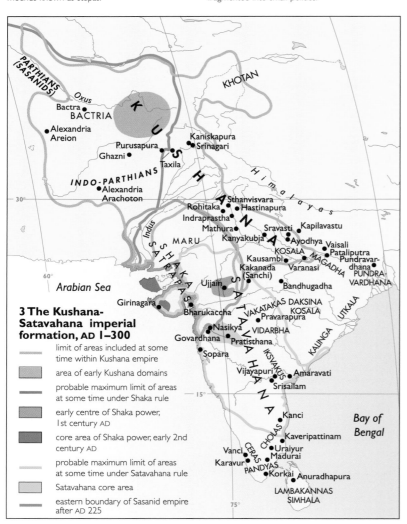

3 The Kushana-Satavahana imperial formation, AD 1–300
limit of areas included at some time within Kushana empire
area of early Kushana domains
probable maximum limit of areas at some time under Shaka rule
early centre of Shaka power, 1st century AD
core area of Shaka power, early 2nd century AD
probable maximum limit of areas at some time under Satavahana rule
Satavahana core area
eastern boundary of Sasanid empire after AD 225

From 500 BC to AD 550 south Asia witnessed a succession of metropolitan empires centred in north India – the Mauryas, the Kushanas and the Guptas. Although centralized political control was often weak, for the first time the entire subcontinent was integrated within a single but diverse cultural field.

BY ABOUT 500 BC NORTH India sustained 16 well-articulated polities, or "mahajanapadas", some of which were still essentially tribal republics and others were already monarchies (see map 1). This region witnessed tremendous change, as the consolidation of settled agriculture led to the emergence of cities and more complex political systems. Such changes made the older sacrificial cult of the Vedas, which had its origins in the pastoral communities of the Aryan tribes, increasingly obsolete. In its place, at the end of the 5th century BC in the heart of the Gangetic plains, the founders of Buddhism and Jainism formulated their radical new teachings.

The first empire

During the 5th century BC the number of mahajanapadas diminished to four – Vajji, Kosala, Kasi and Magadha. After a century of wars, the single kingdom of Magadha dominated, with its splendid new capital of Pataliputra. This was to be the nucleus of the first Indian empire. Shortly after Alexander's incursion into India in 327 BC, the Mauryan prince Chandragupta seized the Magadhan throne. Chandragupta then conquered the land east of the Indus, swung south to occupy much of central India, and in 305 BC decisively defeated Alexander's successor in the northwest, Seleucus Nicator. The Mauryan empire that Chandragupta founded reached its zenith under his grandson, Ashoka, who established his rule over most of the subcontinent (see map 2). Ashoka's empire was composed of a centralized administrative system spread over a number of thriving cities and their hinterlands. After his conquest of Kalinga in 260 BC, Ashoka publicly converted to Buddhism and adopted a policy of "conquest through righteousness", or *dhammavijaya*. In a number of public orders inscribed on pillars and rockfaces throughout the subcontinent, Ashoka called for peace, propagated moral teachings (*dhamma*), and prohibited Vedic animal sacrifices. These edicts, written in Prakrit, are the first specimens of royal decrees in south Asia.

The Kushana empire

Mauryan rule did not long survive Ashoka's death in 232 BC. In the 2nd century BC, the northwest was repeatedly invaded, both by Greeks from Bactria and Parthia, and then by new nomad groups themselves displaced from central Asia. First among these were Scythian tribes called the Shakas who overran Bactria and the Indus valley in the 1st century BC. Then the Kushana branch of the Yüeh-chih horde, who had settled in the Oxus valley after 165 BC, gradually extended their rule inland, subduing the Shakas in western India and reaching Varanasi in the 1st century AD. As well as the Oxus and Indus valleys, large parts of Khotan were included in their cosmopolitan empire, centred in Purusapura.

I HAVE GIVEN THE GIFT OF INSIGHT IN VARIOUS FORMS. I HAVE CONFERRED MANY BENEFITS ON MAN, ANIMALS, BIRDS, AND FISH, EVEN TO SAVING THEIR LIVES, AND I HAVE DONE MANY OTHER COMMENDABLE DEEDS. I HAVE HAD THIS INSCRIPTION OF DHAMMA ENGRAVED THAT MEN MAY CONFORM TO IT AND THAT IT MAY ENDURE.

Second Pillar Edict, Lauriya Nandangarh

Kushana India was a melting pot of cultures. The empire reached its height of power and influence under Kanishka, who patronized Buddhism and became extensively involved in political conflicts in central Asia.

Both the Shakas and the Kushanas took Indian names and were the first kings to adopt Sanskrit at their courts – the first courtly poems in Sanskrit date from this period – though the native kingdom of the Satavahanas of the Deccan continued to use Prakrit. In the northwest Mahayana Buddhism emerged at this time from more conservative teachings known as Theravada, and developed a more eclectic outlook, emphasizing compassion and worship in an enlarged Buddhist pantheon.

In the same period, India's ancient trading links with the west were revitalized and greatly extended as the Roman empire rose to power (see map 5). Ports such as Barbaricum, on the Indus delta, and the entrepot of Barygaza exported turquoise, diamonds, indigo and tortoise-shell, receiving in return a flow of pearls, copper, gold and slaves from the Arab and Mediterranean worlds. Much of the Chinese silk traffic found its way to the city of Taxila, before caravans took it further west. Trade led to other exchanges, as Buddhism spread to central Asia and China.

By the middle of the 2nd century AD the south had also witnessed economic development. The Satavahanas of the Deccan developed a powerful empire and established overland and coastal trading networks and the weaker Tamil-speaking kingdoms of the south established ports on both coasts of the peninsula.

The Guptas

In the 4th century, the native dynasty of the Guptas imposed a new rule, based again in Pataliputra. Following the campaigns of Samudragupta and his son Chandragupta II, their suzerainty was acknowledged over an area almost as great as that of the Mauryan empire. Until repeated Hun incursions ended Gupta power in the 6th century (see map 4), the Gupta period saw the blossoming of earlier cultural trends, and has become known as the "classical" or "epic" age of Indian history.

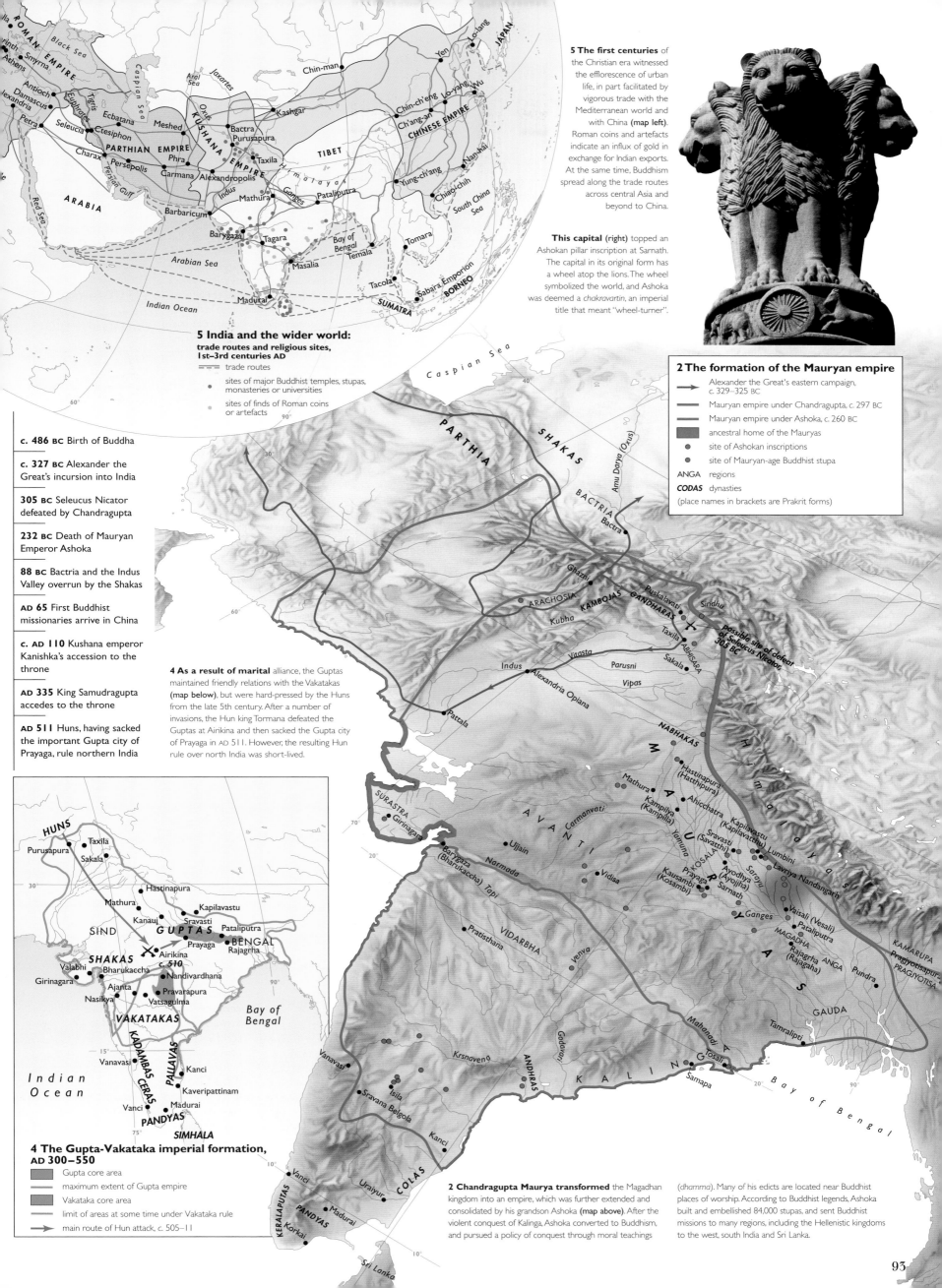

5 The first centuries of the Christian era witnessed the efflorescence of urban life, in part facilitated by vigorous trade with the Mediterranean world and with China (map left). Roman coins and artefacts indicate an influx of gold in exchange for Indian exports. At the same time, Buddhism spread along the trade routes across central Asia and beyond to China.

This capital (right) topped an Ashokan pillar inscription at Sarnath. The capital in its original form has a wheel atop the lions. The wheel symbolized the world, and Ashoka was deemed a *chakravartin*, an imperial title that meant "wheel-turner".

5 India and the wider world:
trade routes and religious sites,
1st–3rd centuries AD
- ═══ trade routes
- • sites of major Buddhist temples, stupas, monasteries or universities
- • sites of finds of Roman coins or artefacts

c. 486 BC Birth of Buddha

c. 327 BC Alexander the Great's incursion into India

305 BC Seleucus Nicator defeated by Chandragupta

232 BC Death of Mauryan Emperor Ashoka

88 BC Bactria and the Indus Valley overrun by the Shakas

AD 65 First Buddhist missionaries arrive in China

c. AD 110 Kushana emperor Kanishka's accession to the throne

AD 335 King Samudragupta accedes to the throne

AD 511 Huns, having sacked the important Gupta city of Prayaga, rule northern India

2 The formation of the Mauryan empire
- → Alexander the Great's eastern campaign, c. 329–325 BC
- ── Mauryan empire under Chandragupta, c. 297 BC
- ── Mauryan empire under Ashoka, c. 260 BC
- ▨ ancestral home of the Mauryas
- • site of Ashokan inscriptions
- • site of Mauryan-age Buddhist stupa
- ANGA regions
- *CODAS* dynasties
- (place names in brackets are Prakrit forms)

4 As a result of marital alliance, the Guptas maintained friendly relations with the Vakatakas (map below), but were hard-pressed by the Huns from the late 5th century. After a number of invasions, the Hun king Tormana defeated the Guptas at Airikina and then sacked the Gupta city of Prayaga in AD 511. However, the resulting Hun rule over north India was short-lived.

4 The Gupta-Vakataka imperial formation,
AD 300–550
- ▨ Gupta core area
- ── maximum extent of Gupta empire
- ▨ Vakataka core area
- ▨ limit of areas at some time under Vakataka rule
- → main route of Hun attack, c. 505–11

2 Chandragupta Maurya transformed the Magadhan kingdom into an empire, which was further extended and consolidated by his grandson Ashoka (map above). After the violent conquest of Kalinga, Ashoka converted to Buddhism, and pursued a policy of conquest through moral teachings (*dhamma*). Many of his edicts are located near Buddhist places of worship. According to Buddhist legends, Ashoka built and embellished 84,000 stupas, and sent Buddhist missions to many regions, including the Hellenistic kingdoms to the west, south India and Sri Lanka.

The peoples of northern Europe

The late Bronze Age saw a number of developments in northern Europe. The use of metals increased, new crops were cultivated, and burial practices were transformed. The "urnfield culture", with which these changes are associated, spread over a large part of Europe and laid the foundations for the rise of the Celts, whose warrior bands briefly threatened the Mediterranean world.

CENTRAL EUROPE had rich supplies of copper ores, which for several centuries had been exploited to produce bronze for tools and weapons. After 1300 BC the extent of bronze-working increased dramatically, and new techniques, including the lost-wax method of casting, led to major developments in art. Delicately worked gold ornaments found in some rich graves indicate that there were also improvements in gold-working at the same time. In agriculture, the staples of wheat and barley were supplemented by legumes and oil-rich crops such as linseed. There was also an increase in the domestication of animals, with horses having a greater presence, especially to the east.

The Urnfield period

The most dramatic change, however, was in burial practices, and it is this that has given the urnfield period its name. Inhumation had been the usual practice in earlier centuries, but from 1300 BC there was a move towards cremation and the burial of ashes in large communal cemeteries known as urnfields. Although there were differences from region to region, and even within cemeteries, there was a considerable decrease in the quantity of grave goods buried with the dead. Some burials, such as the so-called King's Grave at Seddin, were particularly rich, and presumably belonged to local chieftains, but most were simple. A change of practice like this may in part have reflected a change in attitudes to death, but it probably also reflected changes in social organization. Large cemeteries containing graves with little social differentiation suggest the emergence of large communities and more developed social structures.

Another feature that points to social change during this period is the large number of fortified sites. These were centuries in which there was fighting between rival communities, and the archaeological evidence points to a growing warrior culture.

The Celtic world

The 8th century BC saw the re-establishment of contact with the centres of civilization in the eastern Mediterranean and beyond as well as with the new Greek and Phoenician colonies in the western Mediterranean and the emerging Etruscans in Italy. At the same time the techniques of iron-working were widely adopted. This development had little impact on the Atlantic coasts of Europe, which were still characterized by small-scale trade between communities with little interest in Mediterranean luxury goods. But to the east the Rhône valley provided a trade-route from the Mediterranean, especially after the foundation of the Greek colony of Massilia (Marseilles). It was this that led to the development of a "prestige goods economy" in Burgundy, seen in the rich finds from Mont Lassois and Vix, which acted as staging posts between the Mediterranean and central Europe, as well as farther east at the hill fort at the Heuneburg on the upper Danube. Contact with the steppe communities on the eastern flank of the Celtic world also continued, and by this route goods from the Far East could reach central Europe. This is well illustrated by the discovery in a burial mound beside the Heuneburg site of textiles embroidered with Chinese silk.

Among the chief exports to the Mediterranean from this period onwards was slaves, which raised the status of warriors who were able to trade prisoners of war for prestige goods from Etruria and Greece. This "West Hallstatt system" collapsed when the Etruscans started to make direct contact with the area around the Marne and Moselle. The same period also saw the emergence of a distinctive decorative aristocratic style known as "Celtic" art. Spectacular finds have been made at sites such as Somme-Bionne and Basse-Yutz.

The Celts are the first peoples of northern Europe to appear in the historical record. They are mentioned by several Greek and Roman historians, and these writings give us some insight into their social organization and their religious practices – although they

- **c. 2000 BC** High-point of "Únětice" metal-working in north-central Europe
- **c. 1300 BC** Start of Urnfield culture
- **c. 1100 BC** Earliest fortified hilltop sites in western Europe
- **c. 750 BC** Start of "Hallstatt" Iron Age
- **c. 600 BC** Foundation of Greek colony at Massilia (Marseilles)
- **c. 450 BC** Collapse of West Hallstatt system leads to spread of Celtic (La Tène) culture
- **c. 390 BC** Celts sack Rome
- **279 BC** Celts under Brennus attack Delphi
- **58–51 BC** Julius Caesar conquers Gaul

This bronze burial urn (right) is from the "King's Grave" at Seddin in northern Germany. It dates to the 9th or 8th century BC, and the objects with it indicate that the cremated remains it held were of a leading figure in the community. Burial urns from this period were more commonly ceramic and were usually buried with offerings of some sort in them or on the lid.

1 Early Iron Age ("Hallstatt") society emerged in the area between eastern France and the Danube (map far right). It was dominated by an aristocratic elite occupying hillforts, whose wealth was displayed in rich burials. In the later "La Tène" period from the 5th century BC to the 1st century AD, the characteristic curvilinear style of Celtic art appeared throughout Europe, spread by conquest and by exchange. The rapid movement of Celtic warrior bands in the 4th and 3rd centuries BC was followed by increasing settlement in fortified "oppida". Some, such as Manching in Bavaria, were both large and extremely sophisticated. By the 1st century AD, the Celtic world had been almost entirely absorbed within the Roman empire: only Ireland and northern Scotland remained outside Roman control to carry Celtic culture into the Middle Ages.

have to be used with caution. Later Celtic traditions
are recorded in the epic literature of Ireland and
Wales, but it is not clear how much they can tell us
about early Celtic Europe. What is not in question is
the Celtic interest – and skill – in warfare.

After 600 BC, Celtic war-bands spread out from
central Europe into Italy and Greece – Rome was
attacked in 390 BC, Delphi in 279 BC – and settled as
far south as Galatia in Anatolia and Galicia in Spain.
Other areas, such as western France and Britain,
were absorbed into the Celtic world by peaceful
means, with the native aristocracies adopting the
new continental fashions of art and warfare. From
the 3rd century BC fortified urban settlements
known as "oppida" became more common, and unified Celtic states began to appear.

Celtic social organization was increasingly influenced by the growing power of Rome, and the Celts
were the first peoples of northern Europe to be
incorporated within the Roman empire. Already by
the end of the 2nd century BC the Mediterranean part
of Gaul was a Roman province. Julius Caesar's conquests in Gaul then brought the western Celtic world
under Roman control as far as the English Channel by
50 BC. Thus the most economically advanced areas of
the barbarian world were rapidly integrated within
the Roman world.

2 Urnfield culture

Urnfield culture by:

- 14th century BC
- 13th–12th century BC
- 11th–9th century BC
- major urnfields
- major late Bronze Age sites

2 The Urnfield culture was characterized by the appearance
of large cemeteries containing cremated remains in funerary
urns **(map above)**. The spread of these practices over the period
after 1300 BC was probably the result of changing social patterns
rather than movements of populations. The number and
uniformity of urnfield burials indicates an emphasis on
community membership rather than on individual prestige.
Nonetheless the existence of a small number of much richer
graves, such as that at Seddin, show that there were some
powerful chiefs in these communities.

1 Celtic Europe from 800 BC

Celtic sites:
- • "oppidum"
- □ open site
- ■ "Hallstatt" site
- ✠ Celtic religious site
- vehicle burial

Celtic art:
- bronze mirror
- sword scabbard
- ritual figurine
- Situla art
- ◇ other

H "Hallstatt" 8th–5th centuries BC

T "La Tène" 5th century BC–1st century AD

Greek colony from c. 600 BC

Africa

Written sources from this period increasingly help to
reconstruct the history of north Africa, the Nilotic Sudan,
Eritrea and Ethiopia. For the rest of Africa, archaeology
remains the primary source and, since research and
evidence are currently meagre, for large parts of the
continent the past still awaits discovery.

IN THE LAST MILLENNIUM BC, north Africa
was inhabited by the ancestors of the modern
Berbers. At the coast these people came into contact
with a variety of foreigners. The first were the
Phoenicians, seafaring merchants who established
trading settlements westwards from Tripoli and
founded Carthage towards the end of the 9th century
(see map 1). Egypt at this time was politically weak
and succumbed to a variety of foreign powers,
among them the kingdom of Kush, based at Napata
(see map 1), whose kings ruled as the 25th Dynasty
(c. 770–664). From the 3rd century BC, Rome began
to assert its power in the region, successfully
challenging Carthaginian supremacy in the western

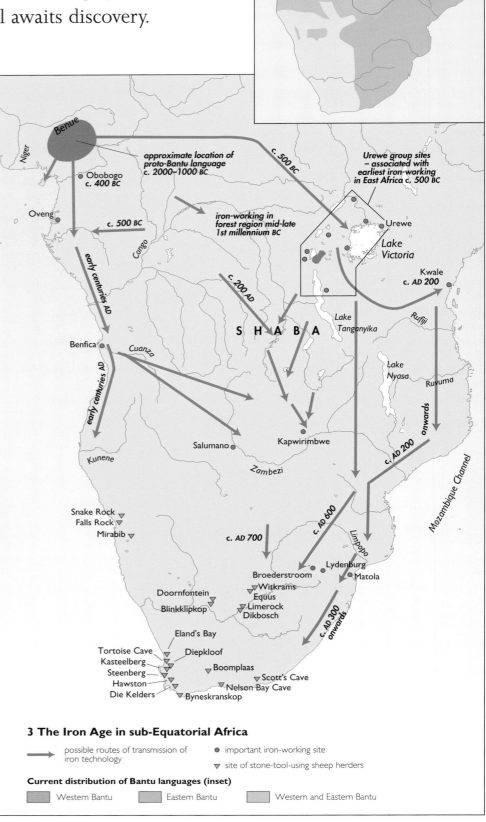

3 The Iron Age in sub-Equatorial Africa

→ possible routes of transmission of
iron technology

● important iron-working site

▽ site of stone-tool-using sheep herders

Current distribution of Bantu languages (inset)

Western Bantu   Eastern Bantu   Western and Eastern Bantu

This Nok terracotta sculpture of a woman with plaited hair is from Rafin Kura in Nigeria (above)
and is known as the Dinya head. It dates from between 500 BC and AD 200. Many Nok sculptures were
shaped by a process similar to carving rather than by the more usual method of adding pieces on. This
may indicate a comparable wood-carving tradition, which has been lost from the archaeological record.
Stylistically, Nok sculpture tends towards the abstract. Heads are proportionately larger than bodies, and
facial features are usually angular with perforated eyes, nostrils, mouths and ears. Other features, such as
elaborate hairstyles and personal ornamentation, are depicted in great detail, giving us tantalizing glimpses
into an otherwise unknown culture. This piece is 36cm (14in) tall.

3 Far too little is known (map above) about the early history of sub-Equatorial
Africa, although research has revealed a correspondence between the current
distribution of Bantu languages (see inset) and the geographical distribution of sites
characterized by iron technology, food production, settled village life and similar types of
pottery. On this basis it is thought that people speaking a proto-Bantu language, located
in the area of eastern Nigeria and Cameroon, began to disperse southwards and
eastwards in a series of migrations that took their new way of life to the Stone Age
communities they encountered. Future research may well modify this interpretation.

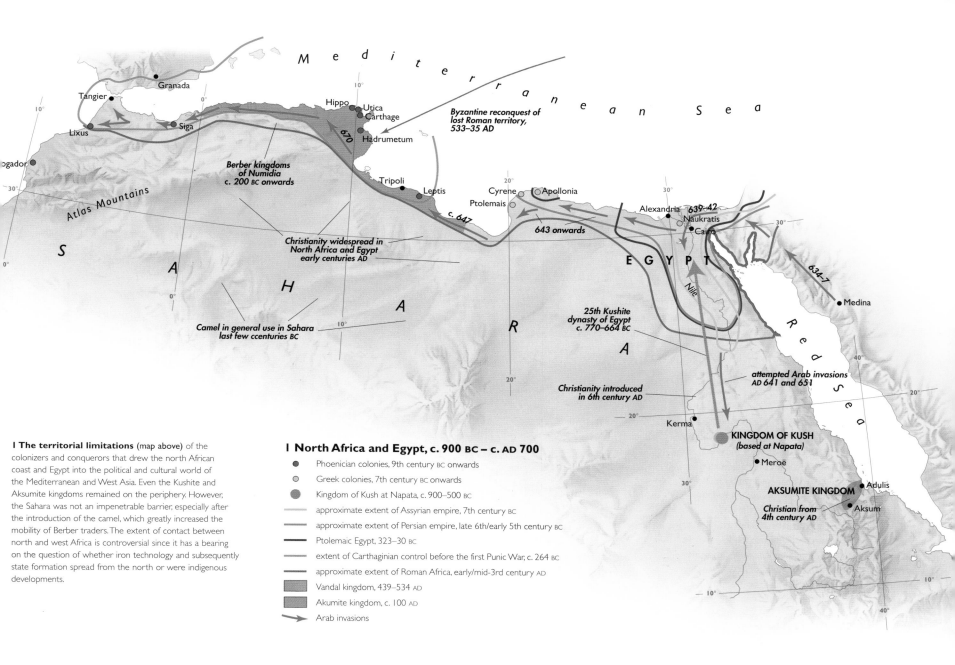

1 North Africa and Egypt, c. 900 BC – c. AD 700

- Phoenician colonies, 9th century BC onwards
- Greek colonies, 7th century BC onwards
- Kingdom of Kush at Napata, c. 900–500 BC
- approximate extent of Assyrian empire, 7th century BC
- approximate extent of Persian empire, late 6th/early 5th century BC
- Ptolemaic Egypt, 323–30 BC
- extent of Carthaginian control before the first Punic War, c. 264 BC
- approximate extent of Roman Africa, early/mid-3rd century AD
- Vandal kingdom, 439–534 AD
- Akumite kingdom, c. 100 AD
- Arab invasions

1 The territorial limitations (map above) of the colonizers and conquerors that drew the north African coast and Egypt into the political and cultural world of the Mediterranean and West Asia. Even the Kushite and Aksumite kingdoms remained on the periphery. However, the Sahara was not an impenetrable barrier, especially after the introduction of the camel, which greatly increased the mobility of Berber traders. The extent of contact between north and west Africa is controversial since it has a bearing on the question of whether iron technology and subsequently state formation spread from the north or were indigenous developments.

Mediterranean. Thereafter Roman control was extended along the north African coast and, in 30 BC, Egypt was conquered. By the time the Roman empire began to weaken in the 4th and early 5th centuries AD, Christianity was widespread in its African provinces and remained unchallenged until the Arab invasions of the 7th century brought Islam to Africa.

By the 4th century BC the Kushite kingdom had moved south to Meroë, where it flourished until the 2nd century AD. Its subsequent decline was probably owed, in part, to the rise of the Aksumite kingdom in northern Ethiopia. In the mid-4th century, Aksum adopted Christianity as its official religion. Although Christian influences must have spread southwards from Egypt into Nubia towards the end of the Meroitic period, it was not until the 6th century that Christianity was introduced into the region. In the

following century, the Arab invasion of Egypt began a process of Islamization that spread slowly southwards into Nubia. The rise of Islam was also a factor in the decline of Aksum, which had ceased to exist as a political entity by about AD 700.

Iron-working and farming

Almost certainly it was the Phoenicians who introduced bronze- and iron-working to north Africa. In west Africa, iron was being used by the mid-1st millennium BC. The development of an urban settlement at Jenne-Jeno from about 250 BC onwards (see map 2), was probably facilitated by the use of iron tools, which helped agriculturalists to till the heavy clay soils of the inland Niger delta. The earliest evidence of iron use in southern west Africa is associated with the Nok culture, famous for its terracotta sculptures. The early

iron-using communities of eastern and southern Africa show such a remarkable degree of homogeneity that they are viewed as a single cultural complex, which first appeared on the western side of Lake Victoria around the mid-1st millennium BC and had spread as far south as Natal by the 3rd century AD. In addition to iron technology, this complex is associated with the beginnings of crop cultivation, livestock herding and settlement. South of Tanzania it is also linked to the manufacture of pottery. In Namibia and Cape Province, which were not settled by these iron-using farmers, some groups had acquired domestic sheep as early as the first two centuries AD. At about the same time a distinctive Cape coastal pottery appears, but others continued with their ancient way of life, living in mobile groups, hunting, gathering and making stone tools.

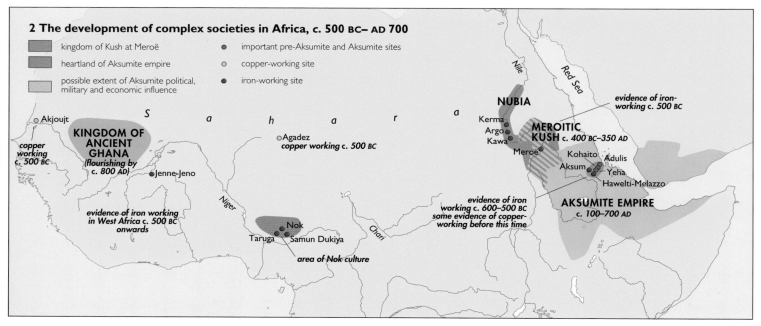

2 The development of complex societies in Africa, c. 500 BC– AD 700

- kingdom of Kush at Meroë
- heartland of Aksumite empire
- possible extent of Aksumite political, military and economic influence
- important pre-Aksumite and Aksumite sites
- copper-working site
- iron-working site

2 Regions with evidence of social complexity (map left), defined by such factors as urbanization, state formation and craft specialization. By 500 BC, Nubia already had a long history of social complexity, but it was at about this time that an urban culture first appears at pre-Aksumite sites such as Yeha, Kohaito and Hawelti-Melazzo. Far less is known about west Africa. Iron-working dates from about 500 BC, while proto-urbanization and craft specialization are attested at Jenne-Jeno and Nok. Ancient Ghana, a powerful kingdom by about AD 800, also had its origins towards the end of this period.

The expansion of Roman power

Rome, a city-state governed by aristocratic families leading an army of peasant soldiers, came to control an empire that stretched from the Atlantic to the Euphrates and from the English Channel to the Sahara. But military success brought social disorder; rivalries between warlords led to civil war; and republican institutions became an autocracy.

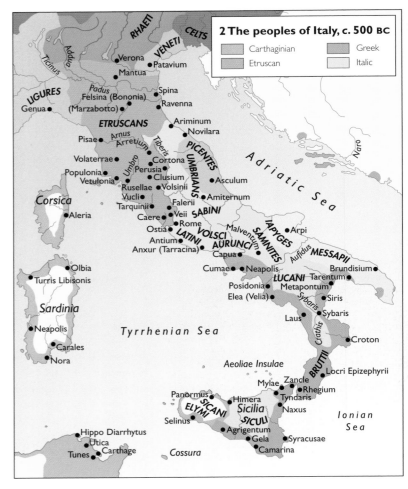

2 The peoples of Italy, c. 500 BC

- Carthaginian
- Etruscan
- Greek
- Italic

THE CITY OF ROME grew up on the Tiber at the lowest point the river could be bridged. Although several of Rome's hills were settled from around 1000 BC, the earliest signs of urbanization date from the 7th century. According to tradition, Rome was ruled by a line of seven kings, and the expulsion of the last of these in 511 BC resulted in the creation of a republic ruled by two annually elected consuls or magistrates. It is probable, however, that the government of the emerging city-state was less formalized than tradition suggests and that republican systems reached their developed form only in the 4th century BC.

Consuls held office for no more than a single year and ruled with the support of the Senate, a council of former magistrates and priests. Legislation proposed by them had also to be ratified by a popular assembly. However, their main task was to protect the city, which in effect meant to lead military campaigns. Success in war brought material gains to the people of Rome and prestige to the commanders making imperialism an inevitable feature of Roman policy.

The Punic Wars

By 264 BC Rome controlled the whole of the Italian peninsula and had emerged as a powerful confederacy

WHO IS SO WORTHLESS OR INDOLENT THAT THEY DO NOT WISH TO KNOW BY WHAT MEANS AND UNDER WHAT POLITICAL SYSTEM THE ROMANS, IN LESS THAN 53 YEARS, HAVE SUCCEEDED IN BRINGING NEARLY THE WHOLE INHABITED WORLD UNDER A SINGLE GOVERNMENT, SOMETHING NEVER BEFORE ACHIEVED?

Polybius (c. 200–c. 118 BC)
Histories

and the principal rival to the other major power in the western Mediterranean, Carthage. The Romans were forced to develop naval skills to defeat Carthage in the First Punic War (264–241 BC), in which Rome drove the Carthaginians out of Sicily; soon after Corsica and Sardinia were seized as well. In the Second Punic War (218–201 BC), Rome was invaded from the north, when Hannibal brought his army and elephants from Spain over the Alps into Italy. Though Rome suffered devastating defeats at Lake Trasimene (217 BC) and Cannae (216 BC) it was able to draw on great reserves of Italian manpower

2 Italy in 500 BC was inhabited by a mixture of peoples (map above). In the south and on Sicily the coastal plains had been settled during the 8th and 7th centuries by colonists from Greece while the city-states of Etruria had long had cultural and economic links with the eastern Mediterranean. As Rome's power spread through Italy, its culture was transformed by its contacts with these older civilizations.

3 The acquisition of overseas provinces by Rome (map below) was seldom by design. Although Roman commanders needed little encouragement to undertake military campaigns, they preferred to make treaties with defeated enemies rather than turn their territories into provinces. However, the wars against Carthage in the 3rd century and against the Hellenistic kingdoms of the eastern Mediterranean in the 2nd and 1st centuries left the Romans with possessions which could yield substantial tribute.

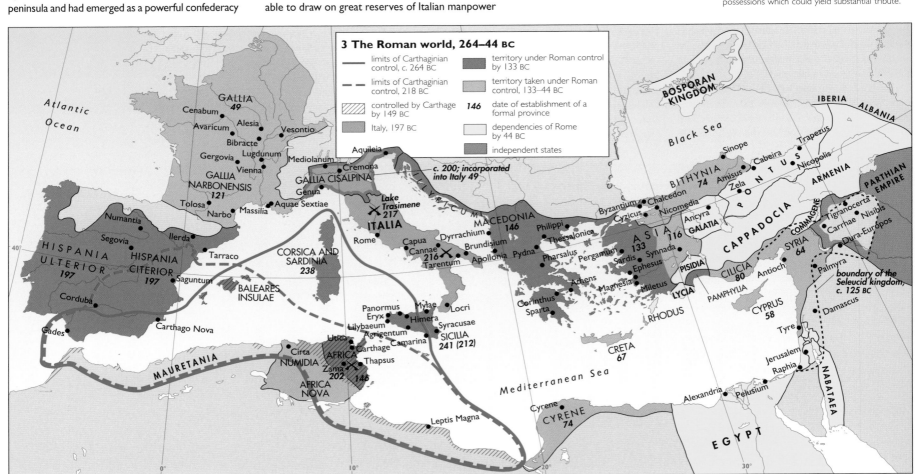

3 The Roman world, 264–44 BC

- limits of Carthaginian control, c. 264 BC
- limits of Carthaginian control, 218 BC
- controlled by Carthage by 149 BC
- Italy, 197 BC
- territory under Roman control by 133 BC
- territory taken under Roman control, 133–44 BC
- **146** date of establishment of a formal province
- dependencies of Rome by 44 BC
- independent states

to drive Hannibal out of Italy and defeat him at Zama in north Africa (202 BC). With Spain added to Rome's provinces, the city now commanded the whole of the western and central Mediterranean.

Expansion to the east

In the following 50 years, Roman commanders turned their attention eastwards, leading expeditions into Greece, but withdrawing their troops once victory was assured, in part from fear that Italy, always most vulnerable to attack from the north, would be invaded. Nonetheless, in 146 BC Macedonia was added to the empire, with the province of Asia following in 133 BC.

Among the consequences of Roman victories abroad was an influx of goods and people into Italy. Works of art were taken from Greek temples to adorn private Roman villas, while Greek literature, rhetoric and philosophy had a profound effect on the nature of Roman politics. Wars also provided cheap slaves, who were brought to Italy as agricultural labourers, threatening the livelihoods of Italian peasant farmers and leading to the rapid growth of the urban population of Rome itself.

From republic to empire

The period from 133 BC saw increasing turbulence within Rome and Italy. Rome's continuing expansion provided opportunities for ambitious men to use their military commands to dominate Roman politics, and the institutions of the republic were powerless to regulate the competition between them. Slave revolts and the Social War with Rome's Italian allies increased disorder within Italy. The last generation of the republic saw the system collapse in a series of civil wars which ended only in 31 BC when Octavian emerged triumphant at the battle of Actium (see p. 100) and found himself in a position of such dominance that he was able to rebuild the government of Rome and make it capable of administering an empire.

c 64 BC Roman Forum laid out

511 BC Expulsion of Tarquinius Superbus, last of Rome's kings

496 BC Battle of Lake Regillus; Rome defeats the Latins

390 BC Sack of Rome by the Gauls

218–201 BC Second Punic War: Hannibal defeated, Spain a Roman province

146 BC Romans sack Carthage and Corinth

91–89 BC Social War: Roman citizenship extended to all Italians

49 BC Julius Caesar crosses the Rubicon and marches on Rome

A silver denarius of 44 BC (above left). The coin bears the image of Julius Caesar. After his conquest of Gaul in 59–49 BC, Caesar used his army to seize power in Rome, his decision to march on Rome marked by his fateful crossing of the river Rubicon. In the civil war that followed, he was victorious over his former ally Pompey, and he was made dictator for life before being stabbed by disaffected senators in 44 BC. The greatest general Rome produced, Caesar was too ambitious to work within the constraints of the republican system.

1 From the 4th century BC the Romans expanded their power in Italy by a combination of alliances and military conquests (map right). The most prolonged resistance came from the Samnites, but by 264 BC the whole of Italy south of the Appenines was under Roman influence. Alliances were made with the Italian communities on various terms, but always included a requirement to supply troops for Roman military campaigns. Territory taken from defeated enemies was occupied either by small garrison colonies of Roman citizens or by larger Latin colonies, whose inhabitants had privileges but not full citizenship of Rome. This left Italy a complicated patchwork of communities each in a different relationship with Rome. As Rome's overseas empire grew, the Italians increasingly resented their lack of equality with Rome and in 91 BC attempted to break away from Roman control in the Social War, setting up a new capital at Corfinium, which they renamed Italia. Though they were defeated, in 90 BC a law was passed granting citizenship to Italians loyal to Rome. By 87 BC almost all the inhabitants of Italy were Roman citizens.

1 The growth of Roman power to 91 BC

- Roman territory and colonies 300 BC
- allies of Rome 300 BC
- additional allies of Rome by 270 BC
- added to Roman territory and colonies by 264 BC
- added to Roman territory and colonies by 200 BC
- territory under Roman control by 91 BC
- □ Roman colonies founded between 338 and 273 BC
- ■ Roman colonies founded after 273 BC
- ⊙ Latin colonies founded before 381 BC
- ◑ Latin colonies founded between 334 and 273 BC
- ○ Latin colonies founded after 273 BC
- • other towns
- — major roads

The height of Roman power

Augustus, the first emperor, transformed the government of the Roman empire. He brought an end to internal conflicts and created a standing army to guard the empire's frontiers and extend its power. As Roman culture and organization spread throughout the empire, it laid the foundations for the development of the Mediterranean world.

REMEMBER, ROMAN, WHERE YOUR SKILLS LIE: IT IS YOUR TASK TO RULE THE PEOPLES BY YOUR POWER, TO ADD CIVILIZATION TO PEACE, TO SPARE THE DEFEATED AND TO BEAT DOWN THE PROUD IN WAR.

Virgil (70–19 BC)
Aeneid

THE AFFAIRS OF THE ROMANS OF THAT TIME [AD 180] DESCENDED FROM A KINGDOM OF GOLD, TO ONE OF IRON AND RUST – AND SO TOO DOES OUR HISTORY.

Cassius Dio (C. AD 164–230)
Roman History

IN 31 BC **OCTAVIAN**, the future emperor Augustus, was undisputed master of Rome. His popularity as adopted son of Julius Caesar and victor over Cleopatra and Mark Antony at the battle of Actium allowed him to rebuild the shattered Roman republic into a system of government capable of controlling a vast empire, reforms which were to bring Rome a new and intense surge of life and two and a half centuries of almost uninterrupted peace and prosperity.

Augustus's reforms were far-reaching. He restored the prestige of the Senate, though not, in practice, its influence. He reorganized the army and, in 27 BC, took command of those parts of the empire where legions were stationed. From then on responsibility for the defence of the empire lay with the emperor alone. At the same time he took the religiously significant name Augustus, and stressed his relationship to the now deified Julius Caesar. Among his many priesthoods was that of Pontifex Maximus, chief priest, and from the time of Augustus onward the emperor became the focus of all Roman religious ritual.

In 19 BC Augustus was given the power to rule by decree, and although he continued to pay due respect to the Senate, whose members he needed to command the legions and to administer the provinces, his authority was now absolute. The vast wealth he had inherited and won (his defeat of Antony and Cleopatra left Egypt as his personal domain) was further increased by bequests from the rich throughout the empire. At his death his property was worth thousands of times as much as that of even the richest senator. That his heir should also inherit his position as head of the empire was inevitable.

In the event, Augustus had great difficulty in finding an heir, eventually settling on his stepson Tiberius (AD 14–37), who had been a successful military commander but took on the role of emperor with reluctance. Neither he nor his successors were able to maintain good relations with the Senate, and the failure

of Nero (54–68) to prevent revolt in the provinces led to his enforced suicide and the end of the Julio-Claudian dynasty. After a year of civil war, Vespasian (69–79) restored order. He was succeeded by his sons, Titus (79–81) and Domitian (81–96). Though the latter was generally regarded as a cruel and probably insane tyrant, many of his imperial policies were adopted by his successors, especially Trajan (98–117), who began the practice of appearing before the Senate not in a toga but in the purple cloak and armour of a triumphant general. This was to become the uniform of the emperor for the next thousand years.

Stability and strife

Domitian's assassination was followed by nearly a century of stability as emperors without sons of their own chose their successors from the Senate. Civil war returned in 193, from which Septimius Severus (193–211) emerged victorious. He ruled with his sons Caracalla (198–217) and Geta (209–12), setting a pattern that was to be followed in the following centuries. Caracalla was murdered, and after him came a series of short-lived emperors, of whom Severus Alexander (222–35) was the last who could claim a dynastic link to his predecessors.

The nature of Rome

The emperor's figure was central to the empire: everywhere statues and coins were constant reminders of his presence. In the former Hellenistic kingdoms the kings had been the objects of religious worship, a practice which continued with the cult of the emperors. In the western provinces, temples and altars dedicated to the emperor became focuses of Romanization.

The early 2nd century saw important cultural developments: Greek and Latin literature flourished; and the distinction between Italy and the provinces dissolved as rich men from all over the empire were admitted to the Senate, with some, such as Trajan and Hadrian (117–38), even becoming emperor. For the poor, there were fewer benefits, and differences in the rights and privileges of rich and poor grew. By the time Caracalla extended Roman citizenship throughout the empire in AD 212, it gave little advantage to the newly enfranchised citizens. Later in the 2nd century, pressures grew on the frontiers. Marcus Aurelius (161–80) spent much of his reign at war with barbarian invaders, and his successors faced threats both from the north, and, after 224, from the rejuvenated Persian empire under the Sasanids.

Relief from the Altar of Peace, the Ara Pacis, in Rome **(below)**. The altar was built by order of the Senate in 13 BC to celebrate the victorious return of Augustus from Gaul and Spain. The imperial family was represented on it, along with symbols of religious piety and agricultural fertility. The decoration of the altar emphasized the importance of Augustus himself in maintaining peace and prosperity for Rome.

I From 27 BC, the emperor himself was responsible for the administration of the imperial provinces (those in which legions were stationed). The others **(map right)** were governed by proconsuls appointed by the Senate. At the start of the imperial period some parts of the empire were ruled by friendly client kings; as they died their lands became Roman provinces. Emperors could gain great glory by extending the empire.

Although campaigns in the 1st century AD in Germany had only limited success, the eastern Balkans, north Africa, Arabia and Britain were all added to Rome while in the following century Trajan added Dacia, Armenia, Assyria and Mesopotamia. Trajan's rule marked Rome's greatest territorial extent. Hadrian, his successor, abandoned Trajan's conquests other than Arabia and Dacia to consolidate more defensible frontiers.

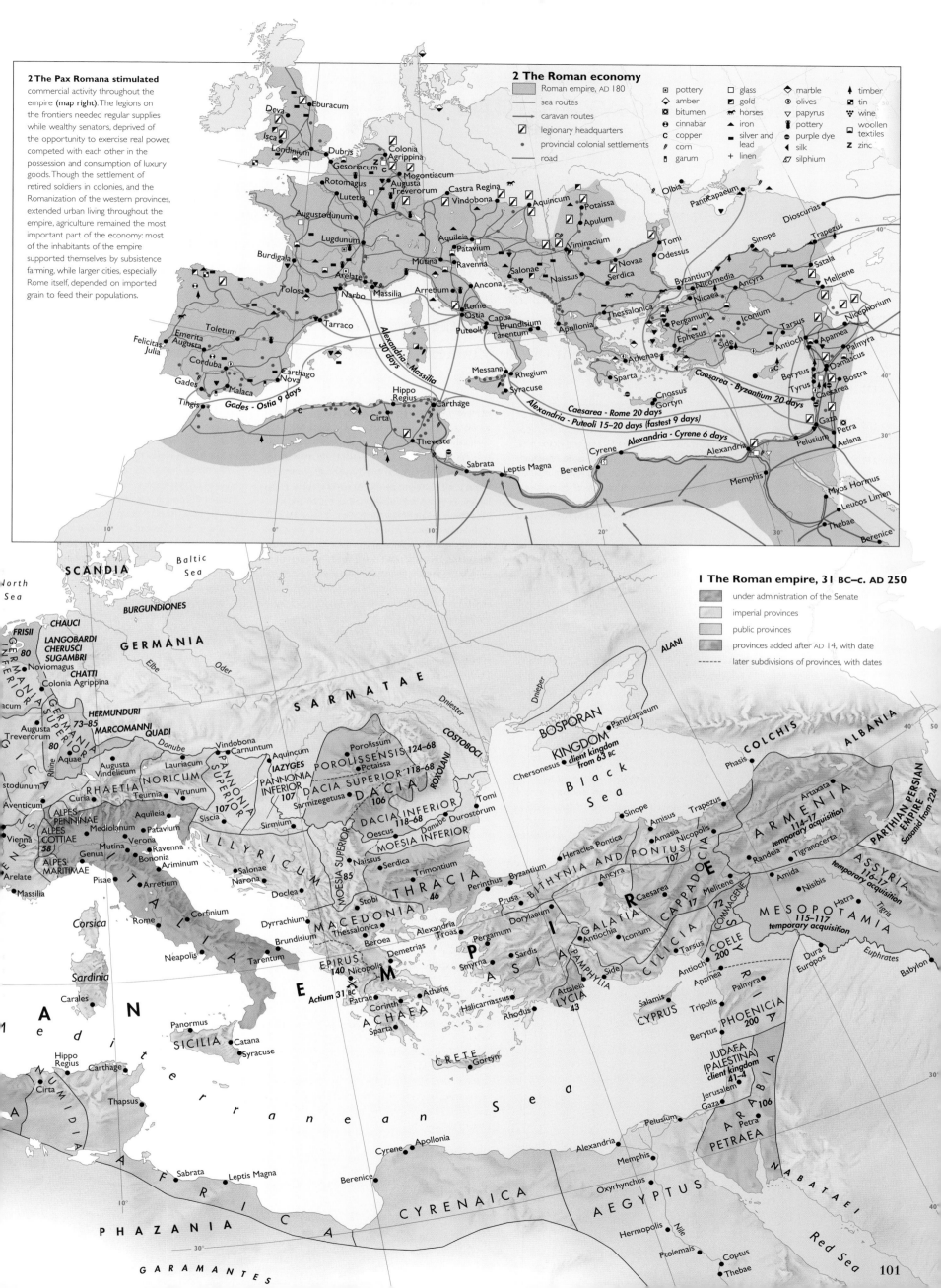

2 The Pax Romana stimulated commercial activity throughout the empire (map right). The legions on the frontiers needed regular supplies while wealthy senators, deprived of the opportunity to exercise real power, competed with each other in the possession and consumption of luxury goods. Though the settlement of retired soldiers in colonies, and the Romanization of the western provinces, extended urban living throughout the empire, agriculture remained the most important part of the economy: most of the inhabitants of the empire supported themselves by subsistence farming, while larger cities, especially Rome itself, depended on imported grain to feed their populations.

2 The Roman economy

- Roman empire, AD 180
- sea routes
- caravan routes
- legionary headquarters
- provincial colonial settlements
- road

- pottery
- amber
- bitumen
- cinnabar
- copper
- corn
- garum
- glass
- gold
- horses
- iron
- silver and lead
- linen
- marble
- olives
- papyrus
- pottery
- purple dye
- silk
- silphium
- timber
- tin
- wine
- woollen textiles
- zinc

1 The Roman empire, 31 BC–c. AD 250

- under administration of the Senate
- imperial provinces
- public provinces
- provinces added after AD 14, with date
- later subdivisions of provinces, with dates

101

From Rome to Byzantium

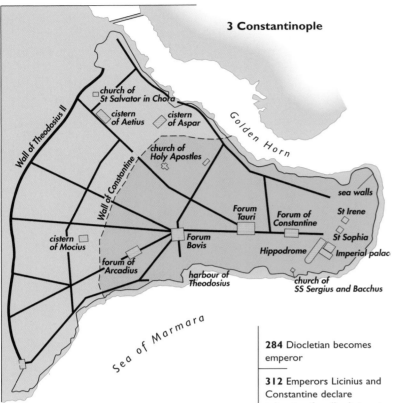

3 Constantinople

3 Constantinople was founded by Constantine in 330, on the site of the Greek city of Byzantium (**map above**) as the base from which to govern the eastern part of his empire. It had its own Senate, and rapidly became the largest city in the eastern empire, with a population reaching 500,000. Although the masses had no formal power, emperors could not afford to antagonize them. The Hippodrome, where chariot-racing took place, was linked to the imperial palace and became the main point of communication between ruler and subjects.

2 Between 235 and 284 the frontiers of the empire were threatened by Germans, Goths and Sasanid Persians (**map below**). The Roman legions struggled to meet the challenge, and there were more than 20 emperors in 50 years, each replaced after failure to stem the barbarian incursions. Under Gallienus (253–68) large parts of the empire broke away. Aurelian (270–5) was able to reunite the empire, and military reorganization enabled him and his successors to repel the invaders. Only Dacia and the Agri Decumates were lost.

The 4th century AD saw Roman emperors still ruling an empire that stretched from Spain to Syria. In the 5th century the two halves of the empire experienced different fortunes. Roman administration in the west dissolved in the face of increasing barbarian settlement, but in the east Byzantine civilization, combining Greek and Roman practices and culture, grew and flourished.

THE EMPIRE EMERGED from the storms of the 3rd century (see map 2) intact but not unchanged. Diocletian and his successors owed their position to the army, not the Senate, and the military now provided most of the provincial governors. Rome itself ceased to be the centre of empire, as the emperors based themselves in cities nearer the frontiers: Mediolanum (Milan) in Italy; and, after AD 330, Constantinople in the east. The emperors were surrounded by large courts, increasingly turning to eunuchs as their closest advisors. To maintain the army, the taxation system was reformed and military service became a hereditary obligation. But as the senators in Italy and other rich landowners were increasingly excluded from power, so they became less inclined to support the emperor, a development which was to have a profound effect on the western half of the empire.

The rise of Christianity

But the greatest change to the empire was religious. In 312 Constantine defeated his rival Maxentius outside Rome, and he came to attribute his victory to the support of the Christian god. In his reign and that of his son Constantius II the churches received many favours from the emperor, and Christianity began to establish itself as the dominant religion of the empire. The last pagan emperor, Julian, died in

AD 363 on campaign against the Persians before he had the opportunity to reverse the trend. Bishops such as St Ambrose in Milan (374–97) became increasingly powerful figures in the empire.

Barbarian incursions continued to erode central control of the empire. The arrival of the Huns in eastern Europe in 376 drove many Goths across the Danube, forcing them into Roman territory. Having in 378 defeated the Romans at Adrianople, in 405 they invaded Italy. In the winter of 406 German tribes then crossed the frozen river Rhine in unstoppable masses. The situation deteriorated throughout the century. The Vandals marched through Gaul and Spain before crossing to Africa where they captured Carthage, the chief city, in 439 and set up their own kingdom.

Where in the 4th century the Roman army had made use of barbarian officers, now the western emperors had little choice but to make grants of land for the invaders to settle on and to employ them in the army. With landowners unwilling to

284 Diocletian becomes emperor

312 Emperors Licinius and Constantine declare toleration for all religions in the empire

361–3 Emperor Julian attempts to restore pagan religion

395 Death of Theodosius I: division between east and west becomes permanent

410 Alaric and Visigoths sack Rome

476 Romulus Augustulus, last western emperor, deposed

527 Justinian becomes emperor in the east

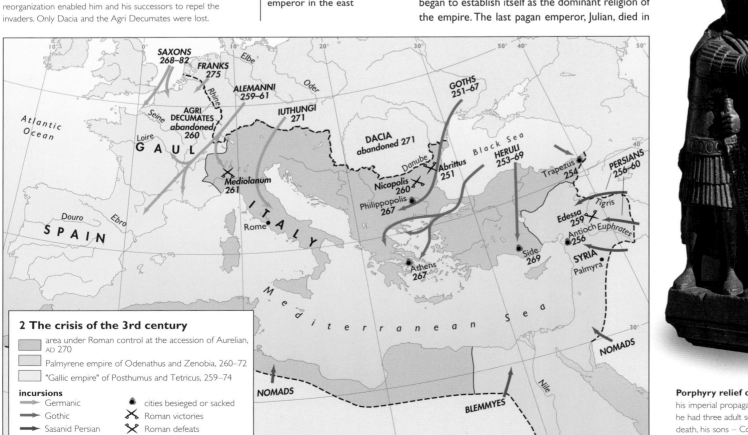

2 The crisis of the 3rd century

	area under Roman control at the accession of Aurelian, AD 270
	Palmyrene empire of Odenathus and Zenobia, 260–72
	"Gallic empire" of Posthumus and Tetricus, 259–74

incursions

→	Germanic	●	cities besieged or sacked
→	Gothic	✗	Roman victories
→	Sasanid Persian	✗	Roman defeats
→	nomadic		

Porphyry relief of Constantine and his sons (**above**). In his imperial propaganda Constantine emphasized the fact that he had three adult sons, a sign of divine favour. After their father's death, his sons — Constantine II (337–40), Constans (337–50) and Constantius II (337–61) — shared control of the empire until Constantius eliminated his brothers and assumed sole power.

allow their tenants to fight, what had been a Roman citizen army became a barbarian mercenary one. Since the frontiers were no longer preventing barbarians from entering the western empire, and since the army was itself largely barbarian, the role of the emperor in the west was effectively redundant.

In 476 the *magister militum* (the chief military officer of the western empire) Odoacer, a German, deposed the emperor Romulus Augustulus, and did not replace him. With the eastern emperor making no attempt to resist this, the western empire ceased to exist (see map 4). In 490 the Ostrogoths took control of Italy, and by 507 the Franks had established an extensive kingdom in Gaul (see p. 118). Yet Roman institutions survived: the Roman Senate continued to sit, and Latin remained the language of government.

The reconquests of Justinian

The eastern part of the empire possessed greater resources than the west, and eastern emperors could use their wealth to persuade would-be invaders to move away westwards. Although Roman culture continued to flourish in the eastern part of the empire (see p. 126), there were growing cultural differences between east and west: when Justinian launched his attempt to reconquer the former western empire, he was trying to impose a Greek-speaking administration on Latin-speaking territories.

Justinian's reign was a mixture of triumph and disaster. In Constantinople it saw the building of the great church of St Sophia (532–63) as well as a devastating plague in 542. His general Belisarius took Africa from the Vandals in 533–4 while in 554, after a campaign lasting 20 years, Ostrogothic rule in Italy was ended. But Justinian's successes in Italy were short-lived: the Lombard invasion of 568 left only Ravenna in Byzantine hands. Meanwhile in the east there was war with Persia (540–62): Antioch was sacked in 540 and peace was eventually bought only at great financial cost. Justinian's wars left Byzantium seriously weakened. The dream of a reunited empire died with him.

4 Southwest Europe at the overthrow of the last western emperor, 476

THUS THE ALMIGHTY SOVEREIGN HIMSELF ACCORDS AN INCREASE BOTH OF YEARS AND OF CHILDREN TO OUR MOST PIOUS EMPEROR, AND RENDERS HIS SWAY OVER THE NATIONS OF THE WORLD STILL FRESH AND FLOURISHING, AS THOUGH IT WERE EVEN NOW SPRINGING UP IN ITS EARLIEST VIGOUR. EVERY ENEMY, WHETHER VISIBLE OR UNSEEN, HAS BEEN UTTERLY REMOVED: AND HENCEFORWARD PEACE, THE HAPPY NURSE OF YOUTH, EXTENDS HER REIGN THROUGHOUT THE WORLD.

Eusebius of Caesarea
Speech in praise of Constantine, AD 336

1 Diocletian (284–305) and Constantine (306–37) oversaw the reorganization of the empire (map below). Military and civil commands were separated and the existing provinces split into smaller units, which were grouped together into 12 dioceses, each headed by a "Vicarius". They in turn were subordinate to up to four "Praetorian Prefects". In the 4th century imperial power was several times divided between two or three senior emperors (called "Augusti"), usually supported by a junior ("Caesar"), a division which became permanent after 395. Milan (Mediolanum), Trier (Treveri), Nicaea, Nicomedia and later Constantinople replaced Rome as centres of imperial administration.

4 By the deposition of Romulus Augustulus by Odoacer in 476, the western empire had already suffered a series of calamitous losses (map above). Spain, Portugal and southwest France were under the control of the Sueves and the Visigoths while the largest Roman-controlled area in France, governed by Syagrius, did not acknowledge the authority of the emperor. Odoacer, until his murder in 493, in fact maintained peace and stability in Italy, which he ruled from Ravenna, retaining Roman administrative structures and rewarding Roman senators for their support. He made some attempts to expand his territory, conquering Dalmatia in 480 after the murder of the imperial claimant, Julius Nepos.

The rise of Christianity

Christianity began as a small sect within Judaism, but gradually established itself as a significant religious and intellectual force throughout the Roman empire. It offered both a promise of eternal salvation to individuals and, from the 4th century onwards, a powerful new vision of an empire united under a Christian ruler which was to be of enormous significance for the future of Europe.

THE EARLIEST CHRISTIANS did not see themselves as founders of a new religion but as witnesses to the fulfilment of God's promise to provide his people, the Jews, with a Messiah or redeemer. By raising him from the dead, they believed that God had shown that Jesus of Nazareth was this Messiah and that the risen Jesus had commissioned his disciples to preach the good news of God's kingdom.

Though the earliest Christians were Jews, they did not interpret the message of Jesus in political or national terms. Christianity was attractive to people besides Jews for its promise of eternal life and for the spiritual benefits of membership of a close-knit, supportive community. So the conversion of gentiles soon began in the cities of the eastern Roman empire and was enthusiastically advocated by Paul, a converted Pharisee and former opponent of Christianity. With the rejection of Christianity's claims by the majority of Jews, Christianity had become a distinct religion by the end of the 1st century. Christian expansion was much slower in the west: while there was a Christian community in Rome by AD 50, the earliest evidence for Christianity in France and north Africa is to be found from the late 2nd century.

At first Christianity was a religion mainly of the urban poor, but it gradually spread to higher social groups. Its growth went largely unnoticed by the Roman authorities. There were sporadic episodes of persecution, such as those under emperors Nero (AD 64) and Decius (250), but these were aimed more at finding scapegoats for major disasters than at systematically eliminating Christianity. Even the "Great Persecution" of 303–12, under the emperors Diocletian and Galerius, had a more profound effect on the leaders of the churches than it did on their followers, as disputes arose over how they had responded to the arrests and confiscations that occurred then.

By this time the church had grown from a network of small communities, meeting in the homes of richer members, into a well-organized body owning buildings and burial grounds, and led by a ministry of bishops, presbyters and deacons. It was well placed to benefit from the changes that began in 312.

Constantine

In that year, the emperor Constantine gained a victory in the civil war against his rival Maxentius, which he came to attribute to the power of the Christian God. In the following year, with his fellow emperor Licinius, Constantine declared toleration for all religions in the Roman empire. These events marked a turning point in the history of Christianity, as Constantine came to see himself as a

Christian ruler endowed with divine authority, and gave privileges to Christian churches. With these privileges came some loss of autonomy for the bishops, as Constantine attempted through a series of Councils to establish orthodoxy of doctrine on the churches. But Constantine did not make Christianity

into the state religion of the empire overnight. This was a gradual process, interrupted by the reign of the pagan emperor Julian (361–3), which was to reach its conclusion – the banning of the pagan rites, which Christians found so offensive – only in the reign of Theodosius (379–95).

I The early Christian churches

main areas of Christian growth, to AD 300

areas largely Christian by AD 600

● important Christian communities of the 1st century

● other important Christian centres, by AD 600

☿ the five patriarchates

+ important bishops with dates of episcopate

◆ other important figures, with dates

I Except in Palestine, 1st-century Christianity was confined mainly to Greek-speaking cities (**map above**). By the early 4th century, Christians may have numbered 10 per cent of the population of the Roman empire, but were still found mainly in the east, in heavily urbanized areas and along trade routes. Following the conversion of Constantine, the expansion of Christianity was helped by imperial support. By 400 it was probably the majority religion of the Roman empire, and by 600 the whole of the empire (including its former territories in the west) was predominantly Christian. Christianity owed much to the writings of its leading bishops and theologians, most of whom lived in the larger cities and were able to express their beliefs in terms drawn from the sophisticated literary and intellectual culture of the Greco-Roman world.

In the 5th century there were still many pagans, even at court, but the empire was gradually Christianized through a programme of church building and the demolition of pagan shrines. Monks took a leading role in evangelization from the 4th century onwards. Meanwhile, Christianity had also spread east to Persia and west among the barbarian tribes which were eventually to invade and destroy the western Roman empire.

Doctrinal development

From its roots in Jewish monotheism, early Christianity underwent a good deal of doctrinal development. Many theologians from the 2nd century onwards attempted to combine the teachings of Christianity with the intellectual assumptions of Greek philosophy. In the 4th and 5th centuries the church embodied its beliefs about God and Jesus in a succession of doctrinal statements intended to prohibit heretical views (see panel right). The statements of faith in the Trinity and the Incarnation produced by the church councils of Nicaea (325) and Chalcedon (451) were especially important. In them, the early church bequeathed to later Christianity a set of doctrinal assumptions that were not to be seriously challenged until the Reformation in the 16th century and which remain the basis of their faith for many Christians even today.

EARLY CHRISTIAN HERESIES AND SCHISMS

In contrast to its later reputation for fostering doctrinal conformity, early Christianity allowed room for intellectual speculation. Not all speculation led to heresy, but some Christians developed ideas which were eventually judged unacceptable by the church as a whole.

In the 2nd century, various forms of **Gnosticism** were the main heresies. Gnostics, such as Valentinus and Basilides, were dualists who taught that matter was evil and distinguished between the creator of the world and the true God – views which most Christians thought inconsistent with the Bible. **Montanism**, a movement of prophetic revival which arose in Asia Minor in the 160s, was also significant. Christians who continued to obey the Jewish law (often called **Ebionites**, from a Hebrew word meaning "poor") also became separated from the mainstream during the 2nd century.

In the 3rd century came the first controversies over the doctrines of the Trinity and the church and sacraments. **Monarchianism**, popular in Rome, taught the unity of God rather than the distinction of the three persons of the Trinity. **Adoptionism**, whose leading representative was Paul of Samosata, stressed the humanity rather than the divinity of Christ. In Rome, **Novatianism** (named after the presbyter Novatian) was a puritan movement which withheld forgiveness from those who had denied the faith in times of persecution or committed other serious sins.

The 4th century was dominated by the **Arian** controversy, which led to the first agreed definition of the relationship between the persons of the Trinity. The Alexandrian presbyter Arius taught that the Son of God was created, and therefore different in nature from the Father. His views were rejected at the Council of Nicaea, which issued a creed stating that the Son is "of one substance with the Father". After further controversy over the interpretation of the creed, this teaching was reaffirmed by the Council of Constantinople in 381.

In the 5th century there were controversies over the doctrine of the Incarnation, or the relationship between the divine and human elements in Jesus. **Nestorianism**, named after Bishop Nestorius of Constantinople, regarded the divine and human elements as distinct in principle, so that the human Jesus could be spoken of as different from the divine Son of God who dwelt in him. Nestorius was accused by his opponents of teaching that Christ was "two Sons". At the Council of Chalcedon Nestorianism was rejected, but the opposite extreme, **Eutychianism**, which denied any distinction between Jesus's divine and human natures, was also avoided. In the west the doctrine of grace and the relationship between faith and works were controversial. **Pelagianism**, which emphasized free will and the capacity of human beings for righteousness, was rejected by Augustine of Hippo, who was more pessimistic about fallen human nature.

By the 5th century many groups of Christians existed whose views had been condemned and who were out of communion with the wider church. Their freedom of worship and action were often restricted by the authorities of the Christian Roman empire. In more recent times it has been generally recognized that the divisions that occurred were often the result of misunderstandings or of different (but equally valid) interpretations of the Bible and Christian tradition, and not just a product of the malice of heretics, as orthodox theologians of the period usually claimed.

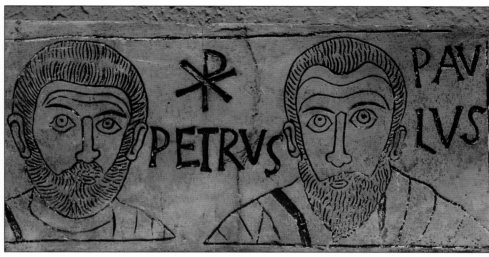

A stone slab of the Apostles Peter and Paul from the sepulchre of the child Amellus dating from after 313 **(above)**. Following the conversion of Constantine, Christian art became more public and explicit representations of Christ and the saints are common from this period. Portraits of Peter and Paul from Rome proudly allude to the connection of the two leading apostles with the city and its powerful bishops. In this example, they are depicted as Roman gentlemen of high social status, as the purple stripe of their togas attests.

2 Almost from the very beginning of organized Christianity, there were Christians who adopted a life of celibacy and renunciation, though they did not at first live in monastic communities separated from society at large. Monasticism originated in Egypt and Syria early in the 4th century, and monasteries were soon found both in desert areas and in villages and towns **(map right)**. By 340 Egyptian monks had visited Rome. Later in the 4th century monasticism spread to Asia Minor, north Africa and France, and in the 5th century to Britain, Ireland and Spain. Women as well as men founded monasteries, though the surviving documentation is biased towards male communities, both anchoritic (groups of hermits) and cenobitic (monks living together under a common rule). Monks and nuns were widely admired and exercised a powerful influence on Christian life and thought.

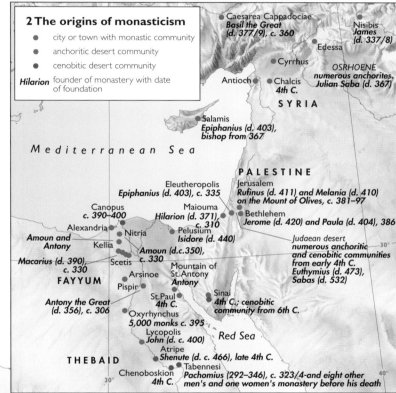

2 The origins of monasticism

- city or town with monastic community
- anchoritic desert community
- cenobitic desert community

Hilarion founder of monastery with date of foundation

Sarcophagus of Livia Primitiva, from the early 3rd century, found in Rome **(below)**. The inscription and decoration on this early Christian gravestone are typical of the period. The former reads:"Livia Nicarus set this up for her sister Livia Primitiva, who lived 24 years 9 months". The incised carvings show Christ as the good shepherd (carrying a sheep on his shoulders) and a fish and anchor, which were popular early Christian symbols. Christ is dressed in Roman style, in a short tunic.

4

THE WORLD
OF DIVIDED
RELIGIONS

THE PERIOD AROUND AD 500 saw upheaval throughout the Eurasian world, when nomads from the steppes of Asia descended upon all the existing centres of civilization. Although the gains of the classical period never entirely disappeared, contacts dwindled between China and the West, between north Africa and Italy and between Byzantium and western Europe. For the next few centuries each region was thrown back on its own resources and forced to fend for itself.

In western Europe this period is traditionally known as 'the Middle Ages'. The description may be appropriate for European history but it makes little sense in the wider perspective of world history. Here, two outstanding events dominated: the rise and expansion of Islam after 632; and the emergence of the Mongol empire in the 13th century. At the same time, important developments transformed hitherto isolated regions. The appearance of the Maya, Aztec and Inca civilizations in America, the creation of the empires of Sri Vijaya and Majapahit in southeast Asia, and the rise of the empires of Ghana, Mali and Songhay in Africa all attested to a new vitality and to the expansion of the area of civilized life.

Europe, by comparison, remained backward. Even here, however, it was a formative age, when primitive societies were welded into feudal monarchies. But the process of consolidation was slow, interrupted by barbarian incursions and by economic setbacks. Not until the second half of the 15th century did Europe begin to draw level with the other world civilizations, laying the foundations for overseas expansion with a series of path-breaking voyages of exploration. Even then, however, it remained overshadowed by the expanding power of the Ottoman Turks for another century.

STUPAS OF BUDDHIST TEMPLES, BAGAN, MANDALAY, MYANMAR.

Germanic settlement in western Europe

With the foundation of barbarian kingdoms within the western Roman empire, Europe began to take on the configurations of the medieval period. The Germanic kingdoms were in a real sense the heirs of Rome, and local populations accommodated the barbarian groups, many of whom originally settled among them as Roman allies or "federates".

THE SETTLEMENT OF GERMANIC and, later, Slav peoples within the former Roman empire was part of a general political and cultural shift within the Mediterranean world in relation to the rest of Europe. Trading and diplomatic relations – both secular and ecclesiastical – between eastern and western Mediterranean and between the Mediterranean and northern Europe were not interrupted.

The origins of the various Germanic tribes are obscured by their own and Roman ethnographers' legends about them, but long before the Christian era West and East Germanic groups (distinguishable on linguistic grounds) probably migrated from the far north of Europe and east central Europe respectively. Between 370 and 470, the build-up of the Asiatic Huns on the eastern fringes of the Roman empire, despite their pastoral economy and lack of

YOU WHO HAVE BEEN RESTORED TO IT AFTER MANY YEARS SHOULD GLADLY OBEY THE ROMAN CUSTOM, FOR IT IS GRATIFYING TO RETURN TO THAT STATE FROM WHICH YOUR ANCESTORS ASSUREDLY TOOK THEIR RISE. AND THEREFORE AS MEN OF GOD'S FAVOUR RESTORED TO ANCIENT LIBERTY, CLOTHE YOURSELVES IN THE MORAL OF THE TOGA, CAST OFF BARBARIAN WAYS, THROW ASIDE SAVAGERY OF MIND, FOR IT IS WRONG OF YOU IN MY JUST TIMES, TO LIVE BY ALIEN WAYS.

King Theodoric of Italy to all the provincials of the Gauls, c. 510

I **In the frontier regions** of the Roman empire, there was much interchange with, as well as raids by, neighbouring peoples (**map above**). On occasion entire peoples were settled as "federates" associated with the army for defence purposes. Other "barbarians" served in the ranks and in the top military posts of the imperial armies. The Huns created a major disruption and pushed groups such as the Goths and Vandals from the frontier regions of the empire. By the early 6th century, especially in the west, a number of successor states of mixed population had emerged on its former territory.

political integration, presented a powerful concentration of force and their attack on the Ostrogoths forced the latter to settle, with Roman permission, south of the Danube in Thrace.

The Huns' advances appear to have forced other groups into Roman territory, some of whom were recruited to defend the Romans and given the notional status of "federates" or allied peoples. The relationship with the Romans on occasion could turn sour: the Goths, for example, inflicted a major defeat on the Emperor Valens at the battle of Adrianople (378), but it was Romans and Germanic tribes who together defeated Attila and his Huns on the Catalaunian Fields near Troyes in Gaul in 451.

Franks and Visigoths

With the cooperation of the Romans among whom they lived in Spain, Gaul and Italy, the military role of the federate groups became a governing role as well. In northern Gaul Clovis, the Frankish leader, ruled over Gallo-Romans and Franks (settled in Toxandria probably since the 4th century) from 486. The Visigoths, military allies of the empire who had briefly set up their own emperor in Rome itself, founded the kingdom of Toulouse in Gaul in 418. They subsequently expanded their territory in Gaul, but were pushed south into Spain by the Franks at the beginning of the 6th century. The Burgundians founded a kingdom around the city of Worms, but were settled in Savoy in 443. The Sueves founded a kingdom in Galicia, though this was in due course absorbed into the Visigothic kingdom. The Vandals and Alans crossed

from Spain into Africa in 429, and in 442 the imperial government recognized their king, Gaiseric, as an independent ruler of the former Roman province.

Ostrogothic Italy

In 476 the last Roman emperor in the west, Romulus Augustulus, was deposed by Odoacer, the commander-in-chief of the Roman army. Odoacer then ruled Italy peacefully until the Ostrogothic leader Theodoric, sent from Constantinople under an arrangement with the Eastern emperor, defeated him and established an Ostrogothic kingdom in Italy in 493. This was effectively destroyed in the middle of the 6th century by the Byzantine emperor Justinian's wars of reconquest, led by the great general Belisarius. He briefly secured the Vandal kingdom of north Africa and the Ostrogothic kingdom until the Byzantines were ousted by the Arabs and Lombards respectively.

The European periphery

Meanwhile in Britain, during the 5th and 6th centuries, Angles and Saxons occupied the eastern and southern coastal areas, from which the Roman garrisons had been withdrawn. The early history of the peoples of southeast Europe is more obscure; but by the end of the 8th century independent Croatian, Serbian and Bulgarian kingdoms were taking shape. In all of these centres of settlement and assimilation, a fusion of Greco-Roman institutions, Germanic traditions and the Judaeo-Christian legacy together transformed the Roman world and heralded the emergence of early medieval Europe.

The votive crown of King Reccesvinth (above) of the Visigoths (649–72), now in the Museo Arqueologico, Madrid. The rich jewels — pearls in cloisonné style — link it with the decorative style of Italian metalwork of the Lombard kingdom in the same period. The pendant letters spell out the name of Reccesvinth and the cross indicates his Christian rulership.

4 The Anglo-Saxon settlement in Britain, c. 449–650

- → lines of Anglo-Saxon advance
- forest
- fenland, swamp
- · Anglo-Saxon burial places c. 450–650
- // British fortifications

4 The first Germanic settlers in Britain were probably mercenaries in Roman service. In the early 5th century the last Roman legions left Britain and the numbers of barbarian incomers increased (map above). According to the Anglo-Saxon Chronicle, the Anglo-Saxons set up their own kingdoms from about the middle of the 5th century, establishing control of most of modern England by about 650.

2 The Visigoths settled in Aquitaine as a Roman allied army from 418 (map below). Gradually their rule extended over a defined area, the kingdom of Toulouse. They invaded Spain in 454, driving out the Sueves. The Visigothic conquest of Spain was consolidated under Euric (466–84), but following their defeat by the Franks at Vouillé, they lost most of Gaul. The Vandals crossed from Spain into North Africa in 429 and in 439 took Carthage. Their kingdom survived until 534.

3 The Germanic kingdoms, c. 493

3 In 493 Theodoric the Ostrogoth overthrew Odoacer to become ruler of Italy. By this time the former territory of the western Roman empire was occupied by Germanic successor kingdoms (map above). These kingdoms were the heirs of Rome in every sense. Much that was Roman — in government, law, social organization, religion and intellectual culture — was maintained and even promoted under Germanic rule.

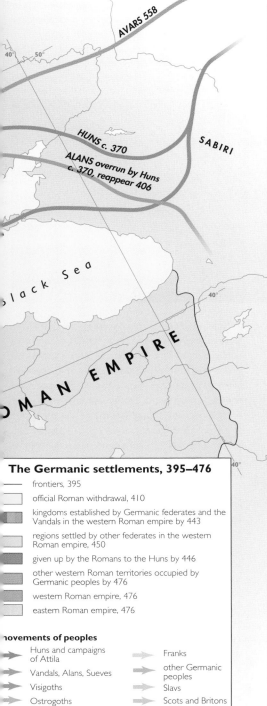

The Germanic settlements, 395–476

- frontiers, 395
- official Roman withdrawal, 410
- kingdoms established by Germanic federates and the Vandals in the western Roman empire by 443
- regions settled by other federates in the western Roman empire, 450
- given up by the Romans to the Huns by 446
- other western Roman territories occupied by Germanic peoples by 476
- western Roman empire, 476
- eastern Roman empire, 476

movements of peoples

- → Huns and campaigns of Attila
- → Vandals, Alans, Sueves
- → Visigoths
- → Ostrogoths
- → Franks
- → other Germanic peoples
- → Slavs
- → Scots and Britons

2 The western Mediterranean: the Visigothic and Vandal kingdoms, 419–555

the Visigoths

- approximate extent of the Visigothic Kingdom from 418
- added by 475
- held temporarily 477–500
- lost in 507
- the Visigothic Kingdom from 555
- dates indicate Visigothic losses

the Vandals

- secured by the Vandals by 429
- added in 439
- added by c. 460
- frontiers, 526

Pre-Islamic Arabia

In ancient times the vast Arabian peninsula was largely inhabited by nomadic tribes, which wandered in search of grazing and water for their camels and sheep. Almost all these nomadic tribes spoke Arabic, and they shared certain customs and systems of kinship. Despite these common ties, they had no political unity and no political organization. Ties of kinship were the essential social cement and, in the absence of any system of law enforcement, each tribe was usually hostile to its neighbours.

WHEN WAHRIZ HAD GONE TO CHOSROES (THE PERSIAN KING) AND MADE SAYF KING OF THE YEMEN, THE LATTER BEGAN ATTACKING THE ETHIOPIANS, KILLING THEM AND SLAYING THE WOMEN WITH CHILD UNTIL HE EXTERMINATED ALL BUT AN INSIGNIFICANT NUMBER OF MISERABLE CREATURES, WHOM HE EMPLOYED AS SLAVES AND RUNNERS TO GO BEFORE HIM WITH LANCES. BEFORE VERY LONG HE WAS OUT WITH THESE ARMED SLAVES WHEN SUDDENLY THEY SURROUNDED HIM AND STABBED HIM TO DEATH.

Ibn Hisham, *Life of Muhammad*

3 In the years before the rise of Islam, most of the Arabian peninsula was inhabited by Bedouin tribes, who lived in tents and had no permanent settlements. In the south-west there were ancient cities which controlled the trade routes which brought the luxury products of the area, especially frankincense, to consumers in the Mediterranean world (**map below**).

WHILE MOST OF THE peninsula was arid desert, there were towns, villages and quite large settled areas. The most important of these was Yemen, in the southwest corner of the peninsula, where the monsoon winds bring water to a mountainous landscape heavily populated with towns and villages. In antiquity Yemen had supported a thriving urban and mercantile community that prospered from the trade in incense between the area of Suhar, where the frankincense trees grew, and the Mediterranean. Cities such as Marib and Shabwa boasted fine stone-built temples and palaces and a developed language and culture.

By the 6th century, this ancient civilization was in decline. The trade routes were bypassed when the Romans and Byzantines discovered how to use the monsoon winds to bring goods by water up the Red Sea. This decline was symbolized by the collapse of the great dam at Marib, which had irrigated a large inland oasis in about 570. It was never repaired. With the break-up of the old states, Yemen became the target for outside invaders: it was conquered first by the Ethiopians, Christian allies of the Byzantines, and then by the Sasanian Persians.

There were other cities and settlements in Arabia. There were Jewish communities, notably at Yathrib (later called Medina) and Khaybar, and Christian ones

The sluice gate at one end of the Marib dam (**right**). This was one of the great engineering works of the ancient world, supplying irrigation water to the oasis on the edge of the Empty Quarter. It was restored many times but finally fell out of use in the late 6th century and its collapse symbolized the end of the settled kingdoms of ancient south Arabia.

3 The States of the Red Sea

- ● capital city
- ⚓ major port
- △ temple remains
- — trade route

area of cultivation
- — myrrh
- — frankincense

at Najran and in the areas bordering the Gulf. There were others, which were pagan shrines. Arabia had a number of ancient holy places where tribesmen who would normally be at war could meet together in the sacred enclave (*haram*) to arrange treaties and trading arrangements. By the late 6th century, the most important of these was the Ka'aba, the shrine at Mecca, whose guardians were the Quraysh tribe. The Prophet Muhammad was born into this tribe in around 570, and the reputation and skills of the Quraysh were an important ingredient in his success.

The old incense trade had been replaced by other forms of commerce, and the merchants of Mecca sent caravans to Syria, especially to Bostra and the Mediterranean port of Gaza, to Iraq, Yemen and Ethiopia. Incense itself had been replaced by gold and silver, and there is both written and archaeological evidence for the mining of precious metals in the hinterland of Mecca.

Arabia lay on the borders of the two great empires of late antiquity, the Byzantine and the Sasanian Persian. Until the early 7th century, both had supported client Arab rulers, known in Greek as phylarchs: the Ghassanids in Syria and the Lakhmids at Hira in Iraq. Their function was to manage the Arab tribes and keep the borders safe. The collapse of these kingdoms left the way open to nomad advance.

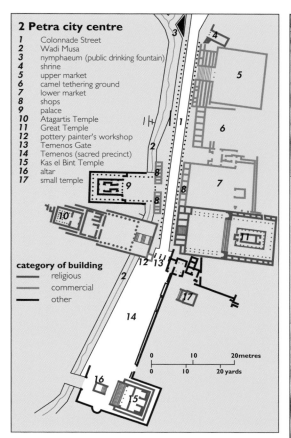

2 Petra city centre

1. Colonnade Street
2. Wadi Musa
3. nymphaeum (public drinking fountain)
4. shrine
5. upper market
6. camel tethering ground
7. lower market
8. shops
9. palace
10. Atagartis Temple
11. Great Temple
12. pottery painter's workshop
13. Temenos Gate
14. Temenos (sacred precinct)
15. Kas el Bint Temple
16. altar
17. small temple

category of building

— religious
— commercial
— other

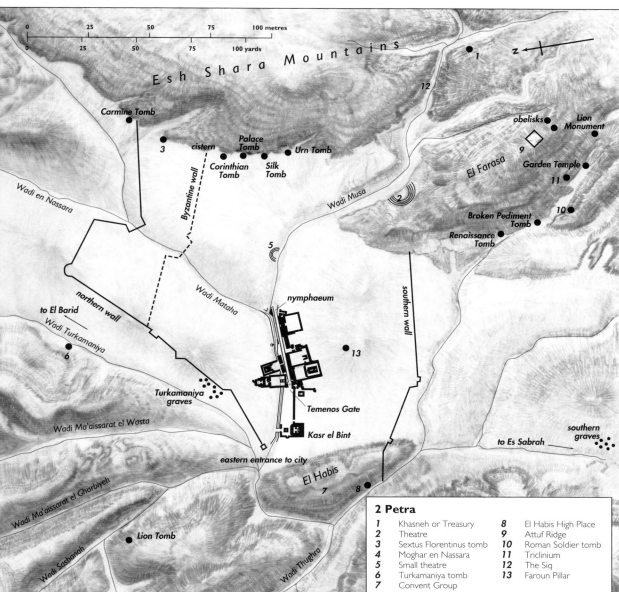

2 The desert city of Petra (above & right) in the southeast corner of the Roman world, carved out of the sandstone mountains to the northeast of the Red Sea, is situated in a cliff-bound valley crossed by numerous wadis. Petra was the capital of the Nabataean kingdom, which at its height controlled a large area on the desert fringe of the Near East reaching from Sinai north towards Damascus. It may have been a trading centre as early as the 5th century BC, but the city reached its greatest prosperity between 100 BC and AD 150, and it is to this period that most of the visible remains belong, such as the monumental tombs cut into the cliffs surrounding the site. Trade was the basis of Petra's prosperity, but when the trade routes between Arabia and the Mediterranean went into decline during the 2nd–3rd centuries, following peaceful occupation by the Romans in AD 106, the city atrophied, and by the mid-6th century was effectively abandoned.

2 Petra

1. Khasneh or Treasury
2. Theatre
3. Sextus Florentinus tomb
4. Moghar en Nassara
5. Small theatre
6. Turkamaniya tomb
7. Convent Group
8. El Habis High Place
9. Attuf Ridge
10. Roman Soldier tomb
11. Triclinium
12. The Siq
13. Faroun Pillar

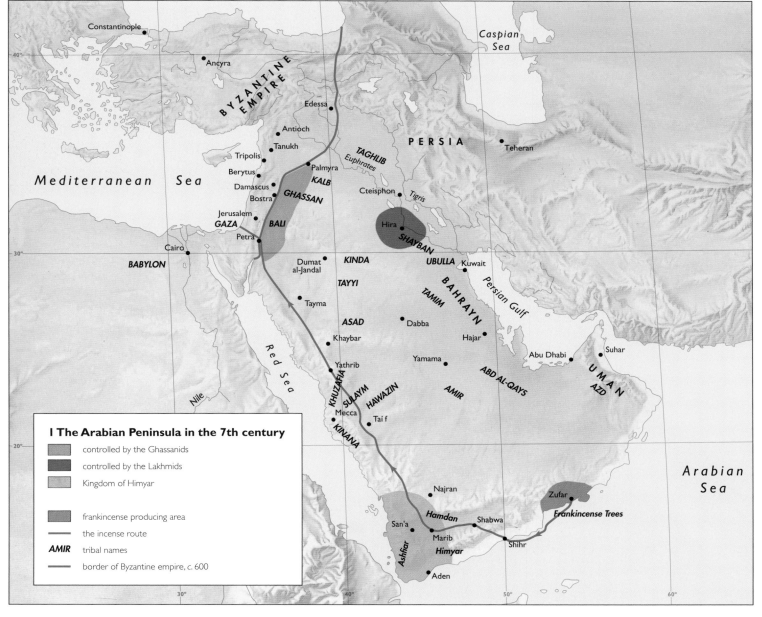

1 The Arabian Peninsula in the 7th century

- controlled by the Ghassanids
- controlled by the Lakhmids
- Kingdom of Himyar
- frankincense producing area
- — the incense route
- **AMIR** tribal names
- — border of Byzantine empire, c. 600

1 The incense states of southern Arabia were linked to the prosperous cities of Egypt and the east Mediterranean by overland routes (map left). Use of the overland routes through arid regions became more regular after the introduction of camels which could travel for longer periods than pack-asses and donkeys. For the most part the routes consisted of dusty desert tracks between settlements or waterholes, but within the kingdoms themselves paved roads were built in some places. These roads performed an important secondary function in channelling the traffic and levying tolls. The road over the Maqlabah pass from the kingdom of Qataban was paved for five kilometres, with a small reservoir for camels and travellers at each end. Another important route linked the principal frankincense areas of Hadhramaut with the port of Qana through the Wadi Harash pass. The small states of the regions were frequently at war with each other and many of the major settlements were fortified with powerful walls and towers. In the early centuries AD the increasing use of shipping, especially along the Read Sea, tipped the balance of power and prosperity in favour of those states with control of the major ports such as Qana, Muza and Aden.

111

The spread of Islam

In the century after the death of Mohammad, Islam was spread by Arab armies through much of the Middle East, North Africa and Spain. This Muslim world retained a considerable degree of cultural unity. In the Middle Ages it conserved much ancient Greek learning, enabling its later transmission to medieval European civilization.

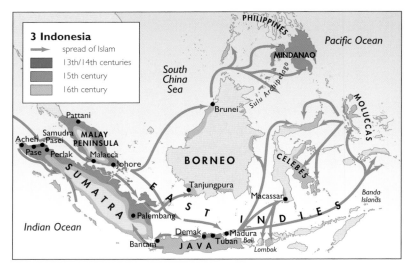

3 Indonesia and the Malay peninsula were converted to Islam by a gradual process of proselytization (map above), probably beginning with Muslim traders from Gujerat who acquired a permanent foothold at Perlak on the northern tip of Sumatra by 1290. From there they spread to the Malay peninsula (c. 1400), Java and the Moluccas (c. 1430–90). By the 16th century most of the archipelago had accepted Islam, as had the southern Philippines.

ISLAM MEANS "submission to the will of God". Muslims believe that God's message to mankind has been expressed through a series of prophets, culminating in Mohammed, the Apostle and Prophet of God; that God has spoken through Mohammed; and that the Koran (meaning "recitation") is the Word of God. Mohammed is the final Prophet, and no others will come after him.

Mohammed was born in Mecca in about AD 570. The city was the principal commercial centre in western Arabia, and was also an important pilgrimage centre because of its shrine, the Ka'ba. Mohammed received his first revelations in about 610 and his followers soon grew in number. However, the hostility of the merchant aristocracy in Mecca developed into persecution, and Mohammed and his followers withdrew to Medina, some 450km (280 miles) northeast of Mecca. This "migration", *hijra* in Arabic, on 16 July 622 marks the beginning of the Islamic era and thus of the Muslim calendar.

The Muslim conquests

In Medina, Mohammed organized the Muslims into a community, and consolidated his base with the assistance of his Medinan hosts. He returned to Mecca in triumph in 630 and cast out the idols from the Ka'ba, transforming it into the focal point of the new religion of Islam. At Mohammed's death in 632, his authority extended over the Hejaz and most of central and southern Arabia.

The first of Mohammed's successors, the caliph Abu Bakr (632–4), completed the conquest of Arabia and entered southern Palestine. Caliph Omar (634–44) advanced to Damascus, and followed victory over the Byzantines at the Yarmuk river in 636 with thrusts east into Mesopotamia and northwest into Asia Minor. By 643 Persia had been overrun, and the last Persian emperor, Yazdigird, was killed in 651 at Merv. The conquest of Herat and Balkh and the fall of Kabul opened the way to India; Sind, in northeast India, fell to the Muslims in 712.

Simultaneously, Arab forces pushed west into Egypt, occupying Alexandria in 643, and advancing across north Africa into Cyrenaica and the Maghreb. Independent Arab forces under the leadership of Tariq ibn Ziyad and Musa crossed the Straits of Gibraltar in 711 and conquered the southern part of Spain (al-Andalus). Raids into southern France, however, were successfully deflected by the Franks. In the east, the Byzantines succeeded in preventing the Arabs from capturing Constantinople and retained control of much of Asia Minor until the 11th century.

Initially, Islam did not particularly encourage, far less insist upon, conversion. The Koran enjoins Muslims to respect the "people of the book", that is, members of the other monotheistic religions with written scriptures. The peaceful co-existence of substantial Christian (and, until comparatively recently, Jewish) communities throughout the Muslim world is ample evidence that this injunction was heeded. Under the Abbasid dynasty (750–1258), however, large-scale conversion to Islam became common.

Politics and culture

From 661 the vast Muslim Empire was ruled from Damascus by the Umayyad Caliphs. The reign of Abd al-Malik (685–705) saw the development of Arabic coinage, the use of Arabic in the administration and the construction of the first great monument of Islamic architecture, the Dome of the Rock in Jerusalem. Many Muslims were dissatisfied with the regime and looked to the family of the Prophet to provide leadership, forming the Shi'ite sect. In 750 the Umayyads were overthrown by the Abbasids, descended from Muhammad's uncle Abbas. Islam continued to expand as a religious force (see maps 2 and 3). This expansion was due to both conquest and, notably in southeast Asia and west Africa, missionary activity by traders and preachers.

1 The spread of Islam outside the Arabian peninsula began almost immediately after the Prophet's death in 632 **(map right)**. By 711, Arab armies were simultaneously attacking Sind in northeast India and preparing for the conquest of the Iberian peninsula. In general, the conquests in the east exceeded those in the west in both size and importance. By 750, when the Abbasids ousted the Umayyad dynasty, the empire to which they succeeded was the largest civilization west of China.

1 The spread of Islam

- growth under Mohammed
- growth under Abu Bakr (632–4)
- growth under Omar (634–44)
- growth under Othman (644–56) and Ali (656–61)
- expansion of Umayyad Caliphate (661–750)
- expansion under the early Abbasids (750–850)
- routes of advance
- 638 date of Muslim conquest

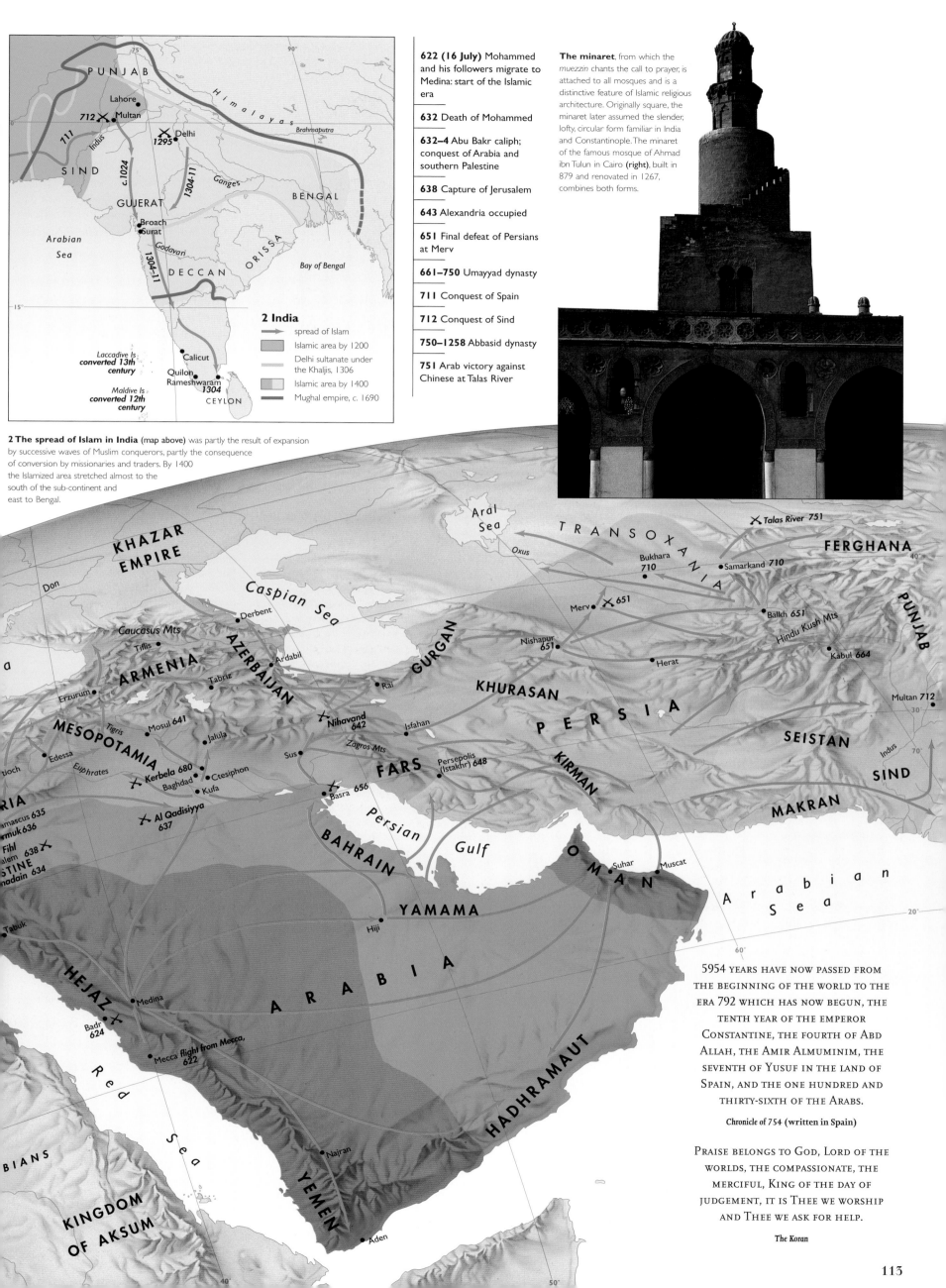

2 India

- → spread of Islam
- Islamic area by 1200
- Delhi sultanate under the Khaljis, 1306
- Islamic area by 1400
- → Mughal empire, c. 1690

Laccadive Is. **converted 13th century**

Maldive Is. **converted 12th century**

2 The spread of Islam in India (map above) was partly the result of expansion by successive waves of Muslim conquerors, partly the consequence of conversion by missionaries and traders. By 1400 the Islamized area stretched almost to the south of the sub-continent and east to Bengal.

622 (16 July) Mohammed and his followers migrate to Medina: start of the Islamic era

632 Death of Mohammed

632–4 Abu Bakr caliph; conquest of Arabia and southern Palestine

638 Capture of Jerusalem

643 Alexandria occupied

651 Final defeat of Persians at Merv

661–750 Umayyad dynasty

711 Conquest of Spain

712 Conquest of Sind

750–1258 Abbasid dynasty

751 Arab victory against Chinese at Talas River

The minaret, from which the *muezzin* chants the call to prayer, is attached to all mosques and is a distinctive feature of Islamic religious architecture. Originally square, the minaret later assumed the slender, lofty, circular form familiar in India and Constantinople. The minaret of the famous mosque of Ahmad ibn Tulun in Cairo (right), built in 879 and renovated in 1267, combines both forms.

5954 YEARS HAVE NOW PASSED FROM
THE BEGINNING OF THE WORLD TO THE
ERA 792 WHICH HAS NOW BEGUN, THE
TENTH YEAR OF THE EMPEROR
CONSTANTINE, THE FOURTH OF ABD
ALLAH, THE AMIR ALMUMINIM, THE
SEVENTH OF YUSUF IN THE LAND OF
SPAIN, AND THE ONE HUNDRED AND
THIRTY-SIXTH OF THE ARABS.

Chronicle of 754 (written in Spain)

PRAISE BELONGS TO GOD, LORD OF THE
WORLDS, THE COMPASSIONATE, THE
MERCIFUL, KING OF THE DAY OF
JUDGEMENT, IT IS THEE WE WORSHIP
AND THEE WE ASK FOR HELP.

The Koran

The expansion of Christianity

Having begun as a Middle Eastern religion, Christianity became a predominantly European one during the Middle Ages. Christianity gave ideological unity to medieval Europe, especially in the west. But by 1500, divisions within the Church and criticism of its teaching and institutions had paved the way for the religious turmoil of the Reformation.

WE LEARN FROM THE WORDS OF THE GOSPEL THAT IN THIS CHURCH AND IN HER POWER ARE TWO SWORDS, THE SPIRITUAL AND THE TEMPORAL.

Pope Boniface VIII, 1302

LET US SEE HOW SUCH PRELATES ARE INFECTED BY THE SPLENDOUR OF THE WORLD AND BY AVARICE ... SO THAT THEY BECOME RICH MEN IN THE WORLD'S EYE.

John Wyclif (1330–84)

IN THE FIRST FIVE CENTURIES OF ITS history, Christianity was largely confined to the Roman empire. The emergent barbarian successor states in the fifth and sixth centuries were also Christian, although some followed the teaching of Arius rather than Catholic doctrine. The Franks, who were pagan, accepted Catholic Christianity between 496 and 508. Nonetheless by AD 600 Christianity had become the dominant religion of the Mediterranean world. However, from the 7th century the Islamic conquests deprived the Christian Byzantine empire of its lands in the Middle East and north Africa: after several centuries of Islamic rule only small Christian minorities remained in these areas. Despite the tolerance extended by Islam to Christians, the rise of Islam isolated the churches of Europe from the Monophysite and Nestorian Christians of the east, who carried out their own missions in Asia in later centuries (see map 1).

In Europe various independent missionary efforts were made by Irish and Frankish missionaires in the lands of their eastern and northern neighbours. After being converted by Roman missionaries sent by Pope Gregory (590–604) the English were also active in propagating the Christian faith. Differences between Irish missionaries already active in England and Roman missionaries over issues such as the date of Easter were the result of over a century of independent development in the Irish church (since c. 450). Nonetheless these disputes were resolved in the 7th century.

Rome and Constantinople
The same was not true of the differences between the Roman and Byzantine churches, which grew steadily greater during the early Middle Ages. Though theology played a part, many of the disputes were over liturgical practices (for example, the use in the west of unleavened bread in the Eucharist) or questions of church government and spheres of influence, especially after the conversion of the Slavs of central Europe had been inaugurated by Cyril and Methodius at the end of the 9th century.

The Byzantines were used to a regime in which the Constantinople patriarchs governed the church under the protection of a Christian emperor, and distrusted the growing power of the western Popes. Although the schism between Rome and Constantinople that occurred in 1054 was not technically a permanent breach, it was an important symbol of the gradual separation of the two churches. The Orthodox church in Byzantium eventually came under the authority of an Islamic ruler when Constantinople fell to the Turks in 1453. From then on, Russia, converted to Christianity from 988, was the most important Orthodox Christian power in Europe.

The power of the Papacy
From the 11th century the Papacy assumed a position of leadership in western Europe, which included presiding over the organization of the crusades (see p. 124). Gregory VII (1073–85) campaigned to end simony (the purchase of ecclesiastical office) and to enforce clerical celibacy. Innocent III (1198–1216) continued his work and was probably the most powerful Pope of the Middle Ages. Papal pretensions to superiority over secular rulers often led to political conflicts. In 1302 Boniface VIII propounded the theory of the "two swords", which held that both temporal and spiritual leadership in Christendom should be under the control of the papacy.

The wealth and political pretensions of the church in the west also led to opposition at a popular level. From the 11th century, heretical movements existed in western Europe. The Cathars of southern France revived the ancient gnostic and Manichaean belief that the flesh was evil, but attracted popular support because of their holiness of life and rejection of the power of the Church. Though the Cathars, like other heretics, were brutally suppressed, some churchmen realized that reform of the church, rather than the violence of the Inquisition, was the answer to heresy. The

I The medieval expansion of Christianity into central and east Asia **(map below)** was largely the work of Nestorian and Monophysite Christians, who had been separated from the rest of the church since the 5th century. Their work along the trade routes of central Asia and the Persian Gulf was tolerated by non-Christian rulers until the 14th century. China was also the scene of missionary work by the Manichees, whose dualist religion (founded in the 3rd century) had been banned and persecuted in the Christian west. Nestorianism and Manichaeism in China eventually died out, but Nestorianism survives in modern Iraq and Monophysitism remains the indigenous form of Christianity in Egypt (the Coptic church), Ethiopia and India (the Syrian Orthodox or St Thomas Christians), where distinctive traditions of worship and theology are preserved.

A section from the 8th-century Ruthwell Cross in Scotland **(above)**, one of the most important surviving Anglo-Saxon sculptures and a fascinating example of early medieval Christian art. The figures represent different aspects of the divine power of Christ. The runic characters on the borders contain an excerpt from *The Dream of the Rood*, an Old English Christian poem.

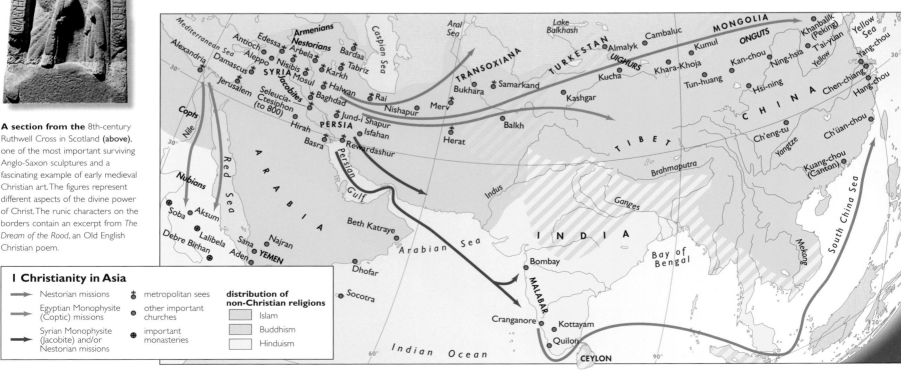

I Christianity in Asia

- → Nestorian missions
- → Egyptian Monophysite (Coptic) missions
- → Syrian Monophysite (Jacobite) and/or Nestorian missions
- ⊕ metropolitan sees
- ● other important churches
- ⊛ important monasteries

distribution of non-Christian religions
- Islam
- Buddhism
- Hinduism

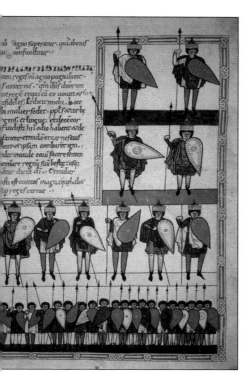

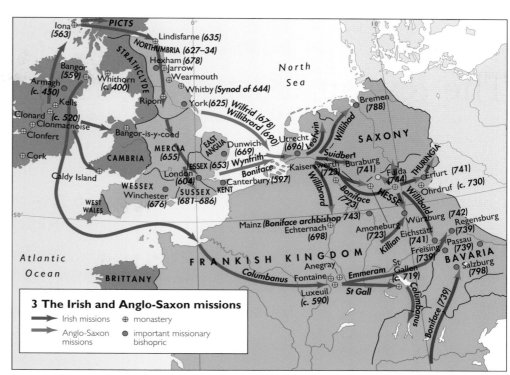

3 Irish missionaries such as Columba (c. 521–97) and Aidan (d. 651) were instrumental in converting Scotland and northern England to Christianity; Columbanus (d. 615) founded monasteries in the Frankish kingdom **(map right)**. The Anglo-Saxon kingdoms also sent missionaries (with Roman and Frankish support) to western Germany. The most important were Willibrord (658–739) and Boniface (c. 675–754), bishops of Utrecht and Mainz.

The ten kings and their troops from the 11th-century *Beatus of Liébana Apocalypse* **(left)**. The important 8th-century commentary on the Book of Revelation (or the Apocalypse) by Beatus of Liébana was usually copied with a series of illustrations, some of which originally alluded to political events such as the Muslim conquest of Spain. The "ten kings" (probably, in the New Testament, representing enemies of the Roman empire) are mentioned in Revelation 17.12–14.

3 The Irish and Anglo-Saxon missions

→ Irish missions   ⊕ monastery
→ Anglo-Saxon missions   ● important missionary bishopric

foundation of orders of friars by Dominic (1172–1221) and Francis of Assisi (1181–1226) was a response to the need of the Church for anti-heretical preachers. The friars played an important role in preaching the gospel in later medieval Europe, as well as leading a few attempts at converting Muslims to Christianity.

In the 14th century there were further challenges to the church in western Europe. The English scholar John Wyclif (1330–84) led a movement of protest against both its wealth and some of its teachings, and there were similar protests elsewhere. The papal schism of 1378 to 1415, when two rival claimants to the papacy were supported by different secular rulers, did much to encourage calls for reform. Though such proposals came to nothing during the Middle Ages, hostility to the papacy played a large part in the Reformation of the 16th century (see p. 204). Nonetheless, by 1500 Europe was a wholly Christian civilization. Despite protests against the papacy, there is little to suggest that the Catholic church did not continue to provide adequately for the spiritual needs of most west Europeans.

2 From about 700, Christianity began to expand into Germany and, from the 9th century, into central Europe, where the Roman and Byzantine churches competed for the allegiance of newly converted rulers **(map right)**. The conversion of Scandinavia began in the mid-10th century, that of Russia in 988. Most of Spain was overrun by Islam in 711 but slowly reconquered by Christian rulers during the rest of the Middle Ages. From 1096, crusader armies from western Europe campaigned to recover the Holy Land from Islam: Christian rule was established in Jerusalem and Antioch, but these territories were lost by 1291. With the conversion of Prussia and Lithuania in the 14th century most of Europe had become at least nominally Christian, though the Church had been permanently divided between Catholic west and Byzantine east.

2 Christianity in Europe

- Roman-rite Christians, c. 1400
- Byzantine-rite Christians, c. 1400
- Monophysite Christians
- Islam
- extent of Catholic (Frankish) Christianity, c. 700
- maximum extent of crusader states in the east in the 12th century
- ● important bishoprics
- (743) date of foundation of a bishopric or of conversion of a region to Christianity

The Jewish diaspora

After their persecution in Palestine by the Romans in the 1st century AD, Jews settled across much of north Africa and then Europe, contributing decisively to the cultural, intellectual and economic development of their new countries. Further expulsions in the Middle Ages led to a new round of enforced Jewish migrations, above all to Poland and Lithuania.

THESE JEWISH MERCHANTS SPEAK ARABIC, PERSIAN, THE LANGUAGES OF THE ROMAN EMPIRE, OF THE FRANKS, THE SPANISH AND THE SLAVS. THEY GO FROM WEST TO EAST BY LAND AND SEA. FROM THE WEST THEY CARRY EUNUCHS, FEMALE AND MALE SLAVES, SILKEN CLOTH, VARIOUS KINDS OF FURS, AND SWORDS. THEY SHIP OUT FROM FRANKISH TERRITORY ON THE MEDITERRANEAN SEA AND HEAD FOR FARAM IN THE NILE DELTA.

Ibn Kurradadhbah
Treatise on the Routes and the Kingdoms, 9th century

FOR OVER 2000 YEARS the history of the Jews has combined external dispersal with internal cohesion. The decisive dispersal of the Jewish people took place under Rome. Although the Jewish revolts of AD 66–73 and 132–5 and their vigorous suppression by the Romans, as well as Hadrian's measures to de-Judaize Jerusalem, caused rapid deterioration in the position of the Jews in Judaea, elsewhere in the Roman world their legal and economic status and the viability of their communities remained unaffected. This stimulated a constant flow of migration from Palestine, Mesopotamia and Alexandria to the western and northern shores of the Mediterranean. Consequently, widely scattered but internally cohesive Jewish communities developed all

over the west and north of the Roman empire: in Italy, in Spain and as far north as Cologne. The Cairo community was a major element in Mediterranean commerce and has left its detailed records (the Cairo "Genizah") of life there during the Middle Ages.

Medieval Jewry and the expulsions

The resilience of Judaism can be chiefly ascribed to the evolution of the Jewish religion following the destruction of the First Temple in Jerusalem in 586 BC, and the gradual emergence of a faith based on synagogue and communal prayer. New local leaders of Jewish life, the men of learning, or rabbis, emerged. Jewish religious and civil law was gradually codified in the *Mishnah* (AD 200) and the

commentary and discussions systematized as the *Talmud* (AD 500).

During the High Middle Ages Jews from the Near East and north Africa settled in southern Italy, Spain, France and southern Germany. They flourished in Spain under the first Umayyad caliph of Córdoba, 'Abd ar-Rahman III (912–61), and continued to play a major role in society, learning and commerce until 1391. Despite the massacres which attended the First Crusade in the 1090s, the 11th and 12th centuries constituted the golden age of medieval German Jewry.

A series of expulsions from western Europe, beginning in England in 1290, led to a steady eastwards migration of German Jews (*Ashkenazim*) to

63 BC Judaea becomes Roman protectorate

AD 66–73 First Jewish revolt

AD 70 Destruction of the Temple in Jerusalem

AD 132–5 Second Jewish revolt under Bar Kokhba

1290 Expulsion of Jews from England

1394 Expulsion from France

1492 Expulsion from Spain

1497 Expulsion from Portugal

1499–1552 Expulsion from many German states

The seven-branched candlestick (right) from the Temple in Jerusalem was taken to Rome by Titus when the Romans destroyed the Temple in AD 70 during the suppression of the Jewish revolt. A second revolt in AD 132–5 was similarly crushed.

1 & 2 The Jews in medieval Europe were tolerated by the authorities for economic reasons, but were subjected to restrictions and frequent persecution. They formed two major sub-groups (**map right**): *Sephardim* from the Hebrew word *Sepharad* (for Spain) who lived in Spain until 1492; and *Ashkenazim* (from the Hebrew word *Ashkenaz*, for the Germanic lands) who originally lived in the Rhineland until, as a result of migration and expulsion (**map far right**), by the late 15th century they flourished primarily in Poland and Lithuania. By 1500 much of Europe, including England, France, Spain and Portugal was closed to Jews.

Prague (from the 11th century) and Vienna. Jewish communities arose in Cracow, Kalisz, and other towns in western and southern Poland in the 13th century and, further east, at Lvov, Brest-Litovsk and Grodno in the 14th. The period of heaviest immigration from the west into Poland-Lithuania came in the late 15th and 16th. Most of the expelled Spanish and Portuguese Jews (*Sephardim*) settled in the Ottoman empire and north Africa, though in the late 16th century a trickle migrated to Rome and northern Italy.

The revival of Jewish life

After the disruption of the Thirty Years' War (1618–48), Jews from central and eastern Europe, as well as the Near East, were once again able to settle, usually in ghettos, with the permission of both trading cities and princely governments, in northern Italy, Germany, Holland and, from the 1650s, in England and the English colonies in the New World (first those in the Caribbean and later in North America). Small groups also migrated from Germany to Denmark and Sweden. In the central European cities of Vienna, Berlin, Hamburg and Budapest, Jewish communities grew considerably during the 18th and 19th centuries and made major contributions to the development of their countries, in particular engaging in financial enterprises forbidden to Christians. During the 17th and 18th centuries, some of the largest and wealthiest, as well as culturally most sophisticated, communities in the Jewish world lived in

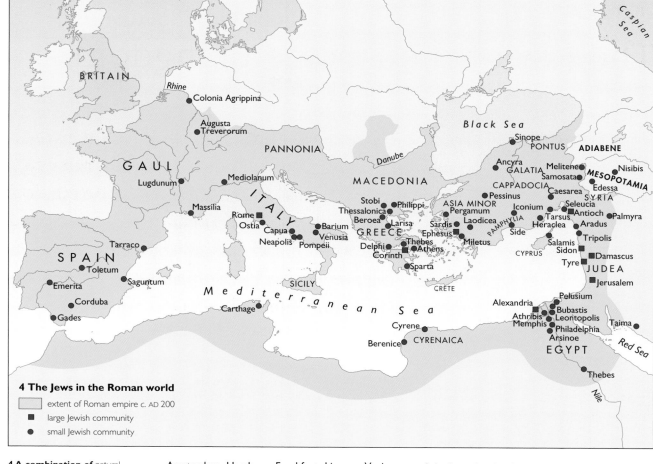

4 The Jews in the Roman world
☐ extent of Roman empire *c*. AD 200
■ large Jewish community
● small Jewish community

4 A combination of natural factors and successive invasions and occupations of Judaea by the neighbouring Ptolemaic and Seleucid rulers (c. 312–165 BC) encouraged sustained emigration of Jews all over the Mediterranean world **(map above)**. Not subject to any restrictions, and with their favoured status confirmed by the Roman emperors, most fared well until the Christianization of the Roman empire from the 4th century AD onwards.

Amsterdam, Hamburg, Frankfurt, Livorno, Venice, Rome, Berlin and London. Amsterdam's Jews were especially important in the areas of commerce, finance, printing and book production.

Eastern Europe

Nevertheless until the 1940s by far the greater proportion of world Jewry continued to live in eastern Europe. The small Jewish populations in Hungary and Romania in 1700 increased in the 18th and 19th centuries through immigration from Poland and Czech lands. Under the tsars, the bulk of the Jewish population in the Russian empire was confined by law to western areas (the "Pale of Settlement"). The demographic preponderance of eastern Europe in world Jewry ended with the Nazis: Jewish life in Poland, Czechoslovakia and the old Pale of Settlement was largely destroyed though large Jewish populations survived in the USSR, Romania, Bulgaria and Hungary.

3 In 140 BC an independent Jewish state emerged under Simon the Hasmonean. It became a Roman protectorate in 63 BC. Herod I (37–4 BC) divided it in his will among his three sons. Judaea was governed by Roman procurators from AD 6 to 66 **(map right)**, with an interlude when the whole of Herod's kingdom was reunited under his grandson Agrippa I (AD 41–4). After Agrippa's death, the rule of the procurators provoked an unsuccessful revolt by Jewish nationalists in AD 66–73, who made a last stand at the fortress of Masada.

1 The Jews in medieval Europe
cultural areas:
▨ Ashkenazi
▨ South Italian
▨ Islamic
▨ Sephardi
▨ "Pale of Settlement" at end of 19th century
→ medieval migrations
→ Early Modern migrations
● principal centres of Jewish settlement, c. 1200
● principal centres of Jewish settlement, c. 1500

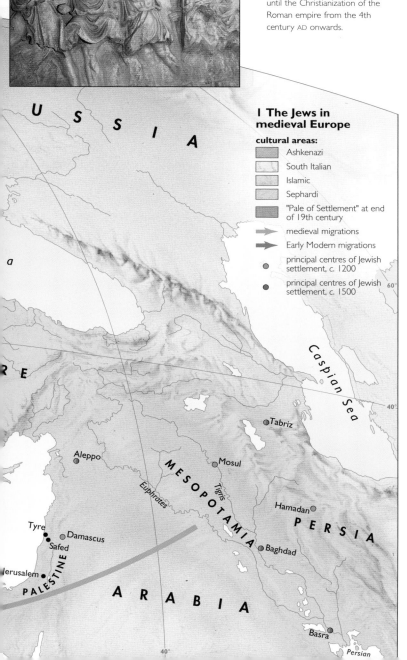

3 Judaea in the 1st centuries BC and AD
☐ area of Roman procuratorial rule in Judaea
▨ Agrippa II's kingdom AD 61
╌╌ areas of major revolt at start of AD 66
── area of revolt at end of AD 69
→ Roman armies

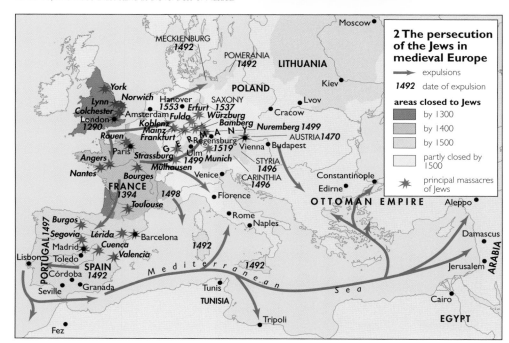

2 The persecution of the Jews in medieval Europe
→ expulsions
1492 date of expulsion
areas closed to Jews
▨ by 1300
▨ by 1400
▨ by 1500
☐ partly closed by 1500
✳ principal massacres of Jews

The rise of the Frankish kingdom

The kingdom of the Franks in Gaul was the most enduring of the barbarian successor states to the Roman empire. Under the Carolingians the Franks dominated western Europe. They combined remarkable political and cultural coherence with crucial developments in kingship and government, culture, education, religion and social organization.

A STRONG REPORT HAS COME TO US THAT YOU HAVE TAKEN OVER THE ADMINISTRATION OF THE SECOND BELGIC PROVINCE. THERE IS NOTHING NEW IN THAT YOU BEGIN TO BE WHAT YOUR PARENTS ALWAYS WERE. YOU SHOULD DEFER TO YOUR BISHOPS AND ALWAYS HAVE RECOURSE TO THEIR ADVICE. IF YOU ARE ON GOOD TERMS WITH THEM YOUR PROVINCE WILL BE BETTER ABLE TO STAND FIRM.

Bishop Remigius of Rheims
Letter to King Clovis of the Franks, 481

THE MEROVINGIAN KINGDOM of the Franks in Gaul (so called because the kings claimed Meroveus, a sea monster, as their legendary ancestor) proved to be the most enduring of the barbarian successor states to the Roman empire. The conquests of Clovis and his sons and grandsons created a powerful basis for Frankish hegemony and one which was built on by their Carolingian successors who later dominated western Europe. Frankish rule in western Europe was a time of remarkable political and cultural coherence, combined with crucial, diverse and formative developments in almost every sphere of life.

The Merovingians

The splendid grave of Clovis's father, Childeric (*d.* 481), discovered at Tournai in 1653, shows that, although a pagan, he had ruled as Roman military governor in the north of Gaul. Clovis's conversion to Catholicism was a major factor in winning over the Gallo-Roman population to acceptance of his rule. Gallo-Romans and Franks merged; by the 7th century it is not possible to determine who among the counts and bishops who were so prominent in Merovingian administration and politics was descended from Gallo-Romans and who from Franks. It is symptomatic of the assimilation of peoples in Gaul that the French language has developed from Latin, though it was not until the 9th century that the first small adjustments to the orthography of the written language began to be made. For the whole of the period of Frankish domi-

nance in Europe, Latin was the language of law, religion and education. West of the Rhine it was the vernacular as well.

Under Clovis's descendants, Frankish power was largely concentrated north of the Loire and especially in the areas known as Neustria and Austrasia. From 613 the kings increasingly relied on officials known as the "mayors of the palace" and other aristocrats who governed the far flung regions of the realm. It was from Austrasia's most powerful family, the Arnulfings, later known as the Carolingians, that

the most concerted challenge to Merovingian rule emerged. It was led by Pippin II, mayor of the palace, for whom the Battle of Tertry in 687 was a crucial short-term victory. It was Pippin II's son Charles Martel, however, who rebuilt the family's and Frankish fortunes in the face of opposition from the

2 The Frankish empire reached its greatest extent by the time of Charlemagne's coronation as emperor in Rome (**map below**). The Lombard kingdom of Italy had been seized in 774; large parts of Germany were added, in the face of prolonged and determined resistance, after 772; and a march, or boundary province, was created across the Pyrenees between 795 and 812.

An image of Charlemagne from his tomb at Aachen (**below**). The tomb was endowed by Frederick Barbarossa in the 12th century. The masterpiece of gold enamels and gems shows that, for the later emperor, Charlemagne was a saint and a personal patron, able to confer political legitimacy.

Map

2 The empire of Charlemagne

- Frankish realm 714
- added to Frankish empire by 814
- Frankish dependencies (with date of formation)
- ⊞ Frankish royal residences
- ✚ archbishoprics
- ⊕ important monasteries
- **GASCONY 769** province with date of acquisition

North Sea

BRITAIN

Quentovic · Boulogne · Tournai

St Riquier
Corbie
St. Wandrille · Rouen × *Tertry 687* · Attigny
Bayeux · Quierzy · Rheims
Seine · St Denis · Paris
NEUSTRIA · Chartres · Sens
Orléans
Loire
BRITTANY · BRETON MARCH
778 march organized, 799 surrender of all Brittany to the Franks
Tours × *733/4*
Bourges

Bay of Biscay

Clermont · BURGUN

Limoges

AQUITANIA
768–9

Bordeaux
Dordogne

GASCONY
769 · Toulouse · SEPTIMANIA · Aniane
Pyrenees
Roncesvalles × · 759
778 · Narbonne
SPANISH MARCH 795

added 812

Ebro

UMAYYAD CALIPHATE

Barcelona
801

Tortosa 811

Medit

Neustrian mayors of the palace, the Frisians, Aquitainians and Saracens. By the time of his death in 741 Charles, although still nominally only the mayor of the palace, handed on to his sons Pippin and Carloman a greatly enlarged and strengthened realm.

It was Pippin III who in 751, on the advice and with the consent of the Frankish magnates, made himself king and so established the new Carolingian dynasty. Pippin's position was further strengthened in 754 when the Pope crossed the Alps and anointed him and his sons as the rightful rulers of the Franks. The realm was again expanded under Pippin III to include Alemannia and Aquitania.

Charlemagne

Pippin's son Charlemagne conquered the Lombard kingdom and annexed Bavaria. In a series of bloody campaigns he then beat the Saxons into submission and obliged them to accept Christianity. Despite the setback at Roncesvalles (778) immortalized in the *Chanson de Roland*, Charlemagne established control of the Spanish march. He also achieved a celebrated victory against the Avars (796). Charlemagne's rule over many peoples was recognized in his coronation as emperor on Christmas Day 800, though this event was largely symbolic and did not materially affect Charlemagne's status or power: it had more to do with the role of the Frankish king in relation to Italy and his protection of Rome. Later generations, however, were to capitalize on its implications. The arrangements for the succession, devised in 806 but never put into effect, did not in fact preserve the imperial title. However, with the death by 813 of all his sons save one, Louis,

Charlemagne crowned him as his successor. The triumphalist narratives of the 9th century created a strong image of Carolingian continuity and success which inspired later rulers in Europe.

Carolingian government

The Carolingian conquests were accompanied by the consolidation of the Christian church. The support as well as the protection of the Papacy, the close relationship with the church, the clerics' key role in all aspects of government alongside lay magnates and the status of the Carolingian ruler as Christian king, responsible for the faith and welfare of the Christians under his dominion, are hallmarks of the Carolingian regime. Scholars, poets and artists from all over Europe were gathered at the court, centred on Aachen from the end of the 8th century, and at other cultural centres throughout the realm. Many innovations were made in government, not least the reform of the coinage and of weights and measures, and a restructuring of the administration, relying heavily on written communications, to rule the vast territories effectively. Laws were compiled and officials charged to ensure justice in society. Christian learning and education, church and monastic life were all regulated and supported systematically. Copies of specified liturgical books for use in the churches, as well as of a corrected Bible text and canon law (ecclesiastical law) were prepared by Carolingian scholars under court auspices for dissemination throughout the kingdom. Although many may have come reluctantly under the Frankish yoke, the Carolingian realm knit together a great diversity of peoples in a remarkable way and laid the foundations of modern western Europe.

1 Frankish expansion: the first phase, 486–561

- Frankish territory at the accession of Clovis, 486
- Merovingian territory before the Battle of Vouillé, 507
- conquered following Battle of Vouillé
- acquired by 560
- Merovingian territory, 560
- area of Merovingian overlordship in Germany

1 The Franks under Clovis and his sons extended their kingdom from their homeland near the Rhine at remarkable speed (map above). Most of this came at the expense of Roman ambitions and barbarian rulers, notably Visigoths and Burgundians. By 560 the Franks were masters of the greater part of Gaul and had extensive tribute-paying regions in the east.

3 Francia in 587 (map above). The treaty of 587 was one of many agreements which divided the Frankish kingdom between the descendants of Clovis. Childebert's portion was in effect ruled by his mother, the Visigoth Brunhild, who dominated Frankish politics until she was executed in 613.

4 Francia in 768 (map above). The custom of partitioning the kingdom was continued by the Carolingians: on the death of Pippin III (768) his two sons divided their inheritance. The elder, Charlemagne, held most of the key area of Austrasia until Carloman died (771), when he inherited the whole.

Magyars, Saracens and Vikings in 9th and 10th century Europe

Three main groups – Magyars, Saracens and Vikings – launched raids on Europe in the 9th and 10th centuries, as well as being involved in trade. It was the Vikings who proved the most adaptable colonists. Settlements established by them in the north Atlantic and North Sea, Russia and the Mediterranean developed into strong independent states.

THE RELATIVELY EFFECTIVE RULE of the Carolingians in western Europe (see p. 118) and of the various kings in Britain gave some assurance of security from attacks both to religious communities and merchants. By the 8th century abbeys and markets were not fortified and the masonry from Roman defences was often used for other building work. The wealth accumulated in such places offered tempting bait to external raiders. They came from countries whose rulers and people were often also partners in trade, the objects of missionary activity and political overtures or attempts at control, and who interacted with the politics of the countries their countrymen raided by entering into political agreements with them or acting as mercenaries. In the 9th and 10th centuries western Europe suffered attacks in particular from bands of Saracens, Magyars and Vikings.

After the Muslim occupation of Sicily, begun in 827 (though conquest was not complete until 902), Saracen pirates, possibly mainly from Crete and the eastern Mediterranean, established temporary bases such as Bari and Taranto on the coast of southern Italy, and later in southern Gaul, from which they were able to attack centres in the western Mediterranean until ousted by Byzantine armies in the late 9th century. Corsica and Sardinia were frequently attacked and many monasteries and towns in central and southern Italy (including Rome itself) were pillaged.

The Magyars

The nomadic Magyars, who may have moved into the Hungarian Plain from the east in the last years of the 9th century, plundered the neighbouring areas: northern Italy, Germany and even France. Their skill as horsemen and their advantages of speed and surprise made opposition difficult. They also acted as mercenaries against the Moravians and the Bulgars. Major defeats were inflicted on east Frankish armies between 899 and 910, but thereafter the German rulers achieved important successes, culminating in the defeat of the Magyars at the Lechfeld in 955. In the east, the threat of Magyar raids was halted by a joint enterprise by the ruler of Kiev and the Byzantine emperor. A Magyar embassy to the German emperor Otto I in 973 marked the beginning of a more settled way of life for the Magyars. Missionary activities thereafter from Regensburg and Passau resulted in Stephen (977–1038), the first Christian king of Hungary, being given the right to set up the Hungarian church with its own bishoprics.

The Viking raids

Frankish expansion into Frisia and Saxony in the 8th century may have prompted defensive aggression on the part of the Danes. Franks and Danes were able to conclude various agreements in the first half of the 9th century, including the conversion to Christianity of a number of leading Danes and the settlement of Viking groups at strategic points to defend outlying regions of the Carolingian empire. However, raids on Lindisfarne in 793 and on the important trading emporium of Dorestad in 834 were the beginning of a grim record of attacks on both France and England until the end of the 9th century. Although the raids were no doubt described in exaggerated terms by survivors, they undoubtedly caused much misery and distress; for example the bishop of Nantes and all his clergy were murdered in 842. Increasingly effective defence (including buying time with tribute payments and the building of new fortifications) against the raids was mounted by the Frankish and English

2 Scandinavian colonies in Britain and France

- areas of Scandinavian settlement
- the Danelaw in England, c. 902
- Norman frontier at end of 10th century
- extent of earldom of Orkney, c. 1000
- ■ forts with "armies" 876–954
- ● trading centres

Shetland Is.

EARLDOM OF ORKNEY — Orkney Is.
CAITHNESS
SUTHERLAND
ROSS
MORAY

Atlantic Ocean

KINGDOM OF THE ISLES

SCOTLAND

North Sea

Derry

IRELAND   Isle of Man

Kells   Clonard
Clonmacnoise   Clonard
Clonfert   Dublin

Limerick

NORTHUMBRIA
York

FIVE BOROUGHS
877–942   Humber
Chester   Torksey   Lincoln
Derby   Stamford
Nottingham
MERCIA   Leicester   EAST ANGLIA   Norwich
878–917
Huntingdon   Thetford
Northampton   Cambridge   Ipswich
Bedford   Colchester
ENGLAND   Maldon
Chippenham   London
Thames

Waterford   Wexford
Cork

WALES   Pembroke

Carhampton

WESSEX   Winchester   Canterbury

English Channel

Bayeux   Rouen   FRANCIA
NORMANDY   Seine
Paris

2 The first Viking colonists were Norwegians who settled in Ireland and Scotland, whence they raided the coast of Britain. Other Norwegians settled in Iceland, Greenland and the Scottish islands. The Danes, who had tended to raid the rich lowlands of England and France, settled in East Anglia, the Midlands and north of the Humber from 876 onwards, leaving a permanent linguistic mark on eastern and northern areas (**map right**). In England, control of the area of Viking settlement – the "Danelaw" – was only finally secured by the kings of Wessex in the mid-10th century. In Scotland, the earldom of Orkney encompassed much of the highlands and islands by 1000 and it was only in the 15th century that Denmark finally ceded Orkney and Shetland to Scotland.

1 Viking, Magyar and Saracen Invasions
Saracen attacks
Magyar attacks
Viking routes
Viking bases
main Viking raids (with dates)
areas most affected by Saracen raiders (with dates)
areas most affected by Magyar raiders (with dates)
areas of Viking settlement:
Danish
Norwegian
Swedish
ICELAND
to Greenland 982
c.870
Faroe Is.
Shetland Is.
Orkney Is.
Atlantic Ocean
Hebrides
Iona
North Sea
NORWEGIANS
SWEDES
SCANDINAVIA
GÖTAR
DANES
Baltic Sea
Staraya Ladoga
Novgorod
Derry 856
Inishmurray
Dumbarton
Lindisfarne 793
Jarrow 794
IRELAND
Kells
Armagh
Isle of Man
BRITAIN
Clonmacnoise
Clonard
Dublin 838
York 866
Limerick
Wexford
Cork
Waterford
Nottingham
Chester 893
Derby
Lincoln
Leicester
Stamford
WALES
Northampton
Thetford
London
WESSEX
Winchester 860
Canterbury
FRISIA
Bremen
Hamburg 845
Dorestad 834
SAXONY (906–38)
Nijmegen 881
Ghent
KIEVAN RUSSIA
Kiev
Cologne
THURINGIA (908–33)
Aachen
Quentovic 820
Louvain 884
St-Lô 889
Arras
Cambrai
Prüm
Rouen 841
Clermont 864
St Malo 872
BRITTANY
Trier
Chartres
Rheims
BAVARIA (907–54)
937
Bavarian army destroyed by Magyars, 907
Le Mans 865
Paris 845, 885–6
799, 842, 891 Nantes
Orléans
SWABIA (909–54)
Regensburg
Noirmoutier 799
Angers
Tours
Passau
Poitiers 864
Lechfeld 955
926
954
Pressburg 907
FRANCE (GAUL)
Angoulême
Hungarian Plain
MAGYARS
Bordeaux
937
926
844
Santiago de Compostela 968
Gijón 844, 1013
859
Valance
Pavia
Toulouse
Nîmes 844
Arles 844
Luna 844
Narbonne 844
Pisa 844
Fraxinetum 890–973
Black Sea
859
CALIPHATE OF CÓRDOBA
Corsica
Rome 936
Constantinople 907, 944
Lisbon 844
ALGARVE 971
Bari 841–71
Agropoli 890
BYZANTINE EMPIRE
859
Balearic Is.
Taranto 840–80
Sardinia 1015
Otranto
Karmona (Córdoba)
Seville 844
Santa Severina c. 840–86
Mediterranean Sea
859
Sicily (occupied 827)
SARACENS (ARABS)
Tunis
Malta 824

rulers. The practice of ceding the Vikings territory in order to act as a buffer culminated in the granting of the county of Rouen in 911 to Rollo, which with hindsight can be recognized as the foundation of Normandy.

The Vikings were highly adaptable colonists as well as traders and raiders and their shipbuilding and seafaring prowess enabled them to journey far afield. The Danes settled in England as well as France. The Norse ventured to Ireland, Man, Scotland, the Orkneys, the Faroes, Iceland, Greenland and even as far as Newfoundland. The Swedes travelled down the great rivers of Russia and founded the kingdom of the Rus based at Kiev and Novgorod where they formed links with Byzantium.

1 No part of the Christian west was immune from either internal war or external attack in the 9th and 10th centuries **(map above)**. The Magyars traversed vast distances, but as they moved on quickly, the disruption they caused was short-lived. In contrast, Saracens and Vikings established bases in the west. The Saracens were expelled, but the Norwegians, Danes and Swedes were in time assimilated.

3 The settlement of Iceland by Norwegians began in about 870 and was completed in two generations **(map below)**. Later emigrants found limited opportunities there, but after the discovery of Greenland in the last years of the 10th century, some went on to create new settlements which survived for some five centuries. The Vikings later reached Newfoundland, but only temporary settlements have been found there and further south.

A carved wooden head (above) from the Oseberg cart (c. 800) depicts a fearsome Viking warrior. Viking success was in large part achieved not through superior organization or tactical skill, but depended on their greater mobility. They were able to launch lightning attacks on undefended coastal settlements and penetrate far inland in shallow boats or on horseback.

3 Viking voyages in the Atlantic from 870
Arctic Ocean
NORTH AMERICA
HELLULAND
GREENLAND
Western settlement 984
Eastern settlement 982
ICELAND 870–930
Faeroes 825
SCANDINAVIA
British Isles
MARKLAND
L'Anse aux Meadows
VINLAND (Newfoundland) 1000
Atlantic Ocean
Mediterranean Sea

Northern and eastern Europe

Stable political regimes in some northern and eastern European regions outside the former Roman empire emerged only in the period from 850 to 1050. Their conversion to Christianity created essential bonds with the rest of Latin Christendom, despite political tensions and enmities between them.

POLITICAL CONDITIONS WERE not as favourable to political consolidation in northern and eastern Europe as they were further south and west. In England the kings of Wessex were only gradually able to absorb the Scandinavian-controlled Danelaw and most settlers were apparently able to retain their land, giving a partly Scandinavian character to the customs and place-names of the region. The conquest of the Danelaw and an expanding economy paved the way for the unification of "England" and for the religious reforms introduced by Eadgar (959–75). Nonetheless England remained subject to Danish attacks, and these culminated in the reign of the Danish king, Cnut, who ruled Norway and Denmark as well as England and introduced many Danish and "Norman" connections into English politics. Emma of Normandy, descended from Vikings, married first Aethelred "the Unready" and then Cnut. It was her son by Aethelred, Edward the Confessor, who succeeded to the English throne

in 1042. Emma symbolizes the international sphere of politics at this time. In the wake of the Norman Conquest of England in 1066, links with France, Flanders and the Mediterranean were strengthened still further at the expense of those with the Scandinavian world.

Ireland, Scotland and Wales
Ireland at this time was characterized by political fragmentation. The Irish were rarely united and much of the period was punctuated by war between the various Irish and Viking dynasties, notably the northern and southern Uí Néill. Brian Boru became king of Munster in 976 and then made himself king of Ireland. But the Vikings of Ireland, Orkney, the Hebrides and Man together with the Leinstermen defeated Brian in 1014. His successors, concentrating on the possession of Dublin, still attempted to establish their rule over the whole country until defeated by the Norman invasion of the 12th century.

The Jelling stones (above) are both a symbol and a proof of the unity of Denmark and its official conversion to Christianity in the 10th century. The inscription reads "King Harald had this monument made in memory of Gorm his father and in memory of Thyre his mother. That Harald who won for himself all Denmark and Norway and made the Danes Christian." Harald died c. 986.

In Scotland, too, Scandinavian control hampered the consolidation of political power. Vikings settled in the western and southern parts of Scotland from the beginning of the 10th century, and different groups of Picts, Scots (originally from Ireland) and Norsemen formed many shifting alliances until a measure of stability and unity was achieved under the Scottish king Malcom II (1005–34). Relations with England fluctuated; there was frequent border warfare, and a firm boundary was fixed only in the 13th century. In Wales a similar process of consolidation took place: the dynasty of Rhodri Mawr established their rule over much of Gwynedd and Dyfed. Ultimately the instability of the conglomeration of Welsh kingdoms made them vulnerable to Norman attack.

Scandinavia
In Scandinavia itself, powerful kingdoms began to emerge out of the disarray of the Viking age. Most notable was the emergence of Denmark under three kings, Gorm, Harald and Sven. By the 10th century Denmark had become a powerful kingdom, and, under Cnut (1014–35), the centre of an Anglo-Scandinavian empire. Much of southern Norway was united under the rule of Harald Finehair after the battle of Hafrsfjord in the 890s, but after his death in the 930s Norway occasionally came under Danish lordship. Sweden, meanwhile, was united only at the end of the 11th century under the kings of Uppland. On the fringes of the Scandinavian world Iceland was, by 930, an independent commonwealth (without a king) while Greenland was colonized by Norwegians from about 985.

Eastern Europe
In eastern Europe, Moravia was attacked in 906 by Magyar invaders, but a new phase of political consolidation began shortly thereafter, probably in response to pressure from the Saxon kings Henry I and Otto I. Although the Slav peoples along the Elbe successfully resisted the Germans in the great Slav revolt of 983, they remained disunited and loosely

3 Poland under Bolesław Chrobry

- Polish territory from 960
- lands added by Bolesław Chrobry, 992–1025
- lands temporarily under Polish occupation
- Hungarian territory
- German territory
- ◉ bishopric
- ◉ archbishopric
- **1000** date of foundation of bishopric
- wasteland (forest and swamp)

3 After the unification of the tribes of Great (northern) Poland under Mieszko I, his son Bolesław Chrobry ("the Brave") attempted to carve out a larger kingdom (map left). Most of the gains were temporary and involved long debilitating wars on all frontiers; but Little Poland, centred on Cracow, was permanently acquired, and became the royal residence under Casimir I (1038–58).

Map labels: Baltic Sea · Gdańsk founded before 990 · Kołobrzeg 1000 · Wolin · POMERANIA (Polish c. 980–1033; thereafter independent) · Szczecin · KIEVAN RUSSIA · Havelberg 948–83 · Oder · Kruszwica · MASOVIA · Bug · Brandenburg 948–83 · Poznań 968 · Gniezno 1000 · Vistula · Magdeburg 968 · Elbe · POLAND · LUSATIA (Polish 1002–5, 1007–31) · Merseburg 968 · Bautzen · Wrocław 1000 founded 920 · (981–1018 Russian; 1018–33 Polish; 1033 Russian) · Zeitz 968 · Meissen 968 castle built 929 · SILESIA (to Poland 990–1038; to Bohemia 1038–50; 1054 Polish) · MEISSEN · Opole · LITTLE POLAND (incorporated, c. 992–9) · Libice · Prague 973 fortified c.890 · Cracow 1000 · BOHEMIA (Polish 1003–4) · Olomouc 975 · MORAVIA (to Poland 1003–20; to Bohemia 1020) · Regensburg 739 · BAVARIA · Danube · Esztergom 1001 · Visegrád capital of Hungary and seat of monarchy before Pest · HUNGARY

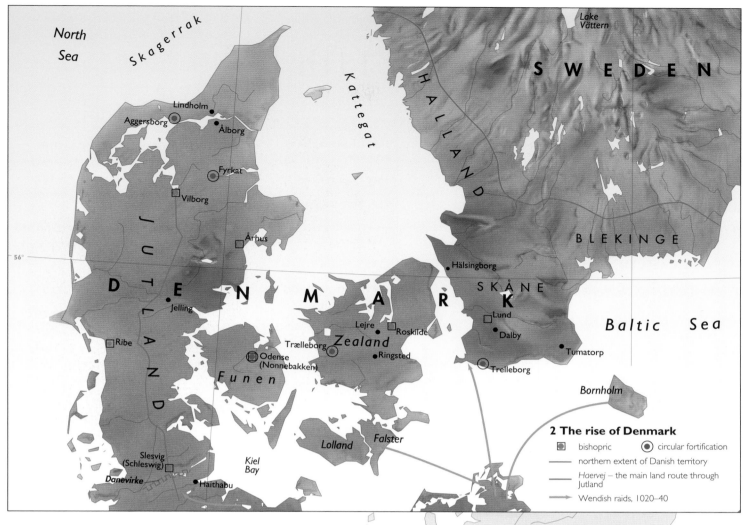

North Sea

Skagerrak

Kattegat

SWEDEN

HALLAND

BLEKINGE

Lindholm
Aggersborg
Ålborg
Fyrkat
Vilborg
Århus

JUTLAND

56°

DENMARK

Jelling

Ribe

SKÅNE

Hälsingborg

Lund
Dalby

Tumatorp

Lejre
Roskilde
Trælleborg
Zealand
Ringsted

Odense
(Nonnebakken)

Funen

Trelleborg

Baltic Sea

Bornholm

Slesvig
(Schleswig)

Kiel Bay

Lolland **Falster**

Danevirke
Haithabu

Lake Vättern

2 The rise of Denmark
◼ bishopric   ◉ circular fortification
— northern extent of Danish territory
— *Haervej* – the main land route through Jutland
→ Wendish raids, 1020–40

844–78 Rule of Rhodri Mawr in Wales

906 Destruction of Moravia by the Magyars

948 Three bishops appointed to sees in Denmark

954 Erik Bloodaxe, last Scandinavian king of York, killed

960–92 Mieszko of Poland expands territory

c. 986 Harald Bluetooth, who restored Danish overlordship in Scandinavia, dies

992–1025 Bolesław I forms kingdom of Poland

999 Revolt of Sitric Silkenbeard, Norse king of Dublin

1013 Sven Forkbeard, king of Denmark, attacks England and makes himself king

1019–54 Kievan Russia at height of its political influence under Jaroslav the Wise

1047 Harald Hardrada establishes control over Norway

organized. It was in Poland that a major Slav state arose: Mieszko I (960–92) united the tribes of northern Poland, and his son, Bolesław Chrobry (992–1025), extended control to the south. Meanwhile the Magyars, led by Duke Geisa (972–97) and his more famous son, King Stephen (997–1038), the first Christian king of Hungary, established their kingdom. Bohemia, caught between Germany and Poland, had also emerged as a political unit by the time of the Přemyslid prince Bolesław I (929–67). The creation of Bohemia, Poland and Hungary – by the Přemyslid, Piast and Arpád dynasties respectively – was based on agricultural development, suppression of tribal differences and independent tribal aristocracies, and on the organizing and civilizing influence of the Church. All three dynasties made use of western institutions and connections to strengthen their position, though a notable feature in eastern Europe in the succeeding centuries was the power of the nobility as distinct from that of the monarchs. Nonetheless Bohemia, Poland and Hungary did not lose their identities, although it was only in the 14th century that a restoration of royal power took place there.

937: IN THIS YEAR KING AETHELSTAN, LORD OF NOBLES, DISPENSER OF TREASURE TO MEN, AND HIS BROTHER ALSO, EDMUND AETHELING, WON BY THE SWORD'S EDGE UNDYING GLORY IN THE BATTLE AROUND BRUNANBURH ... THERE LAY MANY A MAN DESTROYED BY THE SPEARS, MANY A NORTHERN WARRIOR SHOT OVER HIS SHIELD AND LIKEWISE MANY A SCOT LAY WEARY, SATED WITH BATTLE.

1030: IN THIS YEAR KING OLAF WAS KILLED IN NORWAY BY HIS OWN PEOPLE AND WAS AFTERWARDS HOLY. AND PREVIOUSLY IN THIS YEAR THE BRAVE EARL HAKON DIED AT SEA.

from the *Anglo-Saxon Chronicle*

2 Denmark was the first Scandinavian kingdom to achieve full statehood in the Latin Christian tradition **(map above)**. Four kings were responsible: Gorm the Old (c. 940–c. 58), Harald Bluetooth (c. 958–c. 86), Sven Forkbeard (c. 986–c. 1014) and Cnut the Great (c. 1014–35). Harald was instrumental in persuading the Danes to accept Christianity, while politically he countered a German threat and brought Norway under his sway. Sven concentrated largely on campaigns in England from which he drew large amounts of tribute ("Danegeld"), while his son Cnut ruled an empire which stretched from northern Norway to the English Channel. In the 10th and 11th centuries a number of towns developed in Denmark, some on the basis of the earlier 8th- and 9th-century emporia such as Ribe and Haithabu. Also a remarkable series of fortifications was constructed – including at least part of the Danevirke (the fortified southern frontier) and the fortresses at Trælleborg, Odense, Fyrkat and Aggersborg.

1 By his death in 899, Alfred, who had styled himself king of the Anglo-Saxons, had successfully consolidated the kingdom of Wessex **(map right)**; was in effect the overlord of Mercia; reached a *modus vivendi* with the Danes in the Danelaw; and in 886 occupied London. His sons and grandsons, Edward the Elder (899–924), Aethelstan (924–39), Edmund (939–46) and Eadred (946–55) extended and consolidated the English kingdom. Edward established his rule over the entire area south of the Humber; and east of the Welsh and secured Mercia. His successors pushed north: the last Viking ruler of York, Erik Bloodaxe, fell in battle in 954.

ALBA (KINGDOM OF PICTS AND SCOTS)

Dumbarton
Edinburgh

LOTHIAN (added to Wessex by 954; ceded to Scots, 973)

STRATHCLYDE (submitted to English, 924–45)

IRISH KINGDOMS

Durham

KINGDOM OF YORK
York
Humber

Chester

GWYNEDD
POWYS
WEST MERCIA
DANISH MERCIA (FIVE BOROUGHS)
Nottingham

RHWNG GWY A HAFREN
SEISYLLWG
DYFED
GWENT
Worcester
Gloucester

EAST ANGLIA
Thetford
Ely
Cambridge

BRYCHEINIOG
MORGANNWG

London
Canterbury
KENT

WEST WALES
WESSEX
Winchester
Exeter

North Sea

English Channel

1 England after Alfred the Great, 899–1018
— extent of Danelaw, 886
— frontiers, 899
▨ Wessex and dependencies, 899
▨ Welsh principalities
▢ added to Wessex by 924
▨ added to Wessex by 954
— northern and western limits of England in 1018

Crusading in Europe from the 11th to the 15th century

A Crusade was a Christian war concerned with the recovery and defence of lost lands. For those taking part it was a means of salvation. Starting with the First Crusade in 1096–9, the crusaders altered the political balance in the eastern Mediterranean for many centuries. Christian holy war also remained a recurrent feature of northern European politics.

CHRISTIANS HAD MADE pilgrimages to the Holy Land since the 2nd century AD. The combination of religious tourism and spiritual inspiration offered by pilgrimage had greatly increased the number of visitors after the conversion of Constantine and the discovery by his mother, Helena, of the supposed True Cross in Jerusalem. Many new churches and monasteries were built in the Holy Land, often on newly identified holy sites of both Old and New Testament events. Jerusalem in particular held pride of place in the imagination and hearts of Christians everywhere, which not even its conquest by Arab forces in the 7th century could overturn. Indeed, access thereafter was far from denied and throughout the 8th, 9th and 10th centuries there are reports from travellers from Britain, France and Italy who prayed at the holy sites. A constant stream of souvenirs and holy relics, furthermore, reached the west and were treated with great reverence in churches across Europe. Allied to the importance of pilgrimage to the Holy Land were the missionary endeavours to convert pagans conducted in western Europe. Between the 6th and 11th centuries this saw the conversion of the English, the Frisians, Saxons, Slavs, Scandinavians, Bulgars and Rus by Irish,

Roman, English, Frankish, Saxon and Byzantine missionaries. Within the Christian church, moreover, there were intense bouts of eradication of heresy. Pilgrimage, the striving to achieve orthodoxy and the conversion of pagans, coupled with the religious piety and devotion of the laity, came together in the crusading movement of the central and later Middle Ages.

The movement was concerned not only with the recovery of the Holy Land from those who were regarded by the Christian church as "infidels". There were also crusades against the Albigensian heretics in southern France from 1208, the pagan Slavs in Livonia in the Baltic from the end of the 12th century and the Reconquista of Spain from the Arabs by the Catholic monarchs of northern Spain which became a national liberation movement. Even such European rulers as the Emperor Frederick II of Germany and King Beta of Aragon were the objects of crusades to defend the Catholic faith and liberty of the church against their rulers' alleged depredations.

The First Crusade

The crusading movement was precipitated by a plea from a Byzantine embassy to Pope Urban II in

1099 Crusaders capture Jerusalem	
1119 Templars founded	
1142 Krak des Chevaliers built	
1144 Edessa falls to Turks	
1146–8 Second Crusade	
1187 Saladin takes Jerusalem and Acre	
1189–91 Third Crusade	
1199 Livonian Crusade in Baltic	
1204 Fourth Crusade; sack of Constantinople	
1212 Muslims defeated at Las Navas de Tolosa	
1291 Fall of Acre	
1312 Templars suppressed	
1453 Constantinople falls to Turks	
1492 Granada captured by Christians	

3 Norman invasions and Crusader penetration encouraged western ambitions against Byzantium. Fostered by Venice, eager to destroy her main commercial rival, the Fourth Crusade **(map below)** sacked Constantinople, dismembered the Byzantine empire and established a short-lived Latin empire (1204–61).

BOHEMUND GAVE ORDERS SAYING "CHARGE AT TOP SPEED, LIKE A BRAVE MAN AND FIGHT VALIANTLY FOR GOD AND THE HOLY SEPULCHRE, FOR YOU KNOW IN TRUTH THAT THIS IS NO WAR OF THE FLESH, BUT OF THE SPIRIT. SO BE VERY BRAVE, AS BECOMES A CHAMPION OF CHRIST."

Anon. *Gesta Francorum*, VI

WE CONCEDE TO ALL FIGHTING IN THIS EXPEDITION [IN SPAIN] THE SAME REMISSION OF SINS WHICH WE HAVE GIVEN TO THE DEFENDERS OF THE EASTERN CHURCH.

Pope Calixtus II, 1123

1095 for help to defend the eastern church against the Turks who had overrun Asia Minor. In November of that year the Pope preached the First Crusade at the Council of Clermont. The enthusiasm for the call to wage Christian holy war was remarkable. Nobles and knights made considerable sacrifices which affected both themselves and their families in order to go on crusade, for it was a genuinely popular devotional activity. Many sold their patrimonies to raise money for the expeditions, though only a minority actually "took the Cross" and went to fight. Only a few noble families from France joined the First Crusade, though kings, notably Richard I (the Lionheart) of England and Louis IX of France, were involved in later expeditions to the east.

The crusaders

Crusaders made a public, formal vow to join a military expedition in response to an appeal by the Pope on Christ's behalf. It was a legal obligation and crusaders became subject to the jurisdiction of the ecclesiastical courts. In return special privileges were granted to a crusader including the protection of their families' interests and assets while they were absent, and major spiritual privileges in the form of Indulgences to reduce the time spent in purgatory atoning for sins on earth. Closely associated with the crusading movement were the military orders, such as the Templars and Hospitallers, whose members had made a permanent commitment to wage holy war. Both the Templars and Hospitallers had their headquarters in Jerusalem, but soon acquired extensive properties in the west. The rulers of the crusader states, frequently starved of manpower, entrusted great strongholds and large stretches of land to the military orders and by the 13th century they formed the backbone of the military strength of the crusading states.

The later Crusades

The First Crusade led to the foundation of the Latin kingdom of Jerusalem following the crusaders' capture of Antioch and Jerusalem in 1098 and 1099 respectively. The focus of subsequent expeditions was the defence, ultimately unsuccessful, of these gains against Muslim attack. The Second Crusade (1146–8) was inspired by the loss of the city of Edessa to al-Din Zengi, the Muslim ruler of Aleppo, while the Third Crusade (1189–91) was launched as a response to the conquest by Saladin of most of the crusader territories in the Levant, including the catastrophic loss of Jerusalem. Although the city

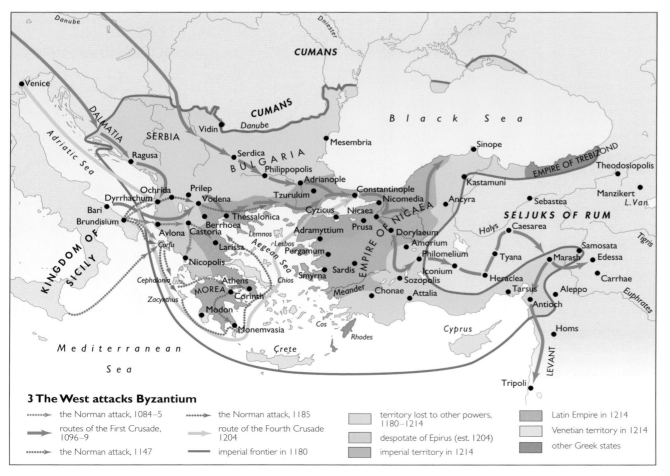

3 The West attacks Byzantium

┄┄┄► the Norman attack, 1084–5	┄┄┄► the Norman attack, 1185
──► routes of the First Crusade, 1096–9	──► route of the Fourth Crusade 1204
┄┄┄► the Norman attack, 1147	── imperial frontier in 1180

territory lost to other powers, 1180–1214	Latin Empire in 1214
despotate of Epirus (est. 1204)	Venetian territory in 1214
imperial territory in 1214	other Greek states

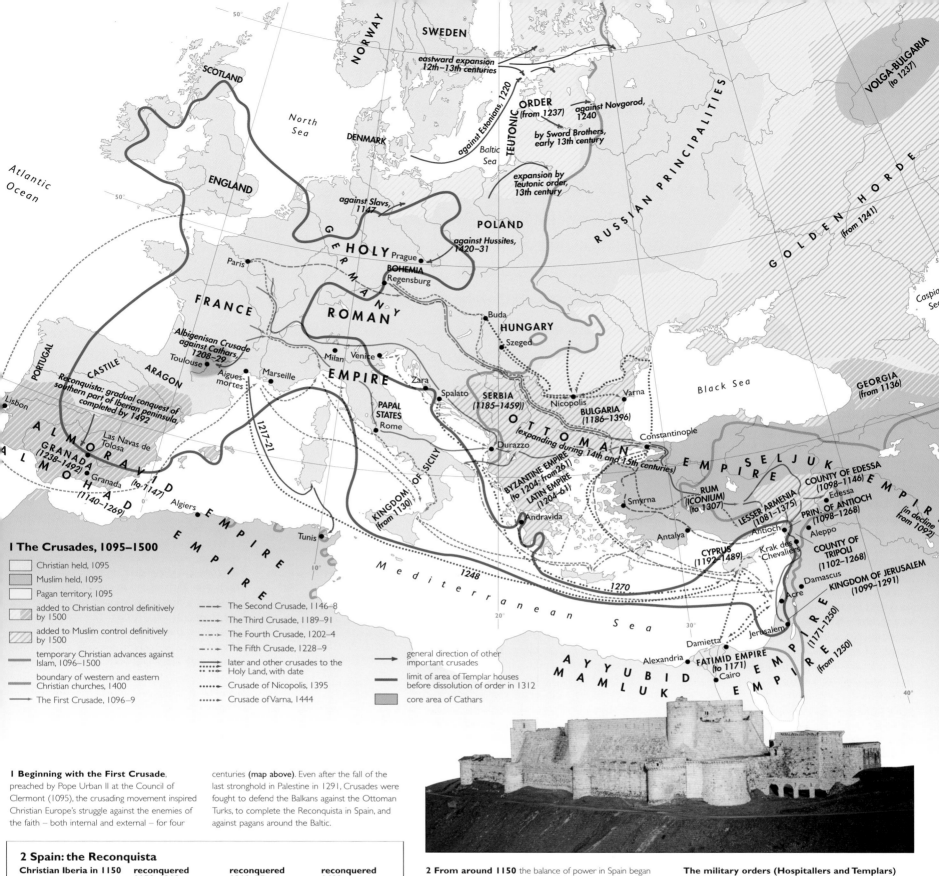

1 The Crusades, 1095–1500

- ☐ Christian held, 1095
- ▨ Muslim held, 1095
- ☐ Pagan territory, 1095
- ▨ added to Christian control definitively by 1500
- ▨ added to Muslim control definitively by 1500
- temporary Christian advances against Islam, 1096–1500
- ---- boundary of western and eastern Christian churches, 1400
- → The First Crusade, 1096–9
- --- The Second Crusade, 1146–8
- ······ The Third Crusade, 1189–91
- ·─·─ The Fourth Crusade, 1202–4
- ─··─ The Fifth Crusade, 1228–9
- ── later and other crusades to the Holy Land, with date
- ······ Crusade of Nicopolis, 1395
- ······ Crusade of Varna, 1444
- → general direction of other important crusades
- ── limit of area of Templar houses before dissolution of order in 1312
- ▨ core area of Cathars

1 Beginning with the First Crusade, preached by Pope Urban II at the Council of Clermont (1095), the crusading movement inspired Christian Europe's struggle against the enemies of the faith – both internal and external – for four centuries (map above). Even after the fall of the last stronghold in Palestine in 1291, Crusades were fought to defend the Balkans against the Ottoman Turks, to complete the Reconquista in Spain, and against pagans around the Baltic.

2 From around 1150 the balance of power in Spain began to favour the Christian states. In the 1140s Alfonso VII of Léon expanded his power to the Tagus and in 1147 the Portuguese took Lisbon, aided by a fleet on its way to the Second Crusade. The Reconquista gathered pace in the 13th century (map left). In 1212 Alfonso VIII of Castile heavily defeated Caliph al-Nasir at Las Navas de Tolosa. The subsequent collapse of the Almohad empire helped the Christians overrun most of southern Spain by 1275, including Córdoba in 1235 and Seville in 1248.

The military orders (Hospitallers and Templars) held a series of important strongholds in the Holy Land, commanding strategic locations such as ports, valleys and passes. Perhaps the most impressive was the Hospitaller castle of Krak des Chevaliers (above). Its imposing fortifications were strengthened at the beginning of the 13th century, but in the end, isolated by the Mamluks' occupation of the surrounding territories, the castle surrendered to them in 1271 after a siege of barely more than a month.

2 Spain: the Reconquista

Christian Iberia in 1150
- ▨ León and Castile
- ▨ Aragon
- ▨ Portugal
- ☐ Navarre

reconquered 1150–1212
- ▨ by Castile
- ▨ by Aragon
- ▨ by Portugal

reconquered 1212–75
- ☐ by Castile
- ☐ by Aragon
- ☐ by Portugal

reconquered 1492
- ☐ by Castile and Aragon

was not recovered, the crusaders reoccupied most of the coastal ports, so ensuring the survival of the crusader states.

In Spain the Reconquista or recovery of land from the Muslims was given impetus by crusading ideals. In contrast to the Crusades to the east this was a local affair, with little help received from outside. Yet in Spain, too, military orders such as Calatrava (from 1158) and Santiago (from 1170) contributed vitally to the war against Islam. In 1212 the armies of Castile, Navarre and Aragon crushed the Muslim army at Las Navas de Tolosa, winning the most important victory of the whole Reconquista. In 1492 Christian armies took Granada, the last remaining Muslim stronghold in Spain.

The crusading movement was seriously compromised in 1204 by the bloodshed of the capture of Constantinople by an army of Latin Christians, who diverged from a planned campaign in Palestine. They dismembered the Byzantine empire and, together with the Genoese and Venetians, set up Latin states around the Aegean. The crusading ideal, however, lived on. Further Crusades targeted Egypt and the Levant. The crusader states in the east survived until the late 13th century, with the loss of the last stronghold at Acre in 1291. Even then further Crusades were still mounted against the Muslims as late as 1444 (the Crusade of Varna), and the language of crusading was employed to describe the struggle against the Ottoman Turks and Spanish incursions into north Africa in the 16th century. Crusades were launched against heretics, such as the Hussites in Bohemia (1420–31) and by the Teutonic Knights in the Baltic against pagan Prussians from 1309 (see p. 160).

The Byzantine empire

The Roman empire in the east continued – as Byzantium – long after the political transformation of the west by the barbarian successor states. Its distinctive, Greek-speaking, Christian and culturally diverse civilization dominated the east Mediterranean, exerting a crucial cultural influence on western Europe despite the steady loss of territory to the Turks.

4 Byzantium and the Slavs

- northern Imperial frontier, c. 628
- northern Imperial frontier, c. 1030
- Slavs within Byzantine borders
- Bulgarian frontier, c. 814
- first Bulgarian empire, 893–1018
- second Bulgarian empire, c. 1200
- Serbia, c. 1217
- other areas within empire

ALTHOUGH **HERACLIUS** (610–41) had ended the struggle with the Sasanid rulers of Persia, for so long Rome's most formidable rival, before his death the southern and eastern frontiers of the empire came under attack from the forces of Islam. Constantinople withstood two Arab sieges, in 674–8 and again in 717–8. At the same time the Bulgars settled in the Balkans with armed outposts less than 100km (60 miles) from Constantinople itself.

Renewal and retreat

Within Byzantium major disruption to society between 726 and 843 was caused by the controversy over the banning of Christian images, known as iconoclasm. Not long after images in churches were restored, a fresh and vigorous Macedonian dynasty of emperors embarked on a new era of expansion. Between 863, when a strong force of Arabs was annihilated at Poson, on the Halys river in Anatolia, and the death of the great warrior-emperor Basil II (976–1025), a series of dramatic victories pushed back the frontiers, often close to where they had been in the heyday of Rome. In the southeast the Arabs at one stage (976) retreated to the very gates of Jerusalem; the Rus were held and routed at Silistra on the Danube (971); and

Bulgaria, after long bitter campaigning, became a group of Byzantine provinces. But the new frontiers, exhaustingly won, proved indefensible, especially as the previously invincible Byzantine armed forces now found themselves starved of funds by a civilian administration fearful of a military coup. In 1071, the Byzantine army was heavily defeated by Seljuk Turks at the battle of Manzikert (see p. 150). The Turks then established a permanent occupation of the Anatolian plateau. In the same year, the empire's last Italian possession fell to the Normans.

The Comeneni and the Crusades

Paradoxically, the 11th and 12th centuries proved to be among the most fertile in Byzantine history in artistic and theological terms. Yet for all their genius, the emperors Alexius I (1081–1118), John II (1118–43) and Manuel I (1143–80) ultimately proved unable to recover much of the vast territory that had been lost, though they succeeded by diplomatic means in maintaining a strong balance of the various interests between themselves and their neighbours. The First Crusade (1096–9) had certainly created serious difficulties for the Byzantine rulers while the ferocious assault of the Christian Latin

4 By 600, Slavic peoples had settled most of the Balkans. Though they were driven back, by the 10th century the first Bulgarian empire became a serious rival to Byzantium (**map above**). Symeon of Bulgaria (d. 927) brought effective rule to Bulgaria: in 904 Byzantium recognized his possession of Thrace and Macedonia. A Byzantine counter-offensive began in 1001. Basil II (976–1025) annexed Bulgaria in 1018 after bitter campaigning. In 1180 a revolt against Byzantine rule led to the rise of a new Bulgarian empire based at Trnovo. Serbia under Stefan Nemanja (1168–96) also carved out a large independent territory. The introduction of Orthodox Christianity helped pacify Slav peoples, and took strong root despite the conflicts.

Crusaders in 1204 inflicted great damage on both Constantinople and the empire.

Byzantium's strength, apart from its religious cohesion, was two-fold: the *themes* (see map 3) with their independent freeholding peasantry, ready both to farm and to defend its land; and an army and a navy often manned by native officers and troops. By the 11th and 12th centuries, mercenaries – themselves often Seljuk, Muslim or Norman – came to form the bulk of the armed forces, and the important civilian posts in the

1 Byzantine greatness and decline

— Imperial frontier, c. 628	**general territorial losses**
— Imperial frontier, c. 1030	to Arabs, 636–41
— Imperial frontier, c. 1143	to Arabs after 641
— Imperial frontier, 1328	to Seljuk Turks from 1065
	Sultanate of Rum from 1071

temporary reconquests: | **special areas:**

- Africa, 685–710 — Exarchate of Ravenna to Lombards, 751
- Syria, 975–6 — Exarchate of Africa to Arabs from 670
- Sicily, 1038–43 — Catapanate of Italy to Normans from
- Ani, 1054
- Edessa, 1052
- Rum, c. 1118

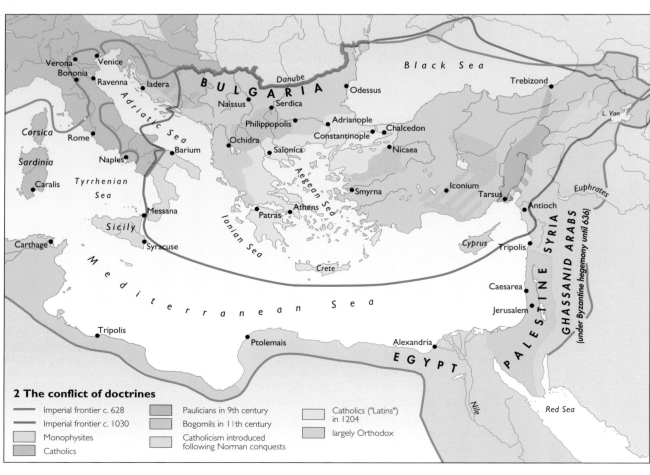

2 The conflict of doctrines

— Imperial frontier c. 628	Paulicians in 9th century	Catholics ("Latins") in 1204
— Imperial frontier c. 1030	Bogomils in 11th century	largely Orthodox
Monophysites	Catholicism introduced following Norman conquests	
Catholics		

2 Doctrinal disputes helped weaken central imperial control (**map left**). The areas where Monophysitism (a heterodox view of the nature of Christ) was strong were conquered by the Arabs in the 7th century. Paulicians and Bogomils (9th–10th centuries) preached varieties of the dualistic heresy of Manichaeism (holding there to be a good god and an evil one) and their adherents occupied key areas of Asia Minor and the Balkans. A large part of the empire came under Catholic "Latin" control after 1204 but this was the faith of the new rulers, not of the people.

civilian bureaucracy fell more and more under the control of a few rich dynasties. These owed much of their new wealth and power to the *pronoia* system, under which key state functions, including tax collection, were handed over to large local landowners – originally for their lifetime, but increasingly on a hereditary basis. In religious matters, Rome and Constantinople moved even further apart. There had been tension, if not actual schism, between the Roman and Orthodox churches since 1054 (*see* p. 114).

The last centuries

Both Seljuks and Normans resumed full-scale frontier aggression in the 1170s and many Byzantine provinces were lost. The immediate beneficiary of the Fourth Crusade (1204) was the rising power of Venice, whose fleets had carried the Crusaders and who established colonies on the Aegean islands and Crete. A Latin empire was created with many principalities in Thessaly, Athens and Achaia and Greek enclaves at Nicaea and Epirus. The Greeks still constituted a majority within the truncated empire and in 1261, aided by Genoa, a rival of Venice, they drove out the westerners. But the Greek empire was only a shadow of the Byzantium of the past and was unable to prevent the steady advance of the Ottoman empire into Anatolia, Thrace, Macedonia and Bulgaria in the 14th century and the conquest of Constantinople itself by Mehmet the Conqueror in 1453.

1 In 641 the old Roman frontiers which Heraclius had largely inherited were everywhere under attack. They retreated, almost without interruption, until the mid-9th century **(map below)**, but then re-expanded, reaching their greatest extent around 1030. The final boundary shows them in 1328, at the accession of the emperor Andronicus III.

628 Heraclius defeats Persians at Nineveh

726 Leo III declares all images to be idols; images finally restored in 843

976–1025 Reign of Basil II, the Bulgar slayer

1054 Schism between Orthodox and Catholic churches

1071 Seljuk Turks defeat Byzantines at Manzikert

1096–9 First Crusade

1204 Constantinople sacked by Fourth Crusade; Latin empire established

1261 Greek empire re-established

1438–9 Council of Florence; attempt to unify eastern and western churches

1453 Fall of Constantinople

3 The themes were administrative districts in which peasants were granted farms in exchange for service in the local army (map above right). They prevented Arab settlement, although they could not stop raids.

The emperor Constantine IV Pogonatus and his brothers hand privileges to the Ravenna church of San Apollinare in Classe and to archbishop Mauro **(right)**. During his reign Constantinople withstood a four year siege by Arab armies (674–8), although much of the Balkans was overrun by Slav tribes and the Bulgars. He summoned the sixth ecumenical Council of Constantinople (680–1) which condemned Monothelitism.

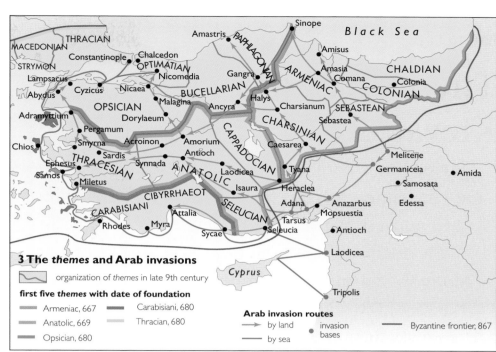

3 The *themes* and Arab invasions

organization of *themes* in late 9th century

first five *themes* with date of foundation
- Armeniac, 667
- Carabisiani, 680
- Anatolic, 669
- Thracian, 680
- Opsician, 680

Arab invasion routes
→ by land
— by sea
invasion bases
— Byzantine frontier, 867

The first Russian state: Kievan Russia

Russia first emerged under the Vikings (or Rus) in the 9th century. Steppes, forests and rivers determined the course of the history of Kievan Rus. It received Christianity from Byzantium, was attacked by Mongols and split into various principalities. When the Kievan Rus lost their southern steppe territory to nomads they resumed eastward colonization.

THE RIVERS BETWEEN the Baltic and the Black Sea assumed great importance from the 9th century with the coming of the Vikings or Rus, who established, dominated and exploited trade routes along these rivers and adjoining lands. The polity the Rus established ran north and south across forests and steppes; these barriers ultimately proved too strong for a river-based north–south alignment to survive. The main waterway route established ran from the Gulf of Finland up the river Neva, the river Volkhov and thence by portages to the Dnieper and on across the Black Sea to Byzantium. As Viking control spread south, Novgorod, Smolensk and Kiev (in 882) became headquarters. Kiev grew rapidly from the early 10th century, and strong links developed with Byzantium, its chief trading partner. It was from Byzantium that Christianity was introduced to Kiev during the reign of Vladimir Svyatoslavich (980–1015).

Expansion of Kievan Rus

At the time of the Viking incursions the Khazars and the Magyars held the steppes. The Rus succeeded in dominating the lands of the lower Prut, Dniester and Bug, and in controlling the upper Dnieper route to the Black Sea and thence to Byzantium. Grand Prince Svyatoslav (c. 962–72) determined to strengthen and expand Rus power by crushing the relatively peaceful Khazars. But by destroying them, he opened the way to the fierce Pechenegs (Turkic nomads) who dominated the south Russian steppes until displaced by the equally warlike Polovtsy in the 12th century. Vladimir I had some defensive success against the Pechenegs,

THE CHUDS, THE SLAVS, THE KRIVICHIANS AND THE VES THEN SAID TO THE PEOPLE OF THE RUS, "OUR LAND IS GREAT AND RICH, BUT THERE IS NO ORDER IN IT. COME TO RULE AND REIGN OVER US."

Russian Primary Chronicle, 1113

I HAVE NEVER SEEN MORE PERFECT PHYSICAL SPECIMENS, TALL AS DATE PALMS, BLOND AND RUDDY. EACH MAN HAS AN AXE, A SWORD AND A KNIFE, AND KEEPS THEM BY HIM AT ALL TIMES ... THEY ARE THE FILTHIEST OF GOD'S CREATURES.

Ibn Fadlan, of Rus traders at Itil, 922

constructing a steppe-frontier south of Kiev, and the Rus princes held the initiative over the nomads during most of the 11th and first half of the 12th centuries.

The southern Rus lands, relatively secure and prosperous, became the bone of contention between rival branches of Vladimir's offspring and from the mid-12th century disputes proliferated. But the resulting multiplication of princely seats opened up outlying areas to Christianity and commerce. Uniquely, Novgorod's oligarchy was powerful enough to "hire and fire" princes and to organize the collection of tribute in the form of furs from as far north as the Arctic Ocean.

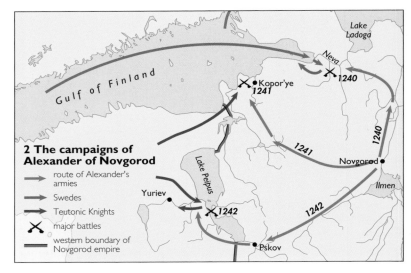

2 The campaigns of Alexander of Novgorod

→ route of Alexander's armies
→ Swedes
→ Teutonic Knights
✕ major battles
━━ western boundary of Novgorod empire

2 An attempt by the Swedes and Germans in 1240 to drive Russia from the Baltic was frustrated by Prince Alexander of Novgorod (map above). His decisive victory on the Neva earned him the title "Nevsky". Two years later he defeated the Teutonic Knights at Lake Peipus, thus effectively stopping Swedish and German attempts at eastward expansion.

3 The first Russian state was established by the Vikings with the Dnieper as its axis (map right). It lay athwart the northern forest and the southern steppe. Kiev was a natural capital.

3 Vegetation belts and early migrations

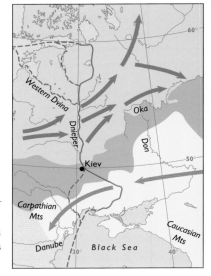

☐ forest belt with marshes
☐ wooded steppe
☐ open steppe
— Viking route
┄┄ associated waterway trade route
→ movement of nomadic peoples
→ early movements of Russians and other East Slavs

750 Settlement at Staraya Ladoga

862 Vikings seize Kiev

882 Oleg unites Novgorod and Kiev

922 Ibn Fadlan's visit to the middle Volga

941 Rus attack on Constantinople

after 987 Vladimir of Kiev converts to Christianity

1019–54 Reign of Iaroslav the Wise

1041 Expedition of Ingvar the Widefarer

1237–8 Mongols attack Vladimir-Suzdal

1240 Mongols sack Kiev

1240 Alexander defeats Swedes at River Neva

4 Until 1236, northern Russia was relatively immune from the steppe nomads' raids, and its cities prospered. But in the winter of 1237–8, the Mongols struck north into the forest and subjugated its princes (map left). An exploratory raid in 1221, and a larger incursion which defeated a combined Russian and Polovtsy force at the Kalka river in 1223 was followed by the massive invasion of 1237.

However, in the early 13th century, Novgorod increasingly came under the sway of the princes of Vladimir-Suzdal, who were emerging as the dominant Rus princes. On the eve of the Mongol attack of 1237, Vladimir-Suzdal was about to challenge the Volgar Bulgars whose stranglehold on the middle Volga obstructed further Russian expansion eastward. Nizhniy Novgorod was built as a first move in this campaign.

The Mongol invasions

The Mongols, led by Khan Batu, attacked the middle and upper Volga regions in 1237–8. They displaced the Polovtsy who fled to Hungary where they settled between the Tisza and the Danube rivers and came to be known as Kuns. That winter, when the protective rivers were frozen, the Mongols overcame the Volga Bulgars and set upon Vladimir-Suzdal, destroying its wealthy towns. Only the approach of spring saved Novgorod, as the invaders dared not be caught by the thaw among its surrounding marshes. In 1239 it was the turn of the southern principalities of the Rus. Kiev itself was sacked in 1240. Novgorod escaped the Mongol fury but was threatened by incessant attacks from Swedes and Germans in the Baltic region. Its prince, Alexander Nevsky, beat the Swedes decisively on the River Neva (1240) and the Teutonic Knights on the ice of Lake Peipus (1242).

The Mongols established the Kipchak Khanate or Golden Horde which came to control the lucrative trade routes between central Asia and the Black Sea. Much of western Rus, however, came under Lithuanian or Polish rule in the 14th century. At first based in Kiev, the metropolitan of the Orthodox church moved to Moscow in the early 14th century. This lent prestige to the princes of Moscow and contributed to Moscow's emergence as the predominant Rus polity in the northeast.

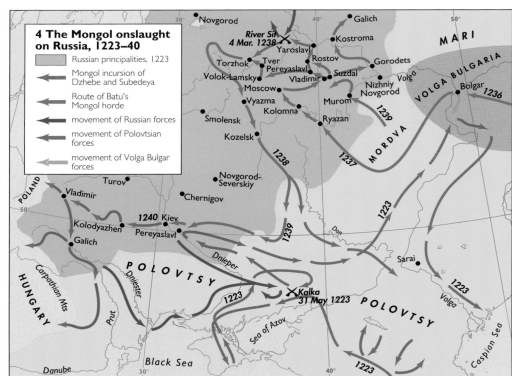

4 The Mongol onslaught on Russia, 1223–40

☐ Russian principalities, 1223
← Mongol incursion of Dzhebe and Subedeya
← Route of Batu's Mongol horde
← movement of Russian forces
← movement of Polovtsian forces
← movement of Volga Bulgar forces

A scene from **Novgorod's** victory over Suzdal in 1169 (**left**). Novgorod was the capital of the Rus until Oleg moved his capital to Kiev in 882. In 1019 Iaroslav I granted Novgorod a charter of self-government, and thereafter the town elected its own prince. Grown rich on the trade in furs, Novgorod became pre-eminent in northern Russia. During the 12th century it came into conflict with the growing power of Vladimir-Suzdal to the south. However, Novgorod defeated Vladimir-Suzdal in 1169 and 1216. It avoided the Mongol destruction and defeated the Germans and Swedes in 1240–2. A struggle for supremacy with Moscow in the 14th and 15th centuries saw the eclipse of Novgorod.

1 In 1054 there was still a unified Russian state, but by the early 13th century it had disintegrated (**map below**). Southern centres, such as Kiev, were weakened by nomadic attack, while northern towns, such as Novgorod, Vladimir and Moscow, exploited their positions on river trade routes in the security of the forest. Novgorod established a vast fur-trading empire stretching to the Arctic and the Urals.

I Kievan Russia, 964–1242

	Kievan Russia, 1054
Yatvagi	tribes of the East Slavs
MARI	other peoples
→	movements of steppe nomads in the 11th century
➤	campaigns of Svyatoslav, 964–71
- - -	waterway trade routes
∿∿∿	defensive works built against nomads
♛	Russian principalities, c.1200
➤	Prince Igor Svyatoslav's campaign against Polovtsy, 1185

Arctic Ocean

White Sea

SAMOYED

Pinega

Mezen

Northern Dvina

Onega

KARELA

CHUD

PERM

YUGRA

Ural Mts

Vychegda

Pechora

L. Onega

N O V G O R O D   E M P I R E

VYATKA TERRITORY

L. Ladoga

Beloozero

Sukhona

Gulf of Finland

Baltic Sea

Staraya Ladoga

Neva

Yes

Kama

ESTS

Vod

Volkhov

Galich

M A R I

Ilmen

Yaroslavl

Kostroma

L. Peipus

Yuriev

Slavs

Novgorod

L. Ilmen

Rostov

Merya

Gulf of Riga

Pskov

Izborsk

Torzhok

Tver

VLADIMIR -SUZDAL

Nizhniy Novgorod

ORDER

Riga

Kukeynoys

Toropets

Pereyaslavl

Dmitrov

KURS

LIVONIAN

Western Dvina

Gertsike

Polochanye

Lovat

K r i v i c h i

Moscow

Suzdal

Vladimir

Klyazma

ZHMUD

Polotsk

SMOLENSK

Golyad

Moskva

Murom

966

Bilyar

TEUTONIC ORDER

Vitebsk

Smolensk

Oka

Kolomna

Muroma

Bolgar

LITVA

POLOTSK

Orsha

Kopys

Ryazan

Suvar

VOLGA BULGARIA

Gorodno

Minsk

Koselsk

Meshchera

Yatvagi

Nesvizh

Klechesk

Vyatichi

MUROM -RYAZAN

MORDVA

Berestye

Drogochin

TUROV -PINSK

Radimichi

Bryansk

CHERNIGOV

Desna

Karachev

Novosil

Pinsk

Turov

Rechitsa

1024

Listen

Ural

VLADIMIR- VOLYNSK

Volynyane

Drevlyane

Lyubech

Novgorod-Severskiy

Kursk

Kholm

Vruchy

NOVGOROD -SEVERSK

Vladimir

Cherven

Korosten

Chernigov

Rylsk

Belz

1036

Gorodets

KIEV

Kiev

Severyane

Peremyshl

Polyane

Rodiya

PEREYASLAV

Terebovl

Ros

Pereyaslavl

Donets

Galich

Poltava

GALICH

Kamenets

Kolomyya

White Khorvaty

Tivertsy

PECHENEGS

P O L O V T S Y (in 1200)

Donets

Don

TORKI

966

POLOVTSY (in 1054)

HUNGARIAN KINGDOM

Peresechen

Prut

Dniester

K H A Z A R S

965

965

Sarkel

Volga

SAKSINY

Belgorod

Dnieper

Bug

Oleshe

Kuma

Carpathian Mts

Pereslavets

Itil

Dorostol

971

Sea of Azov

Sugdeya

Tmutarakan

966-7

Caspian Sea

Danube

Khersones (Korsun)

KASOGI

YASI

Kuban

Terek

BULGARIA

970

Black Sea

The German empire and the Papacy

The right to allocate the Imperial title, to consecrate kings and nominate new bishops or the Pope was vital in medieval Europe. Individual German emperors or popes attempted to assert either Imperial or Papal prerogatives. Popes ultimately sought to promote the authority of the bishops, while the Emperors' priority was to rule their vast territories.

FOR ALL THEIR DIFFERENCES, the separate Frankish kingdoms created between 840 and 843 were nonetheless bound together by many cultural, religious and kinship ties, as well as by the retention of the Imperial title in the Carolingian family. In 911, however, the Carolingians were replaced in the East Frankish (German) kingdom first by the Franconian noble Conrad and then by a member of the Saxon Liudolfing family, Henry I (911–36). Henry I's son, Otto I (936–73), consolidated his position, extended his influence over the German duchies and into Italy and defeated the Magyars. His Imperial coronation in 962 was the symbol of his aspirations and the southern and Italian orientation of his policies.

Imperial government

Government in the German empire was intensely personal with the king constantly on the move with his court. Only 13th-century Sicily possessed a centralized administrative system. The Ottonians stayed in their royal residences, supplied by the produce of their estates, as well as at royal convents, presided over by female members of the royal house. Bishops, notably those from the reformed monastic houses of Gorze in Lorraine, played a major role in government. The rulers themselves were devoted supporters of the church and were behind many of the missionary efforts and founding of new bishoprics, where Christianization and political expansion went hand in hand. It was the royal women, many of whom became abbesses, on the other hand, who appear, together with the bishops, to have done most to patronize culture and learning. The Salian and Staufen emperors continued these traditions.

The Papacy and the empire

The connection forged between Church reformers and the Papacy inaugurated a long dispute between the Emperors and the popes over who had the authority to appoint bishops or depose kings (the Investiture controversy). The conflict came to a head under Pope Gregory VII (1073–85). Gregory excommunicated and

911 Death of Louis, last Carolingian king of east Frankish kingdom

932 Election of Otto I

962 Otto I crowned emperor in Rome

1076 Pope Gregory VII excommunicates Emperor Henry IV

1095 Pope Urban II preaches the First Crusade

1122 Concordat of Worms concludes Investiture controversy

1197 Death of Emperor Henry VI

1215 Lateran Council on doctrine and church reform

1305 Pope takes up residence in Avignon – the "Babylonian captivity"

HENRY, KING NOT BY USURPATION BUT BY THE PIOUS ORDINATION OF GOD, TO HILDEBRAND, NOT NOW POPE, BUT FALSE MONK. OUR LORD, JESUS CHRIST, HAS CALLED US TO THE KINGSHIP, BUT HAS NOT CALLED YOU TO THE PRIESTHOOD. FOR YOU HAVE RISEN BY THESE STEPS: NAMELY, BY CUNNING, WHICH THE MONASTIC PROFESSION ABHORS, TO MONEY; BY MONEY TO FAVOUR; BY FAVOUR TO THE SWORD. BY THE SWORD YOU HAVE COME TO THE THRONE OF PEACE AND FROM THE THRONE OF PEACE YOU HAVE DESTROYED THE PEACE.

Letter of Emperor Henry IV to Pope Gregory VII, 1076

2 Otto I established a firm grip on the East Frankish lands (**map below left**). After the ducal revolts of 938–9 he was able to exercise power even in the more prosperous south and west. Magyar raids were halted. The drive eastward against the Slavs was normally left to the margraves, while Otto himself ranged more widely.

3 Monastic reform movements (**map below**), designed to promote the Rule of Benedict as *the* guide to the monastic life, built on the reforming zeal of the Carolingian period and gathered strength in the later 10th century, mainly in eastern France, Lorraine and Flanders. The principal centres were Cluny, Brogne and Gorze; their influence extended into Germany, Spain and England.

deposed the emperor Henry IV in 1076, forced him to perform public penance at Canossa, and allied with the Emperor's enemies – the Normans of southern Italy, the recalcitrant German nobility, and a chain of states around the periphery which feared German power. Although Gregory failed in his immediate objectives, the launching of the First Crusade (see p. 124) by Pope Urban II (1088–99) testified to the success of the claims for papal authority. The Investiture dispute was settled in 1122 by the Concordat of Worms when the emperor granted canonical election and the free consecration of bishops.

The political involvement of the Papacy in the struggle for the control of Italy became clear when Pope Alexander III (1154–81) allied with the Lombard League to resist the attempts of Frederick I (1152–90) to restore German Imperial authority in Italy. The issue was settled by a compromise but the Papacy failed to prevent the Hohenstaufen from acquiring the Norman Kingdom of Sicily in 1194.

2 The East Frankish kingdom in the reign of Otto I
- ▲ royal mint under Otto I
- → Otto's main campaigns
- ⚕ new bishopric with date of foundation
- ♀ bishopric destroyed in Slav rising of 983
- ☩ archbishopric
- o known to have been visited more than once by Henry I
- → main Magyar raids
- MILIZI Slav tribes
- —— East Frankish kingdom, c. 950

3 Monastic reform
- → Cluny; main influence c. 950–c. 1050
- → Dijon and Marseilles (Cluny-derived); main influence 1000 onwards
- → Lorraine reforms (Brogne and Gorze); main influence 10th and early 11th century
- → Hirsau, Siegburg and St Blasien; from c. 1060, these Cluny-derived influences spread rapidly in Germany

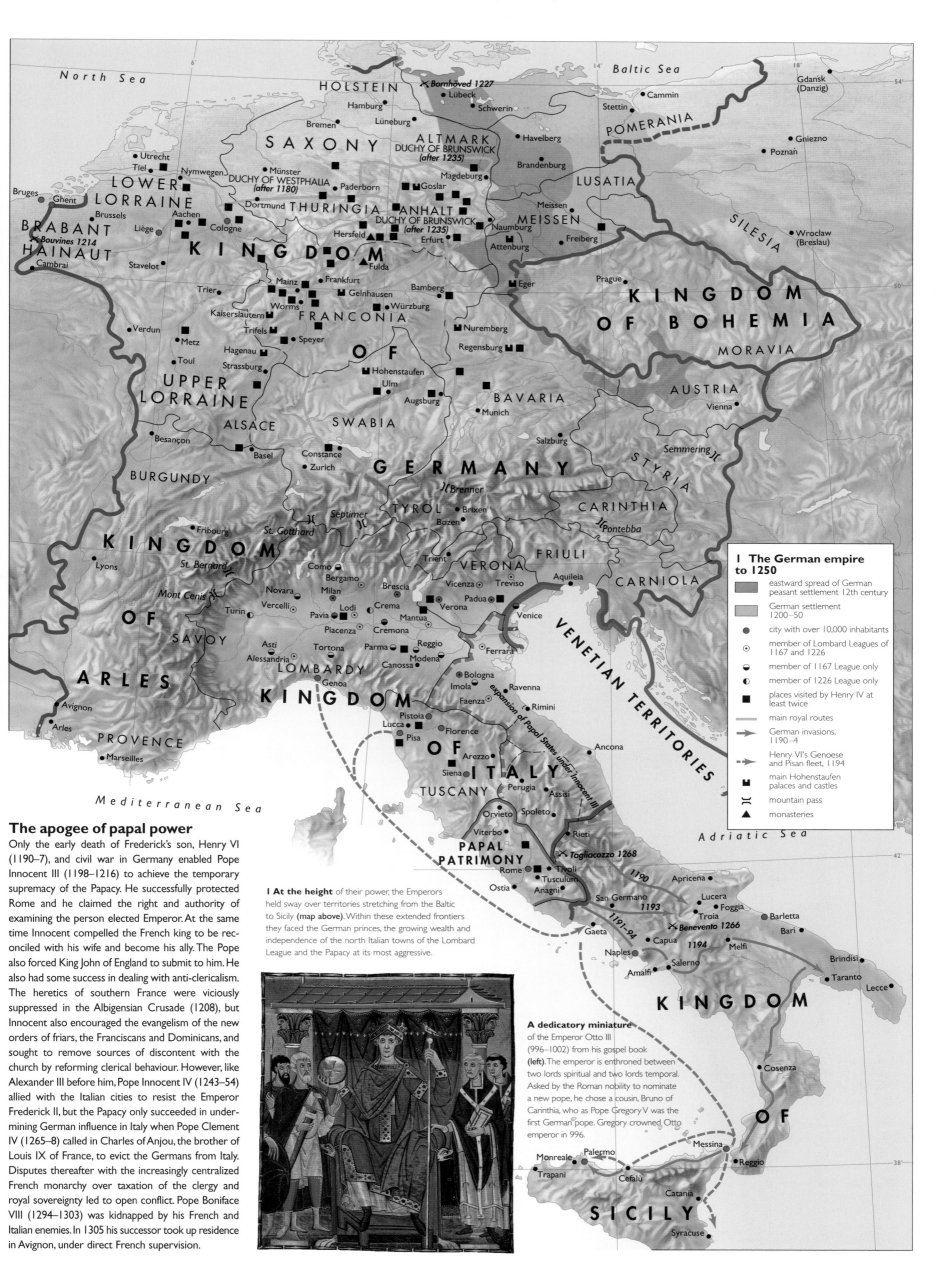

North Sea
Baltic Sea
Mediterranean Sea
Adriatic Sea
HOLSTEIN
✕ Bornhöved 1227
Lübeck
Schwerin
Hamburg
Bremen
Lüneburg
Cammin
Stettin
Gdańsk (Danzig)
POMERANIA
Gniezno
Poznań
SAXONY
ALTMARK
DUCHY OF BRUNSWICK (after 1235)
Havelberg
Brandenburg
Utrecht
Tiel
Nymwegen
Münster
DUCHY OF WESTPHALIA (after 1180)
Magdeburg
LUSATIA
LOWER LORRAINE
Bruges
Ghent
Brussels
Aachen
Cologne
Paderborn
Goslar
Dortmund
THURINGIA
ANHALT
DUCHY OF BRUNSWICK (after 1235)
Meissen
MEISSEN
Naumburg
SILESIA
Wroclaw (Breslau)
BRABANT
✕ Bouvines 1214
Liège
HAINAUT
Cambrai
Stavelot
KINGDOM OF GERMANY
Hersfeld
Erfurt
Freiberg
Attenburg
Fulda
Mainz
Frankfurt
Gelnhausen
Bamberg
Eger
Prague
Trier
Worms
Würzburg
KINGDOM OF BOHEMIA
Kaiserslautern
FRANCONIA
Verdun
Metz
Trifels
Speyer
Nuremberg
Regensburg
MORAVIA
Toul
Hagenau
Strassburg
Hohenstaufen
Ulm
Augsburg
UPPER LORRAINE
BAVARIA
Munich
AUSTRIA
Vienna
ALSACE
SWABIA
Besançon
Basel
Constance
Zurich
Salzburg
Semmering
STYRIA
BURGUNDY
Brenner
TYROL
Brixen
Bozen
CARINTHIA
Septimer
St. Gotthard
Pontebba
Fribourg
KINGDOM OF ARLES
Lyons
St. Bernard
Trient
VERONA
FRIULI
Aquileia
CARNIOLA
Como
Bergamo
Brescia
Vicenza
Treviso
Mont Cenis
Novara
Milan
Padua
Vercelli
Lodi
Crema
Verona
Turin
Pavia
Mantua
Venice
Piacenza
Cremona
SAVOY
Asti
Tortona
Parma
Reggio
Alessandria
Modena
Ferrara
LOMBARDY
Canossa
Genoa
Bologna
Imola
Ravenna
Faenza
Rimini
KINGDOM OF ITALY
VENETIAN TERRITORIES
expansion of Papal States under Innocent III
Avignon
Arles
PROVENCE
Marseilles
Pistoia
Lucca
Florence
Pisa
Ancona
Arezzo
Siena
TUSCANY
Perugia
Assisi
Orvieto
Spoleto
Viterbo
Rieti
PAPAL PATRIMONY
✕ Tagliacozzo 1268
Rome
Tivoli
Tusculum
Ostia
Anagni
1190
Apricena
San Germano
1193
Lucera
Foggia
Troia
Barletta
✕ Benevento 1266
Bari
Gaeta
1191–94
Capua
1194
Melfi
Naples
Salerno
Brindisi
Amalfi
Taranto
Lecce
KINGDOM OF SICILY
Cosenza
Messina
Reggio
Monreale
Palermo
Trapani
Cefalù
Catania
Syracuse
1 The German empire to 1250
eastward spread of German peasant settlement 12th century
German settlement 1200–50
city with over 10,000 inhabitants
member of Lombard Leagues of 1167 and 1226
member of 1167 League only
member of 1226 League only
places visited by Henry IV at least twice
main royal routes
German invasions, 1190–4
Henry VI's Genoese and Pisan fleet, 1194
main Hohenstaufen palaces and castles
mountain pass
monasteries

The apogee of papal power

Only the early death of Frederick's son, Henry VI (1190–7), and civil war in Germany enabled Pope Innocent III (1198–1216) to achieve the temporary supremacy of the Papacy. He successfully protected Rome and he claimed the right and authority of examining the person elected Emperor. At the same time Innocent compelled the French king to be reconciled with his wife and become his ally. The Pope also forced King John of England to submit to him. He also had some success in dealing with anti-clericalism. The heretics of southern France were viciously suppressed in the Albigensian Crusade (1208), but Innocent also encouraged the evangelism of the new orders of friars, the Franciscans and Dominicans, and sought to remove sources of discontent with the church by reforming clerical behaviour. However, like Alexander III before him, Pope Innocent IV (1243–54) allied with the Italian cities to resist the Emperor Frederick II, but the Papacy only succeeded in undermining German influence in Italy when Pope Clement IV (1265–8) called in Charles of Anjou, the brother of Louis IX of France, to evict the Germans from Italy. Disputes thereafter with the increasingly centralized French monarchy over taxation of the clergy and royal sovereignty led to open conflict. Pope Boniface VIII (1294–1303) was kidnapped by his French and Italian enemies. In 1305 his successor took up residence in Avignon, under direct French supervision.

1 At the height of their power, the Emperors held sway over territories stretching from the Baltic to Sicily **(map above)**. Within these extended frontiers they faced the German princes, the growing wealth and independence of the north Italian towns of the Lombard League and the Papacy at its most aggressive.

A dedicatory miniature of the Emperor Otto III (996–1002) from his gospel book **(left)**. The emperor is enthroned between two lords spiritual and two lords temporal. Asked by the Roman nobility to nominate a new pope, he chose a cousin, Bruno of Carinthia, who as Pope Gregory V was the first German pope. Gregory crowned Otto emperor in 996.

Monarchy in Britain and France

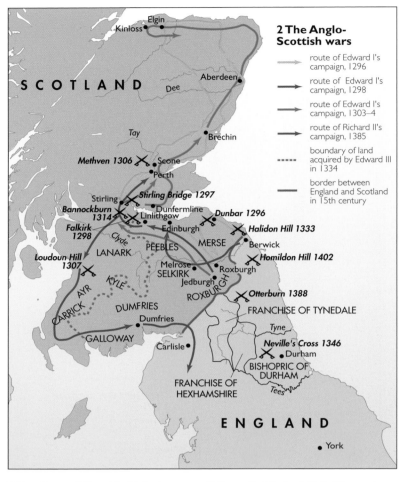

Map 2: The Anglo-Scottish wars

2 The Anglo-Scottish wars

- route of Edward I's campaign, 1296
- route of Edward I's campaign, 1298
- route of Edward I's campaign, 1303–4
- route of Richard II's campaign, 1385
- boundary of land acquired by Edward III in 1334
- border between England and Scotland in 15th century

2 The efforts of Edward I of England (1272–1307) to subjugate Scotland culminated in Edward II's disastrous defeat by the Scots under Robert the Bruce (1282–1327) at Bannockburn (map above). Throughout the century and beyond, the Scots, often fighting in alliance with France, were a significant threat to England's security.

3 Henry II of England (1154–89) created a powerful empire spanning the English Channel (map below). His marriage to Eleanor of Aquitaine brought him control over most of western France. Combined with his Norman and Angevin inheritance this made him the most powerful ruler in France. In 1157 he acquired Cumbria and settled the Scottish border and in 1171 invaded Ireland.

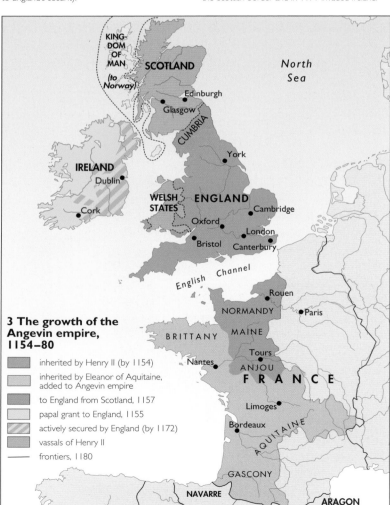

3 The growth of the Angevin empire, 1154–80

- inherited by Henry II (by 1154)
- inherited by Eleanor of Aquitaine, added to Angevin empire
- to England from Scotland, 1157
- papal grant to England, 1155
- actively secured by England (by 1172)
- vassals of Henry II
- frontiers, 1180

Within a distinctive blend of public office and landholding in medieval Britain and France, great stress was laid on authority, especially that of kings. Contemporaries did not think in terms of borders or national entities so much as of territorial and legal jurisdictions, where varied social bonds and political obligations and rights were interdependent.

DESPITE THE GROWTH of principalities in France and the strength of the earls in England in the 10th and 11th centuries, kingship survived. The king's position at the apex of the social hierarchy was hallowed by religious and legal sanctions which might bear little relationship to the realities of political power. In the 12th century kings used their position and fortuitous agglomerations of territory to assert their prerogatives. In the hands of the Emperor Frederick Barbarossa and later of the French Capetians, Roman law became a powerful instrument of royal authority. But the main weapons used by 12th- and 13th-century kings were the king's rights as "liege lord"; the duty of tenants-in-chief to render service; the theory that all land was held of the king; and all rights of justice were delegations of royal authority, which therefore reverted, or "escheated", to the crown in case of abuse or treason. Grave misdemeanours (felonies) were reserved to the king's courts or "pleas of the crown". Much of this process was piecemeal; but by the middle of the 13th century the great lawyers (Bracton in England, Beaumanoir in France) had created a systematic theory of royal government, which kings such as Edward I of England (1272–1307) and Philip IV of France (1285–1314) proceeded to implement.

The Normans and England

The process was most rapid in the Norman kingdoms of England and Sicily, both of which were acquired by conquest. In England this enabled William the Conqueror (1066–87) to retain and build up the fiscal and jurisdictional prerogatives inherited from his Anglo-Saxon predecessors. Henry II's coronation as king of England meant that Anjou, Normandy, the Touraine, Aquitaine and Gascony also came under his rule, creating an Angevin "empire" which, at least initially, held together quite successfully.

The consolidation of France

In France, on the other hand, Louis VI (1108–37) spent his reign asserting authority over the petty barons of the Ile de France, and it was scarcely before the reign of Philip Augustus (1180–1223) that expansion of the royal demesne began in earnest. The turning point was the conquest of Normandy in 1204 which effectively meant the destruction of the Angevin empire. After 1214 English continental possessions were limited to Gascony while a third of France was now under royal control. Much of Languedoc was subdued in a campaign against the Albigensian heretics (1209–29) and royal authority was extended south of the Loire.

Kings exercised powers of taxation and legislation (often in consultation with parliaments or "estates of the realm") and controlled the administration of justice. Nowhere was the network of overlapping rights and

THE DUKE OF NORMANDY OR THE PRINCE IS THE ONE WHO HOLDS THE LORDSHIP OVER THE ENTIRE DUCHY. THIS DIGNITY THE LORD KING OF FRANCE HOLDS TOGETHER WITH THE OTHER HONOURS TO WHICH, WITH THE AID OF THE LORD, HE HAS BEEN RAISED. FROM THIS IT PERTAINS TO HIM TO PRESERVE THE PEACE OF THE LAND, TO CORRECT THE PEOPLE BY THE ROD OF JUSTICE, AND BY THE MEASURE OF EQUITY TO END PRIVATE DISPUTES. THEREFORE HE SHOULD THROUGH THE JUSTICIARS SUBJECT TO HIM SEE TO IT THAT THE PEOPLE UNDER HIS AUTHORITY REJOICE IN THE RULE OF JUSTICE AND THE TRANQUILLITY OF PEACE.

The Summa de legibus of Normandy, c. 1258

jurisdictions more complex than in France. Indeed, the determination of the French kings to assert their lordship over these lands and over Flanders gave rise to a series of major wars.

The limits of royal power

Meanwhile the English kings were asserting similar claims in Scotland, Wales and Ireland. Henry II's attempt to conquer Ireland (1171) achieved only a precarious foothold, but in 1284 Edward I subdued Wales. He tried to repeat the process in Scotland in 1296, but met with resistance under Wallace and Bruce, and his son Edward II suffered a crushing defeat at Bannockburn in 1314 (see map 2).

Edward's failure in Scotland was matched by Philip IV's failure in Flanders. Defeated by the Flemings at Courtrai (1302), the French king, who had seized Gascony in 1294, was compelled to restore it to the English in 1303. In England Edward I was compelled in 1297 to confirm and extend the concessions wrested by the barons from his grandfather, King John, in 1215. In France the Estates-General met for the first time in 1302. Everywhere, nobles, many of them well versed in the law, were challenging royal jurisdictions and prerogatives.

Harlech Castle (right). The castle was the symbol of the conquering monarchies of western Europe in the 13th century. During the reign of Henry III of England (1216–72) much of Wales had become autonomous under Llewelyn ap Gruffydd, but Edward I, infuriated by Llewelyn's refusal to perform homage, invaded in force in 1277. A subsequent Welsh rebellion ended in the death of Llewelyn and, by the Statute of Wales (1284), Edward completed the reorganization of the Principality on English lines. Harlech Castle is one of the best preserved and most impressive of the series of fortifications built by Edward to hold down the conquered country.

1 The institutional strength of monarchy, developing in the 12th century, expanded rapidly in the 13th century. In France the kings extended the extent of their control from a tiny 10th-century royal domain around Paris and Orléans (map below). By 1300 western kings, like their early medieval predecessors, were acknowledged executors of effective public authority.

I The growth of the French and English monarchies

England, Scotland, Wales and Ireland
- boundary of England and Scotland, 1157
- land claimed by Scotland, 1139–57
- English Marcher lordships in Wales
- Principality of Wales, 1284
- Norman conquests in Ireland, 1171–1215
- Norman conquests in Ireland, 1215–1307
- Irish lands, 1307

France
- French royal domain in 987
- French royal domain at death of Louis VII in 1180
- areas dependent on French monarchy in 1180
- English possessions in France in 1259
- additions to French royal domain before death of Louis IX in 1270
- additions before death of Philip IV in 1314
- additions before death of Charles IV in 1328

987 Hugh Capet, first Capetian king of France

1066 Invasion of England by William, Duke of Normandy

1152 Henry of Anjou marries Eleanor of Aquitaine

1158 Henry II invades Brittany

1204 England loses Normandy

1208–29 Albigensian Crusade

1259 Henry III renounces rights in Normandy, Anjou and Poitou

1284 Edward I subdues Wales

1302 First Estates General meet in France

Map labels:

SCOTLAND
KINGDOM OF MAN (Norwegian to 1266 then Scottish)
INVERNESS
ABERDEEN · Aberdeen
PERTH · Perth · St Andrews
Bannockburn 1314 ✕ · Stirling
AYR
LOTHIAN · Edinburgh · Berwick (to Durham)
· Roxburgh
DUMFRIES
Solway Firth
NORTHUMBERLAND · Bamburgh
· Hexham
CUMBERLAND · Carlisle
COUNTY PALATINE OF DURHAM

IRELAND
TIRCONNELL · Derry
TIROWEN
ULSTER 1205 · Armagh
✕ 1257
✕ 1270
CONNAUGHT 1235
· Galway · Athlone
MEATH 1172 · Clontarf
· Dublin
LEINSTER 1172
· Wexford
· Waterford
✕ 1318 · Limerick
DESMOND · Cork
✕ 1281

Isle of Man
Irish Sea
· Lancaster
· York
YORKSHIRE
Humber
· Lincoln
The Wash
Anglesey
GWYNEDD
CAERNARVON · Harlech
MERIONETH
WALES
MARCHER LORDSHIPS
CARDIGAN
CARMARTHEN
· St David's
· Cardigan
· Llandaff
COUNTY PALATINE OF CHESTER WITH FLINT
STAFFORD-SHIRE · Lichfield
SHROP-SHIRE · Leicester
· Nottingham
NORFOLK · Norwich
ENGLAND
· Ely
SUFFOLK
· Cambridge
Severn
Avon
✕ Evesham 1265
· Gloucester
· Oxford
ESSEX
· Windsor · London
Thames · Runnymede
· Canterbury
SUSSEX ✕ Lewes 1264
· Chichester
· Winchester
Bristol Channel
SOMERSET · Bath
· Salisbury
DORSET
DEVON · Exeter
CORNWALL

North Sea

FRIESLAND
HOLLAND
Waal
Meuse
· Antwerp
· Bruges · Ghent
FLANDERS
Scheldt
BRABANT
· Calais
· Boulogne
Courtrai 1302 ✕
Bouvines 1214 ✕
· Valenciennes
HAINAUT
HOLY ROMAN EMPIRE
· Montreuil
PONTHIEU (to England 1279)
· Agincourt
· Arras · Cambrai
· St Quentin
VERMANDOIS
· Rouen
Seine
Oise
· Compiègne
· Senlis
· Rheims
Moselle
· Nancy
ILE DE FRANCE
· Paris · Meaux
· Evreux
· Bar-le-Duc
NORMANDY
· Cherbourg
Channel Islands
Mont St Michel
· St Malo
· Brest
BRITTANY
· Rennes
MAINE
· Chartres
ORLÉANAIS
CHAMPAGNE
· Troyes
· Langres
· Orléans
· Blois
· Nantes
ANJOU
TOURAINE · Tours
Loire
NIVERNAIS
· Dijon
BURGUNDY
· Bourges
BERRY
SAUMUROIS
· Poitiers
POITOU
MARCHE
BOURBONNAIS
Saône
· Mâcon
LYONNAIS
· La Rochelle
· Limoges
LIMOUSIN
AUVERGNE
· Clermont-Ferrand
· Lyons
Rhône
· Saintes
SAINTONGE & ANGOUMOIS
PÉRIGORD
· Périgueux
Auvergne Mts
· St Flour
· Le Puy
CÉVENNES
DAUPHINÉ
· Bordeaux
Garonne
Dordogne
· Cahors
GUYENNE (AQUITAINE)
GASCONY
LANGUEDOC
· Albi
PROVENCE
BÉARN
BIGORRE
ARMAGNAC (to England 1279)
· Toulouse
· Carcassonne
FOIX
PYRENEES
FRANCE
English Channel
Bay of Biscay
Mediterranean Sea

Economic growth in Europe

As new archaeological evidence reveals, the early
Middle Ages was a vital period of economic activity,
in which important new developments in the northwest,
the opening up of new trade routes,
wealth created by new agricultural land and the
foundation of trading towns all built on the
earlier economic patterns of the Roman empire.

7th century Trading settlement at Dorestad founded

688–726 Hamwic founded

755 Frankish king Pippin takes control of coinage

794 Major coinage, weights and measures reforms of Charlemagne

802 Caliph of Baghdad sends an elephant to Charlemagne at Aachen

830–40 Viking raids on Dorestad

c. 850 Dorestad abandoned due to silting up of Rhine

c. 860 Flanders fairs begin

893 Frisian merchants recorded in Duisberg

992 Venetian merchants accorded special privileges in Constantinople

1096 First Crusade

1 Before AD 1000 perhaps four-fifths of Europe north of the Alps and Pyrenees was covered by dense forest **(map below)**. Over the next 200 years much of this was cleared to make land available for human settlement and agriculture. Even in the Rhineland the highlands bounding the river were still largely uninhabited **(see map 3)**. Forests such as the Ardennes and the Eifel constituted an almost impenetrable barrier to communications. Certain areas – Flanders, Lombardy, and the Rhine valley – became centres of commerce from 1100. But it was only after 1150 that Italian merchants regularly attended the Champagne fairs (Troyes, Provins, Lagny), buying Flemish cloths in exchange for Oriental goods.

FROM THE 7TH CENTURY onwards the northwest of Europe grew in importance as a trading area. In the North Sea and the Baltic region, the Scandinavians built on trading networks already established by the Frisians, Franks and English. The extension of Scandinavian activity overseas coincided with the growing demand for goods that could only be obtained from the north; walrus tusks were at that time the main source of ivory in Europe, and furs from the arctic regions of Scandinavia and Russia were greatly prized. There was a growing commerce in coastal markets called *wics*. The greatest was Dorestad at the mouth of the Rhine, but there were many others, including Quentovic (near Boulogne), Ipswich, London and Hamwic, later to develop into Southampton. Other small trading towns flourished, such as Starya Ladoga in Russia, Birka in Sweden, Wastergarn in Gotland, Kaupang in Norway and Ribe and Haithabu in Denmark.

The Scandinavian world

Scandinavians now sought even further afield for fresh supplies of skin, furs and tusks. A 9th-century contemporary account by a Norwegian, Ottar, narrates the voyage he made from his home in northern Norway into the White Sea in search of walrus. Dublin's fortunes fluctuated politically but her function as the chief of the Scandinavian towns in Ireland (founded in the 9th century) is emphasized by the striking of the first Irish coins there in the 990s. From the late 10th century her economic power and international connections grew apace, and the existence of continuous building and growth up to the 12th century bears witness to her prosperity. The town served as the chief market for the Isle of Man, the Western Isles of Scotland and the Atlantic islands, all of which remained under Scandinavian control throughout the period.

The opening of new regions

By 1000 it is estimated that the population of western Europe may have reached a total of 30 million and 150 years later it may have increased by a further 40 per cent. Most of this was concentrated in France, Germany and England and was probably related to the opening up of new land by clearing forests. It took three main forms: steady encroachment by the peasants of the old villages on the woods which surrounded their fields; the migration of settlers, presumably driven by land-hunger to the uninhabited uplands and mountains, where they carved out scattered fields and enclosures from the forest and scrub; and planned development by lay lords and monasteries, wealthy promoters and speculators who founded villages and towns, at the foot of a castle or outside a monastery gate, with the aim of increasing their income. All three types of clearing are found juxtaposed in all countries, and their history is revealed by field patterns and by place-names – Newport, Neuville, Neustadt, Bourgneuf, Nieuwpoort. In a few regions – the Po valley of northern Italy, Flanders, the country around the Wash in England – marshes were drained and land reclaimed from the sea.

Markets and trade

The agricultural surplus further stimulated the foundation and growth of towns, markets and fairs (notably the fairs of Champagne) which initially served a local market but became internationally renowned after 1150. In the Mediterranean, the survival of silks, pottery and other goods indicated a continuation of connections across the Mediterranean and with northern Europe.

In Italy, Pisa, Genoa and Venice extended their overseas trade, assisted by the opportunities offered by the

LET ALL KNOW THAT FOR THE LOVE OF GOD WE HAVE GRANTED THE PETITION OF ADALDAG, THE REVEREND ARCHBISHOP OF HAMBURG, AND HAVE GIVEN HIM PERMISSION TO ESTABLISH A MARKET IN THE PLACE CALLED BREMEN. IN CONNECTION WITH THE MARKET WE GRANT HIM JURISDICTION, TOLLS, A MINT, AND ALL OTHER THINGS CONNECTED THEREWITH TO WHICH OUR ROYAL TREASURY WOULD HAVE A RIGHT. WE ALSO TAKE UNDER OUR SPECIAL PROTECTION ALL THE MERCHANTS WHO LIVE IN THAT PLACE.

Grant by the Emperor Otto I of Saxony to the archbishop of Hamburg, 965

crusading movement in the eastern Mediterranean. North of the Alps, rivers such as the Rhine, Seine, Danube and Rhône, conveyed bulk transport and connected the cloth towns of Flanders and the Rhineland with the south. The western Alpine passes (Mont Cenis, Great St Bernard) were in regular use. The central passes (St Gotthard, Splügen) and the Brenner in the east were developed in the later 12th century. The Rhineland was a major focus of artistic, intellectual and economic life. Cologne, in particular, was at the height of its prosperity, but the cathedral-building throughout the region, as at Mainz and Worms, is a testimony to the wealth which "the great age of clearing" had made available.

St Michael's church at Hildesheim (right) is a supreme example of Saxon architecture from the early 11th century (1010–30). It was overseen by the cultured Bishop Bernward. The interior is as magnificent as the exterior, complemented by the ornate bronze doors, nearly 5m (16ft) high, carved in relief with scenes from the Old and New Testaments.

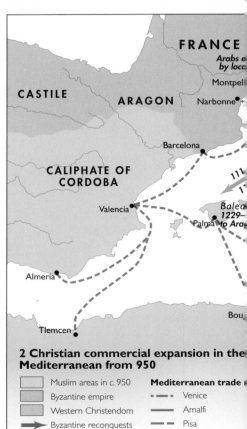

2 In 950 the Mediterranean was in some respects a "Muslim lake" **(map right)**. Trade between western Europe and the Orient was in the hands of traders based in southern Italy, especially Amalfi, and of many independent merchants in lower Egypt, north Africa, Spain and the larger Mediterranean islands. Venice was one of the most important meeting points for trade from the Mediterranean and northern Europe. The weakening of the Saracens' hold on a number of the Mediterranean islands from the 11th century enabled the merchants of Pisa and (later) of Genoa to wrest control of the Ligurian and Tyrrhenian seas. The First Crusade (1096–99) opened up trading stations in the Levant; but it was only after the Venetian naval victory off Ascalon in 1123 that the Italian cities came to dominate the Mediterranean from Spain to Syria.

1 Western Europe, c. AD 1000

— trade routes

areas of forest ▲ fairs

Stamford · The Wash
Norwich
St Ives ▲
London
Winchester · Ipswich
Hamwic · Dorestad
Quentovic · Torhout · Bruges · FLANDERS
St Omer · Ypres · Ghent · Aachen
Lille · Messines · Visé · Cologne
Arras · Douai · Ardennes · RHINELAND
Valenciennes · Eifel · Mainz
CHAMPAGNE · Moselle · Worms
Seine · Meuse · Bamberg
St Denis · Prague
Paris · Lagny · Strassburg
Île-de-France · Provins · Regensburg
Orléans · Sens · Bar-sur-Aube · Rhine · Black Forest · Danube
Loire · Troyes
Cher · Auxerre
Basle
Dordogne · Bern · Brenner
Chalon-sur-Saône · St Gotthard · Splügen
Lot · Great St Bernard · A L P S
Garonne · Milan · Venice
Tarn · Mont Cenis · Pavia · Po
Arles · Rhône · LOMBARDY · Genoa
Marseilles · Pisa
Narbonne
P y r e n e e s

Hildesheim · Magdeburg
Duisberg

2 Christian commercial expansion in the Mediterranean from 950

FRANCE
Arabs e[...] by loca[...]
CASTILE · ARAGON · Montpell[...]
Narbonne
Barcelona
CALIPHATE OF CORDOBA
Valencia
Bale[...] 1229–[...]
Palma to Arag[...]
Almería
Bou[...]
Tlemcen

	Muslim areas in c. 950	**Mediterranean trade [...]**	
	Byzantine empire	▬ ▪ ▬	Venice
	Western Christendom	▬▬▬	Amalfi
	Byzantine reconquests	▬ ▬ ▬	Pisa
	Pisan and Genoese raids and conquests	▪▪▪▪▪	Genoa
	Norman conquests		
Bari 1071	date of Norman conquest		
	Venetian expansion		

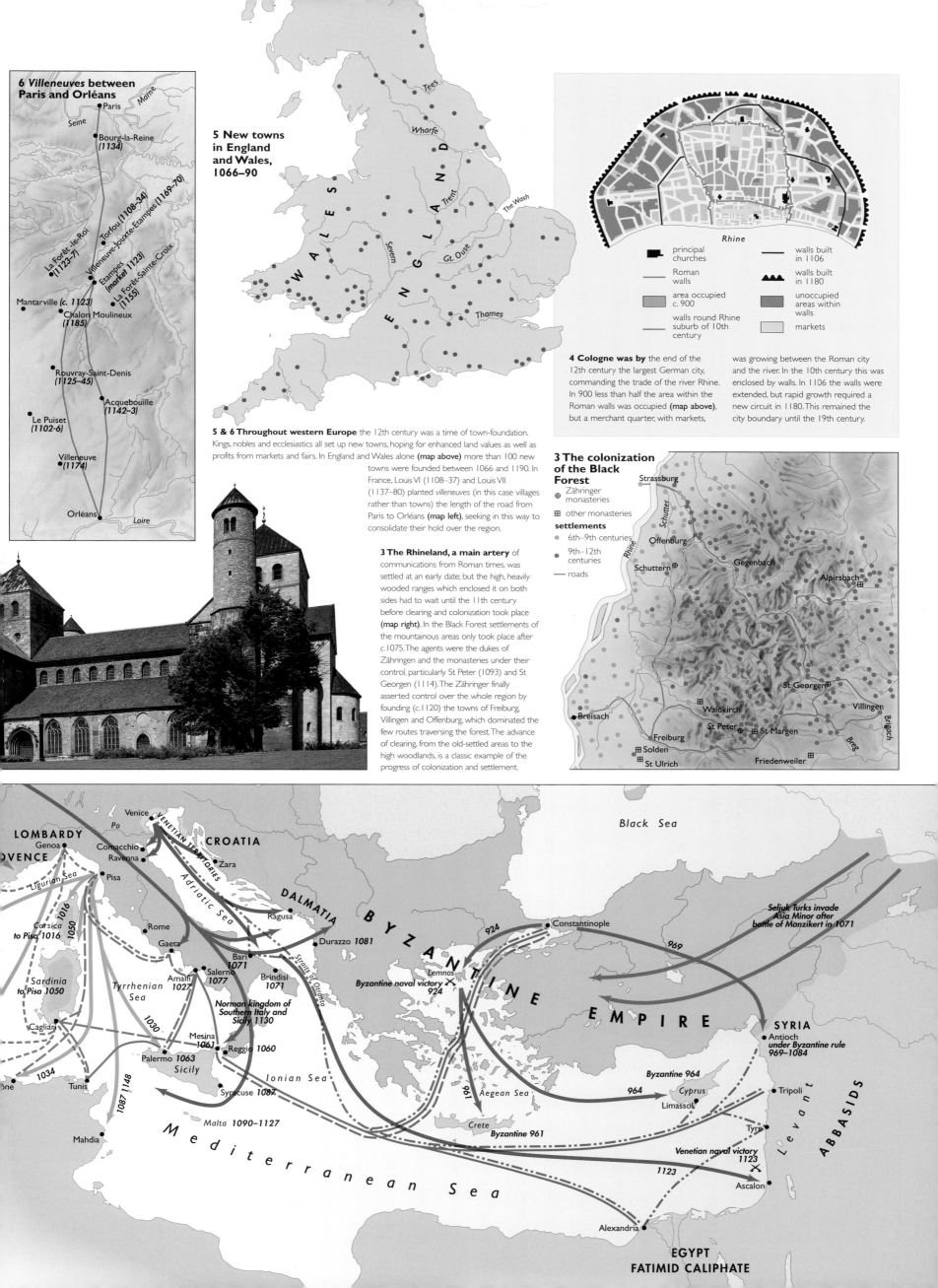

6 Villeneuves between Paris and Orléans

- Paris
- Bourg-la-Reine *(1134)*
- Seine
- Marne
- La Forêt-le-Roi *(1123-7)*
- Torfou *(1108-34)*
- Villeneuve-jouxte-Etampes *(1169-70)*
- Etampes *(market 1123)*
- La Forêt-Sainte-Croix *(1155)*
- Mantarville *(c. 1123)*
- Chalon Moulineux *(1185)*
- Rouvray-Saint-Denis *(1125-45)*
- Acquebouille *(1142-3)*
- Le Puiset *(1102-6)*
- Villeneuve *(1174)*
- Orléans
- Loire

5 New towns in England and Wales, 1066–90

- Tees
- Wharfe
- Trent
- WALES
- ENGLAND
- Severn
- Gt. Ouse
- The Wash
- Thames

5 & 6 Throughout western Europe the 12th century was a time of town-foundation. Kings, nobles and ecclesiastics all set up new towns, hoping for enhanced land values as well as profits from markets and fairs. In England and Wales alone **(map above)** more than 100 new towns were founded between 1066 and 1190. In France, Louis VI (1108–37) and Louis VII (1137–80) planted *villeneuves* (in this case villages rather than towns) the length of the road from Paris to Orléans **(map left)**, seeking in this way to consolidate their hold over the region.

4 Cologne

- Rhine
- principal churches
- Roman walls
- area occupied c. 900
- walls round Rhine suburb of 10th century
- walls built in 1106
- walls built in 1180
- unoccupied areas within walls
- markets

4 Cologne was by the end of the 12th century the largest German city, commanding the trade of the river Rhine. In 900 less than half the area within the Roman walls was occupied **(map above)**, but a merchant quarter, with markets, was growing between the Roman city and the river. In the 10th century this was enclosed by walls. In 1106 the walls were extended, but rapid growth required a new circuit in 1180. This remained the city boundary until the 19th century.

3 The Rhineland, a main artery of communications from Roman times, was settled at an early date; but the high, heavily wooded ranges which enclosed it on both sides had to wait until the 11th century before clearing and colonization took place **(map right)**. In the Black Forest settlements of the mountainous areas only took place after c.1075. The agents were the dukes of Zähringen and the monasteries under their control, particularly St Peter (1093) and St Georgen (1114). The Zähringer finally asserted control over the whole region by founding (c.1120) the towns of Freiburg, Villingen and Offenburg, which dominated the few routes traversing the forest. The advance of clearing, from the old-settled areas to the high woodlands, is a classic example of the progress of colonization and settlement.

3 The colonization of the Black Forest

- ⊕ Zähringer monasteries
- ⊞ other monasteries
- **settlements**
- · 6th–9th centuries
- ● 9th–12th centuries
- — roads
- Strassburg
- Schutter
- Offenburg
- Schuttern ⊞
- Gegenbach
- Alpirsbach ⊞
- Rhine
- Breisach
- Waldkirch ⊞
- St Georgen ⊕
- Villingen
- Freiburg
- St Peter ⊕
- St Margen ⊞
- Breg
- Solden ⊞
- St Ulrich ⊞
- Friedenweiler ⊞
- Brigach

(Mediterranean map)

- LOMBARDY
- PROVENCE
- Venice
- Po
- VENETIAN TERRITORIES
- CROATIA
- Black Sea
- Genoa
- Comacchio
- Ravenna
- Zara
- Pisa
- Adriatic Sea
- DALMATIA
- Ligurian Sea
- Corsica to Pisa 1016
- 1016
- 1050
- Rome
- Gaeta
- Ragusa
- Durazzo 1081
- Straits of Otranto
- 924
- Constantinople
- 969
- Seljuk Turks invade Asia Minor after battle of Manzikert in 1071
- BYZANTINE
- Sardinia to Pisa 1050
- Tyrrhenian Sea
- Amalfi 1027
- Bari 1071
- Salerno 1077
- Brindisi 1071
- Byzantine naval victory 924
- Lemnos
- EMPIRE
- Cagliari
- 1030
- Norman kingdom of Southern Italy and Sicily 1130
- 1034
- Mesina 1061
- Reggio 1060
- Palermo 1063
- Sicily
- Ionian Sea
- Syracuse 1082
- Aegean Sea
- 196
- 964
- SYRIA
- Antioch under Byzantine rule 969–1084
- Byzantine 964
- Cyprus
- Limassol
- Levant
- ABBASIDS
- Tripoli
- 1087 1148
- Tunis
- Malta 1090–1127
- Crete
- Byzantine 961
- Byzantine 961
- Tyre
- Mahdia
- Mediterranean Sea
- Venetian naval victory 1123
- 1123
- Ascalon
- Alexandria
- EGYPT
- FATIMID CALIPHATE

Imperial Japan and the early shogunates

The early Japanese state achieved stability in the 8th century when the great families clustered around the emperor swapped military power for rank in a Chinese-inspired bureauracy. This ruled for four centuries until, in 1185, its own warrior clients founded the first in a series of shogunates, which were to rule Japan until 1868.

645 "Taika" reforms

794 Kyoto established as imperial court

1156–9 Hōgen and Heiji Disturbances pit rival Taira and Minamoto factions against each other

1185 Battle of Dannoura: first shogunate founded

1221 Emperor Go-Toba unsuccessfully attempts to restore imperial authority

1274 & 1281 Mongol invasions defeated

1333–6 Go-Daigo briefly re-establishes imperial rule before being expelled from Kyoto by the new Ashikaga shogunate

1467–77 Ōnin Wars: Japan plunged into civil war

GREAT JAPAN IS THE DIVINE LAND. THE HEAVENLY PROGENITOR FOUNDED IT, AND THE SUN GODDESS BEQUEATHED IT TO HER DESCENDANTS TO RULE ETERNALLY. ONLY IN OUR COUNTRY IS THIS TRUE; THERE ARE NO SIMILAR EXAMPLES IN OTHER COUNTRIES. THIS IS WHY OUR COUNTRY IS CALLED THE DIVINE LAND.

The Jinnō Shōtōki, 1339

JAPAN IS FIRST MENTIONED in Chinese records of the 3rd century AD. These state that the archipelago was divided into a series of small kingdoms, a number of them tributary to the Chinese emperor and most acknowledging the spiritual leadership of the Empress Himiko. Over the next three centuries, a line of emperors, possibly Himiko's descendants, unified most of what is today Japan either by absorbing or destroying other leading families.

The influence of China

Early Japan was consistently overshadowed by its much larger and more powerful neighbour, China – so much so that Japan consciously tried to model itself on China. Embassies were dispatched, imperial records drafted on the Chinese model and Buddhism introduced. The changes culminated in the Taika revolution of 645, when a new emperor, backed by the powerful Fujiwara family, first tried to mirror the role played by the Chinese emperors. Further impetus to reform came in 668 when T'ang Chinese and Sillan armies unified the Korean peninsula, in the process decisively defeating at

Paekmagang River (J. Hakusukinoe) a Japanese fleet sent to help the allied kingdom of Paekche in Korea. Fear of invasion proved a powerful spur to reform.

Early in the following century, Japan accordingly sought to model itself more closely still on the highly centralized Chinese state, continuing the "Taika" process begun in 645. A new Chinese-style capital was established at Nara in 710 and provincial governors and magistrates, all answerable to the emperor, were appointed. At the same time, all rice-growing land was declared the property of the emperor – was in effect nationalized – and then allotted to households on a per capita basis. Farmers paid the government a tax in the form of rice and were obliged to perform military service.

Soon, however, this structure proved unworkable. After smallpox epidemics had slashed the workforce and conscript armies had been mauled by the northern Emishi tribesmen, conscription was abandoned and the tax system simplified. Whereas earlier land had been allocated to farmers by the state only for life, now private individuals owned income-bearing land-rights (*shiki*), which they could pass on to their descendants. The type of *shiki* varied with the

owner's status. At the bottom of the hierarchy, a farmer's *shiki* gave him some of the crop for tilling the soil. A *samurai*'s *shiki* conferred on him a portion of the harvest from the lands he managed. At the top of the scale, an aristocrat's *shiki* gave him income in return for defending the legality of the *shiki* belonging to those below him. Thus the castes were linked by chains of fealty, which were known as *kenmon*.

These changes radically altered the power structure of the country. Previously the imperial family had been dominated by the Fujiwara family, who provided the emperors' consorts. Most emperors were children, very much under the influence of their maternal Fujiwara relatives and, moreover, after coming of age the emperor was required to "retire". However, by the 11th century the imperial family had begun to reassert itself, and the retired emperors had organized themselves as a *kenmon*. With the other new *kenmon* emerging, the Fujiwara now faced real competition, and the scope for factionalism grew.

Now government became merely the arena where *kenmon* heads hammered out their differences. The *kenmon* were largely autonomous, but, when there was a need for military operations beyond the scope of any one *kenmon*, *kenmon* heads would meet and commission as general a Taira or Minamoto, clans who over the generations had acquired a reputation for producing able military commanders. But recurrent factional feuds, culminating in the Genpei Wars (1180–5), allowed one of these generals, Minamoto Yoritomo, to emerge as Japan's first military leader (*shogun*).

The first *shogun*

Yoritomo based his regime not in the existing capital of Kyoto, but far to the east in Kamakura. There, he gave justice and protection to any *samurai* who swore him allegiance. After Yoritomo's death, his two sons were eliminated by his Hōjō in-laws, who then dominated the Kamakura shogunate. Initially, the shogunate deliberately limited its role to defending the interests of its warrior clients within the existing framework of *shiki* and *kenmon*, but in the wake of two major crises, its authority grew: in 1221 a bid by the Emperor Go-Toba to re-establish imperial primacy was crushed in the Jōkyū War; and in 1274 and 1281 two Mongol invasions were thwarted.

But the Hōjō family, with no genealogical rights, overreached themselves in their efforts to control ever-larger swathes of the country. The Hōjō's fall came about in 1333 through an alliance between the Emperor Go-Daigo and Ashikaga Takauji, one of the surviving scions of the Minamoto. Within three years, however, the emperor and Takauji had fallen foul of one another. The emperor was forced to flee with his supporters to the mountain fastness of Yoshino, where he established what came to be

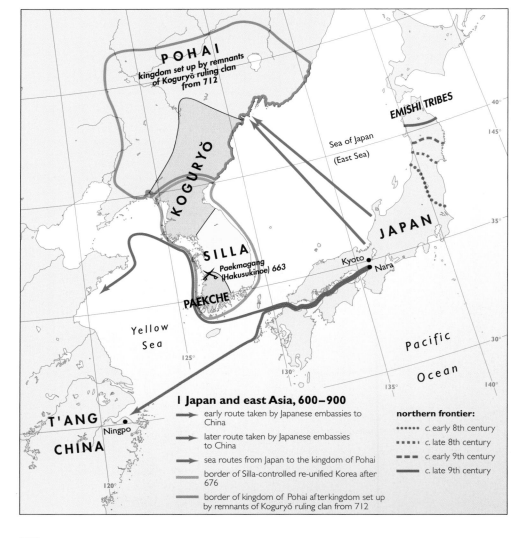

I Japan and east Asia, 600–900

→ early route taken by Japanese embassies to China

→ later route taken by Japanese embassies to China

→ sea routes from Japan to the kingdom of Pohai

— border of Silla-controlled re-unified Korea after 676

— border of kingdom of Pohai after kingdom set up by remnants of Koguryŏ ruling clan from 712

northern frontier:

•••••• c. early 8th century

▪▪▪▪▪ c. late 8th century

- - - - c. early 9th century

——— c. late 9th century

I The resurgence of China under the T'ang and the unification of the Korean peninsula under the Silla in 668-676 faced Japan with a real threat of invasion. The imperial court sought to counter this by borrowing Chinese military and administrative practices, subduing the Emishi tribesmen in the north, and thereby pushing the border of Japanese-controlled territory progressively further north, and establishing itself as an acknowledged peer of the states of the region: China, Korea and Pohai (map left).

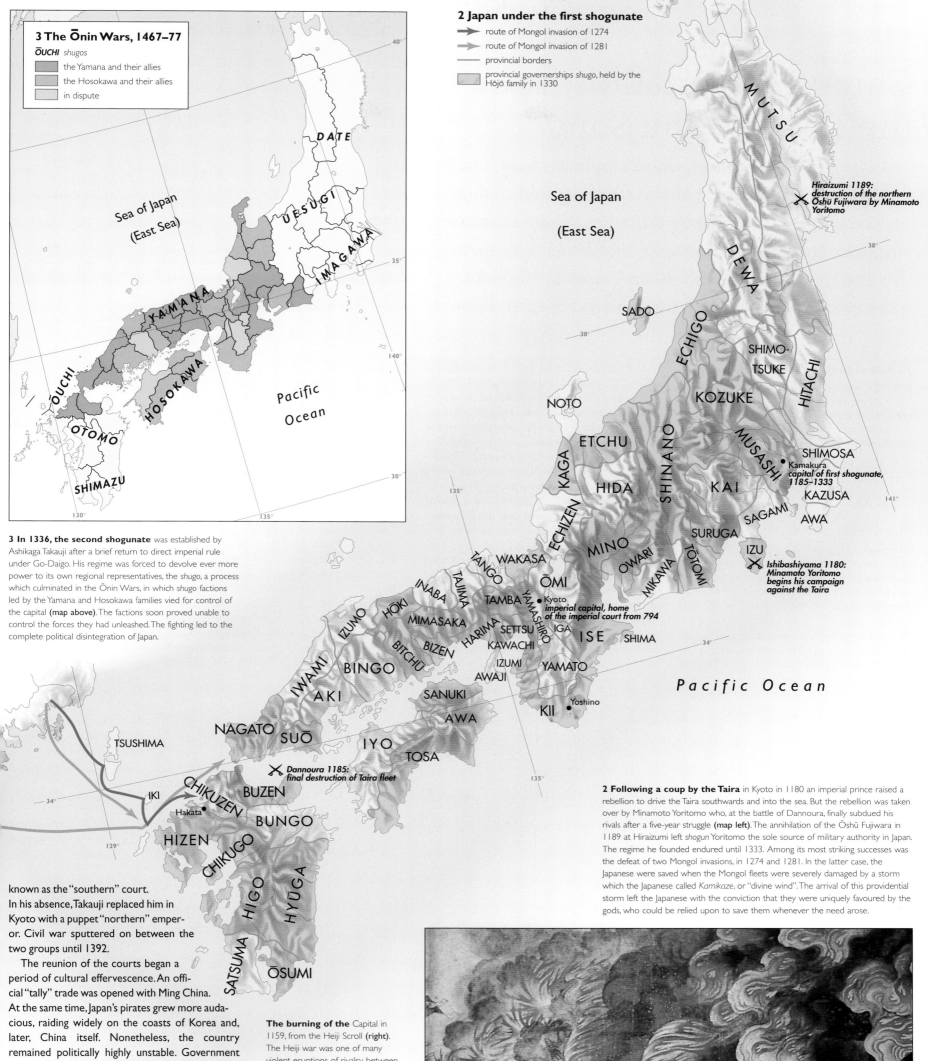

3 The Ōnin Wars, 1467–77

ŌUCHI *shugos*

- the Yamana and their allies
- the Hosokawa and their allies
- in dispute

2 Japan under the first shogunate

- route of Mongol invasion of 1274
- route of Mongol invasion of 1281
- provincial borders
- provincial governorships *shugo*, held by the Hōjō family in 1330

3 In 1336, the second shogunate was established by Ashikaga Takauji after a brief return to direct imperial rule under Go-Daigo. His regime was forced to devolve ever more power to its own regional representatives, the *shugo*, a process which culminated in the Ōnin Wars, in which *shugo* factions led by the Yamana and Hosokawa families vied for control of the capital (**map above**). The factions soon proved unable to control the forces they had unleashed. The fighting led to the complete political disintegration of Japan.

known as the "southern" court. In his absence, Takauji replaced him in Kyoto with a puppet "northern" emperor. Civil war sputtered on between the two groups until 1392.

The reunion of the courts began a period of cultural effervescence. An official "tally" trade was opened with Ming China. At the same time, Japan's pirates grew more audacious, raiding widely on the coasts of Korea and, later, China itself. Nonetheless, the country remained politically highly unstable. Government was possible only when the *shogun* could impose order on what by now had become a series of powerful regional magnates, or *daimyō*. After the assassination of the despotic *shogun* Yoshinori in 1441, feuding between alliances of *daimyō* led by the Yamana and Hosokawa led to open warfare in 1467, the Ōnin Wars. As Japan fragmented, the *daimyō* houses, now cut adrift from the state, themselves found it impossible to maintain internal cohesion and one after another they were brought down by their own retainers. It would be more than a century before Japan was unified again.

The burning of the Capital in 1159, from the Heiji Scroll (**right**). The Heiji war was one of many violent eruptions of rivalry between the Minamoto and Taira families. The history of medieval Japan is punctuated by such civil wars between local warlords, whose armies were composed of hereditary arms-bearing vassals, or *samurai*. A highly developed professional and ethical code developed among the *samurai* at the time, similar to, but more complex than, the chivalric code among European feudal knights. Their exploits were meticulously recorded.

2 Following a coup by the Taira in Kyoto in 1180 an imperial prince raised a rebellion to drive the Taira southwards and into the sea. But the rebellion was taken over by Minamoto Yoritomo who, at the battle of Dannoura, finally subdued his rivals after a five-year struggle (**map left**). The annihilation of the Ōshū Fujiwara in 1189 at Hiraizumi left *shogun* Yoritomo the sole source of military authority in Japan. The regime he founded endured until 1333. Among its most striking successes was the defeat of two Mongol invasions, in 1274 and 1281. In the latter case, the Japanese were saved when the Mongol fleets were severely damaged by a storm which the Japanese called *Kamikaze*, or "divine wind". The arrival of this providential storm left the Japanese with the conviction that they were uniquely favoured by the gods, who could be relied upon to save them whenever the need arose.

Chinese civilization from the T'ang to the Sung

Under the T'ang dynasty, China's military and cultural hegemony in the Far East was firmly entrenched. Its successor dynasty, the Sung, was a less dynamic external power but nonetheless reinforced China's position as the world's most sophisticated country until the disruptions of the Mongol invasions in the 13th century.

> THE BOAT IS LIKE THE MONARCH; AND WATER, THE CITIZENS. WATER IS CAPABLE OF SUPPORTING THE BOAT AS WELL AS CAPSIZING IT.
>
> Emperor T'ang T'ai-tsung (AD 627–49)

I The whole of China, excepting the far southwest, was permanently organized with a centralized administration under the T'ang (map below). The empire was linked by a network of post-roads, while transport of commodities between the rapidly developing regions of the Yangtze valley and the north was provided by an efficient system of canals and waterways. The road system centred on the capital, Ch'ang-an, which remained the political and strategic hub of the empire. However, the northern plain and the area around the Lower Yangtze were the principal economic centres.

AFTER CENTURIES OF DISUNION (see p. 90), China had been reunified in 589 by the Sui dynasty (581–618). This collapsed, partly from the burden imposed by public works like the Grand Canal, partly from expensive attempts to conquer Koguryo (northern Korea).

The Ta ng rose from the widespread rebellions that followed to become a strong centralized empire with an effective administrative system. Underpinning T'ang rule was the Imperial Examination System, which was designed to recruit well-educated citizens to serve the empire. It was to endure until the early 20th century.

After some years of internal consolidation the T'ang began to expand abroad. By the 660s T'ang armies had intervened in India, had occupied the Tarim Basin and Dzungaria and had briefly set up protectorates in Tukharistan, Sogdiana and Ferghana. In the same period Koguryo was finally conquered. By the 660s the Chinese empire reached its greatest extent until the 18th century. Chinese culture and administrative methods were spread alongside its military exploits, establishing a Chinese cultural hegemony in the Far East that would endure long after T'ang power had decayed.

In 755 An Lu-shan, a frontier general, mutinied, severely weakening the T'ang. In the years of turmoil which followed, China withdrew from central Asia and became more inward-looking, in part also as the result of the spread of Islam, which by the 8th century had reached Ferghana and later became dominant in Turkestan (see p. 112). Internally, imperial authority was much reduced. Power passed to the provinces, and many provincial capitals grew into large and wealthy metropolises. At the same time there was a massive movement of population to the Yangtze valley, where new methods of farming developed. Trade boomed, and a network of small market towns grew up.

The rise of the Sung

At the end of the 9th century, massive peasant uprisings reduced central authority to a cipher. China split into ten states with an imperial rump controlled by five successive short-lived dynasties (see map 3). Control was lost of the northeastern area to the Khitan (Liao) who set up an empire in Manchuria and Inner Mongolia. In the northwest another powerful kingdom, the Hsi-hsia, was founded by the Tanguts. These areas remained under foreign domination until 1368.

Following a coup d'état at the palace of the last of the "Five Dynasties", the Later Chou, a new dynasty, the Sung, seized power, led by a skilled military and

618–907 T'ang dynasty

Jan. 960 Coup d'état of General Chao K'unag-yin, later Emperor Sung T'ai-tsu (960–76)

963–79 Sung's war to reunite China

979–1004 Sung-Liao border war

982–1126 Sung-Hsi-hsia border war

1126–7 Tatar (Chin) war to conquer north China

1210–34 Mongol war to conquer Chin-held north China

1235–79 Mongol war to conquer Sung-held south China

2 During the 660s and 670s Chinese military power reached a peak, and briefly extended the power of the T'ang from Sogdiana to north Korea (map right). The Tarim Basin and parts of northwest China fell to the Tibetans in 763–83 after T'ang garrisons were withdrawn. Chinese institutions and literary culture extended over parts of the Far East which although never ruled by China still came under Chinese cultural hegemony.

I T'ang China, 618–907

— canals — roads

▣ metropolitan prefectures

◉ prefectures over 100,000 households

○ prefectures over 40,000 households

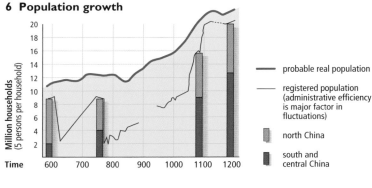

6 Population growth

Time 600 700 800 900 1000 1100 1200

Million households (5 persons per household)

— probable real population

— registered population (administrative efficiency is major factor in fluctuations)

north China

south and central China

4 & 6 The period from 750 to 1250 saw a very rapid growth of the Chinese population, which probably doubled (chart above and map right). At the same time the demographic distribution changed. In the 7th century, 73 per cent of the population lived in the northeast of China, and less than a quarter in south and central China. By the 13th century the situation was reversed and China's economic centre of gravity had shifted from the northern plain to the Yangtze valley.

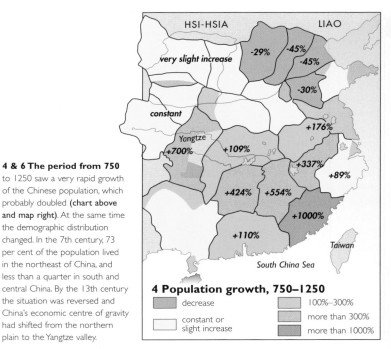

4 Population growth, 750–1250

decrease

constant or slight increase

100%–300%

more than 300%

more than 1000%

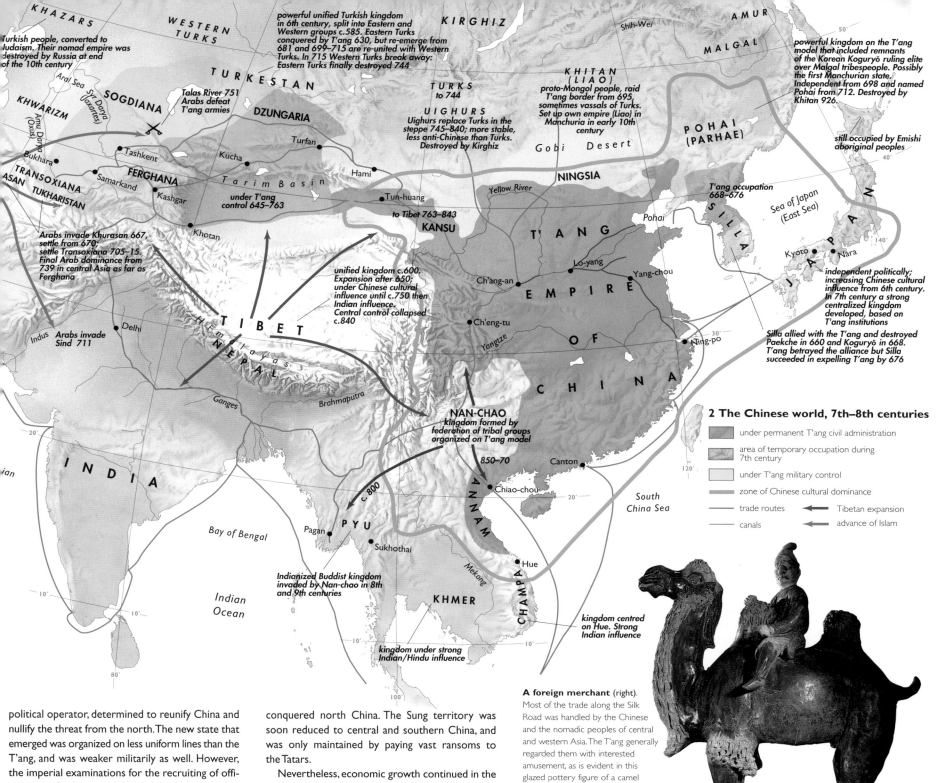

KHAZARS

Turkish people, converted to Judaism. Their nomad empire was destroyed by Russia at end of the 10th century

WESTERN TURKS

TURKESTAN

KIRGHIZ

powerful unified Turkish kingdom in 6th century, split into Eastern and Western groups c.585. Eastern Turks conquered by T'ang 630, but re-emerge from 681 and 699-715 are re-united with Western Turks. In 715 Western Turks break away: Eastern Turks finally destroyed 744

AMUR

MALGAL

Shih-Wei

powerful kingdom on the T'ang model that included remnants of the Korean Koguryŏ ruling elite over Malgal tribespeople. Possibly the first Manchurian state. Independent from 698 and named Pohai from 712. Destroyed by Khitan 926.

Aral Sea

Syr Darya (Jaxartes)

SOGDIANA

Talas River 751 Arabs defeat T'ang armies

DZUNGARIA

KHITAN (LIAO) proto-Mongol people, raid T'ang border from 695, sometimes vassals of Turks. Set up own empire (Liao) in Manchuria in early 10th century

POHAI (PARHAE)

still occupied by Emishi aboriginal peoples

Khwarizm
Amu Darya (Oxus)
Bukhara

TRANSOXIANA
ASAN TUKHARISTAN

Tashkent
Samarkand
FERGHANA

Kashgar

Kucha

Turfan

Tarim Basin

Hami

Gobi Desert

NINGSIA

Yellow River

TURKS to 744

UIGHURS

Uighurs replace Turks in the steppe 745-840; more stable, less anti-Chinese than Turks. Destroyed by Kirghiz

Pohai

T'ang occupation 668-676

SILLA

Sea of Japan (East Sea)

JAPAN

Arabs invade Khurasan 667; settle from 670; settle Transoxiana 705-15. Final Arab dominance from 739 in central Asia as far as Ferghana

Khotan

under T'ang control 645-763

Tun-huang

to Tibet 763-843

KANSU

T'ANG

Ch'ang-an

Lo-yang

Yang-chou

Kyoto
Nara

independent politically; increasing Chinese cultural influence from 6th century. In 7th century a strong centralized kingdom developed, based on T'ang institutions

Arabs invade Sind 711

Indus

Delhi

TIBET

NEPAL

Himalayas

Brahmaputra

Ganges

unified kingdom c.600. Expansion after 650; under Chinese cultural influence until c.750 then Indian influence. Central control collapsed c.840

EMPIRE

Ch'eng-tu

OF

Yangtze

CHINA

Ning-po

Silla allied with the T'ang and destroyed Paekche in 660 and Koguryŏ in 668. T'ang betrayed the alliance but Silla succeeded in expelling T'ang by 676

INDIA

NAN-CHAO kingdom formed by federation of tribal groups organized on T'ang model

850-70

2 The Chinese world, 7th–8th centuries

under permanent T'ang civil administration

area of temporary occupation during 7th century

under T'ang military control

zone of Chinese cultural dominance

trade routes — Tibetan expansion

canals — advance of Islam

c.800

ANNAM

Chiao-chou

Canton

South China Sea

Bay of Bengal

Pagan

PYU

Sukhothai

Indianized Buddist kingdom invaded by Nan-chao in 8th and 9th centuries

Indian Ocean

KHMER

Hue

CHAMPA

kingdom centred on Hue. Strong Indian influence

kingdom under strong Indian/Hindu influence

Mekong

---

political operator, determined to reunify China and nullify the threat from the north. The new state that emerged was organized on less uniform lines than the T'ang, and was weaker militarily as well. However, the imperial examinations for the recruiting of officials were further streamlined and a meritocracy of career bureaucrats became established. This, too, was a period of rapid economic growth. Between 750 and 1100 the population nearly doubled, trade reached new levels with the help of paper currency and a great concentration of industries arose around the early Sung capital, K'ai-feng. But the Sung paid a heavy price for its weak military defence along the northern border. In 1126–7 the Tatar Chin

conquered north China. The Sung territory was soon reduced to central and southern China, and was only maintained by paying vast ransoms to the Tatars.

Nevertheless, economic growth continued in the south. The population continued to increase rapidly, trade and industry boomed and the new capital, Hang-chou, became indisputably the world's greatest city. This was also a period of great cultural achievement ranging from the visual arts to literature and philosophy. New heights were reached in science and technology also, most significantly in metallurgy, porcelain manufacture, ship-building and compass-guided navigation. Education became more widespread, aided by the dissemination of block printing. Merchants established complex commercial organizations with credit systems. In the countryside a free market in land emerged. Since the old overland routes to central Asia and the Middle East were no longer in Chinese hands, the Chinese became a major sea power, regularly trading with southeast Asia, south Asia and the Persian Gulf. A powerful navy was also built.

In the 13th century, the pace of change slowed markedly. This was mainly the result of the immense destruction and social disruption caused by the Mongol invasion and conquest of both Tatar and Sung territory. Nonetheless, 13th-century China remained far more populous and wealthy than contemporary Europe.

A foreign merchant (right). Most of the trade along the Silk Road was handled by the Chinese and the nomadic peoples of central and western Asia. The T'ang generally regarded them with interested amusement, as is evident in this glazed pottery figure of a camel groom or trader with his exaggeratedly large nose.

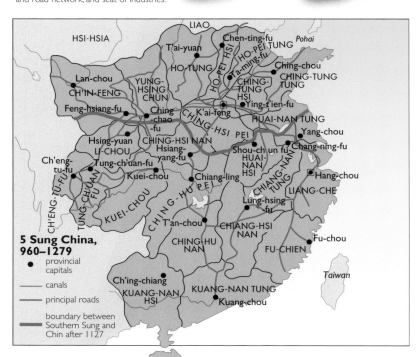

5 The Sung never recovered all of the territory of T'ang China (map below): Annam had broken away; the Khitan state of Liao still occupied the border areas to the northeast; and the Tangut state of Hsi-hsia the northwest. The centre of the Sung state was the great commercial city of K'ai-feng, hub of the canal system and road network, and seat of industries.

---

3 The fragmentation of China: the Five Dynasties and Ten Kingdoms, c. 910

rump of imperial China ruled by the "Five Dynasties"

KAN-CHOU
UIGHURS
LIANG-CHOU TIBETANS
SHA-T'O TURKS
KHITAN
Great Wall
Pohai
STANGUT
CHIN
YEN
CH'ING T'ANG-CH'IANG
TIBET (T'U-PO)
CH'I
LATER LIANG
FORMER SHU
CHING NAN
WU-YUEH
NAN-CHAO MAN
TA-CHANG-HO 902-28
CH'U
WU
MIN
Taiwan
ANNAM
NAN-HAN
South China Sea

3 After the fall of the Tang, a variety of independent local kingdoms developed on the basis of Late T'ang provincial divisions (map left). A rump was left, ruled by five successive dynasties from 907 to 959. Although the area under imperial control expanded after the Later Liang, the last of the "Five Dynasties" emperors still controlled China only north of the Yangtze.

---

5 Sung China, 960–1279

• provincial capitals
— canals
— principal roads
— boundary between Southern Sung and Chin after 1127

LIAO
HSI-HSIA
Chen-ting-fu
Pohai
T'ai-yuan
HO-PEI TUNG
Lan-chou
YUNG-HSING CHUN
HO-TUNG
Ta-ming-fu
CH'IN-FENG
Feng-hsiang-fu
Ching-chao-fu
K'ai-feng
CHING-TUNG HSI
Ying-t'ien-fu
Ching-chou
CHING-TUNG TUNG
HO-PEI HSI
Hsing-yuan
LI-CHOU
Ch'eng-tu-fu
TUNG-CH'UAN FU
Tung-ch'uan-fu
Hsiang-yang-fu
CHING-HSI NAN
HUAI-NAN TUNG
Yang-chou
CHING-HSI PEI
Kuei-chou
Chiang-ling
Shou-ch'un-fu
HUAI-NAN HSI
Chang-ning-fu
CH'ENG-TU-FU
TUNG-CHUAN FU
KUEI-CHOU
CHING-HU PEI
Lung-hsing-fu
CHIANG-NAN HSI
Hang-chou
LIANG-CHE
CHING-HU NAN
T'an-chou
CHIANG-HSI NAN
Ch'ing-chiang
KUANG-NAN HSI
KUANG-NAN TUNG
Fu-chou
FU-CHIEN
Kuang-chou
Taiwan
Hainan

139

Iran and central Asia

1 The Seljuks created the most extensive and impressive Islamic state since the break-up of the Caliphate in the ninth century (**map right**). But in accordance with the nomadic idea that the empire's territories belonged to the ruling dynasty as a whole, the Sultanate granted out provinces as appanages to members of their family: both Kirman and Anatolia (Rum), for instance, were ruled throughout by separate branches of the Seljuk dynasty. In addition, a number of existing dynasties, such as the Shaddadids in Ganja and the Kakuyids in Yazd, were allowed to retain their territories as the Sultan's subordinates.

The Kalyan minaret (below) in Bukhara (12th century) shows Persian brickwork at its most spectacular. It was one of the chief monuments of Islam in this ancient central Asian oasis city and was one of the few to survive the Mongol conquest of 1218. Chingiz Khan preached in its shadow and declared himself "the scourge of God".

The history of Iran was dominated by the interaction between the settled Persian-speaking people of the cities and villages and the repeated invasions of Turkic nomads from the east. The Seljuks in the 11th century, Mongols in the 13th and Timur's followers in the late 14th, all conquered Iran but were in turn converted to Islam and adopted Iranian styles of government. Despite the political chaos, architecture, literature and painting flourished.

OFFICERS WHO HOLD LANDS IN FIEF (*IQTA'*) MUST KNOW THAT THEY HAVE NO AUTHORITY OVER THE PEASANTS EXCEPT TO TAKE FROM THEM, AND THAT WITH COURTESY, THE DUE AMOUNT OF REVENUE WHICH HAS BEEN ASSIGNED TO THEM TO COLLECT. WHEN THEY HAVE TAKEN THAT, THE PEASANTS ARE TO HAVE SECURITY FOR THEIR PERSONS, PROPERTY, WIVES AND CHILDREN AND THEIR GOODS AND FARMS ARE TO BE INVIOLABLE.

Nizam al-Mulk, *Book of Government*

THE CONQUEST OF IRAN by Arab armies between 636 and 650 brought Islamic rule to the lands of the old Persian empire. In medieval times, the area of Iranian culture and civilization extended beyond the borders of modern Iran to include Afghanistan and the central Asian republics of Turkmenistan, Uzbekistan and Tajikistan. Until *c.* 860 the Iranian lands were provinces of the Abbasid Caliphate with its capital in Baghdad. From the end of the ninth century power passed into the hands of local Iranian dynasties, beginning with the Saffarids in Sistan from 867 and the Samanids in Khurasan from 892. These rulers were all Muslim but encouraged the revival of Persian language and culture.

From 1040 Iran was taken over by Ghuzz Turks, originally from the steppes east of the Caspian Sea, led by the Seljuk family. They took Baghdad in 1055 and established an empire which stretched from the Mediterranean to central Asia. The Seljuk period (1055–*c.*1200) also saw the building of the first great monuments of Muslim architecture in Iran, including the great Mosque of Isfahan.

Mongol invasion

This period of comparative peace and prosperity was brought to an end by the invasion of the Mongols under Chingiz (Genghis) Khan (d.1227) from 1218 onwards. Many of the cities of the ancient Khurasan, such as Merv, Nishapur and Balkh, were devastated and never recovered while cities in the south and west, such as Isfahan and Shiraz, were spared the worst ravages. With the arrival of the Mongol khan Hülegü in 1256 Iran

became independent under the rule of his descendants, known as the Il-Khans. They established their centre of power in the uplands of Azerbaijan, around Tabriz and their new capital at Sultaniya. Ghazan Khan (1295–1304) converted to Islam and adopted much of traditional Iranian culture. This was also a period when commercial links with other Mongol successor states along the "Silk Road" flourished and merchants regularly travelled between the Middle East and China.

The collapse of the Il-Khanid empire after 1335 led to another period of political division in Iran. The 1370s saw the growing power of Timur (Tamerlane). Timur was a Turkish tribal leader from the area south of Samarkand. Although a Muslim, he showed himself as brutal and effective a conqueror of Islamic lands as his predecessor, Chingiz Khan. At the same time,

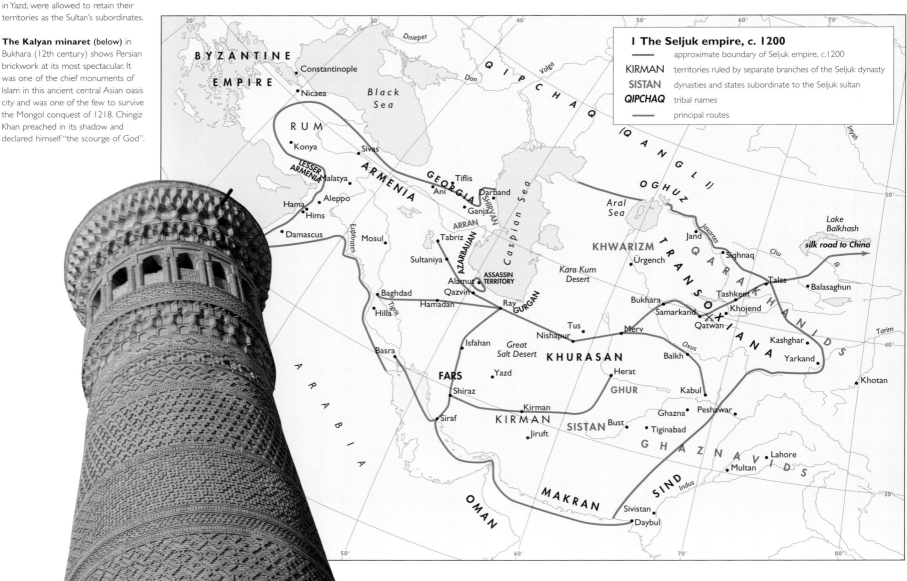

1 The Seljuk empire, c. 1200	
——	approximate boundary of Seljuk empire, *c.*1200
KIRMAN	territories ruled by separate branches of the Seljuk dynasty
SISTAN	dynasties and states subordinate to the Seljuk sultan
QIPCHAQ	tribal names
——	principal routes

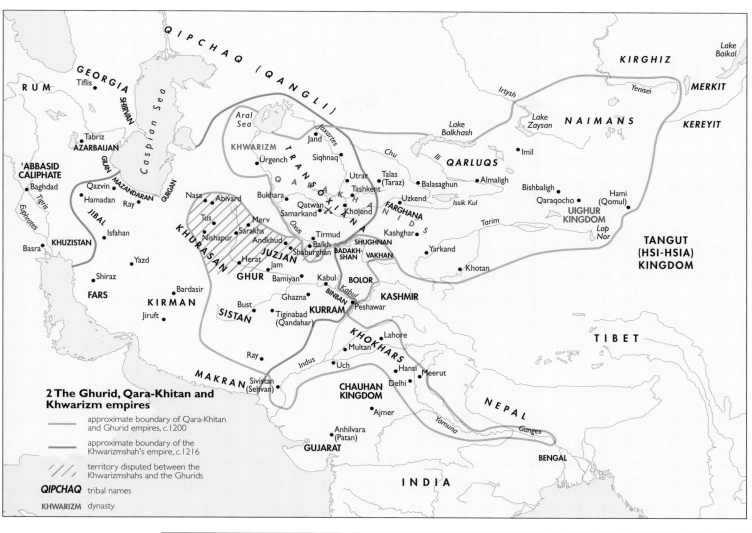

2 The Ghurid, Qara-Khitan and Khwarizm empires

——— approximate boundary of Qara-Khitan and Ghurid empires, c.1200

——— approximate boundary of the Khwarizmshah's empire, c.1216

///// territory disputed between the Khwarizmshahs and the Ghurids

QIPCHAQ tribal names

KHWARIZM dynasty

2 The Ghurids, a dynasty of Iranian stock in an era otherwise dominated by Turks, engaged in a duel for Khurasan with the Khwarizm-shahs and their Qara-Khitan overlords (**map left**). The Qara-Khitan sovereigns were Buddhists, although they appear to have tolerated other faiths and their victories over Muslim princes like Sanjar turned them into candidates for the role of the mythical Christian ruler "Prester John". Their conquests represented the first serious encroachment on Islamic territory by non-Muslims, thereby prefiguring the more cataclysmic advance of the Mongols 100 years later.

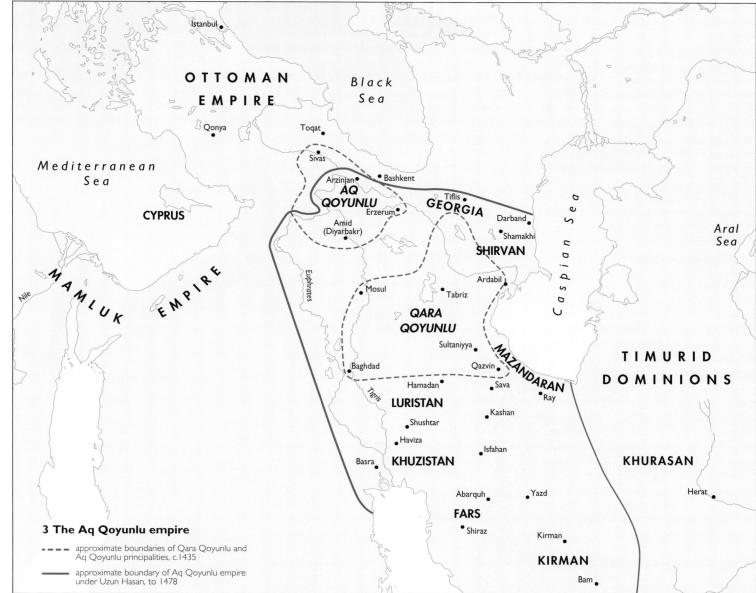

3 The rise of the two Türkmen dynasties – the Qara Qoyunlu and the Aq Qoyunlu – marked the onset of an eastward migration into Iran by tribes that had moved into Anatolia two centuries earlier, during the Seljuq era (**map right**). They had profited, like other tribal groups there, from the collapse of the Il-Khanate. The final phase of this "Türkmen" interlude was the migration of Türkmen tribes that accompanied the takeover of power in Iran by the Safavids from c. 1500 onwards and which was responsible for the ethnic map of Iran in modern times.

3 The Aq Qoyunlu empire

– – – – approximate boundaries of Qara Qoyunlu and Aq Qoyunlu principalities, c.1435

——— approximate boundary of Aq Qoyunlu empire under Uzun Hasan, to 1478

he made his capital Samarkand one of the great cities of Iran and patronized vast building projects in the city. By 1400 all of Iran was under his control but in 1405, just as he was making preparations for an invasion of China, he died.

After his death, his empire began to disintegrate, but the 15th century was a period of great cultural achievements in architecture and book-painting. Under Timur's son Shah Rukh (1405–47), Herat became the capital while his grandson Ulugh Beg (d.1449) built an observatory in Samarkand whose reputation reached western Europe.

The final years of the 15th century saw renewed chaos in western Iran, which opened the way for the rise of the Safavids.

The Mongol Empire

The Mongols, pastoral nomads from the depths of Asia, achieved conquests of unrivalled range, from the eastern frontiers of Germany to Korea and from the Arctic Ocean to Turkey and the Persian Gulf, though their invasions of Japan and Java failed. Whole peoples were uprooted and dispersed, permanently changing the ethnic character of many regions.

THROUGH THEIR DEVASTATING conquests of the 13th century, the Mongols established the largest ever contiguous land empire. Mongol-speaking tribes had lived for centuries in the general area of present-day Mongolia, but it was to take an extraordinary leader to unite not only the Mongols but all the Turco-Mongol tribes of Eurasia and transform them into a world power. Genghis Khan was born Temüjin in around 1167, the son of a minor Mongol tribal chief. In 1206, after years of personal struggle following the murder of his father, he was proclaimed leader of the united Turco-Mongol tribes. Originating in barren lands, the Mongols themselves were relatively few, but from the outset Genghis recruited members of other Turkic tribes. Using traditional battle tactics that relied on light cavalry, he conducted what were initially raids of pillage and plunder from the steppe into the towns. In 1211 he invaded northern China, subduing the independent Chin empire, and crossing the Great Wall aided by the semi-nomadic Khitans. Genghis Khan then turned his attention westward in campaigns against the Kara Khitai, whose Muslim merchants and administrators would form the backbone of his emerging state. Then, reluctantly, he turned against Khwarizm, the first Muslim state to experience the full fury of the Mongol onslaught after their murder of the Great Khan's envoys. Proclaiming himself the "Punishment of God", Genghis Khan unleashed the bloody raids and merciless devastation that have made his name synonymous with barbaric mass slaughter. The trail of blood and massacre led from central Asia through Iran to the Caucasus and north into the plains of Russia. The establishment of the Mongol-led armies throughout Asia and eastern Europe in the first half of the 13th century traumatized the world.

One effect of the Mongol conquests was that trade routes flourished, linking east to west across Asia. Tabriz in northwest Iran became a cosmopolitan centre of trade, culture, and learning. The Venetian merchant Marco Polo came this way in 1271, and after 1300 Italian merchants settled as far away as Zaitun in China. The Great Khan Qubilai opened China to the world and, though his empire was riven by cracks, the Yuan dynasty of China and the Ilkhanate of Persia remained close and became beacons of sophistication, commerce and art.

Mongol conquests in Europe

Genghis Khan died in 1227. Unlike those of other steppe emperors, his sons and successors were able to maintain and extend his power and territories. Before his death, he had appointed Ögödei his successor and divided his empire among his four sons. Batu, son of the eldest son, Jochi, was bequeathed the peoples of the west, and it was he who directed the invasion of Europe (see map 2). The northern Russian principalities

fell in a lightning winter campaign in 1237–8; Kiev was razed in 1240; Poland and Hungary were attacked, Cracow was burned and abandoned; and in 1241 a Silisian army was annihilated at Legnica. Mongol troops even reached the coastline of Croatia near Trogir (Trail). The death of the Great Khan Ögödei in December 1241 saved Europe; Batu withdrew eastwards to immerse himself in affairs of state as a Grand *Quriltai* (council) was convened to decide on the succession.

Mongols, Islam and Christianity

The Mongol conquerors came into contact with three main religions: Buddhism, Islam and Christianity. The Mongol elite was shamanist, although many Turco-Mongols adhered nominally to other faiths. However, they were attracted by the high culture associated with the great religions. Many of their administrators were Muslims, Buddhists and Christians, and the Mongol courts had become truly multi-cultural, multi-ethnic and multi-religious. The Mongols universally exercised religious tolerance, although many have assumed that they were merely hedging their bets with the Almighty. In 1258 the Islamic capital, Baghdad, was captured and plundered, the caliph slain and massacres perpetrated, but the operation was overseen by Muslim advisors, carried out with the assistance of local Muslim rulers and their soldiers and supported by the caliph's Muslim subjects, Kurds and Shi'ites. Even though the Mongols had sometimes promoted Nestorian Christianity and Buddhism in Persia, in 1295 the Mongol ruler, Ghazan Khan, tactically declared his state nominally Muslim. In China meanwhile, the Yuan Mongols had endorsed Buddhism, thereby strengthening the position of that faith in the Far East. Despite their religious differences Iran and China remained politically, commercially and culturally intimate during the first half of the 14th century. With the Christian rulers of western Europe, the Mongol rulers of Iran – the Ilkhans – played up their Christian credentials, which included the presence of Christian queens and princesses at the royal court and the support of their staunchly loyal Christian allies, the Armenians. The Ilkhans made overtures to the Pope, hopeful that a Christian alliance against the Mamluk sultans of Egypt in the Holy Land might emerge.

Just as Europe was saved by the death of Ögödei, it has been said that the death of the Great Khan Möngke in 1259 saved the heartlands of Muslim Asia. Möngke had targeted both Sung China and western Asia for conquest. His brother, Hülegü Khan, returned eastward on hearing news of Möngke's death, leaving only a skeleton military force in Syria – of which the

1206 Temüjin proclaimed Genghis Khan ("universal ruler") of Mongol tribes

1219 Genghis attacks Samarkand

1211–34 Mongol conquest of China

1227 Death of Genghis

1237–8 Moscow and Vladimir fall to Mongols

1241 Mongols invade Poland and Hungary

1258 Mongols destroy Baghdad

1260 Mongol defeat at Ain Jalut

1274–81 Mongol attempts to conquer Japan

c. 1360–1405 Campaigns of Tamerlane

THE TITLE KHAN MEANS IN OUR LANGUAGE "GREAT LORD OF LORDS". AND CERTAINLY HE HAS A RIGHT TO THIS TITLE; FOR EVERYONE SHOULD KNOW THAT THIS GREAT KHAN IS THE MIGHTIEST MAN, WHETHER IN RESPECT OF SUBJECTS OR TERRITORY OR OF TREASURE, WHO IS IN THE WORLD TODAY OR WHO HAS EVER BEEN, FROM ADAM OUR FIRST PARENT DOWN TO THE PRESENT MOMENT ... HE IS INDEED THE GREATEST LORD THE WORLD HAS EVER KNOWN.

Marco Polo
The Travels of Marco Polo, c. 1298

3 The disruption of the Mongol empire after 1259

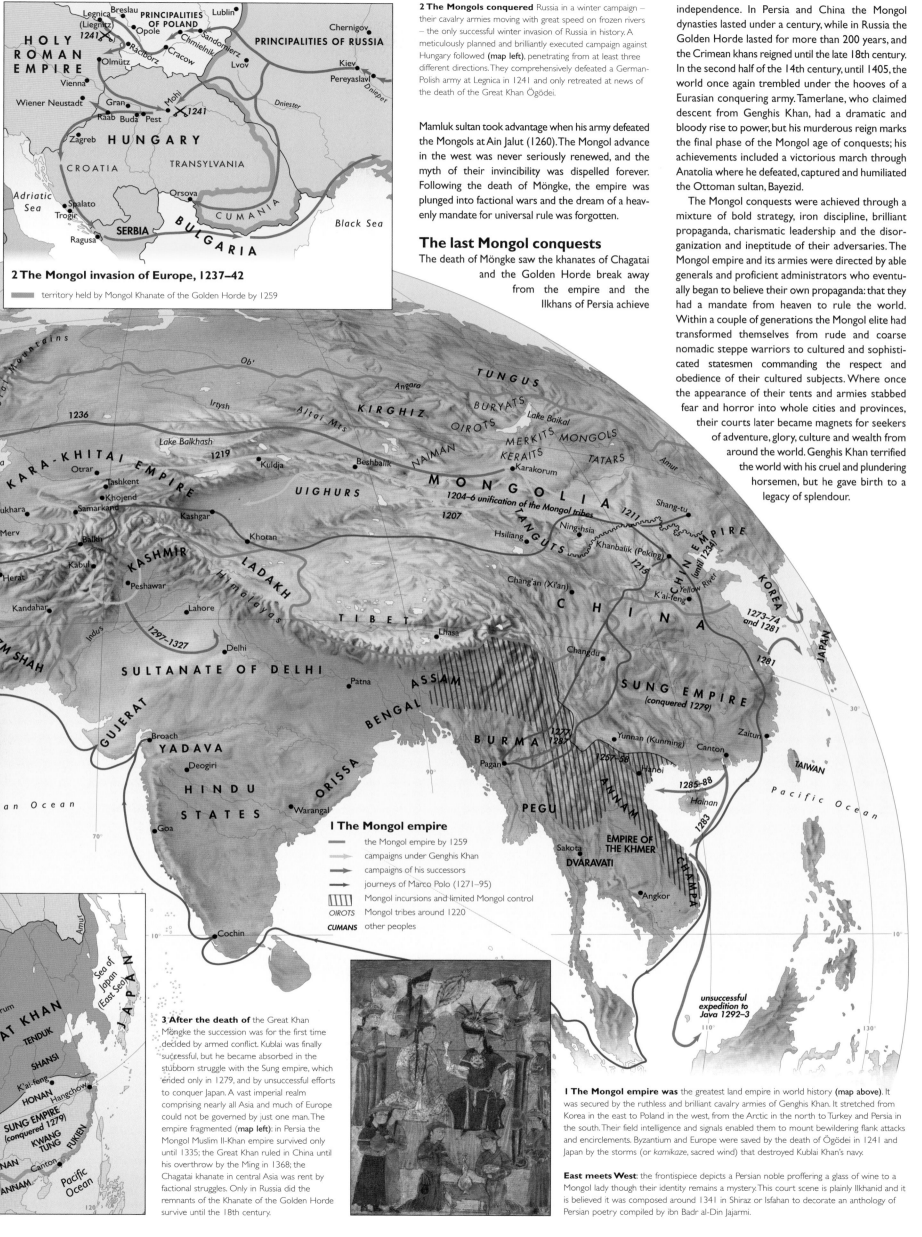

Map 2: The Mongol invasion of Europe

2 The Mongols conquered Russia in a winter campaign – their cavalry armies moving with great speed on frozen rivers – the only successful winter invasion of Russia in history. A meticulously planned and brilliantly executed campaign against Hungary followed (**map left**), penetrating from at least three different directions. They comprehensively defeated a German-Polish army at Legnica in 1241 and only retreated at news of the death of the Great Khan Ögödei.

Mamluk sultan took advantage when his army defeated the Mongols at Ain Jalut (1260). The Mongol advance in the west was never seriously renewed, and the myth of their invincibility was dispelled forever. Following the death of Möngke, the empire was plunged into factional wars and the dream of a heavenly mandate for universal rule was forgotten.

The last Mongol conquests

The death of Möngke saw the khanates of Chagatai and the Golden Horde break away from the empire and the Ilkhans of Persia achieve independence. In Persia and China the Mongol dynasties lasted under a century, while in Russia the Golden Horde lasted for more than 200 years, and the Crimean khans reigned until the late 18th century. In the second half of the 14th century, until 1405, the world once again trembled under the hooves of a Eurasian conquering army. Tamerlane, who claimed descent from Genghis Khan, had a dramatic and bloody rise to power, but his murderous reign marks the final phase of the Mongol age of conquests; his achievements included a victorious march through Anatolia where he defeated, captured and humiliated the Ottoman sultan, Bayezid.

The Mongol conquests were achieved through a mixture of bold strategy, iron discipline, brilliant propaganda, charismatic leadership and the disorganization and ineptitude of their adversaries. The Mongol empire and its armies were directed by able generals and proficient administrators who eventually began to believe their own propaganda: that they had a mandate from heaven to rule the world. Within a couple of generations the Mongol elite had transformed themselves from rude and coarse nomadic steppe warriors to cultured and sophisticated statesmen commanding the respect and obedience of their cultured subjects. Where once the appearance of their tents and armies stabbed fear and horror into whole cities and provinces, their courts later became magnets for seekers of adventure, glory, culture and wealth from around the world. Genghis Khan terrified the world with his cruel and plundering horsemen, but he gave birth to a legacy of splendour.

2 The Mongol invasion of Europe, 1237–42

territory held by Mongol Khanate of the Golden Horde by 1259

1 The Mongol empire

- the Mongol empire by 1259
- campaigns under Genghis Khan
- campaigns of his successors
- journeys of Marco Polo (1271–95)
- Mongol incursions and limited Mongol control
- *OIROTS* Mongol tribes around 1220
- *CUMANS* other peoples

3 After the death of the Great Khan Möngke the succession was for the first time decided by armed conflict. Kublai was finally successful, but he became absorbed in the stubborn struggle with the Sung empire, which ended only in 1279, and by unsuccessful efforts to conquer Japan. A vast imperial realm comprising nearly all Asia and much of Europe could not be governed by just one man. The empire fragmented (**map left**): in Persia the Mongol Muslim Il-Khan empire survived only until 1335; the Great Khan ruled in China until his overthrow by the Ming in 1368; the Chagatai khanate in central Asia was rent by factional struggles. Only in Russia did the remnants of the Khanate of the Golden Horde survive until the 18th century.

1 The Mongol empire was the greatest land empire in world history (**map above**). It was secured by the ruthless and brilliant cavalry armies of Genghis Khan. It stretched from Korea in the east to Poland in the west, from the Arctic in the north to Turkey and Persia in the south. Their field intelligence and signals enabled them to mount bewildering flank attacks and encirclements. Byzantium and Europe were saved by the death of Ögödei in 1241 and Japan by the storms (or *kamikaze*, sacred wind) that destroyed Kublai Khan's navy.

East meets West: the frontispiece depicts a Persian noble proffering a glass of wine to a Mongol lady though their identity remains a mystery. This court scene is plainly Ilkhanid and it is believed it was composed around 1341 in Shiraz or Isfahan to decorate an anthology of Persian poetry compiled by ibn Badr al-Din Jajarmi.

India: the emergence of temple kingdoms

The integration of early India led to agrarian expansion, the proliferation of rival states and the triumph of Hinduism over its rivals. The political centre of India gradually shifted southward to powerful agrarian empires such as the Rashtrakutas and Cholas. As north India fragmented, it became vulnerable to Turkic incursions from the northwest.

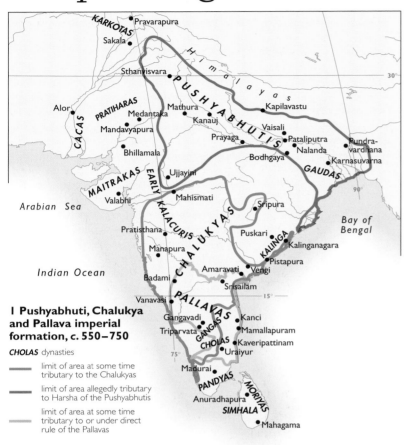

1 Pushyabhuti, Chalukya and Pallava imperial formation, c. 550–750

CHOLAS dynasties

— limit of area at some time tributary to the Chalukyas

— limit of area allegedly tributary to Harsha of the Pushyabhutis

— limit of area at some time tributary to or under direct rule of the Pallavas

1 The famous Pushyabhuti king Harsha of Kanauj, whose court has been detailed by the Sanskrit poet Bana as well as the Chinese traveller Hsüan-tsang, was perhaps the last major king of northern India (map above) as the political centre of India shifted to the south until the establishment of the sultanate (see p. 146). The Chalukyas, who defeated Harsha, and the Pallavas, who developed links with southeast Asia, were powerful dynasties that vied for control of the south throughout this period.

2 Arab travellers in the 9th century reported that the Rashtrakuta king ruled all India, but in fact there were at least two other dynasties that claimed regional paramountcy (map below). The Rashtrakutas, who had arisen to prominence when their king Dantidurga had led a rebellion in the 750s against their Chalukya overlords, met fierce resistance from the Gurjara-Pratiharas, and were able to defeat them only intermittently. The weaker Buddhist empire of the Palas claimed dominance over eastern India.

THE THOUSANDS OF inscriptions that have come down to us from medieval India reveal an intricate mosaic of kings, lords and priests superimposed on an agrarian populace. Overall, civilization and its revenue-extracting agents now penetrated into regions previously beyond the reach of the more urbanized polities of ancient India. The great metropolises of earlier times contracted as the countryside became filled with smaller settlements integrated into local trade networks. Temple Hinduism triumphed over Buddhism and provided the political theology of royal courts as well as the religious sentiments of the peasantry.

Dynastic struggles

Politically, this epoch was composed of successive "imperial formations", hierarchies of dynastic empires in struggle and alliance, vying for paramountcy. After the decline of the power of the Guptas (see p. 92), north India suffered political instability until the Huns were gradually pushed northward from India by local rulers. Not long afterwards, three major dynasties emerged as powerful contenders for imperial paramountcy – the Pushyabhutis of Kanauj, the Chalukyas of Badami and the Pallavas of Kanci. Harsha Pushyabhuti, who hosted the famous Chinese traveller Hsüan-tsang, was defeated in 630 by the Chalukya king Pulakesin II, although the location of this battle is not known. The Chalukyas, who claimed descent from the Satavahana dynasty that had held sway in the south 500 years earlier (see p. 92), gained initial victories against the southern Pallavas, but were later defeated by them and finally faced rebellion by one of their ablest underlords, the Rashtrakutas, who rose to become the chief power in south India for nearly 200 years (c. 750–950). The Rashtrakutas, builders of the famous Kalaisanatha temple at Ellora, were perceived by the Arab traveller Masudi as the most powerful dynasty of India. Their rivals were the Pratiharas to the north and the Palas of eastern India, followers of Mahayana Buddhism and patrons of the Buddhist university at Nalanda.

The rise of the Cholas

By the close of the 10th century these empires had weakened and contracted as the ancient Chola lineage of the south revitalized itself to become the dominant force in a new imperial formation that would last nearly 250 years (c. 950–1200). The Cholas made daring military expeditions to north India, Sri Lanka and southeast Asia, gaining tremendous wealth with which they constructed elaborate imperial temples and patronized Brahmin religious elites. In the Deccan, two families revived the Chalukya dynasty and further north the Pratihara empire fragmented into a number of smaller kingdoms warring amongst themselves, that eventually came to be known as the Rajputs. Perhaps the most

powerful of these smaller dynasties were the Paramaras based in Dhar. The political instability of north India made it particularly vulnerable to the militarily superior Turkic armies, which under the leadership of Mahmud of Ghazni conducted looting raids in the 11th century.

From the time of the Pallavas the dynasties of eastern India – particularly the Palas and the Cholas – established trade links and cultural exchanges with the kingdoms of southeast Asia. Several Buddhist kings of southeast Asia patronized Buddhist institutions in eastern India and maintained trading enclaves at coastal cities. After the decline of Rome, trade links with southeast Asia were further strengthened, as peninsular India eventually became an important depot in a trans-regional trade circuit connecting China to the Arab Middle East. Despite these trading links, medieval Indian empires remained primarily agrarian in nature. Their royal families, courtly officials and ritual specialists enjoyed the revenue extracted from vast tracts of land cultivated by the lower orders, who in turn were divided into hierarchies of cultivators, tenants and labourers. The Cholas, for example, relied on the flourishing wet-cultivation of rice in the Kaveri river delta. Political authority was not directly administered but was sustained through relations of tribute and dependence among a hierarchy of lords, giving India an almost feudal complexion.

Temple Hinduism

Saivism and Vaisnavism, the two main orders of theistic Hinduism, which centred their philosophy and ritual around the exaltation of the gods Shiva and Vishnu respectively, facilitated this chain of medieval lordships. These religions, which had been growing since the time of the Guptas, gained the commitments of most royal courts by the 7th century. Two of the most important early texts of these theistic orders were the *Ramayana*, a tale of the mythical king Rama of Ayodhya (see map 4), and the voluminous *Mahabharata*, recounting the war between two royal families for paramount sovereignty of the earth. The latter contained the *Bhagavad-gita*, which developed the theology of devotion called "bhakti". Through theocentric histories called "Puranas", ancient pedigrees and divine identities were provided for medieval rulers, and images of Hindu gods were housed in royal fashion in hundreds of temples which dotted the countryside, reinforcing the ideology of sovereignty and devotion integral to the authority of kings. Occasionally devotion to god ("bhakti") could be turned against the chain of secular lordships, but such subversions were limited. Temples became the beneficiaries of royal and lordly largesse, accumulating considerable wealth and emerging as significant landholders by the end of the medieval period. This no doubt explains their attraction for the raiding Turks who laid the foundation of Muslim rule in India (see p. 146).

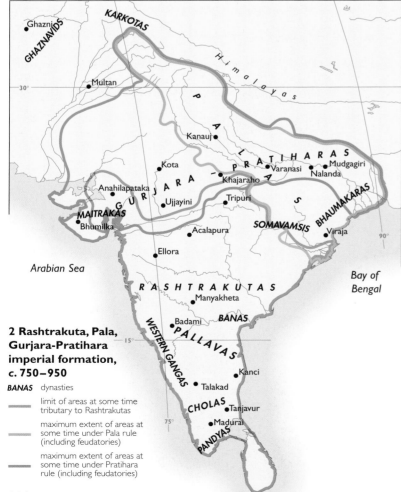

2 Rashtrakuta, Pala, Gurjara-Pratihara imperial formation, c. 750–950

BANAS dynasties

— limit of areas at some time tributary to Rashtrakutas

— maximum extent of areas at some time under Pala rule (including feudatories)

— maximum extent of areas at some time under Pratihara rule (including feudatories)

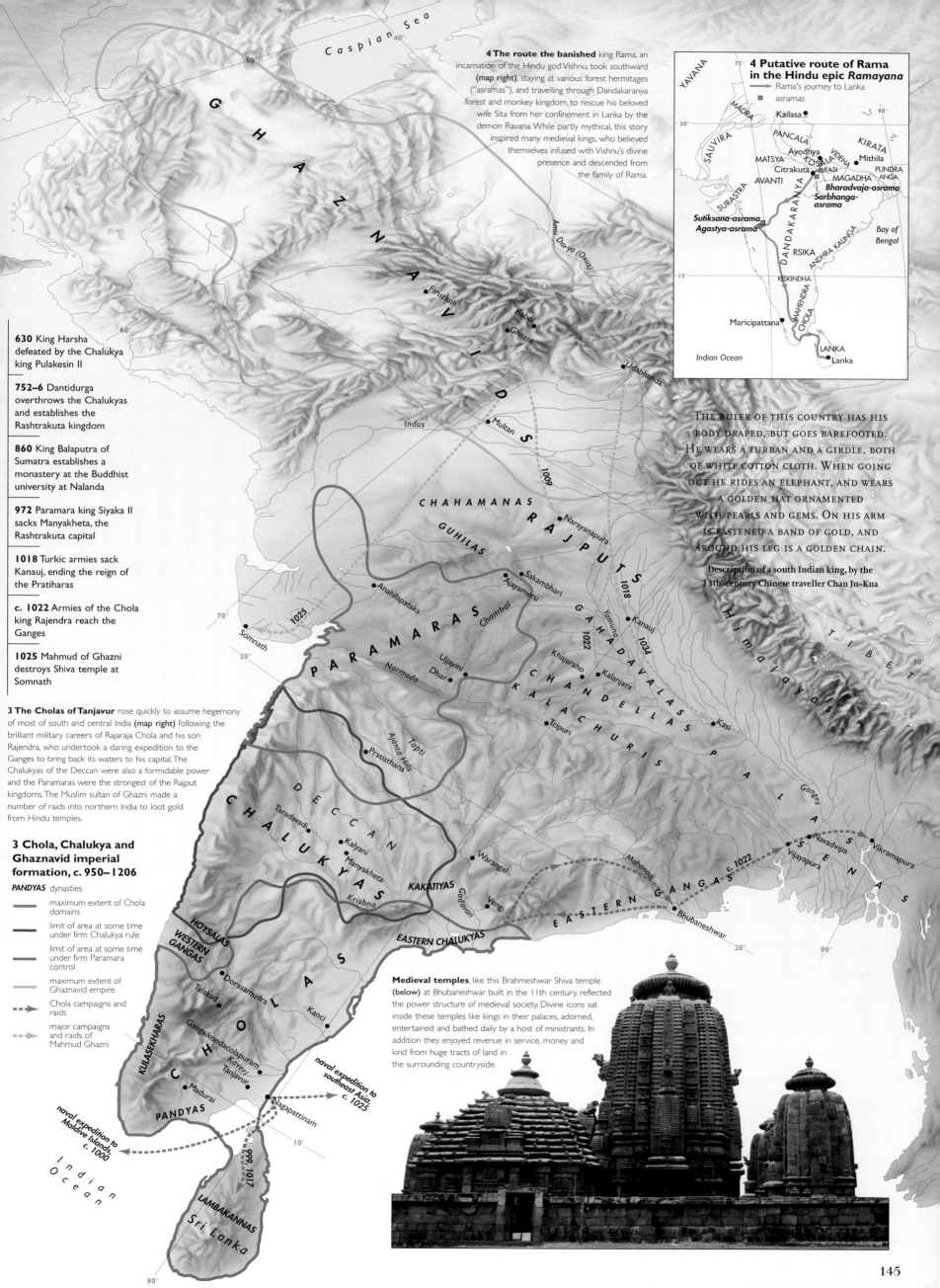

4 **The route the banished** king Rama, an incarnation of the Hindu god Vishnu, took southward (map right), staying at various forest hermitages ("asramas"), and travelling through Dandakaranya forest and monkey kingdom, to rescue his beloved wife Sita from her confinement in Lanka by the demon Ravana. While partly mythical, this story inspired many medieval kings, who believed themselves infused with Vishnu's divine presence and descended from the family of Rama.

4 Putative route of Rama in the Hindu epic *Ramayana*

→ Rama's journey to Lanka
■ asramas

YAVANA
MADRA
SAUVIRA
PANCALA
Kailasa •
Ayodhya KOSALA VIDEHA
Mithila
MATSYA Citrakuta KASI PUNDRA
AVANTI MAGADHA ANGA
Bharadvaja-asrama
Sarbhanga-asrama
Sutiksana-asrama
Agastya-asrama
DANDAKARANYA
RSIKA ANDHRA KALINGA
Bay of Bengal
KISKINDHA
Maricipattana
MAHENDRA
CHOLA
Indian Ocean
LANKA
Lanka

630 King Harsha defeated by the Chalukya king Pulakesin II

752–6 Dantidurga overthrows the Chalukyas and establishes the Rashtrakuta kingdom

860 King Balaputra of Sumatra establishes a monastery at the Buddhist university at Nalanda

972 Paramara king Siyaka II sacks Manyakheta, the Rashtrakuta capital

1018 Turkic armies sack Kanauj, ending the reign of the Pratiharas

c. 1022 Armies of the Chola king Rajendra reach the Ganges

1025 Mahmud of Ghazni destroys Shiva temple at Somnath

3 The Cholas of Tanjavur rose quickly to assume hegemony of most of south and central India (map right) following the brilliant military careers of Rajaraja Chola and his son Rajendra, who undertook a daring expedition to the Ganges to bring back its waters to his capital. The Chalukyas of the Deccan were also a formidable power and the Paramaras were the strongest of the Rajput kingdoms. The Muslim sultan of Ghazni made a number of raids into northern India to loot gold from Hindu temples.

3 Chola, Chalukya and Ghaznavid imperial formation, c. 950–1206

PANDYAS dynasties

——— maximum extent of Chola domains

——— limit of area at some time under firm Chalukya rule

——— limit of area at some time under firm Paramara control

——— maximum extent of Ghaznavid empire

--▶ Chola campaigns and raids

--▶ major campaigns and raids of Mahmud Ghazni

THE RULER OF THIS COUNTRY HAS HIS BODY DRAPED, BUT GOES BAREFOOTED. HE WEARS A TURBAN AND A GIRDLE, BOTH OF WHITE COTTON CLOTH. WHEN GOING OUT HE RIDES AN ELEPHANT, AND WEARS A GOLDEN HAT ORNAMENTED WITH PEARLS AND GEMS. ON HIS ARM IS FASTENED A BAND OF GOLD, AND AROUND HIS LEG IS A GOLDEN CHAIN.

Description of a south Indian king, by the 13th-century Chinese traveller Chau Ju-Kua.

Medieval temples, like this Brahmeshwar Shiva temple (below) at Bhubaneshwar built in the 11th century, reflected the power structure of medieval society. Divine icons sat inside these temples like kings in their palaces, adorned, entertained and bathed daily by a host of ministrants. In addition they enjoyed revenue in service, money and kind from huge tracts of land in the surrounding countryside.

Caspian Sea
GHAZNAVIDS
Firuzkuh
Kabul
Ghazni
Amu Darya (Oxus)
Udabhanda
Indus
Multan
CHAHAMANAS RAJPUTS
Narayanapura
GUHILAS
Sakambhari
Ajayameru
Anahilapataka
GAHADAVALAS
Chambal
Kanauj
Somnath
PARAMARAS Yamuna
Khajaraho
Ujjayini Kalanjara
Narmada Dhar CHANDELLAS
KALACHURIS Kasi
Tripuri PALAS
Ganges
Tapti
Ajanta Hills
Pratisthana
DECCAN
CHALUKYAS EASTERN GANGAS c. 1022
Navadvipa Vikramapura
Taradavadi Warangal Mahanadi Vijayapura
Kalyani KAKATIYAS Bhubaneshwar SENAS
Manyakheta Godavari
Krishna Vengi
EASTERN CHALUKYAS
HOYSALAS
WESTERN GANGAS
Dorasamudra
Talakad
Kanci
CHOLAS
Gangaikondacolapuram
Kaveri Tanjavur
naval expedition to southeast Asia, c. 1025
KULASEKHARAS
Madurai
naval expedition to Maldive Islands, c. 1000
PANDYAS
Nagapattinam
999 1017
Indian Ocean
LAMBAKANNAS
Sri Lanka

India: the Delhi sultanate

The Delhi sultanate spread Muslim rule throughout most of south Asia. It created the circumstances in which large numbers of Indians began to convert to Islam. In the mid-14th century the sultanate reached the peak of its power after which India began to divide into many smaller sultanates, making it an easy target for invaders from the northwest.

2 The mid-14th century (map below) saw the establishment of two major states in southern India, the Muslim Bahmani sultanate and the Hindu Vijayanagar (City of Victory) empire. The two states were involved in almost continuous and inconclusive warfare. In the 15th century the Gajapatis were able to press their rule southward down the east Indian coast. In the 1480s the Bahmani state split into five separate sultanates.

FROM THE BEGINNING of the 11th century the Turkish Muslim rulers of central Asia and Afghanistan had been expanding their power into north India (see p. 144). First Mahmud of Ghazni (927–1030) invaded India 17 times, bringing the Punjab under his sway. Then, from 1175, having overthrown Mahmud's successors, Muhammad Ghuri built his power in northwest India. In 1206, Qutbuddin Aibak, a Ghurid general who had risen from slave status, established in his own name the sultanate of Delhi.

Over the following 320 years northern India was ruled from Delhi by five dynasties of Turkish and Afghan extraction: the Slave Kings (1206–90); the Khaljis (1290–1320); the Tughluqs (1320–1414); the Sayyids (1414–51); and the Lodis (1451–1526). For the first century and a half they strove to spread their rule throughout India. In 1311 the army of Alauddin Khalji (1296–1316) reached the sub-continent's southern tip. Under Muhammad bin Tughluq (1325–51) the sultanate reached its maximum extent, drawing taxes from more than 20 provinces (see map 1). Greater security was promised, more-

over, by the decline of the Mongol threat from the northwest. But controversial decisions by Muhammad to levy higher taxes and to transfer the population of Delhi to a new capital in the Deccan led to the disintegration of the sultanate as it reached its peak. In 1341 Bengal broke away to form a separate sultanate; in 1347 so did the Bahmani rulers of the Deccan. Between 1382 and 1396 Khandesh, Malwa, Jaunpur and Gujerat followed suit. The invasion of Tamerlane in 1398, when Delhi was razed, rendered the sultanate's power nominal, and allowed the emergence of regional powers (see map 3). From the mid-15th century the Afghan Lodis managed to stretch Delhi's sway once more over northern India. Dissensions among them between 1517 and 1526, however, facilitated the final overthrow of the sultanate by Tamerlane's descendant, Babur.

The Hindu south

From the mid-14th to the mid-16th century the south was not disturbed by powers from the north. Here the Bahmani sultanate of the Deccan and its

I ENCOURAGED MY INFIDEL SUBJECTS TO EMBRACE THE RELIGION OF THE PROPHET, AND I PROCLAIMED THAT EVERY ONE WHO REPEATED THE CREED AND BECAME A MUSLIM SHOULD BE EXEMPT FROM THE POLL TAX. INFORMATION OF THIS CAME TO THE PEOPLE AT LARGE, AND LARGE NUMBERS OF HINDUS PRESENTED THEMSELVES, AND WERE ADMITTED TO THE HONOUR OF ISLAM.

Firoz Shah Tughluq

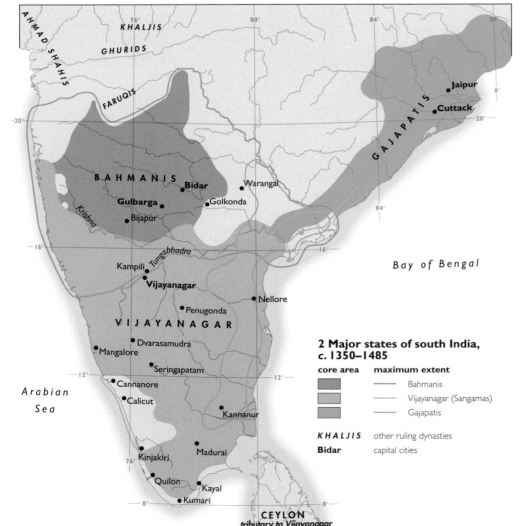

2 Major states of south India, c. 1350–1485

core area	maximum extent
	Bahmanis
	Vijayanagar (Sangamas)
	Gajapatis

KHALJIS other ruling dynasties
Bidar capital cities

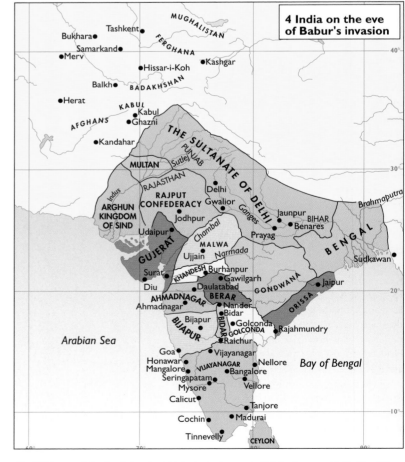

4 In 1526 one of the Lodi dynasty, which had gained power in Delhi in the second half of the 15th century, ruled the Punjab **(map above)** and another controlled the Gangetic plain as far east as Bihar. The Bahmani kingdom in the Deccan had broken up into five warring sultanates. Rajput dynasties controlled Rajasthan and threatened territories to the north.

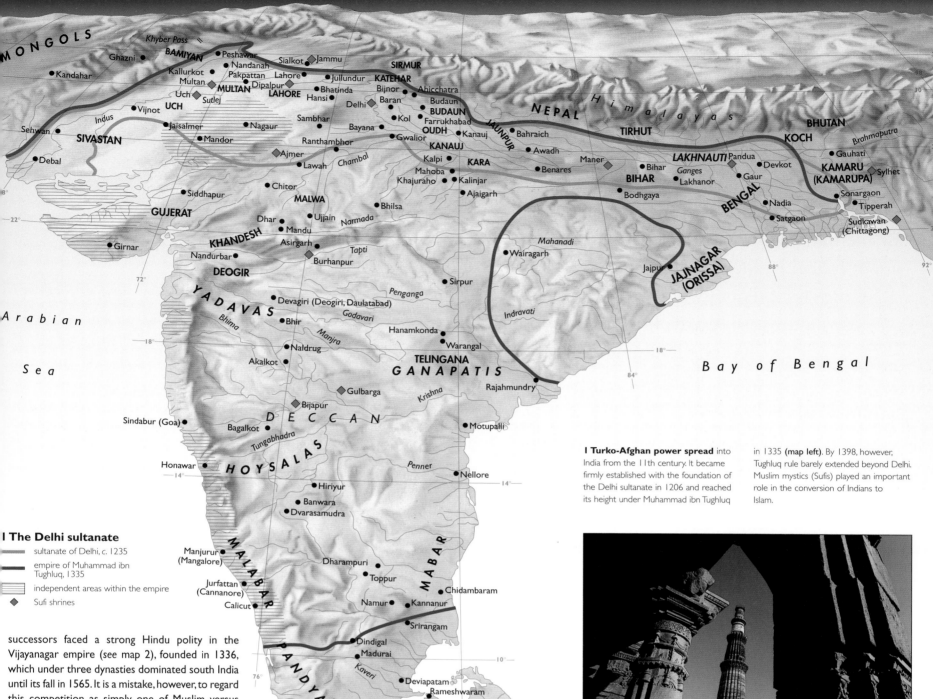

1 The Delhi sultanate

- sultanate of Delhi, c. 1235
- empire of Muhammad ibn Tughluq, 1335
- independent areas within the empire
- ◆ Sufi shrines

successors faced a strong Hindu polity in the Vijayanagar empire (see map 2), founded in 1336, which under three dynasties dominated south India until its fall in 1565. It is a mistake, however, to regard this competition as simply one of Muslim versus Hindu. Men of each faith fought on both sides.

India and Islam

One consequence of the Muslim conquest of much of India was that it came to be linked more closely with central and western Asia. Large numbers of scholars, poets and craftsmen, often uprooted by the havoc wrought by the Mongols and their successors, came to seek their fortunes at Indian courts, providing a great stimulus to Indian arts. Persian became the leading language of literature and government. The dome and the arch became major features of Indian architecture.

Another consequence was the conversion of Indians from all levels of society, but particularly from the lower levels, to Islam. This was a largely peaceful development in which Sufi saints played an important role. One third of the world's Muslims now live in the region.

There was much interaction between Hinduism and Islam, particularly at the mystical level. Teachers emerged who drew from both traditions, for instance Kabir (1440–1518) and Nanak (1469–1539), who founded Sikhism. There was fruitful interaction, too, in literature and architecture, where distinctive traditions developed in the regional kingdoms. Nevertheless, orthodox Muslims continued to find much in Hinduism that offended their belief in the unity of God and His revelation through the Prophet Mohammed.

Hindu culture also saw important achievements. Bhakti devotionalism (love of God) spread from south India to Bengal, leading to a revival of the worship of Vishnu as the Universal God in eastern and northern India. Magnificent temples were built in the rich Hindu civilization of Vijayanagar in the south. Nevertheless, in this period Delhi was established as the political centre of India. It was to remain so until the 19th century.

1 Turko-Afghan power spread into India from the 11th century. It became firmly established with the foundation of the Delhi sultanate in 1206 and reached its height under Muhammad ibn Tughluq in 1335 **(map left)**. By 1398, however, Tughluq rule barely extended beyond Delhi. Muslim mystics (Sufis) played an important role in the conversion of Indians to Islam.

3 The invasion of Tamerlane in 1398–9 had a great impact on the politics of northern India **(map below)**. The power of the Delhi sultanate was greatly reduced and numerous regional powers were able to assert themselves. It was not until the mid-15th century that significant power returned to Delhi under the Lodi sultans.

Quwwat al-Islam Mosque with Qutb Minar in the background (above). The picture shows the arched screen of the Quwwat al-Islam (Might of Islam) mosque built by Qutbuddin Aibak inside a captured Hindu citadel, close to Delhi, on the platform of a demolished Hindu temple. He also built the Qutb Minar as a tower of victory to symbolize the supremacy of Islam in India.

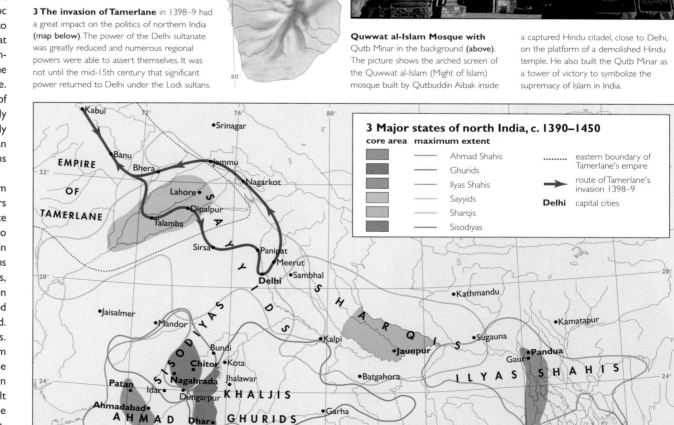

3 Major states of north India, c. 1390–1450

core area	maximum extent	
	Ahmad Shahis	
	Ghurids	
	Ilyas Shahis	
	Sayyids	
	Sharqis	
	Sisodiyas	

- .... eastern boundary of Tamerlane's empire
- → route of Tamerlane's invasion 1398–9
- **Delhi** capital cities

The early civilizations of southeast Asia

Maritime trade routes linked India with southeast Asia from the last few centuries of the pre-Christian era. By the middle of the first millennium AD the influence of Indian Hindu-Buddhist civilization extended throughout the region, but by 1300 Islam was expanding into the island world of Indonesia and the Philippines.

111 BC Han invasion of northern Vietnam under emperor Wu-ti

Early 3rd century AD Earliest Sanskrit writing in southeast Asia in the 'Vo Canh' inscription of central Vietnam

780–850 Construction of Borobudur, Java

802 Foundation of Angkor in Cambodia

849 Pagan (Burma) founded

1287 Mongol attacks on Pagan and elsewhere defeated by Thai-Lao and Viet-Cham alliances

1471 Capture of Cham capital of Vijaya by Vietnamese

1511 Portuguese capture of Melaka

FOLLOWING EARLIER TRENDS (see p. 46), from about the 3rd and 4th centuries AD there was an increasing adoption of Hindu and Buddhist cults among the local rulers of southeast Asia. They adopted Sanskrit titles and personal names, constructed numerous religious monuments and commissioned statuary modelled on Indian prototypes. In addition and largely through local initiative, Indian scripts and languages came to be used for political and religious texts. By the 6th century Buddhist images and votive inscriptions in Sanskrit had spread over continental southeast Asia, Sumatra and Java.

Early kingdoms

By the 6th century AD numerous kingdoms, whose locations are not always easy to identify, seem to have emerged. They were in frequent conflict with one another yet most maintained commercial and political relations with China, which welcomed tribute missions from the south. An ancient port has been found at Oc Eo (3rd–6th centuries AD), and from at least the 7th century Hindu temples were being built in lower Cambodia, notably at Angkor Borei, on the Dieng Plateau in central Java and in the valleys of central Vietnam. Buddhist shrines have been excavated at Beikthano and Sri Ksetra in central Burma (Myanmar) and in Thailand (Siam) at U-Thong, Ku Bua and Nakhon Pathom. The best-studied temple complexes are those of Borobudur and Prambanan in central Java (8th–10th centuries); around Angkor in Cambodia (9th–13th centuries); at Pagan in Burma (11th–13th centuries); and the Cham Shivite temple towers of central Vietnam (7th–13th centuries). All combined Hindu and Buddhist elements to varying degrees.

A centre of Buddhist culture developed from the 7th century at Srivijaya in southeast Sumatra, the capital of the maritime empire of Srivijaya, which for centuries controlled trade passing through the straits of Malacca and Sunda. However, by the 14th century Malacca, on the west coast of Malaya, had replaced Srivijaya as the dominant regional power.

Decline of the temple states

The Salendra kingdom, centred on the temple complexes at Prambanan, was devastated by volcanic ash falls in the early 10th century, and was replaced by a succession of smaller states and, eventually, the Majapahit empire. On the mainland, Pagan was sacked by Mongol invaders in the late 13th century. The Khmer rulers, under pressure from the Thai kingdom of Sukhothai from the 14th century, abandoned Angkor for the greater security of Phnom Penh.

Sukhothai was itself in decline by the late 14th century and the Thai political centre moved south to Ayutthaya and regional capitals were established at Chieng Mai in the northwest and Luang Prabang on the Mekong river. About this time in Burma new political centres emerged at Ava on the upper Irrawaddy and at Toungoo on the Sittang; Pegu became the capital of a new Mon kingdom in the south.

The rise of Vietnam

Northern Vietnam had been incorporated into the Chinese empire following the Han invasions of the 2nd century BC (see p. 88) but broke free at the end of the 10th century. Despite Chinese attempts at reconquest, a new Vietnamese kingdom emerged which gradually absorbed the Cham principalities to the south, annexing their last capital of Vijaya in 1471. However, with the advent of the Ming dynasty in China from the late 14th century Vietnam again fell within China's tributary system (see p. 184).

The political changes of the 14th and 15th centuries were accompanied by significant religious developments and the expansion of the region's international trade. While Theravada Buddhism spread through the mainland, Islam, which had a foothold at Aceh in northern Sumatra before 1300, expanded through the archipelago as far as Mindanao in the Philippines. Rulers of the north Javanese trading ports and those of Ternate and Tidore converted to Islam, whose advance was only halted by the Portuguese capture of the prosperous Sultanate of Melaka in 1511 (see p. 198) and the Spanish settlement in the Philippines from the 1560s.

2 Before the arrival of the Portuguese and Spanish in the 15th century there were many conflicts between the major polities and religions of the region (map below). Hindu cultures were yielding to Islam in Indonesia, the sinicized Dai-Viet rulers were absorbing the remaining Cham kingdoms while Ayutthaya, having driven the Khmer from Angkor, struggled for supremacy with the Burmese to the west.

Prambanan (below) was built between AD 825 and 826 and was the largest and most ambitious temple complex ever constructed in central Java. There are three main temples dedicated to the gods of the Trimurti: Shiva in the centre; Vishnu on the north side; and Brahma on the south.

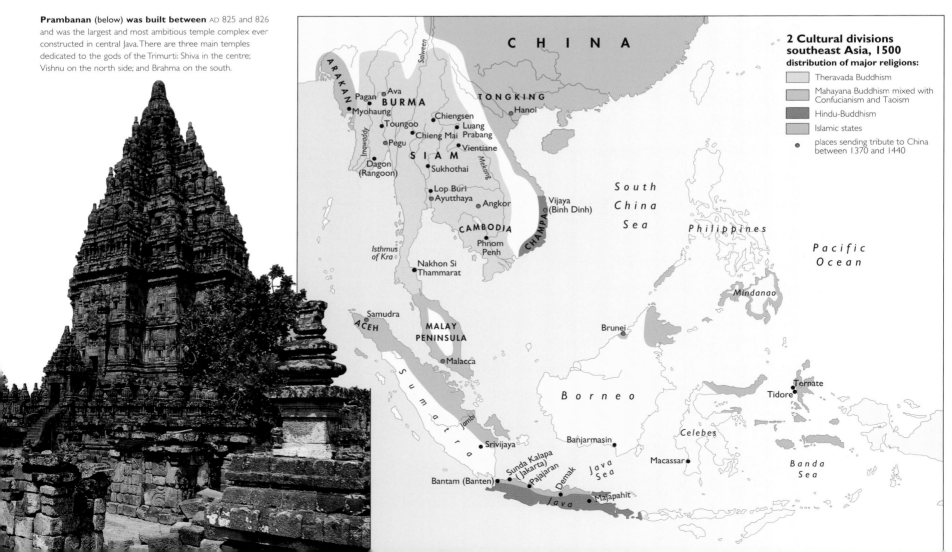

2 Cultural divisions southeast Asia, 1500
distribution of major religions:

- Theravada Buddhism
- Mahayana Buddhism mixed with Confucianism and Taoism
- Hindu-Buddhism
- Islamic states
- places sending tribute to China between 1370 and 1440

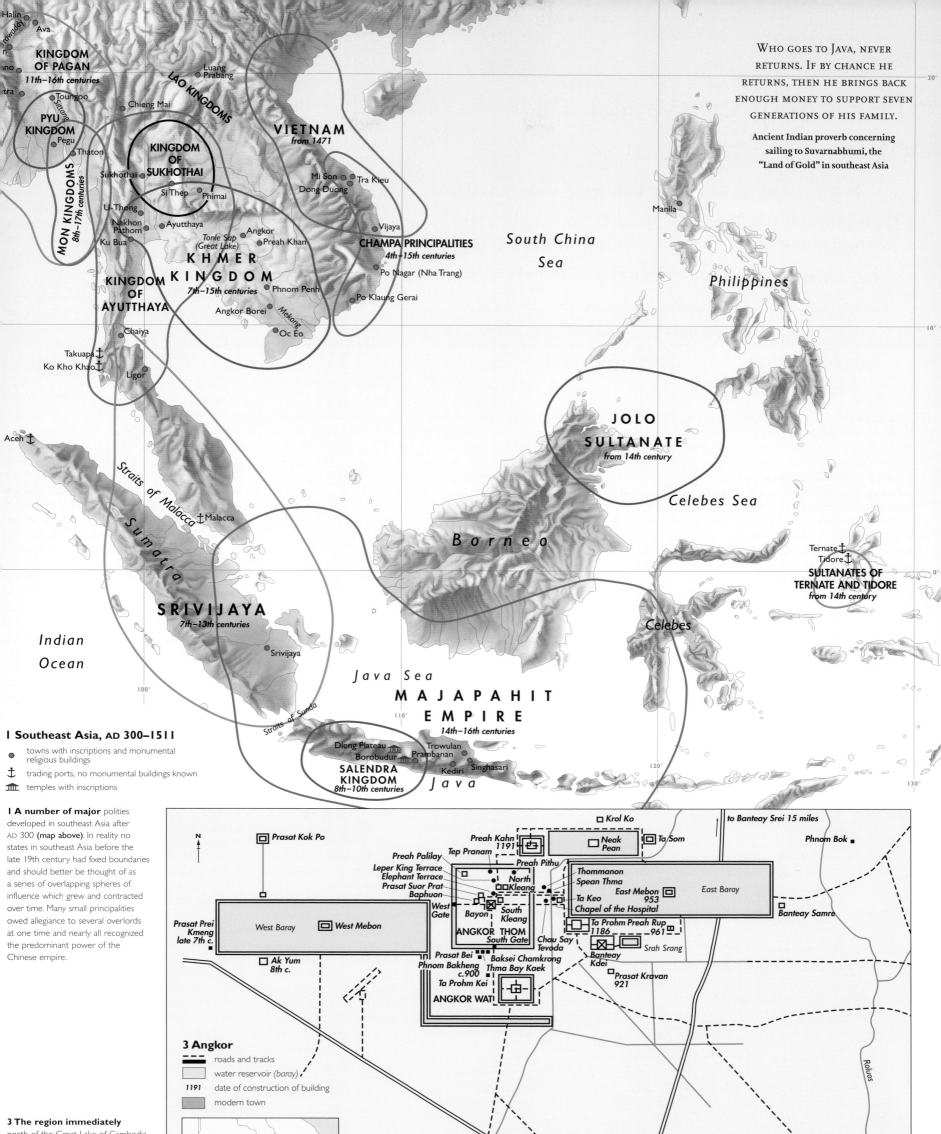

> WHO GOES TO JAVA, NEVER
> RETURNS. IF BY CHANCE HE
> RETURNS, THEN HE BRINGS BACK
> ENOUGH MONEY TO SUPPORT SEVEN
> GENERATIONS OF HIS FAMILY.
>
> Ancient Indian proverb concerning
> sailing to Suvarnabhumi, the
> "Land of Gold" in southeast Asia

KINGDOM OF PAGAN
11th–16th centuries

PYU KINGDOM

LAO KINGDOMS

VIETNAM
from 1471

MON KINGDOMS
8th–17th centuries

KINGDOM OF SUKHOTHAI

CHAMPA PRINCIPALITIES
4th–15th centuries

KHMER KINGDOM
7th–15th centuries

KINGDOM OF AYUTTHAYA

South China Sea

Philippines

Manila

JOLO SULTANATE
from 14th century

Celebes Sea

Aceh ‡

Straits of Malacca

‡ Malacca

Sumatra

Borneo

Ternate ‡
Tidore ‡

SULTANATES OF TERNATE AND TIDORE
from 14th century

SRIVIJAYA
7th–13th centuries

Srivijaya

Indian Ocean

Celebes

Java Sea

MAJAPAHIT EMPIRE
14th–16th centuries

Straits of Sunda

Dieng Plateau
Borobudur
Prambanan
Trowulan
Kediri
Singhasari

SALENDRA KINGDOM
8th–10th centuries

Java

Halin, Ava, Irrawaddy, Toungoo, Pegu, Thaton, Chieng Mai, Luang Prabang, Sukhothai, Si Thep, Phimai, U-Thong, Nakhon Pathom, Ku Bua, Ayutthaya, Angkor, Preah Kham, Tonle Sap (Great Lake), Mi Son, Tra Kieu, Dong Duong, Vijaya, Po Nagar (Nha Trang), Phnom Penh, Angkor Borei, Mekong, Oc Eo, Po Klaung Gerai, Chaiya, Takuapa ‡, Ko Kho Khao ‡, Ligor

1 Southeast Asia, AD 300–1511
- ● towns with inscriptions and monumental religious buildings
- ‡ trading ports, no monumental buildings known
- 🏛 temples with inscriptions

1 A number of major polities developed in southeast Asia after AD 300 (map above). In reality no states in southeast Asia before the late 19th century had fixed boundaries and should better be thought of as a series of overlapping spheres of influence which grew and contracted over time. Many small principalities owed allegiance to several overlords at one time and nearly all recognized the predominant power of the Chinese empire.

3 The region immediately north of the Great Lake of Cambodia witnessed the construction of the greatest complex of monumental religious buildings of the ancient world (plan right). Angkor Wat is the best preserved but far from the largest of these temples. All were planned according to rigid geometric alignments and served by huge reservoirs whose function is still debated.

3 Angkor
- – – – roads and tracks
- ▨ water reservoir (baray)
- *1191* date of construction of building
- ▨ modern town

N

Prasat Kok Po

Krol Ko
to Banteay Srei 15 miles
Phnom Bok

Preah Kahn 1191
Tep Pranam
Neak Pean
Ta Som

Preah Palilay
Leper King Terrace
Elephant Terrace
Prasat Suor Prat
Baphuon

Preah Pithu
North Kleang

Thommanon
Spean Thma
East Mebon 953
East Baray

Prasat Prei Kmeng late 7th c.

West Baray

West Mebon

West Gate
Bayon
South Kleang
ANGKOR THOM
South Gate

Ta Keo
Chapel of the Hospital

Banteay Samre

Ta Prohm 1186
Pre Rup 961

Ak Yum 8th c.

Prasat Bei
Phnom Bakheng c.900
Thma Bay Kaek

Baksei Chamkrong

Chau Say Tevoda
Banteay Kdei
Srah Srang

Prasat Kravan 921

Ta Prohm Kei
ANGKOR WAT

Roluos

Siemreap
Angkor
Phnom Penh
Angkor Borei
Oc Eo
Gulf of Thailand

Siemreap

Lolei 893

to Phnom Krom 10 miles and Tonle Sap

0   1   2   3   4   5 km
0   1   2   3 miles

Preah Ko 879
Bakong 881

Prasat Prei Monti

to Roluos half-mile

to Phnom Krom half-mile

The Muslim World

The three centuries 800–1100 were a period of great political turmoil in the Islamic world: the united Caliphate of the early Islamic period broke up, and a major divide between the Sunni Seljuk Turks and the Shi'ite Fatimids divided the Muslims into two camps. At the same time, this was a period of great cultural and commercial development, especially in Egypt and Iran. Meanwhile, in Spain and Sicily, Christian invaders were gradually conquering Muslim lands.

The choice of Baghdad as capital of the Abbasids pulled the centre of gravity of the Muslim world eastwards **(map below)**. The stiffest challenges to their power came from the west: from Umayyad exiles in Spain and from the Fatimid Caliphs based first in Tunisia and then in Cairo. Syria and Palestine became a battle-ground between Fatimids and the Seljuk Turks, loyal Sunni Muslims who looked towards Baghdad.

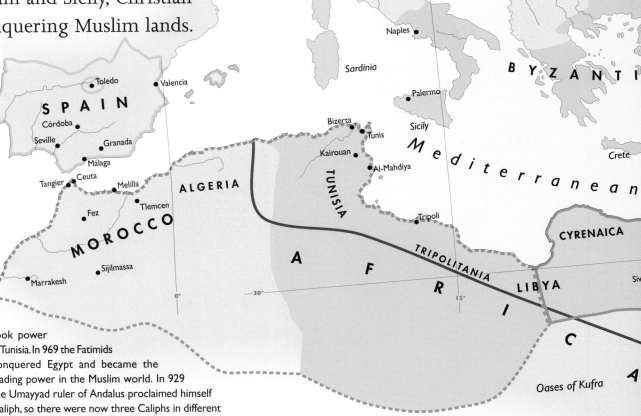

BY 800 THE GREAT MUSLIM conquests were effectively complete. It was only in the area of modern Pakistan and parts of central Asia that Muslim rule expanded during these three centuries. From 1050 onwards, much of Turkey was conquered by the Turks and came under Muslim domination for the first time. At the same time, in Sicily and Spain, Muslim territory was being occupied by Christian powers from the north and Islam was in retreat.

In the *Dar al-Islam* the main change during the three centuries between 800 and 1100 was the break up of the Caliphate and the emergence of successor states. In 800 the whole Muslim world, except for Andalus (Spain and Portugal), was ruled from Baghdad by the Abbasid Caliph Harun al-Rashid. His death in 809 was followed by a civil war, which saw the beginning of the disintegration of this unity. In 868 Egypt became independent under the rule of the Tulunids, and in 900 the Samanids established their independent rule in most of eastern Iran. By 945 the once powerful Abbasid Caliphs were no more than figureheads in their palace in Baghdad: real power in Iraq was seized by Daylamite military adventurers from northern Iran.

The political unity of Islam was further fractured in 909 when a rival Caliph from the Fatimid dynasty, who claimed direct descent from the prophet Muhammad through Muhammad's daughter Fatima, took power in Tunisia. In 969 the Fatimids conquered Egypt and became the leading power in the Muslim world. In 929 the Umayyad ruler of Andalus proclaimed himself Caliph, so there were now three Caliphs in different areas of the *Dar al-Islam*.

These centuries also saw major economic changes in the region. The rich agricultural system of central and southern Iraq was impoverished by the constant disturbances and civil wars, and much of the agricultural land was abandoned as irrigation canals were neglected or destroyed. At the same time, Egypt enjoyed a period of great prosperity under Fatimid rule: the textile industry boomed and Cairo and Alexandria became the entrepots of trade between the Indian Ocean and Mediterranean basins. Cairo, founded by the Fatimids in 969, came to rival Baghdad as a cultural centre, attracting immigrant scholars from Iraq.

The dominance of the Fatimids was challenged in the 11th century by the arrival of the Sunni Seljuk Turks in Iran after 1040. In 1055 they took Baghdad, proclaiming themselves champions of the Sunni Abbasid Caliphs against the Shi'ite Fatimids. The two great powers came into conflict in Syria and Palestine as each tried to control the eastern seaboard of the Mediterranean. In 1071 the Seljuk sultan Alp Arslan defeated the Byzantine army at Manzikert, laying the way open for Turkish penetration of Anatolia.

In the 11th century, Italian merchants began to frequent the ports of Egypt and Syria, buying fine textiles, pepper and spices. Cities such as Alexandria and Tripoli became thriving ports once more. But the Italians were also forerunners of the Crusaders, who took Jerusalem in 1099.

809 Death of Haroun al-Rashid

909 Fatimid Caliphate proclaimed in Tunisia

929 Abd al-Rahman III proclaims Umayyad Caliphate in Cordoba

945 Daylamite Mu'izz al-Dawla takes power in Iraq

969 Fatimids conquer Egypt and found Cairo

1055 Seljuk Tughril beg takes Baghdad

1071 Seljuk Alp Arslan defeats Byzantines at Manzikert

1072 Normans under Roger I take Palermo

1085 Alfonso VI of Castile takes Toledo

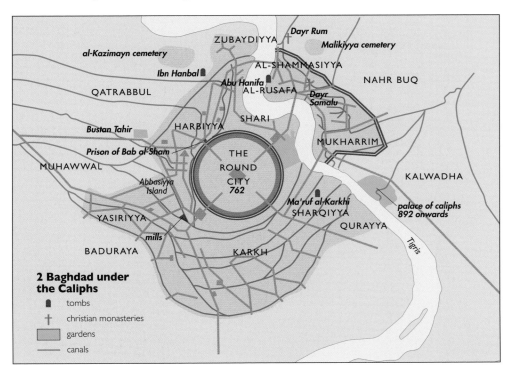

2 Baghdad under the Caliphs
- ⬛ tombs
- ✝ christian monasteries
- ▨ gardens
- — canals

2 The round city of Baghdad, founded in 762 by the Caliph al-Mansur, formed the heart of the Abbasid capital. The circular city **(map left)**, with a diameter of 2.64km was surrounded by a rampart with 360 towers. By the early 9th century, it was one of the world's largest cities.

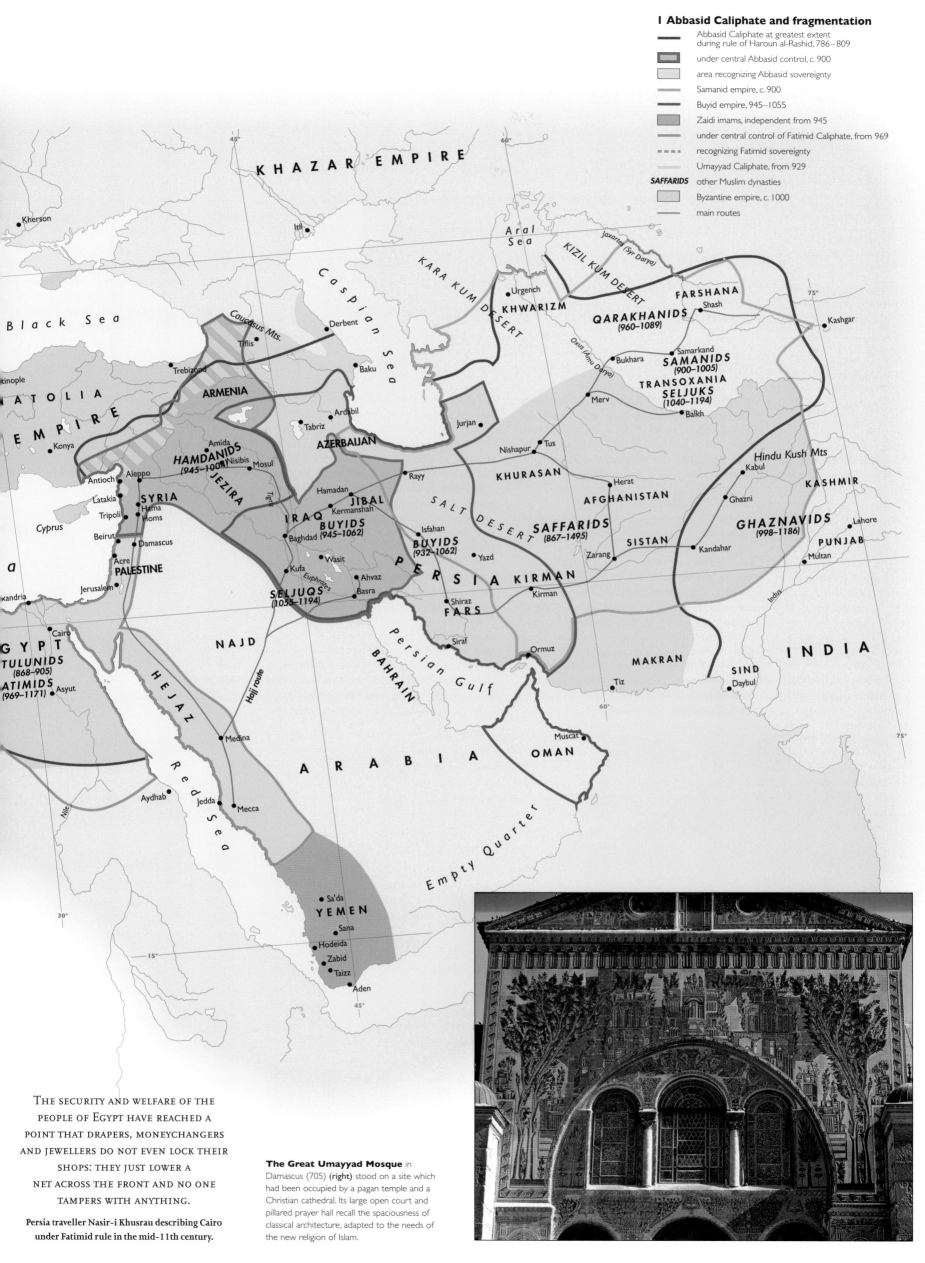

I Abbasid Caliphate and fragmentation

Abbasid Caliphate at greatest extent during rule of Haroun al-Rashid, 786–809

under central Abbasid control, c. 900

area recognizing Abbasid sovereignty

Samanid empire, c. 900

Buyid empire, 945–1055

Zaidi imams, independent from 945

under central control of Fatimid Caliphate, from 969

recognizing Fatimid sovereignty

Umayyad Caliphate, from 929

SAFFARIDS other Muslim dynasties

Byzantine empire, c. 1000

main routes

KHAZAR EMPIRE

Kherson

Itil

Aral Sea

KIZIL KUM DESERT

Jaxartes (Syr Darya)

Black Sea

Caspian Sea

KARA KUM DESERT

KHWARIZM

Urgench

FARSHANA

Shash

Kashgar

Derbent

QARAKHANIDS
(960–1089)

Caucasus Mts.

Tiflis

Baku

Oxus (Amu Darya)

Bukhara

Samarkand

SAMANIDS
(900–1005)

Trebizond

ARMENIA

Ardabil

TRANSOXANIA

SELJUKS
(1040–1194)

ANATOLIA

EMPIRE

Konya

Tabriz

AZERBAIJAN

Jurjan

Merv

Balkh

Amida

HAMDANIDS
(945–1004)

Nisibis

Mosul

Rayy

Nishapur

Tus

Herat

Hindu Kush Mts

Antioch

Aleppo

JEZIRA

Hamadan

JIBAL

KHURASAN

Kabul

KASHMIR

SYRIA

Hama

Homs

Kermanshah

IRAQ

BUYIDS

AFGHANISTAN

Ghazni

Cyprus

Latakia

Tripoli

Beirut

Damascus

Baghdad (945–1062)

Isfahan

SALT DESERT

SAFFARIDS
(867–1495)

SISTAN

GHAZNAVIDS
(998–1186)

Lahore

Acre

PALESTINE

Kufa

Euphrates

Wasit

BUYIDS
(932–1062)

Yazd

Zarang

Kandahar

PUNJAB

Multan

Jerusalem

Ahvaz

Basra

PERSIA

KIRMAN

Indus

SELJUQS
(1055–1194)

Shiraz

Kirman

alexandria

EGYPT

Cairo

NAJD

FARS

Siraf

Ormuz

MAKRAN

INDIA

TULUNIDS
(868–905)

ATIMIDS
(969–1171)

Asyut

Tiz

SIND

Daybul

HEJAZ

Persian Gulf

BAHRAIN

Muscat

Nile

Aydhab

Jedda

Mecca

Medina

Hajj route

Red Sea

ARABIA

OMAN

Empty Quarter

Sa'da

YEMEN

Sana

Hodeida

Zabid

Taizz

Aden

THE SECURITY AND WELFARE OF THE
PEOPLE OF EGYPT HAVE REACHED A
POINT THAT DRAPERS, MONEYCHANGERS
AND JEWELLERS DO NOT EVEN LOCK THEIR
SHOPS: THEY JUST LOWER A
NET ACROSS THE FRONT AND NO ONE
TAMPERS WITH ANYTHING.

Persia traveller Nasir-i Khusrau describing Cairo
under Fatimid rule in the mid-11th century.

The Great Umayyad Mosque in
Damascus (705) **(right)** stood on a site which
had been occupied by a pagan temple and a
Christian cathedral. Its large open court and
pillared prayer hall recall the spaciousness of
classical architecture, adapted to the needs of
the new religion of Islam.

The Muslim World

After 1100 the Muslim countries of the Middle East were subject to attack from the Christian Europeans from the west and the pagan Mongols from the east. In the west, most of Spain was lost to the Christians by 1250, but in the Middle East the Mamluks of Egypt successfully drove the Crusaders from the Levant and resisted the advance of the Mongols.

During the 12th and 13th centuries, the Islamic world was attacked by outsiders from all directions. In some areas, the Muslims were permanently subjugated or expelled but, in others, Muslim forces counter-attacked and repelled or converted the invaders.

The Crusades

On the Iberian peninsula (al-Andalus) the Muslims came under intense pressure. In the east, Zaragoza was taken by the Christians in 1118; in the west they took Lisbon in 1147, and the city immediately became the capital of the emerging kingdom of Portugal. The Christian advance was halted for almost a century by the Almohads, a Berber religio-political movement. From their capital at Marrakesh, the Almohad Caliphs ruled north Africa as far east as Tunis and all of Spain and Portugal, then in Muslim hands. In 1212, however, they were decisively defeated by Alfonso VIII of Castile and his Christian allies. The main cities of Muslim Spain fell rapidly – Corboba and Valencia in 1236, Seville in 1248 – and

Muslim rule was restricted to the mountainous kingdom of Granada, which survived until 1492.

In the Middle East, the Crusaders occupied the lands at the eastern end of the Mediterranean in a long strip from Antioch in the north to Baza and the Red Sea in the south. They were aided by the Muslim world's divisions between the Shi'ite Fatimids of Egypt and the Sunni Turks of Syria and Iraq. In 1174, however, Saladin (d.1193) united Egypt and Syria, and in 1187 he defeated the Crusaders at the Battle of Hattin. Despite the launch of the Third Crusade (1189–91) and subsequent expeditions, the Christians never recovered the territory they had lost. Only a few coastal ports remained in Crusader hands until the fall of Acre in 1291.

A more serious threat to the Muslim world was posed by the invasion from the east by the pagan Mongols under the leadership of Genghis Khan (d.1227). From 1218 they launched a devastating series of attacks on the cities of Iran, and in 1258 they sacked Baghdad, putting an end to the Abbasid Caliphate. In 1260, a Mongol army was defeated at

'Ain Jalut by a force of Mamluk soldiers from Egypt. This setback proved to be a turning point. Mongol rule was confined to Iran and Iraq while the Mamluk sultans ruled Egypt and Syria. The Mongol ruler of Iran, Ghazan Khan (1295–1304), converted to Islam, and his dynasty, known as the Il-Khans, ruled until 1335.

The main rivals of the Mongols were the Mamluks of Egypt. These Turkish soldiers, many of them originally slaves, took power in 1260. They built up a formidable military machine, and it was the Mamluks who destroyed the last vestiges of Crusader power in the Levant. They also prevented further attempts by the Mongols to take Syria and Egypt. Under their rule, Cairo replaced Baghdad as the largest city in the Arab Middle East and became the leading intellectual and cultural centre.

1 After 1100 the Muslim world came under increasing pressure (**map above**) both from Christian European incursions into Palestine and the progress of the Reconquista in Spain, as well as from the pagan Mongols who swept down from central Asia. Yet by the end of the 13th century the Crusaders had been driven from the Levant and the Mongols had been checked at 'Ain Jalut in 1260. Although the Mongols continued to rule Iran, having converted to Islam, they never again posed a serious threat to the Muslim world.

2 By the 11th century, the Ghaznavids and Qarakhanids had been obliged to give ground to the Seljuks, a clan from the Oghuz Turkish confederacy north of the Aral Sea (**map left**). The Qarakhanids acknowledged Turkish overlordship, whilst the Ghaznavids were confined to their easternmost territories. In 1055 the Seljuk leader suppressed the Buyids and assumed protection of the Caliph, who granted him the title of Sultan. The Seljuks conquered the whole of Iran, although they were never able to crush the heterodox Assassins in their strongholds in the Caspian region. From the 12th century the Seljuk empire fell into decline, with the outlying provinces falling under the control of army officers, often nominally acting on behalf of a junior Seljuk prince.

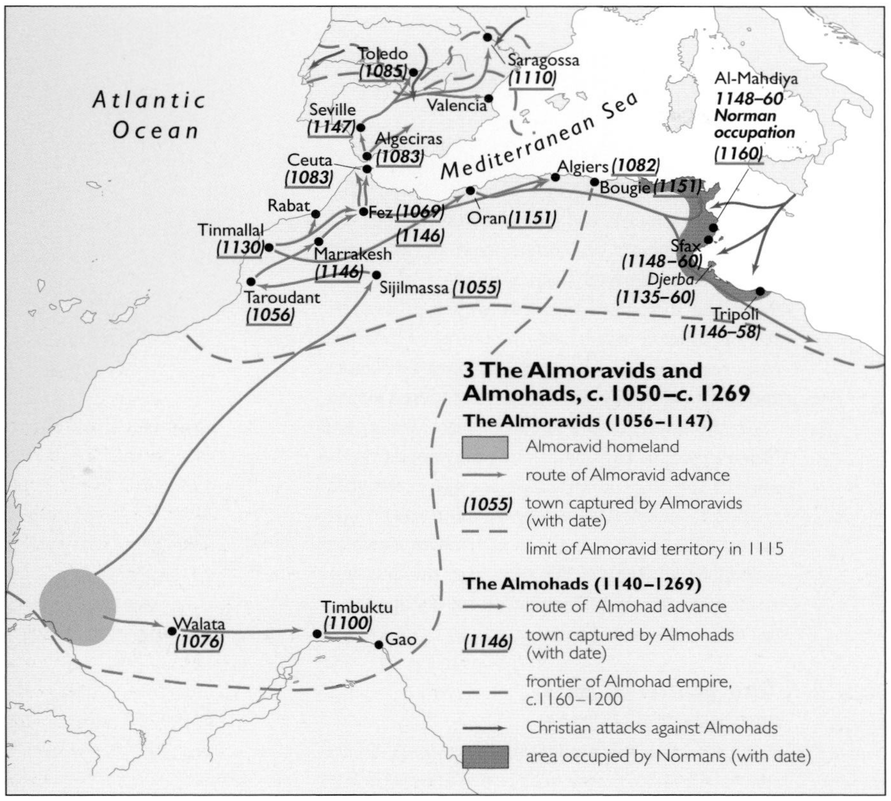
3 The Almoravids and Almohads, c. 1050–c. 1269
The Almoravids (1056–1147)
Almoravid homeland
route of Almoravid advance
(1055) town captured by Almoravids (with date)
limit of Almoravid territory in 1115
The Almohads (1140–1269)
route of Almohad advance
(1146) town captured by Almohads (with date)
frontier of Almohad empire, c.1160–1200
Christian attacks against Almohads
area occupied by Normans (with date)
Atlantic Ocean
Mediterranean Sea
Toledo (1085)
Saragossa (1110)
Valencia
Seville (1147)
Algeciras (1083)
Ceuta (1083)
Rabat
Fez (1069) (1146)
Tinmallal (1130)
Marrakesh (1146)
Taroudant (1056)
Sijilmassa (1055)
Oran (1151)
Algiers (1082)
Bougie (1151)
Al-Mahdiya 1148–60 Norman occupation (1160)
Sfax (1148–60)
Djerba (1135–60)
Tripoli (1146–58)
Walata (1076)
Timbuktu (1100)
Gao

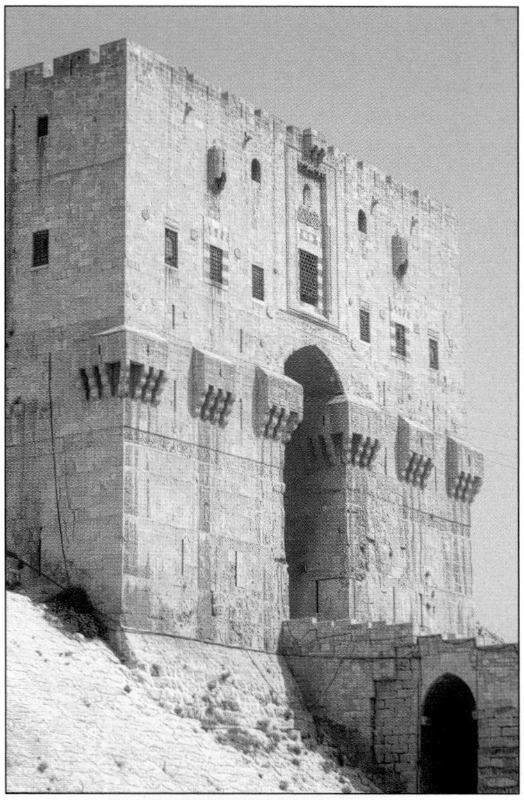

3 The Berbers of North Africa submitted to Islam at the end of the 7th century, but its real penetration among them was slight. In the mid-11th century a radical renewal movement, the Almoravids, imposed strict Sunni Muslim observance on the nomadic tribes of the northwestern Sahara. From a newly founded capital at Marrakesh, the Almoravids seized much of Spain and large areas of Morocco, until they were overthrown in turn by the even more radical Almohads.

The great gate of the citadel at Aleppo **(right)**. Mostly constructed by al-Malik al-Zahir (1186–1216), it is one of the greatest fortresses of the medieval Muslim world. Aimed as much at rival Muslim powers as against the Crusaders, it embodied all the most recent technologies of bend entrances and box-machicolations to deter attack.

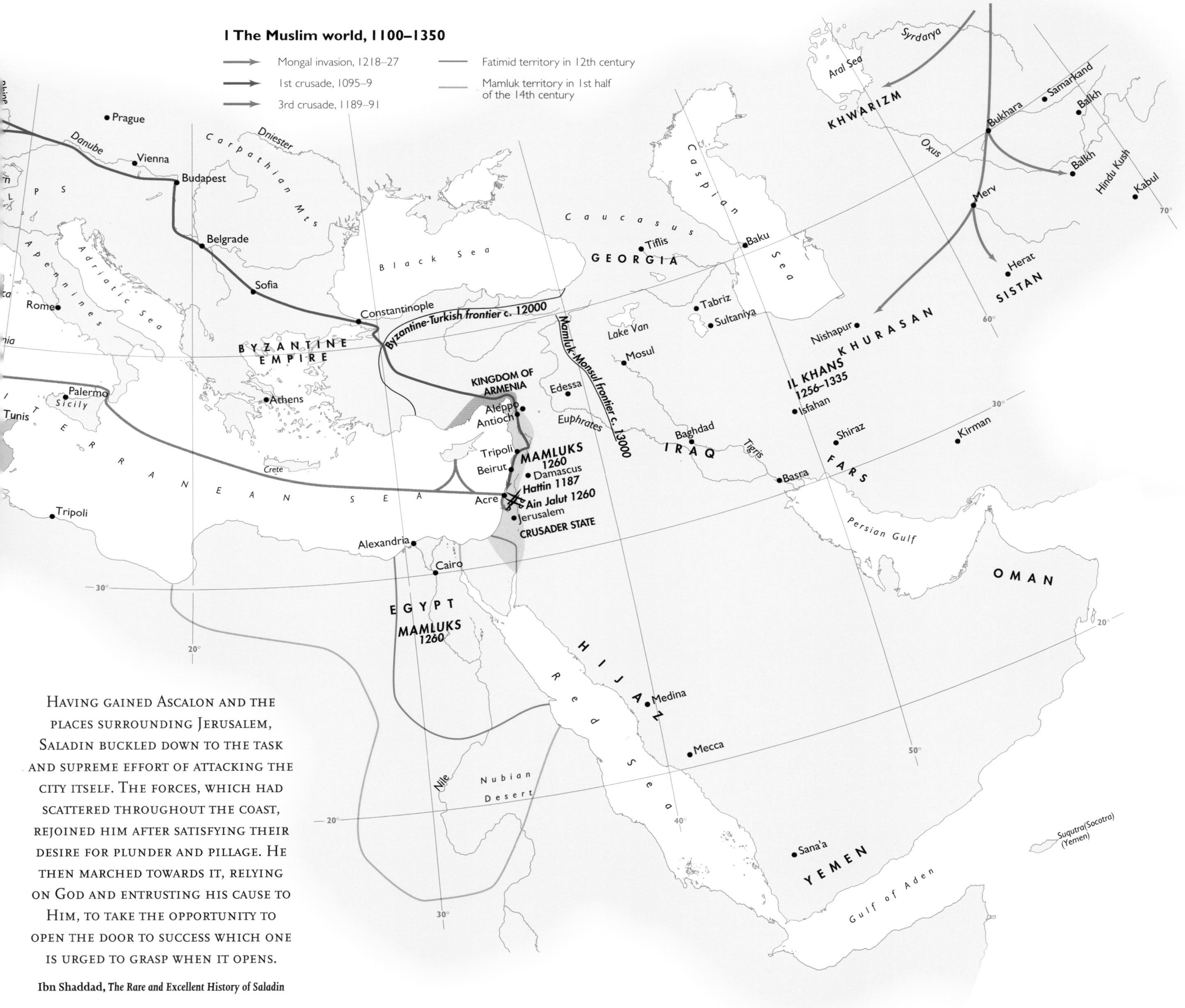
1 The Muslim world, 1100–1350
Mongal invasion, 1218–27
1st crusade, 1095–9
3rd crusade, 1189–91
Fatimid territory in 12th century
Mamluk territory in 1st half of the 14th century
Prague
Danube
Vienna
Budapest
Carpathian Mts
Dniester
Belgrade
Sofia
Adriatic Sea
Apennines
Rome
Black Sea
Constantinople
Byzantine-Turkish frontier c. 12000
BYZANTINE EMPIRE
Athens
Palermo
Sicily
Tunis
Crete
Tripoli
MEDITERRANEAN SEA
KINGDOM OF ARMENIA
Aleppo
Antioch
Edessa
Tripoli
Beirut
MAMLUKS 1260
Damascus
Hattin 1187
Acre
Ain Jalut 1260
Jerusalem
CRUSADER STATE
Alexandria
Cairo
EGYPT
MAMLUKS 1260
Nile
Nubian Desert
Red Sea
HIJAZ
Medina
Mecca
Caucasus
Tiflis
GEORGIA
Baku
Caspian Sea
Tabriz
Sultaniya
Lake Van
Mosul
Mamluk-Monsul frontier c. 13000
Euphrates
Baghdad
IRAQ
Tigris
Basra
Persian Gulf
OMAN
Sana'a
YEMEN
Gulf of Aden
Suqutra(Socotra) (Yemen)
Aral Sea
Syrdarya
KHWARIZM
Bukhara
Samarkand
Balkh
Oxus
Hindu Kush
Kabul
Merv
Herat
SISTAN
Nishapur
KHURASAN
IL KHANS 1256–1335
Isfahan
Shiraz
FARS
Kirman

Having gained Ascalon and the places surrounding Jerusalem, Saladin buckled down to the task and supreme effort of attacking the city itself. The forces, which had scattered throughout the coast, rejoined him after satisfying their desire for plunder and pillage. He then marched towards it, relying on God and entrusting his cause to Him, to take the opportunity to open the door to success which one is urged to grasp when it opens.

Ibn Shaddad, *The Rare and Excellent History of Saladin*

The emergence of states in Africa

The period from 1000 to 1500 saw the emergence of states over much of Africa, crucially assisted by the need to control and secure trading routes and by the wealth which flowed from them. The spread of trade often went hand in hand with the dissemination of Islam. By 1500, sub-Saharan African states had made their first contacts with European explorers.

THE PERIOD FROM 1000 to 1500 saw two principal developments in Africa: the spread of Islam and the emergence of organized states throughout the continent. In many places these were linked. By 1000 the Maghreb (northwest Africa) had been in Islamic hands for over three centuries. Between 1000 and 1500 Islam spread south: up the Nile into the Christian kingdoms of Nubia; along the northern and eastern coasts of the Horn; and across the Sahara into the states of the "Sudanic belt", stretching from the Senegal to the Nile. Muslim merchants crossed the Sahara with caravans of camels which regularly made the hazardous journey from trading depots on either edge of the desert, such as Sijilmassa, south of the Atlas Mountains, and Walata in Mali. This dangerous trade carried luxury goods (and, in time, firearms) and salt to the black African lands of the south. In exchange, leather-work, slaves and gold went northwards: by 1250 the economies of both the Muslim Middle East and Christian Europe depended to a great extent upon African gold.

The states of western Africa

Although the beginnings of urbanism in the Sudanic belt can be traced as far back as the last centuries BC, expanding trans-Saharan trade gave an impetus to the growth of states. Two of the earliest of these were Ghana and Mali. Ghana, an essentially African polity, which flourished from the 8th to the 11th centuries, was established north of the Senegal and Niger rivers, far from the modern state which has taken its name. Its successor, Mali, extended from the Atlantic across the great bend of the Niger. In 1324 the Mali king Mansa Musa went on pilgrimage to Mecca, and is said to have taken so much gold with his retinue that he caused inflation in Cairo. The empire of Mali gave way to that of Songhay, centred on the Niger cities of Gao and Timbuktu. East of Mali lay the city states of Hausaland, some of which – Zaria, Kano, Katsina – became extremely prosperous, although they never united to form a single state. Further east was Kanem, founded by desert people to the east of Lake Chad. Their ruling dynasty, the Kanuri kings, retained authority until their final overthrow in the 19th century.

By the late Middle Ages, at a time of crisis in western Europe (see p. 158), the black kingdoms of the western and central Sudan flourished. A number of African kings, among them Mansa Musa and Sunni Ali (of Songhay), enjoyed renown throughout Islam and Christendom for their wealth, brilliance and the artistic achievements of their subjects. Their capitals were large walled cities with many mosques and at least two, Timbuktu and Jenne, had universities that attracted scholars and poets from far and wide. Their power derived from a mixture of military force and diplomatic alliances with local leaders; their prosperity was based on control of rich local resources; their bureaucracies administered taxation and controlled trade, the life-blood of these empires.

To the south of the Sudanic states, Hausa and Malinke merchants traded among the peoples on the edge of the tropical forests, especially in the gold-producing regions. The prosperity this trade brought led, by 1500, to the foundation of many forest states, such as Benin. Around this time, also, the first contacts occurred with Portuguese sailors exploring the seas of the west African coast.

The states of east and central Africa

In the east, after the decline of Aksum (see p. 42), the centre of political power in Christian Ethiopia shifted southwards, first under the Kushitic-speaking Zagwe dynasty in the 11th century and then, in the 13th century, under the Amharic-speaking Solomonids who later clashed with the Muslim coastal states of the Horn of Africa, notably Adal.

Along the east coast there arose a string of Muslim city states. Kilwa Kisiwani, with its handsome mosques and palaces, prospered as the entrepôt for the gold of Zimbabwe, brought via Sofala. The arrival of the Portuguese in 1498 marked the beginning of European encroachment in this lucrative system of oceanic trade.

Meanwhile, in the interior of the southern half of the continent, many other African peoples coalesced to form states. These processes are best known in two regions: the upper Lualaba where wealth was accumulated in the form of metal, and south of the Zambezi where, from the 10th century, prosperous cattle-herders gave rise to the polity centred at Great Zimbabwe. Other states, many of them Bantu-speaking, emerged south of the lower Congo river, and in the area between the great lakes of east Africa.

2 From the Arab conquest of North Africa, the volume of trade across the Sahara increased significantly. With the wealth generated in the south, stone-built towns developed into market centres and became the nuclei of organized states (map below). By the 14th century Mali was supreme among these. But around 1400, the province of Songhay broke away. With the loss of revenue from the trading post at Gao, Mali declined, and Songhay, under Sunni Ali, became predominant.

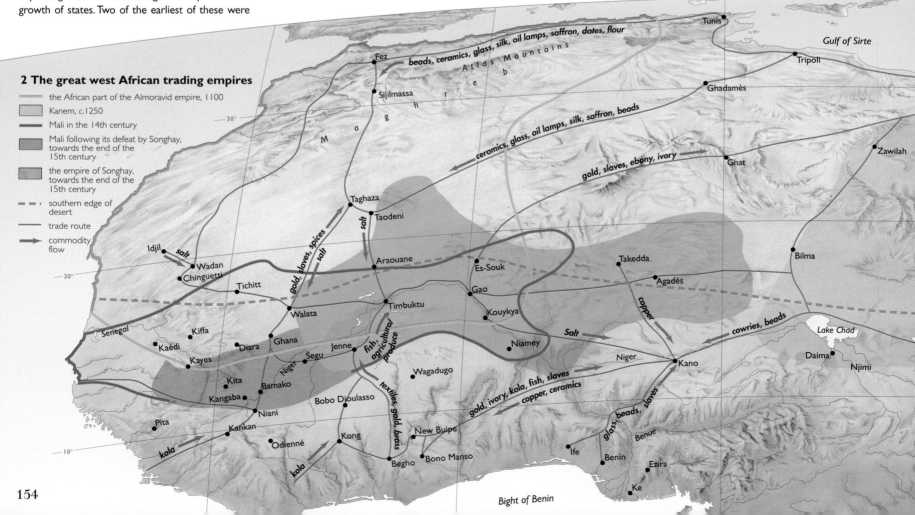

2 The great west African trading empires

- the African part of the Almoravid empire, 1100
- Kanem, c.1250
- Mali in the 14th century
- Mali following its defeat by Songhay, towards the end of the 15th century
- the empire of Songhay, towards the end of the 15th century
- southern edge of desert
- trade route
- commodity flow

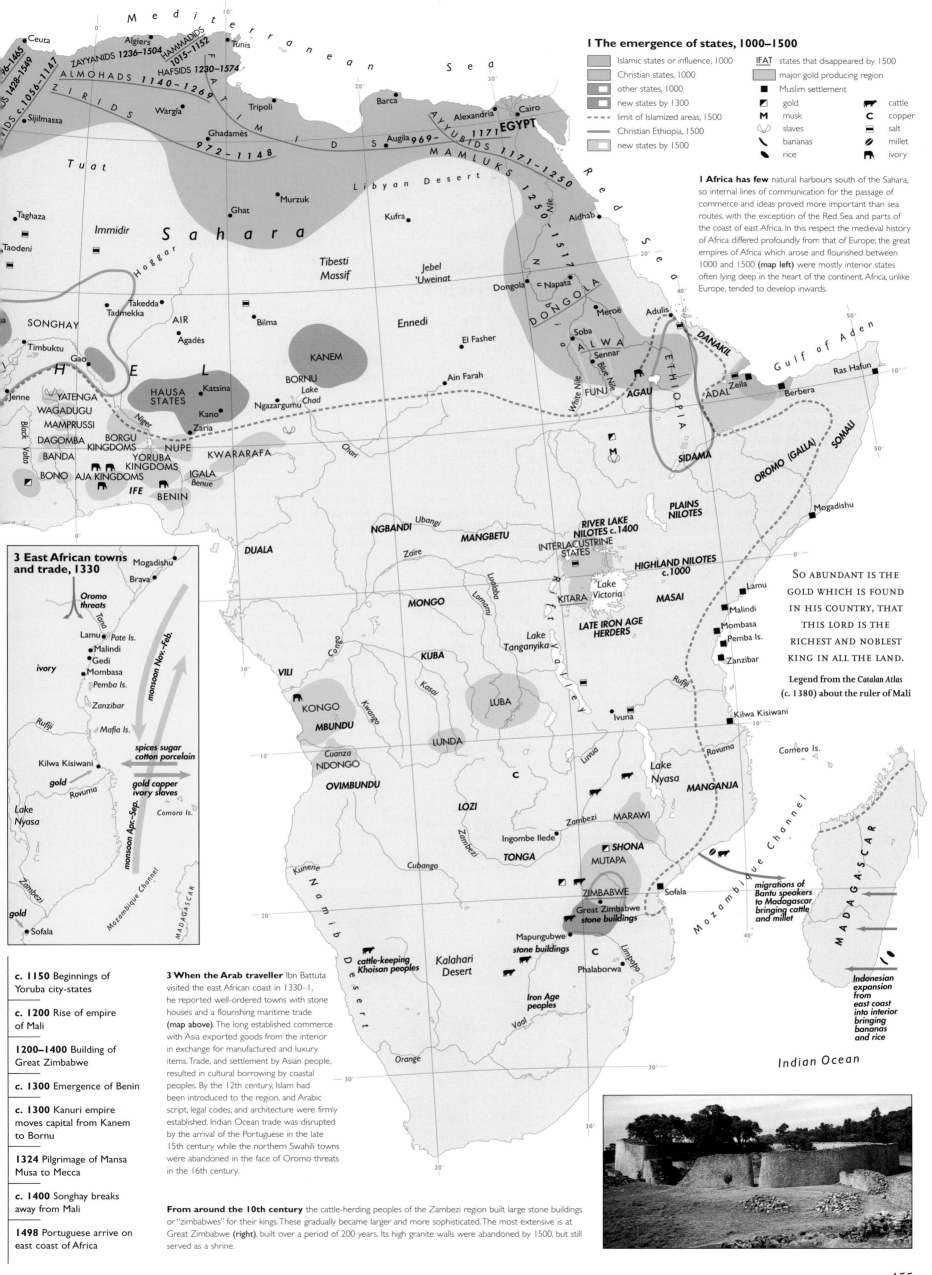

1 The emergence of states, 1000–1500

- Islamic states or influence, 1000
- Christian states, 1000
- other states, 1000
- new states by 1300
- - - limit of Islamized areas, 1500
- Christian Ethiopia, 1500
- new states by 1500
- **IFAT** states that disappeared by 1500
- major gold producing region
- ■ Muslim settlement
- 🌾 gold
- M musk
- 👣 slaves
- 🍌 bananas
- ● rice
- 🐄 cattle
- C copper
- salt
- millet
- 🐘 ivory

1 Africa has few natural harbours south of the Sahara, so internal lines of communication for the passage of commerce and ideas proved more important than sea routes, with the exception of the Red Sea and parts of the coast of east Africa. In this respect the medieval history of Africa differed profoundly from that of Europe; the great empires of Africa which arose and flourished between 1000 and 1500 (map left) were mostly interior states often lying deep in the heart of the continent. Africa, unlike Europe, tended to develop inwards.

> SO ABUNDANT IS THE
> GOLD WHICH IS FOUND
> IN HIS COUNTRY, THAT
> THIS LORD IS THE
> RICHEST AND NOBLEST
> KING IN ALL THE LAND.
>
> **Legend from the *Catalan Atlas* (c. 1380) about the ruler of Mali**

3 East African towns and trade, 1330

Oromo threats

monsoon Nov.–Feb.

monsoon Apr.–Sep.

spices sugar cotton porcelain

gold copper ivory slaves

ivory

gold

gold

3 When the Arab traveller Ibn Battuta visited the east African coast in 1330–1, he reported well-ordered towns with stone houses and a flourishing maritime trade (map above). The long established commerce with Asia exported goods from the interior in exchange for manufactured and luxury items. Trade, and settlement by Asian people, resulted in cultural borrowing by coastal peoples. By the 12th century, Islam had been introduced to the region, and Arabic script, legal codes, and architecture were firmly established. Indian Ocean trade was disrupted by the arrival of the Portuguese in the late 15th century while the northern Swahili towns were abandoned in the face of Oromo threats in the 16th century.

migrations of Bantu speakers to Madagascar bringing cattle and millet

Indonesian expansion from east coast into interior bringing bananas and rice

Indian Ocean

From around the 10th century the cattle-herding peoples of the Zambezi region built large stone buildings or "zimbabwes" for their kings. These gradually became larger and more sophisticated. The most extensive is at Great Zimbabwe (right), built over a period of 200 years. Its high granite walls were abandoned by 1500, but still served as a shrine.

---

c. 1150 Beginnings of Yoruba city-states

c. 1200 Rise of empire of Mali

1200–1400 Building of Great Zimbabwe

c. 1300 Emergence of Benin

c. 1300 Kanuri empire moves capital from Kanem to Bornu

1324 Pilgrimage of Mansa Musa to Mecca

c. 1400 Songhay breaks away from Mali

1498 Portuguese arrive on east coast of Africa

The rise of the Ottoman empire

Originally a petty principality in western Anatolia, from the late 13th century the Ottoman state was transformed into an astonishingly dynamic imperial and military power. By 1522, it had expanded to embrace the Balkans, the Black Sea and the Middle East and had become a major player in the international power politics of the day.

THE RETREAT OF THE Mongols from Anatolia into Iran in the 13th century created a vacuum in Anatolia which a series of rival Turcoman states fought to fill. Among them was a small polity based on Sögüt. With the accession in 1281 of Osman, after whom the Ottoman dynasty came to be called, it began a period of rapid expansion. By 1354 it had gained its first foothold in Europe with the acquisition of Gallipoli. By 1361 the Ottomans had taken Edirne (Adrianople), which they made their capital. The decisive defeat of the Serbians and Bosnians at Kosovo in 1389 then established Ottoman supremacy in the Balkans. By 1393, Bulgaria had been absorbed as had most of the remaining independent emirates of Anatolia. Ottoman rule stretched from the Danube to the Euphrates.

Defeat and reconstruction

The invasion of Tamerlane from the East saw the Ottomans' first serious setback. Though his empire broke up with Tamerlane's death in 1405, his victory at Ankara in 1402 had provided the opportunity for the Balkan states and the Anatolian emirates to escape Ottoman hegemony. But reconstruction of the Ottoman state by Mehmed I (1413–21) and renewed campaigns by his son Murad II (1421–51) again brought most of eastern and central Anatolia

2 On the eve of the Ottoman conquest, invasion and war between Latins, Byzantines, Muslims and Mongols had destroyed the last shred of the former Byzantine and Muslim empires in the Middle East (**map below**). The Balkans and Anatolia, entirely fragmented by the early 14th century, were to become, under the Ottomans, the provinces of a single empire.

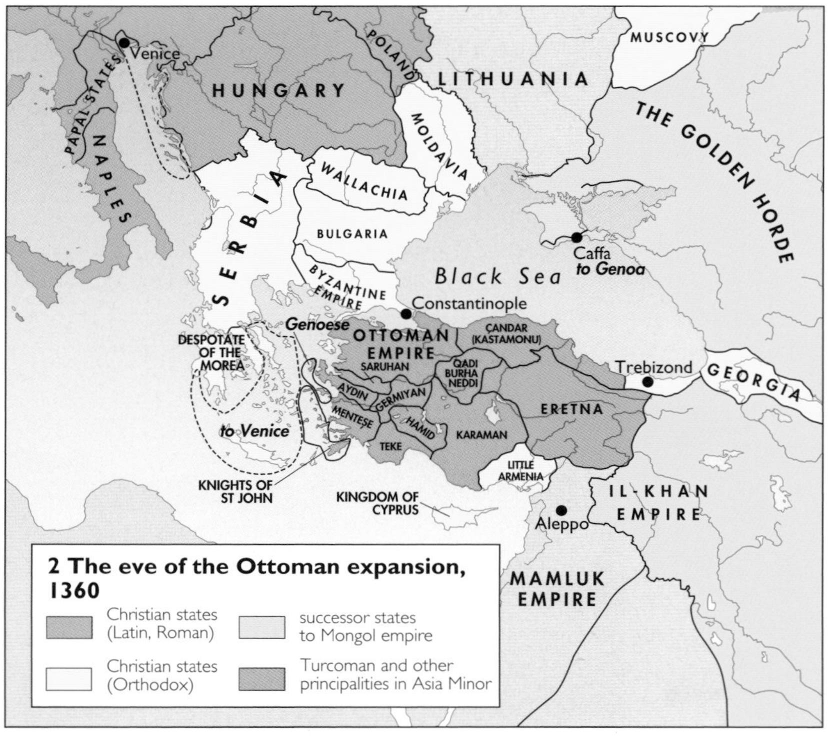

and the southern and eastern Balkans under Ottoman control.

The emergence of the Ottoman state as a world power was the work of Mehmed II, Fatih, "The Conqueror" (1451–81), whose conquest of Constantinople in 1453 made possible Ottoman expansion into northern Anatolia and their dominance of the Straits and southern Black Sea. The conquest of Serbia, Herzegovina and much of Bosnia now left Hungary as the major European power facing the Ottomans. Mehmed's failure to take Belgrade in 1456 established the Danube and lower Sava as the Ottoman boundary with Hungary for over 60 years.

With the final re-absorption of Karaman in 1468 the last of the independent Anatolian emirates disappeared. Farther north, Mehmed established a bridgehead in the Crimea by the capture of Kefe (Caffa) from the Genoese in 1475, bringing the Khanate of the Crimea under Ottoman control.

In Europe, the middle years of Mehmed's reign saw the ending of Byzantine and Frankish control over the Morea, and the erosion of Venetian and Genoese power in the Aegean and the Black Sea. Mehmed's death in 1481, which occurred soon after the Turks overwhelmed Otranto in southern Italy, put paid to his ambition to conquer Rome. The struggle for the succession between Bayezid II (1481–1512) and his brother, Jem, was then skilfully manipulated by the West, protecting it from further Ottoman incursions for many years. However, with the conquests of Akkerman and Kilia the land route from Constantinople to the Crimea was secured in 1484, while the Ottoman-Venetian war of 1499–1502 underlined the growing Ottoman naval power.

I AM GOD'S SLAVE AND SULTAN OF THIS WORLD. BY THE GRACE OF GOD I AM HEAD OF MOHAMMED'S COMMUNITY. GOD'S MIGHT AND MOHAMMED'S MIRACLES ARE MY COMPANIONS. I AM CALIPH IN MECCA AND MEDINA. IN BAGHDAD I AM THE SHAH, IN BYZANTINE REALMS THE CAESAR, AND IN EGYPT THE SULTAN; WHO SENDS HIS FLEETS TO THE SEAS OF EUROPE, NORTH AFRICA AND INDIA. I AM THE SULTAN WHO TOOK THE CROWN AND THRONE OF HUNGARY AND GRANTED THEM TO A HUMBLE SLAVE ...

Inscription celebrating Suleiman the Magnificent (1520–66)

Expansion in the Middle East

The last years of Bayezid II's reign, and most of that of his successor Selim I (1512–20), were taken up with conquests in the Middle East. The rise of the Safavids in Iran after 1501 brought to power a state militarily strong and ideologically hostile to the Ottomans. Risings among the Turcoman tribes of eastern Anatolia in the last years of Bayezid II's reign were a prelude to the war which broke out in the reigns of Selim and Shah Isma'il (1501–24), culminating in the defeat of the Safavids at Çaldiran in 1514. Eastern Anatolia was secured and the threat of religious separatism removed.

Selim's annexation of the emirate of Dhu'l-Qadr in 1515 brought the Ottomans into direct contact with the Mamluk empire for the first time. Over the next two years Selim swept the Mamluks aside, conquering Aleppo and Damascus in 1516 and taking Cairo in 1517. As well as bringing Syria and Egypt under Ottoman control, his campaign added the holy places of Christendom and Islam to the empire. His successor, Suleiman the Magnificent was to continue Ottoman expansion (*see* p. 186).

The siege of Rhodes in 1522 (below), depicting the elite of the Ottoman army storming the walls of the city, defended by knights of St John. The troops shown consisted of the janissaries, the infantry corps founded early in the Ottoman state's history, and the sipahis, the Muslim feudal cavalry. The janissaries were raised by the *Devshirme*, a compulsory levy of Christian boys begun late in the 14th century and which soon became a fundamental institution of the empire. Christian Europe saw them as the most formidable component of the Ottoman army.

Map details:
HOLY ROMA
Danube
Sava
Zag
Venice
VENETIAN REPUBLIC
BOS
Jajce 1528
HERZEGO (14
Dubrovnik
REPUBLIC OF DUBROVNIK (Ottoman vassal 1430–1804)
NAPLES
Avlonya (Vlorë)
Otranto (temporary Ottoman occupation 1480)
Corfu
Cephalonia
Zante
Modon (Ottoman 1500)
Ionian Sea
Adriatic Sea

Map 2 (bottom left):
Venice
PAPAL STATES
NAPLES
HUNGARY
POLAND
LITHUANIA
MUSCOVY
MOLDAVIA
WALLACHIA
SERBIA
BULGARIA
THE GOLDEN HORDE
Caffa to Genoa
Black Sea
BYZANTINE EMPIRE
Constantinople
Genoese
DESPOTATE OF THE MOREA
to Venice
OTTOMAN EMPIRE
SARUHAN
AYDIN
MENTESE
TEKE
HAMID
GERMIYAN
CANDAR (KASTAMONU)
QADI BURHA NEDDI
KARAMAN
LITTLE ARMENIA
Trebizond
GEORGIA
ERETNA
KNIGHTS OF ST JOHN
KINGDOM OF CYPRUS
Aleppo
IL-KHAN EMPIRE
MAMLUK EMPIRE

2 The eve of the Ottoman expansion, 1360
- Christian states (Latin, Roman)
- Christian states (Orthodox)
- successor states to Mongol empire
- Turcoman and other principalities in Asia Minor

1281 Accession of Osman

1354 Ottomans capture Gallipoli and gain first foothold in Europe

1361 Edirne (Adrianople) taken; becomes new Ottoman capital

1389 Battle of Kosovo: Ottoman supremacy in the Balkans established

1402 Tamerlane destroys Ottoman army at Ankara

1413–51 Ottoman control of Balkans and Anatolia reinforced

1453 Constantinople falls to Mehmed II, Fatih

1456 Hungary defeats Ottoman army at Belgrade

1516–17 Ottomans overrun Syria, Egypt and Arabia

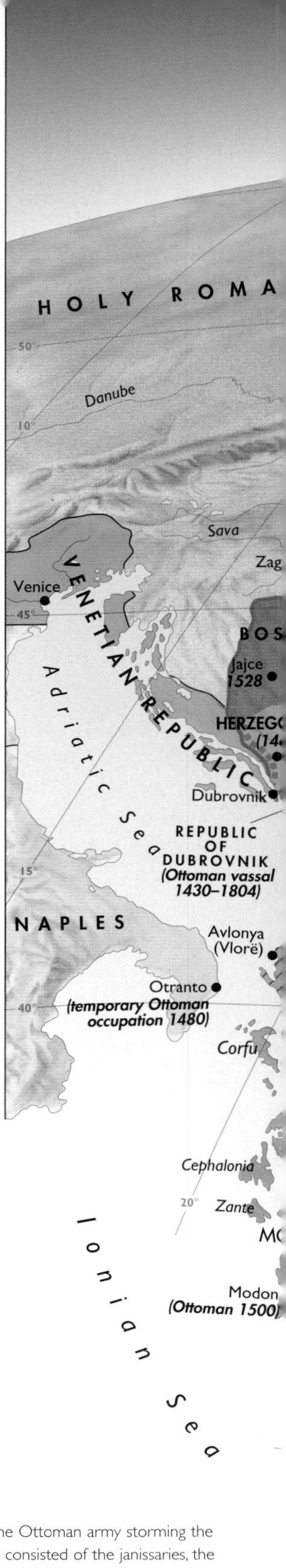

TEUTONIC ORDER

L I T H U A N I A

• Moscow

• Cracow

POLAND

RUSSIA

• Vienna
(Beç)

• Kiev

Carpathian Mountains

Dnieper

Cossack settlements

• Buda

Danube

• Suceava

Dniester

H U N G A R Y

BOĞDAN
(MOLDAVIA)
1455

Prut

Yaş (Jassy)

TRANSYLVANIA

K H A N A T E   O F   T H E   C R I M E A
(vassal 1475)

Akkerman
(1484)

• Belgrade
1456

EFLĂK
(WALLACHIA)
1396

Sea of Azov

• Azov

• Semendire
1444

BUJAK

Kilia

• Bakhchesaray
(Bahçesaray)

Don

aray
o) SERBIA
1389

Vidin

Bükres
(Bucharest)

• Kerç

Morava

Nicopolis
1396

Silistre

Danube

ÇERKES
(CIRCASSIA)

× Kosovo
1389

• Nish

Turnovo

DOBRUJA

1444

Kefe (Caffa)

• Sofia

Yergögü
(Giurgiu)

Varna

Caucasus Mountains

B U L G A R I A

Filibe
(Philippopolis)
1393

B l a c k   S e a

• Manastir
(Bitolj)

Edirne
(Adrianople)
1361

Kastamonu

• Sinop

Selanik
(Salonica)
1430

Gelibolu
(Gallipoli)
1354

Constantinople
1453

CANDAR
(KASTAMONU)
1393 1461

• Samsun

Dardanelles

Bursa
1326

Trabzon
(Trebizond)
1461

• Amasya

Tiflis

Aegean
Sea

KARASI
1345

Söğüt
1265

Eskişehir
1289

Ankara
1402 ×

EMPIRE OF TREBIZOND

Negroponte
(Euboea)
1470

Manisa

SARUHAN
1390 1405

A N A T O L I A
E M P I R E

Chios

GERMIYAN
1380 1428

SIVAS
1398

Otluk-Beli
1473

to Genoa

Izmir
(Smyrna)

Sivas

Erzurum

Athens

Samos

AYDIN
1390 1426

HAMID
1381–90

• Kayseri

KARAKOYUNLU

Naxos

• Konya

Çaldıran
1514

KNIGHTS OF ST JOHN

MENTESE
1390 1426

TEKE
1391 1427

KARAMAN
1390 1468

DHU'L-QADR
1398 1515

AKKOYUNLU

Lake Van

alvasia

Rhodes

Taurus   Mts.

• Diyarbakir

Lake
Urmia

Crete

• Adana

Marj Dabiq
1516

Aleppo
1516

• Raqqa

Tabriz
1514

25°

Cyprus
(Venetian 1489,
Ottoman tributary 1517)

Tigris

Euphrates

• Mosul

M e d i t e r r a n e a n   S e a

SAFAVID EMPIRE
(from 1501)

I Until the mid-15th century, Ottoman
expansion outside western Anatolia was
largely directed into the Balkans (map right).
Although territories were sometimes
recovered or their status within the
empire changed, by 1393 Bulgaria and
Serbia were under Ottoman domination.
After the Mongol invasion in 1402,
progress was halted for a number
of years, but by the time of the
capture of Constantinople
the Ottomans were
definitively established in
Anatolia and re-established
in southeast Europe. The
defeat of the Safavids at
Çaldıran in 1514 opened
the way to further
expansion to the east and
the absorption of the
Mamluk empire in 1517
gave the Ottomans control
of Egypt. The capture of
Belgrade (1521) permitted
the conquest of Hungary,
and the seizure of Rhodes
in 1522 led to Ottoman
naval supremacy in
the eastern basin of
the Mediterranean.

• Tripoli

• Beirut

Damascus
1516

M A M L U K   E M P I R E
1517

• Alexandria

Jerusalem

40°

45°

I The rise of the Ottoman empire, 1301–1520

▨ probable extent of Ottoman state, *c.* 1300	reduced frontiers of Ottoman state after Tamerlane's invasion and civil war of 1403–13
⟵ main routes of Ottoman advance	● Emirates restored by Tamerlane, 1402
---- conquests of Osman, *c.* 1300–26	1427 final reincorporation into Ottoman empire
—— conquests of Orkhan, 1326–62	× Western crusades against the Ottoman state
—— conquests of Murad I, 1362–89	▨ conquests and re-conquests, 1413–51 (Mehmed I 1413–21, Murad II 1421–51)
TEKE 1390 absorbed Emirates with date of first absorption	—— boundary of Ottoman state at the accession of Mehmed II, 1451
—— conquests of Bayezid, 1389–1402	···· additional vassal states by 1451
× major battles	▨ vassal states, 1512
1398 dates of Ottoman control	▨ Ottoman empire, 1512
···· vassal states of Bayezid, 1402	—— western frontiers of Safavid state, *c.* 1512 including tributary states
▨ Venetian territories, 1510	⟵ major campaigns of Selim I, 1512–20
⟵ invasion of Tamerlane, 1402	—— Ottoman sphere of influence, *c.* 1520
◉ successive centres of Ottoman state, with dates of conquest	

× Al-Raydaniyya

• Cairo
1517

• Suez

35°

Nile

to 3rd cataract
of the River Nile

30°

The crisis of the 14th century in Europe

The 14th century saw dramatic change in Europe and Asia as the Black Death spread westward, reaching the Black Sea in 1346, Sicily in 1347 and most of Europe by 1350. In Europe and the Islamic world between a quarter and a half of the population died of plague. The economy and society of East and West underwent radical transformations as a result.

1252 First western European gold coins for 450 years minted in Genoa and Florence

1277 Opening of sea route from Italy to Flanders

1277 Sheep guild or Mesta organized in Castile

1315–17 Great Famine in northern Europe

1346–51 Black Death

1347 Bankruptcy of Peruzzi bankers, Florence

1362–3 Second plague pandemic in Europe

1370 Peace of Stralsund guarantees passage to Hansa merchants

1378 Rebellion of Florentine clothworkers (Ciompi)

1381 Peasants' Revolt, England

2 The function of medieval universities was to train candidates for the upper clergy and parish priests. The first universities were founded in Italy (Bologna, 1088) and France (Paris, late 11th century). The early 14th century saw a new wave of foundations (**map below**) and by the early 15th almost every state in Christian Europe had its own university. In the period after the Black Death the universities played a valuable role in providing new recruits for the priesthood, but they also often became centres of religious dissent.

THE INTENSE PRESSURE on the land of a densely packed population combined with a succession of poor harvests to cause the Great Famine in northern Europe of 1315–17. Yet though Europe was to be afflicted with a series of further harvest failures, this was also a period of expanding markets, meeting the needs of increasingly active regional trade in wine, grain, dyestuffs and raw materials. Further new opportunities grew after the Black Death, when labour, previously in surplus, leading to low wages, suddenly became scarce.

Black Death and economic crisis

Signs of crisis were visible before the Black Death. Textile manufacture in Flemish and Italian cities was in decline on the eve of the plague. Banking failures, beginning with the Buonsignori of Siena (1298), culminated in the collapse of the great Florentine banking houses of Bardi and Peruzzi in the 1340s. The plague struck in 1346, and by 1350 had swept through most of Europe (see map 1). Population levels did not recover until the late 15th century because of the recurrence of plague, which became endemic in Europe, though outbreaks were increasingly localized.

Yet though the effects on the European economy were profound, there were many who benefited from the new economic climate, and this was not necessarily a period of severe depression. Thus English cloth exports expanded greatly, as did Castilian wool exports. Farmland was converted to pasture for sheep in England, Italy and Spain and for cattle in the Netherlands, Spain and northern Germany. New products such as saffron were cultivated in southern Germany, where Nuremberg and Augsburg were front-runners in a new wave of economic expansion, partly based on the mineral resources of the lands to the east.

On the other hand, monopolistic guild restrictions meant that some of the once prosperous cloth towns in northern Europe lost out to more agile competitors in the restructured economy of the late 14th century. Florence, too, lost its pre-eminence in woollen cloth, and attempted to become a major centre of silk production instead; but by now there were several lively competitors. Barcelona

1 Famine, plague and popular unrest

— main sea-trade routes

`wine` important commodities

extent of the spread of the Black Death

1346	end 1349
1347	1350
mid-1348	c. 1351
end 1348	c. 1353
mid-1349	little or no plague mortality

social unrest

areas of disturbance during Peasants' Revolt in England, 1381

● centre of urban revolt

▭ rural uprisings

⊗ defeat of lower orders in battle

religious unrest

spread of Lollardy in England to death of Richard II, 1399

area of Hussite influence

■ Hussite centre

found a market for its upper-middle quality cloths, but financial crises and internal power struggles sapped the city's energy and Valencia took over as the powerhouse of western Mediterranean trade. In the north, the German Hansa became a powerful confederation of trading cities which dominated Baltic and North Sea trade in fish, grain, dairy goods and furs, operating through bases at London, Lynn, Bergen, Bruges and Novgorod; for long it was able to keep competitors such as the Dutch and the English at bay.

Peasant unrest and revolt

Economic change brought new wealth to some and undermined the wealth of others, such as landlords who lost their source of cheap labour. Villages were abandoned in areas as far apart as the English

2 University foundations, 1250–1450

■ universities founded before 1250

■ universities founded, 1250–1378 (with date)

■ universities founded, 1378–1450 (with date)

— borders, 1430

Unlike famine, the pestilence affected every social class, and the psychological impact was profound. Until the early 18th century, scarcely a decade passed without a recurrent outbreak. The disease, spread by infected fleas carried by rats, was particularly virulent, and few who caught it ever recovered. This illustration (above) from the Stiny Codex shows death strangling a plague victim.

Midlands and Russia, as peasants moved – often without permission – to the lands of lords who made less demands on them or which had more fertile soil. Many moved to towns, especially when villages were abandoned to make way for sheep. Yet some peasants were able to accumulate large amounts of land, as relatives died of the plague and left them their possessions. To many it seemed that the world was turned topsy-turvy. Social unrest became strident in town and country, exemplified by the Ciompi rebellion in Florence (1378) or the Peasants' Revolt in England (1381), particularly among those whose depressed social status did not match their rising economic status. Generally, however, serfdom was a thing of the past in much of western Europe by 1400; in eastern Europe it was, in contrast, reinforced, as landlords such as the

Teutonic Knights sought to produce grain for their Hanseatic customers.

The 14th century saw severe readjustment, with the restructuring of economies in the wake of massive depopulation. However, by the end of the century the Hansa was enjoying its Golden Age, the maritime trade routes that linked Italy and Catalonia to England and Flanders (opened around 1277) were flourishing, and Venice and Genoa had secured a strong hold on eastern markets: the Genoese mainly in the Black Sea, from where they brought grain and dried fruits; the Venetians in Egypt and Syria, from where they brought spices and cotton. The Black Death was a dramatic demographic earthquake, with severe aftershocks, yet the European economy was successfully rebuilt on its own shattered remains.

SOME SAY THAT IT DESCENDED UPON THE HUMAN RACE THROUGH THE INFLUENCE OF HEAVENLY BODIES, OTHERS THAT IT WAS A PUNISHMENT SIGNIFYING GOD'S ANGER AT OUR INIQUITOUS WAY OF LIFE. BUT WHATEVER ITS CAUSE, IT HAD ORIGINATED SOME YEARS EARLIER IN THE EAST, WHERE IT HAD CLAIMED COUNTLESS LIVES BEFORE IT UNHAPPILY SPREAD WESTWARD, GROWING IN STRENGTH AS IT SWEPT RELENTLESSLY FROM ONE PLACE TO THE NEXT.

Boccaccio, The Decameron, 1358

I Inadequately financed and weakened by war and internal dissension, western Europe underwent severe strains in the 14th century (map above). Recession, compounded by famine and pestilence, led to conflicts in almost all countries between the autocracy and the urban oligarchies on the one hand and the peasants and urban workers on the other. The effect of the Black Death was particularly severe. After 1346, plague of Asiatic origin spread from the southeast across virtually all of Europe, wiping out between a quarter and a half of the population. As well as economic and social turmoil, Europe saw religious dissent, too, with the Lollard movement in England and the Hussites in Bohemia.

European states in the 14th century

The 14th century was a tumultuous period of state building in which rulers sought to define frontiers and develop centralized bureaucracies. They were challenged by parliaments of nobles, knights and townsmen, seeking concessions in return for taxation. Furthermore, the cost of frontier wars forced rulers back into the arms of their subjects.

WAR ADDED TO THE TURMOIL caused to 14th-century Europe by famine and plague (see p. 158). Italy was particularly affected. The struggle for Sicily after 1282 between the French house of Anjou and Aragonese invaders (the War of the Sicilian Vespers) continued long after its formal ending in 1302 by the Treaty of Caltabellotta. Around 1300 northern Italy remained divided between competing cities, themselves often torn apart by Guelph and Ghibelline factions, the former able to count on the support of Naples or the Papacy. As regional despots gained power over the cities, conflict within their walls died, culminating in the conquest of large areas of Lombardy and Tuscany by Giangaleazzo Visconti, duke of Milan. Few Italian republics stood firm against the trend, though Florence made much capital out of its self-proclaimed dedication to the cause of republican liberty.

The pope himself decamped in 1305 to Avignon in southern France, a more peaceful city than Rome. Papal centralization was visible in the tighter control over Church appointments and taxation, successes that generated bitter criticism from reformers such as Wyclif in Oxford and Hus in Prague. The return of the Papacy to Rome in 1376 led to deep divisions among the cardinals and the outbreak of a schism that lasted nearly 40 years.

The conflict between France and England (see p. 132) for control of France, above all Gascony, erupted again in 1294 and then in 1337 (the Hundred Years' War). Initial English successes coupled with internal strife gravely weakened France and great princes such as the Valois dukes of Burgundy exploited this royal debility to create powerful statelets of their own.

Rulers and subjects

Against this disturbed background, rulers sought to create a sound financial base for themselves. Often this meant, as in Germany and Aragon, negotiating with parliaments that controlled their budget. Conflicts between rulers and their leading subjects led to the deposition of Edward II and Richard II in England (1327, 1399), and of Wenzel in Bohemia (1400). In Germany, the great princely houses vied for the crown, but were more concerned to strengthen their own patrimonies than to stabilize the German monarchy. A web of leagues emerged, of which the Swiss Confederation (from 1291) was the most successful.

In the Mediterranean, the Crown of Aragon consolidated its hold. Sardinia, promised by Pope Boniface VIII to the Aragonese in 1297, was invaded in 1323–4, though it took many decades before Aragonese rule became a reality; Majorca, an autonomous kingdom since 1276, was reconquered in 1343, giving access to prime trade routes; by the end of the century Sicily, too, was under Aragonese

1302	War of Sicilian Vespers ends
1305–76	Papacy in residence at Avignon
1323–4	Aragonese invasion of Sardinia
1337–1453	Hundred Years' War between France and England
1378–1417	Great Schism
1378	Death of Emperor Charles IV
1386	Union of Poland and Lithuania
1397	Union of Kalmar brings together Scandinavian kingdoms
1399	Deposition of Richard II of England
1400	Deposition of Wenzel of Bohemia from imperial throne

IF YOU TAKE THE COAT OF ARMS OF FRANCE, QUARTERING IT WITH THAT OF ENGLAND, AND CALL YOURSELF KING OF FRANCE, WE WILL REGARD YOU AS KING OF FRANCE, AND OBEY YOU AS SUCH; AND WE WILL ... FOLLOW YOU WHEREVER YOU COMMAND.

Flemish petitioners to Edward III of England, 1339

1 The 14th century saw the definitive emergence of many of the European states which were to survive into the modern age. The map **(right)** shows the situation in about 1380. The great German dynasties were consolidating their hold on lands in central Europe, while the Ottoman empire was gaining ever greater authority in the Balkans. France expanded its power in the Rhône valley.

1 European states, c. 1380

- ▬▬ The Holy Roman Empire
- Habsburg possessions
- Luxemburg possessions
- Wittelsbach possessions
- Anjou possessions
- Milanese territory under Giangaleazzo Visconti, 1378–1402

3 Italy after 1282

- Papal states
- ◑ Republican communes
- ◉ cities under Signorial domination c. 1310

the Signori

1. Avvocati	5. Da Camino	9. Este	13. Malatesta
2. Bonacolsi	6. Da Correggio	10. Fissiraga	14. Robert of Anjou
3. Brusati	7. Da Polenta	11. Langosco	15. Scotti
4. Cavalcabo	8. Della Scala	12. Maggi	16. Visconti

3 Papal-imperial controversy and the wealth of the municipalities inhibited consolidation in Italy **(map above)**. After 1250, public power in independent city-states was exercised by republican oligarchies or by despots who often succeeded as alternatives to the factional violence of civic politics.

2 Throughout the 14th century, Prussia was gradually conquered by the Teutonic knights **(map below)**. In 1231 Hermann Balke, provincial master of the Teutonic Order, crossed the river Vistula with a crusading army, swiftly founding new fortified cities such as Königsberg. Eastern expansion was checked by defeat at Lake Peipus and in the west at Tannenberg. Systematic subjection of the pagan Prussian tribes gave way, after 1309, to 100 years of prosperity.

2 The conquest of Prussia by the Teutonic Knights, 1231–1411

- → advance of Teutonic Knights
- occupied before 1309
- occupied, 1309–82 with dates
- occupied, 1382–1411
- swamp and wilderness
- Riga 1201 foundation date of town

Trondhjem

N O R W A Y
(in personal union with Denmark)

S W E D E N

Bergen

Oslo

Åbo

Stockholm

Reval

Gotland

ESTONIA

Riga

Dünaburg

Pskov

PSKOV

O R D E R

N O V G O R O D

Novgorod

MUSCOVY

YAROSLAV

MUSCOVY

Moscow

ROSTOV

TVER

(to Novgorod)

SMOLENSK

Smolensk

SMALL
PRINCIP-
ALITIES

RYAZAN

North
Sea

York

WALES ENGLAND

Bristol Oxford

London

Cherbourg

Calais

Rouen

Seine Paris

Rheims

Tours

Loire Orléans

F R A N C E

Limoges

Dijon

BURGUNDY

Geneva

Lyons

Rhône

VENAISSIN
ORANGE
Avignon

PROVENCE

Montpellier

Marseilles

Nizza

SCONY

Toulouse

ANDORRA

CATALONIA

GON

Barcelona

Aarhus

Copenhagen

Roskilde

Malmö

D E N M A R K

Baltic
Sea

Königsberg

Danzig

Vilnius

Minsk

Hamburg

Bremen

Stettin

BRANDENBURG

Berlin

Poznań

Vistula

Warsaw

T E U T O N I C

L I T H U A N I A

HOLLAND

Utrecht

BRABANT

Brussels

Cologne

Rhine

GERMAN
PRINCIPALITIES

Hanover

Leipzig

Dresden

Oder

Breslau

S I L E S I A

P O L A N D

Kiev

Frankfurt

Elbe

Prague

Cracow

GALICH

Lvov

VLADIMIR

Dnieper

Metz

Strassburg

Nuremberg

BOHEMIA

Brünn

MORAVIA

Dniester

KHANATE OF THE
GOLDEN HORDE

Stuttgart

BAVARIA

Munich

Danube

AUSTRIA

Kassa

Zurich

SWISS
CONFEDERATION
from 1291

Berne

Innsbruck

Salzburg

Vienna

Pozsony

Buda

Debrecen

Suceava

Geneva

TYROL

STYRIA

Graz

H U N G A R Y

Kolozsvár

MOLDAVIA

Turin

Milan

LOMBARDY

Venice

Zágráb

Pécs

Szeged

Temesvár

Brassó

Târgovişta

(to Genoa)

Caffa

REP. OF GENOA

Genoa

TUSCANY

VENETIAN
REPUBLIC

SAN MARINO

D A L M A T I A

Belgrade

WALLACHIA

Corsica

Florence

PAPAL
STATE

Rome

Zara

Spalato

BOSNIA

SERBIAN

Nish

Sofia

l o c a l   r u l e r s

B U L G A R I A N   S T A T E S

Danube

Varna

B l a c k   S e a

(to Genoa)

Majorca

Balearics

Sardinia

N A P L E S

REPUBLIC
OF RAGUSA

STATES

Skoplje

Philippopolis

Adrianople

BYZANTINE
EMPIRE

ÇANDAR

M e d i t e r r a n e a n

Cagliari

Naples

Bari

Taranto

MEGALO-
VLACHIA

BYZANTINE
EMPIRE

O T T O M A N

E M P I R E

Constantinople

Bursa

Angora

Algiers

YYANIDS

H A F S I D S

Tunis

Palermo

SICILY
(to Aragon)

Messina

Catania

Sea

Salonica

DUCHY
OF
ATHENS

Athens

Gallipoli

SARUHAN

Smyrna

(to
Genoa)

AYDIN

HAMID

KNIGHTS OF ST JOHN

MENTEŞE

TEKE

PRINCIPALITY
OF ACHAIA

BYZANTINE
EMPIRE

rule. Castile, on the other hand, was wracked in mid-century by civil war, and social tensions took a brutal toll on the Jewish communities of Spain during the pogroms of 1391. A new dynasty gained power in Portugal, and began to look across to Africa for expansion. In 1415 the Portuguese captured Ceuta.

Scandinavia and eastern Europe

In eastern Europe, the century saw the emergence of large, well-endowed states that escaped many of the economic difficulties afflicting western Europe. Hungary at its peak dominated an area between the Adriatic (acquiring Dalmatia from Venice in 1352) and Poland, though an attempt to gain permanent control of the Polish crown failed. Lithuania had possessions from the Black Sea almost to the Baltic, and the marriage of its newly baptized duke, Jagiello, to the Polish

Robert of Anjou (left) known as "the Wise", ruled Naples for 34 years. He persistently attempted to recover Sicily from the Aragonese after 1282. By the Treaty of Caltabellotta, Aragon agreed to restore the island on the death of the Aragonese ruler of Sicily, Frederick III. Robert fought from 1309 to 1319 on the side of the pro-papal Guelph party against the Visconti of Milan. He ultimately failed to regain Sicily on Frederick's death. However, he was an excellent administrator and patron of leading literary figures such as the poet Petrarch.

heiress in 1386 extended its territories still further. In Bohemia, religious dissent flourished by 1400 among the Hussites of Prague, a city that hugely benefited from the rule of Emperor Charles IV (d.1378), who endowed it with a great university. In Denmark, Norway and Sweden, Margaret of Norway acquired loose control of all three kingdoms by the Union of Kalmar in 1397. Yet they were not permanently united and the supremacy of the aristocracy persisted.

Amid these rivalries, a sense of national identity, generally built more around language than race, was emerging in areas such as Catalonia, Bohemia and England. Frontiers between states were being drawn, some of which lasted into the 20th century.

South America on the eve of European conquest

In 1492 the great diversity of physical environments in South America – which ranged from snow-capped mountains in the Andes, to tropical forest in the east, and desert on the Pacific coast – were home to an equally diverse range of human societies, which encompassed all forms of social organization that had arisen in the course of human history.

c. 1200 Incas establish themselves at Cuzco

1375 Chimú conquests of central Andes begin

1438 Inca expansion begins under Pachacuti

1470 Incas conquer Chimú kingdom

1492 Columbus reaches Americas

mid 1520s Smallpox arrives in the Andes, killing the Inca emperor

1532 Pizarro begins conquest of Inca empire

EUROPEANS BEGAN EXPLORING south from Panama in the late 1520s, but their first contacts with the Incas, who were still extending their empire, did not occur until the early 1530s. The size and sophistication of the Inca empire attracted most Spanish attention, but there were also important chiefdoms in Colombia, Venezuela and Bolivia. Tribal groups dominated most of Amazonia, but even here some societies were becoming larger and more complex. Hunter-gatherers continued to inhabit cold and arid lands to the south.

The Incas

The Inca empire was very different from that of the Aztecs, partly because of its Andean location. However, it was similarly an empire of conquest, and its expansion often met fierce resistance. It has been estimated that in Ecuador perhaps 100,000 people were killed in wars resisting the Incas. Once the Incas had established political control they began to set up an administrative structure that aimed to integrate the empire. To this end they built a road system, more than 20,000km (12,500 miles) in length. They also imposed a common language, Quechua, which is still spoken by large numbers of Indians in the Andes today, and a common religion, which involved the worship of the sun god, Inti, of whom the emperor was regarded an earthly manifestation.

The Incas developed many techniques for enhancing agricultural production, including terracing, irrigation to channel snow-melt from the high Andes, and raised or sunken fields. To straddle such diverse environments the Incas developed a means of internal exchange between peoples living in different zones, so that unlike the Aztecs they needed few markets. The Incas also attempted to maximize production, or increase security, by relocating large populations. In the early 16th century, the Inca ruler Huayna Capac was said to have resettled some 14,000 people in Cochabamba, moving them from areas as far apart as Cuzco and what is now northern Chile. The Incas also developed a system of storehousing; the storehouses were useful in times of food shortage, but they were used primarily to support bureaucratic and religious elites.

Although different in character, the Inca empire revealed some of the structural weaknesses of the Aztec. While the tally of human sacrifice was less extravagant, religion still strained resources as a result of the vast households maintained for the cults of dead rulers. The costs this involved may have contributed to divisions among the elite, which developed into the devastating civil war raging at the time of the Spanish conquest. Also, some subject peoples, particularly in outlying regions, found the burden of Inca rule so oppressive that they were willing to collaborate with the invader. However, in general, the Incas succeeded in creating an empire that was integrated to the extent that resistance to Spanish conquest was greater in the Andes than in Mexico, and the last Inca ruler, Tupac Amaru, was not defeated until 1572.

Amazonia

In 1492 most Amazonians practised shifting cultivation combined with hunting, fishing and gathering along the banks of the large rivers, notably the Amazon itself. However, there is evidence for the emergence of chiefdoms, notably the Tapajós chiefdom at Santarem, whose domain may have covered 25,000 square km (9,500 square miles). Although they had a warlike reputation, the Tapajós were also engaged in more domestic pursuits, producing many items for trade, and in their religion, which involved the worship of idols stored in sacred structures.

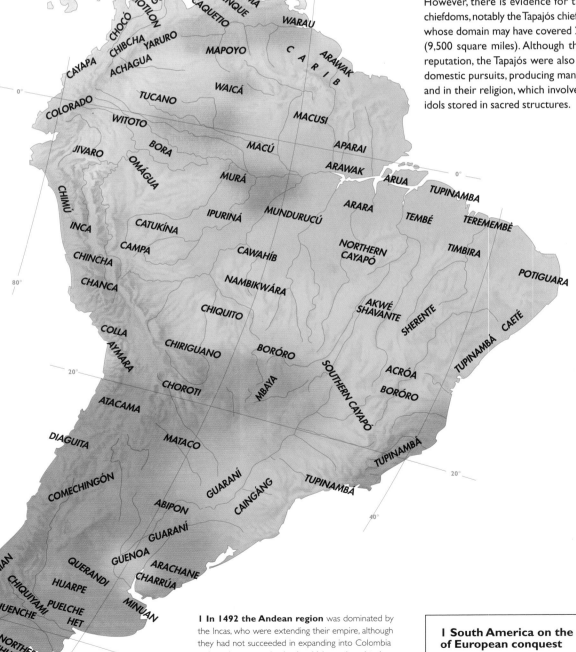

1 In 1492 the Andean region was dominated by the Incas, who were extending their empire, although they had not succeeded in expanding into Colombia or into the eastern lowlands, which continued to be inhabited mainly by tribal peoples (**map above**). Hunter-gatherers and shell-fishers continued to inhabit southern South America where the climate was often too cold or dry for farming to take place.

1 South America on the eve of European conquest
- state civilizations
- theocratic and militaristic chiefdoms
- tropical forest farm villages
- desert farm villages
- nomadic hunting, fishing, and gathering peoples

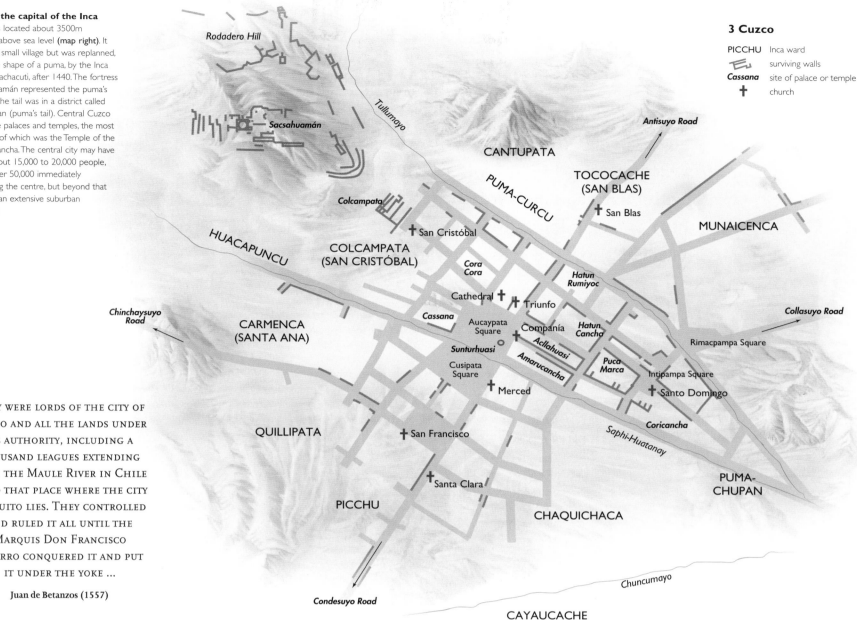

3 Cuzco, the capital of the Inca empire, is located about 3500m (11,600ft) above sea level (map right). It began as a small village but was replanned, to take the shape of a puma, by the Inca emperor, Pachacuti, after 1440. The fortress of Sacsahuamán represented the puma's head, and the tail was in a district called Pumachupan (puma's tail). Central Cuzco housed the palaces and temples, the most important of which was the Temple of the Sun, Coricancha. The central city may have housed about 15,000 to 20,000 people, with another 50,000 immediately surrounding the centre, but beyond that there was an extensive suburban population.

3 Cuzco

PICCHU   Inca ward
         surviving walls
Cassana site of palace or temple
✝   church

THEY WERE LORDS OF THE CITY OF
CUZCO AND ALL THE LANDS UNDER
ITS AUTHORITY, INCLUDING A
THOUSAND LEAGUES EXTENDING
FROM THE MAULE RIVER IN CHILE
UP TO THAT PLACE WHERE THE CITY
OF QUITO LIES. THEY CONTROLLED
AND RULED IT ALL UNTIL THE
MARQUIS DON FRANCISCO
PIZARRO CONQUERED IT AND PUT
IT UNDER THE YOKE …

Juan de Betanzos (1557)

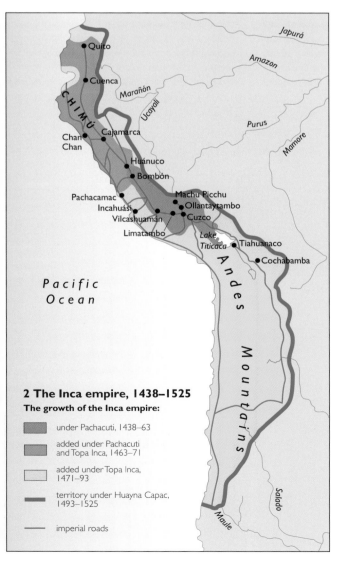

2 The Inca empire, 1438–1525

The growth of the Inca empire:

- under Pachacuti, 1438–63
- added under Pachacuti and Topa Inca, 1463–71
- added under Topa Inca, 1471–93
- territory under Huayna Capac, 1493–1525
- imperial roads

2 The Inca empire expanded rapidly in the 15th century (map left). From Cuzco, the Inca emperor exerted rigid control over this extensive territory by means of a highly trained bureaucracy, a state religion, a powerful army and an advanced communications network. The final expansion under Huayna Capac put the Inca world under great strain, however, and by the arrival of the Spanish conqueror Pizarro, in 1533, civil war had split the empire in two.

Although they did not have a form of writing, the Incas kept account of numerical data, such as populations, contents of warehouses, land measurements and military information, on knotted strings known as *quipus*. The position, number, order, shape and colour of the knots had different meanings. This is a picture (right) of a record keeper drawn by an Inca, Felipe Guaman Poma de Ayala, in the late 16th or early 17th century.

163

Mesoamerica and the Caribbean on the eve of European conquest

c. 1200 The Nicarao arrive in Nicaragua

c. 1250 Mayapán becomes dominant city of Yucatán

1325 Rise of the Aztecs in Mexico

1434 Aztec expansion begins

1441 Mayapán defeated

1492 Columbus reaches the Americas

1519 Cortés begins the conquest of Aztec empire

When Europeans arrived in Mesoamerica they often failed to recognize the profound diversity of societies that existed there and the people's resourcefulness in dealing with their natural environment. Instead they regarded them as technologically backward and as candidates for civilization and conversion to the Catholic faith.

> THERE IS NOTHING LIKE DEATH IN WAR,
> NOTHING LIKE THE FLOWERY DEATH
> SO PRECIOUS TO HIM WHO GIVES LIFE:
> FAR OFF I SEE IT: MY HEART YEARNS FOR IT!
>
> **A Mexican poet**

IN 1492, when Columbus set sail on his historic voyage, the continent he would open to European conquest was already peopled by highly developed societies. In Mesoamerica the Aztec empire had spread its influence throughout much of Mexico and south into Central America. In northern Mexico many other groups still obtained their food by hunting and gathering, while in Panama and on the island of Haiti chiefdoms had emerged.

The Aztec

The origins of the Aztec empire, which dominated the Valley of Mexico at the time of European discovery, are shrouded in myth. It probably began near the beginning of the 14th century with nomads settling among the agrarian states of the Lake Texcoco area. Through military conquest or alliance, their lake-bound city of Tenochtitlán slowly achieved dominance over neighbouring communities. In around 1500, Aztec armies extended the sway of their system of tribute-exaction as far as the Pánuco river in the north and Soconusco province in the south. Borne by trade, their influence reached across the northern deserts into southwest North America, over the Caribbean to the Taino of Haiti (who adopted their ritual ball games with stone courts), and to the east past Xicalango (where the remotest Aztec garrison was stationed) into Yucatán.

The population of Tenochtitlán probably exceeded 150,000 – much greater than any European city at the time. To help meet the needs of such large numbers, the Aztecs developed an elaborate system of drained fields called *chinampas* on which they grew maize and beans, and exploited fish and waterfowl. However, although agriculture was highly productive, the city could not be supported entirely locally, so huge quantities of food, clothing and ritual goods had to be levied and transported from far afield. A surviving tribute-roll (which may itself be incomplete) lists over 225,000 bushels of maize and 123,400 cotton mantles, with corresponding quantities of beans, herbs, such as sage and purslane, as well as chillies, cacao, lime, salt, incense and other precious exotica due every year. Other Aztec cities had comparable rates of consumption. The daily market of Tlatelolco, Tenochtitlán's neighbour, was said to be regularly patronized by 50,000 people.

The Aztec empire was prodigious in other fields. Its material culture featured monumental stone building, vital sculpture, sumptuous goldwork and extravagant featherwork, all requiring intensive labour and expensive raw materials. Its religion exacted a fearful toll in human sacrifices. According to the varying estimates of European colonial sources, between 10,000 and 80,000 sacrifices were offered at the dedication of the main temple of Tenochtitlán in 1487, most of

them acquired through capture in war or ritual exchange of victims with other communities. Human sacrifices were required to give strength to the warrior god, Huitzilopochtli, the empire's patron. The voracious appetites of the Aztec system, while forcing its beneficiaries to be skilled in war, also made it vulnerable to a concerted withdrawal of tribute by suppliers. Isolated by the diplomacy of the Spanish invaders after 1519, the Aztec capital was starved into surrender.

The Maya

Following the decline of the Toltec-Maya, a new Maya-dominated state emerged at Mayapán in northern Yucatán. There its Cocom rulers kept the lords of tributary provinces as virtual prisoners to ensure the payment of tribute, but in 1441 they rebelled and destroyed the city. Subsequently the lowland Maya dissolved into 16 rival states, whose merchants managed a coastal trade in salt, cotton, cloth, cacao, honey, jade, feathers, obsidian and copper.

Outside the Mesoamerican heartland

Hunters and gatherers continued to dominate the vast dry lands of northern Mexico, but further south changes were occurring. Mesoamerican influences spread into Central America through trade and through the migration of the Central Mexican peoples called the Pipil and Nicarao. In 1492 much of Central America was inhabited by militaristic chiefdoms. In Nicaragua the population was supported by the rich volcanic soils found on the Pacific coast. To the east and south the main cultural influences were from

1 By the time the European conquest began, representatives of all types of society inhabited Mesoamerica and the Caribbean. At one extreme were hunter-gatherers of northern Mexico and at the other was the populous and highly sophisticated civilization of the Aztec, but militaristic and theocratic chiefdoms had also emerged in Central America and in Haiti in the Caribbean.

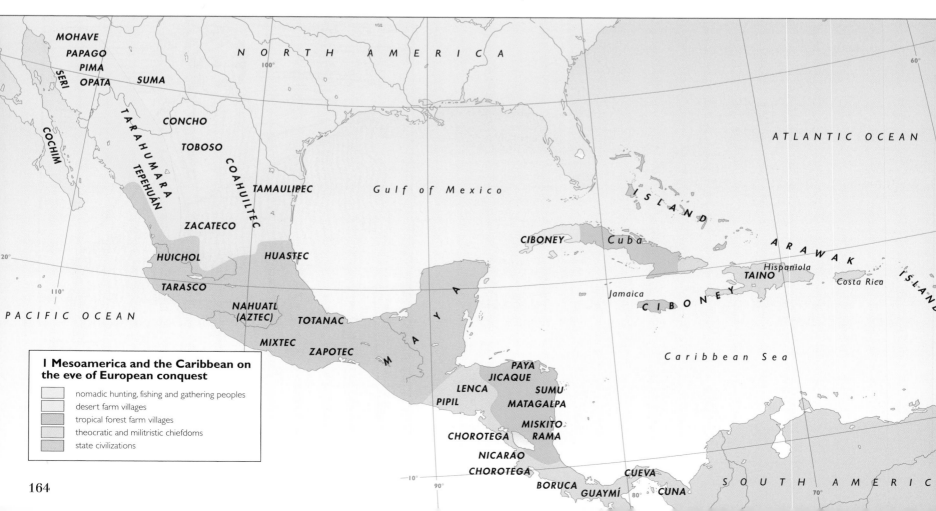

1 Mesoamerica and the Caribbean on the eve of European conquest

- nomadic hunting, fishing and gathering peoples
- desert farm villages
- tropical forest farm villages
- theocratic and militristic chiefdoms
- state civilizations

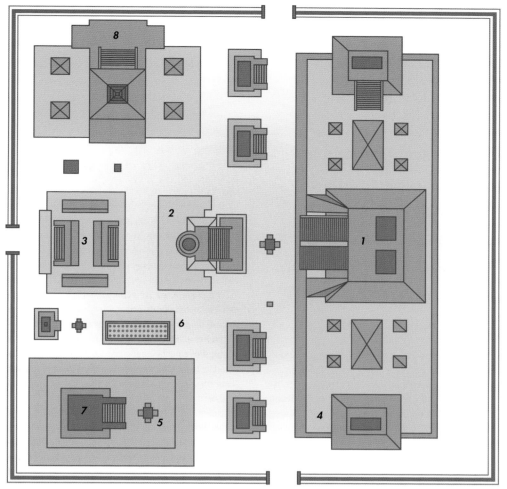

3c The Great Precinct of Tenochtitlán

1 Shrines of Tlaloc and Huitzilopochtli
2 Temple of Quetzalcoatl
3 Ball court
4 Temples of Tezcatlipoca
5 Platform for galditorial combat
6 Skull rack
7 Temple of the Sun
8 Calmecac (school)

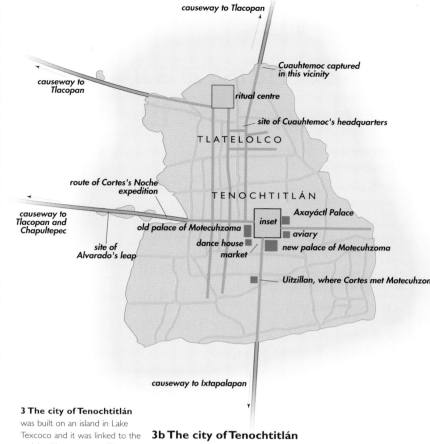

3b The city of Tenochtitlán

3 The city of Tenochtitlán was built on an island in Lake Texcoco and it was linked to the mainland by causeways. The centre of the city possessed a complex of temples where sacrifices took place. It was dominated by the Great Temple, which had the shrines of Tlaloc, the god of rain, and Huitzilopochtli, the god of war. Behind a dyke that ran across the lake the Aztec created drained fields. known as *chinampas*.

South America rather than Mesoamerica. Here many tribal societies continued to practise shifting cultivation, but militaristic chiefdoms, such as the Guaymí and Cuna, had emerged in southern Costa Rica and Panama. They were renowned for their manufacture of pottery, jade, copper and gold, the abundance of which led the Spanish to give these regions names such as "rich land" (Costa Rica).

The Caribbean

At the time of Spanish conquest the Taino were also organized into a complex series of chiefdoms that might encompass as many as 100 villages and tens of thousands of people. Stone-lined ball courts and ceremonial plazas were constructed, and there was a flourishing of art styles in pottery, woodcarving and

stonework. Meanwhile the Lesser Antilles had been occupied by Island Caribs who had migrated there, probably from the Guianas.

An Aztec or Miztec sacrificial knife **(below)**. The Aztecs believed that the continuation of human society required that the sun and earth be nourished with human blood and hearts. War was necessary to provide the sacrificial victims, whose hearts were removed with knives such as this. It is 30cm (12in) long and its handle is inlaid with the form of a warrior costumed as an eagle, or *quauhtli* (which was also a name for the sun).

3a The Valley of Mexico

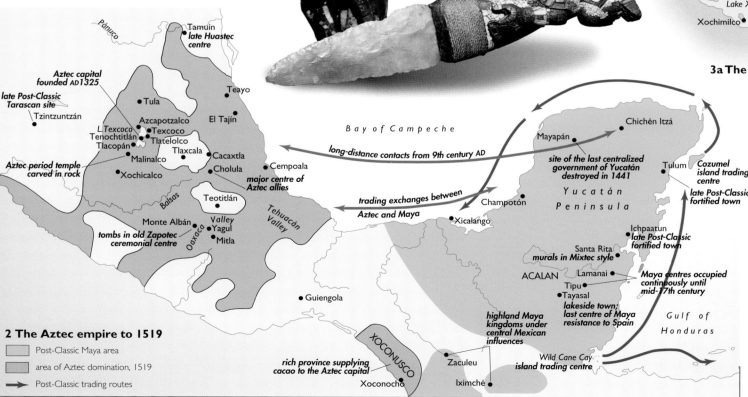

2 The Aztec empire to 1519

  Post-Classic Maya area

  area of Aztec domination, 1519

→ Post-Classic trading routes

2 The Aztecs entered central Mexico from the north. In the course of the 15th century they built a large, tribute-based empire (**map left**) controlled from Tenochtitlán, their capital city, which was founded in the early 14th century. The gargantuan appetite of the Aztec empire for food, gold and sacrificial victims was the source of both its strength and its weakness, explaining both its tentacular reach and its unsustainable consumption. The descendants of the "Classic" Maya civilization still controlled the Yucatán Peninsula in 1535, although the 16 separate provinces were constantly at odds with each other.

The Renaissance and Early Modern state in Europe

Increasing knowledge of the classical past and a desire to return to the Greek and Roman roots of European civilization stimulated the movement known as the Renaissance, which, beginning in Italy, spread rapidly around Europe after the invention of printing. This awakening of interest in its classical past was to affect Europe's politics profoundly.

1 In the early 16th century, more consolidated state structures began to emerge (**map below**). In the east, Muscovy challenged Poland-Lithuania for the inheritance of Kievan Rus, while in the 1520s the Ottomans destroyed the composite monarchy of Hungary and Bohemia which had reached its zenith under Matthias Corvinus in 1485. The collapse of the Scandinavian Union in 1523 was the exception to the rule. Elsewhere, though Italy and the Holy Roman Empire remained fragmented, unions were formed or strengthened: in the Iberian peninsula (between Castile and Aragon in 1479 and Spain and Portugal in 1580); Poland-Lithuania (1569); and Britain (1603).

THE RENAISSANCE SAW a flowering of literature and the arts across Europe. Writers and artists, seeking to emulate the cultures of Greece and Rome, developed new techniques and formulated new ideas in their attempts to apply the knowledge of the Ancients to the very different world of the 16th century. Important scientific and technological advances were made. At the same time, increased exploitation of the invention of printing promoted the emergence of literate secular elites and created a new political environment as secular rulers used artists to display their power visually and written propaganda to appeal directly to their most important subjects.

State consolidation

Such incipient secularization of political life enabled monarchs to challenge the power of the church: in concordats with the Holy Roman Emperor (1448), France (1516) and Spain (1523), the papacy was forced to concede far-reaching rights over the national churches, while in a number of Protestant countries the ruler openly assumed control of spiritual affairs.

These changes aided the internal consolidation of states across Europe after 1450, now recovering from the economic and demographic ravages of the 14th century (*see p. 158*), when so many apparently powerful states had proved ephemeral. The strengthening of the principle of male primogeniture, under which only the eldest son inherited his father's property, thus keeping estates intact, ensured that states could be consolidated more effectively as well as stimulating desires to recover lost territories. Such "reunifications" brought conflict across Europe, since there were inevitably rival claims to be considered and rulers now enjoyed an enhanced capacity to wage war. This was in part the result of increasing economic prosperity and demographic recovery after 1450. By increasing the tax base of all European states, rulers gained greater access to credit, which enabled them to afford the new military technologies made possible by the development of gunpowder. Large artillery trains destroyed the castles of over-mighty subjects, most of whom were usually in no position to compete financially, while only states could afford the new large, infantry-based armies and elaborate fortifications.

The result was a series of large-scale dynastic and territorial wars. In the east, Muscovy, the Ottoman empire and Poland-Lithuania struggled for control; in the west, Burgundy, the rising star of the 15th century, was partitioned after Charles the Bold was killed in 1477 (*see map 2*), while in 1453 the English were expelled from France (except Calais). In Spain, Castile and Aragon were united in 1479 and in 1492 consolidated their rule of Spain when their combined forces completed the conquest of the Muslim kingdom of Granada. In England, though defeat by France in the Hundred Years' War had provoked civil war ("the Wars of the Roses"), after 1485 the new Tudor dynasty restored order and extended royal control in the turbulent north and west. In Germany, a series of dynastic alliances united the Habsburg lands with those of Luxembourg and Burgundy (in 1477). All these possessions, and later those of the Spanish crown, came to Emperor Charles V (1519–56), making him the greatest Christian ruler since Charlemagne.

The modern state

Yet royal dynasticism did not triumph unchecked. Growing interest in the classical past sparked debate

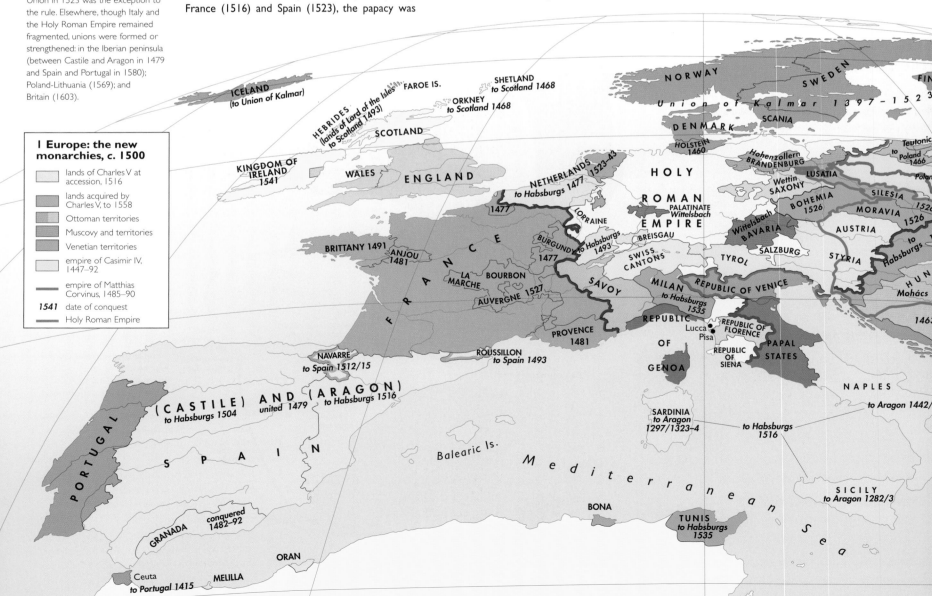

1 Europe: the new monarchies, c. 1500

- lands of Charles V at accession, 1516
- lands acquired by Charles V, to 1558
- Ottoman territories
- Muscovy and territories
- Venetian territories
- empire of Casimir IV, 1447–92
- empire of Matthias Corvinus, 1485–90
- **1541** date of conquest
- Holy Roman Empire

3 The reunification of France 1440–1589

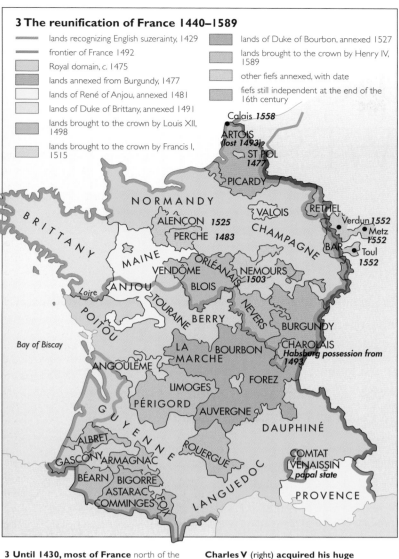

Legend:
- lands recognizing English suzerainty, 1429
- frontier of France 1492
- Royal domain, c. 1475
- lands annexed from Burgundy, 1477
- lands of René of Anjou, annexed 1481
- lands of Duke of Brittany, annexed 1491
- lands brought to the crown by Louis XII, 1498
- lands brought to the crown by Francis I, 1515
- lands of Duke of Bourbon, annexed 1527
- lands brought to the crown by Henry IV, 1589
- other fiefs annexed, with date
- fiefs still independent at the end of the 16th century

Map labels: Calais 1558, ARTOIS (lost 1493), ST POL 1477, PICARDY, NORMANDY, VALOIS, RETHEL, Verdun 1552, Metz 1552, CHAMPAGNE, BAR, Toul 1552, ALENÇON 1525, PERCHE 1483, MAINE, ORLÉANAIS, NEMOURS 1503, VENDÔME, BLOIS, BRITTANY, ANJOU, TOURAINE, BERRY, NEVERS, BURGUNDY, POITOU, Loire, Bay of Biscay, LA MARCHE, BOURBON, CHAROLAIS *Habsburg possession from 1493*, ANGOULÊME, FOREZ, LIMOGES, AUVERGNE, PÉRIGORD, GUYENNE, DAUPHINÉ, ALBRET, ROUERGUE, COMTAT VENAISSIN *papal state*, GASCONY, ARMAGNAC, BÉARN, BIGORRE, ASTARAC, COMMINGES, LANGUEDOC, PROVENCE

3 Until 1430, most of France north of the Loire was in English or Burgundian hands (map above); to the south, the royal domain constituted less than half the total territory. The reconquest in the 1440s of Normandy, Gascony and other lands held by the English doubled the French crown's territory. A series of confiscations and deaths then added the lands of the dukes of Burgundy (1477), Anjou (1481), Brittany (1491) and Bourbon (1527). This left only a handful of fiefs, many of which reverted to the crown when Henry of Navarre became Henry IV in 1589.

Charles V (right) acquired his huge inheritance largely by dynastic accident; after his election as Holy Roman Emperor in 1519, however, he projected himself as the temporal head of Christendom, the successor of Charlemagne and the Roman emperors, arguing that Christian unity was the vital precondition to defeat the Ottomans. Charles's claims were rejected by contemporary monarchs, in particular Francis I of France and Henry VIII of England. Although he remained emotionally attached to the imperial ideal, Charles acted largely as a practical dynastic politician, ruling his various lands as separate entities, conducting vigorous dynastic wars – in particular with Francis I in a vain attempt to reclaim the parts of his Burgundian inheritance lost in 1477 – and dividing his lands upon his abdication.

2 State-building in the low countries

From the late 14th century, the Valois dukes of Burgundy built a powerful state along the northeastern borders of France, its lands among the most prosperous in Europe (map and numbered list below). Charles the Bold (1467–77) overreached himself, however. Defeated at Morat and Grandson (1476), he was killed at Nancy (1477). His French fiefs (Picardy and Burgundy) were confiscated by

Louis XI; the rest passed to Charles's son-in-law Maximilian Habsburg, and thence to Maximilian's grandson Charles V, who added further lands in the Netherlands. In 1548, Charles united his 17 territories in the Low Countries into a single federation. Barely 20 years later, rebellion tore the new state asunder.

1 Friesland: acquired by purchase 1523–4
2 Groningen: acquired by negotiation 1536
3 Overijssel: acquired by negotiation 1536
4 Gelderland: conquered 1473, lost 1477; conquered 1481, lost 1492; conquered again 1543
5 Utrecht: acquired by negotiation 1536
6 Holland: acquired by treaty 1433
7 Zeeland: acquired by treaty 1433
8 Brabant: inherited 1404
9 Limburg: acquired by gift 1396
10 Flanders: acquired by marriage 1384
11 Boulonnais: ceded by marriage treaty 1435, lost 1477
12 Artois: acquired by marriage 1384, lost 1477; regained 1493
13 Hainaut: acquired by treaty 1433
14 Cambrai: conquered 1543
15 Namur: acquired by purchase 1429
16 Luxembourg: inherited 1451
17 Ponthieu: ceded by treaty 1435, lost 1477
18 Amiens: ceded by treaty 1435, lost 1463; regained 1465, lost 1477
19 Vermandois: ceded by treaty 1435, lost 1463; regained 1465, lost 1477
20 Bar: conquered 1475, lost 1476
21 Lorraine: conquered 1475, lost 1476
22 Burgundy: inherited 1363, lost 1477
23 Franche-Comté: acquired by marriage 1384, lost 1477; regained 1493
24 Alsace: partially conquered 1469, lost 1477
25 Tournai: conquered 1521
26 Lingen: acquired 1543

Legend:
- Emperor Charles V's Burgundian possessions, 1548
- Burgundian possessions lost by the death of Charles the Bold, 1477
- Charles the Bold's possessions, 1477
- provincial frontiers

Map labels: RAVENSBURG, English Channel, LIÈGE, PICARDY, Seine, METZ, TOUL, Nancy 1477, Morat 1476, Grandson 1476

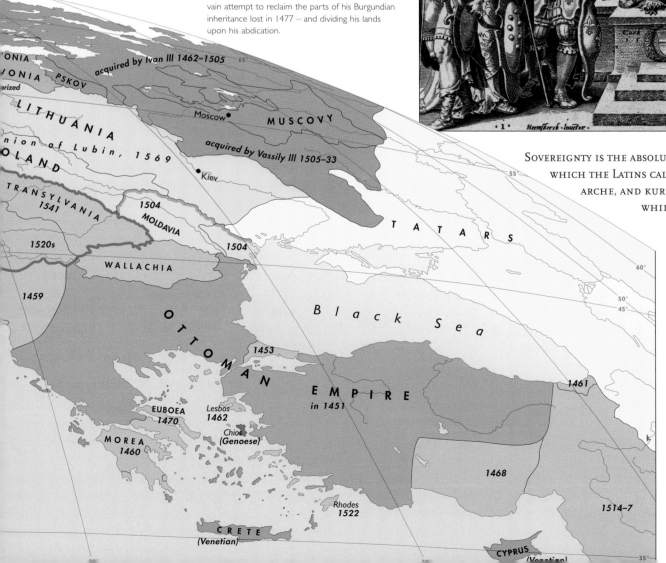

Map labels: PSKOV, acquired by Ivan III 1462–1505, LIVONIA, LITHUANIA, Moscow, MUSCOVY, acquired by Vassily III 1505–33, Union of Lublin, 1569, POLAND, Kiev, TRANSYLVANIA 1541, 1504, MOLDAVIA, 1520s, 1504, WALLACHIA, TATARS, 1459, OTTOMAN EMPIRE, Black Sea, 1453, EMPIRE in 1451, 1461, EUBOEA 1470, Lesbos 1462, Chios (Genoese), MOREA 1460, 1468, Rhodes 1522, CRETE (Venetian), CYPRUS (Venetian), 1514–7

SOVEREIGNTY IS THE ABSOLUTE AND PERPETUAL POWER OF A COMMONWEALTH, WHICH THE LATINS CALL MAIESTAS; THE GREEKS AKRA EXOUISIA, KURION ARCHE, AND KURION POLITEUMA; AND THE ITALIANS SEGNIORIA ... WHILE THE HEBREWS CALL IT TOMECH HÉVET – THAT IS THE HIGHEST POWER OF COMMAND ...

Jean Bodin, *Six Livres de la République,* 1576

about the nature of legitimate authority. Where monarchs sought to justify their claims to absolute power by reference to Roman law and the Roman empire, their opponents sought counter-arguments from the classical past, citing Rome's republican traditions and arguing for a balanced constitution. While most Italian city-republics succumbed to princely power, the republican tradition triumphed to a greater or lesser degree in the northern Netherlands, Poland-Lithuania and in parts of the Holy Roman Empire. This clash of values stimulated the gradual emergence of recognizably modern secular states, in which politics were divorced from religion and organized around an impersonal, centralized and unifying system of government, whether monarchical or republican.

5 THE WORLD OF THE EMERGING WEST

THE INDIAN HISTORIAN K. M. Panikkar described the period from 1498 to 1947, from Vasco da Gama's discovery of the sea route to India to Indian independence, as the European age in history. Others have pointed out the element of exaggeration in this definition: if, in 1750, the Europeans had abandoned their isolated settlements on the coasts of Asia and Africa, they would have left few traces. Nevertheless, around 1500 the balance, which hitherto had weighed on the side of Asia, began to change, and after 1750 that change was momentous.

Before 1500 civilization had been essentially land-centred, and contacts by sea relatively unimportant. If the year 1500 marks a new period in world history it is because thereafter direct sea contact linked the continents. This resulted not only in the integration in a global system of regions which hitherto had developed in isolation,

but in a challenge to the age-old, land-centred balance between the Eurasian civilizations.

Nonetheless, the impact of European expansion should not be exaggerated. The 16th century saw a remarkable resurgence of Muslim power in the Ottoman empire, Safavid Persia and Mughal India. China, meanwhile, remained the world's most advanced state. Indeed to many in 18th-century Europe, Turkey and China were the exemplars of civilized living. The industrial revolution put Europe ahead; but the fruits of that process – some of them poisonous – were only garnered in the 19th century. Europe between 1500 and 1815, for all its thrusting novelty, was still an agricultural society of lords and peasants, closer to its agrarian past than to its industrial future.

ISLAND OF SAN GIORGIO MAGGIORE, VENICE, ITALY.

The world on the eve of European expansion

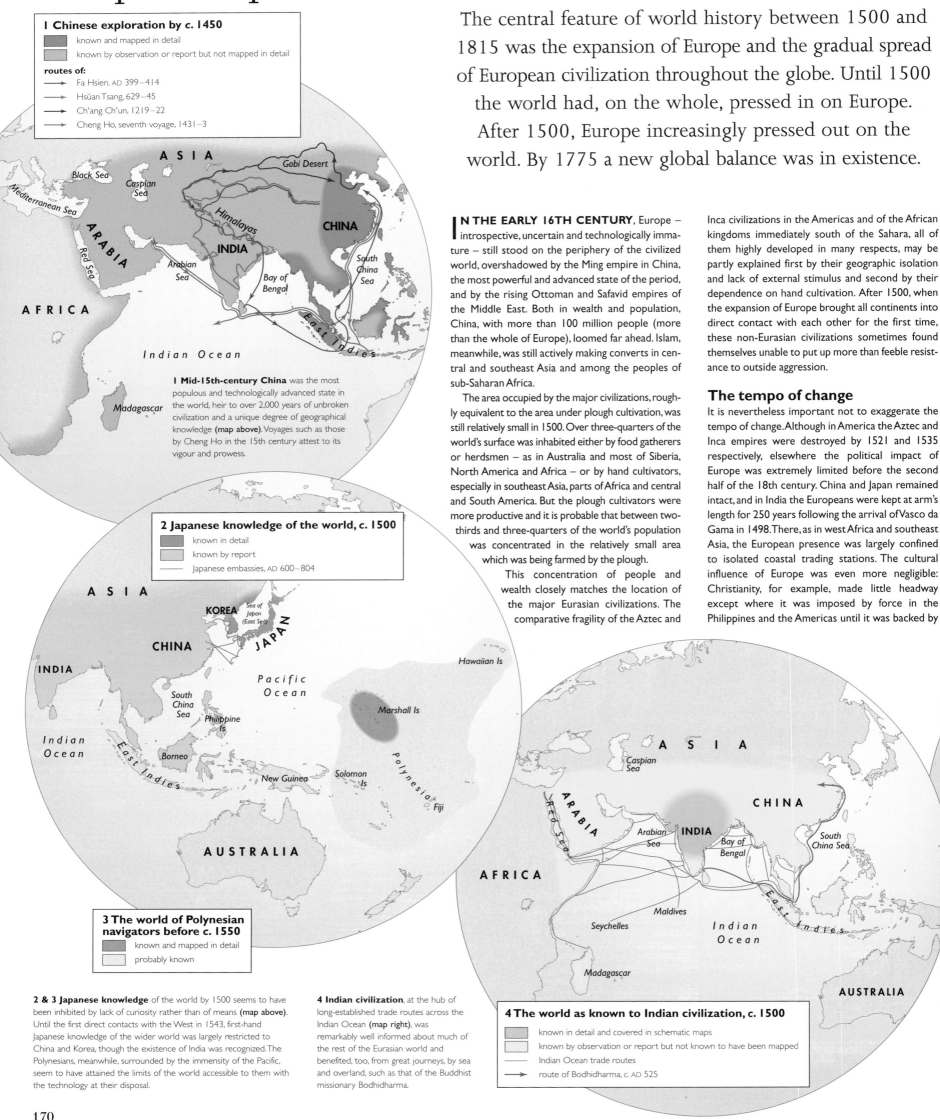

1 Chinese exploration by c. 1450

known and mapped in detail

known by observation or report but not mapped in detail

routes of:

→ Fa Hsien, AD 399–414

→ Hsüan Tsang, 629–45

→ Ch'ang Ch'un, 1219–22

→ Cheng Ho, seventh voyage, 1431–3

1 Mid-15th-century China was the most populous and technologically advanced state in the world, heir to over 2,000 years of unbroken civilization and a unique degree of geographical knowledge **(map above)**. Voyages such as those by Cheng Ho in the 15th century attest to its vigour and prowess.

2 Japanese knowledge of the world, c. 1500

known in detail

known by report

— Japanese embassies, AD 600–804

3 The world of Polynesian navigators before c. 1550

known and mapped in detail

probably known

4 The world as known to Indian civilization, c. 1500

known in detail and covered in schematic maps

known by observation or report but not known to have been mapped

— Indian Ocean trade routes

→ route of Bodhidharma, c. AD 525

The central feature of world history between 1500 and 1815 was the expansion of Europe and the gradual spread of European civilization throughout the globe. Until 1500 the world had, on the whole, pressed in on Europe. After 1500, Europe increasingly pressed out on the world. By 1775 a new global balance was in existence.

IN THE EARLY 16TH CENTURY, Europe – introspective, uncertain and technologically immature – still stood on the periphery of the civilized world, overshadowed by the Ming empire in China, the most powerful and advanced state of the period, and by the rising Ottoman and Safavid empires of the Middle East. Both in wealth and population, China, with more than 100 million people (more than the whole of Europe), loomed far ahead. Islam, meanwhile, was still actively making converts in central and southeast Asia and among the peoples of sub-Saharan Africa.

The area occupied by the major civilizations, roughly equivalent to the area under plough cultivation, was still relatively small in 1500. Over three-quarters of the world's surface was inhabited either by food gatherers or herdsmen – as in Australia and most of Siberia, North America and Africa – or by hand cultivators, especially in southeast Asia, parts of Africa and central and South America. But the plough cultivators were more productive and it is probable that between two-thirds and three-quarters of the world's population was concentrated in the relatively small area which was being farmed by the plough.

This concentration of people and wealth closely matches the location of the major Eurasian civilizations. The comparative fragility of the Aztec and Inca civilizations in the Americas and of the African kingdoms immediately south of the Sahara, all of them highly developed in many respects, may be partly explained first by their geographic isolation and lack of external stimulus and second by their dependence on hand cultivation. After 1500, when the expansion of Europe brought all continents into direct contact with each other for the first time, these non-Eurasian civilizations sometimes found themselves unable to put up more than feeble resistance to outside aggression.

The tempo of change

It is nevertheless important not to exaggerate the tempo of change. Although in America the Aztec and Inca empires were destroyed by 1521 and 1535 respectively, elsewhere the political impact of Europe was extremely limited before the second half of the 18th century. China and Japan remained intact, and in India the Europeans were kept at arm's length for 250 years following the arrival of Vasco da Gama in 1498. There, as in west Africa and southeast Asia, the European presence was largely confined to isolated coastal trading stations. The cultural influence of Europe was even more negligible: Christianity, for example, made little headway except where it was imposed by force in the Philippines and the Americas until it was backed by

2 & 3 Japanese knowledge of the world by 1500 seems to have been inhibited by lack of curiosity rather than of means **(map above)**. Until the first direct contacts with the West in 1543, first-hand Japanese knowledge of the wider world was largely restricted to China and Korea, though the existence of India was recognized. The Polynesians, meanwhile, surrounded by the immensity of the Pacific, seem to have attained the limits of the world accessible to them with the technology at their disposal.

4 Indian civilization, at the hub of long-established trade routes across the Indian Ocean **(map right)**, was remarkably well informed about much of the rest of the Eurasian world and benefited, too, from great journeys, by sea and overland, such as that of the Buddhist missionary Bodhidharma.

the resources of western industrial technology in the mid- to late 19th century.

The global impact

On the other hand, the European discoveries opened the way to a global redistribution of resources: migrations of peoples, diffusions of animals and plants, release of mineral wealth, expansion of cultivation and re-alignment of trade. The spread of food plants – almost all domesticated by prehistoric man in various parts of the world – had proceeded slowly until 1500. Thereafter, they became common to every continent. In addition, the American Indians pioneered two major cash crops: tobacco and cotton (derived largely in its commercial form from varieties they had domesticated, though other species were known and used in the Orient before 1500). Cane sugar, introduced by Europeans into Brazil and the West Indies from the late 16th century, also quickly became a staple of foreign trade.

This interchange of plants produced an enormous surge in food supplies, which made possible the unprecedented population growth after 1500. It also initiated a corresponding increase in intercontinental trade. Before 1500, this trade was limited to Eurasia and Africa and involved

c. 1450 Population of Ming China reaches 100 million

1492 Columbus reaches Americas: European discovery of New World

1493 First Spanish settlement in New World

1498 Vasco da Gama reaches India by sea

1500 Shah Ismail founds Safavid dynasty in Persia

1505 Portuguese establish trading posts in east Africa

c. 1510 First African slaves shipped to Americas

c. 1565 Potato introduced to Europe from South America

8 Though a series of medieval European travellers had made pioneering journeys across Asia (map below), it was not until the end of the 15th century that Europe developed the unique combination of exploring impetus and technical prowess that enabled it to catch up with and surpass its counterparts elsewhere. By the time of Dias's rounding of southern Africa, Europe was poised to open up the world.

8 Exploration from Europe by 1492

- known and mapped in detail
- known by observation or report

routes of:
- John of Piano Carpini, 1245–7, and William of Rubruk, 1253–4
- Marco Polo, 1271–95
- Iberian voyages to the Canaries and Azores, from c. 1330
- John Marignolli, 1338–53
- Bartolomeu Dias, 1487–8

7 Islamic knowledge of the world by c. 1500

- well-established heartlands of Islam
- known by observation or report
- Indian Ocean trade routes

routes of Ibn Battuta:
- 1325–44
- 1352–3

7 Heir, with Europe, to the Greco-Roman legacy of geographical information and imbued with missionary zeal, Islam proved a dynamic exploring culture (map left). Journeys such as those of the indefatigable Ibn Battuta testify to the unified political, religious, social and economic world-system that drew its theoretical and practical precepts from Islam.

5 Mesoamerica, c. 1500

- known and mapped in detail by the Aztecs
- known by observation or report, but not known to have been mapped
- trade routes

5 & 6 A combination of geography and technical deficiencies restricted both Aztec and Inca knowledge of the world (map above). Deserts to their north and no more than basic maritime skills limited Aztec horizons to Mesoamerica. The Incas, meanwhile, hemmed in by the Andes and the Pacific, suffered from possessing no written means of transmitting information.

6 The Inca world, c. 1510

- known in detail and linked by paved roads
- probably known by observation or report, but not reached by the road system
- Inca roads

mostly luxury goods. After 1500, the combination of regional economic specialization and improved sea transport made possible the gradual transformation of the limited medieval luxury trade into the modern mass trade of new bulky necessities – hence the flourishing "triangular trade" of rum, cloths, guns and other metal products from Europe to Africa, slaves from Africa to the New World and sugar, tobacco and bullion from the New World to Europe.

It was not until the 19th century, with the opening of the Suez and Panama canals and the construction of transcontinental railways in Canada, the United States, Siberia and Africa, that areas and lines of commerce which had previously been separate finally blended into a single economy on a world scale (see p. 276). But the first stages of global integration were completed in just over two centuries beginning in 1500.

Descriptions of the volume and direction of maritime trade in the Indian Ocean prove beyond doubt that Arab shipowners and their captains were well able to navigate out of sight of land. This Indian ship from an Iraqi manuscript of 1238 (above) has a square sail ideal for monsoonal winds and ample space for passengers and cargo in its hold.

171

European voyages of discovery

Between 1480 and 1780, European explorers discovered and mapped almost all of the world's seas and the outlines of almost all the continents. Impelled by a variety of motives – trade, personal enrichment, glory and, by the 18th century, scientific knowledge – their legacy is today's world map, a common resource of all mankind.

IN 1480 THE PRINCIPAL SEAFARING peoples of the world were separated not only by great expanses of uncharted sea but by continental landmasses whose extent and shape were unknown. Regular European shipping was still mainly confined to the north Atlantic, the Mediterranean and the Baltic. The west African coast had been explored cursorily and only very recently by Europeans, while the coast from Gaboon to Mozambique was unknown to any regular long-range shipping. In the Americas, limited raft and canoe-borne sailing took place on the Pacific coasts of Ecuador and Peru and in the Caribbean, but there was no communication with Europe nor, so far as is known, with other parts of the Pacific.

In the east, several seafaring peoples overlapped. Indian, Persian and Arab ships plied the northern Indian Ocean. Chinese shipping, which in the past had sailed intermittently to east Africa, by 1480 usually went no farther than Malacca, sharing the shallow seas of the Malay archipelago with local shipping, chiefly Javanese. To the east, it went no farther than the Philippines. No shipping

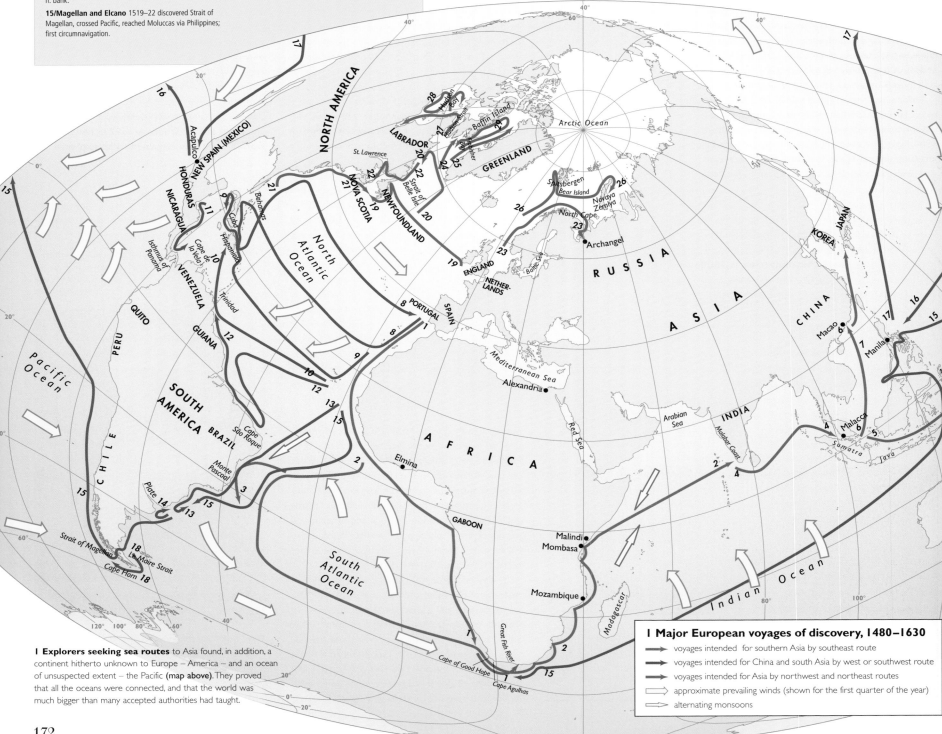

1 Explorers seeking sea routes to Asia found, in addition, a continent hitherto unknown to Europe – America – and an ocean of unsuspected extent – the Pacific **(map above)**. They proved that all the oceans were connected, and that the world was much bigger than many accepted authorities had taught.

1 Major European voyages of discovery, 1480–1630

→ voyages intended for southern Asia by southeast route
→ voyages intended for China and south Asia by west or southwest route
→ voyages intended for Asia by northwest and northeast routes
⇨ approximate prevailing winds (shown for the first quarter of the year)
⇨ alternating monsoons

used the southern Indian Ocean: Javanese contacts with Madagascar had long ceased. The great expanses of the central Pacific were crossed only occasionally and perilously by Polynesian canoes. In the north Pacific, except in Japanese and Korean coastal waters, there were no ships at all.

The Spanish and Portuguese

The European voyages of discovery began early in the 15th century when Portuguese navigators advanced southward, round the west coast of Africa, in search of gold, slaves and spices, until in 1487 Dias and de Covilha brought them into the Indian Ocean. Thenceforth voyages of exploration multiplied, particularly after the resurgence of Islam made the old route to the east via Alexandria and the Red Sea precarious.

While the Spanish sailed west, the Portuguese explored the eastern route to Asia. Once in the Indian Ocean they quickly reached their goal: Malabar (1498), Malacca (1509) and the Moluccas (1512). The Spanish search for a western route to the Spice Islands was less successful but its unintended and momentous result was Columbus's discovery of the New World in 1492 followed by the Spanish conquest of the Americas (see p. 178). But it was not until after 1524, when Verazzano traced the coastline of North America as far north as Nova Scotia, that the existence of the new continent was generally accepted.

Meanwhile the search for a western route to Asia continued, leading to extensive exploration of the Caribbean. Finally, in 1521 Magellan rounded South America, entered the Pacific and reached the Philippines, but his route would prove too long and too hazardous for commercial purposes. In 1557 the Portuguese occupied Macao and after 1571 Spanish galleons traded between Manila and Acapulco in Mexico. The combined effect of these Spanish and Portuguese voyages had been to show that all the oceans of the southern hemisphere were connected. At the same time, for about a century Spain and Portugal

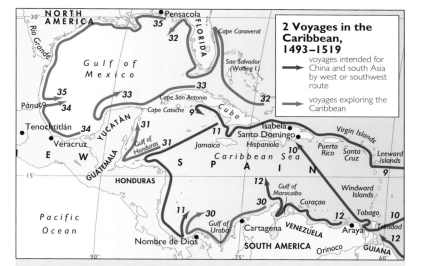

2 Voyages in the Caribbean, 1493–1519
→ voyages intended for China and south Asia by west or southwest route
→ voyages exploring the Caribbean

2 VOYAGES IN THE CARIBBEAN, 1492–1519

Spanish expeditions explored the Caribbean searching for a seaway to China, India and the Golden Chersonese. They found it landlocked on the west; took to slaving, pearling and plunder; encountered settled, city-building peoples; and founded a European empire.

30/Bastidas and La Cosa 1501–2 explored coast from Gulf of Maracaibo to Gulf of Urabá.

31/Pinzón and Solís 1508 sent from Spain to find strait to Asia, perhaps followed e. coast of Yucatán.

32/Ponce de León 1512–3 sailed from Puerto Rico, explored Florida from n. of Cape Canaveral to (possibly)

Pensacola; may have sighted Yucatán on return; first explorer to note force of Gulf Stream.

33/Hernández de Córdoba 1517 sailed from Cuba, explored n. and w. coasts of Yucatán; first report of Maya cities.

34/Grijalva 1518 followed s. and w. coasts of Gulf of Mexico as far as River Pánuco.

35/Pineda 1519 explored n. and w. coasts of Gulf of Mexico from Florida to River Pánuco; ended hope of strait to Pacific in that region.

1434 Portuguese voyages along west coast of Africa begin

1487 Bartolomeu Dias rounds Cape of Good Hope

1492 Columbus reaches New World

1520–1 Magellan makes first crossing of the Pacific

1611 Dutch initiate southerly route across Indian Ocean

1728 Vitus Bering sails through Bering Strait

1768–71 Cook's first voyage to the Pacific

1772–5 Cook's second voyage; first crossing of Antarctic Circle

A pepper harvest in Malabar **(below)**. Pepper accounted for over 70 per cent by volume of the world spice trade in the 16th century. The most valuable variety, *Piper nigrum*, shown here, was native to India and hard to transplant successfully. Demand from Europe and China spread it to selective parts of the East, but Portuguese efforts to introduce it in Africa and America in the 17th century met with little success.

were able to prevent other Europeans from using these connecting sea passages, other than for occasional raids.

The French, British and Dutch

As a result, the exploration of the Pacific was delayed until the 18th century. In part at least it was inspired as much by scientific curiosity as by hope of commercial gain. It was the work of British, Dutch and Russians seeking a navigable passage via the Arctic between the Atlantic and the Pacific and hoping also to locate a hypothetical southern continent. Both proved illusory but the result was the charting of New Zealand and the eastern coast of Australia, both opened in a few years to European colonization.

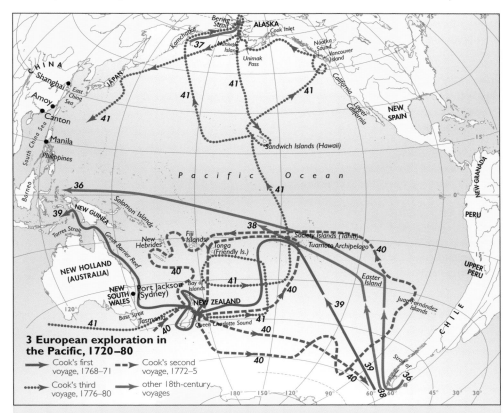

3 European exploration in the Pacific, 1720–80
→ Cook's first voyage, 1768–71
--→ Cook's second voyage, 1772–5
····· Cook's third voyage, 1776–80
→ other 18th-century voyages

3 18TH-CENTURY VOYAGES IN THE PACIFIC:

Most 18th-century voyages of discovery in the Pacific were searches for a habitable southern continent or for a usable northern strait between the Pacific and Atlantic. Both proved imaginary. The expeditions instead confirmed the immensity of the Pacific and revealed the islands of New Zealand, a habitable eastern Australia, numerous islands and a valuable whale fishery.

36/Roggeveen 1722 discovered Easter Island and some of the Samoan group; circumnavigated globe.

37/Bering 1728 sailed from Kamchatka, discovered strait separating ne. Asia and nw. America.

38/Wallis 1766–8 discovered Society Islands (Tahiti), encouraged hope of habitable southern continent; circumnavigated globe.

39/Cook 1768–71 charted coasts of New Zealand, explored e. coast of Australia, confirmed existence of Torres Strait; circumnavigated globe.

40/Cook 1772–5 made circuit of southern oceans in high latitude, charted New Hebrides, discovered many islands, ended hope of habitable southern continent; circumnavigated globe.

41/Cook and Clerke 1776–80 discovered Sandwich Islands (Hawaii), explored nw. coast of N. America from Vancouver Island to Unimak Pass, sailed through Bering Strait to edge of pack ice, ended hope of navigable passage through Arctic to Atlantic.

Meanwhile, England and France, unwilling to recognize the monopoly claimed by Spain and Portugal in the Treaty of Tordesillas of 1494 (see p. 174), had embarked on a series of voyages intended to reach Asia by a northern route. All these proved abortive and were abandoned after 1632, but they resulted in the opening of North America to European settlement. The English, French and Dutch were also unwilling to abandon the profitable trade with south and southeast Asia to the Portuguese and Spaniards and the later years of the 16th and first half of the 17th centuries saw a determined and ultimately successful effort to breach their privileged position (see p. 198).

After 1500 direct sea contact was established between continents and regions which hitherto had developed in isolation. It was necessarily a slow process and for a long time the European footholds in Asia and Africa remained tenuous. But by the time of the death of the last great explorer, James Cook in 1779, few of the world's coastlines remained to be explored.

Expansion of the trading empires

THE DISCOVERIES BY EUROPEAN explorers in the late 15th century were rapidly exploited. By 1500, Portuguese possessions outside Europe included several island groups in the Atlantic and the Gulf of Guinea, and a number of trading stations on the west coast of Africa – above all the fortress-factory of Elmina. A dozen or so ships made the voyage between Portugal and Guinea every year, bartering hardware and cloth for slaves and gold dust.

After the sea route to India was discovered (*see* p. 172), the Portuguese attempted to become the main suppliers of spices to Europe by capturing or leasing trading posts and fortified bases on the east coast of Africa, around the north shores of the Indian Ocean and in the Malay archipelago. By the mid-16th century, they had a tenuous string of more than 50 forts and factories. Strategically, the most important were Mozambique (1507), Goa (1510), Ormuz (1515) and Malacca (1511). East of Malacca, the Portuguese position was precarious and their activity completely commercial. In 1557, with the agreement of the Chinese, they established a base at Macao. From there, they traded to Nagasaki, where they were welcomed as carriers of Chinese goods, since the Chinese themselves were forbidden to trade with Japan. At Ternate, they maintained a warehouse until 1575, when they were expelled by a league of Muslim princes.

Portugal's trading empire

All these Far Eastern enterprises, together with the gold of the Zambezi basin, exported through Sofala, paid for the pepper and other spices shipped annually from Goa to Lisbon for distribution to western Europe. Though the Portuguese never achieved anything like a monopoly, their power was sufficient to channel much of the Indian Ocean trade through harbours under their control, and for 100 years they had no real European rivals. Only the Spanish, whose main interest lay in the Americas, showed a parallel interest in the Far East (*see* p. 178).

Once the Portuguese had started to settle Brazil in the 1530s, the Brazilian demand for slave labour breathed new life into the Portuguese trading stations in west Africa, where the gold trade had dwindled as the gold became exhausted and caused traders to extend their operations from Guinea south to Angola. The Portuguese slave depot of Luanda was founded in 1575 and slave ships shuttled directly between Angola and Brazil, with the slaves paid for by Brazilian tobacco.

Dutch expansion

From the opening years of the 17th century, the Portuguese in the East began to experience significant competition from other European countries. This usually organized itself in the form of joint stock

3 Columbus's first landfall in 1492 was in the West Indies **(map above right)**. On his second visit, in 1493, he encountered the Carib Indians who would subsequently give their name to this region of tropical islands. The Spanish settlement of Hispaniola began in the same year, with the settlers hoping to find gold and to use the island as a launch-pad for trade with China, which they erroneously thought nearby. Hispaniola became the Spanish base for the settlement of Central America, Cuba for that of Mexico. In the 17th century, the British, French and Dutch began to challenge the supremacy Spain had established over the Caribbean. Over the course of time, the West Indies would become famous for their sugar crop (sugar was the most profitable of all the exotic products imported into Europe in early modern times). From the middle of the 17th century until after the end of the 18th, sugar-producing islands in the West Indies were frequently regarded by the British, French and Dutch governments as the most valuable of all their colonial possessions. They were often subjects of dispute between the governments.

Portuguese 16th-century traders established Europe's trading links with Africa, India, the Malay archipelago, China and Japan and dominated the African trade in gold and slaves. But by the 17th century growing Dutch, British and French competition was challenging both Portugal's position and Spain's dominance in the West Indies.

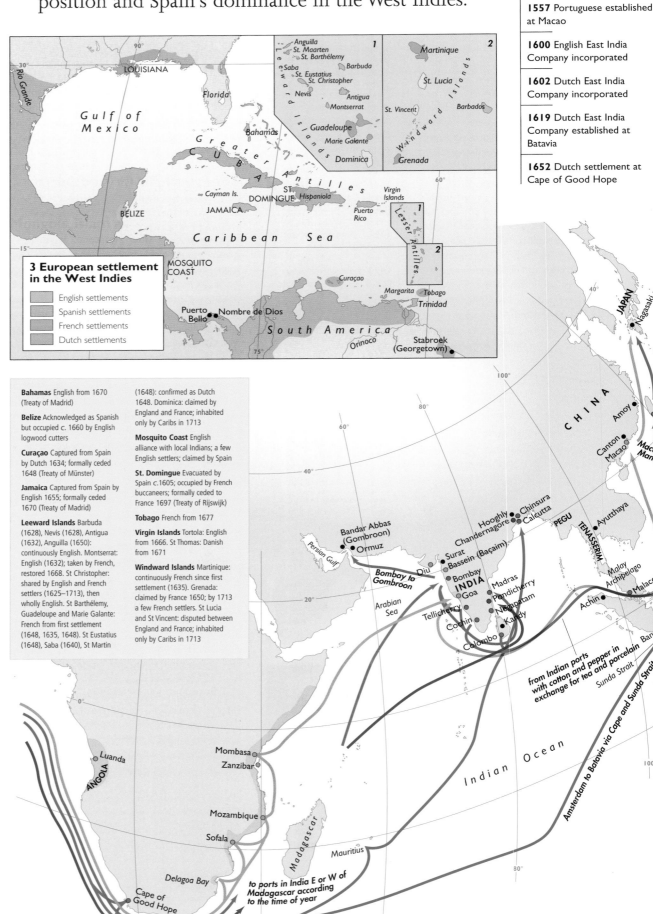

3 European settlement in the West Indies

- English settlements
- Spanish settlements
- French settlements
- Dutch settlements

Bahamas English from 1670 (Treaty of Madrid)

Belize Acknowledged as Spanish but occupied c. 1660 by English logwood cutters

Curaçao Captured from Spain by Dutch 1634; formally ceded 1648 (Treaty of Münster)

Jamaica Captured from Spain by English 1655; formally ceded 1670 (Treaty of Madrid)

Leeward Islands Barbuda (1628), Nevis (1628), Antigua (1632), Anguilla (1650): continuously English. Montserrat: English (1632); taken by French, restored 1668. St Christopher: shared by English and French settlers (1625–1713), then wholly English. St Barthélemy, Guadeloupe and Marie Galante: French from first settlement (1648, 1635, 1648). St Eustatius (1648), Saba (1640), St Martin

(1648): confirmed as Dutch 1648. Dominica: claimed by England and France; inhabited only by Caribs in 1713

Mosquito Coast English alliance with local Indians; a few English settlers; claimed by Spain

St. Domingue Evacuated by Spain c.1605; occupied by French buccaneers; formally ceded to France 1697 (Treaty of Rijswijk)

Tobago French from 1677

Virgin Islands Tortola: English from 1666. St Thomas: Danish from 1671

Windward Islands Martinique: continuously French since first settlement (1635). Grenada: claimed by France 1650; by 1713 a few French settlers. St Lucia and St Vincent: disputed between England and France; inhabited only by Caribs in 1713

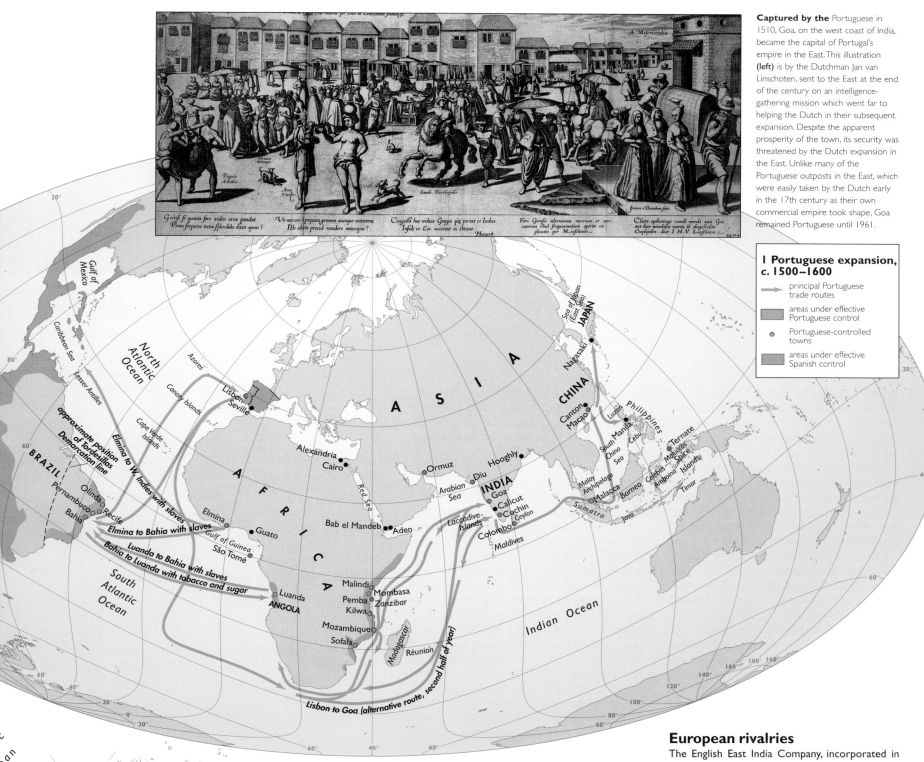

Captured by the Portuguese in 1510, Goa, on the west coast of India, became the capital of Portugal's empire in the East. This illustration (left) is by the Dutchman Jan van Linschoten, sent to the East at the end of the century on an intelligence-gathering mission which went far to helping the Dutch in their subsequent expansion. Despite the apparent prosperity of the town, its security was threatened by the Dutch expansion in the East. Unlike many of the Portuguese outposts in the East, which were easily taken by the Dutch early in the 17th century as their own commercial empire took shape, Goa remained Portuguese until 1961.

1 Portuguese expansion, c. 1500–1600

- → principal Portuguese trade routes
- areas under effective Portuguese control
- ○ Portuguese-controlled towns
- areas under effective Spanish control

2 Commercial expansion to the East, c. 1600–1700

- ● places under Dutch control
- ● places under English control
- ● places under French control
- ● places under Portuguese control
- areas under Portuguese control
- → Dutch trade routes
- → English trade routes
- → French trade routes
- → Portuguese trade routes

1 & 2 The Portuguese empire in the East consisted of fortified bases and trading posts, few of them bigger than a single city and its immediate hinterland (maps above and far left). Some of them were mere warehouse compounds. Nonetheless, by 1600, there were more than 50 such establishments. In the next century, the Dutch, English and French established their own trading stations and gradually supplanted the Portuguese. But as their trading posts in the East were eliminated, so the Portuguese reinforced their position in South America. By 1600, coastal Brazil had become the foremost sugar-producing territory in the western hemisphere.

THE HOLLANDERS SAY WE GO ABOUTE TO REAPE THE FRUITS OF THEIR LABOURS. IT IS RATHER THE CONTRARYE FOR THAT THEY SEEM TO BARRE US OF OUR LIBERTIE TO TRADE IN A FREE COUNTRYE, HAVING MANIE TIMES TRADED IN THESE PLACES, AND NOWE THEY SEEKE TO DEFRAUD US OF THAT WE HAVE SO LONG SOUGHT FOR.

John Jourdain of the English East India Company on Anglo–Dutch rivalry for control of the spice trade, 1613

companies, empowered to trade, settle, conquer, administer and defend. The most formidable, at least to begin with, was the Dutch East India Company, formally incorporated in 1602. In 1619, this vast concern, the biggest trading corporation in Europe, established its eastern headquarters at Batavia, well to the south (and east) of Goa and Malacca, thus acquiring a permanent strategic advantage. Its ships pioneered a direct route to Batavia, provisioning (after 1652) at the new Dutch settlement at the Cape of Good Hope, then running east before the "roaring forties" and entering the archipelago by the Sunda Strait. By acquiring bases in strategic locations, by bringing pressure on local rulers and by squeezing other Europeans out, it established a monopoly of the more valuable trades of the archipelago. Elsewhere in the East it traded in competition with native and European merchants on terms dictated by local rulers, though throughout the 17th century it held its own against all European rivals.

European rivalries

The English East India Company, incorporated in 1600, was a rather smaller concern and usually proved unable to resist Dutch pressure in the archipelago. It engaged principally in trade in cotton goods and pepper from India, first at the Mughal port of Surat, later at stations of its own at Madras, Bombay and Calcutta. In 1685 it began a modest trade with China, purchasing tea and porcelain at Amoy and later at Canton, where from 1698 its agents found themselves in direct competition with the French Compagnie de Chine.

As a result of the commercial competition and naval aggression of these corporations (which continued irrespective of whether there was formal war or peace in Europe), the Portuguese Estado de India shrank both in territorial extent and in commercial profit. The Red Sea and the Persian Gulf both became commercial backwaters as the joint-stock companies carried more and more of the trade between Europe and Asia in their own capacious and well-armed ships. Meanwhile, the Dutch West India Company – less well entrenched than its eastern counterpart, but formidable nonetheless – conquered the Brazilian coastal region of Pernambuco in 1630 and over the next few years seized the Portuguese slaving stations in west Africa, without which the Brazilian plantation system appeared unworkable. But in the 1640s, with the end of the long period of union (1580–1640) of the Spanish and Portuguese crowns, the Portuguese recovered the Angola slave-pens and in 1654 drove the Dutch from Brazil. The West India Company now turned its attention to the Caribbean.

Russian expansion in Europe and Asia

The Grand Duchy of Muscovy emerged in the late 15th century as a powerful state with claims to the legacy of Kievan Rus. Though it spread rapidly east and south, expansion in the west was blocked by Lithuania, which included many of the lands of Kievan Rus. Only after 1648 did Muscovy prevail, laying the foundations of the Russian empire.

Russian woodcut showing a procession of merchants carrying furs at the court of the Holy Roman Emperor c. 1570 (**above**). By the early 17th century the demand for luxury furs fuelled expansion eastwards into Siberia to tap its seemingly inexhaustible supply.

THE EBBING OF MONGOL POWER and the collapse of the Byzantine empire opened the way for the emergence of Muscovy as a European power. Proclaiming Muscovy's independence from the Mongols in 1480, Ivan III (1462–1505) laid claim to the heritage of Kievan Rus and, by marrying the daughter of the last Byzantine emperor and adopting the double-headed eagle as his emblem, to that of Byzantium. The last independent Orthodox state after 1453, Muscovy proclaimed itself the leader of the Orthodox world, with Moscow raised to a metropolitanate in 1448 and a patriarchate in 1589.

Muscovy's growing power was manifested in the ruthless annexations of Novgorod (1478) and Pskov (1510) and the seizure of Smolensk from Lithuania (1514). The conquest of the khanates of Kazan (1552) and Astrakhan (1556) conferred control of the Volga and opened the way to the east and the south. Expansion was not so easy to the west, where the tsars' claim to rule "all the Russias" was challenged by the grand dukes of Lithuania, most of whose subjects were eastern Slavs with elites increasingly attracted by the participative political system of Poland. The 1569 Union of Lublin between Poland and Lithuania, which saw the direct incorporation of Lithuania's Ukrainian territories into the kingdom of Poland, led to the creation of a sophisticated noble democracy with a common *diet* (parliament) and an elective monarchy that was in stark contrast to the centralized Muscovite autocracy.

Between 1558 and 1634, Poland-Lithuania repulsed all Muscovite attempts to expand westwards. Ivan IV's attempts to take Livonia were beaten off, Sigismund III regained Smolensk and Chernigov at the Treaty of Deulino (1618/19), while

during the "Time of Troubles" (1605–13), Sigismund's son Wæadysæaw was elected tsar by a group of boyars, and a Polish garrison occupied the Kremlin (1610–12). A Muscovite attempt to retake Smolensk in 1632–4 was repulsed decisively.

Growth of empire

The turning-point came during the Thirteen Years' War (1654–67). At the 1654 Treaty of Pereyaslav, Tsar Alexis Mikhailovich (1645–76) extended Muscovy's protection to the Zaporozhian Cossacks, who had rebelled against Poland in 1648. Although Alexis failed to hold on to the large areas of Lithuania annexed in 1654–5, the 1667 Treaty of Andrusovo granted Muscovy those areas of the Ukraine on the left bank of the Dnieper and, albeit only for three years, Kiev, though in 1686 the Poles were forced to recognize its permanent loss. The capture of Kiev and left-bank Ukraine made good part of the tsars' claim to rule all the Russias; the Ukraine was dubbed "Little Russia" in contrast to "Great Russia", the empire's Muscovite heartland. Muscovy had become Russia.

As Poland-Lithuania weakened, Russian expansion continued. The military improvements under Alexis were completed by his son, Peter I (the Great), who captured Azov from the Ottomans before turning his attention northwards. In a long war, marked by his great victory at Poltava in 1709, Peter finally wrested Estonia and Livonia from Sweden at the Treaty of Nystad (1721), acquired the ancient port of Riga and founded the new one of St Petersburg.

His successors reverted to the policy of expansion in the south, which was carried to a successful conclusion by Catherine II (the Great) in her first (1768–74) and second (1787–92) Turkish wars. The Crimea was

annexed, and Russia now controlled the northern shore of the Black Sea from the Dniester to the Caucasus. The period from 1772 to 1815 then saw the Russian land frontier advanced by 965km (600 miles) at the expense of Poland. By the partitions of 1772, 1793 and 1795 (see p. 218), Russia obtained much of the former Polish-Lithuanian Commonwealth, in the process acquiring a further 5.5 million inhabitants. Indeed throughout the period as a whole the population of Russia expanded dramatically from an estimated 10 million in 1600 to nearly 43 million in 1812.

3 The Polish-Lithuanian Commonwealth, 1569–1634

Kingdom of Poland, 1562
Grand Duchy of Lithuania, 1562
Poland-Lithuania after the Union of Lublin, 1569
lands taken from Grand Duchy of Lithuania and incorporated into Kingdom of Poland, 1569
fiefs of the Polish Crown
added to Commonwealth 1561/85
eastern border of Commonwealth at Treaty of Deulino, 1618/19

3 The Union of Lublin (1569) between Poland and Lithuania created a formidable barrier to Russian expansion to the west (**map above**). Poland-Lithuania expanded steadily at Muscovy's expense after 1569, until the tables turned following the 1648 Cossack revolt.

2 Russian expansion in Siberia, 1581–1800

Russian territory in 1581
territory added 1581–98
territory added 1598–1618
territory added 1618–89
territory added in 1650s; returned to China 1689
territory added 1689–1725
territory added 1725–62
territory added 1762–1800

● Batsk forts and trading posts 1630 (with date of foundation)

2 Though the Russian population of Siberia was only 200,000 by the mid-17th century, the speed of Russia's expansion was nonetheless prodigious (**map left**). Other than the Amur basin, annexed from China but returned by the 1689 Treaty of Nerchinsk, most of this vast area was acquired from indigenous peoples.

1569 Union of Lublin

1618 Treaty of Deulino: highpoint of Polish-Lithuanian eastward expansion

1648 Revolt of the Zaporozhian Cossacks against Poland-Lithuania

1654 Treaty of Pereyaslav: Tsar Alexis extends protection over Ukraine

1667 Treaty of Andrusovo: Russia acquires Kiev and the Ukraine lands on the left bank of the Dnieper

1703 Foundation of St Petersburg

1772–95 Partitions of Poland-Lithuania

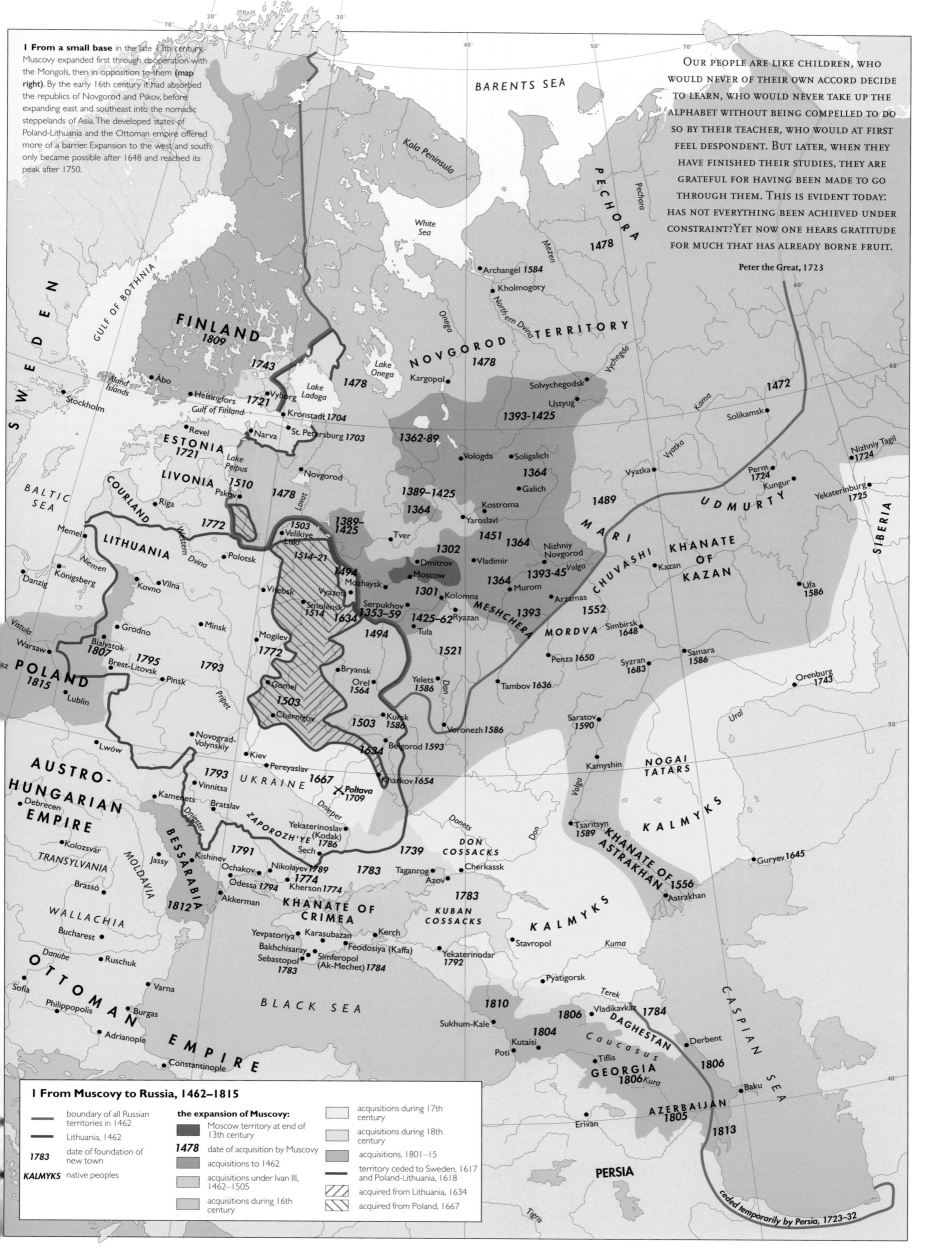

I From a small base in the late 13th century, Muscovy expanded first through cooperation with the Mongols, then in opposition to them (map right). By the early 16th century it had absorbed the republics of Novgorod and Pskov, before expanding east and southeast into the nomadic steppelands of Asia. The developed states of Poland-Lithuania and the Ottoman empire offered more of a barrier. Expansion to the west and south only became possible after 1648 and reached its peak after 1750.

OUR PEOPLE ARE LIKE CHILDREN, WHO WOULD NEVER OF THEIR OWN ACCORD DECIDE TO LEARN, WHO WOULD NEVER TAKE UP THE ALPHABET WITHOUT BEING COMPELLED TO DO SO BY THEIR TEACHER, WHO WOULD AT FIRST FEEL DESPONDENT. BUT LATER, WHEN THEY HAVE FINISHED THEIR STUDIES, THEY ARE GRATEFUL FOR HAVING BEEN MADE TO GO THROUGH THEM. THIS IS EVIDENT TODAY: HAS NOT EVERYTHING BEEN ACHIEVED UNDER CONSTRAINT? YET NOW ONE HEARS GRATITUDE FOR MUCH THAT HAS ALREADY BORNE FRUIT.

Peter the Great, 1723

I From Muscovy to Russia, 1462–1815

	boundary of all Russian territories in 1462
	Lithuania, 1462
1783	date of foundation of new town
KALMYKS	native peoples

the expansion of Muscovy:

Moscow territory at end of 13th century
1478 date of acquisition by Muscovy
acquisitions to 1462
acquisitions under Ivan III, 1462–1505
acquisitions during 16th century

acquisitions during 17th century
acquisitions during 18th century
acquisitions, 1801–15
territory ceded to Sweden, 1617 and Poland-Lithuania, 1618
acquired from Lithuania, 1634
acquired from Poland, 1667

177

North America

While the Spanish and the Portuguese had established large and lucrative empires in the south of the Americas, their northerly European neighbours focused on the lands to the north. John Cabot, commissioned by the English king Henry VII, made the first documented voyage to North America (since the Vikings) in 1497.

> THE NEIGHBORHOOD OF THE FRENCH TO OUR NORTH AMERICAN COLONIES WAS ... THE GREATEST SECURITY FOR THEIR DEPENDENCE ON THE MOTHER COUNTRY, WHICH I FEEL WILL BE SLIGHTED BY THEM WHEN THEIR APPREHENSION OF THE FRENCH IS REMOVED.
>
> **Lord Bedford, British negotiator in 1762**

AFTER JOHN CABOT'S VOYAGE, fishing vessels from England, France, Portugal and the Basque country soon travelled in large numbers to the rich cod grounds off Newfoundland and Nova Scotia. However, these fishing voyages led to relatively little interest in the continent and did not result in settlement. French imperial interest in North America began with Jacques Cartier's voyages in the 1530s. However, unlike Spanish and Portuguese colonization to the south, French and English attempts to colonize the north in the early 16th century failed. Jamestown, Virginia (1607), Quebec (1608), the Mayflower communities of Massachusetts Bay (1620), and New Amsterdam (1626) represented the first successes in establishing European colonies in North America. Beset by many difficulties, these colonies grew slowly and often at the sufferance of surrounding aboriginal groups. Swedish and Scottish attempts at colonization remained small-scale. The more significant Dutch settlement in New Amsterdam (New York) was taken over by the English in 1664. Tobacco, grains and furs proved valuable commodities for export to the mother countries.

The European arrivals brought new military dangers as well as opportunities for the aboriginal peoples. While some groups were exterminated by the Europeans (in the Massachusetts area, for instance), other groups (such as the Iroquois of the Great Lakes region) were able to play one group of foreigners off against another and to expand their areas of influence. North American aboriginal peoples maintained a strong military role – as valued allies or feared opponents – at least until the War of 1812; and some groups, such as the Comanches, continued to resist the incursions of foreigners into their territories until late in the century.

Spain, too, made its presence felt in what is now considered North America – in Florida, Texas, New Mexico, and later Louisiana. Settlers in the British colonies tended to be from minority religions or religious sects, while in the French and Spanish colonies non-orthodox Catholics were strongly discouraged from settling. Relatively few French settlers made their way across the Atlantic, and the majority of these returned home. Nonetheless, given the high birth rate – made possible by living conditions that were better than in the mother country – the population of New France grew dramatically. It did likewise in the British colonies to the south, where a stronger stream of immigrants boosted the population from generation to generation. At the time of the American Revolution, some 2.5 million people lived in the colonies which rebelled against British rule.

In the interior of the continent, more varied communities developed. These combined aboriginal and European bloodlines and cultures. Métis (mixed blood) communities became vitally important to the success of the fur trade, which led the French down the Great Lakes and Ohio and Mississippi systems. However, while diversity reigned in the 18th century, these communities could do little to resist the expansion of American settlement in the 19th century.

3 By 1700, explorers for England, France, Portugal, and Denmark had travelled extensively in eastern North America, mapping out the coastlines with great precision (map right). Inland expeditions had provided much information on the geography and people of the interior of the continent, particularly in the St Lawrence-Great Lakes and Mississippi-Ohio regions. Spanish explorers had charted parts of the west coast of the continent and the areas to the north of New Spain.

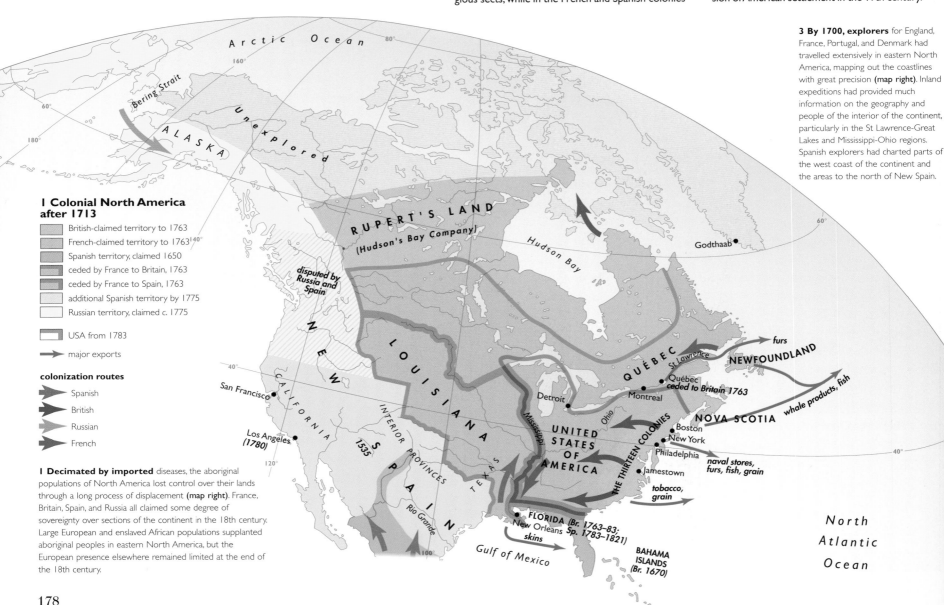

1 Decimated by imported diseases, the aboriginal populations of North America lost control over their lands through a long process of displacement (map right). France, Britain, Spain, and Russia all claimed some degree of sovereignty over sections of the continent in the 18th century. Large European and enslaved African populations supplanted aboriginal peoples in eastern North America, but the European presence elsewhere remained limited at the end of the 18th century.

1 Colonial North America after 1713
- British-claimed territory to 1763
- French-claimed territory to 1763
- Spanish territory, claimed 1650
- ceded by France to Britain, 1763
- ceded by France to Spain, 1763
- additional Spanish territory by 1775
- Russian territory, claimed c. 1775
- USA from 1783
- → major exports

colonization routes
- → Spanish
- → British
- → Russian
- → French

Political hostility and military threat

Despite its small size, the French contingent, with its aboriginal allies, represented an ongoing military threat to the English colonies. In 1713, the Treaty of Utrecht ceded peninsular Nova Scotia to the British, and withdrew French claims to Newfoundland and the Hudson Bay fur-trading posts. With the War of the Austrian Succession (1743–48) and the French and Indian War (1754–60), also known as the Seven Years' War, the battle between British and French interests came to a head. At the battle of the Plains of Abraham, the French were defeated and Britain temporarily unified the eastern half of the continent under its rule.

The costs of this war – and the English government's desire to exact some payment from the American colonists who had ostensibly benefited from the removal of the French threat – contributed to the outbreak of hostilities between Britain and the colonies in the American War of Independence (1775–83). The war's end saw the forced removal of thousands of erstwhile loyalists, many of whom moved to remaining British colonies to the north.

2 By the late seventeenth century, France and England contested control over the eastern part of North America. Earlier Dutch and Swedish settlements had been taken over, and the Spanish presence was limited to the southeast (map left). Permanent European town settlements, following many 16th-century failures, were established on the eastern seaboard and along the St Lawrence and Mississippi/Ohio rivers. Inland and on Hudson's Bay, most Europeans lived near trading posts, trading furs with the aboriginal population that still dominated in those areas.

Despite the illustrations of exotic beasts, this 1550 map (right) by Pierre Desceliers demonstrated the growth in geographic knowledge of North America after the voyages of Cartier and Roberval. The usual north-south cartographic orientation is reversed, and Florida is located at the top of the map.

2 European settlement in North America

- early British settlements and claims
- early French settlements and claims
- early Spanish settlements
- ■ fur trading and military post

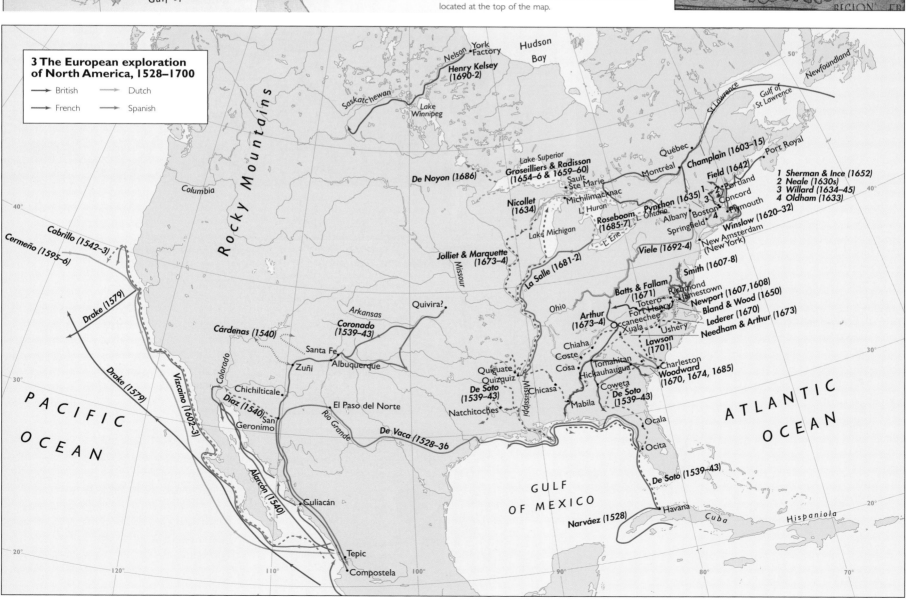

3 The European exploration of North America, 1528–1700

- → British
- → French
- → Dutch
- → Spanish

1 Sherman & Ince (1652)
2 Neale (1630s)
3 Willard (1634–45)
4 Oldham (1633)

179

Latin America and the Caribbean

Within 40 years of Columbus's discovery of America, the Spanish had overturned the rich empires of the Aztec and the Inca. For over a century longer, the Spanish and the Portuguese dominated the "New World", but in the 17th century the French, English and Dutch began to establish footholds in the Caribbean islands and the Guianas. New colonial societies were emerging, however, which sought to cast off European control.

I AND MY COMPANIONS SUFFER FROM A DISEASE OF THE HEART WHICH CAN BE CURED ONLY WITH GOLD.

Hernan Cortés

THEY WERE VERY WHITE, THEIR EYES WERE LIKE CHALK. THEIR ARMAMENTS, THEIR SWORDS, THEIR SHIELDS, THEIR LANCES, WERE ALL OF IRON. THE ANIMALS THEY RODE WERE AS HIGH AS A ROOF TOP AND LOOKED LIKE DEER. THEIR DOGS WERE HUGE, THEIR EYES BLAZED YELLOW LIKE FIRE. THEY MOVED ABOUT WITH THEIR TONGUES HANGING, ALWAYS PANTING.

An Aztec view of Europeans (Florentine Codex)

By 1500, in the wake of Columbus's voyages, around 6,000 Spaniards had already immigrated to the New World. For over a century the Spanish were to dominate the settlement of the Americas. The pace of colonization accelerated enormously after the discovery and conquest of two fabulously rich empires: the Aztec in Mesoamerica and the Inca in the Andean region. Relatively small Spanish forces were able to conquer these societies fairly easily by exploiting existing divisions within them; they were further assisted by the native people's heavy population losses brought about by the introduction of Old World diseases. The Spanish set up a vast bureaucratic system to administer the new colony, and they established many towns, very often on the sites of pre-existing Indian settlements. Mexico and Peru had rich deposits of gold and silver, so they became the main focuses of Spanish settlement in the New World. Few exports could compete with silver, but some sugar, cacao, indigo and cochineal

Aztecs dying of smallpox (below). Owing to the isolation of the continents, in pre-Columbian times the inhabitants of the Americas had not acquired immunity to diseases, such as smallpox, measles or influenza, that were introduced by Europeans and Africans from the Old World. Each epidemic might carry off about a quarter or one third of the population of a region.

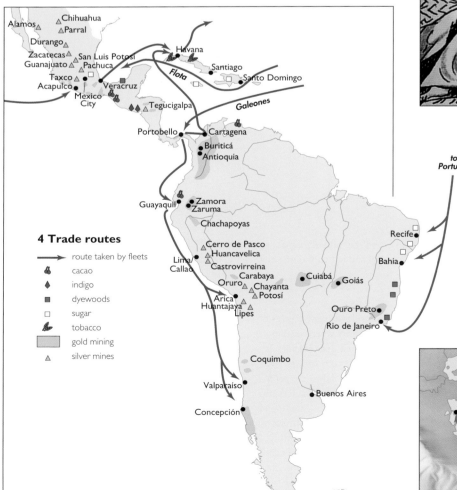

4 Trade routes

- → route taken by fleets
- 🌰 cacao
- 💧 indigo
- ■ dyewoods
- □ sugar
- 🍂 tobacco
- ▨ gold mining
- △ silver mines

4 The Spanish and Portuguese were interested in quick sources of profit, such as gold and silver. High transport costs meant that only goods of high value and little bulk, such as dyestuffs, could be transported to Europe. To protect ships from being attacked by pirates the Spanish set up a fleet system based on a restricted number of ports – Veracruz, Portobello and Cartagena (map left). The fleets were escorted by armed vessels called Armadas.

2 The Spanish invasion of Mexico (map below) showing old Vera Cruz, the first Spanish city; Cempoala, whose ruler was encouraged by Cortés in revolt against the Aztecs; Tlaxcala, home of Cortés's principal allies; and Tenochtitlán, capital of the Aztecs, on its island in Lake Texcoco. The conquest was not easy: Cortés's small force only just escaped destruction in the first stages of the conflict.

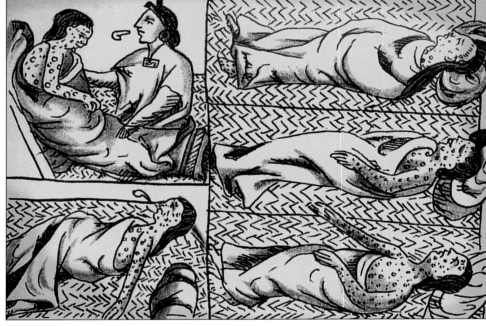

2 The Spanish invasion of Mexico, 1519–20

→ route of Cortés's army, 1519

▬▬▬ defensive wall of Tlaxcala (approx. position)

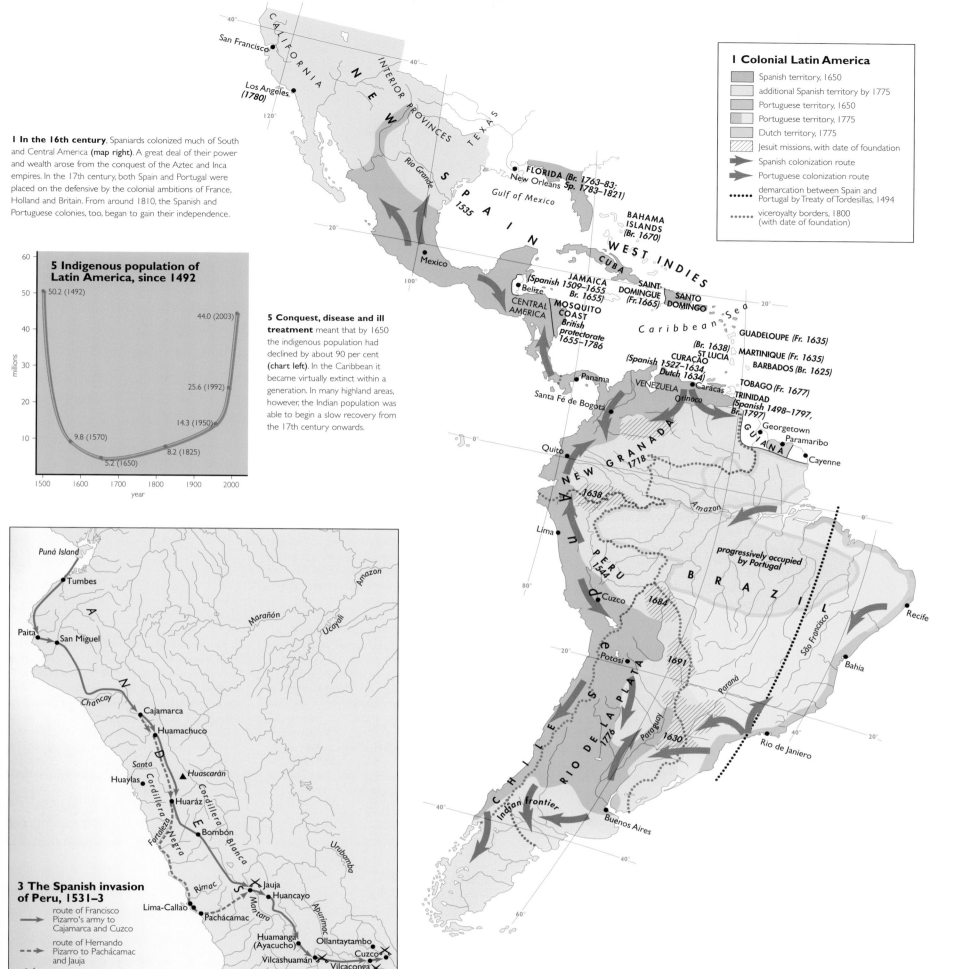

1 In the 16th century, Spaniards colonized much of South and Central America **(map right)**. A great deal of their power and wealth arose from the conquest of the Aztec and Inca empires. In the 17th century, both Spain and Portugal were placed on the defensive by the colonial ambitions of France, Holland and Britain. From around 1810, the Spanish and Portuguese colonies, too, began to gain their independence.

5 Indigenous population of Latin America, since 1492

50.2 (1492)
44.0 (2003)
25.6 (1992)
14.3 (1950)
9.8 (1570)
8.2 (1825)
5.2 (1650)

5 Conquest, disease and ill treatment meant that by 1650 the indigenous population had declined by about 90 per cent **(chart left)**. In the Caribbean it became virtually extinct within a generation. In many highland areas, however, the Indian population was able to begin a slow recovery from the 17th century onwards.

1 Colonial Latin America

- Spanish territory, 1650
- additional Spanish territory by 1775
- Portuguese territory, 1650
- Portuguese territory, 1775
- Dutch territory, 1775
- Jesuit missions, with date of foundation
- Spanish colonization route
- Portuguese colonization route
- demarcation between Spain and Portugal by Treaty of Tordesillas, 1494
- viceroyalty borders, 1800 (with date of foundation)

3 The Spanish invasion of Peru, 1531–3

- route of Francisco Pizarro's army to Cajamarca and Cuzco
- route of Hernando Pizarro to Pachácamac and Jauja
- × battles

3 The Spanish invasion of Peru, 1531–3 (map above) showing Tumbes, where Pizarro landed; Cajamarca, where the Inca ruler, Atahuallpa, was seized at his first meeting with Pizarro; Vilcaconga, where Soto was ambushed; and Cuzco, the Inca highland capital. The small Spanish force took advantage of an opponent split by a civil war. Despite the apparent ease of their victory, active opposition to the Spanish continued until 1572.

were also shipped to Spain. As a result of conquest, disease and ill treatment, the Indian population fell by about 90 per cent within the first 150 years of European arrival.

The Portuguese

By the Treaty of Tordesillas in 1494 the Spanish and Portuguese had established a line of demarcation between them in the New World, with the Portuguese allocated the territories east of the line. However, in the early years the Portuguese traded only on the coast of Brazil for dyewoods, and it was not until 1549 that their administrative capital was established at Bahia (today Salvador). In the absence of a large native workforce, African slaves had to be imported to work the sugar plantations. In the 1690s gold was discovered in the Minas Gerais – meaning General

Mines in Portuguese – and this provoked massive immigration from Portugal and led to the growing importance of Rio de Janeiro.

Beyond the frontiers

Few Europeans ventured outside the main centres of settlement and commercial activity, where the Indian populations were smaller and the opportunities for wealth creation fewer. However, both nations were obliged by papal bulls to convert the indigenous people to Catholicism. They therefore supported the activities of the missionary orders, notably the Jesuits and Franciscans, who through their establishment of missions gradually pushed back the frontier of settlement.

At the same time the French, Dutch and English tried to challenge Spanish and Portuguese power. At first they did this by sponsoring pirates, but later they began promoting settlement in areas where Spanish and Portuguese control was weak, notably in

the Caribbean islands and the Guianas, from where they attempted to undermine them economically through contraband trade.

Moves for independence

Conditioned by the new environment, the mix of traditions brought by the various settlers and the indigenous peoples they encountered, the societies that emerged in the New World were very different from those that the first settlers had left behind in Europe. During the second half of the 18th century, there were increasing moves to gain independence from Spain, with Mexico achieving independence in 1821 and most other countries, apart from Cuba and Puerto Rico, by 1825. Brazil had to wait until 1889 for political independence, although in 1822, when the Portuguese court returned to Europe following the defeat of Napoleon, it acquired considerable economic independence.

Trade and empire in Africa

From 1500 to 1800 African history was dominated by three main processes: the expansion of large political units; the spread of Islam; and the increasing involvement of Europeans. By 1800 Africans had made great progress in evolving distinctive social and political forms, but their independence was already seriously compromised.

FROM THE LATE 15TH CENTURY, large political units multiplied in Africa. In 1464, Sunni Ali became ruler of the Songhay people around Gao in the eastern Niger bend. Under Askia the Great (1493–1528), Songhay became a great empire, incorporating a number of important commercial cities including Timbuktu and Jenne, which developed into centres of learning and Muslim piety. In the savannah and forest country to the south, trading communities gave rise to comparable polities. Well before 1500 Oyo and Benin had emerged in the woodlands to the west of the Niger delta, producing superb terracottas and bronzes.

Elsewhere, similar processes gave rise to centralized states of iron-working agriculturists and cattle-keepers. Increased populations, diversified economies and trade promoted stronger political control. When the Portuguese arrived south of the Congo mouth in 1484, they established close relations with the Kongo kingdom. Inland and to the south were other Bantu-speaking African states including those of the Luba and Lunda, while in the fertile lands between the east African lakes a series of states evolved, notably Rwanda and Buganda.

Equally prosperous was the Zimbabwe plateau with its kingdom based initially at Great Zimbabwe, later replaced by a number of successors including the Mwenemutapa empire centred northeast of modern Harare. At its peak Great Zimbabwe was the political and religious centre of a major state with trade links extending as far as China.

The spread of Islam
Between 1500 and 1800 Islam consolidated its position in the Sudanic lands, and spread southward along the east African coast. Bitter rivalry between

Christian Ethiopia and Muslim coastal states in the Horn then developed: Sultan Ahmad Gran of Adal invaded the Christian highlands in the 1520s, and was only defeated by Portuguese intervention.

Meanwhile, in 1517, the Ottomans conquered the Mamluks in Egypt, and subsequently extended their control over Tripoli and Tunis; Algiers was ruled by corsair princes subject to the Ottomans. Only Morocco remained independent, governed for much of this period by Sharifian dynasties. In 1590, Morocco invaded the Songhay empire and set up a client state, disrupting economic life throughout the region. Later, in the 18th century, the politics and commerce of Muslim west Africa recovered again in a burst of Islamic proselytizing.

Europeans and the slave trade
Throughout the period, Europeans became more involved in Africa, seeking gold, ivory, wood and, above all, slaves to work the mines and plantations of the Americas. Although by 1800 the number of European territorial possessions was small, their domination of oceanic trade had considerable effects in many parts of Africa. In southernmost Africa, Dutch and French Huguenot settlers arrived after 1652 and subjected the Khoisan peoples, but by 1800 they encountered serious resistance from the southeastern Bantu-speakers.

Europeans established "factories" along the coast from Senegal to Angola and bought slaves from Africans. Between 1450 and 1870 some 11,500,000 slaves were exported, first to Europe and then to the Americas. The death rate probably totalled 25 per cent. Most came from west Africa, though by 1800 east Africa, which had long provided slaves to the Muslim world, was contributing to the Atlantic system. The precise effects of the slave trade are unclear. Overall, Europeans gained and Africa's development was inhibited.

2 Under the patronage of Prince Henry the Navigator, Portuguese explorers sailed south in search of gold, spices and slaves **(map right)**. By Henry's death the lower reaches of the Gambia and Senegal had been reached. Fernão Gomes and Diogo Cão pushed the limit of exploration to the river Congo. In 1488 one Portuguese expedition reached the Cape of Good Hope, and another reconnoitred east Africa, preparing the way for Vasco da Gama's journey to India in 1497.

Within the rich artistic traditions of west Africa, the bronzes produced in Benin from the 15th century onwards are outstanding. In court art designed for the *oba* (king), naturalism gave way to stylized designs, emphasizing power. Here **(right)** the *oba*'s butchers sacrifice a cow, the most prestigious animal sacrifice. This form of sculpture may have drawn its inspiration from woodcuts in books shown to the artists by early Portuguese visitors. Benin, which became powerful under Ewuare the Great (1440–73), was first reached by a Portuguese envoy as early as 1486. By the 17th century, Portuguese and Dutch traders were regular visitors.

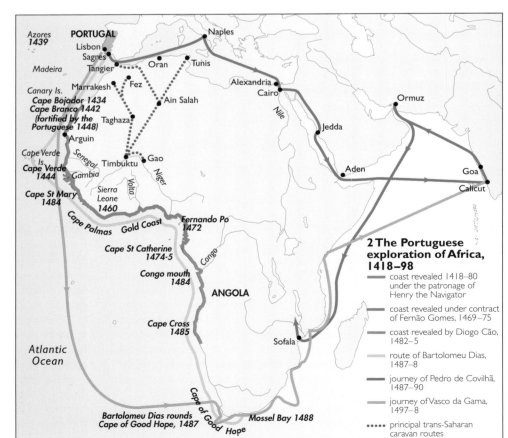

2 The Portuguese exploration of Africa, 1418–98
- coast revealed 1418–80 under the patronage of Henry the Navigator
- coast revealed under contract of Fernão Gomes, 1469–75
- coast revealed by Diogo Cão, 1482–5
- route of Bartolomeu Dias, 1487–8
- journey of Pedro de Covilhã, 1487–90
- journey of Vasco da Gama, 1497–8
- ••••• principal trans-Saharan caravan routes

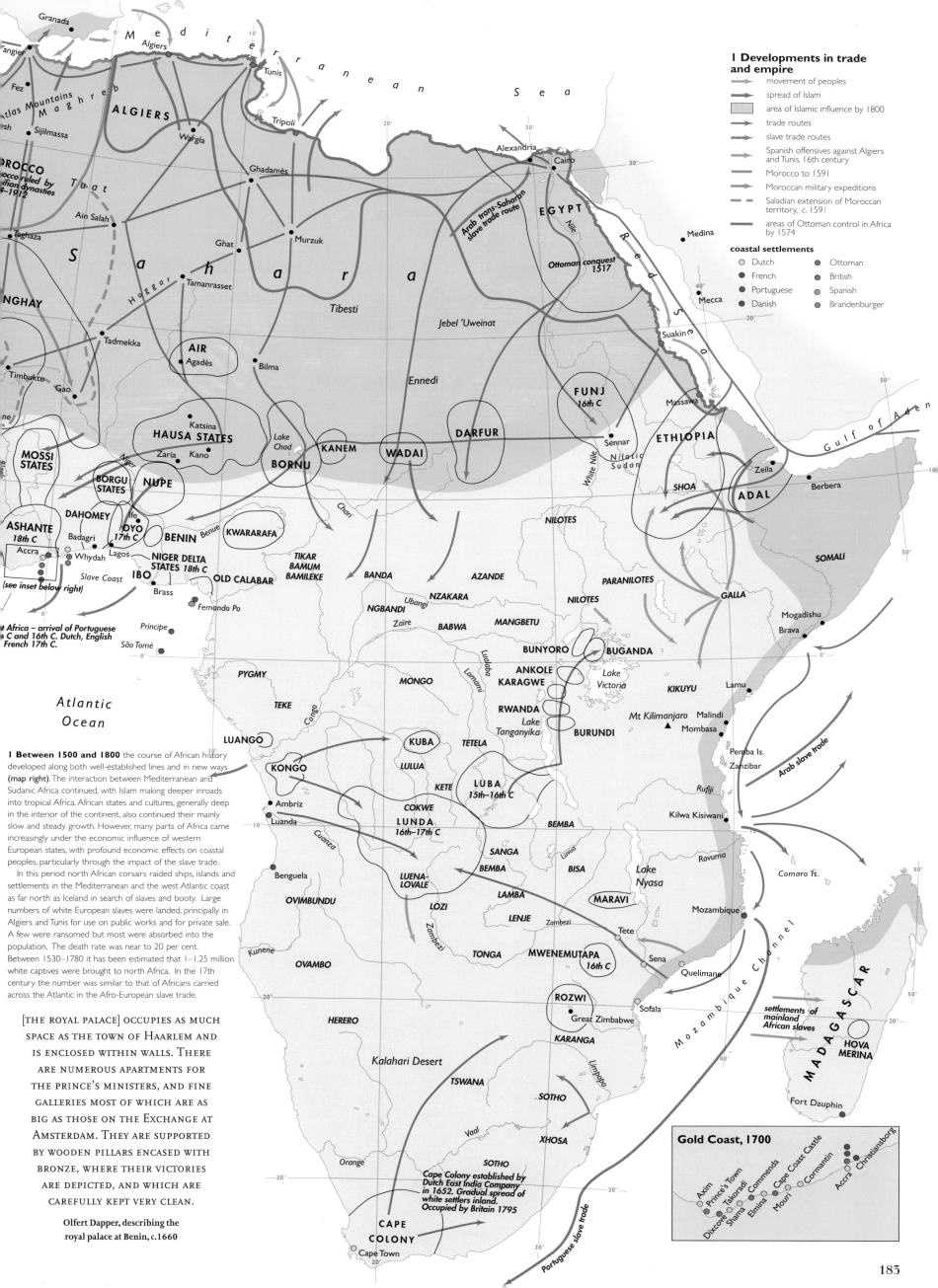

I Developments in trade and empire

- → movement of peoples
- → spread of Islam
- ▢ area of Islamic influence by 1800
- → trade routes
- → slave trade routes
- → Spanish offensives against Algiers and Tunis, 16th century
- → Morocco to 1591
- → Moroccan military expeditions
- - - Saladian extension of Moroccan territory, c. 1591
- — areas of Ottoman control in Africa by 1574

coastal settlements
- ○ Dutch
- ● French
- ● Portuguese
- ● Danish
- ● Ottoman
- ● British
- ○ Spanish
- ○ Brandenburger

I **Between 1500 and 1800** the course of African history developed along both well-established lines and in new ways (map right). The interaction between Mediterranean and Sudanic Africa continued, with Islam making deeper inroads into tropical Africa. African states and cultures, generally deep in the interior of the continent, also continued their mainly slow and steady growth. However, many parts of Africa came increasingly under the economic influence of western European states, with profound economic effects on coastal peoples, particularly through the impact of the slave trade.

In this period north African corsairs raided ships, islands and settlements in the Mediterranean and the west Atlantic coast as far north as Iceland in search of slaves and booty. Large numbers of white European slaves were landed, principally in Algiers and Tunis for use on public works and for private sale. A few were ransomed but most were absorbed into the population. The death rate was near to 20 per cent. Between 1530–1780 it has been estimated that 1–1.25 million white captives were brought to north Africa. In the 17th century the number was similar to that of Africans carried across the Atlantic in the Afro-European slave trade.

[THE ROYAL PALACE] OCCUPIES AS MUCH SPACE AS THE TOWN OF HAARLEM AND IS ENCLOSED WITHIN WALLS. THERE ARE NUMEROUS APARTMENTS FOR THE PRINCE'S MINISTERS, AND FINE GALLERIES MOST OF WHICH ARE AS BIG AS THOSE ON THE EXCHANGE AT AMSTERDAM. THEY ARE SUPPORTED BY WOODEN PILLARS ENCASED WITH BRONZE, WHERE THEIR VICTORIES ARE DEPICTED, AND WHICH ARE CAREFULLY KEPT VERY CLEAN.

Olfert Dapper, describing the royal palace at Benin, c.1660

Cape Colony established by Dutch East India Company in 1652. Gradual spread of white settlers inland. Occupied by Britain 1795

settlements of mainland African slaves

Gold Coast, 1700
Axim · Prince's Town · Dixcove · Takoradi · Shama · Commenda · Elmina · Cape Coast Castle · Mouri · Cormantin · Accra · Christiansborg

China at the time of the Ming dynasty

By the late 14th century a new Chinese dynasty, the Ming, had overthrown the Mongols. For 200 years it brought order and prosperity to much of China. The population more than doubled, new crops were introduced, industry flourished and trade greatly increased. By the early 17th century, corruption, external attack and crop failures conspired to weaken Ming rule and bring about its collapse.

1368 Ming dynasty founded

1392 Korea reduced to vassal status

1405 China sends the first of seven huge fleets into the Indian Ocean

1407 China occupies Annam (Vietnam)

1427 China expelled from Annam

1448 Rebellions in Fukien and Chekiang lead to one million deaths

1449 Chinese invasion of Mongolia ends in the emperor's capture.

1550 Mongol threat re-emerges; Japanese pirate attacks increase

1627 Wave of rebel movements begins

1644 Ming dynasty toppled

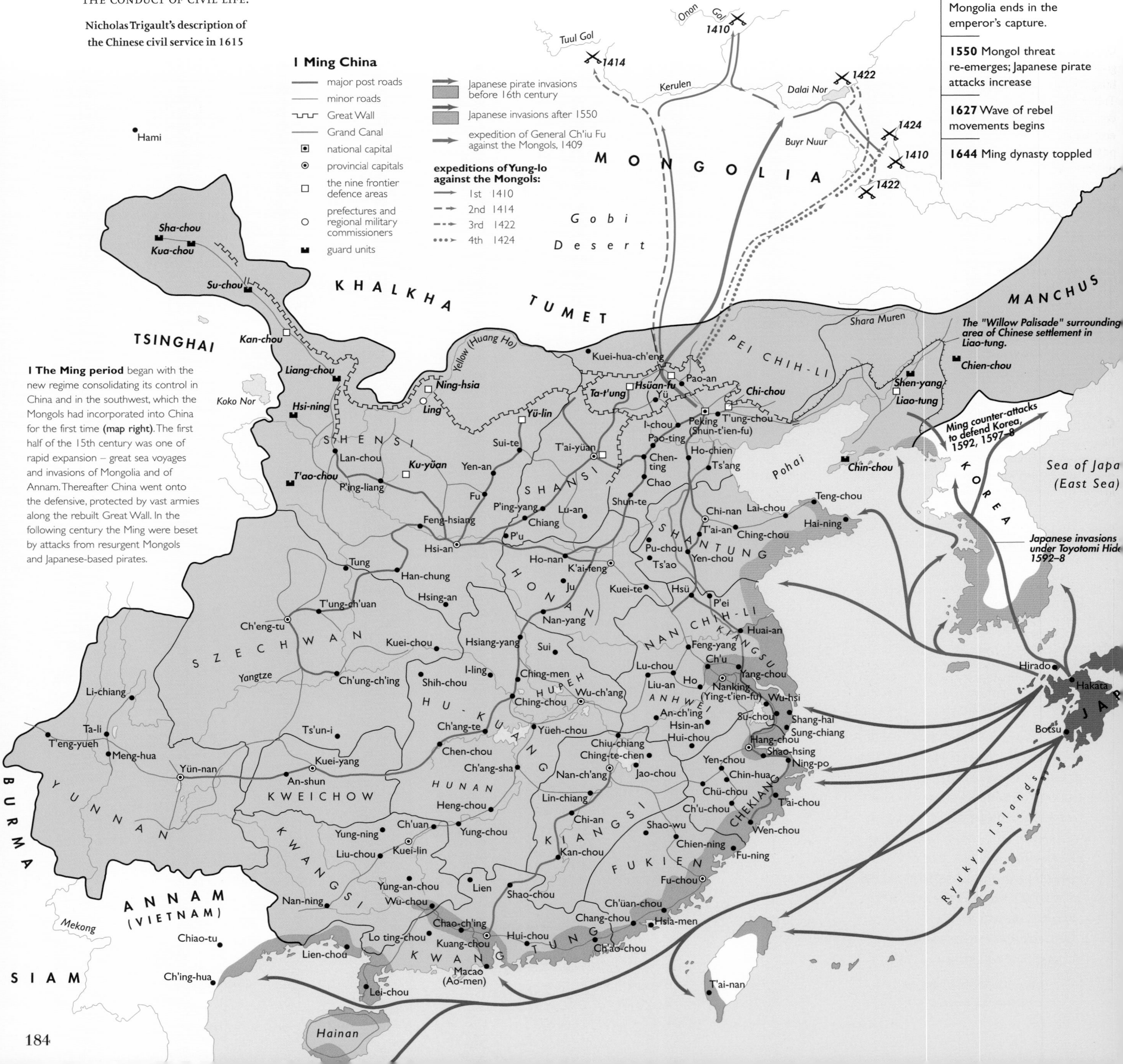

I The Ming period began with the new regime consolidating its control in China and in the southwest, which the Mongols had incorporated into China for the first time (map right). The first half of the 15th century was one of rapid expansion – great sea voyages and invasions of Mongolia and of Annam. Thereafter China went onto the defensive, protected by vast armies along the rebuilt Great Wall. In the following century the Ming were beset by attacks from resurgent Mongols and Japanese-based pirates.

I Ming China

- —— major post roads
- —— minor roads
- ⌐⌐⌐ Great Wall
- —— Grand Canal
- ▣ national capital
- ◉ provincial capitals
- ☐ the nine frontier defence areas
- ○ prefectures and regional military commissioners
- ■ guard units

Japanese pirate invasions before 16th century

Japanese invasions after 1550

expedition of General Ch'iu Fu against the Mongols, 1409

expeditions of Yung-lo against the Mongols:
- —— 1st 1410
- – – 2nd 1414
- – · – 3rd 1422
- ···· 4th 1424

By THE LATE 13th century Mongol rule in China had brought a measure of stability even to the north of the country, which had endured the worst of the Mongol depredations 50 years earlier. But the death of the Mongol emperor Kublai Khan in 1294 sparked further instability as rival claimants fought for the imperial throne. By the 1340s and '50s, dynastic decline was accelerated by floods, droughts and disease. Together with increasing discontent with Mongol rule, these touched off a series of uprisings against the government. The most serious was in central and southeastern China where, in 1368, Chu Yüan-chang, the most powerful of the rebels, proclaimed a new dynasty, the Ming. By 1388, the Mongols were driven back to the steppe and the Ming controlled all China.

Consolidation

Under the Ming, stability was restored and numerous improvements to the country's agricultural base made. Throughout the period, new agricultural techniques enabled the country to feed its rapidly growing population (see chart 5) more efficiently. New crops were introduced – some, such as yams, maize, peanuts and potatoes, by the Portuguese and Spanish – and new areas opened up to cultivation. To facilitate the movements of products and people, the Grand Canal, which would eventually stretch 1600km (1000 miles), from Hang-chou to Peking, was built. Upwards of 20,000 barges carrying 200,000 tons of grain a year used the canal. The administration of the burgeoning Chinese state was simple and practical. Though it discouraged innovation and, being highly centralized, was dangerously dependent on the emperor, it proved effective. Control over the vast population was effected largely through the "gentry", or *shen-shih*, degree-holders who had been through the education system and shared the values of the bureaucracy without actually holding office.

Within the new stability provided by the Ming, industry boomed. The great cities of the Yangtze delta – Nanking, Su-chou, Wu-hsi, Sung-chiang and Hang-chou – developed as major industrial centres, particularly for textiles. The enormous volume of trade that flowed through them gave rise to a number of powerful groups of merchants, whose influence came to extend across the country. By the late 16th century, the economy was further stimulated by inflows of silver from the New World, which were used to pay for Chinese exports of tea, silk and ceramics.

Overseas expansion

Ming China, especially under the Yung-lo emperor, successor to Chu Yüan-chang, was exceptionally expansionist and aggressive. Campaigns against the Mongols in the far north, the occupation of Annam from 1407 to 1427 and a series of immense seaborne expeditions (see map 4) extended China's reach to new and unprecedented limits. But the return on these extravagant ventures was never enough to justify them. Following a further and abortive attack against the Mongols in 1449, which ended with the capture of the Ming emperor himself, China reverted to its traditional defensive posture. Renewed Mongol attacks coupled with a succession of political and economic demands placed the empire under increasing strain. It was made considerably worse by persistent attacks on the south coast by Japanese-based pirates and smugglers. By the 1550s, the seas around China were infested by heavily armed bands who terrorized coastal regions. Exacerbating China's difficulties, at the end of the century Japan launched a costly and destructive invasion of Korea, obliging China to send huge armies to aid their vassal.

These threats both coincided with and were partly responsible for a decline in Ming power, a process made worse by growing government corruption and a series of crop failures in the north. By 1636, much of the country was in rebellion, with the Manchus in the forefront. Though it was to be another rebel leader, Li Tzu-ch'eng, who in 1644 toppled the Ming, his regime was itself overthrown almost immediately by the new Ch'ing dynasty from Manchuria. It was to exercise its iron grip over China until 1911.

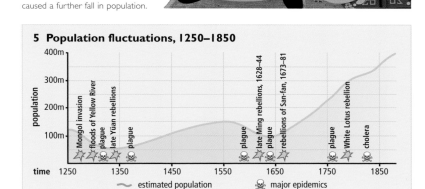

2 The Ming economy

agrarian productivity
relative production of grain (cattle per mou)*

	49–62
	89–115
	160–210

northern limit of rice cultivation

merchant groups
major merchant groups under the Ming all operated on a national scale

merchant groups

trade routes

* 1 cattle = ½kg or 1.1 lb   7 mou = 1 acre

population in 1393
density per sq. mile

- under 20
- 21–40
- 41–90
- 100–200
- over 200

2 China enjoyed an economic boom under the Ming (map left). Silk, cotton textiles and ceramics were exchanged in the Philippines for Spanish silver from the New World. From the early 17th century tea was exported to Europe via Dutch traders. China imported silver, spices, sulphur, sandalwood and copper from Japan. The Grand Canal was crucial to China's economic growth: 160,000 guards were stationed on it to secure this lifeline of empire. At the same time, agricultural productivity was improved as new techniques and crops were introduced.

Chu Yüan-chang (1328–98), founder of the Ming dynasty (right). In 1368 he proclaimed himself the founder of a new imperial dynasty, taking the title Hung-wu, meaning "mightily martial".

5 China's population rose steadily for most of the Ming period (chart below), the result of political stability and rising productivity. By the mid-17th century renewed violence and two outbreaks of plague caused a further fall in population.

5 Population fluctuations, 1250–1850

3 Rural distress produced a number of rebellions during the 15th century, mostly in central and southeastern China (map left). In the early 17th century taxation and economic pressures produced urban risings in the great cities while from the 1620s peasant rebellions broke out in central and northern China. By the 1640s, two rival contenders, both struggling to found new dynasties, had emerged to fill the power vacuum: Li Tzu-ch'eng and Chang Hsien-ch'ung.

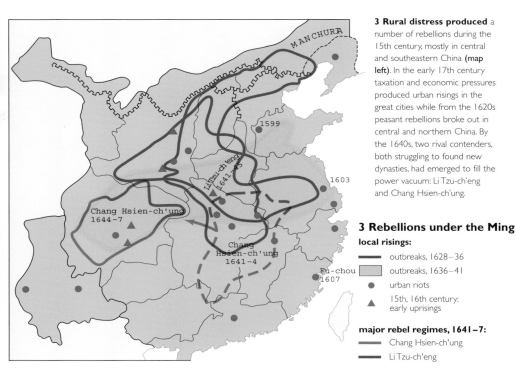

3 Rebellions under the Ming

local risings:
- outbreaks, 1628–36
- outbreaks, 1636–41
- urban riots
- 15th, 16th century: early uprisings

major rebel regimes, 1641–7:
- Chang Hsien-ch'ung
- Li Tzu-ch'eng

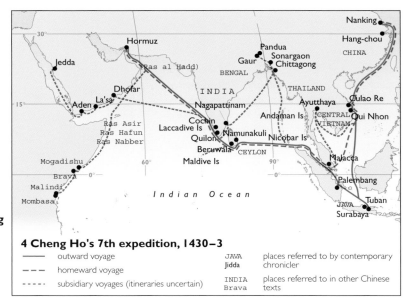

4 Cheng Ho's 7th expedition, 1430–3

- outward voyage
- homeward voyage
- subsidiary voyages (itineraries uncertain)

| JAVA Jidda | places referred to by contemporary chronicler |
| INDIA Brava | places referred to in other Chinese texts |

4 Between 1405 and 1433 China became a significant maritime country, sending seven great fleets under the command of Cheng Ho, a Muslim eunuch, as far as east Africa (map above). In the 1420s these expeditions were attacked as expensive and serving no state interest. They were stopped and China restricted her maritime activity to the southwest coast.

Ottoman Turkey

In the early modern period, the Ottoman sultanate dominated the Balkans, Anatolia, the Middle East and much of north Africa. Despite increasing political paralysis after the death of Suleiman the Magnificent in 1566, the Ottoman army and navy remained formidable. In the 18th century, the sultanate came under increasing threat from Russia and the Habsburg empire, but it was also a period of great cultural achievement.

1526 Ottomans defeat Hungarians at battle of Mohács

1529 Ottomans fail to take Vienna

1571 Ottoman navy defeated by Don John of Austria at Lepanto

1622 Rebellion of the janissaries; Sultan Osman II assassinated

1683 Grand vizier Kara Mustafa defeated at siege of Vienna by John Sobieski of Poland

1696 Russians take Azov on the Black Sea

1703–30 Tulip Age

1774 Treaty of Küçük Kainarji surrenders Crimea to Russians and accepts Russia as guardian of Christian holy places in Palestine

1801–2 Anglo-Ottoman alliance drives French from Egypt

IN THE FIRST THREE decades of the 16th century the frontiers of the Ottoman empire expanded rapidly. In 1514 the defeat of the Safavids (see p.188) at Çaldiran ensured that eastern Anatolia remained under Ottoman rule. In 1517 the troops of the sultan Selim the Grim took Syria and Egypt from the last of the Mamluks. Under his son, Suleiman the Magnificent (1520–66), the empire reached its height. The Ottoman janissaries were the most disciplined and formidable fighting force of the time. The administration, headed by the grand vizier, was both effective and honest. Suleiman embarked on campaigns of conquest in the Balkans, and in 1526 his victory at Mohács led to the incorporation of most of Hungary into the Ottoman empire; in 1529 he came close to taking Vienna. The supremacy of the Ottoman fleet in the Mediterranean made possible the conquest of Rhodes in 1522 and of Algiers in 1529, but they failed to take Malta from the Knights of St John after an epic siege in 1565. Naval bases were established at Suez in 1517 and Basra in 1538 to enable Ottoman ships to sail the Red Sea and the Gulf. Suleiman was also the patron of the great architect Sinan, whose buildings – notably the Suleimaniye mosque and tomb complex – still dominate the skyline of Istanbul.

The empire under pressure

Although the expansion faltered after the death of Suleiman, Ottoman power remained strong. The naval defeat at Lepanto in 1571 was only a temporary setback. The sultans were able to take Cyprus in 1571, Tunis from the Habsburgs in 1574, and Crete from the Venetians in 1662. Campaigns in the east led to the conquest of Yerevan in Armenia in 1635 and the taking of Baghdad from the Persians in 1638. As late as 1683 the Ottoman army, led by the grand vizier Kara Mustafa, was able to lay siege to Vienna.

The years after the death of Suleiman saw the internal administration of the empire becoming increasingly paralysed as palace officials and the harem took over political power. The queen mother or *sultan valide* was often the most important person in the sultanate, and the army was dominated by the janissaries, which were by now an ill-disciplined rabble who resented any attempts at reform and deposed any sultan or grand vizier who threatened their privileged status. The rule of the mad sultan Ibrahim (1640–8) saw the nadir of the sultan's power, but under the Köprülü viziers (1656–76) the administration was once again established on a firm footing.

In the 18th century the empire came under increasing pressure on its European frontiers, and the Ottomans were forced to cede Hungary and Transylvania to the Habsburgs and the lands north of the Black Sea to the Russians. In the east, the collapse of the Safavids in 1722 meant that the frontier with Iran remained largely peaceful. The 18th century was also a period of cultural achievement typified by the "Tulip Age" patronized by the cultivated bibliophile Sultan Ahmet III (1703–30). Nevertheless, in 1800 the Ottoman empire was still the major power in the Middle East and southeast Europe.

Suleiman I receives John Sigismund Zapolya, the ruling Prince of Transylvania, in his camp at Selin in June 1566 **(left)**. Suleiman, known in the west as "The Magnificent" and in Turkey as "the Lawgiver" pushed the frontiers of the empire far into the Balkans, reaching as far as Vienna in 1529. He also seized large parts of Persia and Iraq in the 1540s and his forces unsuccessfully besieged Malta in 1565.

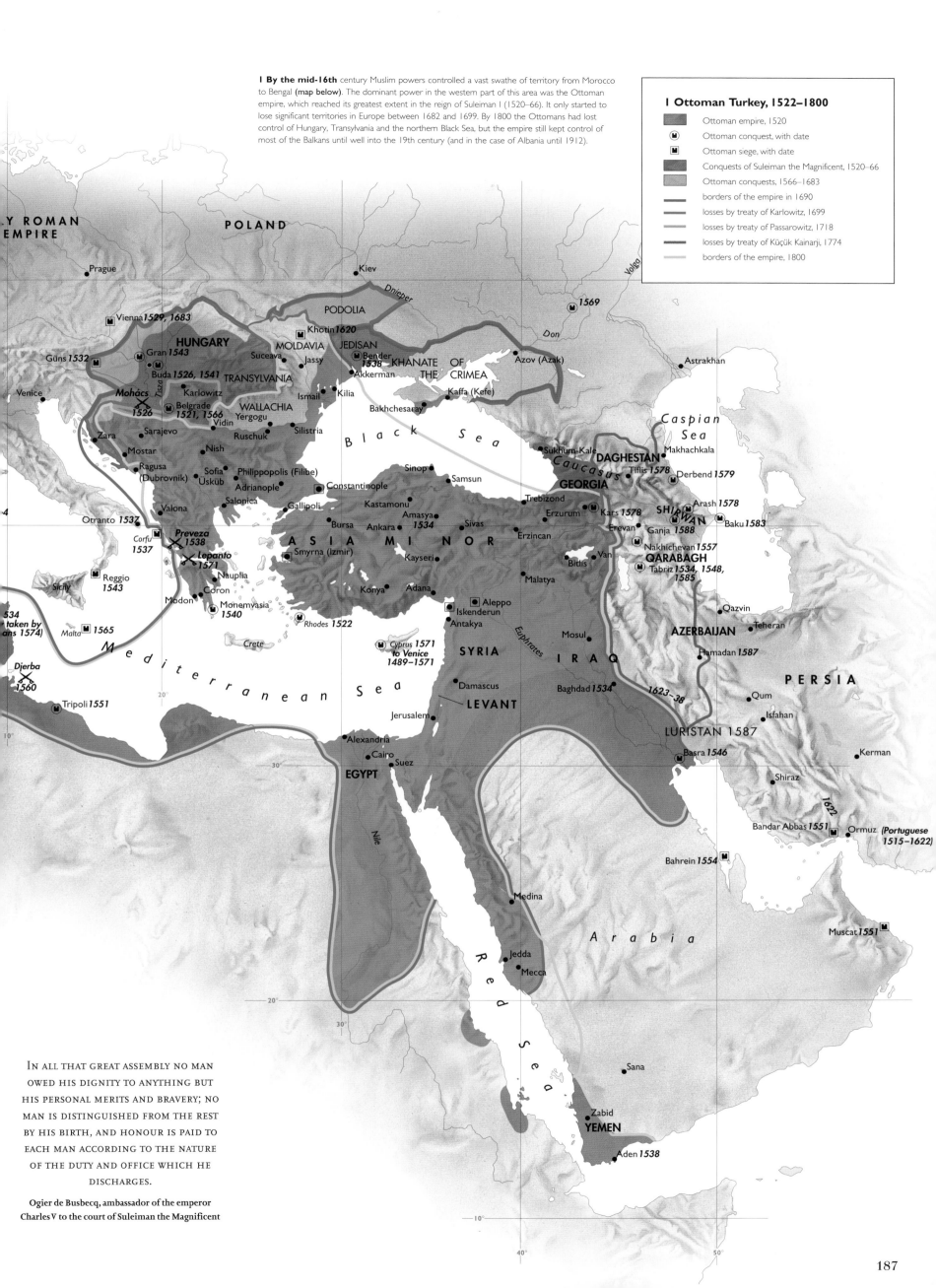

1 By the mid-16th century Muslim powers controlled a vast swathe of territory from Morocco to Bengal (map below). The dominant power in the western part of this area was the Ottoman empire, which reached its greatest extent in the reign of Suleiman I (1520–66). It only started to lose significant territories in Europe between 1682 and 1699. By 1800 the Ottomans had lost control of Hungary, Transylvania and the northern Black Sea, but the empire still kept control of most of the Balkans until well into the 19th century (and in the case of Albania until 1912).

1 Ottoman Turkey, 1522–1800

- Ottoman empire, 1520
- Ottoman conquest, with date
- Ottoman siege, with date
- Conquests of Suleiman the Magnificent, 1520–66
- Ottoman conquests, 1566–1683
- borders of the empire in 1690
- losses by treaty of Karlowitz, 1699
- losses by treaty of Passarowitz, 1718
- losses by treaty of Küçük Kainarji, 1774
- borders of the empire, 1800

HOLY ROMAN EMPIRE

POLAND

Prague

Kiev

Dnieper

1569

Vienna *1529, 1683*

Khotin *1620*

PODOLIA

Don

Volga

Güns *1532*

Gran *1543*

HUNGARY

MOLDAVIA

JEDISAN

Bender *1538*

KHANATE OF THE CRIMEA

Azov (Azak)

Astrakhan

Suceava

Jassy

Akkerman

Buda *1526, 1541*

TRANSYLVANIA

Belgrade *1521, 1566*

WALLACHIA

Kilia

Kaffa (Kefe)

Mohács *1526*

Karlowitz

Venice

Zara

Sarajevo

Yergogu

Silistria

Bakhchesaray

Caspian Sea

Vidin

Mostar

Ruschuk

Nish

Black Sea

Sinop

Samsun

Sukhum-Kale

DAGHESTAN

Makhachkala

Ragusa (Dubrovnik)

Sofia

Philippopolis (Filibe)

Constantinople

Caucasus

Tiflis *1578*

Derbend *1579*

Üsküb

Adrianople

GEORGIA

Valona

Salonica

Gallipoli

Kastamonu

Amasya

Trebizond

Kars *1578*

Arash *1578*

Otranto *1537*

Preveza *1538*

Bursa

Ankara

1534

Sivas

Erzurum

Erevan

SHIRWAN

Ganja *1588*

Baku *1583*

Corfu *1537*

Lepanto *1571*

ASIA MINOR

Erzincan

Van

Nakhichevan *1557*

QARABAGH

Nauplia

Smyrna (Izmir)

Kayseri

Bitlis

Tabriz *1534, 1548, 1585*

Reggio *1543*

Coron

Konya

Adana

Malatya

Qazvin

Sicily

Modon

Monemvasia *1540*

Mosul

AZERBAIJAN

Teheran

Rhodes *1522*

Aleppo

Iskenderun

PERSIA

Malta *1565*

Crete

Cyprus *1571 to Venice 1489–1571*

Antakya

SYRIA

Euphrates

IRAQ

Hamadan *1587*

taken by ns *1574*

Djerba *1560*

Mediterranean Sea

Damascus

Baghdad *1534*

1623–38

Qum

Tripoli *1551*

LEVANT

LURISTAN *1587*

Isfahan

Jerusalem

Kerman

Basra *1546*

Alexandria

Cairo

Suez

EGYPT

Shiraz

1622

Bandar Abbas *1551*

Ormuz (Portuguese 1515–1622)

Bahrein *1554*

Nile

Medina

Red Sea

Arabia

Muscat *1551*

Jedda

Mecca

Sana

Zabid

Aden *1538*

YEMEN

Iran from the Safavids to the Qajars

The rule of the Safavid and Qajar dynasties saw the consolidation of Iran within its modern frontiers and the adoption of Shi'ite Islam as the national religion. The 18th century was a period of great disruption and violence. In the 19th century, the Qajar Shahs struggled to retain their independence from Russian and British influence. Afghanistan became an independent kingdom in the 19th century but the Uzbek Khanates were unable to resist Russian power.

THE LOVE OF WINE, IN WHICH THIS PRINCE OFTEN INDULGED TO EXCESS, WAS THE CAUSE OF ALL THE EVILS OF HIS REIGN. IT WAS IN HIS MOMENTS OF INTOXICATION ALONE THAT HE WAS CAPRICIOUS, CRUEL AND UNJUST: BUT THE DANGER FROM THESE EXCESSES WAS IN A DEGREE LIMITED TO THE CIRCLE OF HIS COURT; THE COUNTRY AT LARGE ONLY KNEW THIS PRINCE AS ONE OF THE MOST GENEROUS AND JUST RULERS THAT EVER REIGNED IN PERSIA. TO THE PUBLIC OFFICERS OF GOVERNMENT HE WAS SEVERE, BUT TO THE POOR, MILD AND LENIENT.

Sir John Malcolm on Shah Abbas II (1642–66)

IN 1501 A NEW ERA in the history of Iran began with the coming to power of the Safavid Isma'il I. The Safavids came from Ardabil in Azerbaijan and their first capital was at Qazvin in northern Iran. Under Isma'il I (d.1524) the frontiers of Iran were consolidated. In the northeast, the lands beyond the Kopet Dag mountains, including Merv, Bukhara and Samarkand, were lost to the Uzbek Shaybani Khans and the modern frontier of Iran was established. In the west, the forces of the Safavids were defeated by the Ottomans at the battle of Çaldiran in 1514 which ensured that eastern Anatolia remained firm-

ly in Turkish hands. It was at this time too that Shi'ite Islam became the state religion, clearly differentiating the Safavid empire from the Ottomans and the Uzbeks, both of whom were Sunnis.

The high point of Safavid power was reached under Shah Abbas I (the Great) (1588–1629) who

2 Isfahan

2 Isfahan was an ancient walled city which had been one of the capitals of the Seljuk empire in the 11th century (map left). Shah Abbas the Great chose it as his capital and began a major development. In contrast to the old city with its narrow winding streets, he laid out a great new square or maydan and a broad straight avenue, the Chahar Bagh or Four Gardens, leading down to the river. Around these he and his successors constructed mosques and palaces, while the river was spanned by eight bridges. New buildings continued to be added down to the end of the Safavid dynasty in 1722, making Isfahan one of the most beautiful cities in the Islamic world.

established a new capital at Isfahan, which was expanded and endowed with a series of mosques, palaces and bridges, forming one of the glories of Persian architecture. In 1623 the Safavids took Baghdad and much of Iraq but this had to be surrendered to the Ottomans in 1639. By the early 18th century the Safavid empire was in decline and in 1722 Isfahan was sacked by the Ghilzai Afghans.

The 18th century was a period of violence and confusion in Iran. The throne was seized by a military adventurer called Nadir Shah, who invaded India and sacked Delhi in 1738–9 but was murdered in 1747. From 1750 to 1779 the main power in the land was the peaceful Karim Khan Zand, ruling from Shiraz.

In 1779 the leader of the Qajar Türkmen of northeastern Iran, Agha Muhammad Khan, established his control over most of the country and the Qajars were to rule as Shahs of Iran until 1924. In 1786 he moved the capital to Tehran which until then had been only a small village. In the period of Qajar rule, Iran came under increasing pressure from Russian influence in the north and the British in India and the Gulf, but the country retained its independence. However, they were forced to cede their claims to sovereignty in the Caucasus to the Russians at the treaty of Turkmenchay in 1828, and Herat to the Afghans in 1857. In 1906 political resistance to the absolutism of the shahs led to the granting of a constitution.

In the east, Dost Muhammad (1819–63) proclaimed himself Amir of Kabul and laid the foundations of modern Afghanistan, playing off the British and the Russians to secure the frontiers of his state. In the lands to the northeast, the Uzbek rulers established the Khanates of Bukhara, Khiva and Kokand, but they were unable to resist Russian encroachment and lost Tashkent in 1865 and Khiva in 1873. By 1900, the Qajars and the Tsarist Russians shared common frontiers in Azerbaijan and northeast Iran.

Coloured tile work at the entrance of the royal mosque in Isfahan, constructed by Shah Abbas the Great (**left**). The use of coloured tiles became characteristic of Persian architecture from the 14th century onwards. The small arches, or muqarnas, above the door were one of the commonest forms of decoration.

1 Iran entered a new phase of political power and prosperity under the Safavids, who originated in a militant Sufi order around the Caspian sea in the late 15th century. Their leader Isma'il I became shah in 1502 and by the mid-16th century the Safavids under rulers such as Shah Abbas rivalled the Ottomans in military and cultural prestige (**map below**). It was also under the Safavids that Shi'ite Islam became the official religion of Iran. After the fall of the Safavids in the early 18th century, Iran suffered a half-century of turbulence until the Qajar dynasty seized power in 1779.

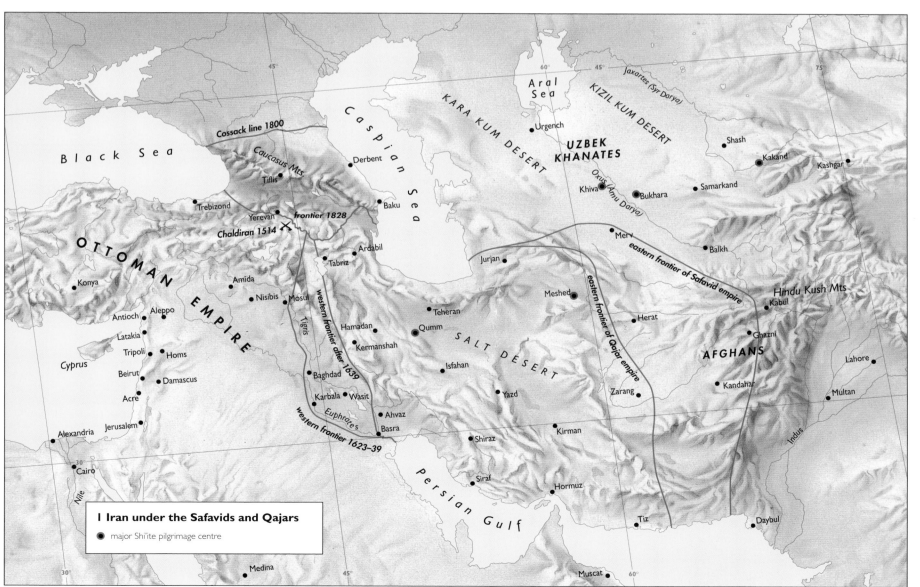

1 Iran under the Safavids and Qajars
- major Shi'ite pilgrimage centre

Mughal India and the growth of British power

Founded in the early 16th century, the Mughal empire was at its height from the 1550s to the 1650s, presiding over a golden age of religious cooperation and cultural synthesis. But in the 18th century it rapidly disintegrated, with the British emerging as the victors over the French and the Maratha Hindus in the struggle for the succession.

1526 Battle of Panipat: Babur conquers the Delhi sultanate and founds Mughal dynasty

1674 Sivaji creates Maratha kingdom

1707 Death of Aurangzeb; decline of Mughal power in India

1739 Nadir Shah invades India and sacks Delhi

1761 Capture of Pondicherry; British destroy French power in India

1765 British granted the revenues of Bengal by the Mughal emperor

1803 British defeat the Marathas at Delhi; the Mughal empire accepts British protection

2 The rich and populous Mughal empire (below) produced many craft goods and cash crops. Textiles from Bengal, Gujerat and Coromandel were the main export, along with sugar to Japan and Iran and pepper and saltpetre to Europe. The main imports were gold and silver.

IN THE 1520s BABUR, who counted both Genghis Khan and Tamerlane among his ancestors, invaded India from Afghanistan. After defeating the Lodi sultan at Panipat in 1526, he began the establishment of the Mughal empire, but died before the foundations were secure. His son, Humayun, was expelled by the Afghans of Bihar under Sher Shah and it took a full-scale invasion, brilliantly consolidated by Babur's grandson, Akbar (1556–1605), to restore Mughal rule. This now stretched from Bengal in the east and the Godavari river in the south, to Kashmir in the north and the Indus Valley in the west (see map 1). Most of the Hindu Rajput princes became tributary allies, and the empire was administered by a new class of bureaucrats, the *mansabdars*, ranked in a military hierarchical system.

Akbar's reign is one of the golden ages of Indian history. A standardized tax system was introduced; there was agricultural prosperity and buoyant trade (see map 2). Policies of tolerance were adopted towards the non-Muslim majority and Akbar himself took wives from Rajput families. His patronage laid the foundations for a remarkable synthesis of Persian and Indian cultural forms. He presided over the development of Mughal miniature painting, which combined the traditions of the Safavid and Rajput schools. Under his son Jahangir (1605–27), Mughal painting reached its peak. Akbar's red sandstone capital at Fatehpur Sikri expressed a striking synthesis of Islamic and Hindu traditions of architecture. The new style reached its climax under his grandson Shahjahan (1628–57), the builder of the Taj Mahal.

Akbar's political inheritance included a ceaseless thrust towards territorial expansion, especially southwards. Under Aurangzeb (1658–1707) this brought confrontation with a new Hindu power, the Marathas, a kingdom founded by Sivaji in 1674. By 1700 the Marathas were ravaging the land from the Deccan to Bengal. There was also open internal disaffection from Rajputs, Sikhs and Jats. It used to be thought that these developments were the outcome of Aurangzeb's revision of Akbar's policies of toleration. It now seems clear that they arose from weaknesses in the economic and administrative structures of the empire.

Mughal decline

After Aurangzeb's death the empire quickly declined. The finishing stroke came from Persia when Nadir Shah's army sacked Delhi in 1739. The former Mughal provinces of Oudh, Bengad and Hyderabad now offered only nominal allegiance to Delhi. In the south the Muslim state of Mysore grew into a formidable power under Haidar Ali and his son, Tipu Sultan. Over the course of the century the Maratha chiefs spread their territories deep into north, west, central and eastern India (see map 4). The Mughal emperor became no more than a Maratha protégé.

The East India Company

Simultaneously, India was undergoing its first major invasion from the sea. By the 1760s the English East India Company, having both defeated the French and been granted control over the revenues of Bengal by the Mughal emperor, was firmly established on the Indian shore. With these resources the Company was now able to sustain an army of over 100,000 men. Through military victories over the Marathas and Mysore, it came to occupy a continuous band of territory from the Gangetic plain to India's southern coasts (see map 3). In addition, by a system of subsidiary alliances, its suzerainty was recognized by many Indian rulers beyond its actual borders. In 1803 the Mughal emperor himself accepted British protection. British supremacy was now widely acknowledged.

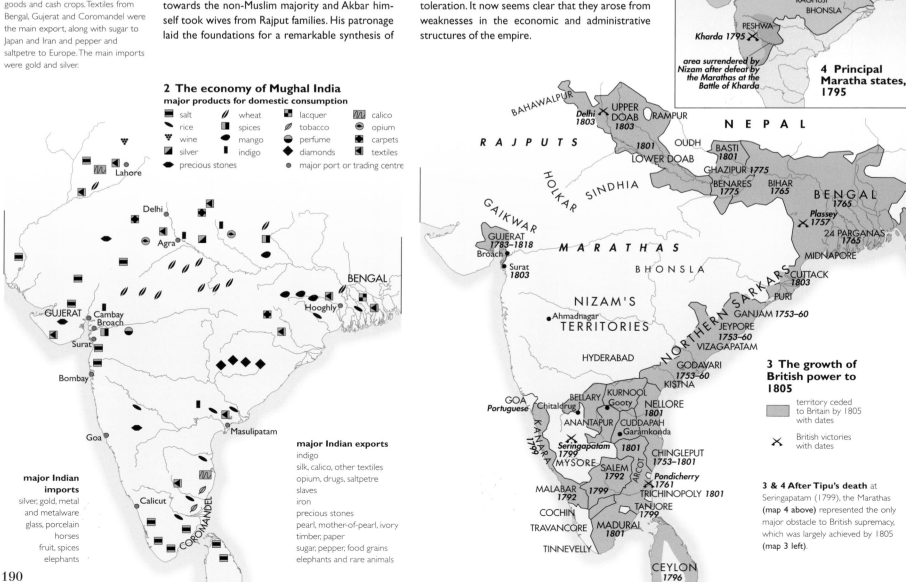

2 The economy of Mughal India
major products for domestic consumption

- salt
- rice
- wine
- silver
- precious stones
- wheat
- spices
- mango
- indigo
- lacquer
- tobacco
- perfume
- diamonds
- calico
- opium
- carpets
- textiles
- major port or trading centre

Lahore
Delhi
Agra
BENGAL
Hooghly
GUJERAT
Cambay
Broach
Surat
Bombay
Goa
Masulipatam
Calicut
COROMANDEL

major Indian imports
silver, gold, metal and metalware glass, porcelain horses fruit, spices elephants

major Indian exports
indigo
silk, calico, other textiles
opium, drugs, saltpetre
slaves
iron
precious stones
pearl, mother-of-pearl, ivory
timber, paper
sugar, pepper, food grains
elephants and rare animals

SINDHIA
MARATHA CONFEDERACY
HOLKAR
GAIKWAR
RAGHUJI
BHONSLA
PESHWA
Kharda 1795 ✕

area surrendered by Nizam after defeat by the Marathas at the Battle of Kharda

4 Principal Maratha states, 1795

BAHAWALPUR
Delhi 1803 ✕
UPPER DOAB 1803
RAMPUR
NEPAL
RAJPUTS
OUDH
LOWER DOAB 1801
BASTI 1801
HOLKAR
SINDHIA
GHAZIPUR 1775
BENARES 1775
BIHAR 1765
BENGAL 1765
GAIKWAR
GUJERAT 1783–1818
Broach
Surat 1803
Plassey ✕ 1757
24 PARGANAS 1765
MARATHAS
BHONSLA
MIDNAPORE
NIZAM'S
Ahmadnagar
TERRITORIES
NORTHERN SARKARS
CUTTACK 1803
PURI
GANJAM 1753–60
JEYPORE 1753–60
VIZAGAPATAM 1753–60
HYDERABAD
GODAVARI 1753–60
KISTNA
GOA Portuguese
Chitaldrug
BELLARY
KURNOOL
Gooty
NELLORE 1801
ANANTAPUR
CUDDAPAH
Garamkonda
KANARA 1799
Seringapatam 1799
MYSORE
SALEM 1792
ARCOT
CHINGLEPUT 1753–1801
Pondicherry ✕ 1761
TRICHINOPOLY 1801
MALABAR 1792 1799
COCHIN
TANJORE 1799
TRAVANCORE
MADURAI 1801
TINNEVELLY
CEYLON 1796

3 The growth of British power to 1805

territory ceded to Britain by 1805 with dates

✕ British victories with dates

3 & 4 After Tipu's death at Seringapatam (1799), the Marathas (map 4 above) represented the only major obstacle to British supremacy, which was largely achieved by 1805 (map 3 left).

A MONARCH SHOULD BE EVER INTENT ON CONQUEST, OTHERWISE HIS NEIGHBOURS RISE IN ARMS AGAINST HIM.

Saying of the Emperor Akbar

I ASSERT THAT IN THE MUGHAL KINGDOM THE NOBLES, AND ABOVE ALL THE KING, LIVE WITH SUCH OSTENTATION THAT THE MOST SUMPTUOUS OF EUROPEAN COURTS CANNOT COMPARE IN RICHNESS AND MAGNIFICENCE WITH THE LUSTRE BEHELD IN THE INDIAN COURT.

Niccolo Manucci, artilleryman and physician at the Mughal Court, c. 1656–86

Much of the early part of Akbar's reign was spent in the conquest of the Hindu Rajputs, who were to become important allies of the Mughals. In this typically sumptuous miniature **(above)** of 1569, Surjan Hara, ruler of the fort of Ranthanbhur, submits to Akbar, offering him the keys to the fort and many gifts.

I The Mughal empire

- ——— the empire at Akbar's death, 1605
- ——— the empire under Shahjahan, 1628–57
- ——— the empire c. 1700
- ▨ Maratha territories at Sivaji's death, 1680
- ● French settlement
- ● Dutch settlement
- ● British settlement
- ○ Danish settlement
- ● Portuguese settlement
- ▬ provinces governed by centralised *zabt* system

I The territory controlled by the Mughal administration grew with each emperor, until the death of Aurangzeb (1707) **(map above)**. But by the end of the 17th century Mughal rule was everywhere under attack, both from within and without. The most important opposition came from the Maratha Hindus, under Sivaji, fanning out from their homeland in the Western Ghats. At the same time, the European trading nations, who had taken serious interest in India's rich resources and markets, had by now established significant footholds along the coast.

191

China under the Ch'ing dynasty

1644 Manchus found the Ch'ing dynasty

1674 Rebellion of the Three Feudatories begins

1689 Treaty of Nerchinsk between China and Russia

1697 China occupies Outer Mongolia

1746 Chin-ch'uan tribal rebellion begins

1751 China overruns Tibet, Dzungaria and Tarim Basin (1756–9)

1793 British embassy under Macartney to the Chinese Court

Under the Ch'ing dynasty China doubled in size and experienced a century of peaceful prosperity. But by the late 18th century economic decline brought about by rapid population growth sparked repeated revolts. The developing crisis was exacerbated by growing government inefficiency and Western economic intervention. By the 1830s China's problems demanded urgent and radical change.

Peaceful rule having lasted now for more than one hundred years, it may be considered of long duration. But if we consider the population, we can see that it has increased five times over what it was thirty years ago, ten times over what it was sixty years ago, and at least twenty times over what it was one hundred and some tens of years ago.

The scholar-official Hung Lian-chi (1746–1809) on China's population problem

3 By the 17th century China had developed considerable regional specialization and a nationwide marketing system **(map below)**. Some cities in the lower Yangtze sustained large and varied handicraft industries, their raw materials and food transported over great distances via the Grand Canal and the Yangtze.

THE CH'ING DYNASTY was founded by a non-Chinese people, the Manchus, who in the early 17th century established a Chinese-style state in Manchuria with its capital at Mukden (see p. 184). When the Ming were toppled by the rebel Li Tzu-ch'eng in 1644, the Manchus invaded China and proclaimed a new dynasty. Though Ming resistance continued in the south and west for several decades, notably in the rebellion of the Three Feudatories of 1674–81, from 1652 Manchu rule was effectively established. The Ch'ing brought to China more than a century of internal peace and prosperity under three rulers of great ability, the emperors K'ang-hsi (1661–1722), Yung-cheng (1722–35) and Ch'ien-lung (1736–96), who also led the expansion of the Chinese empire into central Asia until it was almost doubled in size.

The Manchus maintained their predominant place in government, and above all in the military, but also established good working relationships with their Chinese officials. Only towards the end of the 18th century, as they became more and more influenced by Chinese education and culture, did the distinctive Manchu identity begin to fade. Exploitation by Chinese and Manchu alike led to many rebellions of peoples on the periphery: in Yunnan in 1726–9, among the Chinese Muslim minority in Kansu in 1781–4, among the Yao people of Kwangsi in 1790, among the Miao people of Kweichow in 1795–7, and most notably the massive Chin-ch'uan tribal risings in western Szechwan in 1746–9 and again in 1771–6, when order was finally restored only after ruinously expensive military operations.

Population growth

From the end of the 18th century rebel movements began to take new forms. The background was a developing economic crisis. The area available for agriculture, which had been expanded by the introduction of maize, sweet potato, ground nuts and tobacco in the 16th and 17th centuries, was now fully used. The population, meanwhile, grew inexorably, from 100 million to 300 million between 1650 and 1800 and to 450 million by 1850. This constantly growing population had to be fed by ever-more intensive cultivation of a limited area. By the end of the 18th century, there was widespread hardship and impoverishment which in turn sparked rebellions, usually inspired by secret societies: the rebellions of the Heaven and Earth Society, 1787–8; the White Lotus, 1796–1805; and the Eight Trigrams of 1813, which was accompanied by an attempted coup in Peking. Further risings took place among border peoples.

The crisis of government

The developing economic crisis was exacerbated by the strains that external expansion placed on imperial financial administration and by a sharp decline in the quality of government. Corruption became endemic at every level of administration while the government itself failed to keep up with population growth, delegating more and more power to local gentry. A further factor was the import of opium by foreign powers into China to help pay for their extensive purchases of tea, silk, porcelain and handicrafts. By the 1830s opium imports were leading to a substantial drain of silver from China with concomitant damage to the economy and state finances.

By this time Manchu China was the world's largest and most populous empire, directly controlling vast territories in inner Asia and treating as tributary states still larger areas: Korea, Indo-China, Siam, Burma, Nepal. But within this huge empire, effective Ch'ing administrative and military control was gradually declining, while inexorable economic pressures increased which could be cured only by large-scale technological innovation and radical reorganization. Neither was imminent and in the meantime China faced new pressures from the expansionist Western powers.

furs, gold, ginseng
Peking
SHANSI
CHIHLI
SHANTUNG
Lin-ch'ing
Chi-ning
Grand Canal (Yun Ho)
KANSU
HONAN
KIANGSU
raw cotton, grain
Huai-an
Sian
SHENSI
Yang-chou
Nanking
copper
Su-chou
Ch'eng-tu
HUPEH AND HUNAN
ANHWEI
tea
Hang-chou
SZECHWAN
Yangtze
Nan-ch'ang
CHEKIANG
Ch'ang-sha
KIANGSI
limited Dutch trade
tea, porcelain, silk, cotton
FUKIEN
KWEICHOW
TAIWAN
Amoy
YUNNAN
KWANGSI
Canton
KWANGTUNG
overseas trade with West: tea, silk, fine cottons, porcelain, lacquer
3 The Ch'ing economy
main manufacturing and trading areas, 16th and 17th centuries
major trade routes, with principal traded commodities
iron
gold
silver
copper
lead
tin
mercury
salt
coal
silk textiles
cotton textiles
paper
tea
sugar
iron utensils
ceramics (porcelain)

The most important development of Ch'ien-lung's reign was the expansion of the Chinese empire into central Asia. The new acquisitions were known as "Xingjiang" or the "New Territories". The outcome was that China now established a firm western border with Russia alongside the northern borders settled by the Treaty of Nerchinsk (1689). China also added extra populations of Muslims and Buddhists to its subjects. In this 18th-century scroll **(below)** Kirghiz tribesmen from the western frontier present horses, their most treasured possessions, to the emperor Ch'ien-lung.

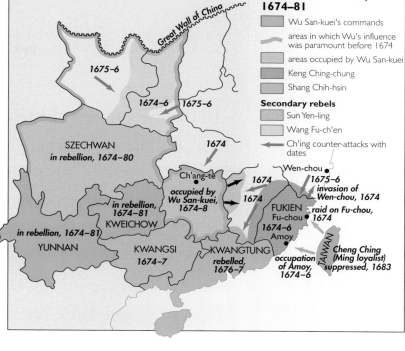

2 The rebellion of the Three Feudatories, 1674–81

- Wu San-kuei's commands
- areas in which Wu's influence was paramount before 1674
- areas occupied by Wu San-kuei
- Keng Ching-chung
- Shang Chih-hsin

Secondary rebels
- Sun Yen-ling
- Wang Fu-ch'en
- Ch'ing counter-attacks with dates

In June 1793, an embassy from Britain arrived off Canton. It lacked nothing which might emphasize its prestige. Among the gifts to the Chinese court were a letter from George III in a gold box and samples of early British industrialization including a globe that needed more than 12 men to carry it (above). The emissary was dismissively received. Europe may have been catching up but the Chinese empire was still the world's largest and most powerful state.

4 Chinese exports of tea increased by over 50 per cent in the first third of the 19th century. Over the same period, silk exports quadrupled. But by the 1830s opium imports by western powers had outstripped Chinese exports and a drain of silver out of China began (chart right). This had increasingly serious effects on the Chinese economy and further impoverished the state finances.

4 The Chinese economy in the 19th century

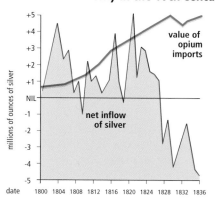

1 Throughout the late 17th and 18th centuries, the Manchus pursued an expansionist policy which left them in control of vast new regions (map below). But these conquests, triggered in part by fear of Russian, French and British expansion, were enormously expensive. Undeterred, Chinese military expeditions went still further: four attacks on Burma in 1766–9, an expedition into Nepal in 1788–92 and a large-scale invasion of Tonking in 1788. All ended in failure. At the same time, a series of peasant revolts began as China struggled with growing economic crisis.

2 Resistance to Ch'ing rule continued for many years after the collapse of the Ming, above all in the southern provinces, which effectively became the personal domains of a series of rebel generals (map above). In 1674, the Ch'ing attempted to reassert control over Kwangtung, provoking a rebellion that lasted until 1681. For a time most of southern and western China was in rebel hands, though by 1677 only the southwest remained. With the death in 1678 of the most prominent rebel, Wu San-kuei, the Ch'ing slowly regained control.

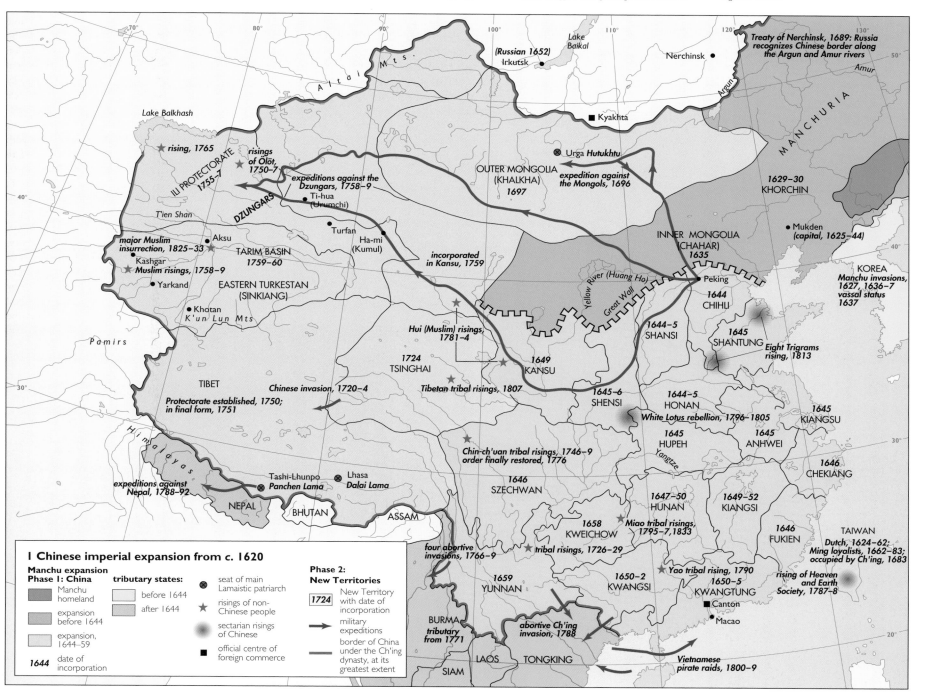

1 Chinese imperial expansion from c. 1620

Manchu expansion
Phase 1: China
- Manchu homeland
- expansion before 1644
- expansion, 1644–59

tributary states:
- before 1644
- after 1644

- ⊗ seat of main Lamaistic patriarch
- ★ risings of non-Chinese people
- sectarian risings of Chinese
- ■ official centre of foreign commerce

1644 date of incorporation

Phase 2: New Territories
- **1724** New Territory with date of incorporation
- → military expeditions
- border of China under the Ch'ing dynasty, at its greatest extent

Korea

The transition from Koryŏ to Chosŏn rule in Korea was essentially smooth, as the same ruling clans retained power, although Chosŏn exchanged Buddhism for Neo-Confucianism. The Chosŏn dynasty survived a Japanese invasion of Korea in 1592, but it was ultimately Japanese imperialism which destroyed it in 1910. The harshness of Japanese rule gave rise to a liberation movement, but ideological divisions within it led to a bitter and damaging war in the 1950s and the division of the peninsula. It was only in the 1960s that economic recovery occurred and then only in the non-communist south.

OUR CRITICAL TASK TODAY LIES ONLY IN SELF-RECONSTRUCTION AND NOT IN THE DESTRUCTION OF OTHERS ... OUR PURPOSE IS TO CORRECT AND REFORM TODAY'S UNNATURAL, ILLOGICAL, AND MALADJUSTED CONDITIONS CREATED BY POWER-HUNGRY AND FAME-SEEKING JAPANESE ... OUR AIM IS TO RESTORE CONDITIONS OF HARMONY WITH JUST PRINCIPLES ... BEHOLD A NEW WORLD UNFOLDS BEFORE OUR EYES. THE AGE OF FORCE IS GONE AND THE AGE OF REASON AND RIGHTEOUSNESS HAS ARRIVED.

1 March 1919: Declaration of Independence

THE CLANS of the Koryŏ era (918–1392) maintained power in the transition to the Chosŏn dynasty (1392–1910), but the new dynasty broke with the past by rejecting other-worldly Buddhism and embracing Sung Neo-Confucianism as the new orthodoxy. The new dynasty brought in a "golden age" of governance. King Sejong (1418–50) commissioned agricultural and medical manuals for general welfare, expanded the world's oldest use of moveable metal type and, in 1446, promulgated a new script that he had a personal hand in producing.

Chosŏn Korea was a model Confucian state. Dress was Ming; law was Ming; government organization and recruitment were Ming; and Korea established its own international order by accepting tribute from Manchurian tribes and Japanese, while the Ming took tribute from Korea. Social ideals derived from *The Family Rites of Zhu-xi* (Chu Hsi): reject Buddhism; practise ancestor rites; establish primogeniture; and enhance clan cohesion. Everyday life was metaphysical, and philosophy became politicized. Chosŏn was not plagued by powerful eunuchs, but court factionalism emerged to produce political gridlock.

In 1590, the Japanese threatened to invade China through Korea. Court opinion split along factional lines and nothing was done. The Japanese came in

1592, and did not withdraw until 1598. East Asia fell into war, with Japanese fighting Chinese in Korea using European arquebuses. Even a Portuguese priest accompanied Christian samurai to Korea. Korea was devastated. Japanese atrocities and pillage left lasting scars, and the war confirmed Korea as the geopolitical pivot of East Asia.

Korea again prospered by the late 1600s, developing balanced agricultural production, cash crops and trade. Because ideology preferred subsistence agriculture, urban centres never developed the commercial focus that they did in China or Japan. Aside from occasional disturbances, peace reigned, and Chinese and Japanese relations were cordial.

From 1800, a succession of boy kings resulted in weak leadership and strong in-laws. Corruption

1 Japanese order of battle for 1592 listed nearly 160,000 troops (**map left**). Admiral Yi Sunsin interdicted shipping, leaving supply vulnerable to guerrillas. In 1593, Ming and Korean troops pushed the Japanese southwards from Pyŏngyang and Seoul. After years of diplomacy, the Japanese launched a second campaign in 1597, but all efforts collapsed after Hideyoshi's death in 1598. Korean noses were taken as trophies; Koreans were sold as slaves (even to Europeans); and the population was decimated.

Resistance to Japanese imperialism reached a watershed in March 1919 when a Declaration of Independence was promulgated. The statement triggered the March First Movement (**below**), a series of nationwide demonstrations (a new experience for most Koreans). More than two million Koreans participated in 1500 gatherings. Resistance was nationalistic, even when it appeared as communism. In Shanghai, liberals established a provisional government and engaged in diplomacy, propaganda, even terrorism. In Manchuria, armed guerrillas enlisted a young Kim II Sung, later to become leader of North Korea.

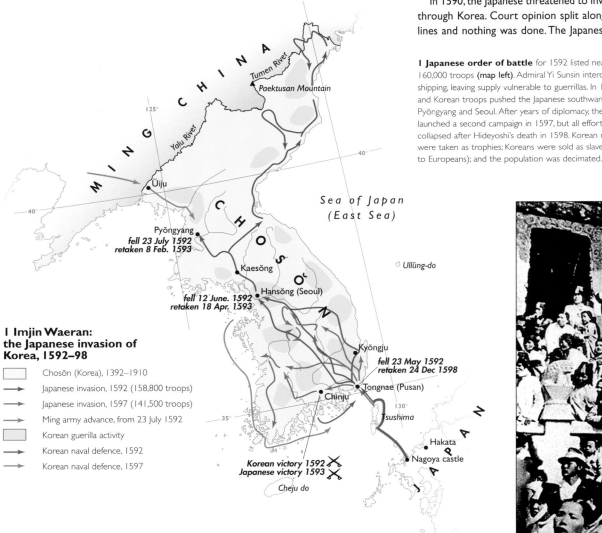

1 Imjin Waeran: the Japanese invasion of Korea, 1592–98

- Chosŏn (Korea), 1392–1910
- → Japanese invasion, 1592 (158,800 troops)
- → Japanese invasion, 1597 (141,500 troops)
- → Ming army advance, from 23 July 1592
- Korean guerilla activity
- → Korean naval defence, 1592
- → Korean naval defence, 1597

Tumen River
Paektusan Mountain
Yalu River

Ŭiju

Pyŏngyang
fell 23 July 1592 retaken 8 Feb. 1593

Kaesŏng

Hansŏng (Seoul)
fell 12 June. 1592 retaken 18 Apr. 1593

Sea of Japan (East Sea)

○ Ullŭng-do

Kyŏngju

fell 23 May 1592 retaken 24 Dec 1598

Chinju

Tongnae (Pusan)

Tsushima

✕ Korean victory 1592
✕ Japanese victory 1593

Hakata

Nagoya castle

Cheju do

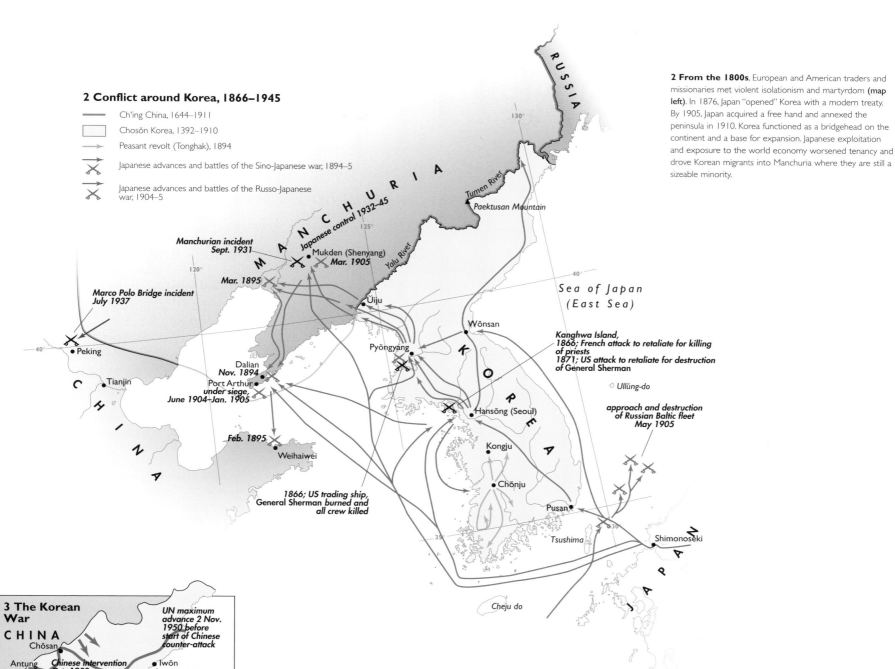

2 Conflict around Korea, 1866–1945

- Ch'ing China, 1644–1911
- Chosŏn Korea, 1392–1910
- Peasant revolt (Tonghak), 1894
- Japanese advances and battles of the Sino-Japanese war, 1894–5
- Japanese advances and battles of the Russo-Japanese war, 1904–5

RUSSIA

MANCHURIA

Japanese control 1932–45

Tumen River

Paektusan Mountain

Manchurian incident Sept. 1931

Mukden (Shenyang) Mar. 1905

Yalu River

Marco Polo Bridge incident July 1937

Mar. 1895

Ŭiju

Sea of Japan (East Sea)

Wŏnsan

Peking

Tianjin

CHINA

Dalian Nov. 1894

Port Arthur under siege, June 1904–Jan. 1905

Pyŏngyang

KOREA

Kanghwa Island, 1866; French attack to retaliate for killing of priests 1871; US attack to retaliate for destruction of General Sherman

Ullŭng-do

approach and destruction of Russian Baltic fleet May 1905

Feb. 1895

Weihaiwei

Hansŏng (Seoul)

Kongju

Chŏnju

1866; US trading ship, General Sherman burned and all crew killed

Pusan

Tsushima

Cheju do

Shimonoseki

JAPAN

2 From the 1800s, European and American traders and missionaries met violent isolationism and martyrdom (map left). In 1876, Japan "opened" Korea with a modern treaty. By 1905, Japan acquired a free hand and annexed the peninsula in 1910. Korea functioned as a bridgehead on the continent and a base for expansion. Japanese exploitation and exposure to the world economy worsened tenancy and drove Korean migrants into Manchuria where they are still a sizeable minority.

3 The Korean War

CHINA

Chŏsan

UN maximum advance 2 Nov. 1950 before start of Chinese counter-attack

Antung

Chinese intervention Oct. 1950

Iwŏn

Unsan

Hungnam

US airborne landings 20 Oct. 1950

NORTH KOREA

Wŏnsan

landing of US 7 Division, 26 Oct. 1950

Pyŏngyang

armistice line 27 July 1953

Panmunjŏm

38th Parallel

Seoul

Inch'ŏn

Chinese and North Korean maximum advance 25 Jan. 1951

landing of US X Corps 15 Sep. 1950

Wŏnju

SOUTH KOREA

Taejŏn

North Korean maximum advance 15 July 1950

Pohang

Taegu

Pusan

Mokp'o

3 The Korean War lasted three years (map left). Estimates put the dead at two million DPRK civilians and 500,000 soldiers; two million ROK civilians and 500,000 soldiers; one to three million Chinese soldiers, including Mao Tse-tung's own son; 54,246 US soldiers; and 3,194 others (including 686 British soldiers). Koreans saw a civil war that became the first international war of the nuclear age, with carpet bombing, atrocities north and south and threats to use nuclear weapons.

The alphabet (today called *hangŭl*) contains cosmic symbols for heaven (circles), earth (horizontal lines), and people (vertical lines) and was an epochal achievement of linguistic science (right). Not only does the script visually represent the shape of the mouth in pronunciation, but it isolates vowels and breaks down human speech into such basic elements that any sound can be represented.

expanded and government became impotent from the 1860s. Systemic decline and climatic disturbance produced vulnerability to Japanese imperialism, which used gunboat diplomacy to obtain an unequal treaty in 1876. In 1882, Korea signed its first treaty with a Western power (USA), opening the country to Christianity and further trade. Economic dislocation and a new religion produced a peasant revolt in 1894. Japanese and Chinese troops intervened and stayed to fight each other in Korea for the first time since 1592. With victory over China, Japan then turned to eliminate a Russian threat and was victorious in the Russo-Japanese War (1904–5). Japan annexed Korea in 1910.

Harsh policies established a compliant agricultural colony and a peaceful independence movement in 1919 was brutally suppressed. Japan industrialized during World War I and relied on Korean rice for Japanese labourers. After 1920, Japanese capital launched Korean industrialization but used it to meet military needs as Japan expanded into Manchuria (1931) and then into China (1937). As the China War

expanded, extreme assimilation policies were imposed on Korea. Names were Japanized, men were abducted as labourers and women abducted as sex slaves.

Korea became the forward base for the China theatre but was never attacked. In 1945, US and Soviet troops divided the country at the 38th parallel and, by October 1948, a communist north, under Kim Il Sung, and a non-communist south (Republic of Korea) had appeared. With Russian and Chinese support, Kim Il Sung attacked southwards in 1950 hoping to reunify Korea. The UN fielded an international (mostly American) force to repel the invasion. As UN forces approached the Yalu River Chinese armies intervened, just as the Ming empire had driven Japanese invaders south in 1593. Seoul exchanged hands four times. Battle lines stabilized near the 38th

parallel, where the truce line runs today. Infrastructure was reduced to rubble. Millions died, and barbed wire still divides the peninsula. Post-war recovery was not apparent until the 1960s, when socialist planning in the north produced surplus, and military dictatorship in the south began an industrialization programme that took the Republic of Korea from US$85 per capita in 1962 to US$20,000 per capita in 2002.

Japan under the shogunate

By 1600, the Tokugawa *shoguns* had pacified Japan. They tamed the feudal barons, controlled Buddhist institutions, disarmed the peasantry, harnessed imperial authority and monopolized diplomacy. Not until 1868 did the Tokugawa fall, powerless in the face of economic crisis, the return of Western powers and new enthusiasm for imperial rule.

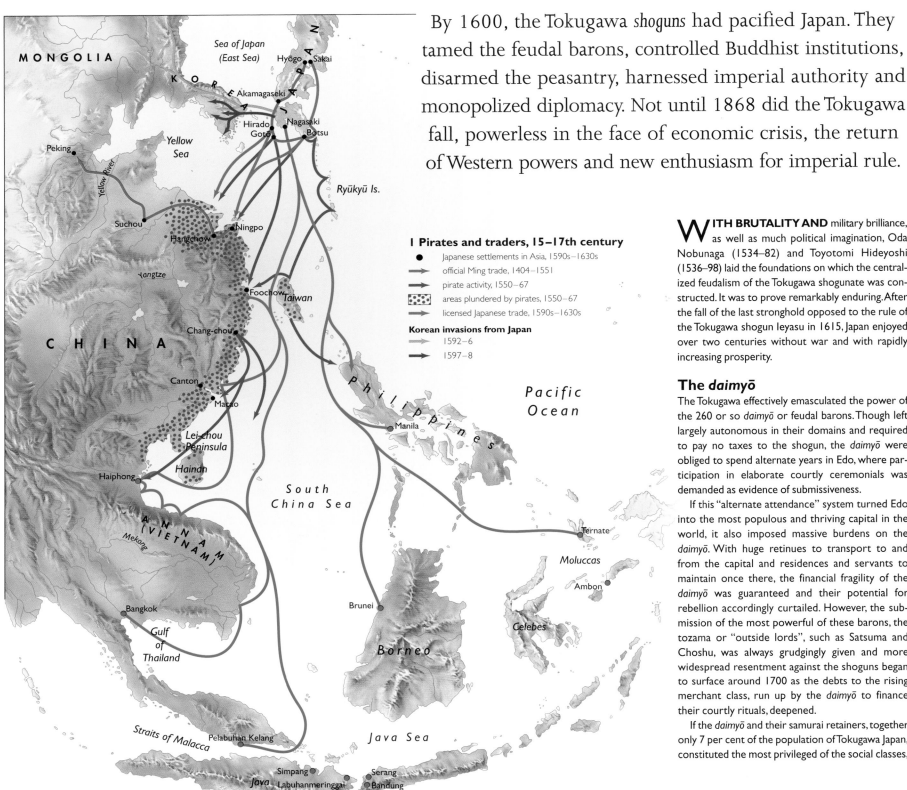

1 Pirates and traders, 15–17th century
- ● Japanese settlements in Asia, 1590s–1630s
- → official Ming trade, 1404–1551
- → pirate activity, 1550–67
- ▨ areas plundered by pirates, 1550–67
- → licensed Japanese trade, 1590s–1630s

Korean invasions from Japan
- → 1592–6
- → 1597–8

WITH BRUTALITY AND military brilliance, as well as much political imagination, Oda Nobunaga (1534–82) and Toyotomi Hideyoshi (1536–98) laid the foundations on which the central-ized feudalism of the Tokugawa shogunate was con-structed. It was to prove remarkably enduring. After the fall of the last stronghold opposed to the rule of the Tokugawa shogun Ieyasu in 1615, Japan enjoyed over two centuries without war and with rapidly increasing prosperity.

The *daimyō*

The Tokugawa effectively emasculated the power of the 260 or so *daimyō* or feudal barons. Though left largely autonomous in their domains and required to pay no taxes to the shogun, the *daimyō* were obliged to spend alternate years in Edo, where par-ticipation in elaborate courtly ceremonials was demanded as evidence of submissiveness.

If this "alternate attendance" system turned Edo into the most populous and thriving capital in the world, it also imposed massive burdens on the *daimyō*. With huge retinues to transport to and from the capital and residences and servants to maintain once there, the financial fragility of the *daimyō* was guaranteed and their potential for rebellion accordingly curtailed. However, the sub-mission of the most powerful of these barons, the tozama or "outside lords", such as Satsuma and Choshu, was always grudgingly given and more widespread resentment against the shoguns began to surface around 1700 as the debts to the rising merchant class, run up by the *daimyō* to finance their courtly rituals, deepened.

If the *daimyō* and their samurai retainers, together only 7 per cent of the population of Tokugawa Japan, constituted the most privileged of the social classes,

IT WAS THE WISH OF TOKUGAWA IEYASU, VENERATED NOW AS THE DEITY WHO SHINES OVER THE EAST, THAT RURAL PEASANTS BE TAXED NOT SO HEAVILY THAT THEY DIE, NOR YET SO LIGHTLY THAT THEY LIVE.

Takano Jodo, 1796

OUR DIVINE REALM IS THE HEAD AND SHOULDERS OF THE GLOBE AND CONTROLS ALL NATIONS. RECENTLY THE FOUL BARBARIANS FROM THE WEST, IGNORANT OF THEIR POSITION AT THE LOWER EXTREMITIES, HAVE BEEN TRAMPLING OTHER NATIONS UNDERFOOT. WHAT MANNER OF IMPUDENCE IS THIS?

Aizawa Seishisai, 1825

1 Japanese pirates responded to Ming China's banning of trade in 1550 by plundering the Chinese coast (**map above**). In 1567, the ban was lifted for all but the Japanese, allowing the Portuguese to take over as middlemen between China and Japan. Later, under Hideyoshi and Ieyasu, Japanese contacts with the region increased markedly. By 1600, 70,000 Japanese were engaged in trade in east Asia and 10,000 lived outside Japan.

3 The extent of Japan's isolation from the wider world under the Tokugawa is much exaggerated (**map right**). While Japan shrank from contact with European powers from the 1630s, it sought to recreate itself as the centre of a new Asian order. Nonetheless, it was mid-19th century American demands that Japan open itself to trade with the West that brought down the Tokugawa.

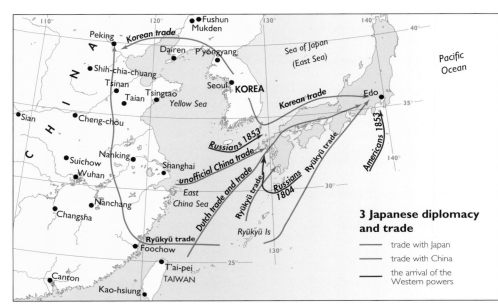

3 Japanese diplomacy and trade
- —— trade with Japan
- —— trade with China
- —— the arrival of the Western powers

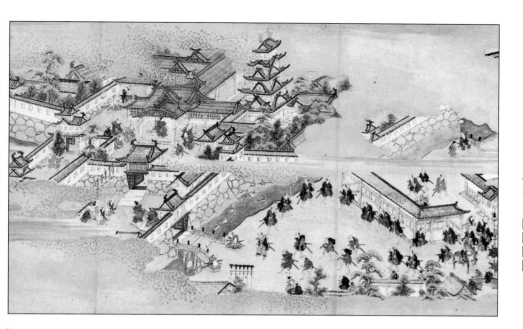

Daimyō and their retinues enter Edo castle (above) to participate in one of the many courtly ceremonials. Edo, now Tokyo, was originally a fishing village, near which a castle was built in 1456 by the daimyō Ota Sukenaga. It rapidly became a powerful centre and in 1590 Tokugawa Ieyasu selected Edo for his residence, building an elaborate castle which remained the seat of the shogunate for 260 years, although it became the capital only in the 19th century.

2 Political consolidation and economic development
five highways
extension to five highways
principal by-ways
MITO domains
major Tozama domains
Tokugawa-related households
land directly controlled by Tokugawa
other important feudal domains
MATSUMAE
MORIOKA
AKITA
SENDAI
Sea of Japan (East Sea)
Ōshū-kaidō
Nikkō
Nikkō-kaidō
MITO
KAGA
Honshū
Nakasendō
Kōshū-kaidō
Edo
Tōkaidō
Sekigahara
Kyoto
Osaka
Sakai
OWARI
KII
CHŌSHŪ
Shikoku
TOSA
HIZEN
Kyūshū
Nagasaki
SATSUMA
Pacific Ocean

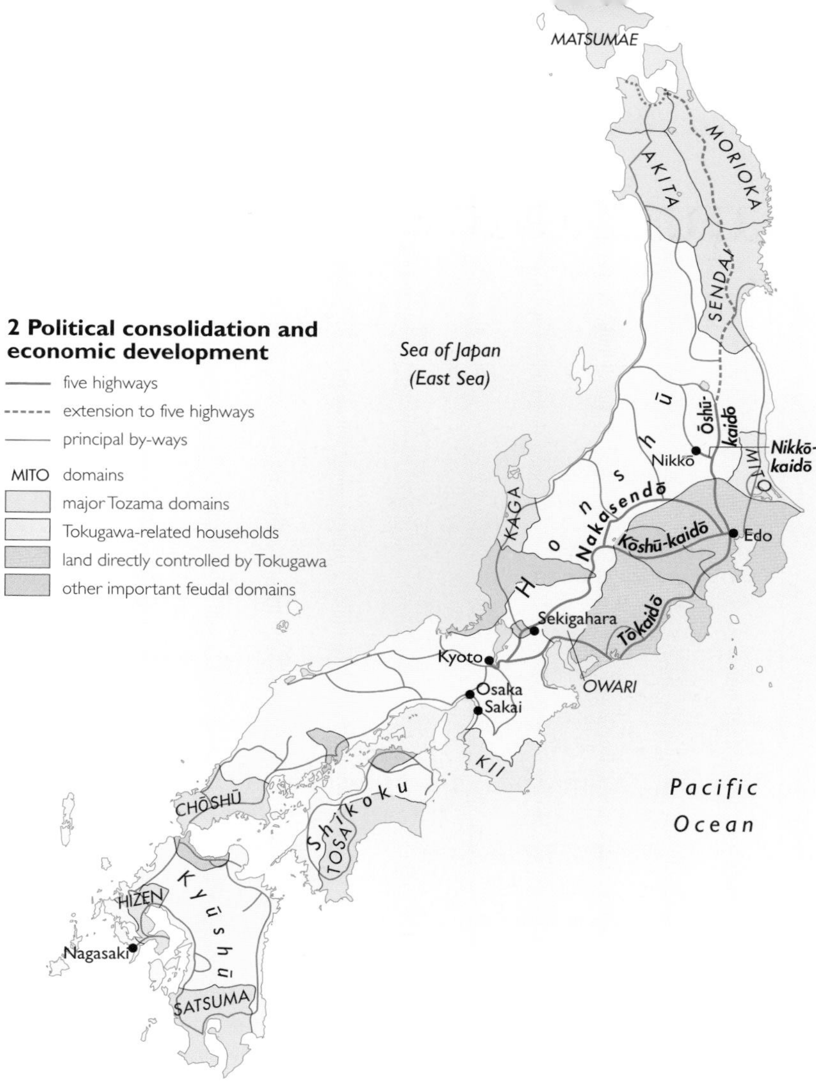

2 Tokugawa Ieyasu and his successors reinforced their rule by using trusted daimyō, or barons, as buffers around the capital, Edo **(map right)**. All daimyō were subject to the "alternate attendance" system, compulsory attendance at court every other year. To facilitate their movements to and from the court five major highways were built. The Tokugawa controlled economic centres, mines and ports; promoted a cult of Ieyasu, centred at Nikko; and effectively sidelined the emperor, confining him to his palace at Kyoto. However despotic, Tokugawa Japan thrived and enjoyed vigorous economic growth.

1467 Ōnin Wars: civil unrest throughout Japan

1543 Portuguese traders arrive

1603 Tokugawa Ieyasu first Tokugawa shogun

1640s Christian missionaries and European traders (except Dutch) expelled

1700 Osaka, Kyoto and Edo flourish as merchant centres

1833–9 Nationwide famine and unrest

1853 Commodore Perry arrives; proposes commercial arrangements between Japan and US

1858 Trade treaties signed with US and Britain

1868 Fall of Tokugawa; Meiji restoration

a comparatively low status was accorded to merchants. This was because Confucianism, used by the Tokugawa as an ideological buttress, despised money-making. Paradoxically, Japanese merchants, based in cities such as Osaka, Kyoto and Edo, were left alone to develop their commercial contacts and a number, such as the Sumitomo family, acquired fabulous wealth. Though excluded from all forms of government, they left an increasingly important mark on the development of Japan. From around 1700, a brilliant and sophisticated alternative culture developed characterized by kabuki drama in Osaka in the 18th century and wood-block prints in Edo in the 18th and 19th centuries.

The bulk of the population, perhaps 80 per cent, consisted of the peasantry. The tax burden they owed their *daimyō* could be crippling, however, especially at times of poor harvests. Rural and urban uprisings in the 1730s, 1780s, 1830s and 1860s were directed at the *daimyō* and the merchant class alike and exposed the contradictions inherent in the Tokugawa system.

Tokugawa control

Aware of the emperors pote ntial as a rival focus of authority, the Tokugawa isolated and carefully controlled the imperial court. The emperor himself, silent and symbolic, served to bestow legitimacy on Tokugawa rule. It was not until the 1850s, when the arrival of Westerners demanding trade with Japan effectively paralysed the Tokugawa, that the imperial court, backed by unrest at the inability of the Tokugawa to stand up to the West, reasserted itself.

But long before this undermining of their authority, the Tokugawa had established complete control over the country, monopolizing foreign trade and diplomacy and expelling most European merchants and missionaries. Yet however self-sufficient and hierarchical, Japan did not withdraw entirely from contact with the wider world. Formal diplomatic and trade relations were maintained only with Korea, but Japan traded with the Chinese and Dutch.

Nonetheless, by the end of the 18th century financial crisis and rural unrest prompted attempts at reform by the Tokugawa. All ended in failure. In 1854 and 1855, the Americans, British, Dutch and Russians extracted "friendship" treaties from the Tokugawa. These aggressive foreign intrusions coupled with the weak Japanese response provoked crisis. For once unsure of itself, the Tokugawa solicited advice from the *daimyō* and authorization from the imperial court, thus drawing both groups on to the political stage. In 1858, the Tokugawa signed trade treaties, with the Americans, then with the British, but without first seeking imperial approval. A wave of radicalism swept Japan which led to the fall of the Tokugawa.

4 Togukawa legitimacy was fatally undermined by the intrusion of the Western powers in the 1850s **(map below)**. The diplomatic crisis prompted outbursts of anti-foreign, pro-imperial violence, which was soon turned on the Tokugawa. When foreign powers flexed their muscles, Tokugawa officials realized that the West could not be repulsed, only accommodated. The sense of social chaos was compounded by widespread millenarian activity in 1867.

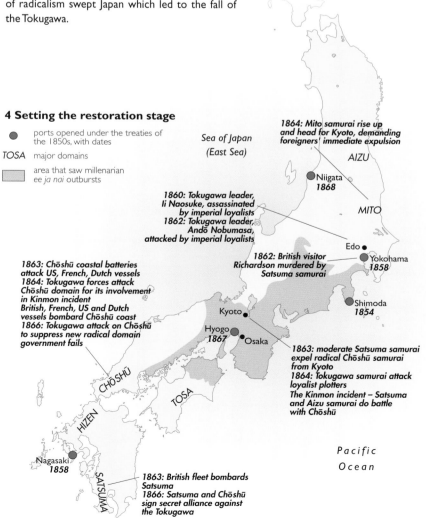

4 Setting the restoration stage
ports opened under the treaties of the 1850s, with dates
TOSA major domains
area that saw millenarian ee ja nai outbursts
Sea of Japan (East Sea)
1864: Mito samurai rise up and head for Kyoto, demanding foreigners' immediate expulsion
AIZU
Niigata 1868
MITO
1860: Tokugawa leader, Ii Naosuke, assassinated by imperial loyalists
1862: Tokugawa leader, Andō Nobumasa, attacked by imperial loyalists
Edo
Yokohama 1858
1862: British visitor Richardson murdered by Satsuma samurai
1863: Chōshū coastal batteries attack US, French, Dutch vessels
1864: Tokugawa forces attack Chōshū domain for its involvement in Kinmon incident
British, French, US and Dutch vessels bombard Chōshū coast
1866: Tokugawa attack on Chōshū to suppress new radical domain government fails
Shimoda 1854
Kyoto
Hyogo 1867
Osaka
1863: moderate Satsuma samurai expel radical Chōshū samurai from Kyoto
1864: Tokugawa samurai attack loyalist plotters
The Kinmon incident – Satsuma and Aizu samurai do battle with Chōshū
CHŌSHŪ
TOSA
HIZEN
Nagasaki 1858
SATSUMA
1863: British fleet bombards Satsuma
1866: Satsuma and Chōshū sign secret alliance against the Tokugawa
Pacific Ocean

Southeast Asia and the European powers

At the beginning of the 16th century the first Europeans, lured by the lucrative spice trade, arrived in southeast Asia. Though the Spanish and Portuguese established the first European settlements, in the longer run the Dutch and the British, exploiting divisions among the southeast Asians themselves, were the major beneficiaries.

1511 Portuguese take control of Malacca

1557 Portuguese become established in Macao (China)

1619 Batavia founded by Dutch; beginnings of Dutch colonial empire in the East Indies

1641 Dutch capture Malacca from the Portuguese

1786 Penang acquired by English East India Company

1819 Singapore founded by Britain as free trade port

1824 Treaty of London formalizes British control of Malaya and Dutch control of East Indies

YOUR HONOURS SHOULD KNOW BY EXPERIENCE THAT TRADE IN ASIA MUST BE DRIVEN AND MAINTAINED UNDER THE PROTECTION AND FAVOUR OF YOUR HONOURS' OWN WEAPONS, AND THAT THE WEAPONS MUST BE PAID FOR BY THE PROFITS FROM THE TRADE; SO THAT WE CANNOT CARRY ON TRADE WITHOUT WAR NOR WAR WITHOUT TRADE.

Jan Pietersz Coen, 1614, founder of Batavia

WHEN EUROPEAN TRADERS and adventurers broke through into the Indian Ocean at the close of the 15th century, the great prize drawing them forward was the spices of southeast Asia. Here was untold wealth to be tapped. But here also, at one of the world's main crossroads, where cultural influences from China and India intermingled, they found themselves in a region of great complexity – politically fragmented and divided between three religions (Buddhism, Hinduism and Islam) and many different types of state.

On the mainland, rival peoples and dynasties competed for hegemony. In the Malayan archipelago, the empires of Srivijaya and Majapahit were little more than memories (see p. 148), having split into many small states with little cohesion between them. This was the situation when Europeans first arrived in the region in the person of Alfonso de Albuquerque who in 1511 conquered the great international emporium of Malacca for the king of Portugal.

The Portuguese presence changed little at first. Albuquerque and his successors were there to dominate the spice trade and to this end built a chain of fortified trading stations linked by naval power. Provided this was accepted, they had no wish to interfere with the native potentates. Far more important, after the arrival on the scene of the Dutch and the English, was the challenge to the Portuguese trading monopoly presented by their European rivals. For most of the 17th century, this rivalry was the dominant factor.

The Dutch and English conquests

The Dutch in particular began a systematic conquest of the Portuguese settlements, capturing Malacca in 1641, before turning against the British. But in doing so, they were drawn into local politics. After establishing a base at Batavia in 1619, they interfered in succession disputes among the neighbouring sultans, to ensure their own position, and in this way gradually extended control over Java, expelling the British from Bantam in 1682. They had already driven them out of the Spice Islands at the "Massacre of Amboina" (1623) and by the seizure of Macassar (1667), as a result forcing the English East India Company to turn instead to the China trade. With this in view, the British acquired Penang on the west coast of Malaya in 1786, the first step in a process which was ultimately to make them masters of the Malay peninsula.

2 European penetration of the Spice Islands was driven by the desire to capture and control the lucrative trade in spices originating in the East Indies (map left). The Portuguese were first on the scene, in 1511. To the east, an early and unsuccessful Spanish expedition to Tidore was followed by their capture of Manila in 1571. By the early 17th century, Dutch and British penetration sparked a continuing struggle between the European powers for control of the region.

3 Dutch territorial expansion in Java began through Sultan Agung of Mataram's attempts to capture Batavia (map below). After his death in 1646 the Dutch East India Company, by intervening in succession disputes, gradually became the strongest political force in the island, with the ruling houses coming under its control and paying their debts by cessions of territory. The maintenance of its trade monopoly played a vital part in this expansion.

But this was still exceptional. Though European activities encroached on the outlying islands they had little impact on the mainland monarchies, which had no direct interest in European trade and were mainly concerned with extending their power at the expense of that of their neighbours. At the same time (see map 1) all the main centres were under pressure from the hill peoples of the interior, always waiting to assert their independence. But the main lines of development include the advance of Annam (Vietnam) at the expense of Cambodia, the rise of a new Burmese empire under Alaungpaya (1735–60) and successful Siamese resistance to Burmese encroachment, in spite of Burmese conquest in 1767.

These events occured for the most part without European involvement even if, during the struggle for empire between France and England in the 18th century (see p. 216), some states were implicated. Already under Louis XIV, France had intervened in Siam against the Dutch. But such was the popular hostility engendered by French meddling in Siam that the dynasty they supported was overthrown and the French themselves were expelled. During the Anglo-French war in India after 1746, France supported the Mon rebellion in Burma, provoking the English East India Company to seize in reply the island of Negrais at the mouth of the Bassein river. Later, when the Burmese, foiled in their attempt to capture Siam, switched their efforts to the north, the British, fearing for the security of Bengal, again intervened. The result was the first Anglo-Burmese War (1824–6) and the British annexation of Assam, Arakan and Tenasserim (see p. 258).

Anglo-Dutch agreement

In Malaya there was similar encroachment on the native states when the British, rulers of Penang since 1786, established Singapore in 1819 as a free trade port after its acquisition by Sir Stamford Raffles, the British Lieutenant-Governor of Benkulen in Sumatra. This led to a conflict of interest with Holland which was only settled by the Anglo-Dutch Treaty of London of 1824, under which the British withdrew from Sumatra in return for Dutch withdrawal from Malacca (see map 4).

But if by the early years of the 19th century the future Dutch and British colonial empires in southeast Asia were taking shape, the control directly exercised by the European powers was still loose, more concerned with trade than with imperial rule. The Portuguese and Dutch had dominated the spice and pepper trades, but they were largely content to receive surpluses produced by local peasants; it was not until 1830 that the Dutch introduced the "Culture System" in which the Javanese were forced to devote one-fifth of their lands to export crops. Only with the impact of the industrial revolution in Europe, and the rapidly expanding market for raw materials and the increased exports of finished goods it created, were the lives and fortunes of the peoples of the region seriously affected by the European presence.

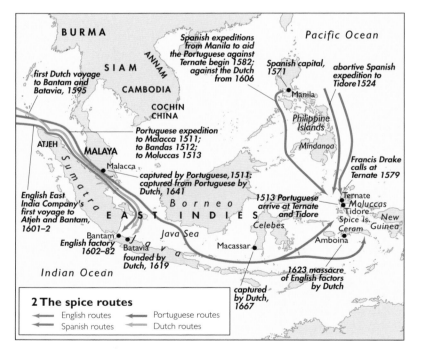

2 The spice routes

← English routes ← Portuguese routes
← Spanish routes ← Dutch routes

3 Dutch expansion in Java

1619 – date of Dutch control

stages of Dutch expansion

under effective Dutch rule from 1830

1 The Europeans in southeast Asia

European possessions, 1826

- British
- Spanish
- Dutch
- Portuguese

trade routes:

- developed by Dutch and English East India Companies
- developed by Arab and Gujerati traders
- developed by the Dutch in the 17th century
- used by English shipping from 1786
- used by the "Manila Galleon"
- local trade routes
- ⊙ principal trading centre

Vietnamese expansion

- Vietnamese border in 1500
- expansion to 1611
- acquisitions from Cambodia in early 18th century
- Vietnamese expansion in 19th century
- kingdom of Luang Prabang, 1707
- area which broke away under Vientiane in 1707
- major Burmese conquests
- Siamese conquests

1 European contact with southeast Asia (map above), though driven initially by demand in Europe for spices, paved the way for the foundation of substantial European empires across the region. The Spanish had ruled the Philippines since the 16th century and, though other European contacts had little impact on mainland societies, by the early 19th century the British had put in place the basis of their subsequent colonial rule in Malaya, while Dutch control of the East Indies was also firmly established.

4 The Malay states in 1826

- Malay states tributary to Siam in 1826
- British possessions

4 Under the Treaty of London of 1824 the Dutch were to withdraw from the Malay peninsula (**map left**). The British settlements there – Penang, Singapore and Malacca – were bound by the doctrine of non-intervention laid down in Pitt's India Act. The immediate danger to the independence of the Malay states in 1826 lay in Siamese expansionism; the Burney Treaty in that year halted Siam's pressure upon them, though only after two incidents in which the Penang government safeguarded Perak's independence.

Javanese culture provided a strong strand of continuity even under Dutch rule. Indeed the new rulers were incorporated into traditional art forms. This 19th-century batik (**right**) depicts a street scene in Jogjakarta – a marriage procession with musicians, street vendors and Dutchmen driven in carriages.

The European economy: agriculture and society

European agriculture as a whole improved only slowly between 1500 and 1800 and with marked regional contrasts. Southern and eastern Europe, the latter severely handicapped by feudalism, saw slow growth. But in northern Europe there were dramatic increases in agricultural productivity, above all in Britain and the Low Countries

FROM THE EARLY 16TH CENTURY Britain and the Low Countries enjoyed an agricultural revolution which by 1800 had produced a highly efficient, commercialized farming system. But elsewhere in Europe agricultural techniques and levels of productivity had hardly changed since Roman times and most peasants produced only about 20 per cent more a year than they needed to feed their families and their livestock and to provide the next year's seed. Consequently, in many countries about 80 per cent of the people worked on the land. In Britain and the Low Countries, however, the proportion fell rapidly during the late 18th century as improved agriculture met the food needs of the growing urban population.

The new crops

Except in Britain and the Netherlands, most improvements came from the introduction of new, more productive crops, mainly from America. Thus the potato became a basic staple in western Europe, starting in Spain and Italy. In Ireland it allowed such a massive increase in population (from 2.5 to 8 million) that disaster struck when the crop failed in 1846. American maize, like the potato, gave a far higher yield than the established cereals – barley, millet and sorghum – and was widely adopted in southern Europe. Buckwheat, useful on poor soils, entered northern Europe from Russia while in the Mediterranean sugarcane, rice and citrus fruits had arrived from Asia before 1500. Sugar production declined after 1550, however, in the face of competition from Madeira, the Canaries and, after 1600, the West Indies and Brazil.

These slow crop changes contrasted strongly with the rapidly developing northwest. The Dutch began the process by pouring capital into reclaiming land from the sea. Naturally wishing to avoid having to leave land fallow every third year (necessary under the traditional system), they discovered that fertility could be maintained by simple crop rotation involving the alternation of arable with artificial grasses and industrial crops such as rapeseed, flax and dyestuffs. Turnips, on which sheep could be grazed in winter to produce manure as well as mutton and wool, were especially important, as were peas, beans and clovers. English farmers copied and developed these innovations. Irrigation, drainage schemes and woodland clearance increased the productive area, while land enclosure and soil treatments encouraged improved husbandry. By the 1740s, grain exports accounted for 10 per cent of England's export earnings, and the old fear of starvation had been banished.

Such techniques gradually spread as the growth of towns encouraged more specialization in food production. Holland concentrated on dairy products and was exporting 90 per cent of her cheese by 1700. The Danes were sending 80,000 head of cattle a year to Germany, and the Dutch, German and Italian cloth industries were sustained by massive imports of Spanish wool. The exchange of northern Europe's cereals and timber for the fruits, wines and oils of the Mediterranean grew apace.

2 The introduction of the potato to Europe

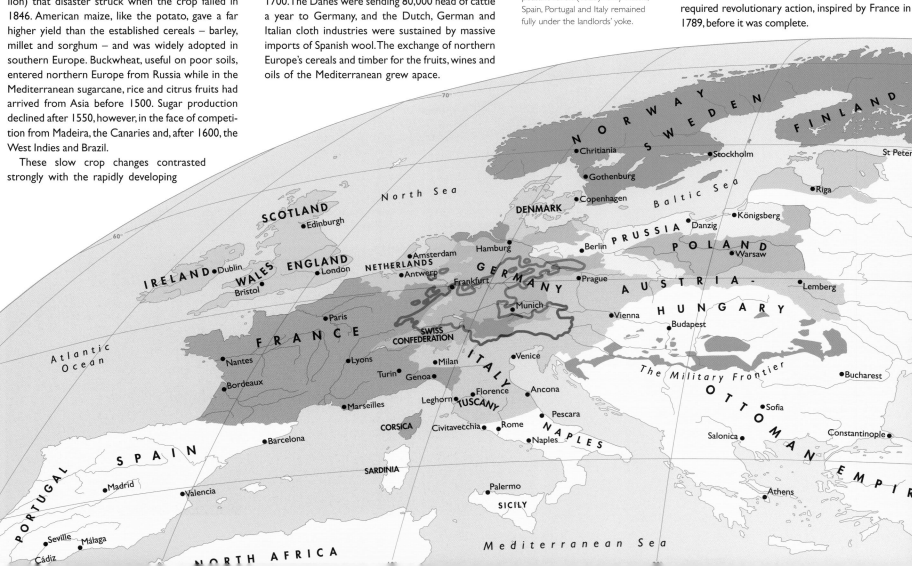

2 Yielding four times as much carbohydrate per hectare as wheat, the potato, a South American import, spread rapidly after its arrival in 1565 – first in gardens, after 1700 as a key field crop (map above).

1 By 1812, the peasants of Britain, Scandinavia and the Netherlands had long been free (map below). Those of Denmark and Austria were encouraged in their efforts by the French revolution, which had revived emancipation movements in Poland and Germany, the latter scene of the most famous peasant revolt (1525). Only Russia, Spain, Portugal and Italy remained fully under the landlords' yoke.

Peasants and feudalism

All improvements in productivity depended on breaking the old feudal relationships which oppressed the peasants, however, and here there was a sharp east-west cleavage. Before 1500 feudalism had been stronger in the older settled areas of western Europe than in the sparsely peopled lands of eastern Europe and Russia. After 1500 this changed completely: peasants in northwest Europe exchanged the traditional labour services on their lords' land for a money rent (especially in England and the Netherlands) or, in France and farther south, for share-cropping tenancies. They also gradually freed themselves from burdensome personal services and dues, though this required revolutionary action, inspired by France in 1789, before it was complete.

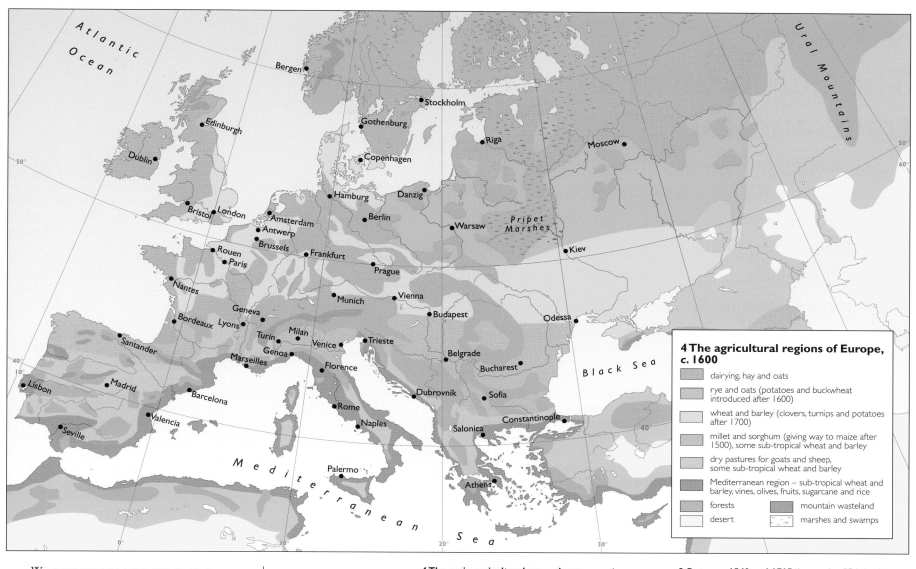

WE RIDE ABROAD A LEAGUE OR TWO INTO THE COUNTRY WHICH THEY CALL GRAVE. [TALKED] WITH A POORE PAISANT'S WIFE. THEIR ORDINARY FOOD RIEBREAD AND WATER. FLESH IS A THING [WHICH] SELDOME SEASONS THEIR POTS, AND, AS SHE SAID, THEY MAKE NO DISTINCTION BETWEEN FLESH AND FAST DAYS; BUT WHEN THEIR MONEY REACHES TO A MORE COSTLY MEALE, THEY BUY THE INWARDS OF SOME BEAST IN THE MARKET AND THEN THEY FEAST THEMSELVES. AND YET THEY SAY IN SAN LONGE AND SEVERALL OTHER PARTS OF FRANCE THE PAISANTS ARE MUCH MORE MISERABLE THAN THESE, FOR THESE THEY COUNT THE FLOURISHING PAISANTS WHICH LIVE IN GRAVE.

John Locke
Travels in France, 1675–9

1525 German peasants revolt

1565 Potato introduced into Europe. Netherlands begins large-scale land reclamation

1594–7 Peasant wars in Austria and Hungary

1649 Serfdom legalized in Russia

1730s Jethro Tull's seed drill invented. Charles Townshend advocates crop rotation

1778 Sardinia frees serfs

1789 The French revolution abolishes feudal privileges in the countryside

1807 Prussia abolishes serfdom

4 The main agricultural areas shown are as they were in 1600 (**map above**). Boundaries are only approximate. Potatoes gradually took over from cereals in many parts of northern and central Europe, while in the south maize replaced millet and sorghum.

In total contrast, feudal power grew and spread in eastern Europe until it approached slavery. Feudal lords increased their power, halting migration to empty lands farther east (as in Russia) and increasing grain-export profits (as in eastern Germany and Poland-Lithuania). Free peasants only survived in newly conquered lands if they performed military service instead of paying rent. The peasants of western Germany occupied a middle position. They had tried to win their freedom in a great revolt in 1525, and briefly controlled most of southern Germany before the rebellion was savagely crushed. Yet the excesses of eastern Europe were averted, and the peasants gradually gained greater freedom by 1800. Their slow emancipation was, however, an important reason why the German industrial revolution came so late.

Improvements in animal husbandry in 18th-century England were remarkable. The average weight of bullocks grew from 168kg (370lb) in 1700 to 381kg (840lb) in 1786, that of sheep from 13kg (28lb) to 45 kg (100lb). *Mr Healey's Sheep* (**below**) graphically illustrates the effects of selective breeding.

3 Between 1540 and 1715 the people of Friesland, Zeeland and Holland wrested 1476 sq. km (364,565 acres) from the sea, and 343 sq. km (84,638 acres) from the edges of the inland lakes (**map below**). Their capital-intensive methods, based on widespread use of windmills and pumps, were adapted with great success in England and, to a lesser extent, in France, Italy and north Germany.

3 Land reclamation in the Netherlands

period of land reclamation
- before 1600
- 1600–1800

FRIESLAND

North Sea

HOLLAND

Zuider Zee

Amsterdam

Rotterdam • Rhine

ZEELAND

Maas

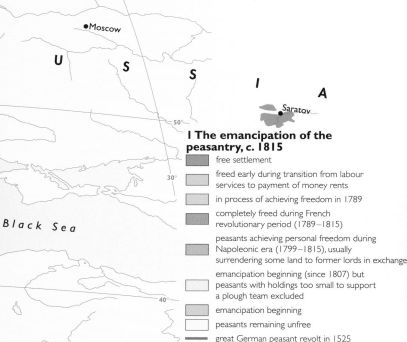

R U S S I A

Saratov

1 The emancipation of the peasantry, c. 1815

- free settlement
- freed early during transition from labour services to payment of money rents
- in process of achieving freedom in 1789
- completely freed during French revolutionary period (1789–1815)
- peasants achieving personal freedom during Napoleonic era (1799–1815), usually surrendering some land to former lords in exchange
- emancipation beginning (since 1807) but peasants with holdings too small to support a plough team excluded
- emancipation beginning
- peasants remaining unfree
- great German peasant revolt in 1525

Black Sea

•Moscow

The European economy: trade and industry

Population growth, expanding industry, the impact of colonial trade and changes to the banking system transformed Europe's economic performance after 1500. At the same time, there was a decisive shift in the economic centre of gravity from southern to northern Europe. The Dutch Republic and, later, Britain emerged as the new economic powerhouses.

EUROPE'S **POPULATION EXPANDED** fast in the 16th century, was retarded by famine, plague and war in the 17th century, but grew rapidly again from the mid-18th century. In 1500 only three cities – Constantinople (by far the largest), Paris and Naples – had more than 200,000 inhabitants. By 1700 this number had doubled, and London, Paris and Constantinople had passed the half-million mark.

The increased complexity of government, an acceleration of trade and finance, a growing taste for conspicuous consumption, and a feeling that survival was better assured in the cities, all helped to hasten this trend. The resulting problems, particularly the need to guarantee reliable urban food supplies, also created new opportunities. Most notably, until the mid-17th century, they generated a massive demand for eastern Europe's wheat and rye, a trade which fed the burgeoning economic strength of Holland, now nearly monopolizing the Baltic carrying trade.

The Netherlands in fact formed the hinge for a gradual but decisive shift in commercial power. In 1500 industry was largely concentrated in the corridor running north–south from Antwerp and Bruges to Florence and Milan. By 1700 this axis had swung through almost 90 degrees. At one end stood Britain and the Dutch Republic, increasingly the most dynamic commercial centres in Europe; eastward the line extended through the metal and woollen districts of the Rhine to the great industrial concentrations of Saxony, Bohemia and Silesia.

Industry, trade and finance

At the same time, however, technology advanced only in patches and much industrial expansion was chiefly achieved by increasing the number of workers while still using the old methods. But even this

helped improve industrial organization, by splitting up production processes, developing production in rural areas free of urban restriction, and drawing on the cheap part-time labour of peasant families. Much industry was controlled by traders who organized a scattered cottage labour force. By the 18th century this had become the typical form of all but local and luxury industry.

More impressive than the erratic spread of industry was the increase in international trade. The maritime powers, with their colonies and ports in Asia and the Americas, imported a fast-growing stream of new products: tea, coffee, sugar, chocolate, tobacco. They were purchased with European manufactures and with the shipping, insurance and merchandising services that built up the wealth of ports such as Bordeaux, London, Amsterdam and Marseilles.

Governments assisted those sectors of economic activity that they favoured. Holland and England waged wars to protect and expand their shipping and trading interests, but did not consistently aid industry. The governments of France and the central European states, by contrast, established new industries and subsidized old ones. Increasingly costly wars, however, had an even more powerful influence. They called for heavy taxation and large borrowings that undermined the precarious stability of Europe's

1545 Discovery of silver mines at Potosí (Peru) and Zacatecas (Mexico)

1559 Tobacco first introduced into Europe

c. 1560 Portuguese begin sugar cultivation in Brazil

1600 English East India Company established

1602 Dutch East India Company founded

1609 Amsterdam Exchange Bank established

1693 Gold discovered in Brazil

1694 Bank of England established

1776 Publication of *The Wealth of Nations*, Adam Smith

Europe was permanently short of silver and gold before the discovery and exploitation by Spain in the 16th century of the New World's more plentiful silver mines. This German silver mine (**right**), painted in 1521, highlights the small-scale and largely rural nature of much pre-industrial European economic activity.

1 Industrial activity in 16th-century Europe was not markedly different from that in the high Middle Ages (**map right**). The traditional commercial and financial centres associated with the great fairs along the rich corridor running south from Flanders to Tuscany still flourished. However, the rise of Seville and Lisbon as centres of the Atlantic trade generated by Spain and Portugal's burgeoning overseas possessions, and of Antwerp as the focus of the North Sea economy, presaged dramatic changes.

1 & 2 Trade and industry in the 16th and 18th centuries

town population		population per sq. km	
⊙	500,000+		40 or more
⊕	200,000+		20 to 40
⊕	100,000+		under 20
○	30,000+		
○	less than 30,000		
●	financial centres	◣	wool
		▶	linen
—	major metallurgical areas	+	cotton
—	major textile areas	◀	silk

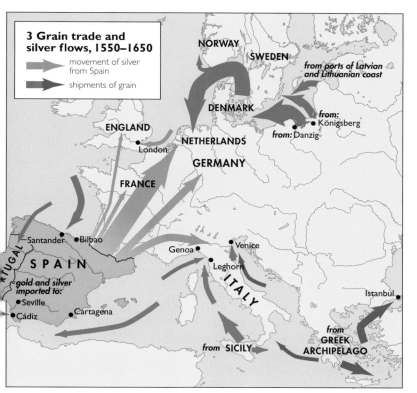

NORWAY
SWEDEN
from ports of Latvian and Lithuanian coast
DENMARK
from: Königsberg
ENGLAND
from: Danzig
London
NETHERLANDS
GERMANY
FRANCE
Santander • Bilbao
Genoa
Venice
SPAIN
Leghorn
ITALY
gold and silver imported to:
• Seville
Cádiz • Cartagena
Istanbul
from SICILY
from GREEK ARCHIPELAGO

4 Russian economic activity, 1600–1815

land growing predominantly rye, flax and hemp
— important 17th-century trade routes
— Russia, 1699

economic activity by:
♦ 1600   ♦ 1725   ♦ 1815

+ linen industry
◆ glass making
◀ silk industry
▬ woollen industry
▾ leather industry

■ salt mining
| copper mining, and smelting
▲ iron mining
▾ iron working
— gold mining

□ paper
✕ soap, tallow and candles industry
○ rope and sailcloth
◆ ship and boat building

White Sea
• Ust-Tsilma
• Berezov
• Archangel
Kholmogory
S W E D E N
• Yarensk
• Shenkursk
• Sol-Vychegodskaya
• Ust-Yug
• Sol-Kamskaya
• Verkhoturye
• Perm
• Tyumen
• Helsingfors
Olonets • Kargopol
• Vologda
R U S S I A N
St. Petersburg
• Reval
• Novgorod
Vyatka
Izhevsk
• Pskov
Yaroslavl
Nizhniy Novgorod
• Ufa
Tver
Kazan
Moscow
E M P I R E
Mozhaysk
Kolomna
Volga
Simbirsk
LITHUANIA
Smolensk
Tula
Murom
• Minsk
Bryansk
Kozlov
Orel • Yelets
Tambov
Saratov
Dnieper
Kursk
Don
Voronezh
• Kiev
Tsaritsyn
P O L A N D
• Kharkov
Dniester
Lugansk
• Azov
KHANATE OF CRIMEA

3 From the mid-16th century, the bullion-bearing galleons from the Indies brought a flood of liquid funds to Spain (map above). But it flowed out as fast as it arrived – to finance Habsburg imperialism and to pay for the Baltic grain for a Mediterranean largely unable to feed itself.

4 Russia was a late developer economically (map above right). By 1600 economic activity, concentrated around Moscow, consisted mainly of the processing of animal and vegetable products. By 1725, the extensive smelting of copper and iron was established in the Urals. By 1815, a third important industrial area, around St Petersburg, had developed.

gradually evolving monetary systems. The wars were ruinous to Spain and damaging to France and many smaller states; only Britain and the Dutch Republic coped successfully thanks to their expanding economies and new credit systems.

Trade and war also generated an unprecedented demand for money. Gold and silver were amply provided from Spanish Mexico and Peru after 1545, supported from the 1690s by Brazilian gold. This bullion was redistributed across Europe by merchants and by Spanish government transactions, much of it financing Europe's trade deficits with the East Indies and the Levant. The money supply was also supple-

mented by the growth of banking. In contrast to the established German and Italian banks, which were heavily engaged in government lending, Dutch and English banks served private interests with giro and foreign-exchange facilities and short-term credits. In the century after its opening in 1609, the Amsterdam Exchange Bank was the undisputed focus of continental trade; Britain could compete only after 1694, when the Bank of England provided a focus for older private banking firms. With low interest rates, free capital movement, secure international payments and an assured savings flow, the foundations of modern finance were firmly laid.

2 Dramatic changes in 18th-century European trade and industry occurred even before the industrial revolution (map right). Italy and Spain lost ground, while England (with major metal-working and mining interests), Holland (building ships for the whole of Europe), France (behind a high protective wall) and Sweden (exploiting her mineral resources), all forged ahead fast. At the same time, the increasing sophistication of her banking mechanisms gave Britain an important and growing advantage.

Atlantic Ocean
St Petersburg
Stockholm
Moscow
Glasgow
Edinburgh
North Sea
Vilna
Dublin
Baltic Sea
Königsberg
Danzig
Birmingham
Norwich
Hamburg
Warsaw
Bristol
Haarlem
Leiden
Amsterdam
Berlin
London
Rotterdam
Ghent
Antwerp
Cologne
Leipzig
Breslau
SILESIA
Lille
Liège
Rhine
Brussels
Frankfurt
SAXONY
Prague
Rouen
Paris
BOHEMIA
Strasbourg
Nantes
Vienna
Budapest
Bordeaux
Lyons
Milan
Verona
Turin
Venice
Bilbao
Bayonne
Toulouse
Genoa
Bologna
Marseilles
Leghorn
Florence
Black Sea
Madrid
Barcelona
Sofia
Adrianople
Rome
Istanbul
Lisbon
Valencia
Naples
Salonica
Córdoba
Seville
Granada
Cádiz • Málaga
Palermo
Messina
Mediterranean

Reformation and Catholic Reformation

The shattering of the unity of Latin Christendom altered the course of European history. The rise of assertive Protestant churches and the reaction of the Catholic church stimulated a battle for the consciences of ordinary Europeans which disrupted traditional loyalties and political arrangements. It was 150 years before an uneasy religious balance was restored.

IN 1500 THE CATHOLIC CHURCH seemed stronger than ever. Paganism was vanquished; the Iberian Reconquista had destroyed the last Islamic state in western Europe and the overthrow of the Byzantine empire in 1453 had weakened the Orthodox church. Lay piety was booming, as was popular interest in the church's promise of salvation. Yet this very success brought profound problems. The moral and spiritual quality of many clergy left much to be desired. There was widespread concern at the state of the church and of popular religious belief which, although often enthusiastic, was frequently characterized by ignorance or heterodoxy. Attempts at reform, however, were often undermined by the unresolved problem of authority within the Church, while the invention of the printing press, by dramatically quickening the pace of debate, facilitated the questioning of established truth by clergy and laity alike.

The Reformation

The Reformation began as a revolt of the clergy, as Martin Luther (1483–1546), Huldrych Zwingli (1484–1531), Martin Bucer (1491–1551) and many others rejected the authority of the Catholic church, attacking the Papacy and basing their challenge on the authority of scripture, increasingly available in vernacular translations. These ideas proved attractive to many princes, who embraced reform. With the emergence of a second wave of Protestant reform spearheaded by the followers of the French reformer John Calvin (1509–64), an increasing number turned Protestant. Protestantism was already the official religion in large parts of northern Germany, Sweden, Denmark, Scotland and England, and Calvinism, which developed sophisticated theories justifying resistance to political authority, was spreading rapidly in the Netherlands, Poland-Lithuania, Hungary and France, where there were perhaps 1200 Calvinist churches by 1570.

Challenges to Protestantism

Yet confessional divisions were by no means fixed, and Protestantism faced growing problems. The Catholic church began a vigorous recovery after the Council of Trent reaffirmed its doctrine in response to the Protestant challenge and launched an ambitious programme of reform. Protestantism, by rejecting Catholic mechanisms for sustaining orthodoxy, could not establish the universal church to which the early reformers had aspired while discipline was always a problem, with radical sects such as Anabaptists and Antitrinitarians surviving vigorous persecution.

The second half of the 16th century was a period of adjustment, as rulers switched between brands of Protestantism, or even considered reunification with Rome, as in England under Mary Tudor (1552–8) or, more ambiguously, in Sweden under John III (1568–92). In eastern Europe, Catholicism outflanked Protestantism by negotiating the 1596 Union of Brest, in which most

1517 Luther launches debate over church reform

1520 Luther burns papal bull of excommunication

1541–64 Calvin reforms Genevan Church

1563 End of the Council of Trent

1589 Independent Orthodox patriarchate established in Moscow

1596 Union of Brest establishes Greek Catholic (Uniate) church in Poland-Lithuania

1598 Edict of Nantes: religious peace in France (revoked 1685)

1648 Peace of Westphalia: religious peace in the Holy Roman Empire

2 By 1670, the religious dividing lines were much firmer (map right). Most striking was the recovery of Catholicism after the Council of Trent. Where Protestantism had failed to win support from state authorities, it had withered. In France in 1685, Louis XIV revoked the Edict of Nantes, forcing thousands of Huguenots into exile. In eastern Europe, Calvinism had all but been eradicated in Poland-Lithuania, although Lutheranism was still strong in Prussia. Meanwhile, the Uniate Church had begun to blossom in Poland-Lithuania.

2 Religion in Europe, c. 1670

1 & 2 Reformation and Catholic Reformation

Roman Catholic	Lutheran
Orthodox	Calvinist
Greek Catholic (Uniate)	Anabaptist
Islam	Anglican
	Hussite

3 delegates sent to last session of Council of Trent

■ date of change from Catholicism to Lutheranism

▲ date of change to Calvinism, Zwinglianism or Anglicanism

— borders, 1572 **(map 1)** and 1683 **(map 2)**

Of the 250,000 or so works printed in Europe between 1447 and 1600, about 75 per cent concerned religion. The Reformation and the Catholic response would have been impossible without printing presses like this one **(right)**, from the cover of a book printed in Frankfurt in the early 17th century.

1 Protestantism at its height, 1560–1600

1 In 1570, **Catholicism appeared** to be in retreat on virtually every front (**map above**). Yet Protestantism, despite its introduction as the official religion in England, Scotland, Denmark, Sweden and much of north Germany and its rapid spread in France, Poland and Hungary, was not yet firmly rooted anywhere. It took time for people to be educated in the new faith, especially where rulers had not turned Protestant and church land had not been secularized.

of the Orthodox hierarchy in Poland-Lithuania accepted papal authority in return for keeping the Orthodox rite. Orthodox resistance to this Uniate (Greek Catholic) church was powerful, and it was only after 1650 that it began to flourish; similar Unions were established with the Ruthenians of northeast Hungary (1646) and the Romanian Orthodox church (1697). In such unstable circumstances, it took time for new religious convictions to take root among the ordinary people and Protestant rulers found that old beliefs died hard even where people welcomed the destruction of the power of the Catholic clergy. Nevertheless, the religious differentiation of Europe proceeded apace and was accompanied by vicious civil wars and widespread persecution. It was only after 1660 that the religious map took on a more permanent shape, as the success of evangelization made it difficult for rulers to challenge the religious beliefs of their subjects. Only now were the religious divisions of the continent accepted, if not welcomed.

THE PEOPLE AS A WHOLE, OR THE OFFICERS OF THE KINGDOM WHOM THE PEOPLE HAVE ESTABLISHED … VERY GRAVELY SIN AGAINST THE COVENANT WITH GOD IF THEY DO NOT USE FORCE AGAINST A KING WHO CORRUPTS GOD'S LAW OR PREVENTS ITS RESTORATION, IN ORDER TO CONFINE HIM TO HIS PROPER BOUNDS.

Philippe du Plessis-Mornay (1549–1623)
Vindiciæ contra Tyrannos (A Defence of Liberty against Tyrants), 1579

Europe: the state and its opponents

Before 1688 European rulers struggled to impose their authority. Nobles, townspeople and peasants fought to protect privileges and to resist the fiscal demands of the state. The Dutch and Portuguese revolts led to independence while in France and Spain monarchs could only increase their power by working with the elites. In England cooperation with Parliament was essential, as Charles I discovered.

LET HIM [PHILIP II] BE A KING IN CASTILE, IN ARAGON, AT NAPLES, AMONGST THE INDIANS, AND IN EVERY PLACE WHERE HE COMMANDS AT HIS PLEASURE; YEA LET HIM BE A KING, IF HE WILL, IN JERUSALEM, AND A PEACEABLE GOVERNOR IN ASIA AND AFRICA, YET FOR ALL THAT I WILL NOT ACKNOWLEDGE HIM IN THIS COUNTRY FOR ANY MORE THAN A DUKE AND A COUNT, WHOSE POWER IS LIMITED ACCORDING TO OUR PRIVILEGES, WHICH HE SWORE TO OBSERVE.

William of Orange
"Apology" for the Dutch Revolt, 1584

DESPITE THEIR APPARENT strength, the monarchies of Europe continued to govern through the personal ties of clientage which had characterized monarchy in the feudal period (see p. 132). The state still relied on the goodwill of its nobles for the enforcement of its policies, and failure to retain the support of the landed classes could provoke major revolts. The French aristocracy staged several rebellions against the crown, culminating in the Fronde (1648–53); a section of the English aristocracy rebelled against Elizabeth I in 1569–70 (the "Northern Rising") and many English peers supported Parliament's stand against Charles I after 1640. Similarly, nobles in the Netherlands opposed their "natural prince", Philip II of Spain, in 1566, 1572 and 1576 while those in Portugal rose against Philip IV in 1640.

These were only the most important rebellions of the period. Uprisings against the state were a continuing fact of life throughout the 16th and 17th centuries. Some revolts arose from attacks on the privileges of the "estates"; others were caused by economic hardship – from taxes imposed at a time of high prices and widespread unemployment, as was the case in most French popular revolts, or from the enclosing of common land, which caused the revolts of 1549 and 1607

in England. Other uprisings – the Pilgrimage of Grace in England in 1536 and the Covenanting Movement in Scotland in 1638 – were triggered by unpopular religious policies. In all cases the revolts were a response to attempts at innovation. Governments everywhere were endeavouring to create what James I of England described as: "one worship to God, one kingdom entirely governed, one uniformity of laws". The problem, however, was one of means, not ends. Neither James nor any of his fellow sovereigns had the resources to enforce such ambitions. They simply lacked the revenues and the officials required.

The age of revolt

The barriers to centralization in Early Modern Europe were formidable. Many subjects did not speak the same language as their government (Breton and Provençal in France, Catalan and Basque in Spain, Cornish in England, Frisian in the Netherlands); certain "corporations", notably the Church, possessed privileges which protected them against state interference; and many provinces possessed charters guaranteeing their traditional way of life.

Serious political upheavals occurred when the state tried to undermine these rights: the Dutch

rebelled largely because they believed that the central government, controlled from Madrid, threatened their traditional liberties. They continued their armed opposition until 1609, when Spain, in effect, recognized the independence of the seven provinces still in rebellion. In England, Parliament began a civil war against Charles I in 1642 because it believed that he intended to destroy the established rights of "free-born Englishmen". They, too, maintained their armed resistance until the power of the king was shattered in battle, and Charles himself was tried and executed in 1649. Although Charles's son was restored in 1660 with full powers and even a small standing army, another revolt, in 1688, supported by the Dutch, drove James II into exile.

While opposition in France did not go to such lengths, the absolutist policies and fiscal exactions of Cardinal Mazarin, chief minister of the boy king Louis XIV, so alienated the crown's officials, the nobles and the people of Paris that in 1649 they drove Louis from his capital and forced him to make major concessions. Royal control was not fully restored until 1655. Philip IV of Spain pushed the Portuguese aristocracy to revolt in support of the House of Braganza and by 1668 Portugal was independent. The Spanish king was fortunate not to lose Catalonia in a similar fashion during the revolt of 1640 to 1652.

The structure of the state

Despite these upheavals, however, the structure of the state survived. None of the rebels seriously questioned the need for strong government, only the location of it. After 1660, and even more after 1688, power in England was shared between Parliament, representing merchants and landowners, and the crown. The last major effort to resist the rise of central power and defend local autonomy had failed. In France, the Fronde was a frightening lesson for Louis XIV whose re-establishment of royal authority was based upon a policy of compromise with aristocratic and office-owning elites (see p. 214). A more sensitive government, combined with a rapidly expanding standing army after 1661, ensured that France saw no repetition of the Fronde before 1789.

The Dutch Revolt, on the other hand, achieved its primary goal of protecting local independence against central encroachment. Despite the preponderance of Holland within the Republic, the other six provinces retained a large measure of autonomy within a decentralized political system reminiscent of the 15th century. It was to leave the Dutch at a permanent disadvantage in a world which permitted no profit without power and no security without war. The 18th century and its profits – particularly in the colonial world – would belong to their rivals, France and Britain.

2 Philip II's inheritance of the Portuguese throne in 1580 united the Iberian peninsula (**map right**). Yet the authority of the Spanish monarchs was fragile. Charles I had been threatened in 1520 by the revolt of the Castilian towns (the Comuneros) and that of the peasants of Valencia, the Germaniá, the same year. Philip II's persecution of the Moriscos provoked the revolt of the Alpujarras of 1568–70. Fear of centralization from Madrid then sparked the revolts of Aragon (1591) and Catalonia (1640–52). The Portuguese revolt of 1640–68 marked the end of Iberia's brief union.

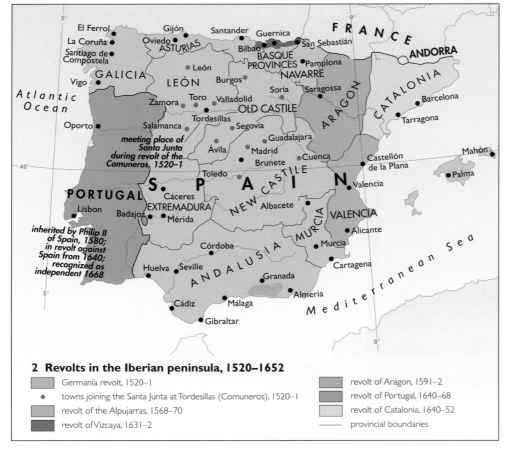

2 Revolts in the Iberian peninsula, 1520–1652

- Germaniá revolt, 1520–1
- towns joining the Santa Junta at Tordesillas (Comuneros), 1520–1
- revolt of the Alpujarras, 1568–70
- revolt of Vizcaya, 1631–2
- revolt of Aragon, 1591–2
- revolt of Portugal, 1640–68
- revolt of Catalonia, 1640–52
- provincial boundaries

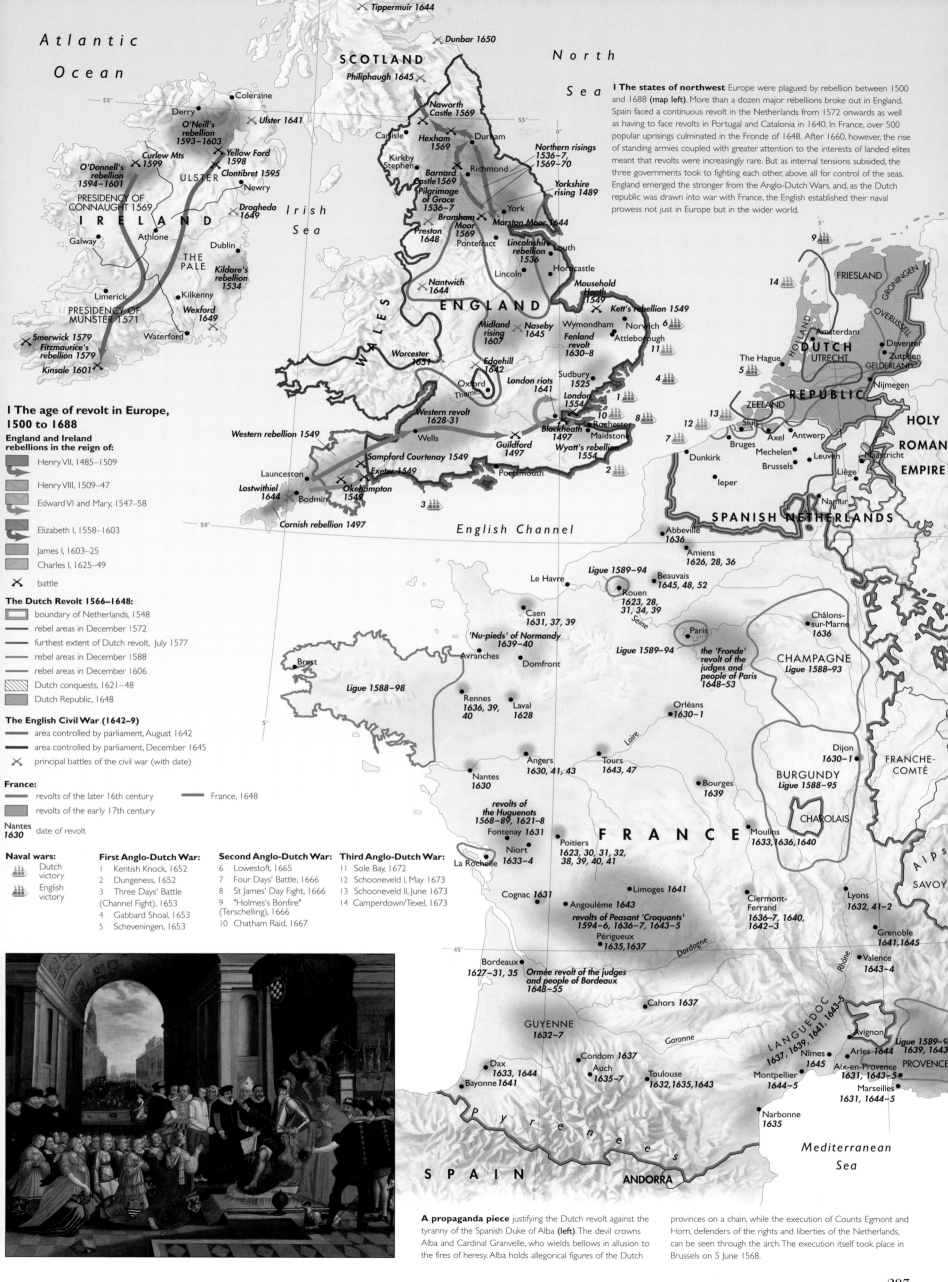

× Tippermuir 1644

Atlantic Ocean

North Sea

× Dunbar 1650

SCOTLAND

Philiphaugh 1645 ×

Coleraine
Derry
O'Neill's rebellion 1593–1603
× Ulster 1641
Naworth Castle 1569
Carlisle
Hexham 1569
Durham
Kirkby Stephen
Richmond
Northern risings 1536–7, 1569–70
Curlew Mts × 1599
Yellow Ford 1598
Clontibret 1595
O'Donnell's rebellion 1594–1601
PRESIDENCY OF CONNAUGHT 1569
Barnard Castle 1569
Pilgrimage of Grace 1536–7
Yorkshire rising 1489
× Bramham Moor 1569
× Marston Moor 1644
York
Preston 1648
Pontefract
Lincolnshire rebellion 1536
Louth
Horncastle
Lincoln
Newry
Drogheda 1649
I R E L A N D
Galway
Athlone
Dublin
THE PALE
Kildare's rebellion 1534
Irish Sea
Nantwich 1644
W A L E S
E N G L A N D
Mousehold Heath 1549
Kett's rebellion 1549
Norwich
Attleborough
Wymondham
Fenland revolt 1630–8
Midland rising 1607
× Naseby 1645
Sudbury 1525
Worcester 1651
Edgehill 1642
Oxford
Thames
London riots 1641
London 1554
Rochester
Blackheath 1497
Maidstone
Guildford 1497
Wyatt's rebellion 1554
Western revolt 1628–31
Wells
Western rebellion 1549
Sampford Courtenay 1549
Exeter 1549
Portsmouth
Lostwithiel 1644
Bodmin
Okehampton 1549
Launceston
Cornish rebellion 1497
Limerick
Kilkenny
Wexford 1649
Waterford
Smerwick 1579
Fitzmaurice's rebellion 1579
Kinsale 1601
PRESIDENCY OF MUNSTER 1571

English Channel

1 The states of northwest Europe were plagued by rebellion between 1500 and 1688 (map left). More than a dozen major rebellions broke out in England. Spain faced a continuous revolt in the Netherlands from 1572 onwards as well as having to face revolts in Portugal and Catalonia in 1640. In France, over 500 popular uprisings culminated in the Fronde of 1648. After 1660, however, the rise of standing armies coupled with greater attention to the interests of landed elites meant that revolts were increasingly rare. But as internal tensions subsided, the three governments took to fighting each other, above all for control of the seas. England emerged the stronger from the Anglo-Dutch Wars, and, as the Dutch republic was drawn into war with France, the English established their naval prowess not just in Europe but in the wider world.

FRIESLAND
GRONINGEN
OVERIJSSEL
Amsterdam
Deventer
DUTCH
The Hague
Zutphen
UTRECHT
GELDERLAND
Nijmegen
REPUBLIC
ZEELAND
Sluis
Bruges
Axel
Antwerp
Dunkirk
Mechelen
Leuven
Maastricht
Brussels
Ieper
Liège
Namur
HOLY ROMAN EMPIRE
SPANISH NETHERLANDS

I The age of revolt in Europe, 1500 to 1688

England and Ireland rebellions in the reign of:

- Henry VII, 1485–1509
- Henry VIII, 1509–47
- Edward VI and Mary, 1547–58
- Elizabeth I, 1558–1603
- James I, 1603–25
- Charles I, 1625–49
- × battle

The Dutch Revolt 1566–1648:

- boundary of Netherlands, 1548
- rebel areas in December 1572
- furthest extent of Dutch revolt, July 1577
- rebel areas in December 1588
- rebel areas in December 1606
- Dutch conquests, 1621–48
- Dutch Republic, 1648

The English Civil War (1642–9)

- area controlled by parliament, August 1642
- area controlled by parliament, December 1645
- × principal battles of the civil war (with date)

France:

- revolts of the later 16th century
- France, 1648
- revolts of the early 17th century
- Nantes 1630   date of revolt

Naval wars:

First Anglo-Dutch War:
1 Kentish Knock, 1652
2 Dungeness, 1652
3 Three Days' Battle (Channel Fight), 1653
4 Gabbard Shoal, 1653
5 Scheveningen, 1653

Second Anglo-Dutch War:
6 Lowestoft, 1665
7 Four Days' Battle, 1666
8 St James' Day Fight, 1666
9 "Holmes's Bonfire" (Terschelling), 1666
10 Chatham Raid, 1667

Third Anglo-Dutch War:
11 Sole Bay, 1672
12 Schooneveld I, May 1673
13 Schooneveld II, June 1673
14 Camperdown/Texel, 1673

Abbeville 1636
Amiens 1626, 28, 36
Le Havre
Ligue 1589–94
Beauvais 1645, 48, 52
Caen 1631, 37, 39
Rouen 1623, 28, 31, 34, 39
Seine
Châlons-sur-Marne 1636
'Nu-pieds' of Normandy 1639–40
Avranches
Domfront
Paris
Ligue 1589–94
the 'Fronde' revolt of the judges and people of Paris 1648–53
CHAMPAGNE Ligue 1588–93
Brest
Ligue 1588–98
Rennes 1636, 39, 40
Laval 1628
Orléans 1630–1
Loire
Dijon 1630–1
FRANCHE-COMTÉ
Angers 1630, 41, 43
Tours 1643, 47
BURGUNDY Ligue 1588–95
Nantes 1630
Bourges 1639
CHAROLAIS
F R A N C E
revolts of the Huguenots 1568–89, 1621–8
Fontenay 1631
Niort
La Rochelle 1633–4
Poitiers 1623, 30, 31, 32, 38, 39, 40, 41
Moulins 1633, 1636, 1640
Limoges 1641
Lyons 1632, 41–2
Cognac 1631
Angoulême 1643
Clermont-Ferrand 1636–7, 1640, 1642–4
revolts of Peasant 'Croquants' 1594–6, 1636–7, 1643–5
Périgueux 1635, 1637
Grenoble 1641, 1645
Valence 1643–4
Bordeaux 1627–31, 35
Ormée revolt of the judges and people of Bordeaux 1648–55
Dordogne
Cahors 1637
GUYENNE 1632–7
Garonne
Rhône
Dax 1633, 1644
Bayonne 1641
Condom 1637
Auch 1635–7
Toulouse 1632, 1635, 1643
LANGUEDOC 1637, 1639, 1641, 1643–5
Avignon
Nîmes 1645
Arles 1644
Aix-en-Provence 1631, 1643–5
Marseilles 1631, 1644–5
Montpellier 1644–5
Ligue 1589–9 1639, 1643
PROVENCE
Narbonne 1635
S P A I N
ANDORRA
SAVOY
A L P S
P y r e n e e s
Mediterranean Sea

A propaganda piece justifying the Dutch revolt against the tyranny of the Spanish Duke of Alba (left). The devil crowns Alba and Cardinal Granvelle, who wields bellows in allusion to the fires of heresy. Alba holds allegorical figures of the Dutch provinces on a chain, while the execution of Counts Egmont and Horn, defenders of the rights and liberties of the Netherlands, can be seen through the arch. The execution itself took place in Brussels on 5 June 1568.

The Mediterranean world

The Ottoman conquest of the eastern Mediterranean and the French invasion of Italy in 1494 opened a new phase in Mediterranean history. Both the sea and the Italian peninsula became the focus for power-struggles between states whose interests were only partly Mediterranean. Meanwhile, Europe's economic centre of gravity shifted northwest.

AFTER 1500, EVEN AS the civilization of the Italian Renaissance was spreading round Europe, Italy and the Mediterranean were losing their dominant position within the cultural and economic worlds of Europe. The invasion of Italy by Charles VIII of France in 1494 (see map 2) initiated over 60 years of warfare between the Habsburgs and the French Valois for control of Italy which undermined the political primacy of the Italian cities, just as the Ottoman drive into the eastern Mediterranean threatened their economic dominance. The loss of Italian primacy was precipitated in part, too, by the creation of the Habsburg empire. Charles V, elected Holy Roman Emperor in 1519, ruled not only the Habsburg lands in Austria, south Germany and the Netherlands, but also the realms bequeathed by his maternal grandparents, Ferdinand and Isabella, in Spain, Italy and north Africa. His inheritance was soon expanded: in 1526 his brother and close ally Ferdinand succeeded to the crowns of Bohemia and Hungary, creating a huge Habsburg power block running from the Adriatic almost to the Baltic. In 1535 Charles himself acquired both Milan and Tunis.

By the peace of Câteau-Cambrésis (1559), France was excluded from Italy, which now came under the domination of the Habsburgs. Although Charles V divided his empire on his death, his son Philip II of Spain retained Milan and the kingdoms of Naples and Sicily. Henceforth, Spanish viceroys ruled in Naples, Sicily and Sardinia, with a Spanish governor in Lombardy.

The Ottoman threat
Even Italy's largest states lacked room for manoeuvre in the face of Spain's overwhelming dominance. 80 per cent of Genoese seaborne trade was conducted with Spain, and Venice, whose eastern Mediterranean empire was falling gradually into Ottoman hands, was surrounded by Habsburg territory. Papal attempts to oppose the Habsburgs ended in catastrophe: the sack of Rome itself in 1527 and a humiliating invasion in 1556–7. Yet the Spaniards at least provided effective defence against the Ottomans who, despite their successful advance along the north African coast with the capture of Algiers (1529), Tripoli (1551) and Bugia (1555), were unable to secure a foothold in Italy. The climactic moment came with the unsuccessful siege of Malta in 1565, although the Spanish victory at Lepanto (1571) could not prevent the fall of Cyprus the same year.

Italy and the Holy Roman Empire
The fading of the Turkish threat after the Ottoman-Spanish truce of 1577 ensured that the new status quo lasted until the 1790s. Southern Italy and Sardinia were ruled by Spain, the Papal States dominated central Italy, while the north, apart from Venice, was still part of the Holy Roman Empire, and was a

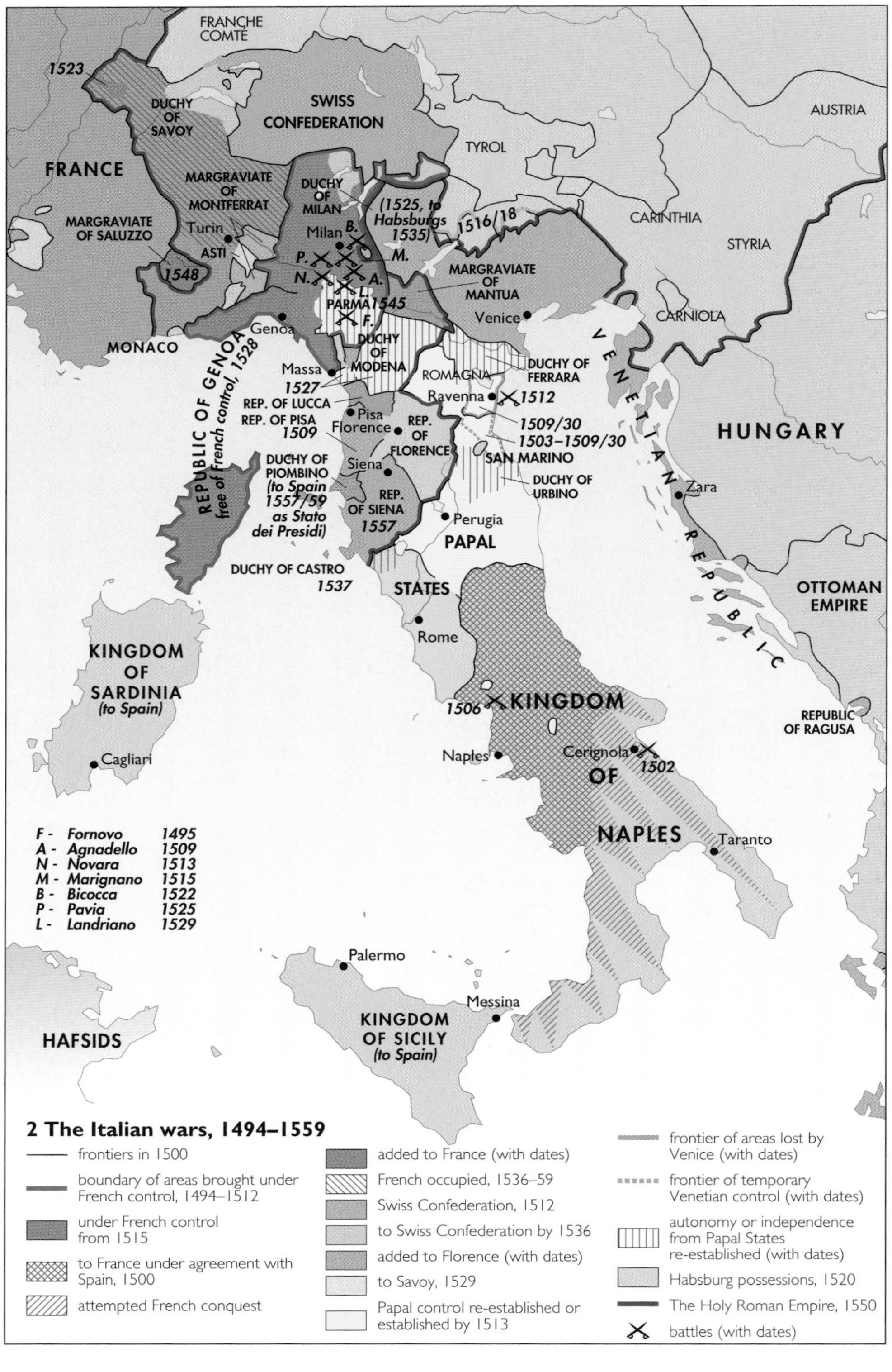

1 Spanish-Ottoman rivalry dominated the Mediterranean until 1577 (map right), as each state sought to expand along the north African coast. The climax came with the Ottoman failure to seize Malta, the gateway to the western Mediterranean (1565). Philip II and Murad III, both preoccupied with other imperial concerns, concluded an uneasy but lasting peace in 1577. Spain turned northwards, to the Netherlands and the Holy Roman Empire, while the Ottomans attacked Persia.

2 In the late 15th century increased rivalry between the major Italian states sucked in foreign powers (map left). In 1494 Charles VIII of France intervened in the Milanese succession. By 1495 he had occupied the kingdom of Naples. The Habsburgs (in alliance with the Papacy, the Emperor and Venice) then acted to halt the French advance, driving the French from the south by 1504 and taking Naples for themselves. Habsburg influence continued to grow: at the Battle of Pavia (1525) Charles V drove out the French from Milan, and restored the native duke, but in 1535 he occupied the duchy himself. Florence and Venice kept or expanded their territories, but by 1559 the French were excluded from Italy and the Habsburgs were effective arbiters of the whole peninsula.

Map labels (map 2)
FRANCHE COMTÉ · 1523 · DUCHY OF SAVOY · SWISS CONFEDERATION · AUSTRIA · FRANCE · MARGRAVIATE OF MONTFERRAT · DUCHY OF MILAN · (1525, to Habsburgs 1535) · 1516/18 · TYROL · MARGRAVIATE OF SALUZZO · Turin · Milan · B. · P. · M. · CARINTHIA · STYRIA · 1548 · ASTI · N. · A. · MARGRAVIATE OF MANTUA · PARMA 1545 · Venice · CARNIOLA · MONACO · Genoa · F. · REPUBLIC OF GENOA (free of French control, 1528) · Massa 1527 · DUCHY OF MODENA · ROMAGNA · DUCHY OF FERRARA · REP. OF LUCCA · REP. OF PISA 1509 · Pisa · Florence · Ravenna · 1512 · 1509/30 · 1503–1509/30 · HUNGARY · DUCHY OF PIOMBINO (to Spain 1557/59 as Stato dei Presidi) · Siena · REP. OF FLORENCE · SAN MARINO · DUCHY OF URBINO · Zara · REP. OF SIENA 1557 · Perugia · PAPAL · DUCHY OF CASTRO 1537 · STATES · Rome · OTTOMAN EMPIRE · KINGDOM OF SARDINIA (to Spain) · Cagliari · KINGDOM · 1506 · REPUBLIC OF RAGUSA · Naples · Cerignola · 1502 · OF · NAPLES · Taranto · Palermo · Messina · KINGDOM OF SICILY (to Spain) · HAFSIDS

Battles (map 2)
F -	Fornovo	1495
A -	Agnadello	1509
N -	Novara	1513
M -	Marignano	1515
B -	Bicocca	1522
P -	Pavia	1525
L -	Landriano	1529

2 The Italian wars, 1494–1559 (legend)
- frontiers in 1500
- boundary of areas brought under French control, 1494–1512
- under French control from 1515
- to France under agreement with Spain, 1500
- attempted French conquest
- added to France (with dates)
- French occupied, 1536–59
- Swiss Confederation, 1512
- to Swiss Confederation by 1536
- added to Florence (with dates)
- to Savoy, 1529
- Papal control re-established or established by 1513
- frontier of areas lost by Venice (with dates)
- frontier of temporary Venetian control (with dates)
- autonomy or independence from Papal States re-established (with dates)
- Habsburg possessions, 1520
- The Holy Roman Empire, 1550
- X battles (with dates)

Map 1 labels
PORTUGAL annexed to Spain 1580–1640 · Madrid · CASTILE including New V... · SPAIN · GRANADA · Tangier · Gibraltar · Portuguese · Ceuta · Peñón de Vélez · Melilla 1497 · 40

Timeline
1494 Charles VIII of France invades Italy; temporary French capture of Naples

1535 Habsburgs take Milan

1559 Treaty of Câteau-Cambrésis ends Habsburg-Valois wars

1565 Failed Ottoman siege of Malta

1571 Battle of Lepanto

1577 Habsburg-Ottoman truce

1629–31 War of the Mantuan Succession

1702–13 War of the Spanish Succession

1797 Napoleon conquers Austrian Lombardy and Venice

> IN SUCH A STATE OF MIND AND IN SUCH A CONFUSION OF AFFAIRS ... BEGAN THE YEAR 1494 – A MOST UNHAPPY YEAR FOR ITALY, AND IN TRUTH THE BEGINNING OF THOSE YEARS OF MISFORTUNE, BECAUSE IT OPENED THE DOOR TO INNUMBERABLE HORRIBLE CALAMITIES, IN WHICH ... FOR VARIOUS REASONS, A GREAT PART OF THE WORLD WAS SUBSEQUENTLY INVOLVED.
>
> **Francesco Guicciardini**
> **The History of Italy, 1540**

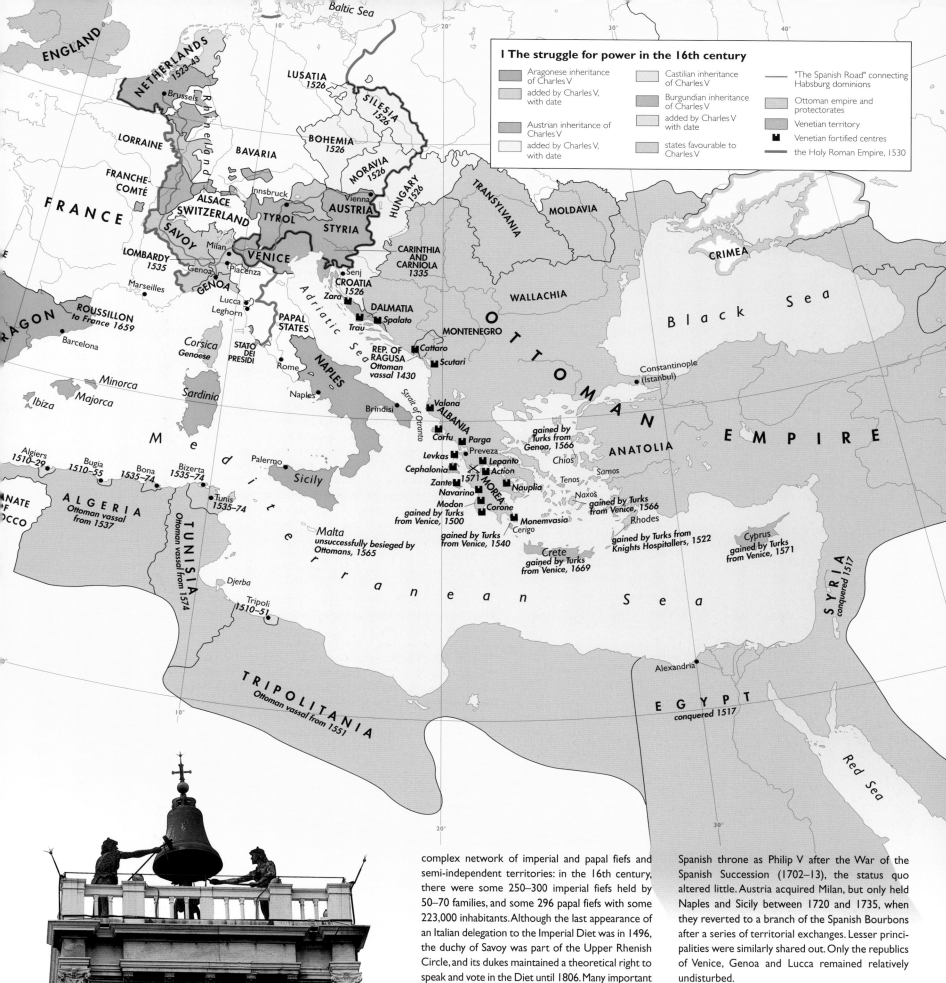

The struggle for power in the 16th century

- Aragonese inheritance of Charles V
- added by Charles V, with date
- Austrian inheritance of Charles V
- added by Charles V, with date
- Castilian inheritance of Charles V
- Burgundian inheritance of Charles V
- added by Charles V with date
- states favourable to Charles V
- "The Spanish Road" connecting Habsburg dominions
- Ottoman empire and protectorates
- Venetian territory
- Venetian fortified centres
- the Holy Roman Empire, 1530

Baltic Sea

ENGLAND

NETHERLANDS 1523–43
• Brussels

LUSATIA 1526

SILESIA 1526

LORRAINE

BOHEMIA 1526

BAVARIA

MORAVIA 1526

FRANCHE-COMTÉ

Innsbruck

ALSACE SWITZERLAND TYROL

AUSTRIA STYRIA

HUNGARY 1526

TRANSYLVANIA

MOLDAVIA

FRANCE

SAVOY

Milan

VENICE

CARINTHIA AND CARNIOLA 1335

LOMBARDY 1535

Genoa Piacenza

CROATIA 1526

CRIMEA

Marseilles

GENOA

Lucca Leghorn

Zara

DALMATIA

Spalato

Trau

WALLACHIA

Black Sea

ARAGON

ROUSSILLON to France 1659

PAPAL STATES

Rome

MONTENEGRO

Cattaro

REP. OF RAGUSA
Ottoman vassal 1430

Scutari

Barcelona

Corsica Genoese

STATO DEI PRESIDI

NAPLES

Constantinople (Istanbul)

Minorca

Sardinia

Naples

Brindisi

Valona
ALBANIA

Corfu Parga

Preveza

gained by Turks from Genoa, 1566

ANATOLIA

Ibiza Majorca

M
e
d
i
t
e
r
r
a
n
e
a
n

S
e
a

Strait of Otranto

Levkas

Cephalonia

Lepanto
Action

× 1571

Chios

Samos

Algiers 1510–29

Bugia 1510–55

Bona 1535–74

Bizerta 1535–74

Palermo

Sicily

Zante

Navarino

MOREA

Nauplia

Tenos

Naxos

Rhodes

Cyprus gained by Turks from Venice, 1571

NATE OCCO

Tunis 1535–74

ALGERIA
Ottoman vassal from 1537

TUNISIA
Ottoman vassal from 1574

Modon Corone
gained by Turks from Venice, 1500

Cerigo

Monemvasia

gained by Turks from Venice, 1540

gained by Turks from Venice, 1566

gained by Turks from Knights Hospitallers, 1522

SYRIA conquered 1517

Malta
unsuccessfully besieged by Ottomans, 1565

Crete
gained by Turks from Venice, 1669

Djerba

Tripoli 1510–51

TRIPOLITANIA
Ottoman vassal from 1551

Alexandria

EGYPT
conquered 1517

Red Sea

The Venetian Republic controlled extensive territories in the eastern Mediterranean and its symbol, the Lion of St Mark (above), stood guard on coastal fortresses in Greece, the Balkans, Crete and Cyprus. The Venetian empire was not purely maritime, however: there were extensive Venetian territories in Italy itself. Nonetheless its lifeline was the Adriatic and, despite territorial losses elsewhere in this period, chiefly to the Ottomans, and the decline throughout the 18th century of its once dominant trading position in the eastern Mediterranean, Venice was able to cling on to its fortresses guarding the entrance to the Adriatic – Cattaro, Corfu, Levkas, Cephalonia, Zante – until the extinction of the republic itself by Napoleon in 1797.

complex network of imperial and papal fiefs and semi-independent territories: in the 16th century, there were some 250–300 imperial fiefs held by 50–70 families, and some 296 papal fiefs with some 223,000 inhabitants. Although the last appearance of an Italian delegation to the Imperial Diet was in 1496, the duchy of Savoy was part of the Upper Rhenish Circle, and its dukes maintained a theoretical right to speak and vote in the Diet until 1806. Many important north Italian families, such as the Doria or the Spinola, were imperial princes, and the Imperial Aulic Council heard 1500 cases involving Italians between 1555 and 1806 (400 in the 16th century; 490 in the 17th; and 540 in the 18th). Northern Italy was strategically vital to Spain during the Dutch Revolt and the Thirty Years' War: with the sea-route to the Netherlands through the English Channel dominated by the Dutch and the English, Milan was the mustering-ground for Spanish troops sent overland down the "Spanish Road" through the Valtellina, Alsace and the Rhineland to the Netherlands. Thus Italy was vital to Spain's long war against the Dutch rebels; this led to a renewal of Franco-Spanish war in Italy during the War of the Mantuan Succession (1629–31), which saw the victory of the French-backed candidate, Charles Gonzaga, Duke of Nevers.

Even when the Spanish Habsburgs died out in 1700, and the grandson of Louis XIV secured the Spanish throne as Philip V after the War of the Spanish Succession (1702–13), the status quo altered little. Austria acquired Milan, but only held Naples and Sicily between 1720 and 1735, when they reverted to a branch of the Spanish Bourbons after a series of territorial exchanges. Lesser principalities were similarly shared out. Only the republics of Venice, Genoa and Lucca remained relatively undisturbed.

Britain in the Mediterranean

The principal guardian of this stability was Great Britain, attracted to the Mediterranean by trading opportunities in the late 16th century, when the Levant Company established a base in Istanbul (1581). In the 1650s, British fleets entered to pursue royalist vessels and punish the Barbary pirates. From 1662 to 1683, Britain held Tangier, guarding the entrance to the Mediterranean; in 1704 it took Gibraltar on the other side of the straits. Sardinia was a British base between 1708 and 1714, as was Minorca from 1708 to 1783. On the whole, though, Britain preferred diplomacy to force; it was only when Napoleon's invasion of Italy and annexation of Egypt and Malta in the late 1790s destroyed the status quo and convulsed the eastern and western Mediterranean alike that British naval power came to dominate both.

The struggle for the Baltic

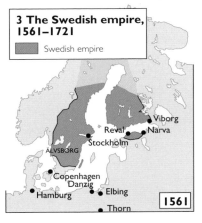

3 The Swedish empire, 1561–1721

▨ Swedish empire

1561 Reval, threatened by Ivan IV and the commercial rivalry of Viborg and Narva, put itself under Swedish protection, rejecting Polish and Danish claims to overlordship and giving Sweden its first foothold across the Gulf of Finland.

1595 Peace of Teusina with Muscovy added Narva and effectively all Estonia, turned the Gulf of Finland into a Swedish waterway and pushed the northern border across the Arctic circle.

1617 Peace of Stolbovo with Muscovy confirmed possession of Estonia, added Ingria (Ingermanland), and Karelia cutting off Russia, including its great trading centre of Novgorod (occupied by Sweden, 1610–6) from the Baltic.

1645 De facto Swedish possession of Livonia by truces of Altmark (1629) and Stuhmsdorf (1635) with Poland-Lithuania. Peace of Brömsebro with Denmark-Norway (1645) transferred Ösel, Gotland, Jämtland, Härjedalen and (for 30 years) Halland.

1648 At the Peace of Westphalia, which ended the Thirty Years' War, Sweden gained West Pomerania, including the important ports of Stettin and Wismar, and the bishoprics of Bremen and Verden.

1658 Peace of Roskilde with Denmark. Sweden acquired Scania, Blekinge, Bohuslän, Trondheim and Bornholm; possession of Halland confirmed. Renewed Swedish attack in summer of 1658 led to Danish-Dutch alliance, rebellion in Scania and defeat on Funen in 1659.

1660 Fighting ceased after the death of Charles X. Treaty of Copenhagen returned Trondheim and island of Bornholm to Denmark and formally abandoned Swedish attempts to close the Baltic to foreign warships.

1721 The treaties ending the Great Northern War (1700–21) dismantled Sweden's Baltic empire. In the east, Karelia, Ingermanland, Estonia and Livonia were lost, as were Bremen & Verden and most of West Pomerania in the Holy Roman Empire.

The growing economic importance of the Baltic after 1500 coincided with the decay of the political status quo as the powers which had dominated the sea in the medieval period entered terminal decline or were seriously weakened. The resultant struggle for control of the Baltic Sea lasted two centuries before Russia emerged as the most significant Baltic power.

FROM 1500 THE BALTIC provided most of the timber, tar, pitch, hemp and flax for the ships with which European powers built their world empires, as well as copper and huge supplies of cheap grain. This increasingly lucrative trade provoked serious rivalry, as neighbouring powers sought to control ports at the mouths of the great rivers which bore goods from the interior, while Denmark's control of both sides of The Sound, the narrow entrance to the Baltic, enabled it to impose the hotly contested Sound Tolls on most of the commerce passing through. After 1500, no power was strong enough to dominate the Baltic or its trade; the resultant conflicts constantly interlocked with wider European affairs.

In 1523 Sweden under Gustav Vasa broke away from the Scandinavian Union of Kalmar (see p. 166). Meanwhile, the Hanseatic League of Baltic trading towns began to unravel, while the Teutonic Order, which controlled the southern Baltic shore from Pomerania to Estonia, slowly decayed. A rebellion led by the burghers of Thorn, Danzig and Elbing in alliance with Poland had already seen the Order lose much of Prussia by the Peace of Thorn (1466); in 1525, Grand Master Albrecht of Hohenzollern then secularized the Order, creating the Duchy of Prussia as a Lutheran fief of the Polish crown. The decaying rump of the Order held on in Livonia, but ancient claims and a desire to profit from Baltic trade led Ivan IV of Muscovy to invade in 1558.

Sweden's Baltic empire

Ivan failed to establish Muscovite power on the Baltic. The early beneficiaries of the Order's collapse were Poland-Lithuania and Sweden. Poland accepted the overlordship of Livonia in 1561 and granted Courland to Gotthard Kettler, Grand Master of the Order, as a fief of the Polish crown. Sweden, meanwhile, seized Reval and Estonia and became involved in the Nordic Seven Years' War with Denmark (1563–70), in which Denmark struggled to re-establish the Union of Kalmar and Sweden sought to expand its foothold on the North Sea at Älvsborg, on the site of the future city of Gothenburg. The Muscovite armies could terrorize but not conquer; they were driven back by determined resistance from the Poles and the Swedes under John III (1568–92), who then married a Polish princess and had his son Sigismund elected king of Poland in 1587. Muscovy gradually subsided into anarchy after Ivan's death in 1584; by 1619, it was cut off from the Baltic, as Sweden secured Karelia, Ingria (Ingermanland) and Estonia, and Poland-Lithuania took Livonia and regained Smolensk. Denmark, despite seizing Älvsborg in the War of Kalmar (1611–13), was unable to secure a decisive advantage, and had to remain content with control of The Sound, returning Älvsborg for a large ransom.

But the Polish-Swedish alliance was short-lived. Sigismund, raised a Catholic, was driven off the Swedish throne in 1599; for 60 years, Poland-Lithuania and Sweden were locked in a dynastic struggle which gave Muscovy time to recover.

Under the brilliant Gustavus Adolphus (1611–32) Sweden seized Livonia in the 1620s, while the powerful military system which matured in his reign enabled Sweden to play a leading role in the Thirty Years' War (see p. 212) after his brilliant victory at Breitenfeld (Sep. 1631). By 1648, despite Gustavus Adolphus's death in the battle of Lützen (Nov. 1632), Sweden had gained substantial territories in northern Germany and, after a devastating war with Denmark (1643–5), had widened its bridgehead on the North Sea.

Under Charles X (1654–60) Swedish power reached its zenith. Charles invaded Poland-Lithuania in 1655 and pushed the Muscovites back from Riga. Denmark, keen for revenge, attacked Sweden in 1657, but was defeated and made peace at Roskilde (Feb. 1658). Charles's decision to attack Denmark again in

the summer of 1658 proved rash, however: he lost the chance to secure concessions from Poland-Lithuania or Russia, while England, the United Provinces and France, fearing Swedish domination of the Baltic, supported Denmark. After the Peace of Copenhagen (1660), though Denmark's grip on the Sound was broken, Sweden had failed to find security.

The decline of Swedish power

Sweden's success brought it many enemies. Swedish support of the house of Holstein-Gottorp, a junior branch of the Danish royal family which shared control of the duchy of Holstein, ensured that relations with Denmark remained tense. Attacked by Brandenburg and Denmark in the Scanian War (1676–9), Sweden's precarious control of its scattered Baltic empire was revealed: it only preserved its southern Baltic holdings thanks to the intervention of Louis XIV of France.

Charles XI (1660–97) adopted a pacific policy after 1679 and revived the army, but when he was succeeded by his teenage son Charles XII (1697–1718), Denmark, Saxony-Poland and Russia formed an alliance which attacked Sweden in 1700, launching the Great Northern War (1700–21). Although Charles immediately knocked Denmark out of the war, smashed the Russian army at Narva (1700) and forced Saxony to make peace at Altranstädt (1706), he became bogged down in Poland. Peter I, given breathing-space after Narva, built a formidable army and fleet; by 1704, Ingermanland and much of Livonia was in his hands. After Charles's crushing defeat at Poltava (1709), Brandenburg-Prussia, Hanover and Denmark joined Russia in a struggle for Sweden's Baltic empire. By 1721, Sweden was once more a second-rank power, and Russia was the dominant force in the region.

> HE CARRIED ALL THE HEROIC VIRTUES TO EXTREMES, AT WHICH TIME THEY BECAME AS DANGEROUS AS THE OPPOSING VICES ... HIS GREAT QUALITIES, ANY ONE OF WHICH WOULD HAVE IMMORTALIZED ANOTHER PRINCE, WERE THE RUIN OF HIS NATION.
>
> Voltaire, *Lion of the North: Charles XII of Sweden*, 1731

1 At the Peace of Brömsebro in 1645, Denmark was forced to cede Halland to Sweden, marking the beginning of Denmark's loss of control of the strategic Sound **(map below)**. Denmark's efforts in 1657 to recover Halland were unsuccessful, and further territorial concessions had to be made to Sweden in February 1658. But Sweden then overreached herself. An attempt to storm Copenhagen in February 1659 was repulsed, and when Swedish forces then occupied Funen in October, they were defeated the next month at Nyborg by a Danish-Dutch force and half the Swedish army was destroyed.

2 Sweden's aggressive empire-building made it many enemies. When Sweden was attacked by Russia, Denmark and Saxony-Poland in 1700, Charles XII launched a series of brilliant campaigns **(map right)** which saw him defeat Denmark, devastate Poland and invade Saxony before catastrophic defeat at Poltava ended his invasion of Russia. Charles spent five years in Turkish exile, before returning to die on campaign in Norway in 1718, thus opening the way to a peace settlement and the loss of Sweden's Baltic empire.

The march over the ice in February 1658 **(right)**. In 1657 Frederick III of Denmark took advantage of Sweden's involvement in Poland during the Second Northern War to attempt to recover Halland, lost in 1645. Charles X responded by moving rapidly through Germany into Jutland, then astonished the Danes by marching his army across the frozen Baltic Sea via the island of Funen to threaten unprotected Copenhagen (see map left), thereby forcing Frederick to accept the humiliating Peace of Roskilde. Erik Dahlbergh, on whose drawing this engraving is based, was an eyewitness; he investigated the thickness of the ice before the army crossed.

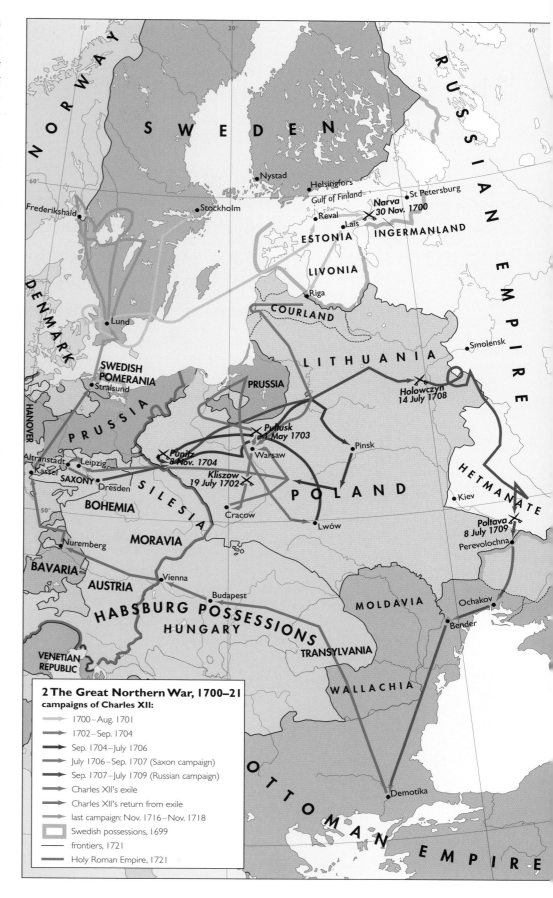

2 The Great Northern War, 1700–21
campaigns of Charles XII:
- 1700–Aug. 1701
- 1702–Sep. 1704
- Sep. 1704–July 1706
- July 1706–Sep. 1707 (Saxon campaign)
- Sep. 1707–July 1709 (Russian campaign)
- Charles XII's exile
- Charles XII's return from exile
- last campaign: Nov. 1716–Nov. 1718
- Swedish possessions, 1699
- frontiers, 1721
- Holy Roman Empire, 1721

1 Denmark's Baltic empire, 1618–60
- Denmark-Norway, 1618
- lost to Sweden, 1645
- lost to Sweden, 1658
- Swedish lands in Germany, 1648
- Charles X's march over the ice, 1658

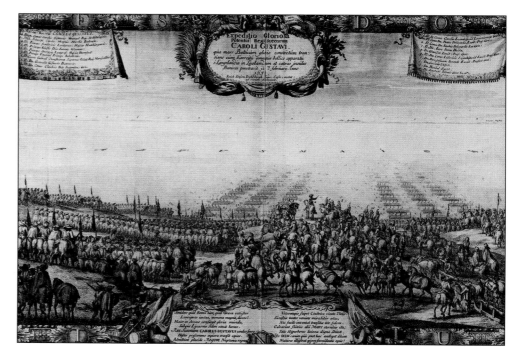

1493 to 1806

The Holy Roman Empire

The Holy Roman Empire was a decentralized confederal system. While undoubtedly complex, it was effective enough to maintain a common currency and robust enough to survive religious division and the Thirty Years' War. After 1648, its institutions revived and it was regarded as the natural political framework for Germany until, undermined from outside, it collapsed in 1806.

> [IT] IS RIGHT TO CONSIDER THE EMPIRE AS A MODEL OF THE CHRISTIAN SOCIETY. IN THE EMPIRE, SUBJECTS CAN PLEAD AGAINST THEIR PRINCES, OR AGAINST THEIR MAGISTRATES ... JUDGES ARE NOT DEPENDENT UPON THE INSTRUCTIONS OF PRINCES, OR OF THE STATES WHICH HAVE APPOINTED THEM: THEY HAVE ONLY TO FOLLOW THE MOVEMENTS OF THEIR CONSCIENCE.
>
> Leibniz
> Observations on the Abbé de St Pierre's Project for Perpetual Peace, 1715

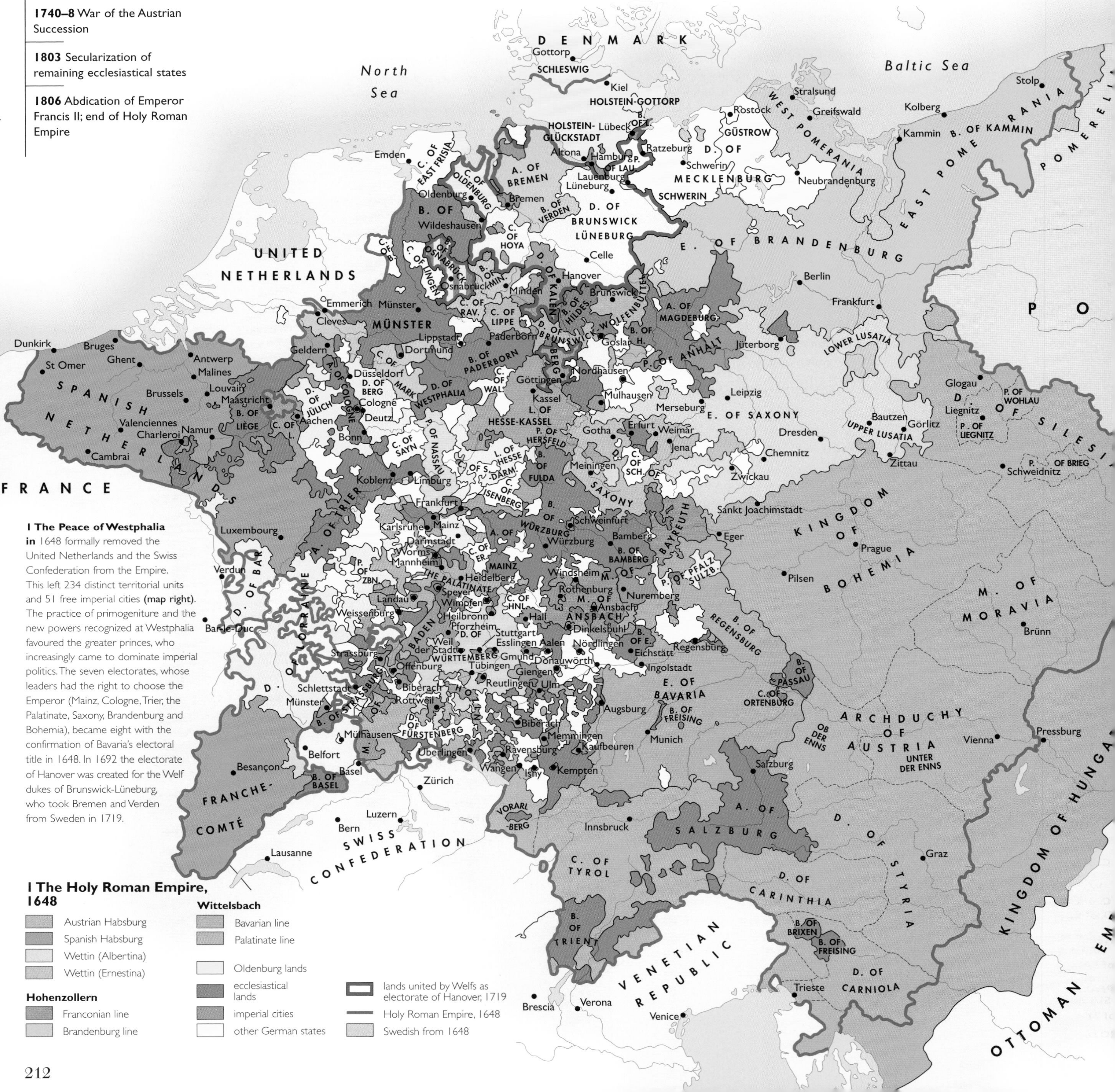

I The Peace of Westphalia in 1648 formally removed the United Netherlands and the Swiss Confederation from the Empire. This left 234 distinct territorial units and 51 free imperial cities (**map right**). The practice of primogeniture and the new powers recognized at Westphalia favoured the greater princes, who increasingly came to dominate imperial politics. The seven electorates, whose leaders had the right to choose the Emperor (Mainz, Cologne, Trier, the Palatinate, Saxony, Brandenburg and Bohemia), became eight with the confirmation of Bavaria's electoral title in 1648. In 1692 the electorate of Hanover was created for the Welf dukes of Brunswick-Lüneburg, who took Bremen and Verden from Sweden in 1719.

I The Holy Roman Empire, 1648

- Austrian Habsburg
- Spanish Habsburg
- Wettin (Albertina)
- Wettin (Ernestina)

Hohenzollern
- Franconian line
- Brandenburg line

Wittelsbach
- Bavarian line
- Palatinate line
- Oldenburg lands
- ecclesiastical lands
- imperial cities
- other German states

- lands united by Welfs as electorate of Hanover, 1719
- Holy Roman Empire, 1648
- Swedish from 1648

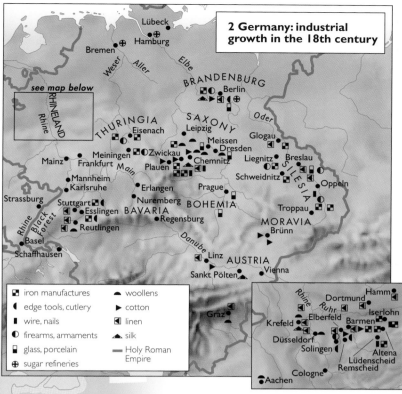

2 Germany: industrial growth in the 18th century

Legend:
- ▣ iron manufactures
- ◀ edge tools, cutlery
- ▌ wire, nails
- ◐ firearms, armaments
- ▣ glass, porcelain
- ⊕ sugar refineries
- ▲ woollens
- ◧ cotton
- ◩ linen
- ▲ silk
- — Holy Roman Empire

2 Although some formerly wealthy areas of Germany stagnated after 1648, new industries sprang up in rural districts where they could escape crippling guild restrictions. Mining, iron and textiles developed in Silesia (maps left) and Saxony, while water power provided the foundations of the new prosperity of the lower Rhineland.

Frederick II of Prussia (1740–88) inspects his troops (above). When Emperor Charles VI died in 1740 leaving only a daughter, Maria Teresa, Frederick invaded Silesia, launching the War of the Austrian Succession. Although Frederick could not prevent the election of Maria Teresa's husband Franz as Emperor, he secured Silesia when peace was made in 1748.

AT FIRST SIGHT, the Holy Roman Empire appears incoherent, with a high degree of political fragmentation and competing jurisdictions. In fact, considerable institutional consolidation took place after 1493 within what was a confederal system, with varying levels of authority which kept political control close to those affected by it. The Empire's division into ten "Circles" improved its administration, with the Circles organizing taxation, regulating disputes and supervising the common currency, the Imperial thaler. The revival of the Imperial Cameral Tribunal and the Imperial Diet and the introduction of a common criminal code provided the empire with a complex but not unworkable constitution. From the election of Maximilian I (1493), the position of emperor became all but hereditary in the Habsburg dynasty, with a brief interlude in the reign of the Wittelsbach Charles VII (1742–5) during the War of the Austrian Succession.

The wars of religion

After 1517 two factors put the Empire under immense strain: the Reformation and the dramatic increase in Habsburg power following the election of Charles V (1519). Religion became a central issue, as princes sought to limit the Emperor's power while the secularization of church property in much of northern and western Germany sparked bitter disputes. Although the formation of the Protestant Schmalkaldic League in the 1530s brought a series of brief civil wars, all sides recoiled from all-out confrontation. At the peace of Augsburg (1555), a compromise was reached based on the principle that princes should determine the religion of their subjects.

Augsburg kept the peace for 60 years, but bitter disputes arose over its interpretation. Further instability was caused by conflict between the Habsburgs and their Austrian and Bohemian subjects, who by 1600 were largely Protestant. In 1618, the Bohemians rebelled, deposing Ferdinand II as their king in 1619. The rebels were defeated, but the war spread into the Empire after 1620. The Thirty Years' War devastated the empire, reducing a population in 1618 of between 20 and 25 million by a third.

3 In the first phase of The Thirty Years' War (map right) the Habsburgs extirpated Protestantism in their patrimonial lands and reclaimed church lands in Germany secularized by Protestants (the Edict of Restitution, 1629). This provoked a Swedish invasion supported by French subsidies and German Protestant princes (1630–2). Spanish intervention helped check the Protestant revival, but increasing involvement of foreigners brought the conciliatory Peace of Prague (1635) between the emperor and leading Protestant princes, although Calvinists were excluded. French intervention to shore up Sweden in 1635 ensured it was not until 1648 that peace was attained at Westphalia.

The Peace of Westphalia (1648), which ended it, brought religious compromise and established a new political framework. The power of the Emperor and the princes was better defined, and the Diet sat in permanent session at Regensburg from 1663; the way was opened for political and economic recovery. Nevertheless, Westphalia brought new problems. The more powerful princes soon created standing armies and played a more prominent role in European relations. The electors of Brandenburg built a new power-base in Prussia, while in 1697 the elector of Saxony turned Catholic to secure election to the Polish throne as Augustus II. In 1714, the elector of Hanover became king of England as George I.

Economic growth

Despite its problems, most Germans still saw the empire as their natural political framework, and the 18th century saw economic expansion in many areas, particularly Silesia, where major landowners combined with government to invest in mining, iron and textiles, and the lower Rhineland and Saxony, which was probably the most advanced of all. But farming remained dominant, with three-quarters of Germany's population still rural in 1815, and towns and cities small compared with those of England and France: Berlin's 140,000 inhabitants in 1777 compared with 260,000 in Vienna, 670,000 in Paris and over 850,000 in London. Nevertheless, this reflected the empire's decentralized constitution, and in cities such as Weimar, Karlsruhe, Mannheim and Stuttgart attempts were made to implement Enlightenment ideas in ambitious reform programmes, often strikingly successful precisely because the principalities were so small. Germany experienced a literary revival in which Goethe and Schiller were figures of international significance. Yet with the import of French revolutionary ideas after 1789, the empire's institutions proved incapable of absorbing new ideas or adjusting to meet the challenge of Napoleon. In 1806, Francis II's abdication as Holy Roman Emperor ended a line which had begun 850 years earlier.

Abbreviations

- **A.** Archbishopric
- **B.** Bishopric
- **C.** County
- **D.** Duchy
- **E.** Electorate
- **L.** Landgraviate
- **M.** Margraviate
- **P.** Principality

- **B. of E.** Bishopric of Erchstätt
- **B. of H.** Bishopric of Halberstadt
- **B. of HILDES.** Bishopric of Hildesheim
- **B. of L.** Bishopric of Lübeck
- **B. of MIN.** Bishopric of Minden
- **C. of B.** County of Bentheim
- **C. of ER.** County of Erbach
- **C. of HNL.** County of Hohenlohe
- **C. of RAV.** County of Ravensberg
- **C. of SCH.** County of Schwarzburg
- **C. of S.** County of Solms
- **C. of WAL.** County of Waldeck
- **C. of L.** County of Limburg
- **D. of C.** Duchy of Cleves
- **L. of HESSE-DARM** Landgraviate of Hesse-Darmstadt
- **of LAU.** Principality of Lauenburg
- **P. of PFALZ-SULZB** Principality of Pfalz-Sulzbach
- **of ZBN.** Principality of Zweibrücken
- **HOZLN.** Hohenzollern

3 The Thirty Years' War, 1618–48

- → route of Gustavus Adolphus, 1630–2
- → route of the Spanish army, 1634
- ✕ Imperial (Catholic) victory
- ✕ Imperial (Catholic) defeat
- — Holy Roman Empire
- — affected by Edict of Restitution, 1629
- ■ date region became Lutheran
- ▲ date region became Calvinist

the religious position in 1640:
- Lutheran
- Calvinist
- Catholic
- regained by Roman Catholics

The ascendancy of France

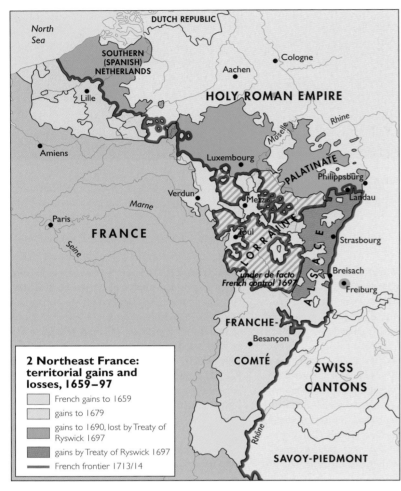

2 Northeast France: territorial gains and losses, 1659–97

	French gains to 1659
	gains to 1679
	gains to 1690, lost by Treaty of Ryswick 1697
	gains by Treaty of Ryswick 1697
—	French frontier 1713/14

Louis XIV's France was the most powerful state in Europe. By 1680 the king was acclaimed as "Louis the Great" and military victories were matched by a flowering of the arts and economic and colonial expansion. Yet French success pushed the other great powers, England, the Dutch Republic and the Austrian Habsburgs, into a coalition which, by 1709, had brought France close to invasion and defeat.

3 Carlos II, ruler of Spain, Spanish America, the south Netherlands and half of Italy, died childless in 1700, bequeathing his empire to Philip, grandson of Louis XIV. This concentration of territory in Bourbon hands overturned the balance of power in Europe, provoking war with Britain, the Dutch Republic, the Holy Roman Empire, Portugal and Savoy (map below). Bourbon victories were followed by a string of defeats. By the peaces of Utrecht (1713) and Rastatt (1714), Philip kept Spain and Spanish America; Savoy and the Austrian Habsburgs partitioned the rest.

2 With Paris and later Versailles vulnerable to invasion from the northeast, Louis was anxious to expand into the Spanish Netherlands and to fortify the frontier defences (map above). This can be partly explained by Louis's fear that at the death of Carlos II of Spain, Spanish possessions on Louis's northeast frontier would be left to the Austrian Habsburgs, raising the spectre of a resurrection of the empire of Charles V. For the same reason, he conquered Franche-Comté, widened his hold on Alsace, occupied Lorraine and in 1681 annexed Strasbourg.

DURING THE REIGN OF Louis XIV France became so powerful that other states feared her ascendancy, regarding her as a danger to the balance of power on the Continent. Louis was suspected of plans to oust the Austrian Habsburgs from their traditional position as elected Holy Roman Emperor and of spearheading a second Catholic counter-reformation. He was generally held to be seeking French hegemony in Europe.

Such fears rested upon solid ground. After a century of foreign war and internal strife, Louis XIV and his able ministers took advantage of the peaceful years between 1659 and 1672 to make great progress in manufacturing, in trade, in overseas expansion and in ship-building. At the same time the French army was greatly expanded. The richness of French resources, including a population estimated at 20 million (Great Britain, in comparison, had a population of less than 8 million), played a significant part in these developments, but so did conscious effort and directives from the centre.

Territorial consolidation

Louis' objectives were at first quite limited and concerned the security of France's frontiers. Habsburg encirclement, forged by the family compacts of the Austrian and Spanish Habsburgs, was still felt to be pressing round France though the Peace of Westphalia (1648) brought sovereignty over Metz, Toul and Verdun and possession of the landgravates of Upper and Lower Alsace. The Peace of the Pyrenees (1659) plugged the gap in the southern frontier with Spain ceding Roussillon and northern Cerdagne. Yet France was still vulnerable from the Spanish Netherlands and Franche-Comté as well as through Lorraine and the Belfort Gap. This helps to explain the two aggressive wars of Louis' reign: the War of Devolution, fought to lay claim to part of the Spanish Netherlands in 1667–8; and the attack on the Dutch Republic in 1672. The latter, much to Louis' discomfiture, escalated into a European-wide war not settled until 1678–9.

Famine and war

Louis tried to avoid large-scale war after 1679 by resort to arbitration and treaties to settle European problems, but the memories of his early wars and the enormous power of France made the rest of Europe suspicious. He caused further unease by his "reunion" policy to expand his control of German border areas and he lost the sympathy of all Protestant powers for his persecution of the Huguenots. The deleterious economic effects of the exodus of over 200,000 French Calvinists in the 1670s and 1680s have been greatly exaggerated, but the international consequences of Louis' revocation of the Edict of Nantes (1685) (see p. 204) were far-reaching, and contributed to the outbreak of the Nine Years' War (1688–97) and the War of the Spanish Succession (1701–14) (see map 3).

The defensive element in Louis' foreign policy is still disputed among historians, but can be demonstrated by the construction of a *barrière de fer* of

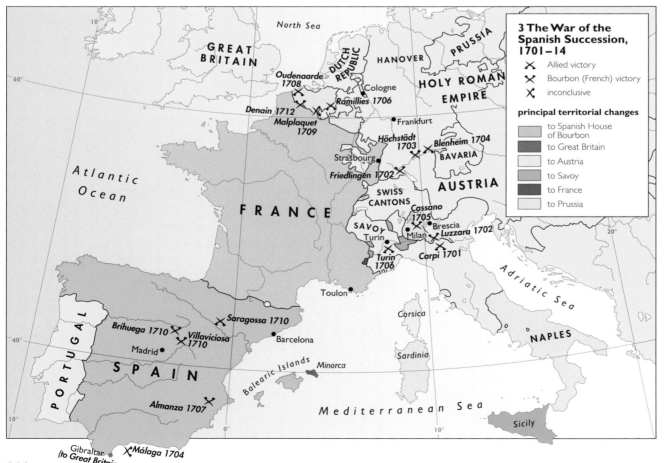

3 The War of the Spanish Succession, 1701–14

✕	Allied victory
✕	Bourbon (French) victory
✕	inconclusive

principal territorial changes

	to Spanish House of Bourbon
	to Great Britain
	to Austria
	to Savoy
	to France
	to Prussia

HE UNITED IN HIS PERSON GREAT MAJESTY AND AFFABILITY. WHILE COMMANDING MEN HE REMEMBERED THAT HE WAS A MAN HIMSELF, AND HE HAD A TALENT FOR WINNING THE HEARTS OF ALL THOSE WHO HAD THE HONOUR OF APPROACHING HIM. IN HIM ALSO WERE GREAT PIETY AND JUSTICE ... IN THE MIDST OF THE DISORDERS OF WAR HE MADE GOOD GOVERNMENT FLOURISH AND SPREAD THE SCIENCES AND ARTS THROUGHOUT HIS KINGDOM ... ALL QUALITIES WORTHY OF FORMING THE PERFECT MODEL OF A GREAT KING ...

Papal Nuncio on the death of Louis XIV, 1715

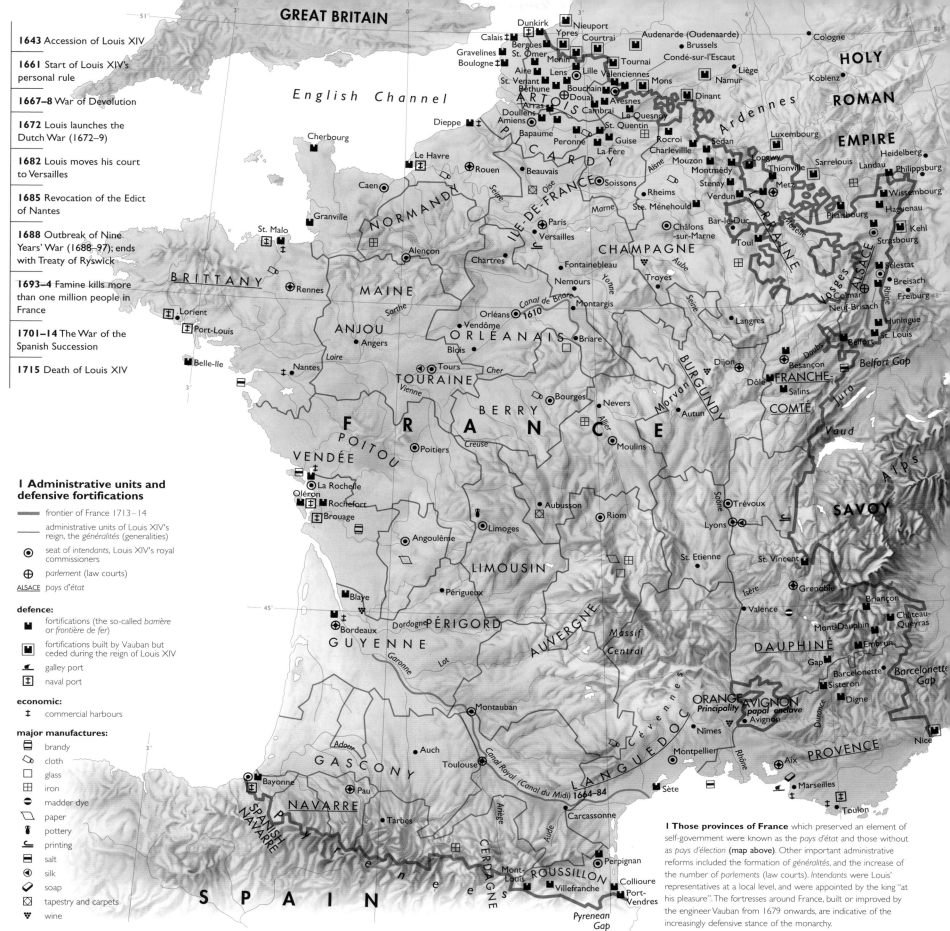

1 Administrative units and defensive fortifications

— frontier of France 1713–14

| administrative units of Louis XIV's reign, the *généralités* (generalities)

◉ seat of *intendants*, Louis XIV's royal commissioners

⊕ *parlement* (law courts)

<u>ALSACE</u> *pays d'état*

defence:

◼ fortifications (the so-called *barrière* or *frontière de fer*)

◼ fortifications built by Vauban but ceded during the reign of Louis XIV

⚓ galley port

⊞ naval port

economic:

‡ commercial harbours

major manufactures:

▯ brandy

◇ cloth

☐ glass

⊞ iron

◖ madder dye

▱ paper

🍶 pottery

⬒ printing

▭ salt

◔ silk

◇ soap

⊠ tapestry and carpets

🍇 wine

1 Those provinces of France which preserved an element of self-government were known as the *pays d'état* and those without as *pays d'élection* (map above). Other important administrative reforms included the formation of *généralités*, and the increase of the number of *parlements* (law courts). *Intendants* were Louis' representatives at a local level, and were appointed by the king "at his pleasure". The fortresses around France, built or improved by the engineer Vauban from 1679 onwards, are indicative of the increasingly defensive stance of the monarchy.

---

fortresses around the whole of France (*see* map 1) and by his willingness to promote a peaceful partition of the Spanish empire before the death of Carlos II. When that policy failed and the dying Spanish king offered the crown to his grandson, the future Philip V, Louis had no alternative but to accept. While understandable, it was a fateful decision for his subjects. Over a million had starved during the terrible famine of 1693–4 and nearly as many would perish as war combined with natural disaster to exact a terrible toll.

Cultural ascendancy

French ascendancy between 1648 and 1715 was not apparent only in the fields of politics, diplomacy and war. Louis' work for French architecture, learning, and for science and the arts in general, and his pensions paid to a great number of European poets, artists and scholars, whether they studied in France or not, may seem more important than his wars. His court at Versailles and his support for academies became models for other princes. French became the language of the educated classes all over Europe and helped to create the the country's cosmopolitan civilization of the late 17th and the early 18th centuries. France also made progress during his reign in the number of colleges and hospitals; in the codification of laws; in administrative practices and efficiencies; and in a range of practical improvements from street lighting and policing in Paris to the digging of the Canal Royal (completed by 1684), which provided cheap and efficient communication between the Atlantic and the Mediterranean. Taken as a whole, the reign fixed the French frontiers in Europe (though colonial cessions had to be made to Great Britain) and in the history of French civilization, the period is deservedly honoured with the title *Le Grand Siècle*.

In the vast palace of Versailles, seen (right) in the background behind Jean-Baptiste Tuby's bronze sculpture of Apollo rising from the waters, Louis XIV directed the fortunes of France. The court was household to the king, the centre of government and a source of inspiration – and envy – to monarchs throughout Europe.

The struggle for empire

From 1713 until 1815 Great Britain and France fought for global supremacy in India, North America and the Caribbean. Britain, with her great naval strength, was always at an advantage because France was first and foremost a continental power. Control of the seas allowed the British to defeat her enemy in North America and India.

2 The capture of Madras by the French under Dupleix in 1746 began the struggle for India (map below). As in America, British sea power proved decisive. Dupleix was checked at Trichinopoly in 1752, and after the capture of Bengal in 1757 the British could reinforce the Carnatic at will. The capture of Pondicherry in 1761 destroyed French power, and with control of the sea the British were able to hold off all subsequent challenges.

EUROPEAN TERRITORIAL EXPANSION

overseas continued throughout the 18th century and led to serious clashes between Portugal and Spain in the Banda Oriental (Uruguay), between Spain and Great Britain in Georgia and between Great Britain and France elsewhere in North America. Trading monopolies proved an even greater source of friction. Spanish attempts to suppress British and Dutch smugglers reduced the Caribbean to a state of undeclared war. Further north, British efforts to enforce similar restrictions upon its American colonists provoked resistance and finally, from 1775, open revolt.

The Anglo-French struggle

During 1739–40 the fragile peace brought about by the Treaty of Utrecht in 1713 (see p. 214) collapsed as Great Britain and Spain went to war in defence of their trading rights, while Frederick the Great's invasion of Silesia began the struggle for supremacy in eastern Europe (see p. 218). The outbreak of hostilities between Great Britain and France in 1744 brought the colonial conflict and the war for Silesia together into a single conflict that extended from

North America to India and from the West Indies to Russia. This struggle, which lasted intermittently until 1815, rapidly became a duel between Great Britain and France for global supremacy. European states, American settlers, Native American chiefs and Indian princes all fought as subsidized and dependent allies of these two great powers.

Conflict in North America

The Treaty of Aix-la-Chapelle (1748) settled none of the outstanding questions, and fighting began again in North America in 1754. France quickly achieved local military superiority with its strategically sited forts preventing further British expansion. The outbreak of the Seven Years' War in Europe (1756–63) transformed the situation. France was handicapped by its continental commitments and Britain took control of the Atlantic, decisively defeating the French fleet at Quiberon Bay and Lagos in 1759. With French forces in Canada cut off from reinforcements Louisbourg fell in 1758, Quebec in 1759 and Montreal in 1760.

The British triumph was short-lived. Between 1763 and the American War of Independence

(1776–83: see p. 224), France rebuilt both its navy and its alliances in pursuit of revenge. By 1781, confronted in home waters by a hostile coalition of France, Spain and the Dutch Republic and over-strained by the need to defend an empire stretching from Canada to India, Great Britain was forced to surrender control of North American waters. The French blockade of Yorktown forced a major British army to surrender, and in 1783 Great Britain was obliged to recognize American independence.

Rivalry in India

During these same years the British founded a new

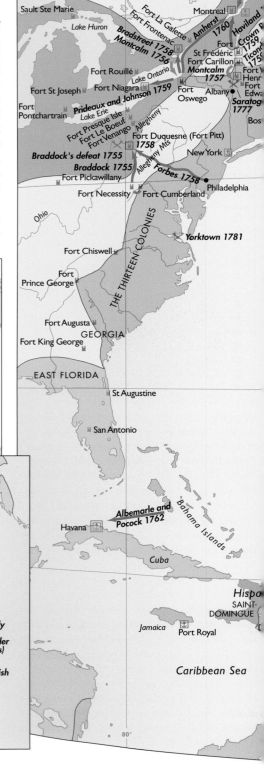

empire in India. The emergence of independent princes from the ruins of the Mughal empire in the early 18th century gave the English and the French East India companies opportunities to intervene in local politics. Here again sea power was decisive. Thus, after early French successes, Great Britain's ability to reinforce its position by sea enabled it to check France's ambitious designs in the Carnatic. But the real foundation of the British empire in India followed Clive's victory at Plassey (1757) which gave the British control of the rich province of Bengal (see p. 190). Reinforcements from Bengal enabled the British to eliminate French influence in the Carnatic and become the predominant European power in India.

The French revolution of 1789 shattered the French navy and left British naval power preeminent. This ruined Napoleon's plans for the invasion of Great Britain. By 1815, the French, Spanish, Dutch and Danish fleets were defeated, their colonies mostly in British hands. With the acquisition of the Cape, Ceylon and Mauritius, Great Britain secured the route to India, and laid the foundations for the second British empire.

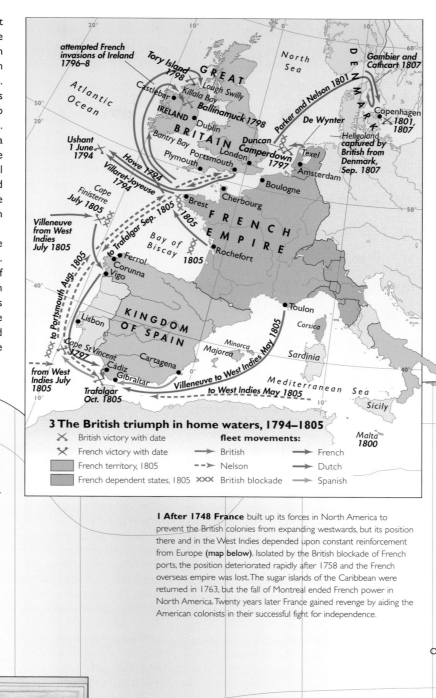

3 The British triumph in home waters, 1794–1805

- ✕ British victory with date
- ✕ French victory with date
- French territory, 1805
- French dependent states, 1805

fleet movements:
- → British
- --→ Nelson
- XXX British blockade
- → French
- → Dutch
- → Spanish

1 After 1748 France built up its forces in North America to prevent the British colonies from expanding westwards, but its position there and in the West Indies depended upon constant reinforcement from Europe **(map below)**. Isolated by the British blockade of French ports, the position deteriorated rapidly after 1758 and the French overseas empire was lost. The sugar islands of the Caribbean were returned in 1763, but the fall of Montreal ended French power in North America. Twenty years later France gained revenge by aiding the American colonists in their successful fight for independence.

ENGLAND IS THE DECLARED ENEMY OF YOUR POWER AND OF YOUR STATE; SHE ALWAYS WILL BE. HER AVIDITY IN COMMERCE, THE HAUGHTY TONE SHE TAKES IN THE WORLD'S AFFAIRS, HER JEALOUSY OF YOUR POWER, THE INTRIGUES THAT SHE HAS MADE AGAINST YOU, MAKE US FORESEE THAT CENTURIES WILL PASS BEFORE YOU CAN MAKE A DURABLE PEACE WITH THAT COUNTRY WHICH AIMS AT SUPREMACY IN THE FOUR QUARTERS OF THE GLOBE.

Duke of Choiseul, French foreign minister, to Louis XV, 1765

3 In the final confrontation between Great Britain and France the decisive battles were fought in European waters **(map left)**. Weakened by the revolution, the French fleet was no match for the British, and as successive invasion attempts foundered against British superiority at sea, Britain occupied its rival's possessions. By 1815, and the final defeat of Napoleon, British control of the key strategic colonies left it as the supreme imperial power.

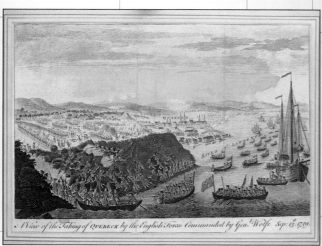

The fall of Quebec (above) in October 1759 signed the death warrant of the French empire in North America. The city was taken after a daring assault by British troops, commanded by General James Wolfe, who scaled the reputedly impregnable cliffs to surprise French forces led by General Montcalm. Both generals died in the battle. It was British control of the seas that made the triumph possible.

1 The struggle in the North Atlantic and North America, 1754–82

- → British operations and date
- → French operations and date
- ✕ British victory
- ✕ French victory
- British fort
- French fort
- Spanish fort
- British naval base
- French naval base
- Spanish naval base
- British capture and date
- French capture and date
- British possessions
- French possessions
- Spanish possessions

The age of partition: eastern Europe

After 1648, a new balance of power in eastern Europe was brought about by the decline of both Poland-Lithuania and the Ottoman empire. Turkish resilience preserved the Ottoman empire from collapse, but Poland's internal weakness was cynically exploited by its neighbours to block reform and to destroy and partition the state.

> CATHERINE AND I ARE SIMPLY BRIGANDS, BUT I WONDER HOW THE QUEEN-EMPRESS MANAGED TO SQUARE HER CONFESSOR! … SHE WEPT AS SHE TOOK; THE MORE SHE WEPT, THE MORE SHE TOOK.
>
> **Frederick II of Prussia on Maria Theresa during the First Partition of Poland**

1652 First use of the *liberum veto* in the Polish *Sejm*

1669 Ottoman conquest of Crete

1672 Peace of Buczacz: Ottomans take Podolia from Poland

1683 Siege of Vienna

1699 Peace of Carlowitz: Poland regains Podolia; Habsburgs gain all of Hungary

1772 First Partition of Poland-Lithuania

1791 Polish Constitution of 3rd May

1793 Second Partition of Poland-Lithuania

1795 Third Partition of Poland-Lithuania

POLAND'S FAILURE TO CRUSH the revolt of the Zaporozhian Cossacks after 1648 (see p. 176) opened a new chapter in east European history. Poland-Lithuania was torn by foreign invasion in the Second Northern War (1655–60) and although it recovered it could not prevent the loss of Kiev and the left-bank Ukraine to Muscovy at the treaty of Andrusovo (1667) or rebuild its military system, with the result that the Ukraine remained a battleground for Poland, Russia and the Ottomans. The Cossacks divided into pro-Polish, pro-Russian and pro-Ottoman factions in the period known in Ukraine as "the Ruin".

Ottoman revival and decline

The renewed opportunities in Ukraine tempted the Ottoman empire, which pursued an expansionist policy under a succession of Grand Viziers from the Köprülü family. It reconquered Tenedos and Lemnos from Venice (1657) and seized Crete (1669). At the peace of Buczacz (1672) Podolia was then taken from Poland, before Grand Vizier Kara Mustafa led a huge army to besiege Vienna (1683). A combined Imperial and Polish army led by King John III Sobieski of Poland-Lithuania (1674–96) drove the Ottomans from the city wall. Thereafter the establishment in 1684 of the Holy League of Venice, Austria and

Poland-Lithuania, supported by the Papacy, marked the start of a long campaign to push the Ottomans back. In 1686 Russia, too, joined the alliance.

The Ottomans could not combat the new military sophistication of European armies. At the peace of Carlowitz (1699), Podolia was returned to Poland, and Austrian possession of Hungary was confirmed. Yet division and distractions among the allies ensured that until 1739 the Ottoman empire, far from collapsing, was able to reverse some of its defeats. Azov, seized by Russia in 1696, was returned in 1711 after Peter I's army was surrounded on the river Prut, while Serbia and parts of Wallachia, ceded to Austria at Passarowitz in 1718, were regained in 1739 at the Peace of Belgrade. It was only after 1770 that Russian expansion to the Black Sea and the Caucasus was triumphantly resumed. Nonetheless Ottoman resilience was still enough to ensure that retreat was gradual. Only after 1815 did the balance tip decisively against the Ottomans and their final decline begin.

Sobieski's triumph at Vienna, however, marked the Commonwealth of Poland-Lithuania's last major victory as a significant European power, as the political problems which increasingly paralysed its institutions became clear to its neighbours. The Commonwealth's

diet (the *Sejm*) was composed of delegates from provincial dietines (*sejmiki*). Decisions were consensual; in 1652, this saw the first acceptance of the *liberum veto*, by which a sole delegate had the right to block *Sejm* decisions. Henceforth, *Sejm* sessions regularly broke up without deciding anything, including the levying of taxes with which to pay the army.

The partitions of Poland

The first plans to partition Poland-Lithuania were drawn up in 1656–7, but after 1660 its neighbours recognized that there were advantages to be drawn from preserving it politically divided and weak. The *liberum veto* proved the perfect instrument: deputies could always be bribed to break the *Sejm*. Hopes of revival after the election of King Augustus II, elector of Saxony, (1697–1733) were dashed during the Great Northern War (1700–21), when Peter I's political acumen enabled him to establish a virtual Russian protectorate over the Commonwealth from 1717, when its army was limited to 24,000, tiny by 18th-century standards.

This situation suited Austria and Prussia, fighting for control of Silesia after the Prussian invasion of 1740. The War of Austrian Succession (1740–8) and the Seven Years' War (1756–63) left Prussia with

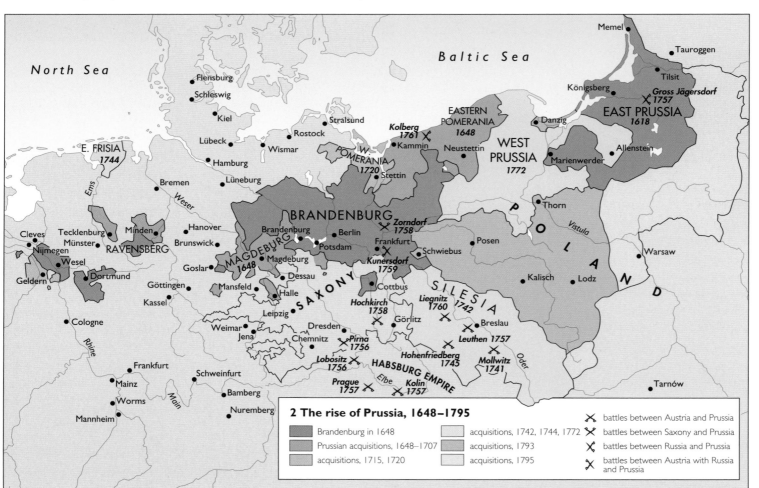

2 The rise of Prussia, 1648–1795

▓ Brandenburg in 1648	░ acquisitions, 1742, 1744, 1772
▓ Prussian acquisitions, 1648–1707	░ acquisitions, 1793
▓ acquisitions, 1715, 1720	░ acquisitions, 1795

✕ battles between Austria and Prussia
✕ battles between Saxony and Prussia
✕ battles between Russia and Prussia
✕ battles between Austria with Russia and Prussia

2 & 3 The electors of Brandenburg acquired a series of scattered territories in the 17th century (**map left**). Frederick William (the Great Elector) gained recognition of his full sovereignty from Poland in 1657; his son Frederick I was crowned king in Prussia in 1701. Frederick II (the Great) seized Silesia from the Habsburgs. Prussia's participation in the Partitions of Poland sealed its position as a Great Power. In three Partitions (1772, 1793, 1795), Russia, Austria and Prussia divided up the whole of Poland (**map above**). Austria gained 4,150,000 inhabitants, Russia 5,500,000 inhabitants and Prussia 2,600,000 inhabitants.

1 The growth of the Habsburg empire

- hereditary Habsburg lands, 1525
- acquisitions, 1526
- acquisitions, 1648–99
- acquisitions, 1699–1772
- acquisitions, 1772–1805
- boundary of the Holy Roman Empire, 1789
- military frontier

1 The Austrian branch of the Habsburg dynasty was founded by Charles V's brother Ferdinand, elected king of Bohemia and Hungary in 1526. For 200 years, the Habsburgs disputed possession of Hungarian territory with the Ottomans (map left). After the Turkish defeat at the siege of Vienna (1683), the Habsburgs extended control rapidly down the Danube, consolidating their gains at the treaties of Carlowitz (1699) and Passarowitz (1718), though some territory was lost at the Peace of Belgrade (1739). Austria lost Silesia to Prussia in the War of the Austrian Succession (1740–8) and failed to recover it in the Seven Years' War (1756–63); compensation came in the shape of the land won in the First and Third Partitions of Poland, though Austrian possession of west Galicia was short-lived.

The Siege of Vienna in 1683 marked both the climax of the long Ottoman wars of expansion in the Balkans and the last great triumph of Polish arms (picture below). The siege of Vienna by a massive Turkish army from July to September was lifted by a combined Imperial and Polish force, led by King John III Sobieski of Poland-Lithuania, which swept down the slopes of the Wienerwald on 12 September to win a dramatic victory.

3 The partitions of Poland-Lithuania

- —— Poland before the partitions
- Russian, Prussian and Austrian acquisitions in the First Partition, 1772
- Russian and Prussian acquisitions in the Second Partition, 1793
- Russian, Prussian and Austrian acquisitions in the Third Partition, 1795

Silesia; the two powers soon found common ground in the east where the election of Stanislaw Poniatowski as king of Poland in 1764 heralded the breakdown of the Russian protectorate over Poland as Poniatowski, inspired by Enlightenment teaching, sought to reform the unworkable Polish constitution. This provoked dangerous opposition: after the anti-Russian Confederation of Bar (1768–72) reduced the Commonwealth to political anarchy, Austria's seizure of the small territory of Zips (Spiz) stimulated Prussia and Russia to join in the First Partition.

Taking advantage of Russian distraction in the Turkish war of 1788–92 Poniatowski summoned the Four-Year *Sejm* (1788–92) which passed the Constitution of 3rd May 1791. This abolished the *liberum veto* and radically restructured the Commonwealth. The prospect of a revived Poland was too much for Russia and Prussia, who in 1793 agreed the Second Partition, in which Prussia secured Danzig. When the following year Tadeusz Kosciuszko led a rising in protest, Russia, Austria and Prussia combined to wipe Poland-Lithuania from the map in the Third Partition.

4 From the mid-17th century the western powers began to realize that the Ottoman empire was no longer an invincible force and had indeed become dangerously weak. As Austria and Russia sought advantage from Turkish disintegration, Prussia expanded, and France and Sweden tried to maintain the traditional balance (map right). With France increasingly paralysed and Britain preoccupied beyond Europe, the eastern powers were able to contrive the Partitions of Poland.

4 Territorial gains and losses in eastern Europe 1648–1795

- Russian gains from Poland, 1667–1795
- Russian gains from Sweden, 1700–43
- Russian gains from Ottomans, 1768–92
- Prussian gains from Austria, 1742
- Prussian gains from Sweden, 1720
- Prussian gains from Poland, 1772–95
- Habsburg gains from Ottomans, 1683–1775
- Habsburg gains from Poland, 1772–95
- Ottoman gains from Venice, 1669–1718

The emerging global economy

During the 18th century international trade made rapid strides, fuelled by the demand for luxury goods and foodstuffs from a Europe growing in wealth. The core of the trading system was the Atlantic triangle, dominated by Britain and France, which was based on the sale of slaves from Africa and the export of sugar and tobacco from the New World.

WHAT WAS THE SOLE CAUSE OF THE REVIVAL OF SLAVERY BY CHRISTIANS, BUT THE DISCOVERY OF WASTE COUNTRIES, AND THE DISPROPORTION WHICH HAS EVER SINCE EXISTED IN THOSE COUNTRIES BETWEEN THE DEMAND AND SUPPLY OF LABOUR? AND WHAT IS IT THAT INCREASES THE NUMBER OF SLAVES OF CHRISTIAN MASTERS, BUT THE INCREASE OF CHRISTIAN CAPITALISTS WANTING LABOURERS, BY THE SPREADING OF CHRISTIAN PEOPLE OVER REGIONS HERETOFORE WASTE?

Edward Gibbon Wakefield,
A Letter from Sydney, 1820

DURING THE COURSE of the 18th century, European and American merchants developed an extensive system of intercontinental trade routes which laid the foundation for the evolution of a sophisticated global economy in the next century. Trade on such a scale encouraged the development of large ocean-going merchant fleets, and the gradual development of modern commercial practices, particularly in the supply of insurance and trade credits. Nonetheless most trade in Europe and in the rest of the world remained local. In 1800 extra-European trade contributed an estimated 4 per cent to Europe's aggregate gross national product.

Mercantilism

For much of the century trade was still governed by mercantilist principles: trade should always be in surplus to provide a stream of bullion, and trade was always a war between states for a fixed quantity of commerce. In reality European merchants could see that trade was growing rapidly over the century, and bullion increasingly being replaced by bills of exchange. Nevertheless states still played an important part in inhibiting trade by pursuing mercantilist policies. British tariffs rose sharply over the 18th century, averaging 30 per cent, while British colonies were banned from producing industrial products that competed with domestic manufactures. Britain's Navigation Acts prevented any other power from engaging in trade in Britain's empire. Bullion was also essential for western European trade with the Baltic, Turkey and Asia, which supplied goods much in demand in Europe but had little market for European products.

There were other factors that made trade difficult. Piracy was widespread, and not until the defeat of the Mediterranean corsairs after 1815 and the elimination of Caribbean pirates by 1830 was trade in these seas secure. Piracy remained endemic in the Indian Ocean and the China Sea. War also interrupted trade

development, for states permitted official piracy in time of war. Trade security could only be guaranteed by those states that possessed large navies, which meant that Britain, France and the Netherlands profited most from the growth of world commerce.

The slave economy

Trade growth owed a great deal to the emergence of the Atlantic economy, where most trans-oceanic trade was conducted. Much of this was based on the Spanish and Portuguese empires which still played an important part in the 18th century, chiefly through the mining of gold and silver and its shipment exclusively to the Iberian peninsula. But the growth of the American colonies, the Caribbean and Canada promoted a new trade. The most important commodity was slaves, and more than 8 million Africans were shipped to the New World between the 17th and 19th centuries. Although outlawed by the United States and Britain in 1807, the slave trade continued until the 1860s.

The rise of the Atlantic slave economy was based on the growing demand in Europe for tobacco, sugar and cotton, all of which were produced in plantations in the New World. British trade in sugar grew six-fold over the 18th century, and the supply of tobacco, much of which was re-exported to Europe, grew from 14,500,000kg (32,000,000lb) to 22,700,000kg (50,000,000lb). Europeans brought manufactured goods to the west African coast to trade for slaves which were then taken to the New World and sold. Plantation products were then exported to Europe. Half of the slaves died before shipping, perhaps a quarter more on board ship, another fifth in the first year of work. It was a brutal and inefficient trade, but it kept Europe supplied with cheap luxury products which it could not afford from Asia.

Trade with Asia

Trade with the rest of the world was small. Asian and African traders kept to inland routes, or engaged in coastal trade. Europeans bought silk, spices, coffee and china, but often paid with gold or silver. Trade was conducted through local chartered companies such as the East India Company, which enjoyed a monopoly of Britain's south Asia trade until 1813. The consolidation of British power in Bengal opened the way in the late 1700s to the opening up of Asian trade. In 1700 Britain imported 32,000kg (70,000lb) of teas; by 1800 the figure had risen to 6,800,000kg (15,000,000lb). The development of Britain's cotton textile industry in the last third of the century produced a trading revolution. By then, the rapid pace of industrialization was poised to open the way for the domination of world markets by European traders in the 19th century and the development of a global system of communication, finance and production.

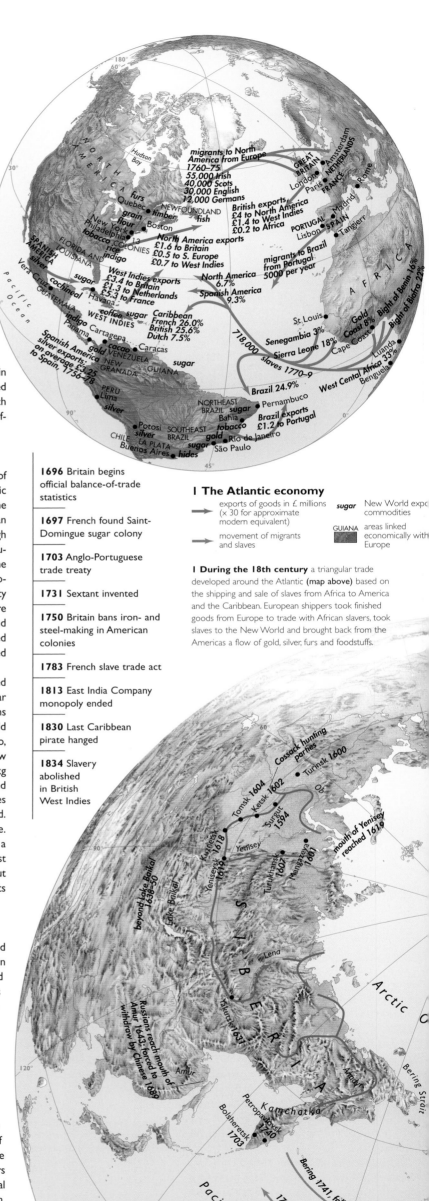

1696 Britain begins official balance-of-trade statistics

1697 French found Saint-Domingue sugar colony

1703 Anglo-Portuguese trade treaty

1731 Sextant invented

1750 Britain bans iron- and steel-making in American colonies

1783 French slave trade act

1813 East India Company monopoly ended

1830 Last Caribbean pirate hanged

1834 Slavery abolished in British West Indies

1 The Atlantic economy
→ exports of goods in £ millions (× 30 for approximate modern equivalent)
→ movement of migrants and slaves
sugar New World export commodities
GUIANA areas linked economically with Europe

1 During the 18th century a triangular trade developed around the Atlantic (map above) based on the shipping and sale of slaves from Africa to America and the Caribbean. European shippers took finished goods from Europe to trade with African slavers, took slaves to the New World and brought back from the Americas a flow of gold, silver, furs and foodstuffs.

4 & 5 French trade grew remarkably over the course of the 18th century, at an average of 3 per cent a year (**chart near right**). By the 1780s 40 per cent of the Bordeaux trade was colonial, and the French merchant fleet plied the Atlantic routes in increasing numbers (**chart far right**): to Senegal for slaves; and from Saint-Domingue, Guadeloupe and Martinique laden with sugar. In 1792 the total tonnage of the French fleet was exceeded only by Britain's.

4 French exports and imports 1716–79

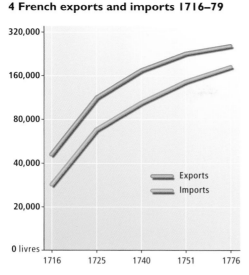

Exports
Imports

320,000
160,000
80,000
40,000
20,000
0 livres

1716 1725 1740 1751 1776

5 Foreign destinations of the French merchant fleet, 1788

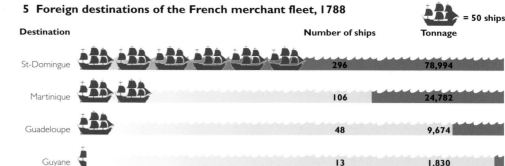

= 50 ships

Destination	Number of ships	Tonnage
St-Domingue	296	78,994
Martinique	106	24,782
Guadeloupe	48	9,674
Guyane	13	1,830
Other American	47	6,997
Africa	60	9,087
Indies	51	19,041

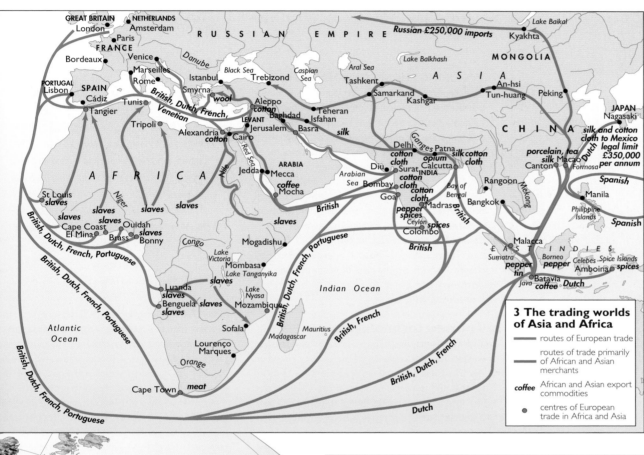

3 The trading worlds of Asia and Africa

—— routes of European trade

—— routes of trade primarily of African and Asian merchants

coffee African and Asian export commodities

● centres of European trade in Africa and Asia

6 Slave prices in Africa, Brazil and the Caribbean

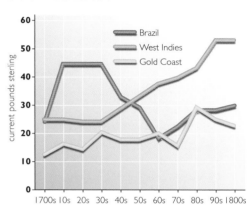

Brazil
West Indies
Gold Coast

current pounds sterling

60
50
40
30
20
10
0

1700s 10s 20s 30s 40s 50s 60s 70s 80s 90s 1800s

6 Slave prices (chart above) rose most sharply with increased demand from the Americas, particularly with the Brazilian gold rush of the early 18th century and the sugar boom in the Caribbean from the mid-century. In the 1770s prices paid for slaves in Africa expanded much faster than the selling price in the New World as African slavers exploited their monopoly.

3 European trade in Africa and Asia (**map left**) was restricted to high-value products bought mainly for silver since there was little demand for Europe's own products. In 1800 British trade with Africa and the Far East was only 10 per cent of her overseas trade. European trade was largely dominated by chartered companies which established forts and entrepôts around the rim of Africa and southern Asia.

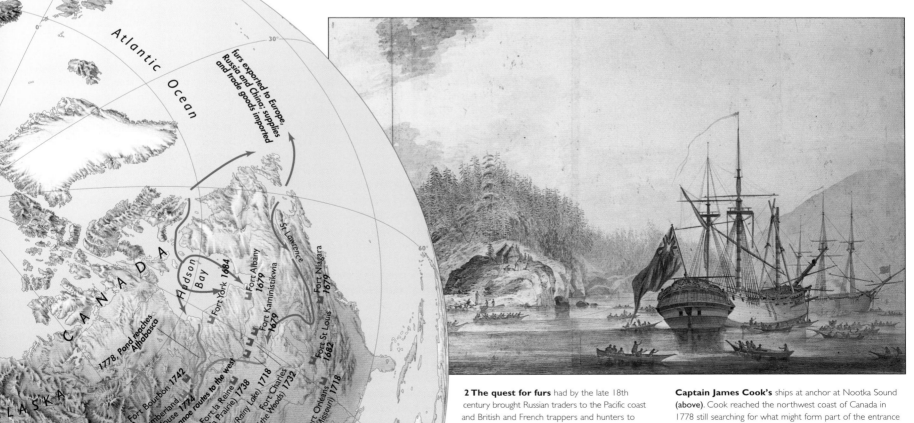

2 The quest for furs had by the late 18th century brought Russian traders to the Pacific coast and British and French trappers and hunters to the Rockies (**map left**). In the 1780s sea trade linked up Kamchatka and Alaska, which became a Russian outpost until sold to the USA in 1867. Furs made up only 3 per cent of American-British trade in the 18th century, but the search for pelts opened up trade for other commodities.

Captain James Cook's ships at anchor at Nootka Sound (**above**). Cook reached the northwest coast of Canada in 1778 still searching for what might form part of the entrance to a Northwest Passage allowing seaborne trade to pass directly from the Atlantic to the Pacific. He did not locate the route he sought, but surveyed an area which was to become a point of severe conflict between the British, Spanish and Russians, all intent on expansion, the security of their existing territories and the dominance of trade in the north Pacific. The British were in the end to prevail.

2 The fur trade

→ 17th-century routes
→ 18th-century routes
🏰 French fort
🏰 British fort

The industrial revolution begins: Great Britain

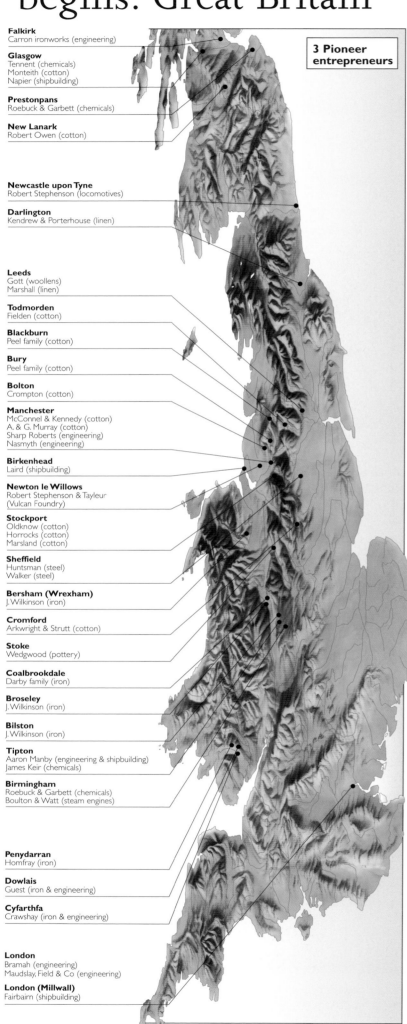

Falkirk
Carron ironworks (engineering)

Glasgow
Tennent (chemicals)
Monteith (cotton)
Napier (shipbuilding)

Prestonpans
Roebuck & Garbett (chemicals)

New Lanark
Robert Owen (cotton)

Newcastle upon Tyne
Robert Stephenson (locomotives)

Darlington
Kendrew & Porterhouse (linen)

Leeds
Gott (woollens)
Marshall (linen)

Todmorden
Fielden (cotton)

Blackburn
Peel family (cotton)

Bury
Peel family (cotton)

Bolton
Crompton (cotton)

Manchester
McConnel & Kennedy (cotton)
A. & G. Murray (cotton)
Sharp Roberts (engineering)
Nasmyth (engineering)

Birkenhead
Laird (shipbuilding)

Newton le Willows
Robert Stephenson & Tayleur
(Vulcan Foundry)

Stockport
Oldknow (cotton)
Horrocks (cotton)
Marsland (cotton)

Sheffield
Huntsman (steel)
Walker (steel)

Bersham (Wrexham)
J. Wilkinson (iron)

Cromford
Arkwright & Strutt (cotton)

Stoke
Wedgwood (pottery)

Coalbrookdale
Darby family (iron)

Broseley
J. Wilkinson (iron)

Bilston
J. Wilkinson (iron)

Tipton
Aaron Manby (engineering & shipbuilding)
James Keir (chemicals)

Birmingham
Roebuck & Garbett (chemicals)
Boulton & Watt (steam engines)

Penydarran
Homfray (iron)

Dowlais
Guest (iron & engineering)

Cyfarthfa
Crawshay (iron & engineering)

London
Bramah (engineering)
Maudslay, Field & Co (engineering)

London (Millwall)
Fairbairn (shipbuilding)

**3 Pioneer
entrepreneurs**

3 The expansion of manufacturing
depended on the emergence of an entrepreneurial
class (map above). The pioneering enterprises
shown here all played significant roles in the
industrial revolution. Men from a variety of social

backgrounds became inventors and businessmen.
At the same time landowners and merchants also
played their part by investing in new processes or
developing the supply of raw materials and an
improved transport system.

During the 18th century, Britain experienced the world's first industrial revolution as new technologies and overseas markets developed. British industry began to meet a growing demand for cheap consumer goods. It was a revolution that ushered in the mass market and paved the way for the economic transformation of the globe.

DURING THE SECOND HALF of the 18th century, the British economy was slowly transformed by the development of new industrial technologies that permitted cheaper production on a larger scale to meet the demands of a growing mass market. In fact the term "industrial revolution" is misleading. The British economy had been growing steadily since the late 17th century, while much of the success of the new industries depended on changes in agriculture, transport and financial services and on the accelerated growth of the population. Nonetheless, at the heart of Britain's late 18th-century industrial transformation lay changes in the production of iron, textiles and machinery and a shift from wood to coal as the primary source of energy.

The new technologies

The key lay in steam power. Steam engines had existed since the beginning of the century, but when the Scottish scientist James Watt developed a more reliable and powerful version in the 1760s it was rapidly applied in mining, then in the iron industry. The invention of a rotative motion engine in 1781 opened the way for steam power to drive machinery. By 1800 the cotton and brewing industries were regular users of steam power. When Watt's patents lapsed in 1800, steam power spread throughout the industrial economy and the transport system. In 1825 the first steam railway was opened, ushering in another new period of economic development.

Innovation was also important in manufacturing. In the cotton textile industry, production was slowly mechanized from the 1760s to the 1790s, though hand-loom weaving was not challenged by machines until the 1820s. Mechanization permitted the shift from small-scale craft output to factory production: by 1816, for example, Arkwright's mill at Cromford in northwest England employed over 700 people. In the iron industry the inventions of Henry Cort in 1784 permitted coal to be used as the main refining fuel for iron, while the steam engine was used to produce rolled and bar-iron for working. Large production units developed which both smelted the ore and produced the finished iron products. Better quality iron could be used in all forms of construction work. Innovation became a continuous process, producing a stream of cheaper and better products.

The conditions for growth

Britain was by no means the only country to produce industrial inventions, but it enjoyed a number of advantages which explain its rapid industrial development. In the first place agriculture experienced its own "revolution", making it more prosperous and more productive. Improvements in patterns of land cultivation, greater use of fertilizers and improved stock breeding all contributed to raising farm incomes. The enclosure of common land accelerated

> THE WHOLE OF THE ISLAND ... SET AS
> THICK WITH CHIMNEYS AS THE MASTS
> STAND IN THE DOCKS OF LIVERPOOL;
> THAT THERE SHALL BE NO MEADOWS IN
> IT; NO TREES; NO GARDENS ... THAT, THE
> SMOKE HAVING RENDERED THE LIGHT
> OF THE SUN UNSERVICEABLE, YOU WORK
> ALWAYS BY THE LIGHT OF YOUR OWN
> GAS: THAT NO ACRE OF ENGLISH
> GROUND SHALL BE WITHOUT ITS SHAFT
> AND ITS ENGINE.
>
> **John Ruskin**
> *The Two Paths,* 1859

after 1760 with Parliamentary Enclosure Acts, and had the effect of creating large integrated farms where modern practices could be introduced and yields and incomes raised. Farming generated growing demand for industrial goods and encouraged the creation of a wider market for farm products.

Agrarian change also encouraged the development of better transport and a more sophisticated capital market to meet the costs of farm improvement and canal-building. Both helped the emergence of early industry. Many businessmen came from humble social backgrounds with little access to finance. Landlord and merchant capital, derived largely from Britain's prosperous overseas and colonial trade, was mobilized for investment in expanding industries and in the building of canals, roads, ports and, from 1825, railways. The rapid growth of a largely unregulated capital market brought a serious bank crisis in 1825 which prompted bank reform in 1826 and, in 1844, the creation of a central bank and clearing-bank system. Without the emergence of this modern credit structure, the pace of industrial change might well have been much slower.

The social revolution

By 1820 Britain was in the throes of rapid social and economic transformation. Population growth produced a flow of cheap labour to the new cities and provided a large new market for mass-produced consumer goods. There were few social barriers to labour mobility or a business career, while governments favoured legislation that encouraged economic growth. It was between 1820 and 1851, when Britain hosted the Great Exhibition to trumpet its economic triumphs, that the industrialization of Britain finally overturned the agrarian social structure and traditional landlord rule. The new business class became an important political force, while the new urban workforce, toiling in appalling conditions with little security, laid the foundations for organized labour protest. "Class" in its modern sense was the direct offspring of industrial change.

(mail port for N

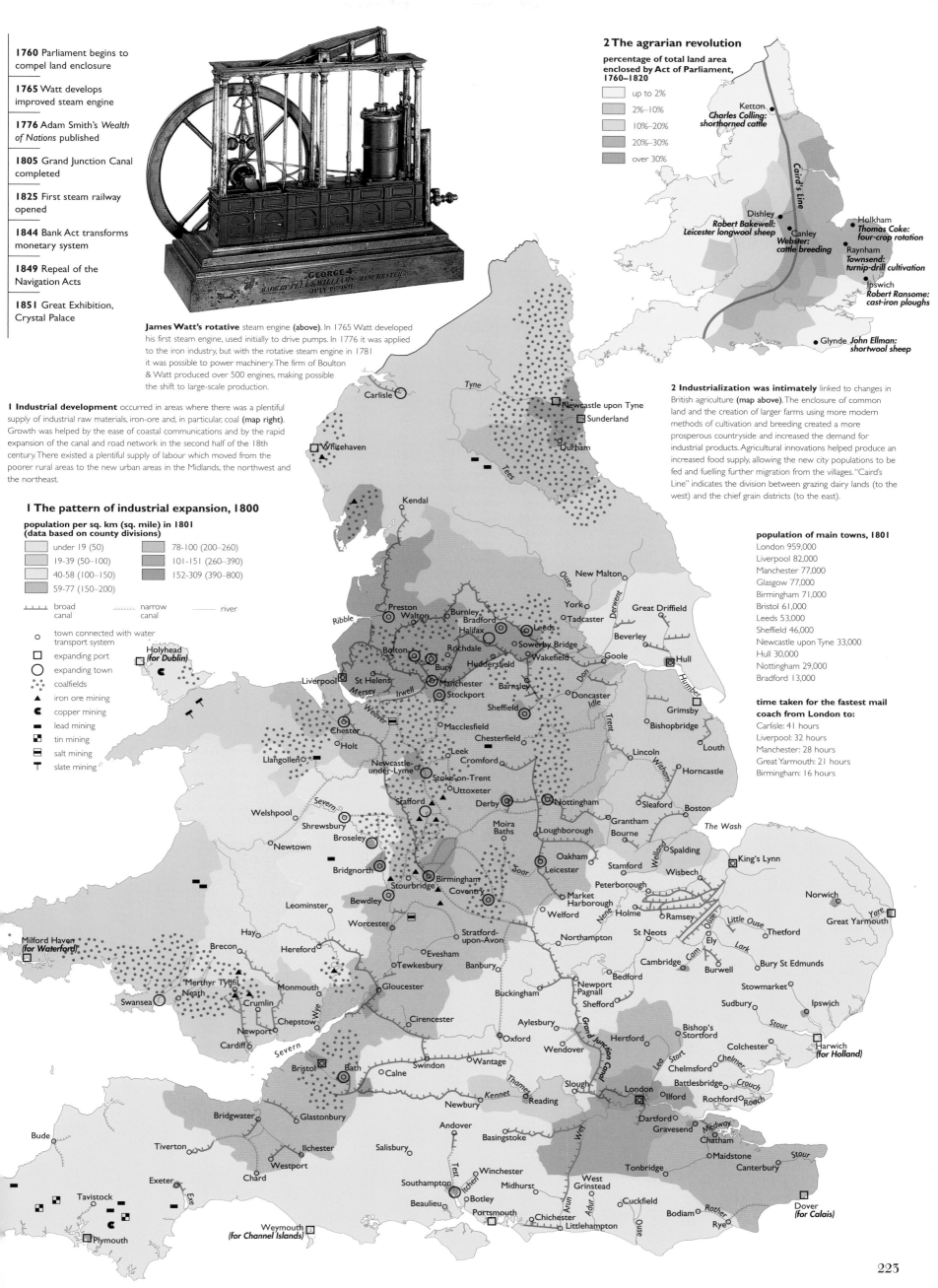

1760 Parliament begins to compel land enclosure

1765 Watt develops improved steam engine

1776 Adam Smith's *Wealth of Nations* published

1805 Grand Junction Canal completed

1825 First steam railway opened

1844 Bank Act transforms monetary system

1849 Repeal of the Navigation Acts

1851 Great Exhibition, Crystal Palace

James Watt's rotative steam engine (above). In 1765 Watt developed his first steam engine, used initially to drive pumps. In 1776 it was applied to the iron industry, but with the rotative steam engine in 1781 it was possible to power machinery. The firm of Boulton & Watt produced over 500 engines, making possible the shift to large-scale production.

1 Industrial development occurred in areas where there was a plentiful supply of industrial raw materials, iron-ore and, in particular, coal (map right). Growth was helped by the ease of coastal communications and by the rapid expansion of the canal and road network in the second half of the 18th century. There existed a plentiful supply of labour which moved from the poorer rural areas to the new urban areas in the Midlands, the northwest and the northeast.

1 The pattern of industrial expansion, 1800

population per sq. km (sq. mile) in 1801
(data based on county divisions)

- under 19 (50)
- 19-39 (50–100)
- 40-58 (100–150)
- 59-77 (150–200)
- 78-100 (200–260)
- 101-151 (260–390)
- 152-309 (390–800)

⊥⊥⊥ broad canal ⋯⋯ narrow canal — river

○ town connected with water transport system
□ expanding port
◯ expanding town
⋰ coalfields
▲ iron ore mining
C copper mining
▬ lead mining
⊡ tin mining
⊟ salt mining
⊤ slate mining

2 The agrarian revolution

percentage of total land area enclosed by Act of Parliament, 1760–1820

- up to 2%
- 2%–10%
- 10%–20%
- 20%–30%
- over 30%

Ketton — *Charles Colling: shorthorned cattle*
Caird's Line
Dishley — *Robert Bakewell: Leicester longwool sheep*
Canley — *Webster: cattle breeding*
Holkham — *Thomas Coke: four-crop rotation*
Raynham — *Townsend: turnip-drill cultivation*
Ipswich — *Robert Ransome: cast-iron ploughs*
Glynde — *John Ellman: shortwool sheep*

2 Industrialization was intimately linked to changes in British agriculture (map above). The enclosure of common land and the creation of larger farms using more modern methods of cultivation and breeding created a more prosperous countryside and increased the demand for industrial products. Agricultural innovations helped produce an increased food supply, allowing the new city populations to be fed and fuelling further migration from the villages. "Caird's Line" indicates the division between grazing dairy lands (to the west) and the chief grain districts (to the east).

population of main towns, 1801
London 959,000
Liverpool 82,000
Manchester 77,000
Glasgow 77,000
Birmingham 71,000
Bristol 61,000
Leeds 53,000
Sheffield 46,000
Newcastle upon Tyne 33,000
Hull 30,000
Nottingham 29,000
Bradford 13,000

time taken for the fastest mail coach from London to:
Carlisle: 41 hours
Liverpool: 32 hours
Manchester: 28 hours
Great Yarmouth: 21 hours
Birmingham: 16 hours

223

The age of revolt

A wave of revolutions swept over Europe and the Americas in the late 18th century, inspired in part by ideas of freedom promoted in the Enlightenment. New social forces challenged the old royal regimes and traditional privileges. Revolutions in France and America symbolized the struggle against despotism and the triumph of a new ideal of citizenship.

IN THE *SOCIAL CONTRACT* (1762), the French philosopher Rousseau claimed "Man is born free, but everywhere he is in chains". He was writing at the height of the European Enlightenment, an intellectual revolt against tradition and superstition. The spirit of the Enlightenment was the emancipation of the individual and the rational organization of society. Both ideas had deep political implications. Over the next 30 years much of the political order of Europe and America was overturned by revolutionaries who drew inspiration from the idea of political liberty and civil rights embodied in Enlightenment political philosophy.

The pattern of revolt was unpredictable and diverse. It owed something to early stirrings of nationalism, evident in Corsica, Poland and Ireland. But the chief revolutions in the American colonies and in France were responses to royal authority which came to be regarded as arbitrary, inefficient and unjust. In 1775 Britain's American colonies rebelled against the existing tax regime and under George Washington fought a six-year war against British-led forces, finally winning independence in 1783. The "founding fathers" of American liberty established a modern constitutional republic based on ideas on human rights culled from Enlightenment Europe.

WHAT WERE FORMERLY CALLED REVOLUTIONS, WERE LITTLE MORE THAN A CHANGE OF PERSONS, OR AN ALTERATION OF LOCAL CIRCUMSTANCES. THEY HAD NOTHING ... THAT COULD INFLUENCE BEYOND THE SPOT THAT PRODUCED THEM. BUT WHAT WE NOW SEE IN THE WORLD, FROM THE REVOLUTION OF AMERICA AND FRANCE, ARE A RENOVATION OF THE NATURAL ORDER OF THINGS, A SYSTEM OF PRINCIPLES AS UNIVERSAL AS TRUTH AND THE EXISTENCE OF MAN, AND COMBINING MORAL WITH POLITICAL HAPPINESS AND NATURAL PROSPERITY.

Tom Paine, *Rights of Man*, 1791

The spread of revolution

The American revolution had a great impact in Europe and many of those involved in it subsequently played a part in the many European revolts. Benjamin Franklin was an important influence in France, while the Polish nationalist Tadeusz Kosciuszko, who fought in the American revolution, returned to lead the Polish revolt against the two powers – Russia and Prussia – which had partitioned Poland in 1792. The revolution in Poland was typical of the popular reaction to the ideal of liberty and independence expressed in the newly-created

1762 Rousseau's *Social Contract* published

1773–4 Pugachev revolt in Russia

1776 American Declaration of Independence

1789 Fall of Bastille signals revolution in France

1791 Slave revolt in Haiti

1793 Execution of Louis XVI

1794–5 Dutch revolt creates Batavian Republic

1798 Irish rebellion under Wolfe Tone

1808 Spanish revolt against French rule

1815 Congress of Vienna imposes "legitimism" on Europe

3 In 1775 the Thirteen Colonies on the eastern coast of North America revolted against British rule (**map below**). Attempts by the British to reassert control over the colonists, such as the 1763 declaration of the "Proclamation Line", forbidding settlement west of the Appalachians, had ended in failure. In 1774 the boundaries of the new Canadian province of Quebec had been enlarged to the Mississippi and Ohio rivers, a move bitterly resented in Virginia and Pennsylvania. When the situation escalated into warfare, the American army under George Washington suffered early defeats until Saratoga in 1777. With French assistance from 1778 a war of attrition set in which culminated in Franco-American victory at Yorktown in 1781. The Treaty of Versailles in 1783 granted independence to the colonies which organized themselves as the United States.

2 The Batavian Republic

- annexed by France after 1794
- ceded to France by Treaty of Hague, 1795
- The Batavian Republic, 1795

2 In 1794-5 French revolutionary armies drove the Coalition from Belgium and the Netherlands. Belgium was annexed to France (**map left**), but in the Netherlands a revolution brought to power pro-French republicans who organised a Batavian Republic, the first to use the words 'liberty, equality and fraternity' as their official slogan. For three years provincial rivalries made it difficult to agree a constitution. In 1798 a unitary state, organised in departments, was established, but six months later a military coup overthrew the government. The republic lasted until 1806 when it was transformed into the Napoleonic Kingdom of Holland.

3 The American War of Independence

- the Thirteen Colonies, 1763
- Indian Reserve, 1763
- Quebec, 1763–74
- Quebec under Quebec Act, 1774
- other British possessions
- Spanish territory
- 1763 Proclamation Line

American War of Independence, 1775–83

- ✕ colonists' victory
- ✕ British victory

USA. In the spring of 1794 thousands of Poles, drawn mainly from the educated and gentry classes, under the military leadership of Kosciuszko, drove the Russian army from Warsaw. Many of those involved were "Jacobins" who modelled themselves on the more radical social reformers and democrats of the French Revolution. The Polish revolution was destroyed by Russian and Prussian forces late in 1794. Attempts to spread the revolution further into eastern Europe failed. Small groups of Jacobins in Budapest were organized by Ignaz Martinovics in 1794 to imitate the Polish revolt, but the leaders were arrested and imprisoned. Only in the Netherlands and northern Italy did the revolutionary example have greater success, not only because ideas of "democracy" were more widely understood and broadcast, but because revolutionary groups there enjoyed the protection of the French.

The French example inspired hope of liberty around the world. In India Tipu Sultan planted a symbolic "Tree of Liberty" and declared himself an ally of revolutionary France against the British. In Haiti a slave revolt in 1791 freed the island from colonial rule. In Latin America the growing local hostility to Spanish rule was fuelled by news of the French revolution. Jacobin conspirators were discovered by the authorities in Quito and Buenos Aires. In Bogotá in 1793, 100 copies of the *Rights of Man* were printed, copied from the French declaration of 1789. In eastern Europe Jacobin activity was stamped out in Vienna and Budapest, while the 1794 Polish revolt, though led by the Polish nobility, used the French cry of "liberty and equality" against its Russian and Prussian oppressors.

Counter-revolution

The wave of political revolt produced a strong counter-revolutionary reaction. Many of the revolutionaries in America and France were themselves conservative in outlook and worked to eliminate more radical or utopian revolutionary movements. Slave revolts in America were brutally suppressed in the 1790s. The revolutionary Directory unleashed a "white terror" against the Jacobins in France, and Napoleon restored a strong centralist and authoritarian state after 1800. In eastern and central Europe reform introduced by so-called Enlightened despots was reversed or suspended and revolt in Poland, Hungary, Bohemia and the Ukraine violently quashed. Though Britain possessed the most liberal political system, the regime stamped hard on Irish nationalism and on any domestic threat of republicanism or domestic agitation.

In 1815 the Vienna Congress, summoned after the defeat of Napoleon, restored much of pre-1789 Europe by adopting the principle of "legitimism". But although monarchy was returned in France, the new ideas of liberty and nationhood were to find fertile ground throughout Europe and the Americas over the following century.

THE AGE OF REVOLT (maps below)

1755, 1793 Corsica Local clans led by Paoli rebelled against Genoese rule. France bought the island from Genoa in 1768 and crushed the revolt. A second attempt by Paoli to secure independence from (revolutionary) France in 1793, led to a brief British occupation; the rise of Bonaparte, himself a Corsican, put an end to the separatist movement.

1768 Geneva Middle-class citizens of the small city-state rebelled against domination by a few patrician families; with French support the latter reasserted predominance in 1782.

1773 Southeast Russia Cossacks, peasants and Asiatic tribes rebelled in the Volga and Ural regions under Pugachev, a Don Cossack. After fierce fighting, the Russian army put down the rebellion in autumn 1774.

1775 America Prolonged resistance by the Thirteen Colonies to Britain's financial policies resulted in open warfare and the Declaration of Independence, 1776. The defeat of Britain led to the formation of the United States in 1783. Numerous slave revolts from the 1790s.

1785, 1794–5 Dutch Netherlands Three-cornered struggle for power between the "Stadholder", patrician families who controlled the Estates General, and the middle-class Patriot party which aimed to democratize the government. In 1787 Prussian troops defeated the Patriot army and restored the "Stadholder" with greater powers. In 1794–5 the Patriot movement revived and with French help a republic was declared.

1787 Austrian Netherlands (Belgium) A revolt against the centralizing policy of Emperor Joseph II led to the proclamation of the Republic of the United Belgian Provinces in 1790. Austrian emperor re-took the area at the end of 1790.

1789 France In 1789 Louis XVI called the Estates General to try to solve the financial crisis, but the gathering turned into a national assembly and with army support royal authority was overturned. In 1791 a constitution was introduced loosely based on the "rights of man", and in 1793 the king was executed and a republic declared. A moderate republic under the Directory ruled from 1795–9 until Napoleon assumed power in 1799.

1789 Liège Middle-class citizens, workers and peasants expelled the prince-bishop. The bishop was restored by Austrian troops in 1790.

1790 Hungary Magyar nobles rejected edicts of Austrian emperor and demanded greater independence for Hungary within Habsburg empire; later, frightened by peasant disturbances, they accepted a compromise with the monarchy.

1791 Poland The king, supported by patriotic nobles, adopted a constitution to modernize government. Catherine II of Russia organized a counter-revolution with the support of some of the greater nobles to restore the old regime, invaded Poland and divided large areas with Prussia. In 1794 a popular revolt led by patriotic nobles under Kosciuszko was brutally crushed by Russian armies and Poland was partitioned between Russia, Prussia and Austria.

1791 Haiti A slave rising in the western (French) part of the island (Saint-Domingue) resulted in the rise of a black leader, Toussaint l'Ouverture; by 1801 he had conquered the rest of the island from the Spaniards and secured virtual independence. The island was then seized by the French, the rising suppressed and independence not fully secured until 1825.

1793 Sardinia Islanders demanded autonomy within combined kingdom of Piedmont-Sardinia. The king reasserted his authority when the French threat subsided in 1796.

1798 Ireland The rebellion of United Irishmen seeking independence from England was put down by the British army. Leading conspirator, Wolfe Tone, committed suicide.

1804 Serbia Revolt against Ottoman atrocities led to demands for autonomy within the Ottoman empire and later for independence. Rebels under Kara George fought until the Ottoman reoccupation of Serbia in 1813.

1808 Spain A national rising against the French provided an opening for an expeditionary force under Wellington. A liberal constitution was proclaimed by Cortes of Cádiz in 1812, but did not survive the restoration of the Bourbon king in 1814.

1809 Tyrol Tyrol had been taken from Austria by Napoleon in 1805 and given to Bavaria. Peasants rebelled against the new rulers. In spite of a brave stand under Andreas Hofer, an innkeeper, the revolt was crushed by Bavarian and French troops.

1810 Spanish America Discontent increased after 1808 when the colonists were faced with the prospect of new imperialist policies from either Napoleon or Spanish liberals; beginning of the revolutionary movement which secured independence by 1826 (*see* p. 250).

The Polish patriot Tadeusz Kosciuszko (1746–1817) at the Battle of Bemis Heights during the War of American Independence in which he volunteered to fight for the American cause. He was military commander of the abortive Polish national revolt in 1794, but following its defeat he finally settled in revolutionary France, where he later died.

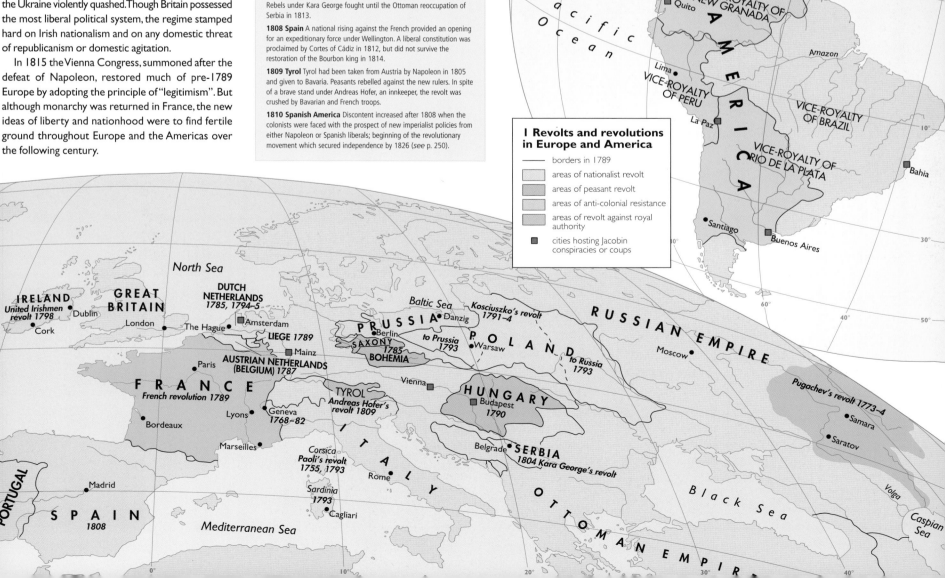

1 Revolts and revolutions in Europe and America

— borders in 1789
areas of nationalist revolt
areas of peasant revolt
areas of anti-colonial resistance
areas of revolt against royal authority
■ cities hosting Jacobin conspiracies or coups

The French Revolution

In the summer of 1789 the most powerful monarchy in Europe was overthrown by a popular revolution in favour of constitutional rule. There followed ten years of political turmoil as moderate parliamentarians and radical republicans fought over the political future of France. The many different ideals represented by the revolution were impossible to reconcile, and in 1799 a new era of authoritarian rule began under the dashing revolutionary general, Napoleon Bonaparte.

THE FRENCH REVOLUTION had many causes, some long-term, some more immediate. For 30 years there had been growing peasant hostility to rising rents and declining common rights as gentry and bourgeois landowners tried to cope with inflation and falling incomes by tightening the screw. For much of the century France was the hub of new ideas about liberty, citizenship and patriotism, and a powerful intellectual demolition of royal authority and clerical influence. By the 1780s the language of liberty had permeated much of the educated elite, gentry and bourgeois, and had filtered down into popular politics. Craftsmen and shopkeepers came to articulate their social and economic grievances in terms of civil rights and economic justice.

The actual events that came to be known as the French Revolution were precipitated by a crisis of

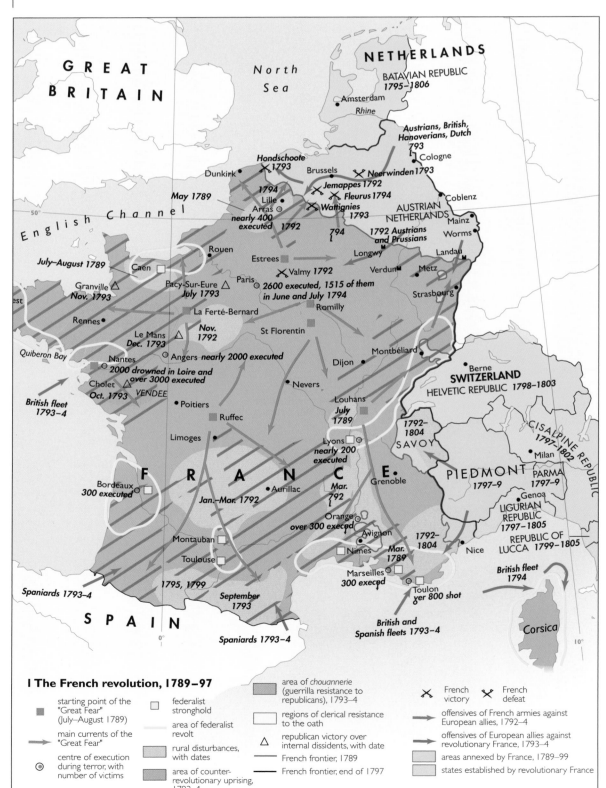

3 The Terror

death sentences passed, by département

- over 100
- 50–100
- 10–50
- fewer than 10

3 In 1793–4 the Committee of Public Safety prompted a wave of violence against alleged counter-revolutionaries (map above). An estimated 16,000 were executed by the revolutionary tribunals, but up to 240,000 victims may have died in the civil war in the Vendée and the areas of federalist revolt. The Prairial Law of June 1794 gave revolutionary tribunals the right to condemn prisoners to death without proof or a defence lawyer. By summer 1794 executions ran at ten times the level of the previous year, but by August the leaders of the Terror had been executed in turn and the Thermidorian reaction ended the savage counter-revolutionary violence.

1 The revolution that began in Paris quickly engulfed the whole of France (map left). By 1792–3 economic crisis and revolutionary wars prompted the radicalization of the revolution and initiated what became known as the Great Terror across France, during which thousands were executed. Opposition existed, particularly in northwestern and southern France, but by 1795 the more moderate Directorate came to power and set about a period of consolidation and reform.

1 The French revolution, 1789–97

- starting point of the "Great Fear" (July–August 1789)
- main currents of the "Great Fear"
- centre of execution during terror, with number of victims
- federalist stronghold
- area of federalist revolt
- rural disturbances, with dates
- area of counter-revolutionary uprising, 1793–4
- area of *chouannerie* (guerrilla resistance to republicans), 1793–4
- regions of clerical resistance to the oath
- republican victory over internal dissidents, with date
- French frontier, 1789
- French frontier, end of 1797
- French victory
- French defeat
- offensives of French armies against European allies, 1792–4
- offensives of European allies against revolutionary France, 1793–4
- areas annexed by France, 1789–99
- states established by revolutionary France

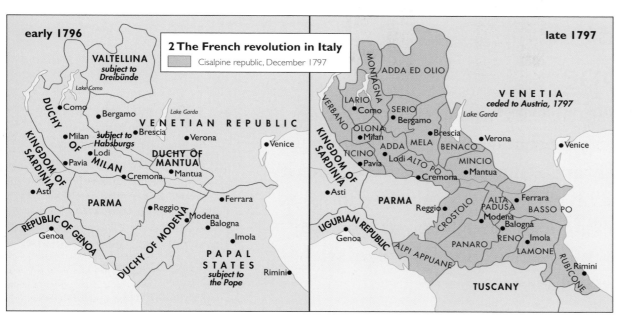

2 The French revolution in Italy

Cisalpine republic, December 1797

early 1796

VALTELLINA
subject to Dreibünde

Lake Como

DUCHY OF MILAN

KINGDOM OF SARDINIA

• Como
• Bergamo
• Milan
• Lodi
• Pavia
• Asti
• Cremona
• Mantua

VENETIAN REPUBLIC
subject to Habsburgs

• Brescia
• Verona
• Venice

DUCHY OF MANTUA

PARMA

REPUBLIC OF GENOA

• Genoa
• Reggio
• Modena
• Balogna
• Imola
• Ferrara

DUCHY OF MODENA

PAPAL STATES
subject to the Pope

Rimini

late 1797

MONTAGNA
ADDA ED OLIO
LARIO
SERIO
OLONA
VERBANO
TICINO
ADDA
MELA
ALTO PO
MINCIO
BENACO
ALTA PADUSA
CROSTOLO
PANARO
RENO
LAMONE
RUBICONE
ALPI APPUANE

• Como
• Bergamo
• Milan
• Brescia
• Verona
• Lodi
• Pavia
• Cremona
• Mantua
• Asti
• Reggio
• Modena
• Balogna
• Imola
• Ferrara
• Rimini
• Genoa
• Venice

VENETIA
ceded to Austria, 1797

Lake Garda

KINGDOM OF SARDINIA

LIGURIAN REPUBLIC

PARMA

BASSO PO

TUSCANY

2 The French revolutionaries hoped to export their revolution to neighbouring regions. Belgium and the Netherlands were annexed and new republics installed. In northern Italy **(map left)** French armies under Bonaparte drove the Austrians from the northern and central provinces in 1796. In June 1797 the various republics set up with French co-operation merged into a Cisalpine Republic, organized, like France, in administrative departments. In Lombardy, revolutionaries used a green, white and red flag, which later became the national flag of united Italy. In spring 1799 Austrian, Russian and Turkish forces defeated the French and the republic disappeared under a brutal counter-revolutionary occupation.

WE WISH TO SUBSTITUTE IN OUR COUNTRY …
THE EMPIRE OF REASON FOR THE TYRANNY OF
CUSTOM … A PEOPLE MAGNANIMOUS, POWERFUL
AND HAPPY FOR A PEOPLE LOVABLE, FRIVOLOUS
AND WRETCHED – THAT IS TO SAY, ALL THE
VIRTUES AND MIRACLES OF THE REPUBLIC
FOR ALL THE VICES AND PUERILITIES
OF THE MONARCHY.

Maximilien Robespierre, 1794

state. For much of the century the monarchy had increased levels of central control and fiscal demands, undermining local privilege and raising taxes. The moral authority of the old order was eroded by the rising tide of political criticism and the spread of scurrilous libels of the monarchy and court life. Faced with severe financial crisis, failure in war and poor harvests, Louis XVI tried to stave off criticism by calling the Estates General. This assembly, representing the clergy (known as the First Estate), the gentry (Second Estate) and commoners (Third Estate), had not been summoned since 1614. However, in the summer of 1789 a group of deputies representing the Third Estate (the overwhelming majority of Frenchmen) declared themselves to be a National Assembly and overturned centuries of royal absolutism. On 14 July the royal prison at the Bastille was stormed. In August feudal privilege was abolished throughout France, and the *Declaration of the Rights of Man*, which promised individual liberty in place of royal despotism, was published. Louis was forced to accept a parliamentary constitution and the abolition of much of the structure of privilege that sustained the monarchy and the aristocratic elite.

In December 1792 Louis XVI was brought before the National Convention that would put him on trial during January 1793. The assembly's final decision in favour of execution was carried by one vote. On 21 January 1793 he was executed **(below)**. As he waited for death he was heard to say: "I hope that the shedding of my blood will contribute to the happiness of France."

4 The revolution and administration

administrative divisions pre-1790

Parlements
Pays d'Etat

FLANDERS
ARTOIS
CAMBRÉSIS
NORMANDY
BRITTANY
• Paris
LORRAINE
FRANCHE COMTÉ
BURGUNDY
Corsica
GUIENNE
MARSAN
LABOUR
NÉBOUZAN
DAUPHINE
LOWER NAVARRE
SOULE
BÉARN
BIGORRE
QUATRE VALLÉES
FOIX
LANGUEDOC
PROVENCE

administrative divisions post-1790

département boundary
border of France pre-1789

• Brest
• Paris
• Nantes
• Dijon
Corsica
• Bordeaux
• Lyon
• Toulouse
• Toulon

4 On the eve of the revolution France was a decentralized state divided between different administrative systems, tax regimes and customs areas **(map above)**. Fourteeen *parlements* held local independent judicial rights. The state was also divided into intendancies, run by representative "intendants" of the king. In 1790 France was reorganized into a unitary state, with 83 departments and 41,000 communes, and a common system of courts. The new geography was organized in such a way that no commune would be more than a day's ride from a department capital.

From reform to terror

A new constitution, finally accepted by the king in September 1791, established a constitutional, parliamentary monarchy. The Catholic Church lost many of its privileges, and priests were compelled in November 1790 to swear allegiance to the new order. Thousands refused, and were forced from office, or led local resistance to the Paris-based revolutionary regime in Brittany and large parts of southern France. The revolutionary assembly also reformed local administration into "departments" in 1791, and began a programme of legal reform and land redistribution.

The revolutionary leadership was never unitary. Divisions emerged over the utopian ideals of some revolutionaries, who wanted to create a new social and moral order and develop a "new man" on the enlightenment model. The more moderate Girondin faction launched a revolutionary war in April 1792 against Austria and other counter-revolutionary forces. The ensuing economic crisis, the rhetoric of patriotic mobilization and fear of conspiracy in France, produced a radical transformation of French politics. Under the leadership of the Jacobin faction, any pretence at representative government vanished. The constitutional monarchy was abolished in September 1792 and a republic declared. A Committee of Public Safety was set up in April 1793, and a little later a Committee of General Security, which launched a nationwide hunt for traitors to the revolution. Thousands of nobles, clergymen, merchants, as well as numbers of peasants and workers, were executed in 1793 and 1794 on the strength of often trumped-up charges. Growing popular revulsion against terrorism led to the execution in July 1794 of leading Jacobins, including their chief spokesman, Maximilien Robespierre. A reaction against the utopianism of the revolutionary elite produced a more moderate revolutionary Directorate in November 1795, which savagely crushed radical political circles while consolidating the reforms of the revolution.

The legacy of the revolution

The French Revolution failed to turn France into a democratic state, and the civil rights enshrined in its opening declaration were subject to constant abuse; but the programme of legal, administrative and educational reform was enduring. The revolution provided an inspiration to political opposition, and the symbols of the new French order were widely imitated. The French parliamentary system established in 1791 gave rise to new political terms: left and right (derived from the physical make-up of the new French assembly building) came to define the battle-lines of European politics, while the term communism was coined by popular radicals in the mid-1790s. For conservatives, the revolution represented for decades to come the unbridled political appetites of the mob.

Napoleon and the reshaping of Europe

Between 1799 and 1815 Napoleon blazed across Europe, plunging the continent into near permanent war and ruthlessly imposing on it French Revolutionary institutions and his own tirelessly cultivated image as a latter-day Julius Caesar. Though he was ultimately defeated and exiled, the world of the *ancien régime* was swept aside for ever.

1799 Napoleon appointed First Consul

1804 *Code Napoléon* published

1805 Battle of Trafalgar; Britain's naval supremacy uncontested

1806 Battle of Jena; Germany reshaped into French-dominated client states

1809–14 Spanish uprising against France drains French resources

1812 Russia invaded; Napoleon suffers catastrophic defeat

1813 Battle of the Nations, Leipzig; Napoleon defeated and exiled

1815 Battle of Waterloo; Napoleon's final defeat followed by exile to South Atlantic

2 Napoleonic institutions (map below), including the system of departments and local prefects and the famous *Code Napoléon*, were introduced in many of the areas conquered by France. Though Napoleon won the support of local reformers, there was little real social change. In Spain the reforms lasted less than five years and were soon reversed.

NAPOLEON, BORN IN 1769 to minor gentry in Corsica, was barely 30 years old when, in November 1799, he became First Consul and de facto ruler of the French First Republic. He had made his name as a Revolutionary general in northern Italy in 1796–7, where his defeat of Austria allowed him to create a new state, the Cisalpine Republic, run on French lines by pro-French Italian notables, a pattern reproduced throughout the areas later conquered by him.

Though Napoleon as First Consul inherited a system with an element of popular participation, within three years the Revolution's democratic aspirations had been smothered and France had been ruthlessly centralized. This concentration of power in his own hands reached its logical conclusion in 1804 with the creation of a French empire over which Napoleon presided as self-appointed emperor.

The primacy of the military
Napoleon's centralization of power took many forms – notably the *Code Napoléon* of 1804 which, in codifying and rationalizing French law, swept away *ancien régime* privilege and increased the power of the French state; the agreement with the Pope in 1802, which ended the dispute for primacy between state and church, again very much in the former's favour; and the creation of a paramilitary police force, the

gendarmerie, which mercilessly suppressed opposition to the Revolution. But its overriding characteristic was the mobilization of France on an unprecedented scale in support of the army. With more than 1.5 million Frenchmen under arms, the French economy came to be dominated by the needs of the military.

This was not yet "total war", but the demands of more than 20 years of conflict turned the Napoleonic empire into a militarized society. The military priorities explain the long string of military triumphs. In 1800 Italy was reconquered and French power extended in Germany. In 1805 Russia and Austria were defeated at Austerlitz and in 1806 Prussia humiliated at Jena. At Eylau in 1807 Russia was again defeated. Under the terms of the subsequent Treaty of Tilsit, French power was extended as far as Poland, where Napoleon established yet another puppet regime, the Grand Duchy of Warsaw.

Napoleon appointed kings, princes and dukes to enforce French rule throughout his empire. In the Kingdom of Westphalia he installed his youngest brother, Jerome. In Naples his brother Joseph was made king. When Joseph was transferred to Spain as its monarch in 1808, Naples was placed under the rule of Napoleon's brother-in-law, Joachim Murat. Holland was ruled by another brother, Louis, from 1806 to 1810. In all these areas, French officials introduced conscription and new taxes, helping finance the almost permanent state of war Napoleon faced.

By 1807 only Britain, at war with France almost continuously since 1792, remained undefeated. Britain's chief weapon was its navy, largely unchallenged by Napoleon after its defeat of the combined French and Spanish fleets at Trafalgar in 1805. But unable to defeat Napoleon on land, Britain then blockaded French ports. Napoleon responded by

BETWEEN OLD MONARCHIES AND A YOUNG REPUBLIC THE SPIRIT OF HOSTILITY MUST ALWAYS EXIST. IN THE EXISTING SITUATION EVERY TREATY OF PEACE MEANS TO ME NO MORE THAN A BRIEF ARMISTICE: AND I BELIEVE THAT, WHILE I FILL MY PRESENT OFFICE, MY DESTINY IS TO BE FIGHTING ALMOST CONTINUALLY.

Napoleon, 1802

I WISHED TO FOUND A EUROPEAN SYSTEM, A EUROPEAN CODE OF LAWS, A EUROPEAN JUDICIARY: THERE WOULD BE BUT ONE PEOPLE IN EUROPE.

Napoleon, writing in exile on St Helena

1 By 1812 Napoleon dominated most of Europe west of Russia. In western Europe **(map right)** French administrators and local notables tried to modernize law and government. The persistent hostility of Britain undermined the empire. The British supported a series of shifting coalitions against Napoleon. Spain rebelled in 1809 and Russia refused to collaborate in 1812. The failure to conquer Russia weakened France and led to Napoleon's fall in 1814–5. The Congress of Vienna in 1815 tore up the Napoleonic empire.

2 Napoleonic institutions

areas which experienced **Napoleonic institutions in full:**
- for more than 10 years
- for less than 5 years

areas which experienced **modified forms of Napoleonic institutions:**
- for more than 8 years
- for less than 5 years
- departments of the French empire

1 Napoleon and the reshaping of Europe
- French territories ruled directly from Paris, c. 1812
- states ruled by members of Napoleon's family, c. 1812
- other dependent states, c. 1812
- British or British-occupied territory
- ☒ French victory   ☒ French defeat
- ☒ battles in the Italian campaign
- ☒ battles in the War of the Second Coalition
- ☒ battles in the War of the Third Coalition
- ☒ battles in the Austrian War of 1809
- ☒ battles in the Peninsular War
- ☒ battles in the Russian campaign
- ☒ battles in the War of Liberation from French rule
- ☒ battles in the defence of France
- ☒ battles in the War of the 100 Days

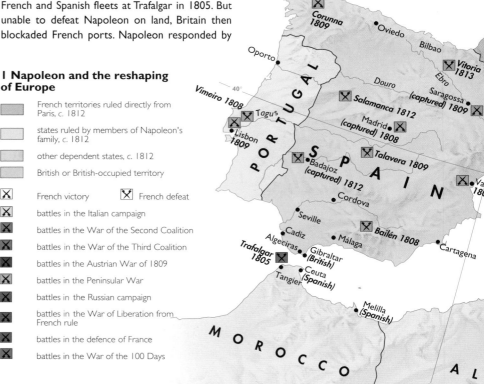

The remnants of Napoleon's army struggled across the Berezina river in November 1812 on the disastrous retreat from Moscow (left). Thousands of wounded French soldiers had to be abandoned. Napoleon's catastrophic failure in Russia was decisive in his eventual defeat.

forbidding trade with Britain in any of the territories of his empire. But though this, the Continental System, brought hardship to Britain, its effects on France were hardly less severe. The political crisis that followed was made all the more serious when in 1809 Spain revolted against French rule. The "Spanish Ulcer" drained France of 70 million francs a year. In 1810, Tsar Alexander refused to exclude British trade. In June 1812 Napoleon invaded Russia.

Defeat and exile

It was a fatal miscalculation. With widespread unrest against French rule in much of northern Europe as well as in Spain, Napoleon had over-reached himself. As his troops retreated from Moscow, ravaged by hunger, disease and cold, they were harried

relentlessly by the Russians. About 450,000 began the campaign; only 40,000 survived.

The cost broke the empire. Steep tax rises and conscription caused bitter popular protest. At the same time, Napoleon's enemies, realizing that he could after all be defeated, reformed the coalition against him. At Leipzig in October 1813, the French army was overwhelmed. The following year Napoleon was exiled and the Bourbon monarchy restored. Though Napoleon contrived a final throw, escaping from exile in 1815 and regrouping his army, this time his defeat, at Waterloo, was decisive and he was exiled to St Helena in the South Atlantic, where in 1821 he died.

The treaty drawn up by the Great Powers to decide the fate of Napoleon's empire – the Vienna Settlement of 1815 – aimed not just to overthrow his legacy but to make any further revolutionary upsurge impossible. In the longer term, it failed. Napoleon's reforms had shaken Europe's traditional structures to their foundations, creating the conditions for the emergence of recognizably modern states across Europe.

The Legion of Honour (below) was created in 1802 to reward soldiers and civilians for outstanding service to the state. By 1814 more than 32,000 had been awarded, almost all to soldiers. There were only 1,500 civilian awards, the bulk of them to judges, bishops and prefects.

6 THE AGE OF EUROPEAN DOMINANCE

BETWEEN 1815 AND 1914 EUROPE thrust out into the world, impelled by the force of its own industrialization. Millions of Europeans poured overseas and into Asiatic Russia, seeking and finding new opportunities in the wider world. Between 1880 and 1900 Africa, a continent four times the size of Europe, was parcelled out among the European powers. And when in 1898 the United States of America, following Europe's lead, annexed Puerto Rico, the Philippines and other islands of the Pacific, and asserted a controlling voice in Latin American affairs, it seemed as though Western expansion had secured the domination of the white race over the non-white majority. But expansion carried with it the seeds of its own destruction. Even before European rivalries plunged the continent into the war of 1914–18, the beginnings of anti-European reaction were visible in Asia and Africa, and no sooner had the USA occupied the Philippines than they were met by a nationalist uprising.

Today, in retrospect, we can see that the age of expansive imperialism was a transient phase of history. Nevertheless, it left a lasting European imprint. The world in 1914 was utterly different from the world in 1815, the tempo of change during the preceding century greater than in the entire millennium before it. Though industry in 1914 was only beginning to spread beyond Europe and North America, and life in Asia and Africa was still regulated by age-old traditions, the 19th century inaugurated the process of transformation which dethroned agricultural society as it had existed for thousands of years, replacing it with the urban, industrialized, technocratic society, which continues to spread into even the most remote parts of the globe – for good or ill – more than a century later.

EIFFEL TOWER, PARIS, FRANCE.

Population growth and movements

The 19th century witnessed the beginning of the remarkable population explosion which has continued ever since. Europe was at the centre of the surge, sending millions overseas to America, Africa and Australasia. Millions more left the land to work in the bustling cities whose populations grew faster than at any point in their history.

IN EXAMINING THE PRINCIPAL STATES OF MODERN EUROPE, WE SHALL FIND, THAT THOUGH THEY HAVE INCREASED VERY CONSIDERABLY IN POPULATION SINCE THEY WERE NATIONS OF SHEPHERDS, YET THAT, AT PRESENT, THEIR PROGRESS IS BUT SLOW. THE CAUSE OF THIS SLOW PROGRESS IN POPULATION CANNOT BE TRACED TO A DECAY OF THE PASSIONS BETWEEN THE SEXES … WHY THEN DO NOT ITS EFFECTS APPEAR IN A RAPID INCREASE IN THE HUMAN SPECIES?

Thomas Malthus
An Essay on the Principle of Population, 1798

WHEN THOMAS MALTHUS wrote his *Essay on the Principle of Population* at the end of the 18th century the population of Europe, and of much of the rest of the world, had been stagnant for two centuries. Yet Malthus's belief that populations were always restricted – by famine, war and disease – was destroyed by the sudden explosion of world population in the century that followed.

The population explosion

It is estimated that the world's population grew in the 19th century from 900 million to 1,600 million. Much of the increase came from the expansion of the population of Europe, from 123 million to 267 million (excluding Russia). Europe also provided emigrants whose descendants populated the huge areas of the Americas, Australasia, southern Africa and Siberia. The population of these areas increased from 5.7 million to over 200 million between 1810 and 1910. The most heavily industrialized states grew fastest: the populations of the United States, Germany and Britain multiplied fivefold across the century.

Part of the explanation for this sudden burst of population growth lay in the decline of Malthusian checks. There were few major wars in the century after 1815; the spread of cultivation worldwide gradually overcame the regular incidence of famine or poor nutrition; above all, the effects of epidemic disease, particularly in Europe and America, declined significantly.

Smallpox, one of the major killers, was successfully combated with the introduction of Jenner's vaccination. Bubonic plague, still endemic in the Ottoman empire and in Asia, almost disappeared from Europe after 1816. The poor state of urban living produced a new cluster of epidemics – typhus and tuberculosis chiefly – but over the century better public-health measures and quarantine methods, and a general rise in living-standards in Europe and areas of European settlement reduced the general impact of disease. The crisis death-rates of the previous century receded. In France in 1801 only 5,800 out of every 10,000 lived to the age of 20; by 1901 7,300 reached that age.

The rapid growth of cities in Europe and America saw them overtake the greatest cities of India and China in size. In 1800 5.5 million Europeans lived in cities of more than 100,000; by 1900 the figure was 46 million. In cities people tended to marry younger and have more children. Legal controls over the age of marriage disappeared, while larger families provided a stream of young workers and a kinship group which could support the interests of the family as a whole. The rising birth-rate and the slowly falling death-rate produced a "demographic gap", an excess of births over deaths that created a favourable cycle for further high growth.

3 World population movements, 1821–1910
→ emigration from Europe
→ emigration from Japan
→ emigration from China
→ emigration from India
→ migration from European Russia

4 New York: urban growth, 1870–1914
▉ city and suburbs c. 1870
▨ city and suburbs c. 1914
— railways 1914

4 By 1810 New York (map above) had outstripped its rivals to become the most dynamic urban centre in the New World. In 1810 its population was 100,000. By 1871 it had grown to more than a million, and by 1914 had reached over 3 million. More than two-thirds of all 19th-century immigrants to the United States passed through the city. The Statue of Liberty (below) symbolized to immigrants the promise of a new and better life held out to them by the New World.

6 European population growth, 1800–1910

Year	Population
1800	123m
1820	140m
1830	156m
1840	170m
1850	184m
1860	194m
1870	210m
1880	225m
1890	244m
1900	267m
1910	

(scale: 100m — 200m)

6 Population growth in Europe (chart above) accelerated in the first four decades of the 19th century, slowed in the mid-century period of famine and revolution and revived strongly from the 1860s, when the peak of births over deaths was reached. From 1910 rates of growth slowed and have declined steadily since.

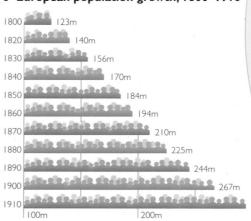

The movement of population

High population growth produced many pressures to migrate. In rural areas migration increased rapidly as peasants left their villages to find city work. In Russia and Spain migrant workers were a traditional source of labour throughout the century. Elsewhere, workers flocked to where mines and factories were springing up. Polish workers moved to the Ruhr mines; Irish workers travelled to Scotland and Lancashire; Italians worked in France and Germany. By 1914 there were an estimated 3 million migrant workers in Europe.

The promise of economic opportunity also lured millions overseas. Between 1801 and 1840 only 1.5 million left Europe, mainly for the United States; between 1841 and 1880 the figure leapt to 13 million; and between 1880 and 1910 it leapt again to 25 million. Some migrants returned (estimates suggest as many as 25 per cent), but those who stayed in the vast expanses of America or Australia or southern Africa became buoyant population groups with high growth rates, better diets and more opportunities than Europe could provide. Some migrants were the victims of coercion – the threat of famine took millions from Ireland; political or racial persecution pushed out thousands more, particularly from eastern Europe – but most were lured by the promise of wealth, freedom or adventure. Between 1800 and 1930 the white proportion of the world's population expanded from 22 to 35 per cent.

Europeans were not the only ones on the move. Chinese and Indian emigrants reached the Caribbean and Africa in search of work and business openings. Japanese workers crossed the Pacific to west-coast America. Until the 1820s slaves were still shipped from Africa to the plantations of the New World, and continued to be shipped to the Middle East until the major slave markets of Zanzibar and Madagascar were closed in the 1870s. Gradually the movement of populations became regulated by governments as local labour forces, once migrants themselves, began to protest at the further flow of fresh recruits.

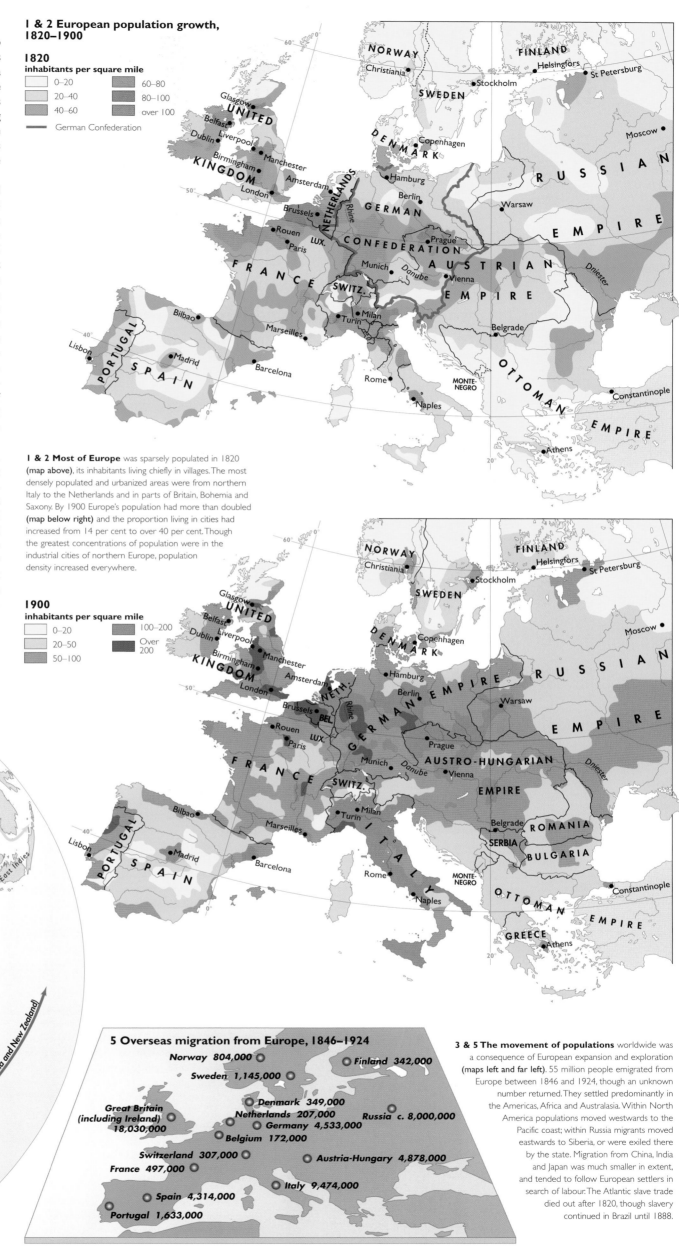

1 & 2 European population growth, 1820–1900

1820
inhabitants per square mile
- 0–20
- 20–40
- 40–60
- 60–80
- 80–100
- over 100
- German Confederation

1 & 2 Most of Europe was sparsely populated in 1820 (map above), its inhabitants living chiefly in villages. The most densely populated and urbanized areas were from northern Italy to the Netherlands and in parts of Britain, Bohemia and Saxony. By 1900 Europe's population had more than doubled (map below right) and the proportion living in cities had increased from 14 per cent to over 40 per cent. Though the greatest concentrations of population were in the industrial cities of northern Europe, population density increased everywhere.

1900
inhabitants per square mile
- 0–20
- 20–50
- 50–100
- 100–200
- Over 200

5 Overseas migration from Europe, 1846–1924

- Norway **804,000**
- Sweden **1,145,000**
- Finland **342,000**
- Denmark **349,000**
- Great Britain (including Ireland) **18,030,000**
- Netherlands **207,000**
- Germany **4,533,000**
- Russia c. **8,000,000**
- Belgium **172,000**
- Switzerland **307,000**
- Austria-Hungary **4,878,000**
- France **497,000**
- Spain **4,314,000**
- Italy **9,474,000**
- Portugal **1,633,000**

3 & 5 The movement of populations worldwide was a consequence of European expansion and exploration (maps left and far left). 55 million people emigrated from Europe between 1846 and 1924, though an unknown number returned. They settled predominantly in the Americas, Africa and Australasia. Within North America populations moved westwards to the Pacific coast; within Russia migrants moved eastwards to Siberia, or were exiled there by the state. Migration from China, India and Japan was much smaller in extent, and tended to follow European settlers in search of labour. The Atlantic slave trade died out after 1820, though slavery continued in Brazil until 1888.

The industrial revolution in Europe

The 19th century witnessed a fundamental transformation of the European economy with the spread of modern forms of industrial organization and production. Industrial regions grew up around major ore- and coalfields, drawing in millions of workers from the villages to form a new class of labouring poor. Marx called them the proletariat and defined the new era as the age of capitalism.

1781 Steam engine first used in Europe

1828 First modern blast furnace in Silesia

1834 Zollverein formed

1837 First French railway, Paris to St-Germain

1846 Central Bank established in Prussia

1857 Danube and Danish Sound opened to free navigation

1885 Benz develops first petrol-driven car

1888 Hoechst develops first chemical painkiller

1890 First electric tram, in Florence

1896 Marconi builds first radio transmitter

INDUSTRIALIZATION IN EUROPE was a slow and uneven process over the course of the 19th century. Europe had a rich commercial heritage and was far from an undeveloped region in 1800, but most production was still small-scale and craft-based, and most workers were on the land. Poor communications and shortages of capital allowed the traditional economy to survive until mechanized production, the coming of the railways and a modern banking system created the conditions for the rapid industrial growth of the late century.

Proto-industrialization
The early stages of industrial change have been described as "proto-industrialization". The term reflects an economy in transition, with traditional production methods and marketing existing alongside large merchants and new experimental factories borrowing the technology of early industrial development in Britain. The textile industry was typical. The mechanization of spinning and weaving developed very slowly: in Saxony British engineers introduced mechanical spinning in 1807 and the first steam machinery in 1831, yet handloom weaving survived until long into the century in much of Europe. Only by 1900 was the bulk of textile production mechanized.

Heavy industry also developed slowly. Coke-fired iron production had revolutionized British industry, but as late as the 1850s charcoal furnaces supplied

THE BOURGEOISIE HAS CREATED MORE MASSIVE AND MORE COLOSSAL PRODUCTIVE FORCES THAN HAVE ALL PRECEDING GENERATIONS TOGETHER. SUBJECTION OF NATURE'S FORCES TO MAN, MACHINERY, APPLICATION OF CHEMISTRY TO INDUSTRY AND AGRICULTURE, STEAM-NAVIGATION, RAILWAYS, ELECTRIC TELEGRAPHS ... CANALISATION OF RIVERS ... WHAT EARLIER CENTURY HAD EVER A PRESENTIMENT THAT SUCH PRODUCTIVE FORCES SLUMBERED IN THE LAP OF SOCIAL LABOUR?

Karl Marx
Manifesto of the Communist Party, 1848

70 per cent of German iron production. The first coke furnace appeared in France in 1823, yet by 1850 only two-fifths of iron was smelted by coke. Only in Belgium was the new technology embraced, and the Belgian coalfield became the second major industrial region of Europe until the 1860s. After 1850 the situation changed sharply: a long boom based on coal, iron and steel and modern engineering turned much of Europe within 25 years into industrial states.

The mid-century boom
Industrial development crucially depended on changes in the wider economic framework. The transport revolution was vital. Railways and steam-shipping meant fast and reliable delivery, and cheaper food from the major food producers outside Europe. In 1850 there were 24,150km (15,000 miles) of railway, most of it in Britain and Belgium; by 1870 another 80,450km (50,000 miles) had been added. By 1914 railways smothered the European area. Russia had less than 2000km (1240 miles) of rail track in 1860; more than 65,000km (40,000 miles) 50 years later. The reform of the banking system in the 1850s and 1860s stabilized national currencies and created credit and mortgage banks that invested heavily in new technologies in industry and agriculture. The creation of the Gold Standard in the 1870s made trade and currency conversion easy; the subsequent boom in international trade encouraged another wave of industrial growth.

The "second industrial revolution"
By the 1870s Europe had been transformed as Britain had been from the late 18th century. Over the next 40 years there began what has been called the "second industrial revolution" based on the application of modern science in electricity, chemicals and motor

2 European trade was severely hampered in the pre-industrial age by thousands of local tariffs and tolls. Internal duties were scrapped in revolutionary France in 1791 and were progressively reduced in the German and Habsburg lands. In 1834 Prussia reached agreement with six other German states to establish a German free trade area or Zollverein (**map below**). Trade between states, however, continued to be dominated by protective tariffs.

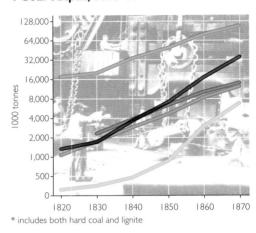

4 Coal output, 1820–70*

* includes both hard coal and lignite

5 Pig iron output, 1820–70

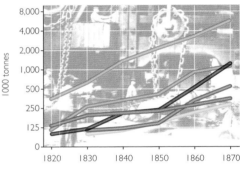

6 Length of railway line open, 1840–70

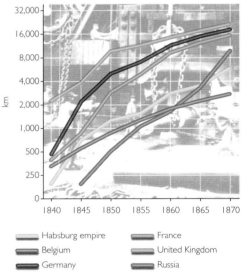

Habsburg empire	France
Belgium	United Kingdom
Germany	Russia

4–6 Until 1870, Britain dominated Europe's output of coal and iron and, despite its relative smallness, enjoyed a lead in railway development (**charts above**). In 1850 there were 1.7km of railway for every 100 sq. km in Britain (2.1 miles/60 square miles): the equivalent figures in France and Germany were 0.33km (0.4 miles) and 0.57km (0.7 miles) respectively. Railway-building in turn boosted iron and coal output, while the rail networks carried foodstuffs, fuel and raw material to hitherto inaccessible markets.

vehicles. Iron gave way to high quality steel: in 1861 steel output in Europe was 125,000 tons; by 1913 it had reached 38 million. Germany became the heart of the new industrial boom, producing half of the world's trade in electrical goods and 80 per cent of the world's dyestuffs. The motor-car was pioneered in Germany by the engineers Gottlieb Daimler and Karl Benz.

Alongside the technical and scientific breakthroughs came a revolution in commerce. Department stores, chains of high-street shops and popular advertising made goods available to all and created global markets for the new products. Rising productivity produced a long boom in real wages down to 1914, freeing many workers from primary poverty and creating a culture of popular consumption. Only in the countryside, where over half of Europeans worked in 1914, was progress slower and poverty widespread.

joined German customs union 1888

NORWAY AND SWEDEN customs union 1874–90

DENMARK customs union 1853

Russo-Polish customs frontier abolished 1851

SCHLESWIG HOLSTEIN

Hamburg Bremen

Tax Union

Berlin

united with the Tax Union 1854

Dresden

RUSSIA

CONGRESS POLAND

Kiev

Prague

Cracow

LUXEMBOURG

Paris

FRANCE internal duties abolished 1791

Munich

Vienna Buda

HABSBURG

Pest

SWITZERLAND internal duties abolished 1848–74

EMPIRE Austro-Hungarian customs frontier abolished 1850

Zagreb

MOLDAVIA-WALLACHIA 1847

Milan

ITALY political and economic unification 1860–70

Zara

Spalato

Mostar

Danube

Sofia

Black Sea

Corsica

Rome

Sardinia

Cagliari

OTTOMAN EMPIRE

Istanbul

Sicily Catania

Mediterranean Sea

2 European customs unions from 1848

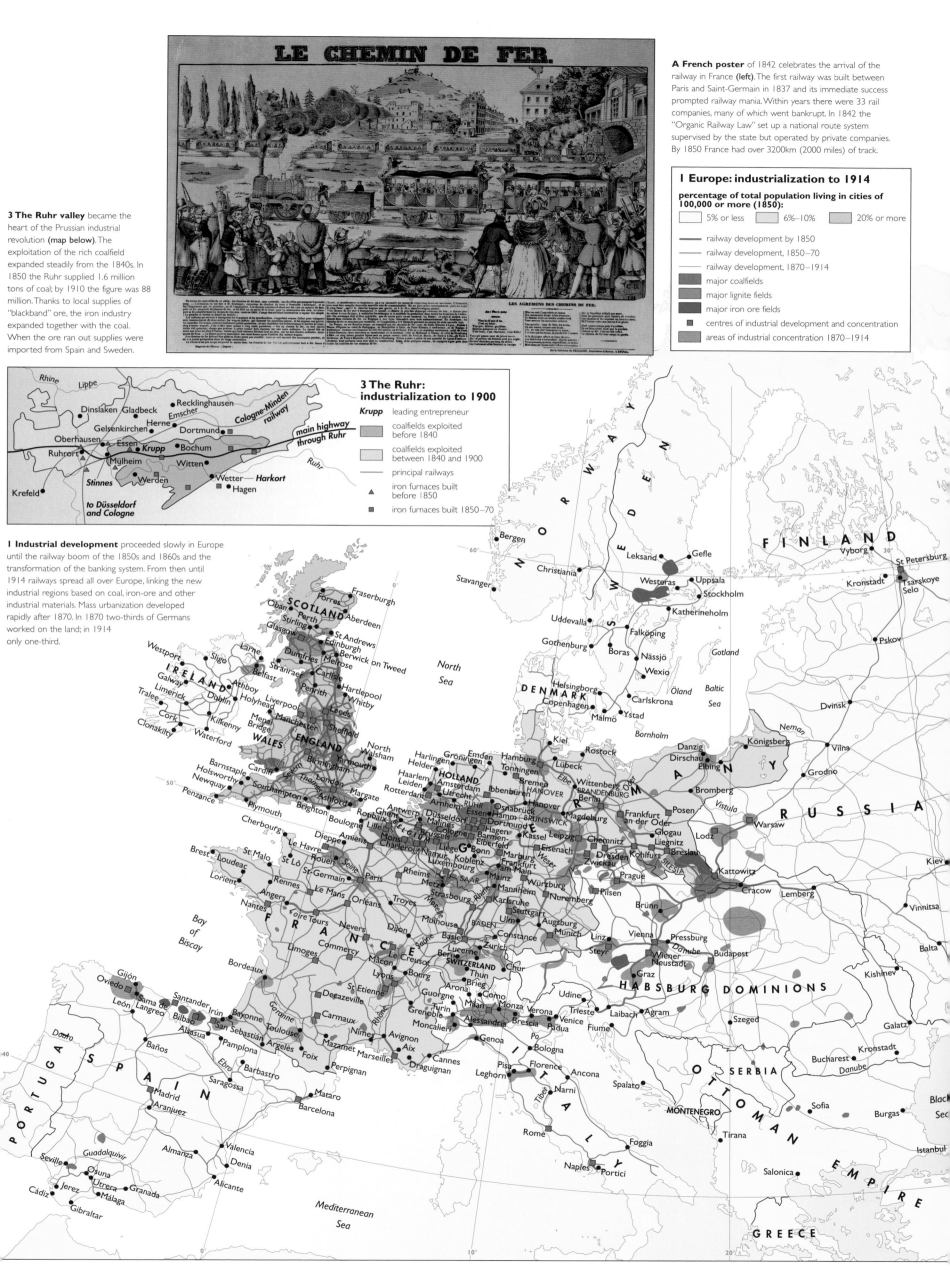

LE CHEMIN DE FER.

LES AGREMENS DES CHEMINS DE FER.

A French poster of 1842 celebrates the arrival of the railway in France **(left)**. The first railway was built between Paris and Saint-Germain in 1837 and its immediate success prompted railway mania. Within years there were 33 rail companies, many of which went bankrupt. In 1842 the "Organic Railway Law" set up a national route system supervised by the state but operated by private companies. By 1850 France had over 3200km (2000 miles) of track.

3 The Ruhr valley became the heart of the Prussian industrial revolution **(map below)**. The exploitation of the rich coalfield expanded steadily from the 1840s. In 1850 the Ruhr supplied 1.6 million tons of coal; by 1910 the figure was 88 million. Thanks to local supplies of "blackband" ore, the iron industry expanded together with the coal. When the ore ran out supplies were imported from Spain and Sweden.

1 Europe: industrialization to 1914

percentage of total population living in cities of 100,000 or more (1850):

- 5% or less
- 6%–10%
- 20% or more

— railway development by 1850
— railway development, 1850–70
— railway development, 1870–1914

- major coalfields
- major lignite fields
- major iron ore fields
- centres of industrial development and concentration
- areas of industrial concentration 1870–1914

3 The Ruhr: industrialization to 1900

Krupp leading entrepreneur

- coalfields exploited before 1840
- coalfields exploited between 1840 and 1900
- principal railways
- ▲ iron furnaces built before 1850
- ■ iron furnaces built 1850–70

1 Industrial development proceeded slowly in Europe until the railway boom of the 1850s and 1860s and the transformation of the banking system. From then until 1914 railways spread all over Europe, linking the new industrial regions based on coal, iron-ore and other industrial materials. Mass urbanization developed rapidly after 1870. In 1870 two-thirds of Germans worked on the land; in 1914 only one-third.

The rise of nationalism in Europe

The French revolution paved the way for the modern nation-state. Across Europe radical intellectuals questioned the old monarchical order and encouraged the development of a popular nationalism committed to re-drawing the political map of the continent. By 1914 the days of the old multi-national empires were numbered.

> NO PEOPLE EVER DIE, NOR STOP SHORT UPON THEIR PATH, BEFORE THEY HAVE ACHIEVED THE ULTIMATE AIM OF THEIR EXISTENCE, BEFORE HAVING COMPLETED AND FULFILLED THEIR MISSION. A PEOPLE DESTINED TO ACHIEVE GREAT THINGS FOR THE WELFARE OF HUMANITY MUST ONE DAY OR OTHER BE CONSTITUTED A NATION.
>
> **Giuseppe Mazzini, 1861**

1815 The Congress of Vienna

1822 Greek declaration of national independence

1848 Nationalist revolts in Hungary, Italy and Germany

1859–61 Italy unified

1863 Polish national revolt

1866–71 Germany unified

1867 Hungary granted autonomy

1878 Congress of Berlin: Serbia, Romania, Montenegro granted independence

1908 Bulgaria becomes independent

THE FRENCH REVOLUTION, by destroying the traditional structures of power in France and territories conquered by Napoleon, was the instrument for the political transformation of Europe. Revolutionary armies carried the slogan of "liberty, equality and fraternity" and ideas of liberalism and national self-determinism. National awakening also grew out of an intellectual reaction to the Enlightenment that emphasized national identity and developed a romantic view of cultural self-expression through nationhood. The key exponent of the modern idea of the nation-state was the German Georg Hegel (1770–1831). He argued that a sense of nationality was the cement that held modern societies together in an age when dynastic and religious allegiance was in decline.

In 1815, at the end of the Napoleonic wars, the major powers of Europe tried to restore the old dynastic system as far as possible, ignoring the principle of nationality in favour of "legitimism", the assertion of traditional claims to royal authority. With most of Europe's peoples still loyal to their local province or city, nationalism was confined to small groups of intellectuals and political radicals. Furthermore, political repression, symbolized by the Carlsbad Decrees published in Austria in 1819, pushed nationalist agitation underground.

The struggle for independence

Nevertheless there began to develop a strong resentment of what came to be regarded as foreign rule. In Ireland, Italy, Belgium, Greece, Poland, Hungary and Norway local hostility to alien dynastic authority started to take the form of nationalist agitation. Nationalism came to be seen as the most effective way to create the symbols of resistance and to unite in a common cause.

Success came first in Greece where an eight-year civil war (1822–30) against Ottoman rule led to an independent Greek state; in 1831 Belgium obtained independence from the Netherlands. Over the next two decades nationalism developed a more powerful voice, spurred by nationalist writers championing the cause of national self-determination. In 1848 revolutions broke out across Europe, sparked by a severe famine and economic crisis and mounting popular demands for political change. In Italy Giuseppe Mazzini used the opportunity to encourage a war for national unification; in Hungary Lajos Kossuth led a national revolt against Austrian rule; in the German Confederation a National Assembly was elected at Frankfurt and debated the creation of a German nation.

1 Political and linguistic frontiers, above all in central and eastern Europe, were rarely the same. Many linguistic minorities, even some majorities, found themselves under alien rule (map right): the creation of ethnically homogeneous states would bedevil Europe for many years to come. The map highlights Europe's major languages, though some are too scattered to be included: Sorb (or Wendish, Lusatian) in Prussia and Saxony; Masurian in East Prussia; Vlach in Macedonia, Epirus and Transylvania; and Yiddish, spoken throughout the broad area of Jewish settlement in central and eastern Europe.

1 Languages, peoples and political divisions of Europe, 1815–1914

— frontiers, 1914

— frontiers, 1815 (where different)

— boundary of Ottoman empire, 1815

⋅⋅⋅ Pale of Jewish Settlement

▨ Romansch and Ladin

▧ Macedonian Slavs

2 The Balkans, 1830–1908

- - - frontier of Ottoman empire, 1800
——— boundaries agreed by the Treaty of San Stefano, 1878

territories lost by Ottoman empire by Treaty of Berlin, 1878

to Romania

to Serbia

to Montenegro

——— frontier of Ottoman empire, 1908

——— frontiers, 1908

None of the nationalist revolts in 1848 was successful, any more than the two attempts to win Polish independence from Russian rule in 1831 and 1846 had been. Conservative forces proved too strong, while the majority of the populations little understood the meaning of national struggle. But the 1848 crisis had given nationalism its first full public airing, and in the 30 years that followed no fewer than seven new national states were created in Europe. This was partly the result of the recognition by conservative forces that the old order could not continue in its existing form. Conservative reformers such as Cavour and Bismarck (see pp. 238–9) made common cause with liberal political modernizers to create a consensus for the creation of conservative nation-states in Italy and Germany. In the Habsburg empire a compromise was reached with Hungarian nationalists in 1867 granting them a virtually independent state. In the Balkans (see map 2) the Greek example had inspired other national awakenings. Native history and culture were rediscovered and appropriated for the national struggle. Following a conflict between Russia and Turkey, the Great Powers met at Berlin in 1878 and granted independence to Romania, Serbia and Montenegro.

Nationalism exported

The invention of a symbolic national identity became the concern of racial or linguistic groups throughout Europe as they struggled to come to terms with the rise of mass politics, popular xenophobia and the decline of traditional social elites. Within the Habsburg empire the different races developed a more mass-

based, violent and exclusive nationalism, even among the Germans and Magyars, who actually benefited from the power-structure of the empire. The Jewish population of eastern and central Europe began to develop radical demands for their own national state in Palestine. In 1897, inspired by the Hungarian-born nationalist Theodor Herzl (1860–1904), the First Zionist Congress was held in Basle. On the European periphery, especially in Ireland and Norway, campaigns for national independence became more strident. In 1905 Norway won independence from Sweden, but attempts to grant Ireland the kind of autonomy enjoyed by Hungary foundered on the national divisions in the island between the ethnic Irish and British migrants.

By this time the ideals of European nationalism had been exported worldwide and were now beginning to threaten the colonial empires still ruled by European nation-states.

Seeing the Greeks as the modern heirs of the classical civilization of ancient Greece, the Great Powers put aside their instinctive desire to maintain the existing order and contributed decisively to their fight for independence. At the battle of Navarino **(right)**, fought in October 1827, a combined British, French and Russian force annihilated the Ottoman fleet, paving the way for Greek independence three years later.

2 In 1815 the Balkan peninsula (above) was still within the increasingly decrepit Ottoman empire. The combination of weakening Ottoman control, Russian and Austrian designs on the region and the rise of Balkan nationalism in territories far less ethnically homogeneous than those in western Europe destabilized the region well into the 20th century. Only Greek independence proved relatively trouble free. Bulgaria's bitter fight

for liberation, helped by Russia, was followed by the Russian-imposed Treaty of San Stefano. The huge Bulgarian state this created was unacceptable to the other Great Powers, who feared Russian influence in the region. The Treaty of Berlin, signed the same year, overturned it: Bulgarian resentment festered for years. The treaty also confirmed the independence of Serbia, Romania and Montenegro.

Germany and Italy: the struggles for unification

The French revolution laid the foundation for a romantic nationalism in Italy and Germany that was harshly suppressed after 1815. The two regions were united in the end not by popular nationalism but by the ambitions of the major powers and the machinations of statesmen who preferred to unify from above rather than risk revolutionary demands.

1831 Mazzini founds Young Italy movement

1848 Italian states revolt against Austrian rule

1848–9 German national assembly tries to build united German state

1852 Cavour prime minister of Piedmont

1858 National Society established in Germany

1859–60 Piedmont leads drive to unify Italy

1862 Bismarck minister-president of Prussia

1866 War between Prussia and Austria

1867 North German Confederation founded

1871 William of Prussia crowned emperor of Germany

The unification of Italy, and in particular the exploits of Garibaldi, excited artists all over Europe. This French painting (above), entitled "The Defenders of Italian Independence" shows from left to right, Garibaldi (holding his hat aloft), Victor Emmanuel II (on a white horse, wearing a green sash) and Napoleon III (on a black horse, wearing a red sash). Great efforts were made to portray the events leading to unification as heroic, rather than as the result of Great Power politics.

THE ROOTS OF ITALIAN and German nationalism lay in the reaction to French domination under the Napoleonic empire. In both regions the experience of French revolutionary rule stimulated the emergence of a nationalist intelligentsia committed to the development of a native culture and language. National development was seen as the key to political freedom and economic success.

The struggle for nationhood

In 1815 the Vienna Settlement restored the conservative order in Germany and Italy. Secret societies kept nationalist aspirations alive – the *carbonari* in Italy, the student *Burschenschaften* in Germany – but the Habsburg empire, guided by Chancellor Metternich, smothered demands for national unification. What protest there was, for example in Italy in 1820–1 and 1830–1, was more anti-Austrian than actively nationalist in character. Most German and Italian liberals looked for constitutional reform, civil rights and economic freedoms rather than for unity.

The revolutionary upheavals of the 1840s gave impetus to the infant nationalist movements. Economic crisis combined with increasing resentment at the absence of political reform to produce growing demands for nationhood. In Italy Mazzini, who founded the Young Italy movement in 1831, inspired a generation of young nationalists. When revolt broke out in 1848, Mazzini was among the revolutionaries demanding a new national Italian state. Austrian forces crushed the revolutions and defeated the army of Charles Albert of Piedmont-Sardinia, who had briefly placed himself at the forefront of Italian revival, the *risorgimento*.

In Germany the 1848 crisis gave nationalist circles, drawn largely from the educated bourgeoisie, the opportunity to overturn the Habsburg-dominated German Confederation, which had been revived in 1815, and to replace it with a united German nation. Though a national assembly met at Frankfurt, it found itself split between those who wanted a Germany which included Austria (*Grossdeutschland*) and those who wanted a smaller Germany free of Habsburg interference (*Kleindeutschland*). The debate proved academic: in 1849 Prussian troops disbanded the parliament and reimposed the old order.

The failure of 1848 pushed nationalism to the margins again. Mazzini launched nationalist revolts in the 1850s, but with no success. It took ten years before a National Society was founded in Germany, and its numbers never exceeded 25,000. In the event the unification of Italy and Germany was made possible not through nationalist agitation but as a result of the changing character of the conservative order, both at home and abroad. In Germany and Italy conservative reformers emerged who were hostile to the continuation of Austrian dominance but fearful of mass

politics and revolution. A programme of "reform from above" was initiated, led by the major regional states, Prussia in Germany, Piedmont-Sardinia in Italy.

Unification from above

In Italy the lead was taken by Count Cavour, who became Piedmontese prime minister in 1852. He introduced economic, military and constitutional reforms that made Piedmont the most advanced state in the peninsula. When Austria found itself isolated internationally after the Crimean War

2 The unification of Italy, 1859–70

- French from 1768, formerly Genoese
- Kingdom of Sardinia in 1815
- territory annexed 1859
- territory annexed March 1860
- territory annexed November 1860
- territory lost to France 1860
- territory annexed 1866
- territory annexed 1870
- Austrian empire, 1815
- Italian border, 1914

2 Italy was unified (map above) by war and revolution. In 1848 Charles Albert of Piedmont-Sardinia tried to expel Austria from northern Italy but was defeated at Custoza and Novara. Ten years later, with Napoleon III's France as an ally, Piedmontese forces together with nationalist volunteers defeated Austria at Magenta and Solferino. In return, Napoleon obtained Nice and Savoy, but Lombardy was joined to Piedmont, followed swiftly by the smaller central Italian duchies. When Sicily rose in revolt against the Kingdom of Naples in 1860, Garibaldi led a nationalist army southwards which defeated the Bourbon king. The northern states then joined with the liberated south to form a Kingdom of Italy ruled by the Piedmontese king, Victor Emmanuel.

(1853–5), Cavour opportunistically allied with Napoleon III of France to drive Austria out of northern Italy. Defeated at Magenta and Solferino, Austria signed the Treaty of Villafranca with France, giving up Lombardy but keeping Venetia. Lombardy then joined with Piedmont, and was followed by Tuscany, Parma, Romagna and Modena, where plebiscites overwhelmingly favoured a union with Piedmont. When Garibaldi, a flamboyant nationalist, lent his support to a peasant revolt against the Bourbon Kingdom of Naples, nationalists flocked to join him. Fearful that Garibaldi's success would result in popular uprisings throughout Italy, Cavour skilfully imposed Piedmontese control over Garibaldi, and in 1861 the Kingdom of Italy was declared with the Piedmont-Sardinian monarch, Victor Emmanuel II, its first king. Venetia was added in 1866, when Austria was defeated by Prussia, while in 1870 Rome was taken over from papal rule to become the new capital.

German unification

A similar process occurred in Germany, where Prussia embarked on a programme of conservative modernization, building up a strong industrial economy and reforming the army. With Bismarck as minister-president from 1862, Prussia began to dominate northern Germany. Following war with Denmark in 1864 over the duchies of Schleswig and Holstein, Prussian-Austrian relations deteriorated sharply. In 1866 Austria declared war on Prussia to prevent a repeat of her loss of influence in Italy. Defeated at Sadowa, Austria was effectively excluded from northern Germany and in 1867 Prussia established a North German Confederation. Napoleon III's ambition to revive French influence in the Rhineland then led to a crisis in Franco-Prussian relations which resulted in war in 1870 in which Germany decisively defeated the French, in the process occupying Paris. The southern German states, Bavaria, Baden and Württemberg,

then allied with Prussia, and in 1871 agreed to join a larger federal structure, a German empire, rather than remain isolated and economically dependent on their much more powerful northern neighbour.

Nationalists in both Italy and Germany welcomed the new states, but in neither case had mass nationalism brought about unification. The old orders took the initiative to avoid popular revolution. When, later in the century, mass nationalism did develop in Italy and Germany it eventually led to fascism and the collapse of the conservative order that had ushered in the new nation states.

1 The economic unification of Germany, 1828–88

	Prussian-Hessian Customs Union 1828
	Deutscher Zollverein (German Customs Union) 1834
	New *Zollverein*, 1867
	additions to 1888 (with dates)

1 In 1834 Prussia established a customs union (*Zollverein*) between a number of the German states with the object of removing restrictions on trade (map above). Austria was deliberately excluded, while northern Germany became the main area of trade and industrial expansion. Membership of the *Zollverein* did not stop most of Prussia's major economic partners, led by Saxony, from fighting on the side of Austria against Prussia in 1866.

3 In 1815 the German Confederation (map below) was a patchwork of city-states and principalities dominated by Prussia and Austria. From the 1850s relations between the two powers deteriorated, and after 1864 they squabbled over the administration of the annexed territory of Schleswig-Holstein. In 1866 Austria led the Confederation in a war against Prussia. After victory at Sadowa, Prussia absorbed Hanover, Hesse-Nassau and Frankfurt. In 1867 the North German Confederation was established, and following war with France in 1870, the southern states joined the Prussian-dominated federation in a new German empire.

3 The unification of Germany, 1815–71

	Prussia in 1815
	acquired by Prussia 1815–66
	German Confederation, 1815
	North German Confederation, 1867
	Imperial territory of Alsace-Lorraine, 1871
●	free city
—	German Empire, 1871
←	Austro-Prussian forces attack on Denmark, 1864
←	Prussian armies in the war with Austria, 1866
←	German armies in the Franco-Prussian war, 1870–1

The making of the United States: westward expansion

At independence in 1783 most Americans lived on the eastern seaboard of the new country. Over the next 100 years there was a vast movement of population westwards into new lands acquired through treaty and exploration. It was a century of frontier towns, gold rushes and Indian wars. By 1890 railroads crossed the USA and the "frontier" was closed.

1783 American independence officially recognized

1803 Louisiana Purchase

1838–9 Final removal of the southern Cherokee tribes ("Trail of Tears")

1845 Annexation of Texas

1849 California Gold Rush

1862 The Homestead Act

1869 First trans-continental railroad completed

1876 Battle of the Little Big Horn

1890 US Bureau of Census declares the frontier closed

1 There were several separate frontiers in American history (map below): the frontier of the explorer, the fur trader, the miner, the cattleman and sheep-herder, and finally the farmers' frontier. Each of those westward movements had its own special rhythm, its own settlements and its own routes. By the 1850s settlers were crossing the Great Plains in vast numbers. In 1890 the Bureau of the Census deemed the frontier closed; by then San Francisco's population approached 300,000.

OUR MANIFEST DESTINY IS TO OVERSPREAD THE CONTINENT ALLOTED BY PROVIDENCE FOR THE FREE DEVELOPMENT OF OUR YEARLY MULTIPLYING MILLIONS.

John L. O' Sullivan, 1845

TELL YOUR PEOPLE THAT SINCE THE GREAT FATHER [THE PRESIDENT] PROMISED THAT WE WOULD NEVER BE REMOVED, WE HAVE BEEN MOVED FIVE TIMES ... I THINK YOU HAD BETTER PUT THE INDIANS ON WHEELS AND YOU CAN RUN THEM ABOUT WHEREVER YOU WISH.

Chief Spotted Tail of the Sioux

GO WEST, YOUNG MAN, AND GROW UP WITH THE COUNTRY.

Horace Greeley's advice to the poor of New York City, 1850

WHEN IN 1783 THE INDEPENDENCE of the USA was at last recognized, most Americans – apart from a small settlement in Kentucky – lived between the eastern seaboard and the Appalachian mountains. Soon after independence, however, a vast westward movement of population began. This was assisted by improvements in communications – first roads, later canals, and finally railroads. It was also encouraged by a series of political decisions through which, between the Louisiana Purchase of 1803 and the Gadsden Purchase of 1853 (see map 2), the new republic acquired vast new territories in the west and pushed its continental boundary as far as the Pacific Ocean.

After the political acquisition of new territory, 19th-century explorers – following in the footsteps of colonial predecessors such as Louis Joliet, James Marquette and Daniel Boone – visited and mapped the vast new lands. Many of these men, including William Clark, Meriwether Lewis, John C. Frémont and Zebulon Pike, were army officers. In their wake flowed pioneering settlers.

By 1820, the frontier of western settlement had reached the Mississippi River. It carried on shifting until by the 1840s it had reached the 100th meridian (bisecting present-day North Dakota and passing down through the middle of Texas). There, for a time, expansion faltered: the Great Plains to the west had too little rainfall to support mixed farming. It was only in the generation after the civil war and with the assistance of new technology – the railroads, barbed wire and steel ploughs – that this part of the west was finally settled and the region became the heart of American wheat production.

The move westwards

Beginning in the 1840s, sizeable wagon trains set out from Missouri and Midwestern states such as Illinois in order to cross the Rocky Mountains and settle near the Pacific coast. There were two basic routes: the Oregon Trail and, diverging away from it after the junction with the Snake River, the California Trail. It took most migrants about six months to complete the journey in ox-drawn, canvas-covered wagons. Often, they were under constant pressure from Indian attack or infectious disease. Some turned back. Others failed to reach the Far West – the notorious Donner party of 1846–7 experienced many fatalities when trapped by snow in the Rocky Mountains.

There were many different motives for western migration. The desire for cheap land was clearly a major one – especially in the wake of the Homestead Act of 1862 (which offered 160 acres (65ha) of land free to anyone settling it). But not just farmers moved west. There were also professional folk interested in a new career in booming towns. Some of those booming towns went on to become great cities: Chicago, a small community on the shore of Lake Michigan when first incorporated as a city in 1837, had become a huge metropolis with a

1 Westward expansion

- →→ explorers' routes
- —— settlers' routes
- —— cattle trails
- ⊙ cow town
- →→ fur traders' routes
- ◼ fur station
- ◈ pass
- ⋏ mining sites
- ♀ Catholic mission
- ♁ Protestant mission

240

3 The fate of the Indians

major indian Battles

⚔	1521–1700	⚔	1801–45
✕	1701–1800	✕	1846–90

— Indian reservation, 1875   ➡ removal of southern tribes ("The Trail of Tears")

◼ Indian reservation, 1930   ▲ village of the Delaware Indians

CREEK principal Indian tribes   ➡ route of retreat of the Delaware Indians

3 The main victims of the western movement by whites were Indians (map above). In the Great Plains and Far West, there were perhaps a quarter of a million Indians. As settlers moved into Indian areas there was a series of wars. The Indians had some temporary successes, for example, the defeat of General Custer's force at Little Big Horn by Sioux and Cheyenne in 1876. But, by 1890 Indian resistance had effectively been brought to an end and the Indians themselves were largely confined to their reservations.

2 In 1783 the new nation extended from the Atlantic coast to the Mississippi river. Its territory was enlarged in just two great spates of expansion (map right). During the first (1803–19), three Virginian presidents acquired Louisiana and the Floridas. During the second, the heyday of "manifest destiny" (1845–53), Texas, Oregon, California and the remainder of the southwest were added, thereby completing the area occupied by the 48 contiguous states of today.

population of a million by 1890. Miners also moved west – especially during the California "Gold Rush" of 1849. Some groups, such as the Mormons, who migrated to the Utah Territory in the 1840s, were in search of not simply economic opportunity but religious freedom as well. Others who moved west did so involuntarily, like the Cherokee Indians compelled to trek to Oklahoma in 1838. There were also large ethnic minorities, including blacks and Asians, in the west.

The development of communications

The story of the west was also one of faster communications. In 1851, a stagecoach service started between Independence, Missouri, and Salt Lake City. It was buttressed in 1857 by the Overland Mail between St Louis and San Francisco. In 1860, the Pony Express mail service was introduced – only to become immediately obsolete when the telegraph service between Kansas and California began just 18 months later. In 1869, the stagecoach suffered the same fate with the completion of the first transcontinental railroad. Abraham Lincoln thought that the settlement of the whole west would take 100 years. It was the railroads that proved him wrong. In 1890, only 21 years after the opening of the first transcontinental service, the US Census Bureau announced that it could no longer locate a continuous area of free land for settlement in the west. With the final disappearance of the frontier line, the western stage of American development effectively came to an end.

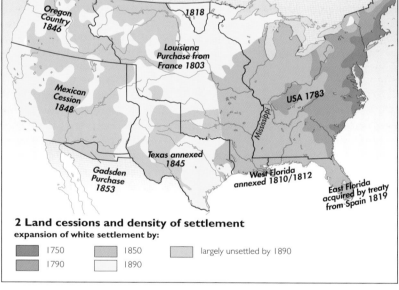

2 Land cessions and density of settlement

expansion of white settlement by:

◼ 1750	◼ 1850	largely unsettled by 1890
◼ 1790	◻ 1890	

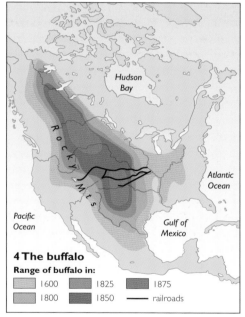

4 The buffalo

Range of buffalo in:

1600	1825	1875
1800	1850	— railroads

4 On the Great Plains, the economic and spiritual base of Indian culture was destroyed when the buffalo herds (map above right) were cut in two by the first transcontinental railroad (1869) and then slaughtered in a deliberate campaign to starve out the Sioux. By the 1890s, the buffalo, like the Indians, survived only on reservations.

In the wake of the first settlers, railroads, stagecoaches and covered wagons brought reinforcements. The lithograph (right), from a painting of 1872 by John Gast, shows the figure of Progress (clasping a schoolbook under her arm and looping telegraph wires behind her) leading settlers westwards, where they drive darkness, buffaloes and Indians alike before them with peaceful but firm resolution.

The market revolution in the United States

The century between 1800 and 1900 witnessed a "market revolution" in the USA. Small farms and workshops gave way to a national economy where manfacturers produced for a distant marketplace. Better transportation, vast resources and favourable government policies were all crucial in creating, by 1900, the world's most productive economy.

I CANNOT AVOID REFLECTING WITH PLEASURE ON THE PROBABLE INFLUENCE THAT COMMERCE MAY HEREAFTER HAVE ON HUMAN MANNERS AND SOCIETY IN GENERAL.

George Washington, 1785

WE HOLD IT BEST THAT THE LAWS SHOULD FAVOUR THE DIFFUSION OF PROPERTY AND ITS ACQUISITION, NOT THE CONCENTRATION OF IT IN THE HANDS OF THE FEW.

George Bancroft, historian, 1835

IN 1800, THE USA had been internationally recognized as a nation for only 17 years. Most of its estimated population of 5,298,000 dwelt in small communities or on farms: there were only 73 towns and cities with a population of over 2500, of which just one – New York – had over 50,000 inhabitants. By 1900, the nation had been transformed. The estimated population of the USA had grown to 76,094,000 (an increase of 1337 per cent). There were now 827 settlements with a population between 2500 and 50,000, and 75 cities of more than 50,000 people (including three of more than 1,000,000). The statistics of economic growth during the century show equally large increases: the net tonnage entering US ports grew by 3400 per cent; total imports by 922 per cent; and exports by 2011 per cent.

In 1800, not only was the USA primarily an agricultural nation, but most farm crops were grown for local consumption. Farming families produced either for themselves, or for their neighbours. There was little chance, because of the high cost of internal transportation, of moving towards a more national market-oriented type of economy. According to one estimate of 1816, shipping a ton of goods from Europe to America cost approximately $9; the same amount would enable it to be transported only 14.5km (9 miles) by land.

Better transportation made possible a "market revolution". After 1800, there were many improvements in communications. The building of the Cumberland Road (1811–18) between Cumberland, Maryland, and Vandalia on the Ohio river, symbolized the drive to build turnpike roads that, by the time the road construction boom collapsed in 1821, had seen 6400km (4,000 miles) of such roads constructed. Return voyages by the *Clermond* between New York and Albany in 1807 and the *Washington* between Louisville and New Orleans in 1817 inaugurated an era of steamship navigation on rivers and inland lakes. The successful completion of the Erie Canal in 1825 also prompted a major boom in canal-building in subsequent years.

The arrival of the railroad

Most crucial of all was the arrival of the railroad. By 1840, the USA had 5355km (3328 miles) of railroad track (compared to 2896km/1800 miles for the whole of Europe). A further 46,660km (29,000 miles) were built during the next 20 years. The last four decades of the 19th century saw a great expansion in railroad construction and the completion of five new transcontinental railroads. By 1900, the USA had 311,094km (193,346 miles) of rail track carrying about 142 billion ton-miles of freight (compared to 39 billion in 1866). The railroads, which had

played so significant a part in creating a national market, both recognized it and regularized it with the introduction of standard time zones (1883) and a common track gauge.

Industrialization

During the 19th century, smaller-scale manufacturing gave place to industrial production in ever larger economic units. This process began during the war of 1812–14 between the USA and Britain, which saw considerable capital transferred from foreign trade into manufacturing. The organization of the first path-breaking cotton factory at Waltham, Massachusetts, was followed by the spread of the factory system throughout cotton manufacturing and then to other industries. The USA had a large pool of labour drawn from mass immigration, seemingly endless natural resources (for example, the huge iron ore fields around Lake Superior, the vast coal reserves of Appalachia, and the oil-fields of Pennsylvania), and great native inventiveness and ingenuity. It also had a class of entrepreneurs who, particularly towards the end of the century, organized themselves into larger and larger business corporations.

For most of the 19th century, Federal and state governments – while often paying lip service to laissez-faire principles – actively promoted the

3 Underpinning America's economic growth in the 19th century were the country's natural reserves (**map right**). Some of these – the vast Appalachian anthracite coal fields, the bituminous coal fields of the west and the iron ore reserves near Pittsburgh, in northern Michigan and in Minnesota – helped the enormous growth in iron and steel production in the 19th century. Others saw the beginnings of new industries, with a huge oil industry growing out of the discovery of petroleum by Edwin L. Drake in Pennsylvania in 1859. Many discoveries of precious metals were also made in the West, starting with the California "Gold Rush" of 1849. In subsequent years, discoveries were also made in Colorado, Nevada (the location of the fabulous Comstock Lode), Idaho, Arizona and Montana.

3 Industrial growth and mineral wealth, 1799–1901

- counties with 1000 or more factory employees in 1899
- principal coalfields

oil and mineral finds (with date)
- gold
- copper
- oil
- silver

I The growth of railroad and canals in the east, 1825–60

— railroads built by 1840
— railroads built, 1840–50
⊢⊢⊢ canals, 1825
⊢⊢⊢ canals built, 1825–60

I The completion of the Erie Canal stimulated a great boom in canal construction (map above). Although the boom itself collapsed after 1837, the canals already built – and later extensions to them – played a major role in spreading the market revolution to the west. Most canals and railroads were in New England and the Middle Atlantic States. By 1860, there were still comparatively few major railroads in the south.

Pig iron production, 1810–1900

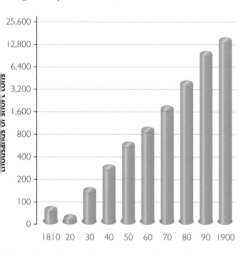

Production and consumption of bituminous coal, 1800–1900

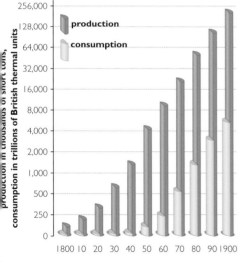

production
consumption

Manufacturing production in the USA, 1860–1900

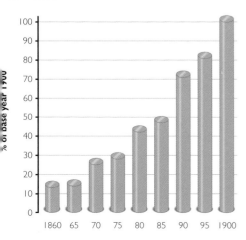

4, 5 & 6 The importance of iron to the 19th-century market revolution cannot be underestimated (charts left). It literally provided the foundation for transportation (not for nothing was the railroad called the "Iron Horse") and the construction industries. Industrialization also depended on the use of anthracite coal and, increasingly, on bituminous coal, which was considerably better for making the coke used to smelt iron.

2 When, in 1893, the Great Northern Railroad from Duluth and St Paul finally reached Seattle, the USA had five transcontinental railroads, all built since 1862 (map right). Beginning in 1866, enterprising Texas cattle ranchers drove their herds north to railheads, since beef would command a much higher price in northern markets. In subsequent years, as railroads and the farming frontier moved to the west, the cattle trails followed. Under the impact of the availability of cheap range cattle, the spread of railroads and the introduction of the refrigerator car, beef became an American staple.

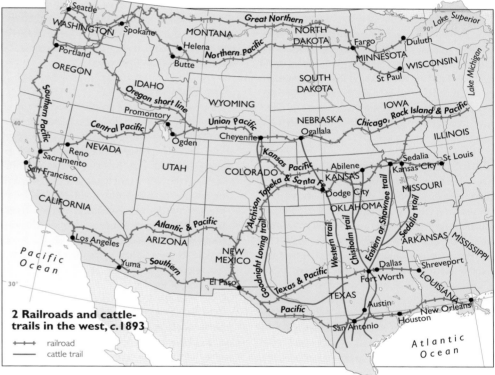

2 Railroads and cattle-trails in the west, c.1893
↤⊶↦ railroad
—— cattle trail

growth of industry and a market economy. The Erie Canal was built by the state of New York. The Federal government, which had financed the Cumberland Road, later took over the policy begun by the state of Illinois in the 1850s of promoting railroad construction through grants of land.

In 1800, the USA was a largely provincial and non-market economy. As the 19th century progressed, it not only developed a national marketplace, but also became part of the international economy. In terms of industrial production, by the end of the 19th century it was leading the world, with the most rapid developments coming in the last decades of the 19th century. In 1880, the USA produced less steel than Britain. By 1900, it was producing more than the combined total of Britain and Germany, its nearest rivals. As the 20th century dawned, the USA was well on the way to developing into an economic colossus.

Pittsburgh, Pennsylvania (left), surrounded by huge coal-fields and beds of iron and at the confluence of two important rivers, became the leading centre of iron and steel production in the USA. So vast and dramatic was the sight of its blast furnaces and coke ovens at work that early 20th-century artists and commentators began to refer to it as "Hell with the lid off."

Slavery, civil war and Reconstruction

The civil war was the most dramatic event in American history. It caused the deaths of 620,000 men – more casualties than in all other American wars combined. The roots of the conflict lay in slavery. Where the North sought to abolish it, the South was determined on its preservation, as well as on protecting its rights in the Union as a whole.

SLAVERY WAS AN EMBARRASSMENT to many of the early leaders of the American republic. Although they launched their new nation on the basis that everyone had a right to "life, liberty, and the pursuit of happiness", many of them – including Thomas Jefferson – themselves owned slaves. In the northern states, slavery did begin to disappear at the start of the 19th century. In the South, however, the invention of the cotton gin by Eli Whitney in 1793 made cotton, grown principally by black slaves, a lucrative crop. Far from declining, slavery consolidated in the South.

The South and slavery

During the early 19th century, Southern slavery became intimately bound up with the issues raised by westward expansion. Southerners felt politically disadvantaged if new states were forbidden to enter the Union with slaves. In 1819 Missouri applied for admission to the Union as a slave state and the North refused. The problem was solved by the Compromise of 1820, which sought to balance the two interests by admitting Missouri as a slave state at the same time as Maine as a free one. It also drew a line at the latitude of 36 degrees 30 minutes across the Louisiana territory purchased in 1803 (see p. 240): future states entering the Union north of that line would be free, whereas south of it they could be slave states.

The Compromise of 1820 was finally brought down by a rising abolitionist clamour in the North and by the territories gained by the USA as a result of the war with Mexico (1846–8). California threatened to upset the sectional balance by applying to enter the Union in 1849 as a free state. This was opposed by the South, which feared Northern political dominance. Another compromise resulted: California was allowed into the Federal Union as a free state, but the territories of Utah and New Mexico were organized on a new principle: popular or squatter sovereignty. The decision on whether or not to have slavery was left to the settlers themselves. But this Compromise lasted less than four years: in 1854 an attempt was made to extend the same principle of popular sovereignty to the territories of Kansas and Nebraska. These lay north of the line of 36 degrees 30 minutes, so the possibility arose that they might decide to have slavery in an area from which it was banned by the Missouri Compromise of 1820.

The consequences of the Kansas-Nebraska Act were disastrous for the Union. Armed conflict broke out in Kansas between pro- and anti-slavery forces. A new political party, the Republicans, was born to resist any further expansion of slavery into the territories. Relations between the North and the South deteriorated rapidly. Finally, in 1860, when Abraham Lincoln, as the Republican candidate, was elected president solely on the basis of northern votes, the South began to secede from the Union. In spring 1861, war broke out between the 11 seceded Southern

states, which formed a new collective government known as the Confederacy, and the Federal Union, which refused to accept the legality of secession. Eighteen months later, Lincoln added another war aim to the salvation of the Union when he issued his provisional proclamation emancipating the slaves, to become effective on 1 January 1863.

The Civil War

During the first months of the war, volunteer armies on both sides were neither very disciplined nor very effective. Serious military operations really began in spring 1862. The North's strategy was based on denying the South vital resources by a naval blockade, controlling key river routes and capturing the Confederate capital of Richmond. Despite overwhelming superiority in manpower and resources, however, the Union took four years to win the war. There were two principal reasons: first, the South had superior generalship during the war's first two years; second, the North's goals demanded the occupation of the South and the destruction of its armies, while the South fought on home ground to defend its own territories. General Robert E. Lee thwarted two invasions of Virginia in 1862, and carried the war into the North, only to be stopped at Antietam, Maryland, in September 1862 and defeated at Gettysburg, Pennsylvania, in July 1863. By then, in the west, the Union had gained control of the Mississippi and Tennessee rivers and opened the way for an invasion of the lower South. In 1864, with the Union blockade increasingly effective, General Ulysses S. Grant began his invasion of Virginia which, combined with General Philip T. Sherman's march through Georgia and South Carolina, had destroyed the South's armies by the spring of 1865.

Reconstruction

With Lincoln's assassination and the end of the war, a political conflict arose between Congress and the new president, Andrew Johnson, over "Reconstruction" – the process of re-admitting the South to the Union. Johnson wanted to be as lenient to the South as possible. Many Republicans, however, dismayed by the continuing intransigence of the Southern states, wished to follow a more radical policy centred around the enfranchisement of blacks in the South. In 1867, the Republicans imposed their version of Reconstruction on the South. But attempts to promote real equality for blacks were hampered by Southern resistance, through organizations such as the Ku Klux Klan, and the failure to provide land for the freed slaves. One by one, the Republican regimes supported by black voters in the South were overthrown. By 1876, only three states – South Carolina, Florida and Louisiana – were still undergoing Reconstruction. The withdrawal of Federal troops from these states, in the wake of the elections of 1876, caused the Republican regimes there to fall and Reconstruction finally came to an end.

1820 Missouri Compromise bans slavery north of 36 degrees 30'

1846–8 War with Mexico; USA annexes California, Utah and New Mexico

1854 The Kansas-Nebraska Act

1860 Abraham Lincoln elected to the presidency; The South secedes

1861 Civil War begins

1863 Emancipation of the slaves

14 April 1865 Lincoln assassinated

26 April 1865 The South surrenders; Reconstruction begins

1877 Reconstruction formally comes to an end

2 On the eve of the Civil War, cotton-producing areas stretched from eastern Texas to North Carolina (map below). Sixty per cent of slaves worked in the fields producing cotton, which accounted for two-thirds of US exports. Other Southern crops – often also cultivated by slaves – included sugarcane, rice and tobacco.

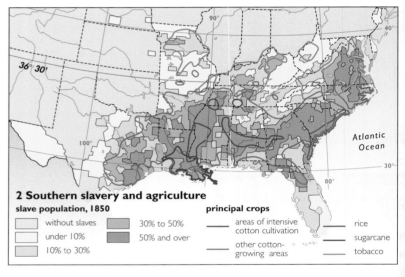

2 Southern slavery and agriculture

slave population, 1850

- without slaves
- under 10%
- 10% to 30%
- 30% to 50%
- 50% and over

principal crops

- areas of intensive cotton cultivation
- other cotton-growing areas
- rice
- sugarcane
- tobacco

3 Some states, though they had slaves, declined to join the Confederacy (map below). At the start of the Civil War, West Virginia split from Virginia in order to stay with the Union. Once the war was over, "Reconstruction" governments were established in the South, backed by northern Republicans. The last of these survived until 1877.

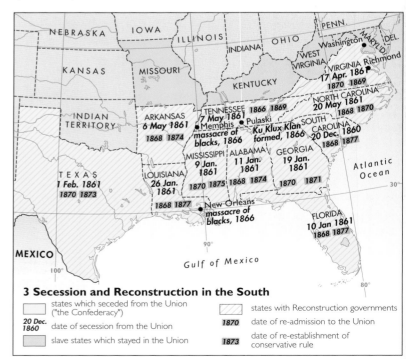

3 Secession and Reconstruction in the South

- states which seceded from the Union ("the Confederacy")
- 20 Dec. 1860 date of secession from the Union
- slave states which stayed in the Union
- states with Reconstruction governments
- 1870 date of re-admission to the Union
- 1873 date of re-establishment of conservative rule

Dead soldiers at Gettysburg (above). The small market town of Gettysburg, Pennsylvania, was the scene of the greatest battle of the war. Lee, advancing into the North for a second time to force Lincoln to negotiate peace on the basis of Southern independence, attacked General Meade's Union army, but in the course of a three-day battle was comprehensively beaten. The Union lost 23,000 men, the Confederacy 28,000. Four months after the battle, at a ceremony dedicating a national cemetery on the Gettysburg site, Lincoln made perhaps his finest speech, declaring that the war would bring "a new birth of freedom" and vowing that "government of the people, by the people, for the people, shall not perish from the earth."

4 Comparative resources: Union and Confederate states, 1861

Union States   Confederate States

Total population: 2.5 to 1	Naval ship tonnage: 25 to 1
Male population 18–60 yrs.: 4.4 to 1	Factory production value: 10 to 1
Free men 18–60 yrs in military service: 1864 — 44% / 90%	Textile goods production: 17 to 1
Wealth produced: 3 to 1	Iron production: 20 to 1
Railroad mileage: 2.4 to 1	Coal production: 38 to 1
Merchant ship tonnage: 9 to 1	Firearms production: 32 to 1
Farm acreage: 3 to 1	
Draft animals: 1.8 to 1	
Livestock: 1.5 to 1	
Wheat production: 4.2 to 1	
Corn production: 2 to 1	
Cotton production: 1 to 24	

4 Because the South lacked the North's industrial capacity (chart above), the Confederacy was obliged to import or capture most of its arms. As the Union blockade tightened and the Confederate transport system broke down through inability to replace equipment, the agricultural South experienced difficulty even in feeding itself. The only area where the South had a decisive advantage was in the production of cotton.

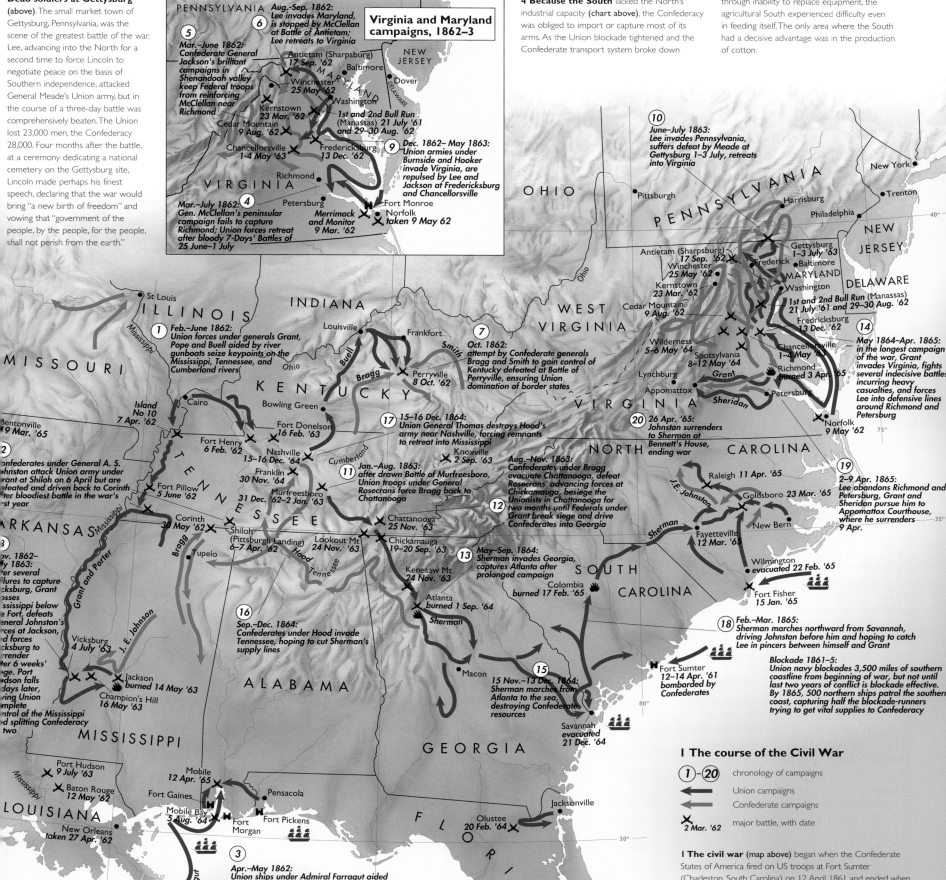

Virginia and Maryland campaigns, 1862–3

⑤ Mar.–June 1862: Confederate General Jackson's brilliant campaigns in Shenandoah valley keep Federal troops from reinforcing McClellan near Richmond

⑥ Aug.–Sep. 1862: Lee invades Maryland, is stopped by McClellan at Battle of Antietam; Lee retreats to Virginia

Antietam (Sharpsburg) 17 Sep. '62 — Baltimore — Winchester 25 May '62 — Kernstown 23 Mar. '62 — Cedar Mountain 9 Aug. '62 — Washington — 1st and 2nd Bull Run (Manassas) 21 July '61 and 29–30 Aug. '62 — Chancellorsville 1–4 May '63 — Fredericksburg 13 Dec. '62 — Richmond — Petersburg — Fort Monroe — Merrimack and Monitor 9 Mar. '62 — Norfolk taken 9 May 62

⑨ Dec. 1862– May 1863: Union armies under Burnside and Hooker invade Virginia, are repulsed by Lee and Jackson at Fredericksburg and Chancellorsville

④ Mar.–July 1862: Gen. McClellan's peninsular campaign fails to capture Richmond; Union forces retreat after bloody 7-Days' Battles of 25 June–1 July

NEW JERSEY — Dover — DELAWARE — PENNSYLVANIA — VIRGINIA — MARYLAND

Map — main labels

NEW YORK — Trenton — New York — PENNSYLVANIA — Pittsburgh — Harrisburg — Philadelphia — NEW JERSEY — OHIO — Frankfort — Louisville — Gettysburg 1–3 July '63 — Frederick — Baltimore — MARYLAND — Washington — DELAWARE — Antietam (Sharpsburg) 17 Sep. '62 — Winchester 25 May '62 — Kernstown 23 Mar. '62 — Cedar Mountain 9 Aug. '62 — 1st and 2nd Bull Run (Manassas) 21 July '61 and 29–30 Aug. '62 — Fredericksburg 13 Dec. '62 — Wilderness 5–6 May '64 — Spotsylvania 8–12 May '64 — Chancellorsville 1–4 May '63 — Richmond burned 3 Apr. '65 — Lynchburg — Appomattox — Grant — Petersburg — Sheridan — Norfolk 9 May '62 — WEST VIRGINIA — VIRGINIA

⑩ June–July 1863: Lee invades Pennsylvania, suffers defeat by Meade at Gettysburg 1–3 July, retreats into Virginia

⑭ May 1864–Apr. 1865: in the longest campaign of the war, Grant invades Virginia, fights several indecisive battles incurring heavy casualties, and forces Lee into defensive lines around Richmond and Petersburg

⑦ Oct. 1862: attempt by Confederate generals Bragg and Smith to gain control of Kentucky defeated at Battle of Perryville, ensuring Union domination of border states

⑰ 15–16 Dec. 1864: Union General Thomas destroys Hood's army near Nashville, forcing remnants to retreat into Mississippi

⑪ Jan.–Aug. 1863: after drawn Battle of Murfreesboro, Union troops under General Rosecrans force Bragg back to Chattanooga

⑫ Aug.–Nov. 1863: Confederates under Bragg evacuate Chattanooga, defeat Rosecrans' advancing forces at Chickamauga, besiege the Unionists in Chattanooga for two months until Federals under Grant break siege and drive Confederates into Georgia

⑳ 26 Apr. '65: Johnston surrenders to Sherman at Bennett's House, ending war

⑲ 2–9 Apr. 1865: Lee abandons Richmond and Petersburg, Grant and Sheridan pursue him to Appomattox Courthouse, where he surrenders 9 Apr.

① Feb.–June 1862: Union forces under generals Grant, Pope and Buell aided by river gunboats seize keypoints on the Mississippi, Tennessee, and Cumberland rivers

St Louis — ILLINOIS — INDIANA — MISSOURI — Island No.10 7 Apr. '62 — Cairo — Bowling Green — Fort Donelson 16 Feb. '63 — Fort Henry 6 Feb. '62 — Nashville 15–16 Dec. '64 — Knoxville 2 Sep. '63 — Perryville 8 Oct. '62 — Smith — Bragg — Buell — Ohio

⑧ Nov. 1862– May 1863: after several failures to capture Vicksburg, Grant crosses Mississippi below the Fort, defeats General Johnston's forces at Jackson, and forces Vicksburg to surrender after 6 weeks' siege. Port Hudson falls 5 days later, giving Union complete control of the Mississippi and splitting Confederacy in two

Confederates under General A. S. Johnston attack Union army under Grant at Shiloh on 6 April but are defeated and driven back to Corinth after bloodiest battle in the war's first year

Fort Pillow 5 June '62 — Corinth 30 May '62 — Shiloh (Pittsburg Landing) 6–7 Apr. '62 — Tupelo — Franklin 30 Nov. '64 — Murfreesboro 31 Dec. '62–2 Jan. '63 — Chattanooga 25 Nov. '63 — Lookout Mt 24 Nov. '63 — Chickamauga 19–20 Sep. '63 — Kenesaw Mt 24 Nov. '63 — Atlanta burned 1 Sep. '64 — Sherman — TENNESSEE — ARKANSAS — Grant and Porter — Hood — Tennessee — J. E. Johnston — Sherman — Raleigh 11 Apr. '65 — Goldsboro 23 Mar. '65 — New Bern — Fayetteville 12 Mar. '65 — Wilmington evacuated 22 Feb. '65 — Fort Fisher 15 Jan. '65 — NORTH CAROLINA — SOUTH CAROLINA — Columbia burned 17 Feb. '65

Bentonville 19 Mar. '65 — Vicksburg 4 July '63 — Jackson burned 14 May '63 — Champion's Hill 16 May '63 — MISSISSIPPI — ALABAMA — GEORGIA — Macon — Savannah evacuated 21 Dec. '64 — Fort Sumter 12–14 Apr. '61 bombarded by Confederates

⑯ Sep.–Dec. 1864: Confederates under Hood invade Tennessee, hoping to cut Sherman's supply lines

⑬ May–Sep. 1864: Sherman invades Georgia, captures Atlanta after prolonged campaign

⑮ 15 Nov.–13 Dec. 1864: Sherman marches from Atlanta to the sea, destroying Confederate resources

⑱ Feb.–Mar. 1865: Sherman marches northward from Savannah, driving Johnston before him and hoping to catch Lee in pincers between himself and Grant

Blockade 1861–5: Union navy blockades 3,500 miles of southern coastline from beginning of war, but not until last two years of conflict is blockade effective. By 1865, 500 northern ships patrol the southern coast, capturing half the blockade-runners trying to get vital supplies to Confederacy

Port Hudson 9 July '63 — Baton Rouge 12 May '62 — Mobile 12 Apr. '65 — Fort Gaines — Pensacola — Mobile Bay 3 Aug. '64 — Fort Morgan — Fort Pickens — LOUISIANA — New Orleans taken 27 Apr. '62 — FLORIDA — Jacksonville — Olustee 20 Feb. '64 — Farragut

③ Apr.–May 1862: Union ships under Admiral Farragut aided by troops under General Butler capture forts at mouth of the Mississippi, force New Orleans to surrender, and gain control of the Mississippi as far north as Port Hudson

1 The course of the Civil War

①–⑳ chronology of campaigns

⟵ Union campaigns

⟵ Confederate campaigns

✕ 2 Mar. '62 major battle, with date

1 The civil war (map above) began when the Confederate States of America fired on US troops at Fort Sumter (Charleston, South Carolina) on 12 April 1861 and ended when the main Confederate armies surrendered in April 1865. Nearly 3 million Americans served in the Union and Confederate forces — two-thirds of them under 23 years of age. Some 200,000 Union soldiers were black, mostly emancipated slaves. Over 21 per cent of the civil war soldiers died (and 35 per cent of Confederate troops), a much higher proportion even than in any of the armies of the First World War, and twice as many of them died of disease as were killed in battle.

The United States:
a nation of immigrants

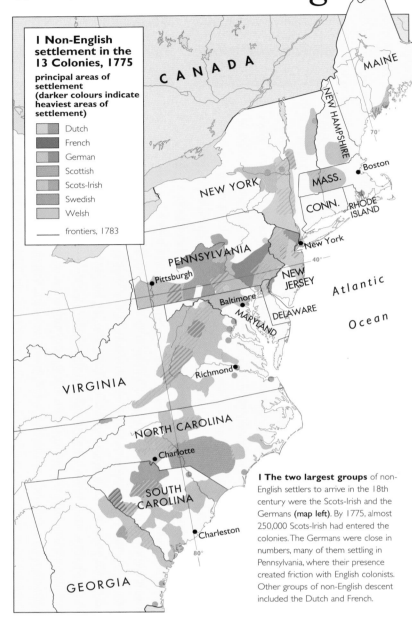

1 Non-English settlement in the 13 Colonies, 1775

principal areas of settlement
(darker colours indicate heaviest areas of settlement)

Dutch
French
German
Scottish
Scots-Irish
Swedish
Welsh

frontiers, 1783

1 The two largest groups of non-English settlers to arrive in the 18th century were the Scots-Irish and the Germans (map left). By 1775, almost 250,000 Scots-Irish had entered the colonies. The Germans were close in numbers, many of them settling in Pennsylvania, where their presence created friction with English colonists. Other groups of non-English descent included the Dutch and French.

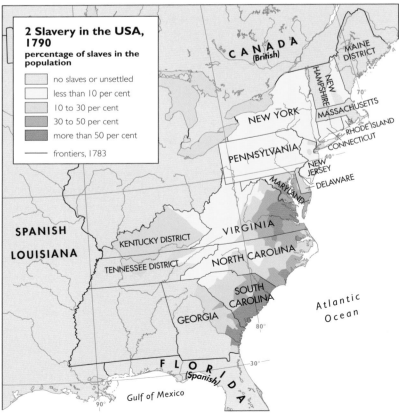

2 Slavery in the USA, 1790

percentage of slaves in the population

no slaves or unsettled
less than 10 per cent
10 to 30 per cent
30 to 50 per cent
more than 50 per cent

frontiers, 1783

2 The numbers of black slaves rose sharply after 1700, partly as a result of the thriving slave trade (map above). In 1700 there were perhaps 20,000 slaves; by 1763, there were over a third of a million. While slavery was to be found in the north, it never made up more than a small proportion of the population. In the South, on the eve of independence, two out of every five inhabitants were slaves.

Although the USA is not the only country to have been founded – and to have had much of its subsequent history shaped by – immigrants and their descendants, it is the most powerful, populous and ethnically diverse of such countries. Between 1820 and 1920 the USA received a total of over 34 million immigrants.

UNTIL AROUND 1700, the great majority of immigrants to the British American colonies were English, Welsh or Scottish. Thereafter, as British governments discouraged voluntary emigration, the ethnic composition of the population changed, as growing numbers of German, Swiss, French, Dutch, Swedish and, above all, Ulster Scotch-Irish migrants arrived. Britain continued to transport involuntary emigrants to the American colonies, including around 200,000 slaves from Africa and 30,000 British convicted felons. As ethnic groups tended to settle in particular areas and (outside towns) there was comparatively little intermingling between them, the population of late colonial America very much resembled a mosaic.

The early 19th century

In the early years following independence, immigration was on a comparatively small scale. But, after the Napoleonic Wars in 1815, more Europeans started to emigrate to the USA, thereby beginning a mass migration that would last for more than a century. Between 1820 and 1880, largely unaffected by the Civil War of 1861–5, over 10 million immigrants entered the USA. Most came from northern and western Europe – mainly Germany, Ireland, Britain and Scandinavia. They sailed for America to better themselves economically, to escape (in the case of the Irish) the famine of the 1840s, or – more rarely – as political refugees (German "Forty-Eighters", for example). Scandinavian immigrants often became farmers in Minnesota and Wisconsin, Germans in Illinois, Wisconsin, Iowa and Ohio. The Irish were the most urban of all immigrant groups: less than one in ten took up farming and New York, Philadelphia and Boston soon contained large Irish populations.

From the 1830s many native-born Americans were becoming increasingly disturbed by the extent of immigration. An anti-immigrant movement culminated in the 1850s in the emergence of a short-lived but, for a time, relatively successful "nativist" party: the Know Nothings. But anti-immigrant feeling dissipated during the Civil War and in the years following it, when immigrants were welcomed as contributing to the American economy. It revived in the 1880s and '90s, in part in response to economic stresses and the huge increase in the numbers of immigrants (from 2.8 million in 1871–80 to 5.2 million in 1881–90), in part because of a perceived change in the origins of immigrants themselves.

The "new" immigrants

The bulk of immigrants after 1880 came from southern and eastern Europe. These areas had suffered the collapse of the old agricultural order, huge population increases and anti-semitic pogroms. The immigrants, taking advantage of the easier and cheaper travel offered by steamships, arrived in a growing flood in the

THERE SHE LIES, THE GREAT MELTING POT. LISTEN! CAN'T YOU HEAR THE ROARING AND THE BUBBLING? THERE GAPES HER MOUTH, THE HARBOUR WHERE A THOUSAND MAMMOTH FEEDERS COME FROM THE ENDS OF THE WORLD TO POUR IN THEIR HUMAN FREIGHT. AH, WHAT A STIRRING AND SEETHING! CELT AND LATIN, SLAV AND TEUTON, GREEK AND SYRIAN, BLACK AND YELLOW.

The Melting Pot, 1909

USA. Total immigration soared to 8.8 million in 1901–10 and 5.7 million in the subsequent decade. "New" immigrants – to a far greater extent than the "old" (other than the Irish) – tended to settle in cities. Cities like New York and Chicago developed a mosaic of ethnic neighbourhoods. Many Americans, between the 1880s and 1914, became increasingly uneasy over whether such groups could be assimilated and began to support demands for immigration restriction. The First World War, making Americans newly aware of their ethnic disunity, and the reaction against Europe that followed the war and the postwar recession, drove Congress, in 1921 and 1924, to impose ceilings on total immigrant numbers and introduce a "quota" system that was heavily biased against the nations that had produced most of the "new" immigration.

Controls and continuity

The legislation of the 1920s banned immigration from most Asian countries, but exempted the western hemisphere from its provisions since many southwestern employers regarded Mexican labour as essential. In 1943, the US government introduced the *braceros* system, allowing large numbers of Mexican agricultural labourers to enter the country. Meanwhile, immigration laws were relaxed to allow successive waves of refugees to enter: fugitives from communism in eastern Europe; Cubans after the revolution of 1959 and Vietnamese after the collapse of South Vietnam in 1975. The law was liberalized in 1965, allowing increased immigration from Asia. Indeed, throughout the 1970s, Asia (especially the Philippines and Korea) contributed more immigrants than Europe.

The poet Walt Whitman, writing in the 1850s, described America as "not merely a nation but a teeming of nations." Immigrants have made a massive contribution to American finance, society, politics and culture. American society today is recognizably and irreversibly multi-cultural. Yet anxieties persist among some Americans towards immigration both legal and illegal (the so-called "wetbacks") from Mexico that has transformed much of the South-West and Far West into predominantly Spanish-speaking areas.

3 Between 1840 and 1930, the USA accepted millions of immigrants from European countries (map below). In the first decades of this tremendous migration, most immigrants came from northern and western Europe (Britain, with Ireland, Germany and Scandinavia). From about 1890, the main source of immigrants came from southern and eastern Europe (especially Italy, Austria-Hungary and Russia). After the passage of the restrictive legislation of 1921 and 1924, total immigration into the USA fell sharply.

4 The total of immigrants from different nationalities over the period from 1820 to 1930 (chart right) demonstrates that, during this period, English-speaking immigrants from Ireland, Britain and Canada contributed a good proportion of total immigration. But to think of immigrants solely in terms of their "national origins" is slightly misleading. There was comparatively little immigration from Russia or Poland before the 1880s, for example, and many of those who came from these countries thereafter were Jewish and identified themselves in this way rather than as Russian or Poles.

4 Total immigrants to the USA, 1820–1930

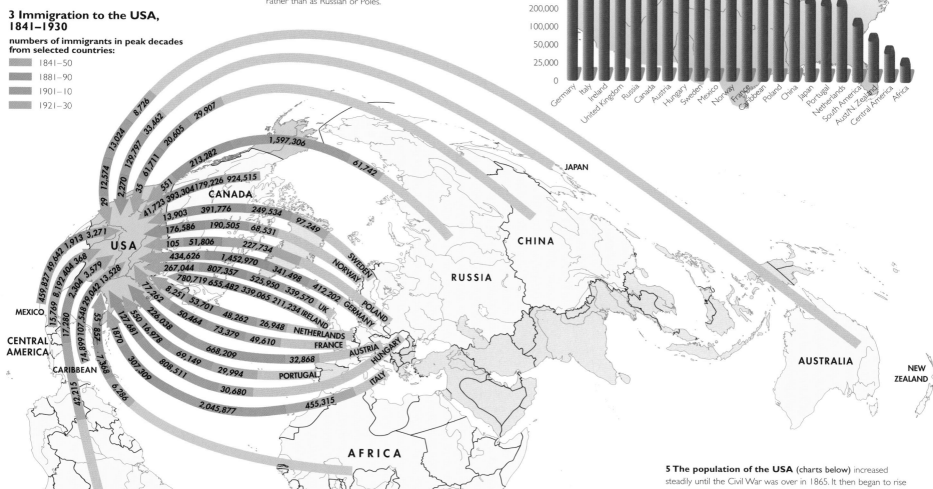

3 Immigration to the USA, 1841–1930

numbers of immigrants in peak decades from selected countries:

- 1841–50
- 1881–90
- 1901–10
- 1921–30

5 The population of the USA (charts below) increased steadily until the Civil War was over in 1865. It then began to rise much more sharply. Until around 1880, population grew fastest in towns. Stimulated by industrialization and mass immigration, some cities then expanded very fast: Chicago doubled in size between 1880 and 1890, to reach a population of a million for the first time. Because of the vast geographical size of the USA and its territorial expansion during the 19th century, the massive population increase since 1790 is only partly reflected in figures for population density.

5 Population of the USA, 1790–1995

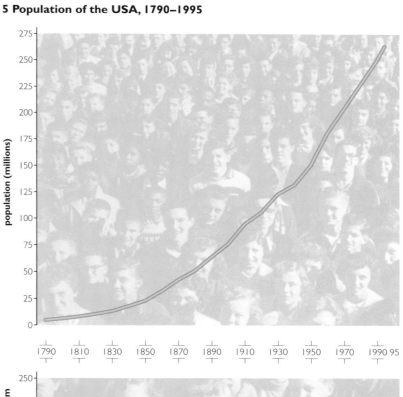

1619 Arrival in Virginia of the first black slaves

1840s Irish potato famine

1848 Failed revolutions in Germany; "liberals" leave for USA

1882 First Federal immigration law. First Chinese Exclusion Act

1892 Ellis Island becomes New York's immigrant reception depot

1924 Johnson-Reed Act introduces quota system based on national origins to limit immigration

1943 Introduction of *braceros* system

1965 Abolition of national origins system

Children at Ellis Island (right). In 1892 Ellis Island became New York's main reception depot for immigrants. Its immigration officers had the task of weeding out and excluding those regarded as undesirables. The first federal immigration law in 1882 began the task of defining exactly who was undesirable.

Canada

In 1867 Canada became the first British colony to govern its internal affairs. Like other "New World" countries, it relied on immigration for most of its population growth. Many migrants came from western and northern Europe, but in the early 20th century – and especially since the 1960s – sources of immigrants have become much more diversified. Canada is now one of the few countries to declare itself as officially multicultural.

FOR A SHORT TIME – beginning with the British conquest of New France (1759–60) – all of eastern North America formed part of the British empire, while through the Hudson's Bay Company's claim to the vast area of Rupert's Land, British influence was felt, via the fur trade, in much of central North America. Aboriginal peoples continued to dominate the population of the west through the 19th century, but their lands were gradually taken away from them, often, but not always, through treaty negotiations.

Territory

Québec, Nova Scotia and Newfoundland were not drawn into the War of 1812, although the influx of loyalist refugees in the aftermath of the conflict reinforced pro-British sentiment in these colonies. At the time of the war, British troops, local volunteers and aboriginal warriors repulsed the American threat. The separate British colonies of eastern North America maintained strong local identities. On a number of occasions, proposals to unite the various colonies met with failure. In 1867, Nova Scotia, New Brunswick and the Canadas (present-day southern Ontario and southern Québec) were brought together as the self-governing Dominion of Canada, still under formal British control. Over the next 80 years, Canada subsumed the rest of the British territories in North America. The Rupert's Land territory was acquired from the Hudson's Bay Company in 1867, the Arctic Islands were transferred from British control to Canadian in 1880, and other colonies joined the new country. Newfoundland, whose decision to become a Canadian province in 1949 was determined in a close-run referendum, was the last to join.

Population

Through much of its history, this region had difficulty attracting immigrants, and much of the population growth depended on natural increase. The size of the aboriginal population, beset by epidemic diseases against which it had no immunity, declined through the 19th century. British and Irish immigration transformed many parts of eastern North America between the 1810s and the 1850s. Economic difficulties during the first decades of Canada's dominion status reduced the flow of migrants. But at the very end of the 19th century, immigration to Canada expanded tremendously, at a pace that was sustained until just before the First World War. This population influx derived from Britain and northwest Europe as well as from southern and eastern Europe. Immigration of black Americans and Asians was discouraged by the Canadian government from the early 20th century, although sizeable Chinese, Japanese and Sikh communities developed in British Columbia. Despite the hostility they faced, black populations continued to live in Nova Scotia and southern Ontario.

I British North America comprised the colonies and territories of North America that had not joined the War of 1812 (map below). In the second half of the 19th century, most of these parts were joined together in the Dominion of Canada. After many decades of separate existence, Newfoundland and Labrador joined Canada in 1949.

I The Territorial development of Canada, 1867–2000

Alberta	Nova Scotia
British Columbia	Nunavut
British Possessions	Ontario
District of Keewatin	Prince Edward Island
Manitoba	Québec
New Brunswick	Saskatchewan
Newfoundland	Yukon Territory
Northwest Territories	

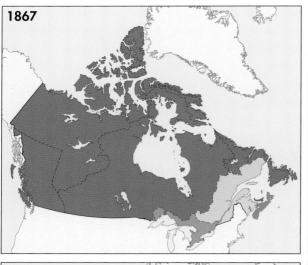

1867

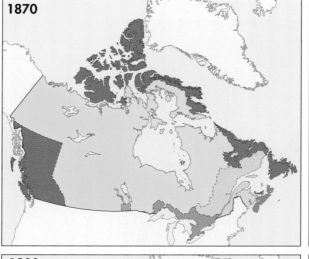

1870

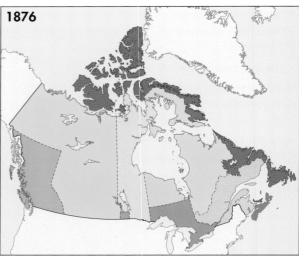

1876

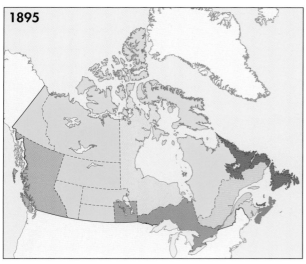

1895

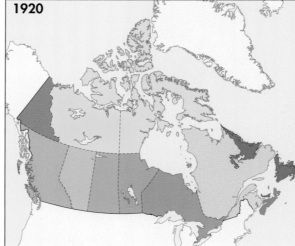

1920

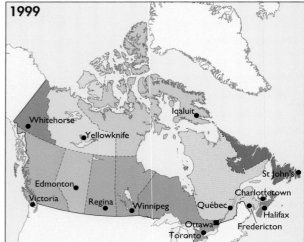

1999

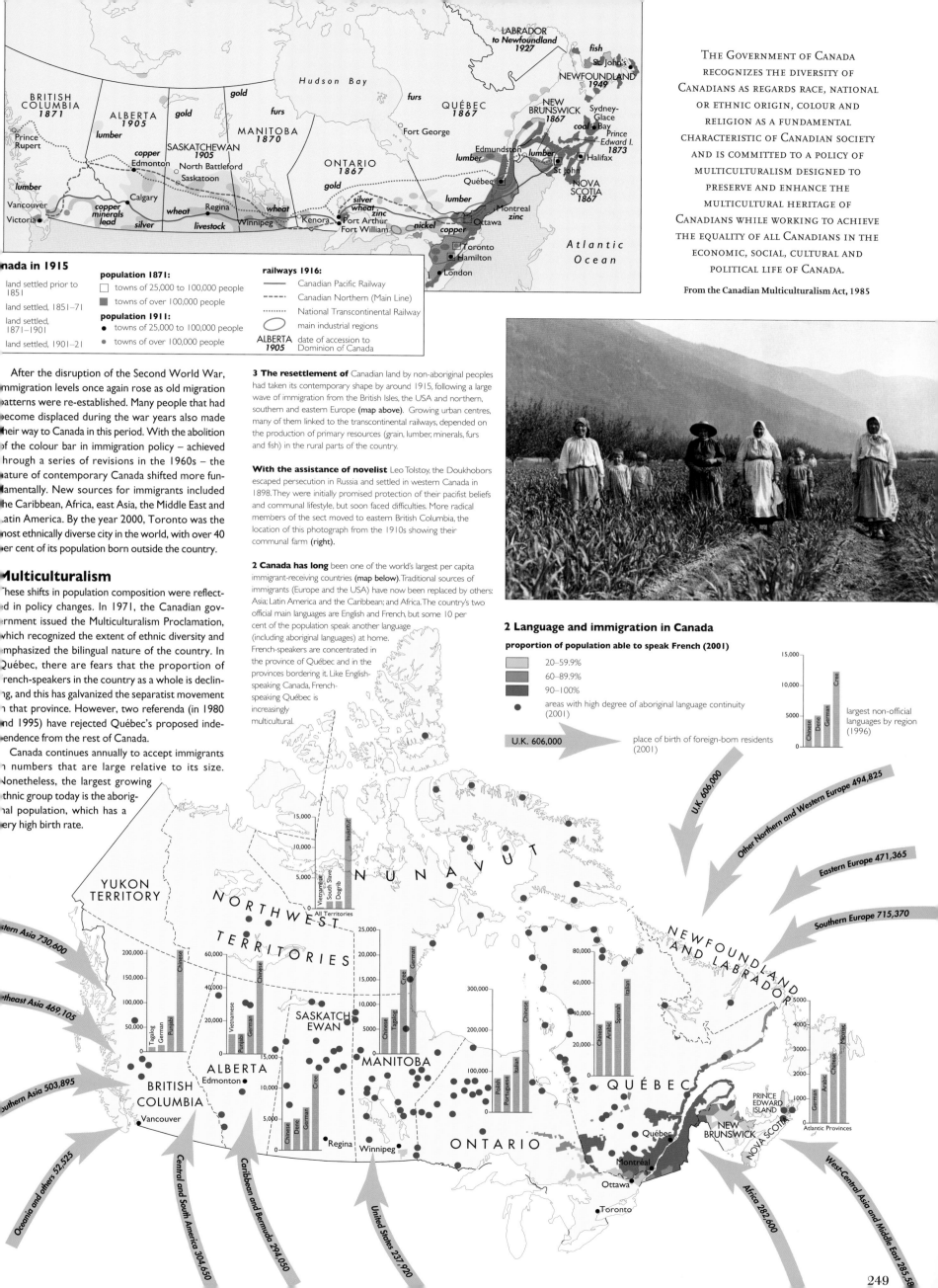

Map (top): Canada in 1915

Hudson Bay

BRITISH COLUMBIA 1871
ALBERTA 1905
SASKATCHEWAN 1905
MANITOBA 1870
ONTARIO 1867
QUÉBEC 1867
NEW BRUNSWICK 1867
NOVA SCOTIA 1867
Prince Edward I. 1873
NEWFOUNDLAND 1949
LABRADOR to Newfoundland 1927

Atlantic Ocean

Prince Rupert, Vancouver, Victoria, Edmonton, Calgary, North Battleford, Saskatoon, Regina, Winnipeg, Kenora, Port Arthur, Fort William, Fort George, Québec, Montreal, Ottawa, Toronto, Hamilton, London, Edmundston, St John, Halifax, Sydney-Glace Bay, St John's

Resources: gold, furs, lumber, copper, wheat, silver, livestock, minerals, lead, nickel, zinc, coal, fish, silver

Canada in 1915 (legend)

land settled prior to 1851
land settled, 1851–71
land settled, 1871–1901
land settled, 1901–21

population 1871:
☐ towns of 25,000 to 100,000 people
■ towns of over 100,000 people

population 1911:
● towns of 25,000 to 100,000 people
● towns of over 100,000 people

railways 1916:
— Canadian Pacific Railway
- - - Canadian Northern (Main Line)
······ National Transcontinental Railway
◯ main industrial regions
ALBERTA 1905 date of accession to Dominion of Canada

THE GOVERNMENT OF CANADA RECOGNIZES THE DIVERSITY OF CANADIANS AS REGARDS RACE, NATIONAL OR ETHNIC ORIGIN, COLOUR AND RELIGION AS A FUNDAMENTAL CHARACTERISTIC OF CANADIAN SOCIETY AND IS COMMITTED TO A POLICY OF MULTICULTURALISM DESIGNED TO PRESERVE AND ENHANCE THE MULTICULTURAL HERITAGE OF CANADIANS WHILE WORKING TO ACHIEVE THE EQUALITY OF ALL CANADIANS IN THE ECONOMIC, SOCIAL, CULTURAL AND POLITICAL LIFE OF CANADA.

From the Canadian Multiculturalism Act, 1985

After the disruption of the Second World War, immigration levels once again rose as old migration patterns were re-established. Many people that had become displaced during the war years also made their way to Canada in this period. With the abolition of the colour bar in immigration policy – achieved through a series of revisions in the 1960s – the nature of contemporary Canada shifted more fundamentally. New sources for immigrants included the Caribbean, Africa, east Asia, the Middle East and Latin America. By the year 2000, Toronto was the most ethnically diverse city in the world, with over 40 per cent of its population born outside the country.

Multiculturalism

These shifts in population composition were reflected in policy changes. In 1971, the Canadian government issued the Multiculturalism Proclamation, which recognized the extent of ethnic diversity and emphasized the bilingual nature of the country. In Québec, there are fears that the proportion of French-speakers in the country as a whole is declining, and this has galvanized the separatist movement in that province. However, two referenda (in 1980 and 1995) have rejected Québec's proposed independence from the rest of Canada.

Canada continues annually to accept immigrants in numbers that are large relative to its size. Nonetheless, the largest growing ethnic group today is the aboriginal population, which has a very high birth rate.

3 The resettlement of Canadian land by non-aboriginal peoples had taken its contemporary shape by around 1915, following a large wave of immigration from the British Isles, the USA and northern, southern and eastern Europe (map above). Growing urban centres, many of them linked to the transcontinental railways, depended on the production of primary resources (grain, lumber, minerals, furs and fish) in the rural parts of the country.

With the assistance of novelist Leo Tolstoy, the Doukhobors escaped persecution in Russia and settled in western Canada in 1898. They were initially promised protection of their pacifist beliefs and communal lifestyle, but soon faced difficulties. More radical members of the sect moved to eastern British Columbia, the location of this photograph from the 1910s showing their communal farm (right).

2 Canada has long been one of the world's largest per capita immigrant-receiving countries (map below). Traditional sources of immigrants (Europe and the USA) have now been replaced by others: Asia; Latin America and the Caribbean; and Africa. The country's two official main languages are English and French, but some 10 per cent of the population speak another language (including aboriginal languages) at home. French-speakers are concentrated in the province of Québec and in the provinces bordering it. Like English-speaking Canada, French-speaking Québec is increasingly multicultural.

2 Language and immigration in Canada

proportion of population able to speak French (2001)
☐ 20–59.9%
▨ 60–89.9%
■ 90–100%
● areas with high degree of aboriginal language continuity (2001)

U.K. 606,000 → place of birth of foreign-born residents (2001)

largest non-official languages by region (1996): Chinese, Dene, German, Cree

Map (bottom): Canada — language and immigration

YUKON TERRITORY
NORTHWEST TERRITORIES
NUNAVUT
BRITISH COLUMBIA (Vancouver)
ALBERTA (Edmonton)
SASKATCHEWAN (Regina)
MANITOBA (Winnipeg)
ONTARIO (Toronto)
QUÉBEC (Québec, Montréal, Ottawa)
NEWFOUNDLAND AND LABRADOR
NEW BRUNSWICK
NOVA SCOTIA
PRINCE EDWARD ISLAND

Immigration source regions (arrows):
- Eastern Asia 730,600
- Southeast Asia 469,105
- Southern Asia 503,895
- Oceania and others 52,525
- Central and South America 304,650
- Caribbean and Bermuda 294,050
- United States 237,920
- Africa 282,600
- West-Central Asia and Middle East 285,5..
- U.K. 606,000
- Other Northern and Western Europe 494,825
- Eastern Europe 471,365
- Southern Europe 715,370

Bar chart languages by province:
- All Territories: Vietnamese, South Slave, Dogrib, Inuktitut
- British Columbia: Tagalog, German, Punjabi, Chinese
- Alberta: Vietnamese, Punjabi, German, Chinese
- Saskatchewan: Chinese, Dene, German, Cree
- Manitoba: Chinese, Tagalog, Cree, German
- Ontario: Polish, Portuguese, Italian, Chinese
- Québec: Chinese, Arabic, Spanish, Italian
- Atlantic Provinces: German, Arabic, Chinese, Mi'kmaq

Latin America: independence and national growth

The early 19th century saw the Portuguese and Spanish colonies break away from their mother countries, in the latter case after a bitter military struggle. The new states that emerged were at first unstable; initial confederations soon broke up and military dictatorships flourished. By the early 20th century comparative stability had returned.

BY THE LATE 18TH CENTURY, demands for political freedom, administrative autonomy and economic self-determination were growing throughout Latin America. Yet, while they were encouraged by the American and French revolutions, it was the Napoleonic invasion of Spain and Portugal in 1808 that enabled them to develop into successful movements for independence. Having fled from Lisbon to Rio de Janeiro, which then became the centre of their empire, the Portuguese royal family presided over the relatively peaceful transition of Brazil from colony to independent nation. After his father had returned to Portugal, Pedro I, renouncing his claims to the Portuguese throne and assuming the title emperor, declared the independence of Brazil. This, together with the fact that the planter elite were too fearful of slave revolts to split into factions, made for considerable political and institutional continuity.

The revolt against Spain

Spain, on the other hand, tried to crush revolts in her own Latin American colonies, and several years of conflict were necessary before her government acknowledged defeat. A southern revolution was carried by San Martín's Army of the Andes from Buenos Aires to Chile and beyond. A northern revo-

IT IS NOTORIOUS THAT THE MORE WE RELY ON FOREIGN INTERESTS TO SUPPLY OUR NEEDS, THE MORE WE DIMINISH OUR NATIONAL INDEPENDENCE; AND OUR RELIANCE NOW EVEN EXTENDS TO DAILY AND VITAL NEEDS.

Rafael Revenga, Venezuelan economist, 1829

MANY TYRANTS WILL ARISE ON MY TOMB.

Simón Bolívar, 1830

lution, more vigorously opposed by Spain, was led by Bolívar from Venezuela to the battlefield of Boyacá in Colombia (then called New Granada). Both, by 1822, had converged on Peru, the fortress of Spain in South America. In the north, insurgency in Mexico followed a course of its own – frustrated social revolution, then prolonged counter-revolution and finally the seizure of power by Iturbide, an army officer, who proclaimed himself Emperor Agustín I.

The independence movement as a whole was essentially political. It involved a transfer of authority, but little social or economic change. Its leaders were mostly drawn from the Creole population, Iberians born in America. They were mainly politically inexperienced and, in many of the new Latin American

1808 Napoleonic invasion of Portugal and Spain effectively begins the movement for independence

1819 Battle of Boyacá leads to independence of Colombia

1821 Battle near Carabobo finally secures Venezuelan independence

1822 Brazil declares independence

1824 Peru and Bolivia become independent

1879 War of the Pacific (Chile, Bolivia, Peru)

1888 Brazil becomes the last Latin American country to abolish slavery

1910 Start of Mexican revolution

Simón Bolívar (1783–1830) (picture above right) became known as "The Liberator" for his role in the emancipation of South America from Spanish rule. After participating in several unsuccessful revolts, he and his army defeated the Spanish at Boyacá in 1819 and organized the republic of Gran Colombia. In 1821, he defeated the Spanish near Carabobo, ensuring Venezuelan independence. Between 1822 and 1824 he also helped free Ecuador and Peru. Southern Peru became a new republic, named Bolivia in his honour.

3 The new nations of Latin America were classic export economies, exploiting cheap land and labour to produce raw materials for a world market **(map below)**. After independence, they carried on exporting the same products to Europe as during the colonial period: silver, cacao, sugar, coffee, hides and tobacco. Economic development was discouraged for several decades by the survival of slavery, small domestic markets and foreign competition. But the last years of the 19th century saw an influx of foreign capital, above all from Britain and the USA, that improved communications and encouraged the exploitation of new products.

republics, the decades between independence and mid-century were characterized by violent political conflicts. With the masses excluded from political decision-making, politics became a matter of rivalries amongst oligarchic families and military cliques. *Caudillos* – military leaders – fought with one another for political power without greatly affecting the mainly rural and traditional societies surrounding them.

Political stability

From the mid-19th century, there was greater stability, marked by the emergence of new institutional arrangements, "oligarchic republics", essentially based on alliances of regional elites. (Brazil remained an Empire until the monarchy fell in 1889.) The consolidation of nation-states at this point was driven by export-led growth. Politics was no longer the zero-sum game of the immediate post-Independence period. Rapid growth in the world economy meant an increasing demand for Latin American exports and an inflow of foreign investment, notably from Britain. Foreign capital helped rejuvenate the mining sector, and financed railway construction, the modernization of ports and domestic market consolidation. Associated with greater political stability and economic opportunity, mass migration from southern Europe transformed agriculture in temperate zones, such as southern Brazil, the Argentinian pampas, Uruguay, and central Chile and Colombia. Cuba, Spanish until 1898, also received large numbers of immigrants. Commodity booms – Peruvian guano, Chilean nitrates, Brazilian coffee and rubber, River Plate cereals and meat – underwrote the new political order.

The early 20th century

By the beginning of the 20th century, the socio-political fabric of many republics was radically different from a century earlier. Economic growth, urbanization and, less so, industrial growth in countries like Argentina, Chile, Brazil and Mexico fostered the consolidation of a fairly large middle class clamouring for greater political representation, and the appearance of vocal working-class organizations. These groups sought political change at about the time when volatility in the world economy limited the capacity of oligarchic regimes to accommodate those demands. The result, in Mexico, was violent social protest involving disaffected segments of the oligarchy, middle-class intellectuals, small farmers and peasant communities whose land had been alienated during the dictatorship of Porfirio Díaz (1876–1910). Elsewhere (eg Uruguay, Argentina and Chile), electoral reform enabled newer social constellations to obtain political power via the ballot box.

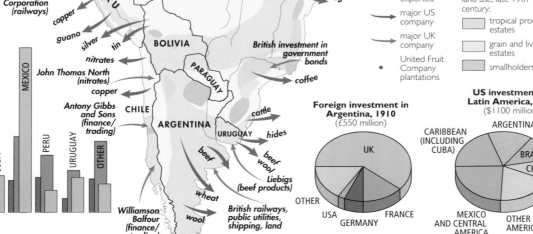

3 Export economies and foreign investment to 1910

commodities exported
major US company
major UK company
United Fruit Company plantations

principal agricultural land use, late 19th century:
tropical produce estates
grain and livestock estates
smallholders

Foreign investment in Argentina, 1910 (£550 million)
UK
OTHER
USA GERMANY FRANCE

US investment in Latin America, 1910 ($1100 million)
ARGENTINA
BRAZIL
CHILE
CARIBBEAN (INCLUDING CUBA)
MEXICO AND CENTRAL AMERICA
OTHER SOUTH AMERICAN

Total British investment in Latin America
1910, total £1000 million
1890, total £427 million
1880, total £179.5 million

Guggenheim (mining)
Standard Oil
J. P. Morgan (railways)
Weetman Pearson (contracting/oil)
United Fruit Company (plantations)
Peruvian Corporation (railways)
John Thomas North (nitrates)
Antony Gibbs and Sons (finance/trading)
Williamson Balfour (finance/trading)
Liebigs (beef products)
British investment in government bonds
British railways, public utilities, shipping, land

MEXICO
CUBA
VENEZUELA
COLOMBIA
ECUADOR
PERU
BRAZIL
BOLIVIA
PARAGUAY
CHILE
ARGENTINA
URUGUAY

oil, tobacco, sugar, coffee, cacao, cattle, bananas, rubber, cacao, sugar, copper, guano, silver, tin, nitrates, copper, cattle, hides, beef, wool, wheat, wool, cotton, sugar, coffee, beef

ARGENTINA
BRAZIL
MEXICO
CHILE
CUBA
PERU
URUGUAY
OTHER

1 Latin American nationalists fought not only Spain and Portugal, but also each other. Uruguay split from Brazil in 1828, but otherwise Brazil preserved its territorial integrity. Elsewhere, fragmentation quickly followed emancipation from Spanish rule (map below). In 1823, Central America seceded from Mexico and in 1839 itself split into five republics. In 1830, Venezuela and Ecuador seceded from Gran Colombia, the republic created by Bolívar. Subsequent boundary disputes led to several major wars, including the war between Mexico and the USA (1846–8) and the war of the Pacific (1879–83) between Chile, Peru and Bolivia.

2 In 1817, José de San Martín wrested Chile from Spanish forces (map left). Simón Bolívar defeated the Spanish to free Colombia in 1819 and Venezuela in 1821. By 1824 their armies had liberated all of Spanish America.

Independence campaigns, 1810–25
- viceroyalties, 1800
- anti-Spanish forces
- principal battle (with date)
- 25 date of independence

1 Latin America: political development from 1824

A	AGUASCALIENTES
C	CAMPECHE
G	GUANAJUATO
H	HIDALGO
ME	MÉXICO
M	MORELOS
N	NUEVO LEÓN
P	PUEBLA
Q	QUERÉTARO
S	SAN LUIS POTOSÍ
T	TLAXCALA
V	VERACRUZ

- boundary of Mexico 1824
- Mexico 1867
- 1821 date of independent statehood
- Republic of Gran Colombia, 1821–30
- United Provinces of Central America, 1823–38
- later Brazilian acquisitions
- areas affected by Mexican revolution, from 1910
- disputed between Ecuador and Peru
- disputed between Bolivia and Paraguay
- caudillismo
- revolutionary movements
- constitutionalism
- radical reformism
- French territory
- British territory
- Dutch territory
- Spanish territory

4 Population and immigration, 1825–1910

million people

racial profiles 1825
- whites
- mestizos, mulattos
- Indians
- blacks
- date of abolition of slavery
- unconquered Indians

population

	1825	1880	1910
Cuba	700,000	1.5m	2.2m
Mexico	6.8m	11.5m	15.2m
Guatemala	850,000*	1.2m	1.5m
El Salvador	370,000*	1.1m	1.4m
Honduras	350,000*	350,000	750,000
Nicaragua	300,000*	300,000	510,000
Costa Rica	100,000*	200,000	400,000
Brazil	4m	12.0m	26.0m
Colombia	1.3m	3.0m	5.1m
Peru	1.4m	2.8m	4.2m
Venezuela	800,000	1.9m	2.5m
Ecuador	550,000	900,000	1.9m
Bolivia	1.1m	1.2m	1.9m
Argentina	630,000	3.9m	7.8m
Chile	1m	2.4m	3.3m
Uruguay	50,000	700,000	1.5m
Paraguay	180,000	450,000	800,000

*1850

4 During the 19th century, most Latin American societies were composed of three main elements (map above): a Creole elite of Iberians born in the Americas, many owning large landed estates or *haciendas*; a small, mostly urban middle class; and a huge mass of landless and largely illiterate Indians, mestizos (persons of mixed Indian and European ancestry), Blacks (predominantly slaves or the descendants of slaves) and mulattos (descendants of Blacks and another race).

slave trade from Africa to Cuba 1822–67 400,000

slave trade from Africa 1800–55 1.2 million

immigrants to Brazil: country of origin
- PORTUGAL 28%
- ITALY 35%
- SPAIN 13%
- GERMANY 5%
- JAPAN 3%
- OTHERS 16%
(1881–1910)

immigrants to Argentina: country of origin
- ITALY 53%
- SPAIN 37%
- FRANCE 5%
- OTHERS 5%
(1857–1910)

immigrants to Chile: country of origin
- SPAIN 29%
- FRANCE 23%
- ITALY 21%
- SWITZERLAND 8%
- GREAT BRITAIN 7%
- GERMANY 6%
- OTHERS 6%
(1882–97)

FALKLAND IS. (Islas Malvinas) claimed by Spain to 1811, subsequently claimed by Argentina; colonized by Britain 1765–74; British from 1833

United Provinces of Rio Plata 1819–25
Argentine confederation 1825–53
Argentine republic from 1853

settled by Argentina by late 19th C

settled by Chile through 19th C

The disintegration of the Ottoman empire

During the 19th century, the Ottoman empire – "the sick man of Europe" – slowly disintegrated under the impact of foreign encroachment, popular anti-Turkish nationalism and a powerful reform movement. Defeat in the First World War brought complete collapse and the emergence of a modern Turkish national state under Kemal Atatürk.

BY THE END OF THE 18TH CENTURY, the Ottoman empire was no longer the military and cultural force it had once been. In 1798, the Ottoman province of Egypt was invaded and occupied by Napoleon. This was the first time since the Crusades that a European power had encroached directly on the Ottoman heartlands. Although Napoleon was ousted by the British, Egypt was seized by the Albanian general Muhammad Ali, who had been sent to attack the French by the Ottoman sultan, Selim III. From 1805, Egypt became independent of the empire, beginning a century-long process of territorial decline and persistent intervention by the European powers.

The Tanzimat reforms
Defeat at the hands of the Greeks and their European allies in 1827–9 (see p. 236) forced the Ottoman empire to modernize. The failure of the traditional janissary warriors during the war led to far-reaching military reforms based on European models. In 1839 a young generation of liberal officers and bureaucrats launched the Tanzimat reform movement, culminating in 1876 with the granting of a parliamentary constitution. Following Turkish defeat in war with Russia in 1877, which led a year later to the independence of Serbia, Montenegro and Romania, the new sultan, Abdulhamid II, suspended the constitution and ruled for 30 years as a modern authoritarian monarch.

Abdulhamid introduced further reforms and tried to modernize the economy while suppressing popular politics. The chronic financial instability of the sultanate was helped by granting European powers tax-raising privileges within the empire in 1881. Any popular nationalism was brutally repressed. When Armenian nationalists, representative of the large Christian community living in Anatolia, developed their own national awakening, the Zartonk, it sparked the revival of popular Islam. In 1895–6 the state orchestrated a series of massacres of 200,000 Armenians at the hands of Muslim Turks.

The creation of modern Turkey
Abdulhamid was overthrown in 1908 by a revolution of "Young Turks" drawn from among the new liberal intelligentsia and nationalist army officers organized through the Paris-based Committee of Union and Progress, founded in 1889. The sultanate was suspended and a modernizing regime installed. In 1913 the moderate liberals were overthrown by a military coup and hardline nationalists and Islamicists under Enver Pasha came to dominate Ottoman politics.

In October 1914 Enver Pasha brought Turkey in on Germany's side in the First World War and in November 1914 a *jihad*, or Holy War, was declared. On the grounds that Armenians in eastern Anatolia were a threat to the Turkish war effort, the regime unleashed a wave of savage violence against the Christian community. An estimated 1.5 million Armenians died, others were forced into slavery or made to convert to Islam. A fraction of the population arrived in deportation centres in Mesopotamia after enduring long "death marches".

Following Turkish defeat in 1918, the Young Turk regime was overthrown and the sultan briefly restored as an Allied puppet. But in 1920, Turkish nationalists led a war of liberation against the Allied occupying forces. Under the army officer Kemal Atatürk, and with the support of the emerging Turkish middle classes, the Turkish army re-conquered Anatolia. The rest of the former empire was divided up between France and Britain by the League of Nations as mandated territories. In the Treaty of Lausanne in 1923, Turkish independence was recognized, and Atatürk began the process of building a modern nation state based on secular rule, mass education and economic reform.

2 In the 19th century relations between Muslims and Armenian Christians in the empire slowly deteriorated. In the 1890s, a modest Armenian revolt was mercilessly crushed by the Ottomans. In 1915 under the impact of war and defeat a serious crisis erupted in eastern Anatolia which led to the deportation of the Christian population and the deaths of an estimated 1.5 million Armenians by 1923 **(map left)**. As Armenian populations were driven south towards Mesopotamia most were killed or died of hunger on the way. When the Turks regained eastern Anatolia in 1923, thousands of Armenians fled to join their co-religionists in the USSR.

4 Between 1750 and 1914 the territory of the Ottoman empire declined by almost 50 per cent as distant provinces were taken over by European colonial powers or lost to nationalist revolts **(chart below)**. By 1914 Turkey ruled only a fraction of its former European territory together with a swathe of territory from Anatolia to Arabia.

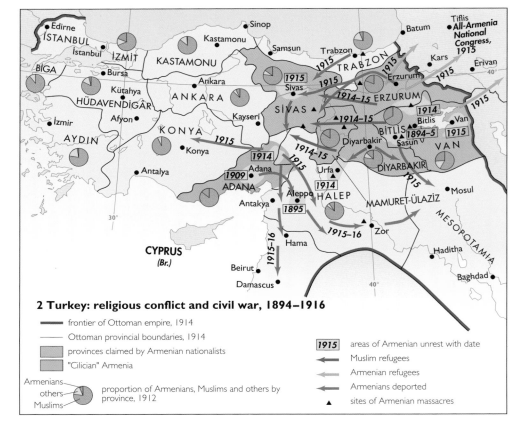

2 Turkey: religious conflict and civil war, 1894–1916

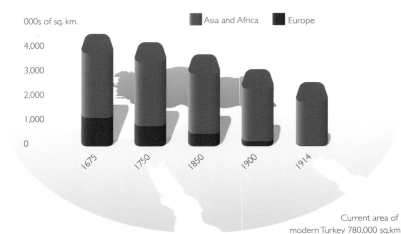

4 The contraction of the Ottoman empire

1 The Ottoman empire
slowly disintegrated in the 19th and early 20th centuries (map right). Egypt won its autonomy in 1805 while the Balkan nationalities broke away or had their independence confirmed one by one: Greece in 1830, Serbia, Romania and Montenegro in 1878, Bulgaria in 1908, Albania in 1912. Anatolia, the Ottoman heartland, became modern Turkey in 1923.

5 Ethnic composition of Ottoman empire, 1914

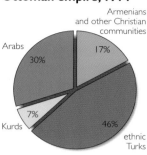

- Arabs 30%
- Kurds 7%
- ethnic Turks 46%
- Armenians and other Christian communities 17%

5 The Ottoman empire was a mix of ethnic groups in which Turks remained a minority (chart above). Most of the empire's inhabitants were Muslim but there were almost 3 million Christians and Jews in Anatolia.

Abdul Hamid II (1876–1909) was the last Ottoman sultan to wield effective power over the empire (below). A fierce opponent of political liberalization, he nonetheless encouraged educational, legal and economic reforms. In 1897, Abdul Hamid appointed a special court martial under General Reshid Pasha to crush the freedom movement among the educated and westernized youth of the empire. His reign witnessed the early stirrings of a women's movement within the region, but polygamy remained in force.

3 Under the Allied-imposed Treaty of Sèvres, the remnants of the Ottoman empire were to be dismembered leaving a rump Turkish state (map right). Parts of Anatolia were to be under Greek, French and British control and an independent Armenia and Kurdistan created. Greek occupation prompted a nationalist revival. The army overthrew the pro-Allied sultan and drove the Greeks out, recaptured parts of Armenia and defeated a Franco-Armenian force in Cilicia.

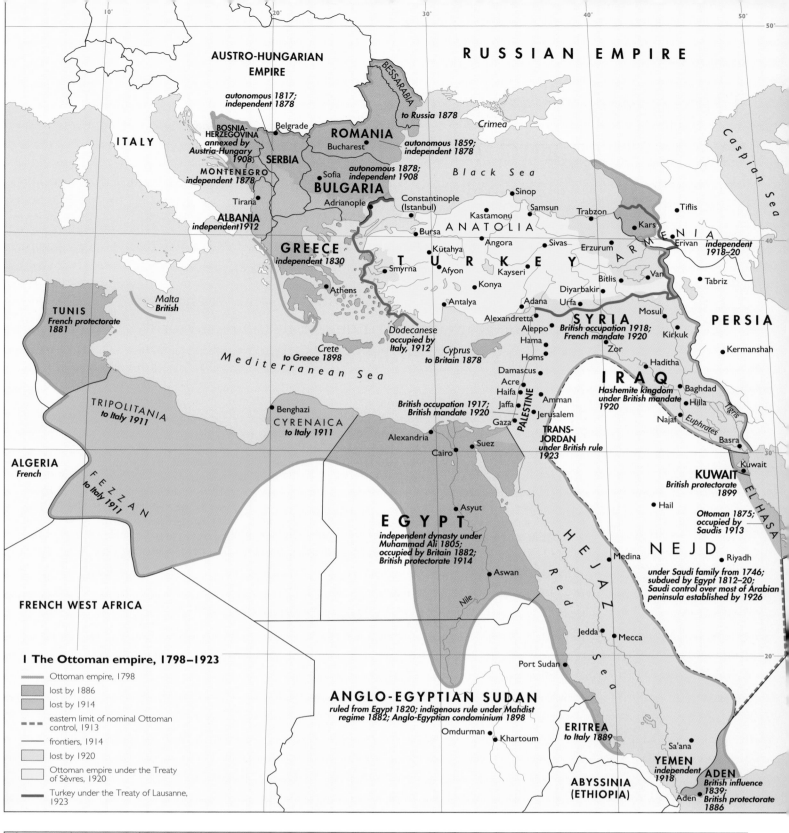

1 The Ottoman empire, 1798–1923

- Ottoman empire, 1798
- lost by 1886
- lost by 1914
- --- eastern limit of nominal Ottoman control, 1913
- frontiers, 1914
- lost by 1920
- Ottoman empire under the Treaty of Sèvres, 1920
- Turkey under the Treaty of Lausanne, 1923

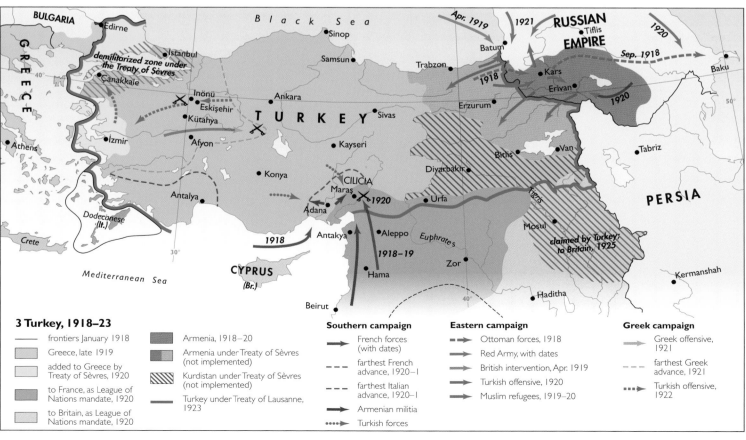

3 Turkey, 1918–23

- frontiers January 1918
- Greece, late 1919
- added to Greece by Treaty of Sèvres, 1920
- to France, as League of Nations mandate, 1920
- to Britain, as League of Nations mandate, 1920
- Armenia, 1918–20
- Armenia under Treaty of Sèvres (not implemented)
- Kurdistan under Treaty of Sèvres (not implemented)
- Turkey under Treaty of Lausanne, 1923

Southern campaign
- → French forces (with dates)
- --- farthest French advance, 1920–1
- --- farthest Italian advance, 1920–1
- → Armenian militia
- ⋯ Turkish forces

Eastern campaign
- ⇢ Ottoman forces, 1918
- ⇢ Red Army, with dates
- → British intervention, Apr. 1919
- → Turkish offensive, 1920
- → Muslim refugees, 1919–20

Greek campaign
- → Greek offensive, 1921
- --- farthest Greek advance, 1921
- ⋯ Turkish offensive, 1922

The Russian empire: expansion and modernization

Though Russia emerged in the 19th century as one of the European Great Powers, her international status was compromised by economic backwardness and military failure. Efforts to modernize created demands for revolutionary change, and when Russia failed again on the battlefield in the First World War the monarchy collapsed in revolution.

WITH EVERY DAY THE NEED AND MISERY OF THE PEASANTS GREW. THE SCENES OF STARVATION WERE DEEPLY DISTRESSING, AND IT WAS ALL THE MORE DISTURBING TO SEE THAT AMIDST ALL THIS SUFFERING AND DEATH THERE SPRAWLED HUGE ESTATES, BEAUTIFUL AND WELL-FURNISHED MANORS, AND THAT THE GRAND OLD LIFE OF THE SQUIRES, WITH ITS JOLLY HUNTS AND BALLS, ITS BANQUETS AND ITS CONCERTS, CARRIED ON AS USUAL.

Sergei Semenov, peasant leader, 1912

I N 1815 RUSSIA WAS widely regarded as the foremost power in Europe. Its role in the defeat of revolutionary France had left it the largest military power on the continent and greatly reinforced the prestige of the ruling elite, which was able to reassert its own power while stifling liberal reform and modernization.

Under the tsars Alexander I (1801–25) and Nicholas I (1825–55) Russia remained a predominantly rural society, dominated by the crown, the nobility and corrupt bureaucrats and gendarmes. Attempts at political liberalization were ruthlessly suppressed. In December 1825, opponents of the autocracy, strongly influenced by Western models, tried to overthrow the tsar and install a modernizing regime. The "Decembrists", drawn mainly from the army, were easily crushed, and Nicholas I, whose one-day-old reign they had tried to destroy, imposed a harsh regime of censorship and political oppression. The instrument of control, a forerunner of the secret police empires of the 20th century, was the notorious Third Department, set up in 1826 to suppress threats to the crown and any flirtation with Western ideas.

Abroad, Russia was seen as a force for conservatism in international affairs. Under Nicholas Russia tried to increase its influence in the Balkans and the Middle East, while opposing revolutionary and nationalist threats. In 1849 Russian troops put down revolution in Hungary, and in 1853 Russia seized the provinces of Moldavia and Wallachia from Ottoman Turkey and destroyed the Turkish Black Sea Fleet at Sinop. Alarmed by Russian ambitions in the Holy Land, France and Britain declared war and invaded the Crimean peninsula. In a campaign notable for military ineptitude on both sides, Russia was nonetheless defeated. Rebuffed in Europe, Russia thereafter turned her attentions more to expansion in Asia (see map 2). But the humiliation of defeat on her own soil had exposed Russian backwardness. The new tsar, Alexander II (1855–81), embarked on a widespread programme of reform.

The reforming tsars

Alexander's intention was not to liberalize Russia but to make it more efficient. Both he and his successor, Alexander III, were wedded to the idea of royal autocracy and saw reform as necessary to strengthen it rather than to alter its essential nature. Nonetheless, in 1861, following growing unrest, the serfs were emancipated while in 1864 new institutions of local government, the *zemstvo*, were introduced to stem the demand for liberal constitutional reform. In the same year Russia's legal system was overhauled on Western lines. Army reforms created a more effective fighting force. But Alexander set his face against political concessions or widespread industrialization. Radical groups turned to violent terrorism and in 1881, after three attempts, the "People's Will" group succeeded in assassinating the tsar.

Regicide produced a backlash. Alexander III introduced industrialization schemes and encouraged modern banking and transport in order to build a strong Russia capable of resisting internal demands for change or pressure from the West. A conservative nationalism was whipped up against Westernizers and Jews, while reform groups were savagely repressed. In 1881 the Okhrana secret police was established. In 1889 Land Captains were instituted in the countryside to restore the influence of the gentry. In the new industrial centres trade unions were outlawed and

3 Serfdom in Russia, 1860

serfs as a percentage of the population

■ over 50	10–30
30–50	under 10

— boundary of Russia, 1871

serfs' obligations

◆ *obrok*: dues in kind or cash
◇ *barshchina*: labour service to landlord
◕ both *obrok* and *barshchina* dues

3 In 1858 there were over 10 million serfs in Russia, 45 per cent of the adult male population **(map left)**. Many serfs paid dues (*obrok*) in kind or cash to their landlords; others were tied to the land through labour service (*barshchina*). By the 1850s there was widespread rural protest against serfdom and mass migrations from the major serf areas in western central Russia. In 1861 Tsar Alexander II granted emancipation to the serfs as part of a programme of modernization.

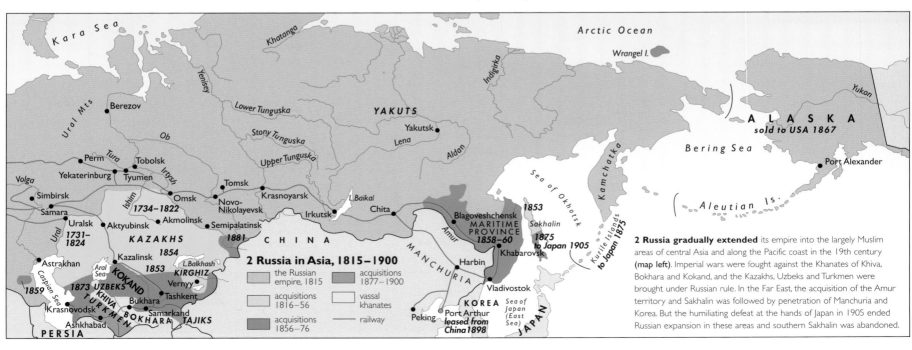

2 Russia gradually extended its empire into the largely Muslim areas of central Asia and along the Pacific coast in the 19th century **(map left)**. Imperial wars were fought against the Khanates of Khiva, Bokhara and Kokand, and the Kazakhs, Uzbeks and Turkmen were brought under Russian rule. In the Far East, the acquisition of the Amur territory and Sakhalin was followed by penetration of Manchuria and Korea. But the humiliating defeat at the hands of Japan in 1905 ended Russian expansion in these areas and southern Sakhalin was abandoned.

2 Russia in Asia, 1815–1900

the Russian empire, 1815	acquisitions 1877–1900
acquisitions 1816–56	vassal khanates
■ acquisitions 1856–76	— railway

"**It is better to abolish serfdom** from above than wait for it to abolish itself from below" declared Alexander II (**above**) in 1857. Four years later Alexander did indeed free the serfs. He soon found that it was one thing to emancipate them, another to feed, clothe and educate them. Radical though they were in Russian terms, Alexander's reforms failed to address the core problems facing his country.

socialist movements persecuted. Russia in 1900 was more modern and militarily stronger, but its political system remained reactionary and unreformed.

Revolution and war

Under the last tsar, Nicholas II (1894–1917), the tension between the unreformed system and the new social forces thrown up by modernization reached a climax. Defeat in the Far East by Japan in 1905 saw protest reach a crisis-point. Revolt broke out across Russia. Sergei Witte, the leading architect of modernization, persuaded the tsar to grant a constitution. The October Manifesto of 1905 instituted a parliament, or *Duma*, a restricted franchise and the promise of civil rights.

Nicholas soon reverted to type. The *Duma* was prorogued twice until he got deputies he could work with; civil rights were never fully granted; the franchise became ever more narrow. The tsar still ruled by decree and through the vast police and bureaucratic apparatus. By 1914, when Russia entered the First World War, there was wide expectation of revolution. Defeat in battle, hunger in the cities and corrupt management of the home front produced irresistible pressure for a radical break. In February 1917 Nicholas abdicated, and the tsarist empire collapsed.

I European Russia, 1815–1914
- ● urban population increase, 1861–1914 the circle is proportionate to the size of growth
- economic activity to 1861
- economic activity 1861–1914
- ⊗ metallurgical and metalworking industry
- · coal mining
- ▲ iron ore mining
- ▶ textile industry
- ⊓⊓ sugar refining
- ⊓ oil industry
- railway
- frontiers 1914

5 Foreign investment in Russia, 1861–1913

year	state bonds	private shares & bonds	total
1861	400*	8	408*
1881	2345*	115	2460*
1893	2713	238	2951
1900	3995	911	4910
1913	5461	1960	7585

in millions of roubles   * estimated

5 Russia was short of capital to begin the industrial modernization drive of the 1890s and relied on overseas loans (**chart above**), much of them from France. By 1913 an estimated one-third of all capital in Russia was foreign-owned, concentrated in the oil, iron and steel and chemical sectors.

I Despite her vast size Russia remained economically underdeveloped for most of the 19th century. Railway building and industrial development expanded from the 1880s with the help of foreign capital (**map above**). Under the influence of the finance minister, Sergei Witte, Russia experienced high rates of industrial growth from the 1890s, particularly in the Donbass region of the Ukraine. But living-standards remained well below European levels and social tensions worsened as industry developed.

4 In 1853 Britain and France declared war on Russia following a dispute about who had custody of the Christian Holy Places in Ottoman-ruled Palestine (**maps below and right**). Though the Anglo-French force was poorly equipped and undermined by disease and inter-allied squabbles, the Russian forces proved even more incompetent. Russian defeats at Balaklava and Inkerman in 1854 opened the way to the loss of the Black Sea base of Sevastopol in 1855. By highlighting Russian weaknesses, the war led to widespread reforms.

4 The Crimean War, 1853–5
- Anglo-French forces
- raids on Russian coast
- Turkish forces
- Russian forces
- ceded by Russia to Turkey, 1856

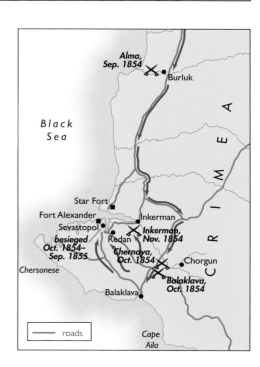

The collapse of the Chinese empire

1839–42 Opium War. China cedes Hong Kong to Britain and opens Treaty Ports

1850–64 T'ai-p'ing rebellion; immense loss of life

1858 Treaty of Tientsin; further Treaty Ports opened to foreign trade

1860 Treaty of Peking confirms Russian control of Maritime Province

1894–5 Sino-Japanese War: Japan occupies Taiwan

1898 Abortive "Hundred Days" reform.

1900 Boxer uprising

1911 Revolution: Sun Yat-sen proclaimed provisional president of Chinese Republic in 1912

2 During the 19th century China was forced to cede Hong Kong to Great Britain and to open to foreign trade ever more regions in which foreigners enjoyed extra-territorial rights (map below). It also lost extensive territories in the north and northeast to the expansionist Russian empire, and was challenged in peripheral states which had been her vassals. With the collapse of the Ch'ing empire in 1911 China also lost control of Tibet and Mongolia.

During the 19th century China experienced a systemic crisis, with rebellions and humiliations by foreign powers. The Chinese leadership was slow to grasp how much internal change was needed. Realization came in the 1890s leading to sweeping reforms along Western lines and the overthrow of a dynastic system which had lasted over 2000 years.

FOR MUCH OF THE 19th century the Chinese failed to understand the challenge presented by Western powers. After a peak of prosperity under the Ch'ing in the 18th century, they regarded themselves as the centre of world civilization and were slow to realize that Western power, with its superior technology, productivity and wealth, had overtaken them. Such attitudes informed their negative responses to British attempts to develop diplomatic relations from 1793. Matters came to a head when the Chinese tried to end the illicit trade in opium with its damaging economic effects. They were defeated by the British in the First Opium War and in 1842 forced to cede Hong Kong and five treaty ports in which foreigners were permitted to trade free from Chinese jurisdiction.

Defeat in the Opium War weakened imperial authority and exacerbated the systemic crisis which had been developing since the 18th century (see p. 192). Major rebellions broke out all over China, the most important of which was the T'ai-p'ing in which, together with the Nien rebellion, 25 million died (see map 1). Nevertheless, imperial support for traditional attitudes and institutions continued.

Foreign penetration

These serious disorders allowed further foreign penetration of China and her satellites (see map 2). From 1858 the Russians pressed forward their interests in northern China, and in 1860 Peking was occupied by the British and French. In 1884–5 the French defeated the Chinese over Indo-China. In 1894–5 the Japanese, having already intervened in Taiwan, the Ryukyu islands and Korea, overwhelmed China in a full-scale war.

Although this last defeat led in 1898 to an attempt at comprehensive reform headed by the Emperor, it was foiled by a reactionary coup. Meanwhile, foreign powers, believing China about to collapse, scrambled for further concessions. This in turn produced a wave of local xenophobia, leading to the Boxer uprising and finally to the siege of foreign legations in Peking. The uprising was suppressed by foreign armies at the cost of further concessions and a huge indemnity.

After 1901 it was at last accepted that modernization was required throughout China's state and society. When the reformers, now including many foreign-educated young Chinese, realised the Manchu were still determined to cling on to power, they turned to revolution. A small army revolt at Wu-ch'ang in 1911 won support throughout China. The 2000-year-old imperial system came to an end, and the leader of the revolutionary alliance, Sun Yat-sen, was proclaimed provisional president on 1 January 1912.

A SURVEY OF ALL STATES IN THE WORLD WILL SHOW THAT THOSE STATES WHICH UNDERTOOK REFORMS BECAME STRONG WHILE THOSE STATES WHICH CLUNG TO THE PAST PERISHED. THE CONSEQUENCES OF CLINGING TO THE PAST AND THE EFFECTS OF OPENING UP NEW WAYS ARE THUS OBVIOUS. IF YOUR MAJESTY, WITH YOUR DISCERNING BRILLIANCE, OBSERVES THE TRENDS IN OTHER COUNTRIES, YOU WILL SEE THAT IF WE CAN CHANGE, WE CAN PRESERVE OURSELVES, BUT IF WE CANNOT CHANGE, WE SHALL PERISH.

K'ang Yu-wei, Confucian reformer
Memorial to the imperial throne,
submitted 29 January 1898

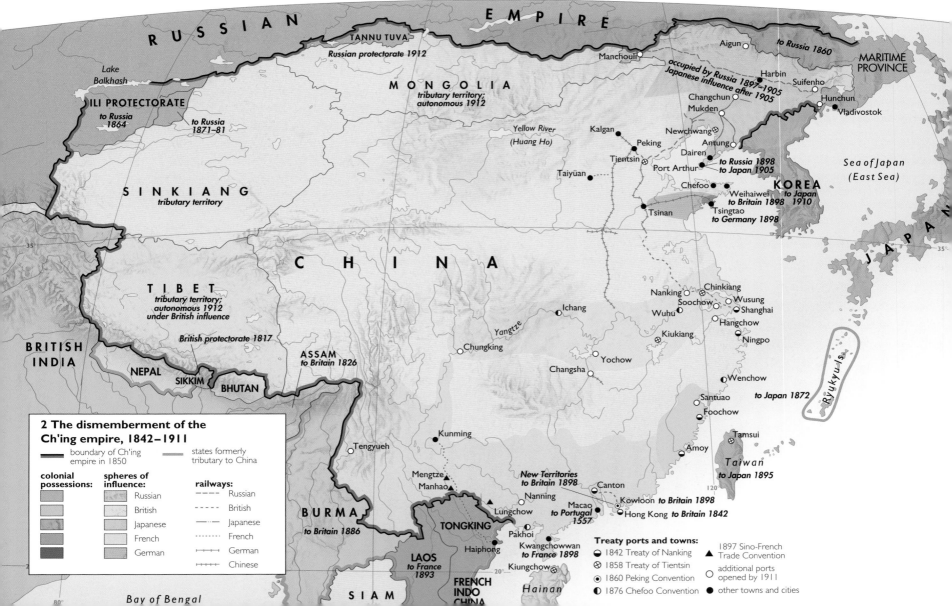

2 The dismemberment of the Ch'ing empire, 1842–1911

- boundary of Ch'ing empire in 1850
- states formerly tributary to China

colonial possessions:

spheres of influence:
- Russian
- British
- Japanese
- French
- German

railways:
- Russian
- British
- Japanese
- French
- German
- Chinese

Treaty ports and towns:
- 1842 Treaty of Nanking
- 1858 Treaty of Tientsin
- 1860 Peking Convention
- 1876 Chefoo Convention
- 1897 Sino-French Trade Convention
- additional ports opened by 1911
- other towns and cities

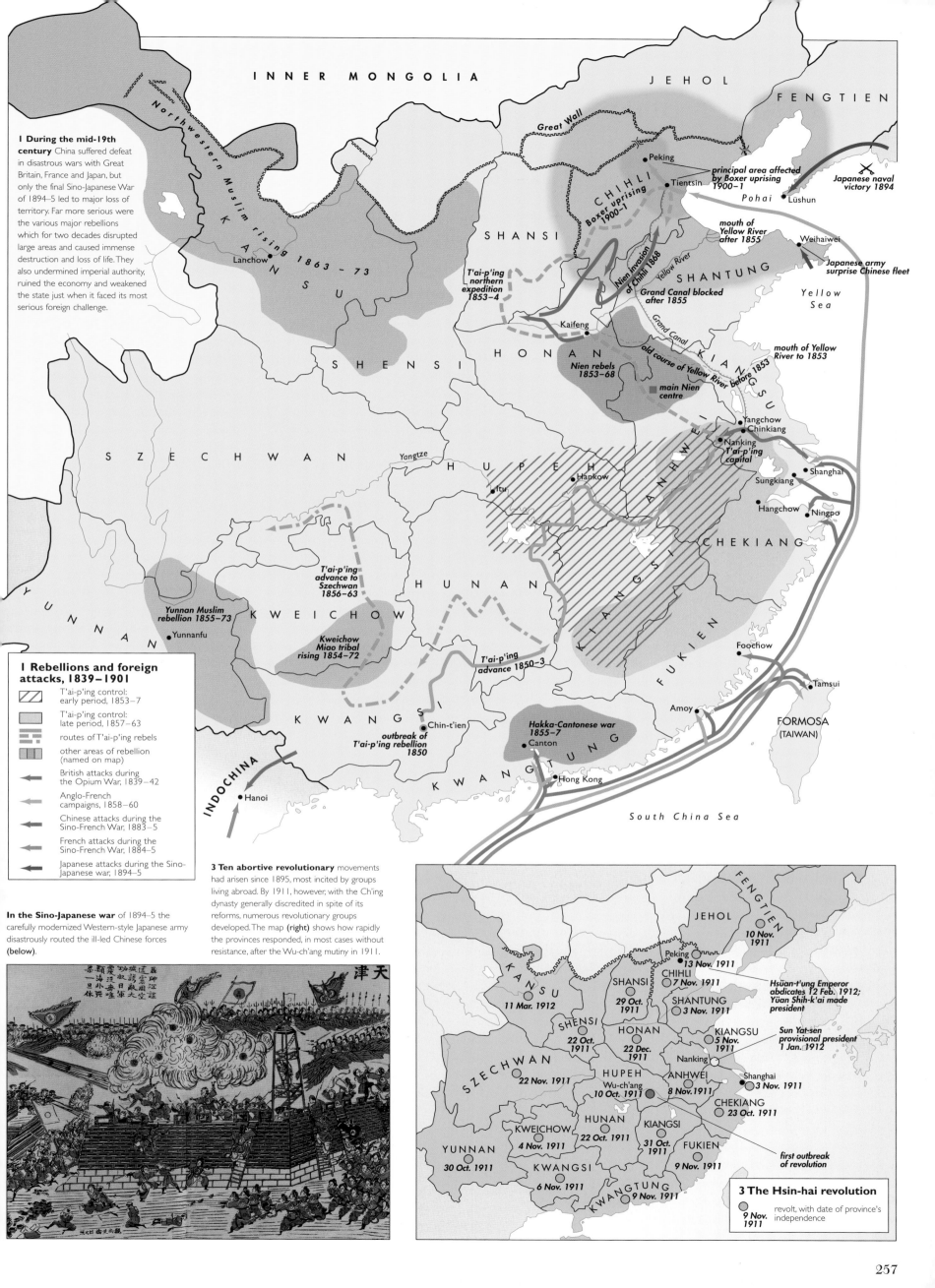

INNER MONGOLIA

JEHOL

FENGTIEN

1 During the mid-19th century China suffered defeat in disastrous wars with Great Britain, France and Japan, but only the final Sino-Japanese War of 1894–5 led to major loss of territory. Far more serious were the various major rebellions which for two decades disrupted large areas and caused immense destruction and loss of life. They also undermined imperial authority, ruined the economy and weakened the state just when it faced its most serious foreign challenge.

Northwestern Muslim rising 1863–73

K A N S U

Lanchow

Great Wall

Peking

CHIHLI
Boxer uprising
1900–1

Tientsin

principal area affected by Boxer uprising 1900–1

Japanese naval victory 1894

Pohai Lüshun

SHANSI

T'ai-p'ing northern expedition 1853–4

Nien invasion of Chihli 1868

Yellow River

SHANTUNG

mouth of Yellow River after 1855

Weihaiwei

Japanese army surprise Chinese fleet

SHENSI

HONAN

Kaifeng

Grand Canal blocked after 1855

Grand Canal

old course of Yellow River before 1853

mouth of Yellow River to 1853

Yellow Sea

Nien rebels 1853–68

main Nien centre

KIANGSU

SZECHWAN

Yangtze

HUPEH

Itu Hankow

ANHWEI

Yangchow
Chinkiang

Nanking
T'ai-p'ing capital

Sungkiang Shanghai

Hangchow Ningpo

HUNAN

KIANGSI

CHEKIANG

T'ai-p'ing advance to Szechwan 1856–63

Yunnan Muslim rebellion 1855–73

YUNNAN

Yunnanfu

KWEICHOW

Kweichow Miao tribal rising 1854–72

T'ai-p'ing advance 1850–3

FUKIEN

Foochow

1 Rebellions and foreign attacks, 1839–1901

- ▨ T'ai-p'ing control: early period, 1853–7
- ▦ T'ai-p'ing control: late period, 1857–63
- routes of T'ai-p'ing rebels
- ▨ other areas of rebellion (named on map)
- ➤ British attacks during the Opium War, 1839–42
- ➤ Anglo-French campaigns, 1858–60
- ➤ Chinese attacks during the Sino-French War, 1883–5
- ➤ French attacks during the Sino-French War, 1884–5
- ➤ Japanese attacks during the Sino-Japanese war, 1894–5

KWANGSI

Chin-t'ien

outbreak of T'ai-p'ing rebellion 1850

Hakka-Cantonese war 1855–7

Canton

KWANGTUNG

Amoy

Tamsui

FORMOSA (TAIWAN)

INDOCHINA

Hanoi

Hong Kong

South China Sea

In the Sino-Japanese war of 1894–5 the carefully modernized Western-style Japanese army disastrously routed the ill-led Chinese forces (**below**).

3 Ten abortive revolutionary movements had arisen since 1895, most incited by groups living abroad. By 1911, however, with the Ch'ing dynasty generally discredited in spite of its reforms, numerous revolutionary groups developed. The map (**right**) shows how rapidly the provinces responded, in most cases without resistance, after the Wu-ch'ang mutiny in 1911.

FENGTIEN

JEHOL

10 Nov. 1911

Peking
13 Nov. 1911

KANSU
11 Mar. 1912

SHANSI
29 Oct. 1911

CHIHLI
7 Nov. 1911

SHANTUNG
3 Nov. 1911

Hsüan-t'ung Emperor abdicates 12 Feb. 1912; Yüan Shih-k'ai made president

SHENSI
22 Oct. 1911

HONAN
22 Dec. 1911

KIANGSU
5 Nov. 1911

Nanking

Sun Yat-sen provisional president 1 Jan. 1912

SZECHWAN
22 Nov. 1911

HUPEH
Wu-ch'ang
10 Oct. 1911

ANHWEI
8 Nov. 1911

Shanghai
3 Nov. 1911

CHEKIANG
23 Oct. 1911

KWEICHOW
4 Nov. 1911

HUNAN
22 Oct. 1911

KIANGSI
31 Oct. 1911

FUKIEN
9 Nov. 1911

first outbreak of revolution

YUNNAN
30 Oct. 1911

KWANGSI
6 Nov. 1911

KWANGTUNG
9 Nov. 1911

3 The Hsin-hai revolution

- ⬤ *9 Nov. 1911* revolt, with date of province's independence

India under British rule

In the early 19th century, Britain consolidated its rule in south Asia as India became the focus of its imperial system. The authoritarian style of British rule encouraged many different types of anti-imperial political organization. By 1935 anti-imperial forces had seriously weakened British power.

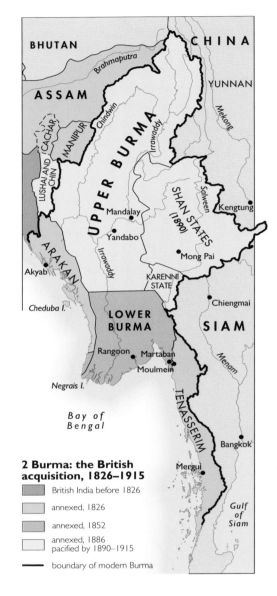

2 Burma: the British acquisition, 1826–1915

- British India before 1826
- annexed, 1826
- annexed, 1852
- annexed, 1886 pacified by 1890–1915
- ⸻ boundary of modern Burma

IN THE 50 YEARS after 1805 the supremacy of the English East India Company on the subcontinent was steadily consolidated. The third Anglo-Maratha War, ending in 1818, eliminated the most serious threat to Company rule. The conquest of the Gurkhas (1816), the Sindhis (1843) and the Sikhs (1849) then saw the empire become coterminous with its natural frontiers in the north and west (see map 1). To the east the British clashed with the Burmese kingdom and from 1824 began the process of annexing all its territories (see map 2). In addition, within the subcontinent dependent states such as Awadh and some Maratha kingdoms were brought under direct rule.

However, British policy was seen by many in south Asia as a serious challenge to Indian ways of life. Growing resentment resulted in the uprising of 1857. Beginning as a mutiny of the Company's army, the rebellion soon involved princes, landlords and peasants in north and central India. The insurrection was bloody; its suppression, during 14 months of bitter fighting, as brutal. From 1858, the administration of India was taken over by the British Crown.

India then became the focus of the British imperial system, the source of rivalries with Russia in central Asia and France in southeast Asia, and a factor, too, in British involvement in the partition of Africa. From Abyssinia to China the Indian army protected British interests. Simultaneously India was absorbed into the world economy as a dependant of Britain. Indian communications, largely in the form of railways, were developed to facilitate the import of British manufactures and the export of raw materials.

Exploitation and dependency

As a result of this development and the opening of the Suez canal, India's foreign trade increased sevenfold from 1869 to 1929 and, despite severe British competition, some modern industries developed (see map 3). But by 1853 India had lost her worldwide market for textiles and was actually importing cloth from Britain. GNP per capita increased only slowly and, with sustained population growth (see maps 4 & 5), from 1921 even declined. India increasingly took on the typical characteristics of an underdeveloped economy while at the same time contributing substantially to Britain's balance of payments.

Administrative developments also contributed to India's absorption into a world order dominated

1818 British defeat the Marathas and become the effective rulers of India

1824 British begin conquest of Burma

1833 Death of Ram Mohan Roy (born 1772), father of modern Indian nationalism

1843 British conquer Sind

1849 British conquer the Punjab

1853 First railway and telegraph lines in India

1857 Outbreak of the Indian Mutiny

1877 Queen Victoria proclaimed Empress of India

1885 Foundation of Indian National Congress

1920–2 Non-Cooperation Movement against the British

1935 Government of India Act; Indians gain provincial autonomy

1 The Indian Mutiny (map below) began at Meerut on 10 May 1857 and spread swiftly to other parts of northern India. Hindus and Muslims alike rose against their British overlords. Sikh loyalty in the Punjab, coupled with passivity in the Deccan and the south, turned the tide in favour of the British after an orgy of bloodletting.

4 & 5 India: population growth, 1872–1931

1872

2 Burma (above left) was annexed, along with her dependencies of Arakan, Manipur and Assam, as a result of three wars fought in 1826, 1852 and 1885. The Shan States were acquired in 1890.

4 & 5 Between 1872 and 1931 (maps left) India's population rose from 253.9 million to 352.8 million, with a slight acceleration at the beginning of the 1920s. Over the same period the proportion of literates grew only from 35 per thousand to 80 per thousand while a mere 101 people in every 10,000 were able to read and write in English. Nevertheless, the spread in education was such as to encourage the conditions in which the beginnings of a modern economy could emerge.

1931

inhabitants per sq km:

- over 250
- 150 to 250
- 100 to 150
- 50 to 100
- 25 to 50
- under 25

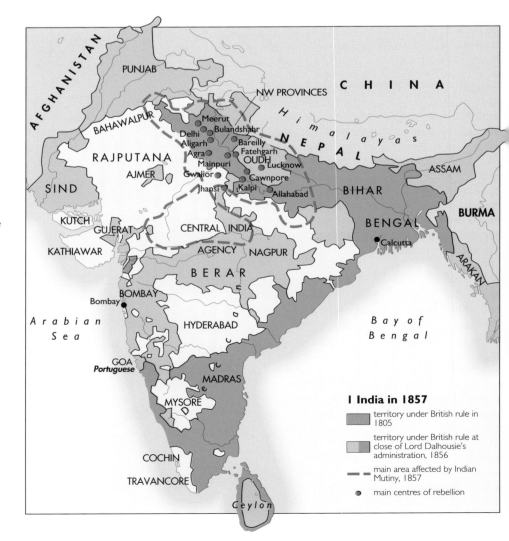

1 India in 1857

- territory under British rule in 1805
- territory under British rule at close of Lord Dalhousie's administration, 1856
- ⸺ main area affected by Indian Mutiny, 1857
- ● main centres of rebellion

3 British India, 1931

- territory under British rule
- territories permanently administered by Government of India (mostly tribal)
- states and territories administered by local Indian rulers
- Portuguese enclave
- French enclave
- Hindu majority provinces
- Muslim majority provinces
- area of Buddhist predominance
- area of large Sikh population

manufacturing products

- cotton textiles
- woollens
- tea
- chemicals
- tobacco
- sugar
- rice mills
- iron and steel (large scale)
- metals
- machinery and transport material
- shipping
- mills (various grains)

Map labels: RUSSIA · AFGHANISTAN · NORTH WEST FRONTIER PROVINCE · JAMMU AND KASHMIR · Peshawar · Srinagar · Rawalpindi · Quetta · Kalat · BALUCHISTAN AGENCY · KALAT · Lahore · Amritsar · Multan · PUNJAB · Simla · PUNJAB STATES · GARWHAL KUMAON · RAJPUTANA · Delhi · Karachi · Hyderabad · SIND · AGENCY · Jodhpur · Jaipur · Agra · Ajmer · Chambal · GWALIOR · Cawnpore · Oudh · Lucknow · UNITED · PROVINCES · Allahabad · Patna · Benares · Bhagalpur · Ganges · CHINA · TIBET · SIKKIM · BHUTAN · Darjeeling · TARAI · NAGA HILLS · ASSAM · Shillong · CACHAR · MANIPUR · NORTHERN SHAN STATES · *Arabian Sea* · Gulf of Kutch · KUTCH · STATES OF W. INDIA · Ahmedabad · Indore · Narmada · Baroda · Surat · Damao · DIU · Taptī · CENTRAL INDIAN AGENCY · BUNDELKHAND · CHOTA NAGPUR · CENTRAL · BIHAR · Jamshedpur · AND · ORISSA · Chandernagore · Calcutta · Dacca · BENGAL · TRIPURA · Chittagong · NORTHERN SHAN STATES · SOUTHERN SHAN STATES · BURMA · ARAKAN · Salween · Godavari · BERAR · PROVINCES · Nagpur · Sambalpur · Mahanadi · Cuttack · BASTAR · *Bay of Bengal* · Bombay · Poona · BOMBAY · SATARA · HYDERABAD · Sholapur · Kolhapur · Hyderabad · Kistna · Yanaon · Masulipatam · Nova Goa (Panjim) · GOA · DECCAN · MYSORE · Mangalore · Bangalore · Mysore · Madras · Pondicherry · Mahe · NILGIRIS · Calicut · Coimbatore · Karkal · Trichinopoly · Negapatam · Cochin · Madurai · Rangoon · Gulf of Martaban · Andaman Islands · Trivandrum · Gulf of Mannar · CEYLON Crown Colony · Colombo · Indus

---

by Europe. Britain's colonial administrators set out to refashion Indian society along European lines. The net results are still debated. Probably the rural propertied classes benefited, but at the cost of the mass of producers who were subjected, while commercial agriculture flourished, to deadly famines. The beneficiaries of the new order – landlords, civil servants and professional men – formed the new elite of colonial India, and sought Western-style education. The bridges this elite built between Western knowledge and indigenous cultural resources inspired a host of religious, social and intellectual movements. Among them was the Brahmo Samaj founded by Ram Mohan Roy in the 1820s, which aimed at restoring Hindu monotheism, and the Aligarh movement founded by Saiyid Ahmad Khan in the 1870s, which aimed to reconcile India's Muslims to modernity.

Anti-Imperial politics

Many different forms of anti-imperial politics flourished in the late 19th and early 20th centuries, as Indians attempted to assert their identity against British racism in many different ways. The Indian National Congress was founded in 1885 to lobby for Indians to have greater involvement within the imperial administration. It soon developed a vociferously anti-imperial wing that asserted the superiority of Indian culture and questioned Britain's right to rule. In 1905, nationalists resisted the decision to partition the province of Bengal. Many techniques adopted by them later on were first used in the *swadeshi* ("our country") agitation of that year. By 1917, Congress demanded Home Rule. British politicians promised eventual self-government and allowed some expansion of Indian involvement in local and provincial government. But repressive legislation after the First World War led many to question British intentions.

Congress was perceived by many Muslims as a purely Hindu organization, as many Congress politicians defined "India" to be an exclusively Hindu nation. The years after the First World War saw both the rise of mass, popular nationalist campaigning and the emergence of Hindu and Muslim separatist politics. Fuelled by Muslim fury at the destruction of the Ottoman sultan's power in the Middle East, Muslims and Hindus worked together in the *Khilafat* and Non-Cooperation Movements (1920–2), in which Gandhi deployed his weapon of *satyagraha* or non-violent direct action. As Congress retreated from direct action, the mid-1920s saw the rise of Hindu–Muslim riots. Gandhi led a civil disobedience movement in 1930–4, which forced the British to concede full autonomy to Indians at a provincial level with the 1935 Government of India Act.

3 The racial and religious balance of the Indian empire – a crucial issue before and after independence – is shown **(above)** at the moment when the negotiations leading to the 1935 Government of India Act began. The almost equal weight of Muslims and Hindus in Bengal and the Punjab held the seeds of later violence.

King George V was crowned King Emperor of India at a durbar, or assembly of notables, in Delhi in 1911 **(right)**. In an attempt to placate nationalist emotions, the decision to annul the unpopular partition of Bengal was announced at the durbar.

THERE IS MORE POWER IN HIS LOIN CLOTH THAN IN ALL THE GUNS IN THE BRITISH ARMY.

Saying about Gandhi in the 1920s

WE DIVIDE, YOU RULE.

Maulana Mohamed Ali, 1930

HE IS TAKING THE MASSES WITH HIM, NOT MERELY CONVERTING THE ELECT.

Jawaharlal Nehru on Gandhi

Australia

European settlement of Australia began in the late 18th century. Soon, settlers pushed the Aborigines by force from the most productive land. By 1900 a rich economy had emerged, still, however, dependent on British capital. Only in the late 20th century did new economic and immigration policies and circumstances signal a complete sense of independence.

AUSTRALIA CAME INTO intermittent contact with Europeans from the 16th century, but neither the Portuguese nor the Dutch had any use for what they found there. The Englishman James Cook mapped the east coast extensively in 1770, though it was only in 1788 when Britain wanted to make use of the overflow from its prisons to establish a naval base on an alternative trade route to China, that European settlement in Australia began. New South Wales and Van Diemen's Land (Tasmania) were essentially convict colonies until the 1850s, though by then there were "respectable free settlements" in Western Australia and South Australia. The search for staple products produced whaling and sealing, and later wool, in great quantity. Graziers succeeded gaolers and traders as the elite in the eastern colonies. Wool came to the fore in Australia and it continues today to be a major export.

The Aborigines

Highly successful in the arts of survival off the land, there were about 750,000 Aborigines in Australia in 1788. But in the face of European invasion, they retreated, their numbers decimated by a falling birthrate, disease, dispossession and the bullet. The Australian pastoral frontier witnessed much violence and bloodshed, most of it in guerrilla-type skirmishes, as it swept inland, not coming to a final halt until it reached the north of Western Australia and the Northern Territory in the 1930s. By then the Aboriginal population had been reduced to 10 per cent of its original size.

Economic development

Gold rushes in eastern Australia in the 1850s led to a huge population influx and a vast expansion of wealth. On this basis, self-government was assured. Grain, frozen beef, sugar, dairy products and a range of minerals were also exported, as rail and steam "tethered the mighty bush to the world". By 1900 Australia was labelled a "working man's paradise", boasting the highest living standards in the world. Despite the wealth of agricultural produce, most Australians then, as now, were living in cities.

I Settlement and development

- native land rights claims, Jan. 1997
- more than 2 persons per square mile 1961 (by statistical division)
- no significant use, c. 1960
- ■ penal settlements
- ● settlements

minerals

⬯ gold		◣ iron ore
⬯ copper		⬙ silver
⬯ lead		◣ zinc
⬠ natural gas		▲ oil
T tungsten		N nickel
⬮ tin		A alumina/bauxite
U uranium		M manganese
⊕ blast furnace		

Designed by the convict architect, Francis Greenway, the elegantly classical, three-storey Female Factory at Parramatta (above) was opened in 1821. It housed 300 women and combined the roles of workhouse, marriage bureau, female refuge and orphanage. Inmates earned their keep by spinning and weaving, and occasionally rioted when their rations were cut. Only a fifth of the convicts transported were women, and the Australian gender-ratio did not reach parity until the end of the 19th century.

I **After 1820 settlement** spread inland from scattered coastal towns, but vast arid areas remained sparsely populated even in 1961 (**map above**). Extensive mineral discoveries have contributed to a high standard of living, but many of these are on lands subject to aboriginal land claims.

THE AUSTRALIAN NATION IS WOVEN TOGETHER OF PEOPLE FROM MANY ANCESTRIES AND ARRIVALS. OUR VAST ISLAND CONTINENT HAS HELPED TO SHAPE THE DESTINY OF OUR COMMONWEALTH AND THE SPIRIT OF ITS PEOPLE. SINCE TIME IMMEMORIAL OUR LAND HAS BEEN INHABITED BY ABORIGINES AND TORRES STRAIT ISLANDERS, WHO ARE HONOURED FOR THEIR ANCIENT AND CONTINUING CULTURES. IN EVERY GENERATION IMMIGRANTS HAVE BROUGHT GREAT ENRICHMENT TO OUR NATION'S LIFE ... WE VALUE EXCELLENCE AS WELL AS FAIRNESS, INDEPENDENCE AS DEARLY AS MATESHIP. AUSTRALIA'S DEMOCRATIC AND FEDERAL SYSTEM ... EXISTS ... TO PRESERVE AND PROTECT ALL ... IN AN EQUAL DIGNITY WHICH MAY NEVER BE INFRINGED BY PREJUDICE OR FASHION OR IDEOLOGY NOR INVOKED AGAINST ACHIEVEMENT.

Extract from PM John Howard's draft Preamble to the Australian Constitution in 1999, which recognized current multicultural orthodoxies, but did not fully acknowledge Aboriginal custodianship of the soil and was seen by some as too "blokey" to reflect the aspirations of women.

Map labels

Melville Island 1824–9
Darwin
Port Essington 1838–49
Raffles Bay 1827–9
all Torres Strait and Barrier Reef Islands included in Queensland 1879
Groote Eylandt
Gulf of Carpentaria
Cooktown
Coral Sea
Yampi Sound
Kimberley Plateau
Derby
Broome
Cairns
Normanton
Croydon
Great Barrier Reef
Townsville
NORTHERN TERRITORY
overland telegraph line
129°E
133°E
138°E
141°E
Barrow I.
Port Hedland
Great Sandy Desert
part of NSW to 1863
part of SA 1863–1910
to Commonwealth of Australia 1911
Cloncurry
Mount Isa
Mackay
Dampier
Pilbara
Winton
Longreach
Rockhampton
Gibson Desert
Alice Springs
Simpson Desert
1862
QUEENSLAND
separated from NSW 1859
WESTERN AUSTRALIA
26°S
Charleville
Big Bell
Wiluna
Great Victoria Desert
Oodnadatta
SOUTH AUSTRALIA
29°S
1859
Brisbane /Moreton Bay 1824–42
Toowoomba
N
Geraldton
Kalgoorlie
N
Nullarbor Plain
1825
1836
1788
1859
NEW SOUTH WALES
Broken Hill
Port Macquarie 1821–36
Perth
Fremantle 1829
A
Esperance
Great Australian Bight
Port Augusta
Port Pirie
Whyalla
Bathurst 1814
Newcastle 1801–2
1804–23
Augusta
Albany 1826
Port Lincoln
Mildura
Adelaide 1836
Canberra: capital from 1927
Sydney 1788–1840
Botany Bay
Australian Capital Territory
VICTORIA
Bendigo
separated from NSW 1851
Ballarat
Melbourne 1835
Portland 1834
T Van Diemen's land [renamed Tasmania 1853]
Launceston
Macquarie Harbour 1821–34
Maria I. 1825–32
Hobart 1803–53
Port Arthur 1830–77
40°

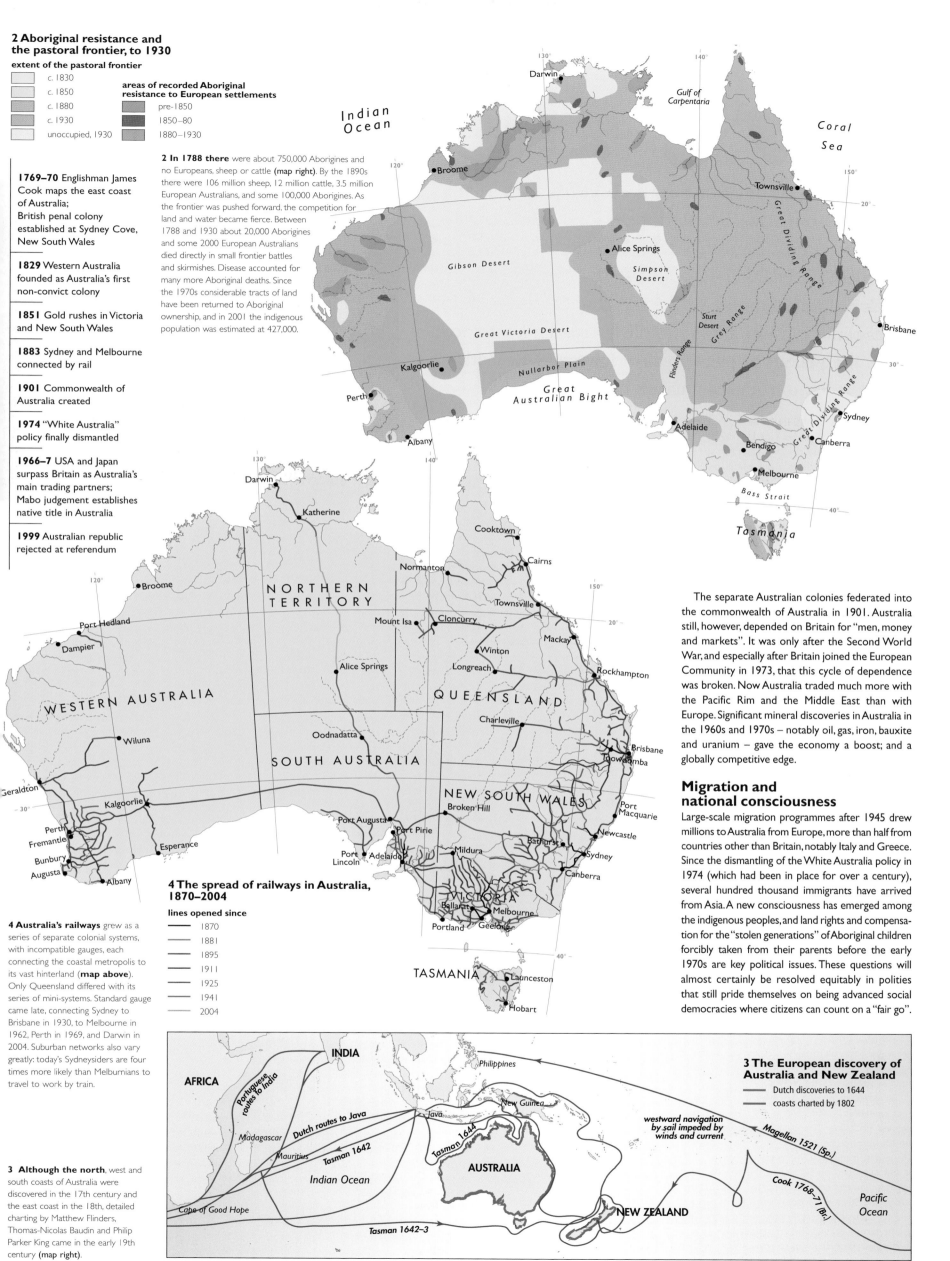

2 Aboriginal resistance and the pastoral frontier, to 1930

extent of the pastoral frontier

- c. 1830
- c. 1850
- c. 1880
- c. 1930
- unoccupied, 1930

areas of recorded Aboriginal resistance to European settlements

- pre-1850
- 1850–80
- 1880–1930

1769–70 Englishman James Cook maps the east coast of Australia; British penal colony established at Sydney Cove, New South Wales

1829 Western Australia founded as Australia's first non-convict colony

1851 Gold rushes in Victoria and New South Wales

1883 Sydney and Melbourne connected by rail

1901 Commonwealth of Australia created

1974 "White Australia" policy finally dismantled

1966–7 USA and Japan surpass Britain as Australia's main trading partners; Mabo judgement establishes native title in Australia

1999 Australian republic rejected at referendum

2 In 1788 there were about 750,000 Aborigines and no Europeans, sheep or cattle (map right). By the 1890s there were 106 million sheep, 12 million cattle, 3.5 million European Australians, and some 100,000 Aborigines. As the frontier was pushed forward, the competition for land and water became fierce. Between 1788 and 1930 about 20,000 Aborigines and some 2000 European Australians died directly in small frontier battles and skirmishes. Disease accounted for many more Aboriginal deaths. Since the 1970s considerable tracts of land have been returned to Aboriginal ownership, and in 2001 the indigenous population was estimated at 427,000.

4 The spread of railways in Australia, 1870–2004

lines opened since

- 1870
- 1881
- 1895
- 1911
- 1925
- 1941
- 2004

4 Australia's railways grew as a series of separate colonial systems, with incompatible gauges, each connecting the coastal metropolis to its vast hinterland (**map above**). Only Queensland differed with its series of mini-systems. Standard gauge came late, connecting Sydney to Brisbane in 1930, to Melbourne in 1962, Perth in 1969, and Darwin in 2004. Suburban networks also vary greatly: today's Sydneysiders are four times more likely than Melburnians to travel to work by train.

3 Although the north, west and south coasts of Australia were discovered in the 17th century and the east coast in the 18th, detailed charting by Matthew Flinders, Thomas-Nicolas Baudin and Philip Parker King came in the early 19th century (**map right**).

The separate Australian colonies federated into the commonwealth of Australia in 1901. Australia still, however, depended on Britain for "men, money and markets". It was only after the Second World War, and especially after Britain joined the European Community in 1973, that this cycle of dependence was broken. Now Australia traded much more with the Pacific Rim and the Middle East than with Europe. Significant mineral discoveries in Australia in the 1960s and 1970s – notably oil, gas, iron, bauxite and uranium – gave the economy a boost; and a globally competitive edge.

Migration and national consciousness

Large-scale migration programmes after 1945 drew millions to Australia from Europe, more than half from countries other than Britain, notably Italy and Greece. Since the dismantling of the White Australia policy in 1974 (which had been in place for over a century), several hundred thousand immigrants have arrived from Asia. A new consciousness has emerged among the indigenous peoples, and land rights and compensation for the "stolen generations" of Aboriginal children forcibly taken from their parents before the early 1970s are key political issues. These questions will almost certainly be resolved equitably in polities that still pride themselves on being advanced social democracies where citizens can count on a "fair go".

3 The European discovery of Australia and New Zealand

- Dutch discoveries to 1644
- coasts charted by 1802

Since 1800

New Zealand

European settlement of New Zealand from the 1840s led to two major wars with the Maoris over the next quarter century. Thereafter New Zealand became a rural "Britain of the South", supplying the mother country with primary produce. An advanced social and political laboratory, it was among the first to extend votes to its indigenous population and to women. Recently, it has introduced a native title tribunal and liberalized and internationalized its economy.

Maori peaceful protests for some redress over Waitangi issues started in the 1970s with marches and sit-ins, and they continue to this day (above). The initially toothless Waitangi Tribunal was given real power in 1985 and several important judgments followed, including the ruling that all sales of state assets had to take Maori claims into consideration. In 1995 the Tainui fisheries and Ngai Tahu claim transferred assets worth NZ$400 million.

NEW ZEALAND HAD ITS first European visitors in the 17th century and attracted itinerant whalers and sealers in the wake of James Cook's visit in 1769. Missions to the Maoris started in 1814, but European colonization did not start there in earnest until the 1840s. A number of distinct Wakefieldian "scientifically planned" colonies of free settlers were established in Wellington, New Plymouth, Nelson and Christchurch. These settlements were injected into a seething cauldron of internecine Maori warfare, exacerbated by the introduction of the musket in the 1820s. With the new European element in the equation, competition for land and other resources soon became even more intense.

The New Zealand Wars
The Maoris were doughty warriors with a sophisticated military tradition. Though apparently guaranteed possession and use of their lands by the Treaty of Waitangi, signed with the British Crown in 1840, they were soon fighting bloody campaigns against regular British forces in defence of their land. The first phase of the wars was the Flagstaff War around Kororareka and the Bay of Islands in 1844–6, then in the Hutt Valley near Wellington soon afterwards. A second phase came in the 1860s in the Taranaki and Waikato areas. Ultimately, the Maoris were successful in keeping title to some of their land and in making headway in European society.

Economic and political development
As in Australia, wool became a staple export early on in New Zealand's colonization. Then gold-rushes in the South Island in the 1860s led to huge population influxes and vast expansion of wealth. Grain, frozen beef, dairy products and a range of minerals were added to the export list. By 1900 New Zealand was a social laboratory, with high wages and state-of-the-art social welfare provision. Despite the wealth of agricultural produce, however, most New Zealanders then, as now, were living in cities.

Self-government was achieved in 1856, Maori representation in 1867, and in 1893 New Zealand women (including Maoris) were the first in the British Empire to win the vote. New Zealand changed its name from colony to dominion in 1907. It still depended on Britain on the one hand for migrants, investment and imported manufactures and on the other as the main market for its pastoral and agricultural exports. In both world wars New Zealanders fought and died in considerable numbers in Europe and north Africa to protect their mother country. Only after Britain joined the European

I The New Zealand Wars
- proposed confiscations of Maori land, 1864–7
- 1st aukati (border), 1862
- 2nd aukati (border), 1866

Aukati was a border proclaimed by the Maori king to limit European penetration from the south.

I The steady influx of British colonists following the Treaty of Waitangi led to intense competition between the colonists and the Maoris for land. The British assumed the treaty granted them full sovereignty while the Maoris maintained they still had their own autonomy. The wars of the 1840s (map left) were small-scale, involving 1300 British troops and fewer Maori, and ended in a stand-off. Those of the 1860s, known as te riri pakeha (white man's anger) were much larger in scale and shattered traditional Maori society.

By the 1870s New Zealand had four cities of roughly equal size – Auckland (right), Wellington, Christchurch and Dunedin – and the South Island was more populous than the North. By 1936 the North Island had twice the South's population and by 1996 three times. Auckland, which drew ahead after the Panama Canal in 1914 made it closer to Britain, is now three times the size of its nearest rival and the only city with nearly a million people.

> I, AS PRIME MINISTER, NEVER WENT TO WASHINGTON, CERTAINLY NEVER WENT TO A PRESIDENTIAL RANCH. I DECIDED THAT I WASN'T GOING TO BE THE PILOT FISH TO A SHARK, WHEREAS AUSTRALIA QUITE HAPPILY BOBBED ALONG LIKE A HAPPY LITTLE PILOT FISH WITH A SHARK WHO WAS A MESSY EATER. AND I JUST COULDN'T FEEL LIKE THAT.
>
> David Lange, the New Zealand leader who banned visits by US nuclear warships, Radio Australia interview, 16 March 2004

Community in 1973 was this cycle of dependence broken. Today, New Zealand trades much more with the Pacific Rim and the Middle East than with Europe. New Zealand's government reforms in the 1980s again gave its economy a globally competitive edge.

Migration and national consciousness

New Zealand's prime source of recent immigration has been the Pacific Islands, making Auckland the world's largest Polynesian city with over 77,000 Polynesians in its population of 367,000 in 2001. A new consciousness has emerged among the Maoris, and land rights and compensation are key political issues. These questions are being resolved carefully

2 & 3 New Zealand's food exports (maps right and below) to Britain took off in the 1880s with the first exports of butter, cheese and frozen meat in 1882. By 1901 there were 259 dairy export factories and over 20 meat-freezing works. By the 1930s, chilling was replacing freezing and the "protein bridge" from New Zealand was supplying half of Britain's combined imports of dairy products and lamb. Britain's joining the EEC in 1973 severely dented this relationship but New Zealand's superb protein products are still found on British supermarket shelves.

4 By the early 21st century, New Zealand's population was increasingly mixed and the long-standing dominance of European settlement was being challenged (chart below) both by the indigenous Maoris and by incomers from Asia and the Pacific Islands. In North Island this was particularly the case, with non-Europeans making up close to 40% of the population of Auckland, whilst in South Island over 90% of the population of Dunedin and Invercargill claimed European descent.

4 Racial diversity in New Zealand

city	European	Maori	Pacific	Asian
Whole of NZ	80.1	14.7	6.5	6.6
North Island				
Auckland	66	8.4	14	18.7
Rotorua	71	35.6	4.1	3.2
Hamilton	78	19	3.5	7.2
Wanganui	84	20.7	2.2	1.7
Palmerston North	85	13.5	3.1	6.2
Wellington	81	7.6	5.3	10.8
South Island				
Nelson	94	8	1.5	2.1
Christchurch	89	7.1	2.5	5.7
Dunedin	92	5.9	2	4
Invercargill	92	13.1	2.2	1.1

totals more than 100% as some recipients identified with more than one group

by the Waitangi Tribunal, which is a world model for its kind. Recently, New Zealand has defined itself against its larger allies, the USA and Australia, by banning nuclear warship visits and refusing to participate with them in the War in Iraq in 2003, although it has participated internationally elsewhere, notably in Rwanda, East Timor, Afghanistan, and the Solomons.

1840 Treaty of Waitangi; Wellington settled

1844–6 The Flagstaff War in the Bay of Islands

1860–5 The Waikato and Taranaki Wars

1867 Maori seats introduced in Parliament

1882 First frozen meat exports from New Zealand

1893 New Zealand women (including Maoris) win the vote

1907 New Zealand becomes a Dominion

1975 Waitangi Tribunal established

1985 Visits by nuclear warships banned

1993 Mixed Member Proportional voting introduced

2004 A New Zealand, "Wellywood"-made, film *Return of the King* wins a record number of Oscars and boosts the national economy

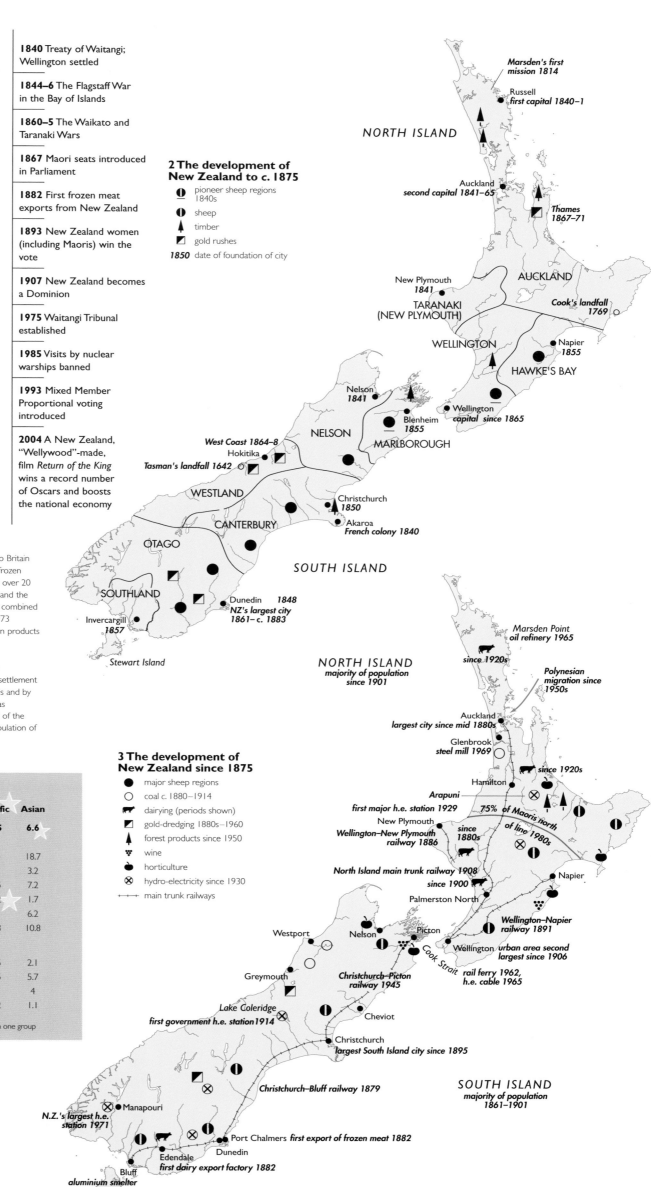

2 The development of New Zealand to c. 1875

3 The development of New Zealand since 1875

263

Africa before the partition by the European powers

THE AFRICANS ARE ALL DEEPLY IMBUED WITH THE SPIRIT OF TRADE. WE FOUND GREAT DIFFICULTY IN GETTING PAST MANY VILLAGES. EVERY ARTIFICE WAS EMPLOYED TO DETAIN US THAT WE MIGHT PURCHASE OUR SUPPERS FROM THEM ... THEY ARE ENTIRELY DEPENDANT ON ENGLISH CALICO FOR CLOTHING ... MANY OF THEIR VILLAGES WERE MODELS OF NEATNESS, AND SO WERE THEIR GARDENS & HUTS. MANY WERE INVETERATE MUSICIANS, AND MADE ONE REMEMBER HOW MUCH OF OUR ANGLO-SAXON ENERGY IS EXPENDED IN DRESS & IN THE HOWLING OF PIANOS.

David Livingstone to Arthur Tidman (Secretary, London Missionary Society), 12 October 1855

Africa between 1800 and 1880 was shaped by indigenous societies and their rulers, intent as ever on pursuing their own ambitions. Europeans occupied little more than the tiniest of coastal footholds, and the commercial and political developments of the period represented more than the prelude to an inevitable European partition.

IN THE EARLY NINETEENTH CENTURY much of west Africa was profoundly affected by an Islamic religious revival manifested in Holy Wars (*jihads*) waged mainly against backsliding Muslim or partly-Islamicized communities. The great warriors of the *jihad* were the widely-scattered Fulani cattle-keepers of the Sudanic region. In the 18th century they had established theocracies in Futa Toro, Futa Jallon and in Masina on the upper Niger. Much larger, however, was the 19th-century Fulani state set up in Hausaland. In 1804 a Fulani religious leader, Usuman dan Fodio, was proclaimed Commander of the Faithful, and declared a *jihad* against the infidel. His formidable army of horsemen soon conquered the Hausa city states, and struck out into Adamawa, Nupe and Yorubaland. His son became the sultan of Sokoto, an empire still in existence in the 1890s.

An even fiercer *jihad* was conducted by al-Hajj Umar from Futa Jallon. Conquering the Bambara kingdoms and Masina, he was only kept from the Atlantic by the French on the Senegal river. In fact, Islam increasingly became a counterforce to European advance, especially in the case of the Mandinka leader Samory who carved out another empire south of the Niger; he was finally defeated by the French only in 1898.

New trade

In the forest states further south, the slave trade had long flourished but the British in particular began to try to replace it with "legitimate trade". Although a government-sponsored mission in 1841–2 to establish "Christianity, commerce and civilization" inland failed, African responses to Europe's new commercial demands for palm oil and other products encouraged change.

Likewise in east and west central Africa new commercial patterns brought disruption. There the western world's almost insatiable appetite for ivory (for billiard balls and piano keys) caused the hunting and trading of elephant tusks to become a major economic activity, enriching many states and peoples – the Cokwe and King Msiri in central Africa, for instance, and Buganda and the Nyamwezi in east Africa. Foreign traders in central Africa were frequently Portuguese from Angola and Mozambique, and in east Africa Swahili-Arabs from Zanzibar, who often brought their Islamic religion with them. Some peoples, particularly around lakes Nyasa and Tanganyika, suffered severely from the Arab slave trade, which went hand-in-hand with that in ivory.

In northeast Africa, the expansion of Egypt, ruled by Khedives, nominally viceroys of the Ottoman sultan, brought a foretaste of the later European conquest. Muhammad Ali's armies conquered the northern Nilotic Sudan, founding the provincial capital at Khartoum in 1821, and his grandson, Ismail, consolidated Egyptian control over much of the Red Sea coast and Horn of Africa, as well as pushing south up the Nile towards the Great Lakes. Partly in response to this Egyptian activity, Ethiopian political power revived.

European colonization

Only two areas of Africa were colonized by European powers during this period. In 1830 France invaded Algeria and in a long and bitter struggle conquered and settled the territory. The British took the Cape from the Dutch during the Napoleonic wars and the south saw the presence of increasing numbers of Europeans, including the Boers – white farmers who left Cape Colony in the "Great Trek" of 1836 to avoid British rule. In the 1850s Britain recognized the Transvaal and Orange Free State republics which the Boers founded, but by the 1870s were again in dispute with them.

2 Early European explorers (map left) generally travelled with African trading groups and proved remarkably receptive to the cultures they encountered. David Livingstone was the most able scientist among them and was also motivated by religious zeal and hatred of the slave trade. Later explorers, notably H. M. Stanley, were far more aggressive and exploitative, their expeditions resembling military campaigns.

The Battle of Isandhlwana (below) on 22 January 1879 was the first major engagement of the Zulu war. A British force of 1700 white and African troops under Lord Chelmsford was routed by 20,000 Zulu, the consequence rather of British arrogance and carelessness than of overwhelming numbers. It demonstrated the continuing possibility that African tactics and weaponry could triumph over well-armed European forces.

2 European exploration within Africa

- Bruce, 1768–73
- Browne, 1792–6
- Mungo Park, 1795–7
- Hornemann, 1798–9
- Hornemann, 1799–1801
- Mungo Park, 1805–6
- Burckhardt, 1812–14
- Mollien, 1818
- Clapperton, 1822–5
- Clapperton and Lander, 1825–7
- Réné Caillé, 1828
- Barth, 1850–5
- Livingstone, 1853–6
- Burton and Speke, 1857–9
- Livingstone, 1858–64
- Speke and Grant, 1860–3
- Livingstone, 1866–73
- Nachtigal, 1869–74
- Stanley, 1871–2
- Stanley, 1874–7
- de Brazza, 1875–9
- Wissmann, 1880–7
- Stanley, 1887–9

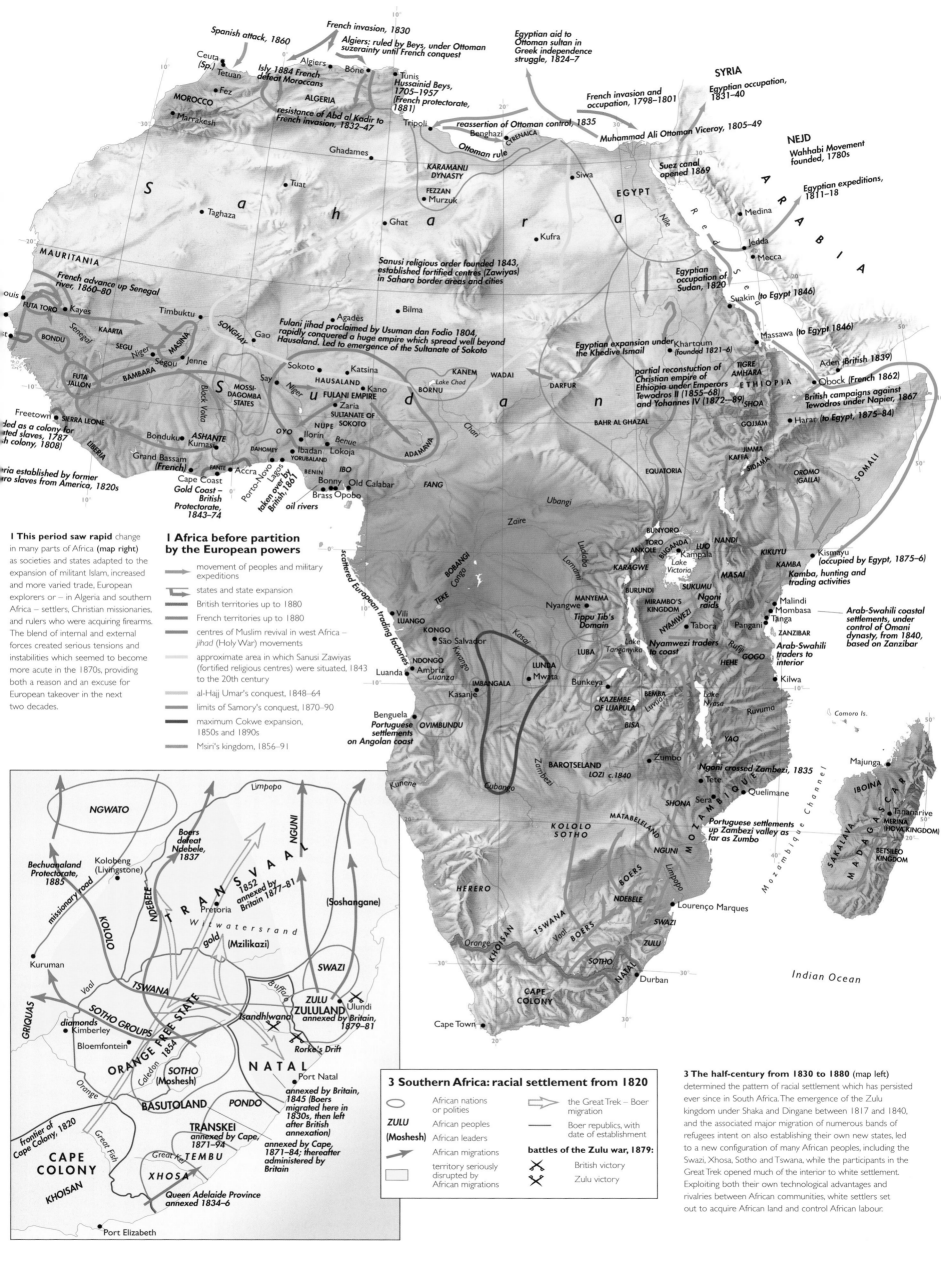

1 This period saw rapid change in many parts of Africa (map right) as societies and states adapted to the expansion of militant Islam, increased and more varied trade, European explorers or – in Algeria and southern Africa – settlers, Christian missionaries, and rulers who were acquiring firearms. The blend of internal and external forces created serious tensions and instabilities which seemed to become more acute in the 1870s, providing both a reason and an excuse for European takeover in the next two decades.

1 Africa before partition by the European powers

- movement of peoples and military expeditions
- states and state expansion
- British territories up to 1880
- French territories up to 1880
- centres of Muslim revival in west Africa – jihad (Holy War) movements
- approximate area in which Sanusi Zawiyas (fortified religious centres) were situated, 1843 to the 20th century
- al-Hajj Umar's conquest, 1848–64
- limits of Samory's conquest, 1870–90
- maximum Cokwe expansion, 1850s and 1890s
- Msiri's kingdom, 1856–91

3 Southern Africa: racial settlement from 1820

- African nations or polities
- ZULU African peoples
- (Mosesh) African leaders
- African migrations
- territory seriously disrupted by African migrations
- the Great Trek – Boer migration
- Boer republics, with date of establishment

battles of the Zulu war, 1879:
- British victory
- Zulu victory

3 The half-century from 1830 to 1880 (map left) determined the pattern of racial settlement which has persisted ever since in South Africa. The emergence of the Zulu kingdom under Shaka and Dingane between 1817 and 1840, and the associated major migration of numerous bands of refugees intent on also establishing their own new states, led to a new configuration of many African peoples, including the Swazi, Xhosa, Sotho and Tswana, while the participants in the Great Trek opened much of the interior to white settlement. Exploiting both their own technological advantages and rivalries between African communities, white settlers set out to acquire African land and control African labour.

The partition of Africa

Once Europe's partition of Africa began in the 1880s, the continent was carved up remarkably rapidly: 30 years later only Abyssinia and Liberia remained wholly independent. The scramble was completed with the redistribution of Germany's colonies after the First World War, when, for the first time, colonial administration began to be imposed effectively.

LITTLE OF AFRICA was directly ruled by Europeans in 1880: the French had been subjugating Algeria since 1830; there were small French and British colonies in west Africa; and there were moribund Portuguese settlements in Angola and Mozambique. Only in the south, where the British Cape colonists were in competition with the Afrikaners of the Transvaal and Orange Free State, did political control extend far inland. Yet within two decades the continent had been seized and partitioned. Of the 40 political units to which it was reduced by 1913, 36 were completely under European control. France was the largest beneficiary, ruling nearly one-third of Africa's 30.3 million sq. km (11.7 million sq. miles).

The scramble begins

Many ingredients contributed to this imperial explosion, among them the search for raw materials and new markets for Europe's rapidly expanding industries. At the same time, rivalries between European states were partly played out outside Europe, especially in Africa. As a result, often trivial incidents in Africa between competing European traders precipitated major international crises, accelerating the undignified scramble for the continent. Yet ironically, few European powers actively sought partition. At the Berlin West Africa Conference in 1884 the powers had agreed to avert partition and maintain access for all. Yet whatever their official hesitations, the process had acquired a momentum of its own.

In west Africa, French army officers, eager to recover their honour after their humiliating defeat by Germany in 1870 (see p. 238), sought glory advancing inland from Senegal in the late 1870s. This created conflict with the British in Gambia and Sierra Leone, and with African rulers such as al-Hajj Umar and Samory. Intense British-French rivalry developed in the Gold Coast, Togo, Dahomey and Yorubaland and hardened after Britain's unilateral occupation of Egypt in 1882.

King Leopold of the Belgians' determination to become involved in Africa led him to recruit the explorer H. M. Stanley after his epic journey down the Congo River in 1877. In 1879 Stanley returned to the lower Congo to lay the foundations of the huge private domain the king eventually acquired in the Congo basin. His activities stimulated others in the region. The French naval officer de Brazza concluded vital protection treaties with African chiefs,

3 The single-most effective resistance to the spread of white imperialism in Africa came not from native Africans but from existing European settlers, the Dutch farmers known as Boers. The discovery of gold in Boer-held territory saw Britain determined to bring the Boer republics under its control. Though eventually defeated, the Boer's brilliant guerrilla tactics came close to inflicting a humiliating defeat. Britain was forced to field 300,000 troops against 75,000 Boers **(map below)**.

1881 France establishes protectorate over Tunisia

1882 Britain occupies Egypt

1884–5 Berlin West Africa Conference: Berlin Act and recognition of the Congo Free State

1883–6 Discovery of gold in the Transvaal

1896 British reconquest of Sudan begins; Italy defeated at Adowa

1898 Fashoda Crisis: France confronts Britain on the Nile

1899–1902 South African War: Britain conquers Boer republics, Transvaal and Orange Free State

1904–7 Herero Revolt against German rule in South West Africa

War between Britain and France in 1898 over their claims to Fashoda in the Sudan was only narrowly averted. The incident aroused nationalist fervour on both sides. Here **(right)** a French newspaper portrays an innocent France as Red Riding Hood confronted by Britannia as the wolf.

1 Despite the rapidity and apparent ease of the partition, nearly everywhere Europeans encountered resistance to their invasion of Africa **(map right)**. Much of this was local and could be dealt with piecemeal, often using other African groups as allies. Some resistance was sustained, such as that of Samori against the French in west Africa in the 1880s. In all cases, the policy of the Europeans was to divide and rule. Certainly by the 1890s the white man had an overwhelming technological superiority: machine-guns, telegraphs and transport were the handmaidens of partition.

2 Colonial rule took many forms **(map below)**: the self-governing white territories of the Cape Colony and Natal; the manipulation of nominally independent local governments in the manner of the British in Egypt; and the incorporation of indigenous authorities into the autocratic administrations of French West Africa. Intended to be peaceful and cheap, colonial rule was often neglectful and oppressive.

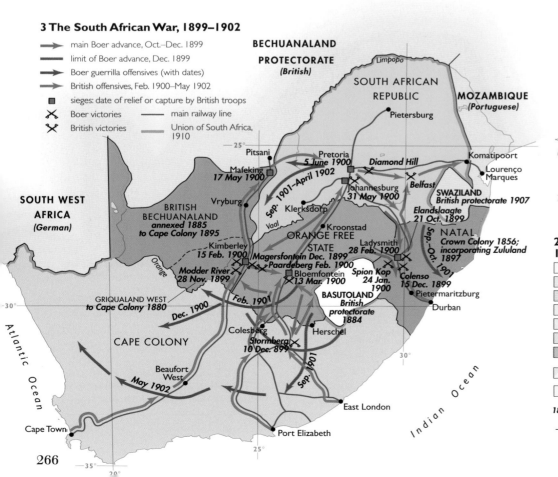

3 The South African War, 1899–1902

- → main Boer advance, Oct.–Dec. 1899
- — limit of Boer advance, Dec. 1899
- → Boer guerrilla offensives (with dates)
- → British offensives, Feb. 1900–May 1902
- ■ sieges: date of relief or capture by British troops
- ✕ Boer victories   — main railway line
- ✕ British victories   Union of South Africa, 1910

2 Alien rule in Africa, 1913

- French
- British
- German
- Portuguese
- Belgian
- Spanish
- Italian
- Anglo-Egyptian condominium
- independent
- **1882–95** date of determination of colonial boundary
- — frontiers, 1914

which the government in Paris readily took up. Germany also entered the race, grabbing territory in Togoland, the Cameroons, southwest and east Africa. French and German commercial and political initiatives in west Africa provoked British intervention, especially in securing the lands which became Nigeria. The far interior was left to the French, who by 1900 had swept right across the western Sudan.

Germany's presence in southern Africa revived Portuguese ambitions, and threats of Afrikaner expansion led to British thrusts into central Africa, aided decisively by the Cape politician Cecil Rhodes. Likewise, German colonization in Tanganyika prompted British claims to what became Uganda and Kenya. French conquest of Dahomey (1893) and her drive towards Lake Chad drew Britain and the Royal Niger Company into protecting its trading sphere, which in turn led to armed clashes with African states. Multiple tensions reached their height in 1898 at Fashoda on the White Nile where the two countries narrowly avoided war.

Conflict and war

Partition caused increasing bloodshed. Abyssinia routed the Italians at Adowa in 1896; some 120,000 Sudanese died in Britain's reconquest of the Mahdist state; and Rhodes' settlers fought bitterly with Ndebele and Shona as they moved north. Conflicts climaxed with the South African War (1899–1902) in which Britain with difficulty won the Transvaal gold fields and absorbed the Afrikaner republics (see map 3). Elsewhere black Africans, although bitterly opposing the European powers, could never offer concerted resistance and for the most part were easily overcome.

I The partition of Africa
colonies or settlements, 1880

- French
- British
- Portuguese

★ anti-European resistance

African states or empires

colonial penetration
→ French
→ British
→ Portuguese
→ German
→ Italian
→ Spanish
→ Belgian

The expansion and modernization of Japan

1868 Tokugawa shogunate ends and the Meiji emperor is restored

1891 Construction of the Trans-Siberian railway begins

1894–5 Sino-Japanese War; Japan occupies Formosa

1904–5 Russo-Japanese War; Japanese success stimulates Asian nationalism

1910 Japan annexes Korea

1914 Japan takes over German concessions in China

1920 Japan given permanent seat on the League of Nations

Between the 1850s and the 1920s Japan emerged from isolation to become a major world power. Western pressure was the spur which led to the destruction of the feudal system and the unleashing of her great potential for rapid modernization. But by 1920 there were signs that her rapid growth was causing dangerous internal stresses.

> THE ONE OBJECT OF MY LIFE IS TO EXTEND JAPAN'S NATIONAL POWER. COMPARED WITH CONSIDERATIONS OF THE COUNTRY'S STRENGTH, THE MATTER OF INTERNAL GOVERNMENT AND INTO WHOSE HANDS IT FALLS IS OF NO IMPORTANCE AT ALL. EVEN IF THE GOVERNMENT BE AUTOCRATIC IN NAME AND FORM, I SHALL BE SATISFIED WITH IT IF IT IS STRONG ENOUGH TO STRENGTHEN THE COUNTRY.
>
> **The leader of Japan's Liberal Party in the late 19th century**

5 The three decades from 1888 to 1918 saw both a substantial growth in Japan's population (charts below right) from 39.5 to 55 million, and a significant shift from country to town. The proportion living in cities of over 100,000 people more than doubled in the period, and that in urban settlements of between 10,000 and 100,000 trebled. But the villages still remained preponderant.

JAPAN AVOIDED EXCESSIVE interference by expansionist Western powers during the latter half of the 19th century by implementing successful policies for rapid modernization. The very countries that had threatened her independence became models for her own development and hence fuelled her own imperialist ambitions. The process began in the 1850s and by 1920 the Japanese empire was firmly established.

The spur to modernization was the demand from Western powers, led by the USA, for access to Japan's ports. The "unequal treaties" concluded under threat in 1858 prompted the restoration of direct imperial rule in 1868 in the name of the Meiji emperor (see p. 196). Already the country had considerable strengths: an extensive network of commerce and credit; an agricultural sector capable of feeding the nation and providing exports of tea and raw silk; reserves of copper, coal and iron; and scholars who, in spite of Japan's enforced isolation, had studied Western science and technology.

It was crucial to Japan's rapid modernization to bring these strengths into play. The abolition of feudalism, and the replacement in 1873 of feudal dues with cash payments based on the value of land, enabled wealth to be redirected to the purposes of central government. To encourage the transfer of technology and to stimulate investment, the government used this land tax to build model factories in strategic and import-saving industries, such as steel and textiles, and became directly involved in the development of transport and communications. There was also indirect encouragement in the form of subsidies and tax privileges.

The new leaders introduced complementary administrative reforms: feudal domains were replaced by modern bureaucracy (1871); the feudal army was replaced by a conscript one (1873); a bicameral legislature provided the basis for political unity and stability (1889); a national education system was instituted (1872); and legal codes based on those of France and Germany were introduced (1882).

Industrialization and trade

Within this framework capitalism advanced rapidly; Japan became the outstanding example of large-scale industrialization in the non-Western world. By 1918, when she had achieved major penetration of markets in China, the USA and elsewhere, she had become a major importer of raw materials and exporter of finished goods. Such developments meant considerable changes for Japanese society: by 1918 the population had risen to 55 million (from 35 million in 1873) and nearly one-third lived in towns of 10,000 or more.

National strength brought expansion overseas, motives being both strategic and economic. Japan began by claiming neighbouring islands such as the Ryukyus and Kuriles. The "unequal treaties" were revoked in 1894. Then concerns that China was too weak to keep Russia out of Korea led to war (1894–5) in which Japan destroyed the Chinese forces and acquired Formosa (Taiwan). The Russian threat, however, was only resolved by Japan's overwhelming defeat of Russia on land and sea in 1904–5, which led to Japanese control over the Liaotung peninsula, extensive rights in southern Manchuria and the acquisition of southern Sakhalin (see map 2). There followed the annexation of Korea (1910), the acquisition of former German territories in China (1914), and the "Twenty-one Demands" (1915), which made sweeping, though not wholly successful, claims over China. In 1919 the Paris Peace Conference confirmed most of these gains and granted Japan mandates to German colonies in the Pacific.

The cost of success

There was, however, another side to the story: the army was beginning to act independently of civil control, politicians were becoming too beholden to business, traditionalists objected to the sacrifice of Japanese values to the West, and the farmer and the labourer began to resent the subjection of their well-being to capital. The end of the war brought economic disruption, major disturbances in town and countryside, and the assassination in 1921 of the prime minister by a fanatic. These events presaged turbulent years ahead.

5 Japanese population
- in towns of over 100,000
- in towns of 10,000–100,000
- in small towns and rural areas

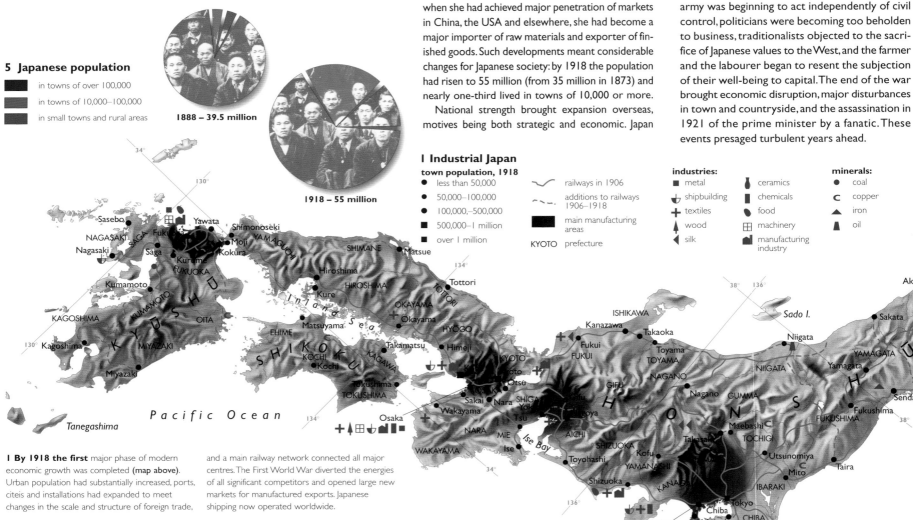

1888 – 39.5 million

1918 – 55 million

1 Industrial Japan
town population, 1918
- ● less than 50,000
- ● 50,000–100,000
- ● 100,000,–500,000
- ■ 500,000–1 million
- ■ over 1 million

- ∿ railways in 1906
- ∿ additions to railways 1906–1918
- ▬ main manufacturing areas
- KYOTO prefecture

industries:
- ■ metal
- ⊥ shipbuilding
- + textiles
- ▲ wood
- ◄ silk

- ◊ ceramics
- chemicals
- food
- ⊞ machinery
- ▦ manufacturing industry

minerals:
- ● coal
- C copper
- ▲ iron
- ▮ oil

1 By 1918 the first major phase of modern economic growth was completed (map above). Urban population had substantially increased, ports, cities and installations had expanded to meet changes in the scale and structure of foreign trade, and a main railway network connected all major centres. The First World War diverted the energies of all significant competitors and opened large new markets for manufactured exports. Japanese shipping now operated worldwide.

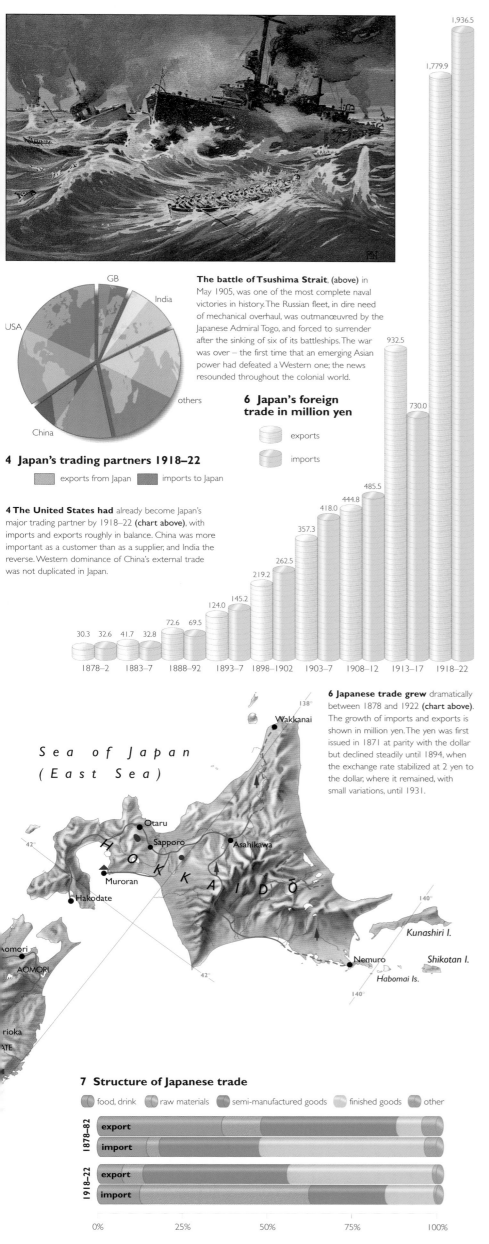

The battle of Tsushima Strait, (above) in May 1905, was one of the most complete naval victories in history. The Russian fleet, in dire need of mechanical overhaul, was outmanœuvred by the Japanese Admiral Togo, and forced to surrender after the sinking of six of its battleships. The war was over – the first time that an emerging Asian power had defeated a Western one; the news resounded throughout the colonial world.

6 Japan's foreign trade in million yen

exports
imports

4 Japan's trading partners 1918–22

exports from Japan   imports to Japan

4 The United States had already become Japan's major trading partner by 1918–22 (chart above), with imports and exports roughly in balance. China was more important as a customer than as a supplier, and India the reverse. Western dominance of China's external trade was not duplicated in Japan.

Japan's foreign trade in million yen:
1878–2: 30.3 / 32.6
1883–7: 41.7 / 32.8
1888–92: 72.6 / 69.5
1893–7: 124.0 / 145.2
1898–1902: 219.2 / 262.5
1903–7: 357.3 / 418.0
1908–12: 444.8 / 485.5
1913–17: 932.5 / 730.0
1918–22: 1,779.9 / 1,936.5

6 Japanese trade grew dramatically between 1878 and 1922 (chart above). The growth of imports and exports is shown in million yen. The yen was first issued in 1871 at parity with the dollar but declined steadily until 1894, when the exchange rate stabilized at 2 yen to the dollar, where it remained, with small variations, until 1931.

Sea of Japan (East Sea)

Wakkanai
Otaru
Sapporo · Asahikawa
Muroran
Hakodate

H O K K A I D Ō

Kunashiri I.
Nemuro
Shikotan I.
Habomai Is.

Aomori
AOMORI
rioka
ATE

7 Structure of Japanese trade

food, drink   raw materials   semi-manufactured goods   finished goods   other

1878–82
export
import

1918–22
export
import

0%   25%   50%   75%   100%

7 The structure of Japanese foreign trade (chart left) changed strikingly between 1878–82 and 1918–22. In the earlier period, manufactured goods represented half of all imports, but only 7.2 per cent of exports. Within 40 years the ratio had reversed: manufactures now accounted for over 40 per cent of sales and only 15 per cent of purchases.

3 The Russo-Japanese War, 1904–5

southern limit of Russian sphere of influence in China, 1900

Trans-Siberian railway, constructed 1891–1903

frontiers, 1904

northern limit of 1903 Russian-proposed Japanese sphere of influence

Japanese troop movements

Russian frontline at end of war, 10 Aug. 1905

★ battle or siege, with date

occupied by Russia 1900; returned to China by Portsmouth Treaty, Sep. 1905

Russian territory ceded to Japan by Portsmouth Treaty

Japanese protectorate from 1905

limit of Chinese territory under Japanese occupation, end 1905

2 Japanese expansion, 1875–1918

Japan's possessions at the end of 1875 with dates of acquisition

territorial acquisitions 1894–1914 with dates

spheres of Japanese influence in 1918

2 The 1868 revolution was followed by an upsurge of Japanese interest in the West and in her neighbours (map above). By 1875, Japan had asserted her claims to a number of Pacific islands including the Kurile, Ryūkyū and Bonin islands. By 1918 her holdings included Korea, Taiwan and half of the island of Sakhalin.

European colonial empires

In the first 50 years after 1815, there was a gradual extension of the European colonial empires as exploration opened up new regions to European traders and missionaries. But the late 19th century saw a heightening of imperial ambitions and rivalries that resulted in the partition of almost all of Africa, southeast Asia and the Pacific.

1823 US Monroe Doctrine warns European powers against intervention in America

1830 French conquest of Algiers

1833 Slavery abolished in British empire

1836 Afrikaners begin "Great Trek" in southern Africa

1839–42 First Opium War in China

1856–60 Second Opium War in China

1857–8 Indian mutiny sparks widespread rebellion

1869 Suez Canal opens

1884–5 Conference of Berlin on the partition of Africa

1899–1902 The South African ("Boer") War

I FEEL SURE THAT THE TIME FOR SMALL KINGDOMS HAS PASSED AWAY. THE FUTURE IS WITH THE GREAT EMPIRES AND IT RESTS WITH US TO SAY WHETHER OUR OWN SHALL BE COUNTED FOR MANY YEARS TO COME AS ONE OF THE GREATEST OR WE SHALL SPLIT UP INTO MINOR COMPARATIVELY UNIMPORTANT NATIONALITIES.

Joseph Chamberlain
letter to Sir George Reid (prime minister of Australia 1904-5) 13 June 1902

IN 1815 **BRITAIN ALONE** remained a great overseas power: France, Spain and the Netherlands had all lost colonial territories to the British. The decade after 1815 even saw a contraction of European colonial empires as South and Central American Spanish and Portuguese colonies broke free. With Britain holding undisputed naval preeminence and discarding mercantilism (the theoretical underpinning of imperialism) in favour of free trade, the first half of the 19th century seemed unlikely to witness further British expansion.

Yet European colonial empires grew almost continuously between 1815 and 1914. The West Indies, with the decline of the Atlantic slave trade and failing economically, lost their 18th-century importance, but in India further British conquests and, in Australia and New Zealand, emigration, pushed forward the boundaries of British imperialism. Britain also acquired Singapore (1819), Malacca (1824), Hong Kong (1842), Natal (1843), Lower Burma (1852) and Lagos (1861), and claimed sovereignty over Australia (1829) and New Zealand (1840). Many of these were to secure British commercial interests and to protect Britain's position in India; others were defensive reactions against France or necessitated by settler activity. Other European countries also steadily expanded. Russia sold Alaska to the United States in 1867, but continued its continental expansion: between 1801 and 1914 over 7 million Russians emigrated to Asiatic Russia. France, determined to replace the empire lost in 1815, conquered Algeria in the 1830s, annexed Tahiti and the Marquesas in the 1840s, expanded its colony in Senegal in the 1850s and began the conquest of Indo-China in 1858–9. Over and beyond the extension of formal empires, European technology and industrialization opened up other areas of the world – from Turkey and Egypt, to Persia and China,

South America and even Japan – to European, particularly British, trade and finance. As Europe continued to disgorge missionaries, explorers and settlers overseas, relations with, and knowledge of, the wider world was transformed.

The scramble for empire

After 1880, the pace of imperial expansion, fuelled by commercial competition, rivalries between imperial powers and changing conditions in Asia and Africa, quickened hugely. By 1914, Europe had engrossed nine-tenths of Africa and a large part of Asia. Between 1871 and 1914 the French empire grew by nearly 10 million sq. km (4 million sq. miles) and 47 million people. Defeat in Europe by Germany in 1870 redoubled French efforts to regain prestige through overseas conquests. Germany herself acquired 2.6 million sq. km (1 million sq. miles) and 14 million subjects in southwest Africa, the Cameroons, east Africa and the Pacific islands. Italy, eager for reasons of prestige to enter the colonial race, obtained Tripoli and Libya, Eritrea and Italian Somaliland, though in 1896 failed to conquer Abyssinia. But the greatest gains of all were made by Britain, who, partly to secure areas for free trade, established control over Nigeria, Kenya, Uganda, Rhodesia, Egypt and the Sudan, Fiji and parts of Borneo and New Guinea. Nonetheless, India remained the keystone of the British empire and many of these acquisitions were made with a view to bolstering British control over and access to India.

Imperialism was not confined to Europe. The United States and Japan joined the race as well, the former acquiring the Philippines (from Spain) in 1898, the latter taking Formosa in 1895 and Korea in 1910. Of the great European trading nations, the Netherlands almost alone remained content with its existing rich possessions in the East Indies.

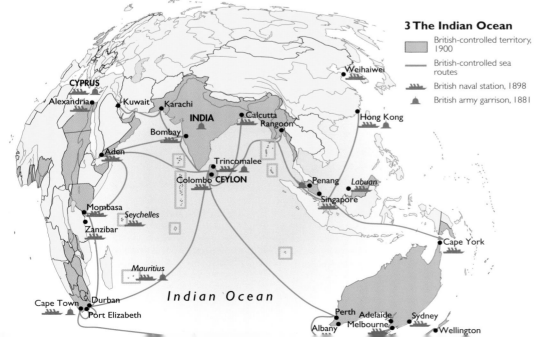

3 The Indian Ocean

- British-controlled territory, 1900
- British-controlled sea routes
- British naval station, 1898
- British army garrison, 1881

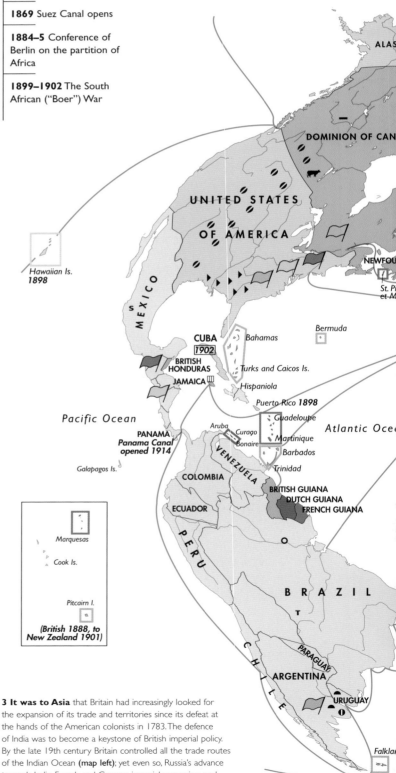

3 It was to Asia that Britain had increasingly looked for the expansion of its trade and territories since its defeat at the hands of the American colonists in 1783. The defence of India was to become a keystone of British imperial policy. By the late 19th century Britain controlled all the trade routes of the Indian Ocean (map left); yet even so, Russia's advance towards India, French and German imperial expansion, and European, US and Japanese naval expansionism sparked new concerns about British paramountcy.

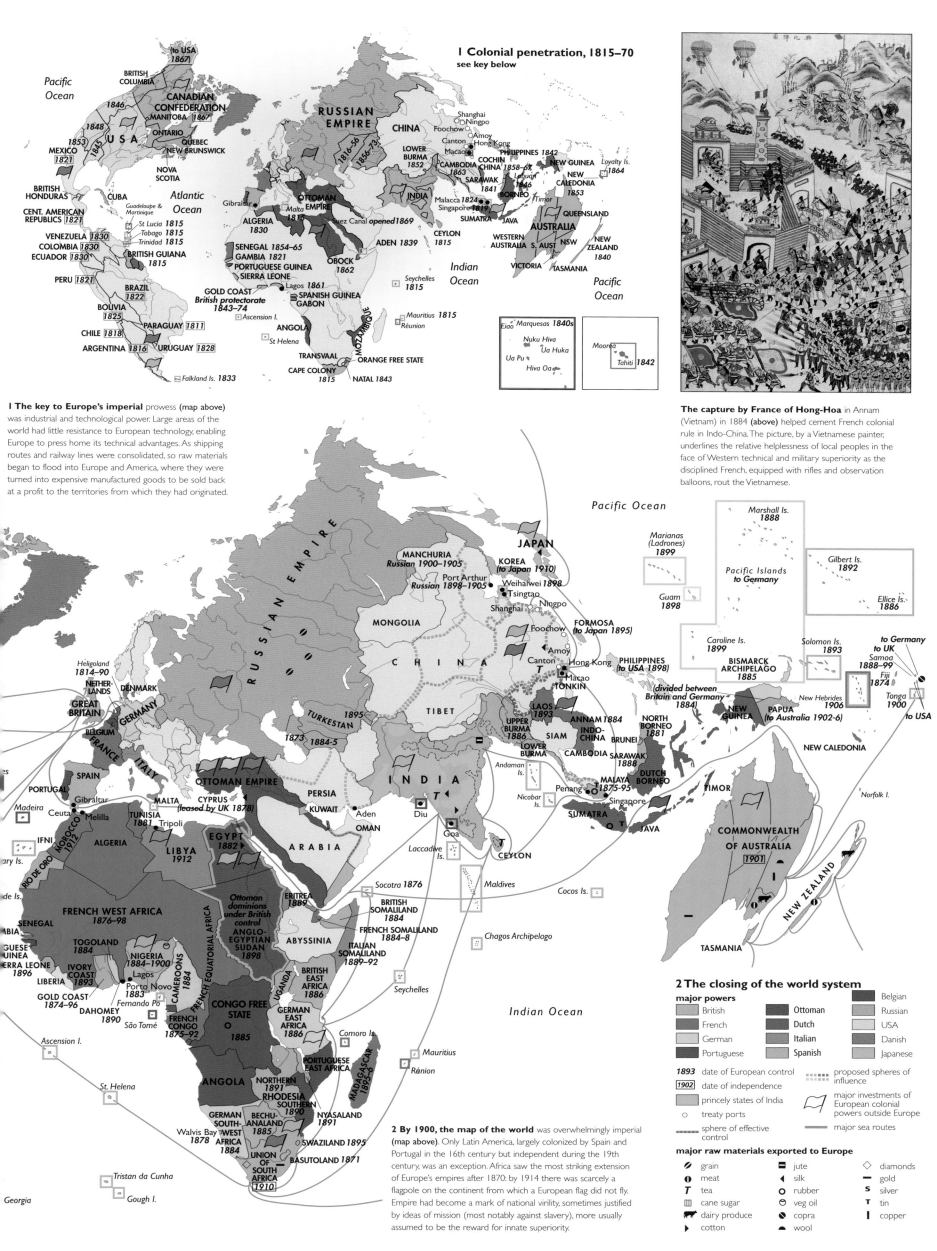

1 Colonial penetration, 1815–70
see key below

Map 1 labels:

Pacific Ocean

(to USA 1867)
BRITISH COLUMBIA
CANADIAN CONFEDERATION
1846
1848
MANITOBA 1867
ONTARIO
QUEBEC
NEW BRUNSWICK
NOVA SCOTIA
1853
1845
USA
MEXICO 1821
BRITISH HONDURAS
CUBA
CENT. AMERICAN REPUBLICS 1821
Atlantic Ocean
Guadeloupe & Martinique
St Lucia 1815
Trinidad 1815
Tobago 1815
VENEZUELA 1830
COLOMBIA 1830
ECUADOR 1830
BRITISH GUIANA 1815
PERU 1821
BRAZIL 1822
BOLIVIA 1825
PARAGUAY 1811
CHILE 1818
ARGENTINA 1816
URUGUAY 1828
Falkland Is. 1833

RUSSIAN EMPIRE
1815–56
1856–73
CHINA
Shanghai
Ningpo
Foochow
Canton
Amoy
Macao
Hong Kong
PHILIPPINES 1842
LOWER BURMA 1852
CAMBODIA 1863
COCHIN CHINA 1858–67
SARAWAK 1841
NEW GUINEA
Loyalty Is. 1864
NEW CALEDONIA 1853
LABUAN
BORNEO
Timor
INDIA
Malacca 1824
Singapore 1819
SUMATRA
JAVA
QUEENSLAND
AUSTRALIA
WESTERN AUSTRALIA
S. AUST.
NSW
VICTORIA
NEW ZEALAND 1840
TASMANIA
Pacific Ocean

OTTOMAN EMPIRE
Gibraltar
Malta 1815
Suez Canal opened 1869
ALGERIA 1830
ADEN 1839
CEYLON 1815
Indian Ocean
SENEGAL 1854–65
GAMBIA 1821
PORTUGUESE GUINEA
SIERRA LEONE
Lagos 1861
SPANISH GUINEA
GABON
GOLD COAST British protectorate 1843–74
OBOCK
OBOCK 1862
Seychelles 1815
Ascension I.
ANGOLA
Mauritius 1815
Réunion
St Helena
MOZAMBIQUE
TRANSVAAL
ORANGE FREE STATE
CAPE COLONY 1815
NATAL 1843

Eiao
Marquesas 1840s
Nuku Hiva
Ua Huka
Ua Pu
Hiva Oa
Moorea
Tahiti 1842

1 The key to Europe's imperial prowess (map above) was industrial and technological power. Large areas of the world had little resistance to European technology, enabling Europe to press home its technical advantages. As shipping routes and railway lines were consolidated, so raw materials began to flood into Europe and America, where they were turned into expensive manufactured goods to be sold back at a profit to the territories from which they had originated.

The capture by France of Hong-Hoa in Annam (Vietnam) in 1884 (above) helped cement French colonial rule in Indo-China. The picture, by a Vietnamese painter, underlines the relative helplessness of local peoples in the face of Western technical and military superiority as the disciplined French, equipped with rifles and observation balloons, rout the Vietnamese.

Map 2 labels:

Pacific Ocean

JAPAN
MANCHURIA Russian 1900–1905
KOREA (to Japan 1910)
Port Arthur Russian 1898–1905
Weihaiwei 1898
Tsingtao
MONGOLIA
Ningpo
Shanghai
FORMOSA (to Japan 1895)
Foochow
Amoy
Canton
Hong Kong
Macao
TONKIN
PHILIPPINES (to USA 1898)
Marshall Is. 1888
Marianas (Ladrones) 1899
Pacific Islands to Germany
Gilbert Is. 1892
Guam 1898
Caroline Is. 1899
Solomon Is. 1893
Ellice Is. 1886
to Germany to UK
BISMARCK ARCHIPELAGO 1885
Samoa 1888–99
(divided between Britain and Germany 1884)
New Hebrides 1906
Fiji 1874
Tonga 1900
to USA
Heligoland 1814–90
NETHERLANDS
DENMARK
GREAT BRITAIN
GERMANY
RUSSIAN EMPIRE
TURKESTAN 1895
1873
1884–5
TIBET
LAOS 1893
UPPER BURMA 1886
ANNAM 1884
INDO-CHINA
NORTH BORNEO 1881
NEW GUINEA
PAPUA (to Australia 1902–6)
New Guinea (divided between Britain and Germany 1884)
BELGIUM
FRANCE
ITALY
SPAIN
PORTUGAL
Gibraltar
MALTA
CYPRUS (leased by UK 1878)
PERSIA
SIAM
LOWER BURMA
CAMBODIA
BRUNEI
SARAWAK 1888
MALAYA 1875–95
DUTCH BORNEO
TIMOR
NEW CALEDONIA
Norfolk I.
Madeira
Ceuta
Melilla
TUNISIA 1881
Tripoli
INDIA
Andaman Is.
Penang
Singapore
SUMATRA
JAVA
COMMONWEALTH OF AUSTRALIA 1901
IFNI
MOROCCO 1912
ALGERIA
LIBYA 1912
EGYPT 1882
ARABIA
KUWAIT
Aden
OMAN
Nicobar Is.
Diu
Goa
Laccadive Is.
CEYLON
NEW ZEALAND
RIO DE ORO
Canary Is.
OTTOMAN EMPIRE
Socotra 1876
Maldives
Cocos Is.
TASMANIA
Indian Ocean
FRENCH WEST AFRICA 1876–98
SENEGAL
TOGOLAND 1884
NIGERIA 1884–1900
Lagos
IVORY COAST 1893
GOLD COAST 1874–96
LIBERIA
DAHOMEY 1890
Porto Novo
Fernando Po
CAMEROONS 1884
FRENCH EQUATORIAL AFRICA
FRENCH CONGO 1875–92
São Tomé
CONGO FREE STATE 1885
UGANDA
BRITISH EAST AFRICA 1886
GERMAN EAST AFRICA 1886
Ottoman dominions under British control ANGLO-EGYPTIAN SUDAN 1898
ERITREA 1889
ABYSSINIA
BRITISH SOMALILAND 1884
FRENCH SOMALILAND 1884–8
ITALIAN SOMALILAND 1889–92
Chagos Archipelago
Seychelles
GUINEA
SIERRA LEONE 1896
PORTUGUESE GUINEA
Ascension I.
St Helena
ANGOLA
NORTHERN RHODESIA 1891
SOUTHERN RHODESIA 1890
GERMAN SOUTH-WEST AFRICA 1884
Walvis Bay 1878
BECHUANALAND 1885
NYASALAND 1891
SWAZILAND 1895
PORTUGUESE EAST AFRICA
Comoro Is.
Mauritius
Réunion
MADAGASCAR 1895–9
UNION OF SOUTH AFRICA 1910
BASUTOLAND 1871
Tristan da Cunha
Gough I.
Georgia

2 By 1900, the map of the world was overwhelmingly imperial (map above). Only Latin America, largely colonized by Spain and Portugal in the 16th century but independent during the 19th century, was an exception. Africa saw the most striking extension of Europe's empires after 1870: by 1914 there was scarcely a flagpole on the continent from which a European flag did not fly. Empire had become a mark of national virility, sometimes justified by ideas of mission (most notably against slavery), more usually assumed to be the reward for innate superiority.

2 The closing of the world system

major powers

British	Ottoman	Belgian
French	Dutch	Russian
German	Italian	USA
Portuguese	Spanish	Danish
		Japanese

1893 date of European control
1902 date of independence
princely states of India
o treaty ports
sphere of effective control
proposed spheres of influence
major investments of European colonial powers outside Europe
major sea routes

major raw materials exported to Europe

grain	jute	diamonds
meat	silk	gold
tea	rubber	silver
cane sugar	veg oil	tin
dairy produce	copra	copper
cotton	wool	

The anti-Western reaction

From 1881 the European scramble for global power provoked new and widespread resistance throughout Asia and Africa. Elsewhere, in China and the Ottoman empire, intense European commercial and political penetration was undermining the old order. By 1917 modern nationalist movements were emerging in many European colonies.

RESISTANCE TO EUROPEAN colonialism existed well before 1881. Furthermore, patterns of resistance were shaped just as much by struggles for economic advantage and by local and inter-state rivalries as by the imposition of European political control. Resistance took many forms, from mass migrations to, among African Christian converts, the establishment of indigenous Christian churches. Nevertheless, the unprecedented scale of the annexations of the "new imperialism" after 1881 unleashed an anti-colonial wave that was bigger and more significant than anything that had preceded it. Nowhere was independence surrendered passively. Throughout Africa and Asia, Europeans met prolonged and often bitter armed resistance.

In Annam the emperor, Ham Nghi, took to the mountains and resisted French occupation; Russia encountered Muslim resistance when it invaded central Asia; the USA became embroiled in a costly war with nationalist forces under Emilio Aguinaldo

after it occupied the Philippines in 1898; and the Italians were defeated by the Abyssinians at Adowa in 1896. In Africa, Europeans faced resistance movements of varying strength. In many cases local groups alternated between diplomacy and armed opposition. Before and after mounting military resistance against the French, a west African leader, Samory, unsuccessfully sought British protection. Meanwhile oppressive German rule in South-West Africa and Tanganyika provoked the Herero and Maji-Maji revolts. In the Philippines resistance to the USA continued among the Islamic population of Mindanao while in Indo-China the "Black Flags" and later De Tham took up the struggle after the emperor Ham Nghi was captured in 1888.

| 1884–5 Berlin Conference on the partition of Africa |
| 1890 Brussels Convention forbids export of European arms to Africa |
| 26 Jan. 1885 Khartoum falls to the Mahdi; General Gordon killed |
| 1898 Battle of Omdurman |
| 1899–1902 South African ("Boer") War |
| 1900 Boxer Rebellion in China |
| 1911 Chinese revolution |
| 1914 Outbreak of First World War |

IT SEEMS TO ME THAT THERE IS A CHANGE COMING OVER THE EAST ... IN CHINA THERE IS A MARKED MOVEMENT AGAINST THE FOREIGNERS ... IN EGYPT AND NORTH AFRICA IT IS SIGNALIZED BY A REMARKABLE INCREASE IN FANATICISM, COUPLED WITH THE SPREAD OF THE PAN-ISLAMIC MOVEMENT. PERHAPS THE EAST IS REALLY AWAKENING FROM ITS SECULAR SLUMBER, AND WE ARE ABOUT TO WITNESS THE RISING OF THESE PATIENT MILLIONS AGAINST THE EXPLOITATION OF AN UNSCRUPULOUS WEST.

E. G. Browne
The Persian Revolution of 1905–1909 (1910)

1 The reaction against European imperialism took many forms (**map right**). In areas such as French Indo-China and the Dutch East Indies, native populations took up arms to fight for their independence. In the great Asian empires – the Ottoman empire and China – whose territorial integrity was threatened, the result of European intervention was revolt against the ruling dynasties and the beginnings of modernization so as to be able to confront the West on more nearly equal terms. In Africa, meanwhile, the partition of the continent by the European powers, a process inaugurated at the Berlin Conference of 1884, provoked resistance which was never quelled, despite harsh repression. Almost every one of the colonial powers was confronted by violent threats to its continued rule.

2 Britain's occupation of Egypt led to intervention in the Sudan. When Khartoum was threatened by local Islamic forces under the "Mahdi", General Gordon was sent there to evacuate the garrison. But he stayed and himself came under siege by the Mahdists. The failure of the relief attempt under Sir Garnet Wolseley (**map right**), bedevilled by complacency and incompetence, caused outrage at home. In the second half of the 19th century Britain was almost continually involved with fighting small colonial wars. Sudan was not finally reconquered until 1898.

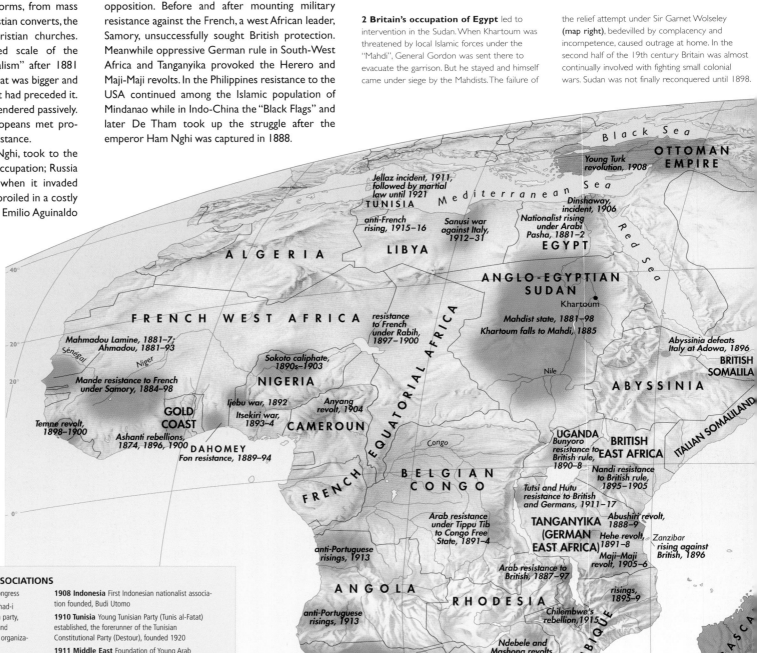

NATIONALIST PARTIES AND ASSOCIATIONS

1885 India Foundation of Indian National Congress

1889 Ottoman empire Ottoman Union (Ittihad-i Osmani), the first organized Turkish opposition party, established; name changed in 1895 to Union and Progress (Ittihat ve Terakki), henceforward the organization of the Young Turk movement

1897 Egypt Egyptian National Party (al-Hizb al-Watani) established, headed by Mustafa Kamil

1905 China Sun Yat-sen founds the secret revolutionary organization T'ung Meng Hui, transformed in 1912 into the Nationalist Party (Kuomintang)

1906 India Foundation of All-India Muslim League

1907 Egypt People's Party (Hizb al-Umma) established, organ of Saad Zaghlul, precursor of the Egyptian nationalist party, the Wafd (1919)

1908 Indonesia First Indonesian nationalist association founded, Budi Utomo

1910 Tunisia Young Tunisian Party (Tunis al-Fatat) established, the forerunner of the Tunisian Constitutional Party (Destour), founded 1920

1911 Middle East Foundation of Young Arab Association (al-Jamiya al-Arabiya al-Fata); headquarters moved to Syria in 1913

1912 Indonesia Foundation of Indonesian nationalist party, the Islamic Association (Sarekat Islam)

1912 South Africa South African National Congress established, later the African National Congress

1913 Vietnam Foundation by Phan Boi Chau of the revolutionary Association for the Restoration of Vietnam (Viet Nam Quang Phuc Hoi)

② *Sep. 1884 Wolseley leaves Cairo (c. 600 miles to the north) for Khartoum relief expedition*

2nd cataract
Sarras
• Wadi Halfa
③ *6 Nov. Wolseley leaves Sarras*

ANGLO-EGYPTIAN SUDAN

⑧ *24 Feb. river column ordered to return to Korti*

3rd cataract

river column • Abu Hamed

• Dongola
Kirbekan
11 Feb. ✕
4th cataract
5th cataract

• Korti
④ *28 Dec. at Korti, Wolseley sends small "flying column" across desert to Metemmeh*
• Berber
• Atbara

② *2 May British forces ordered to leave Sudan*

Abu Klea
17 Jan. ✕
Abu Kru
19 Jan. ✕

⑤ *24 Jan. small reconnaissance force proceeds to Khartoum*
Gumbat ✕ ✕
Metemmeh
21 Jan.

⑦ *28 Jan. flying column arrives; turns back under attack when it is clear the town has fallen*
6th cataract

① *18 Mar. 1884 siege begins*
Khartoum
Blue Nile

⑥ *26 Jan. 1885 Khartoum falls; death of Gordon*
White Nile

2 The attempted relief of Khartoum, 1884–5

Even in areas not under colonial rule, European commercial and political penetration created local instability and provoked anti-Western resistance. In China the disastrous wars with Japan in 1894–5, and the subsequent threat of partition, led to the abortive Hundred Days' Reform of 1898 and, after its failure, the anti-foreign Boxer Rebellion. In Turkey the Russian assault in 1877 and the dismemberment of the Ottoman empire's Balkan territories by the European powers at the Congress of Berlin fanned the patriotism of the Young Turks, who rose in revolution in 1908. In Egypt a revolt led by Arabi against the western-influenced Khedive provoked British occupation in 1882.

Many of these movements were strongly religious in character. Religion offered a powerful language of resistance. The Mahdiyya, which effectively controlled the Sudan from 1881 to 1898, was a Muslim revivalist movement, directed against Egyptians and Europeans alike. Hinduism played a similar role in articulating resistance in India, as did Confucianism in China. Other movements were "proto-nationalist" rather than nationalist in character: the disparate elements they brought together lacked unity and clearly defined objectives.

The consequences of resistance

But if African and Asian armed resistance was ultimately no match for European weaponry, technology and communications, its significance cannot be measured only in terms of its immediate military outcome. For the participants it often had important local political and economic consequences, and there were considerable continuities in rural resistance and in the ideologies of protest between the movements of this period and later anti-colonial opposition.

Even before 1914, "modern" nationalist movements, characterized by the formation of nationalist associations and political parties, were emerging. Many of these were little more than small groups of disaffected intelligentsia whose impact was negligible, but a few, such as the Indonesian Sarekat Islam, quickly gained a mass following. In the First World War, with the European colonial powers simultaneously preoccupied with the war and forced to demand more from their colonies, new impetus was given to this incipient nationalism.

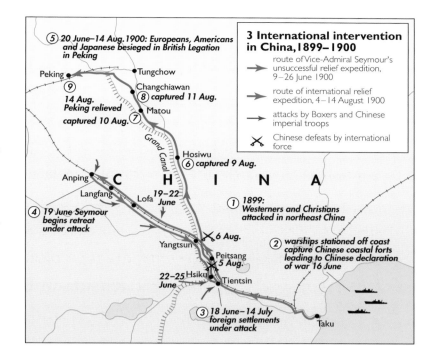

3 International intervention in China, 1899–1900

⑤ *20 June–14 Aug. 1900: Europeans, Americans and Japanese besieged in British Legation in Peking*

→ route of Vice-Admiral Seymour's unsuccessful relief expedition, 9–26 June 1900
→ route of international relief expedition, 4–14 August 1900
→ attacks by Boxers and Chinese imperial troops
✕ Chinese defeats by international force

Peking
• Tungchow
⑨
• Changchiawan
⑧ *captured 11 Aug.*
14 Aug. Peking relieved
• Matou
captured 10 Aug.
⑦
Grand Canal

Hosiwu
⑥ *captured 9 Aug.*

C H I N A

Anping
Langfang
Lofa
19–22 June
④ *19 June Seymour begins retreat under attack*

① *1899: Westerners and Christians attacked in northeast China*

Yangtsun ✕ *6 Aug.*
Peitsang ✕ *5 Aug.*
Hsiku ✕
22–25 June
Tientsin

② *warships stationed off coast capture Chinese coastal forts leading to Chinese declaration of war 16 June*

③ *18 June–14 July foreign settlements under attack*
• Taku

3 Western territorial encroachment provoked a violent uprising in northeast China. By early 1900 the "Boxers" – practitioners of the martial arts who believed themselves to be invulnerable – had won the support of the Imperial court and Christians were attacked and representatives of 11 countries besieged in Peking **(map above)**. Peking was relieved in August at the second attempt as an international force brushed aside the imperial troops and the virtually unarmed Boxers. The uprising had revealed the extent of popular resistance to the foreign presence in China, but in 1901 further concessions had to be made to the Western powers. Such a striking display of impotence by the imperial government could not go unremarked by its subjects.

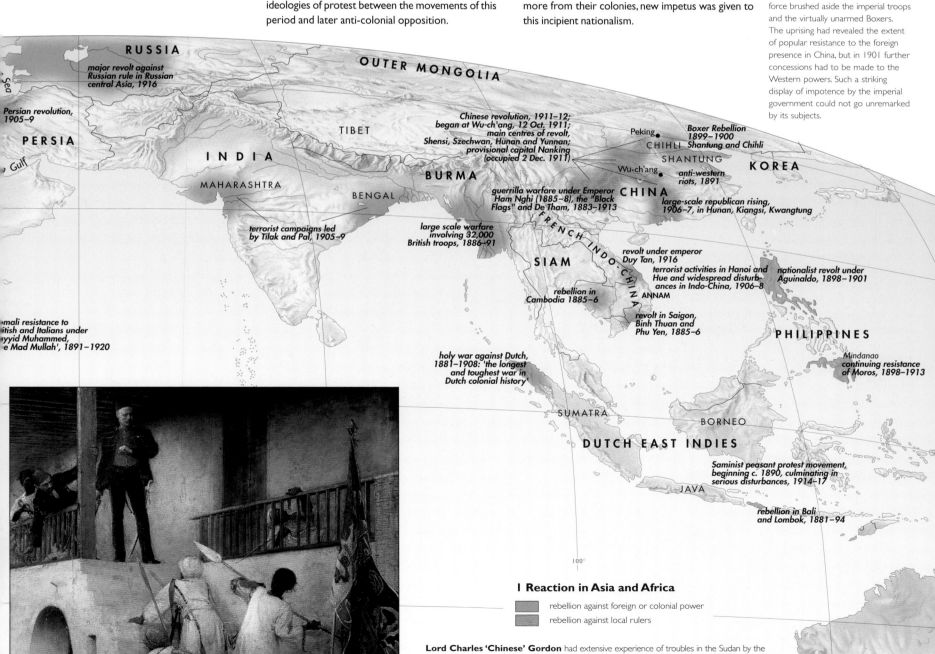

RUSSIA
major revolt against Russian rule in Russian central Asia, 1916

OUTER MONGOLIA

Persian revolution, 1905–9

PERSIA

TIBET
Chinese revolution, 1911–12; began at Wu-ch'ang, 12 Oct. 1911; main centres of revolt, Shensi, Szechwan, Hunan and Yunnan; provisional capital Nanking (occupied 2 Dec. 1911)

Peking •
Boxer Rebellion 1899–1900
CHIHLI *Shantung and Chihli*

INDIA

MAHARASHTRA

BURMA

Wu-ch'ang •
SHANTUNG
KOREA
anti-western riots, 1891

BENGAL
guerrilla warfare under Emperor Ham Nghi (1885–8), the "Black Flags" and De Tham, 1883–1913
CHINA
large-scale republican rising, 1906–7, in Hunan, Kiangsi, Kwangtung

terrorist campaigns led by Tilak and Pal, 1905–9

large scale warfare involving 32,000 British troops, 1886–91

FRENCH INDO-CHINA

SIAM
revolt under emperor Duy Tan, 1916
terrorist activities in Hanoi and Hue and widespread disturbances in Indo-China, 1906–8

nationalist revolt under Aguinaldo, 1898–1901

rebellion in Cambodia 1885–6
ANNAM
revolt in Saigon, Binh Thuan and Phu Yen, 1885–6

PHILIPPINES

...mali resistance to ...itish and Italians under ...yyid Muhammed, ...e Mad Mullah', 1891–1920

holy war against Dutch, 1881–1908: 'the longest and toughest war in Dutch colonial history'

SUMATRA

Mindanao continuing resistance of Moros, 1898–1913

BORNEO

DUTCH EAST INDIES

Saminist peasant protest movement, beginning c. 1890, culminating in serious disturbances, 1914–17

JAVA

rebellion in Bali and Lombok, 1881–94

1 Reaction in Asia and Africa

▮ rebellion against foreign or colonial power
▮ rebellion against local rulers

Lord Charles 'Chinese' Gordon had extensive experience of troubles in the Sudan by the time he was dispatched in 1884 to relieve the Khartoum garrison. A victory over Egyptian forces at El Teb in February 1884 had emboldened the Mahdist forces sweeping through Sudan and by May 1884 Gordon found himself isolated. The relief force was too slow in coming and in February 1885 Khartoum fell to the Mahdi and Gordon was killed. His death, depicted in a romanticized fashion **(left)** made him a Victorian archetype of heroic defiance in the face of overwhelming odds.

European rivalries and alliances

1878	The Congress of Berlin
1879	Austro-German alliance
1884	Berlin conference partitions Africa
1894	Franco-Russian alliance
1904	Anglo-French entente ends colonial rivalry
1905	First Moroccan crisis
1907	Anglo-Russian entente
1908	Bosnian crisis
1912–13	Balkan Wars: Turkey loses bulk of remaining European territory

WHAT ARE THE FUNDAMENTAL MOTIVES THAT EXPLAIN THE PRESENT RIVALRY OF ARMAMENTS IN EUROPE? THEY ARE BASED ON THE UNIVERSAL ASSUMPTION THAT A NATION, IN ORDER TO FIND OUTLETS FOR EXPANDING POPULATION AND INCREASING INDUSTRY, IS NECESSARILY PUSHED TO TERRITORIAL EXPANSION AND THE EXERCISE OF POLITICAL FORCE AGAINST OTHERS; THAT NATIONS BEING COMPETING UNITS, ADVANTAGE, IN THE LAST RESORT, GOES TO THE POSSESSOR OF PREPONDERANT MILITARY FORCE, THE WEAKER GOING TO THE WALL, AS IN OTHER FORMS OF THE STRUGGLE FOR LIFE.

Norman Angell
The Great Illusion, 1909

Under the impact of mass nationalism and economic rivalry, relations between the Great Powers of Europe moved away from the balance-of-power politics practised since 1815 to a system based on rival alliance blocs. Rapid rearmament fuelled a growing tension in Europe which finally exploded in 1914 with the outbreak of the First World War.

IN THE FORTY YEARS before 1914 the major European powers dominated the international order as never before. With military superiority assured, the search for security and economic expansion was expressed through a wave of imperialism and conquest. This sharpened rivalries between the powers and reduced the spirit of collaboration and collective settlement of disputes which had characterized the period since 1815.

Within Europe the traditions of "concert diplomacy" were undermined by the sharp changes in the relative strength of the major players. The rise of Germany and Italy as major powers coincided with the decline of the Habsburg empire and the fatal weakening of the Ottomans. Under Bismarck Germany had played a cautious, even conservative role in Europe. After Bismarck's dismissal in 1890 German leaders began to pursue *Weltpolitik*, a global foreign policy, which brought them into conflict with the established colonial powers.

From the 1890s both Britain and France began a steady rearmament in response to the German threat. Russia, which since 1879 had been party to the League of the Three Emperors with Germany and Austria-Hungary, abandoned its traditional conservatism for an alliance with republican, democratic France, which was signed in 1894. By 1907 Britain had sealed a Triple Entente with them both to resolve colonial tensions.

The weakness of some countries was as much a source of instability as the growing strength of others. The Ottoman empire had been shored up by the Great Powers since 1815 in preference to their allowing any one of them to achieve a dominant position in the Middle East. But from the 1870s Ottoman influence declined sharply. Defeated by Russia in 1876–7 and then forced to grant independence to Romania, Serbia and Bulgaria, Ottoman Turkey found itself threatened all across the Middle East and north Africa.

The Balkan crisis

As Ottoman strength declined the Powers sought to reach agreement to prevent the "Eastern Question" from precipitating a wider crisis. In 1887 Britain, Italy and Austria combined to limit French and Russian encroachments on Turkish territory. In 1897 Russia and Austria agreed to limit their ambitions in the Balkan region and this fragile collaboration lasted until 1908.

No other issue so divided the Powers in the years immediately before 1914 as the future of

the Balkan peninsula. It was the one area of Europe where territorial and political advantage was still to be won as Ottoman imperialism waned. For Russia it had been an axis of advance since at least the 18th century; for Austria-Hungary it was the one region where Habsburg ascendancy could be maintained after defeat in Germany and Italy. When in 1908

2 In October 1912 the Balkan states (Bulgaria Greece, Serbia and Montenegro) drove Turkey from its remaining European territory (**map right**). The Balkan states divided up the spoils between them. In 1913 a second Balkan war broke out between Bulgaria and Serbia, Greece and Turkey, leading to a rapid Bulgarian defeat. Macedonia was divided between Greece and Serbia, leaving an enlarged and ambitious Serb state on the borders of the Habsburg empire.

HMS *Temeraire* (below), depicted on a pre-war postcard. Britain responded to Germany's increased warship building after 1900 with a rival programme based on the most modern Dreadnought battleships. The Royal Navy was fully mobilized for exercises at the outbreak of war.

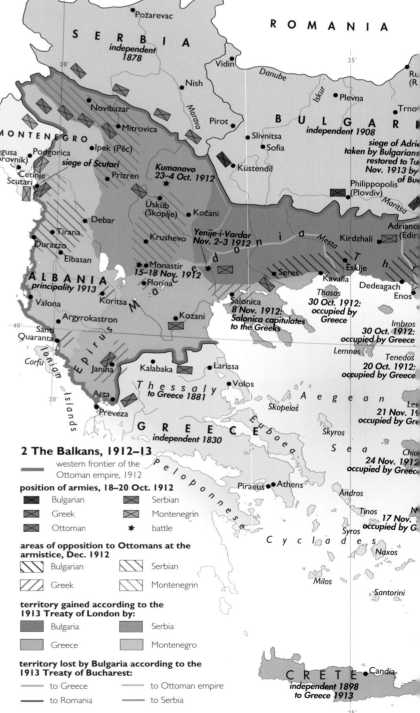

2 The Balkans, 1912–13

western frontier of the Ottoman empire, 1912

position of armies, 18–20 Oct. 1912

◨	Bulgarian	⊠	Serbian
⊠	Greek	⊠	Montenegrin
⊠	Ottoman	✱	battle

areas of opposition to Ottomans at the armistice, Dec. 1912

▨	Bulgarian	▧	Serbian
▨	Greek	▨	Montenegrin

territory gained according to the 1913 Treaty of London by:

	Bulgaria		Serbia
	Greece		Montenegro

territory lost by Bulgaria according to the 1913 Treaty of Bucharest:

—	to Greece	—	to Ottoman empire
—	to Romania	—	to Serbia

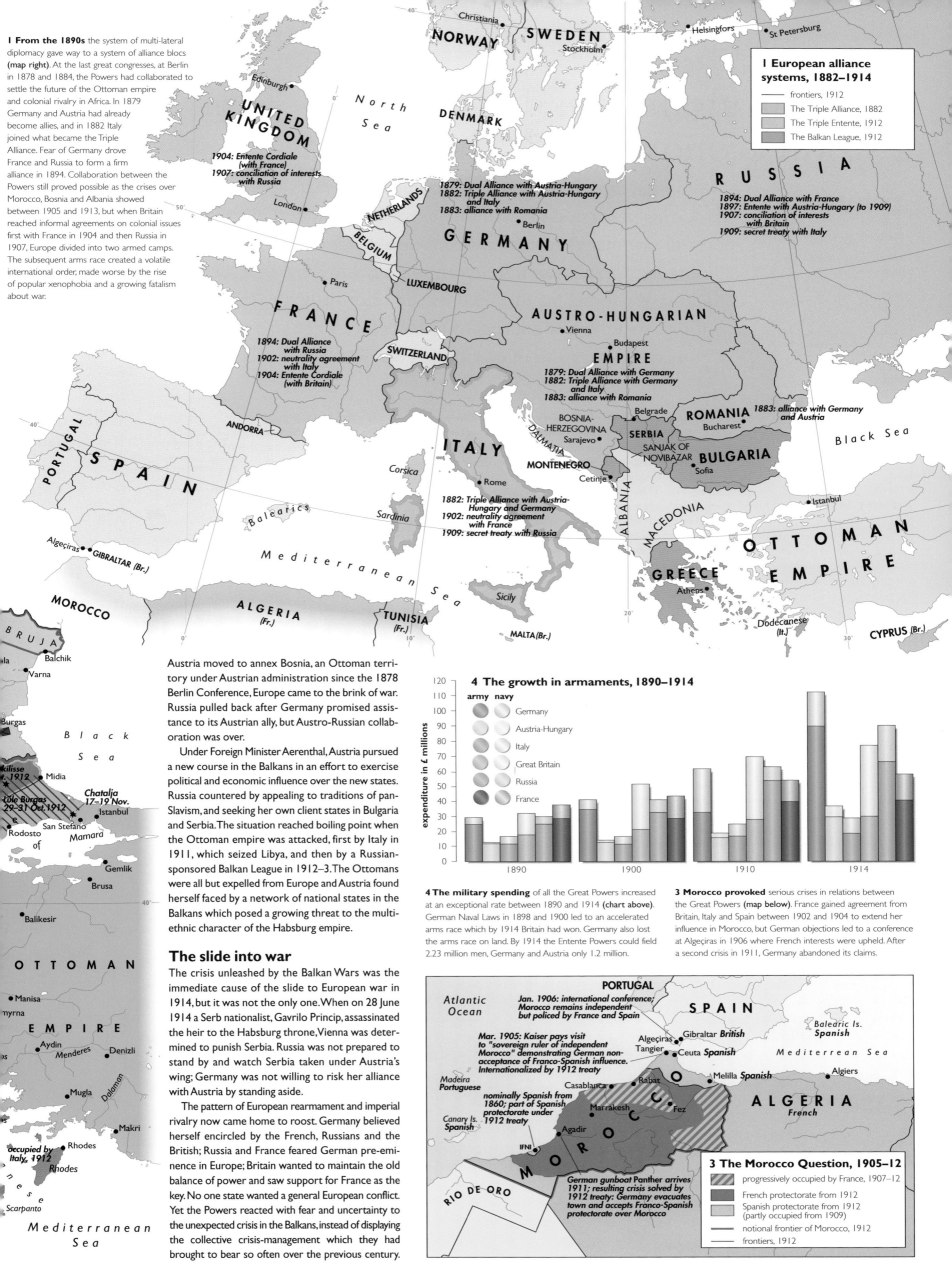

1 From the 1890s the system of multi-lateral diplomacy gave way to a system of alliance blocs **(map right)**. At the last great congresses, at Berlin in 1878 and 1884, the Powers had collaborated to settle the future of the Ottoman empire and colonial rivalry in Africa. In 1879 Germany and Austria had already become allies, and in 1882 Italy joined what became the Triple Alliance. Fear of Germany drove France and Russia to form a firm alliance in 1894. Collaboration between the Powers still proved possible as the crises over Morocco, Bosnia and Albania showed between 1905 and 1913, but when Britain reached informal agreements on colonial issues first with France in 1904 and then Russia in 1907, Europe divided into two armed camps. The subsequent arms race created a volatile international order, made worse by the rise of popular xenophobia and a growing fatalism about war.

1 European alliance systems, 1882–1914

— frontiers, 1912

The Triple Alliance, 1882
The Triple Entente, 1912
The Balkan League, 1912

1904: Entente Cordiale (with France)
1907: conciliation of interests with Russia

1879: Dual Alliance with Austria-Hungary
1882: Triple Alliance with Austria-Hungary and Italy
1883: alliance with Romania

1894: Dual Alliance with France
1897: Entente with Austria-Hungary (to 1909)
1907: conciliation of interests with Britain
1909: secret treaty with Italy

1894: Dual Alliance with Russia
1902: neutrality agreement with Italy
1904: Entente Cordiale (with Britain)

1879: Dual Alliance with Germany
1882: Triple Alliance with Germany and Italy
1883: alliance with Romania

1883: alliance with Germany and Austria

1882: Triple Alliance with Austria-Hungary and Germany
1902: neutrality agreement with France
1909: secret treaty with Russia

Chatalja 17–19 Nov.

Lüle Burgas 29–31 Oct. 1912

occupied by Italy, 1912

Austria moved to annex Bosnia, an Ottoman territory under Austrian administration since the 1878 Berlin Conference, Europe came to the brink of war. Russia pulled back after Germany promised assistance to its Austrian ally, but Austro-Russian collaboration was over.

Under Foreign Minister Aerenthal, Austria pursued a new course in the Balkans in an effort to exercise political and economic influence over the new states. Russia countered by appealing to traditions of pan-Slavism, and seeking her own client states in Bulgaria and Serbia. The situation reached boiling point when the Ottoman empire was attacked, first by Italy in 1911, which seized Libya, and then by a Russian-sponsored Balkan League in 1912–3. The Ottomans were all but expelled from Europe and Austria found herself faced by a network of national states in the Balkans which posed a growing threat to the multi-ethnic character of the Habsburg empire.

The slide into war

The crisis unleashed by the Balkan Wars was the immediate cause of the slide to European war in 1914, but it was not the only one. When on 28 June 1914 a Serb nationalist, Gavrilo Princip, assassinated the heir to the Habsburg throne, Vienna was determined to punish Serbia. Russia was not prepared to stand by and watch Serbia taken under Austria's wing; Germany was not willing to risk her alliance with Austria by standing aside.

The pattern of European rearmament and imperial rivalry now came home to roost. Germany believed herself encircled by the French, Russians and the British; Russia and France feared German pre-eminence in Europe; Britain wanted to maintain the old balance of power and saw support for France as the key. No one state wanted a general European conflict. Yet the Powers reacted with fear and uncertainty to the unexpected crisis in the Balkans, instead of displaying the collective crisis-management which they had brought to bear so often over the previous century.

4 The growth in armaments, 1890–1914

army navy

Germany
Austria-Hungary
Italy
Great Britain
Russia
France

expenditure in £ millions

1890   1900   1910   1914

4 The military spending of all the Great Powers increased at an exceptional rate between 1890 and 1914 **(chart above)**. German Naval Laws in 1898 and 1900 led to an accelerated arms race which by 1914 Britain had won. Germany also lost the arms race on land. By 1914 the Entente Powers could field 2.23 million men, Germany and Austria only 1.2 million.

3 Morocco provoked serious crises in relations between the Great Powers **(map below)**. France gained agreement from Britain, Italy and Spain between 1902 and 1904 to extend her influence in Morocco, but German objections led to a conference at Algeçiras in 1906 where French interests were upheld. After a second crisis in 1911, Germany abandoned its claims.

Jan. 1906: international conference; Morocco remains independent but policed by France and Spain

Mar. 1905: Kaiser pays visit to "sovereign ruler of independent Morocco" demonstrating German non-acceptance of Franco-Spanish influence. Internationalized by 1912 treaty.

nominally Spanish from 1860; part of Spanish protectorate under 1912 treaty

German gunboat Panther arrives 1911; resulting crisis solved by 1912 treaty: Germany evacuates town and accepts Franco-Spanish protectorate over Morocco

3 The Morocco Question, 1905–12

progressively occupied by France, 1907–12
French protectorate from 1912
Spanish protectorate from 1912 (partly occupied from 1909)
notional frontier of Morocco, 1912
frontiers, 1912

The formation of a world economy

In the last third of the 19th century international trade, migration and capital flows expanded rapidly. Food and raw materials were now produced worldwide using European wealth. In return came a flow of industrial goods. This market operated informally, without state regulation. The 40 years before 1914 marked the zenith of economic liberalism.

IN THOSE DAYS WHEN YOU LEFT THE SHORES OF EUROPE YOU ENTERED A KIND OF MERCANTILE REPUBLIC. ECONOMIC MANAGEMENT ON A WORLDWIDE BASIS ACTUALLY EXISTED. EUROPE DEVISED IT AND EUROPE LARGELY BENEFITED BY IT. ONE COULD RELY ON A GENERAL STABILITY IN ALMOST EVERYTHING.

Andre Siegfried (1875–1959), French economist

THE 40 YEARS BEFORE the First World War witnessed a remarkable flowering of worldwide commerce, which in turn led to the establishment of an integrated and interdependent global economy. The creation of this world market derived from the economic expansion of Europe and North America, the wealthiest and most technically advanced areas of the world by 1870. Their search for markets and for new sources of raw materials and cheap food produced a restless economic imperialism at the expense of traditional native economies.

The transport revolution

To a large extent, this growth was governed by the spread of modern communications. The most significant development was the expansion of world shipping following the development of steamships. In 1850 most of the world's tonnage consisted of sailing ships; by 1914 only 8 per cent was still powered by sail. Between 1870 and 1910 European steam tonnage expanded from 1.5 million tons to over 19 million. Steam travel was faster, safer and allowed for much larger ships and cargoes. The average British steamship in 1914 was ten times the size of the average sailing ship in 1850.

There was also a remarkable expansion of the world rail network after 1870. While Europe possessed 97,200km (60,400 miles) of track in 1870 and the USA and Canada 90,600 (56,300), the rest of the world had only 14,650 (9100). By 1911 this had grown to 281,500km (175,000 miles). The American continent was first crossed by rail in 1869 and Canada in 1886, while the Russian empire completed the Trans-Siberian railway in 1904. Railways were essential in providing Europe with easy access to new sources of materials and food in the wider world.

The railway and the steamship also revolutionized commerce throughout the southern hemisphere.

The development of effective means of refrigeration allowed meat, fruit and dairy produce to be sent across the equator to European customers. The first refrigerated cargo reached London from Australia in 1880. By the 1890s ships capable of carrying 150,000 frozen carcasses had been developed.

World commerce and banking

This revolution in transport produced an exceptional expansion of world trade. Between 1880 and 1913 the value of the world's imports and exports increased almost six-fold, from $7 billion to $40 billion. Europe dominated foreign trade, accounting for 57 per cent in 1913, of which Britain provided over one-quarter. But Europe's trade was overwhelmingly with other European states. The significant change since 1870 was the rising share of wider global trade, particularly inter-American trade and Japanese trade with Asia.

Trade expansion was closely linked with the development of foreign investment from Europe and America. The lead was taken by the world's wealthiest states, Britain and France. By 1914 they had invested the equivalent of 25 per cent and 15 per cent respectively of their national wealth abroad.

I Between 1870 and 1914 a genuinely global economy developed **(map right)**. A transport and communications revolution was fundamental to this new global economic boom. Shipping routes and telegraph lines linked continents; railways linked interiors to ports. Finance from Europe and the USA helped to fuel economic activity worldwide while world trade was helped, too, by the adoption of the Gold Standard and the development of an international banking network. Trade between European states and their overseas empires played a major role for Britain, France, Belgium and the Netherlands.

The Kaiser-Wilhelm dock in Hamburg c. 1900. Hamburg grew rapidly in the late 19th century, exporting the goods of central Europe worldwide and receiving a stream of colonial products in return. By 1914 one-quarter of the German workforce derived its livelihood from exports.

I The development of the world economy

foreign investment, 1914 (in $ million)

| 535 | United Kingdom | 420 | United States |
| 3180 | France | 1050 | Germany |

—— busiest shipping routes

—— other major shipping routes, c. 1900

—— international telegraph cables

Colonial empires in 1900

Belgian		Japanese	
British		Ottoman	
Danish		Portuguese	
Dutch		Russian	
French		Spanish	
German		USA	
Italian		other countries	

2 Average tariffs on industrial goods, 1914

United Kingdom	0%
Holland	4%
Switzerland	9%
Belgium	9%
Germany	13%
Denmark	14%
Austria-Hungary	18%
Italy	18%
France	20%
Sweden	20%
Russia	38%
Spain	41%

2 Though Britain encouraged freer trade in the 19th century, from the 1870s other states found that competition from Britain forced them to protect their trade by means of tariffs (chart above).

3 The opening of the Suez and Panama canals transformed world trade: journey times were dramatically cut and the dangerous routes around the Cape Horn and the Cape of Good Hope eliminated (charts right).

3 The Suez and Panama canals: journey times

Suez canal

London	via Cape 10,667 nautical miles / via Suez 6,274 nautical miles	41% saved	to Bombay
London	via Cape 11,900 nautical miles / via Suez 8,083 nautical miles	32% saved	to Calcutta
London	via Cape 11,740 nautical miles / via Suez 8,362 nautical miles	29% saved	to Singapore
London	via Cape 13,180 nautical miles / via Suez 9,799 nautical miles	26% saved	to Hong Kong

Panama canal

Liverpool	via Magellan 13,502 nautical miles / via Panama 7,836 nautical miles	42% saved	to San Francisco
New York	via Magellan 13,135 nautical miles / via Panama 5,262 nt. mls.	60% saved	to San Francisco
Liverpool	via Magellan 8,747 nautical miles / via Panama 7,207 nautical miles	18% saved	to Valparaiso
New York	via Magellan 8,385 nautical miles / via Panama 4,633 nautical miles	45% saved	to Valparaiso
New York	via Magellan 16,579 nautical miles / via Panama 11,530 nautical miles	30% saved	to Hong Kong
New York	via Magellan 13,000 nautical miles / via Panama 9,332 nautical miles	29% saved	to Sydney

Much of this money went to the USA and the settler colonies where it was used to promote railway building, farming and mining.

The rapid expansion of trade also raised issues of payment. From the 1860s, encouraged by the British example, most major states came to adopt the common Gold Standard against which their currencies could be valued. This was made possible by a great increase in gold production following discoveries in the USA in 1848, Australia in 1851 and South Africa in 1886. During the 1870s most European states adopted a Gold Standard. Japan followed in 1886, India in 1892, Russia in 1895–7 and the USA in 1900. The core measurement became the British pound, fixed at 113 grains of gold. The result was long-term stability in exchange rates and prices.

The regulation of commerce relied largely on the City of London, which became the world's financial and commercial centre in the half century before 1914, confidently exporting the virtues of free enterprise and economic liberalism. The growth of world trade and investment benefited the developed economies very substantially. Their share of world income in 1860 was 44 per cent; by 1913 it was 60.4 per cent. Though earnings in the developed world grew steadily, in the areas opened up by Europe and America they remained low, while native industries were often undermined by foreign imports. Only Japan succeeded in adopting modern technology and enterprise without becoming an economic satellite of the richer economies. Elsewhere local elites largely came to depend for their wealth and power on their links with the new world market, a relationship which in time provoked popular political resistance.

4 The rapid increase in the size and speed of Atlantic liners (chart below) was the result of the enormously improved efficiency of the new steam engines and of the greatly increased demand for travel. The fastest crossing times decreased from almost nine days in 1874 to just over four days in 1904.

4 The *Britannic* and *Mauretania*

	date	tonnage	length (metric/imperial)	indicated horse power	fuel consumption (tons per day)	speed (knots)	passengers	time to cross Atlantic
Britannic	1874	5,004	139/455	5,500	75	16	1,100	8 days 20 hours
Mauretania	1907	31,938	241/792	70,000	1,000	25	2,000	4 days 10 hours

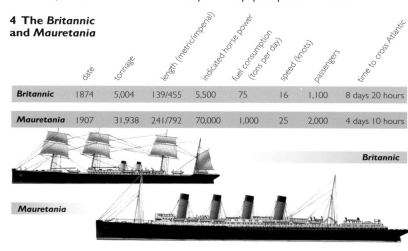

5 Foreign investment, 1914 (mill. of US dollars)

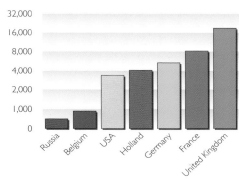

Russia	
Belgium	
USA	
Holland	
Germany	
France	
United Kingdom	

5 Though its relative lead may have been declining, by 1914 British investment overseas was still twice as great as that of France, its nearest competitor and more than five times as great as that of the USA (chart left).

6 The period between 1860 and 1914 was one of remarkable price stability in which economies grew rapidly (chart below). The main beneficiaries were in Europe and the USA, which between them had two-thirds of the world's income in 1914.

6 Distribution of world income, 1860 and 1913

	1860 aggregate income ($ millions)	%	1913 aggregate income ($ millions)	%
North America	14,400	14.8	100,300	32.0
Oceania	500	0.5	4,100	1.4
Northwest Europe	28,500	20.4	84,000	27.5
Russia	7,000	7.0	22,500	7.4
Southeast Europe	9,500	9.7	26,000	8.5
Latin America	3,700	4.0	13,300	4.1
Japan	1,300	1.6	4,600	1.5
Near East	–	–	–	–
Far East	1,300	1.4	5,700	1.8
Central Africa	–	–	–	–
Southeast Asia	11,500	11.8	21,000	6.9
China	19,500	19.8	24,000	8.0
Total	95,900	100.0	304,800	100.0

The First World War

In 1914, for the first time since the Napoleonic wars, most of Europe was convulsed by warfare. Expected to be short, the conflict became a long and bloody "total war", mobilizing civilians as well as soldiers and killing millions. By 1918, the war had become a global conflict. Its legacy was economic dislocation, political violence and heightened nationalism.

WHEN ARCHDUKE FRANZ Ferdinand, heir to the Habsburg throne, and his wife were shot by Serb nationalists in Sarajevo on 28 June 1914, few Europeans expected the major powers to be locked in war within five weeks. Yet deeper fears for the balance of power and the preservation of national interest turned a minor incident into a diplomatic crisis. Once Austria-Hungary had decided to punish Serbia for the outrage it proved impossible to contain the conflict. German support for Austria and Russian support for Serbia created an explosive confrontation in which neither side would give way. When Austria invaded Serbia in late July, the two European blocs found themselves within a week fighting the first major European war since 1815.

Stalemate

Neither side thought the war would last more than six months. Germany expected to be able to quickly conquer Belgium and France – the Schlieffen Plan – by sweeping round Paris and encircling French troops before swinging its forces east to confront the more slowly mobilizing Russian army. But the decision to hold forces in reserve in the industrial regions of Alsace-Lorraine and the Saar reduced the number of troops available and the weakened German offensive was blunted by Anglo-French forces on the

3 The war was fought between the Central Powers – Germany, Austria-Hungary, Bulgaria and the Ottomans – and the Allies – the British, Russian, French and Japanese empires (map below). Italy joined the Allies in 1915; Romania, Greece and the USA also later joined them. Almost 70 million were mobilized, more than 9 million were killed, millions more were maimed or psychologically scarred.

Marne between 5 and 8 September. By November both sides had dug in along a 650km (400-mile) front from the English Channel to Switzerland. Behind a tangle of barbed wire, machine-guns and artillery each side confronted the other for almost four years of attritional warfare.

The war in the east

In the east the war was at first more mobile. The Russians pushed back German and Austro-Hungarian armies at Gumbinnen and Lemberg. Then, at the end of August, German forces defeated the Russians at Tannenberg and the Masurian Lakes. But trapped in a two-front war, Germany never had sufficient resources to consolidate its victories in the east. Elsewhere, the Central Powers found a decisive breakthrough similarly elusive. When Italy opened up a front against the Central Powers in 1915, Austro-Hungarian forces were stretched to the limit until German intervention helped crush the Italians at Caporetto in 1917. The conquest, with Bulgarian help, of Romania and Serbia by Austrian and German forces in 1916 was balanced by the Russian Brusilov offensive in June. The real breakthrough in the east for the Central Powers came with the overthrow of Russia's tsarist regime in February 1917, precipitating Russia's withdrawal from the war. In March 1918 the Treaty of Brest-Litovsk ended the war against Russia, allowing Germany to concentrate its efforts in the west.

Both sides had repeatedly tried to break the stalemate on the Western Front, launching offensives at terrible cost. In February 1916 German forces tried to seize the French fortress of Verdun with no greater strategic object than to bleed the enemy white. More

than 600,000 died. Verdun was saved in July 1916 by a British offensive on the Somme but at the cost of over 400,000 British casualties. By 1917, the constant blood-letting had produced protests. French units mutinied until concessions were granted; the German parliament passed a Peace Resolution to force the military to seek an honourable settlement. But by then Germany was under the virtual military dictatorship of Field Marshal Hindenburg and General Ludendorff, both determined on victory in what was now seen as a "total war". In February 1917 the German government authorized unrestricted submarine warfare to combat the Allied naval blockade. Outraged, in April the USA joined the war on the Allied side.

Victory in the west

The US decision to fight not only created a real world war, it tipped the balance against the Central Powers. America loaned over $10 billion to its allies and sent much equipment and food. In March 1918 Ludendorff gambled on a last offensive. German forces broke through towards Paris until, exhausted and short of weapons, they ground to a halt. With clear superiority in arms, the Allies pushed German and Austrian forces back in France and Italy. In September, Ludendorff sued for peace. When granted, on 11 November, Austria, Turkey and Bulgaria were already beaten. A prostrate Germany and revolution in Russia transformed Europe and led to an age of violent social unrest.

Sep. 1914 First Battle of the Marne

1915 Italy enters war on the side of the Allies

1916 Siege of Verdun leaves 600,000 dead

June 1916 Battle of the Somme fails to break German line

1917 German Navy begins unrestricted submarine warfare

1917 USA enters war on Allied side

Mar. 1918 Treaty of Brest-Litovsk ends war on Eastern Front

May 1918 German "Spring Offensive" halted

Sep. 1918 Germans sue for armistice

Nov. 1918 Armistice on 11 Nov. ends the war

1 The Great War in Europe 1914–18

- Allied Powers
- Central Powers
- major Allied Power offensive
- major Central Power offensive
- ★ battles
- ★ battles costing over 250,000 killed
- ⊤ naval mutinies
- army mutinies
- ⊥ naval bases
- ✳ major naval battle
- German raids on English coast

all battles, offensives, mutinies etc. coloured according to year

- 1914
- 1915
- 1916
- 1917
- 1918

- – – farthest German advance in West, 1914
- —— trench line, November 1914
- – – – farthest Russian advance in east, 1914–15
- —— Russian front, November 1915
- territory held by Central Powers, December 1917
- —— front line at time of Brest-Litovsk armistice between Germany and Russia, December 1917
- – – – German penetration of Russia, March 1918
- —— armistice line in West, November 1918

1 The war in Europe was fought on four fronts, but most resources were concentrated on the Western and Eastern fronts (map above right). In the west the superiority of defensive systems led to a static war of attrition dominated by the machine-gun and the artillery barrage. In the

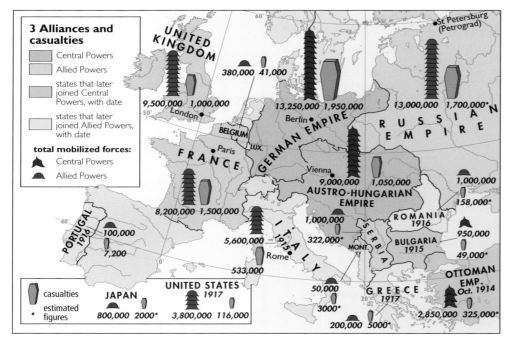

3 Alliances and casualties

- Central Powers
- Allied Powers
- states that later joined Central Powers, with date
- states that later joined Allied Powers, with date

total mobilized forces:
- Central Powers
- Allied Powers

UNITED KINGDOM
St Petersburg (Petrograd)
380,000 41,000
9,500,000 1,000,000   London ●
BELGIUM   Berlin ●   GERMAN EMPIRE   13,250,000 1,950,000   RUSSIAN EMPIRE   13,000,000 1,700,000*
FRANCE   LUX.   Paris ●
Vienna ●
AUSTRO-HUNGARIAN EMPIRE   9,000,000 1,050,000   1,000,000
8,200,000 1,500,000   1,000,000   158,000*
ROMANIA 1916
PORTUGAL 1916   ITALY 1915   322,000*   950,000
100,000   5,600,000   MONT.   SERBIA   BULGARIA 1915   49,000*
7,200   Rome ●   533,000   GREECE 1917   OTTOMAN EMP. Oct. 1914
50,000
3000*   2,850,000 325,000*
UNITED STATES 1917   200,000 5000*
JAPAN   800,000 2000*   3,800,000 116,000

- casualties
- ● estimated figures

On most fighting fronts soldiers' lives were dominated by the trench (above). Conditions were at their worst on the Western Front. Prey to disease, living in damp, poorly ventilated bunkers, constantly shelled and occasionally gassed, the soldier's life was cheerless and brutal.

Lisbon ● Togus
PORTUG
Cad
Gibr (Br.)

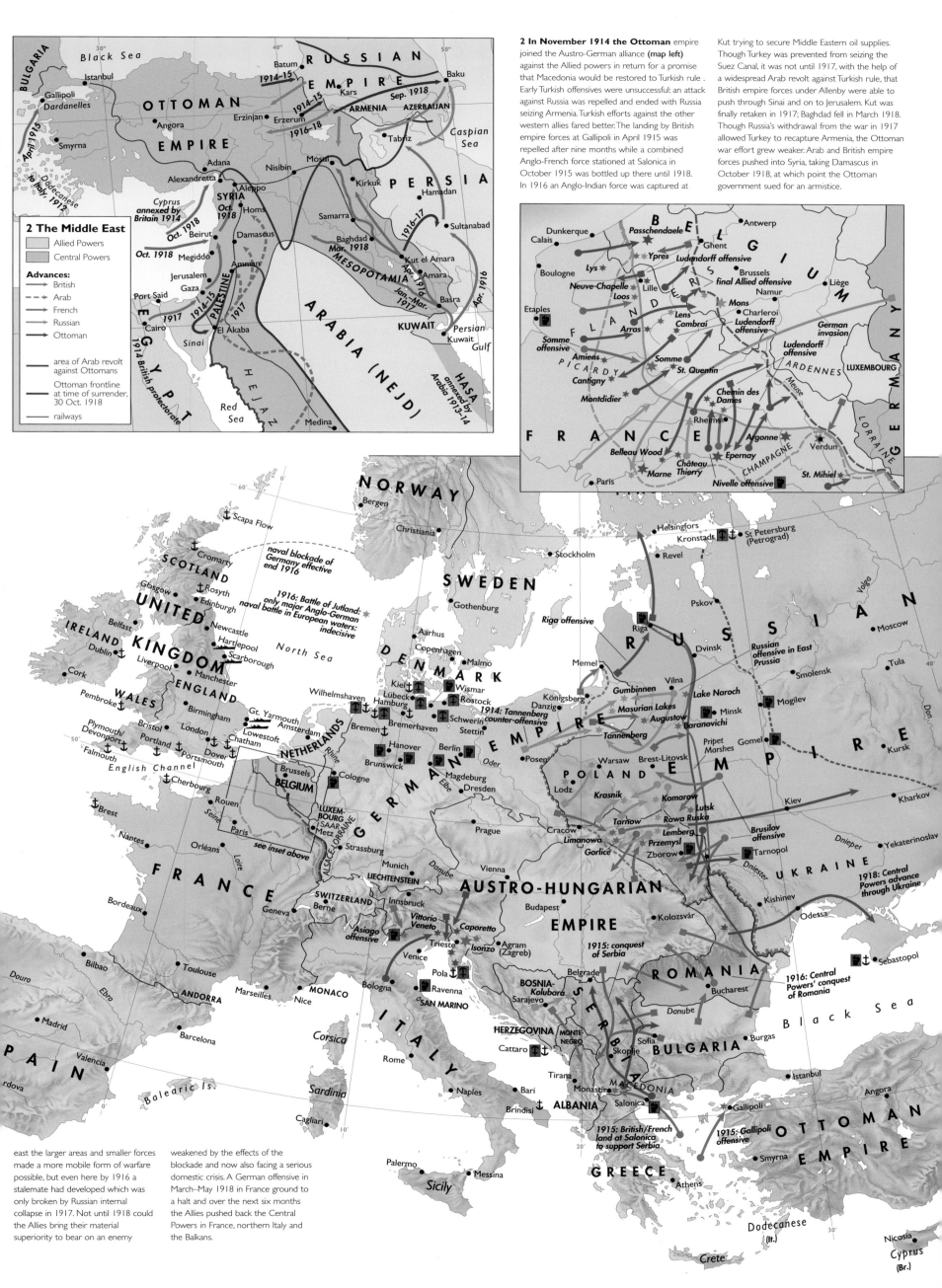

see inset above

2 In November 1914 the Ottoman empire joined the Austro-German alliance **(map left)** against the Allied powers in return for a promise that Macedonia would be restored to Turkish rule . Early Turkish offensives were unsuccessful: an attack against Russia was repelled and ended with Russia seizing Armenia. Turkish efforts against the other western allies fared better. The landing by British empire forces at Gallipoli in April 1915 was repelled after nine months while a combined Anglo-French force stationed at Salonica in October 1915 was bottled up there until 1918. In 1916 an Anglo-Indian force was captured at Kut trying to secure Middle Eastern oil supplies. Though Turkey was prevented from seizing the Suez Canal, it was not until 1917, with the help of a widespread Arab revolt against Turkish rule, that British empire forces under Allenby were able to push through Sinai and on to Jerusalem. Kut was finally retaken in 1917; Baghdad fell in March 1918. Though Russia's withdrawal from the war in 1917 allowed Turkey to recapture Armenia, the Ottoman war effort grew weaker. Arab and British empire forces pushed into Syria, taking Damascus in October 1918, at which point the Ottoman government sued for an armistice.

2 The Middle East

Allied Powers
Central Powers

Advances:
→ British
--→ Arab
→ French
→ Russian
→ Ottoman

— area of Arab revolt against Ottomans

— Ottoman frontline at time of surrender, 30 Oct. 1918

— railways

east the larger areas and smaller forces made a more mobile form of warfare possible, but even here by 1916 a stalemate had developed which was only broken by Russian internal collapse in 1917. Not until 1918 could the Allies bring their material superiority to bear on an enemy weakened by the effects of the blockade and now also facing a serious domestic crisis. A German offensive in March–May 1918 in France ground to a halt and over the next six months the Allies pushed back the Central Powers in France, northern Italy and the Balkans.

7 THE AGE OF GLOBAL CIVILIZATION

THE DATE AT WHICH THE EUROPEAN age gave way to the age of global civilization is a matter of debate. Some historians have picked out 1917 as a year of destiny. Others have seen 1947, the year of Indian independence, and 1949, the year of the Chinese revolution, as the decisive turning points. Certainly, America's declaration of war in 1917 turned a European conflict into a world war while the Bolshevik revolution in Russia split the world into two conflicting ideological camps. Similarly, the independence of India and the revolution in China symbolized the resurgence of Asia and the gathering revolt against the West.

Today it is obvious that we live in a post-European age. By making the world one, the European powers stirred up forces which spelled their own eclipse. The world wars between 1914 and 1945 whittled away the resources of the European powers, and only the healing of the wounds, in acts such as the formation of the European Economic Community in 1957, restored their fortunes. Europe's exhaustion after 1945 benefitted the

Soviet Union and the USA, the two superpowers on the eastern and western flanks, whose rivalry produced an age of bipolarity. But bipolarity, too, proved to be a temporary phenomenon. The recovery of Europe, the emancipation of Asia and Africa, the rise of Japan and finally the collapse of the Soviet empire brought a new constellation into being, and with it the threat of confrontation between rich and poor nations and of the exhaustion of global resources through overpopulation. The world is now dominated by a single major power – the USA – whose massive economic and military strength is challenged by a new wave of anti-Western violence not unlike the reaction that eventually undermined the age of European empire.

PUDONG SKYLINE, SHANGHAI, CHINA.

The Russian revolution

The architect of the October Revolution was the lawyer-turned-revolutionary Lenin (**far right**). Leader of the Bolsheviks in Russia since 1903, Lenin was a convinced Marxist who saw the collapse of the tsarist monarchy as the signal for worldwide communist revolution.

2 The Bolsheviks were convinced that their revolution would be the signal for a European revolt against the old imperialist order. At the end of the war communism surfaced in Hungary, Germany and other areas of eastern Europe, and social unrest was widespread in the west (**map below**). But the revolution was bloodily suppressed outside Russia, leaving the new revolutionary state dangerously isolated by 1921.

In 1917 the Russian monarchy collapsed. For eight months liberals and moderate social democrats tried to set up a parliamentary regime, but in October radical communists under Lenin seized power and established a dictatorship which survived military intervention, civil war and economic crisis to forge the world's first communist state, the Soviet Union.

THE TSARIST SYSTEM in Russia was faced with intolerable strains by the First World War. While Nicholas II did little to dispel hostility to his regime, the war effort went from bad to worse. Land was left untilled, the cities went hungry. The railway system threatened to collapse, towns were swamped with new workers who could not be adequately paid or housed. In February 1917 there were strikes and demonstrations in Petrograd. The army withdrew support from the tsar, and the Duma (parliament) called for a new order. In the face of the revolution, Nicholas abdicated. He was succeeded by a Provisional Government under the liberal Prince Lvov.

The second revolution

The first revolution in February solved none of Russia's problems. The Provisional Government had to work with a system of "Dual Power", which it exercised with the Petrograd Soviet, an elected assembly representing workers and soldiers in the capital. A constitution was promised but constantly delayed and the economic situation deteriorated sharply. Soviets sprang up all over Russia, claiming to be the authentic voice of the people. When the war could not be

continued effectively, the clamour for change pushed the population towards a more radical solution.

The main beneficiaries were the Social Revolutionaries and the Bolsheviks (Marxist Social-Democrats). In May a mainly socialist government was appointed under the leadership of a Social Revolutionary, Kerensky, but he was unable to stem the radical tide. By October land had been seized by the peasantry, the cities were in chaos, the authority of the government a hollow sham. The Bolshevik leader, Lenin, called for a second, communist revolution, and when Bolsheviks stormed the government building on 25 October 1917, resistance crumbled. The Bolsheviks seized power and established an emergency dictatorship.

Civil war

Bolshevik power extended only over the heartland of Russia; the rest of the empire broke into a series of smaller national states. On the fringes anti-Bolshevik forces gathered to destroy Russian socialism. After the new regime had agreed to end Russian participation in the First World War at Brest-Litovsk in March 1918, the Bolsheviks fought a three-year civil war against the "White" counter-revolutionary armies, foreign forces sent to crush the revolution, and armed nationalist movements in the Ukraine, the Baltic states and the Caucasus.

A period of extraordinary confusion followed. By organizing a war effort on lines even more authoritarian than the tsar's, the Bolsheviks defeated one enemy after another. By 1920 the civil war was over, and by 1922, when the new state of the USSR was established, its power extended over the Ukraine, the far eastern territories and the Caucasus. In 1921 the regime allowed private trade and farming under the New Economic Policy, but the political system stayed a tight Party dictatorship. During the 1920s an uneasy social peace reigned, but the issue of how to establish an industrial state in a peasant-based society had only been postponed. Under Stalin, General Secretary from 1922, the problem of modernizing Russia was addressed in 1928 in a savage "revolution from above".

3 The Bolshevik message appealed much more to peasants than to workers, and the revolution spread rapidly across central Asia and into China, where a communist party was established in 1921 (**map below**). Autonomous communist states were set up in the east but, except for Mongolia, they were brought into the Soviet Union when it was established in 1922 as a federation of Bolshevik-dominated socialist republics.

3 Red Star over Asia

- Bolshevik held, Aug. 1918
- USSR Oct. 1922
- nominally independent communist states from 1920 (with date of incorporation into USSR)
- other nominally independent communist states, (with dates of Bolshevik control)
- Trans-Siberian and Trans-Caspian railways
- limit of temporary Japanese occupation during Russian civil war
- frontiers, 1921

2 Red Star over Europe

- Bolshevik held, end October 1918
- added to Bolshevik control by 1921
- temporary communist control, 1918–20
- **24 Feb. 1919** date communist government declared
- states where communist-led or inspired uprisings took place, with date **(1923)**
- post-settlement frontiers

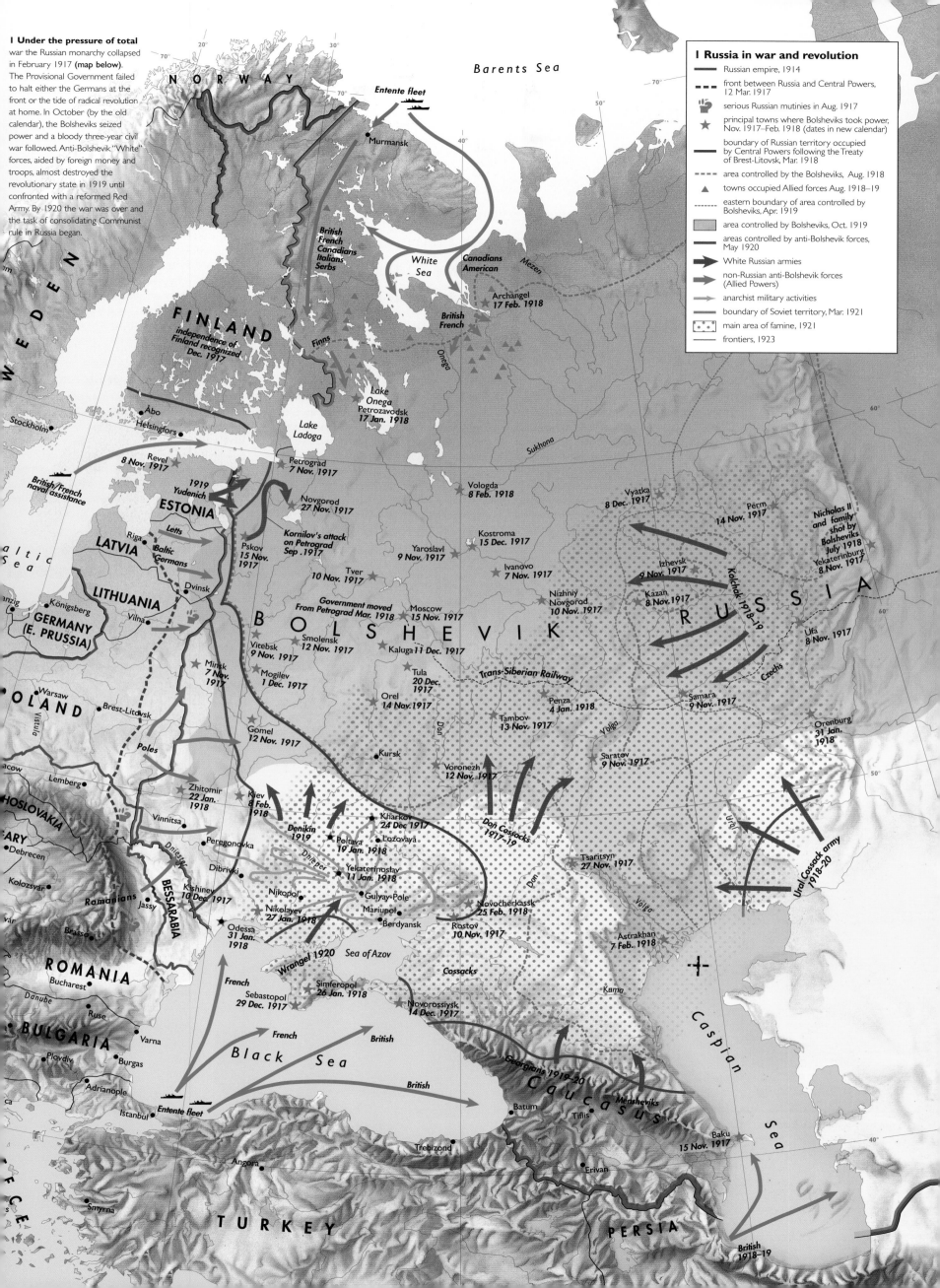

1 Under the pressure of total war the Russian monarchy collapsed in February 1917 (**map below**). The Provisional Government failed to halt either the Germans at the front or the tide of radical revolution at home. In October (by the old calendar), the Bolsheviks seized power and a bloody three-year civil war followed. Anti-Bolshevik "White" forces, aided by foreign money and troops, almost destroyed the revolutionary state in 1919 until confronted with a reformed Red Army. By 1920 the war was over and the task of consolidating Communist rule in Russia began.

Barents Sea

NORWAY

Entente fleet

Murmansk

White Sea

Canadians American

British French Canadians Italians Serbs

Archangel 17 Feb. 1918

British French

FINLAND
independence of Finland recognized Dec. 1917

Finns

Mezen

Onega

Lake Onega Petrozavodsk 17 Jan. 1918

Lake Ladoga

Sukhona

SWEDEN

Åbo

Stockholm

Helsingfors

British/French naval assistance

Revel 8 Nov. 1917

1919 Yudenich

ESTONIA

LATVIA

Riga

Letts

Baltic Germans

Dvinsk

LITHUANIA

Vilna

Königsberg

GERMANY (E. PRUSSIA)

Danzig

Petrograd 7 Nov. 1917

Novgorod 27 Nov. 1917

Pskov 15 Nov. 1917

Kornilov's attack on Petrograd Sep. 1917

Tver 10 Nov. 1917

Vologda 8 Feb. 1918

Kostroma 15 Dec. 1917

Yaroslavl 9 Nov. 1917

Ivanovo 7 Nov. 1917

Government moved From Petrograd Mar. 1918

Moscow 15 Nov. 1917

Nizhniy Novgorod 10 Nov. 1917

Vyatka 8 Dec. 1917

Perm 14 Nov. 1917

Izhevsk 9 Nov. 1917

Kazan 8 Nov. 1917

Nicholas II and family shot by Bolsheviks July 1918 Yekaterinburg 8 Nov. 1917

RUSSIA

Kolchak 1918-19

BOLSHEVIK

Smolensk 12 Nov. 1917

Vitebsk 9 Nov. 1917

Kaluga 11 Dec. 1917

Mogilev 1 Dec. 1917

Tula 20 Dec. 1917

Orel 14 Nov. 1917

Trans-Siberian Railway

Penza 4 Jan. 1918

Tambov 13 Nov. 1917

Don

Samara 9 Nov. 1917

Ufa 8 Nov. 1917

Czechs

Orenburg 31 Jan. 1918

Warsaw

Brest-Litovsk

POLAND

Vistula

Minsk 7 Nov. 1917

Gomel 12 Nov. 1917

Poles

Kursk

Voronezh 12 Nov. 1917

Saratov 9 Nov. 1917

Volga

Cracow

Lemberg

CZECHOSLOVAKIA

HUNGARY

Debrecen

Kolozsvár

Brasso

Zhitomir 22 Jan. 1918

Kiev 8 Feb. 1918

Vinnitsa

Peregonovka

Dibrivki

Denikin 1919

Kharkov 24 Dec 1917

Poltava 19 Jan. 1918

Lozovaya

Dnieper

Yekaterinoslav 11 Jan. 1918

Don Cossacks 1917-19

Tambov

Tsaritsyn 27 Nov. 1917

Don

Volga

Ural

Ural Cossack army 1918-20

Kishinev 10 Dec 1917

BESSARABIA

Nikopol

Gulyay-Pole

Mariupol

Berdyansk

Novocherkassk 25 Feb. 1918

Rostov 10 Nov. 1917

Astrakhan 7 Feb. 1918

Nikolayev 27 Jan. 1918

Odessa 31 Jan. 1918

Wrangel 1920

Sea of Azov

Cossacks

Kama

ROMANIA

Ramanians

Jassy

Bucharest

Danube

Ruse

BULGARIA

Varna

Burgas

Plovdiv

Adrianople

Istanbul

French

Sebastopol 29 Dec. 1917

Simferopol 26 Jan. 1918

Novorossiysk 14 Dec. 1917

French

British

British

Black Sea

Entente fleet

Georgians 1919-20

Caucasus

Batum

Mensheviks

Tiflis

Baku 15 Nov. 1917

Caspian Sea

Angora

Trebizond

TURKEY

Erivan

PERSIA

British 1918-19

Smyrna

Imperialism and nationalism

Though the First World War destroyed the German and Ottoman empires, the British and French empires reached their greatest territorial extent after 1919. Nevertheless, the war had eroded the foundations of imperialism in Asia and the Middle East while by the 1930s the stability of Europe's empires was being shaken by the Depression.

THE IMPERIAL CONTRIBUTION to the Allied cause during the First World War led Lloyd George to reflect that "the British empire was not an abstraction but a living force to be reckoned with". Britain, like France, then consolidated the strategic underpinning of its empire by the acquisition of new Middle East territories and expansion in Africa. This was possible because the new League of Nations distributed former Ottoman and German dependencies in the form of "mandates" among the victorious powers. Britain gained trusteeships for Palestine, Iraq and Transjordan, as well as former German colonies in Tanganyika and, with France, Togoland and German Cameroon. France also gained Syria and Lebanon. Germany's Pacific islands and New Guinea (see p. 271) went to New Zealand and Australia respectively and German South West Africa went to South Africa.

Ironically, by 1919 the British faced significant challenges. National identities had been consolidated in the white self-governing colonies, and after the war these countries, termed "dominions" since 1907, pressed for a definition of their status as independent countries within the British Commonwealth. At the same time, there was growing criticism of colonialism from the United States and the Soviet Union, while, despite the real economic rewards they brought with them, the empires were increasingly expensive to maintain.

Nationalist opposition

Above all the European empires faced growing opposition from within their territories, led by educated elites who sought a role in local administration or even national autonomy. The war lubricated the existing nationalist movements in India and Egypt, and intensified opposition in Ireland. Between 1920–2 and again in the early 1930s Mahatma Gandhi led the first nationalist Congress All-India campaigns for self rule. Confronted by mass opposition, in 1919 and 1935

Britain greatly extended Indian participation in government. Egypt, although Britain retained great influence and military rights, was given independence in 1922, while, after violently suppressing guerrilla warfare, Britain conceded "dominion status" in 1921 to a new state created in southern Ireland. Meanwhile postwar uprisings in the newly acquired territories of the Middle East presaged problems to come. In Palestine, where Britain had committed itself to supporting the creation of a Jewish homeland, Jewish immigration after Hitler came to power in Germany led to a widespread Arab uprising after 1936. Iraq meanwhile had secured independence by 1932.

In other European colonies the 1920s were less troubled. In tropical Africa, a "thin white line" of officials administered the colonies acquired in the late 19th century, and African chiefs were incorporated into colonial structures of local governance. Large settler communities developed in east and central Africa, especially in Kenya and southern Rhodesia.

Imperialism in the 1930s

The 1930s saw a last burst of imperialism as Japan invaded Manchuria in 1931 and Italy conquered Abyssinia in 1935–6. The League of Nations, however ineffective in practice at dealing with such aggression, had nonetheless, through its mandate system, introduced the idea of international accountability in colonial affairs. Together with the British idea of progress towards "dominion status", it gave rise to a new conception of colonial rule as something temporary and limited. Other colonial powers also faced mounting opposition. In north Africa, Italy experienced

continuous resistance while nationalist movements mushroomed in the French territories of Tunisia, Algeria and Morocco. In the Dutch East Indies, a phase of revolutionary movements, beginning with the communist revolt of 1926, was seen off with only limited changes in provincial government, but in Indo-China the preservation of firm French control led to unrest in the 1930s and the creation of a nationalist guerrilla organization, the Viet Minh, by Ho Chi Minh in 1941.

Differing political and social conditions meant that there were fewer challenges in sub-Saharan Africa; nonetheless, discontent with colonial rule took a variety of forms, and the Depression in particular, hitting colonial economies vulnerable to changes in world trade, saw widespread unrest. Cocoa farmers in the Gold Coast were stirred to protest. In the West Indies, meanwhile, unemployment and falling export prices led to a series of strikes and riots between 1935 and 1938.

By 1939 the development of nationalism in Asia and north Africa and the rise of new, more radical nationalist leaders – Sukarno in Indonesia, Nehru in India, Bourguiba in Tunisia – was placing strains on the European colonial empires. It was the Second World War, however, which was to deliver the fatal blow to European colonialism.

1 The material advantages of the European overseas empires were offset by growing political and social conflict **(map below)**. Some of this was the result of impoverishment and trade decline but much came from nationalists hostile to colonial rule. Though concessions were made in the Middle East, India and the British Dominions, by 1939 the long-term prospects for the survival of colonial empires were bleak.

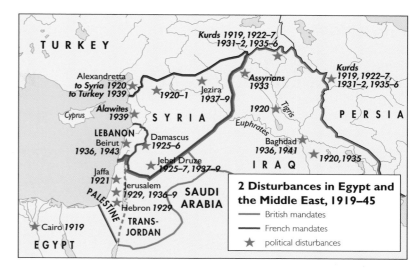

2 Disturbances in Egypt and the Middle East, 1919–45
- British mandates
- French mandates
- ★ political disturbances

2 The Middle East saw numerous instances of opposition to British and French imperialism **(map above)** and attempts by rural or minority populations to resist the newly created central governments. Palestine experienced frequent anti-British disturbances and an Arab uprising (1936–9) in protest at Jewish immigration. Two national revolts in Syria-Lebanon (1925–7, 1943–5) sought to force the French to grant independence. In Egypt in 1919 the Wafd party organized a nationwide revolt in an attempt to overturn the British protectorate, which finally ended in 1922.

> THEY TALK TO ME ABOUT PROGRESS, ABOUT "ACHIEVEMENTS", DISEASES CURED, IMPROVED STANDARDS OF LIVING. I AM TALKING ABOUT SOCIETIES DRAINED OF THEIR ESSENCE, CULTURES TRAMPLED UNDERFOOT, INSTITUTIONS UNDERMINED, LANDS CONFISCATED, RELIGIONS SMASHED, MAGNIFICENT ARTISTIC CREATIONS DESTROYED, EXTRAORDINARY POSSIBILITIES WIPED OUT.
>
> **Aimé Césaire**
> *Discourse on Colonialism, 1950*

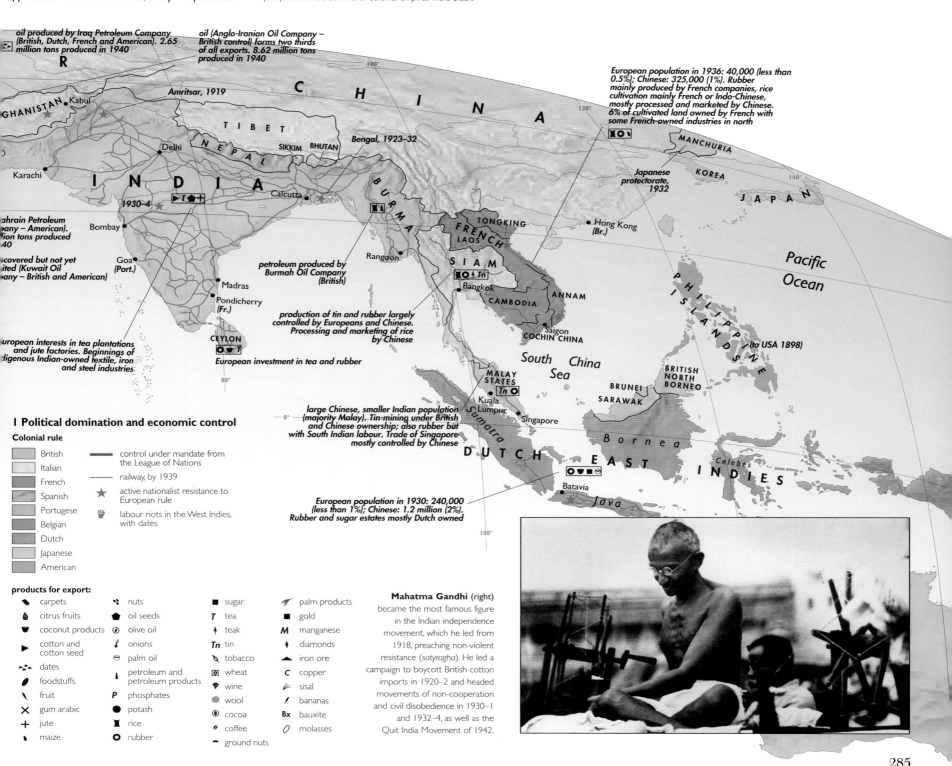

1 Political domination and economic control

Colonial rule
- British
- Italian
- French
- Spanish
- Portuguese
- Belgian
- Dutch
- Japanese
- American

― control under mandate from the League of Nations
― railway, by 1939
★ active nationalist resistance to European rule
✊ labour riots in the West Indies, with dates

products for export:
- ↘ carpets
- ⬤ citrus fruits
- ⬤ coconut products
- ▶ cotton and cotton seed
- ⋅⋅⋅ dates
- ⬤ foodstuffs
- ↘ fruit
- ✕ gum arabic
- ✚ jute
- ↘ maize
- ✕ nuts
- ⬤ oil seeds
- ⬤ olive oil
- ✓ onions
- ⬤ palm oil
- **T** tea
- ↑ teak
- **Tn** tin
- ↘ tobacco
- ☑ wheat
- ❀ wine
- ⬤ wool
- ⬤ cocoa
- ✕ rice
- ⬤ coffee
- ⬤ rubber
- ■ sugar
- ■ gold
- **M** manganese
- ◆ diamonds
- ⬤ iron ore
- **C** copper
- ⧈ sisal
- ∕ bananas
- **Bx** bauxite
- *O* molasses
- ▿ palm products
- ― ground nuts

Mahatma Gandhi (right) became the most famous figure in the Indian independence movement, which he led from 1918, preaching non-violent resistance (*satyagraha*). He led a campaign to boycott British cotton imports in 1920–2 and headed movements of non-cooperation and civil disobedience in 1930–1 and 1932–4, as well as the Quit India Movement of 1942.

The Chinese revolution

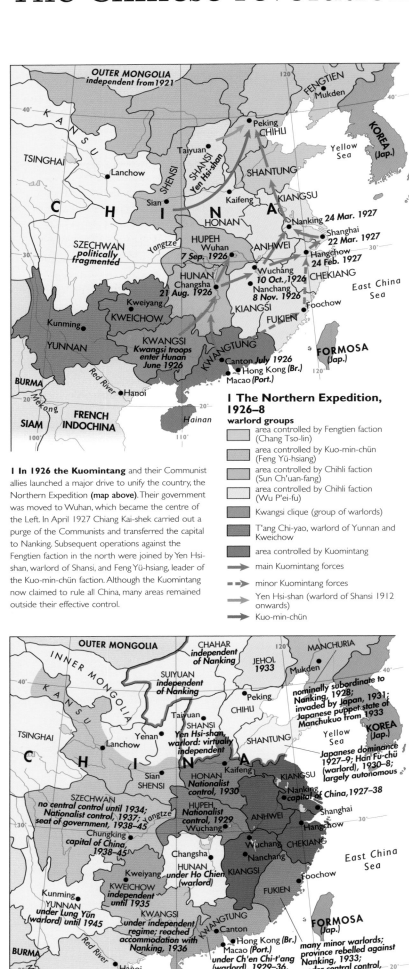

1 In 1926 the Kuomintang and their Communist allies launched a major drive to unify the country, the Northern Expedition (map above). Their government was moved to Wuhan, which became the centre of the Left. In April 1927 Chiang Kai-shek carried out a purge of the Communists and transferred the capital to Nanking. Subsequent operations against the Fengtien faction in the north were joined by Yen Hsi-shan, warlord of Shansi, and Feng Yü-hsiang, leader of the Kuo-min-chün faction. Although the Kuomintang now claimed to rule all China, many areas remained outside their effective control.

1 The Northern Expedition, 1926–8
warlord groups

- area controlled by Fengtien faction (Chang Tso-lin)
- area controlled by Kuo-min-chün (Feng Yü-hsiang)
- area controlled by Chihli faction (Sun Ch'uan-fang)
- area controlled by Chihli faction (Wu P'ei-fu)
- Kwangsi clique (group of warlords)
- T'ang Chi-yao, warlord of Yunnan and Kweichow
- area controlled by Kuomintang
- → main Kuomintang forces
- ⇢ minor Kuomintang forces
- → Yen Hsi-shan (warlord of Shansi 1912 onwards)
- → Kuo-min-chün

2 The Kuomintang regime after 1928 controlled only part of China (map above). The northeast was occupied by Japan from 1931, warlords ruled supreme in many provinces while other areas fell into anarchy. Large tracts of Kiangsi were under Communist control after 1931 while by 1936 the Communists possessed a new base in the northwest, at Yenan.

2 The Nationalist (Kuomintang) regime, 1928–37

- occupied by Japan by 1933
- area in which Japan attempted to establish a puppet North China state, 1935

areas of effective control of Chiang Kai-shek's Nationalist government at Nanking

- 1928
- 1929–34
- 1935–7
- brought under Nanking influence 1935–7

China from 1912 entered a phase of brutal internal anarchy. With no effective central government, warlords, Nationalists and Communists struggled for control while imperialist Japan occupied increasingly large areas of the north. Japan's defeat in 1945 saw a further civil war from which the Communists emerged victorious in 1949.

THE FOUNDATION OF THE REPUBLIC

in 1912 (see p. 256) failed to produce a lasting solution to China's problems. Within weeks Sun Yat-sen, the revolutionary who had been elected China's provisional first president, was replaced by Yüan Shih-k'ai, the most powerful general of the imperial era. China's continuing weakness was clear: the government had to borrow huge sums abroad to offset the lack of a modern revenue system; the satellite states of Tibet and Mongolia fell under British and Russian dominance respectively; and Japan expanded her influence on Chinese territory. At the outbreak of the First World War Japan seized the German-leased territory in Shantung and presented "Twenty-one Demands" which would have reduced China to a Japanese dependency. Though Yüan was able to resist most, he was forced to acknowledge Japanese dominance in Shantung, Manchuria and Inner Mongolia.

After Yüan died in 1916 power passed increasingly into the hands of provincial generals. For the next decade, although the Peking government claimed to rule China, it was the puppet of one group of generals or another. Some of these warlords established stable and reforming regimes, as in Shansi, Kwangsi and Manchuria, others, as in Szechwan, presided over anarchy. In the 1920s warlord coalitions fought devastating campaigns against each other. Only the Treaty Ports (see p. 256), under foreign protection, remained secure.

Nationalist reaction

After the First World War there was an upsurge of revolutionary activity driven by widespread popular reaction against foreign interference and economic exploitation, as well as disgust at the terms of the Paris Peace Conference, which reinforced Japan's position in Shantung. In 1919 the reaction erupted into the nationalist "May 4th Movement" in which a new generation of Western-oriented students and intellectuals, joined by urban workers, became a force in politics for the first time. The Movement even succeeded in preventing the government from signing the Treaty of Versailles. There followed the transformation in 1923 of Sun Yat-sen's revolutionary party into the Nationalist (Kuomintang) Party.

With Sun's death in 1925, the Nationalists were headed by Chiang Kai-shek, who in 1926 led the "Northern Expedition" from the Nationalist base in Canton to eliminate the warlords and unify the nation. By 1928 Chiang's armies had taken Peking. For much of this period the Nationalists operated in alliance with the Communist Party, which had been founded in 1920. The Communists showed themselves most effective at organizing support in the industrial cities until Chiang, in April 1927, decided he was strong enough to do without them, and they were ruthlessly purged.

... A REVOLUTION IS NOT A DINNER PARTY, OR WRITING AN ESSAY, OR PAINTING A PICTURE, OR DOING EMBROIDERY; IT CANNOT BE SO REFINED, SO LEISURELY AND GENTLE, SO TEMPERATE, KIND, COURTEOUS, RESTRAINED AND MAGNANIMOUS. A REVOLUTION IS AN INSURRECTION, AN ACT OF VIOLENCE BY WHICH ONE CLASS OVERTHROWS ANOTHER.

Mao Zedong
Report on an investigation of the peasant movement in Hunan, March 1927

Although the Nationalists now dominated China, serious competitors for power remained. With warlords still flourishing, Chiang's government had firm centralized control over only the rich provinces of the lower Yangtze (see map 2). There it modernized the administration and the army, built a road and railway system and established new industries.

The Japanese, meanwhile, remained full of imperial ambition: in 1931 they occupied Manchuria, which they industrialized to great effect; in 1933 they occupied the neighbouring province of Jehol; and in 1935 they attempted, without success, to turn the whole of northern China into a puppet state. At the same time, the Communists were beginning to establish themselves effectively in the countryside. From 1929–34 they had made a great success of the Kiangsi Soviet at Jui-chin, where they pioneered a revolution in Marxist theory, developing reform programmes as a peasant-based party rather than as one of the urban proletariat. After the Nationalists forced them to leave the region in 1934, the Communists embarked on what they later saw as the achievement which established their national reputation, the "Long March" to Yenan in northern China (see map 3). During the march, Mao Zedong, who had pioneered the peasant-based theory, came to dominate the Party.

Japanese advance

From 1936 a three-cornered struggle for power developed between the Nationalists, the Communists and the Japanese. In that year the Nationalists and Communists formed a united front against the Japanese, who responded by invading in force. By the end of 1938 the Japanese controlled most of north and central China, the main coastal ports and all the centres of modern industry. The Nationalist retreat to the far west of China provided the Communists with their opportunity. Using their reform policies they won support in the countryside of occupied China, and with this new peasant base they waged guerrilla warfare against the Japanese. By the end of

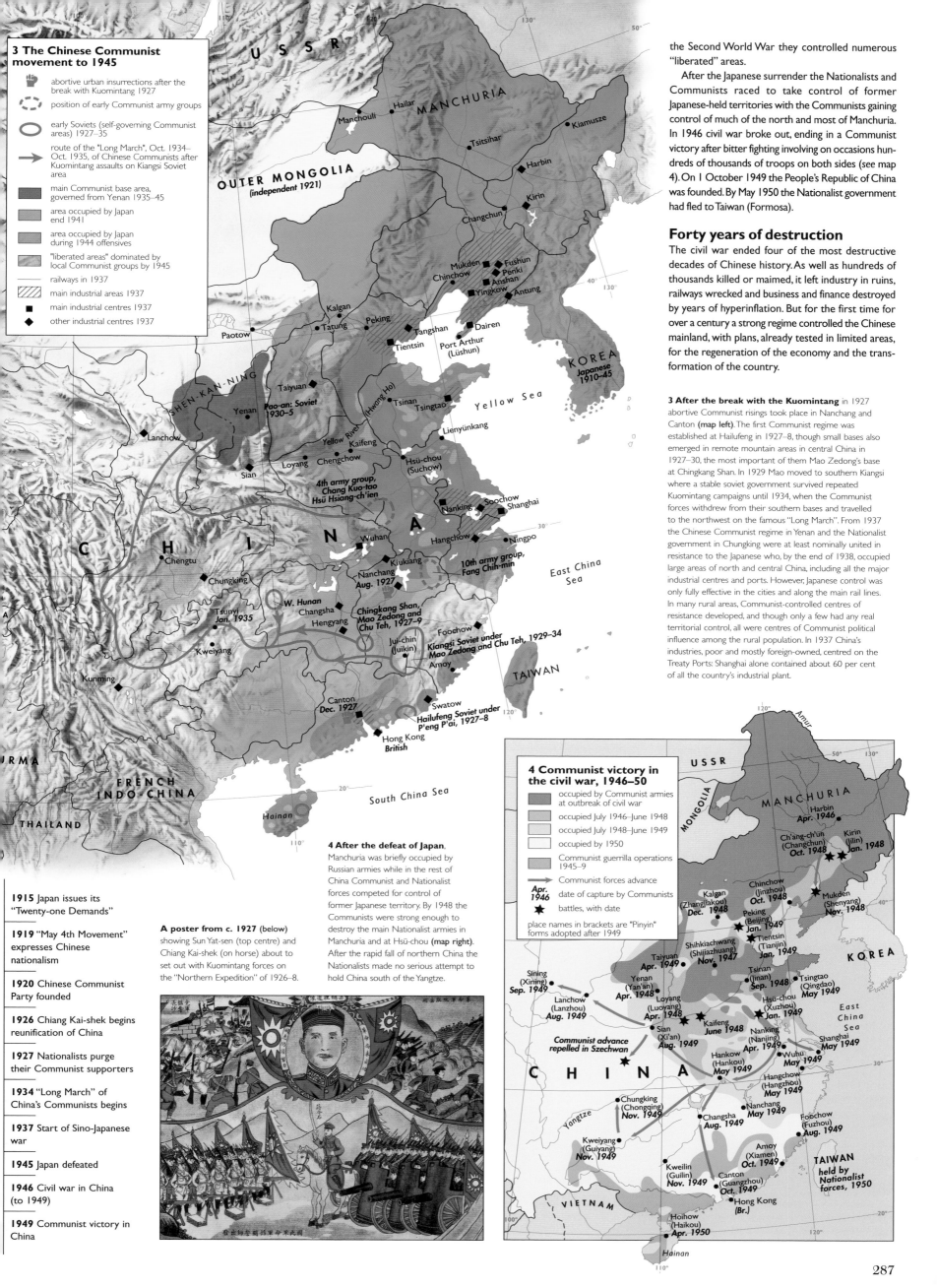

3 The Chinese Communist movement to 1945

Legend:
- abortive urban insurrections after the break with Kuomintang 1927
- position of early Communist army groups
- early Soviets (self-governing Communist areas) 1927–35
- route of the "Long March", Oct. 1934–Oct. 1935, of Chinese Communists after Kuomintang assaults on Kiangsi Soviet area
- main Communist base area, governed from Yenan 1935–45
- area occupied by Japan end 1941
- area occupied by Japan during 1944 offensives
- "liberated areas" dominated by local Communist groups by 1945
- railways in 1937
- main industrial areas 1937
- main industrial centres 1937
- other industrial centres 1937

the Second World War they controlled numerous "liberated" areas.

After the Japanese surrender the Nationalists and Communists raced to take control of former Japanese-held territories with the Communists gaining control of much of the north and most of Manchuria. In 1946 civil war broke out, ending in a Communist victory after bitter fighting involving on occasions hundreds of thousands of troops on both sides (see map 4). On 1 October 1949 the People's Republic of China was founded. By May 1950 the Nationalist government had fled to Taiwan (Formosa).

Forty years of destruction

The civil war ended four of the most destructive decades of Chinese history. As well as hundreds of thousands killed or maimed, it left industry in ruins, railways wrecked and business and finance destroyed by years of hyperinflation. But for the first time for over a century a strong regime controlled the Chinese mainland, with plans, already tested in limited areas, for the regeneration of the economy and the transformation of the country.

3 After the break with the Kuomintang in 1927 abortive Communist risings took place in Nanchang and Canton (map left). The first Communist regime was established at Hailufeng in 1927–8, though small bases also emerged in remote mountain areas in central China in 1927–30, the most important of them Mao Zedong's base at Chingkang Shan. In 1929 Mao moved to southern Kiangsi where a stable soviet government survived repeated Kuomintang campaigns until 1934, when the Communist forces withdrew from their southern bases and travelled to the northwest on the famous "Long March". From 1937 the Chinese Communist regime in Yenan and the Nationalist government in Chungking were at least nominally united in resistance to the Japanese who, by the end of 1938, occupied large areas of north and central China, including all the major industrial centres and ports. However, Japanese control was only fully effective in the cities and along the main rail lines. In many rural areas, Communist-controlled centres of resistance developed, and though only a few had any real territorial control, all were centres of Communist political influence among the rural population. In 1937 China's industries, poor and mostly foreign-owned, centred on the Treaty Ports: Shanghai alone contained about 60 per cent of all the country's industrial plant.

4 After the defeat of Japan, Manchuria was briefly occupied by Russian armies while in the rest of China Communist and Nationalist forces competed for control of former Japanese territory. By 1948 the Communists were strong enough to destroy the main Nationalist armies in Manchuria and at Hsü-chou (map right). After the rapid fall of northern China the Nationalists made no serious attempt to hold China south of the Yangtze.

4 Communist victory in the civil war, 1946–50

Legend:
- occupied by Communist armies at outbreak of civil war
- occupied July 1946–June 1948
- occupied July 1948–June 1949
- occupied by 1950
- Communist guerrilla operations 1945–9
- Communist forces advance
- date of capture by Communists
- battles, with date
- place names in brackets are "Pinyin" forms adopted after 1949

A poster from c. 1927 (below) showing Sun Yat-sen (top centre) and Chiang Kai-shek (on horse) about to set out with Kuomintang forces on the "Northern Expedition" of 1926–8.

1915 Japan issues its "Twenty-one Demands"

1919 "May 4th Movement" expresses Chinese nationalism

1920 Chinese Communist Party founded

1926 Chiang Kai-shek begins reunification of China

1927 Nationalists purge their Communist supporters

1934 "Long March" of China's Communists begins

1937 Start of Sino-Japanese war

1945 Japan defeated

1946 Civil war in China (to 1949)

1949 Communist victory in China

European political problems

The end of the Great War was supposed to usher in an age of peace and disarmament, but the conflict had undermined economic stability, opened up the threat of communist revolt and left a generation of veterans alienated from parliamentary politics. The slump of 1929 left European capitalism in deep crisis and opened the way to political extremism.

THE WHOLE OF EUROPE IS FILLED WITH THE SPIRIT OF REVOLUTION. THERE IS A DEEP SENSE NOT ONLY OF DISCONTENT BUT OF ANGER AND REVOLT. THE WHOLE EXISTING ORDER IN ITS POLITICAL, SOCIAL AND ECONOMIC ASPECTS IS QUESTIONED ... FROM ONE END OF EUROPE TO THE OTHER. THERE IS A DANGER THAT WE MAY THROW THE MASSES OF THE POPULATION THROUGHOUT EUROPE INTO THE ARMS OF THE EXTREMISTS.

David Lloyd George, Versailles, 1919

1919 Germany signs the Treaty of Versailles

1920 Polish-Russian war ends with Treaty of Riga

1922 Mussolini appointed prime minister in Italy

1923 Treaty of Lausanne settles conflict between Turkey, Greece and the Allies

1923 Hyperinflation in Germany

1925 Treaty of Locarno seals brief Franco-German friendship

1928 Kellogg-Briand Pact outlaws war

1932 Lausanne Conference suspends German reparations

1933 Hitler appointed Chancellor

1934 February riots in Paris overthrow government

I N 1919 THE POLITICAL map of Europe was transformed. The defeat of the German and Austro-Hungarian empires in 1918 (and the collapse of the Tsarist system in Russia the year before) brought to an end the long period of dynastic empires that had dominated central and eastern Europe. The victorious Allies met at Versailles in January 1919 to try to replace the imperial regimes with a system of independent states.

The Allies brought with them conflicting ambitions: the American president, Woodrow Wilson, hoped to broker a peace that would end war for ever and establish a liberal, democratic Europe of national states; the French wanted to punish Germany and prevent her revival; Italy, Serbia and Romania sought territorial concessions. The outcome was a messy compromise. Weak new democratic states were created, based loosely on the principle of national self-determination, but the defeated countries were heavily penalized and their national territories dismembered. The political instability of the post-war years can be traced back to the bitter legacy imposed by the peace settlement.

The settlement itself took four years to complete. New states were created (see map 1): Finland, Estonia, Latvia and Lithuania freed themselves from Russian rule; a Polish state was reconstituted after a bitter conflict with the new Soviet armies in the east and with German nationalist militia in the west; Czechoslovakia was carved out of the northern territories of the Habsburg empire, and Yugoslavia was created (see map 2). The defeated powers were forced to relinquish territory, to pay substantial reparations and to disarm. The German army was reduced to a mere 100,000 men, the Austrian forces to 30,000 and the Hungarian to 35,000.

The League of Nations

Europe was now dominated by France, the most heavily armed state in the world in the 1920s. She played a key role with Britain in running the League of Nations, which was established in 1920 as a forum for the conduct of international politics on peaceful lines. The French aim was to find a system of "collective security" which could protect her from any revival of German power. In 1926 Germany was admitted to the League and in 1928 the Kellogg-Briand Pact was signed in Paris by all the powers, committing them to the settlement of disputes without resort to war.

The collective system was a superficial one. The League had no agreed procedures for enforcing settlement and no military back-up. The Soviet Union did not join until 1934, and the United States refused to join at all. The expectation that Europe would embrace democracy as a foundation for collaboration soon evaporated. Economic crisis and bitter social conflict, engendered by the rise of socialism and the revolutionary activity of European communists, could not be contained within weak parliamentary systems by liberal politicians often quite out of touch with popular social and nationalist agitation. Between 1922 and 1926 democracy was torn up in Italy by Mussolini and the Fascist party; Spain had military rule imposed in 1923 by Primo de Rivera and, after a brief republican interlude between 1931 and 1936, the army imposed Franco's dictatorship. In Poland, Austria, the Baltic states, Yugoslavia, Hungary, Romania, Greece and Bulgaria, democracy was eventually suspended and nationalist regimes installed based on royal dictatorship, military coup or single-party rule.

Even in the victor powers democracy was challenged. In Ireland a bloody civil war led to the creation of an independent Irish state and the break up

The Versailles Conference (below) convened in Paris in January 1919. In all 32 states were invited to attend (but not the defeated powers or the infant Soviet Union). 70 plenipotentiaries were sent, but most decisions were taken by the three major powers, Britain, the USA and France, whose leaders can be seen at the centre of the picture.

2 The formation of Yugoslavia, from 1918

- Serbia and Montenegro, 1913
- annexed by Serbia and Montenegro from Ottoman empire, 1913
- frontiers, 1914
- annexed from Bulgaria, 1919
- Austro-Hun. territory united with Serbia and Montenegro, 1920, to create the Kingdom of Serbs, Croats and Slovenes
- remained Austrian by plebiscite, 1920
- Kingdom of Serbs, Croats and Slovenes in 1929, when renamed Yugoslavia

2 The collapse of the Habsburg empire in 1918 created conditions for the establishment of a south Slav state (map above). In December 1918 the Kingdom of the Serbs, Croats and Slovenes was set up in Belgrade, but arguments between the different national groups over the nature of the new state delayed until 1921 the full establishment of what was to be called Yugoslavia. The state was dominated by Serbs, who made up 43 per cent of the population.

I National conflicts and frontier disputes, 1919–36

――― German empire, 1914	new states
――― Austro-Hungarian empire, 1914	areas of dispute
――― Russian empire, 1914	areas temporarily autonomous or independent
――― post-settlement frontiers	areas under armed occupation
▲ plebiscites held	areas under League of Nations High Commissioners

PLEBISCITES AND TERRITORIAL DISPUTES

1 plebiscite Feb. 1920: divided between Denmark and Germany
2 occupied by France 1923–5
3 to Belgium 1919
4 to Belgium 1919
5 evacuated 1930, remilitarized 1936
6 League of Nations Mandate by plebiscite to Germany 1935
7 to France 1919
8 divided between Germany and Poland by plebiscite Mar. 1921
9 Allied occupation 1920–3, annexed by Lithuania 1923, autonomous 1924, to Germany 1939
10 to Germany July 1920
11 to Poland Dec. 1918
12 partitioned between Czechoslovakia and Poland 1920
13 to Hungary 1921
14 to Austria 1920
15 occupied by Poland 1920, annexed by Poland following elections 1922
16 to Greece from Bulgaria 1919
17 demilitarized 1924, remilitarized 1936
18 Greek-Bulgarian conflict, 1925

I At the end of the war the victorious powers tried to redraw the political map of Europe **(map above)** by creating new states in the east at the expense of the defeated states: Germany, Austria-Hungary, Bulgaria and the Ottoman empire. Though not party to the peace settlement, the Soviet Union also lost extensive territories which had once formed part of the Tsarist empire. Millions of Europeans were expelled or fled from oppression, but there remained many areas where national aspirations were not satisfied, or where national minorities remained under the rule of another nationality. Irredentist conflict and national revolt created an unstable continent, marred by persistent violence and racial tension.

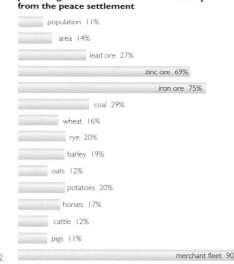

4 German reparations, 1920–32
(reparations suspended at Lausanne Conference 1932)

Versailles/ Spa Plan	(no fixed schedule)	132bn marks
Dawes Plan	(no fixed amount)	2bn marks/annum
Young Plan	(total to be paid by 1988)	37bn mks
Total payments	(including in kind)	17bn marks
Loans from US and UK		27bn marks

1920 1922 1924 1926 1928 1930 1932

percentage losses to the German economy from the peace settlement

population 11%
area 14%
lead ore 27%
zinc ore 69%
iron ore 75%
coal 29%
wheat 16%
rye 20%
barley 19%
oats 12%
potatoes 20%
horses 17%
cattle 12%
pigs 11%
merchant fleet 90%

4 Reparations (charts above) were demanded from Germany by the victor powers in 1919. A final sum was agreed at Versailles in 1921 after much had been taken in kind. German economic problems led to the rescheduling of payments in 1924 (Dawes Plan) and in 1929 (Young Plan). They were finally suspended in 1932, though they were set to run to 1988.

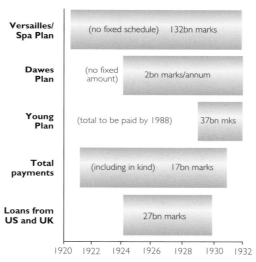

1930

1933

3 Electoral performance of the Nazi Party in Sep. 1930 and Mar. 1933

NSDAP % share of vote

50–59	20–29
40–49	10–19
30–39	0–9

3 The NSDAP (Nazi Party) made spectacular gains between 1929 and 1933, when it won the largest vote any party had obtained in German history (44 per cent). Hitler's promise of national awakening, moral revival and social peace drew support from across German society, from workers to the aristocracy.

of the Anglo-Irish Union. In 1926 a General Strike provoked sharp social conflict in Britain. In France conflicts between right and left led to growing violence, which culminated in the storming of the French parliament in 1934 and the overthrow of the government. Yet democracy survived in both states despite the noisy agitation of right and left.

The rise of Hitler

In Germany democracy was overcome by extremism. Despite efforts to make the new system work through coalition rule, the slump of 1929, which hit Germany harder than anywhere else, created an economic catastrophe that the government was powerless to ameliorate. German society was politically polarized. Communist support doubled, but millions of Germans turned to Adolf Hitler's Nazi Party (see map 3) with its promise of a New Order, neither socialist nor parliamentary. Hitler was committed to overturning Versailles, and his appointment as German chancellor in January 1933 challenged not only the German peace settlement but the whole system set up across Europe in 1919–20. Hitler emboldened radical nationalists and irredentists everywhere who rejected liberalism and collective security in favour of dictatorship and the violent revision of the peace treaties.

The United States: the rise of the federal state

Ever since the Revolution, American political tradition regarded a strong central government as a threat to liberty. The states regulated the lives of their citizens and the main contact Americans had with the federal government was the post office. This began to change in the late 19th century as the United States faced new challenges and problems which demanded a nation solution.

THE START OF THE CIVIL WAR marked the beginning of a new role for the federal government.

The 1863 National Bank Act created a national banking system and established a national currency. Millions of former slaves began to depend on the US army and the Freedmen's Bureau for help and protection. The Civil War Pension system eventually provided support for all disabled veterans of the Union army and their widows or orphans. It gradually developed into a pension system for all Northern veterans which at its peak benefited a majority of all men in the North and many women and consumed nearly half of all federal revenues. When the last Union soldier to receive a pension died in 1956, over 5,700 widows and orphans were still receiving payments from the federal government.

The new State, War and Navy Building (now called the Eisenhower Executive Office Building) next to the White House epitomized the growing size and role of the federal government. Built over a period of 17 years in the style of the French Second Empire, it provided a sharp contrast to the other buildings in Washington DC and housed three major government departments when it was finished in 1888. Today, it is just big enough to accommodate some of the president's staff.

Slowly, the federal civil service became more professional. The 1883 Pendleton Act for the first time introduced competitive written exams to fill some government jobs based on merit rather than patronage. The act initially covered only 10 per cent of the 132,000 federal employees, but its reach was gradually extended and a Civil Service Commission created to enforce it. Today, more than 90 per cent of the 2.7 million federal employees are covered.

The armed forces also modernized. The 1898 war with Spain exposed severe weaknesses, especially in the army, and triggered widespread reforms. The size of the regular army grew from 27,865 in 1897 to 101,713 in 1900. Training schools for officers and federal standards for the National Guard were established. A Joint Army and Navy Board was created in 1903, followed by the Joint Chiefs of Staff in the 1940s.

1 Until the Civil War, the Mall in Washington DC had no special symbolic value **(map below)**. Its main features were a smelly canal, the unfinished Washington Memorial (construction started in 1848 and stopped in 1854) and railroad tracks and a train station. As the role of the federal government changed, so did the appearance of the Mall. The canal was filled up in 1872, Congress appropriated funds to resume construction on the Washington Memorial in 1876 (finished in 1884), and the tidal flats south and west of the Washington Memorial were reclaimed between 1882 and 1900. Led by Senator James McMillan, the Park Commission proposed a plan for the redevelopment of the Mall in 1902, based on L'Enfant's original vision. The railroad tracks and train station were removed in 1907, and the Mall gradually filled up with monuments, museums and official buildings, creating a symbolic space for the nation

4 The growing importance of the federal government is also reflected in the rising number of civilian employees, active military personnel and veterans from the start of the 20th century to the early 1990s **(chart right)**.

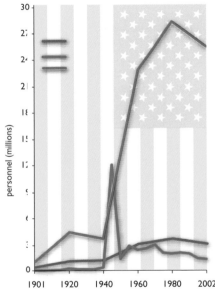

4 Federal government employment, 1901–2002

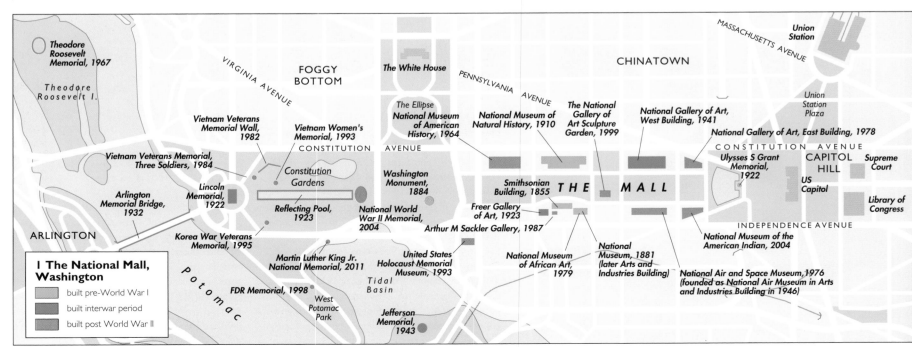

1 The National Mall, Washington

- built pre-World War I
- built interwar period
- built post World War II

Theodore Roosevelt Memorial, 1967

Theodore Roosevelt I.

FOGGY BOTTOM

VIRGINIA AVENUE

The White House

PENNSYLVANIA AVENUE

CHINATOWN

MASSACHUSETTS AVENUE

Union Station

The Ellipse

National Museum of American History, 1964

National Museum of Natural History, 1910

The National Gallery of Art Sculpture Garden, 1999

National Gallery of Art, West Building, 1941

Union Station Plaza

National Gallery of Art, East Building, 1978

Vietnam Veterans Memorial Wall, 1982

Vietnam Women's Memorial, 1993

CONSTITUTION AVENUE

Vietnam Veterans Memorial, Three Soldiers, 1984

Constitution Gardens

Washington Monument, 1884

Smithsonian Building, 1855

THE MALL

CONSTITUTION AVENUE

Ulysses S Grant Memorial, 1922

CAPITOL HILL

Supreme Court

Lincoln Memorial, 1922

US Capitol

Arlington Memorial Bridge, 1932

Reflecting Pool, 1923

National World War II Memorial, 2004

Freer Gallery of Art, 1923

Library of Congress

ARLINGTON

Korea War Veterans Memorial, 1995

Arthur M Sackler Gallery, 1987

INDEPENDENCE AVENUE

National Museum of the American Indian, 2004

Martin Luther King Jr. National Memorial, 2011

United States Holocaust Memorial Museum, 1993

National Museum of African Art, 1979

National Museum, 1881 (later Arts and Industries Building)

Potomac

FDR Memorial, 1998

West Potomac Park

Tidal Basin

National Air and Space Museum, 1976 (founded as National Air Museum in Arts and Industries Building in 1946)

Jefferson Memorial, 1943

The growing and increasingly integrated American economy also strengthened the role of the federal government, as many economic and social issues could no longer be addressed through state legislation alone. This took place against the resistance of the US Supreme Court which would only end in the second half of the 1930s.

The farmers' demand for regulation of the railroads led to the passing of the Interstate Commerce Act in 1887 and the creation of a commission to administer it. A growing popular pressure to ensure competition in the market also led to the passing of the Sherman Antitrust Act three years later, but the federal courts weakened both pieces of legislation. The US Supreme Court also struck down the federal income tax in 1895, a decision which was eventually overturned by the 16th Amendment in 1913. The 1894 march of "Coxey's Army" from Ohio to Washington DC and similar marches of other groups of unemployed Americans laid the problem of the workless at the doorstep of Congress. The federal government would only accept this responsibility during the New Deal of the 1930s, but the march provided a precedent for many subsequent protest events in the national capital, such as the National Woman's Suffrage Parade in 1913 or the Bonus Army in 1932.

Theodore Roosevelt and Woodrow Wilson

The federal government became more active in the "progressive" drive for social, political and economic reform when Theodore Roosevelt became president in 1901. Roosevelt mediated in the 1902 anthracite coal strike instead of using troops to break it, successfully pursued antitrust action against JP Morgan's Northern Security Company and promoted a range of reform measures. His successor Taft was much more cautious, causing Roosevelt to run again in 1912 on a ticket of the Progressive Party. He lost against another Progressive, the Democrat Woodrow Wilson.

Wilson lowered the protective tariff, reformed the American banking system and created the Federal Trade Commission to supervise business. The federal government also started to use its existing powers creatively, such as in the 1916 attempt to end child labour through the use of the interstate commerce clause. Although the Keating-Owen Act (and a subsequent attempt to tax goods produced by child labour out of existence) was ruled unconstitutional by the US Supreme Court, the reforms of the late 19th and early 20th centuries showed that the role and power of the federal government in American life was changing.

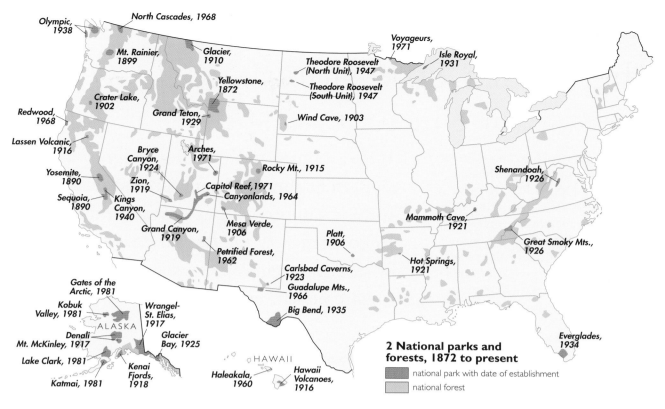

2 National parks and forests, 1872 to present

- national park with date of establishment
- national forest

2 The Progressive Era saw a growing concern with conservation (**map above**). Under President Theodore Roosevelt, the executive branch started to create new National Parks or Forests or added land to existing ones, and his successors continued this trend.

3 State pledge of allegiance requirements for schools, 2003

- schools required
- schools have option
- no law

5 & 6 As the federal government assumed ever more commitments at home and abroad, its budget also steadily increased over the years (**charts below**). This was partly financed by a federal income tax through which Washington directly touched the lives of a growing number of American citizens, especially for the 1940s onwards.

3 The growing number of immigrants from southern and eastern Europe in the late 19th century created anxiety and gave rise to the belief that public schools should encourage and train patriotism in immigrant children (**map above**). In the late 1880s, the Grand Army of the Republic, a very influential organization of Civil War veterans, supported the drive to fly the US flag over every schoolhouse in America. The Pledge of Allegiance, written by Francis Bellamy for the National Columbian Public School Celebration in 1892, originated from this movement and served the same purpose.

Few other buildings reflect the growth of the federal government so vividly as the Pentagon in Virginia. When Congress was asked to approve the massive new building for the War Department in 1941, concerns were raised about what to do with it after the war. Suggestions included its use as a record storage facility or to allow civilian government departments to move in. The post-war military establishment, however, remained more than large enough to make full use of the building.

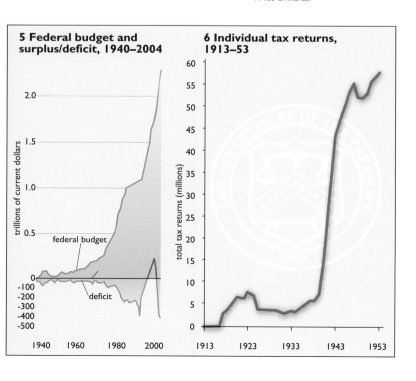

5 Federal budget and surplus/deficit, 1940–2004

6 Individual tax returns, 1913–53

The Great Depression

> THE DEFECTS OF THE CAPITALIST SYSTEM HAVE BEEN INCREASINGLY ROBBING IT OF ITS BENEFITS. THEY ARE NOW THREATENING ITS EXISTENCE. A PERIOD OF DEPRESSION AND CRISIS IS ONE IN WHICH ITS GREAT MERIT, THE EXPANSION OF PRODUCTIVE CAPACITY UNDER THE STIMULUS OF COMPETITIVE GAINS, SEEMS WASTED; AND ITS MAIN DEFECT, AN INCREASING INABILITY TO UTILISE PRODUCTIVE CAPACITY FULLY AND TO DISTRIBUTE WHAT IT PRODUCES TOLERABLY, IS SEEN AT ITS WORST.
>
> Arthur Salter
> *Recovery*, 1932

In 1929 the world was plunged into the worst slump in modern history. Trade and prices collapsed, millions were thrown out of work. As governments took responsibility for economic revival, the old economic order was replaced by state intervention. At the same time, the crisis provoked extreme nationalism, paving the way to dictatorship.

THE GREAT INTER-WAR SLUMP is usually dated from 29 October 1929 when the New York stock market crashed. When in July 1933 the index at last stopped falling, shares stood at 15 per cent of their 1929 value. Thousands of Americans were bankrupt, millions unemployed and impoverished. In the developed world alone over 23 million were out of work by 1932. At its peak, unemployment affected one in four of the American workforce; in Germany almost 9 million were thrown out of work in a workforce of 20 million.

The causes of the crisis

The crash of 1929 was a symptom as much as a cause of the worldwide slump that followed. The world economy had been weakened by the First World War and the massive debts it generated. It proved impossible to re-introduce the Gold Standard system (see p. 276) fully, or to revive an effective multilateral trading system. Overproduction led to falling prices and declining profits. Despite the boom

in America, business confidence elsewhere had been low and investment sluggish. When the US stock market crashed, it was against the background of an already declining and fragile world economy.

The effects of the slump

The effects unfolded slowly. Protective tariffs were set up worldwide to save domestic industry. Even laissez-faire Britain adopted Imperial Preference in 1932, a protected trading bloc within the empire. World trade in the 1930s never recovered its 1929 level, and bilateral trade agreements came to replace the liberal system of multilateral trade and exchange. Germany in 1934 adopted a "New Plan" for state-regulated trade, and in 1936 a programme of "autarky", or self-sufficiency.

Declining trade encouraged domestic sources of economic revival. In Britain, Sweden, Germany and the USA, experiments in state work-creation projects soaked up some of the millions of unemployed. In 1933 Roosevelt introduced a package of recovery

---

Oct. 1929 New York stock market crashes

1930 Hawley-Smoot Tariff in USA

1931 Banks collapse in Germany and Austria

1931 National Government formed in Britain to combat slump

1932 Lausanne Conference suspends German reparations

1933 Roosevelt launches "New Deal"

1933 World Economic Conference fails to find solution

1934 German "New Plan" for controlling trade

1936 Large-scale rearmament begins in Germany, Britain and France

2 The slump radicalized European politics, pushing electorates towards the extreme right and left (**map below**). Democracy was strong enough to survive in Britain and France, but in Spain, Germany and much of eastern Europe authoritarian anti-Marxist regimes appeared which violently repressed communism and abandoned the liberal parliamentary model.

SOCIAL AND POLITICAL CHANGE IN EUROPE, 1929–39

Protest movements of the left and right arose in almost every country in response to the slump, severely testing the social and political fabric. In countries where democratic traditions were weak – including most eastern and central European countries – some form of right-wing dictatorship resulted.

Albania Nov. 1927, virtual Italian protectorate established.

Austria Mar. 1933, Dollfuss dictatorship established; Feb. 1934, all parties banned, destruction of Austrian Socialists.

Belgium Mar. 1935, Government of National Union formed; June 1936, Social Improvement Programme stimulates reform.

Bulgaria May 1933, army coup; 1936, King Boris establishes royal dictatorship.

Estonia Mar. 1934, Päts dictatorship established.

France June 1936, Popular Front government installed; Mar. 1937, "Breathing Spell" from reform proclaimed.

Germany Jan. 1933, Hitler chancellor; Mar., Enabling Act passed.

Greece 1935, George II restores monarchy; Aug. 1936, Metaxas establishes dictatorship.

Hungary 1931–5, Gömbös dictatorship.

Ireland 1932, De Valera president, oath of allegiance repudiated; 1932–3, tariff war with United Kingdom.

Latvia May 1934, Ulmanis coup establishes dictatorship.

Lithuania Dec. 1926, Smetona coup; Feb. 1936, all parties banned.

Netherlands 1933–9, Crisis Cabinet formed.

Norway 1935, Labour government institutes major reforms.

Poland 1926–35, Pilsudski dictatorship; 1935–9, Colonels' regime.

Portugal 1928, Salazar finance minister; 1930, National Union becomes only party; 1932, Salazar premier.

Romania 1930–40, King Carol II builds dictatorship; 1938, all parties banned, Front of National Rebirth founded.

Spain 1931, new constitution; Feb. 1936, Popular Front government elected; July 1936, civil war (to Mar. 1939).

Sweden 1932–6, socialists introduce public works programme; 1936–40, Socialist Agrarian Coalition.

Switzerland 1931, Labour largest party.

Turkey 1923–38, Kemal Atatürk modernizing programme; 1934, Five Year Plan adopted.

United Kingdom Aug. 1931, National Government formed to carry through economy measures.

Yugoslavia Jan. 1929, Alexander establishes royal dictatorship.

2 Social and political change in Europe, 1929–39

political regimes

- democratic
- democratic, became fascist
- fascist or communist
- authoritarian
- democratic, became authoritarian

23.2 percentage of industrial workers unemployed, 1932

major movements of protest and dissatisfaction, 1929–39

- ◆ strike wave
- ● right-wing activity
- ■ riot or demonstration
- —— frontiers, 1937

1931: fascist "Blueshirts" organized
1937, 1938: wave of strikes and union organization

1932–9: Oswald Mosley's "Blackshirts"
1935–6: miners' "stay-down" strikes against company unions

1931–3: serious strikes and riots

1932, 1935–7: strike waves

1934: growing fascist (Rexist) activity
Feb. 1934: Stavisky riots
1936: wave of sit-down strikes – 2.5 million workers participate
1938: communist general strike

1932: serious labour disturbances

1929–36: unstable, pre-revolutionary situation, marked by right- and left-wing strikes, demonstrations and uprisings
1936–9: Spanish Civil War won by army and nationalist right

1932: Salazar dictatorship declared
1934: general strike

Oct. 1930 and Feb. 1932: attempted fascist (Lapua) coup

1934: Päts dictatorship established

1928 onwards: state-organized wave of mass annihilation of civilians and party cadre

1931, 1936–8: strike waves

1933: North Schleswig German agitation

1934: Ulmanis coup establishes dictatorship

1926: Smetona coup

1930–2: clashes between Nazis and communists
1933: Nazis come to power; one-party state created
1933: concentration camps established
1938: anti-Jewish pogrom

1926–35: Pilsudski dictatorship
1935–9: Colonels' regime
1930–8: major strike waves affecting peasants and workers

1933–8: Nazi activity amongst Germans in Sudetenland
1938: Sudetenland annexed
1939: Bohemia annexed

1920: Horthy becomes regent and virtual dictator
April 1933: pro-Nazi demonstrations

1930–8: fascist "Iron Guard" tolerated and financed by King Carol II
1933: Bucharest railway strike bloodily suppressed

1932: attempted fascist coup in Styria
1934: unsuccessful Nazi coup
1938: annexed by Germany

1929: Alexander establishes army-backed royal dictatorship
1935–8: strike wave

1933: army coup
1935: King Boris establishes dictatorship

1926: Mussolini head of one-party state

May 1937: Muslim insurrection

1933: attempted republican coup
1935: Venizelist riot
1936–41: Metaxas dictator

1923–38: Kemal Atatürk modernizes Turkey

Dec. 1930: Dervish rising near Izmir

30.8
22.8
31.7
29.5
23.5
13.5
24.3
30.1
21.3
26.1
23.2
22.5

I The Depression in the United States

population decrease or increase:

decrease	10–15%
0–5%	15–20%
5–10%	20% and over

percentage of families on relief from October 1933:

⚭ below 8% ⚭ 8–15%

⚭ over 15%

■ riot, demonstration, or other protest action

◆ strike

Map labels:
- farm workers begin organizing, 1933
- San Francisco general strike, May–July 1934
- farmers' strike, Sep.–Oct. 1932
- Minneapolis general strike, 1934
- Kansas City sitdown, GM, Dec. 1934
- farmers' strike, Aug. 1932
- Farmers' Holiday Association formed, May 1932
- Wisconsin milk strikes, Feb.–May 1933
- Chicago Memorial Day Massacre, Republic Steel, 1937
- Bendix, Nov. 1936; Anderson, GM, Jan.–Feb. 1937
- Flint sitdown, GM, Dec. 1936–Feb. 1937; Chrysler sitdown, Mar. 1937
- general strike, 1934
- GM, Dec. 1934
- left-wing demonstration of 100,000; riot in Harlem, 1935
- textile strikes, 1934
- Camden RCA strike, 1936
- Veterans' Bonus March on Washington DC, Mar. 1932
- miners' strike, 1931; anti-union terrorism, 1937
- marching strikes against cotton planters, 1935–6
- GM, 18 Nov. 1936
- Alabama Sharecroppers Union organized, 1931

1 Following a burst of speculative investment in the late 1920s, the US stock market collapsed in October 1929. The crash produced a banking crisis and sharp industrial decline (**map above**). By 1932 over 11 million Americans were unemployed. The US government reacted by imposing prohibitive tariffs under the Hawley-Smoot Tariff of 1930 and using federal funds to try to halt the slide. After Roosevelt's election in 1932 a "New Deal" was introduced to create work, protect labour and reform the banking system. But by 1939 there was still much idle capacity in the US economy.

By 1932 17 million Americans were on public relief. For many the only source of food was to queue for meals and handouts organized by charities (**above**). In May 1933 an Emergency Relief Act was passed to provide federal funds to tackle the desperate poverty and hunger.

4 The world economy during the slump

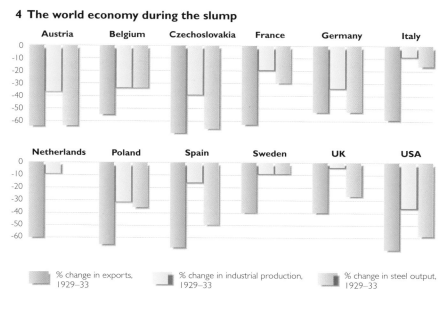

Austria Belgium Czechoslovakia France Germany Italy

Netherlands Poland Spain Sweden UK USA

% change in exports, 1929–33
% change in industrial production, 1929–33
% change in steel output, 1929–33

4 & 5 By 1932 there were more than 23 million people registered as unemployed worldwide (**chart right**). Millions more disappeared off the registers, and millions of others were thrown onto short-time working. Industrial production and trade slumped (**chart above**), causing severe price-falls and a further slump in output and profits. In Germany in 1932 some 40 per cent of the workforce was unemployed and production declined to the levels of the 1890s.

5 World unemployment, 1928–35

% of industrial workforce — 30%, 20%, 10%, 0 — 1930, 1932, 1934, 1936, 1938

Registered unemployment (thousands)

	1928	1932	1935
Germany	1,400	5,775	2,151
Austria	182	378	349
Belgium	5	71	66
Czechoslovakia	39	554	686
Denmark	50	100	76
France	16	301	464
Italy	324	1006	964
Netherlands	22	271	385
Poland	126	256	385
UK	1,217	2,745	2,036
USA	1,982	11,586	12,830

policies known as the "New Deal", which extended state regulation of the economy in a country with little tradition of such government activity. In Britain and Germany state regulation by the late 1930s had produced what was called a "managed economy", a forerunner of the mixed economies of the post-1945 era.

The political cost

The severity of the slump produced a political backlash. In more vulnerable economies such as Germany or Japan, radical nationalist groups argued for economic empire-building and an end to the old liberal capitalist order. In France and Spain economic crisis stimulated communism or anarchism, sparking prolonged social conflict. Only in Britain, with its large empire markets, did democracy survive and a modest prosperity set in during the 1930s. In much of Europe and Latin America various forms of dictatorship came to replace parliamentary systems now irrevocably associated with economic disaster.

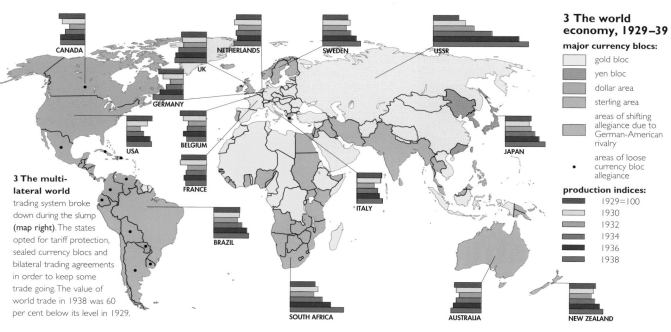

3 The multi-lateral world trading system broke down during the slump (**map right**). The states opted for tariff protection, sealed currency blocs and bilateral trading agreements in order to keep some trade going. The value of world trade in 1938 was 60 per cent below its level in 1929.

3 The world economy, 1929–39

major currency blocs:

- gold bloc
- yen bloc
- dollar area
- sterling area
- areas of shifting allegiance due to German-American rivalry
- areas of loose currency bloc allegiance

production indices:
- 1929=100
- 1930
- 1932
- 1934
- 1936
- 1938

The outbreak of the Second World War

In the 1930s the world order was violently challenged by states committed to establishing a "New Order" based on military conquest and brutal imperial rule. As the post-war system dissolved, bitter political conflicts between democrats, communists and fascists tore Europe apart and sent the world spiralling once again to war.

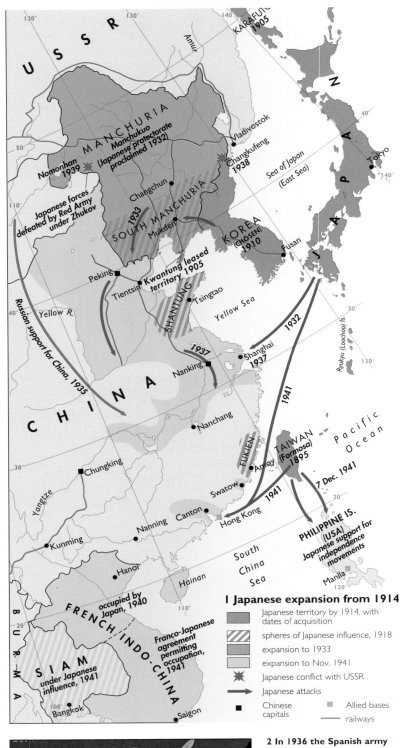

I Japanese expansion from 1914

- Japanese territory by 1914, with dates of acquisition
- spheres of Japanese influence, 1918
- expansion to 1933
- expansion to Nov. 1941
- ✱ Japanese conflict with USSR
- → Japanese attacks
- ■ Chinese capitals
- Allied bases
- railways

IN THE 1930s the international order constructed after the First World War, based upon the League of Nations and "collective security", collapsed under the violent impact of major revisionist powers bent on building a "New Order" in their favour.

The crisis of the international system owed much to the effects of the worldwide slump, which encouraged strident nationalism and militarism in the weaker economies. In Japan the economic crisis provoked the military into seizing economic resources and markets by force to compensate for their declining trade. In 1931 the Chinese province of Manchuria was conquered and soon turned into a Japanese satellite state, Manchukuo, ruled by the last Manchu emperor, Pu Yi. Japan left the League and declared a "New Order" in East Asia. With the League of Nations powerless in the face of this aggression, Japan continued to encroach on Chinese sovereignty until full-scale war broke out in 1937, bringing much of northern China under direct Japanese rule.

In Europe Mussolini's Italy also looked for a new economic empire. In 1935, expecting little reaction from the other major powers, Italy invaded Ethiopia.

I Growing nationalist and militarist pressure at home pushed Japan into a policy of open imperialism in Asia **(map left)**. In 1931 Manchuria was occupied and over the next six years Japan encroached farther into China, exploiting its political disintegration. In 1932 Japan threatened the port of Shanghai with its large European population. After a restless peace, in 1937 Japan and China became embroiled in a brutal war. Japan then seized much of northern and eastern China.

Though sanctions were half-heartedly applied by the League, by 1936 the conquest was complete. Italy, too, pulled out of the League.

German expansion

In 1935 Hitler began the process of overturning the Versailles settlement, declaring German rearmament in defiance of the Treaty. In March the following year, he ordered German troops back into the Rhineland. When the expected protest from Britain and France failed to materialize, his ambitions widened. In March 1938 Austria was occupied and united into a Greater Germany. In May Hitler's plans for the conquest of Czechoslovakia were frustrated only by belated protests from Britain and France. At the Munich conference in September that year, called to discuss the crisis, Britain and France nonetheless agreed to the incorporation of the Sudetenland, the German-speaking areas of Czechoslovakia, into Germany.

Far from marking an end to "legitimate" German territorial aspirations, the Munich Pact encouraged Hitler further. In March 1939, in clear defiance of the Pact, Germany occupied Bohemia and Moravia. Slovakia, all that remained of Czechoslovakia, became a German puppet state. At the same time, Hitler forced Lithuania to agree the return of Memel on the Baltic coast to Germany. Hitler then formally demanded the return of Danzig, which had been made a Free City under League jurisdiction after the war.

The failure of Britain and France to respond to Hitler's aggression was largely the result of their

2 In 1936 the Spanish army under Franco rebelled against the Republic established in 1931 **(map right)**. The result was a bitter and sanguinary civil war between the nationalist right and the liberal and socialist left which came to symbolize the wider struggle between fascism and communism. Hitler and Mussolini sent help to the rebels; Stalin gave assistance to the left. Britain and France, in the face of widespread criticism, initiated an international non-intervention agreement to prevent the spread of the war. The fall of Madrid in spring 1939 brought Franco final victory in a conflict which left 600,000 dead.

A poster from the Spanish civil war **(left)** calls on republicans to defend Madrid and Catalonia. In 1933 the Catalans were granted partial autonomy from the capital but found themselves fighting on the same side in 1936. Catalonia and Madrid were the last areas to fall to Franco.

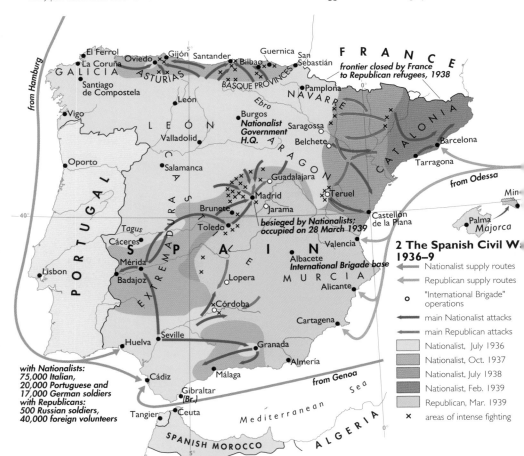

2 The Spanish Civil War 1936–9

- → Nationalist supply routes
- → Republican supply routes
- ○ "International Brigade" operations
- → main Nationalist attacks
- → main Republican attacks
- Nationalist, July 1936
- Nationalist, Oct. 1937
- Nationalist, July 1938
- Nationalist, Feb. 1939
- Republican, Mar. 1939
- ✕ areas of intense fighting

with Nationalists:
75,000 Italian,
20,000 Portuguese and
17,000 German soldiers
with Republicans:
500 Russian soldiers,
40,000 foreign volunteers

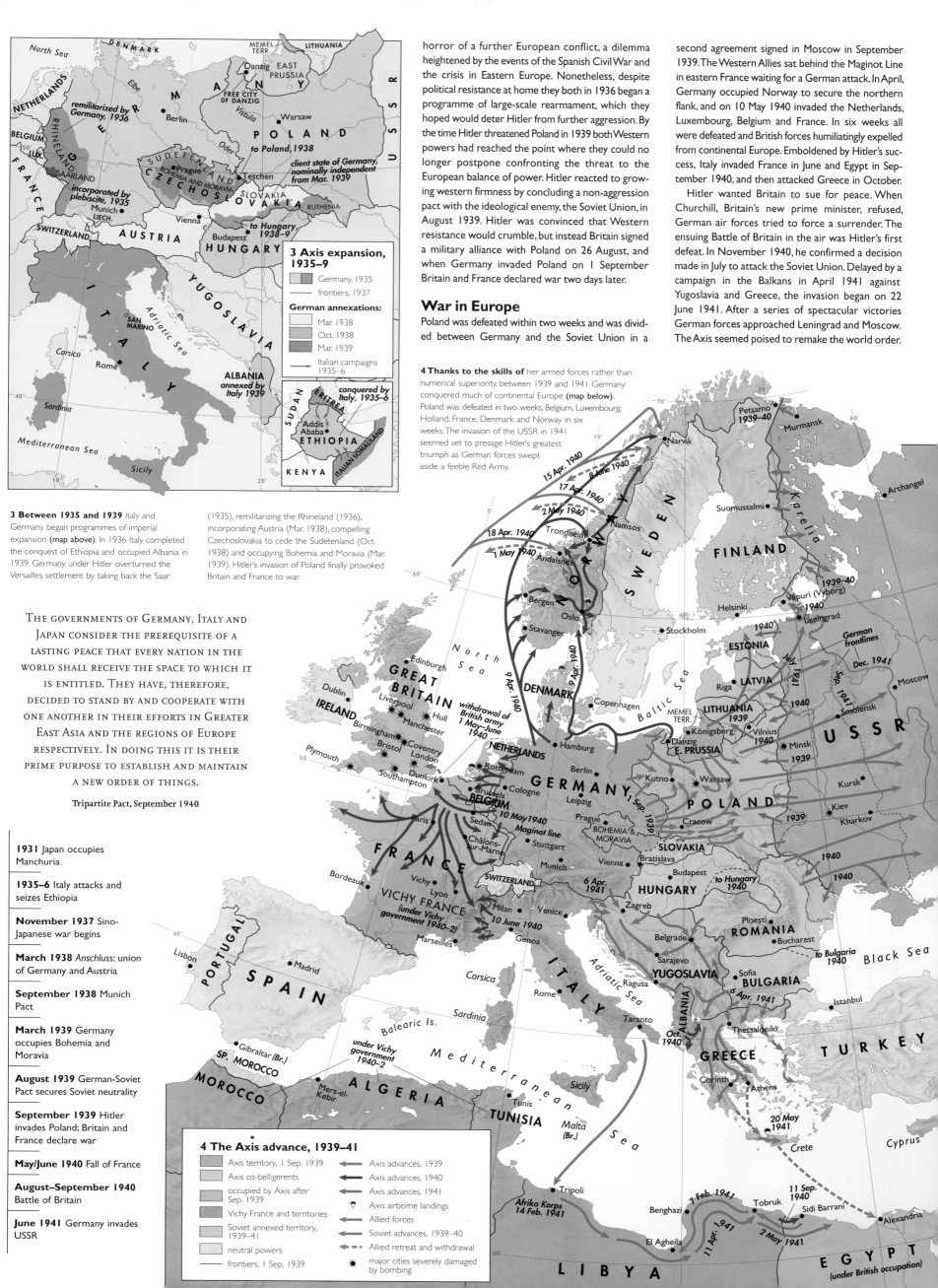

horror of a further European conflict, a dilemma heightened by the events of the Spanish Civil War and the crisis in Eastern Europe. Nonetheless, despite political resistance at home they both in 1936 began a programme of large-scale rearmament, which they hoped would deter Hitler from further aggression. By the time Hitler threatened Poland in 1939 both Western powers had reached the point where they could no longer postpone confronting the threat to the European balance of power. Hitler reacted to growing western firmness by concluding a non-aggression pact with the ideological enemy, the Soviet Union, in August 1939. Hitler was convinced that Western resistance would crumble, but instead Britain signed a military alliance with Poland on 26 August, and when Germany invaded Poland on 1 September Britain and France declared war two days later.

War in Europe

Poland was defeated within two weeks and was divided between Germany and the Soviet Union in a second agreement signed in Moscow in September 1939. The Western Allies sat behind the Maginot Line in eastern France waiting for a German attack. In April, Germany occupied Norway to secure the northern flank, and on 10 May 1940 invaded the Netherlands, Luxembourg, Belgium and France. In six weeks all were defeated and British forces humiliatingly expelled from continental Europe. Emboldened by Hitler's success, Italy invaded France in June and Egypt in September 1940, and then attacked Greece in October.

Hitler wanted Britain to sue for peace. When Churchill, Britain's new prime minister, refused, German air forces tried to force a surrender. The ensuing Battle of Britain in the air was Hitler's first defeat. In November 1940, he confirmed a decision made in July to attack the Soviet Union. Delayed by a campaign in the Balkans in April 1941 against Yugoslavia and Greece, the invasion began on 22 June 1941. After a series of spectacular victories German forces approached Leningrad and Moscow. The Axis seemed poised to remake the world order.

3 Axis expansion, 1935–9

Germany, 1935
frontiers, 1937

German annexations:
Mar. 1938
Oct. 1938
Mar. 1939

Italian campaigns 1935–6

ALBANIA annexed by Italy 1939

conquered by Italy, 1935–6

3 Between 1935 and 1939 Italy and Germany began programmes of imperial expansion (map above). In 1936 Italy completed the conquest of Ethiopia and occupied Albania in 1939. Germany under Hitler overturned the Versailles settlement by taking back the Saar (1935), remilitarizing the Rhineland (1936), incorporating Austria (Mar. 1938), compelling Czechoslovakia to cede the Sudetenland (Oct. 1938) and occupying Bohemia and Moravia (Mar. 1939). Hitler's invasion of Poland finally provoked Britain and France to war.

THE GOVERNMENTS OF GERMANY, ITALY AND JAPAN CONSIDER THE PREREQUISITE OF A LASTING PEACE THAT EVERY NATION IN THE WORLD SHALL RECEIVE THE SPACE TO WHICH IT IS ENTITLED. THEY HAVE, THEREFORE, DECIDED TO STAND BY AND COOPERATE WITH ONE ANOTHER IN THEIR EFFORTS IN GREATER EAST ASIA AND THE REGIONS OF EUROPE RESPECTIVELY. IN DOING THIS IT IS THEIR PRIME PURPOSE TO ESTABLISH AND MAINTAIN A NEW ORDER OF THINGS.

Tripartite Pact, September 1940

1931 Japan occupies Manchuria

1935–6 Italy attacks and seizes Ethiopia

November 1937 Sino-Japanese war begins

March 1938 *Anschluss*: union of Germany and Austria

September 1938 Munich Pact

March 1939 Germany occupies Bohemia and Moravia

August 1939 German-Soviet Pact secures Soviet neutrality

September 1939 Hitler invades Poland; Britain and France declare war

May/June 1940 Fall of France

August–September 1940 Battle of Britain

June 1941 Germany invades USSR

4 Thanks to the skills of her armed forces rather than numerical superiority, between 1939 and 1941 Germany conquered much of continental Europe (map below). Poland was defeated in two weeks, Belgium, Luxembourg, Holland, France, Denmark and Norway in six weeks. The invasion of the USSR in 1941 seemed set to presage Hitler's greatest triumph as German forces swept aside a feeble Red Army.

4 The Axis advance, 1939–41

Axis territory, 1 Sep. 1939
Axis co-belligerents
occupied by Axis after Sep. 1939
Vichy France and territories
Soviet annexed territory, 1939–41
neutral powers
frontiers, 1 Sep. 1939

Axis advances, 1939
Axis advances, 1940
Axis advances, 1941
Axis airborne landings
Allied forces
Soviet advances, 1939–40
Allied retreat and withdrawal
major cities severely damaged by bombing

The war in Asia and the Pacific

In 1941 Japan embarked on an ambitious programme of expansion in the Pacific and Southeast Asia. War with the USA and Britain, together with the ongoing war with China, proved more than Japanese resources could cope with. In 1945, after the US air force had reduced many of her cities to ruin, two by atomic weapons, Japan capitulated.

WHEN AIR RAIDS GOT SEVERE, AND THERE WAS NO OPPOSITION BY OUR PLANES, AND FACTORIES WERE DESTROYED, I FELT AS IF WE WERE FIGHTING MACHINERY WITH BAMBOO. WE COULD HARDLY STAND IT. THE GOVERNMENT KEPT TELLING US THAT THEY WOULD DEFEAT THE UNITED STATES FORCES AFTER THEY LANDED HERE, BUT AS MY HOUSE WAS BURNED DOWN AND I HAD NO FOOD, CLOTHING OR SHELTER, I DIDN'T KNOW HOW I COULD GO ON.

Japanese bombing victim, 1946

THE GERMAN VICTORIES in the Soviet Union in 1941 prompted Japanese leaders to establish a new order in Southeast Asia and the Pacific while the colonial powers were weakened and before the United States began serious rearmament. The object was to create a southern zone which could be defended by the formidable Japanese navy while resources, particularly oil, were seized and shipped north to help the Japanese war economy and stiffen the Japanese army in its war with China.

The decision for war with the United States was taken in November 1941 and on 7 December Japanese aircraft attacked the Pearl Harbor naval base in the Hawaiian islands, crippling part of the US Pacific Fleet. Japan then occupied European colonial territories to the south – Burma, Malaya, Singapore, the East Indies – and captured a string of Pacific Islands stretching to the Solomons north of Australia. Though Japanese warships threatened Ceylon and Madagascar, there were no plans to occupy any larger region despite the rapid and comprehensive success of the original campaign.

The Japanese attack on Pearl Harbor brought the United States fully into the war. Within a year the USA was turning out more vehicles, ships and aircraft than all the other combatant powers together. Japan could not hope to compete with American industrial might on this scale and planned instead to inflict a crippling defeat on what was left of the US Pacific Fleet, severing American communications across the Pacific and forcing a compromise peace. The naval battle sought by Admiral Yamamoto was fought off Midway Island between 3 and 6 June and resulted in a major Japanese defeat. In August 1942 US forces, commanded by General MacArthur, invaded Tulagi and Guadalcanal in the Solomons.

The Allied build-up

Though the Allies could not afford to allow the Pacific campaign to divert resources from the European theatre, sufficient supplies were made available to push the Japanese back island by island, using a combination of massive air power, fast carriers and submarines. The Japanese merchant fleet, on which the whole southern campaign relied, was reduced from over 5 million tons in 1942 to 670,000 tons in 1945. Communications were cut when US forces reoccupied the Philippines in 1944 and seized the Marianas. Japan threw its final air and naval reserves into these battles. Defeated in the Philippine Sea in June 1944 and at Leyte Gulf in October, the remaining Japanese forces were stranded in what was left of the

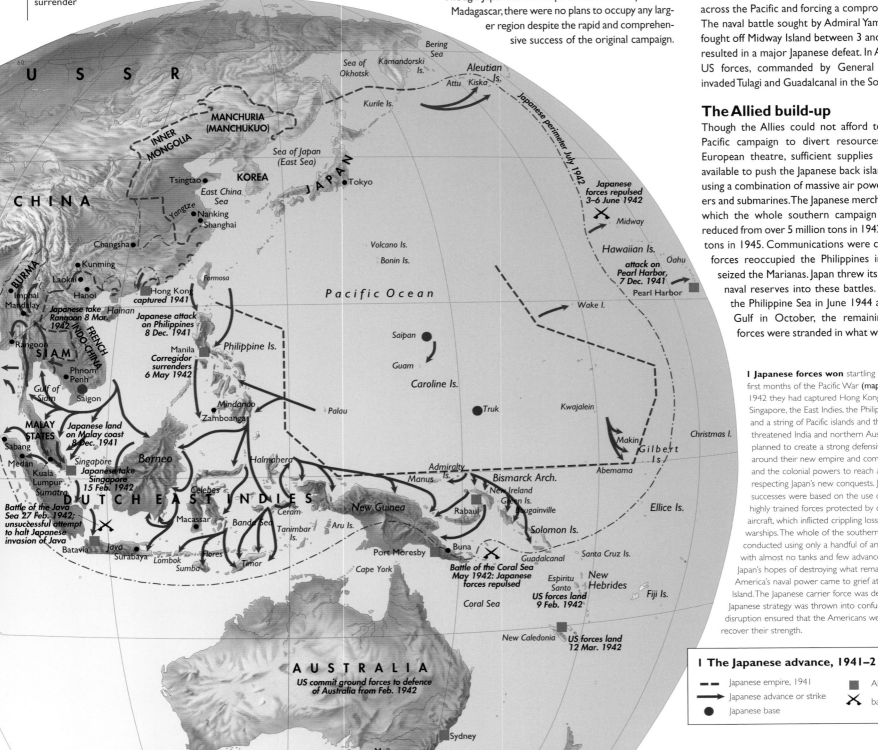

1 Japanese forces won startling victories in the first months of the Pacific War (map left). By April 1942 they had captured Hong Kong, Malaya, Singapore, the East Indies, the Philippines, Burma and a string of Pacific islands and their armies threatened India and northern Australia. Japan planned to create a strong defensive perimeter around their new empire and compel the USA and the colonial powers to reach an agreement respecting Japan's new conquests. Japan's successes were based on the use of small but highly trained forces protected by carrier-borne aircraft, which inflicted crippling losses on enemy warships. The whole of the southern campaign was conducted using only a handful of army divisions with almost no tanks and few advanced weapons. Japan's hopes of destroying what remained of America's naval power came to grief at Midway Island. The Japanese carrier force was destroyed and Japanese strategy was thrown into confusion. The disruption ensured that the Americans were able to recover their strength.

1 The Japanese advance, 1941–2

- – – Japanese empire, 1941
- → Japanese advance or strike
- ● Japanese base
- ■ Allied base
- ✗ battle

southern empire. Only fanatical resistance held up the Allied advance. By the spring of 1945, with the fall of Iwo Jima and Okinawa, America was in a position to attack mainland Japan.

The final defeat

The war in Asia made slower progress. In March 1944 Japan's forces in Burma attacked India, but were decisively defeated at Imphal with the loss of 53,000 men out of 85,000. In China, Japanese forces in the north fought both the Chinese Nationalists and the Communists under Mao Zedong. A million men were tied down in the Chinese war, which soaked up far more resources than the southern campaign. In 1944 Japan launched its last major offensive, Ichi-Go, which brought a large area of south-central China under Japanese rule, opened up a land-link with Indo-China and destroyed the Nationalist armies.

But victory in China came just as Allied forces in the Pacific could bring mainland Japan into their sights. Between March and June 1945, a series of devastating air raids were launched in which heavy B-29 bombers destroyed 58 Japanese cities, killing more than 393,000 Japanese civilians. Within the Japanese government arguments continued through the summer about surrendering, but the military refused to countenance such a dishonour. Suicide pilots (*kamikaze*) were sent out to attack Allied shipping, sinking or damaging 402 ships. America planned Operation Downfall for the invasion of the Japanese home islands, using 14,000 aircraft and 100 aircraft carriers, but the decision to drop atomic bombs on Hiroshima and Nagasaki in August 1945 ended Japanese resistance. On 15 August, with her cities in ruins and her economy devastated, Japan surrendered unconditionally to the Allies.

The devastation inflicted by the first atomic bomb (above). It was dropped on the city of Hiroshima by the United States on 6 August 1945. Nagasaki suffered the same fate three days later. The immediate death toll was over 200,000. Japan finally surrendered. The world had entered the atomic age.

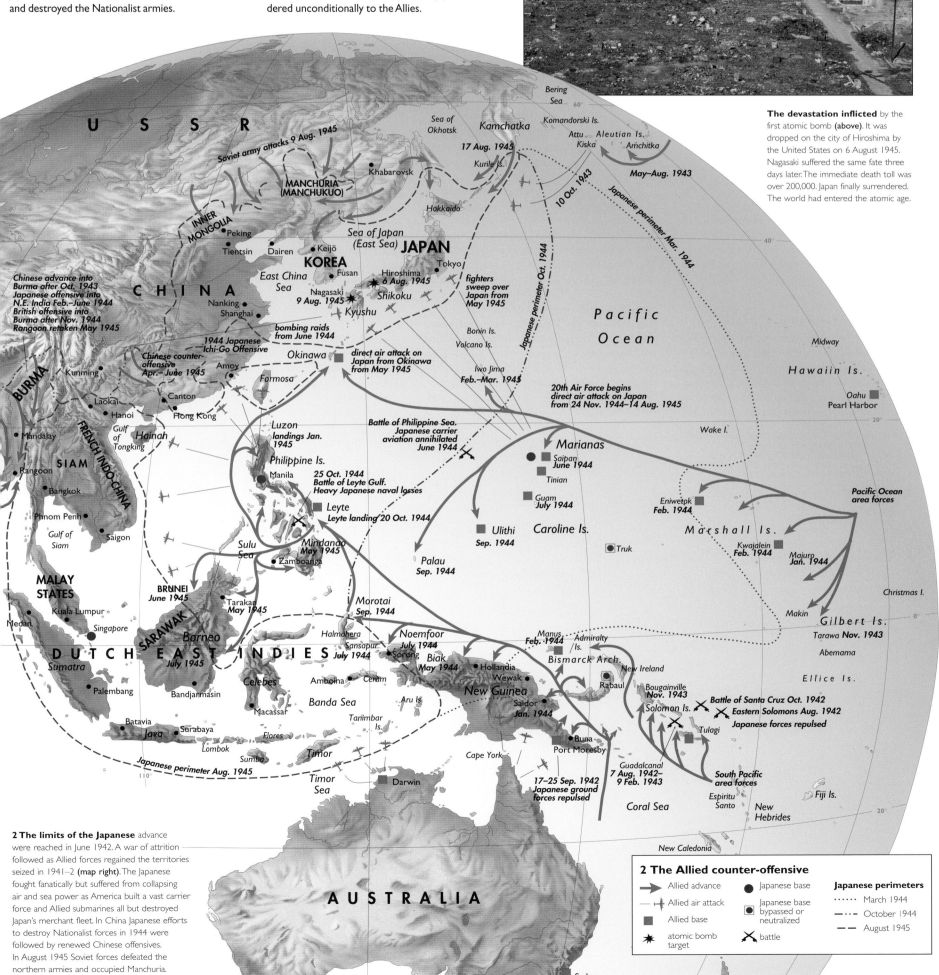

2 The limits of the Japanese advance were reached in June 1942. A war of attrition followed as Allied forces regained the territories seized in 1941–2 (map right). The Japanese fought fanatically but suffered from collapsing air and sea power as America built a vast carrier force and Allied submarines all but destroyed Japan's merchant fleet. In China Japanese efforts to destroy Nationalist forces in 1944 were followed by renewed Chinese offensives. In August 1945 Soviet forces defeated the northern armies and occupied Manchuria.

2 The Allied counter-offensive

→ Allied advance	● Japanese base
⊣ Allied air attack	■ Japanese base bypassed or neutralized
■ Allied base	
✳ atomic bomb target	✕ battle

Japanese perimeters
······ March 1944
–·–·– October 1944
– – – August 1945

297

The European war

The Second World War was the largest and bloodiest conflict in human history, bringing the deaths of more than 55 million people and transforming the international order. In Europe, the main land battle was won in the East but the bombing offensive in the West destroyed German air power, paving the way for the invasion of German-held Western Europe.

> IT WAS THE BLOODIEST AND MOST FEROCIOUS DAY OF THE WHOLE BATTLE. ALONG A FRONT OF FOUR TO FIVE KILOMETRES, THEY THREW IN FIVE BRAND-NEW INFANTRY DIVISIONS AND TWO TANK DIVISIONS, SUPPORTED BY MASSES OF INFANTRY AND PLANES. THAT MORNING YOU COULD NOT HEAR THE SEPARATE SHOTS OR EXPLOSIONS; THE WHOLE THING MERGED INTO ONE CONTINUOUS DEAFENING ROAR.
>
> **General Chuikov on Stalingrad, 1942**

July 1941 "Final solution" initiated

Sep. 1942–Feb. 1943 Battle of Stalingrad

Nov. 1942 Anglo-American landings in north Africa

June 1943 Combined Bomber Offensive launched

July 1943 Battle of Kursk: USSR defeats Germany

Sep. 1943 Italy surrenders to Allies

6 June 1944 D-Day: Allied invasion of France

2 May 1945 Fall of Berlin

7 May 1945 German surrender

BY THE AUTUMN OF 1941 Hitler's empire in Europe had reached its zenith. German forces, buttressed by the industrial resources of a whole continent, seemed unconquerable. Yet within a year the balance began to tilt towards the Allies. Despite his failure to defeat the USSR in 1941, in December that year Hitler nonetheless declared war on the USA. Germany now faced not only a two-front war but enemies who were rapidly learning from their earlier mistakes and, above all in the shape of the USA, could claim immense and increasing military and industrial potential.

The turn of the tide

But in early 1942, the prospects for the Allies looked bleak. The Soviet Union had suffered catastrophic losses, American rearmament was in its infancy and the U-Boat war in the Atlantic was strangling British trade. The Allied cause was saved by a remarkable resurgence of Soviet fighting power and morale in the face of the most barbarous conflict of the war and by the prodigious manufacturing record of American industry. In 1944 Allied aircraft production reached 168,000 against only 39,000 German.

Allied victory was also aided by German treatment of the conquered areas. Instead of winning the conquered peoples over to Hitler's European "New Order" and to his crusade against communism, German rule was terroristic and exploitative. More than seven million Europeans, from France to Russia, were taken as forced labour to Germany. One-third of Germany's war costs was met by tribute extracted from occupied Europe. Thousands were executed or imprisoned for their ideological beliefs. Nazi racism was directed at the so-called lower races in the East, who were to be enslaved, and against Jews, Gypsies and the disabled. Around 6 million Jews were murdered in a state-sponsored campaign of genocide.

At the end of 1942 German forces suffered their first reverses, at El Alamein in north Africa and at Stalingrad. Anglo-American forces landed in Morocco and Algeria in November 1942, and in the same month the Red Army began an offensive on the Don river which initiated almost three years of continuous Soviet victories. The following spring the submarine offensive in the Atlantic was ended by the use of combined air and sea power, allowing American assistance to pour into Europe on a massive scale. In July 1943 the Western Allies invaded Sicily, opening up a major southern front which drained German resources, while at Kursk on the Russian steppe the largest pitched battle in history was won by an increasingly well-organized Red Army.

The defeat of Germany

In June 1943 Anglo-American forces in Britain and the Mediterranean began the Combined Bombing Offensive, which by the spring of 1944 had imposed crippling destruction on the German urban population, undermined further expansion of German war

1 During the war German leaders planned a European "New Order" (map below). At its core was an enlarged "Greater Germany", around it a ring of dependent and satellite states. In the east a vast colonial empire was to be established, economically exploited and ethnically cleansed. A continent-wide economy was to be centred on Berlin and Vienna.

1 MEDJIMURJE and PREKMURJE (to Hungary 1941)
2 NORTHERN SLOVENIA (to Germany 1941)
3 PROTECTORATE OF BOHEMIA AND MORAVIA (to Germany, semi-autonomous, 1939)
4 WESTERN POLAND (to Germany 1939)
5 BIALYSTOK (to Germany 1941)
6 SPIŠ and ORAVA (to Slovakia 1939)
7 GALICIA (to General Government 1941)
8 NORTHERN BUKOVINA (lost by Romania 1940, regained 1941)
9 NORTHERN TRANSYLVANIA (to Hungary 1940)
10 BESSARABIA (lost by Romania 1940, regained 1941)
11 TRANSNISTRIA (to Romania 1941)

production and almost destroyed the German air force. The campaign also paved the way for the massive Allied seaborne invasion of northern France in June 1944. France was liberated in four months, while Soviet forces continued their push into Eastern Europe.

Soviet victories raised the issue of the post-war order. As the likelihood of German defeat increased, the Western powers found themselves facing a second authoritarian system in the form of their Soviet ally. Conferences at Teheran in 1943 and Yalta in 1945 exposed these growing divisions over the future of Europe. Yet this potential split, though it would come to dominate the post-war world, was never great enough to break up the alliance, and in the last bitter months of fighting the Allies remained united in their determination to defeat Hitler. In 1945 a final assault on Germany brought Western and Soviet forces face to face across central Germany. On 2 May Berlin fell, two days after Hitler had committed suicide. By 7 May German forces had surrendered.

The war was enormously costly. Worldwide, at least 55 million lost their lives, including an estimated 17 million Soviet citizens. Some 10 million Germans fled Eastern Europe in 1944–5; millions of Soviet citizens were forced into internal exile or sent to Soviet labour camps (see p. 300). After four years of destruction, Europe lay in ruins, its economy shattered. The Second World War had exceeded by far the terrible cost of the First.

3 An estimated 6 million European Jews were slaughtered, worked to death or starved between 1941 and 1945 to fulfil Hitler's fanatical vision of a "Jew-free" continent **(map above right)**. The Jews were deported first to transit camps or herded into ghettos. Then, in 1941, the invasion of the USSR led to widespread massacres of Jews by German SS *Einsatzgruppen*, security police and soldiers. In 1942 extermination was organized in death-camps in Poland. Millions of Gypsies and Slavs were also murdered or starved.

2 Hitler's failure to defeat Britain by bombing and the Atlantic submarine campaign coupled with the reverse of German fortunes at Stalingrad left Germany fighting a two-front war **(map right)**. While the German army in the east was worn down by Soviet forces in a series of gigantic battles, Anglo-American armies invaded North Africa in 1942, Italy in 1943 and France in 1944. Western air forces undermined the German war effort through bombing, while partisans and resistance movements challenged German occupation.

German soldiers in the ruins of a factory in Stalingrad **(right)**. The battle was the most horrendous conflict of the war. The city was reduced to rubble, 40,000 civilians died in air raids and 624,000 Soviet and German soldiers perished.

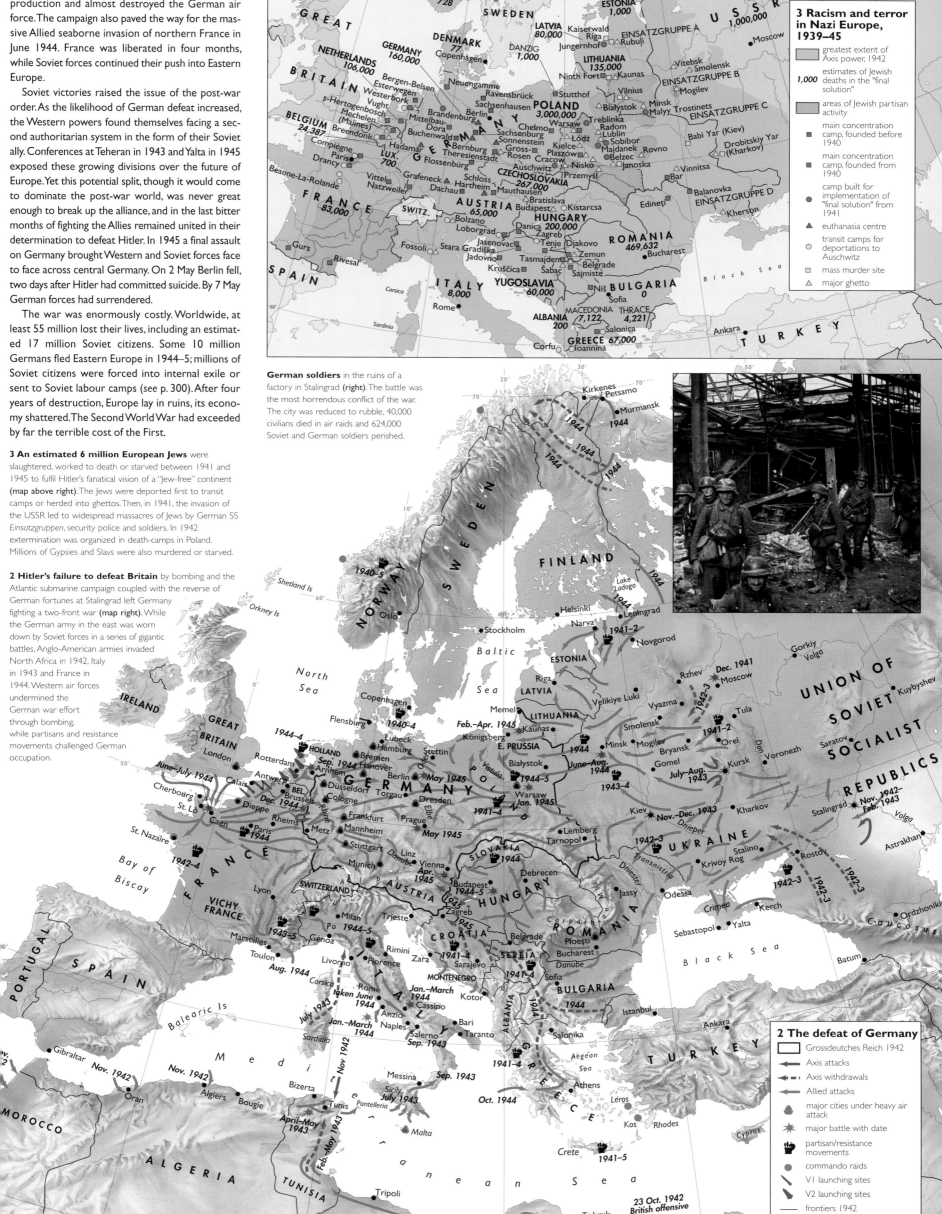

Racism and deportations

For almost 40 years Europe witnessed an exceptional period of forced population transfers, mass asylum-seeking, savage racial discrimination and genocide. Millions were forced from their homeland through political revolution, irredentism or social exclusion; millions more were murdered in the name of narrow nationalist ideologies or scientific racism.

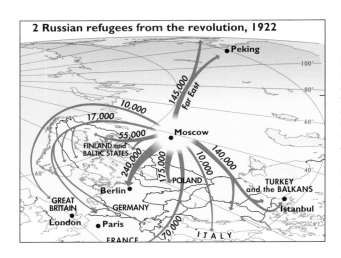

2 Russian refugees from the revolution, 1922

2 Following the Bolshevik revolution of October 1917 an estimated 863,000 Russians fled abroad to seek asylum from communism (**map left**). By 1937 over 400,000 still remained unassimilated refugees and the decision to set up a League of Nations High Commission for Refugees owed much to émigré Russian pressure to be granted official legal status as refugees.

1916 Massacre of Armenian Christians in Turkey

1922–4 Greeks expelled from Turkey, Turks from Greece

1935 Nuremberg Laws against German Jews

1937 National deportations begin in USSR

1941 Start of "Final Solution"

1942–4 Murder of European Gypsies

1945–7 Germans driven from Eastern Europe

ONE OF THE DIRECT causes of the First World War was an upsurge in extreme forms of nationalism and xenophobia. The post-war peace settlements not only failed to stem the tide, but in many cases encouraged it by leaving ethnic enclaves in states dominated by a different nationality. Millions of Germans ended up living in the newly created states of Czechoslovakia and Poland. Hundreds of thousands of Hungarians ended up under Romanian rule. Germans in the South Tyrol were ruled by Italians. In the Near East a war between Greece and Turkey ended in 1921 with the transfer of thousands of Greeks and Turks living on alien territory.

The new nationalism had a strong racial basis to it. Theories of scientific racism common before 1914 were adopted to justify policies of racial exclusion and to encourage a process of biological selection to ensure that racial stock remained pure and uncontaminated. The target of much of this racism was Europe's Jewish population. Popular anti-Semitism in the 1920s developed the idea of a world Jewish conspiracy to weaken the nation and pollute its gene pool. In many states in Central and Eastern Europe popular hostility was followed by legislation to restrict Jewish rights and economic opportunities.

Deportation and exile

The Bolshevik Revolution of 1917 provoked a bitter civil war inside the new Soviet state, which resulted in a mass exodus of almost one million former Russians to Europe and overseas. The deep ideological divisions inspired by communism and anti-communism led to further waves of exile, voluntary and otherwise. In the 1920s thousands of Italian opponents of Mussolini's fascism fled abroad; after 1933 hundreds of thousands of Germans fled from Hitler's Third Reich, including more than half Germany's Jewish population.

In the 1930s the Soviet regime began to deport sections of its own population, at first removing nationalities from the borderlands who were thought to be sympathetic to the Soviet Union's enemies – Koreans, Finns, Poles, Greeks. Then in 1939–41 millions were deported from the new lands acquired under the terms of the German-Soviet agreements of August and September 1939. From 1941, when Axis forces invaded, millions more were deported to Siberia and central Asia, including almost one million Soviet Germans, because their loyalty to the Soviet war effort was in doubt. At the end of the war more deportations removed potential anti-communist resistance in the states of Eastern Europe and nationalists in the Ukraine or Belarus who had used German occupation to extend their influence.

The murder of European Jews

The Hitler regime regarded the Soviet state as a haven for "Jewish-Bolshevism" and linked its anti-Marxism and anti-Semitism together. In the 1930s German Jews were encouraged to emigrate, stripped of their citizenship, and subjected to economic discrimination and social exclusion. As German power spread into the states of Central Europe, so the anti-Semitism became more strident. With the conquest of Poland in 1939 there began a deliberate programme of isolation and ghettoization of the Jews in the East.

In 1941 with the invasion of the USSR, the German regime began a systematic programme of murder directed at certain categories of Soviet Jews, then at

1 Under Stalin's dictatorship around three million non-Russians were deported to harsh special settlements in Siberia, Kazakhstan and Uzbekistan (**map below**) where they were forced to work under the supervision of the Soviet security apparatus. The first wave of deportations occurred in the 1930s against nationalities close to vulnerable borders. In 1939/41 and again after the war a second wave of alleged counter-revolutionaries were deported from Eastern Europe. During the war millions of Soviet Germans and Caucasian peoples were deported for alleged political unreliability and were allowed back only after Stalin's death in 1953.

1 Deportations within the Soviet Union

🏃 deported minorities (with numbers and dates of deportation)

➡️ direction of deportation

— frontiers, 1940

— maximum German advance, 1942

— Soviet Union, 1945

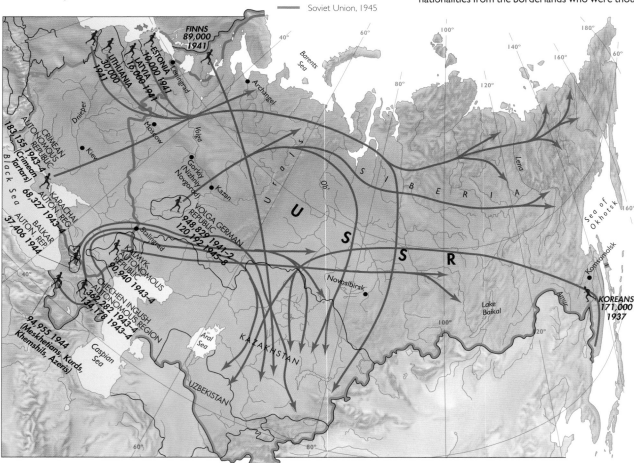

5 Jewish deaths in the Holocaust

Poland	up to 3,000,000
USSR	over 700,000
Romania	270,000
Czechoslovakia	260,000
Hungary	over 180,000
Lithuania	up to 130,000
Germany	up to 120,000
Netherlands	over 100,000
France	75,000
Latvia	70,000
Yugoslavia	60,000
Greece	60,000
Austria	over 50,000
Belgium	24,000
Italy (including Rhodes)	9000
Estonia	2000
Norway	under 1000
Luxembourg	under 1000
Danzig	under 1000
countries as of 1937	**Total 5,100,000**

3 Between 1941 and 1945 around one half of the Jews living in Europe were deliberately murdered by Nazi Germany and a number of German wartime allies and collaborators. Their geographical distribution was researched by the German secret police (*Gestapo*) and German agents were sent to occupied countries to coordinate the collection and deportation of the Jewish populations **(map left)**. They were imprisoned in holding camps in the west, or herded into ghettoes in the east, and were then shipped to a group of seven extermination camps set up in occupied Poland and Ukraine. Around 1.2 million were murdered in the east in 1941 and 1942 by mobile killing units (*Einsatzgruppen*) organized by Himmler's SS, assisted by local anti-Semites in the Baltic States and the western Soviet Union.

3 The deportation and murder of European Jews, 1941–5

- —— greatest extent of Axis power, 1942
- ○ main concentration camp, with date of foundation
- ☠ camp built for implementation of Final Solution (from 1942)
- ■ mass murder site
- ▲ major ghetto

AS AN OLD NATIONAL SOCIALIST I MUST SAY, IF THE JEWISH TRIBE WERE TO SURVIVE THE WAR, WHEREAS WE SACRIFICED OUR BEST BLOOD FOR THE PRESERVATION OF EUROPE, THEN THIS WAR WOULD REPRESENT ONLY A PARTIAL VICTORY. THEREFORE, AS REGARDS THE JEWS, I START FROM THE BASIC ASSUMPTION THAT THEY SHALL DISAPPEAR. THEY HAVE GOT TO GO.

Hans Frank, Governor of Poland, 1941

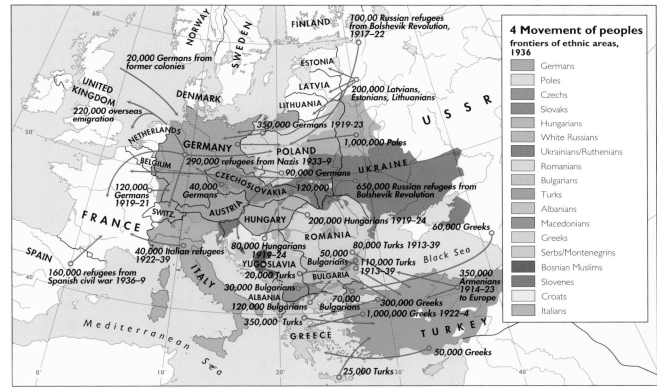

4 Movement of peoples

frontiers of ethnic areas, 1936

- Germans
- Poles
- Czechs
- Slovaks
- Hungarians
- White Russians
- Ukrainians/Ruthenians
- Romanians
- Bulgarians
- Turks
- Albanians
- Macedonians
- Greeks
- Serbs/Montenegrins
- Bosnian Muslims
- Slovenes
- Croats
- Italians

Heinrich Himmler and his deputy, Reinhard Heydrich (left). Himmler was the architect of the genocide of the Jews. As head of the Reich Security Main Office, he organized the isolation and ghettoization of the Jews under German control, and in 1941 at Hitler's insistence began the mass murder of Soviet Jews. In 1942 he operated the entire programme for the identification, deportation and murder in extermination camps of the Jewish population of Europe. In 1944, worried about the attitude of the victorious Allies, the programme was wound down. Himmler killed himself when he was captured in 1945.

4 The First World War peace settlements drawn up between 1919 and 1921 left many Europeans living in states occupied by another, dominant ethnic group **(map above)**. There occurred large transfers of population either under agreement, as in the case of Greek-Turkish population transfers, or because minority groups sought the safety of their own national homelands. In the 1930s there were renewed waves of political exiles, from Mussolini's Italy, Hitler's Germany and nationalist Spain following the civil war.

whole Jewish populations. In reaction to the coming of global war in late 1941, Hitler ordered the murder of all Europe's Jews in revenge for their alleged efforts to destroy the new Germany. A system of extermination camps was set up and more than three million Jews from all over occupied and Axis Europe were murdered in gas chambers. Some countries resisted German demands; in Bulgaria, Denmark and Italy large numbers of Jews were saved. Elsewhere local anti-Semites encouraged the programme of deportation and murder. At the end of the war the populations in the East turned on the Germans still living in their midst and around 13 million were driven westward, many ending up in America or Britain. This marked the end of a short and savage period of ethnic cleansing in Europe which resulted in the death of well over ten million people and the uprooting of millions more.

Europe

War-devastated Europe after 1945 was a continent on an ideological fault-line: capitalist and democratic in the West, communist and authoritarian in the East. The division was clear, too, in the West's superior economic performance. Despite the confrontation, the continent also experienced a growing stability and prosperity.

EUROPE WAS A REGION of extraordinary desolation in 1945. More than 30 million people had been killed and 16 million permanently displaced from their homes. Many of Europe's greatest cities lay in ruins. Industrial production had sunk to one-third of the pre-war level, agricultural production to half. The war also left a legacy of bitterness. Collaborators with fascism were ostracized, imprisoned or murdered while the revival of communism brought real fears of social collapse in the areas of Europe not under Soviet rule.

New frontiers

The first task was to dismantle Hitler's New Order in Europe (see p. 298). The new frontiers of Germany were agreed by the Allied powers at Yalta (February 1945) and Potsdam (July 1945). Germany lost its eastern territories to Poland and was separated from Austria. Czech and Yugoslav sovereignty was restored. In the East, however, the German New Order was replaced by a Soviet one. The USSR moved westward to absorb most of the territories of the former Tsarist empire – Eastern Poland, the Baltic States, Bessarabia. Czech democracy, briefly restored in 1945, was overturned in 1948. Only Yugoslavia, under the rule of Tito's communists, retained real independence from Moscow. The other states of Eastern Europe had traded one dictatorship for another.

Economic revival

The economic and social revival of Europe depended on the two superpowers: the USA and the Soviet Union. In Western Europe revival was linked to American economic strength. Through the UN and

A UNION BETWEEN FRANCE AND GERMANY WOULD GIVE NEW LIFE AND VIGOUR TO A EUROPE THAT IS SERIOUSLY ILL. IT WOULD HAVE AN IMMENSE PSYCHOLOGICAL AND MATERIAL INFLUENCE AND WOULD LIBERATE POWERS THAT ARE SURE TO SAVE EUROPE ... THE AMERICAN PEOPLE WOULD SEE SOME REAL RETURNS FOR THE BILLIONS OF DOLLARS THEY HAVE GIVEN TO EUROPE, BECAUSE THERE WOULD BE A GENUINE AND SIGNIFICANT CONTRIBUTION FROM WITHIN TO THE RECONSTRUCTION AND UNIFICATION OF EUROPE.

Konrad Adenauer, 1950

3 As the Cold War confrontation hardened after 1945, Europe was divided into two armed camps (map right). NATO was formed with the USA and Canada in 1949 as the centrepiece of Western security. In 1955 the Soviet Union created the Warsaw Pact, linking the states of the Communist bloc in a single defence pact. Economic union divided the continent along the same lines. In the West the EEC (1957) and EFTA (1960) created capitalist trading blocs matched by COMECON (1949) in the Soviet bloc.

3 European military and economic trading blocs, 1947–73

military partitions

- Nato 1949– (including United States and Canada)
- Warsaw Pact 1948–91

economic blocs

- Benelux customs union, 1947
- original European Economic Community (EEC) members, 1957
- joined EEC, 1973
- founder members of European Free Trade Association (EFTA), 1960
- subsequent EFTA members
- Council for Mutual Economic Assistance (COMECON) members, 1949
- subsequent COMECON members

2 The Marshall Plan

- applied for and received Marshall aid, with amounts (in US$)
- applied for Marshall aid but withdrew application
- did not apply

14.0% net Marshall aid as percentage of national income 1948–9

5 Rates of growth of selected European economies (average percentage per year)

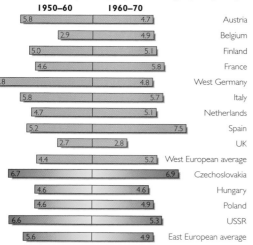

	1950–60	1960–70	
	5.8	4.7	Austria
	2.9	4.9	Belgium
	5.0	5.1	Finland
	4.6	5.8	France
	7.8	4.8	West Germany
	5.8	5.7	Italy
	4.7	5.1	Netherlands
	5.2	7.5	Spain
	2.7	2.8	UK
	4.4	5.2	West European average
	6.7	6.9	Czechoslovakia
	4.6	4.6	Hungary
	4.6	4.9	Poland
	6.6	5.3	USSR
	5.6	4.9	East European average

5 During the 1950s and 1960s all European states enjoyed exceptionally high rates of economic growth (chart above) thanks to expanding trade and a technological revolution that pushed chemicals, cars and electronics to a central role in the continent's industrial economies. West Germany above all emerged as Europe's economic powerhouse.

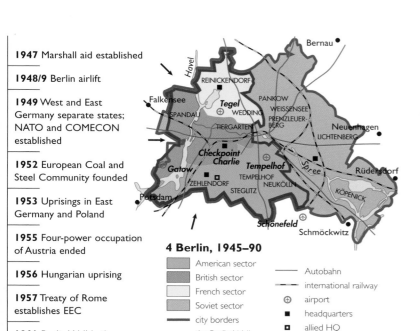

4 Berlin, 1945–90

- American sector
- British sector
- French sector
- Soviet sector
- city borders
- the Berlin Wall, 1961–89
- Autobahn
- international railway
- ⊕ airport
- ■ headquarters
- ◻ allied HQ
- → air corridor

4 Post-war Berlin (map above), though wholly within the Soviet sector of Germany, was divided into four zones administered separately by the victorious Allies. As the Cold War intensified, so the city became the focus of East-West tensions. Soviet attempts to drive the other Allies from the city in 1948 by blockading it were thwarted by a year-long airlift organized by the Western powers. A further Soviet attempt to isolate the city in 1958 also failed. In 1961, exasperated by the flood of refugees fleeing to the Western zones, the Soviets divided the city physically in two, erecting a wall across it overnight (**picture above right**).

2 In the spring of 1947 US Secretary of State George Marshall put his name to a European Recovery Programme backed by American finance. The Marshall Plan (**map left**) sought to get the European economy back on its feet by enabling Europe to purchase goods from the dollar area, and to promote a more stable political situation. The aid was intended for all European countries, capitalist and communist alike. However, Stalin refused to allow any countries of Soviet-dominated Eastern Europe to accept it and the $11.8 billion went entirely to West and Southern Europe.

6 Unemployment as a percentage of the labour force

	1950–60	1960–70
Austria	3.9	1.9
Belgium	4.0	2.2
France	1.3	1.4
West Germany	4.2	0.8
Italy	7.9	3.3
Netherlands	1.9	1.1
Norway	1.0	1.0
Sweden	1.7	1.7
Switzerland	0.2	0.0
UK	1.2	1.6

6 Unemployment was almost eliminated in the post-war boom (**chart above**). Spending and tax policies boosted employment while training schemes produced a more employable workforce.

1 War and its aftermath drove millions of Europeans from their homelands (**map right**). An estimated 30 million people became refugees, most of them permanently displaced. Territorially, the Soviet Union emerged as the major victor, its borders shifted dramatically to the west. Politically, it also dominated Eastern Europe. Germany, greatly reduced, became two states in 1949, those areas occupied by the Western Allies becoming the Federal Republic, the Soviet zone becoming the German Democratic Republic, a division which endured until 1990.

the International Bank for Reconstruction and Development the USA pumped $17 billion into Europe's economy. In 1947 a European Recovery Programme was set up which released another $11.8 billion. In 1948 the 16 nations qualifying for aid set up the Organization for European Economic Cooperation to coordinate the aid programme, the harbinger of much closer economic collaboration over the following decades. In 1952, France, Germany,

Italy and the Benelux countries set up the European Coal and Steel Community to coordinate industry in their countries. In 1957 they moved to a full customs union, the European Economic Community.

Western Europe underwent the greatest economic boom in its history. By 1950 output of goods was 35 per cent higher than in 1938; by 1964 it was 250 per cent higher. Even in Eastern Europe's command economy there was sustained economic growth though the price was high: low living standards, pollution and police oppression. The gap between the two economic systems widened greatly in the 1950s and 1960s, fuelling popular unrest in the East. There were strikes and political protests in East Germany and Poland in 1953, in Hungary in 1956 and Czechoslovakia in 1968, all violently suppressed by the USSR.

In the West, the EEC made another war between France and Germany virtually unthinkable and the two countries' relationship lay at the heart of the continent's new political alignment from the 1950s onwards. Economic growth encouraged political stability, too. Democracy was restored in Italy in 1946, in West Germany in 1949, in Austria in 1955. Authoritarianism survived in Portugal and Spain, and emerged briefly in Greece after 1967, but it remained the exception. Local independence movements in Northern Ireland, the Basque region of Spain and in Corsica produced sporadic violence, but the nationalist tensions that brought war twice since 1914 finally evaporated.

1 Post-war population movements and territorial change

Territorial change and population movements, 1945–9
- ▪▪ cities divided into four occupation zones
- frontiers, 1949
- border of Germany, 1937
- Allied control zones of Germany and Austria
- annexed by Soviet Union 1940–5
- states which became Communist 1945–8
- Yugoslav gains from Italy, 1945
- Federal Republic of Germany from 1949
- German Democratic Republic from 1949

peoples resettled, evacuated or expelled (with numbers):
- → Germans
- → Finns driven from area bordering Russia
- → Baltic peoples
- → Russians
- → Russians forcibly repatriated
- → Poles
- → Czechs
- → peoples settled by International Refugee Organisation

The Cold War

At the end of the Second World War, the world was dominated by the USA and the USSR. Their ideological differences produced a complete polarization between the capitalist West and the communist bloc. Both sides developed nuclear arsenals but the fear of nuclear destruction led to a "Cold War", a confrontation short of armed conflict.

AFTER 1945 THE INTERNATIONAL order was dominated by the division between the capitalist West and communist East, each side grouped around the two new "superpowers" that emerged from the defeat of Hitler: the United States in the West, the Soviet Union in the East. Yet though their hostility produced persistent confrontation, open conflict was avoided, a state described by the American journalist Walter Lippmann as "Cold War".

The source of the conflict

The roots of the Cold War lay in the Russian revolution of 1917. Communism, with its belief in its own inevitable domination of the world, was seen as a profound threat to the world capitalist system, of which the USA was taking the leadership. The United States and the other Western Allies had found themselves allied to the Soviet Union in the Second World War through force of circumstance: the imperatives of defeating Hitler overrode all other considerations, though this did not prevent persistently strained relations throughout the war. But with Hitler beaten, the underlying tensions resurfaced. The West saw in Soviet communism the spectre of a second expansionist authoritarian system, while for its part the USSR believed it had helped defeat one form of capitalist imperialism only to be confronted with an even more powerful one in the form of the USA.

The height of the Cold War

With both sides eager to avoid open conflict, the Cold War was fought out in a world of spies and secrets, political threat and subversion. In large measure it was a war fought by proxy. Both camps exploited

CONSCIOUS OF THE SPECIAL RESPONSIBILITY OF THE USSR AND THE US FOR MAINTAINING PEACE, [THEY] HAVE AGREED THAT A NUCLEAR WAR CANNOT BE WON AND MUST NEVER BE FOUGHT. RECOGNIZING THAT ANY CONFLICT BETWEEN THE USSR AND THE US COULD HAVE CATASTROPHIC CONSEQUENCES, THEY EMPHASIZE THE IMPORTANCE OF PREVENTING ANY WAR BETWEEN THEM, WHETHER NUCLEAR OR CONVENTIONAL.

Reagan-Gorbachev Joint Statement, 1985

or entered local conflicts in which they armed, equipped and trained the opposing sides, each seeking to extend their spheres of influence without coming to blows directly.

Tension was most acute in the period between 1947 and 1963, as the new political order in Europe and Asia was being fashioned, above all in Central and Eeastern Europe where the USSR sought to impose itself on those territories it had liberated in the war. The consolidation of communist regimes in the region combined with the success of the communist revolution in China in 1949 under Mao Zedong created an apparently solid communist bloc from Europe to the Pacific, though by 1960 an open rift developed in Sino-Soviet relations.

America in 1947 committed itself to "containing" communism (the Truman Doctrine) and lent support to countries fighting wars against the communist

threat, in Greece (1947), in Korea (1950–3) and then in the long and draining conflict in Vietnam (1961–73). At the same time, the United States tried to bolster these efforts by creating security blocs – NATO in Europe in 1949, SEATO in Southeast Asia in 1954 and CENTO in the Middle East in 1959. The Soviet Union and China retaliated by giving military aid and political support to anti-colonial and nationalist struggles against "world imperialism" throughout Asia, Latin America and Africa. In 1955 the Soviet Union also sponsored a military alliance of its own, the Warsaw Pact.

The shadow of the bomb

The most important factor preventing the shift to "hot war" was the existence of nuclear weapons. First used in 1945 against Japan, America's monopoly of the weapon was broken by the Soviet Union in 1949. In 1952 the USA developed thermonuclear weapons, with still more destructive power, and by 1953 the Soviet Union had them, too. By 1958 the American arsenal of warheads was estimated to be able to kill 200 million on a first strike. The development of intercontinental ballistic missiles and

2 Following Castro's quasi-communist revolution in Cuba in 1959, the USA boycotted the new regime and in 1961 backed a failed counter-revolutionary invasion. Castro turned to the USSR for help, who in 1962 began to install nuclear missiles on the island. On 14 October the sites were spotted by a US reconnaissance plane, and President Kennedy ordered a quarantine of Cuba, to be enforced by the US Navy, while asking the USSR to withdraw the nuclear bases (**map left**). On 26 October, following the most dangerous confrontation of the Cold War, Khrushchev ordered the withdrawal.

1947 Greek Civil War; Truman Doctrine announced

1948–9 Berlin airlift

1949 NATO formed

1949 Soviet Union detonates first nuclear bomb

1950–3 Korean War

1955 Warsaw Pact formed

1962 Cuban missile crisis

1964–73 USA intervenes militarily in Vietnam

1979 Soviet Union invades Afghanistan

1987 INF treaty: phased elimination of intermediate range nuclear weapons

1991 Collapse of USSR; Cold War ends

2 The Cuban missile crisis, 1962

- US blockade zone
- range of Soviet missiles
- Soviet missile and jet bomber bases
- US Air Force base
- US naval base

UNITED STATES OF AMERICA

Ft. Worth · Dallas · · Atlanta
Birmingham
Jacksonville
Houston · New Orleans
San Antonio
Tampa
Gulf of Mexico
Monterrey
Homestead · Miami
Key West
1,100 miles
Guanajay · Nassau
Sagua la Grande · THE BAHAMAS
San Cristóbal · Havana · Remedios
Tampico
Bay of Pigs
Santa Clara · CUBA
1,100 miles
Atlantic Ocean
Veracruz
Guantánamo
DOMINICAN REP.
Mexico City
Puebla
HAITI
San Juan
PUERTO RICO (USA)
JAMAICA · Kingston · Santo Domingo
ANTIGUA
BELIZE
Belmopan
DOMINICA
HONDURAS
GUAT.
Guatemala · Tegucigalpa
Caribbean Sea
ST LUCIA
ST VINCENT
EL SALVADOR · NICARAGUA
Managua
GRENADA
BARBADOS
TRINIDAD & TOBAGO
Barranquilla
COSTA RICA
San José
Panama City
Caracas
Port of Spain
Pacific Ocean
PANAMA · COLOMBIA
VENEZUELA
Orinoco

The age of bipolarity / map labels

Pacific Ocean — Midway, Hawaii, Wake, Kwajelein, Iwo Jima, Guam

US 7th fleet

JAPAN
Okinawa
S. KOREA 1950–53
TAIWAN 1954–55, 1958
Quemoy, Matsu 1954–55, 1958
PHILIPPINES
MALAYSIA
SOUTH VIETNAM 1945–54, 1957–73
LAOS
THAILAND
EAST PAKISTAN
CHINA — left Soviet bloc, 1960
MONGOLIA
SOVIET UNION
INDIA
PAKISTAN
AFGHANISTAN
IRAN
IRAQ 1958
SAUDI ARABIA
Arctic Ocean
Indian Ocean
NORWAY
E. GERMANY
DENMARK
POLAND
CZECH.
HUNGARY
ROMANIA
YUGO. 1948–53 BULGARIA
ITALY
ALBANIA
GREECE 1946–9
TURKEY 1945–7
LEBANON 1958
US 6th fleet
LIBYA
EGYPT
Suez, 1956
FRANCE
SPAIN
PORTUGAL
UNITED KINGDOM
BELGIUM
HOLLAND
GERMANY
ALASKA

1 The age of bipolarity

- USA and allies, 1958
- USSR and allies, 1958
- Soviet ICBM bases (11,250 km / 7000 mile range)
- other Soviet missile sites, 1961
- principal Soviet military airfields
- US ICBM bases (8000 km / 5000 mile range)
- US heavy bomber bases (capable of reaching USSR with airborne refuelling)
- US nuclear and other major bases (Oct. 1962)
- strategic US fleets
- points of conflict in the Cold War
- uprisings in the communist world

Czechoslovakia
1948
1968

East Germany
Berlin 1948–9, 1958–62
Berlin 1953

Hungary
1956

Poland
1945–8, 1956

Lithuania (L)
1945–7

Ukraine (U)
1945–50

---

1 The world order after 1945 was divided into a bi-polar confrontation between the US-led capitalist states and the Soviet-dominated communist bloc (**map left**). The NATO system and the Warsaw Pact created an armed camp in Europe either side of an "Iron Curtain". A network of bases was set up by the USA to hem in the USSR with the threat of nuclear missile attack, but the subsequent development of intercontinental missiles which could directly attack the enemy's territory created the prospect of mutual assured destruction. This threat prevented the Cold War from slipping into open nuclear conflict, despite conventional wars in the Middle East, Korea, Indo-China and central Asia.

submarine-launched missiles in the 1950s then gave both sides the ability to destroy the other almost entirely, indeed to obliterate much of the globe. By the 1960s, Britain, France and China had also developed a nuclear capability. The prospect of mutual destruction on a horrific scale acted as a deterrent to conflict. The closest the world came to war was the Cuban missile crisis of 1962 (see map 2). The experience so alarmed the two sides that from 1963 a slow thaw set in with the signing of a partial test-ban treaty.

It was followed in 1969 with the opening of strategic arms limitation talks (SALT) and, in 1970, by a nuclear non-proliferation treaty (though France, China, India, Pakistan and Israel refused to sign). Although relations improved again in the early 1970s with the advent of détente, tensions increased with the communist victory in Vietnam and the Soviet military intervention in Afghanistan in 1979. The USA responded in the early 1980s with renewed anti-Soviet rhetoric and a massive rearmament programme, calculating that the cost of matching it would be more than the already impoverished Soviet economy could bear.

The expense of maintaining their unwinnable war in Afghanistan coupled with the costs of this renewed arms race was to prove too great a burden for the USSR. In 1985 President Gorbachev announced Soviet willingness to disarm and between 1985 and 1987 negotiations proceeded for the progressive reduction of nuclear arsenals. The collapse of the Soviet communist bloc in 1989–91 and reform in Asian communist states brought the Cold War to an end.

US inspectors at a Soviet nuclear weapons site 20km (12 miles) from Saratov (**below**). Under the terms of the disarmament agreement of 1987 both sides agreed to decommission a large proportion of their nuclear stockpiles and to a system of mutual inspections.

3 The nuclear monopoly enjoyed by the USA in 1945 was ended in August 1949 when the USSR tested its first bomb. Britain, France and China subsequently developed their own nuclear forces, but the two superpowers had vastly greater arsenals (**chart below left**). The USA kept a lead in intercontinental nuclear capability; the USSR had more short-range missiles for use in Europe. The warheads available by the 1950s were capable of obliterating either side.

---

3 The nuclear balance, 1955–80

USSR intercontinental
- bombers
- land missiles
- sea missiles
- warheads

1955 1960 1965 1970 1975 1980

USA intercontinental
- bombers
- land missiles
- sea missiles
- warheads

1955 1960 1965 1970 1975 1980

USSR regional
- bombers
- missiles
- warheads

1955 1960 1965 1970 1975 1980

USA regional
- bombers
- missiles

1955 1960 1965 1970 1975 1980

Retreat from empire

1939–45 Second World War: 1940, fall of France; 1942, Japan overruns Europe's Far Eastern colonies; 1943, Italy surrenders; 1945, Allied victory

1947 India partitioned; India and Pakistan independent

1954 Communist Vietnamese defeat French at Dien Bien Phu; start of the Algerian War

1956 Britain and France unsuccessfully invade Egypt after President Nasser seizes Suez Canal

1957–68 Independence for British African colonies

1960 Independence for all French sub-Saharan colonies and Belgian Congo

1962 France withdraws from Algeria

1965 Rhodesian white settlers declare UDI (Unilateral Declaration of Independence), resulting in guerrilla war

1975 Portuguese rule in Africa ends

1997 Hong Kong returned to China

In 1939 European colonial powers still controlled much of Asia, the Caribbean and the Pacific and almost all of Africa. The dissolution of their empires after 1945, frequently accompanied by violence, was one of the most remarkable transformations of the modern world. By the 1990s only a handful of European dependencies remained.

> THE WIND OF CHANGE IS BLOWING THROUGH THIS CONTINENT, AND, WHETHER WE LIKE IT OR NOT, THIS GROWTH OF NATIONAL CONSCIOUSNESS IS A POLITICAL FACT.
>
> Harold Macmillan, 1960

> NATIONAL LIBERATION, NATIONAL RENAISSANCE, THE RESTORATION OF NATIONHOOD TO THE PEOPLE, COMMONWEALTH: WHATEVER MAY BE THE HEADINGS USED OR THE NEW FORMULA INTRODUCED, DECOLONIZATION IS ALWAYS A VIOLENT PHENOMENON.
>
> Franz Fanon
> *The Wretched of the Earth*, 1961

BY 1939 THERE WERE already significant nationalist movements in some European colonies. Britain, France and the Netherlands were also, to varying degrees, committed to the evolution of their colonial territories towards self-government, and this commitment was reinforced, in the case of Great Britain and France, by the terms under which they had been granted mandates by the League of Nations over territories formerly part of the German and Ottoman empires.

The Second World War accelerated these developments. The Italian empire was dismembered entirely, while after the war the remaining European colonial powers no longer had the economic muscle to enforce imperial rule. Furthermore, international politics were dominated by the two avowedly anti-colonial superpowers, the United States and the USSR. In addition, in east Asia, where the British, French and Dutch set about attempting to restore control of colonies overrun by the Japanese in the war, nationalists were unwilling to return to dependence. Similarly, in north Africa, Anglo-American occupation of French colonies during the war revitalized the independence movements there, while in British India independence had already been promised during the war in an unsuccessful attempt to secure the cooperation of the nationalist Congress.

Asia

It was in Asia that nationalists and, in some colonies, communists, presented the greatest challenges to European colonialism. The British, knowing they could not hold India on pre-war terms, advanced the subcontinent rapidly towards independence in 1947. Neither Britain nor Congress was able to resist the Muslim campaign for a separate state of Pakistan, and India was partitioned in circumstances of great violence. The following year Britain abandoned its mandate in Palestine, and withdrew from Ceylon and Burma. In Malaya a long struggle against communist insurgents culminated in Britain granting independence in 1957. The Dutch never regained control of the Dutch East Indies after the Japanese left and independence was finally achieved in 1949. In Vietnam communists and nationalists opposed the restored French administrations. After prolonged conflict and military defeat at Dien Bien Phu, the French abandoned their Far Eastern empire.

2 In the 30 years after the end of the Second World War the colonial territories were given up by the European powers **(map right)**. Though American and Soviet hostility to colonialism put pressure on war-weakened Europe to relinquish its empires, it was the impossibility of defending the empires against nationalist movements within the colonial areas that finally eroded Europe's imperialism. The British Commonwealth, however, endured as a largely non-political association, while some small islands **(map below)**, for reasons of economic or political pragmatism, have so far opted to remain as dependencies.

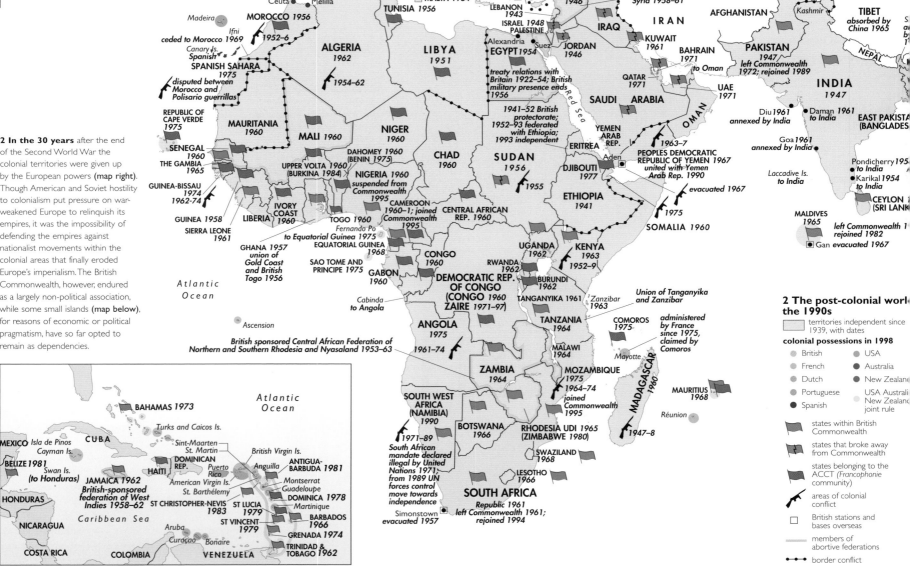

2 The post-colonial world in the 1990s

☐ territories independent since 1939, with dates

colonial possessions in 1998

- British
- French
- Dutch
- Portuguese
- Spanish
- USA
- Australia
- New Zealand
- USA Australia New Zealand joint rule

🏴 states within British Commonwealth

🏴 states that broke away from Commonwealth

🏴 states belonging to the ACCT (Francophonie community)

⚔ areas of colonial conflict

☐ British stations and bases overseas

━ members of abortive federations

•━•━• border conflict

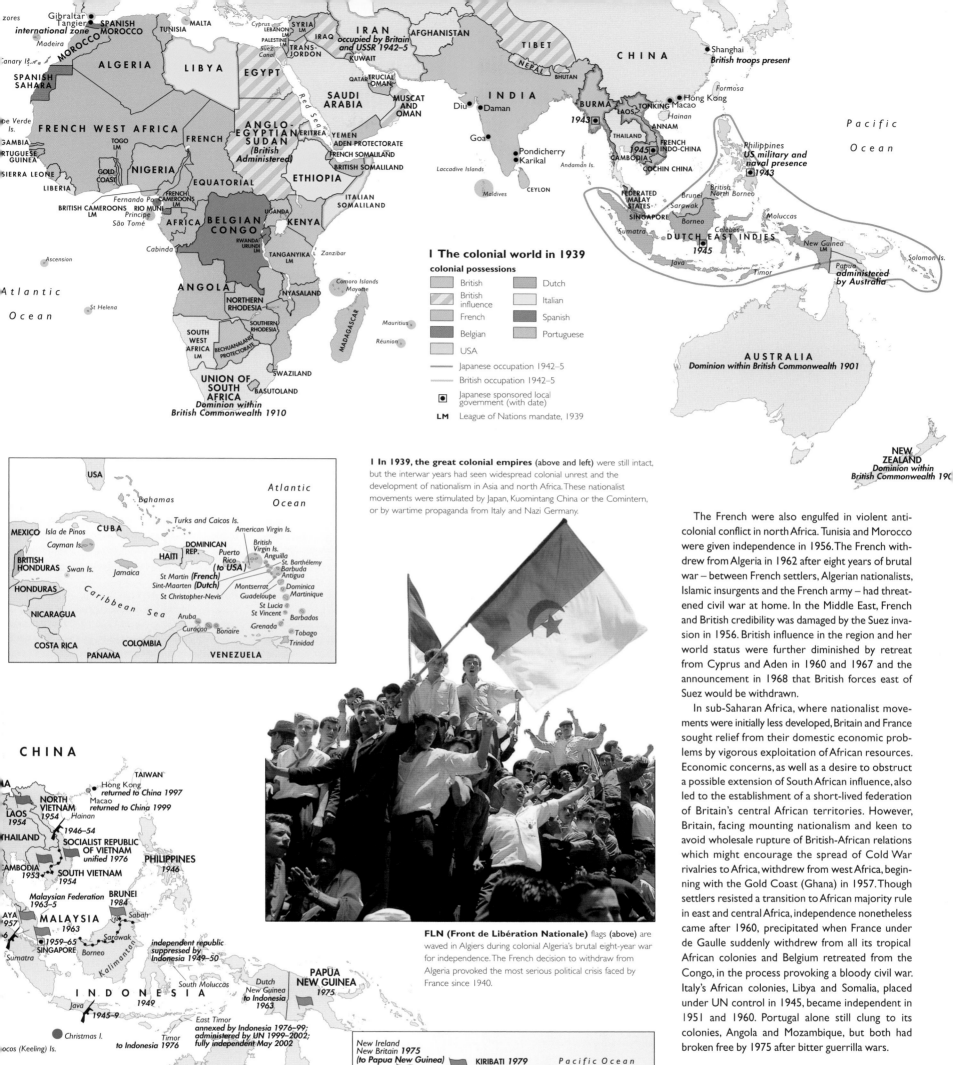

I The colonial world in 1939

colonial possessions

British	Dutch
British influence	Italian
French	Spanish
Belgian	Portuguese
USA	

Japanese occupation 1942–5

British occupation 1942–5

◉ Japanese sponsored local government (with date)

LM League of Nations mandate, 1939

I In 1939, the great colonial empires (above and left) were still intact, but the interwar years had seen widespread colonial unrest and the development of nationalism in Asia and north Africa. These nationalist movements were stimulated by Japan, Kuomintang China or the Comintern, or by wartime propaganda from Italy and Nazi Germany.

FLN (Front de Libération Nationale) flags (above) are waved in Algiers during colonial Algeria's brutal eight-year war for independence. The French decision to withdraw from Algeria provoked the most serious political crisis faced by France since 1940.

The French were also engulfed in violent anti-colonial conflict in north Africa. Tunisia and Morocco were given independence in 1956. The French withdrew from Algeria in 1962 after eight years of brutal war – between French settlers, Algerian nationalists, Islamic insurgents and the French army – had threatened civil war at home. In the Middle East, French and British credibility was damaged by the Suez invasion in 1956. British influence in the region and her world status were further diminished by retreat from Cyprus and Aden in 1960 and 1967 and the announcement in 1968 that British forces east of Suez would be withdrawn.

In sub-Saharan Africa, where nationalist movements were initially less developed, Britain and France sought relief from their domestic economic problems by vigorous exploitation of African resources. Economic concerns, as well as a desire to obstruct a possible extension of South African influence, also led to the establishment of a short-lived federation of Britain's central African territories. However, Britain, facing mounting nationalism and keen to avoid wholesale rupture of British-African relations which might encourage the spread of Cold War rivalries to Africa, withdrew from west Africa, beginning with the Gold Coast (Ghana) in 1957. Though settlers resisted a transition to African majority rule in east and central Africa, independence nonetheless came after 1960, precipitated when France under de Gaulle suddenly withdrew from all its tropical African colonies and Belgium retreated from the Congo, in the process provoking a bloody civil war. Italy's African colonies, Libya and Somalia, placed under UN control in 1945, became independent in 1951 and 1960. Portugal alone still clung to its colonies, Angola and Mozambique, but both had broken free by 1975 after bitter guerrilla wars.

The colonial legacy

Though the winding up of colonial empires continued through the 1970s and 1980s in the Caribbean and the South Pacific and into the 1990s – Hong Kong was returned to China by the British in 1997 – by the beginning of the 1970s the age of European overseas empires was effectively past. In the process of decolonization, not only had many former dependencies faced rapid, sometimes violent, political change, a number then had to reconcile the demands of rival ethnic or religious divisions within their new borders. In varying degrees, most also confronted economic problems that for some would prove all but insuperable.

Japan and east Asia

In the years after 1945 east Asia struggled to throw off the legacy of the Second World War. After 1948, United States support for Japan, South Korea and Taiwan, perceived as its first line of defence in east Asia, transformed their economies. Until the late 1990s they seemed to form the core of one of the world's most dynamic economic regions.

FOR THE NEW AGE, THERE IS ONLY ONE PATH OPEN TO JAPAN. INSTEAD OF ARMS, WE MUST CHOOSE CULTURE. THROUGH OUR EDUCATION AND TRUE MORALITY, WE MUST CONTRIBUTE TO THE WORLD'S PROGRESS.

Maeda Tamon, Japan's Minister of Education, 1945

AS A RESULT OF DEFEAT, THE WALL THAT SECLUDED THE JAPANESE MIND FROM THE OUTSIDE WORLD BROKE DOWN. THE JAPANESE PEOPLE COULD SEE THE WORLD AS IT WAS FOR THE FIRST TIME.

Iyama Ikuo
Japan's Future Course, 1948

IN THE AUTUMN OF 1945 the future for Japan looked grim. The economy was in ruins; most of the towns and industrial plant had been destroyed; the navy had been sunk; nearly all foreign assets had been lost; domestic capital was run down; the victorious enemy demanded large reparations; all the necessities of life were short.

The reconstruction of Japan

The rebuilding of the country was led by the American occupation administration. Japan had to accept a new constitution which ended the divinity of the emperor and gave sovereignty to the people. An independent judiciary was established, free labour unions were permitted and war was renounced as a means of settling disputes. From 1948, with the advance of the Chinese communists, the USA increasingly came to see Japan not only as the key bulwark of Western power in east Asia but also as one whose effectiveness depended on the reconstruction of its economic power. In September 1951 the American occupation was ended.

For Korea Japan's defeat ended the harsh Japanese colonial regime imposed in 1910. But it also brought a division of the country between a communist state in the north backed by the Soviet Union and an anti-communist state in the south backed by the USA. In June 1950 war broke out and, when it came to an end in 1953, Korea was divided along the armistice line.

The Korean War provided the first boost to the Japanese recovery. There followed a period of exceptionally high economic growth – well over 10 per cent a year throughout the 1960s – which turned her into an economic superpower. In the years 1974–85 her economy grew at 4.3 per cent per annum, faster than that of any other OECD country. A key feature of Japan's growth was her flexibility in pursuing economic objectives: in the 1950s she emphasized heavy industry, shipbuilding and iron and steel; in the 1960s she moved into high-technology consumer manufactures largely for export; from the 1970s she concentrated on technological innovation and higher value-added products while transferring the production of lower value-added goods overseas. There began an era of massive Japanese investment in Asia, Europe and North America (see map 3). In the early 1990s Japan had the world's strongest economy

with the largest per capita GNP and the largest holding of foreign assets and debt. Amongst the causes of this remarkable success were: Japan's surplus labour in the 1950s–60s which kept prices down; the role of government intervention (and support); the high levels of domestic saving; and the distinctive character of employee-company relations which emphasized extensive consultation and group loyalty.

Korea and Taiwan

Korea epitomized the relative success of the communist and capitalist projects. Until 1970 North Korea had the higher GNP per capita. By the 1990s GNP was declining at 5 per cent and the state, still communist, was close to economic and humanitarian disaster. From the mid-1960s South Korea embarked on rapid industrialization under Park Chung Hee and emerged as one of the "little tigers" amongst the Asian economies. By the 1990s it was the world's 13th-largest economy with great strengths in car manufacture, shipbuilding and semiconductors. For much of this period of rapid economic growth, however, its regime showed little tolerance of political dissent: open protest was forcefully crushed.

Taiwan, where the Chinese Nationalists established their government in 1949 after the communist

4–6 The economic progress of Japan has been startling since the 1960s **(charts below and right)**. As the level of Japanese exports grew after the war, so Japanese investment overseas increased. By the end of the 1980s the country was a long-established economic superpower. But however impressive Japan's economic performance since 1945, the country has had to contend with a sharp economic slowdown since the early 1990s. The end of the "bubble economy" has brought depressed land prices, banking collapses and a series of less-than-successful attempts by successive Japanese governments to kick-start the economy. The Asian economic crisis of 1997–8 made the Japanese government's task in restoring growth to the economy even more difficult. By 2004 Japan had endured almost a decade of low or negative growth, a stagnant stock exchange and rising unemployment.

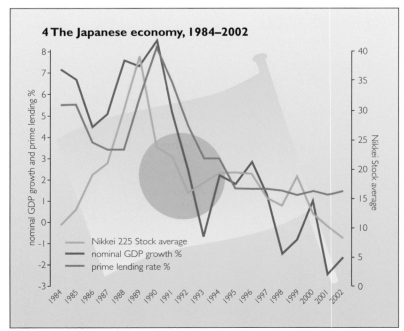

4 The Japanese economy, 1984–2002

Nikkei 225 Stock average
nominal GDP growth %
prime lending rate %

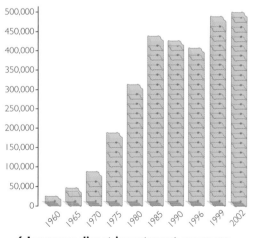

5 Japanese exports, 1960–2002 (millions US $)

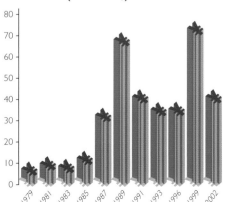

6 Japanese direct investment overseas, 1979–2002 (billions US $)

EUROPE NETH.
33,500   800   WEST GERMANY 400
8,424 34,710
2,500
1,800 LUX. UK
FRANCE 330
SOVIET
860
MIDDLE EAST
12,000
54
AFRICA
27,100
SAUD ARABI
LIBERIA 267 4,162 4,244 272

In 1948 the new state of North Korea was set up by the Korean Workers' Party led by Kim Il Sung (left). Kim imposed his own brand of communism on North Korea. Political dissidents were sent to concentration camps. The rest of the populace led strictly regimented lives. The economy was sealed off from the outside world and a personality cult of bizarre proportions arose. By his death in 1994, North Korea was impoverished. Its economic and political isolation continued under his son and successor, Kim Jong Il, when the country's military nuclear programme provoked confrontation with the international community. From 2008, the region faced new uncertainty with rumours of Kim Yong Il's illness which brought the question of political succession once more to the fore.

1 From the devastation at the end of the Second World War, Japan emerged as an economic powerhouse (map below), by the 1980s challenging even the USA. South Korea, though far from a model democratic state for much of the post-war period, has developed a thriving industrial base. Like Japan in the same period, it has specialized in high-tech industries. An economic crisis in 1997–8 showed that continued success would depend on financial reforms.

1 Japan and Korea

major industries

- ⊚ major industrial areas
- ⚛ research and development
- ⦿ heavy engineering
- 🖵 consumer goods
- 🏭 vehicle manufacturing
- ⛴ shipbuilding
- iron and steel
- 🗄 electronics
- ⚱ chemicals
- textiles
- ☎ telecommunications
- — major roads
- ✈ airports
- bullet trains
- railways

takeover on the mainland, experienced economic success similar to that of South Korea. A one-party state to 1986, it subsequently become a fully functioning multi-party democracy. The growing diplomatic recognition from the 1970s of communist China, which saw Taiwan as a province, has left it isolated. Since 1990, however, Taiwan has been responsible for more than 60 per cent of inward investment into China.

The economic turmoil which hit the east Asian economies in 1997 exposed serious structural weaknesses, particularly in the inefficient and debt-laden finance and banking sectors. Yet the vast underlying strength of Japan suggests that the region, together with China and southeast Asia, will continue to play a critical role in the world economy in the early 21st century.

3 During the 1970s and 1980s Japan's economic presence abroad expanded dramatically (map below). By 1987 overseas investments were worth $139 billion. Foreign trade totalled only 7 billion Yen in 1970 but was 40 billion by 1993. The US trade deficit with Japan reached $60 billion by 1987, over a third of the total trade deficit. The great bulk of Japanese exports was made up of machinery and equipment.

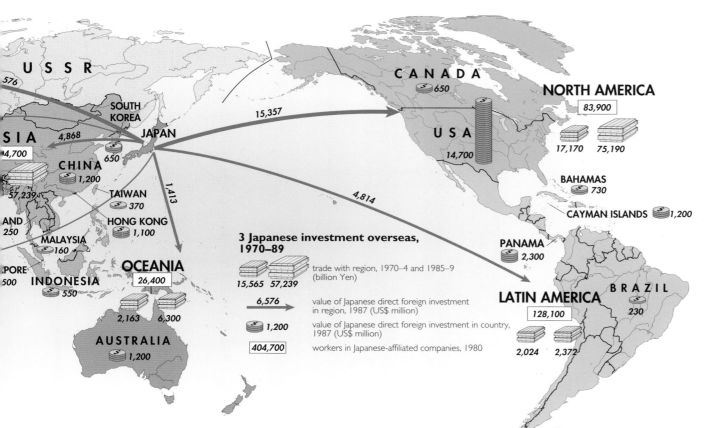

3 Japanese investment overseas, 1970–89

- 15,565 57,239 — trade with region, 1970–4 and 1985–9 (billion Yen)
- 6,576 → value of Japanese direct foreign investment in region, 1987 (US$ million)
- 1,200 — value of Japanese direct foreign investment in country, 1987 (US$ million)
- 404,700 — workers in Japanese-affiliated companies, 1980

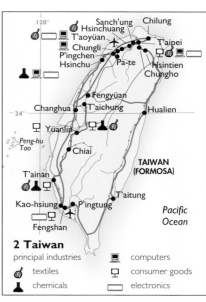

2 Taiwan

principal industries

- textiles
- ⚱ chemicals
- 🖵 computers
- consumer goods
- electronics

2 Taiwan — the Republic of China — (map above) was established in 1949 by Chiang Kai-Shek's Kuomintang, whose government in Beijing had been overthrown by Mao Zedong. The Kuomintang still claim to be the sole legitimate rulers of China, while communist China considers Taiwan to be one of its provinces. Taiwan has had one of the world's most successful economies since the 1950s, with growth rates over the period second only to those of Japan (and 6.6 per cent a year between 1985 and 1995).

Maoist China

Under Mao Zedong, the Chinese Communist Party revolutionized China. Mao launched the "Great Leap Forward", broke with the Soviet Union, and embarked on the Great Proletarian Cultural Revolution. But his radical programme of industrial and social transformation, though delivering some benefits, often had catastrophic consequences for China's people.

THE ESTABLISHMENT OF the People's Republic of China in 1949 marked a decisive turning point in China's modern history. After a century of internal conflict and disintegration, exacerbated by external aggressors, China now experienced strong centralized government. Despite the excesses and failures of the Maoist era, not least the systematic repression of much of the population, this was a fundamental achievement.

Establishment of a communist state

Maoist China was characterized by violence and tumult. Mass campaigns in the early years targeted suspected opponents of the regime, such as supporters of the exiled Nationalist Party and "bad classes" like landlords and capitalists. Until 1956, though, the Communists placed pragmatic change ahead of revolutionary zealotry, and social reforms brought real benefits to women, peasants and other marginalized groups. But thereafter Mao, eager to accelerate the pace of socialist transformation and demonstrate his leadership of global communism, took a more radical line. Though his own authority in the party sometimes ebbed, he was able to reshape China fundamentally prior to his death in 1976.

The central concern of the new regime was the economy, crucially the raising of agricultural production and the creation of a heavy industrial base. China's First Five-Year Plan in 1953 was strongly influenced by its Cold War ally, the USSR. The alliance with Moscow brought scores of Soviet technicians to China and sent Chinese students in the other direction. Industrial production grew in leaps and bounds, reaching an average annual rate of 19 per cent between 1952 and 1957.

But by the late 1950s, Mao was growing impatient with the gradualism of revolutionary change. He saw the seeds of counter-revolutionary revisionism in the denunciation of Stalin by the new Soviet leader Nikita Khrushchev, and this shaped his decision to beat a different path. Mao initially invited intellectuals to speak openly about Communist rule in the "Hundred Flowers" campaign of 1957, but when this led to a wave of criticism of the regime, he turned on the dissenters. In February 1958, he launched the "Great Leap Forward" which aimed to modernize China in three years by mobilizing the energy of the masses. Rural China was divided into 26,000 communes which were required to abolish private property and to meet huge targets in agricultural and industrial production. 600,000 backyard furnaces sprang up across the country. The experiment was an unmitigated disaster: production declined sharply and 20–30 million died from starvation or malnutrition. In 1961, the project – by some measures the largest man-made disaster in human history – was abandoned. This failure strengthened the hands of moderates in the Chinese Communist Party (CCP) under Liu Shaoqi and Deng Xiaoping, who preferred a return to a more centrally planned, Soviet-style development. Mao responded by forming an alliance with the People's Liberation Army (PLA) under General Lin Biao. Lin helped to build a cult of personality around Mao that served to mobilize Chinese students as ideologically driven "Red Guards".

The Cultural Revolution

With this new base of support Mao was able to launch the Great Proletarian Cultural Revolution in 1966. Red Guards were set loose to prevent the development of "vested interests" and careerism in party and state. They pursued a permanent revolution that would not succumb to the stultified "bureaucratism" of the Soviet Union. In struggle sessions, Mao's foot-soldiers waged war on tradition

OF ALL THE IMPORTANT THINGS, THE POSSESSION OF POWER IS THE MOST IMPORTANT. SUCH BEING THE CASE, THE REVOLUTIONARY MASSES, WITH A DEEP HATRED FOR THE CLASS ENEMY, MAKE UP THEIR MIND TO UNITE, FORM A GREAT ALLIANCE, [AND] SEIZE POWER! SEIZE POWER!! SEIZE POWER!!! ALL THE PARTY POWER, POLITICAL POWER, AND FINANCIAL POWER USURPED BY THE COUNTER-REVOLUTIONARY REVISIONISTS AND THOSE DIEHARDS WHO PERSISTENTLY CLING TO THE BOURGEOIS REACTIONARY LINE MUST BE RECAPTURED!

Editorial in pro-Cultural Revolution newspaper, 22 January 1967

3 In 1966, threatened by growing opposition in the Party and bureaucracy, and tired of their careerism and autocratic methods, Mao launched the Great Proletarian Cultural Revolution. In July 1966, he set his Red Guards loose. They rampaged through cities attacking the "Four Olds" (old ideas, culture, customs and habits) and took over many parts of the establishment. By mid-1968, rampant chaos led Mao to call in the PLA to restore order.

Between August and November 1966, 13 million students travelled to Beijing for a glimpse of the Chairman **(right)**. Mao held nine rallies in Tiananmen Square, the first of which saw a million students turn out to see him at sunrise. Here, he called on Chinese youth to advance the Cultural Revolution.

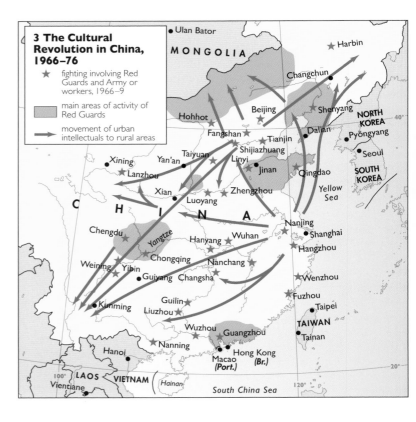

3 The Cultural Revolution in China, 1966–76

★ fighting involving Red Guards and Army or workers, 1966–9

▨ main areas of activity of Red Guards

→ movement of urban intellectuals to rural areas

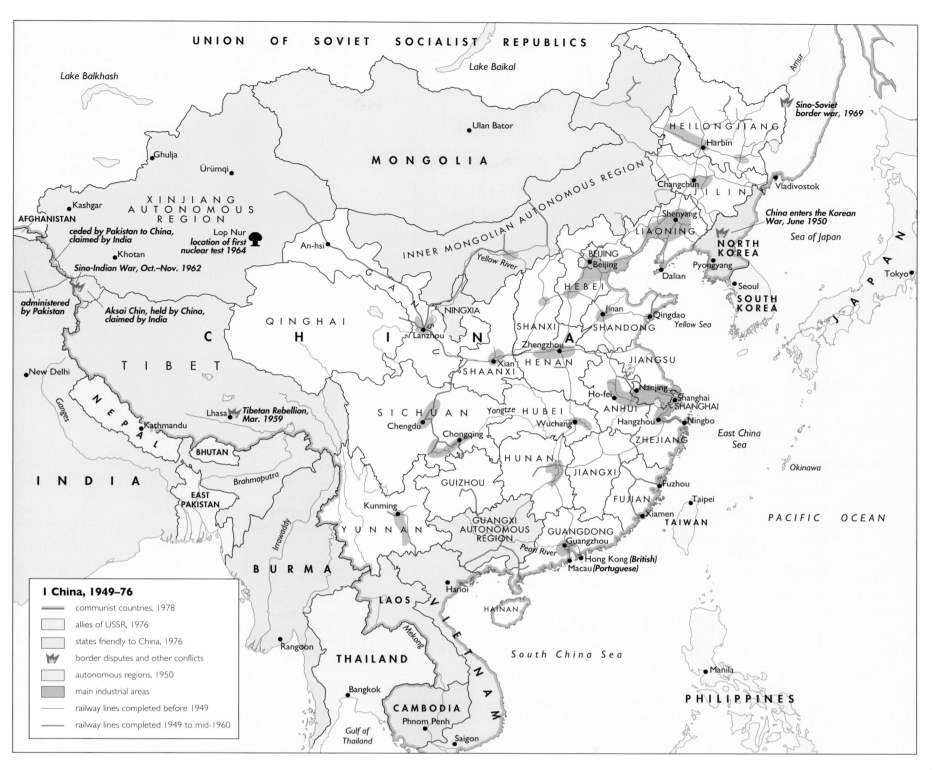

UNION OF SOVIET SOCIALIST REPUBLICS

Lake Balkhash
Lake Baikal
Amur

Sino-Soviet
border war, 1969

Ghulja
Ulan Bator
HEILONGJIANG

MONGOLIA
Harbin

Ürümqi
Changchun
JILIN
Vladivostok

AFGHANISTAN
Kashgar
XINJIANG
AUTONOMOUS
REGION
Shenyang
China enters the Korean
War, June 1950

*ceded by Pakistan to China,
claimed by India*
Lop Nur
*location of first
nuclear test 1964*
INNER MONGOLIAN AUTONOMOUS REGION
LIAONING
NORTH
KOREA
Sea of Japan

Khotan
An-hsi
Yellow River
Dalian
Pyongyang

Sino-Indian War, Oct.–Nov. 1962
BEIJING
Beijing
Seoul
SOUTH
KOREA

*administered
by Pakistan*
QINGHAI
NINGXIA
HEBEI

*Aksai Chin, held by China,
claimed by India*
C H I N A
Lanzhou
SHANXI
Jinan
Qingdao
Yellow Sea

New Delhi
SHANDONG

T I B E T
Zhengzhou
JIANGSU

Xian
HENAN

SHAANXI
Ho-fei
Nanjing
Shanghai
SHANGHAI

NEPAL
SICHUAN
Yangtze HUBEI
ANHWEI
Hangzhou
Ningbo

Kathmandu
Lhasa
*Tibetan Rebellion,
Mar. 1959*
Chengdu
Wuchang
ZHEJIANG

BHUTAN
Chongqing
East China
Sea

Brahmaputra
HUNAN
JIANGXI

EAST
PAKISTAN
GUIZHOU
Fuzhou
Okinawa

I N D I A
Kunming
FUJIAN
Taipei

Irrawaddy
YUNNAN
GUANGXI
AUTONOMOUS
REGION
GUANGDONG
Xiamen
TAIWAN
PACIFIC OCEAN

Guangzhou
Pearl River
Hong Kong *(British)*
Macau *(Portuguese)*

Hanoi
HAINAN

LAOS
South China Sea

BURMA

1 China, 1949–76

— communist countries, 1978

allies of USSR, 1976

states friendly to China, 1976

border disputes and other conflicts

autonomous regions, 1950

main industrial areas

railway lines completed before 1949

railway lines completed 1949 to mid-1960

THAILAND
Rangoon
Manila

Bangkok
PHILIPPINES

CAMBODIA
Phnom Penh
Saigon
Gulf of
Thailand

by subjecting authority figures, from Liu Shaoqi (the CCP's second-in-command) to school teachers, to humiliation and torture. Many victims – most estimates indicate well over a million – were killed. If Mao succeeded in using the Cultural Revolution (1966–72) to restore his pre-eminence in the Communist Party, though, it led to chaos throughout China, and he was forced to call on the PLA to restore order. Many of the revolutionaries were sent to the countryside where they could do less damage.

Ironically, the radicalism of the Cultural Revolution enabled a diplomatic pivot towards the US. Mao's estrangement from Moscow, first evident in the late 1950s, became more pronounced over the following decade; in 1969, a border conflict came close to escalating into full-scale war between China and the USSR. Seizing the opportunity presented by this rift in the Communist bloc, President Richard Nixon made overtures to the PRC, and visited Beijing in 1972. A few years later, the US officially recognized the PRC as China's legitimate government: a privilege hitherto granted to the Republic of China's government-in-exile on Taiwan.

On 9 September 1976 Mao died. His wife Jiang Qing, along with three conspirators – the "Gang of Four" – tried to seize power. But their ties to the Cultural Revolution made them unpopular with more moderate leaders who were tired of constant upheaval. The Gang of Four were arrested, tried and convicted.

Mao's leadership fundamentally altered China's society, economy and international position. His Communist Party had united the nation, developed its resources, and steered it away from its seemingly natural alliance with the USSR. Literacy rates improved markedly and many prospered from the Revolution. But these benefits came at immense human cost, and the revolutionary upheavals of the Great Leap Forward and Cultural Revolution retarded economic growth.

1 and 2 The Chinese Communist Party,
like its Nationalist Party predecessor, aimed to unite China through infrastructure and industry (map above). With Soviet assistance, the new government built railroads and factories. By 1958, though, Mao was eager to use the revolutionary energy of the people to leapfrog other major powers. His Great Leap Forward – a mass campaign to collectivize agriculture, increase production, and use the surplus extracted from the land to fund industrialization – proved a catastrophic failure and led to a famine that killed an estimated 20–30 million rural Chinese (map below).

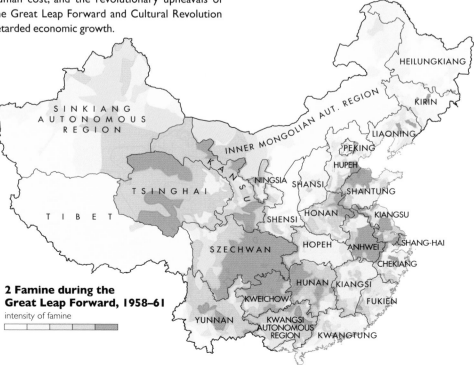

**2 Famine during the
Great Leap Forward, 1958–61**

intensity of famine

Southeast Asia's long war

For the first three decades of the post-war period, much of Southeast Asia was embroiled in conflict. After the end of colonial rule, the Western powers tried to establish supportive regimes in the region. But left-wing forces with strong rural support inflicted heavy losses. The late 1960s and early 1970s saw the Cold War played out on Southeast Asian soil, with disastrous consequences.

ONCE JAPAN WAS DEFEATED in 1945, the Western powers sought to return to their territories, but with differing ambitions and different consequences. At first they tried to return as colonial rulers, but a brief period of rule proved this to be unrealistic and led the way to European and American attempts to hand power to friendly, moderate nationalist regimes that could block the rise of communism. This in turn gave rise to more radical nationalism.

In July 1946, the USA left the Philippines but provided military training and financial support against peasant insurgencies between 1946 and 1954. Throughout the period the Philippines remained one of the USA's most loyal allies. The country was one of only three Asian states to join the US-dominated South East Asian Treaty Organization in 1954.

Sukarno and non-alignment

In Indonesia and French Indo-China, the Netherlands and France sought to reimpose their direct authority forcefully. Both became embroiled in bloody wars. In Indonesia, the Dutch almost defeated the republic declared in 1945, but withdrew in December 1949 once world opinion had turned against them. Attempting to forge a non-aligned path between capitalism and communism, Sukarno's Indonesian regime initially attempted to direct a planned economy with a multi-party parliament. Sukarno called this "guided democracy". Yet by the late 1950s, Sukarno's regime was moving closer to the Soviet Union and taking a hard-line stance against internal enemies and the Indonesian Chinese population. His regime was brought down by a US-backed coup in

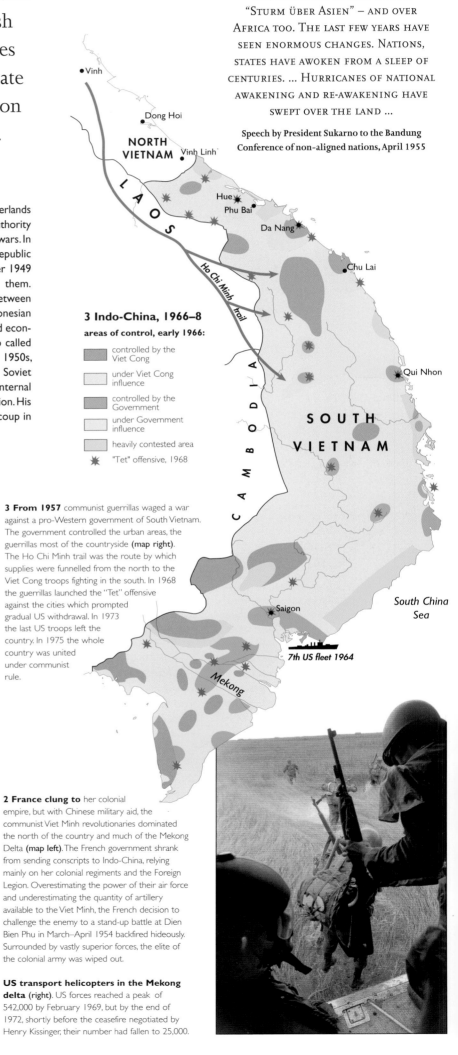

3 Indo-China, 1966–8
areas of control, early 1966:

- controlled by the Viet Cong
- under Viet Cong influence
- controlled by the Government
- under Government influence
- heavily contested area
- ✳ "Tet" offensive, 1968

3 From 1957 communist guerrillas waged a war against a pro-Western government of South Vietnam. The government controlled the urban areas, the guerrillas most of the countryside (map right). The Ho Chi Minh trail was the route by which supplies were funnelled from the north to the Viet Cong troops fighting in the south. In 1968 the guerrillas launched the "Tet" offensive against the cities which prompted gradual US withdrawal. In 1973 the last US troops left the country. In 1975 the whole country was united under communist rule.

2 France clung to her colonial empire, but with Chinese military aid, the communist Viet Minh revolutionaries dominated the north of the country and much of the Mekong Delta (map left). The French government shrank from sending conscripts to Indo-China, relying mainly on her colonial regiments and the Foreign Legion. Overestimating the power of their air force and underestimating the quantity of artillery available to the Viet Minh, the French decision to challenge the enemy to a stand-up battle at Dien Bien Phu in March–April 1954 backfired hideously. Surrounded by vastly superior forces, the elite of the colonial army was wiped out.

US transport helicopters in the Mekong delta (right). US forces reached a peak of 542,000 by February 1969, but by the end of 1972, shortly before the ceasefire negotiated by Henry Kissinger, their number had fallen to 25,000.

2 Indo-China, 1949–54
- ▨ Viet Minh-dominated zones, 1949
- ✕ major battles
- ·········· demilitarized zone, 22 July 1954

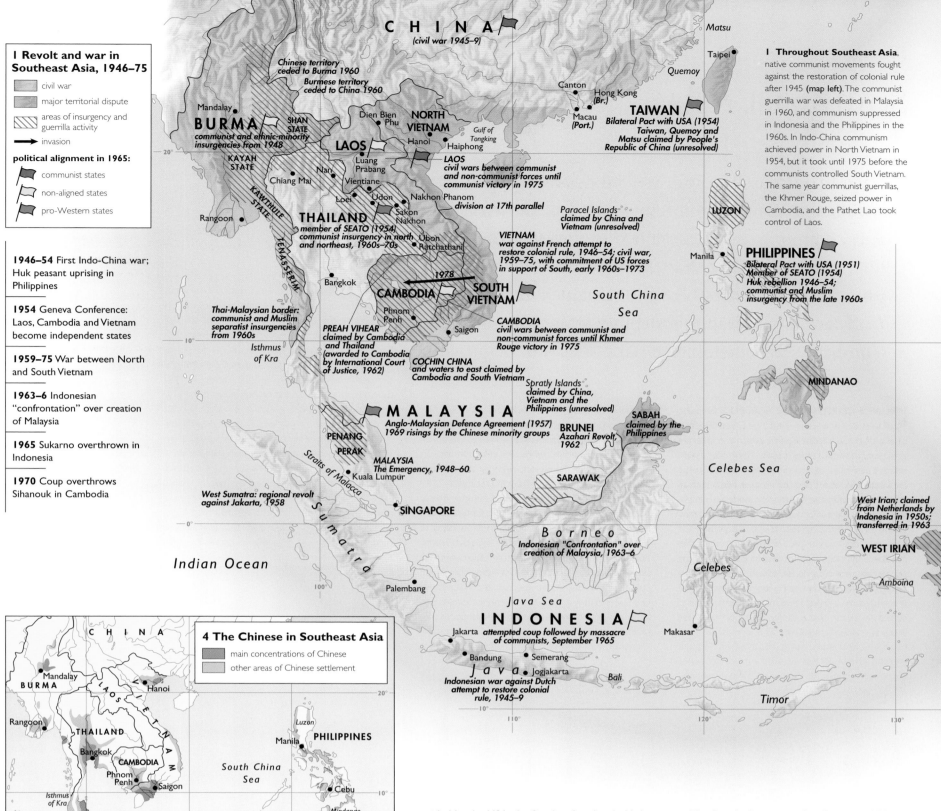

1 Revolt and war in Southeast Asia, 1946–75

- civil war
- major territorial dispute
- areas of insurgency and guerrilla activity
- invasion

political alignment in 1965:
- communist states
- non-aligned states
- pro-Western states

1946–54 First Indo-China war; Huk peasant uprising in Philippines

1954 Geneva Conference: Laos, Cambodia and Vietnam become independent states

1959–75 War between North and South Vietnam

1963–6 Indonesian "confrontation" over creation of Malaysia

1965 Sukarno overthrown in Indonesia

1970 Coup overthrows Sihanouk in Cambodia

1 Throughout Southeast Asia, native communist movements fought against the restoration of colonial rule after 1945 (map left). The communist guerrilla war was defeated in Malaysia in 1960, and communism suppressed in Indonesia and the Philippines in the 1960s. In Indo-China communism achieved power in North Vietnam in 1954, but it took until 1975 before the communists controlled South Vietnam. The same year communist guerrillas, the Khmer Rouge, seized power in Cambodia, and the Pathet Lao took control of Laos.

4 Many Chinese emigrated because of civil war or economic difficulties. The demand from European entrepreneurs for cheap labour also drew many Chinese abroad. By the 1980s there were over 20 million overseas Chinese, many of them in Southeast Asia (map above). The largest number was in Thailand, some 6 million, with over 4 million in Malaysia and more than 3 million in Indonesia. Although contributing greatly to the dynamism of the economies where they settled, they often suffered political discrimination. At the time of Sukarno's overthrow in 1965 in Indonesia, thousands were massacred.

1966, which led to a bloody battle in the countryside. Suharto, his successor, adopted a much more pro-Western stance.

The Vietnam War

The French struggle in Vietnam was bitter. After the Japanese defeat, Ho Chi Minh established a nationalist regime in the north while the French reasserted their authority in the south. War broke out between the two in 1946. After colossal losses on both sides, the war ended in the humiliating defeat of the French at Dien Bien Phu in 1954, and Vietnam was temporarily partitioned at the 17th parallel. The communist North Vietnamese expected that the country would be reunited once elections were held in 1956; but fearing a communist victory, and

guided by the USA, the South refused to hold the scheduled elections. Vietnam became a major battlefield of the Cold War. The anti-communist South received massive US support, which from 1965 took a directly military form, while the North was supplied by China and the Soviet Union. In the late 1960s, after sending half a million troops to the region, the Americans realized they could not prevent a communist victory. By 1973 the USA had negotiated a withdrawal but continued to supply the South. After almost 30 years of division and conflict, a North Vietnamese victory brought unity and peace under communist rule to the two Vietnams in 1975.

After gaining its independence from France in 1954, Cambodia initially maintained its independence from the wars raging around it. Governed by the magnetic personality of Prince Sihanouk between 1954 and 1970, Cambodia was successful at maintaining a non-aligned path. Cambodia's neutrality was undermined by Vietnamese incursions and US bombing, which led to a pro-American regime in 1970.

Throughout the post-war period, Thailand managed to retain its independence by gaining US protection. Thailand joined SEATO and sent troops to support the South in the Vietnam War. Like other states in the region, it faced a rurally based communist resistance movement that was suppressed with US assistance.

The British also returned to Burma and Malaya, committed to re-establishing colonial rule. But post-war Britain could not afford to defend an empire in Asia, and accepted quickly that withdrawal was inevitable. After civil order broke down rapidly after the end of the Second World War the British quit Burma in January 1948. Throughout Southeast Asia, pro-Soviet communists had allied with Britain against Japanese occupation. In the post-war period many Southeast Asian communists found themselves opposing their former allies. In Malaya, between 1948 and 1960, communist insurgents based in the countryside violently opposed British rule and its Malaysian successor state. The Malayan "emergency" ended after troops were sent from Britain, and potential rebel supporters in the villages resettled. The separate peninsular states of Malaya achieved independence in 1957, uniting with Sabah, Sarawak and the city-state of Singapore to form the Federation of Malaysia in 1963. Tension between ethnic Chinese and Malays led to Singapore's breaking away to become an independent republic in 1965. The Malay-dominated regime faced risings by Chinese minority groups in 1969.

By the late 1960s, Southeast Asia was divided between Indo-China, Burma and the Philippines, which were beset by internal conflict or embroiled in international war, and Malaysia, Thailand, Singapore, and even Indonesia, which had achieved a degree of political stability, had begun to reap the beneficial economic consequences of peace.

Southeast Asia

In 1975, Southeast Asia was divided between communist states allied to China and the Soviet Union, and virulently anti-communist countries allied to the USA. The late 1970s and 1980s were years of political violence – even genocide – and unrest. Poverty remained endemic in many areas, but despite instability many parts of the region have seen phenomenal rates of economic growth.

IN 1975 **COMMUNIST REGIMES** achieved political dominance in Vietnam, Cambodia and Laos. All three regimes were rooted in peasant protest against colonial and then pro-Western rule, yet the paths each state took were very different. In Cambodia, Pol Pot's anti-Vietnamese faction gained control of the communist party. A French-educated intellectual, Pol Pot knew little about the countryside, but his Khmer Rouge (the communist movement founded in the 1960s) attempted to create a self-sufficient rural utopia by forcibly moving people from the cities to the countryside. Estimates of the number of people who lost their lives to the resulting famine, disease and maltreatment vary, but at least a million and a half people may have died in the Cambodian genocide. The world's first war between communist states began when Vietnam invaded Cambodia and installed a pro-Vietnamese puppet government in 1979, and China's invasion of

Vietnam followed. The Vietnamese announced their withdrawal from Cambodia in 1988, and elections were held in 1993, but the Khmer Rouge continued their guerrilla war until 1998, when Pol Pot died.

Communist rule

Vietnam suffered from diplomatic isolation and from the economic impact of its war with Cambodia and China after the end of the Vietnam War. Many of the South Vietnamese middle class, including a large number of Vietnamese Chinese, fled the country in boats rather than face communist repression. These "boat people" found refuge across the globe. Since the late 1980s Vietnam has developed closer ties with Europe and, eventually, the USA. Undergoing a process of economic but not political liberalization, Vietnam's economy was, by the late 1990s, among

2 Much of Southeast Asia's economic miracle was based on Japanese investment (**map below**). Initially, the region was seen as supplying raw materials. Later, Southeast Asia became the production base for Japanese manufacturing. During the 1990s, Japan increasingly concentrated on investing in its own backyard. In 1990 only 30 per cent of Japanese investment flowed to Asia; by 1996 it stood at 47 per cent.

the fastest growing in the region. Neighbouring Laos became increasingly dependent on Vietnam after the communists took over in 1975. Like Vietnam, Laos abandoned economic communism in the 1990s while the communist party retained control of the country's political institutions.

Asian "tigers"

Since 1975, Thailand has been governed by fervently anti-communist regimes, alternating between military rule and periods of democracy. Despite an unstable and violent political culture, Thailand appeared to have Indo-China's strongest economy for many years. But economic growth obscured the extent of corruption and unsustainable speculation. In 1997 the collapse of the Thai currency plunged the Thai economy into deep recession and started a crisis across Asia's financial markets. But, like other countries hit by Asia's economic crash, Thailand's recovery has been quicker than most people predicted.

Along with Singapore, Malaysia and Indonesia, Thailand has been described as one of Asia's "tiger economies". Each country achieved an annual growth rate well in excess of 5 per cent by creating an export-oriented industrial base. Many factors contributed: massive Japanese investment; cheap

labour; and a close relationship between investors, industrialists and the state. Southeast Asia's "tigers" have developed closer ties with each other through ASEAN, an organization that promotes free trade and closer communication – but not political integration – within the region. By 1999, ASEAN had expanded to include Cambodia, Laos, Myanmar (Burma) and Vietnam. Along with Japan and Taiwan, southeast Asia offered an example of planned capitalism. This allowed high rates of growth to occur. But the close relationship between the state and business made corruption an endemic problem.

Singapore is Asia's most prosperous state. Its economy was built upon political stability, a close relationship between business and government and a strict – some would say repressive – social order. Prime Minister Lee Kuan Yew held office continually between 1959 and 1990. Similarly, Malaysia's transformation occurred under a stable administration. In the 1960s its economy was based on agriculture and rubber production. By 2000 manufacturing and the service sector played a much greater role.

Some estimates say 1.7 million or 21 per cent of the population were killed in the Cambodian genocide. As well as those dying of starvation, many were massacred in the "killing fields" and buried in mass graves. Others were taken to schools converted into prisons where they were photographed and then shot. The Tuol Sleng museum documents and commemorates the 1000s of murders that took place during the Pol Pot regime (**above**).

The Petronas Towers (above right) symbolize Kuala Lumpur's claim to be a global financial centre. From 1996 to 2003 the 452m (1,483ft) towers were the world's tallest building.

Map

SOVIET UNION
Sea of Okhotsk
MONGOLIA
Peking
N. KOREA
S. KOREA Seoul
JAPAN
Tokyo
CHINA Shanghai
4478
Osaka
Canton
Taipei TAIWAN
Bonin Is.
BURMA
Hanoi
Chiang Mai
Hong Kong
Rangoon
THAILAND
VIETNAM 129
Bangkok Phnom
1978 Penh
1240
PHILIPPINES
718
Caroline Is.
1979
Pep-ang
575
Kota Kinabalu
Pacific
Ocean
MALAYSIA
Johor Bahru BRUNEI
1982
Medan
1978
SINGAPORE
1185
Borneo
Celebes
1605
KIRIBATI
Bismarck Arch.
Kuala Lumpur
Sumatra
INDONESIA
New Guinea
PAPUA NEW GUINEA
TUVALU
Jakarta
Java Bali
SOLOMON IS.
Timor
Santa Cruz Is.
Timor Sea
Cape York
Port Moresby
VANUATU
Darwin
Coral Sea
FIJI
Townsville
New Caledonia
AUSTRALIA
Brisbane
Perth
Adelaide
Sydney
Auckland
Melbourne
Wellington
NEW ZEALAND
Christchurch
Hobart

2 Japan, Australia and Asia to 1996

- 631 Japanese direct investment, 1996 (US$ million)
- Bangkok 1978 major Japanese transport/infrastructure project, with date
- ▲ pilot Japanese transport/infrastructure projects
- ✈ major international airports
- —— principal air routes
- ▨ development corridors

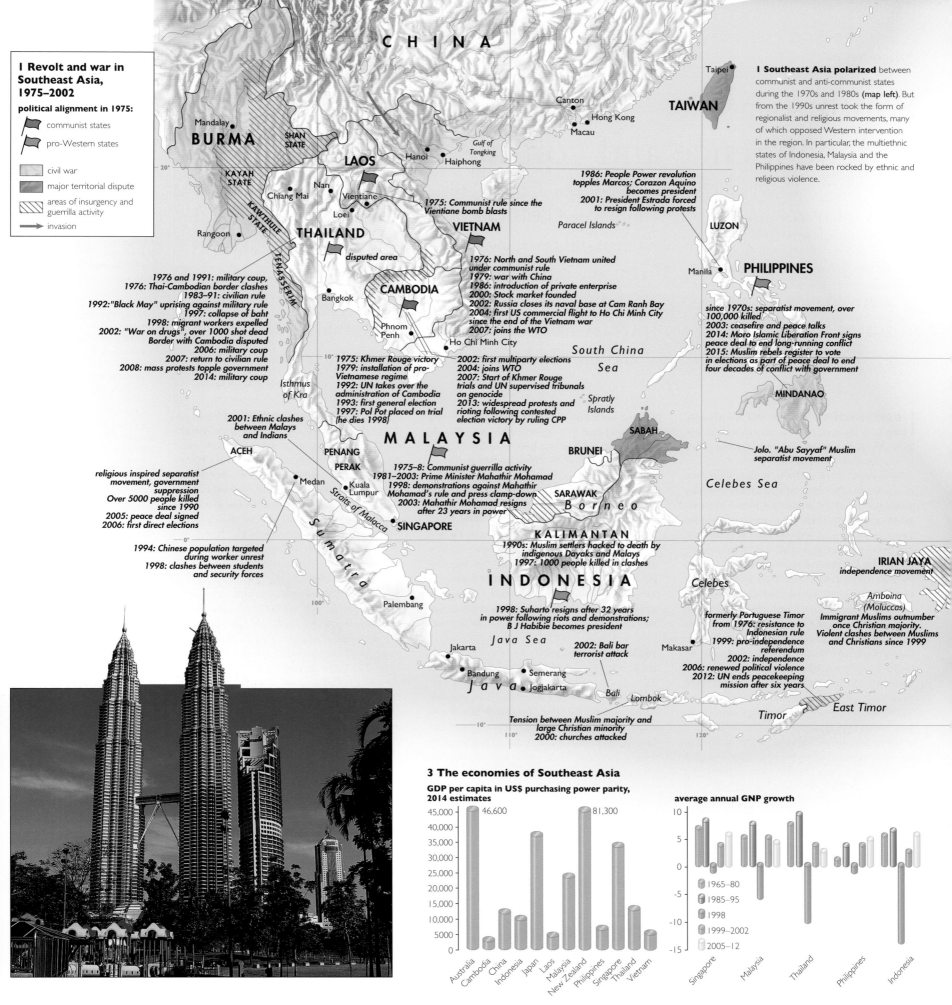

1 Revolt and war in Southeast Asia, 1975–2002

political alignment in 1975:

- communist states
- pro-Western states
- civil war
- major territorial dispute
- areas of insurgency and guerrilla activity
- invasion

1 Southeast Asia polarized between communist and anti-communist states during the 1970s and 1980s (map left). But from the 1990s unrest took the form of regionalist and religious movements, many of which opposed Western intervention in the region. In particular, the multiethnic states of Indonesia, Malaysia and the Philippines have been rocked by ethnic and religious violence.

CHINA

TAIWAN — Taipei

BURMA — Mandalay, SHAN STATE, KAYAH STATE, Chiang Mai, Nan, Rangoon

LAOS — Hanoi, Haiphong, Vientiane, Loei, Gulf of Tongking

KAWTHULE STATE — TENASSERIM

THAILAND — Bangkok — disputed area

Canton, Hong Kong, Macau

1986: People Power revolution topples Marcos; Corazon Aquino becomes president
2001: President Estrada forced to resign following protests

1975: Communist rule since the Vientiane bomb blasts

VIETNAM

1976: North and South Vietnam united under communist rule
1979: war with China
1986: introduction of private enterprise
2000: Stock market founded
2002: Russia closes its naval base at Cam Ranh Bay
2004: first US commercial flight to Ho Chi Minh City since the end of the Vietnam war
2007: joins the WTO

Paracel Islands

LUZON

Manila — PHILIPPINES

1976 and 1991: military coup,
1976: Thai-Cambodian border clashes
1983–91: civilian rule
1992:"Black May" uprising against military rule
1997: collapse of baht
1998: migrant workers expelled
2002: "War on drugs", over 1000 shot dead
Border with Cambodia disputed
2006: military coup
2007: return to civilian rule
2008: mass protests topple government
2014: military coup

CAMBODIA — Phnom Penh — Ho Chi Minh City

South China Sea

since 1970s: separatist movement, over 100,000 killed
2003: ceasefire and peace talks
2014: Moro Islamic Liberation Front signs peace deal to end long-running conflict
2015: Muslim rebels register to vote in elections as part of peace deal to end four decades of conflict with government

Isthmus of Kra

1975: Khmer Rouge victory
1979: installation of pro-Vietnamese regime
1992: UN takes over the administration of Cambodia
1993: first general election
1997: Pol Pot placed on trial (he dies 1998)

2002: first multiparty elections
2004: joins WTO
2007: Start of Khmer Rouge trials and UN supervised tribunals on genocide
2013: widespread protests and rioting following contested election victory by ruling CPP

Spratly Islands

MINDANAO

Jolo. "Abu Sayyaf" Muslim separatist movement

2001: Ethnic clashes between Malays and Indians

ACEH — PENANG, PERAK

MALAYSIA

SABAH
BRUNEI
SARAWAK
Borneo

Celebes Sea

religious inspired separatist movement, government suppression
Over 5000 people killed since 1990
2005: peace deal signed
2006: first direct elections

Medan, Kuala Lumpur

Straits of Malacca

1975–8: Communist guerrilla activity
1981–2003: Prime Minister Mahathir Mohamad
1998: demonstrations against Mahathir Mohamad's rule and press clamp-down
2003: Mahathir Mohamad resigns after 23 years in power

SINGAPORE

KALIMANTAN

IRIAN JAYA
independence movement

1994: Chinese population targeted during worker unrest
1998: clashes between students and security forces

Sumatra

1990s: Muslim settlers hacked to death by indigenous Dayaks and Malays
1997: 1000 people killed in clashes

INDONESIA

Celebes

Amboina (Moluccas)
Immigrant Muslims outnumber once Christian majority.
Violent clashes between Muslims and Christians since 1999

Palembang

1998: Suharto resigns after 32 years in power following riots and demonstrations; B J Habibie becomes president

2002: Bali bar terrorist attack

Makasar

formerly Portuguese Timor from 1976: resistance to Indonesian rule
1999: pro-independence referendum
2002: independence
2006: renewed political violence
2012: UN ends peacekeeping mission after six years

Jakarta, Java Sea, Bandung, Semerang, Java, Jogjakarta, Bali, Lombok, Timor, East Timor

Tension between Muslim majority and large Christian minority
2000: churches attacked

3 The economies of Southeast Asia

GDP per capita in US$ purchasing power parity, 2014 estimates

45,000 — 46,600 — 81,300
40,000
35,000
30,000
25,000
20,000
15,000
10,000
5000
0

Australia, Cambodia, China, Indonesia, Japan, Laos, Malaysia, New Zealand, Philippines, Singapore, Thailand, Vietnam

average annual GNP growth

10
5
0
-5
-10
-15

- 1965–80
- 1985–95
- 1998
- 1999–2002
- 2005–12

Singapore, Malaysia, Thailand, Philippines, Indonesia

EXTERMINATE THE 50 MILLION VIETNAMESE ... AND PURIFY THE MASSES OF THE PEOPLE.

Pol Pot, 1 May 1978, radio broadcast.

People power

Throughout much of the 1970s and 1980s, both the Philippines and Indonesia were governed by stable but repressive regimes that only survived in power with US support. Each eventually succumbed to populist democratic aspirations. In the Philippines Ferdinand Marcos was overthrown by Corazan Aquino's People Power movement in 1986. Unlike other anti-communist regimes in Southeast Asia, Marcos's government was not effective at developing the economy in the Phillipines. In Indonesia the premier Suharto (who had replaced Sukarno in 1967) survived until the Asian crash when he handed over power to a loyal ally, B J Habibie. Unemployment soared, violence increased, and in the wake of the independence of the region of East Timor, Habibie's government lost support. After general elections in 1999, the Islamic reformer Abdurrah-man Wahid became president, only to be replaced less than two years later by Sukarno's daughter Megawati Sukarnoputri, amid continuing unrest. The situation only stabilised after Susilo Bambang Yudhoyono won Indonesia's first-ever direct presidential elections in September 2004. Continued growth and democratic optimism led Yudhoyono to be re-elected by a landslide victory in 2009. However, he was faced by a corruption scandal which questioned the extent of his government's achievements. By the same year, the region's economy had largely recovered.

Years of opposition to authoritarian rule meant Islamist politicians in both Indonesia, the most populous Muslim country in the world, and the Philippines tended to be fervent supporters of democracy. But since democratization, more radical Islamic organizations in Southeast Asia have allied themselves with groups from outside the regime in a series of violent confrontations with Christian populations. In the wake of the tsunami of 2004, a peace deal was signed by separatists in Aceh, but political violence continued in Mindanao, East Timor and southern Thailand. In 2006, a military coup in Thailand jeopardized the country's democratic progress, and much of Southeast Asia was still overshadowed by the conflict between national states and movements for regional and religious autonomy.

3 Economic growth in much of Southeast Asia was exceptionally high from 1965 to 1995, and the region's economies have recovered quickly from the slump following the financial crisis of 1997 (charts above). Rapid growth in some areas and stagnation in others have meant there are enormous inequalities in the region, both between different states and within each state.

South Asia: independence and conflict

ALL OVER ASIA WE ARE PASSING THROUGH TRIALS AND TRIBULATIONS. IN INDIA ALSO YOU WILL SEE CONFLICT AND TROUBLE. LET US NOT BE DISHEARTENED BY THIS; THIS IS INEVITABLE IN AN AGE OF MIGHTY TRANSITION. THERE ARE A NEW VITALITY AND CREATIVE IMPULSES IN THE PEOPLES OF ASIA ... LET US HAVE FAITH IN THESE GREAT NEW FORCES AND THE DREAM WHICH IS TAKING SHAPE. LET US, ABOVE ALL, HAVE FAITH IN THE HUMAN SPIRIT WHICH ASIA HAS SYMBOLIZED FOR THESE LONG AGES PAST.

Jawaharlal Nehru, 1947

The politics of south Asia since the early 1940s has been dominated by conflict between the nation-state and the demand for regional autonomy and separation. This struggle drove the partition of British India in 1947. It has influenced the course of south Asian politics between parliamentary democracy and – in Pakistan, Bangladesh and Burma (Myanmar) – military intervention since.

INDEPENDENCE CAME TO British-ruled India with the creation of independent India and Pakistan in August 1947, to Burma in January 1948 and to Ceylon in February 1948.

Partition occurred as British and nationalist politicians were unable to agree to a balance of power between a united Indian government and provincial governments. Indian National Congress and Muslim League politicians reluctantly agreed to partition British India on religious lines, with Pakistan being created as the "homeland" for India's Muslims. Partition included the division of the populous provinces of Punjab in the west and Bengal in the east (*see* maps 1 & 2). Independence took place on 14 and 15 August, but the border between Pakistan and India was only announced on 17 August. As large numbers of Hindus and Muslims found themselves on the wrong side of the border, 15 million trekked from one state to the other. Law and order entirely broke down while political power was transferred. Over 500,000 were slaughtered in wave after wave of religious killings in an atmosphere of panic and fear.

Newly independent India and Pakistan had quickly to define the relationship between their new governments and the different communities living within their borders. The new regimes needed to determine the role of the 600 princely states, surviving from the period of British rule. Most chose to join India or Pakistan. The Muslim-ruled state of Hyderabad was forcibly integrated into India in 1948.

Kashmir had a majority Muslim population but was ruled by a Hindu dynasty. India and Pakistan fought a war for control of the state between October 1947 and January 1949, before the UN imposed a ceasefire and divided the area. The solution satisfied neither side. War broke out in 1965 and a peace settlement was signed in 1966. Escalating tension almost saw war again over Kashmir in 1999, as India accused Pakistani troops of infiltrating into Indian territory. India and Pakistan's explosion of nuclear devices in 1998 made many fear nuclear catastrophe, and in 2001–2 war came close to breaking out. Although tensions receded after peace talks began in 2004, Kashmir remained part of the unfinished business of Partition, and hostilities flared again in 2014.

Nation or Region? a struggle for identity

Throughout south Asia, regional politicians have accused the nation-state (whether Indian, Pakistani, Bangladeshi, Burmese or Sri Lankan) of failing to accommodate regional identities. In India, early conflicts were over language, even after 1956 when prime minister Jawaharlal Nehru agreed to reorganize state boundaries on provincial lines. Tribal groups in India and Bangladesh fought with both state administrations and central governments for separate statehood and independence, leading to the division of northeast India into seven separate states in the 1970s, and the creation of the new states of Chattisgarh,

Jharkhand and Uttaranchal in 2000, and Telangana in 2014. Serious religious conflict began to emerge from the 1970s. Sikh demands for the independent state of Khalistan led to the assassination of Prime Minister Indira Gandhi in 1984. In response to what was perceived as the erosion of Indian identity since 1947 by regional separatism and the rise of lower castes, many middle-class Hindu Indians asserted the Hindu-ness (Hindutva) of the Indian state. In 1992 the growth of Hindu nationalism saw the demolition of a 16th-century Muslim mosque built on what many believed to have been the birthplace of the Hindu god Ram. By then, India's Muslim population exceeded that of Pakistan. But the continued rise of Hindu nationalism, which culminated in the victory of the Hindu nationalist party, BJP, in parliamentary elections in 2014, meant India's Muslim minority felt ever more insecure.

Conflict between centre and region dominated the politics of other areas of south Asia. In Ceylon there was little friction until 1972, when a new constitution renamed it Sri Lanka and institutionalized the pursuit of a state dominated by the Buddhist religion and Sinhala language. The Tamil minority made up 15 per cent of the island's population, and began to demand their separate state of Eelam. Between 1983 and the 1990s Tamils fought the Sri Lankan army for control of the northeast of the island (see map 4), a situation hardly helped by the intervention of an Indian peacekeeping force in 1987–90. In 1991 the LTTE (Tamil Tigers) assassinated the ex-prime

3 Since independence the countries of south Asia (map right) have suffered from internal conflicts as well as major confrontations between states. There have been three wars between India and Pakistan and one between India and China. Both Pakistan and Sri Lanka have endured civil war, and key areas of India have spent long periods under martial law or president's rule. Boundaries inherited from colonial rule have been one factor in international disputes, but domestic and regional conflict has also arisen from migration, demands for greater autonomy from centralizing states and attempts by religious, linguistic and ethnic minorities to assert their own identities or resist incorporation into larger political and cultural units. For instance, the Tamil speakers of the Dravidian language group of southern India have steadily resisted the imposition of Indo-European Hindi as a national language in their part of India. The tension between Pakistan and India, the most serious threat to the stability of the region, was heightened in 1998 when India tested nuclear devices, prompting Pakistan to test her own nuclear capabilities.

1947 India and Pakistan independent

1948 Mohandas Gandhi assassinated

1962 China invades northern India

1965 War between India and Pakistan

1971 War between India and Pakistan leads to the creation of Bangladesh

1977 Military coup ends civilian rule in Pakistan (restored 1988)

1979–89 USSR occupies Afghanistan

1983 Tamil revolt in Sri Lanka

1984 Sikhs assassinate Indira Gandhi

1990 Free elections in Burma; results annulled by military dictatorship

1992 Hindu zealots demolish Babur's mosque at Ayodhya

1998 India and Pakistan test nuclear devices

1 & 2 The division of the Indian subcontinent in 1947 particularly affected Punjab and Bengal (maps left). The result of partition was a great exodus. Six million Muslims migrated from Punjab to the new Pakistan and about 4.5 million Sikhs and Hindus to the areas between Amritsar and Delhi. In Bengal over 2 million Hindus left the eastern sector (now Bangladesh); thousands of Muslims from Bihar, Calcutta and elsewhere sought shelter in East Bengal.

I East Pakistan, 1947–71
— national boundaries
— state boundaries after 1960

2 The partition of Punjab, 1947
— national boundaries
— state boundaries after 1960

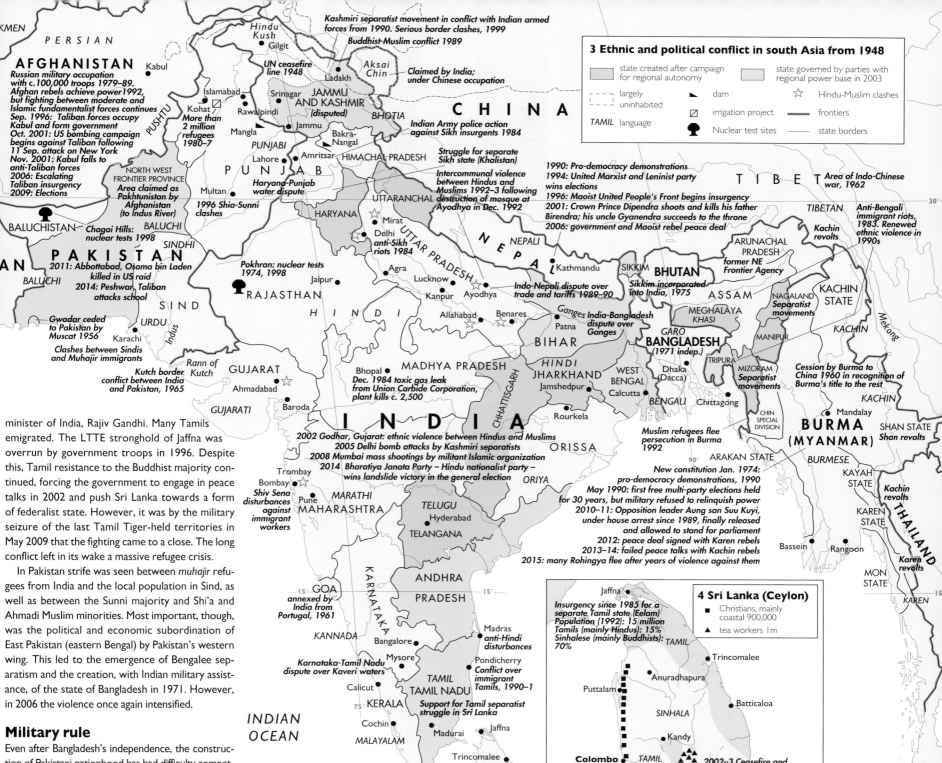

KMEN

P E R S I A N

AFGHANISTAN
Russian military occupation with c.100,000 troops 1979–89. Afghan rebels achieve power 1992, but fighting between moderate and Islamic fundamentalist forces continues Sep. 1996: Taliban forces occupy Kabul and form government Oct. 2001: US bombing campaign begins against Taliban following 11 Sep. attack on New York Nov. 2001: Kabul falls to anti-Taliban forces 2006: Escalating Taliban insurgency 2009: Elections

Kabul

Hindu Kush
Gilgit

Kashmiri separatist movement in conflict with Indian armed forces from 1990. Serious border clashes, 1999
Buddhist-Muslim conflict 1989

UN ceasefire line 1948
Ladakh
Aksai Chin

Claimed by India; under Chinese occupation

Islamabad
Srinagar   JAMMU AND KASHMIR *(disputed)*
Rawalpindi   Jammu
Kohat
More than 2 million refugees 1980–7
Mangla   Bakra-Nangal
BHOTIA

C H I N A

PUSHTU
PUNJAB
Lahore   Amritsar   HIMACHAL PRADESH
Indian Army police action against Sikh insurgents 1984

NORTH WEST FRONTIER PROVINCE
Area claimed as Pakhtunistan by Afghanistan (to Indus River)

P U N J A B
Haryana-Punjab water dispute

Struggle for separate Sikh state (Khalistan)

Multan
HARYANA
Intercommunal violence between Hindus and Muslims 1992–3 following destruction of mosque at Ayodhya in Dec. 1992

UTTARANCHAL

1990: Pro-democracy demonstrations 1994: United Marxist and Leninist party wins elections 1996: Maoist United People's Front begins insurgency 2001: Crown Prince Dipendra shoots and kills his father Birendra; his uncle Gyanendra succeeds to the throne 2006: government and Maoist rebel peace deal

T I B E T
Area of Indo-Chinese war, 1962

BALUCHISTAN
Chagai Hills: nuclear tests 1998
BALUCHI

BALUCHI   SINDHI

A N   P A K I S T A N
2011: Abbottabad, Osama bin Laden killed in US raid 2014: Peshwar, Taliban attacks school

1996 Shia-Sunni clashes

S I N D

URDU

Pokhran: nuclear tests 1974, 1998
RAJASTHAN
Jaipur

Mirat
Delhi
1984 anti-Sikh riots 1984

Agra
Lucknow
Kanpur
U T T A R   P R A D E S H

1990: Pro-democracy demonstrations

TIBETAN

Anti-Bengali immigrant riots, 1983. Renewed ethnic violence in 1990s

ARUNACHAL PRADESH
former NE Frontier Agency

Kachin revolts

Gwadar ceded to Pakistan by Muscat 1956
Clashes between Sindis and Muhajir immigrants
Karachi

Kutch border conflict between India and Pakistan, 1965
Rann of Kutch
GUJARAT
Ahmadabad
Baroda
GUJARATI

H I N D I
Allahabad
Benares

Ayodhya

Kathmandu
N E P A L
NEPALI

Indo-Nepali dispute over trade and tariffs 1989–90

SIKKIM
Sikkim incorporated into India, 1975

BHUTAN

MEGHALAYA
KHASI
GARO

ASSAM

NAGALAND
Separatist movements

KACHIN STATE

Ganges India-Bangladesh dispute over Ganges

KACHIN

Mekong

BIHAR
Patna

HINDI
JHARKHAND
Jamshedpur

WEST BENGAL
Calcutta
BENGALI

BANGLADESH
(1971 indep.)
Dhaka *(Dacca)*
TRIPURA
MIZORAM
Separatist movements

Chittagong

Cession by Burma to China 1960 in recognition of Burma's title to the rest

KACHIN

Bhopal
MADHYA PRADESH
Dec. 1984 toxic gas leak from Union Carbide Corporation, plant kills c. 2,500

CHHATISGARH

Rourkela

Muslim refugees flee persecution in Burma 1992

CHIN SPECIAL DIVISION

Mandalay

BURMA *(MYANMAR)*

SHAN STATE *Shan revolts*

I N D I A

2002 Godhar, Gujarat: ethnic violence between Hindus and Muslims 2005 Delhi bomb attacks by Kashmiri separatists 2008 Mumbai mass shootings by militant Islamic organization 2014 Bharatiya Janata Party – Hindu nationalist party – wins landslide victory in the general election

ORISSA
ORIYA

ARAKAN STATE
BURMESE

New constitution Jan. 1974: pro-democracy demonstrations, 1990 May 1990: first free multi-party elections held for 30 years, but military refused to relinquish power 2010–11: Opposition leader Aung san Suu Kuyi, under house arrest since 1989, finally released and allowed to stand for parliament 2012: peace deal signed with Karen rebels 2013–14: failed peace talks with Kachin rebels 2015: many Rohingya flee after years of violence against them

KAYAH STATE
Kachin revolts

KAREN STATE

Trombay
Bombay
Pune
Shiv Sena disturbances against immigrant workers

MARATHI
MAHARASHTRA

TELUGU
Hyderabad
TELANGANA

ANDHRA PRADESH

Bassein
Rangoon

MON STATE
Karen revolts

THAILAND

GOA
annexed by India from Portugal, 1961

KARNATAKA

KANNADA
Bangalore
Mysore
Calicut

Karnataka-Tamil Nadu dispute over Kaveri waters

Madras
anti-Hindi disturbances

Pondicherry
Conflict over immigrant Tamils, 1990–1

TAMIL
TAMIL NADU

KERALA
MALAYALAM
Cochin
Madurai
Jaffna
Trincomalee

Support for Tamil separatist struggle in Sri Lanka

Cape Comorin

Colombo
Kandy

SRI LANKA
(Ceylon to 1972)
see inset

INDIAN OCEAN

Legend box:

3 Ethnic and political conflict in south Asia from 1948

- state created after campaign for regional autonomy
- state governed by parties with regional power base in 2003
- largely uninhabited
- dam
- Hindu-Muslim clashes
- TAMIL language
- irrigation project
- frontiers
- Nuclear test sites
- state borders

Sri Lanka inset:

4 Sri Lanka (Ceylon)

- ▪ Christians, mainly coastal 900,000
- ▲ tea workers 1m

Insurgency since 1985 for a separate Tamil state (Eelam) Population (1992): 15 million Tamils (mainly Hindus): 15% Sinhalese (mainly Buddhists): 70%

Jaffna
Puttalam
TAMIL
Trincomalee
Anuradhapura
SINHALA
Batticaloa
Kandy
Colombo   TAMIL

1987 India-Sri Lanka accord permits Indian Army intervention in northern Sri Lanka, withdrew in 1990 May 1993 Tamil bomb attack kills President Ranasinghe

2002–3 Ceasefire and Norwegian-sponsored peace talks between Tamil Tigers and government 2006 Renewed fighting and further peace talks 2009 Government seizes last Tamil Tiger stronghold

---

minister of India, Rajiv Gandhi. Many Tamils emigrated. The LTTE stronghold of Jaffna was overrun by government troops in 1996. Despite this, Tamil resistance to the Buddhist majority continued, forcing the government to engage in peace talks in 2002 and push Sri Lanka towards a form of federalist state. However, it was by the military seizure of the last Tamil Tiger-held territories in May 2009 that the fighting came to a close. The long conflict left in its wake a massive refugee crisis.

In Pakistan strife was seen between *muhajir* refugees from India and the local population in Sind, as well as between the Sunni majority and Shi'a and Ahmadi Muslim minorities. Most important, though, was the political and economic subordination of East Pakistan (eastern Bengal) by Pakistan's western wing. This led to the emergence of Bengalee separatism and the creation, with Indian military assistance, of the state of Bangladesh in 1971. However, in 2006 the violence once again intensified.

Military rule

Even after Bangladesh's independence, the construction of Pakistani nationhood has had difficulty competing with entrenched regional Sindhi, Punjabi, Pashtun, Kashmiri, Baluchi or *muhajir* identities. Only two forces have been capable of binding the nation together – Islam and the military. The Islamization of politics during the 1970s and 1980s occurred as politicians used Islam as a rallying cry to unite a fragmenting nation. Military government occurred in Pakistan – as also in Burma and Bangladesh – when soldiers believed civilian rule was incapable of maintaining the unity of the state. In Burma, despite promises in the 1990s of free multi-party elections to end 30 years of increasingly repressive rule, the military remained in power. Ethnic tensions persisted in Burma as groups such as the Karens and Shans struggled for regional autonomy against an authoritarian state. Burma's military regime justified its rule by claiming that it alone was capable of maintaining the "sovereign and territorial integrity of the Burmese state". Since 2010, there have been moves towards liberalization, including the release of the pro-democracy leader Aung San Suu Kyi from house arrest, but sectarianism – not least the intensification of persecution of the Muslim minority – has persisted.

India has avoided military rule while its parliamentary system has been able to accommodate (often uncomfortably) tension between regional identities and the nation-state. The BJP is a party which asserts the existence of a very strong, national Hindu Indian identity. Yet it survived in power during the early 2000s by allying with regional parties from outside its north Indian heartland. Despite a government with a strongly nationalist ideology, during the early 2000s a large number of Indian states were governed by regionalist parties (see map 3).

South Asia in global politics

During the initial phases of the Cold War, non-alignment was a feature of the external relations of south Asian states. The Chinese invasion of India in 1962 showed the limits of that policy. For the rest of the War, India tilted towards the Soviet Union while Pakistan was backed by the USA. Since the Soviet occupation of Afghanistan in 1979, south Asia has been on the frontline in the Cold War and subsequent global conflict. The USA funded the Islamic opposition to the Soviet-backed communist state in Afghanistan. Soviet forces left Afghanistan in 1989, but were replaced with a power struggle between Afghani politicians from different regions. The weakness of the Afghan state allowed the Taliban, a group of Islamists supported by Pakistan's intelligence services, to win power in the mid-1990s by presenting themselves as a force for stability. The Taliban regime's support for those seen as responsible for terror attacks in the USA led to the second occupation of Afghanistan – by the USA and its allies. From 2005, NATO forces faced a large-scale Taliban insurgency against the US-backed regime of Hamid Karzai. August 2009 elections gave Karzai a second term as president, but the process was widely disputed. In the same year, US troops numbers were escalated by President Barack Obama prior to the beginning of a withdrawal in 2011. But Taliban resistance remained tenacious and the path to peace and stability is uncertain.

4 In Ceylon, the Hindu Tamils (map above) have resisted pressures, institutionalized in the new Sri Lankan Constitution of 1972, from the Sinhalese Buddhist majority. Tamil leaders demanded a separate state in a loose federation and after 1983 guerrilla activity by the Tamil Tigers and other militants precipitated a full-scale clash with the Sri Lankan army, with civilian massacres on both sides. Sinhala-Tamil tensions increased dramatically after 1985 and the Indian army intervened in 1987 to try to reimpose order.

The Golden Temple, Amritsar (below). The principal place of worship in the Sikh faith, the temple was begun by Arjan, the fifth Sikh guru, in 1589. It subsequently became a symbol of Sikh political as well as religious aspirations and in June 1984 was the scene of a five-day gun battle between the Indian Army and Sikh extremists. The severely damaged temple complex was later restored.

Africa

Africa's development since the ending of European colonial control was anything but smooth. Poverty, corruption and ethnic rivalry dogged parts of the continent, while wars, repressive one-party governments, disease and famine meant that the lives of many Africans were a mockery of the optimistic goals proclaimed at independence.

BY **1975 MOST AFRICAN STATES** were independent of European colonial control. Decolonization was sometimes peaceful, although there were major wars in Algeria and in the Portuguese colonies, as well as anti-colonial rebellions from Madagascar to Morocco. South Africa's policy of apartheid, introduced in 1948, legally segregated people by race and colour. African social, economic and political advance was blocked.

At independence Africa inherited weak economies and fragile political systems. After 1950 population and urbanization grew rapidly. Increased pressure on land caused ecological problems. Times of serious drought, as in the Sahelian region in 1972–3, led to famine and political instability, which in turn created refugees. Endemic tropical diseases were joined in the late 1980s by the scourge of AIDS. African states had low levels of capital accumulation, small markets, inadequate public utilities and limited welfare services. Widespread corruption discouraged foreign investment. Many educated people left the continent, and the gulf between rich and poor steadily widened.

Ethnic and political conflict

Independence arrived in Africa on a wave of optimism. Newly formed independent governments promised their citizens development, modernization, and an end to poverty and exploitation, but these promises went largely unfulfilled. At independence most African states hastily created systems of parliamentary government that were short-lived. In many

WE ARE AT WAR ... A WAR AGAINST
POVERTY AND OPPRESSION ...;
HIS STRUGGLE IS AIMED AT MOVING THE
PEOPLE OF TANZANIA FROM THE STATE
OF POVERTY TO A STATE OF PROSPERITY ...
NOW WE WANT A REVOLUTION –
A REVOLUTION WHICH BRINGS TO AN END
OUR WEAKNESS, SO THAT WE ARE NEVER
AGAIN EXPLOITED, OPPRESSED,
OR HUMILIATED.

Julius Nyerere, President of Tanzania.
Speach to launch the Arusha Declaration on
Socialism and Self-Reliance, January 1967

states ruling politicians suppressed opposition parties and declared one-party rule, giving rise to a wave of authoritarian regimes from late 1960 to the 1980s. Arbitrary government could be removed only by force and thus, in many sub-Saharan states, the military seized power from civilians, sparking a wave of coups and counter-coups across the continent.

The new states of Africa had inherited colonial frontiers. Ethnic, religious and political rivalries across and within these borders resulted in secessionist movements and civil wars. Major wars of secession occurred in the southern Sudan (see p. 322), in Ethiopia against Amharic rule in the 1970s and 1980s, and in Nigeria where the Igbo tried to secede Biafra (1967–70). Nigeria, the most populous state in Africa, faced acute problems in nation-building, with over 250 ethnicities, three major competing ethnic and regional blocs, and a divide between the Muslim North and predominantly Christian South.

From the 1960s sub-Saharan Africa saw the rapid growth of both Christianity and Islam. New Protestant heartlands developed, and Pentecostalism spread widely. Islam also grew in militancy, encouraged by the creation of an Islamic Republic in Iran after the revolution in 1979 (see p. 331). Religious fervour led to communal tension, particularly in Nigeria where ethnic and political differences met along the religious fault line dividing the mainly Christian south and the mainly Islamic north.

2 During the 1980s the apartheid government in South Africa operated a "total strategy" against African nationalism, destabilizing her northern neighbours through intervention in Angola and Mozambique's civil wars (**map left**). Cuban troops aided the MPLA government in Angola and reached a stalemate with South African forces at Cuito Cuanavale. Unrest within South Africa, increasing international pressure and economic crisis helped bring about the end of the apartheid regime.

Economic failure

The state dominated early economic development schemes, but with limited success. Governments' economic ambitions were rarely able to match their administrative capabilities. Even plans that focused on rural development, such as Tanzania's "Ujamaa" policies, introduced in 1967, were largely failures. Several countries adopted economic policies modeled on those of communist countries, a particular example being that of Ethiopia's Marxist regime (1975–91).

African states relied on the export of primary products in a global economy where prices were determined by industrial countries. They were weak players in a system dominated by Western capitalist powers upon whom they depended for capital and markets. Rises in prices of manufactured imports, vital for African development, rapidly increased in the 1970s and 1980s, while prices of primary export materials declined. Foreign loans and global inflation led to increased indebtedness so that the annual income of some countries amounted to less than the cost of servicing their debt.

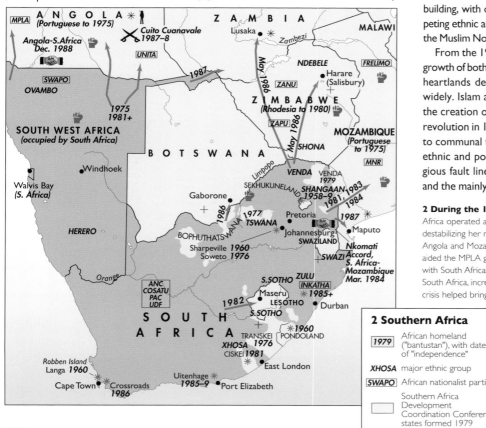

2 Southern Africa

1979	African homeland ("bantustan"), with date of "independence"	✳	ANC bases
		+	ANC offices
XHOSA	major ethnic group	1986	South African Defence Force attacks, with date
SWAPO	African nationalist parties		agreements
	Southern Africa Development Coordination Conference states formed 1979		guerrilla campaigns
			Cuban troops
		✳	violent clashes, with dates

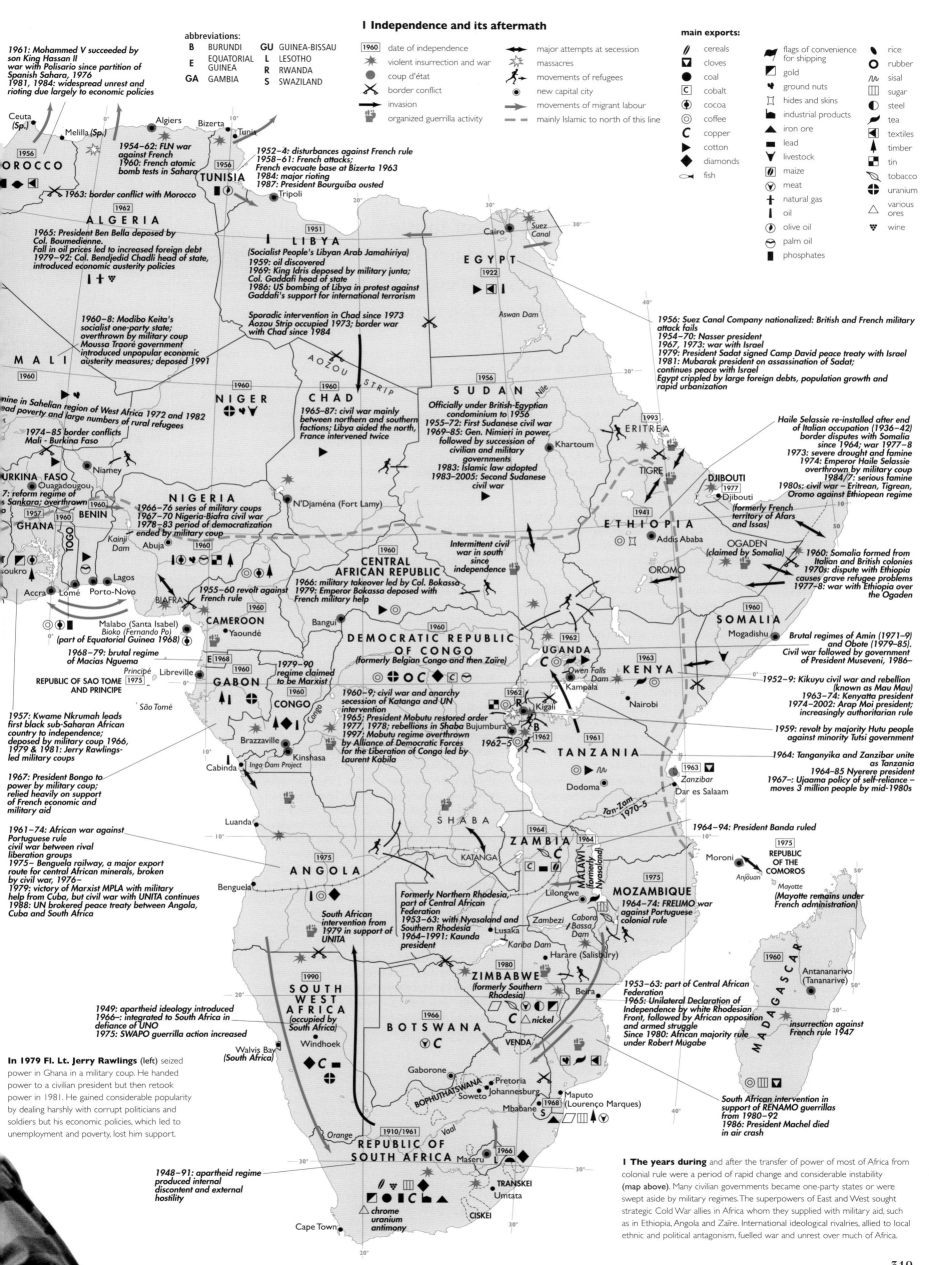

I Independence and its aftermath

abbreviations:
B BURUNDI
E EQUATORIAL GUINEA
GA GAMBIA
GU GUINEA-BISSAU
L LESOTHO
R RWANDA
S SWAZILAND

1960 date of independence
✳ violent insurrection and war
● coup d'état
✗ border conflict
→ invasion
organized guerrilla activity
major attempts at secession
massacres
movements of refugees
new capital city
movements of migrant labour
mainly Islamic to north of this line

main exports:
cereals
cloves
coal
C cobalt
cocoa
coffee
C copper
cotton
diamonds
fish
maize
meat
natural gas
oil
olive oil
palm oil
phosphates
flags of convenience for shipping
gold
ground nuts
hides and skins
industrial products
iron ore
lead
livestock
rice
rubber
sisal
sugar
steel
tea
textiles
timber
tin
tobacco
uranium
various ores
wine

1961: Mohammed V succeeded by son King Hassan II war with Polisario since partition of Spanish Sahara, 1976
1981, 1984: widespread unrest and rioting due largely to economic policies

Ceuta (Sp.)
Melilla (Sp.)
Algiers
Bizerta
Tunis
1956

1954–62: FLN war against French
1960: French atomic bomb tests in Sahara
1963: border conflict with Morocco

1952–4: disturbances against French rule
1958–61: French attacks; French evacuate base at Bizerta 1963
1984: major rioting
1987: President Bourguiba ousted

TUNISIA
Tripoli

ALGERIA
1962
1965: President Ben Bella deposed by Col. Boumedienne.
Fall in oil prices led to increased foreign debt
1979–92: Col. Bendjedid Chadli head of state, introduced economic austerity policies

LIBYA
1951
(Socialist People's Libyan Arab Jamahiriya)
1959: oil discovered
1969: King Idris deposed by military junta; Col. Gaddafi head of state
1986: US bombing of Libya in protest against Gaddafi's support for international terrorism

EGYPT
1922
Cairo
Suez Canal
Aswan Dam

1956: Suez Canal Company nationalized: British and French military attack fails
1954–70: Nasser president
1967, 1973: war with Israel
1979: President Sadat signed Camp David peace treaty with Israel
1981: Mubarak president on assassination of Sadat; continues peace with Israel
Egypt crippled by large foreign debts, population growth and rapid urbanization

1960–8: Modibo Keita's socialist one-party state; overthrown by military coup
Moussa Traoré government introduced unpopular economic austerity measures; deposed 1991

MALI
1960

Sporadic intervention in Chad since 1973
Aozou Strip occupied 1973; border war with Chad since 1984

AOZOU STRIP

NIGER
CHAD
1960
1965–87: civil war mainly between northern and southern factions; Libya aided the north, France intervened twice

SUDAN
1956
Officially under British-Egyptian condominium to 1956
1955–72: First Sudanese civil war
1969–85: Gen. Nimieri in power, followed by succession of civilian and military governments
1983: Islamic law adopted
1983–2005: Second Sudanese civil war

Khartoum
Nile

ERITREA 1993
TIGRE 1941
DJIBOUTI 1977
Djibouti

Haile Selassie re-installed after end of Italian occupation (1936–42) border disputes with Somalia since 1964; war 1977–8
1973: severe drought and famine
1974: Emperor Haile Selassie overthrown by military coup
1984/7: serious famine
1980s: civil war – Eritrean, Tigrean, Oromo against Ethiopian regime

(formerly French territory of Afars and Issas)

famine in Sahelian region of West Africa 1972 and 1982
spread poverty and large numbers of rural refugees
1974–85 border conflicts Mali – Burkina Faso

BURKINA FASO
1987: reform regime of Sankara; overthrown
Ouagadougou
Niamey

NIGERIA
1966–76 series of military coups
1967–70 Nigeria-Biafra civil war
1978–83 period of democratization ended by military coup
N'Djaména (Fort Lamy)
Abuja
1960

ETHIOPIA
Addis Ababa
OGADEN (claimed by Somalia)
OROMO

1960: Somalia formed from Italian and British colonies
1970s: dispute with Ethiopia causes grave refugee problems
1977–8: war with Ethiopia over the Ogaden

GHANA 1957
1960 BENIN
TOGO
Kainji Dam
Lagos
Accra Lomé Porto-Novo
BIAFRA
1955–60 revolt against French rule
1960

Intermittent civil war in south since independence

SOMALIA 1960
Mogadishu

Brutal regimes of Amin (1971–9) and Obote (1979–85). Civil war followed by government of President Museveni, 1986–

CENTRAL AFRICAN REPUBLIC
1966: military takeover led by Col. Bokassa
1979: Emperor Bokassa deposed with French military help
Bangui

Malabo (Santa Isabel)
Bioko (Fernando Po)
(part of Equatorial Guinea 1968)
CAMEROON
1960
Yaoundé

1968–79: brutal regime of Macias Nguema

REPUBLIC OF SAO TOME AND PRINCIPE
Principé 1975
Libreville
E 1968
1960
Príncipe
São Tomé
GABON
1960

DEMOCRATIC REPUBLIC OF CONGO
(formerly Belgian Congo and then Zaïre)
1960

1979–90 regime claimed to be Marxist

CONGO
Brazzaville
Kinshasa
Cabinda
Inga Dam Project

1960–9: civil war and anarchy secession of Katanga and UN intervention
1965: President Mobutu restored order
1977, 1978: rebellions in Shaba
1997: Mobutu regime overthrown by Alliance of Democratic Forces for the Liberation of Congo led by Laurent Kabila

UGANDA 1962
Owen Falls Dam
Kampala
R Kigali
B Bujumbura
1962–5
1962

KENYA 1963
Nairobi

1952–9: Kikuyu civil war and rebellion (known as Mau Mau)
1963–74: Kenyatta president
1974–2002: Arap Moi president; increasingly authoritarian rule

1959: revolt by majority Hutu people against minority Tutsi government

1964: Tanganyika and Zanzibar unite as Tanzania
1964–85 Nyerere president
1967–: Ujaama policy of self-reliance – moves 3 million people by mid-1980s

1957: Kwame Nkrumah leads first black sub-Saharan African country to independence; deposed by military coup 1966, 1979 & 1981: Jerry Rawlings-led military coups

1967: President Bongo to power by military coup; relied heavily on support of French economic and military aid

1961–74: African war against Portuguese rule
civil war between rival liberation groups
1975– Benguela railway, a major export route for central African minerals, broken by civil war, 1976–
1979: victory of Marxist MPLA with military help from Cuba, but civil war with UNITA continues
1988: UN brokered peace treaty between Angola, Cuba and South Africa

TANZANIA
Dodoma
Dar es Salaam
Zanzibar 1963
Tan-Zam 1970–5

SHABA
ANGOLA
Luanda
1975
Benguela

KATANGA

ZAMBIA 1964
1964
MALAWI (formerly Nyasaland)
Lusaka
Lilongwe

Moroni
Anjouan
REPUBLIC OF THE COMOROS 1975
Mayotte
(Mayotte remains under French administration)

1964–94: President Banda ruled

Formerly Northern Rhodesia, part of Central African Federation
1953–63: with Nyasaland and Southern Rhodesia
1964–1991: Kaunda president

South African intervention from 1979 in support of UNITA

SOUTH WEST AFRICA
(occupied by South Africa)
1990
Windhoek
Walvis Bay (South Africa)

1949: apartheid ideology introduced
1966–: integrated to South Africa in defiance of UNO
1975: SWAPO guerrilla action increased

MOZAMBIQUE
1975
1964–74: FRELIMO war against Portuguese colonial rule
Cabora Bassa Dam
Zambezi
Kariba Dam
Harare (Salisbury)
Beira

ZIMBABWE
(formerly Southern Rhodesia)
1980

1953–63: part of Central African Federation
1965: Unilateral Declaration of Independence by white Rhodesian Front, followed by African opposition and armed struggle
Since 1980: African majority rule under Robert Mugabe

BOTSWANA 1966
C nickel
Gaborone

VENDA

BOPHUTHATSWANA
Pretoria
Johannesburg
Soweto
Maputo (Lourenço Marques)
Mbabane S 1968
Maseru L 1966

MADAGASCAR 1960
Antananarivo (Tananarive)
insurrection against French rule 1947

In 1979 Fl. Lt. Jerry Rawlings (left) seized power in Ghana in a military coup. He handed power to a civilian president but then retook power in 1981. He gained considerable popularity by dealing harshly with corrupt politicians and soldiers but his economic policies, which led to unemployment and poverty, lost him support.

South African intervention in support of RENAMO guerrillas from 1980–92
1986: President Machel died in air crash

REPUBLIC OF SOUTH AFRICA
1910/1961
Orange
Vaal
Cape Town
TRANSKEI
Umtata
CISKEI
chrome
uranium
antimony

1948–91: apartheid regime produced internal discontent and external hostility

I The years during and after the transfer of power of most of Africa from colonial rule were a period of rapid change and considerable instability (map above). Many civilian governments became one-party states or were swept aside by military regimes. The superpowers of East and West sought strategic Cold War allies in Africa whom they supplied with military aid, such as in Ethiopia, Angola and Zaïre. International ideological rivalries, allied to local ethnic and political antagonism, fuelled war and unrest over much of Africa.

319

Africa since 1989

The end of the Cold War brought political change to Africa. Elected governments replaced authoritarian rule, and South Africa's system of apartheid finally fell apart. However, wars continued to ravage areas of the continent, and Africa's social and economic future was blighted by heavy debt and the scourge of AIDS.

WITH THE END OF THE COLD WAR, Africa lost its former global strategic significance. Corrupt military rulers and one-party states, increasingly challenged by civic groups, churches and trade unions, surrendered power in multi-party elections during an era of democratization. From 1991, elected governments gained power in more than 30 countries, including Zambia and Nigeria, but some countries such as Côte d'Ivoire experienced political violence and conflict following elections, whilst others like Kenya saw incumbent regimes control voting to retain power. Democratization was incomplete in many areas, with corruption, human rights violations and single-party dominance of the state remaining pressing issues.

The collapse of the USSR also ended South Africa's weak claim to be a bastion against communism in the region. The country's economy was fragile, international pressure against white-minority rule increased and apartheid was crumbling internally under assault from anti-apartheid forces. President FW de Klerk freed Nelson Mandela and unbanned the African National Congress (ANC) – the central political party in the campaign against apartheid. After a tense transition period, in 1994 the ANC won a majority in the country's first full democratic elections, and Nelson Mandela became the country's first black African president.

Since 1990, Africa's economies have experienced considerable difficulty, with many becoming increasingly dependent on foreign aid. Sustainable development is hindered by unequal terms of trade, food shortages and heavy debts. Structural adjustment programmes imposed by the International Monetary Fund (IMF) since the 1980s to regularize African debt made life harder for many Africans. African initiatives for economic renewal include the New Economic Partnership for African Development (NEPAD) of 2001. The problems to be tackled are many and severe, not least the scourge of HIV/AIDS, particularly in southern regions. Poverty, drought, economic mismanagement and conflict have also contributed to the eruption of famine in some countries, such as in Ethiopia, Malawi and Angola around 2002. Economic collapse also contributed to growing political opposition to the Mugabe regime in Zimbabwe. The illegal exploitation of natural resources like diamonds and coltan has also driven conflict in Sierra Leone and the Democratic Republic of Congo (DRC). The 2014–15 Ebola epidemic highlights how vulnerable Africa's populations and economies still are, with 11,000 people confirmed dead and an estimated $1.6 billion foregone GDP in Guinea, Sierra Leone and Liberia alone. Overall however, in 2000–8 resources helped drive annual real GDP growth of 4.9 per cent across Africa.

Conflict and genocide

In many parts of Africa, democratization was stalled by conflict. War persisted in Sudan between the largely Arab government in Khartoum and Christian and animist African rebels in the south, exacerbated by oil reserves and regional tensions, until South Sudan gained its independence in 2011 (see p. 322). The continent witnessed one of its worst crises with the Rwandan genocide in 1994. Ethnic and communal violence between Hutu and Tutsi populations resulted in the killing of over 800,000 mainly Tutsi people, and the flight of over two million refugees, sparking conflict in the DRC (see p. 324). During complex civil wars from 1989-2003 in Liberia and Sierra Leone, rival warlords inflicted great brutality on civilians and created many refugees.

Across northern Africa in the 1990s, the rise of Islamism led to clashes with political authorities. In Algeria, civil war and an Islamist terror campaign left over 100,000 people dead. Since 2011, the "Arab Spring", ethno-political tensions and international terrorist networks have driven conflict in countries like Libya and Mali. Kenya and Somalia have suffered terrorist attacked and bombings by Al-Shabaab, whilst the Nigerian government has faced a growing threat in the north from Boko Haram.

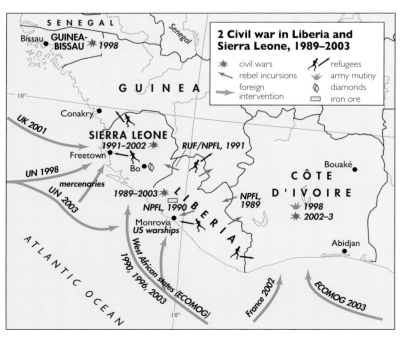

2 Civil war in Liberia and Sierra Leone, 1989–2003

- civil wars
- rebel incursions
- foreign intervention
- refugees
- army mutiny
- diamonds
- iron ore

Map labels:
SENEGAL
Bissau GUINEA-BISSAU 1998
Senegal
GUINEA
UK 2001
Conakry
SIERRA LEONE 1991–2002
Freetown RUF/NPFL, 1991
UN 1998
Bo
mercenaries
UN 2003 1989–2003
NPFL, 1990
LIBERIA
Monrovia US warships
ATLANTIC OCEAN
West African states (ECOMOG) 1990, 1996, 2003
France 2002
NPFL, 1989
CÔTE D'IVOIRE
Bouaké
1998
2002–3
Abidjan
ECOMOG 2003

2 Civil war and communal violence in Liberia and Sierra Leone (map left) spread into neighbouring countries. Unrest began with an attack by the National Patriotic Front of Liberia. In Sierra Leone rebels of the Revolutionary United Front (RUF) gained control of the valuable mining areas, using "blood diamonds" to fund campaigns. Government and rebel forces waged brutal campaigns to control territory, until foreign intervention helped to end the wars.

Kenyans queuing (right) to cast their votes in the 1997 multi-party election, which was marred by violence and irregularities in the voting. It was not until the 2002 elections that the authoritarian rule of President Arap Moi of Kenya was ended. Violence again erupted in the 2007 elections with over one thousand killed and 250,000 displaced.

Map labels:
Canary Islands (Sp.)
1991: ceasefire between Morocco and Polisario. Large defensive sand walls built on eastern border with Mauritania
2001: UN proposal that W. Sahara be autonomous for 4 years and then a referendum for integration with Morocco or independence
Dakhla (Villa Cisneros)
W. SAHARA
MAURITANI
2008: military coup Gen. Abdel Aziz to
REPUBLIC OF CAPE VERDE
Cape Verde Islands
1991
Nouakchott
Dakar
SENEGAL 2000
Banjul 1994 GA
Casamance conflict
Bissau GU 1999
Senegal
Bamako
GUINEA 2008
2005: drug trade seizes control of economy
Conakry 2007
UN, UK
Freetown
SIERRA LEONE
1991–2002: ethnic violence and civil war
Monrovia
1989–2003: ethnic civil war to overthrow Doe regime degenerates into conflicts between rival warlords
2007: Johnson-Sirleaf becomes Africa's first elected female head of state
LIBERIA
UN, US
1998: army mutiny and coup
2002: French troops into in civil war

We enter into a covenant that we shall build the society in which all South Africans, both black and white, will be able to walk tall, without any fear in their hearts, assured of their inalienable right to human dignity – a rainbow nation at peace with itself and the world.

Nelson Mandela
From his speech at his inauguration as President of South Africa, 10 May 1994

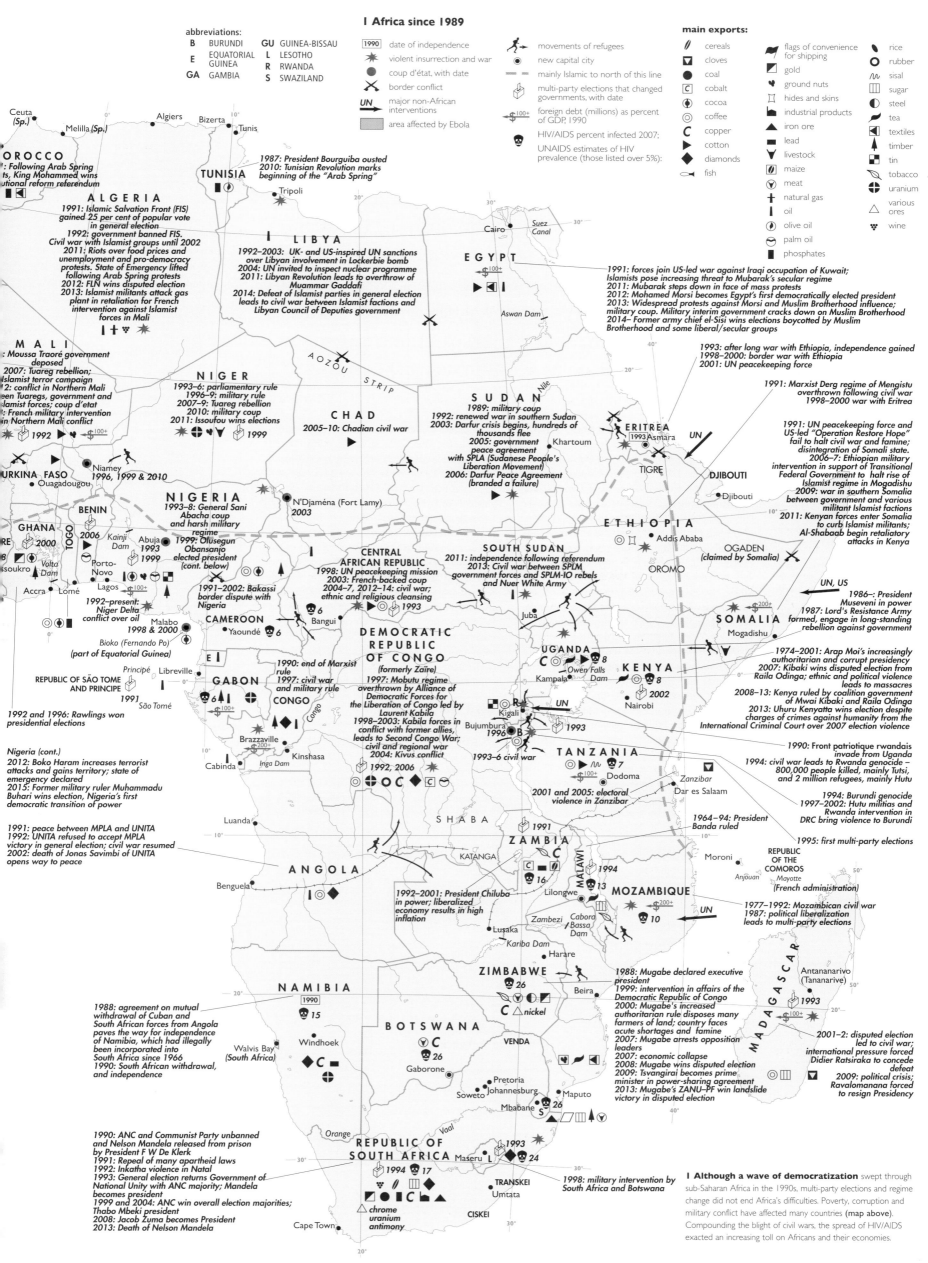

abbreviations:

B	BURUNDI	**GU**	GUINEA-BISSAU
E	EQUATORIAL GUINEA	**L**	LESOTHO
		R	RWANDA
GA	GAMBIA	**S**	SWAZILAND

1990 date of independence

violent insurrection and war

coup d'état, with date

border conflict

UN major non-African interventions

area affected by Ebola

movements of refugees

new capital city

mainly Islamic to north of this line

multi-party elections that changed governments, with date

foreign debt (millions) as percent of GDP, 1990

HIV/AIDS percent infected 2007; UNAIDS estimates of HIV prevalence (those listed over 5%):

main exports:

cereals	flags of convenience for shipping	rice
cloves	gold	rubber
coal	ground nuts	sisal
C cobalt	hides and skins	sugar
cocoa	industrial products	steel
coffee	iron ore	tea
C copper	lead	textiles
cotton	livestock	timber
diamonds	maize	tin
fish	meat	tobacco
	natural gas	uranium
	oil	various ores
	olive oil	wine
	palm oil	
	phosphates	

Ceuta (Sp.)
Melilla (Sp.)
Algiers
Bizerta
Tunis

OROCCO
: Following Arab Spring
ts, King Mohammed wins
tional reform referendum

TUNISIA
1987: President Bourguiba ousted
2010: Tunisian Revolution marks beginning of the "Arab Spring"

Tripoli

ALGERIA
1991: Islamic Salvation Front (FIS) gained 25 per cent of popular vote in general election
1992: government banned FIS. Civil war with Islamist groups until 2002
2011: Riots over food prices and unemployment and pro-democracy protests. State of Emergency lifted following Arab Spring protests
2012: FLN wins disputed election
2013: Islamist militants attack gas plant in retaliation for French intervention against Islamist forces in Mali

LIBYA
1992–2003: UK- and US-inspired UN sanctions over Libyan involvement in Lockerbie bomb
2004: UN invited to inspect nuclear programme
2011: Libyan Revolution leads to overthrow of Muammar Gaddafi
2014: Defeat of Islamist parties in general election leads to civil war between Islamist factions and Libyan Council of Deputies government

Cairo
Suez Canal

EGYPT
1991: forces join US-led war against Iraqi occupation of Kuwait; Islamists pose increasing threat to Mubarak's secular regime
2011: Mubarak steps down in face of mass protests
2012: Mohamed Morsi becomes Egypt's first democratically elected president
2013: Widespread protests against Morsi and Muslim Brotherhood influence; military coup. Military interim government cracks down on Muslim Brotherhood
2014– Former army chief el-Sisi wins elections boycotted by Muslim Brotherhood and some liberal/secular groups

Aswan Dam

MALI
: Moussa Traoré government deposed
2007: Tuareg rebellion;
Islamist terror campaign
2: conflict in Northern Mali een Tuaregs, government and Islamist forces; coup d'etat
: French military intervention in Northern Mali conflict
1992

AOZOU STRIP

NIGER
1993–6: parliamentary rule
1996–9: military rule
2007–9: Tuareg rebellion
2010: military coup
2011: Issoufou wins elections

CHAD
2005–10: Chadian civil war

N'Djaména (Fort Lamy) 2003

Nile
Khartoum

SUDAN
1989: military coup
1992: renewed war in southern Sudan
2003: Darfur crisis begins, hundreds of thousands flee
2005: government peace agreement with SPLA (Sudanese People's Liberation Movement)
2006: Darfur Peace Agreement (branded a failure)

1993: after long war with Ethiopia, independence gained
1998–2000: border war with Ethiopia
2001: UN peacekeeping force

ERITREA
1993 Asmara
UN
TIGRE

1991: Marxist Derg regime of Mengistu overthrown following civil war
1998–2000 war with Eritrea

DJIBOUTI
Djibouti

1991: UN peacekeeping force and US-led "Operation Restore Hope" fail to halt civil war and famine; disintegration of Somali state.
2006–7: Ethiopian military intervention in support of Transitional Federal Government to halt rise of Islamist regime in Mogadishu
2009: war in southern Somalia between government and various militant Islamist factions
2011: Kenyan forces enter Somalia to curb Islamist militants; Al-Shabaab begin retaliatory attacks in Kenya

URKINA FASO
Ouagadougou
Niamey 1996, 1999 & 2010

NIGERIA
1993–8: General Sani Abacha coup and harsh military regime
1999: Olusegun Obansanjo elected president (cont. below)

CENTRAL AFRICAN REPUBLIC
1998: UN peacekeeping mission
2003: French-backed coup
2004–7, 2012–14: civil war; ethnic and religious cleansing

SOUTH SUDAN
2011: independence following referendum
2013: Civil war between SPLM government forces and SPLM-IO rebels and Nuer White Army

Juba

OGADEN (claimed by Somalia)
OROMO

ETHIOPIA
Addis Ababa

GHANA
TOGO
2000
2006
Kainji Dam
Abuja
1993
1999
Porto-Novo
BENIN
Volta Dam
Accra
Lomé
Lagos

1991–2002: Bakassi border dispute with Nigeria
Bangui 1993

Yaoundé 6

CAMEROON
Malabo
Bioko (Fernando Po) (part of Equatorial Guinea)

1992–present: Niger Delta conflict over oil

UN, US

1986–: President Museveni in power
1987: Lord's Resistance Army formed, engage in long-standing rebellion against government

1974–2001: Arap Moi's increasingly authoritarian and corrupt presidency
2007: Kibaki wins disputed election from Raila Odinga; ethnic and political violence leads to massacres
2008–13: Kenya ruled by coalition government of Mwai Kibaki and Raila Odinga
2013: Uhuru Kenyatta wins election despite charges of crimes against humanity from the International Criminal Court over 2007 election violence

E
GABON
Libreville
Principé

REPUBLIC OF SÃO TOME AND PRINCIPE
1991
São Tomé

1992 and 1996: Rawlings won presidential elections

DEMOCRATIC REPUBLIC OF CONGO
(formerly Zaïre)
1990: end of Marxist rule
1997: civil war and military rule
1997: Mobutu regime overthrown by Alliance of Democratic Forces for the Liberation of Congo led by Laurent Kabila
1998–2003: Kabila forces in conflict with former allies, leads to Second Congo War; civil and regional war
2004: Kivus conflict
1992, 2006

CONGO
Brazzaville
Kinshasa
Cabinda
Inga Dam
Congo

Nigeria (cont.)
2012: Boko Haram increases terrorist attacks and gains territory; state of emergency declared
2015: Former military ruler Muhammadu Buhari wins election, Nigeria's first democratic transition of power

UGANDA
8
Owen Falls Dam
Kampala

KENYA
8
2002
Nairobi

1990: Front patriotique rwandais invade from Uganda
1994: civil war leads to Rwanda genocide – 800,000 people killed, mainly Tutsi, and 2 million refugees, mainly Hutu

R
Kigali
UN
Bujumbura 1996
B
1993
1993–6 civil war

1994: Burundi genocide
1997–2002: Hutu militias and Rwanda intervention in DRC bring violence to Burundi

TANZANIA
7
Dodoma
Zanzibar
Dar es Salaam

2001 and 2005: electoral violence in Zanzibar

1995: first multi-party elections

1991: peace between MPLA and UNITA
1992: UNITA refused to accept MPLA victory in general election; civil war resumed
2002: death of Jonas Savimbi of UNITA opens way to peace

Luanda
SHABA

1964–94: President Banda ruled

REPUBLIC OF THE COMOROS
Moroni
Anjouan
Mayotte (French administration)

1977–1992: Mozambican civil war
1987: political liberalization leads to multi-party elections

ANGOLA
Benguela

ZAMBIA
1991
KATANGA
16

MALAWI
1994
13
Lilongwe

MOZAMBIQUE
10
Zambezi
Cabora Bassa Dam
UN

1992–2001: President Chiluba in power; liberalized economy results in high inflation

Lusaka
Kariba Dam
Harare

1991: peace between MPLA and UNITA

NAMIBIA
1990
15

ZIMBABWE
26
C nickel
Beira

1988: Mugabe declared executive president
1999: intervention in affairs of the Democratic Republic of Congo
2000: Mugabe's increased authoritarian rule disposes many farmers of land; country faces acute shortages and famine
2007: Mugabe arrests opposition leaders
2007: economic collapse
2008: Mugabe wins disputed election
2009: Tsvangirai becomes prime minister in power-sharing agreement
2013: Mugabe's ZANU-PF win landslide victory in disputed election

MADAGASCAR
Antananarivo (Tananarive)
1993

2001–2: disputed election led to civil war; international pressure forced Didier Ratsiraka to concede defeat
2009: political crisis; Ravalomanana forced to resign Presidency

1988: agreement on mutual withdrawal of Cuban and South African forces from Angola paves the way for independence of Namibia, which had illegally been incorporated into South Africa since 1966
1990: South African withdrawal, and independence

Walvis Bay (South Africa)
Windhoek

BOTSWANA
C
26
Gaborone

VENDA

Pretoria
Johannesburg
Soweto
Maputo
Mbabane
S 26

1990: ANC and Communist Party unbanned and Nelson Mandela released from prison by President F W De Klerk
1991: Repeal of many apartheid laws
1992: Inkatha violence in Natal
1993: General election returns Government of National Unity with ANC majority; Mandela becomes president
1999 and 2004: ANC win overall election majorities; Thabo Mbeki president
2008: Jacob Zuma becomes President
2013: Death of Nelson Mandela

Orange
Vaal

REPUBLIC OF SOUTH AFRICA
1994
17
Maseru L
1993 24

1998: military intervention by South Africa and Botswana

chrome uranium antimony

TRANSKEI
Umtata
CISKEI

Cape Town

I Although a wave of democratization swept through sub-Saharan Africa in the 1990s, multi-party elections and regime change did not end Africa's difficulties. Poverty, corruption and military conflict have affected many countries (map above). Compounding the blight of civil wars, the spread of HIV/AIDS exacted an increasing toll on Africans and their economies.

The Horn of Africa

The Horn of Africa is one of the world's most complex and conflict-ridden regions. Each of the countries – Somalia, Ethiopia, Eritrea, Djibouti, Sudan and South Sudan – has suffered protracted political strife, arising from local and national grievances, identity politics and regional inter-state rivalries. War, lawlessness, famine, humanitarian crisis and the rise of Islamic extremism and terrorism have driven regional crisis.

THE RECENT HISTORY of the Horn of Africa has been characterized by conflict, political authoritarianism and humanitarian crisis, with local grievances interacting with wider regional tensions. In Sudan, civil war raged from 1983 to 2005 between southern rebels led by John Garang's Sudan People's Liberation Movement/Army (SPLM/SPLA) and the northern government in Khartoum. Conflict was driven by tensions between a largely Muslim "Arab" north and an "African" south, but also by southern claims to political autonomy, by ethnic tensions, and competition over land and Sudan's new-found oil wealth. A Comprehensive Peace Agreement in 2005 granted autonomy to southern Sudan, but tensions persisted. Another conflict erupted in 2003 in the Darfur region of western Sudan, when Sudan Liberation Army (SLA) and Justice and Equality Movement (JEM) rebels protesting against Khartoum's oppression of black Africans and neglect of the region attacked government targets. Tensions between Fur, Masalit and Baqqara communities over land and grazing rights also fuelled conflict. Government-sponsored Janjaweed militias massacred thousands of civilians and over two million people were displaced, leading to accusations of genocide. President Omar al-Bashir was indicted on war crimes charges by the International Criminal Court (ICC) in 2009. In 2011, South Sudan voted for independence in a referendum, but since late 2013 the country has descended into civil war between the Salva Kiir's SPLM government and Riek Machar's SPLM-IO rebels and the Nuer White Army.

Neighbouring Ethiopia underwent its own long-running civil war, with revolts by Tigrayan, Oromo and Eritrean rebel groups against the Marxist Derg government under Mengistu Haile Mariam. Mengistu was overthrown in 1991 by an Ethiopian People's Revolutionary Democratic Front (EPRDF) force, a coalition of rebels, and Eritrea gained its formal independence in 1993. War erupted between Ethiopia and Eritrea in 1998–2000 over border disputes, with tensions ongoing despite United Nations (UN) intervention. Neighbouring Djibouti also faced civil war in 1991–94 between Afar and Issa forces.

Civil war in Somalia

Somalia has suffered a long-running civil war since the overthrow of Mohammed Siad Barre's dictatorial regime in 1991. The central state collapsed, with Somaliland and Puntland seceding. Rival clans and warlord militias fought for control of the capital Mogadishu, displacing millions, despite UN and American intervention. Localized conflict, law-

WE BELIEVE THE PROBLEM BETWEEN OURSELVES AND ERITREA CAN BE RESOLVED THROUGH DIALOGUE. AND SO EVERYTHING WE DO IS CALCULATED TO REINFORCE THIS MESSAGE; INCLUDING THE TROOP MOVEMENT. THE TROOP MOVEMENT IS DESIGNED TO SEND A MESSAGE TO OUR BROTHERS THAT THE OPTION OF VIOLENCE IS NOT AN ATTRACTIVE OPTION TO ANY SIDE.

**Meles Zenawi,
Ethiopian Prime Minister, 2008**

A RADICAL INSURGENCY WITH LINKS TO AL-QAEDA ARE PRESENTING A REAL THREAT TO THE STATE OF SOMALIA TODAY AND THEY ARE STARTING TO SPREAD REGIONALLY IN THE HORN OF AFRICA. SOMALIA HAS FOR DECADES HAD INTERNAL POWER STRUGGLES, AND THE MOST RECENT INSURGENCY ... IS GROWING IN A CLIMATE OF ECONOMIC POVERTY AND LACK OF GOVERNANCE.

**Omar Abdirashid Ali Sharmarke,
Prime Minister of Somalia, 2009**

2 Food security remains a major problem in the Horn of Africa with over 13 million people dependent upon food aid for survival in 2011 (**map below**). Drought, rising food prices and harsh environments combine with poverty, conflict, population displacement and weak political response to create a devastating humanitarian crisis.

3 Piracy in Somali Waters: The collapse of Somalia's government allowed foreign fishing vessels into Somali waters, initially spurring piracy to defend maritime resources (**map below left**). Piracy soon became increasingly criminal, bringing wealth to Somali's maritime communities. Since 2005, Somali pirates have attacked or hijacked hundreds of vessels, but attacks decreased after 2011, due to the presence of an international naval task force.

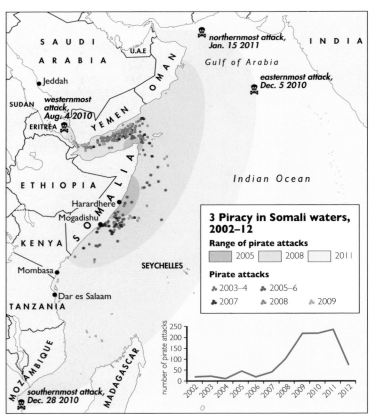

3 Piracy in Somali waters, 2002–12

Range of pirate attacks
2005　2008　2011

Pirate attacks
2003–4　2005–6
2007　2008　2009

northernmost attack, Jan. 15 2011

easternmost attack, Dec. 5 2010

westernmost attack, Aug. 4 2010

southernmost attack, Dec. 28 2010

2 Food security in the Horn of Africa, 2011

Famine/Humanitarian crisis

Emergency

Crisis

Moderately/borderline food secure

Generally food secure

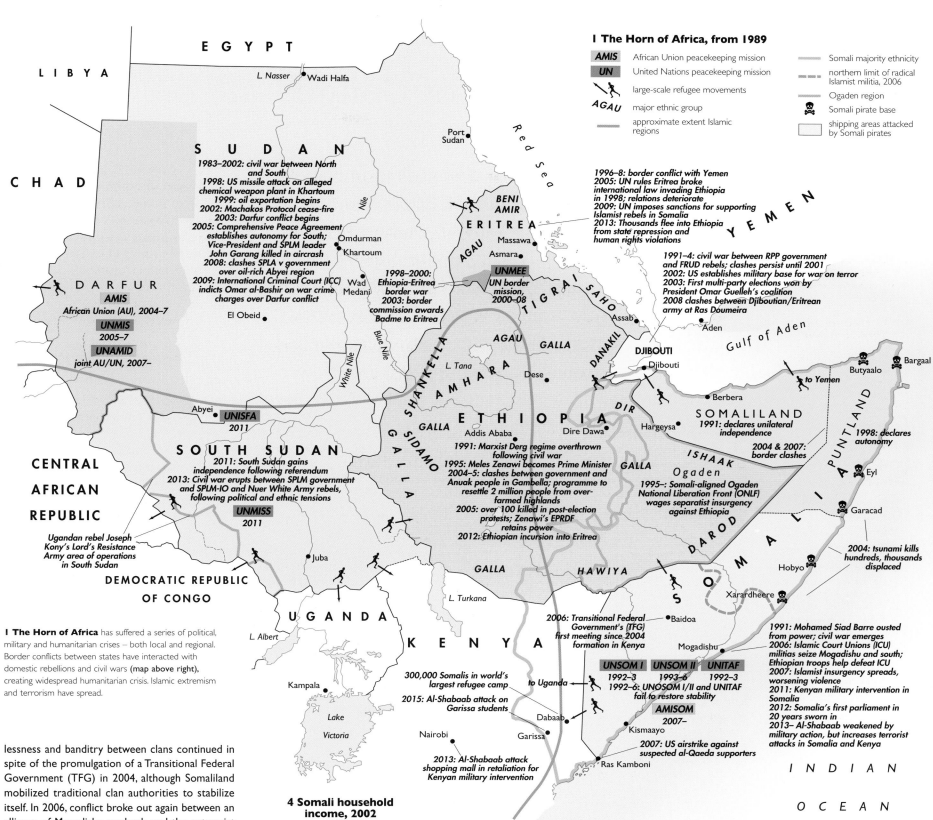

1 The Horn of Africa, from 1989

AMIS African Union peacekeeping mission
UN United Nations peacekeeping mission
large-scale refugee movements
AGAU major ethnic group
approximate extent Islamic regions
Somali majority ethnicity
northern limit of radical Islamist militia, 2006
Ogaden region
Somali pirate base
shipping areas attacked by Somali pirates

EGYPT

LIBYA

L. Nasser • Wadi Halfa

CHAD

Port Sudan

Red Sea

S U D A N

1983–2002: civil war between North and South
1998: US missile attack on alleged chemical weapon plant in Khartoum
1999: oil exportation begins
2002: Machakos Protocol cease-fire
2003: Darfur conflict begins
2005: Comprehensive Peace Agreement establishes autonomy for South; Vice-President and SPLM leader John Garang killed in aircrash
2008: clashes SPLA v government over oil-rich Abyei region
2009: International Criminal Court (ICC) indicts Omar al-Bashir on war crime charges over Darfur conflict

Omdurman •
Khartoum •
Wad Medani •
El Obeid •

Nile

D A R F U R
AMIS
African Union (AU), 2004–7
UNMIS
2005–7
UNAMID
joint AU/UN, 2007–

Blue Nile
White Nile

BENI AMIR
ERITREA
AGAU
Massawa •
Asmara •

SAHO
TIGRAI

1996–8: border conflict with Yemen
2005: UN rules Eritrea broke international law invading Ethiopia in 1998; relations deteriorate
2009: UN imposes sanctions for supporting Islamist rebels in Somalia
2013: Thousands flee into Ethiopia from state repression and human rights violations

YEMEN

UNMEE
UN border mission, 2000–08

1998–2000: Ethiopia-Eritrea border war
2003: border commission awards Badme to Eritrea

Assab •
Aden •

DANAKIL

AGAU
GALLA

DJIBOUTI
Djibouti •

Gulf of Aden

1991–4: civil war between RPP government and FRUD rebels; clashes persist until 2001
2002: US establishes military base for war on terror
2003: First multi-party elections won by President Omar Guelleh's coalition
2008 clashes between Djiboutian/Eritrean army at Ras Doumeira

CENTRAL AFRICAN REPUBLIC

Abyei •
UNISFA
2011

SHANKELLA
AMHARA
L. Tana •
Dese •

SIDAMO
GALLA

E T H I O P I A
Addis Ababa •
Dire Dawa •

1991: Marxist Derg regime overthrown following civil war
1995: Meles Zenawi becomes Prime Minister
2004–5: clashes between government and Anuak people in Gambella; programme to resettle 2 million people from over-farmed highlands
2005: over 100 killed in post-election protests; Zenawi's EPRDF retains power
2012: Ethiopian incursion into Eritrea

DIR
Berbera •
Hargeysa •

SOMALILAND
1991: declares unilateral independence
2004 & 2007: border clashes

ISHAAK

Ogaden
1995–: Somali-aligned Ogaden National Liberation Front (ONLF) wages separatist insurgency against Ethiopia

PUNTLAND
1998: declares autonomy

Butyaalo
Bargaal

Eyl

Garacad

DAROD

GALLA

2004: tsunami kills hundreds, thousands displaced

SOUTH SUDAN
2011: South Sudan gains independence following referendum
2013: Civil war erupts between SPLM government and SPLM-IO and Nuer White Army rebels, following political and ethnic tensions
UNMISS
2011

Ugandan rebel Joseph Kony's Lord's Resistance Army area of operations in South Sudan

Juba •

DEMOCRATIC REPUBLIC OF CONGO

UGANDA
L. Albert
Kampala •

Lake Victoria

L. Turkana

HAWIYA

Hobyo

Xarardheere

K E N Y A

Baidoa •

2006: Transitional Federal Government's (TFG) first meeting since 2004 formation in Kenya

Mogadishu •

UNSOM I **UNSOM II** **UNITAF**
1992–3 1993–6 1992–3
1992–6: UNOSOM I/II and UNITAF fail to restore stability

AMISOM
2007–

1991: Mohamed Siad Barre ousted from power; civil war emerges
2006: Islamic Court Unions (ICU) militias seize Mogadishu and south; Ethiopian troops help defeat ICU
2007: Islamist insurgency spreads, worsening violence
2011: Kenyan military intervention in Somalia
2012: Somalia's first parliament in 20 years sworn in
2013– Al-Shabaab weakened by military action, but increases terrorist attacks in Somalia and Kenya

300,000 Somalis in world's largest refugee camp
2015: Al-Shabaab attack on Garissa students

to Uganda

Dabaab •
Nairobi •
Garissa •
Kismaayo •

2007: US airstrike against suspected al-Qaeda supporters

2013: Al-Shabaab attack shopping mall in retaliation for Kenyan military intervention

Ras Kamboni •

INDIAN OCEAN

---

1 The Horn of Africa has suffered a series of political, military and humanitarian crises – both local and regional. Border conflicts between states have interacted with domestic rebellions and civil wars (map above right), creating widespread humanitarian crisis. Islamic extremism and terrorism have spread.

lessness and banditry between clans continued in spite of the promulgation of a Transitional Federal Government (TFG) in 2004, although Somaliland mobilized traditional clan authorities to stabilize itself. In 2006, conflict broke out again between an alliance of Mogadishu warlords and the extremist Islamic Courts Union (ICU) militia, which sought to institute shari'a law. Ethiopia intervened in support of the TFG to defeat the ICU, but Islamic extremist groups like al-Shabaab continue to threaten stability in the region. Links between increasing numbers of Islamic extremists and international terrorist networks, including al-Qaeda, have made the Horn a major front in the "war on terror". In 2005–11 in particular, lawlessness and economic collapse saw piracy proliferate in Somali waters, with a multinational naval task force established in 2008 to combat hijackings. Following Kenyan military intervention in 2011, al-Shabaab has increased terrorist attacks in Kenya, including attacks on a Nairobi mall in 2013 and on Garissa students in 2015.

Humanitarian Crisis

Conflict and political insecurity have combined with drought, poverty and harsh environmental conditions to create sustained humanitarian crisis in the region. Amidst war, famine in Somalia killed some 280,000 people and displaced two million more in 1991–3. In 2009, some two million Somalis and three to four million Sudanese were internally displaced or refugees as a result of fighting. A severe drought in 2011 intensified the crisis, with 13 million people in the Horn in need of emergency assistance for survival.

4 Somali household income, 2002

- 50% self employment
- 13.5% others (rent & aid)
- 22.5% remittances
- 14% wage employment

4 Decades of conflict in the Horn have weakened formal economies, and left many communities reliant on foreign aid or remittances from diasporic communities in the Middle East, North America, Europe and Eastern Africa (above).

Since 2003, conflict has raged in Darfur, Western Sudan, between the Khartoum government and rebel forces, with ethnic tensions and struggles over land also driving the violence. The conflict has resulted in some 300,000 deaths and over two million people displaced (right). Government-sponsored "Janjaweed" militias have been implicated in ethnic cleansing and human rights abuses. The international community is split over whether the mass killing constitutes a "genocide".

The Democratic Republic of Congo: conflict and crisis

One of the bloodiest, and most complex, conflicts in modern history has unfolded in the Democratic Republic of the Congo since the 1990s. Wars of armed conflict and atrocities against civilians have resulted in some five million casualties. Resistance against dictatorship, the collapse of the Congolese state, ethnic tensions, nationalism, warlord struggles to control territory and resources, international intervention and local power disputes all shaped Congo's wars. The conflicts have been characterized by the plundering of Congo's vast natural resources, and high civilian casualties.

THE WAR AGAINST THE DEVIL CONTINUES. BUT THERE IS STILL MUCH WORK TO BE DONE AND TO FINISH THE JOB WE MUST GET TO KINSHASA.

Laurent-Désiré Kabila, 1997

FROM THE TIME OF BELGIAN COLONIAL RULE, THE INHABITANTS OF THE REGION HAVE DERIVED LITTLE IF ANY BENEFIT FROM ITS NATURAL WEALTH. INSTEAD, THEY HAVE SUFFERED AN UNBROKEN SUCCESSION OF ABUSIVE POLITICAL ADMINISTRATIONS, MILITARY AUTHORITIES AND ARMED POLITICAL GROUPS THAT HAVE LOOTED THE REGION AND COMMITTED HUMAN RIGHTS ABUSES WITH IMPUNITY

Amnesty International, 2003

AFTER INDEPENDENCE and the Congo Crisis, Joseph Mobutu seized control of the Congo in a 1965 coup, and established one-party rule and an autocratic regime which lasted until 1997. Mobutu renamed the country Zaïre and embarked on a policy of "Zaïrianization" of society and the economy. Mobutu became known as the "king of the kleptocrats" due to his corrupt and patrimonial regime, amassing a fortune of some $5 billion. Resistance against his dictatorship grew in the 1980s, as the state collapsed and the economy declined, but Mobutu resisted international and domestic pressure to step down and allow democratization.

First Congo War, 1996–7
In 1994, genocide erupted in neighbouring Rwanda (see p. 320). Hundreds of thousands of Hutu refugees – including genocidaires (perpetrators of genocide) – fled to Zaïre in its aftermath, destabilizing the eastern regions. In 1996, Rwanda launched an invasion, partly in retaliation for Zaïre's sheltering of genocidaires. The invasion was presented as drive by a coalition of anti-Mobutu elements, the Alliance of Democratic Forces for the Liberation of the Congo

(AFDL) and the Banyamulenge, Kinyarwanda-speaking Tutsi herders living in Congo's South Kivu province. After seven months of fighting, Mobutu was overthrown and replaced by the coalition's leader, Laurent-Désiré Kabila, and the country renamed the Democratic Republic of the Congo.

Second Congo War, 1998–2002
Rwanda soon lost patience with Kabila's attempts to limit its influence on his government, and in August 1998 launched another invasion under cover of the opposition coalition Congolese Rally for Democracy (RCD). The attempt to overthrow Kabila was foiled by intervention from Angola, Zimbabwe and Namibia, but sparked the second Congolese war. This conflict became "Africa's First World War" as numerous surrounding states became involved and rebel factions splintered. Forces loyal to Kabila held southern regions, including most of Katanga and the capital Kinshasa. With oil from the coast, diamonds from the Kasais, and cobalt and other minerals from Katanga, this proved an adequate base for Kabila to control the south and pay off his African partners. By 2000, much of the north was held by the Uganda-

3 Annual growth rate, 1980–2011

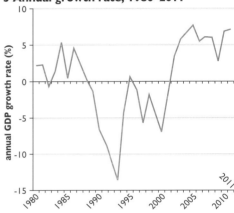

3–5 The DRC's economy has been stifled by decades of corruption and conflict, yet its mineral resources are a vast source of potential wealth (above and below). Competition to control resources including "blood diamonds", oil, gold and cobalt has driven much of the fighting. The diamond industry is worth an estimated $700 million per annum, but ordinary miners earn less than $1 per day working in dangerous conditions. Despite UN resolutions against illicit trading in conflict resources, western firms, African governments and rebel forces have all profited from exports.

Thomas Lubanga (right), leader of the Union of Congolese Patriots, was a key actor in the Ituri conflict (1999–2007). In 2006 he was arrested on war crimes charges and sent to face trial at the International Criminal Court in the Hague. After a 3-year trial, he became in 2012 the first person convicted by the ICC for the crime of recruiting child soldiers, and was sentenced to 14 years in prison.

4 Key development indicators
Source: UNDP and CIA Factbook

Human Development Index	0.338 (2014)
Population below poverty line	71% (2006)
Infant mortality rate	7.315% (2014)
GDP per capita (USD)	$400 (2013)

5 Composition of exports, 2004 (US dollars)

3% copper
1% coffee
14% cobalt
20% crude oil
16% other
46% diamonds

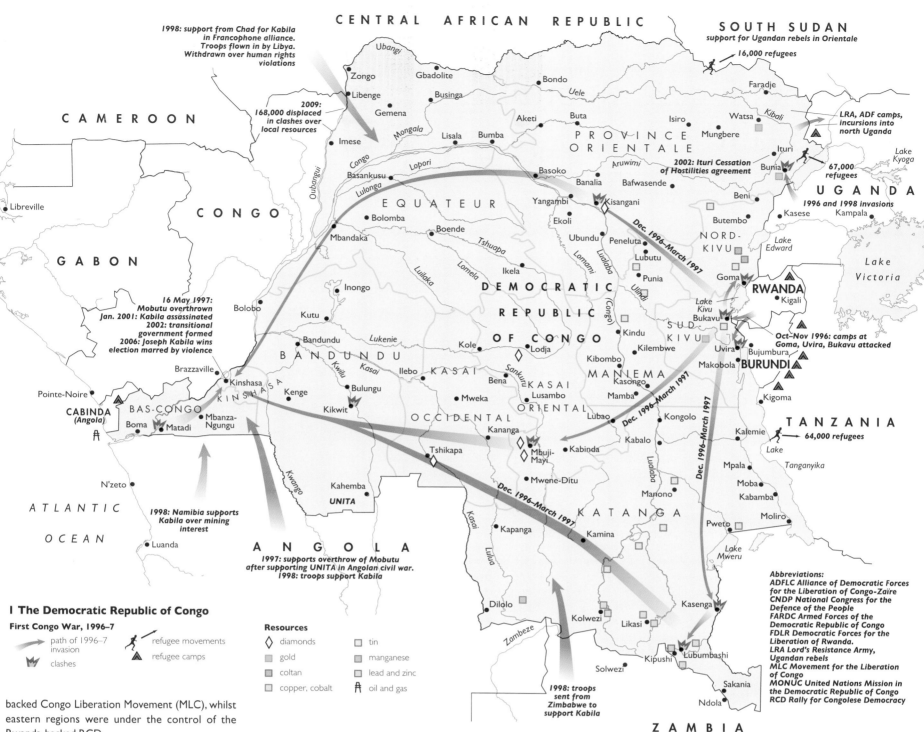

1998: support from Chad for Kabila in Francophone alliance. Troops flown in by Libya. Withdrawn over human rights violations

2009: 168,000 displaced in clashes over local resources

South Sudan
support for Ugandan rebels in Orientale

16,000 refugees

LRA, ADF camps, incursions into north Uganda

2002: Ituri Cessation of Hostilities agreement

67,000 refugees

1996 and 1998 invasions

16 May 1997: Mobutu overthrown Jan. 2001: Kabila assassinated 2002: transitional government formed 2006: Joseph Kabila wins election marred by violence

Oct–Nov 1996: camps at Goma, Uvira, Bukavu attacked

1998: Namibia supports Kabila over mining interest

1997: supports overthrow of Mobutu after supporting UNITA in Angolan civil war. 1998: troops support Kabila

64,000 refugees

1998: troops sent from Zimbabwe to support Kabila

Oct. 1998: peace talks fail at Lusaka

1 The Democratic Republic of Congo

First Congo War, 1996–7

- path of 1996–7 invasion
- clashes
- refugee movements
- refugee camps

Resources
- ◇ diamonds
- ☐ tin
- ☐ gold
- ☐ manganese
- ☐ coltan
- ☐ lead and zinc
- ☐ copper, cobalt
- ⚒ oil and gas

Abbreviations:
ADFLC Alliance of Democratic Forces for the Liberation of Congo-Zaire
CNDP National Congress for the Defence of the People
FARDC Armed Forces of the Democratic Republic of Congo
FDLR Democratic Forces for the Liberation of Rwanda.
LRA Lord's Resistance Army, Ugandan rebels
MLC Movement for the Liberation of Congo
MONUC United Nations Mission in the Democratic Republic of Congo
RCD Rally for Congolese Democracy

backed Congo Liberation Movement (MLC), whilst eastern regions were under the control of the Rwanda-backed RCD.

In 2001, Laurent Kabila was assassinated and replaced as president by his son, Joseph. A stalemate ensued and the war dragged on to 2003. Millions of Congolese died due to fighting, population displacement and the resultant humanitarian emergency. The transitional government faced continuous instability, and elections in 2006 – won by Joseph Kabila – were marred by violence.

Continuing conflict in Eastern Congo

Conflict has continued in eastern Congo, particularly in North and South Kivu, Ituri and Equateur. Mai-mai (local militia groups) have been heavily involved in the fighting, which continues despite the presence of the United Nations peacekeeping force (MONUSCO). Human rights violations, including ethnic cleansing, the employment of child soldiers and the use of rape as a weapon of war against women, have occurred on all sides. In 2012, rebel leader Thomas Lubanga became the first person convicted by the International Criminal Court, for the war crime of recruiting child soldiers in Ituri. Regional instability continues, despite 2013 peace agreements with M23 rebels in the Kivus, with clashes between Lendu and Hema groups in Ituri, and Ugandan rebel Joseph Kony's Lord's Resistance Army also operating in the northern DRC. Attempts to control the country's vast mineral and resource wealth have directly contributed to this continuing conflict. Despite UN resolutions against such illicit trade, Western firms, Rwanda, Uganda, Zimbabwe and Congolese forces have profited from the export of gold, cobalt, tin ore, diamonds and timber.

1 The Democratic Republic of Congo (DRC) covers over two million km², with some 66 million inhabitants (map above). There are five major languages – French, KiKongo, Lingala, Tshiluba and KiSwahili – and over two hundred different ethnic groups. Competing claims to land, resources and citizenship have fuelled the most devastating conflict since the Second World War. Regional destabilization worsened fighting, with conflict spilling over from Uganda, Rwanda, Burundi, the Republic of Congo and Angola.

2 Conflict continued in eastern Congo after 2003 (map right), particularly in Ituri, northern Katanga and the Kivus, where General Laurent Nkunda's CNDP rebel forces were the government's major opponents before Nkunda's arrest in 2009. Competition for land and resources, ethnic tensions and regional instability fuelled warfare.

1993: Masisi ethnic clashes kill 10,000

2004: massacre of Banyamulenge

2 Conflict in eastern Congo

- major clashes
- deployment of Mai-Mai forces
- deployment of RCD forces
- *FNL* foreign rebel groups

Human rights violations
perpetrator:
- ☠ Mai-Mai
- ☠ FDLR
- ☠ RCD
- ▲ Tutsi refugee camps

Palestine, Zionism and the origins of the Arab-Israeli conflict

The Arab-Israeli conflict has proved among the most bitter, protracted, violent and seemingly intractable of the last 60 years. Its historical origins are rooted in the early twentieth century when, in the context of world war and declining empire, both the Zionist movement and the Arab population were courted by the British government in an effort to secure an Allied victory and gain a foothold in the future Middle East. Palestine became a land twice-promised.

IN 1896, THE AUSTRIAN JOURNALIST Theodore Herzl published *Der Judenstaat* (The Jewish State). His book formalized a growing belief among world Jewry about the need for a Jewish state. The rise of Zionism was part of the general movement of ethnic and linguistic nationalism in the 19th century. In the case of the Jews, the idea was particularly audacious: they were widely dispersed, they did not speak the same language; in conventional terms they were not even a people. But at the first Zionist Congress in 1897 it was nonetheless agreed that a Jewish homeland should be created. It was subsequently agreed that this should be in Palestine, or biblical Israel, then within the Ottoman Empire.

Broken promises

In November 1914, the Ottoman Empire entered the First World War on the side of Germany. The war would be fought as much in the Middle East as in Europe, and the Ottomans found themselves pitted against Britain, France and Russia, all of whom had territorial aspirations in the region. The Ottoman Empire also faced rebellion from its Arab citizens. The ruler of Mecca, Sherif Hussein, saw the war as an opportunity to attain Arab self-rule from its imperial masters. Britain, at first, supported the creation of an independent Arab state in return for Hussein's galvanization of Arab rebels against their Ottoman rulers. However, while Britain and France were allied against the Germans and their Ottoman supporters, they also competed against each other for territorial control of as much land in the declining empire as possible. The Sykes-Picot Agreement of 1916 saw Britain, France and Russia agreeing to partition the Middle East between them, at the expense of the original territory Hussein to be part of his independent Arab state. In addition, to further political and strategic wartime aims, Britain also courted the Zionists, resulting in a web of double diplomacy and contradictory promises. The Balfour Declaration of 1917 implied a British goal of establishing in Palestine a national home for the Jewish people. Yet any attempt to fulfil this promise would undoubtedly prejudice the rights of the Palestinian Arabs currently residing in the territory.

Today the land where the British forces were active during the First World War lies in Egypt, Palestine/Israel, Jordan, Saudi Arabia, Iraq and Syria, at the time part of the Ottoman Empire. In 1917 an offensive was launched which took British troops, commanded by General Edmund Allenby, into the Holy Land and Syria. It ended in victory for the British, and on 11 December 1917 Allenby rode triumphantly into Jerusalem through the Jaffa Gate (**below**). With the Ottoman Empire destroyed, Russia paralyzed by military intervention and civil war, and French influence limited somewhat by their minor military role in the Middle East, Britain's military success made it the dominant power in the region.

I The ruler of Mecca, Sherif Hussein, saw the First World War as an opportunity to attain Arab self-rule. Corresponding with Sir Henry McMahon, British High Commissioner in Egypt, Hussein felt assured that, in return for an Arab revolt against their Ottoman rulers, Britain would support the creation of an independent Arab state stretching from the Indian Ocean in the southeast to what is today the northern border of Iraq, with the exception of the Syrian/Lebanese coast, the Holy Places in Palestine, and with special access for Britain to Baghdad and Basra. However, the Sykes-Picot Agreement of 1916 saw Britain, France and Russia agreeing to partition the Middle East between them, at the expense of the original territory Hussein believed to be part of his independent Arab state (**map right**).

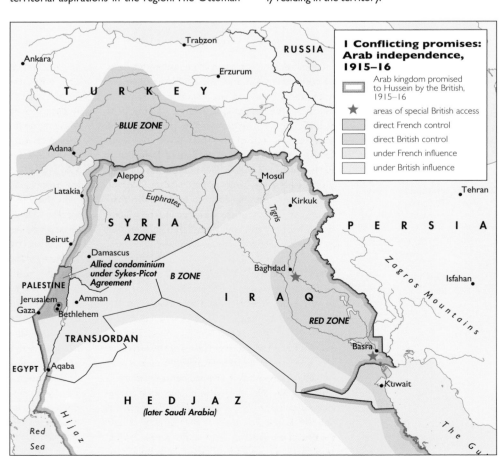

I Conflicting promises: Arab independence, 1915–16

- Arab kingdom promised to Hussein by the British, 1915–16
- ★ areas of special British access
- direct French control
- direct British control
- under French influence
- under British influence

2 Palestinian Arab and Jewish population in Palestine, 1878–1946

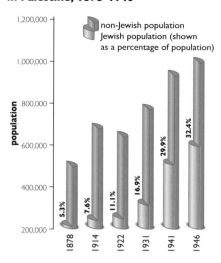

non-Jewish population

Jewish population (shown as a percentage of population)

population

1,200,000
1,000,000
800,000
600,000
400,000
200,000

1878	1914	1922	1931	1941	1946
5.3%	7.6%	11.1%	16.9%	29.9%	32.4%

Jewish immigration into Palestine grew over the first decades of the 20th century, especially during the 1930s **(left)**. The Arab population also grew during this period as a result of high birth-rates and economic migration from Syria and Transjordan. As the Jewish population in Palestine increased, the Palestinian Arabs put pressure on the British authorities to control immigration and land purchase. However, both sides felt let down by the British response which led to rising tensions and sporadic violence. In 1947 the UN proposed to partition Palestine into two separate states: the land allocated to the Arab state consisted of about 43 per cent of Mandatory Palestine; the Jewish state was to receive 56 per cent to accommodate the increasing numbers of Jews who would migrate there.

3 In the San Remo Conference of April 1920, Great Britain was assigned the mandate for Palestine (map 3a). It included the territory that the Zionists hoped would create a Jewish homeland. The first partition of Palestine took place in 1922 when the area of Transjordan was assigned a separate administration. It was within the remaining territory that the competing triangle of interests was to be played out, often violently. As a result of the 1936–9 "Great Arab Rebellion" the British recommended partition in the form of the Peel Commission Report **(map 3b)**. However, increasing inter-communal tensions and the impact of the Second World War resulted in Britain handing over the Mandate to the fledgling United Nations who re-stated partition in the form of separate Jewish and Palestinian Arab states. **(map 3c)**. Rejected by the Palestinian Arabs, Palestine descended into war.

3a Palestine, 1920–2

British mandate granted at San Remo Conference, 1920

approximate area of Jewish National Home

subsequent British mandate of Palestine, 1921

subsequent British mandate of Transjordan, 1921–2

Mediterranean Sea

Damascus

S Y R I A (French mandate)

Haifa

Golan Heights ceded to French mandate of Syria, 1923

I R A Q

PALESTINE

Tel Aviv
Jaffa

Jerusalem

Amman

Gaza

Bethlehem

Beersheba

Dead Sea

Karak

Negev

TRANSJORDAN

British mandate of Transjordan given to Emir Abdullah

E G Y P T

Sinai

Ma'an

Aqaba

SAUDI ARABIA

4 The war of 1948

Jewish State as proposed by the United Nations, Nov. 1947

principal Arab attacks, May 1948

Jewish territory overrun by Arab attacks

territory conquered by Israel, 1948–9

Israel according to armistice agreements, 1949

destroyed Palestinian villages

officially registered refugee movement by 1951

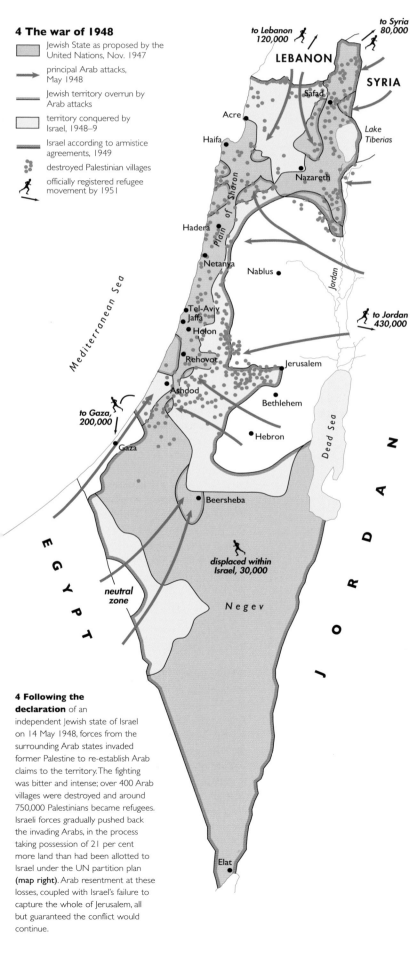

to Lebanon 120,000

to Syria 80,000

LEBANON

Safad

SYRIA

Acre

Haifa

Lake Tiberias

Nazareth

Plain of Sharon

Hadera

Netanya

Nablus

Jordan

to Jordan 430,000

Tel-Aviv
Jaffa
Holon

Rehovot

Jerusalem

Ashdod

Bethlehem

to Gaza, 200,000

Hebron

Gaza

Dead Sea

Beersheba

displaced within Israel, 30,000

neutral zone

Negev

E G Y P T

J O R D A N

Mediterranean Sea

Elat

4 Following the declaration of an independent Jewish state of Israel on 14 May 1948, forces from the surrounding Arab states invaded former Palestine to re-establish Arab claims to the territory. The fighting was bitter and intense; over 400 Arab villages were destroyed and around 750,000 Palestinians became refugees. Israeli forces gradually pushed back the invading Arabs, in the process taking possession of 21 per cent more land than had been allotted to Israel under the UN partition plan **(map right)**. Arab resentment at these losses, coupled with Israel's failure to capture the whole of Jerusalem, all but guaranteed the conflict would continue.

SYRIA

Haifa

Lake Tiberias

Nazareth

Jenin

Nablus

Tel-Aviv
Jaffa

Ramallah

Jerusalem

Jericho

Ashdod

Bethlehem

Gaza

Hebron

Dead Sea

Beersheba

JORDAN

Negev

E G Y P T

3b The Peel Commission Partition Plan, 1937

proposed Jewish state

proposed Arab state

to remain under British mandate

Elat

SYRIA

Haifa

Lake Tiberias

Nazareth

Jenin

Nablus

Tel-Aviv
Jaffa

Ramallah

Jerusalem

Jericho

Ashdod

Bethlehem

Gaza

Hebron

Dead Sea

Beersheba

JORDAN

Negev

E G Y P T

3c The UN Partition Plan, 1947

proposed Jewish state

proposed Arab state

proposed international zone of Jerusalem

Elat

It was within this triangle of competing interests – Palestinian Arab, Zionist and British – that Britain attempted to manage the Mandate of Palestine awarded at the San Remo Conference in April 1920. In 1922 the first partition of Palestine took place when the area east of the Jordan River was identified as a separate administration of Transjordan. Furthermore, the Balfour Declaration was formally integrated into the terms of the Mandate. Palestine was therefore the only mandate set up in the post-war period not to prepare the indigenous population for self-determination but instead to reconstitute an entirely new community – a Jewish state.

Termination of the Mandate

British policy during the Mandate tended to vacillate according to which groups demanded most. The early 1930s were characterized by a rapid increase in Jewish immigration and land purchases. The rise to power of Adolf Hitler in Germany and increased anti-Semitism in Poland, Hungary and Romania led to a massive influx of immigrants from these countries. By 1936 the Jewish population made up approximately thirty per cent of the total population of Palestine. Palestinian Arab frustration at both the British and Zionists eventually exploded in what would later be called the "Great Arab Rebellion"

which lasted for three years. In 1937, with the situation in Palestine still volatile, Britain sent a Royal Commission to investigate. The Peel Commission Report recommended the partition of Palestine. Accepted by the Zionists, it was rejected outright by the Palestinian Arabs. However, tensions in Palestine were soon overshadowed by the Second World War where, in the Holocaust, Jews faced the ultimate expression of anti-Semitism.

In the aftermath of the Second World War a weakened Britain struggled to retain control of an increasingly anarchical Palestine. Reviled by both sides, Britain turned the problem over to the United Nations. In November 1947, it divided Palestine into separate Jewish and Arab states. Sporadic but fierce violence erupted between Jews and Palestinian Arabs, and tensions ran high. The following May, Britain withdrew and the State of Israel was proclaimed. It was immediately invaded by Arab armies. After fierce fighting, a cease-fire was agreed in early 1949. It left an uneasy truce. Israel had beaten off the Arab forces, but had failed to take East Jerusalem. Equally important, over 400 Arab villages had been destroyed and up to 750,000 Palestinians had become refugees, crowded into the Gaza Strip and the West Bank. The name "Palestine" had been wiped off the map.

The Arab-Israeli conflict

The Arab-Israeli conflict has been the defining issue in the Middle East since 1948. It has impacted upon every Arab country and remains a central feature of global politics. After decades of violent conflict, a glimmer of resolution emerged in the early 1990s when the Israeli government and the Palestine Liberation Organization (PLO) agreed the Oslo Accords. However, the road to peace has since been stalled amid an atmosphere of injustice, distrust and recrimination. Sporadic violence in Lebanon, Israel and Gaza have demonstrated the distance that remains from a lasting resolution of this conflict.

I In the first Arab-Israeli war of 1948, Israel succeeded in significantly expanding the borders of the nascent Israeli state (**map right**). This was the first of three major wars between Israel and various Arab forces over the next 25 years. These subsequent wars saw Israel annex the West Bank, Gaza Strip, Golan Heights and the Sinai Peninsula. More recently, Israel has responded to perceived threats to their borders with Lebanon and Gaza by devastating land and air invasions commenced in July 2006 (Lebanon) and December 2008 (Gaza). Since then, Israeli airstrikes against Gaza and cross-border violence have reoccurred, most recently in the summer of 2014.

FOR ISRAEL THE WAR OF 1948 became known as the War of Independence, for the Arabs "al-Nakba" or "the catastrophe". The armistice of 1949 reflected the status quo positions of each belligerent and, as such, Israel was awarded significantly more territory than it had been designated in the UN partition plan of 1947. An independent Palestine was not created. Instead the West Bank was under the control of Jordan, and Egypt occupied the Gaza Strip. Israel and Jordan assumed joint control of Jerusalem. Relations between Israel and its neighbours following the war remained volatile.

Wars after 1948

The hostility that followed became a prime cause of instability within the Middle East as well as a major focus of Cold War rivalry. To Egypt, Syria and Iraq – buttressed by the Soviet Union – Israel represented

FOR MORE THAN 60 YEARS [THE PALESTINIANS] HAVE ENDURED THE PAIN OF DISLOCATION. MANY WAIT IN REFUGEE CAMPS IN THE WEST BANK, GAZA, AND NEIGHBOURING LANDS FOR A LIFE OF PEACE AND SECURITY THAT THEY HAVE NEVER BEEN ABLE TO LEAD. THEY ENDURE THE DAILY HUMILIATIONS – LARGE AND SMALL – THAT COME WITH OCCUPATION ... FOR DECADES, THERE HAS BEEN A STALEMATE: TWO PEOPLES WITH LEGITIMATE ASPIRATIONS, EACH WITH A PAINFUL HISTORY THAT MAKES COMPROMISE ELUSIVE. IT IS EASY TO POINT FINGERS – FOR PALESTINIANS TO POINT TO THE DISPLACEMENT BROUGHT BY ISRAEL'S FOUNDING AND FOR ISRAELIS TO POINT TO THE CONSTANT HOSTILITY AND ATTACKS THROUGHOUT ITS HISTORY FROM WITHIN ITS BORDERS AS WELL AS BEYOND. BUT IF WE SEE THIS CONFLICT ONLY FROM ONE SIDE OR THE OTHER, THEN WE WILL BE BLIND TO THE TRUTH: THE ONLY RESOLUTION IS FOR THE ASPIRATIONS OF BOTH SIDES TO BE MET THROUGH TWO STATES, WHERE ISRAELIS AND PALESTINIANS EACH LIVE IN PEACE AND SECURITY.

US President Barack Obama's keynote speech on US-Muslim relations at Cairo University, 4 June 2009

not only an affront to Arab nationalism but, with its support from the USA, an extension of American imperialism in the region. Three further full-scale Arab-Israeli wars broke out after 1949: in 1956, over Suez, when Israel inflicted a humiliating defeat on Egypt; in 1967, when in the face of renewed Arab hostility Israel achieved a crushing pre-emptive strike against Egypt and then routed Jordanian, Syrian and Iraqi forces; and in 1973, when a combined Egyptian-Syrian attack was repulsed by Israel after days of desperate fighting. In all three cases, not only did Israel extend its territorial domination, occupying the West Bank, Gaza Strip, Sinai and the Golan Heights, but huge numbers of new Palestinian refugees were created in Jordan and Lebanon, increasing the Palestinian sense of injustice and giving rise to militant Arab movements dedicated to winning back the lost territories. The misery and humiliation of life in the refugee camps yielded a disgruntled mass receptive to revolutionary rhetoric. In 1967, the PLO assumed leadership of the struggle, using the refugee camps as a base for cross-border raids into Israel.

The search for peace

While defeat in 1973 had hardened the resolve of some Arab states to continue the war against Israel, Egypt, under President Sadat, sought to make peace. In 1978 the two sides agreed terms at Camp David in the USA, provoking outrage in the Arab world. The PLO, meanwhile, stepped up its attacks on Israel from new bases in Lebanon, sparking an Israeli invasion of southern Lebanon in 1982. Although the Israeli army withdrew from Beirut it continued to occupy a "security zone" in southern Lebanon until May 2000. This, in turn, galvanized internal Lebanese resistance – Hezbollah. Life in the Occupied Territories had continued to decline, and by the late 1980s the failure of any international movement to secure peace and the increasingly oppressive nature of the occupation combined to create a powder keg of Palestinian frustration which exploded in the form of the first

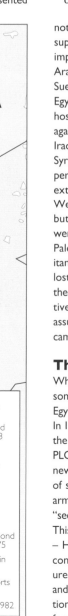

Mediterranean Sea

Israeli invasion of Lebanon, 12 July–14 Aug. 2006

Israeli military operations in Gaza: Operation Cast Lead, 27 Dec. 2008–18 Jan. 2009 (invasion); Operation Returning Echo, 9–14 Mar. 2012 (air strikes); Operation Pillar of Defense, 14–21 Nov. 2012 (air strikes); Operation Protective Edge, 8 July–26 Aug. 2014 (invasion)

Rafah salient: 11 Israeli settlements established by 1978, with Jewish population of 2,000

Sinai Peninsula returned to Egypt 1982

I Arab-Israeli conflicts, 1948–2014

- Israel after Arab invasion and War of Independence, 1948
- Israeli conquests, 1967
- Land that would have been annexed
- Egyptian re-conquests, and Israeli conquests, 1973

Sinai, the Israeli withdrawal:

- Egyptian frontline under second Sinai agreement, 1 Sept 1975
- Israeli settlements given up in 1982
- Israeli military and civil airports given up in 1982
- Israeli oil wells given up in 1982

Intifada – "uprising" – in 1987. Early successes led directly to the declaration of a State of Palestine by the PLO leader Yasser Arafat in November 1988. In the Declaration he publicly endorsed the two-state solution, recognizing Israel's right to exist as a state.

The Gulf War in 1991 was also a defining moment in the Arab-Israeli conflict, undermining the position of both Israel and the PLO. In 1993 Israel and the PLO agreed a Declaration of Principles on interim self-government for the West Bank and Gaza Strip (the Oslo Accords). The following year, the Palestinian National Authority (PA) assumed responsibility for both areas with an understanding that further Israeli withdrawals and an extension of Palestinian self-rule would follow. In 1994 Jordan also agreed peace with Israel, while the following year Syria agreed to open talks with Israel.

However, in the years since Oslo little progress has been made. The Accords were never fully implemented despite a series of later agreements all designed to move the process forward. Fifty years after the partition of Palestine, the Palestinians had autonomous control of less than four per cent of historic Palestine. This disappointment, along with increasingly harsh conditions in the Occupied Territories, led to the rise in popularity of the Islamic resistance movement, Hamas, which began a series of attacks against Israeli targets. Since 2001, under prime ministers Ariel Sharon, Ehud Olmert and Benjamin Netanyahu, the Israeli government has taken a more aggressive approach towards the Palestinians and other Arab adversaries. In 2006, Israeli forces attacked Hezbollah bases in Lebanon causing widespread damage and loss of life. Despite an Israeli withdrawal from the Gaza Strip in 2005, its Palestinian inhabitants have been subjected to a virtual blockade since Hamas seized control in June 2007. In an effort to destroy Hamas, responsible for rocket attacks against Israel, a devastating three-week conflict was launched against Gaza in 2008. Since then, repeated offensives have taken place; the most

recent, in 2014, resulted in the death of over 2,200 Palestinians (of whom almost 1,500 were civilians) and 71 Israelis (including 66 soldiers). In the occupied West Bank, settlements continued to be built and the 'fence/wall' has constituted the biggest change in landscape, in Israel's favour, since 1967. In November 2012, in response to UN approval of the Palestinian bid for the status of non-member observer state, the Israeli government announced that it had approved the building of 3,000 settler homes in the West Bank. Despite US President Barack Obama's apparent early-term commitment to trying a new approach to peacemaking, US influence has waned in recent years. The Arab Spring that began in 2011, the crises in Iraq and Syria, the rise of the Islamic State, and the return of hardline Likud leader, Benjamin Netanyahu, as Israel's prime minister, have all restricted US efforts to move forward on Israeli-Palestinian peace talks. The conflict shows no signs of ending.

2 The Gaza Strip is a narrow strip of arid coastal plain that is the most densely populated piece of land on the planet, home to around 1.7 million people, the majority of whom are Palestinian refugees (map right). Occupied by Israel since the third Arab-Israeli war of 1967 (Six-Day War), governance was transferred to the PA in 1994. In June 2007 a brief civil war between Hamas and Fatah culminated in a decisive victory for Hamas, with whom Israel refuses to negotiate. As a result, Gaza has been under blockade in an attempt to weaken Hamas, and in December 2008 Israel launched a full-scale invasion in an attempt to remove them. Israel retains control of most access to the Gaza Strip. The 2014 Israeli invasion caused unparalleled devastation and has further exacerbated the humanitarian crisis. In the context of the on-going blockade, it presents an almost impossibly challenging environment for Palestinians in Gaza.

3 In 1993 the Israeli government and the PLO agreed at Oslo to limited Palestinian self-rule and a phased Israeli withdrawal from Gaza and the West Bank (map below). While Israel did withdraw from Gaza in 2005, in 2003 the government of Sharon began to construct a "fence/wall" to separate Jewish and Arab settlements on the West Bank. Its proposed length is twice that of the 1949 Armistice Line, and 87 per cent is in the West Bank. The population of Jewish settlers in the West Bank has been growing at a rate of 5–6 per cent since 2001. The continued expansion of existing settlements and the construction of new ones in the West Bank remains a constant bone of contention between the two sides.

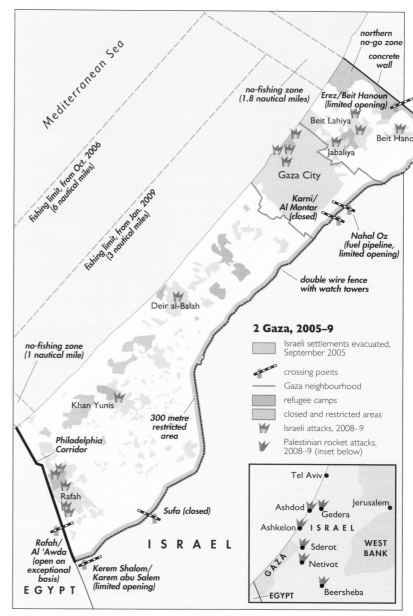

2 Gaza, 2005–9

- Israeli settlements evacuated, September 2005
- crossing points
- Gaza neighbourhood
- refugee camps
- closed and restricted areas
- Israeli attacks, 2008–9
- Palestinian rocket attacks, 2008–9 (inset below)

On 22 September 2009, 16 years after the signing of the Oslo Accords, President Barack Obama watched Israeli prime minister Benjamin Netanyahu (**left**) and Palestinian President Mahmoud Abbas (**right**) shake hands during a trilateral meeting at the Waldorf Astoria Hotel, New York (**above**). The meeting was an attempt to restart the peace process, floundering since the mid-1990s. Despite some progress regarding Palestinian self-rule and the evacuation of Gaza by Israeli settlers, the political will on both sides to arrive at a lasting and just settlement has generally been conspicuous by its absence.

4 There are a number of Middle Eastern states that are suspected of possessing chemical and biological weapons programmes, and a larger number that possess ballistic missile capabilities. The two major problems in the Middle East with respect to WMD are Israel's unacknowledged possession of nuclear weapons, which provides a powerful incentive for other states in the region to arm themselves, and the evolving Iranian nuclear programme which Israel uses to justify its own self-defence.

4 Nuclear power in the Middle East

Country	WMDs	Signatory to the 1968 Nuclear Non-Proliferation Treaty (NPT)?
Egypt	Missiles; Chemical and Biological programmes.	Yes..
Iran	Missiles; Chemical and Biological programmes.	Yes. Subject to NPT safeguard agreements.
Israel	Missiles; Chemical and Biological programmes. (Widely assumed to possess 75–200 nuclear warheads but has never confirmed it publicly.)	No.
Syria	Missiles; Chemical and Biological programmes.	Yes.

3 The failing Israeli-Palestinian peace process, 1993–2008

- – – – 1967 borders of Israel
- under full Palestinian control from May 1994
- under full Palestinian control from 1995–7
- under Palestinian administrative control from 1995
- Jewish settlements in occupied territories
- patrolled by the Israeli military
- patrolled by joint Israeli-Palestinian forces
- Israeli police posts
- co-ordination offices
- East Jerusalem
- Completed sections of fence/wall, Dec. 2007
- Completed/planned sections of fence/wall Dec. 2007
- Palestinian villages behind fence/wall
- settlements established prior to March 2001
- settlements established after March 2001

Nationalism, Islam and reform in the Middle East

Since the end of the Second World War, Arab countries of the Middle East have journeyed from colonial subjects towards their 21st-century incarnations: largely authoritarian states that are opening up to political reform and opposition. This passage has not been easy and has consisted of nationalist revolts, independence struggles, Islamic revival, military interventions, coups and repression, exacerbated by global and regional conflicts and fuelled by oil riches and extremes of wealth and poverty.

IN THE IMMEDIATE POST-WAR period, war weariness, financial pressure and local opposition led Britain and France to abandon their colonial possessions in the Middle East, as elsewhere in the world. Despite efforts to keep a European military presence in an area of vital strategic importance to the West, by 1956 the Arab world was largely independent of European power.

But while the Europeans retreated, the USA and the Soviet Union advanced, both anxious to increase their influence in the region and to secure access to the region's oil resources. In the process, the Middle East rapidly became a key theatre of the Cold War. Fearing Soviet expansion, the USA underpinned Israel, Saudi Arabia and, until 1979, Iran, all of which became the principal surrogates of American interests. For its part, the Soviet Union, keen to protect its southern borders, supported Egypt, Iran and Syria, portraying itself as the champion of anti-imperialism, the Palestinian cause, revolutionary socialism and Arab nationalism.

Nationalism

It was nationalism that formed the keynote of Arab political goals in the period, with President Nasser of Egypt its principal standard bearer. Having led a military coup against the British-sponsored Egyptian monarchy in 1952, within two years he had become president of Egypt and the most charismatic Arab leader of the period. Whilst Nasser's vision of Arab unity was only achieved for short periods, and even then it was never very effective, the sentiment behind pan-Arab nationalism remained significant.

With the active support of the Soviet Union, Nasser's influence was crucial to the development, not just of Egypt, but of Iraq, Sudan, Syria, South Yemen, Algeria and Libya, all of which owed much to eastern European economic and political models. In every case, the ruling regime was backed by the military while their economies were dominated by the state and all of them introduced ambitious land reforms and nationalized most of industry, banking and foreign trade, with varying degrees of success. In common with most other Arab states, they all also maintained huge armies, supposedly to counter the threat posed by Israel, in reality to maintain the ruling regimes in power.

Rivalries and war

Regional tensions also led to a series of Middle Eastern wars, manipulated and exacerbated by superpower rivalry and self-interest. In Lebanon, divisions between Christian and Muslims, between Lebanese and Palestinians, and between Sunni and Shi'a Muslims created a microcosm of the tensions in the wider Arab world. In 1975 full-scale civil war broke out in which both Israel and Syria became deeply involved. In 1980 Iraq's president Saddam Hussein launched a pre-emptive assault on Iran, then in the throes of revolutionary turmoil. The conflict turned into a lethal eight-year campaign of attrition costing an estimated 450,000 dead and 750,000 wounded. Undaunted, in 1990 Hussein survived Iraq's defeat in 1991 at the hands of a US-led United Nations coalition force. In the ensuing decade, the country endured international isolation and further chaos following the next US-UK coalition invasion and overthrow of Hussein's regime in 2003.

Perhaps the only group to benefit from the 2003 war and subsequent occupation were the Kurds. United by geography and a common history, the formation of a state of Kurdistan was another promise made and quickly lost in the aftermath of the First World War. Spread across Turkey, Iran, Iraq and Syria, Kurdish nationalists have been subjugated by the nation-states they have found themselves within. They have also been held back by internal divisions and rivalry, and denied direct assistance at crucial moments from the international community. Kurdish uprisings occurred in Iraq since the 1920s, and

Popular protest played a key role in the fall of the Shah of Iran in 1979 and the assumption of power by Ayatollah Khomeini (1900–89) in February that year. More recently, the country is showing signs of entering another era of political and social transformation, again with popular protest at its heart **(above)**. President Mahmoud Ahmadinejad's controversial re-election in June 2009 has further widened the rift between conservatives and reformists, resulting in tens of thousands of Iranians taking to the streets in protest.

2 The Lebanese crisis

	Sunni majority
	Christian majority
	Shi'a majority
——	frontiers
– – –	Israeli security zones
———	limit of Syrian occupation, 1976
▲	Palestinian refugee camp

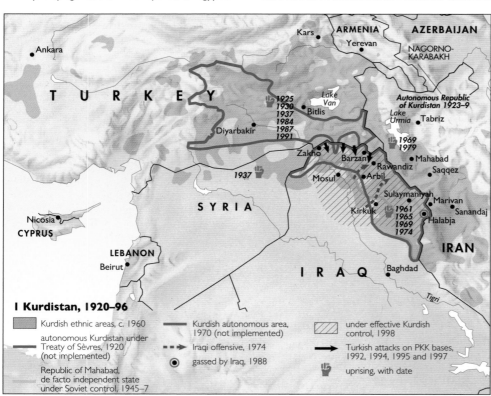

1 Kurdistan, 1920–96

	Kurdish ethnic areas, c. 1960
	autonomous Kurdistan under Treaty of Sèvres, 1920 (not implemented)
	Republic of Mahabad, de facto independent state under Soviet control, 1945–7
——	Kurdish autonomous area, 1970 (not implemented)
– –▷	Iraqi offensive, 1974
⊙	gassed by Iraq, 1988
▨	under effective Kurdish control, 1998
➤	Turkish attacks on PKK bases, 1992, 1994, 1995 and 1997
✊	uprising, with date

1 The Kurds, now divided between Turkey, Iran, Iraq and Syria, were promised an independent homeland under the post-First World War settlement. Like the Palestinians, they too were disappointed. Largely confining their struggle to demands for autonomy within national frontiers **(map left)**, the Kurds of Turkey fought against their government in the 1920s and 1930s, and have renewed their activities since the early 1970s. The Kurds of Iraq have waged an almost equally bitter struggle for most of the 20th century. After the 1991 war, an autonomous Kurdish region was created in northern Iraq.

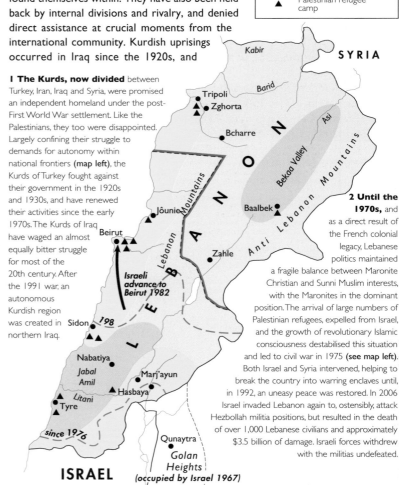

2 Until the 1970s, and as a direct result of the French colonial legacy, Lebanese politics maintained a fragile balance between Maronite Christian and Sunni Muslim interests, with the Maronites in the dominant position. The arrival of large numbers of Palestinian refugees, expelled from Israel, and the growth of revolutionary Islamic consciousness destabilised this situation and led to civil war in 1975 **(see map left)**. Both Israel and Syria intervened, helping to break the country into warring enclaves until, in 1992, an uneasy peace was restored. In 2006 Israel invaded Lebanon again to, ostensibly, attack Hezbollah militia positions, but resulted in the death of over 1,000 Lebanese civilians and approximately \$3.5 billion of damage. Israeli forces withdrew with the militias undefeated.

at the end of the 1991 Gulf War the Allies established a safe haven in northern Iraq. Iraqi Kurdistan emerged as an autonomous entity inside Iraq, with its own local government and parliament in 1992.

Islam and political reform

If the politics of the Arab world in the 1950s and 1960s were dominated by Cold War tension between conservative and radical Arab states, in the 1970s they gave way to a new development: the rise of revolutionary Islam. The Islamic movement dated back to the foundation of the Muslim Brotherhood in 1928 but was given new life partly by the military failures against Israel in 1967 and 1973, resentment towards western manipulation of Arab politics, and by a general sense of hopelessness and despair which pervaded the region. In such an atmosphere, militant Islamic activity seemed to give new hope, however illusory, for the future.

In 1978–9, an alliance of Islamic radicals overthrew the US-backed regime of the Shah in Iran and an Islamic republic was installed under the guidance of Ayatollah Khomeini. Islamic radicalism took root in other parts of the Muslim world, leading to a savage civil war in Algeria and Sudan and widespread Islamic terrorism in the rest of North Africa and the Middle East. With the collapse of Saddam Hussein's regime in Iraq a new crisis appeared. The profound division between Sunni and Shi'ite Muslims was exposed and a vicious religious civil war erupted from 2003 onwards which threatened to spread beyond the borders of Iraq. However, in Iran, the stability of the Islamic regime was tested in the immediate aftermath of President Mahmoud Ahmadinejad's controversial re-election in June 2009. Tens of thousands took to the streets of Tehran to protest. While conservatives continue to retain power, significant signs of political and social transformation have emerged. Furthermore, it is distracting to simply label conflict in the Middle East a result of irreconcilable religious and ethnic differences. Other factors, notably continued Western influence and denial of self-determination, oil, displaced peoples, and inadequate access to the region's precious water supplies, remained serious challenges for policymakers in the region.

4 Population, GNP and oil reserves, 2008

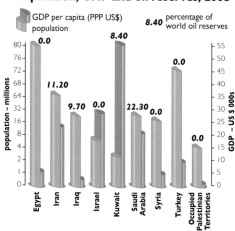

4 The tensions caused by Western interference and political repression have been reinforced by differences in wealth between states (above). Iran, Iraq, Kuwait, Saudi Arabia and the UAE possess over 50 per cent of the world's oil reserves. Though they have become enormously rich, their dependence on oil has left them vulnerable to stagnation or even decline in world oil prices. In countries with little or no oil reserves, average per capita incomes are no higher than $800. Subsistence agriculture remains the occupation of most of the region's working populations.

3 Between the 1930s and the 1960s, the states of the Middle East freed themselves from British and French colonial rule and established themselves as independent nations. The region has been plagued by instability, partly because of the Arab-Israeli conflict, partly because of its role in the power struggle of the Cold War and its aftermath, and more recently because of the upheavals caused by the rise of revolutionary Islam (map below). In addition, it contains some 65 per cent of the world's oil reserves.

3 The Middle East, 1945–2007

→ invasion

✳ major conflicts

✊ guerrilla activity

1955: Anti-Soviet Baghdad Pact
1958: Hashemite dynasty overthrown in military coup; power seized by General Abdel-karim Kassem
1963: Kassem overthrown in military coup
1968: Ba'th Party seizes power
1972–5: Intermittent fighting between Kurds and government
1974–5: Iraq-Iran War; Iran withdraws support from Kurds; Kurdish rebellion collapses
1979: Saddam Hussein becomes president
1980–8: Iraq-Iran War
1990: Invasion of Kuwait by Iraq
1991: UN coalition expels Iraqi army from Kuwait;
1991–8: Western sanctions remain in place. UN weapons inspectors seek to locate and neutralize Iraqi weapons of mass destruction
1998: UN weapons inspectors withdraw. Operation "Desert Fox": large-scale airstrikes against Iraq
2002: UN weapons inspectors return to Iraq
2003: US-led forces invade and overthrow Saddam Hussein
2003–4: continuing insurgency against US coalition forces
2005: limited sovereignty restored
2006: escalating religious civil war
2006: Saddam Hussein executed

1946: Withdrawal of French troops
1958–61: Union with Egypt (United Arab Republic)
1963: Ba'th Party seizes power
1967: Six Day War; Syria loses Golan Heights
1970: General Hafiz al-Assad seizes power
1973: October (Yom Kippur) War; Syria and Egypt attack Israel; Syrian forces expelled from Golan Heights and Israeli forces occupy Syrian territory
1976: Syrian forces intervene in Lebanese civil war
1980: Treaty of Friendship and Co-operation with USSR
1991: Peace made with Lebanon
2000: Death of President Hafiz al-Asad, succeeded by his son Bashir al-Asad

1963–74: Intermittent intercommunal clashes
1974: Turkish invasion and occupation of northern part of island
2004: joins EU

1969: Increase in Palestinian guerrilla activity
1975: Lebanese civil war breaks out
1976: Syrian invasion
1978: Israeli invasion
1982: Attack on Beirut by Israel
1985: Formal withdrawal of Israeli troops
1992: Christians boycott first elections for 20 years
2002: Israeli forces withdraw from buffer zone in South Lebanon
2006: Hizbollah bases bombed

1941: Abdication of Shah Reza Pahlavi following Anglo-Russian occupation of Iran; his son Mohammed Reza Pahlavi becomes Shah
1951: Nationalization of oil industry; deterioration in relations with UK
1953–4: Prime Minister Mossadeq becomes de facto ruler; the Shah flees but is later reinstated by royalist military forces with covert US support; oil dispute settled
1975: Algiers Agreement with Iraq acknowledges Iran's supremacy in Gulf
1978–9: Revolution; the Shah is exiled; Ayatollah Khomeini returns from exile; Iran becomes an Islamic Republic
1980–8: Iran-Iraq War
1989: Khomeini dies, Rafsanjani president
1995: USA imposes economic sanctions
1997: Moderate Khatami elected president
2001: Khatami re-elected president
2005: Mahmoud Ahmadinejad elected president
2007: Declares nuclear capability

1952: Accession of King Hussein
1970: Attempted destruction of PLO by Jordanian Army (Black September)
1990: King Hussein refuses to join coalition against Iraq
1994: Peace accord and full diplomatic relations with Israel
1999: Death of King Hussein

1990: Invaded by Iraq; Gulf Crisis
1991: Liberated by UN coalition forces

1948: Leads Arab coalition against Israel
1952: Monarchy overthrown; military government led by Nasser after 1952
1956: Nationalization of Suez Canal Company; tripartite invasion by Britain, France, Israel
1958–61: Union with Syria (United Arab Republic)
1967,1973: Wars with Israel
1970: Nasser dies; Sadat becomes president
1979: Egyptian-Israeli peace treaty
1981: Sadat assassination; Mubarak becomes president
1989: Egypt readmitted to Arab League
1990: Egypt sends troops to anti-Iraq coalition

1971: Created from former British-protected Trucial States after British evacuation

1951: Mutual Defence Assistance Agreement with USA
1960: Organization of Petroleum Exporting Countries formed
1981: Gulf Co-operation Council formed (with Bahrain, Kuwait, Oman, Qatar and UAE)
1973: Saudi Arabia embargos oil exports to USA; oil price soars
1990: Base for UN Coalition attacks against Iraq
1992: Tentative steps towards political openness
1996: King Fahd temporarily steps down

1965–75: Marxist insurgency by People's Democratic Republic of Yemen defeated with British and Iranian help
1970: Accession of Sultan Qaboos
1999: "Basic Statues of the State" promulgated; Oman's first written constitution

1953: Anglo-Egyptian agreement on ending British condominium of 1899
1956: Sudan gains independence
1958: Coup by General Ibrahim Abboud
1963–72: Civil war between Arab Muslim rulers in north and Christian and animist Africans in south
1969: Abboud deposed; Colonel Gaafar Mohammed el-Nimeiri seizes power
1983: Civil war re-erupts; food shortages increase
1985: Military coup ousts Nimeiri
1989: Military coup; National Islamic Front in effective control
1990–1: Famine worsens; reports of military aid from Iran
1994–5: Cease-fire between feuding anti-government forces
1998: US attacks suspected chemical weapons plant
1999–2001: Parliament suspended
2001: Arrest of Hassan al-Turabi, speaker of parliament and founder of National Islamic Front
2002: Machakos agreement with SPLA ends civil war in south
2003–: Civil war continues in Darfur and other western regions

1962–9: Civil war
1972–9: Intermittent war with Aden

1967: Coup by National Liberation Front; civil war; Britain withdraws troops from Aden
1968: Ali Nasar Muhammad overthrown as president by Haidar al Attas

YEMEN
1948: Assassination of Imam Yahya; his son takes power
1959: Creation of the Arab Emirates of the South (later the Federation of South Arabia)
1962: Civil war and revolution in San'a; Yemen Arab Republic (North Yemen) established
1967: Withdrawal of British forces; declaration of People's Democratic Republic of Yemen (South Yemen)
1990: YAR and PDRY united
1994: Civil war breaks out; Democratic Republic of Yemen declares secession (suppressed July)
1999: First direct Presidential elections held; Ali Abdallah Salih elected

TURKEY
Aleppo
Hama
SYRIA
Beirut
CYPRUS
LEBANON
Damascus
ISRAEL
Jerusalem
Amman
Cairo
EGYPT
JORDAN
Euphrates
IRAQ
Baghdad
Tigris
Tehran
IRAN
AFGHANISTAN
USSR
Kuwait
KUWAIT
Persian Gulf
PAKISTAN
BAHRAIN
QATAR
Doha
Abu Dhabi
UAE
Muscat
SAUDI ARABIA
Riyadh
Medina
Mecca
Red Sea
Nile
SUDAN
Khartoum
OMAN
Arabian Sea
YEMEN ARAB REPUBLIC
PEOPLE'S DEMOCRATIC REPUBLIC OF YEMEN
San'a
Aden

South America: search for stability and development

For much of the twentieth century Latin America was subject to recurrent cycles of economic boom and bust, and alternating periods of political opening and authoritarian rule. There appeared to be a trade-off between anti-democratic politics and stable growth, and democracy and macroeconomic volatility. Only towards the end of the first decade of the 21st century did the region appear to enter a phase of sustainable growth and democratic consolidation.

> AND NOW I HAVE GIVEN MY
> LAST LECTURE ... THE NEXT
> WILL BE GIVEN BY A COLONEL.
>
> Bernardo Houssay, renowned
> Argentinian physiologist, 1943

> [MILITARY RULE AIMED] TO MAKE
> CHILE NOT A NATION OF PROLETARIANS,
> BUT A NATION OF ENTREPRENEURS.
>
> General Augusto Pinochet, dictator of Chile, 1973–89

> WE ARE TAKING OUR OWN PATH
>
> President Hugo Chávez of Venezuela at the first ever
> All Latin America Summit
> (from which the USA and Canada were excluded),
> February, 2010

3 Latin America's traditional primary-export economy (map below) was modified, though not transformed, by the Great Depression, which reduced demand and lowered prices, and the Second World War, which cut it off from foreign goods and capital. Industrialization met with a degree of success in some countries and impetus was given to import substitution. However, the area continued to depend upon the developed world for markets for its raw material exports, for imports of industrial capital goods, for technology and for finance.

War and depression

The pre-1910 order was shattered by war and depression. Although prices of strategic exports rocketed, import scarcity and the evaporation of investment inflows in 1914 destabilized Latin America. While the world economy appeared to recover in the 1920s, the 1930 depression hit Latin America hard. Between 1929 and 1932, governments failing to cope with crisis collapsed. In Chile and Brazil, new regimes applied Keynesian-style measures to stimulate activity. Populist leaders – Getúlio Vargas, in Brazil, and Juan D. Perón, in Argentina – encouraged industrialization. Around 1948, ad hoc responses to crisis were synthesized into a strategy for development by the UN Economic Commission for Latin America: "structuralism" advocated industrialization to substitute imports, agrarian reform and regional economic integration in order to promote national, state-led capitalist development. Nevertheless, primary commodities dominated exports until c. 1990.

Urbanization, populism and violence

Democratic aspirations, often frustrated by violent reaction, characterized the decades from 1910 to the 1970s. The 1920s witnessed democratic openings in the Southern Cone republics (Argentina, Chile and Uruguay), although these were curtailed by crisis. The late 1940s saw another brief wave of democratization. The main political expressions were populism and nationalism, which overlaid societal tensions driven by competition for land (notably in the Andean republics and Brazil), and unemployment and poverty in burgeoning cities. Land reform was achieved in Bolivia (1952), in Peru (1968) and in Chile (1970 – reversed in 1973). The Cuban Revolution, 1959, triggered a wave of hope and fear – and the reality of Havana-directed insurgency. Christian democratic and constitution-

alist left-wing parties enjoyed some success in the 1960s, culminating in the 1970 election of Marxist President Salvador Allende in Chile, although the pendulum was already swinging in the other direction. Threats of terrorism and the need for "discipline" to deepen industrialization were invoked to justify military interventions. The Brazilian military regime of 1964 lasted until 1985. In Chile (1973) and Argentina (1976) military administrations applied bloody repression: "disappearances" and violation of human rights were widespread. An alliance of the military and civilian technocrats – bureaucratic-authoritarian regimes of the 1960s and 1970s – were undermined by economic mismanagement (culminating in Debt Crisis), political miscalculation and sheer incompetence (the Argentine invasions of the Falklands in 1982), and a groundswell of civic protest. A reappraisal of the statist model of industrialization resulted.

Violence, democracy, neo-liberalism and globalization

The neo-liberal Washington Consensus promised growth with macroeconomic-based state shrinkage (privatization of government corporations and pension funds, and "pruning" of social spending), decentralization, balanced budgets, capital market deregulation, trade liberalization and labour reforms. Liberal experiment sometimes followed failed heterodox efforts at stabilization – Austral Plan (Argentina), Cruzado Plan (Brazil) and Inti Plan (Peru) – that ended in hyperinflation. In some republics, neo-liberalism was applied as a "surprise" economic reorientation after the election of candidates who had advocated populist strategies during presidential campaigns; for example, in Argentina, Peru and Venezuela. Elsewhere, in Brazil and Uruguay, victorious candidates explicitly advanced a Washington Consensus agenda. The difference between the late 1980s and 1990s, and the earlier neo-liberal experiments in the 1970s, was

Juan Domingo Perón and his wife Eva (known as "Evita") (right) at the height of their popularity in 1951. Perón became president of Argentina in 1946 through an alliance of workers and dissident soldiers. After Eva's death in 1952 and a prolonged economic downturn, he was overthrown in a military coup. In 1973 he returned from exile in Spain and became president once again.

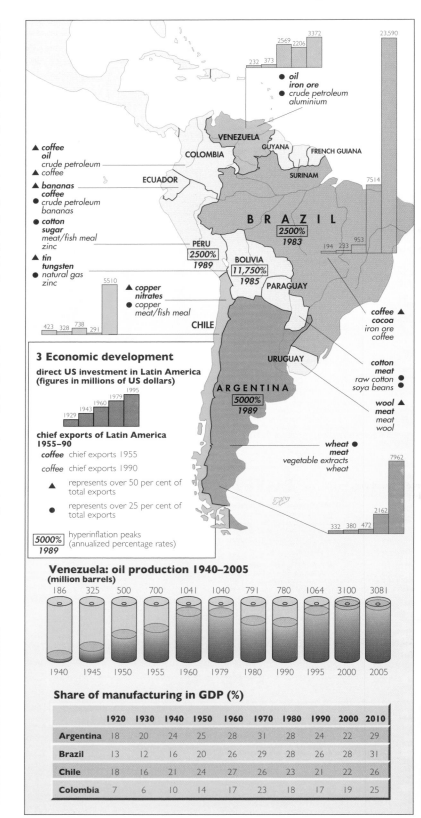

3 Economic development

direct US investment in Latin America (figures in millions of US dollars)

chief exports of Latin America 1955–90
- *coffee* chief exports 1955
- *coffee* chief exports 1990
- ▲ represents over 50 per cent of total exports
- ● represents over 25 per cent of total exports

| 5000% |
| 1989 | hyperinflation peaks (annualized percentage rates)

Venezuela: oil production 1940–2005
(million barrels)

| 186 | 325 | 500 | 700 | 1041 | 1040 | 791 | 780 | 1064 | 3100 | 3081 |
| 1940 | 1945 | 1950 | 1955 | 1960 | 1979 | 1980 | 1990 | 1995 | 2000 | 2005 |

Share of manufacturing in GDP (%)

	1920	1930	1940	1950	1960	1970	1980	1990	2000	2010
Argentina	18	20	24	25	28	31	28	24	22	29
Brazil	13	12	16	20	26	29	28	26	28	31
Chile	18	16	21	24	27	26	23	21	22	26
Colombia	7	6	10	14	17	23	18	17	19	25

Fundamental change (attempted or achieved) in economic and social structure by nationalist or Marxist/Maoist movements

Moderate socio-economic change or modernization by democratic or other process

Revolutionary change by dictatorships appealing to popular forces, especially urban labour

Radical socio-economic change by Christian Democrat parties

Military dictatorship of the right, with or without social or modernizing programme

Urban guerillas from late 1960s following failure of Cuban-inspired rural guerillas

Introduction of neo-liberalism, with date

1930–1 Revolutions in Argentina, Bolivia, Brazil, Chile, Ecuador and Peru

1955 Overthrow of Perón regime in Argentina

1959 Cuban revolution

1964–8 Military coups in Brazil, Argentina and Peru

1973 Overthrow of Allende regime in Chile

1976 Overthrow of "Isabel" Martínez de Perón in Argentina

1982 Falklands War

1983 Democratic rule in Argentina

1998 Hugo Chávez elected president of Venezuela

2011 Community of Latin American and Caribbean States formed

2011 Dilma Rousseff elected president of Brazil

I Between 1930 and 1998 Latin America experienced many military regimes, most of them dedicated to the preservation of the status quo (map right). It also witnessed radical or left-wing movements that were directed towards ending the backwardness of the region and its marked economic inequalities. By the 1980s most countries had abandoned military rule for democratic politics.

Liberal-Conservative Pact, 1957

intermittent militarism to 1978

election of reformist government 1978

radical militarism 1968

Sendero Luminoso from 1980

return to civilian rule 1980 President Fujimori suspends constitution 1992

Bolivian revolution 1952–64

Che Guevara (killed 1967)

military 1980; democratization 1985

CUBA

Cuban-inspired guerrilla movements 1959–68

Rómulo Betancourt 1945–8, 1959–64; Carlos Andrés Pérez 1974–9

Rafael Caldera 1969–74; Luis Herrera Campins 1979; Jaime Lusinchi 1984;

Hugo Chávez 1998

Getúlio Vargas 1930–45; 1950–4 João Goulart 1961–4

modernizing militarism 1964

civilian rule 1985; democratization 1986

Dilma Rousseff 2011

VENEZUELA ☆ 1989

Grenada

Cartagena
Caracas
Georgetown
Paramaribo
Cayenne
SURINAM FRENCH GUIANA
GUYANA
Macapá
Belém
Gurupá
Bogotá
Amazon
COLOMBIA ☆ 1990–1
Rio Negro
Manaus
Fortaleza
Quito
ECUADOR ☆ 1992–3
Guayaquil
Purus
BRAZIL ☆ 1989–96
Recife
Piura
PERU ☆ 1990
Salvador (Bahia)
Trujillo
Huánco
Brasília
Callao
Lima Cuzco
Belo Horizonte
Arequipa
La Paz
BOLIVIA ☆ 1985–6
Rio de Janeiro
Sucre
São Paulo
PARAGUAY ☆ 1988–9
Santos
Antofagasta
military dictatorship Stroessner 1954 Rodriguez 1989
Asunción
Florianópolis
San Miguel de Tucumán
Porto Alegre
Copiapó
Uruguay
Eduardo Frei 1964–70
Rio Grande
Santa Fé
URUGUAY ☆ 1989
Batllismo 1903–33
Salvador Allende (Popular Unity) 1970–3
Córdoba
Fray Bentos
Rosario
Montevideo
Tupamaros
Mendoza
Valparaíso 1974–5 ☆
Buenos Aires
military 1973
Santiago
ARGENTINA ☆ 1989–91
Pinochet 1973–89
Concepción
Bahia Blanca
civilian rule 1985; democratization 1986
Valdivia
Montoneros
democratization 1989
Osorno
Rawson
Juan Domingo Perón 1946–55, 1973–4
Comodoro Rivadavia
military 1976–83
democratization and civilian rule 1983
Santa Cruz
Falkland Islands (Islas Malvinas) occupied by Argentina 1982: occupation ended by UK Task Force June 1982
Tierra del Fuego

---

2 Population growth and social structure

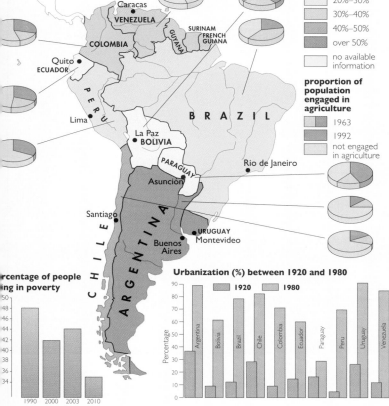

middle class as % of total population (1963)
- 5%–20%
- 20%–30%
- 30%–40%
- 40%–50%
- over 50%
- no available information

proportion of population engaged in agriculture
- 1963
- 1992
- not engaged in agriculture

Caracas
VENEZUELA
SURINAM
FRENCH GUIANA
GUYANA
COLOMBIA
Quito
ECUADOR
PERU
BRAZIL
Lima
La Paz
BOLIVIA
PARAGUAY
Rio de Janeiro
Asunción
Santiago
CHILE
ARGENTINA
URUGUAY
Montevideo
Buenos Aires

Percentage of people living in poverty

1990 2000 2003 2010

Urbanization (%) between 1920 and 1980

1920 1980

Argentina, Bolivia, Brazil, Chile, Colombia, Ecuador, Paraguay, Peru, Uruguay, Venezuela

2 Population growth in Latin America (map above) has been so rapid that industrialization has been unable to provide employment for the growing multitude. Within the space of about two generations, between the 1920s and 80s, rapid population growth and rural-urban migration transformed most of South America from an overwhelmingly rural to a predominantly urban society. Agrarian reform has failed significantly to improve conditions in the countryside or to halt the migration of rural people to the cities.

that structural reform was applied in a democratic context. Electoral support for neo-liberalism was strong among the urban poor, who had gained least from post-Second World War industrialization. Late 20th-century liberalism yielded contending models of international and intra-Americas economic relations: the MERCOSUR (Argentina, Brazil, Paraguay and Uruguay) – evolving from a trade association into a common market – sought closer collaboration with the European Union and broader international engagement; the Free Trade Area of the Americas, fitfully fostered by Washington, was envisaged as a

trade zone stretching from Alaska to Tierra del Fuego. Since the turn of the twenty-first century, there has been a sustained move to develop less market-orientated policies, initially led by the Venezuelan president Hugo Chávez, elected in 1998. In 2010 at a summit in Mexico, Latin American states agreed to set up the Community of Latin American and Caribbean States. Founded in 2011, the community was set up to challenge the United States-dominated Organization of American States. The inclusion of Cuba was a direct challenge to the American boycott of the island. Most Latin American states now belong to the new organization.

This change accompanied the efforts of the continent to cope with the world financial crisis in 2007–10 which the major economies in Latin America survived more successfully than they did the crash of 1929. Brazil has now become a major player on the world economic stage and, together with Argentina, is a member of the G20 economic group set up in 1999. Social inequality remains a pressing problem, as does drug-related violence in Colombia and Mexico. But in Brazil and Chile, prudent management coupled with fiscal stimulation packages have helped to reduce poverty and unemployment, as well as promote

democratic institution-building. In such countries, market-friendly policies have been combined consciously with redistributive social programmes. Further indications of change are provided by the election of Michelle Bachelet in Chile in 2005, the first woman in the history of Latin America to be elected president, the election of President Cristina Fernández de Kirchner in the Argentine in 2007, who succeeded her husband, and the election of Evo Morales in 2005 as the first fully indigenous president of Bolivia. Yet other indications of democratic consolidation are provided by the rotation of political parties – indicated for example by the election of conservative Sebastian Piñera as president of Chile in 2010, ending the electoral dominance of the left-of-centre coalition which has held power since the return of democracy in 1990.

Mexico, Central America and the Caribbean

The "backyard" proximity of Mexico, Central America and the Caribbean to the USA has given rise to much anxiety. Relations have been dynamic and destructive – shaped by political interventions and economic integration, by ideological conflict, by equivocal US support for dictatorships and democracy, and by Washington's preoccupation with trade, finance, revolution, insurgency, migration and drugs – and by the continuing blockade of Cuba.

Revolution and intervention

By the early 20th century, agrarian reform was a pressing issue, featuring in the revolutionary upheavals that punctuated the period. Such upheaval culminated in the Mexican Revolution (began 1910) and the Cuban Revolution (1959), and frustrated reform in Guatemala in the 1950s. The aims of the Mexican Revolution, encapsulated in the 1917 Constitution, were nationalist, socially reformist and broadly pro-capitalist, promising land to peasants, workers' rights, political democracy

and stability for business. The apogee of radicalism occurred under president Lázaro Cárdenas (1934–40), who embarked on massive land redistribution projects and the nationalization of British and US oil companies. Factors that prompted protest in Mexico also existed elsewhere: before 1914, US companies had established dominant positions in plantation agriculture and mineral extraction across the Isthmus and circum-Caribbean. Corporations such as United Fruit virtually functioned as states within states – with transport systems that crossed

international boundaries, and running hospitals and schools for workers and their families. Foreign corporations appeared to function with little reference to national governments. Collaborating with landed and commercial elites, international businesses – their position guaranteed by US might – seemed secure, certainly in dynastic kleptocracies run by the Somoza clan in Nicaragua, or Duvalier in Haiti.

Economic development and violence

The 1959 Cuban Revolution, headed by Fidel and Raúl Castro and Argentine émigré Ernesto "Che" Guevara, sought national solidarity through social progress and economic growth. With Soviet subsidies, welfare gains were impressive until the 1990s; the record regarding political and civil rights was decidedly less so. Nevertheless, Cuba became a beacon. Peasant demand for land and student-inspired pressure for political reform generated tensions in Central America. Anxiety about communist agitation and threats to business, as well as fear of Cuban-style revolution, led to Washington-inspired *golpes* designed to pre-empt political radicalization. The action was counter-productive: uprisings occurred in every republic between Panama and Mexico, save Costa Rica. The 1970s and 1980s witnessed the operation of CIA-trained military death squads, massive human rights abuses by government forces

1910	Start of Mexican Revolution
1924–28	Reformist uprising led by Agusto César Sandino, Nicaragua
1945–50	Socially reformist, democratically elected regime of Juan José Arévalo Bermejo, Guatemala
1954	US-inspired coup against reformist administration of Jacobo Arbenz Guzmán, Guatemala
1959	Cuban revolution
1961–79	Sandinista armed struggle, Nicaragua
1965–90	Guerrilla war in Guatemala
1975–92	Guerrilla war in El Salvador
2009	Constitutional crisis and coup d'etat in Honduras
2000	PRI loses Mexican presidential elections after 79 years on power
2006	Felipe Calderón launches anti-drug war in Mexico
2015	President Obama and Raúl Castro meet in Panama

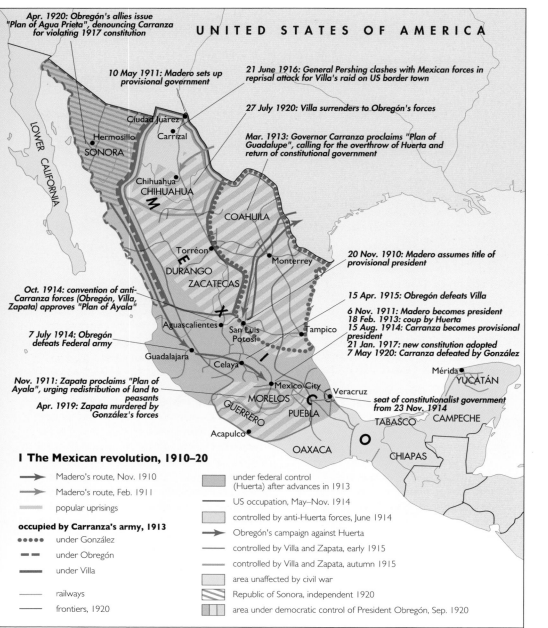

I The Mexican revolution, 1910–20

→ Madero's route, Nov. 1910
→ Madero's route, Feb. 1911
— popular uprisings

occupied by Carranza's army, 1913
●●●●● under González
– – – under Obregón
— under Villa

— railways
— frontiers, 1920

under federal control (Huerta) after advances in 1913
— US occupation, May–Nov. 1914
— controlled by anti-Huerta forces, June 1914
→ Obregón's campaign against Huerta
— controlled by Villa and Zapata, early 1915
— controlled by Villa and Zapata, autumn 1915
area unaffected by civil war
Republic of Sonora, independent 1920
area under democratic control of President Obregón, Sep. 1920

Instrumental in the overthrow of the Porfirian order, Pancho Villa and Emiliano Zapata, seen here (above) celebrating their victory in the presidential palace in Mexico City, represented quite different groups. Villa, sometimes described as a Robin Hood type figure, drew support from small ranchers and vaqueros ("cowboys") in the north. Zapata led a peasant uprising in the southwestern state of Morelos, a region that had witnessed widespread seizure of village land during the Díaz period.

I For the quarter century until 1910, Mexico had been dominated by the dictatorship of Porfirio Díaz. Following a challenge to his re-election in 1910 by the northern landowner-turned-radical, Francisco Madero, political resistance to Díaz hardened. A peasant civil war erupted, led by the ex-bandit Pancho Villa in Chihuahua and by Emiliano Zapata in the central state of Morelos (map left). The unlikely alliance of northern landowners and peasant radicals led to the fall of Díaz in 1911 and Madero's election as president. Over the next nine years Mexico descended into political confusion and further civil war. On the one side the old elites of the Díaz years (urban modernizers and rural bosses) rallied together; against them were ranged the constitutionalists of the northern states in a loose and often hostile alliance. The older forces were finally defeated in 1914, but their opponents split into warring factions. The northern elites, led by Venustiano Carranza and Alvaro Obregón, defeated the radical Zapatist forces in Mexico City in August 1916. The following year a new constitution was drawn up to establish a democratic Mexico, but not until the election of Plutarco Calles as president in 1920 was the period of revolutionary crisis finally ended.

UNITED STATES OF AMERICA
US intervention
Washington
Mexico 1914, 1916
Guatemala 1954
Nicaragua 1912–33
Panama 1903–18, 1989
Cuba 1921–23, 1933, 1961
Haiti 1915–34, 1944, 1994
Dominican Republic 1916–24, 1965–6
Grenada 1983
Atlantic Ocean
Miami
Bahama Islands
Havana
CUBA
Cuban revolution 1959
1917; 1921–2; 1933
HAITI
DOMINICAN REPUBLIC
Cuban-inspired guerrilla movements 1959–68
1916–22; 1964–6
1915–34
Grenada
MEXICO
Mexican revolution 1910–40
Mexico City
Puebla
Veracruz
Acapulco
BELIZE
GUATEMALA
HONDURAS
EL SALVADOR
NICARAGUA
1912–33
Guatemala City
Managua
COSTA RICA
San José
Panama City
PANAMA
Zapatista revolt, 1994
Guatemalan revolution 1944–54
Military Junta 1979
Figueres 1948
Sandinista revolution 1979–90; democratization 1990
2 Mexico and Central America, 1910–94
fundamental change (attempted or achieved) in economic and social structure by nationalist or Marxist/Maoist movements
moderate socio-economic change or modernization by democratic or other process
military dictatorship of the right, with or without social or modernizing programme
urban guerrillas from late 1960s following failure of Cuban-inspired rural guerrillas
US occupations and "protectorates"

and reprisals by guerrilla forces. There was an ethnic component to violence: elites regarded Indian communities as sources of subversion. Gradually guerrillas consolidated their position in the countryside and, in the case of Nicaragua, toppled regimes. Elsewhere, changes in attitude in Washington, and peace deals brokered by Costa Rica, Colombia, Mexico and Venezuela, led to cease-fires and reasonably fair elections. But decades of war and terrorism had resulted in massive population movements and emigration.

Democratization

Central America and Mexico began a fragile process of democratization in the mid-1980s. A mixture of exhaustion, regime-collapse and external aid (and pressure) fostered stability in Central America, while in Mexico the combination was growth, followed by inflation and crisis, and a remarkable transition within the single party, the PRI, which dominated politics after the 1920s. Attempts at political liberalization in the late 1960s were thwarted by internal resistance within the governing party apprehensive at student-led demands for change that led to a crackdown in 1968. After the collapse of oil prices, inflation and default in 1982, the ground was laid for economic reorganization and democratic opening. Export-oriented manufacturing and commodity diversification were prioritized. Elected president in 1988, Carlos Salinas announced that Mexico would enter the North American Free Trade Area and the GATT. The 1994 elections, which took place at a time of armed struggle in the southern state of Chiapas and economic crisis, were possibly the freest in Mexican history. Further institutional democratization allowed Vicente Fox, from the rightist National Action Party (PAN), to take the presidency in 2000. The PAN won again in 2006, but in 2012 the Institutional Revolutionary Party regained the presidency once more under Peña Nieto and began to rein back the democratic process. The continued political crisis in Mexico highlighted widespread corruption and the continuing war against drug barons. Beginning in 2006, the anti-drug war and rival gang killings have resulted in more than 100,000 deaths. Attempts by Mexicans keen to escape the poverty and chaos by migrating to the United States have been undermined by the building of the US "Border Wall"; migration peaked earlier in the 21st century at well over a million a year, but has fallen to a fraction of this figure by 2014. In that year, more non-Mexicans were stopped at the border than Mexicans.

Another factor making for instability in the region was the relationship between Cuba and the United States. Cuba had been embargoed by the United States since the 1959 revolution. In 2008, Raúl Castro replaced his brother, Fidel, as president and began a modest economic liberalization, but the Communist Party of Cuba retained its grip on power. In 2014, American president Barack Obama began overtures to heal the rift, and in April 2015 Castro and Obama met at the Summit of the Americas in Panama, the first time Cuba had attended. Progress in this case, as in the reform of Mexican politics, is likely to be slow and difficult.

ALAS POOR MEXICO: SO FAR FROM GOD, SO CLOSE TO THE UNITED STATES.

President Porfirio Díaz, Mexico, c.1910

THE NICARAGUAN PEOPLE HAVE NOT THROWN ME OUT. I WAS REMOVED BY AN INTERNATIONAL CONSPIRACY ... OF COMMUNISTS THAT DESIRES NICARAGUA TO BE A COMMUNIST COUNTRY.

Ex-president Somoza, in exile, 1979

2 Between 1930 and 1998 Central America experienced many military regimes, most of them dedicated to the preservation of the status quo **(map above)**. It also witnessed radical or left-wing movements that were directed towards ending the backwardness of the region and its marked economic inequalities. By the 1980s most countries had abandoned military rule for democratic politics.

3 Population growth in Central America (map right) has been so rapid that industrialization has been unable to provide employment for the growing multitude, many of them attracted to sprawling cities with inadequate housing and social services. Agrarian reform has failed significantly to improve conditions in the countryside or to halt the migration of rural people to the cities.

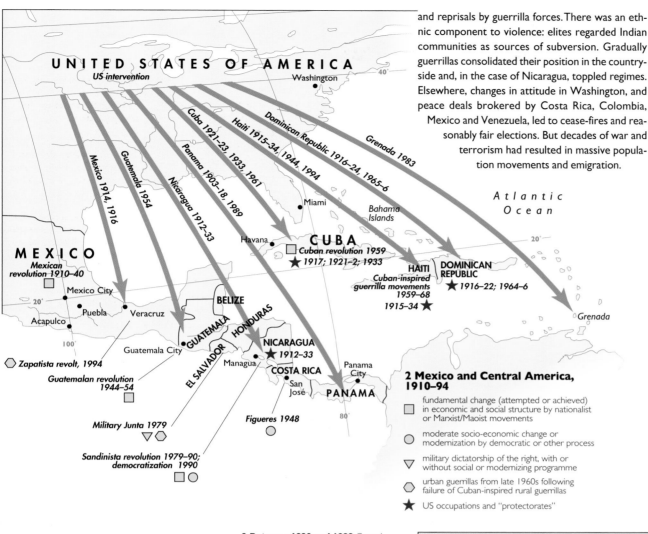

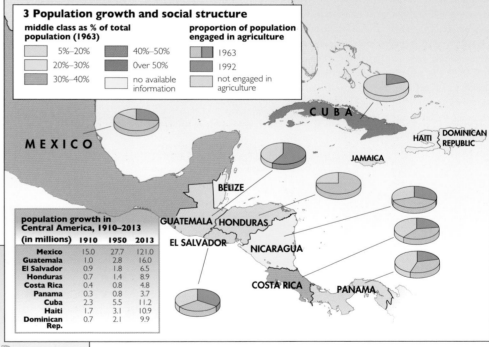

3 Population growth and social structure
middle class as % of total population (1963)
5%–20%
20%–30%
30%–40%
40%–50%
Over 50%
no available information
proportion of population engaged in agriculture
1963
1992
not engaged in agriculture
MEXICO
CUBA
HAITI
DOMINICAN REPUBLIC
JAMAICA
BELIZE
GUATEMALA
HONDURAS
EL SALVADOR
NICARAGUA
COSTA RICA
PANAMA

population growth in Central America, 1910–2013 (in millions)

	1910	1950	2013
Mexico	15.0	27.7	121.0
Guatemala	1.0	2.8	16.0
El Salvador	0.9	1.8	6.5
Honduras	0.7	1.4	8.9
Costa Rica	0.4	0.8	4.8
Panama	0.3	0.8	3.7
Cuba	2.3	5.5	11.2
Haiti	1.7	3.1	10.9
Dominican Rep.	0.7	2.1	9.9

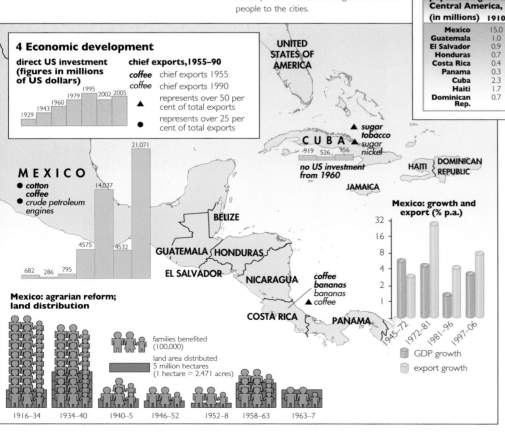

4 Economic development
direct US investment (figures in millions of US dollars)
1929
1943
1960
1979
1995
2002
2005
chief exports, 1955–90
coffee chief exports 1955
coffee chief exports 1990
represents over 50 per cent of total exports
represents over 25 per cent of total exports
UNITED STATES OF AMERICA
CUBA
919
526
956
sugar
tobacco
sugar
nickel
no US investment from 1960
HAITI
DOMINICAN REPUBLIC
JAMAICA
MEXICO
cotton
coffee
crude petroleum
engines
21,071
14,037
4575
4532
682
286
795
BELIZE
GUATEMALA
HONDURAS
EL SALVADOR
NICARAGUA
coffee
bananas
bananas
coffee
COSTA RICA
PANAMA
Mexico: growth and export (% p.a.)
32
16
8
4
2
1
1945–72
1972–81
1981–96
1997–06
GDP growth
export growth
Mexico: agrarian reform; land distribution
families benefited (100,000)
land area distributed 5 million hectares (1 hectare = 2.471 acres)
1916–34
1934–40
1940–5
1946–52
1952–8
1958–63
1963–7

4 Central America's traditional primary-export economy **(map left)** was modified, though not transformed, by the Great Depression, which reduced demand and lowered prices, and the Second World War, which cut it off from foreign goods and capital. Industrialization met with a degree of success in some countries and impetus was given to import substitution. However, the area continued to depend upon the developed world for markets for its raw material exports, for imports of industrial capital goods, for technology and for finance.

The United States: the affluent society

After the Second World War, the USA experienced a period of exceptional economic growth and consumer-led prosperity. The economic boom changed the character of American society as well as the landscape of the United States through the construction of highways and suburbs. However, a significant share of the population was and remains excluded from the affluent society.

> AMERICA'S FUTURE WILL INEVITABLY BRING BETTER THINGS FOR MORE PEOPLE.
>
> **General Motors Advertisement, May 1945**

> WHAT I WANT TO SEE ABOVE ALL IS THAT THIS REMAINS A COUNTRY WHERE SOMEONE CAN ALWAYS GET RICH.
>
> **President Ronald Reagan, 1981**

IN 1945, THE UNITED STATES was by far the strongest economy in the world. While its traditional competitors had been devastated during the war, the USA possessed nearly two-thirds of the world's gold reserves and produced a third of the world's goods. And the boom continued in the post-war period. The American gross national product grew from nearly $212 billion in 1945 to over $503 billion in 1960 and $977 billion in 1970. The American population also increased during the "baby boom" after the war, from nearly 140 million in 1945 to over 180 million in 1960. By the end of the decade, the population had crossed the 200 million mark.

The post-war boom

A combination of consumer demand, government spending and technological innovation fuelled the fast economic growth. The construction and car industry greatly benefited from the exodus of the white middle class to the suburbs. Between 1950 and 1970, the suburban population grew from 36 million to 74 million. Suburban growth was facilitated by the Federal Housing Administration (FHA) and Veterans Administration insured-loan programmes,

which significantly reduced the down payment required to buy a home, as well as by the Federal Highway Act of 1956.

Motor transport was essential for suburban living, and the number of registered cars increased from over 25 million in 1945 to over 52 million ten years later. By 1968, there were well over 100 million cars, buses and trucks on America's streets. The increasingly dense network of highways made it quicker and more economical to move passengers and goods on the road and started the decline of the American railroads. The automobile not only allowed Americans to live at greater distance from their workplace, but also led to the rise of large supermarkets, shopping malls and business parks outside of cities, and the proliferation of motels and fast-food chains. Manufacturing jobs were also increasingly located outside of metropolitan areas.

By 1972 the percentage of American families owning homes had risen to 63 per cent, and the FHA ensured that the new homes conformed to certain minimal standards. Ownership of durable consumer goods also increased after the war. While there were only 17,000 television sets in the entire

country in 1946, there were over 50 million by 1960. Private demand was stimulated by a growing consumer culture as well as the expansion of consumer credit. The first real credit cards, for example, were issued during the 1950s.

In 1955, the USA, with just 6 per cent of the world's population, was producing and consuming half of its goods. By 1970s, with the same proportion of the total population, it accounted for two-thirds of the world's goods.

The other side

Not all benefited from the economic boom to the same degree, and large pockets of poverty continued to exist, especially in the South, Appalachia, along the border with Mexico and on Native American reservations. The growing Black and Hispanic

I Starting with the Federal Highway Act in 1956, a large-scale road-building programme began in the USA (map below). By the 1980s the interstate highway network, built at a cost of over $76 billion, totalled about 64,350 km (40,000 miles). It encouraged the growth of suburbs and later "exurbs", "edge cities" or "technoburbs" along the highway corridors.

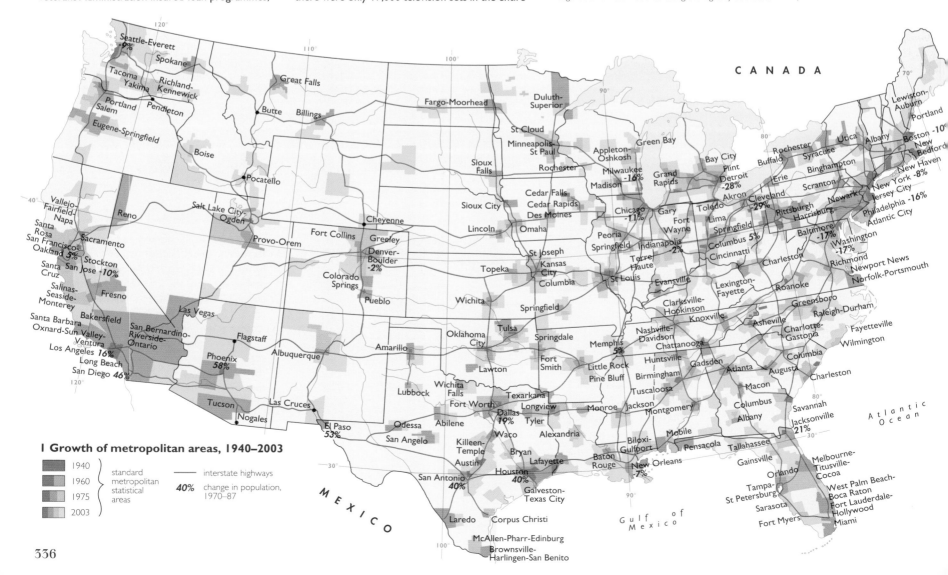

I Growth of metropolitan areas, 1940–2003

- 1940
- 1960
- 1975
- 2003

standard metropolitan statistical areas

—— interstate highways

40% change in population, 1970–87

population in America's inner cities also suffered economic hardships as job opportunities diminished due to the relocation of businesses outside of metropolitan areas or even abroad. These minorities often lacked the means to leave the ghettos or were not welcome in better areas. The FHA also supported residential segregation by refusing to provide mortgages to African-Americans trying to move into white neighbourhoods.

Television and advertising promoted the values and lifestyle of the white middle class as the norm, which increased feelings of exclusion and alienation among the poor. Even those who benefited experienced the affluent society as a mixed blessing. Married middle-class women often felt unfulfilled and isolated by domestic life in their suburban homes, while many members of the younger generation grew alienated by the sterility, homogeneity and materialism of mainstream American culture. The resulting tension came to the surface during the 1960s and 70s.

The end of economic dominance

By the late 1960s, America's economic competitors were catching up, and in 1971 the USA registered its first trade deficit since the Second World War. Two years later, the OPEC oil embargo demonstrated that access to cheap raw materials abroad had become more difficult in the post-colonial world. High inflation and the declining competitiveness of America's manufacturing industries were the dominant economic problems of the 1970s and early 80s. The long process of deindustrialization had painful social consequences, as many workers were ill-suited to transfer into the newly created jobs of the service and information technology sector.

The 1980s saw an economic recovery but also a severe fiscal crisis. In his two terms in office, President Reagan accumulated more debt than all governments before him combined since the founding of the USA. Nevertheless, the period of growth which started in late 1983 continued until 2000, with the exception of a brief recession in 1992–3. The benefits of this boom were very unevenly distributed. The average family income of the wealthiest quintile (fifth) of the population increased by 20 per cent between 1980 and 2000, the second quintile saw an increase by more than 8 per cent, whereas most of the remaining 60 per cent saw no increase and those at the bottom even saw their average income decline.

The burst of the "dot.com" bubble in 2001 and collapse of the home mortgage market which began in September 2008 also had serious repercussions for the many who already lived a precarious economic existence.

2 Migration patterns, 1935–2000

1935–40
gain
108.6 to 30.0
29.9 to 0.0
-0.1 to -30.0
-30.1 to -94.9
loss

1965–70
gain
108.6 to 30.0
29.9 to 0.0
-0.1 to -30.0
-30.1 to -94.9
loss

1995–2000
gain
108.6 to 30.0
29.9 to 0.0
-0.1 to -30.0
-30.1 to -94.9
loss

The "Levittowns" of developer William Levitt came to epitomize the post-war housing boom and the growth of suburbia after the Second World War **(left)**. Levitt and his sons used mass-production techniques to build thousands of almost identical affordable detached homes to satisfy the great demand for housing.

2 Americans have always been very mobile and continued to be so during the 20th century **(maps above)**. Interstate migration patterns shifted regularly, often depending on economic circumstances such as the drought in the Midwestern "dust bowl" between the World Wars, deindustrialization in the north or the rise of the "sunbelt".

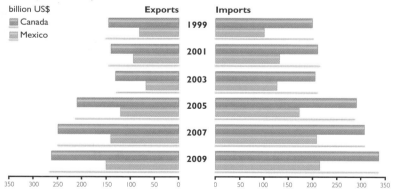

4 North American trade and NAFTA
US imports and exports to NAFTA countries

billion US$
- Canada
- Mexico

Exports | Imports
1999
2001
2003
2005
2007
2009

350 300 250 200 150 100 50 0   0 50 100 150 200 250 300 350

5 Growth of consumer durables, 1950–2000

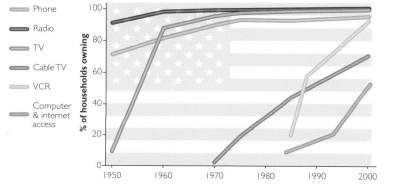

- Phone
- Radio
- TV
- Cable TV
- VCR
- Computer & internet access

% of households owning

1950 1960 1970 1980 1990 2000

3 The growth of home ownership, 1940–2000

percentage rise in growth, 1940–2000
- above 220
- 190
- 160
- 130
- below 100

WASHINGTON, MONTANA, NORTH DAKOTA, MINNESOTA, VERMONT, MAINE, OREGON, IDAHO, WYOMING, SOUTH DAKOTA, WISCONSIN, MICHIGAN, NEW YORK, N.H., MASS., R.I., CONN., NEVADA, UTAH, NEBRASKA, IOWA, PENNSYLVANIA, N.J., DEL., M.D., CALIFORNIA, COLORADO, KANSAS, ILLINOIS, IND., OHIO, W. VA., VIRGINIA, MISSOURI, KENTUCKY, NORTH CAROLINA, ARIZONA, NEW MEXICO, OKLAHOMA, ARKANSAS, TENNESSEE, SOUTH CAROLINA, TEXAS, MISS., ALABAMA, GEORGIA, LOUISIANA, FLORIDA

3 At the start of the 20th century, less than half of all householders (46.5 per cent) owned the home they lived in **(map above)**, and due to the Great Depression, home ownership dropped to its lowest level of the century in 1940 (43.6 per cent). After the Second World War, however, a booming economy, favorable tax laws and easier financing led to a rapid growth, especially in the south. By 2000, more than 66 per cent of all householders owned their own homes.

4 On 1 January 1994 Mexico joined the North American Free Trade Agreement (NAFTA), creating, with Canada and the USA, the largest free-trade bloc in the world. NAFTA's total GNP was over $6 trillion, with a market of over 360 million people. Trade in the area has increased **(chart above left)**, but the US is importing more than it is exporting.

5 Consumerism boomed in the USA after 1945. Before the Second World War, only 25 per cent of the farming population even had electricity; by 1960 over 80 per cent had not just lighting but televisions and telephones as well **(chart left)**. By 1990 almost every household had these, while an increasing number had cable television, video recorders and computers, too. Between 1945 and 1980 consumer expenditure in the USA increased almost fourfold.

The United States as a superpower

The struggle with international communism after the Second World War led the United States into two major military conflicts in Korea and Vietnam and frequent military and diplomatic interventions in other areas. The break-up of the Soviet Union in 1991 left the USA as the sole surviving superpower, but one facing new threats and challenges.

IN 1920, THE USA declined to join the League of Nations and continued its policy of avoiding "entangling alliances" with foreign powers until the Second World War. The Washington Treaty of 1 January 1942 with Great Britain, the Soviet Union, China and 22 other nations was the country's first military alliance since the 18th century. The long-established antagonism between the United States and the Soviet Union and their respective political philosophies re-emerged near the end of the war, despite the founding of the United Nations (UN) in 1945. Over the next decades, both sides tried to consolidate and expand their sphere of influence through alliances, aid and interventions.

Containment

The installation of pro-Soviet governments in Eastern Europe, Soviet pressure on Turkey and the British announcement of an end to its support for the anti-communist forces in the Greek civil war led the United States to adopt a policy of "containing" communist expansion in 1947. Economic aid was an important part of this strategy, which remained the basis of American foreign policy until the late 1980s, alongside the creation of regional military alliances such as the North Atlantic Treaty Organization (NATO) in 1949.

The communist victory in the Chinese Civil War and the detonation of the first Soviet atomic bomb

3 In the 1970s the United States entered a long period of deindustrialization, relative economic decline, and negative trade balances. Nevertheless, economic and military aid remained a vital tool to expand or consolidate American influence around the world and continues to do so. While the largest share of US military aid traditionally goes to the Middle East, Afghanistan has also become a major recipient during the "war on terror". US economic aid to sub-Saharan Africa has also increased very significantly since the 1990s.

in 1949 shocked many Americans. President Truman responded in 1950 by ordering the construction of the hydrogen bomb and accepting NSC-68, a document calling for the rearmament of America's conventional forces and for the USA to "organize and enlist the energies and resources of the free world" in order to "frustrate the Kremlin design for world domination". When communist North Korea invaded South Korea in 1950, the USA committed American forces against it and its Chinese allies under a UN mandate.

Under the Eisenhower administration from 1953, secretary of state John Foster Dulles talked not of containing communism but of the "liberation" of Eastern Europe. The hollowness of this rhetoric was demonstrated when Soviet forces suppressed the protest against the communist regime in East Germany in 1953 and the Hungarian uprising of 1956. On both occasion, the United States refrained from intervening.

After an abortive US-backed attempt to overthrow the Castro regime in Cuba in 1961, Cuba was the site of the most dangerous moment of the Cold War in October the following year. When the USSR started to install nuclear missiles on Cuba, President Kennedy ordered a naval blockade on the island. Both sides seemed on the brink of nuclear war until the Soviets agreed to withdraw their missiles in return for concessions over US missiles in Turkey. From 1962, relations between the two "superpowers" – the USA and the USSR – began slowly to improve, as symbolized by the 1963 treaty banning nuclear testing in the atmosphere and the first Strategic Arms Limitation Treaty (SALT) agreed in 1972. The Nixon Administration (1969–74)

also began a process of rapprochement with the communist People's Republic of China.

The attempt to contain the spread of communism also led to US involvement in Vietnam after the Second World War. After initially providing only aid and advisors to the anti-communist regime in South Vietnam, the USA began to commit combat troops in 1965 to help fight the communist insurgency. The conflict continued for another eight years, cost 58,000 American lives, and had profound repercussions on domestic politics. It also failed: in April 1975, North Vietnam unified the country under communist rule.

The post-Vietnam era and the collapse of communism

Elected in 1976, President Carter had promised to shift the emphasis of American foreign policy to the defence of human rights. His greatest success was the brokering of a peace treaty between Israel and Egypt, but he found no effective response to the taking of hostages by Iranian revolutionaries in Tehran or the Soviet invasion of Afghanistan in 1979.

Ronald Reagan, elected in 1980, was determined to restore America's prestige and leadership in the world and followed a two-prong strategy: large-scale rearmament directed at the Soviet Union; and intervention, either open (as in Grenada in 1983) or covert (as in Nicaragua in the early 1980s) to overthrow left-wing regimes.

The collapse of communism in Eastern Europe and the demise of the Soviet Union itself in 1991 left the United States as the sole remaining superpower. With the ending of the Cold War, a whole series of ethnic, nationalist and separatist conflicts emerged, and the USA played a crucial role in many of these.

1947 Truman administration launches policy of containment

1948 Marshall Aid launched. Berlin airlift

1949 Communist takeover in China. USSR explodes an atomic bomb. Foundation of NATO

1950–3 The Korean War

1962 The Cuban Missile Crisis

1965–73 US combat operations in Vietnam

1989 Collapse of communism in eastern Europe

1991 The Gulf War. Demise of the Soviet Union

2001 US intervention against Taliban in Afghanistan

2003 Second Gulf War: large-scale US troop commitment in Iraq

2015 Airstrikes again Islamic State in Iraq and Syria

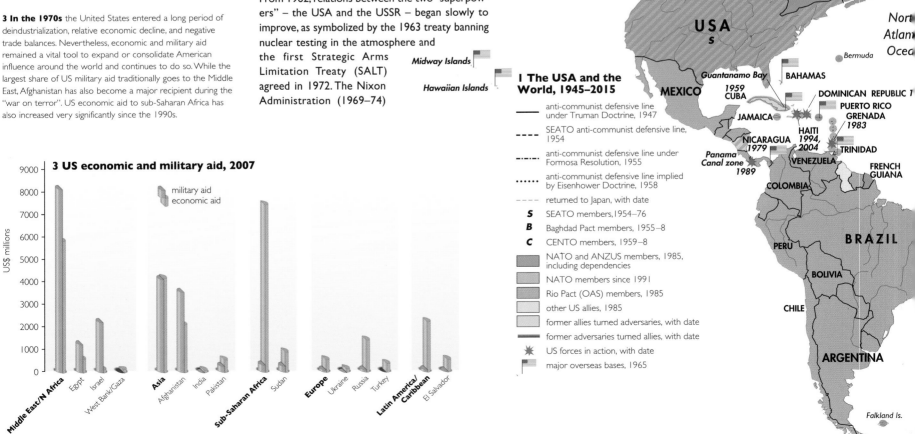

3 US economic and military aid, 2007

military aid
economic aid

US$ millions

Middle East/N Africa · Egypt · Israel · West Bank/Gaza · Asia · Afghanistan · India · Pakistan · Sub-Saharan Africa · Sudan · Europe · Ukraine · Russia · Turkey · Latin America/Caribbean · El Salvador

1 The USA and the World, 1945–2015

⸺ anti-communist defensive line under Truman Doctrine, 1947

- - - - SEATO anti-communist defensive line, 1954

–·–·– anti-communist defensive line under Formosa Resolution, 1955

······ anti-communist defensive line implied by Eisenhower Doctrine, 1958

- - - - returned to Japan, with date

S SEATO members, 1954–76

B Baghdad Pact members, 1955–8

C CENTO members, 1959–8

NATO and ANZUS members, 1985, including dependencies

NATO members since 1991

Rio Pact (OAS) members, 1985

other US allies, 1985

former allies turned adversaries, with date

former adversaries turned allies, with date

✳ US forces in action, with date

🏴 major overseas bases, 1965

The 1990s saw US troops deployed in many conflict regions overseas, and America also led the coalition against Iraq in the Gulf War of 1991.

New challenges

Following the al-Qaeda attacks on New York and Washington on 11 September 2001 President George W. Bush declared a "war on terror" which brought US-led interventions in Afghanistan in October 2001 and – in defiance of world opinion – in Iraq in March 2003. New challenges arose from the start of the so-called "Arab Spring" in December 2010: a series of protests and revolutions which challenged or ended authoritarian regimes across North Africa and the Middle East. The USA participated in airstrikes which contributed to the fall of Gaddafi in Libya in 2011 and was prepared to intervene in Syria two years later over the use of chemical weapons by the Assad regime. The ongoing civil wars in Syria and Libya, and persistent instability in Iraq led to the rise of the so-called "Islamic State" in the region. Attempts by the USA and its allies to stop its advance with the help of air strikes in 2015 have shown only limited results.

The growing proliferation of nuclear weapons also raised concerns. While some nations voluntarily dismantled or abandoned their nuclear weapons arsenal or programme (South Africa and Libya), others have entered the once exclusive club of nuclear powers (Pakistan and North Korea). The conflict over Iran's nuclear programme, which had started in 2002, was resolved by a provisional agreement in 2015 limiting Iran primarily to the development of nuclear energy.

Russia's and China's drive to modernize their conventional armed forces and their willingness to use as well as display their might also poses challenges for the United States. Russia's occupation of Crimea in 2014 and its subsequent support for separatists in Eastern Ukraine as well as China's assertive behaviour in the conflict with Japan over the Senkaku/Diaoyu islands since 2013 indicate that the era of unilateral hegemony has come to an end.

April 9 2003, a US serviceman drapes the Stars and Stripes over a statue of the Iraq dictator Saddam Hussein in Baghdad **(below)**. Arguing that Iraq had weapons of mass destruction (WMDs) and was trying to enhance its arsenal in defiance of the UN, a US-led coalition invaded Iraq on 20 March 2003 and occupied the capital within three weeks. Saddam himself was captured in December 2003 and executed three years later, but no WMDs were ever found.

2 The USA and Latin America, 1945–2015

- ▨ overthrow, or attempted overthrow, of left-wing regime by US or US-supported forces, with date
- ▨ other left-wing regimes, with date
- ● diplomatic relations with USA suspended during the 1960s
- ━ countries where Cuban-inspired guerrillas were active in the 1960s
- ■ OAS members, 1961
- ▲ joined OAS by 1965
- ━ contributed to Inter-American Peace Force in Dominican Republic, 1965
- + recipients of US aid under Alliance for Progress programme, 1961–70

2 US policy towards Latin America was guided by a number of considerations: the Monroe Doctrine (1823), which asserted that non-American powers should not intervene in the Western hemisphere; the desire to protect regional American economic and strategic interests (including the Panama Canal, completed in 1914); and by the attempt to overthrow, by a variety of means, governments which were considered left-wing or Soviet backed **(map right)**. The human rights records of anti-commmunist regimes became a secondary consideration.

UNITED STATES OF AMERICA

Los Angeles

1961: US-supported émigré invasion
1962: US blockade forces removal of Soviet nuclear missiles; OAS membership suspended until 2009
2014: US restore full diplomatic ties

HAITI
1994: US intervention to reinstate President Jean-Bertrand Aristide
2004: International force, including US soldiers, arrives after President Aristide resigns
2010: Humanitarian aid after earthquake

MEXICO
Mexico City
Gulf of Mexico
THE BAHAMAS
Nassau
Havana
CUBA
Bay of Pigs
DOMINICAN REP.
invaded by US forces to restore order, 1965
JAMAICA 1972–80
HAITI
Kingston
PUERTO RICO (USA)
Santo Domingo
San Juan
ANTIGUA
DOMINICA
Belmopan
GUAT. 1954
BELIZE
HONDURAS
Guatemala City
Tegucigalpa
ST LUCIA
ST VINCENT
BARBADOS
EL SALVADOR
NICARAGUA 1981–90
Caribbean Sea
GRENADA 1983
Managua
COSTA RICA
San José
Panama City
PANAMA 1968–82
TRINIDAD & TOBAGO
Port of Spain
VENEZUELA 1998
Caracas
Georgetown
Paramaribo
GUYANA
SUR.
FR. GUIANA

US support in civil wars against leftist guerrillas, 1979–92

Treaty signed 1977: Bi-national Panama Canal Commission administered canal from 1979–9, handover to Panama on 31 Dec. 1999
1989: Invasion to out General Manuel Noriega

COLOMBIA
Quito
ECUADOR 1972–6
Lima
PERU 1968–75
BRAZIL
1982–8
1968–92
2009: Military agreement allows US personnel to be stationed at seven military bases
La Paz
Brasilia
BOLIVIA 1970–1
Rio de Janeiro
PARAGUAY
Asunción
São Paulo
Santiago
CHILE 1973
Buenos Aires
Montevideo
URUGUAY
ARGENTINA
Falkland Islands (UK)
Stanley
Cape Horn

LIKE THE IDEOLOGY OF COMMUNISM, OUR NEW ENEMY PURSUES TOTALITARIAN AIMS ... AND LIKE THE IDEOLOGY OF COMMUNISM, ISLAMIC RADICALISM CONTAINS INHERENT CONTRADICTIONS THAT DOOM IT TO FAILURE ... OUR NEW ENEMY TEACHES THAT INNOCENT INDIVIDUALS CAN BE SACRIFICED TO SERVE A POLITICAL VISION.

George W. Bush, 11 November 2005

GREENLAND
ICELAND
NORWAY
WEST GERMANY
EAST GERMANY
RUSSIAN FEDERATION
Nato command
US occupation zone, 1945–55
UK B,C,S
POLAND
FRANCE S
1995
YUGOSLAVIA (KOSOVO 1999 SERBIA 1999)
KAZAKHSTAN
MONGOLIA
SPAIN
ITALY
GREECE
TURKEY B,C
2015
MOROCCO
LEBANON 1958,1982
ISRAEL
SYRIA
IRAQ B 2003–11
1979
IRAN 1979 B,C
AFGHANISTAN 1998, 2001–14
CHINA
N. KOREA
1950–3 S. KOREA
JAPAN
LIBYA 1969
1986
2011
EGYPT 1973
KUWAIT 1991
PAKISTAN B,C,S
BANGLADESH B,C,S
Okinawa
Amami-Oshima Is. 1953
administered by USA under peace treaty with Japan, 1945
Bonin Is. 1968
Ryukyu Is. 1972
Volcano Is.
Marcus I.
SAUDI ARABIA
OMAN
INDIA
BURMA 1964–73
NORTH VIETNAM
Parece Vela I.
SUDAN 1998
NIGERIA
2000
SOMALIA 1977
1974 ETHIOPIA
LAOS 1975
1962–75
THAILAND 1975
SOUTH VIETNAM 1975
CAMBODIA 1970–3
PHILIPPINES *independent from USA, 1946*
Guam
TRUST TERRITORY OF THE PACIFIC ISLANDS *brought under US control as UN trusteeship, 1947*
LIBERIA
KENYA 1992
ZAÏRE
Indian Ocean
Ascension I.
British Indian Ocean Territory
Mayotte
St Helena
ANGOLA
Madagascar
South Atlantic Ocean
SOUTH AFRICA
Tristan da Cunha
AUSTRALIA S
NEW ZEALAND S

1 The USA after 1945 maintained a world presence through a network of military bases and defence pacts in Europe, the Middle East and Asia **(map left)**. The desire to contain the threat of communism forced the USA into the role of the world's policeman, intervening militarily on numerous occasions. Many states saw the USA's role as a new imperialism, replacing the defunct colonial empires of Europe.

eorgia

The Soviet Union: modernization and crisis

In 1929 Stalin led the drive to modernize the Soviet Union through a programme of forced industrialization, collectivization, and a wide range of social and cultural reform, generating a "second revolution" and a wave of state-sponsored terror. The Stalin era culminated in the defeat of the Axis invasion and following his death in 1953, the USSR experienced years of both liberalization and repression, cultural flourishing and economic stagnation, which paved the way for Mikhail Gorbachev's attempted reform of the system in the mid-1980s.

A panorama of the Magnitogorsk iron and steel works in the 1930s (**above**), the largest in the Soviet Union. The new city became the centre of a large industrial complex in the Urals region set up under the Five-Year Plans.

I N THE LATE 1920s, the Stalinist state launched a "second revolution", designed to modernize the Soviet Union rapidly and complete the social transformation begun in 1917. This renewed modernization drive was necessary, Stalin believed, in order to reduce the size and economic preponderance of the peasantry – still around 80 per cent of the population – something that was essential to the achievement of communism, and to strengthen the country against the threat of international conflict. Although this involved a wide range of reforms, it is epitomized by a focus on industrialization and the collectivization of agriculture.

The First Five-Year Plan was launched in 1928, and was followed by two more, each one setting ambitious targets for the expansion of heavy industry in particular. The whole enterprise rested on the ability to extract a grain surplus from the countryside to feed the growing cities. In the second half of 1929, the state began a programme of collectivizing peasant landholdings and, although this policy was met with widespread resistance, by 1935 around 90 per cent of the land previously owned by peasants had been taken, often by force, and amalgamated into state-owned farms. The social cost was considerable: millions were deported, imprisoned, or executed for being kulaks ("rich" peasants) and millions more died as a result of famines created by draconian grain quotas, with Ukraine and Kazakhstan being the areas hardest hit. The economic consequences of these modernization policies were mixed but even allowing for Soviet hyperbole, industrial output expanded remarkably in the 1930s. The social goal was also achieved, with the urban population expanding by 30 million between 1926 and 1939, and the peasantry declining to around half the Soviet population.

The costs of modernization

These policies of modernization went hand-in-hand with the increased policing of society, as citizens were called on to be vigilant for spies and saboteurs intent on wrecking the Soviet project. This campaign against the "enemies of the people" was marked by a

I Although the term Gulag is synonymous with the Stalin era, thinking about the camp system as one entity hides a great deal of complexity. Several different types of camps existed across the Soviet Union – including the Special Settlements, where those labelled as kulaks were sent – although the purpose of each was the same: to correct perceived deviant behaviours or ideologies through labour. The number of camps also varied hugely across the period, as did the number of prisoners held within each camp, most of whom were "ordinary" criminals rather than those incarcerated for political reasons. It would also be a mistake to see the Gulag as being completely divorced from Soviet life: as the map shows (**below**), the vast majority were in the populated areas of European Russia rather than in the remote regions of Siberia.

I Distribution of prisoners in the Gulag, 1931–41

- 0
- 1–10,000
- 10,001–50,000
- 50,001–100,000
- 100,001–200,000
- 200,001–300,000

Major Soviet administrative divisions:
ASSR autonomous Soviet Socialist Republic
AO autonomous Oblast
SSR Soviet Socialist Republic
AD autonomous district (Okrug)

series of show trials, the execution of high-profile party members and the purging of the Red Army leadership. By 1937, this had turned into a terror which massively affected the lives of ordinary people: millions were arrested, imprisoned, and transported to the Gulag, with many dying either at the hands of the NKVD (People's Commissariat of Internal Affairs) or as a result of the inhumane conditions in the camps. The late 1930s also saw the deportation of millions of the country's smaller national groups – most notably the Volga Germans, Chechens, Ingush, and Crimean Tatars – away from the western border regions and into the interior of the country, a policy that would continue through the war years and also cost many lives. Although figures remain debatable, it is estimated that there were around 10 million excess deaths between 1927 and 1938.

Despite this turmoil, the Soviet Union was to face its greatest challenge following the Axis invasion of June 1941. The cost of the war for the USSR was tremendous: in addition to those wounded, disabled, and brutalized by the experience, around 27 million people died – more than half of whom were civilians – and 25 million people were left homeless. Tens of thousands of towns, villages and factories were destroyed and huge tracts of the most valuable agricultural land were left desolated by the scorched earth policy. Still, the country emerged from the war victorious and over the coming years consolidated its domination of Eastern Europe, rebuilt its economy, and developed its own atomic bomb.

Attempts at reform

The death of Stalin was followed by a period of liberalization, which saw the denunciation of the former leader by Nikita Khrushchev in 1956 and the attempted de-Stalinization of society. In 1954, control of Crimea was transferred from the Russian Federation to the Ukrainian SSR to commemorate the 300th anniversary of Russian-Ukrainian "reunification" The Khrushchev years also witnessed massive industrial and agricultural growth, with particular attention being given to housing construction and the development of science and technology, leading to a hugely successful space programme. Difficulties in foreign policy and the slowing of the economy were among the key issues that led to Khrushchev's resignation in 1964.

After this period of reform, the regime of Leonid Brezhnev looked to restore stability and order to the political system, but as a result these years have been labelled an "age of stagnation". Yet the era was one of contradiction: economic decline went hand-in-hand with prosperity, détente was mixed with military aggression, and repression was paralleled by a growing dissident and human rights movement. By the early 1980s, though, it was clear that restoration had failed; the country was in economic decline and the party leadership had lost its dynamism, now being dominated by old men who had been in positions of power unchecked for years. Reform had to be introduced in an attempt to save the Soviet system and this came in the form of Mikhail Gorbachev's *Perestroika* (see p. 356).

3 Distribution of Soviet population, 1929–59

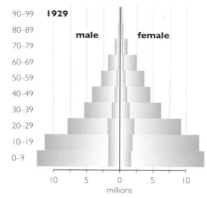

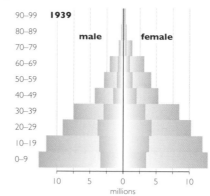

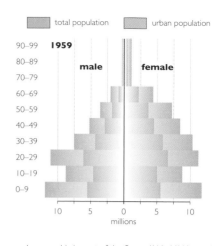

total population urban population

2 One of the consequences of the Soviet Union's massive industrialization was a huge expansion of pre-existing cities and the emergence of new ones, such as the steel-town of Magnitogorsk, which grew from just 25 inhabitants in 1929 to 250,000 by 1932 **(map below)**. Such an enormous influx of people naturally put pressure on both infrastructure and resources: housing could not be built quickly enough and many new workers found themselves living in poorly constructed dormitories, often sharing a bed with other workers on different shift patterns. Levels of crime, disease, drunkenness and violence were high; standards of living

and the availability of food was low. In 1932, the average living space for a Soviet citizen was just 4.6m² (49.5 ft²) The growth of the urban population put increasing pressure on the countryside to hand over more grain, a policy which ultimately led to famine in 1933.

3 The population pyramids (above) have been constructed using data collected in the Soviet censuses of 1926, 1939 and 1959. These diagrams clearly chart the huge expansion of the urban population during this 30-year period, along with the subsequent decline of the peasant class. The 1959 pyramid illustrates the

demographic impact of the Second World War on the Soviet Union. It shows the severe loss of men in the 40–70 age range – those who would have been aged between 20 and 50 at the outbreak of war – with the males making up almost 10 per cent less of the total population than they did in 1939. Of the estimated 27 million deaths caused by the war, around 20 million of these were men. The small number of children born in the war years is also reflected: birth rates fell from 34.6 per 1,000 people in 1940 to 26.0 in 1946 and it is estimated that around 11.5 million fewer Soviet children were born as a result of the war.

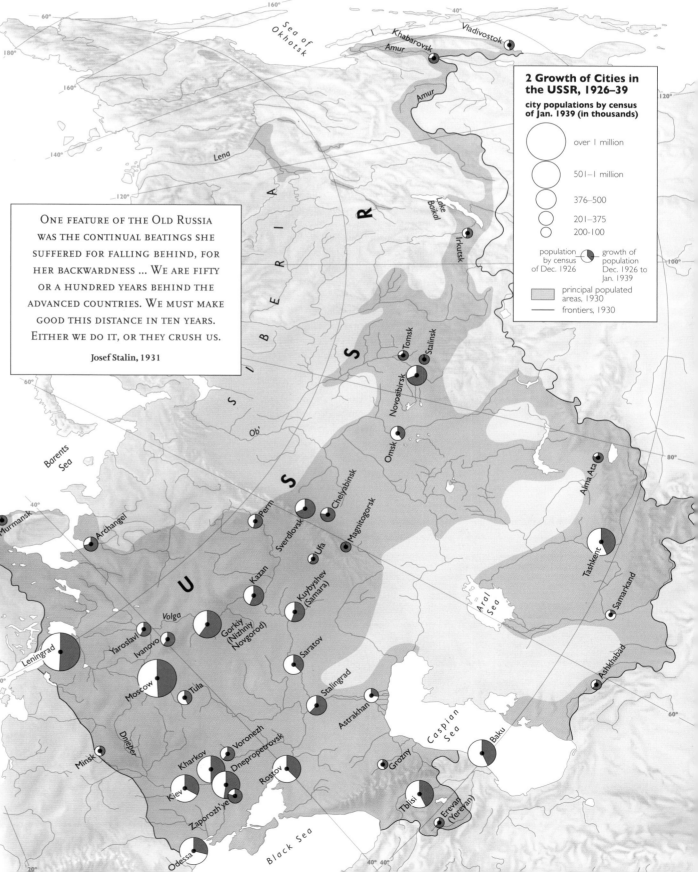

2 Growth of Cities in the USSR, 1926–39

city populations by census of Jan. 1939 (in thousands)

- over 1 million
- 501–1 million
- 376–500
- 201–375
- 200–100

population by census of Dec. 1926 / growth of population Dec. 1926 to Jan. 1939

principal populated areas, 1930

frontiers, 1930

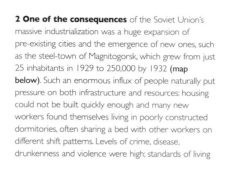

ONE FEATURE OF THE OLD RUSSIA WAS THE CONTINUAL BEATINGS SHE SUFFERED FOR FALLING BEHIND, FOR HER BACKWARDNESS ... WE ARE FIFTY OR A HUNDRED YEARS BEHIND THE ADVANCED COUNTRIES. WE MUST MAKE GOOD THIS DISTANCE IN TEN YEARS. EITHER WE DO IT, OR THEY CRUSH US.

Josef Stalin, 1931

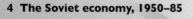

4 The Soviet economy, 1950–85

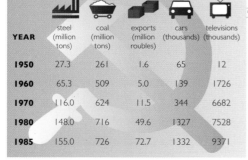

YEAR	steel (million tons)	coal (million tons)	exports (million roubles)	cars (thousands)	televisions (thousands)
1950	27.3	261	1.6	65	12
1960	65.3	509	5.0	139	1726
1970	116.0	624	11.5	344	6682
1980	148.0	716	49.6	1327	7528
1985	155.0	726	72.7	1332	9371

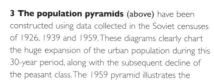

Europe

With the oil crisis of 1973, the post-war boom was replaced by more unstable growth and high inflation. While Western Europe became more united through the EU, the Soviet bloc collapsed. Renewed economic growth after 2000 brought an enlarged union, linking East and West.

1973 Oil crisis

1974 Salazar dies; democracy restored to Portugal

1975 Franco dies; democracy restored to Spain

1980–1 Solidarity campaign begins in Poland

1985 Gorbachev becomes Soviet leader; EEC agrees to create single market

1989 Communist bloc in eastern Europe disintegrates

1990 Germany reunified

1991 Maastricht Treaty signed

1992–5 Civil war in former Yugoslavia

1995 European Union formed

1999 Single European currency launched

1999 Kosovo crisis

2001 Nice Treaty signed

2009–12 Widespread protests against austerity measures

2010 Polish President Lech Kaczynski killed in air disaster

2013 EU expands to 28 members

2014 Scotland votes against independence from the UK

IN 1973 THE OIL-PRODUCING states almost trebled the price of oil in a year, triggering worldwide price inflation. In Europe, the crisis coincided with a general slowdown in productivity and profit growth and mounting unemployment. The 1970s saw the onset of "stagflation" – low rates of growth and soaring inflation. Unemployment, which had been almost eradicated in the 1960s, rose sharply, producing widespread labour unrest. Oil prices in the USSR affected the Soviet bloc as well. Economic performance stagnated behind the Iron Curtain, and in some cases actually declined.

Economic integration

Across much of Western Europe, the crisis was confronted by continuing the trend to greater economic integration. By the late 1960s, the original six members of the EEC (European Economic Community) had established themselves as the economic vanguard of the continent. Fearful that they were being left behind by their more dynamic neighbours, in 1973 Britain, Ireland and Denmark joined them. They were followed in 1981 by Greece, in 1986 by Spain and Portugal and in 1995 by Austria, Finland and Sweden.

Underpinning the EEC (renamed the EU, European Union, in 1995) was the belief, first proposed in the 1950s (see p. 303), that integrating the nations of Western Europe was the only effective means of guaranteeing continued economic success. The massive economic bloc thereby created would allow Europe to compete effectively with the world's other leading economies, the USA and Japan. Such integration should in time evolve into full political union, with the aim of creating a single state. In 1985, the EEC agreed to create a single market and free-trade zone. The subsequent Maastricht Treaty of 1991 also committed what became known in

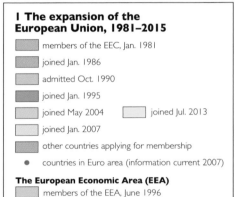

1 The expansion of the European Union, 1981–2015

- members of the EEC, Jan. 1981
- joined Jan. 1986
- admitted Oct. 1990
- joined Jan. 1995
- joined May 2004 / joined Jul. 2013
- joined Jan. 2007
- other countries applying for membership
- countries in Euro area (information current 2007)

The European Economic Area (EEA)
- members of the EEA, June 1996

1995 as the European Union to a single currency. The Euro was introduced into most of the EU in 2002, though Britain declined to join at that time. The EU drew up proposals for a European Constitution in 2003, but no firm agreement resulted. In the ten years following, a further thirteen states joined the EU. In 2007 a treaty was agreed at

1 The EC in 1973 began a long-term programme of expansion **(map above)**. By 1995 it embraced most of western, southern and central Europe and, with reservations on the part of some member states, had agreed to create a single currency and to admit the former communist states of eastern Europe.

3 The rapid expansion in size of the European Union has raised problems about how to allocate voting weights to the new members that reflect fairly on their population size and economic contribution. In 2015, a new system was adopted to replace the existing weighting, based on population size **(chart below)**. This favours the four largest states at the expense of the smallest.

4 Natural gas is one of Europe's major energy sources and over one-quarter of the supply comes from the major gasfields in Russia **(map below)**. In recent years, control of gas pipelines and energy companies has become a major concern, particularly as Russia has the option of restraining supply, as it did with Ukraine in 2007 and 2009 for non-payment. Russia is developing two major new pipelines that avoid Ukraine, the North Stream and South Stream. Gas supply threatens to become a major issue for Europe and an important element in the EU's relationship with Russia.

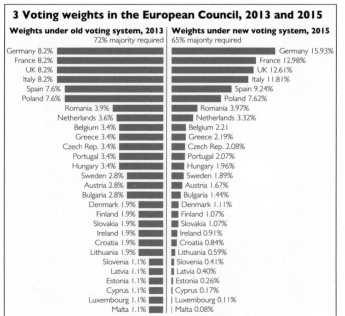

3 Voting weights in the European Council, 2013 and 2015

Weights under old voting system, 2013 (72% majority required)	Weights under new voting system, 2015 (65% majority required)
Germany 8.2%	Germany 15.93%
France 8.2%	France 12.98%
UK 8.2%	UK 12.61%
Italy 8.2%	Italy 11.81%
Spain 7.6%	Spain 9.24%
Poland 7.6%	Poland 7.62%
Romania 3.9%	Romania 3.97%
Netherlands 3.6%	Netherlands 3.32%
Belgium 3.4%	Belgium 2.21
Greece 3.4%	Greece 2.19%
Czech Rep. 3.4%	Czech Rep. 2.08%
Portugal 3.4%	Portugal 2.07%
Hungary 3.4%	Hungary 1.96%
Sweden 2.8%	Sweden 1.89%
Austria 2.8%	Austria 1.67%
Bulgaria 2.8%	Bulgaria 1.44%
Denmark 1.9%	Denmark 1.11%
Finland 1.9%	Finland 1.07%
Slovakia 1.9%	Slovakia 1.07%
Ireland 1.9%	Ireland 0.91%
Croatia 1.9%	Croatia 0.84%
Lithuania 1.9%	Lithuania 0.59%
Slovenia 1.1%	Slovenia 0.41%
Latvia 1.1%	Latvia 0.40%
Estonia 1.1%	Estonia 0.26%
Cyprus 1.1%	Cyprus 0.17%
Luxembourg 1.1%	Luxembourg 0.11%
Malta 1.1%	Malta 0.08%

4 Major European gas pipelines
- → pipeline
- --→ pipeline under construction
- ···→ proposed pipeline
- onshore gas field
- offshore gas field

Lisbon to strengthen economic and political ties and this became law in 2009 at exactly the time when the world financial crisis was putting severe strain on the Eurozone countries.

The coming of democracy

The combined effects of the economic slowdown after 1973 and the realization that by clinging to their pre-war authoritarian governments they were increasingly being pushed to the margins of Europe were sufficient to see the reintroduction of democracy to Portugal (1974) and Spain (1975). Greece also embraced democracy in 1974.

But these changes paled in comparison with events in Eastern Europe in the late 1980s. These involved nothing less than the disintegration of the Soviet Union and the fall of communism in every one of its satellite states as well as in Yugoslavia and Albania.

IN 1989 WE EXPERIENCED UPHEAVALS ON OUR CONTINENT WHICH HAVE BEEN UNPARALLELED IN PEACETIME SINCE 1848, WHICH WAS ALSO A YEAR OF REVOLUTIONS DRIVEN BY A DESIRE FOR POLITICAL LIBERTY AND NATIONAL SELF-EXPRESSION. FOR THE MOST PART THE REVOLUTIONS OF 1848 ENDED IN VIOLENCE AND DISAPPOINTMENT. IN 1989, AS THIS ASTONISHING PACE OF CHANGE CONTINUES, WE HAVE BEGUN TO HOPE THAT IT MIGHT PROVE LASTING. THERE MAY BE HALTS AND REVERSES, BUT IT WOULD BE HARD NOW TO RECREATE THE IRON CURTAIN.

Douglas Hurd, British Foreign Secretary, November 1989

As remarkable as the collapse of this apparently permanent system was the creation in its wake of no less than 15 new countries. The reasons for this transformation were as much economic as political. Throughout the 1970s and 1980s, the economies of the communist bloc had declined to the point where the region was effectively bankrupt. Unable to guarantee the survival of its client states, the Soviet Union under President Gorbachev abandoned them. By 1991 free elections had been held in every country of the region, including the Soviet Union, and the two Germanys had been reunited. Except for a short surge of violence in Romania, the transformation had been relatively peaceful.

The revival of nationalism

The euphoria which greeted the end of communism was followed swiftly by a fresh set of economic problems as the new regimes struggled to come to terms with democracy and economic liberalization. In the atmosphere of crisis old ethnic or religious conflicts revived. Slovakia won its independence from the Czechs in 1993. In 1991 Moldova declared independence and a brief civil war followed between the differing ethnic groups making up the new state.

But the most bloody and prolonged struggle took place in Yugoslavia, which in 1991 disintegrated under pressure from the long-suppressed rivalries of its ethnic groups, despite Serbian resistance. Between 1991 and 1995 Serbia fought first against Slovenian, then Croatian and finally Bosnian independence, declared in 1992 by its Muslim majority. Only the intervention of NATO in 1995 prevented further bloodshed in what had become the most barbarous European conflict since the Second World War. In 1998 civil war broke out in Serbia itself when ethnic Albanian separatists in Kosovo fought for independence.

A student demonstration outside the Greek parliament on 6 March 2013 protesting against government plans for education **(above)**. The financial crisis in Greece led to widespread anti-austerity campaigns and violent protests, and the election in 2015 of a far-left government under Alexis Tsipras.

Nationalist conflict continued in Western Europe, too. Basque separatism in Spain and Irish nationalism in Ulster were both sustained by terrorism from the 1970s. In Ireland political agreement for closer cooperation between nationalists and Unionists was secured in 1998. Since the millennium the greatest problem facing Europe has been the increased number of political and economic refugees. Fear of "asylum seekers" fuelled radical right-wing movements in Europe and heightened racial tension. In France this exploded in 2006 in major urban riots among frustrated and impoverished immigrant communities. The issue of internal European migration has heightened calls for reform of the EU structure and encouraged the emergence of political movements committed to complete withdrawal.

2 Between 1989 and 1991 communist eastern Europe was transformed **(map below)** from a Soviet-dominated bloc of authoritarian dictatorships to a patchwork of new regimes and states, most of them multi-party democracies. Growing popular dissatisfaction with the absence of civil rights and political freedom coupled with the region's poor economic performance produced widespread popular protest in 1989. Beginning in Hungary and Poland, the protests spread to East Germany. The fall of the East German government, precipitated by a mass emigration through Hungary, was a signal, like the Paris revolution in 1848, for the rest of eastern Europe to follow suit. By 1990, 50 years of Soviet domination of eastern Europe had ended.

2 The collapse of communism, 1985–91

- ─── Soviet-dominated Eastern Europe to 1989
- ─── Soviet Union to 1991
- ─── Yugoslavia to 1991
- ☐ united with the Federal Republic of Germany, 1990
- ☐ achieved independence, 1991
- ▨ other former communist states, 1991
- ▨ de facto independent states, late 1991, on former territory of the Soviet Union, internationally unrecognized
- ▨ overrun by Yugoslav army, July–Dec. 1991
- ─── borders, 1991

Mar. 1990: Congress of Estonia formed, declares Soviet rule illegal
Mar. 1991: referendum endorses independence
Aug. 1991: independence declared
Sep. 1991: independence recognized by USSR

Mar. 1985: Mikhail Gorbachev becomes leader of Communist Party; initiates Perestroika and Glasnost, loosens Soviet control of satellite states
June 1991: Boris Yeltsin elected president of Russian Federation
Aug. 1991: hard-line Communist coup against Gorbachev fails
Nov. 1991: Communist Party declared illegal
Dec. 1991: USSR dissolved

1989: mass anti-Communist demonstrations
Mar. 1991: referendum endorses independence
Aug. 1991: independence declared
Sep. 1991: independence recognized by USSR

1989: mass anti-Communist demonstrations
Mar. 1991: independence declared
Apr.–June 1990: economic embargo imposed by USSR
Sep. 1991: independence recognized by USSR

from 1985: Solidarity leads opposition to communism
June 1989: partially free elections
Sep. 1989: Solidarity-led government takes office
Jan. 1990: Communist Party dissolved
Oct. 1991: free elections

Sep. 1989: mass exodus of political refugees reach the West via Hungary; Communist leadership in crisis
Oct.–Nov. 1989: widespread demonstrations against leadership
9 Nov. 1989: Berlin Wall breached
Mar. 1990: free elections
July 1990: currency union with West Germany
Oct. 1990: reunited with West Germany

June 1989: Popular Front founded
Aug. 1991: independence declared
Dec. 1991: founder member of Commonwealth of Independent States

from 1988: anti-government demonstrations
Nov. 1989: mass demonstrations end Communist rule
Apr. 1990: new constitution adopted; becomes a federation
June 1990: free elections

1989: opposition mass-movements emerge
Aug. 1991: independence declared
Dec. 1991: referendum endorses independence; founder member of Commonwealth of Independent States

from 1987: Communist regime relaxes control
Sep. 1989: allows East Germans to travel to the West
Oct. 1990: Communist rule ends peacefully
Mar.–Apr. 1990: free elections

June 1989: Popular Front wins 75% of votes in election
Aug. 1991: independence declared

Dec. 1989: economic war between Belgrade government and Slovenia
Apr. 1990: free elections
June 1991: independence declared; Yugoslav army attempts to regain control of Slovenia
July 1991: Brioni Agreement ends fighting in Slovenia; Yugoslav army withdraws

Apr.–May 1990: free elections
Dec. 1990: Serb-inhabited areas declare independence
June 1991: independence declared; fighting in Slovenia spreads to Croatia as Serbs attempt to extend territory in Croatia and Bosnia

Dec. 1989: mass demonstrations lead to armed uprisings and overthrow of Ceausescu regime
June 1991: free elections
Nov. 1991: new constitution adopted

Nov. 1989: President Zhivkov removed from office
June 1990: free elections
July 1991: fresh elections following adoption of new constitution

1987: mass strikes against wage freeze and falling living standards; growing Serb militancy against minorities
July 1990: provincial autonomies abolished
1990–1: increasing tension between Belgrade government and Slovenia and Croatia

Jan.–May 1990: democratic reforms initiated by leadership
Mar. 1991: free elections

Jan. 1990: state of emergency declared; Soviet troops intervene
Oct. 1991: independence declared

Nov. 1991: independence declared

Nov. 1988: mass demonstrations against Russification
Mar. 1991: referendum endorses independence
Apr. 1991: independence declared

Sep. 1989: economic embargo imposed by Azerbaijan
Sep. 1991: referendum endorses independence; independence declared

Sep. 1991: independence declared

Labels on map: FINLAND, SWEDEN, Baltic Sea, DENMARK, ESTONIA, Tallinn, LATVIA, Riga, LITHUANIA, Vilnius, RUSSIAN FED., Moscow, TATARSTAN, UNITED KINGDOM, North Sea, NETHERLANDS, BELGIUM, GERMANY, Berlin, Bonn, POLAND, Warsaw, BELARUS, Minsk, RUSSIAN FEDERATION, Prague, CZECHOSLOVAKIA, Bratislava, Kiev, UKRAINE, SWITZ., AUSTRIA, Budapest, HUNGARY, SLOVENIA, Zagreb, CROATIA, MOLDOVA, TRANSNISTRIA, GAGAUZIA, FRANCE, ITALY, Sardinia, ROMANIA, Belgrade, Bucharest, Sarajevo, YUGOSLAVIA, KOSOVO, BULGARIA, Sofia, Black Sea, CHECHNYA, Grozny, GEORGIA, Mediterranean Sea, Tirana, Skopje, ALBANIA, Sicily, ARMENIA, AZERBAIJAN, NAGORNO-KARABAKH

The United States: crisis and response

The United States emerged from the Second World War as the largest economic and military power in the world. Yet the country remained divided along economic, racial, ethnic and political lines and began to experience serious conflict and change from the 1950s onwards which polarized society and led into the "culture wars" of the 1990s.

DESPITE THE REMARKABLE economic growth of the post-war years, poverty continued to exist in the United States. In the early 1960s, 22 per cent of the population in America lived below the poverty line. African-Americans were three times more likely to live in poverty than white people. Many poor Black people were trapped in inner-city areas while the white middle-class continued its move to the suburbs.

The question of poverty was closely linked with the issue of civil rights, as the 1963 March on Washington for Jobs and Freedom showed. President John F. Kennedy began to devise a series of measure to improve the situation and prospects of the poor and to revitalize decaying cities. Lyndon B. Johnson continued this policy and outlined his vision of "The Great Society" with "an end to poverty and racial injustice". The urgency of the problem was further underlined by a series of race riots in Black ghettos, starting with Watts, Los Angeles, in 1965. Public spending on transfer programmes to the poor increased significantly from the early 1960s to the second half of the 1970s.

Growing militancy and protest

Johnson's decision to escalate the war in Vietnam, however, limited his ability to fund the "War on Poverty" at home. Disappointed with slow pace of reform at home, outraged by the often violent resistance against the civil rights movement in the South and inspired by the colonial liberation movements in Africa and Asia, a growing number of African-Americans adopted the philosophy of Black Power and Black Nationalism in the mid-1960s. Their militancy and separatism led to a decline of white support for the civil rights movement, but the latter encouraged other marginalized groups to campaign more forcefully for their rights. Native Americans, Hispanic Americans, feminists, gays and lesbians and others began publicly to express their grievances and demand redress.

The civil rights movement also greatly influenced the "New Left" which emerged with the funding of the Students for a Democratic Society (SDS) in 1960. The students of the New Left questioned the values, politics and organization of American society and were part of a new youth or counter-culture which openly expressed its rejection of traditional

THIS IS OUR BASIC CONCLUSION: OUR NATION IS MOVING TOWARDS TWO SOCIETIES, ONE WHITE, ONE BLACK – SEPARATED AND UNEQUAL.

National Advisory Commission on Civil Disorders, 1968

THERE IS A RELIGIOUS WAR GOING ON IN THIS COUNTRY. IT IS A CULTURAL WAR, AS CRITICAL TO THE KIND OF NATION WE SHALL BE AS THE COLD WAR ITSELF. FOR THIS WAR IS FOR THE SOUL OF AMERICA.

Patrick Buchanan at the Republican National Convention in Houston, Texas, 1992

5 The increase in prison population, 1950–2009

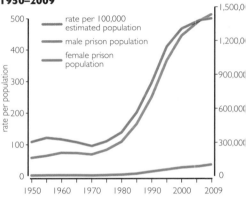

- rate per 100,000 estimated population
- male prison population
- female prison population

5 The desire for order and stability led to a "tough on crime" policy in the 1980s and a sharp rise in the prison population. Non-white males are sentenced to jail at a disproportionate rate and therefore especially affected: In 2008, African-Americans and Hispanics comprised 58 per cent of all prisoners, even though both groups only make up approximately one quarter of the US population.

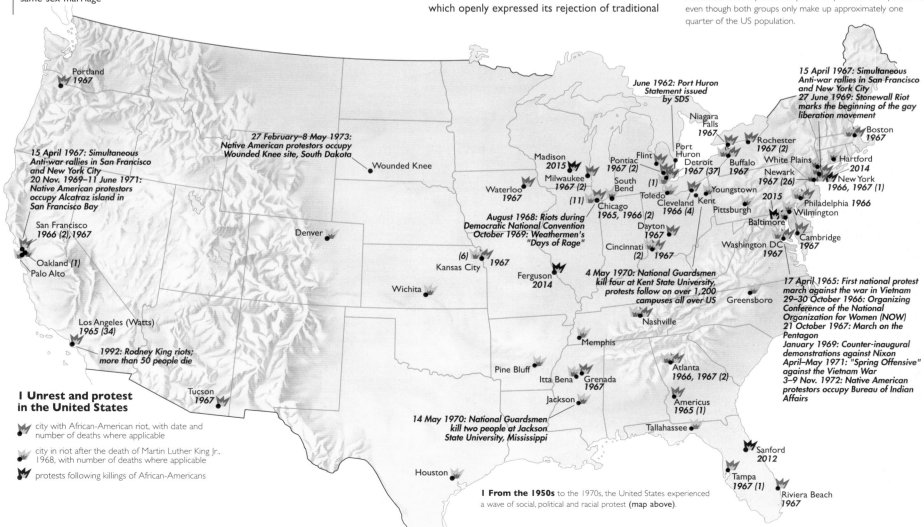

I Unrest and protest in the United States

- city with African-American riot, with date and number of deaths where applicable
- city in riot after the death of Martin Luther King Jr., 1968, with number of deaths where applicable
- protests following killings of African-Americans

I From the 1950s to the 1970s, the United States experienced a wave of social, political and racial protest (**map above**).

morals and conventions through the use of drugs and other means. The New Left was also at the heart of the growing public protest against the war in Vietnam which increasingly polarized American society in the second half of the 1960s. University campuses became places of conflict, starting with the Free Speech Movement in Berkeley in 1964.

The conservative reaction

The change and turmoil of the 1960s and 70s created a conservative backlash. Many Americans were critical of the expensive Great Society programmes, and affirmative action measures designed to actively promote racial equality, such as minority quotas or the forced "busing" of children to integrate schools, also triggered resentment. "Big government" was denounced as contrary to American values and as a cause of the nation's social and economic problems rather than the solution to it. Many Americans also disapproved of the protest against the war in Vietnam as unpatriotic and disorderly and were concerned by the rise in political and social violence in American cities.

The conservative resurgence had its strongholds in the expanding "Sunbelt" and the suburban communities. Evangelical Christians formed an important part of the "New Right" which began to organize itself after the defeat of Barry Goldwater in the 1964 presidential election and experienced a rapid growth during the 1970s.

President Richard Nixon had already begun to dismantle some social programmes during the 1970s, but the New Right found its most charismatic leader in Ronald Reagan and a popular cause in attacking high taxes. The Reagan administration initiated the restructuring of the welfare state and promoted the de-regulation of the economy.

The conservative resurgence also led to an attempt to reverse many of the cultural and social changes of the 1960s and 70s. The resulting "culture wars" raged on a number of high-profile battlegrounds, such as the campaign to reverse or undermine the 1973 *Roe v. Wade* decision of the U.S. Supreme Court which legalized abortions in the early stages of pregnancy. A constitutional amendment to ban gender discrimination

The Promise Keepers *"Stand in the Gap: A Sacred Assembly of Men"*. On 4 October 1997, the all-male Christian organization held a day-long revival service at the Mall in Washington DC, (below), which was attended by hundreds of thousands of participants.

was approved by Congress in 1972 but failed to get ratified by enough states. Equal rights for gays and lesbians was another controversial issue, as were school prayers or the question of America's role in the world. The conservative attack on "revisionist" historians led, among other things, to the cancellation of the Enola Gay exhibition in the National Air and Space Museum in 1995. Fierce resistance against gun control, the denial of man-made climate change, the emergence of the "Tea Party" movement, an umbrella for dogmatic anti-government and fiscally ultra-conservative grass root groups in 2009, or the ongoing conservative opposition against mandatory health insurance show that the long-standing conflict over "the soul of America" continues.

Police Violence

The well-documented killing of a number of unarmed African-Americans by law enforcement officers or armed civilians, and the frequent failure to persecute the perpetrators, has also re-ignited the debate about race in recent years. Despite the election of a black President, African-Americans still have a high chance of becoming victims of police violence. In 2014, they were nearly three times more likely to be killed by police than white Americans, while 40 per cent of all unarmed people killed by police in that year were African-American.

2 Despite the efforts to eradicate poverty in the 1960s, the problem persisted and continued to affect minority groups disproportionately (maps above right). In 1960, poverty was concentrated in the South and Southwest, Native American lands and inner cities. Forty years later, it had spread more evenly throughout the country, reflecting in part the changed demographic distribution of the Black and Hispanic population.

3 Work is no protection against poverty (map right). Over 30 per cent of families in more than 30 states were working but poor in 2000.

4 The various conflicts of the 1960s and 70s led to a growth of Christian fundamentalism in the United States. (map below). This trend is exemplified in the growth and spread of the Southern Baptist Convention which is now the largest Protestant denomination in the United States with over 16 million members and 45,000 churches.

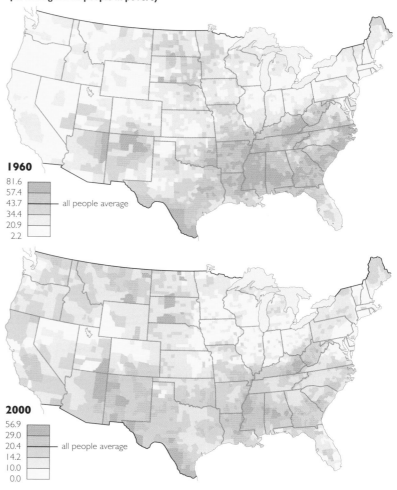

2 Poverty in America, 1960/2000
percentage of all people in poverty

1960

| 81.6 |
| 57.4 |
| 43.7 |
| 34.4 | all people average |
| 20.9 |
| 2.2 |

2000

| 56.9 |
| 29.0 |
| 20.4 | all people average |
| 14.2 |
| 10.0 |
| 0.0 |

3 Working poor families, 2000

percentage of families who are working but poor

| 61.0 |
| 54.2 |
| 49.4 |
| 46.3 |
| 27.2 |
| 23.9 |

4 Southern Baptist Convention, 1990

percentage of total population

| 34.0 |
| 14.0 |
| 3.0 |
| 1.5 |
| 0.4 |
| 0.1 |

Europe's civil wars

The collapse of communism in Russia and Eastern Europe in 1989–90 provoked serious conflict between national minorities which now sought independence or ethnic cleansing. In Armenia, Azerbaijan and Moldova there were brief ethnic wars, but in Chechnya and in Yugoslavia there developed major conflicts which resulted in wide destruction and a high death toll. Yugoslavia fragmented into five separate states. Chechnya was forced to stay within the Russian Federation and remains a focus of terrorist violence.

THE LONG PERIOD of peace in Europe after 1945, a product of the Cold War divisions and Soviet domination of the eastern bloc, came to an end with the collapse of the Soviet system and the eclipse of European communism. In the former Soviet Union there were violent clashes in Moldova which led to the establishment of an autonomous region in Transnistria. The new states established in the Caucasus also provoked ethnic violence in Georgia, Armenia and Azerbaijan. The Armenian enclave of Nagorno-Karabakh in Azerbaijan rejected Azeri rule and war broke out between the two new states which ended in a cease-fire in 1994 and virtual autonomy for the contested area.

War over Chechnya

When the Russian province of Chechnya, whose population had returned from deportation in the 1960s, declared its right to become an independent state in 1991, the Russian army intervened. Between 1994 and 1996 a bitter civil war was waged, with heavy losses on both sides. The Chechen capital Grozny was destroyed. A cease-fire in 1996 granted virtual autonomy, but in 1999 Russia again sent in troops to occupy the whole region which had descended into rival warlord provinces and was host to a rising tide of Islamic fundamentalism. The War officially ended in 2001, but Chechen guerrillas loyal to the idea of an independent state continued to fight against Russian occupation and spread a terror campaign into the Russian heartland, carrying out bomb attacks on the Moscow metro and instigating a siege at a theatre in the capital which left around 130 of the 850 hostages dead. Most infamously, Chechen separatists were behind the siege at a school in Beslan, North Ossetia, in September 2004 in which more than 1,000 people were held hostage and more than 300 people were killed. It was this attack that prompted President Putin

to institute new security measures, to give the central government more control over the region, and also to carry out pre-emptive strikes against some of the separatists' more high-profile leaders.

Following a referendum, a new constitution was introduced in 2003, which brought the troubled region back into the Russian Federation but gave it limited powers of autonomy. The republic is now led by Ramzan Kadyrov, a pro-Russian former rebel and son of the previous president.

While the situation in Chechnya has remained relatively stable in recent years, the neighbouring republic of Dagestan has witnessed an upsurge of violence since 2010, leading some to believe the region is on the verge of civil conflict. The most ethnically diverse republic in the Russian Federation, Dagestan has also suffered from high levels of poverty and corruption. It has come under the growing influence of Islamic extremism, culminating in frequent violent attacks against both security forces and civilians. Although Dagestani militants were blamed for the bombing of the Moscow metro in 2010 which killed 40 people, the rise of fundamentalism in Dagestan was brought to the world's attention by the attack at the Boston marathon in 2013.

The Chechen capital Grozny (above) became the scene of bitter fighting between Russian and Chechen forces in 1994–6. When war broke out again in 1999 Grozny was encircled in December by Russian forces, heavily shelled and finally taken in February 2000. Chechen forces fled south to the mountains where they continued to wage an intermittent guerrilla war against Russian forces.

1989 Milosevic elected Serbian president

1990 Slovenia declares independence

1991 Croatia and Macedonia break away from Yugoslavia

1991 Chechnya declares independence from Russian Federation

1992 Serbia declares new Yugoslavia

1992–5 Civil war in Bosnia

1995 Bosnian state created by Dayton Agreement

1994–6 First civil war in Chechnya

1999 Civil war in Kosovo

1999–2000 Second Chechen War

2003 New constitution for Chechnya

2008 Russo-Georgian War

I The break-up of the Soviet Union in 1991 led to widespread ethnic and political violence in the Caucasus. In addition to Russia's two wars against separatists in Chechnya, Armenia and Azerbaijan clashed over the Christian Armenian enclave of Nagorno-Karabakh, and Georgia fought to keep both South Ossetia and Abkhazia within its borders (map left). All three of these wars are examples of "frozen conflicts", as no peace treaty has been signed and no long-term resolution to the territorial disputes has been found, meaning that the region remains prone to instability and violence.

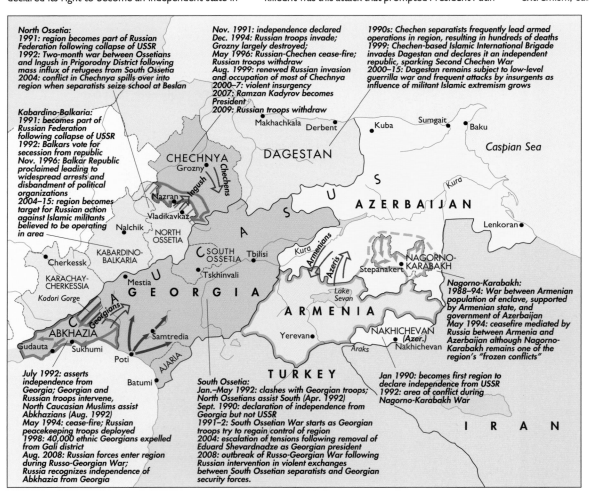

North Ossetia:
1991: region becomes part of Russian Federation following collapse of USSR
1992: Two-month war between Ossetians and Ingush in Prigorodny District following mass influx of refugees from South Ossetia
2004: conflict in Chechnya spills over into region when separatists seize school at Beslan

Kabardino-Balkaria:
1991: becomes part of Russian Federation following collapse of USSR
1992: Balkars vote for secession from republic
Nov. 1996: Balkar Republic proclaimed leading to widespread arrests and disbandment of political organizations
2004–15: region becomes target for Russian action against Islamic militants believed to be operating in area

Nov. 1991: independence declared
Dec. 1994: Russian troops invade; Grozny largely destroyed;
May 1996: Russian-Chechen cease-fire; Russian troops withdraw
Aug. 1999: renewed Russian invasion and occupation of most of Chechnya
2000–7: violent insurgency
2007: Ramzan Kadyrov becomes President
2009: Russian troops withdraw

1990s: Chechen separatists frequently lead armed operations in region, resulting in hundreds of deaths
1999: Chechen-based Islamic International Brigade invades Dagestan and declares it an independent republic, sparking Second Chechen War
2000–15: Dagestan remains subject to low-level guerrilla war and frequent attacks by insurgents as influence of militant Islamic extremism grows

Nagorno-Karabakh:
1988–94: War between Armenian population of enclave, supported by Armenian state, and government of Azerbaijan
May 1994: ceasefire mediated by Russia between Armenia and Azerbaijan although Nagorno-Karabakh remains one of the region's "frozen conflicts"

Jan 1990: becomes first region to declare independence from USSR
1992: area of conflict during Nagorno-Karabakh War

July 1992: asserts independence from Georgia; Georgian and Russian troops intervene, North Caucasian Muslims assist Abkhazians (Aug. 1992)
May 1994: cease-fire; Russian peacekeeping troops deployed
1998: 40,000 ethnic Georgians expelled from Gali district
Aug. 2008: Russian forces enter region during Russo-Georgian War; Russia recognizes independence of Abkhazia from Georgia

South Ossetia:
Jan.–May 1992: clashes with Georgian troops; North Ossetians assist South (Apr. 1992)
Sept. 1990: declaration of independence from Georgia but not USSR
1991–2: South Ossetian War starts as Georgian troops try to regain control of region
2004: escalation of tensions following removal of Eduard Shevardnadze as Georgian president
2008: outbreak of Russo-Georgian War following Russian intervention in violent exchanges between South Ossetian separatists and Georgian security forces.

I The Caucasus, 1988–2015

- notional extent of Georgia at independence
- advance of pro-Gamsa-khurdia forces, Oct. 1993
- Georgian advance into Abkhazia, Aug. 1992
- areas of Georgia under Abkhazian control, Oct. 1993
- evacuated by Georgia, Oct. 1994
- notional extent of Azerbaijan at independence
- Armenia at independence
- limit of Armenian control, May 1992
- Azerbaijani advance into Karabakh, Oct. 1993
- secured by Armenia and Karabakh by Nov. 1993
- Chechnya-Ingushetia at independence
- seceded from Chechnya, joined Russian Fed. Mar. 1992
- claimed by Ingushetia, 1992
- mass movements of refugees
- autonomous within Russian Federation

Map labels: Makhachkala, Derbent, Kuba, Sumgait, Baku, Caspian Sea, CHECHNYA, Grozny, Chechens, DAGESTAN, Nazran, Ingush, Vladikavkaz, AZERBAIJAN, Kura, Nalchik, NORTH OSSETIA, KABARDINO-BALKARIA, Cherkessk, SOUTH OSSETIA, Tbilisi, Armenians, Azeris, NAGORNO-KARABAKH, Stepanakert, Lenkoran, KARACHAY-CHERKESSIA, Mestia, Tskhinvali, Lake Sevan, GEORGIA, Kodori Gorge, ARMENIA, Yerevan, NAKHICHEVAN (Azer.), Nakhichevan, Araks, ABKHAZIA, Georgians, Samtredia, Gudauta, Sukhumi, Poti, AJARIA, Batumi, TURKEY, IRAN

The collapse of Yugoslavia

Although Yugoslavia was not formally a member of the Soviet bloc, the collapse of the Soviet Union hastened the collapse of Yugoslav communism. A weak economy, growing nationalist sentiment and the assertion of Serb predominance over the six federal republics that made up Yugoslavia provoked the collapse of the state in 1991. In December that year Croatia and Slovenia declared their independence. After a brief civil war Slovenia successfully seceded. Full-scale war broke out between Croatia and Serbia, which ended in 1992 with Croat independence. Serbia and Montenegro formed a new Yugoslav Federation of their own.

In between the two warring groups lay the provinces of Bosnia-Herzegovina, which were inhabited by a mixture of Croats, Christian Serbs and Muslim Bosnians. All but the Serbs wanted an independent Bosnian state, and this was formally recognized abroad in 1992. Both Croats and Serbs had ambitions to partition the region and add it to their territory. There followed a confused and savage civil war between the three groups, which left the Bosnian Serbs under Radovan Karadzic in control of 70 per cent of the region by 1993. The Bosnian Serb army surrounded the Bosnian capital of Sarajevo and laid it to siege for three years. International efforts to end the fighting proved abortive, but in 1995, as the Serbs seemed poised for victory, NATO forces compelled an end to hostilities and, under the Dayton Agreement, Bosnia was divided into three ethnically distinct republics in a federal Bosnian state. There existed thereafter a fragile truce.

In the southern Yugoslav province of Kosovo fighting broke out between Serbs and ethnic Albanians which escalated into a full civil war in 1998–9. Serb rejection of international pressure to grant autonomy to the province provoked a wave of NATO bombings between March and May 1999 which ended with Serbian agreement. Within a year the hardline Serbian president, Slobodan Milosevic, was voted out and sent for trial in 2001 to the International Criminal Court in The Hague on charges of genocide, where he died before the trial ended. In 2003 Serbia and Montenegro became independent states and in February 2008 Kosovo declared its independence, although Serbia has not yet accepted it.

2 The Chechen War, 1994–2003

- ····· Chechen-Ingush Autonomous Soviet Socialist Republic, 1936–44
- ──── Chechen-Ingush Autonomous Soviet Socialist Republic, 1957–91
- Ingushetia, seceded from Chechnya-Ingushetia, 1991
- Chechnya, independent after declining to join Russian Federation (created 1991)
- main lines of Russian attack on Chechnya, Dec. 1994
- approximate route of Chechen campaign to Budennovsk and return to Chechnya, June 1995
- attack by Muslim irregulars on Dagestan with aim of detaching it from Russia, August 1999
- under Chechnya's control at end of Nov. 1999 after Russian invasion in September despite Khasavyurt treaty
- main Russian attacks by the beginning of 2000
- approximate extent of area where Russian control remains contested by Chechnya's forces by Autumn 2003
- frontier of constituents of the Russian Federation

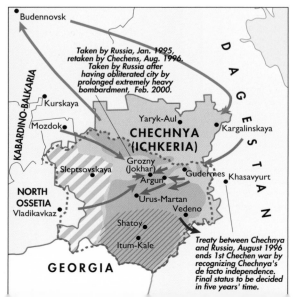

Taken by Russia, Jan. 1995, retaken by Chechens, Aug. 1996. Taken by Russia after having obliterated city by prolonged extremely heavy bombardment, Feb. 2000.

Treaty between Chechnya and Russia, August 1996 ends 1st Chechen war by recognizing Chechnya's de facto independence. Final status to be decided in five years' time.

3 The Yugoslav civil war, 1991–5

- → Croatian advances, Jan. 1993
- → Federation of Bosnia and Herzegovina advances, Oct.–Nov. 1994
- ⇢ Croatian and Federation of Bosnia and Herzegovina advances, spring 1995
- → Bosnian Serb advances, summer 1995
- → Croatian and Federation of Bosnia and Herzegovina advances, Aug.–Oct. 1995

- Croatia, June 1991
- overrun by the Yugoslav army and Croatian Serb forces by Dec. 1991
- Bosnia-Herzegovina, Mar. 1992
- secured by Yugoslav army and Bosnian Serb forces by Dec. 1992
- controlled by Bosnian Croat forces, Dec. 1992
- under Bosnian government control, Dec. 1992
- overwhelmingly or largely Serb, 1991. No significant Serb presence by the end of 1995
- overwhelmingly or largely Muslim, 1991. No significant Muslim presence by the end of 1995
- Autonomous Province of Western Bosnia, Sep. 1993–Aug. 1994, opposed to the government in Sarajevo
- remained under control of breakaway Serbian forces, Oct. 1995
- returned to Croatian control in Jan. 1998 under Erdut agreement of Nov. 1995
- **UN** UN-designated "safe areas"
- ──── UN routes

3 In 1991 Croatia and Slovenia both broke away from the central Yugoslav state, provoking a savage civil war between Croat and Serb, and then between Croats, Serbs and the Muslim population of Bosnia (**map left**). The war was ended only in 1995 following the intervention of NATO forces, and a separate Bosnian state established with distinct ethnic areas.

5 The siege of Sarajevo, 1992–5

- ──── frontline

5 The Bosnian capital of Sarajevo (map above) was subjected to a siege by the Serb army for three years from 1992 to 1995, when the Dayton Agreement in December 1995 finally ended the war. A 900m (2950ft) tunnel was built in 1992 under the airport to link the besieged city with the outside world. The population was subjected to regular shelling from Serb forces.

LET MILOSEVIC TAKE THE LARGER PART; HE CONTROLS IT ANYWAY. WE CAN DO WITH LESS THAN 50 PER CENT. WE'RE WILLING TO LEAVE THE MUSLIMS A SMALL AREA AROUND SARAJEVO. THEY MAY NOT LIKE IT, BUT A STABLE BALKANS IS POSSIBLE ONLY IF THERE'S A SMALL CHANGE IN BOSNIA'S BORDERS, NO MATTER WHAT THE MUSLIMS THINK. THERE'S NOTHING SACRED ABOUT THOSE BORDERS. BOSNIA ISN'T AN OLD STATE, LIKE CROATIA.

Franjo Tudman, 1992

4 The war in Kosovo

- ← flight of Kosovan Albanian refugees, Mar.–May 1999
- ✷ bombed by NATO forces, Mar.–June 1999
- → NATO bombing raid
- ✛ sites of religious significance to Serbs
- ──── NATO zone of occupation with nationality of Multi-national Brigade, 2003
- KLA strongholds
- ☠ major massacres

2 In December 1994

Russian armed forces occupied Chechnya to prevent its attempt to break away from the Russian Federation (**map left**). After two years in which much of the urban area was destroyed, an uneasy truce was reached, giving Chechnya wide autonomy. In 1999 Russia invaded again, anxious about the growth of militant Islam in the area. Although the new war lasted until 2000, insurgent violence has continued throughout the northern Caucasus ever since, as the region has increasingly come under the influence of radical Islam.

4 The Yugoslav province of Kosovo became in 1998 the centre of an ethnic conflict between Albanians and Serbs (**map right**). Albanian requests for Western aid resulted in an 11-week NATO air campaign against military and infrastructure targets in Serbia. Serb forces abandoned Kosovo in June 1999 and the province was occupied by NATO forces.

Warfare

Though there has been no major war since 1945 there have been smaller regional wars throughout the past half-century. Conventional weaponry has been transformed and armed forces reorganized to meet the reality of the small war. Many of the conflicts have been asymmetrical, a major state using armed power to enforce its political will. Other regional or civil wars have been fuelled by the worldwide sale of modern armaments from developed states which have tried at the same time to limit the violence their trade stimulated.

THE FIRST HALF of the 20th century saw the two largest and costliest wars in history, waged by the world's most militarily powerful and economically advanced states. The First and Second World Wars were total wars, absorbing huge resources and mobilizing manpower in tens of millions. By contrast the 60 years since 1945 experienced no major war between the developed states, largely because the nuclear and missile technologies that emerged after the Second World War made war between the major states too costly and terrifying to risk.

The nuclear standoff did not prevent hundreds of smaller conflicts. The typical wars after 1945 were civil wars, or wars of insurgency or national liberation, often not limited to defined state territories. Many of these smaller wars and civil wars were asymmetrical conflicts, the imbalance widening remarkably if a major state was involved, as with the French in Algeria and Vietnam, or the USA in Korea, Vietnam and the Middle East. Asymmetry as such did not guarantee victory to the stronger power. France was forced to withdraw from Algeria; the USA withdrew from Vietnam; and the Korean conflict ended with the peninsula permanently divided.

New ways of warfare

The nature of modern warfare produced two entirely contradictory developments. The developed states created the scientific and technical means to wage a sophisticated land, air and sea war. The three services became increasingly integrated, and the technology of modern radio, satellite and electronic communication, high-quality air power, rockets, chemical agents, laser guided weapons and, more recently, the extensive "electronic battlefield" to direct the massive and destructive firepower available, have all produced modern armed forces of exceptional striking power and flexibility, exemplified by the war against Iraq in 2003 and the new "drone" technology.

Yet most wars have involved forces with limited, simple and easily portable weaponry adaptable for use by poorly trained militia and proved ideal for the many guerrilla conflicts since 1945. The chief weapons for the irregular forces were the sub-machine gun, the mine,

CONFLICT REMAINS COMMONPLACE IN THE MODERN WORLD WITH LITTLE CLEAR DISTINCTION BETWEEN WAR AND PEACE. EVEN LOCALISED CONFLICTS MAY HAVE IMPLICATIONS FOR WORLD PEACE, STABILITY AND TRADE. THEREFORE MANY NATIONS NOT DIRECTLY ENGAGED IN CONFLICT ARE INVOLVED IN EFFORTS TO MONITOR, MANAGE AND RESOLVE ACTUAL OR POTENTIAL CONFLICTS. A FEATURE OF MODERN CONFLICT IS THE INCREASINGLY STARK ASYMMETRY BETWEEN THE OPPONENTS. THIS IS CHARACTERISED BY STATES WITH MODERN, POWERFUL, WELL-EQUIPPED FORCES SET AGAINST OPPONENTS WHO ARE LESS OR MUCH LESS WELL-EQUIPPED …

RAF Air Power Doctrine Manual, 2002

booby traps and primitive bombs, and hand-held rocket launchers. This arsenal was easily available worldwide. More sophisticated weaponry also spread to developing areas, usually to the local armies trying to maintain domestic control. This produced a further paradox. While the industrially developed states fed the growing appetite of the rest of the world for weapons of all kinds, they also promoted a more interventionist approach to conflict through the United Nations and the growth of a body of international law and the institutions to enforce it.

Peacekeeping and modern warfare

Ever since its foundation in 1945 the United Nations has been involved in efforts to keep warring sides apart. In many cases intervention only occurred after the damage had been done. In others intervention has made little difference to a situation of perennial conflict – for example in the Congo or Israel. Since the 1980s the United Nations has taken a larger role in policing conflict and compelling reconciliation. At the same time, the international community drew up agreements to define and proscribe a whole range of potential war crimes and crimes against humanity, beginning with the Genocide Convention of 1948. In 1977 at Geneva a set of Protocols was signed to protect the civilian population in conflicts of all kinds, but its provisions have largely been ignored, even by major states. In 2001 an International Criminal Court was established where cases related to war crimes and crimes against humanity could be heard, but the failure to secure American agreement to the court weakened its influence. NATO forces continue to violate international law on the protection of civilians in the conduct of anti-insurgency operations.

1 In June 1967 Israel responded to the growing threat from her Arab neighbours by launching a pre-emptive strike against Egypt. Using fast-moving armoured forces and modern strike aircraft, victory was achieved in six days (map below). Syrian and Jordanian forces intervened but were rapidly defeated.

1944	First rocket missiles
1945	First jet aircraft in combat
1948	First UN intervention
1950–3	Korean War
1957–75	Vietnam War
1967	Six-Day War in Middle East
1977	Geneva protocols signed
1980	USA launches "strategic defence initiative"
1982	Falklands War
1991	First use of "electronic battlefield": UN coalition expels Iraq from Kuwait
2003	War against Iraq
2013	Islamic State launches religious war in Iraq
2014	War in Ukraine

1 The Six Day War, June 1967
- frontiers before the war
- ★ Israeli air strikes
- ← Israeli advances
- airborne landings

frontlines
- 5 June
- 6 June
- 7 June
- 8 June
- 9–10 June

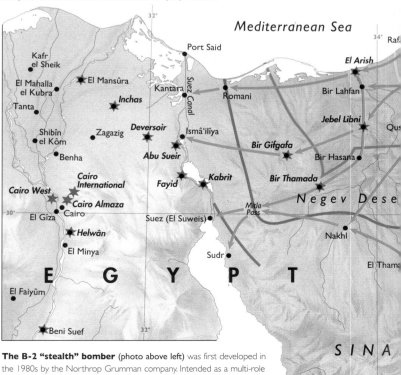

The B-2 "stealth" bomber (photo above left) was first developed in the 1980s by the Northrop Grumman company. Intended as a multi-role bomber capable of carrying conventional and nuclear weapons, the B-2 came into service with the US Air Force in 1997. It has a range of 9650km (6000 miles), and its unique design and materials make it very difficult for conventional radar to detect. Each aircraft costs approximately $2.1 billion.

5 There has been no reduction in the level of state and non-state violence in the 21st century. The regions most prone to conflict are Africa and Asia, where local power struggles, civil wars and insurgencies are more difficult for peacekeepers to control. In 2012, violence reached a new peak with 77 separate conflicts worldwide.

5 Armed conflicts worldwide, 2003–2012

- state-based conflicts
- non-state conflicts

number of conflicts (y-axis: 0, 5, 10, 15, 20, 25, 30, 35, 40, 45, 50)

x-axis: 2003, 2004, 2005, 2006, 2007, 2008, 2009, 2010, 2011, 2012

- Middle East
- Europe
- Asia
- Americas
- Africa

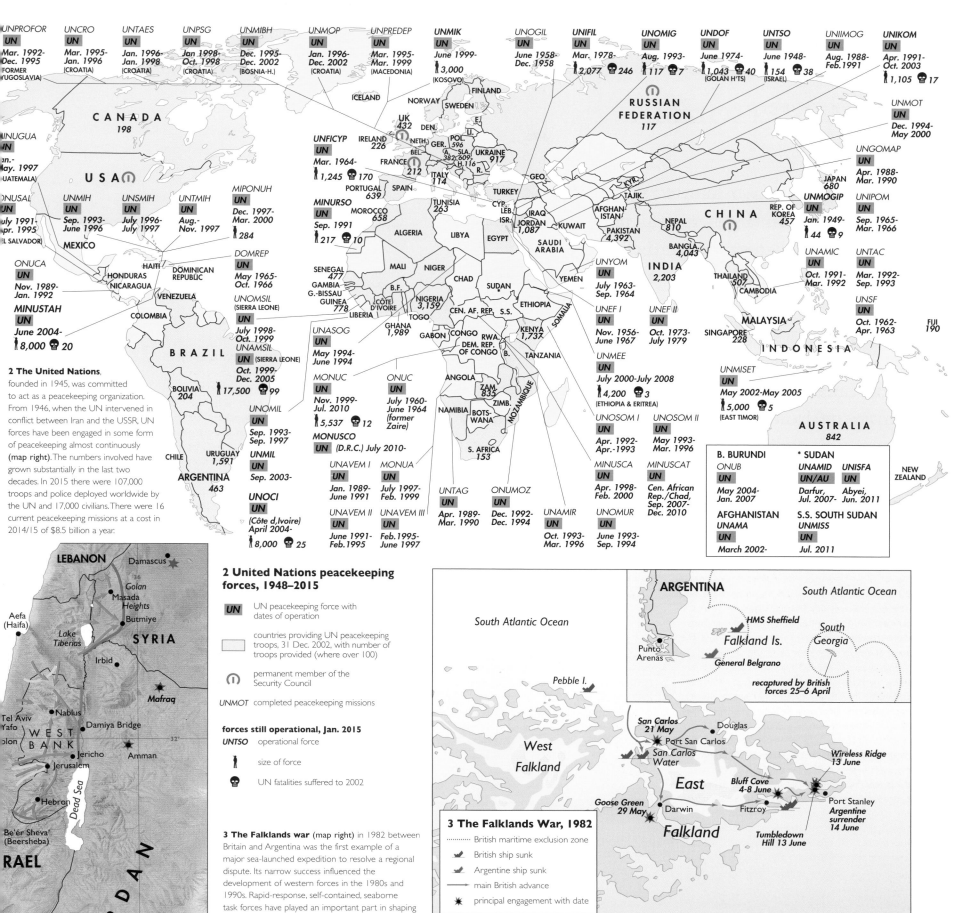

UNPROFOR UN Mar. 1992–Dec. 1995 (FORMER YUGOSLAVIA)

UNCRO UN Mar. 1995–Jan. 1996 (CROATIA)

UNTAES UN Jan. 1996–Jan. 1998 (CROATIA)

UNPSG UN Jan. 1998–Oct. 1998 (CROATIA)

UNMIBH UN Dec. 1995–Dec. 2002 (BOSNIA-H.)

UNMOP UN Jan. 1996–Dec. 2002 (CROATIA)

UNPREDEP UN Mar. 1995–Mar. 1999 (MACEDONIA)

UNMIK UN June 1999– ♦ 3,000 (KOSOVO)

UNOGIL UN June 1958–Dec. 1958

UNIFIL UN Mar. 1978– ♦ 2,077 ☠ 246

UNOMIG UN Aug. 1993– ♦ 117 ☠ 7

UNDOF UN June 1974– ♦ 1,043 ☠ 40 (GOLAN H'TS)

UNTSO UN June 1948– ♦ 154 ☠ 38 (ISRAEL)

UNIIMOG UN Aug. 1988–Feb. 1991

UNIKOM UN Apr. 1991–Oct. 2003 ♦ 1,105 ☠ 17

UNMOT UN Dec. 1994–May 2000

CANADA 198

USA

ICELAND NORWAY SWEDEN FINLAND

RUSSIAN FEDERATION 117

UK 432 IRELAND 226 DEN. EJ. U. GER. 596 POL. A. SLA. H. 116 UKRAINE 917

UNFICYP UN Mar. 1964– ♦ 1,245 ☠ 170

FRANCE 212 ITALY 114 382 609 BEL. NETH.

PORTUGAL 639 SPAIN TURKEY GEO. KYR. TAJIK. AFGHANISTAN

JAPAN 680

UNGOMAP UN Apr. 1988–Mar. 1990

UNMOGIP UN Jan. 1949– ♦ 44 ☠ 9

UNIPOM UN Sep. 1965–Mar. 1966

CHINA

REP. OF KOREA 457

MINURSO UN Sep. 1991 ♦ 217 ☠ 10

MOROCCO 658 ALGERIA LIBYA EGYPT TUNISIA 263 CYP. LEB. ISR. IRAQ JORDAN KUWAIT SAUDI ARABIA YEMEN PAKISTAN 4,392 NEPAL 810 BANGLA. 4,043 INDIA 2,203 THAILAND 507 CAMBODIA

UNAMIC UN Oct. 1991–Mar. 1992

UNTAC UN Mar. 1992–Sep. 1993

UNUSAL UN July 1991–Apr. 1995 EL SALVADOR

UNMIH UN Sep. 1993–June 1996

UNSMIH UN July 1996–July 1997

UNTMIH UN Aug.–Nov. 1997

MIPONUH UN Dec. 1997–Mar. 2000 ♦ 284

MEXICO HAITI DOMINICAN REPUBLIC VENEZUELA COLOMBIA HONDURAS NICARAGUA

DOMREP UN May 1965–Oct. 1966

SENEGAL 477 GAMBIA G.-BISSAU GUINEA 778 LIBERIA COTE D'IVOIRE GHANA 1,989 TOGO B.F. MALI NIGER NIGERIA 3,159 CHAD SUDAN CEN. AF. REP. S.S. ETHIOPIA SOMALIA KENYA 1,737

UNYOM UN July 1963–Sep. 1964

UNEF I UN Nov. 1956–June 1967

UNEF II UN Oct. 1973–July 1979

MALAYSIA SINGAPORE 228

UNSF UN Oct. 1962–Apr. 1963

FIJI 190

INDONESIA

ONUCA UN Nov. 1989–Jan. 1992

MINUSTAH UN June 2004– ♦ 8,000 ☠ 20

UNOMSIL (SIERRA LEONE) UN July 1998–Oct. 1999

UNASOG UN May 1994–June 1994

MONUC UN Nov. 1999–Jul. 2010 ♦ 5,537 ☠ 12

ONUC UN July 1960–June 1964 (former Zaire)

GABON CONGO RWA. DEM. REP. OF CONGO B. ANGOLA ZAM. 835 ZIMB. TANZANIA NAMIBIA BOTSWANA MOZAMBIQUE S. AFRICA 153

UNMEE UN July 2000–July 2008 ♦ 4,200 ☠ 3 (ETHIOPIA & ERITREA)

UNOSOM I UN Apr. 1992–Apr. 1993

UNOSOM II UN May 1993–Mar. 1996

UNMISET UN May 2002–May 2005 ♦ 5,000 ☠ 5 (EAST TIMOR)

AUSTRALIA 842

BRAZIL BOLIVIA 204 CHILE URUGUAY 1,591 ARGENTINA 463

UNAMSIL (SIERRA LEONE) UN Oct. 1999–Dec. 2005 ♦ 17,500 ☠ 99

UNOMIL UN Sep. 1993–Sep. 1997

UNMIL UN Sep. 2003–

MONUSCO UN (D.R.C.) July 2010–

UNAVEM I UN Jan. 1989–June 1991

MONUA UN July 1997–Feb. 1999

MINUSCA UN Apr. 1998–Feb. 2000

MINUSCAT UN Cen. African Rep./Chad, Sep. 2007–Dec. 2010

NEW ZEALAND

B. BURUNDI ONUB UN May 2004–Jan. 2007

* SUDAN UNAMID UN/AU Darfur, Jul. 2007–

UNISFA UN Abyei, Jun. 2011

AFGHANISTAN UNAMA UN March 2002–

S.S. SOUTH SUDAN UNMISS UN Jul. 2011

UNOCI UN (Côte d,Ivoire) April 2004– ♦ 8,000 ☠ 25

UNTAG UN Apr. 1989–Mar. 1990

ONUMOZ UN Dec. 1992–Dec. 1994

UNAVEM II UN June 1991–Feb. 1995

UNAVEM III UN Feb. 1995–June 1997

UNAMIR UN Oct. 1993–Mar. 1996

UNOMUR UN June 1993–Sep. 1994

2 The United Nations, founded in 1945, was committed to act as a peacekeeping organization. From 1946, when the UN intervened in conflict between Iran and the USSR, UN forces have been engaged in some form of peacekeeping almost continuously (map right). The numbers involved have grown substantially in the last two decades. In 2015 there were 107,000 troops and police deployed worldwide by the UN and 17,000 civilians. There were 16 current peacekeeping missions at a cost in 2014/15 of $8.5 billion a year.

2 United Nations peacekeeping forces, 1948–2015

UN — UN peacekeeping force with dates of operation

☐ — countries providing UN peacekeeping troops, 31 Dec. 2002, with number of troops provided (where over 100)

Ⓜ — permanent member of the Security Council

UNMOT — completed peacekeeping missions

forces still operational, Jan. 2015

UNTSO — operational force

♦ — size of force

☠ — UN fatalities suffered to 2002

3 The Falklands war (map right) in 1982 between Britain and Argentina was the first example of a major sea-launched expedition to resolve a regional dispute. Its narrow success influenced the development of western forces in the 1980s and 1990s. Rapid-response, self-contained, seaborne task forces have played an important part in shaping US and NATO intervention in distant conflicts.

Israel/Lebanon/Syria/Jordan inset map

LEBANON Damascus ★ Golan Masada Heights Butmiye Aefa (Haifa) Lake Tiberias SYRIA Irbid Mafraq Nablus Tel Aviv Yafo Damiya Bridge WEST BANK Jericho Amman Jerusalem JORDAN Hebron Dead Sea Be'ér Sheva' (Beersheba) ISRAEL Eilat SAUDI ARABIA

3 The Falklands War, 1982

ARGENTINA South Atlantic Ocean Punto Arenas HMS Sheffield South Georgia Falkland Is. General Belgrano recaptured by British forces 25–6 April Pebble I.

San Carlos 21 May Douglas Port San Carlos San Carlos Water West Falkland Goose Green 29 May Darwin East Falkland Wireless Ridge 13 June Bluff Cove 4–8 June Fitzroy Tumbledown Hill 13 June Port Stanley Argentine surrender 14 June

.... British maritime exclusion zone
⚓ British ship sunk
⚓ Argentine ship sunk
→ main British advance
✴ principal engagement with date

4 World expenditure on the military in 2014 totalled more than $1,700 billion, one-third of it accounted for by the United States, the world's single superpower (map right). Modern conventional weapons produced a trade in arms worth $197 billion in the decade 1993–2002, much of it to the world's trouble-spots in the Middle East and Asia. Since the Cold War, Russia has become a much smaller military power; in 2014 its military budget was just 4 per cent of world expenditure.

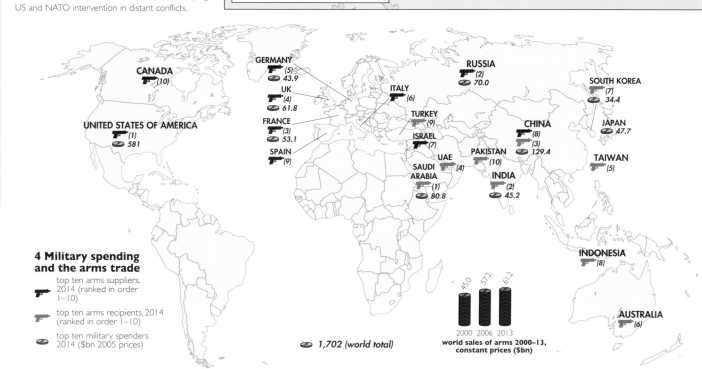

4 Military spending and the arms trade

🔫 top ten arms suppliers, 2014 (ranked in order 1–10)

🔫 top ten arms recipients, 2014 (ranked in order 1–10)

⬭ top ten military spenders 2014 ($bn 2005 prices)

CANADA 🔫(10)
UNITED STATES OF AMERICA 🔫(1) ⬭ 581
GERMANY 🔫(5) ⬭ 43.9
UK 🔫(4) ⬭ 61.8
FRANCE 🔫(3) ⬭ 53.1
SPAIN 🔫(9)
ITALY 🔫(6)
TURKEY 🔫(9)
ISRAEL 🔫(7)
SAUDI ARABIA 🔫(1) ⬭ 80.8
UAE 🔫(4)
RUSSIA 🔫(2) ⬭ 70.0
PAKISTAN 🔫(10)
INDIA 🔫(2) ⬭ 45.2
CHINA 🔫(8) ⬭ 129.4
SOUTH KOREA 🔫(7) ⬭ 34.4
JAPAN ⬭ 47.7
TAIWAN 🔫(5)
INDONESIA 🔫(8)
AUSTRALIA 🔫(6)

⬭ 1,702 (world total)

world sales of arms 2000–13, constant prices ($bn)
450 572 612
2000 2006 2013

World terrorism

The use of indiscriminate violence against military and civilian targets to achieve defined political objectives, generally described as "terrorism", has become a characteristic feature of politics worldwide since 1945. Employed on the right as well as the left of the political spectrum, terrorism has been used as an instrument for national liberation, or to challenge conventional politics or to sustain religious conflict. In 2001 the American President George W. Bush declared a worldwide "war on terror".

I SETTLED IN PAKISTAN IN THE AFGHAN BORDER REGION. THERE I RECEIVED VOLUNTEERS WHO CAME FROM THE SAUDI KINGDOM AND FROM ALL OVER THE ARAB AND MUSLIM COUNTRIES. I SET UP MY FIRST CAMP WHERE THESE VOLUNTEERS WERE TRAINED BY PAKISTANI AND AMERICAN OFFICERS. THE WEAPONS WERE SUPPLIED BY THE AMERICANS, AND THE MONEY BY THE SAUDIS.

Osama bin Laden, 1998

1945–8 Jewish terrorism in Palestine

1969–98 IRA terrorism campaign in UK

1974 Al Jihad founded, Egypt

1978 Red Brigades in Italy kill Prime Minister Aldo Moro

1978–89 Contra terrorist campaign in Nicaragua

1985 Osama bin Laden founds al-Qaeda

1997 Luxor massacre by Al Gamaat terrorists

2001 Al-Qaeda destroys World Trade Center

2002 Bali nightclub bombings

2004 Madrid train bombings

2005 Bus and tube bombings in London

2011 Killing of Osama bin Laden

2013 Islamic State in Iraq and Syria (ISIS) movement founded

TERRORISM EXISTED LONG before 1945, but only in the past 40 years has it become a major element in world politics. In 2001 the American President, George W. Bush, declared war on global terrorism, and the USA has been in a "state of war" against terror ever since. In reality terror is not a movement or a defined political concept. Terrorism describes the means by which, usually small, groups of political dissidents or criminals fight against a potentially stronger political or military opponent. The aims of those who have used terror tactics are extraordinarily diverse. They share only the tactics, using methods of irregular or guerrilla warfare – ambushes, bombings, kidnapping, suicide attacks, assassination – and targeting either representatives of the "enemy" system or ordinary civilians.

Terrorism and nation-building

Many of the longest-running and most violent terrorist campaigns were launched by groups demanding national liberation. In Ireland the Irish Republican Army (IRA) fought a terror campaign against the British authorities from the 1920s, demanding a united Ireland that included the province of Ulster. In Spain, demands for an independent Basque homeland led in 1966 to the onset of a long wave of violence which in 40 years claimed over 800 deaths, more than half of them army or police targets. The organization Euskadi Ta Askatasuna (ETA), founded in 1959, drew on Marxism-Leninism for its inspiration. It has remained uncompromisingly committed to armed struggle.

I Terrorist campaigns have taken place across the world since 1945 **(map below)**. In the developing world many of the early terror campaigns were inspired by Marxist revolutionary struggle, but terrorism also existed in Europe either as struggles for national liberation (Northern Ireland, the Basque province in Spain) or against capitalism (Germany, France, Italy). More recently terrorism has been represented by religious conflict: Hindu against Muslim in India; militant Islam against the West; and westernized native elites throughout the Middle East and north Africa.

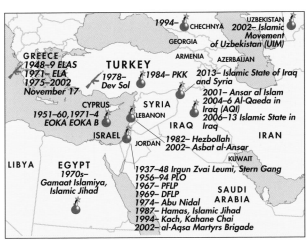

I Terrorist conflicts since 1945

⚒ successful Marxist revolutions involving terrorism, with date

🔫 unsuccessful or ongoing Marxist terrorist challenges, with date and name of group

💣 nationalist, communal and religious terrorist challenges, with date and name of group

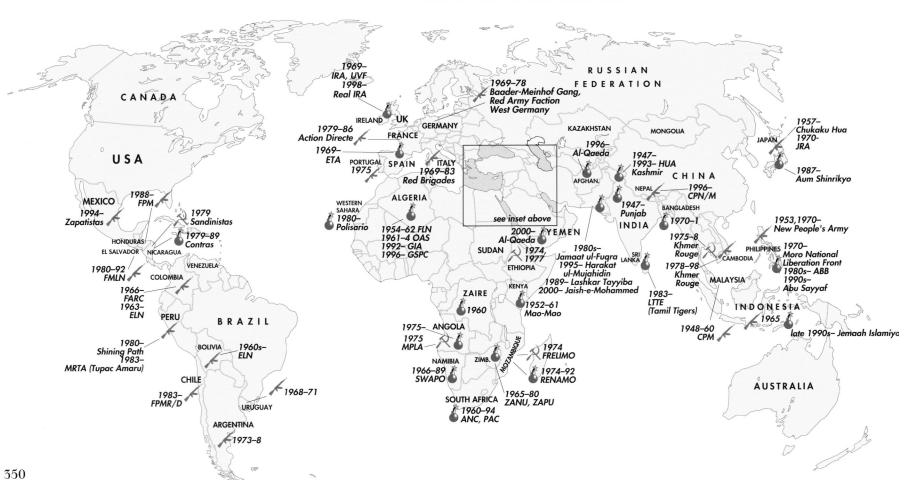

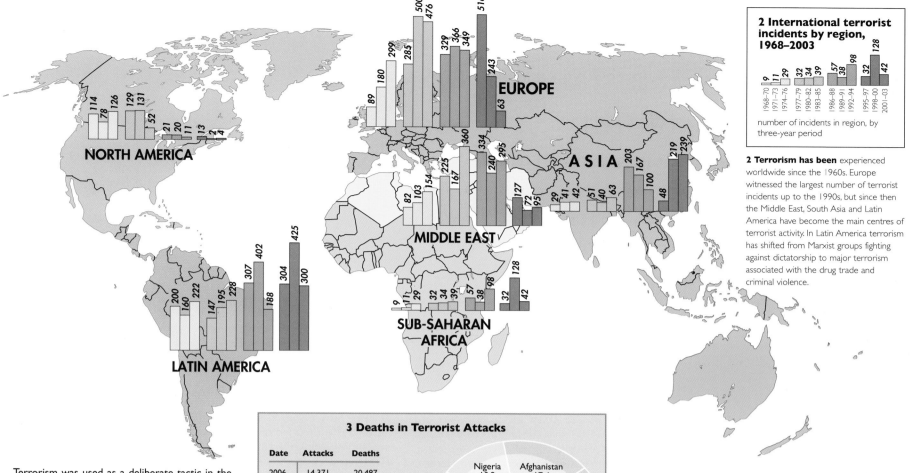

NORTH AMERICA
114 78 126 129 131 52 21 20 11 13 2 4

EUROPE
89 180 299 285 329 366 349 500 476 516 243 63

MIDDLE EAST
82 103 154 167 225 360 334 240 295 127 72 95 29 41 42

ASIA
51 40 63 203 167 100 48 219 239

SUB-SAHARAN AFRICA
9 11 29 32 34 39 57 38 98 32 42

LATIN AMERICA
200 160 222 147 195 228 307 402 188 304 425 300

2 Terrorism has been experienced worldwide since the 1960s. Europe witnessed the largest number of terrorist incidents up to the 1990s, but since then the Middle East, South Asia and Latin America have become the main centres of terrorist activity. In Latin America terrorism has shifted from Marxist groups fighting against dictatorship to major terrorism associated with the drug trade and criminal violence.

Terrorism was used as a deliberate tactic in the struggle to create a Jewish homeland in Israel under British rule in 1945. In 1947 Britain abandoned the effort to maintain control and many former Jewish terrorists became prominent Israeli politicians, facing their own terrorist threat in demands for a Palestinian homeland. In the 1970s and 1980s the Palestine Liberation Organization (PLO) carried out prominent terrorist attacks, and in the 1990s radical Islamic groups, including Hamas and Hezbollah, added a religious dimension to the terror campaigns. Since the late 1990s the al-Qaeda ("The Base") network led by Osama bin Laden, first founded in 1985, added to the conflict, which broadened out into a general campaign of terror by Islamic militants to drive Jews and westernizers out of Islamic territory and to establish fundamentalist Islamic states. In Algeria those very

3 Deaths in Terrorist Attacks

Date	Attacks	Deaths
2006	14,371	20,487
2007	14,414	22,719
2008	11,662	15,708
2009	10,969	15,310
2010	11,604	13,186
2011	10,823	12,533
2012	6,771	11,098
2013	9,707	17,891

Distribution of Deaths in Terrorist Attacks, 2013 (%)

Iraq 35.6
Afghanistan 17.4
Pakistan 12.9
Nigeria 10.2
Rest of the World 9.5
Syria 6
Somalia 2.3
India 2.2
Philippines 1.6
Yemen 1.6
Thailand 0.7

3 Terrorism has reached new heights in the past decade with the deaths worldwide of 129,000 people in terrorist attacks (see chart above). Most of the victims were in Iraq, Afghanistan and Pakistan, which in 2013 accounted for 65.9 per cent of all incidents (see pie-chart). Outside the arc of predominantly Islamic terror attacks from Yemen to the Philippines, the rest of the world suffered only 9.5 per cent of terrorist activity.

On 11 September 2001 two aircraft were flown deliberately into the two towers of the World Trade Center in New York, destroying them both and killing over 2,000 people (right). A third aircraft hijacked by al-Qaeda suicide terrorists crashed onto the edge the Pentagon building in Washington.

4 The terrorist struggle in Northern Ireland (map left) stems from the armed struggle to liberate Ulster from British rule that began in the interwar years. The campaign escalated with the onset of the "Troubles" in 1966. Both Catholic and Protestant communities developed para-military terrorist organizations that carried out a campaign of violence for more than thirty years in Ireland and in mainland Britain. A fragile ceasefire was agreed in 2000.

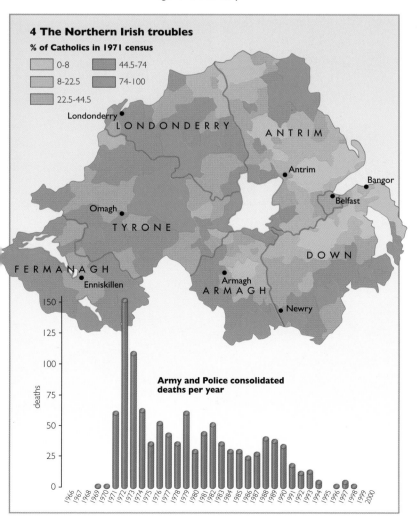

4 The Northern Irish troubles

% of Catholics in 1971 census
- 0-8
- 8-22.5
- 22.5-44.5
- 44.5-74
- 74-100

Londonderry
LONDONDERRY
ANTRIM
Antrim
Bangor
Belfast
Omagh
TYRONE
DOWN
FERMANAGH
Enniskillen
Armagh
ARMAGH
Newry

Army and Police consolidated deaths per year

deaths
150
125
100
75
50
25
0
1966 1967 1968 1969 1970 1971 1972 1973 1974 1975 1976 1977 1978 1979 1980 1981 1982 1983 1984 1985 1986 1987 1988 1989 1990 1991 1992 1993 1994 1995 1996 1997 1998 1999 2000

politicians who had used terrorism to free Algeria from French rule found themselves facing savage terrorism from the Islamic Salvation Front, founded in 1989. These many Islamic groups form the core target for the current "war on terror", declared by President Bush in 2001 following the 9/11 attacks. The invasion and occupation of Iraq in 2003 led to persistent terrorism in the following 12 years, culminating after 2013 in the emergence of the Islamic State movement.

Terrorism and social revolution

Many of the terrorist movements since 1945 have been linked with ideas of social revolution and radical Marxism. In the aftermath of the 1968 youth movement in Europe, there developed small cells of committed revolutionary terrorists, in France the Action Directe movement, in Germany the Baader-Meinhof group and in Italy the Red Brigades. In the 1970s these urban guerrilla movements kidnapped businessmen and politicians, robbed banks and murdered policemen. The Italian interior minister was kidnapped and killed in 1978. The extreme right also used terrorist tactics in Europe and America, where a massive bomb in Oklahoma City was eventually traced to a militant white supremacist group. The European urban terrorists modelled their campaigns on the guerrilla wars in Latin America, where left-wing rebels, inspired by Leninism or Maoism, ran long campaigns of violence against the military and authoritarian regimes that dominated the continent from the 1950s to the 1980s. In Peru in 1980, Abimael Guzman, a philosophy professor, founded the Shining Path movement, a terrorist organization that launched a wave of savage violence against the state and the peasantry it sought to liberate, until Guzman's arrest and imprisonment in 1992. Terrorist activity in Colombia has lasted for more than 40 years, practised by all sides in the many disputes about Colombia's political future and the massive trade in narcotics. Here the divide between political dissidence and crime has been eroded and terrorism has become a way of life.

Iraq and Afghanistan: the arc of instability

Since the early 1980s Afghanistan and Iraq have been at the centre of two separate areas of crisis. Instability has resulted in more than 20 years of civil or guerrilla war in and around Afghanistan and involved Iraq in three wars: against Iran, a UN-led coalition, and a USA-UK invasion force. Western efforts to stabilize the two states have proved costly and resulted in further destabilization across the region, particularly in Iran and Pakistan.

IN THE 1980s Afghanistan and Iraq were united by a common conflict with the revival of fundamentalist Islam. Both were secular states: Afghanistan a pro-Soviet regime, Iraq dominated by Saddam Hussein's Ba'ath Party. In September 1980 Iraq launched a war against the new Islamic state of Iran set up under Ayatollah Khomeini which lasted for eight years and cost more than 400,000 lives. In Afghanistan the pro-communist president Babrak Karmal, followed in 1986 by Mohammed Najibullah (responsible for an estimated 80,000 deaths during his period as head of the secret police), led a savage civil war against muhajeddin rebels with the support of Soviet troops and equipment. The civil war cost 1.5 million lives and produced some 5 million refugees.

Afghanistan after communism

The collapse of communism and the withdrawal of Soviet aid produced political chaos in Afghanistan with fighting between rival warlords, some former communists, some hard-line Muslims. In October 1994 the southern city of Kandahar was captured by a religious militia or Taliban led by Mullah Omar. With increased support and armed from outside, the Taliban captured Kabul in September 1996 where they declared Afghanistan a completely Islamic state and imposed a harsh regime of Islamic law. The region remained in a state of turmoil as anti-Taliban tribal forces continued to fight against radical Islam. In 1998 the USA, which during the Soviet intervention had armed the Islamic guerrilla war, turned against their former allies as American military bases and embassies became the target of militant Islamic terrorism.

By October 2000, with the region still plunged in civil war, the USA was preparing to attack Afghanistan as the perceived base of al-Qaeda, the most dangerous of the new terrorist groups. After the September 11 attacks in 2001 on New York and Washington, American and British forces began a heavy bombardment of Afghanistan to support an offensive by a Northern Alliance of anti-Taliban warlords. In 2002 a new regime was installed in Kabul, but within a year Taliban forces began fighting again in the south and by 2006 had extended their influence in much of the area. In 2009, amid a war that the US and NATO looked increasingly to be losing, President Hamid Karzai won a second term in an election marred by widespread fraud. Despite additional troop commitments from the USA and Britain, Taliban insurgency dominated the majority of the country, spreading across the border into Pakistan, an increasing hotbed of Taliban recruitment and cross-border militancy. Although there was a formal end to combat operations by NATO, the UK and the US in late 2014/early 2015, American forces have increased raids against Islamist militants, moving beyond counterterrorism missions. In March 2015, it was announced that the United States would maintain almost 10,000 service members in Afghanistan until at least the end of 2015, a change from the planned reduction.

The Iraqi wars

In August 1990, in the aftermath of the Iraq-Iran war, Saddam Hussein ordered the invasion of Kuwait. The operation was widely condemned by many Western and Arab states and a coalition force was mobilised to expel Iraq. In January and February 1991 "Operation Desert Storm" forced the expulsion of Iraqi forces

1979 USSR invades Afghanistan

1980 Outbreak of Iran-Iraq War

1989 Soviet forces leave Afghanistan

1990 Iraq invades Kuwait; expelled by UN forces in 1991

1996 Taliban capture Kabul, declare Islamic state

2001 Taliban regime overthrown in Afghanistan by US and allied forces

2003 USA-UK coalition invades Iraq

2005 New constitution ratified in Iraq. Iraq resumes limited sovereignty

2010 Ex-British premier Tony Blair tells the Chilcot inquiry into the UK's role in the Iraq war he has "no regrets"

2011 Osama bin Laden killed by US Navy Seals in Pakistan

2011 US forces declare a formal end to their operations in Iraq

2013 The rise of Islamic State (also known as ISIS or ISIL) transforms the Iraqi insurgency into a regional war

2014 US and UK end combat operations in Afghanistan

2014–15 Islamic State seize control of most of Mosul, Tikrit, Fallujah and Ramadi

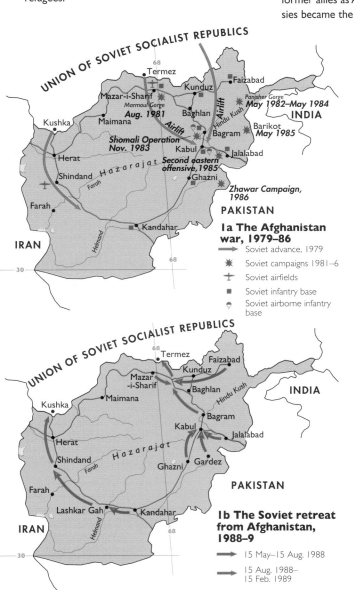

1 In December 1979 Soviet forces were sent to Afghanistan to protect the pro-Soviet government in Kabul (map 1a). They fought a war against Islamic rebels, the muhajeddin, who were funded and armed by the West. After ten years of fruitless fighting and 60,000 casualties, Soviet forces withdrew in 1989, plunging Afghanistan into civil war (map 1b).

2 In 1994 a fundamentalist Taliban regime assumed power in Kabul. A civil war against rival warlords followed, which ended in November 2001 when the US-backed Northern Alliance overthrew the Taliban regime (map 2a). Since 2006, the Taliban has revived, and now heavy insurgency activity dominates Afghanistan and is increasingly active in Pakistan, particularly the Federally Administered Tribal Areas and the North West Frontier Province (map 2b).

1a The Afghanistan war, 1979–86
- → Soviet advance, 1979
- ✳ Soviet campaigns 1981–6
- ✟ Soviet airfields
- ■ Soviet infantry base
- ⚲ Soviet airborne infantry base

1b The Soviet retreat from Afghanistan, 1988–9
- → 15 May–15 Aug. 1988
- → 15 Aug. 1988– 15 Feb. 1989
- ● border crossing points

2a Afghanistan, 2001–2
- held by the Northern Alliance, 9 November
- → main thrust of Northern Alliance forces to 12 Nov.
- brought under Northern Alliance control by 12 Nov.
- Northern Alliance control extended by 13 November
- → seized by Northern Alliance by mid-November
- last Taliban-controlled area towards the end of Nov.

Area held by respective Northern Alliance leaders on 12 November are indicated by names

2b Instability in Afghanistan and Pakistan

Afghanistan
- heavy Taliban/insurgent activity
- substantial Taliban/insurgent activity
- light Taliban/insurgent activity
- 🚚 main supply route

Afghan refugee camps
- ▲ considered Taliban recruiting ground
- ▲ considered Taliban safe haven

Pakistan
- Federally Administered Tribal Area
- North West Frontier Province
- Taliban stronghold
- Taliban presence
- Government controlled
- ● border crossing points

abbreviations
BAG. BAGHLAN
KA. KAPISA
K. KABUL
L. LAGHMAN
NAN. NANGARHAR

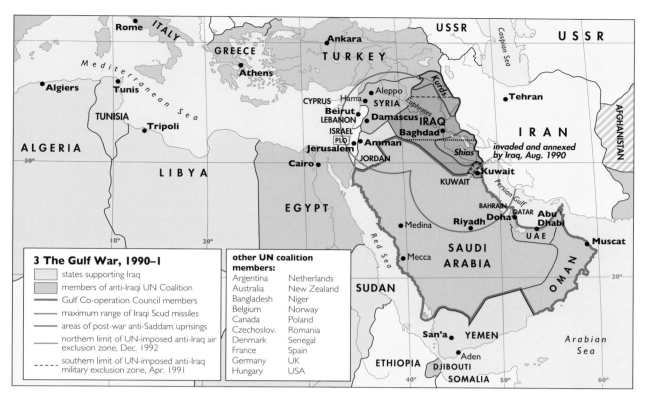

3 The Gulf War, 1990–1

- ☐ states supporting Iraq
- ▨ members of anti-Iraqi UN Coalition
- ── Gulf Co-operation Council members
- ── maximum range of Iraqi Scud missiles
- ── areas of post-war anti-Saddam uprisings
- ······ northern limit of UN-imposed anti-Iraq air exclusion zone, Dec. 1992
- ---- southern limit of UN-imposed anti-Iraq military exclusion zone, Apr. 1991

other UN coalition members:

Argentina	Netherlands
Australia	New Zealand
Bangladesh	Niger
Belgium	Norway
Canada	Poland
Czechoslov.	Romania
Denmark	Senegal
France	Spain
Germany	UK
Hungary	USA

AGAINST ALL ODDS, WE, MEANING THE FREE WORLD AND AFGHANS, HALTED AND CHECKMATED SOVIET EXPANSIONISM A DECADE AGO. BUT THE EMBATTLED PEOPLE OF MY COUNTRY DID NOT SAVOUR THE FRUITS OF VICTORY. INSTEAD, THEY WERE THRUST INTO A WHIRLWIND OF FOREIGN INTRIGUE, DECEPTION, GREAT-GAMESMANSHIP AND INTERNAL STRIFE...

Ahmad Shah Massoud, 2000

3 In August 1990 Iraqi forces occupied Kuwait (map left) to enforce agreements about oil distribution. The United Nations voted to expel Iraq by force and in January and February 1991 a coalition force mounted "Operation Desert Storm", bombing Iraqi installations and driving the Iraqi army from Kuwait City. The UN subsequently imposed sanctions and a demilitarized zone on Iraq.

4 In March 2003, without a second UN resolution, a combined US-UK invasion force attacked and occupied Iraq (map 4) in the belief that Iraq posed a direct threat with "weapons of mass destruction" secretly developed since the 1991 war. Iraqi forces were easily swept aside following heavy bombing of Iraqi cities and strongholds, and no secret weapons were subsequently discovered.

and inflicted enormous damage on Iraq's already impoverished economy. For the following twelve years harsh sanctions and military restrictions were imposed on Iraq, which had also been the victim of a sharp change in American attitudes. From distant support for Iraq's war to contain Islamic fundamentalism, American policy in the 1990s penalized Iraq as a potential threat to peace despite its secular outlook and more westernized society. Sanctions were followed from December 1998 by five years of persistent and heavy bombing of Iraq by US and British aircraft to force Saddam to comply with the terms of his defeat in 1991.

In the spring of 2003, without the sanction of a UN resolution and in the face of international condemnation, Britain and the USA launched an attack on Iraq in the belief that Saddam had WMDs under development. Saddam was deposed (and executed in 2006) and the USA and Britain occupied Iraq, securing its large oil supplies and engaging in brutal acts of pacification against radical Muslim militia and Iraqis hostile to Western intervention. The aim was to turn Iraq into a functioning parliamentary state but the region was no longer a consensual unit. A violent wave of anti-occupation insurgency coincided with a mounting civil war between the rival Sunni and Shia Muslims. Although a constitution was popularly ratified in October 2005, the new Iraqi government was unable to prevent a slide into further instability. Twelve years after the US-led invasion, Allied forces had mostly withdrawn, leaving a bloody legacy. Since the start of the invasion, over 130,000 Iraqi civilians had died as a result of violence and much of the country's infrastructure remained unworkable. The number of Iraqis seeking refuge in other countries rose considerably. The political vacuum left by the fall of Saddam Hussein was rapidly filled by extremist Islamist militants, most notably the Islamic State, although Iraqi Kurds were able to make some gains towards independence. The violent ramifications of western interference in both Iraq and Afghanistan continue to make this the most unstable region in the world.

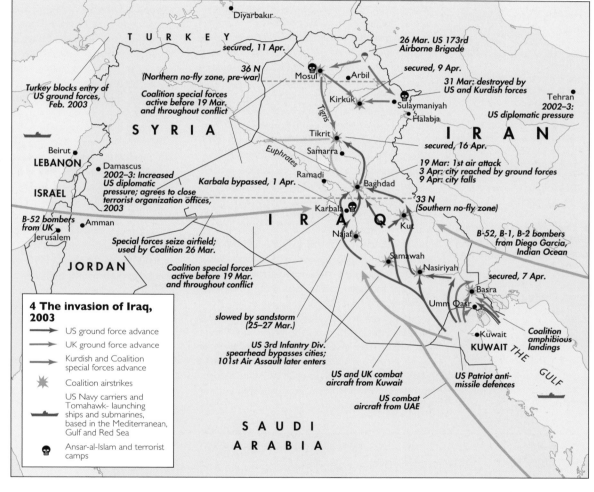

4 The invasion of Iraq, 2003

- → US ground force advance
- → UK ground force advance
- → Kurdish and Coalition special forces advance
- ✳ Coalition airstrikes
- ⚓ US Navy carriers and Tomahawk-launching ships and submarines, based in the Mediterranean, Gulf and Red Sea
- ☠ Ansar-al-Islam and terrorist camps

5 Although the United States-led coalition for the 2003 war in Iraq contained fewer active members than its 1991 counterpart (and no Arab countries), the US government still claimed political support from nearly 50 countries. Fewer nations actually sent troops and the overwhelming bulk of military forces came from the United States itself. The total invasion force amounted to 315,000 troops, of which 250,000 were American. By July 2009, all non-US forces had withdrawn. In March 2009, US President Barack Obama announced a withdrawal of most US troops by the end of August 2010; this was completed on the morning of 18 December 2011. However, an American-led intervention in Iraq started on 15 June 2014, when President Obama ordered US forces to be dispatched to the region, in response to offensives in Iraq conducted by the Islamic State.

In the invasion of Iraq in March 2003 the US air forces unleashed a campaign of bombing against the capital, Baghdad, under the codename "Shock and Awe" (right). Massive coalition air power created extensive damage to the urban areas and infrastructure and hastened an Iraqi defeat. The number of civilian dead is disputed, but estimates in early 2015 stood at over 130,000.

5 Iraq War 2003 in numbers (as of January 2010 unless otherwise indicated)

Population of Iraq	Approx. 27.5 million (as of October 2009)
US 2009 monthly spending in Iraq	$7.3 billion (as of October 2009)
Cost of UK military action in Iraq for the year 2007–2008	£1,457 million (as of 2008)
Number of major US bases in Iraq	75
Troops in Iraq	115,000 US troops (as of November 2009). All other nations have withdrawn their troops.
US troop casualties	4,377
Non-US troop casualties	316, with 179 from the UK
Iraqi civilians killed	Estimates between 50,000 to over 100,000
Iraqis displaced inside Iraq by war	2.7 million (April 2008)
Iraqi refugees in neighbouring countries	2 million (April 2008)

China since 1976

Mao's death created space for reformers to take control of China's destiny. Under Deng Xiaoping, the PRC pursued a course of market-driven liberalization which has made the nation the largest economy in the world. Political liberalization, however, has not kept pace, and simmering conflicts on China's internal and external frontiers are a preoccupation for Communist Party leaders.

FROM THE LATE 1970s the dominant figure in Chinese politics was Deng Xiaoping. Deng had been purged twice under Mao for his lack of revolutionary commitment. Unlike Mao, Deng was a pragmatist rather than an ideologue, and his world-view was summed up in the aftermath of the Great Leap Forward when he remarked "It doesn't matter whether a cat is black or white," for "as long as it catches mice, it's a good cat." His pragmatic outlook led China down the "capitalist road"x after 1976.

A beginning had been made in opening up China to the West with President Nixon's visit in 1972. After 1978, Deng set out plans for the "Four Modernizations": a design to improve the nation's industry, agriculture, defence and science. Economic liberalization stood at the heart of this programme. To induce overseas investment, Deng created special economic zones in areas bordering Hong Kong and Macau, and in Shanghai. By 1992, $36 billion of foreign capital had poured into China. Other reforms followed. Peasants were permitted to lease land that had been collectivized in the Great Leap Forward, and by 1984, 98 per cent did so. With incentives to produce for the market, farmers increased agricultural output by 49 per cent. Private businesses were also permitted. The numbers of these grew from 100,000 in 1978 to 17 million in 1985. However, the success of liberalization brought its own problems: inflation, external deficits, migration to the cities and corruption.

Protest, reform and growth

Economic reforms led to demands for political liberalization. In December 1986, students demonstrated for democracy in 15 cities. Deng responded with repression: "troublemakers" were arrested, and Hu Yaobang, the liberal secretary-general of the CCP, was sacked. When Hu died in April 1989, students marked his passing with demands for democracy. For six weeks they gathered in Tiananmen Square, at times numbering over a million. In June, the PLA was sent in and the movement was ruthlessly crushed.

After the Tiananmen massacre, China moved quickly to reassure the world that it was a stable economic partner; the world largely ignored human rights concerns to assure itself of a share of China's economic boom. There was further economic liberalization: most of China now operated a "socialist market economy" or "socialism with Chinese characteristics", as Deng had put it. Growth rates, which averaged 10 per cent or more for the 1980s and 1990s, were only slightly affected by the economic turmoil which hit east Asia in 1997–8. The economic opening of China was sealed by its joining the World Trade Organization in 2001 and its successful hosting of the 2008 Olympic Games. The

I The world's most populous nation, China developed rapidly after the civil war and communist takeover in 1949 **(map below left)**. But the country's industrial and agricultural expansion was slowed by the Great Leap Forward of the late 1950s and the Cultural Revolution of the mid-1960s. From the 1970s onwards, China has experienced an economic revolution under Deng Xiaoping and his successors. A massive programme of investment produced significant gains in output, but led to high inflation. In the mid-1980s, a policy of retrenchment stabilized the economy, before the regime launched more thorough market reforms and a new expansionary wave from 1990. China's economic transformation has spurred a mass exodus from the countryside to the cities. From 1980 to 2011 the proportion of Chinese living in urban areas increased from 19 per cent to 51 per cent. But the disparities in wealth between the coastal and other regions have remained wide, and major policy drives were launched after 2000 to narrow the gap. In 2006, to help power this internal growth, the world's largest hydro-electric plan, the Three Gorges Dam, was opened amid controversy over its ecological impact, while the government has also invested heavily in transportation to link major cities and remote regions..

economic crisis which hit China in 2009, though not triggering widespread social unrest, showed that the country was no longer insulated from global economic turmoil. Although the PRC weathered the storm better than many western nations, a slowdown in growth over recent years has been seen by some commentators as a prelude to a crash.

China's economic rise has turned it into a major world power. Heavy investment in developing countries in Africa and elsewhere – though this is as much an extension of programmes in the Mao era as a new departure – has gone alongside the pouring of money into the military. Territorial disputes over seas, islands, and borders have threatened to escalate into conflict. Meanwhile, Chinese policymakers have tried to hold the nation together across ethnic and cultural divisions. Indigenous nationalism in Taiwan, claimed by the PRC but governed as the Republic of China, remains a bone of contention and missile testing in the run-up to Taiwan's elections in 1996 led the US to send aircraft carriers to the Taiwan Straits. In the far western provinces of Tibet and Xinjiang, separatist movements have troubled Beijing. In Xinjiang, Muslim separatists have sometimes turned to violence, which has led to fierce repression on the part of Chinese authorities.

Since Deng's death in 1996, China's leadership has been dominated by technocrats. In 2013, 83 dollar billionaires sat in the National People's Congress. Yet if the fruits of economic growth have been distributed unevenly, standards of living across China have improved markedly in the post-Mao era and the government has invested heavily in areas such as transportation and education. Political reform in the post-Tiananmen era, however, has been limited, and in recent years the state has extended control over civil society by carefully monitoring internet usage and targeting dissidents.

I The Chinese economy, 1983–2011

GDP per capita, 2010, in million US$

	<80% of national average
	80–120% of national average
	>120% of national average

$495 foreign investment, 2011, by province, in million US$

○ Special Economic Zones (SEZ), 1980

● open coastal cities, 1984

● inland city with expanded authority, 1984

"golden triangle" development areas, 1985

high-speed railway lines

A view of the China pavilion at the Expo 2015 exhibition in Milan, Italy **(left)**. The lighted strands represent a field of corn, marrying together China's ancient past and modern future.

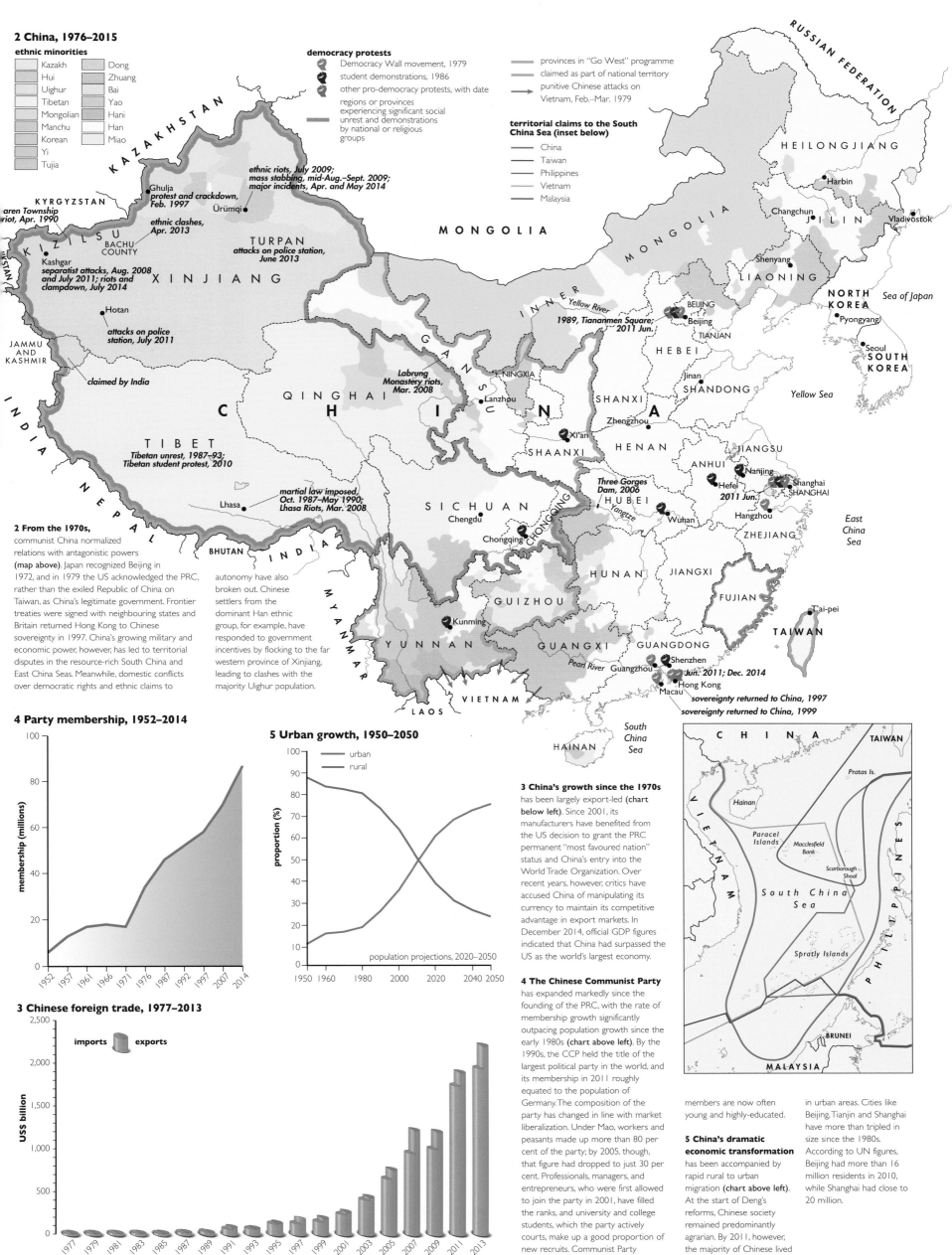

2 China, 1976–2015

ethnic minorities

Kazakh
Hui
Uighur
Tibetan
Mongolian
Manchu
Korean
Yi
Tujia

Dong
Zhuang
Bai
Yao
Hani
Han
Miao

democracy protests

Democracy Wall movement, 1979
student demonstrations, 1986
other pro-democracy protests, with date
regions or provinces experiencing significant social unrest and demonstrations by national or religious groups

provinces in "Go West" programme
claimed as part of national territory
punitive Chinese attacks on Vietnam, Feb.–Mar. 1979

territorial claims to the South China Sea (inset below)

China
Taiwan
Philippines
Vietnam
Malaysia

RUSSIAN FEDERATION

KAZAKHSTAN

KYRGYZSTAN

aren Township riot, Apr. 1990

KIZILSU

Ghulja protest and crackdown, Feb. 1997

ethnic riots, July 2009; mass stabbing, mid-Aug.–Sept. 2009; major incidents, Apr. and May 2014

Ürümqi

ethnic clashes, Apr. 2013

BACHU COUNTY

Kashgar

separatist attacks, Aug. 2008 and July 2011; riots and clampdown, July 2014

XINJIANG

TURPAN

attacks on police station, June 2013

Hotan

attacks on police station, July 2011

JAMMU AND KASHMIR

claimed by India

MONGOLIA

Yellow River

INNER MONGOLIA

HEILONGJIANG

Harbin

Changchun

JILIN

Vladivostok

Shenyang

LIAONING

NORTH KOREA

Sea of Japan

BEIJING
Beijing
TIANJAN

1989, Tiananmen Square; 2011 Jun.

Pyongyang

Seoul

SOUTH KOREA

HEBEI

NINGXIA

Jinan

SHANDONG

Yellow Sea

QINGHAI

GANSU

Lanzhou

Labrung Monastery riots, Mar. 2008

Xi'an

SHAANXI

Zhengzhou

SHANXI

HENAN

C H I N A

TIBET

Tibetan unrest, 1987–93; Tibetan student protest, 2010

Lhasa

martial law imposed, Oct. 1987–May 1990; Lhasa Riots, Mar. 2008

NEPAL

BHUTAN

INDIA

SICHUAN

Chengdu

CHONGQING

Chongqing

Three Gorges Dam, 2006

HUBEI

Yangtze

Wuhan

ANHUI

Hefei

Nanjing

JIANGSU

Shanghai
SHANGHAI

Hangzhou

ZHEJIANG

East China Sea

MYANMAR

HUNAN

JIANGXI

GUIZHOU

Kunming

YUNNAN

GUANGXI

FUJIAN

T'ai-pei

TAIWAN

GUANGDONG

Pearl River

Guangzhou

Shenzhen

Jun. 2011; Dec. 2014

Hong Kong
Macau

sovereignty returned to China, 1997
sovereignty returned to China, 1999

LAOS

VIETNAM

HAINAN

South China Sea

2 From the 1970s,

communist China normalized relations with antagonistic powers (**map above**). Japan recognized Beijing in 1972, and in 1979 the US acknowledged the PRC, rather than the exiled Republic of China on Taiwan, as China's legitimate government. Frontier treaties were signed with neighbouring states and Britain returned Hong Kong to Chinese sovereignty in 1997. China's growing military and economic power, however, has led to territorial disputes in the resource-rich South China and East China Seas. Meanwhile, domestic conflicts over democratic rights and ethnic claims to

autonomy have also broken out. Chinese settlers from the dominant Han ethnic group, for example, have responded to government incentives by flocking to the far western province of Xinjiang, leading to clashes with the majority Uighur population.

4 Party membership, 1952–2014

membership (millions) — vertical axis: 0, 20, 40, 60, 80, 100

horizontal axis: 1952, 1957, 1961, 1966, 1971, 1976, 1987, 1992, 1997, 2007, 2014

5 Urban growth, 1950–2050

proportion (%) — vertical axis: 0, 10, 20, 30, 40, 50, 60, 70, 80, 90, 100

urban
rural

population projections, 2020–2050

horizontal axis: 1950, 1960, 1980, 2000, 2020, 2040, 2050

3 Chinese foreign trade, 1977–2013

US$ billion — vertical axis: 0, 500, 1,000, 1,500, 2,000, 2,500

imports   exports

horizontal axis: 1977, 1979, 1981, 1983, 1985, 1987, 1989, 1991, 1993, 1995, 1997, 1999, 2001, 2003, 2005, 2007, 2009, 2011, 2013

3 China's growth since the 1970s

has been largely export-led (**chart below left**). Since 2001, its manufacturers have benefited from the US decision to grant the PRC permanent "most favoured nation" status and China's entry into the World Trade Organization. Over recent years, however, critics have accused China of manipulating its currency to maintain its competitive advantage in export markets. In December 2014, official GDP figures indicated that China had surpassed the US as the world's largest economy.

4 The Chinese Communist Party

has expanded markedly since the founding of the PRC, with the rate of membership growth significantly outpacing population growth since the early 1980s (**chart above left**). By the 1990s, the CCP held the title of the largest political party in the world, and its membership in 2011 roughly equated to the population of Germany. The composition of the party has changed in line with market liberalization. Under Mao, workers and peasants made up more than 80 per cent of the party; by 2005, though, that figure had dropped to just 30 per cent. Professionals, managers, and entrepreneurs, who were first allowed to join the party in 2001, have filled the ranks, and university and college students, which the party actively courts, make up a good proportion of new recruits. Communist Party members are now often young and highly-educated.

5 China's dramatic economic transformation

has been accompanied by rapid rural to urban migration (**chart above left**). At the start of Deng's reforms, Chinese society remained predominantly agrarian. By 2011, however, the majority of Chinese lived in urban areas. Cities like Beijing, Tianjin and Shanghai have more than tripled in size since the 1980s. According to UN figures, Beijing had more than 16 million residents in 2010, while Shanghai had close to 20 million.

CHINA

TAIWAN

VIETNAM

Hainan

Paracel Islands

Pratas Is.

Macclesfield Bank

Scarborough Shoal

South China Sea

Spratly Islands

PHILIPPINES

BRUNEI

MALAYSIA

The collapse of the Soviet Union and the creation of modern Russia

1986 Disaster at Chernobyl nuclear plant

1989 End of Soviet-Afghan War

1991 (June) Boris Yeltsin elected President of the Russian Federation

1991 (Aug.) Yeltsin defeats unsuccessful coup

1991 (Aug.–Sept.) Estonia, Latvia, Ukraine, Belarus, Moldova and Azerbaijan declare independence

1991 (Dec.) Creation of CIS; resignation of Gorbachev; dissolution of USSR

1996 G7 agrees to admit Russia to become G8

1999 Vladimir Putin replaces Sergei Shepashin as Prime Minister

2000 Putin wins presidential election with 53% of vote

2008 Dmitrii Medvedev becomes President with Putin as Prime Minister

2012 Vladimir Putin secures third term as Russian President

2014 Russian annexation of Crimea. Civil War in Ukraine

Through his programme of reform aimed to revitalize the USSR, Mikhail Gorbachev inadvertently released forces that led to the collapse of the Soviet Union at the end of 1991. While some were hopeful for the future, the early post-Soviet years brought hardship and poverty for many in the new Russian state. The early 21st century has seen many of these domestic problems persist, while Russia has experienced a resurgence on the global stage, largely as a result of the state's attempts to police dissent and its actions in the recent crisis in Ukraine.

Russia established a fragile democracy in 1992. In October 1993 hard-line parliamentary delegates hostile to further reform tried to depose President Boris Yeltsin. He ordered in tanks and special forces and bombarded the White House, the Russian parliament (above). On 4 October, the rebels surrendered. There were 140 deaths in the fighting.

BY THE 1980s, THE SOVIET system was under pressure. In an attempt to solve some of the problems it faced, Mikhail Gorbachev launched a series of reforms commonly known as *Perestroika* ("restructuring") and *Glasnost* ("openness"). *Perestroika* was meant to reform and revitalize the mechanics of the state and the economy, while *Glasnost* was aimed at rooting out corruption and creating new avenues of communication within society. This approach led to greater freedom of speech and more open discussion about the abuses of the past. Voices within the national republics also grew louder, as groups outside the Communist Party claimed to represent the people, and began to push for independence.

Although Gorbachev enjoyed success on the global scene, improving relations with other major powers, particularly with the UK and the USA, problems continued to mount domestically. This came to a head in August 1991, when the so-called Emergency Committee launched an unsuccessful coup against his regime. Over the previous months, a number of Soviet republics had declared their sovereignty and the failure of the coup meant that there was now no

hope of a new union. The biggest blow to the future of the Soviet Union came in December 1991, when Ukraine declared its independence. This was quickly followed by the creation of the Commonwealth of Independent States, made up initially of Russia, Ukraine and Belarus, which claimed to be the successor of the USSR. On Christmas Day 1991, Gorbachev resigned and on 31 December the Soviet Union ceased to exist.

The Russian Federation

The Russian Federation, now a presidential democracy under Boris Yeltsin's leadership, had been the largest state within the USSR in terms of territory, population and wealth, and so assumed the place of the Soviet Union on the UN Security Council and took control of most Soviet nuclear weapons. With abundant natural wealth and a well-educated labour force, Russia seemed poised to develop a new market economy. However, the liberalization and privatization of the market was done very rapidly, leading to hyperinflation, which wiped out people's savings and pensions. In the first five years of independence, Russia suffered an economic downturn

worse than that experienced by the West during the depression of the 1930s. Life expectancy and birth rates fell sharply, while rates of alcoholism and drug addiction soared, as did levels of organized crime. The gap between rich and poor – those who gained massively from the privatization process and those who suffered as a result of the economic collapse – also widened dramatically, creating one of the world's most unequal distributions of wealth. The economic crisis continued into the late 1990s, as the state's ability to gather taxes, provide basic social services, and control corruption declined. The Russian economy hit rock bottom on "Black Monday" (17 August 1998), when the rouble collapsed and the Russian stock exchange lost 88 per cent of its value.

2 One of the most lasting legacies of the Soviet Union is the number of ethnic Russians who continue to live in parts of the former USSR (map left). While much of this is due to organic population movement, some of is the result of deliberate policy. This is especially the case in Kazakhstan, which witnessed a huge wave of immigration from the Slavic parts of the union as a consequence of Stalinist deportations and Khrushchev's Virgin Lands Scheme in particular. For a period in the late Soviet era, this led to the Kazakhs being a minority within their own state, although Russian migration out of the country since 1991 has reversed this. The region with one of the highest concentrations of ethnic Russians is Crimea, which was a part of the Russian Federated Socialist Republic until 1954 when it was gifted to Ukraine.

In people's hearts and minds, Crimea has always been an inseparable part of Russia. This firm conviction is based on truth and justice and was passed from generation to generation, over time, under any circumstances, despite all the dramatic changes our country went through during the entire 20th century.

Vladimir Putin, March 2014

2 Ethnic Russian population in the former Soviet states

percentage of ethnic Russians

- less than 5%
- 5 to 15%
- 15 to 25%
- over 25%
- border of former Soviet Union

RUSSIAN FEDERATION 77.7%

ESTONIA 24.8%
LATVIA 26.2%
LITHUANIA 5.8%
BELARUS 8.3%
UKRAINE 17.3%
MOLDOVA 5.9%
CRIMEA 58%
GEORGIA 1.5%
ARMENIA 0.5%
AZERBAIJAN 1.3%
KAZAKHSTAN 23.7%
KYRGYZSTAN 12.5%
UZBEKISTAN 5.5%
TAJIKISTAN 1.1%
TURKMENISTAN 4.0%

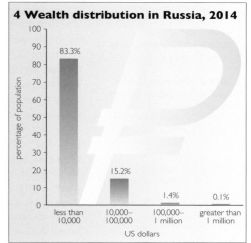

a KARACHAY-CHERKESSIA
b KABARDINO-BALKARIA
c NORTH-OSSETIA
d INGUSHETIA (from June 1992)
e CHECHNYA

1 The Russian Federation

— the Russian Federation

constituent republics within the Russian Federation, Mar. 1992

independence declared, Nov. 1991; at war with Russia from Dec. 1994 to 1996. De facto independent, 1996–9. Re-occupied by Russia 1999

The Commonwealth of Independent States (CIS)

entered into close political and economic union with Russia, 2 Apr. 1996

entered into close economic union with Russia, 30 Mar. 1996

other members of the CIS

The rise of Putin

In August 1999, Yeltsin appointed the relatively unknown former head of the KGB, Vladimir Putin, as Prime Minister. After a series of deadly bomb attacks, one of Putin's early actions was to launch a new offensive in Chechnya and, in the light of the success of this campaign, his popularity soared. Yeltsin resigned shortly after, triggering an election designed to capitalize on Putin's new-found status. Putin won this easily and set about restoring the Russian state, reducing the power of the oligarchs, reforming provincial government, and strengthening central control, all of which was aided by a period of economic boom. Despite this, many of the social problems of the early post-Soviet era remained. After acting as Dmitrii Medvedev's prime minister from 2008 to 2012, Putin was re-elected to the presidency for a third time in 2012, although significant protests occurred both before and after the election. In 2013, Putin's government introduced a law against "homosexual propaganda", a piece of legislation that attracted particular attention in the West in view of the award of the Winter Olympics to Sochi in 2014. However it has been Russia's involvement in Ukraine that has come under most scrutiny in recent times. Following a referendum in March 2014, Russia annexed the ethnically Russian-dominated region of Crimea, prompting several countries to impose economic sanctions. Russia responded to these measures with a series of restrictions of its own, such as banning the import of food from the EU and USA, but the situation in Ukraine is widely seen to have contributed to the declining value of the rouble, prompting fears of a new Russian economic crisis and even a new Cold War.

1 The Russian Federation

was formed in 1991 and consisted of 21 republics and 69 other defined areas (map above). The creation of the Commonwealth of Independent States, an alliance initially between Russia, Belarus and Ukraine, hastened the collapse of the Soviet Union just months later. Since its formation, the Russian Federation has faced a number of challenges from regions wishing to gain independence from Moscow, most significantly in Chechnya, which launched a war of independence in 1994. Although most of the Russian army was withdrawn from the region in April 2009, the region is far from stable. Many of the major terrorist attacks on Russia since the 1990s have had connections with the Chechen cause, most notably the attack on the Dubrovka Theatre in 2002, the Beslan school siege in 2004, and the bombing of the Moscow metro in 2010.

3 The destruction of Lenin statues in Ukraine, 21 Feb.–30 Sept. 2014

- by 22 Feb. 2014
- 23 Feb.–30 March 2014
- from 1 April 2014

4 Modern Russia is characterized

by tremendous disparity in wealth. Although personal wealth has on average increased significantly since the start of the 21st century, driven mainly by an international demand for Russia's natural resources, this economic development has greatly benefited a very small number of the population. Out of a population of approximately 140 million, there are only around 158,000 dollar millionaires. The country also has 111 billionaires, who are estimated to hold almost 20 per cent of household wealth. The other side of this story is that more than 80 per cent of the population has household wealth of less than $10,000 per head.

4 Wealth distribution in Russia, 2014

[bar chart]

percentage of population (y-axis, 0–100)

- less than 10,000: 83.3%
- 10,000–100,000: 15.2%
- 100,000–1 million: 1.4%
- greater than 1 million: 0.1%

US dollars (x-axis)

3 Attacks against remnants

of the old Soviet regime have been relatively commonplace since the collapse of the Soviet Union in 1991, but the statues of Lenin which remained in Ukraine became a particular target for anti-Russian activists during the recent conflict in the region (map right). On 22 February 2014 alone, the day President Viktor Yanukovych was removed from his post, 90 statues of Lenin were destroyed. In this context, the former Soviet leader became symbolic of what was perceived to be a Russian attempt to exercise imperial domination over Ukraine, rather than a reminder of the two countries' shared Communist past. The map also clearly shows the low levels of destruction in eastern Ukraine and the Crimea, parts of the country with a significant Russian population.

The Arab World in transition

On 2 May 2011 Osama bin Laden, the founder and head of the Islamist militant group al-Qaeda, was killed by a group of US Navy Seals. It was the same year that uprisings broke out across much of the Arab world and for many these twin developments marked the end of a period of Islamic militancy that had commenced with the 9/11 attacks. However, the uprisings which were quickly termed the "Arab Spring" appeared to descend into an "Islamist Winter" with Islamists rising to power in several Arab states. The failed promise of the Egyptian revolution, Libya's complete collapse, the savage sectarian repression of Bahrain's demonstrations, and above all the civil war in Syria have long since diverted attention from the possibility of meaningful change through popular mobilization.

ON 17 DECEMBER 2010, 26-year-old Mohamed Bouazizi, a fruit and vegetable seller in Sidi Bouzid, Tunisia, set himself on fire in front of a government building in protest against the confiscation of his cart by the police. His gesture resonated with others and within days protests around Tunisia forced the regime of President Zine el Abidine Ben Ali to step down after 23 years in power. On 14 January 2011, the former president fled with his family to Saudi Arabia.

The Tunisian protests set off uprisings across the Middle East in a movement that became known as the "Arab Spring", a term with echoes of the "Spring of Nations" in 1848 or the "Prague Spring" of 1968. As in those previous "springs" in Europe, it was believed that popular uprisings in the name of democracy would unseat autocratic regimes. Large-scale civilian protests erupted in Egypt, Libya, Yemen, Syria and Bahrain and repercussions were felt in Morocco, Algeria, Saudi Arabia, Jordan, Lebanon and Sudan. The results, as in 1848, were mixed. Some regimes were overturned, notably that of Egypt's longstanding ruler Hosni Mubarak following mass demonstrations in Cairo's Tahrir Square, but Syria descended into civil war, while in Bahrain strong repression blunted the protests. Monarchies in Morocco, Jordan, Saudi Arabia and the Gulf States were able to avoid major crisis; in 2011, the Saudi King Abdullah promised his people benefits worth $37 billion to buy their compliance. The region remains in a state of flux, with an uneven pace of reform and regular and unpredictable violence. Hopes for greater freedom for women have been frustrated by rising sexual violence.

The rise of Islamist militancy

The widespread destabilization of the region opened the way to growing sectarian violence between Sunni and Shia Muslims and between Muslims and Christians. Armed militant groups have emerged, committed to cleansing the faith and establishing world Islamic rule. The most prominent of the new sectarian forces is the Islamic State of Iraq and Syria (known since July 2014 as Islamic State). It grew out of Al-Qaeda activism in Iraq, but following the collapse of Saddam Hussein's regime and the civil war in Syria, opportunities arose to extend IS influence across the region, from central Syria to the Kurdish areas of northern Iraq. In February 2014, the movement's extreme violence and intransigence led to its expulsion from Al-Qaeda. In July 2014, IS declared a worldwide Caliphate with its Sunni leader, Abu Bakr al-Baghdadi as Caliph. Despite a campaign of air strikes initiated by the United States and its allies in the summer of 2014, the movement has made substantial territorial gains in 2015, and has won recruits in Libya and Nigeria.

Atlantic Ocean

Tangier

Algiers

10°

Rabat

Casablanca

MOROCCO
20 Feb. 2011
King Mohammed VI remains in power with only sporadic and modestly sized protests against his rule

30°

ALGERIA

Tunis

Sousse

TUNISIA
Dec. 2010

Former President Zine el Abidine Ben Ali's 23 years in power ended on 14 Jan. 2011, when he fled to Saudi Arabia as the regime collapsed

Tripoli

Ghadames

0°

10°

Ubari

NIGER

I The Arab Spring was a series of anti-government protests, uprisings and armed rebellions that spread across the Middle East in early 2011. Their purpose, relative success and outcome remain hotly disputed in Arab countries, among foreign observers, and between world powers looking to exploit the changing map of the Middle East. Extremist Islamist groups, such as Islamic State – an Iraqi franchise of al-Qaeda – have taken advantage of the chaos caused by political vacuums and sectarian tension, particularly in Syria, to expand beyond Iraq's borders and recruit vast numbers of anti-government rebels. In January 2014, IS took control of the Iraqi city of Fallujah, in the western province of Anbar; in May 2015 it captured the provincial capital Ramadi (map right).

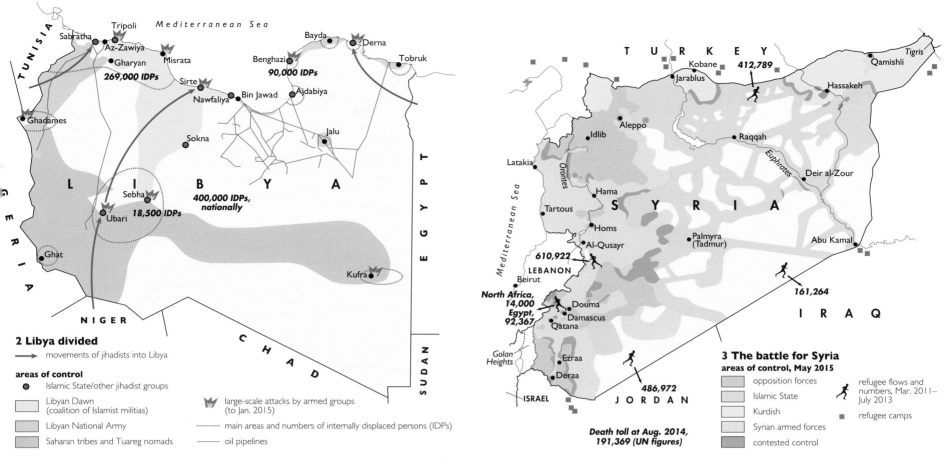

2 Libya divided

→ movements of jihadists into Libya

areas of control

● Islamic State/other jihadist groups

Libyan Dawn
(coalition of Islamist militias)

Libyan National Army

Saharan tribes and Tuareg nomads

♛ large-scale attacks by armed groups
(to Jan. 2015)

·········· main areas and numbers of internally displaced persons (IDPs)

— oil pipelines

269,000 IDPs

90,000 IDPs

400,000 IDPs,
nationally

18,500 IDPs

3 The battle for Syria
areas of control, May 2015

opposition forces

Islamic State

Kurdish

Syrian armed forces

contested control

🏃 refugee flows and
numbers, Mar. 2011–
July 2013

▪ refugee camps

412,789

610,922

North Africa,
14,000
Egypt,
92,367

161,264

486,972

Death toll at Aug. 2014,
191,369 (UN figures)

2 By 2015, more than three years since the fall of Libya's strongman Muammar al-Gaddafi, Islamic State had taken advantage of fighting between Islamist, secular and tribal groups, all jockeying for the country's vast oil riches and arsenal of weapons **(map above)**. Spiralling lawlessness and armed conflict within the country made Libya a very dangerous and unstable place to live. According to UNHCR, 400,000 Libyans were displaced as of 16 January 2015 by fighting between various armed groups. The plight of refugees and migrants in Libya became so desperate that many were driven to risk their lives in treacherous sea crossings in an attempt to reach sanctuary in Europe.

Libya and Syria

In Libya, the Arab Spring took the form of a widespread revolt against the four decades of rule by Muammar al-Gaddafi. The subsequent civil war against Gaddafi's forces, supported by Western states, led to the collapse of the regime and the dictator's death in October 2011. A civil war continued between rival factions representing different tribal groupings, while Islamist militants exploited the instability. The internationally recognized government of Libya in 2015 was confined to the port of Tobruk.

In Syria the civil war that began after peaceful protests in 2011 against the rule of the Assad family, who had held power for 45 years, provoked widespread conflict between the minority Shia, including Bashar al-Assad's own Alawite sect, and the majority Sunnis. The brutal attempts to suppress the revolt led to a civil war that cost almost 200,000 lives and still raged four years later. The United Nations calculated that 16 per cent of Syria's population became refugees, chiefly in neighbouring countries. The violent expansion of the Islamic State movement in 2014–15 brought much of the north and east of the country under the control of militant Sunnis.

The Arab Spring had unpredictable consequences which are still playing out amidst rising religious conflict. The people of Iraqi Kurdistan are no nearer to an independent state, their early gains from a disintegrating unitary state being overshadowed by the encroaching threat of the Islamic State. In Egypt, the election of the Muslim Brotherhood leader, Mohamed Morsi, in 2012, provoked further protests and after a year he was overthrown by the army and in 2015 condemned to death. The role of the United States has been reduced in the Middle East as a result of the crises, while Iran and Turkey, the key regional powers, have been forced to play a larger part. It is impossible to imagine a solution in Syria without Iranian agreement and, much to the alarm of Saudi Arabia and Israel, America is showing readiness to talk to Tehran about Iran's nuclear policy.

3 Opposition groups in Syria have been fighting President Bashar al-Assad for over three years, but have lost ground in recent months. The UN says the number of people fleeing the conflict in Syria escalated to an average of 6,000 a day during 2013 **(map above)** – a rate not seen since the genocide in Rwanda nearly two decades ago. In August 2014, the death toll, as reported by the UN, stood at more than 191,000 people; a figure that, according to the UN human rights chief, Navi Pillay, was "probably an underestimate" owing to "international paralysis" on the issue.

1 From Arab Spring to Islamist Winter

countries most affected by Arab Spring protests

✊ 2011 date protests began

🏃 leader's fate

IS control/influence in Iraq and Syria, May 2015

IS areas of military operations

Iraqi Kurdistan

President Bashar al-Assad remains in power, with some popular support at home; backing from Iran and Russia, but otherwise near-isolation from foreign powers

15 Mar. 2011

14 Feb. 2011
King Hamad bin Isa al Khalifa, Sunni Muslim leader of a tiny Shia-majority island, remains in power after a harsh crackdown

17 Feb. 2011
Muammar al-Gaddafi's 42-year rule ended with NATO-backed rebel capture of Tripoli in August 2011; Gaddafi killed in October 2011

25 Jan. 2011
President Hosni Mubarak forced out after 18-day uprising; military seizes power

March. 2011
King Abdullah faces no national uprising but has issued some pre-emptive reforms and a $37 billion spending programme to rally support

President Ali Abdullah Saleh, badly wounded in assassination attempt in June 2011, pledges in Nov. to step down in Feb. 2012; replaced by his deputy Abd Rabbuh Mansur Hadi, who in turn faces Houthi rebellion and flees the capital in Feb. 2015

27 Jan. 2011

The world in the 21st century

In 2000 the world turned its back on a difficult century torn by massive violence and persistent conflict, but an age capable of extraordinary technical, scientific and economic achievements. The new century has inherited that ambiguous legacy. Wars in Afghanistan and Iraq, civil wars in Africa, the Middle East, Europe and Asia have all shown that the new century will be no less violent. Yet at the same time, the pace of technical and scientific progress has not slackened, while global concerns for the future of the planet have encouraged international collaboration.

THE 20TH CENTURY BEQUEATHED to its successor a number of major issues for humanity to face in the 21st. Some of these are long-term problems about global development that were first identified in the 1960s and 1970s. Population growth has slowed in the first decades of the new century, but it is still high. By 2050, the world may have to sustain 50 per cent more people than it does now; by 2100, perhaps as many as 10 billion. There is already extreme pressure on the world's natural resources, which will worsen as the new populations demand food and basic living standards. Oil, which is essential to today's motorized populations, is a shrinking commodity and most of it is now located in the Middle East, the least stable area in world politics. Scientific breakthroughs may help, but the balance between people and resources is likely to be the century's key problem.

Environmental crisis

Demographic pressure is just one of the problems affecting the global environment. Since the 1990s, when a key international agreement was reached at the Kyoto Summit in Japan, there has been a sustained effort by the world community to find ways of limiting environmental damage caused by deforestation, the burning of fossil fuels and high levels of carbon gas emissions. A summit in Copenhagen in 2009 showed how difficult it would be to persuade rapidly modernizing states to reduce environmental effects when their populations demand rising living standards. In 2014, the two largest contributors to carbon emissions, China and the United States, finally reached agreement about mutual reductions. The result of the man-made damage to the environment is evident in the earth's changing climate. An increase in global temperatures will produce wide-

A Kurdish refugee camp in the Turkish border town of Suruc in January 2015 following the mass flight of Kurds from the scene of the fighting against Islamic State forces **(above)**. Millions of refugees in the Middle East were the victims of civil war in Syria and religious war in northern Syria and Iraq.

1 The emission of large quantities of carbon dioxide and other gases produced by industrial processes and by motor vehicles has raised world temperatures by creating a "greenhouse effect" in the atmosphere **(map below)**. The consequence will be worldwide changes in the location of agricultural surplus areas and widespread flooding of coastal areas. Global temperatures have risen consistently since the 1930s. 1998 was the hottest year since formal records began.

2001 Al-Qaeda attacks New York and Washington

2002 Taliban regime overthrown in Afghanistan; the Euro currency is launched

2003 Second Gulf War and overthrow of Saddam Hussein

2003 Genocidal crisis in Darfur

2004 Indian Ocean tsunami kills estimated 280,000

2007 Property crisis in USA triggers world financial meltdown

2009 North Korea detonates nuclear device

2011 Tunisian revolt launches the Arab Spring

2013 Islamic State in Syria and Iraq founded

2014 Russia annexes Crimea from Ukraine

1 Global warming

- more humid than before
- drier than before
- principal farming regions
- flooding through rise in sea level
- **1C** increase in surface temperature

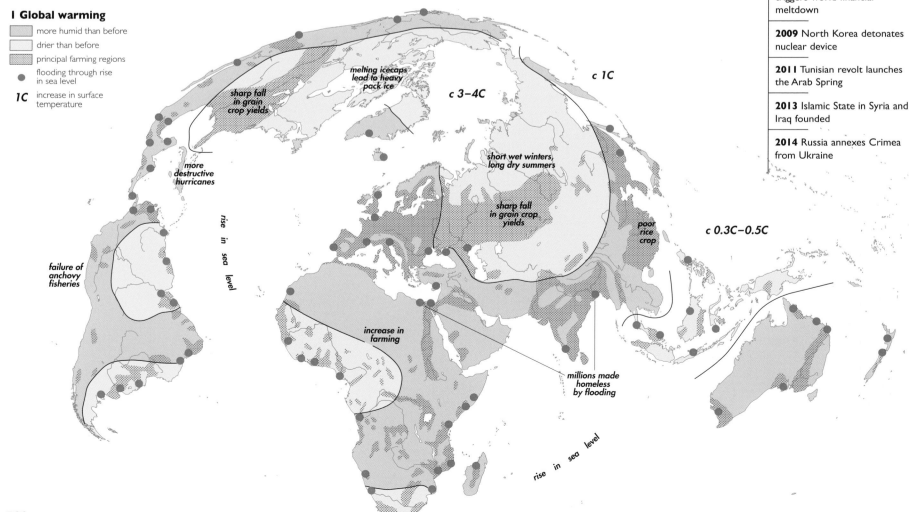

melting icecaps lead to heavy pack ice

sharp fall in grain crop yields

c 3–4C

c 1C

short wet winters, long dry summers

sharp fall in grain crop yields

poor rice crop

c 0.3C–0.5C

more destructive hurricanes

rise in sea level

failure of anchovy fisheries

increase in farming

millions made homeless by flooding

rise in sea level

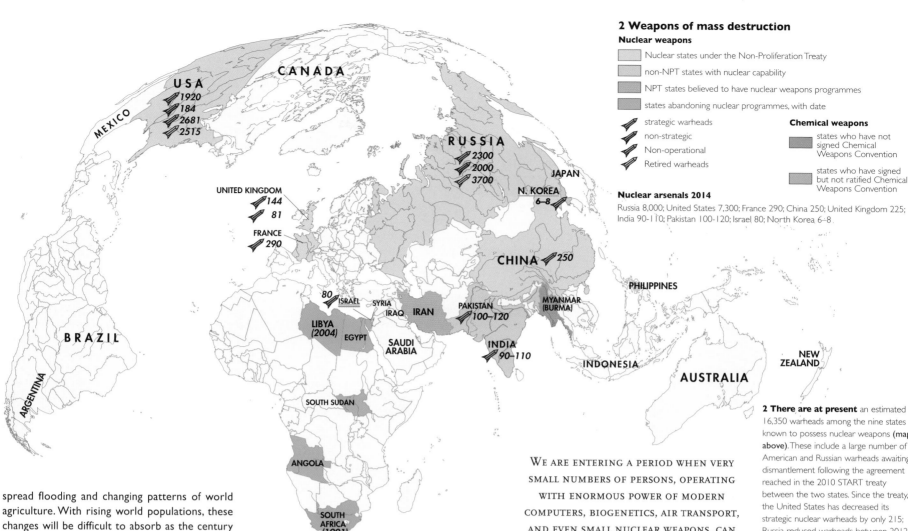

2 Weapons of mass destruction

Nuclear weapons

	Nuclear states under the Non-Proliferation Treaty
	non-NPT states with nuclear capability
	NPT states believed to have nuclear weapons programmes
	states abandoning nuclear programmes, with date

- strategic warheads
- non-strategic
- Non-operational
- Retired warheads

Chemical weapons

- states who have not signed Chemical Weapons Convention
- states who have signed but not ratified Chemical Weapons Convention

Nuclear arsenals 2014

Russia 8,000; United States 7,300; France 290; China 250; United Kingdom 225; India 90–110; Pakistan 100–120; Israel 80; North Korea 6–8

Map labels: USA 1920 184 2681 2515; RUSSIA 2300 2000 3700; UNITED KINGDOM 144 81; FRANCE 290; CHINA 250; N. KOREA 6–8; ISRAEL 80; PAKISTAN 100–120; INDIA 90–110; LIBYA (2004); SOUTH AFRICA (1991)

---

spread flooding and changing patterns of world agriculture. With rising world populations, these changes will be difficult to absorb as the century progresses.

Weapons of mass destruction

The other peril facing the 21st century world is the danger from weapons of mass destruction. The fears expressed by the West about Iraq's possession of these prompted the Second Gulf War in 2003. The international spread of chemical, biological and, above all, nuclear weapons is difficult to control and there is fear of attacks by terrorists or so-called "rogue states" employing toxic agents or even "dirty" bombs using radioactive material. The end of the Cold War has made traditional deterrence strategy no longer workable. In 2002, a crisis between India and Pakistan prompted fears that

they might resort to using their nuclear arsenals; North Korea now has a nuclear capability and leaders whose willingness to resort to nuclear assault is unpredictable. Fears that Iran might develop a nuclear device led to sanctions against the country and in 2015, following prolonged negotiations with the United States and other world powers, a limited commitment by the Iranian government not to develop a nuclear weapons programme.

In truth, the bulk of weapons of mass destruction are held in the hands of a few major states. Russia and the United States could obliterate the planet with their stockpiles of nuclear warheads. China has emerged as a global superpower and also has a

WE ARE ENTERING A PERIOD WHEN VERY SMALL NUMBERS OF PERSONS, OPERATING WITH ENORMOUS POWER OF MODERN COMPUTERS, BIOGENETICS, AIR TRANSPORT, AND EVEN SMALL NUCLEAR WEAPONS, CAN DEAL LETHAL BLOWS TO ANY SOCIETY. BECAUSE THE ORIGIN OF THESE ATTACKS CAN BE EFFECTIVELY DISGUISED, THE FUNDAMENTAL BASES OF THE STATE WILL CHANGE.

Philip Bobbitt, 2002

large nuclear capability. As the post-Cold War order takes shape, there remain risks that an unpredictable international crisis might trigger dangerous tensions backed by the threat of sophisticated modern weaponry. A century after the First World War, widespread commemoration is a reminder of how easily the modern world slipped into global conflict.

2 There are at present an estimated 16,350 warheads among the nine states known to possess nuclear weapons (map above). These include a large number of American and Russian warheads awaiting dismantlement following the agreement reached in the 2010 START treaty between the two states. Since the treaty, the United States has decreased its strategic nuclear warheads by only 215; Russia reduced warheads between 2012 and 2014 by 99. The total available arsenals would still produce a nuclear winter worldwide if they were ever used.

3 The doomsday predictions of massive and unsustainable population growth into the 21st century have given way to more modest estimates (map below). Current trends will produce a global population of nine billion by the mid-century, as smaller family size and the spread of contraception slow down the rate of growth. In Africa disease (particulary AIDS), hunger and war have also helped to slow the fastest area of population expansion. Feeding and resourcing a world population of this size still remains a daunting task.

---

3 World population in the 21st century

Family size and population growth

- very rapid growth (more than 5 children per family)
- intermediate growth (2.1–5 children per family)
- slow growth or decline (fewer than 2.1 children per family)

Fastest-growing populations (% per annum)

- 4.5% 2000–5
- 4.0% 2045–50 (projection)
- 48.6 % of population under 15

Slowest-growing populations (% per annum)

- -4.5% 2000–5
- -4.0% 2045–50 (projection)

JAPAN 9 — countries with population of 50 million or more in 2000, in ranking order

JAPAN (15) — countries with population of 50 million or more in 2050 (projection), in ranking order

JAPAN -13.6 — countries with projected population decrease 2000–50, with percentage

Tokyo 26.4 — cities with populations over 10 million in 2000 (with population)

Tokyo (27.2) — cities with populations over 10 million in 2050 (with projected population)

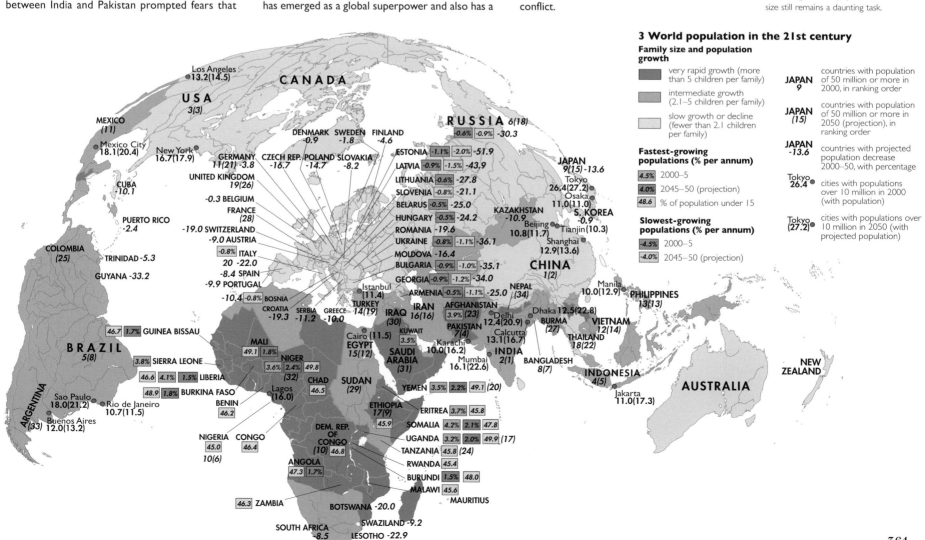

361

The state of the world

The choice of Beijing, capital of China, as the host city for the 2008 Olympic Games produced an extraordinary historic marriage of East and West. The games symbolize the world of classical Greece, whose legacy has played such an exceptional part in the development of the Western world. Greek civilization gave the West professional medicine, geometry, ethical speculation, democracy, an ideal of participatory citizenship, codified law, the first history, a science of politics and an artistic heritage imitated again and again down the ages. Many of our common terms today – from economics to psychiatry – are Greek in origin.

China, on the other hand, is the seat of the most ancient and continuous of civilizations. Always the site of the largest fraction of the world's population, China for thousands of years, despite waves of invasions, sustained a way of life and a social structure which proved remarkably enduring. Chinese values and intellectual life were not, unlike Greek civilization, diffused widely outside the frontiers of what was loosely defined as "China". Western critics in the 19th century regarded China as a stagnant culture, unmoved for centuries, but the artistic, scientific and intellectual life of China, though very different from that of the West, was rich and diverse. A good case can be made for arguing that China has been a fixed point throughout the period of recorded history, where Greek culture has been anything but continuous, relying for much of its survival on the intercession of the Arab cultures of the Middle East that succeeded the Roman Empire, through which aspects of Greek thought were kept alive and then re-exported to late medieval Europe.

The China of the 2008 Olympics is still a central part of the world story, but it has come part way to meet the West. From the late 19th century traditional Chinese society crumbled under Western impact. A nationalist revolution overthrew the emperors and the old way of life after 1911. A second communist revolution transformed China into a more modern industrial state after 1949. Over the past 25 years China has undergone a third revolutionary wave by embracing the fruits of modern global capitalism and becoming one of the world's major economic players. China has not become an Asian "West", but has adapted what the West has had to offer and has turned itself into a world "superpower". The relationship between East and West has come full circle. For centuries the West pushed outwards into the world exporting, usually violently, a version of Western civilization. China was long resistant to this pressure; now China can exert pressure of its own, challenging the monopoly hitherto enjoyed by the remorseless march of Western economics, political models, consumerism and popular culture.

The meeting of Greece and China weaves together two of the central threads of world history. But the Olympics are also a symbolic fusion of ancient and modern. Although the original games are far removed from the glossy, commercialized, technically sophisticated and ruinously expensive modern version, their revival is a reminder that there are easily understood reference points back to the Europe of more than 2,000 years ago. Boxing, wrestling, javelin-throwing and running are simply what they are, the same for a modern audience as they were for the Greeks. Even the marathon, the icon of the current Western obsession with keeping fit, describes a Greek legend, when a soldier-runner covered 26 miles non-stop under a gruelling sun from the Battle of Marathon to Athens to warn of the approaching Persian fleet, only to drop dead from the effort on his arrival. Distant though the ancient world seems, the span of recorded human history is remarkably short in relation to the long history of prehistoric man and the infinitely longer history of the earth. The span can be covered by just a hundred human lives of 60 years, stretched out one after the other. Only 50 human lives will take you back to those first Olympic Games. To think about the past as something connected by a continuous thread of human activity runs the danger of imposing a false sense of unity, but for much of the earth's surface, over long periods of time, fundamental change has been absent. Anthropological evidence has for a long time been able to describe practices and beliefs that are clearly connected with a world so distant that it has been transmuted into myth. One hundred human lives laid end-to-end is not very many. To put it another way: it is possible to house an artefact from every major civilization of the past 5,000 years in a single cabinet and to recognize that until the last few hundred years those artefacts – whether a pot, a fertility doll, an arrow-head, a shoe, a coin – bear a remarkable underlying similarity. The recorded history of the world can be read at one level as a unitary experience, a brief 4 per cent of the time modern hominids have been evolving, a hundred human lives.

The Sphinx and pyramid at Giza, Egypt

Of course these lives were not the same wherever they were lived. Whatever homologies can be detected between peoples and civilizations, the experience of world history over the past 6,000 years is a series of fractured narratives, divided geographically and segmented by differing cultures, religious practices and political orders. The whole course of world history has been a process of cultural exchange and discovery, of imperial expansion and decline: sometimes links once made were then ruptured again; at other times communication enriched both cultures. In the past 500 years that process of discovering, mapping and understanding the world as a whole has accelerated, but for most previous civilizations the "known world" was only what was immediately known. The modern concept of "world history" which this book encapsulates was meaningless to most human civilizations through most of human history. For large areas of the globe there was no written culture so that "history" survived as myth or folk memory, dating was arbitrary or non-existent, and the world was circumscribed by the very limited geographical reach of particular peoples. Rome was an exception, but even for Romans the known world was centred on the Mediterranean and the barbarous (meaning alien) outside was scarcely understood or valued. China for centuries regarded itself as the centre of the universe, and the outside world, to the extent that it intruded at all, was supposed to revolve like so many blighted planets around the Chinese sun. The history of the world is a very Western idea and it has become knowable only in the last century or so as Europeans and their descendants overseas produced sophisticated archaeological techniques and scholarly skills to unlock many of the remaining secrets of the past. When the English novelist H. G. Wells wrote his famous *Outline of History*, published in 1920, he was able to do so only on the foundation of an outpouring of new research in the last decades of the 19th century. Wells was preoccupied, he wrote in his introduction, with "history as one whole", and he was one of the first to attempt it.

The more that came to be known about the many civilizations and cultures that made up human history, the more tempting it was, like Wells, to try to see history as a whole and to explain the process of historical change as a uniform one. This ambition had roots in the 19th century, where it was famously attempted by the German thinkers Georg Hegel and his erstwhile disciple Karl Marx, who both suggested that historical change was dynamic, the result of shifting patterns of thought or the transition from one economic system to another, each stage of human development incorporating the best from the past but each an advance on the one before it, until humankind finally reached an ideal society. The 19th-century view, coloured by the remarkable technical progress of the age, was to try to see a purpose behind historical change – not a mere random set of events, or a set of parables or myths to educate the present, but a triumphant account of the ascent of man. Neither Hegel nor Marx was a historian, and they both regarded China as a backwater that had somehow failed to move like the rest of the world. The 20th century witnessed more historically sophisticated attempts to find a unity in world history. The German philosopher Oswald Spengler published just after the First World War two volumes of an ambitious study of the pattern of all world history. Each civilization, Spengler argued, had a natural life-cycle, like any organism, of birth, growth, maturity and death, a run of approximately 1,000 years each. He called his volumes *The Decline of the West* in order to argue against the optimism of the previous century and to demonstrate that Western civilization, for all its belief that it represented the full flowering of human history, was doomed to go the way of the rest. The British historian Arnold Toynbee thought Spengler's view of history too schematic, but he produced 10 volumes of *A Study of History* between 1934 and 1954 in which he too detected a common pattern in all previous civilizations which explained their birth, rise to cultural fruition and eventual collapse. Both Spengler and Toynbee rejected the idea that the purpose of history was the triumph of the West, but they both thought that history could be understood as a single, repeated pattern, from ancient Egypt to the modern West.

Few historians now accept that world history works like this. The rise and fall of civilizations evidently has causes, but it does not follow from this that history ought to progress, or that it follows internal laws or patterns of development. History does not move forward entirely blindly, but its progress is more often than not accidental, not patterned, and the circumstances of its development contingent rather than purposive – a product of a particular set of circumstances at a particular time rather than a necessary progress from one stage to the next. The same objection can be raised to the popular idea that there are turning points in history, key battles or events that have determined the course of history. Some events are clearly more important than others. History might now be written differently if the Roman army had not defeated Hannibal at Zama in 202 BC, but this was just one event in a much wider world of human activity, insignificant in the India or China of the 3rd century BC. On balance human history moves forward on a broad front, less affected by "turning points" than might be expected. If one set of events had never happened, there would just be a different narrative which would now be accepted as part of the past as readily as any other. History has neither pattern nor purpose. It is simply the record of what has been.

There are nonetheless broad common factors that have shaped the development of human communities wherever they have settled. The most important element has been the continuous and complex relationship between mankind and the natural world. Natural phenomena have defined a great deal of the human story. Until quite recently most natural forces were beyond human capacity to control or mediate or even to understand. Some still remain so. In the spring of 2008 a ferocious cyclone which laid waste large parts of southern Myanmar and a powerful earthquake in China killed at least 150,000 people between them. Natural disasters – earthquakes, tidal waves, volcanic eruptions, soil erosion, rising sea levels, crop failure – have been a constant feature of all history. The shaping of the landscape determined patterns of settlement, forms of husbandry, the possibility of exploration and trade. The seas and rivers have been both barrier and pathway. The siting of cities, artificial

additions to the landscape, has been determined by access to river communications, or the existence of a natural harbour, or the natural defensive walls provided by high outcrops of rock or hillside. For the past 5,000 years and since the introduction of widespread agriculture, the relationship between population size and food supply has added a further natural factor restricting or enhancing the prospects of particular societies, or creating violent tensions between communities that lived by hunting and those with settled pastoral traditions. This competition is not confined to the ancient past, when, for example, waves of hunters from the plains of Eurasia descended on Europe in the 5th and 6th centuries; in the 19th century, the near extermination by white hunters of the North American buffalo, an animal on which some Native American tribal societies depended, opened the way for the vast grain-growing prairie belt and the emasculation of the Native American population.

The supply of food, or its absence, famine, is a constant through human history. It exercised the ancient Egyptians, who developed complex irrigation systems to compensate for a buoyant population surrounded by desert; 3,000 years later Adolf Hitler argued that Germans needed "living space" in Eastern Europe to provide a proper balance between population and food supply; the contemporary world, trying to support a vastly greater population, witnesses famines in Africa side by side with an overabundance of food in the richer West. A new food crisis (in 2008) has prompted the bleak conclusion that food output must expand 50 per cent by 2030 to meet demand. For most people through most of recorded history the search for food has been unyielding. In hunting communities, as long as there existed a wealth of animal life or fish, food was not a problem. In settled, agricultural communities, on the other hand, the supply of food was restricted either by problems of soil or changeable climate or by the maldistribution of food between rich and poor, or both. Tilling the soil was no guarantee of a decent diet; a Roman feast or a groaning Victorian banquet gives no clue as to how inadequate was the food supply for the slaves who grew and garnered it in Roman Italy, or for the Victorian poor, most of them cut off from the land and dependent on a monotonous starch-rich diet. (In post-Renaissance Italy there developed one of the most sophisticated cuisines in the world, informed by a wealth of gastronomic masterworks, but the later peasant workers of the Po Valley suffered debilitating pellagra from eating a stodgy maize-based diet that inflated their abdomens and eventually killed them.) In settled civilizations, an adequate, varied, artistically presented or innovative diet was the preserve of the rich. It was no accident that the Russian Revolution of February 1917 began with a demonstration for bread by hungry women in St Petersburg (Petrograd).

The relationship between humankind and the environment has changed a good deal over the past 200 years. Larger and more regular food supplies, together with changes in healthcare, have provoked a population explosion. Global population was around 800 million in the 18th century; currently it is an astonishing 7 billion. A result has been the massive expansion of the agricultural base, partly from utilising virgin lands, partly from raising yields artificially through plant- and stock-breeding or the addition of chemical fertilizer. These changes have provoked deforestation and the transformation of natural habitat. Heavy hunting has brought thousands of land and sea creatures to the edge of extinction. The world's urban population has grown dramatically since 1900 and now stands at just over 50 per cent of the whole, producing huge sprawling cities and high levels of human pollution. To meet the daily needs of such a population has meant expanding industrial production, depleting the earth's natural resources, and creating a growing chemical imbalance in the atmosphere that has damaged the ozone layer and threatens through so-called "global warming" to undermine the fragile basis on which 7 billion people can subsist. Demands for a higher living standard from Western populations already rich in resources, and for catch-up living standards in much of the rest of the world, have accelerated the depletion of resources, the transformation of the landscape and the unnatural climate change. The rich United States has 5 per cent of the world's population but generates annually 25 per cent of the "greenhouse gases" that cause climate change. The most alarming scenarios are now painted of the capacity of man to forge new natural disasters to which there will be no answer – enough methane gas perhaps to cause a global explosion in a century's time, or the release of bacteria from the frozen icecaps millions of years old, from which current populations would have no prospect of immunity. The relationship between man and nature has about it a profound irony. The attempt to master the natural world has simply given nature new and more terrible powers.

Only in one respect has it proved possible to tame nature sufficiently to alter human society for the good. Over the past 150 years, in itself a fraction of the long history of man, it has proved possible to understand and then prevent or cure most medical conditions. For all the rest of human history, disease and disability were an ever-present reality for which there was almost no effective relief. The establishment of cities and animal husbandry combined to create ideal conditions for the establishment of a cluster of endemic epidemic diseases which periodically killed off wide swathes of the human host. The earliest epidemics in the cities of the first civilizations in China, Egypt or Mesopotamia included smallpox, diphtheria, influenza, chickenpox and mumps. With the opening of trade routes and regular invasions, disease could be spread from populations that had developed some immunity to those biologically vulnerable. Athens was struck by a devastating plague in 430 BC which undermined its political power; the Antonine plague in the late 2nd century AD Roman Empire killed around one-quarter of the populations it infected, probably with smallpox. Bubonic plague, transmitted by fleas carried on rats, killed around two-thirds of its victims. Plague originating in Egypt in AD 540 spread to the Eastern Mediterranean where again one-quarter of the population died. The famous Black Death in the 14th century swept from Asia to Europe, killing an estimated 20 million and reducing Europe's population by one-quarter. Epidemics died out partly because the pathogens had no other victims to kill. Modernity was no safeguard either. Cholera coincided with the industrialization and urbanization of Europe and produced regular pandemics in Asia, the Middle East and Europe between the 1820s and the 1890s. "Spanish influenza" struck Europe at the end of the First World War with populations unnaturally weakened by lack of food; it was the world's worst pandemic, killing 60 million people in just two years.

The attempt to understand and explain the nature of disease, and if possible cure it, goes back to the very earliest periods of recorded history. Classic Chinese medicine (now usually described as Traditional Chinese Medicine or TCM) is thought to date back almost 5,000 years. The standard text on "Basic Questions of Internal Medicine" (known as *Neijing Suwen*) was written, according to legend, by the Yellow Emperor in around 2,600 BC; the earliest surviving version dates from at least 2,000 years ago. Early Chinese medicine was rooted in a broader philosophical system based in one case on Confucianism, in the second on Taoism. Confucianism rejected the idea of anatomical or surgical invasion in the belief that the body was sacred; instead the use of acupuncture or massage was preferred, influencing internal disease by external means. Taoism saw health related entirely to achieving harmony between the different elements of the world, the Yin and the Yang. Disease was a consequence of lack of harmony. Chinese medicine focused on herbal remedies and acupuncture as means to restore that harmony rather than more violent medical intervention. Close observation of morbid symptoms was regarded as essential to understand what combination of remedies was needed. During the brief Sui dynasty (AD 581–618) a group of doctors composed *The General Treatise on the Causes and Symptoms of Disease*, which comprised 50 volumes and described some 1,700 conditions.

The Parthenon on the Acropolis, Athens, 6th century BC

The classic texts retained an enduring influence down to the 20th century when successive modernizing regimes tried to substitute Western medicine with only limited success.

The other classic tradition arose in Greece from the 5th century BC based on the teachings of the secular theorist Hippocrates, born around 460, whose famous "oath", that doctors should at the least do no harm, is still sworn by Western doctors today. Like Chinese medicine, Greek medicine relied on explaining disease as an absence of harmony in the body between four elements or "humours" that composed it. The elements were blood, choler (yellow bile), phlegm and black bile. These humours corresponded to the elements identified by Greek science as universal components – air (blood), fire (choler), water (phlegm) and earth (black bile). Cure for any imbalance was based on a range of options – bleeding, diet, exercise and occasional surgery. These views, revived in medieval Europe, exercized a continuing influence down to the time when modern medical science made its first appearance in the European Renaissance, and even beyond it. The problem for Greek as for Chinese medicine was the strong prejudice against direct anatomical research on human cadavers. In all pre-scientific medical systems an absence of proper understanding of the function of the body and the cause of disease meant that cures were largely accidental. Recent tests on 200 Chinese traditional herbal remedies for malaria found that only one, by chance, contained anything that might contribute to a cure.

Only the onset of serious research on how the body worked – perhaps the most famous example was William Harvey's discovery of the circulation of the blood, published in 1628 – made it possible to understand how the body was affected by particular conditions and to suggest prophylaxis. Even then the growing understanding of the body did little to help prevent epidemics until the onset of vaccination (introduced in late 18th-century Britain for smallpox) and the ground-breaking research of the French chemist, Louis Pasteur, and the German doctor Robert Koch, which by the 1880s had confirmed that disease was caused by bacteria, each different micro-organism responsible for a particular disease. The discovery of antibiotic properties in penicillin mould in 1928 completed the therapeutic revolution. From the mid-19th century onwards the older medical traditions, which had limited or no medical efficacy, were superseded by a science-based medicine which has pushed the frontiers of biochemistry, neurology, physiology and pharmacology almost to their limits and has, at least temporarily, conquered almost all known diseases and a large number of internal medical disorders.

Only the identification of the HIV virus in the 1980s, which attacks the body's immune system, made it clear that even the most scientifically advanced medicine may not in the future be able to stem new and unexpected forms of epidemic. For the fortunate few generations in the West who have been the full beneficiaries of the medical revolution, the transformation has been extraordinary. For all the rest of recorded human history there was no effective cure for most diseases and humans survived only because of a complex struggle between the micro-organisms and the human immune system. Death was ever-present and social attitudes and religious beliefs had to be rooted in the expectation of high levels of mortality. For those who survived there were disfiguring illnesses, crippling medical conditions, poor eyesight, chronic toothache, and so on. For women throughout history there was the debilitating cycle of births and the ever-present risk of maternal death. Pain, like premature death, was a permanent visitor.

To make matters worse, throughout human history both death and pain have been inflicted unnaturally, the product of deliberate violence on the part of human communities. Humankind, and almost always the male of the species, is a uniquely aggressive and punitive creature. Although attempts have been made over the past century to demonstrate that other animal species indulge in deliberate violence, animal violence is instinctive, not conscious. Humankind, on the other hand, has throughout recorded history, and evidently long before that, been able to premeditate the use of violence directed at other humans. Some anthropologists, following the 18th-century French philosopher Jean-Jacques Rousseau, have tried to argue that early humans were most likely peaceable, and that only the tensions generated by more complex forms of social life introduced higher levels of violence. But the range and sophistication of prehistoric weapons, first stone, then iron and bronze, makes the idea of a pacific prehistoric state implausible. It is of course true that with settled communities, centred on cities, violence came to be organized through the use of armies. The evolution of a specialized human function for organizing and legitimating the use of violence is evident in the very earliest recorded history. The soldier, armed with an ever more lethal armoury, runs in an unbroken line from all corners of the ancient world where complex civilizations arose. In tribal communities, without settled urban life, inter-tribal and intra-tribal violence was often ritualized, the young males of the tribe using violence as a rite of passage or a sacred obligation.

There is no single answer to the question of why violence should be such a hallmark of world history, but it can be found on almost every page. The German legal theorist Carl Schmitt, writing in the 1920s, claimed that the human community has always been divided between "friend" and "foe", those who are included in the group and those who are excluded. Simplistic though the distinction might seem, the concept of the alien, the other, the barbarian, the enemy, or the excluded also runs as a thread through all history. Treatment of the "other" has always been harsh, even in the modern age with its vain efforts to impose some kind of restraints or norms on military behaviour and state violence. Yet even this distinction leaves a great deal unexplained. Human beings do not just fight each other in pitched battles using soldiers who know what to expect. They punish human victims in hideously painful and savage ways. Coercive social relationships have been far more common than consensual ones. Victims, even those from among "the included" who are guilty of crime, have been tortured, beaten, imprisoned and executed in ways so ingeniously atrocious and gratuitously cruel that it is difficult not to assume that violence is the normal human condition and the very recent and limited experience of peace and respect for the individual a merciful historical anomaly. Violence is also universal, not some characteristic of "savage society" as self-righteous Victorian imperialists liked to think. Civilizations, however sophisticated, have indulged in violence of every kind. Religions have often led the way in devising grotesque ways to seek out heresies and exorcize devils. At the Museum of Torture Instruments in Guadalest in Spain (by no means the only such museum) are displayed roomfuls of fearful devices designed to extract confessions from across early-modern Europe, including the unhappy victims of the notorious Spanish Inquisition – iron crowns with spikes which tighten around the victim's head, sharp stakes that could impale the whole length of a human body without killing the victim immediately. Human beings have devoted a deplorable amount of effort to inflicting suffering, and seem to have done so with few moral qualms.

There have been many attempts to explain why wars happen, or why human history is so soaked in blood. There is no single concept of war that can embrace all the many forms of war or the thousands of separate historical reasons why particular wars break out. Early 20th-century anthropologists were inclined to argue that war might have had some important function in primitive societies or in the age of early state formation but they could see no justification for it in the modern age. The idea that war, and other forms of violence, were a throwback to a past age now thinly papered over with "civilization" was urged by the Austrian psychoanalyst Sigmund Freud when he reflected on the reasons for the prolonged and deadly fighting in the First World War. Freud thought war rapidly exposed the savage persona inside and later argued that the more "civilized" a people became, the more likely it was that the dam of repression would burst and uncontrollable violence result.

Whether or not this really is the mechanism that releases violence, Freud proved all too right in his prediction. In the late 19th century it was still just possible to imagine that the barbarities of earlier history, when cities were sacked, their populations put to the sword and fine buildings burned, were a thing of the past (though this did not prevent European troops on a punitive expedition from destroying the stunning Summer Palace in Beijing in 1860, an act of wanton vandalism that witnesses compared with the sack of Rome by the Goths). But the 20th century has been the bloodiest in all of human history, witness to somewhere between 85 and 100 million violent deaths, and millions more wounded, maimed, tortured, raped and dispossessed. It includes the deliberate murder of the European Jews which must rank with anything else in scale and horror from the past 6,000 years. It will be difficult for historians in a few hundred years' time to see what separates the Mongol sack of Samarkand in 1220, which left only a few of the inhabitants alive, from the Allies' destruction of Hamburg in 1943, which burnt the city to the ground and killed 40,000 people in hideous ways in just two days. The second was, of course, quicker and more efficient, but the moral defence usually mounted, that war is war, is a maxim as comprehensible in the ancient world as it would have been to Genghis Khan or Napoleon. So-called civilization displays precisely Freud's divided self – capable of self-restraint and social progress, but capable of sudden lapses into barbarism.

The impact of famine, disease and war on human history was famously illustrated by the English 18th-century clergyman, Thomas Malthus, who argued in his *Essay on the Principle of Population*, published in 1798, that throughout history the dangers of overpopulation were always checked by the operation of these three elements. It is tempting to turn this argument on its head and wonder how it is that the human species survived at all under the multiple assault of violence, hunger and epidemic, but it took an English biologist, Charles Darwin, with the publication of *The Origin of Species* in 1859, to explain that species survived through natural selection. The survival of *Homo sapiens* was thus biologically explicable; the stronger survived, the weaker perished. In a crude sense that was true, and for decades thereafter it was assumed that harsh though the realities of history had been, they had been necessary hardships to produce a biologically and intellectually progressive species. Both writers have in the end been confounded by a further paradox of the modern age: population has risen to levels often predicted as insupportable, but growth has scarcely been dented by the incidence of disease or violence or hunger, while natural selection has been overturned by modern medicine and welfare policies. The most violent and deadly century has at the same time been the century with the highest survival rates.

The Taj Mahal, Agra

Grim though the past has often been, history has not been an unmediated story of suffering borne by an uncomprehending and victimized humanity. From the very earliest times human societies needed to make sense of the chaos and dangers around them, or to justify the hardships they faced, or the reality of unpredictable or premature death or to find some wider moral universe which sanctioned acceptable forms of behaviour and penalized others. Religion was able to satisfy all these needs, and religious beliefs, like warfare, have been a constant for at least six millennia. Consideration of religion raises awkward questions about the nature of "world history" because for most human societies through most of time, the material world described by modern historians has only been one part of the universe of human experience. Religious communities are connected to other unseen states and unknowable sites which have been, and for many still are, as profound a part of reality as the political structures and economic systems of the visible world. Belief in a world of spirits or an afterlife, or in unseen and divine guardians, or in a sublime universal "other" has made historical experience multi-dimensional, natural as well as supernatural. For medieval Christians the world was one link in a complex chain between heaven and hell, which included the nether world of purgatory where souls were left to wait for entry to paradise. For ancient Egyptians the other world was so real that kings talked and walked with the gods, and when they died took with them their household, animals and furnishings. So widespread was the belief that the dead, or at least kings, nobles and priests, needed to take possessions with them beyond the grave that modern knowledge of past cultures has been enormously expanded by the votive offerings and funerary furnishings found in excavated graves.

Belief in the supernatural, the divine, a world of the spirit, the reality of a soul that could live on beyond the decay of the earthly body, magic, superstition and witchcraft created for the inhabitants of all but the most recent communities a sphere of experience that was always larger than the material world around them. Belief was used to explain the apparently inexplicable, to ward off evil, to promote well-being, induce harmony of being and to prepare the mortal body for the world or worlds to come. The link with a world beyond mere physical observation has proved remarkably enduring, even in the secular, liberal West. In southern Italy images of saints and the Madonna are still carried through villages to offer protection against floods or volcanic eruptions or to encourage rainfall. The concept of "the Limbo of the Infants", introduced as a term by the Catholic Church in around 1300 to describe a haven for the souls of babies who died before there was time for baptism, in which they enjoyed a natural happiness, but were denied access to heaven, was all but set aside in 2007 when the Church announced that unbaptized infants should be entrusted to the possible mercy of God. Protests from parents anxious that their dead children should have a sure destination forced the Church to admit that Limbo was still a possibility. All attempts to provide a secular alternative to traditional Islam have foundered on the continuing vitality of the values and practices of the faith which is bound to a world beyond this one. Suicide bombers are recruited on the promise that they will be welcomed at once by the souls of the faithful when they cross the threshold of death.

Religions of every kind have exerted an extraordinary psychological power. This has been served in a number of ways. For thousands of years the finest buildings and monuments have been dedicated to religious purposes; in tribal societies the sacred – totems, ancestral graveyards – has exerted powerful fears and provoked an instinctive reverence. The numerous cathedrals, mosques and temples built in Christian, Islamic and Buddhist communities from medieval times onwards as gateways to the divine are among the richest architecture in the world, constructed in societies where for the poor the monumental buildings were awe-inspiring expressions of the spiritual. Religions were also the source of sanctioned behaviour. The rules laid down for social practice, custom, family life or sexual conduct are almost all religious in origin. A great many religions have been vehicles for constructing a male-centred society in which women were compelled to accept an ascribed and restricted gender role or risk severe forms of punishment or social discrimination. Many moral codes or legal systems were constructed by lay authorities – for example, Justinian's *Codex*, or the Code Napoleon – but they relied on a conception of acceptable behaviour that was derived from the core moral teaching of the Church. In traditional Islam there should ideally be no distinction between religious precept and state law. In early Chinese history the emperors were accorded divine status, making the law, but making it as gods. In Japanese society, where the emperors also enjoyed quasi-divine status, to die willingly for the emperor was a moral obligation that overrode all others.

Religious belief was always difficult to challenge because the threat that unbelief or heresy posed was a threat to an entire way of viewing the world. For a great many communities governed by animist or polytheistic systems of belief there were no reasons, and usually no means, for questioning the ground in which such belief was rooted. There was no question of earning salvation; simply obeying the customary rites and endorsing the beliefs of a given system was all that was required. Monotheistic religions, in which respect for the deity and reverence for doctrine earned the right to salvation, were altogether more problematic. Arguments about Christian doctrine brought regular schism, provoking the rift between Orthodox Christianity in Eastern Europe and Western Catholic Christianity in 1054, and further schism between Catholic and Protestant Christianity in the 16th century. Fear of heterodoxy, or of the diabolical, provoked Catholicism into regular heresy hunts and the extraction of confessions through torture. Both Protestants and Catholics were burnt at the stake for their faith in the struggle over the Reformation. Radical Protestantism was also fearful of idolatry or witchcraft and the last witches were famously burnt in Salem, Massachusetts, in 1692. Islam was also schismatic. In AD 680 the faith divided between Sunni and Shiite sects over disagreements on doctrine (including the Shia insistence that Allah could take human form), and the two branches are still engaged in violent confrontation throughout the Middle East.

To claim no religious allegiance has been a recent and limited option, confined largely to the Western world. Atheism became publicly admissible in the 19th century without fear of punishment, but the public denial of God still attracts outrage. Secularists over the past two centuries have been keen to separate Church and state, but have not necessarily been irreligious. The strident rejection of the supernatural was identified with 19th-century socialism whose world view was materialist. Atheism appealed to a progressive intelligentsia hostile to what they saw as stale Christian convention. When the German poet-philosopher Friedrich Nietzsche famously announced in *Thus Spake Zarathustra*, published in 1888, that "God is dead!", he challenged what he saw as the great lie, dating back 2,000 years, and found a limited intellectual audience more than willing to accept a godless reality. In the early 20th century atheism was formally adopted by the Soviet Union, and by communist China after 1949, but in neither case was it possible to eradicate belief. Atheism is now widely regarded as a declining intellectual force in an age of religious revivalism. The wide popular hostility to Richard Dawkins's recently published *The God Delusion* (2006) is testament to how necessary it is even for societies where church attendance is moribund to belive that the material world is not just all there is.

For much of recorded history what was known or believed to be knowable was bound up with religion. Religious institutions and the priesthood were the depositories of knowledge passed down, like the famous Jewish Talmud, from generation to generation. The earliest work of "wisdom literature" in ancient Egypt, perhaps in the world, was attributed to Imhotep, high priest of Heliopolis under Djoser, king between 2654 and 2635 BC. Religious buildings housed valuable manuscripts, not only sacred books but treatises on many subjects. During the early Christian era in Europe, in what used to be known as the "Dark Ages", monasteries and churches kept alive traditions of teaching, writing and recording. The Venerable Bede, based at the monastery in Wearmouth-Jarrow in the northeast of England in the early 8th century, helped to collect together an estimated 300–500 volumes, one of the largest libraries of books in the then Western world. Western education was dominated by the Church until the 18th century. Knowledge of this kind was limited in several ways. First, it was confined to a very small elite who could read and write. A distinct literary or official language was developed which could be fully understood only by the favoured few. Although the earliest writing can be dated back to the Sumerian civilization in present-day Iraq around 5,000 years ago, and then emerged in Egypt and China, the overwhelming majority of all humans who lived between then and the last few centuries were illiterate. Knowledge for them was limited to what could be conveyed orally, or crudely illustrated. For most people information was passed on through rumour, superstition, ritual, songs, sagas and folk tales. Second, it was limited by the theological or philosophical priorities of those who held the key to knowledge, reinforcing existing views of the known world, or of man's relation to the universe, or of social hierarchy. Knowledge was used instrumentally, rather than for its own sake, confirming the existing order rather than encouraging critical or subversive discourse.

Knowledge in this sense did not inhibit technique. From the earliest settled communities onwards rapid strides were made in the practical skills associated with metallurgy, construction, irrigation, sculpture, and the production of artefacts of often stunning originality and beauty. The contrast between the last 6,000 years and the previous tens of thousands of years is remarkable. Early man made painfully slow progress in the development of sophisticated tools of stone or bone; humans in settled communities, with a division of labour and access to trade, could transfer technologies or fashions in a matter of years. By the time of the late Roman Empire, as any visit to a museum of classical archaeology will confirm, the range and sophistication of everything from daily products to major pieces of engineering was as advanced as anything that could be found for another thousand years. Practical skill was not, however, knowledge. Understanding of the natural world, like understanding of the supernatural, was conditional. It was possible to build the most technically remarkable and artistically splendid cathedral but still to believe that the earth was flat and that hell really existed.

The development of a critical, sceptical, speculative science that did not endorse existing beliefs but deliberately undermined them was a historical development of exceptional importance. The foundations of a speculative intellectual life were to be found in ancient Greece, whose philosophers, poets and playwrights produced work of real originality whose central concerns, despite the passage of 2,000 years, engaged the enthusiasm of educated Europeans when the classics were rediscovered in the late medieval period. Nineteenth-century intellectuals could write as if little separated their age from that of Plato or Aristotle or Aeschylus. The principal breakthrough in understanding the nature of material reality was begun during the 16th and 17th centuries, associated mainly with the rise of a body of experimental or deductive science based on close observation. The key names are well known. The Polish astronomer Nicolaus Copernicus dared to argue that the earth revolved around the sun in a book only published in the year of his death, in 1543; the Italian astronomer Galileo Galilei extended these observations and in many other ways paved the way for much modern physical science, utilizing recent developments in the mechanical sciences; the Englishman Thomas Hobbes laid the foundations of modern political science and human psychology in his *Leviathan*, published in 1651; in 1687 the mathematician Isaac Newton in his *Principia Mathematica* announced the law of gravity and ushered in a new age of mechanical physics. The scientific and philosophical revolution precipitated by the late 17th century in Europe opened the way to developing a modern understanding of nature and natural laws and above all accepting that such things were intrinsically knowable, not part of a Divine Plan whose purpose was not to be questioned. The new principle, according to the late 18th-century Prussian philosopher, Immanuel Kant, was *sapere aude* – "dare to know".

Those who pioneered a critical, scientific view of the world ran great risks. In 1616 the Catholic Church banned Copernican teaching, and placed Galileo under house arrest for challenging scripture. Galileo was fortunate: a few years before, in 1600, Giordano Bruno, another Copernican, was burnt at the stake in Rome. Hobbes was forced into exile, suspected of atheism; John Locke, who wrote the founding text of modern liberal representative government in the 1680s, was also forced to write in exile, and his works circulated in parts of Europe in secret, too subversive for open sale. Writers of the 18th-century "Enlightenment", during which critical thinking began to flourish for the first time, had to steer a careful line between what could or could not be said. Rousseau was also banned for life from his native city of Geneva for his radical democratic views. But it was a tide that could not be held back. By the early 19th century most of the modern Western sciences had been established on a firm intellectual basis; political and social theory exploded traditional claims to authority (expressed most clearly in the founding of the American Republic in 1776 and the French Revolution of 1789); organized religion in its Western guise was shown to be unable to defend its major contentions about the nature of the universe and of man's place in it, and an alternative, naturalistic, rational model of the world was substituted. The triumph of free expression now seems irreversible, but the revolution represented by modern thought was not inevitable and its progress was subject to fits and starts. It is still not entirely clear why the prevailing authorities in Europe came to tolerate the new intellectual wave when a century before it might have been violently suppressed. The publication in 1859 of *On Liberty* by the English philosopher John Stuart Mill summed up what had been achieved in modern Europe. There was no other freedom, Mill asserted, more fundamental than the right to say what you like without fear that you will be silenced.

The formal acquisition of scientific, material knowledge about all aspects of the natural world and its application to human societies has been responsible for transforming world history more fundamentally than any other development in the past 6,000 years. Whatever case can be made for showing that there are strong lines of continuity throughout world history, the possibilities opened up by transcending the narrow world view of a God-centred and God-given universe have been unprecedented. It is a story intimately bound to the wider history of the rise of Europe (which with European expansion to America came to be regarded as the Western world) over the past 500 years. Historians have often been tempted to see this is as a happily progressive narrative while the rest of the world stagnated. From a Western perspective the idea of "the triumph of the West" has an evident plausibility. Yet it begs the larger question of why Europe did evolve in very different ways, not only from the other civilizations existing alongside, but from all previous civilizations. What has been distinctive about the West, as Karl Marx argued in the mid-19th century, is the fact that it proved capable of expanding world-wide; Marx thought that no other culture or civilization would be capable of withstanding what Europe had to offer or what it forced upon them.

Holocaust Memorial, site of Second World War concentration camp in Mauthausen, Germany

There is no agreed or straightforward answer to the question "why Europe?" Geography was clearly favourable – a temperate climate, generally adequate food supplies, population growth steady but not excessively large and few of the debilitating, parasite-borne diseases that affected large parts of Africa and Asia with elephantiasis, river-blindness, bilharzia or malaria. The long European shoreline, never very far from any human habitation, encouraged the development of seaborne trade and exploration and the development of early sea power. Seafaring technology was one of the earliest and most important of the technical revolutions and Europeans exploited it fully. Europe also succeeded in stemming the tide of regular invasion which had characterized European history for almost a thousand years from the collapse of the Western Roman Empire. The Tatar invasions of the 13th century and the expansion of the Ottoman Turkish Empire into southeastern Europe during the early modern period were checked sufficiently to allow central and western Europe to consolidate the state system, to build settled cities, and to found a regular trading network. The military organization of Europe was transformed by the application of gunpowder and the development of cannon and musket-fire. Although these innovations were usually used against other Europeans, they gave Europeans a clear advantage whenever they found themselves fighting non-European peoples. It is sometimes argued that post-Reformation Protestantism, with its emphasis on individualism, played an important part in making Europe different, but the earliest explorers and imperialists were Catholic Portuguese and Spanish, while the Americas were discovered by an Italian from Genoa, Cristoforo Colombo. The long history of the Crusades against the Arab Middle East showed that there was nothing passive about Catholic Christianity.

The distinctive characteristic of European societies as they solidified into an early version of the modern states' system was their willingness to look outwards towards the wider world. The voyages of discovery were not isolated examples of a lucky piece of exploration, but rapidly embraced the whole globe, making it clear in the process that the earth was round rather than flat. Only Europeans embraced the world in this way: map-making, navigation, inland exploration, elaborate descriptions of native communities and exotic fauna and flora, all contributed to creating a view of the world fundamentally different from the view from Constantinople or Beijing. Not only did Europeans discover large areas of the hitherto unknown (at least to Europeans) but they began a process of aggressive settlement across the Americas, in parts of Africa and India and into the archipelagos of the western Pacific "spice islands". If occasionally briefly reversed, European expansion proved irresistible and European appetites insatiable. Once the imperial toeholds were established across the oceans, Europeans never abandoned them. They became a source of remarkable wealth, helping eventually to make Europe richer than any rival civilization, and making it possible to defend and extend the imperial frontier.

Wealth itself would not have made Europe distinctive. The rulers of China and India were fabulously rich. What made the difference was how that wealth was used. The application of rational organization and scientific technique made possible a remarkable economic revolution. An important fraction of the wealth generated in Europe was mobile wealth, mobilized to develop yet further wealth by banks and commercial houses, which developed across Europe from the late 17th century. This was the engine that made commercial capitalism possible and it was fuelled by an acquisitive urge that was subject to few customary or religious restrictions. From the late 18th century the mobile wealth was used to fund a second revolution of technique. Although inventiveness was nothing strictly European – Chinese scientists and engineers had anticipated many European discoveries, including gunpowder – the critical difference was the application of invention. The development of steam technology in Britain made possible the mobilization of new and efficient forms of energy quite distinct from the water or horse-powered technologies of other cultures. The development of gas and generated electricity as an energy source, the mastery of turbine technology, the perfection of rail locomotion, were all uniquely Western, a blend of European

and American innovation. In a mere hundred years the gap between Western technique and the rest of the world was unbridgeable, making possible the rapid expansion of European states as imperial powers. The British American colonies won their independence in 1783, and European settlers, enjoying the same technical advantages and territorial ambitions, occupied the whole area of North America between Mexico and Canada by the middle years of the 19th century. The economic and technical revolutions relied on a high level of social and spatial mobility. Europeans moved abroad in large numbers, bringing with them Christianity, guns and trade. In Western Europe there were few barriers to social mobility, allowing new classes of successful bankers, merchants and manufacturers to play an influential part in public affairs. The establishment of secure property rights and respect for individual wealth-making removed any legal inhibitions on the right to make money. The publication of Adam Smith's classic The Wealth of Nations in 1776 provided a sound intellectual basis for the claim that the interests of communities were best served by allowing the free play of market forces and individual pursuit of economic well-being. Economic individualism and belief in the benign concept of the market had no equivalent in other cultures.

The economic revolution was accompanied by other important changes. In Europe and the United States the idea of education for all replaced the traditional distinction between the illiterate mass and the educated few. Education was basic for most people, but opportunities for higher forms of training or for university expanded throughout the 19th century and became general in the 20th. Civil rights and the rule of law were applied in most European states and the settler communities overseas, and limited progress was made towards representative forms of government. One of the most striking aspects of the move to greater emancipation was the gradual recognition in the liberal West that women should have equal rights – social, sexual, political – with men, even if the principle has not always worked as it should. Finally, the idea of the modern nation-state, in which identity was derived from being a citizen of a particular nation, defined by territory, shared culture and language, although far from universal even in Europe in the 19th century (and certainly not applied to Europe's empires), set the model that has been subsequently established worldwide. The United Nations now counts 195 sovereign states, all but three as members.

The impact of Western wealth, military advantage, technology and ambition on the rest of the world was catastrophic. India was conquered, the Mughal emperors overthrown, and British rule imposed. China succeeded in keeping the West at bay, but at the cost of regular punitive expeditions, and the final sapping of China's traditional political system by Western-educated Chinese who wanted China to adopt modern politics and economics. The Ottoman Empire crumbled under the remorseless pressure of Europe, which took over the whole of North Africa and encroached on the Ottoman Middle East. The Empire finally collapsed in 1919 at the end of the First World War. Everywhere else traditional societies, long isolated from any contact with a wider world, were visited, annexed, fought over and incorporated into the Western orbit. What resulted was usually an unstable mix of tradition and novelty, the old order sufficiently challenged or undermined that it could no longer function effectively, the new order mediated by surviving social traditions, religious practices and native cultures. The one exception was Japan. Contact with the West in the 1850s was perceived to be an immediate threat. In 1868 the Tokugawa Shogunate was overthrown, the Meiji emperor restored, and a rapid process of modernization undertaken to shield Japan from Western imperialism. Within 40 years Japan's modern armed forces could defeat the much larger Russian army and navy in the war of 1904–5; in the 1930s Japan invaded large parts of China and in 1941 Japanese forces launched a swift and successful campaign against American and European territories in the Pacific and Southeast Asia which was reversed only by the exploitation of Western technologies yet more advanced.

The changes ushered in by the rise of European and American power have developed exponentially. The history of the past 250 years shows a dizzying transformation: global horizons have narrowed with mass communication

and the development of a homogenized consumer culture; a level of knowledge and technical achievement unimaginable a century ago makes it possible to explore planets millions of miles distant, to revisit the earliest moments of the universe, to understand the genetic codes that dictate human biology, and to harness lasers and micro-electronic components to produce a technical base not only of exceptional sophistication, but one that is also democratic in its reach. Some sense of the sheer speed of change can be illustrated in numerous ways, but few examples are more remarkable than the difference between the colonial wars of the late 19th century, fought with Gatling machine guns, rifles and small artillery pieces, and the Second World War, fought only 40 years later with tanks, high-speed aircraft, radar, radio, missiles, and, in its late stages, with jet aircraft and nuclear weapons.

The Western experience, for all its technical and social achievements, has nonetheless been profoundly ambiguous. There have been perhaps no other civilizations which have been so publicly anxious about the prospects for their survival, so fearful of pride before a fall. The two world wars, both generated in Europe, compromised that claim to be the heartland of modern civilization and a source of social progress and moral authority which had been relayed throughout the last decades of the 19th century. Exporting ideas about civil rights and nationhood accelerated the decline and disappearance of the old European empires. The transfer of the British crown colony of Hong Kong to Chinese rule in 1997 marked a symbolic end to a long history of coercive European expansion and acknowledged China's growing international stature. The export of Western technology and commercial skills resulted in the collapse of many European industries and the transfer of large-scale manufacturing to the rapidly growing economies of eastern and southeastern Asia. The global reach of Western commerce and the remorseless march of English as the global language has produced a backlash against what are perceived to be new forms of imperialism, and against the crass failure of Western states to understand the complex differences that still mark off communities in Asia, Africa, Latin America or the Middle East from the Western model. Islamic terrorism is only one of the many fruits of hostility to the idea that somehow the Western model ought to be appropriate in any cultural or geographical context.

Where, then, is this history going? Accelerated change can be read several ways: it could either mean speeding downhill to the edge of the precipice, or climbing rapidly to a richer, more secure and more peaceable world. Historians would do well to be humble in the face of an unpredictable future. How few commentators and Sovietologists thought in the late 1980s that the Soviet bloc could possibly collapse in a matter of a few years; how many observers thought, wrongly, that HIV/AIDS would provoke an unstoppable pandemic which would decimate the world's population. One thing can be said with certainty: for all the talk of a new unipolar world built around the massive military power of the United States and the appeal of the Western model, the foreseeable future will have China, Russia, India and the Middle East, the great bulk of the world's population, developing in ways that are not consistent with an ideal Western model, capable of exerting a growing influence on global economic structures and the distribution of political influence, and able perhaps to restore at least some of that diversity in historical experience characteristic of all recorded history up to the 19th century.

Taking the longer view there is little to be said. Two hundred human generations of 30 years will take us to AD 8,000. Perhaps the acceleration of history will provoke a sudden crash long before that. There remain the awful paradoxes that the more "progress" there has been, the more violence, discrimination and crime has been generated, and the more economic desires are satisfied, the nearer the earth moves to ecological crisis. Human history may well be finite. On the other hand, the history of the world hitherto has shown humankind to be a remarkably adaptable, ambitious, unscrupulous, technically adept creature. This history so far is no simple parable of survival and triumph; the future of the world may have to be just that.

Richard Overy, 2015

Bibliography

HISTORY ATLASES

Atlas zur Geschichte, 2 vols, Leipzig 1976
Bazilevsky, K V, Golubtsov, A & Zinoviev, M A *Atlas Istorii SSR*, Moscow 1952
Beckingham, C F *Atlas of the Arab World and the Middle East*, London 1960
Bertin, J (*et al.*) *Atlas of Food Crops*, Paris 1971
Bjørklund, O, Holmboe, H & Røhr *A Historical Atlas of the World*, Edinburgh 1970
Cappon, L (*et al.*) *Atlas of Early American History*, Chicago 1976
Channon, J *The Penguin Historical Atlas of Russia*, London 1995
Darby, H C, Fullard, H (eds) *The New Cambridge Modern History*, vol. XIV: *Atlas*, Cambridge 1970
Davies, C C *An Historical Atlas of the Indian Peninsula*, London 1959
Engel, J (ed.) *Grosser Historischer Weltatlas*, 3 vols, Munich 1953–70
Fage, J D *An Atlas of African History*, London 1958
Fernández-Armesto, F (ed.) *The Times Atlas of World Exploration*, London 1991
Gilbert, M *Russian History Atlas*, London 1972
Gilbert, M *Recent History Atlas 1860–1960*, London 1966
Gilbert, M *First World War Atlas*, London 1970
Gilbert, M *Jewish History Atlas*, London 1969
Haywood, J (ed.) *The Cassell Atlas of World History*, London 1997
Hazard, H W *Atlas of Islamic History*, Princeton 1952
Herrmann, *A Historical and Commercial Atlas of China*, Harvard 1935
Herrmann, A *An Historical Atlas of China*, Edinburgh 1966
Jedin, H, Latourette, K S & Martin, J *Atlas zur Kirchengeschichte*, Freiburg 1970
Kinder, H & Hilgemann, W *Atlas zur Weltgeschichte* 2 vols, Stuttgart 1964 (published in English as *The Penguin Atlas of World History*, London 1974 & 1978)
Magosci, P R *Historical Atlas of East Central Europe*, Toronto, revised edn 1995
Matsui & Mori *Ajiarekishi chizu*, Tokyo 1965
May, H G (ed.) *Oxford Bible Atlas*, Oxford 1974
Mackay, A & Ditchburn, D (eds) *Atlas of Medieval Europe*, London 1997
McNeill, W H, Buske, M R & Roehm, A W *The World … its History in Maps*, Chicago 1969
Nelson's Atlas of the Early Christian World, London 1959
Nelson's Atlas of the Classical World, London 1959
Nelson's Atlas of World History, London 1965
Nihon rekishi jiten Atlas vol., Tokyo 1959
Palmer, R R (ed.) *Atlas of World History*, Chicago 1965
Paullin, C O *Atlas of the Historical Geography of the United States*, Washington 1932
Ragi al Faruqi, I (ed.) *Historical Atlas of the Religions of the World*, New York 1974
Roolvink, R *Historical Atlas of the Muslim Peoples*, London 1957
Scarre, C (ed.) *Past Worlds: The Times Archaeology of the World*, London 1999
Schwartzberg, J E (ed.) *A Historical Atlas of South Asia*, Chicago 1978
The Times Atlas of European History, 2nd edn, London 1997
Toynbee, A J & Mers, E D *A Study of History, Historical Atlas and Gazetteer*, Oxford 1959
Treharne, R F & Fullard, H (eds) *Muir's Historical Atlas*, London 1966
Tubinger Atlas der Vorderen Orients, Wiesbaden (various vols) since 1972
Van der Heyden, A M & Scullard, H H *Atlas of the Classical World*, London 1959
Wesley, E B *Our United States … its History in Maps*, Chicago 1977
Westermann Grosser Atlas zur Weltgeschichte, Brunswick 1976
Whitehouse, D & R *Archaeological Atlas of the World*, London 1975
Wilgus, A C *Latin America in Maps*, New York 1943

GENERAL WORKS

Abu-Lughod, J L *Before European Hegemony: The World System AD 1250–1350*, Oxford 1991
Ajayi, J F A & Crowder, M *History of West Africa*, 2 vols, 3rd edn. 1988
Allchin, B & R *The Birth of Indian Civilization*, London 1968
Atkinson, A *The Europeans and Australia*, vol. 1, Melbourne 1997
Australia, Commonwealth of, Department of National Development, *Atlas of Australian Resources*, 3rd series 1980
Bakewell, P J *A History of Latin America: Empires and Sequels, 1450–1930*, Malden Mass. 1997
Bartlett, R *The Making of Europe: Conquest, Colonization and Cultural Change 950–1350*, London 1993
Basham, A L *The Wonder That Was India*, 2 vols, 3rd revised, London 1987
Belich, J *Making Peoples*, Allen Lane, Auckland 1996
Belich, J *Paradise Reforged*, Allen Lane, Auckland 2001
Bellwood, P *Prehistory of the Indo-Malay Archipelago*, Ryde, NSW 1985
Berdan, F F & Anawalt, P R *The Codex Mendoz* (4 vols), University of California Press, Berkeley 1992
Bethel, L (ed.) *The Cambridge History of Latin America*, 11 vols, Cambridge 1984–95
Beresford, M *New Towns of the Middle Ages*, London 1967
Boardman, J (ed.) *The Oxford History of the Classical World*, Oxford 1989
Bolton, G (ed.) *The Oxford History of Australia*, vol. V, 2nd edn, Melbourne 1996
Bonney, R *The European Dynastic States 1494–1660*, Oxford 1991
Braudel, F *The Mediterranean and the Mediterranean World in the Age of Philip II*, 2 vols, London 1972–3
Brown, C (ed.) *Illustrated History of Canada*, Key Porter, Toronto 2002
Brown, P *The Rise of Western Christendom: Triumph and Diversity 200–1000*, Oxford 1996
Burkholder, M A & Johnson, L L *Colonial Latin America* (4th edn), Oxford University Press 2001
Bury, J B, Cook, S A & Adcock, F E (eds) *The Cambridge Ancient History*, Cambridge 1923–; 2nd edn 1982
Cameron, A M *The Mediterranean World in Late Antiquity AD 395–600*, London 1993
Campbell, P R *Louis XIV*, London 1994
Chang, K C *The Archaeology of Ancient China*, 4th edn, New Haven 1986
Chaudhuri, K N *Trade and Civilization in the Indian Ocean: An Economic History From the Rise of Islam to 1750*, Cambridge 1985
Chaudhuri, K N *Asia Before Europe: Economy and Civilization of the Indian Ocean from the Rise of Islam to 1750*, Cambridge 1991
Chungse Omunsŏn (ed.) *"Hunmin chŏngŭm Onhae". In Han'gukŏ munhakho*, Hyŏngsŏl ch'ulp'ansa, Seoul 1988
Cook, M A (ed.) *A History of the Ottoman Empire to 1730*, Cambridge 1976
Coward, B *The Stuart Age*, London, 2nd edn 1996
Crowder, M *West Africa Under Colonial Rule*, London 1968
Cunliffe, B (ed.) *The Oxford Illustrated Prehistory of Europe*, Oxford 1994
Curtin, P D *The Atlantic Slave Trade*, Madison 1972
Curtin, P D *Cross-cultural Trade in World History*, Cambridge 1984
Dalton, B J *War and Politics in New Zealand, 1855–1870*, Sydney 1967
D'Altroy, T N *The Incas*, Blackwell, Oxford 2002
Darby, H C (ed.) *An Historical Geography of England Before AD 1800*, Cambridge 1936 & 1960
Daniels, P & Lever, W *The Global Economy in Transition*, London 1996
Davis, R W *The Industrialization of Soviet Russia*, 3 vols, Cambridge 1989
Demand, N *A History of Ancient Greece*, New York 1996
Denoon, D, (*et al.*) *The Cambridge History of the Pacific Islanders*, Cambridge University Press 1997
East, W G *The Geography Behind History*, London 1965
East, W G *An Historical Geography of Europe*, 5th edn. London 1967
Eckert, C J, (*et al.*) *Korea old and new: a history*, Ilchokak Publishers (for the Korea Institute, Harvard University), Seoul 1990
Edwardes, M *A History of India*, London 1961
Ettinghausen, R. & Grabar, O *The Art and Architecture of Islam, 650–1250*, Pelican Books 1987
Fage, J D & Oliver, R (eds) *Cambridge History of Africa*, Cambridge 1975–86
Ferguson, J *The Heritage of Hellenism*, London 1973
Ferrier, R W *A Journey to Persia: Jean Chardin's Portrait of a Seventeenth Century Empire*, London 1996
Fisher, C A *South-East Asia*, London 1964
Flannery, T *The Future Eaters: An Ecological History of the Australasian Lands and People*, Reed Books, Sydney 1995
Fletcher, A *Tudor Rebellions*, 3rd edn, London 1983
Flood, J *Archaeology of the Dreamtime*, Angus & Robertson, Sydney 1994
Floor, W *Safavid Government Institutions*, Costa Mesa C., 2001
Frye, R N *The Golden Age of Persia*, Weidenfeld 1993
Geelan, P J M & Twitchett, D C (eds) *The Times Atlas of China*, London 1974
Gernet, J *Le Monde Chinois*, Paris 1969; English translation 1982
Goodman, J & Honeyman, K *Gainful Pursuits: The Making of Industrial Europe 1600–1914*, London 1988
Goodwin, G *A History of Ottoman Architecture*, Thames and Hudson 1971
Graff, E & Hammond, H E *Southeast Asia: History, Culture, People*, 5th revised edn, Cambridge 1980
Grousset, R *The Empire of the Steppes: A History of Central Asia*, New Brunswick NJ 1970
Guillermaz, J *Histoire du Parti Communiste Chinois*, Paris 1968; English translation 1972
Hall, D G E *A History of South-East Asia*, 4th edn, London 1981
Hallam, E *Capetian France 987–1328*, London 1980
Harlan, J R "The Plants and Animals that Nourish Man", *Scientific American* 1976
Harlan, J R & Zohary, D "The Distribution of Wild Wheats and Barleys", *Science* 1966
Harley, J B & Woodward, D *The History of Cartography*, 2 vols, Chicago 1987–
Hatton, R M *Europe in the Age of Louis XIV*, London 1969
Hawke, G R *The Making of New Zealand: An Economic History*, Cambridge 1985
Henderson, W O *Britain and Industrial Europe, 1750–1870*, Liverpool 1965
Higham, C F W *The Archaeology of Mainland Southeast Asia from 10000 BC to the Fall of Angkor*, Cambridge 1989
Higham, C F W & Thosarat, R *Prehistoric Thailand from Early Settlement to Sukhothai*, Bangkok 1999
Hillenbrand, C *The Crusades: Islamic Perspectives*, Edinburgh 1999
Historical Atlas of Canada, Vols 1–3, University of Toronto Press, Toronto 1987–93
Holt, P M *The Age of the Crusades*, Longman 1986
Hopkins, A G *Economic History of West Africa*, London 1973
Hørai, S *DNA jinrui shinkagaku, Iwanami shoten*, Tokyo 1997
Horton, D (ed.) *Encyclopedia of Aboriginal Australia*, Aboriginal Studies Press, Canberra 1994
Hourani, A *A History of the Arab People*, Harvard 1991
Howe, K *Where the Waves Fall: A New South Sea Islands History from First Settlement to Colonial Rule*, Allen & Unwin, Sydney 1984
Inalcik, H *The Ottoman Empire: The Classical Age, 1300–1600*, reprint, London 1989
Inikori, J E & Engerman, S L *The Atlantic Slave Trade: Effects on Economy, Society, and Population in Africa, America, and Europe*, Durham, NC 1992
Jeans, D N *An Historical Geography of New South Wales to 1901*, Sydney 1972
Jennings, J D *Prehistory of North America*, 3rd edn, Mountain View, CAS 1989
Johnson, G (ed.) *New Cambridge History of India*, Cambridge 1989–
Jones, G *The Evolution of International Business*, London 1996
Josephy, A M (ed.) *America in 1492: the World of the Indian Peoples before the Arrival of Columbus*, New York 1992
Kahan, A *Russian Economic History*, Chicago 1991
Kelly, P *The End of Certainty*, Sydney 1992
Kennedy, H *Muslim Spain and Portugal*, Longman 1996
Kennedy, H *The Prophet and the Age of the Caliphates*, Longman 2004
Kennedy, J *A History of Malaya, 1400–1959*, London 1967
Kinross, Lord P *The Ottoman Centuries*, Jonathan Cape 1977
Koeningsberger, H G, Mosse, G L & Bowler, G Q *Europe in the 16th Century*, 2nd edn, London 1989
Kuhrt, A T L *The Ancient Near East c. 3000–330 BC*, London 1995
Laird, C E *Language in America*, New York 1970
Lambton, K S *A History of Qajar Persia*, London 1987
Landes, D *The Wealth and Poverty of Nations*, London 1998
Langer, W L (ed.) *An Encyclopedia of World History*, revised edn, London 1987
Lapidus, I M *A History of Islamic Societies*, Cambridge 1988
Lattimore, O *Inner Asian Frontiers of China*, New York 1951
Lossky, A *Louis XIV and the French Monarchy*, London 1995
Lyashchenko, P I *History of the National Economy of Russia to the 1917 Revolution*, New York 1949
Macintyre, S *A Concise History of Australia*, Melbourne 1999
Macmillan's Atlas of South-East Asia, London 1988
Majumdar, R C *The Vedic Age*, Bombay 1951
Majumdar, R C *History and Culture of the Indian People, Age of Imperial Unity*, Bombay 1954
Mantran, R *Histoire de l'Empire Ottoman*, Paris 1989
McCarthy, J *The Ottoman Turks: an Introductory History to 1923*, London 1994
McKitterick, R *The Frankish Kingdoms under the Carolingians 751–987*, London 1983
McKitterick, R (*et al.*) *The New Cambridge Medieval History*, Cambridge 1995
McNeill, W H *The Rise of the West: A History of the Human Community*, Chicago 1991
McNeill, W H *Plagues and Peoples*, New York 1992
McPherson, J M *Battle Cry of Freedom: the Civil War Era*, Oxford 1988
Meining, D W *On the Margins of the Good Earth*, New York 1962, London 1963
Mellaart, J *The Neolithic of the Near East*, London 1975
Milner, C A (*et al.*) *The Oxford History of the American West*, New York 1994
Morgan, D *The Mongols*, Blackwell 1986
Morgan, D *Medieval Persia 1040–1797*, London 1988
Morrell, W P & Hall, D O W *A History of New Zealand Life*, Christchurch 1962
Mulvaney, D J *The Prehistory of Australia*, London 1975
Mulvaney, J & Kamminga, J *Prehistory of Australia*, Allen & Unwin, Sydney 1999
Nahm, A C *Korea: Tradition & Transformation, A History of the Korean People*, Hollym International, Seoul 1988
The National Atlas of the United States of America, Washington DC 1970
Neatby, H *Quebec: The Revolutionary Age 1760–1791*, London 1966
Ogot, B A (ed.) *Zamani: A Survey of West African History*, London 1974–1976
Oliver, R & Fagan, B *Africa in the Iron Age c. 500 BC–AD 1400*, Cambridge 1975
Oliver, R & Atmore, A *Africa Since 1800*, 3rd edn, Cambridge 1981
Oliver, W H & Williams, R R *Oxford History of New Zealand*, Oxford 1981
Osbourne, M E *Southeast Asia: An Introductory History*, 2nd edn. Sydney 1983
Ostrogorsky, G *History of the Byzantine State*, Oxford 1969
Overy, R *Why the Allies Won*, London 1995
Parker, W H *An Historical Geography of Russia*, London 1968
Phillips, J R S *The Medieval Expansion of Europe*, Oxford 1988
Pierce, L *The Imperial Harem*, Oxford University Press 1993
Piggott, S *Prehistoric India to 1000 BC*, London 1962
Pitcher, D E *An Historical Geography of the Ottoman Empire*, Leiden 1973
Postan, M M *Medieval Trade and Finance*, Cambridge 1973
Pounds, N J G *An Historical Geography of Europe 1800–1914*, Cambridge 1985
Powell, J M *An Historial Geography of Modern Australia: the Restive Fringe*, Cambridge 1988
Ragozin, Z *A History of Vedic India*, Delhi 1980
Reuter, T *Germany in the early Middle Ages, 800–1056*, London 1991
Rice, G W (ed.) *The Oxford History of New Zealand*, 2nd edn, Oxford University Press, Auckland 1992
Rizvi, A A *The Wonder That Was India: 1200–1700*, 2 vols, London 1987
Roberts, J M *The Hutchinson History of the World*, revised edn, London 1987
Rouse, I *The Tainos: Rise and Decline of the People who Greeted Columbus*, Yale University Press, New Haven 1992
Sanders, W T & Marino, J *New World Prehistory: Archaeology of the American Indian*, Englewood Cliffs, NJ 1970
Saum, L O *The Fur Trader and the Indian*, London 1965
Sawyer, P (ed.) *The Oxford Illustrated History of the Vikings*, Oxford 1997
Scammell, G V *The First Imperial Age: European Overseas Expansion, c.1400–1715*, London 1992
Seltzer, L E (ed.) *The Columbia Lippincott Gazetteer of the World*, New York 1952
Shaw, I & Nicholson, P *British Museum Dictionary of Europe*, Oxford 1994
Shaw, S *History of the Ottoman Empire*, Cambridge University Press 1976
Shepherd, J & Franklin, S *The Emergence of the Rus*, London 1996
Simkin, C F *The Traditional Trade of Asia*, Oxford 1968
Sinclair, K (ed.) The *Oxford Illustrated History of New Zealand*, Oxford University Press, Auckland 1990
Smith, C D *Palestine and the Arab-Israeli Conflict*, Oxford 1994
Smith, C T *An Historical Geography of Western Europe before 1800*, revised edn, London & New York 1978
Smith, W S *The Art and Architecture of Ancient Egypt*, revised edn. London 1981
Snow, D *The American Indians: Their Archaeology and Prehistory*, London 1976
Sonyel, S R *The Ottoman Armenians*, London 1987
Spate, O *The Spanish Lake*, ANU Press, Canberra 1979
Stark, R *The Rise of Christianity: A Sociologist Reconsiders History*, Princeton 1996
Stavrianos, L S *The World Since 1500: A Global History*, 7th edn, Englewood Cliffs, NJ 1995
Stavrianos, L S *The World to 1500: A Global History*, 7th edn, Englewood Cliffs, NJ 1998
Stokes, M & Conway, S (eds) *The Market Revolution in America: Social, Political and Religious Expressions, 1800–1880*, Charlottesville 1996
Stoye, J *The Siege of Vienna*, London 1964
Tate, D J M *The Making of South-East Asia*, Kuala Lumpur 1971
Thapar, R *A History of India*, London 1967
The Times Atlas of the World, 9th Comprehensive Edition, London 1992
Thompson, E A *The Huns*, Oxford, 1996
Toynbee, A J *Cities of Destiny*, London 1967
Toynbee, A J *Mankind and Mother Earth*, Oxford 1976
Twitchett, D & Loewe, M (eds) *The Cambridge History of China*, Cambridge 1979–
Van Alstyne, R W *The Rising American Empire*, reprint, Oxford 1974
Van Heekeren, H R *The Stone Age of Indonesia*, 2nd revised edn, The Hague 1972
Wadham, S, Wilson, R K & Wood, J *Land Utilization in Australia*, Melbourne 1964
Webster, L & Brown, M (eds) *The Transformation of the Roman World 400–900*, London 1997
Wheatley, P *The Golden Khersonese*, Kuala Lumpur 1966
Wheeler, M *Early India and Pakistan to Ashoka*, London 1968
White, D W *The American Century: the Rise and Decline of the United States as a World Power*, New Haven 1996
Wickins, P L *An Economic History of Africa From Earliest Times to Partition*, New York 1981
Willey, G *An Introduction to American Archaeology*, vols 1 & 2, Englewood Cliffs, NJ 1970
Williams, M *The Making of the South Australian Landscape*, London 1974
Williamson, E *The Penguin History of Latin America*, London 1992
Wilson, M & Thompson, L *Oxford History of South Africa*, vols 1 & 2, Oxford 1969, 1971
Wood, I N *The Merovingian Kingdoms 450–751*, London 1994
Yarshater, E (ed.) *The Cambridge History of Iran*, vol. 3, Cambridge 1983

Glossary

This glossary is intended to provide supplementary information about some of the individuals, peoples, events, treaties and processes which, through lack of space, receive only a brief mention on the maps and accompanying texts. It is not a general encyclopedia of world history. Names in bold type within entries have their own main glossary entries.

ABBAS I, THE GREAT (c. 1557–1629) Shah of Persia. Attaining the throne in 1587, he reorganized and centralized the **Safavid** state. His reign was marked by cultural efflorescence and territorial expansion. Having crushed the rebellious **Uzbeks** (1597) he drove the Ottomans from their possessions in western Iran, Iraq and the eastern Caucasus (1603–7), and extended **Safavid** territories (temporarily) from the Tigris to the Indus. He moved the capital to Isfahan.

ABBASIDS Second major dynasty in Islam, displacing the **Umayyads** in 750. It founded a new capital, Baghdad, in 762, but its political control over the Islamic world, almost complete in the 9th and early 10th centuries, gradually decayed. Its rulers frequently became figureheads for other regimes: the last true caliph was killed by Mongols in 1258 and later Abbasid caliphs, nominally restored in 1260, were merely court functionaries to Egypt's **Mamluk sultans.**

ABD AL KADIR (1808–83) Also known as Abd el-Kader and Abd-al-Qadir. Algerian independence leader. He was elected in 1832 to succeed his father as leader of a religious sect; as emir, he took control of the Oran region, successfully fought the French, and in 1837 concluded the Treaty of Tafna; he extended his authority to the Moroccan frontier; renewed hostilities (1839–47) ended with his defeat and imprisonment, though he was freed in 1852.

ABD ALLAH (1846–99) Khalifa, or religious and political leader, in the Sudan after the death of the Mahdi in 1885. In 1880 he became a disciple of the **Mahdi, Mohammed Ahmed,** whom he succeeded. As leader of the Mahdist movement he launched attacks on Egypt and Ethiopia; he consolidated power within the Sudan, building up an effective centralized state, until invaded by Anglo-Egyptian forces under Kitchener. He lost the battle of Omdurman in 1898, and was killed the following year while resisting Anglo-Egyptian troops.

ABD EL-KRIM (1882–1963) Founded Republic of the Rif (1921–5), the north African precursor of many 20th-century independence movements. His forces defeated major French and Spanish armies until overwhelmed, in May 1926, by 250,000 Franco-Spanish troops. He was exiled to Réunion, but escaped to Egypt where he was given political asylum in 1947.

ABDULHAMID II (1842–1918) Last important Ottoman sultan, 1876–1909. He carried further some lines of modernization already begun, and used Islamic sentiment to resist European encroachments. The revolt by **Young Turks** in 1908 against his autocratic rule led to his deposition, 1909; he was imprisoned at Salonica, 1910, and died in Istanbul eight years later.

ABRAHAM First of three patriarchs of the **Jews** (Abraham, his son Isaac, Isaac's son Jacob). Born in Ur, he migrated via Harran in Syria to Canaan (Palestine), the land promised by God to his descendants. Abraham, Isaac and Jacob have been dated to the early or middle 2nd millennium BC. According to much later tradition, he was considered to be the progenitor of the Arabs through his other son, Ishmael.

ABREU, ANTONIO DE 16th-century Portuguese navigator, who in 1512 discovered the Banda Islands, Indonesia, during an exploratory voyage to the Moluccas.

ABU BAKR (c. 573–634) Close friend and advisor to **Mohammed**, and said to have been the first male convert to Islam. He became Mohammed's father-in-law, and accompanied him on the historic journey to Medina in 622. After Mohammed's death he was selected as caliph – "successor of the Prophet of God". Under his two-year rule, central Arabia accepted Islam and the Arab conquests began, with expansion into Iraq and Syria.

ABUSHIRI REVOLT An insurrection in 1888–9 by the Arab population of those areas of the East African coast which were granted by the sultan of Zanzibar to Germany in 1888. It was eventually suppressed by an Anglo-German blockade of the coast.

ACHAEMENIDS Ancient Persian dynasty of Fars province. **Cyrus II the Great**, a prince of the line, defeated the **Medes** and founded the Achaemenid empire, 550–330 BC. Descended traditionally from Achaemenes (7th century BC), the senior line of his successors included Cyrus I, Cambyses I, Cyrus II and **Cambyses II**, after whose death in 522 BC the junior line came to the throne with **Darius I**. The dynasty was extinguished with the death of Darius III in 330 BC after defeat by **Alexander the Great** (331 BC).

ACHESON, DEAN (1893–1971) US Secretary of State, 1949–53. He was responsible for many important policy initiatives under President **Truman**, including the implementation of the **Marshall Plan**, the **North Atlantic Treaty Organization**, non-recognition of Communist China and the re-arming of West Germany.

ADAMS, JOHN (1735–1826) Second President of the USA, 1797–1801. A leading advocate of resistance to British rule before the American War of Independence, in 1776 he seconded the Declaration of Independence. He was American envoy to Britain, 1785–8, and author of *Thoughts on Government* (1760).

ADAMS, JOHN QUINCY (1767–1848) Sixth President of the USA, 1825–9, and son of **John Adams** (second president). As Secretary of State, 1817–25, he contributed to the shaping of the **Monroe Doctrine**, and in 1843 he led the opposition to the annexation of Texas.

ADENAUER, KONRAD (1876–1967) German statesman. He studied law and served in the Provincial Diet of the Rhineland (1920–33) until dismissed from office in 1933, when he was forced to go into exile and later imprisoned because of his unhidden opposition to the Nazis. After 1945, he became active in the newly formed Christian Democratic Union, becoming chancellor of the Federal Republic of Germany from 1949 until his retirement in 1963. Known affectionately as "der Alte" (the Old Man), he remained deeply committed to close ties with the democratic Christian west.

AESCHYLUS (525/4–456 BC) "The Father of Tragedy" who claimed Dionysus had come to him in a dream and instructed him to write tragedies. He also fought at the **Battle of Marathon**, 490 BC. He wrote at least 80 plays, mostly tragedies, of which seven survive in full, including *The Oresteia* trilogy and *Prometheus Bound.*

ÆTHELRED II (d.1016) King of Wessex, England, from 988 and known by the epithet "the Unready", referring to his selection of poor advisers and his indecision. His reign was marked by a steady increase in Danish influence; in 1013 he fled to Normandy and the English recognized the Danish king, **Sven Forkbeard**, as their ruler.

AFGHANI, JAMAL AD-DIN AL- (1838–97) Muslim agitator, reformer and journalist. Born in Persia, he was politically active in Afghanistan, Istanbul and Cairo. Exiled from Egypt in 1879 for political reasons, he published (1884) *The Firmest Bond*, a periodical attacking British imperialism and advocating Islamic reform. Exiled from Persia in 1892, he spent his remaining years in Istanbul; he instigated the assassination of the Shah in 1896.

AGHLABIDS Muslim Arab dynasty, ruling much of North Africa from 800 to 909. They controlled Tunisia and eastern Algeria, conquered Sicily after 827 and invaded southern Italy. They were finally defeated and ousted by the **Fatimids**.

AGIS IV (c. 262–239 BC) King of Sparta who, in 243 BC, attempted to introduce a "communist" programme of land redistribution and debt cancellation. Tricked by an unscrupulous uncle and unable to complete his reforms quickly enough, he was forced to leave the country for war with the Aetolians in 241; in his absence a counter-revolution put his enemies in power, and after a mock trial he was executed.

AGUINALDO, EMILIO (1869–1964) President of the short-lived Philippine Republic (1898–1901). Of mixed Chinese and Tagalog ancestry, he fought Spanish rule as leader of the revolutionary Katipunan Society. Exiled in 1897, he returned, first to cooperate with US forces, and then to lead a three-year insurrection. He was captured and deposed in 1901. In 1945 he was briefly imprisoned for supporting Japanese occupation. His dream of Philippine independence materialized in 1946, and he became a member of the Philippine Council of State in 1950.

AGUNG, SULTAN Third ruler of Mataram, the Muslim kingdom which, in the 17th century, dominated central and much of eastern Java. He sought an alliance against Bantam and, when this was refused, attacked Batavia (now Jakarta), founded in 1619 by the **Dutch East India Company**. Defeated there in 1629, he undertook the Islamization of eastern Java by force; but failed in all attempts to conquer Bali, which remained loyal to traditional Hindu-Buddhist culture.

AGUSTIN I Emperor of Mexico *see* **Iturbide**.

AHMADU SEFU (1835–97) Son and successor of **al-Hajj Umar** (d.1864), a Tukolor chief whose kingdom was on the Upper Niger. He came to power some years after his father's death, but his kingdom was eventually destroyed by the French in the 1890s.

AHMED GRAN (c.1506–42) Muslim conqueror in 16th-century Ethiopia. He gained control of the Somali Muslim state, Adal, and declared a *jihad* (holy war) against Christian Ethiopia. By 1535, with help from Turkish troops and firearms, he had seized three-quarters of the country, and in 1541 defeated a Portuguese relief force. He was killed in battle against the new Ethiopian leader, Galawdewos.

AHMOSE *see* **Amosis I**.

AIDAN, ST (d.651) Born in Ireland, he trained as a monk at Iona, off the isle of Mull, west Scotland. He was consecrated bishop of the newly-converted Northumbrians in 635, establishing his church and monastery on Lindisfarne, off the northeast coast of England. From here, evangelists set out to convert large areas of northern England, under the protection of kings Oswald and Oswin of Northumbria.

AIUGUN, TREATY OF Agreement reached in 1858 by which China ceded the north bank of the Amur river to Russia. Together with further gains under the **Treaty of Peking** (1860), this gave Russia access to ice-free Pacific waters; the port of Vladivostok was founded in 1860.

AIX-LA-CHAPELLE, TREATY OF Agreement reached in 1748 which concluded the War of the Austrian Succession; Austria ceded Silesia to Prussia, Spain made gains in Italy, and **Maria Theresa** was confirmed in possession of the rest of the Austrian lands.

AKBAR (1542–1605) Greatest of India's **Mughal** emperors. Born in Umarkot, Sind, he succeeded his father, Humayun, in 1556. During his reign he consolidated Mughal rule throughout the sub-continent, winning the loyalty of both Muslims and Hindus; at his death he left superb administrative and artistic achievements, including the fortress-palace at Agra and the magnificent but now deserted city of Fatehpur Sikri.

AKHENATEN 18th Dynasty Egyptian pharaoh, reigned c.1364–1347 BC; the son of Amenhotep III, he took the throne as Amenhotep IV. He promoted the monotheistic cult of Aten, the god in the sun disc; changed his name c.1373 BC and transferred the capital from Thebes to the new city of Akhetaten (el-Amarna). With his wife, Nefertiti, and six daughters, he devoted the rest of his reign largely to the cult of Aten, dangerously neglecting practical affairs.

AKKADIANS Name given to a wave of Semitic-speaking immigrants from the west, of increasing prominence in Mesopotamia from the first third of the 3rd millennium BC. **Sargon** of Agade was of Akkadian origin.

AK KOYUNLU Turcoman tribal federation, ruling eastern Anatolia, Azerbaijan and northern Iraq from c.1378 to 1508. The dynasty, whose name means "white sheep", was founded by Kara Yüllük Osman (ruled 1378–1435), who was granted control over the Diyarbakir region of Iraq by **Tamerlane** in 1402. Under Uzun Jasan (1453–78) they expanded at the expense of the **Kara Koyunlu** ("black sheep") but were defeated by the Ottomans in 1473. They finally succumbed to internal strife and to pressure from the **Safavids.**

AKSUM Ancient city and kingdom of northern Ethiopia, an offshoot of one of the Semitic states of southern Arabia in the last millennium BC. By the start of the Christian era it was the greatest ivory market of northeast Africa. Converted to **Christianity** in the 4th century AD, it was gradually transformed, after the Muslim conquest of the Red Sea littoral in the 10th century, into the modern Amhara state of Ethiopia.

AL- For all Arabic names prefixed by al-, see under following element.

ALANS Ancient people, first noted in Roman writings of the 1st century AD as warlike, nomadic horse-breeders in the steppes north of the Caucasus Mountains. Overwhelmed by the **Huns** in 370, many Alans fled west, reaching Gaul with the **Vandals** and **Suebi** in 406 and crossing into Africa with the Vandals in 429.

ALARIC I (c. 370–410) Visigothic chief and leader of the army that captured Rome in AD 410. Born in Dacia, he migrated south with fellow-tribesmen to Moesia, and briefly commanded a Gothic troop in the Roman army. Elected chieftain in 395, he first ravaged the Balkans and then, in 401, invaded Italy; the "sack" of Rome, following a decade of intermittent fighting, negotiation and siege, was in fact relatively humane and bloodless, as Alaric's main aim was to win land for the settlement of his people.

ALARIC II (d. 507) King of the **Visigoths**. From his accession in AD 484 he ruled Gaul south of the Loire and all Spain except Galicia. He issued a code of laws known as the Breviary of Alaric. He died after being defeated by **Clovis**, king of the Franks, at the Battle of Vouillé, near Poitiers.

ALAUDDIN KHALJI (1255–1316) Sultan of Delhi who usurped the throne in 1296 from the sons of Jalaluddin. He unified much of northern India, thanks to heavy taxes and a standing army, and began the Muslim penetration of the south. He repelled a series of Mongol invasions between 1297 and 1306.

ALAUNGPAYA (1711–1760) King of Burma and founder of the Konbaung dynasty which ruled until the British annexation of 1866. He rose from the position of village headman to lead resistance against invading Mons of Lower Burma; recaptured the Burmese capital, Ava, in 1753, finally seizing Pegu, the Mon capital, in 1757; and massacred staff of the **English East India Company**'s trading settlement on the island of Negrais, 1759. He was mortally wounded during the siege of the Siamese capital, Ayuttha.

ALBIGENSIANS (Albigenses) Members of a heretical Christian sect, following the **Manichaean** or **Cathar** teaching that all matter is evil. Strongly entrenched in southern France around the city of Albi in the 12th century, they were subjected to violent attack by northern French nobles in the Albigensian Crusade after 1208.

ALBUQUERQUE, AFONSO DE (1453–1515) Portuguese empire-builder. Appointed Governor-General of Portuguese India in 1509, he seized Goa and several Malabar ports, 1510; Malacca and the coast of Ceylon, 1511.

ALEMANNI Germanic tribe which in the 5th century AD occupied areas now known as Alsace and Baden; defeated in 496 by the Franks under **Clovis**.

ALEXANDER THE GREAT (356–323 BC) Most famous conqueror of the ancient world. The son of **Philip II of Macedon,** he was taught by **Aristotle**. Succeeding his father in 336, he reaffirmed Macedonian dominance in Greece and between 334 and 323 BC led his armies all but "through to the ends of the earth". He was only 32 when he died in Babylon. His victories, though never consolidated into a world empire, spread Greek thought and culture throughout Egypt, northern India, central Asia and the eastern Mediterranean. His body, sealed in a glass coffin and encased in gold, was preserved in Alexandria, the city he founded as his own memorial, but the tomb has never been located.

ALEXANDER I (1888–1934) King (1921–34) of the Serbo-Croat-Slovene state whose name he changed to Yugoslavia in 1929. Prince Regent of Serbia, 1914–21. Enthroned in 1921, he established a royal dictatorship in 1929. He was assassinated.

ALEXANDER II (1818–81) Tsar of Russia. The son of Nicholas I, he succeeded his father in 1855. He emancipated the serfs in 1861, and introduced legal, military, educational and local government reforms; he extended the Russian frontiers into the Caucasus (1859) and Central Asia (1865–8), and defeated Turkey in the last of the Russo-Turkish wars (1877–8). He was assassinated.

ALEXANDER II (1198–1249) King of Scotland, son of William I the Lion, also known as "the peaceful". He succeeded to the throne in 1214, and sided with the rebel English barons against **King John** in the following year. He paid homage to Henry III in 1217, and in 1217 married his sister Joan. Under the Peace of York, which he concluded in 1237, Scotland abandoned English land claims and the border was fixed in more or less its present position.

ALEXANDER III (d.1181) Pope 1159–81. Distinguished canon lawyer, at one time professor at the University of Bologna. As pope, he opposed secular authority over the Church, allying successfully with the cities of Lombardy against Emperor **Frederick I Barbarossa**, and imposed a penance on **Henry II** of England for the murder of Thomas Becket, Archbishop of Canterbury.

ALEXIUS I COMNENUS (1048–1118) Byzantine emperor who seized the imperial throne in 1081. He was victorious over the Normans of Italy and the **Pecheneg** nomads; revived the Byzantine economy; founded the Comnene dynasty; and reluctantly accepted the arrival of the first **Crusade** in the East (1096–7).

ALFONSO X, THE WISE (1221–84) King of Castile and León, succeeding to the throne in 1252. He promulgated the *Siete Partidas*, Spain's great medieval code of laws; captured Cádiz and the Algarve from the Moors.

ALFRED THE GREAT (849–99) King of Wessex, England, succeeding his brother, Æthelred I, in 871. The early part of his reign was spent in hard struggle against Danish (Viking) invaders, in which he was gradually successful; Wessex itself was freed by 878, London retaken in 885, and the country divided on the line London–Chester. A notable lawgiver, he encouraged learning, vernacular translations of Latin classics and the compilation of an historic record, the *Anglo-Saxon Chronicle*; he also created many fortifications, a fast, mobile army and the beginnings of a fleet. He is the only English monarch to carry the title "the Great".

ALI (c. 600–61) Mohammed's cousin, second convert and son-in-law (married to the Prophet's daughter, **Fatima**), who became fourth caliph after the murder of Othman in 656. His accession led to civil war, he was murdered by a dissident supporter, Ibn Muljam. His descendants' claim to be imams, heirs of the Prophet as leaders of the community, still divides Islam (*see* **Shi'ism**).

ALLENBY, EDMUND HENRY HYNMAN (1861–1936) 1st Viscount; British field marshal. After service in France he commanded British forces in Palestine, 1917–18; he conducted a successful campaign against the Ottoman Turks culminating in the capture of Jerusalem (9 December 1917), victory at Megiddo (September 1918), and the capture of Damascus.

ALLENDE GOSSENS, SALVADOR (1908–73) Chilean statesman, elected president 1970, becoming the world's first democratically chosen Marxist head of state. He instituted a major programme of political, economic and social change, but ran into increasing opposition both at home and abroad, and was killed during the successful right-wing military *coup d'etat* which brought to power General **Pinochet** in 1973.

ALMOHADS Berber dynasty ruling North Africa and Spain, 1130-1269, inspired by the religious teachings of Ibn Tumart. It defeated the **Almoravids**, 1147, and established its capital at Marrakesh; captured Seville, 1172. Its control over Islamic Spain was largely destroyed by the Christian victory of Las Navas de Tolosa in 1212.

ALMORAVIDS Saharan Berbers who built a religious and military empire in northwest Africa and Spain in the 11th and 12th centuries, after halting the advance of Castilian Christians near Badajoz, 1086; they ruled all Muslim Spain except El Cid's Christian Kingdom of Valencia. Their sober, puritanical style of art and architecture replaced the exuberant work of the **Umayyads** whose Córdoba government collapsed in 1031.

ALTAN KHAN (1507–82) Mongol chieftain who terrorized China during the 16th century. He became leader of the Eastern Mongols in 1543; in 1550 he crossed the Great Wall into northern China, and established his capital, Kuku-khoto (Blue City), just beyond the Wall; he concluded a peace treaty with China in 1570. In 1580 he converted the Mongols to the *Dge-bugs-pa* (Yellow Hat) sect of Lamaism, a mystical Buddhist doctrine originating in Tibet, and gave the head of the sect the title of Dalai ("all-embracing") Lama.

ALTMARK, ARMISTICE OF Truce concluded in May 1629 ending the war (since 1621) between Sweden and Poland. Sweden won the right to levy tolls along the Prussian coast, but renounced this when the agreement was renewed for 26 years in 1635.

AMBROSE, ST (c. 339–97) He served as governor of Aemilia-Liguria, in northern Italy, *c.* 370–4; appointed Bishop of Milan in 374, he was frequently in conflict with imperial authority. His writings laid the foundation for medieval thinking on the relationship between Church and state.

AMHARIC The most widely spoken language of Ethiopia, of Semitic origin, derived from Geez, a southern Arabian tongue related to Arabic and Hebrew, and still used in the liturgy of the Ethiopian Orthodox Church. It displaced and partially absorbed the indigenous Cushitic languages of the western highlands.

AMIN DADA, IDI (1925–2003) President of Uganda. He joined the British army in 1946, and was promoted to commander of the Ugandan army in 1965. He seized power in 1971 during the absence of President Milton Obote, and subsequently expelled all Asians (1972) and most Britons (1973). Having survived revolts against his repressive and bloody regime, he was overthrown in 1979 when Ugandan exiles seized power and (1980) restored Dr Obote.

AMORITES Immigrants from Syria into Mesopotamia, where they took over political supremacy from the **Sumerian** and **Akkadians** at the beginning of the 2nd millennium BC. Babylon's first dynasty was Amorite; to this belonged Hammurabi (1792–1750 BC). In the Bible, the term "Amorite" is used to describe the pre-Israelite inhabitants of Palestine.

AMOSE I Founder of Egypt's 18th Dynasty. He completed the expulsion of **Hyksos** after the death of his brother, **Kamose**. Reigned *c.* 1550–1525 BC; with the aid of his mother, Queen Ahhotep, who may have acted as co-regent early in his reign, he extended Egyptian control into Palestine and Nubia, and reopened trade with Syria. He died leaving the country prosperous and reunited.

AMSTERDAM EXCHANGE BANK Important early financial institution founded in 1609 with an official monopoly of foreign currency dealings in the city. It played a key part in the development of monetary instruments and commercial credit in western Europe.

ANAXAGORAS (c. 500–c. 428 BC) Greek philosopher. He taught a theory of cosmology based on the idea that the universe was formed by Mind; his particulate theory of matter opened the way to atomic theory. He was exiled as part of a political attack on his friend **Pericles**, perhaps *c.* 450 BC, after suggesting that the sun was an incandescent stone.

ANGEVINS Dynasty of English kings, often known as the Plantagenets, beginning with **Henry II** (reigned 1154–89). Descended from Geoffrey, Count of Anjou, and Matilda, daughter of Henry I; the direct line ended with **Richard II** (reigned 1377–99).

ANGLO-SAXONS Term originally coined to distinguish the Germanic tribes ruling England from 5th to 11th centuries AD, from the Saxons of continental Europe, the Angles and the Saxons being the most prominent of the invaders; later extended to mean "the English" and their descendants all over the world.

AN LU-SHAN (703–57) Rebel Chinese general. Of Sogdian and Turkish descent, in 742 he became military governor of the northeast frontier districts. After the death of his patron, the emperor's chief minister Li Lin-fu, in 752, great rivalry developed between him and the courtier Yang Juo-chung; in 755 he turned his 160,000-strong army inwards and marched on the eastern capital, Lo-yang, proclaiming himself emperor of the Great Yen dynasty in 756 and capturing the western capital, Ch'ang-an. He was murdered the next year. The rebellion petered out by 763, but resulted in the serious weakening of the authority of the **T'ang** dynasty.

ANNAN, KOFI (1938–) Seventh Secretary General of the United Nations (1997–). Born in Ghana, Annan studied economics and management in Ghana, the USA and in Geneva. He joined the UN as an administrative officer for the World Health Organization (WHO) in 1960, and rose rapidly through the ranks to become the first Secretary General to be elected from UN staff, and the first black African. He is seen to be very independent, as well as an innovator. As Secretary General, he initiated a plan for reforming and renewing the organization, created a global AIDS and health fund, and has promoted women to achieve higher posts in the organization. He has also had to preside over some very dark periods in the UN's history, including its management of the atrocities committed in Bosnia and Rwanda, for which the UN was harshly criticised, and the political difficulties of the Iraq war. In 2001, Annan and the UN received a Nobel Peace Prize.

ANSKAR or Ansgar (801–65) Frankish saint, known as "the Apostle of the North", who conducted missions to the Danes (826) and Swedes (829); first archbishop of Hamburg, 834.

ANTI-COMINTERN PACT Joint declaration by Germany and Japan, issued on 25 November 1936, that they would consult and collaborate in opposing the **Comintern** or Communist International. It was acceded to by Italy in 1937, and later became the instrument by which Germany secured the loyalty of its Romanian, Hungarian and Bulgarian satellites and attempted to bind Yugoslavia.

ANTIGONUS III DOSON (c. 263–221 BC) King of Macedonia from 227 BC, who created and led the Hellenic League (founded 224 BC) which defeated **Cleomenes III** of Sparta.

ANTIOCHUS III (242–187 BC) Seleucid king of Syria, who succeeded his brother, Seleucus III, in 223. After an inconclusive war with Egypt, he conquered Parthia, northern India, Pergamum and southern Syria, and invaded Greece (192), but was decisively driven back by the Romans at Thermopylae and defeated at Magnesia in Asia Minor (190). By his death the empire had been reduced to Syria, Mesopotamia and western Persia.

ANTONY (c. 82–31 BC) Marcus Antonius, best known as Mark Antony. A member of a prominent Roman family, he became joint consul with **Julius Caesar** in 44 BC; after Antony's defeat of Caesar's assassins, Brutus and Cassius, at Philippi, he controlled the armies of the Eastern empire; started liaison with **Cleopatra**; war broke out between him and Octavian, 32 BC. He committed suicide after naval defeat at Actium.

APACHE Indian hunters and farmers, located in the North American southwest. They probably originated in Canada, reaching their main hunting grounds, west of the Rio Grande, some time after the year 1000. The main groupings were the Western Apache, including the Mescalero and Kiowa tribes, and the Eastern Apache, including the Northern and Southern Tonto. In the colonial period they proved an effective barrier to Spanish settlement, and under such leaders as Cochise, Geronimo and Victorio in the 19th century, figured largely in the frontier battles fought in the American advance westward. After Geronimo's surrender in 1886, the remaining survivors became prisoners of war in Florida and Oklahoma; after 1913 they were allowed to move to reservations in Oklahoma and New Mexico.

APAMEA, PEACE OF Agreement ending the Syrian War between Rome and Seleucia; signed in 188 BC after the battle of Magnesia (190 BC). The Seleucid king, **Antiochus III**, paid an indemnity of 15,000 talents, surrendered his elephants and ships, and ceded all Asia Minor west of the Taurus Mountains.

APOLLONIUS (c. 295–c. 230 BC) Poet and director of the library at Alexandria in the 3rd century BC; known as "Rhodius", because he chose to retire to the island of Rhodes. His four-book epic, the *Argonautica*, tells the story of Jason's quest for the Golden Fleece.

ARABIAN AMERICAN OIL COMPANY (ARAMCO) Joint venture, set up in 1936 by **Standard Oil** of California and Texaco to exploit petroleum concessions in Saudi Arabia. It is now among the most powerful oil groups in the world, with additional partners Exxon and Mobil. In 1974 the Saudi Arabian government acquired a 60 per cent stake in the company and in 1979 took complete control. The services of the four US companies were retained to operate the production facilities on behalf of the government.

ARABI PASHA (1839–1911) Egyptian military leader. After service in the Egyptian-Ethiopian War, 1875–6, he was made a colonel; he joined the officers' mutiny, 1879, against **Ismail** Pasha, and in 1881 led the movement to oust Turks and Circassians from high army posts. Minister of War, 1882, he quickly became a national hero with his slogan *Misr lil Misriyin* ("Egypt for the Egyptians"); he was commander-in-chief, 1882, when the British navy bombarded Alexandria, and was defeated on 13 September at Tell-el-Kebir by British troops under Sir Garnet Wolseley. He was captured and sentenced to death, but instead was exiled to Ceylon.

ARAB LEAGUE Association of Arab states, with its headquarters in Cairo. Founded in 1945, by Iraq, Trans-Jordan, Lebanon, Saudi Arabia, Egypt, Syria and Yemen, it was later joined by other states as they became independent: Algeria, Bahrain, Djibouti, Kuwait, Libya, Mauritania, Morocco, Oman, Qatar, Somalia, Sudan, Tunisia, United Arab Emirates. The PLO has been a full member since 1976. Egypt was expelled between 1978 and 1989.

ARAUCANIANS (also known as the Mapuche). A warlike Indian tribe in southern Chile which successfully resisted many Inca and Spanish incursions. The first native group to adopt the Spaniards' horses, they became brilliant cavalry fighters, and in 1598 300 mounted Araucanians wiped out a major Spanish punitive expedition. They retained effective independence, despite numerous Spanish and Chilean attempts to subdue them, until the late 19th century.

ARBENZ GUZMAN, JACOBO (1913–71) Guatemalan political leader of Swiss immigrant parentage. He rose to the rank of colonel in the Guatemalan army; played a leading role in the democratic revolution of 1945, and President of Guatemala, 1951; he inaugurated a radical leftwing land reform programme. He was overthrown in a US-backed military coup in 1954, fleeing to Mexico and Cuba.

ARCHILOCHUS Greek satirical poet, writing about 700 BC; many fragments of his work survive.

ARCHIMEDES (c. 287–212 BC) Greek mathematician and scientist. Born in Syracuse, he studied in Alexandria. He calculated the upper and lower limits for the value of ϖ; devised a formula for calulating the volume of a sphere; invented, among many other things, Archimedes' Screw, for raising large quantities of water to a higher level, and also Archimedes' Principle, which enabled him to discover, with a cry of "Eureka!", the impurity in King Hiero's crown by weighing it in and out of water in comparison with pure gold and pure silver. He returned to Sicily to design weapons and defence strategies for King Hiero, and was killed during the Roman siege of his native city.

ARDASHIR I (d.241) Founder of the Sasanid empire of Persia; born in the late 2nd century AD. Ardashir took the crown of Persis in 208. He rapidly extended his territory, defeating his Parthian overlords at Hormizdagan in 224, and occupying their capital, Ctesiphon. He made Zoroastrianism the state religion.

ARIANISM *see* **Arius**

ARISTOPHANES (c. 450–c. 380 BC) Athenian comic dramatist. Eleven of some 40 plays survive, including *The Frogs*, *The Birds*, and *Lysistrata*. They are highly political, brilliant in language and verse, dramatic situation, parody, satire, wit and farce, sparing neither men nor gods.

ARISTOTLE (384–322 BC) Greek philosopher and scientist. Born in Thrace, he studied in Athens under Plato. He taught the young **Alexander the Great**, then established his Lyceum in Athens, 335, and founded the Peripatetic school of philosophy. He was an outstanding biologist. His voluminous works, covering almost every aspect of knowledge, survive mainly in the form of lecture notes, edited in the 1st century AD.

ARIUS (c. AD 250–336) Originator of the Christian doctrine known as Arianism, later condemned as the Arian heresy. A pupil of Lucian of Antioch, he taught that the son of God was a creature, not consubstantial or coeternal with the Father. He was excommunicated for these views by the provincial synod of Alexandria in 321, unsuccessfully defended his belief in 325 before the **Council of Nicaea** and was banished. He died on the point of being reinstated by the Emperor **Constantine.** His controversial teachings divided the Church for many centuries.

ARKWRIGHT, SIR RICHARD (1732–92) English inventor and pioneer of the factory system, who invented the water-frame (1769) and other mechanized spinning processes.

ARMENIANS Indo-European people occupying in ancient times, the area now comprising northeast Turkey and modern Armenia. They were converted to Christianity in the late 3rd century. Armenians boast a highly distinctive culture, which flowered particularly during periods of independence and reached peaks in the 10th and 14th centuries. During the First World War the Ottoman government deported most Armenians in Asia Minor (about 1,750,000 people) to the Syrian and Mesopotamian provinces. Armenians claim that over 1 million deportees were systematically killed at this time in a policy of genocide.

ARMINIUS (c. 18 BC–AD 21) German tribal chief and early national hero, known also as Hermann. He became leader of the Cherusci after service and honour with Roman forces; in AD 9 he defeated and massacred three Roman legions at the Battle of Teutoburg Forest; held off Roman attacks, AD 16–17, but was murdered by his own people during a war with the Marcomanni, another German tribe. Described by Tacitus as *liberator haud dubie Germaniae* ("undoubtedly the liberator of Germany").

ARNOLD OF BRESCIA (c. 1100–55) Radical theologian and religious reformer who studied under Peter Abelard and was condemned with him at the Council of Sens in 1140. He later moved to Italy where, in alliance with the citizens of Rome, he strongly attacked Pope **Eugenius III** and forced him to leave the city. He was captured and executed at the pope's request by **Frederick Barbarossa**. His leading anti-clerical argument was that spiritual persons should not possess temporal goods.

ARPAD Magyar dynasty, ruling Hungary from late 9th century to 1301; named after Arpád, who was chosen in 889 to lead seven Magyar tribes westward from their homeland on the river Don. Under Béla III (1172–96), Hungary was established as a major central European power, but was later weakened by the Mongol invasion (1241–2); the dynasty died out with Andrew III (1290–1301), who left no heir.

ARTAXERXES II MNEMON (c. 435–358 BC) King of Persia, son of Darius II (reigned 423–404); he changed name from Arsaces on his accession in 404. He was challenged by his brother, Cyrus the Younger (c.430–401), but defeated and killed him at Cunaxa, near Babylon, 401.

ARTEVELDE, JACOB VAN (c. 1295–1345) Flemish leader during the early phases of the **Hundred Years' War.** In 1338 he emerged as one of five "captains" governing the town of Ghent; formed an alliance with the English king, **Edward III**, against France and the Count of Flanders; ruled as chief captain until killed in a riot.

ARYAN Contentious term used at various times to describe a member of the Caucasian race from which the Indo-European peoples supposedly sprang; in **Hitler**'s Germany, a member of the so-called "master" or "Nordic" race. Correctly applied to the Indo-Iranian branch of the eastern Indo-European group of languages, and at one time to the hypothetical parent language of that group.

ARYA SAMAJ Hindu reform movment; its followers reject all idolatrous and polytheistic worship and insist on the sole authority of the **Vedas**.

ASHANTI (Asante) One of several states of Akan-speaking peoples of southern Ghana, Togo and Ivory Coast. Also an independent kingdom in southern Ghana in the 18th and 19th centuries, taking an active part in the Atlantic slave trade. Ultimately failing to resist British penetration, it was annexed in 1901, and is now an administrative region of Ghana.

ASHANTI WARS Engagements fought in 1824–7, 1873–4, 1895–6 between the west African kingdom of Ashanti, which originated in the 17th century, and the British, at first to prevent Ashanti expansion into the British (coastal) colony of the Gold Coast and subsequently as resistance by the Ashanti to the attempted imposition of British rule over them. Final annexation of Ashanti came in 1901; it is now a province of independent Ghana.

ASHKENAZIM From the Hebrew word *Ashkenaz*, meaning Germany. It refers to the Jews of the Germanic lands, many of whom emigrated eastward in the Middle Ages. Today it represents most of the Jews of Europe, the British Commonwealth, the USA, the USSR, South America and approximately half the Jewish population of Israel. The word is used in distinction to **Sephardim**, who have slightly different customs and rites.

ASHOKA (Asoka) (d.232 BC) Greatest of the Mauryan emperors of early India, succeeding his father, **Bindusara**, in 272 BC. In 260 BC he inflicted a crushing defeat on Kalinga (modern Orissa), the last major independent Indian state. He was converted to **Buddhism** and from then developed a policy of toleration and non-violence, renouncing conquest.

ASHURNASIRPAL II (d.859 BC) King of Assyria, 883–859 BC, who began the 1st-millennium expansion of the Assyrian empire to the Mediter-ranean. Monuments and inscriptions describe with great frankness the harsh treatment of conquered peoples in ancient warfare. He created Calah (Nimrud) as his new capital.

ASIENTO Monopoly granted to an individual or company for the exclusive supply of Negro slaves to the Spanish colonies in America. The first asiento was signed by the Spanish court with Genoese entrepreneurs in 1517, later it passed mainly to the Portuguese until 1640, and then in succession to the French Royal Guinea Company and to the British South Sea Company (until 1750). It was finally extinguished in 1793, when all Spanish colonial trade was freed from central control.

ASKIA THE GREAT (d.1538) Founder of the Askia dynasty, rulers of the Songhay empire, centred round the capital of Gao in present day Mali, from 1492–1591. He rose to power in 1493, reigning as Mohammed I Akia; he promoted the spread of Islam in his domains and made a pilgrimage to Mecca in 1495–7. He was deposed in 1528 by his sons, led by Askia Musa.

AL-ASSAD, BASHAR (1965–) Syrian president since 2000 when he succeeded his father, Hafez al-Assad, who had ruled Syria from 1971 until his death. Despite promises of transformational reform, there was little change once Bashar al-Assad took office. For nearly a decade, he successfully suppressed internal dissent, due mostly to the close relationship between the Syrian military and intelligence agencies. Beginning in 2011, Assad faced a major uprising in Syria that evolved into a civil war.

ASSASSINS European name given to the Nizari branch of the Ismailis, organized by the leader of the "new preaching", Hadan-i Sabbah (d.1124). They ruled parts of northern Persia and coastal Syria from strongholds of which Alamut in Persia was the most important, and played a part in the general history of Persia and Syria, partly because of their practise of killing opponents (hence "assassination"). The leader of the Syrian group was known to Crusaders as the "Old Man of the Mountains". Their political power was ended by the Mongols in Persia, and by the **Mamluks** in Egypt.

ASSYRIANS Warlike people of northern Mesopotamia, remarkable for fighting prowess, administrative efficiency (after 745 BC) – which made possible the control of an empire of unprecedented size – and for the magnificent bas-reliefs in their palaces. They formed an independent state in the 14th century BC, and under the Neo-Assyrian empire dominated much of the Near East until destroyed by a Chaldaean-Mede coalition in 612 BC. In modern times the term is applied to an ancient Christian sect, found chiefly in Turkey, Iraq and Iran, whose members claim to be descended from the ancient Assyrians.

ASTURIAS, KINGDOM OF Founded in 718 in the extreme north of Spain by a group of Visigoth nobles after the Muslim invasions. Expanded and established on a firm basis under Alfonso I (739–57), it included northwest Spain and northern Portugal. For almost 200 years it remained the sole independent Christian bastion in Iberia; it survived many attacks and, particularly under Alfonso III (866–910), began to push its frontier further south. After 910 it continued as the kingdom of León.

ATAHUALLPA (c. 1502–33) Last independent ruler of the **Inca** empire in Peru. He was given the subsidiary kingdom of Quito on the death of his father, **Huayna Capac**; he fought a war with his brother **Huascar**, and deposed him in 1532, just before the Spaniards invaded the Inca realms. Taken prisoner by **Francisco Pizarro,** he was accused of complicity in his brother's murder and executed.

ATATÜRK (1881–1938) Founder and first president of the republic of Turkey. Originally named Mustafa Kemal, he was born in Salonica; he graduated from Istanbul Military Academy, in 1902. He resigned from the army in 1919 to support the Turkish independence movement, and in the same year was elected president of the National Congress. After British and Greek occupation (1920), he opened the first Grand National Assembly, was elected first president and prime minister, and directed operations in the Greco-Turkish War of 1920–2. After the peace treaty of 1923 he abolished the Ottoman caliphate and began a far-reaching reform and modernization programme. He took the name Atatürk, "Father of the Turks', in 1934.

ATHANASIUS (c. 296–373) Theologian, statesman and saint, born in Alexandria (Egypt). He attended the **Council of Nicaea**, 325, and was appointed bishop of Alexandria in 328. He became both Egyptian national leader and the chief defender of orthodox Christianity against the heresy of Arianism. His major writings include a *Life of St Antony*, a short treatise *On the Incarnation of the Word* and *Four Orations against the Arians*.

ATTALUS III (d.133 BC) Last independent king of Pergamum, reigning 138–133 BC. On his deathbed he bequeathed his kingdom to Rome, which then (129) organized it into the province of Asia.

ATTILA (c. 406–453) Sole rule of the vast **Hun** empire after the murder of his brother Bleda c. 445. He overran much of the Roman empire, reaching Orléans in Gaul, 451, and the river Mincio in Italy, 452; his empire collapsed after his death.

ATTLEE, CLEMENT (1883–1967) British prime minister. Educated at Oxford university, he briefly practised law, then spent 1907–22 (apart from war service) working among the poor in London's East End. He became Mayor of Stepney, 1919, and a Member of Parliament, 1922; a junior minister in the Labour governments of 1924 and 1929–31, leader 1935–55; and was a member of **Churchill**'s War Cabinet. As prime minister, 1945–51, he presided over the establishment of the Welfare State in Britain and the granting of independence to India, Pakistan, Burma and Ceylon; he relinquished British control of Egypt and Palestine. He was created Earl Atlee in 1955.

AUGUSTINE OF HIPPO, ST (354–430) Leading thinker of the early Christian Church. After a restless youth, recorded in his *Confessions*, he was converted in 386, baptized by **St Ambrose** the following year, and in 396 appointed Bishop of Hippo, in North Africa. His greatest work, *The City of God*, was written between 413 and 426 as a philosophic meditation on the sack of Rome by the **Visigoths** in 410.

AUGUSTUS (63 BC–AD 14) First emperor of Rome, born Gaius Julius Caesar Octavianus; great-nephew, adopted son and heir of **Julius Caesar**. With **Antony** and Lepidus he emerged victorious in the civil war against Brutus and Cassius, after Caesar's murder. He broke with Antony and defeated him at Actium in 31 BC; offered sole command in Rome, he brought peace and prosperity to the empire, over which he effectively ruled from 27 BC until his death.

AURANGZEB (1618–1707) Last of India's great Mughal emperors. Son of the emperor **Shahjahan**; he succeeded in 1658 after a struggle with his brothers. Up to 1680 he successfully consolidated power over Hindu and Muslim subjects, but later his empire began to disintegrate through rebellions, wars with the **Rajputs** (erstwhile allies) and the **Marathas**.

AUSTRO-SERBIAN "PIG WAR" Tariff conflict in 1906–11 between Austria-Hungary and Serbia, which also exacerbated anti-Habsburg agitation in Bosnia (occupied by Austria in 1878, annexed in 1908).

AVVOCATI (or Avogadro) Prominent family of medieval Vercelli, Italy. Supporters of the **Guelph** (anti-imperial) party, they engaged in a semi-permanent feud with their Ghibelline (pro-imperial) rivals until in 1335 the city came under the control of the **Visconti** of Milan.

AYLWIN, PATRICIO (1918–) Chilean lawyer and politician. He served as president of the Christian Democratic Party (PDC) in 1973 and 1987–91. He led the opposition coalition formed to reject General Pinochet in a national plebiscite in October 1988 and was President of Chile 1990–3.

AYYUBIDS Sunni Muslim dynasty, founded by **Saladin**. It ruled Egypt, Upper Iraq, most of Syria and Yemen from Saladin's death in 1193 until the **Mamluk** rise to power (1250).

BABUR (1483–1530) Founder of the **Mughal** dynasty of Indian emperors. Son of the ruler of Ferghana, central Asia, he lost this territory while seeking to conquer Samarkand (1501–4). He captured Kandahar, strategic point on the northern road to India, 1522; occupied Delhi, 1526, and established himself on the imperial throne. He wrote poetry and his memoirs.

BACSONIAN AND HOABINHIAN Stone Age cultures of southeast Asia, characterized by the fact that their typical implements and artefacts are worked on one side only. They were named after two provinces of northern Vietnam, Bac Son and Hoa Binh, where the largest concentration of examples have been found.

BAFFIN, WILLIAM (c. 1584–1622) English navigator; sailed (1612) with Captain James Hall's expedition in search of the Northwest Passage; in 1615 and 1616, with Captain **Robert Bylot**, he penetrated the waters between Canada and Baffin Island, and deep into Baffin Bay, both named after him. Working for the **English East India Company** he surveyed the Red Sea and the Persian Gulf.

BAGHDAD PACT *see* **Central Treaty Organization**

BAIBARS (1223–77) Mamluk sultan, ruling Egypt and Syria, 1260–77. Born among the **Kipchak** Turks north of the Black Sea, he was sold as a slave to an Egyptian soldier. He fought and defeated both crusaders and Mongols before seizing the throne.

BAKEWELL, ROBERT (1725–95) English animal-breeder who revolutionized the development of meat-bearing strains in sheep and cattle. His successes included the Leicester Longhorn cow (now superseded by the Shorthorn) and the heavy, barrel-shaped, Leicester sheep. He was the first man to commercialize large-scale stud-farming.

BALAIADA Revolutionary uprising, 1838–41, in Maranhão province, Brazil; it was finally suppressed by the imperial general, Duque de Caxias.

BALBAN (1207–87) Sultan of Delhi, originally a junior member of the Forty, made up from personal slaves of Itutmish, who divided the kingdom after his death. He acted as deputy to Sultan Nasiruddin Mahmud (reigned 1246–66), whom he succeeded; he ably consolidated Muslim power, despite continual war with **Rajputs**, Mongols and Hindu states.

BALFOUR DECLARATION Letter from Britain's foreign secretary, Arthur Balfour, dated 2 November 1917, to Lord Rothschild, a leader of British Jewry, stating British support for the establishment in Palestine of a national home for the Jewish people, provided that the rights of the non-Jewish communities be respected. Approved at the San Remo Conference in 1920, it was incorporated into the mandate over Palestine granted to Britain by the **League of Nations** in 1922.

BALKAN LEAGUE The outcome of bilateral agreements made by Bulgaria with Serbia, Greece and Montenegro, leading to the Balkan Wars against Turkey, 1912–13. It collapsed completely in June 1913 when Bulgaria attacked Greece and Serbia in the hope of preventing them from acquiring the bulk of Macedonia.

BALKAN WAR, FIRST War that largely expelled the Ottomans from Europe. Montenegro, Bulgaria, Greece and Serbia attacked the Ottoman empire in October 1912; by December only the fortresses of Adrianople (Edirne), Scutari (Shkodër) and Yannin (Ioannina) remained in Turkish hands, and they too were lost to Turkey by the Treaty of London (May 1913) which also, at Austrian insistence, created the Albanian state to keep Serbia from the Adriatic.

BALKAN WAR, SECOND War among the victors of the First Balkan War over the division of Macedonia, June–Aug. 1913. Romania intervened on the side of Greece and Serbia against Bulgaria, which suffered a heavy defeat reflected in the Treaty of Bucharest (10 Aug. 1913); meanwhile, the Turks took the opportunity of regaining Adrianople (Edirne) from Bulgaria.

BALKE, HERMANN (d.1239) Provincial master of the **Teutonic Order**, who began the conquest of the pagan Prussians in 1231, at the head of a crusading army.

BAMBARA Also known as Banmana, west African people from the Upper Niger region of the Re-public of Mali. Their spoken language is derived from the **Mande** group, but their method of writing is distinctive, as is its associated cosmological system. The Bambara states, Segu (founded c. 1600) between the Senegal River and the Niger, and Kaarta (c. 1753) on the Middle Niger, flourished until the mid-19th century.

BANDARANAIKE, SOLOMON (1899–1959) Prime minister of Ceylon, 1956–9. He resigned from the Western-oriented United National Party in 1951 to form the nationalist Sri Lanka Freedom Party; in 1956 his People's United Front, an alliance of four nationalist-socialist groups, won a sweeping electoral victory. As prime minister he replaced English with Sinhala as the official language, fostered **Buddhism**, and established diplomatic relations with Communist states. He was assassinated and succeeded by his widow.

BANK OF ENGLAND Central financial institution of Great Britain. It was founded in 1694 with the initial object of lending King William III £1,200,000 at 8 per cent. Originally a private, profit-making institution, its public responsibilities were extended and defined by Bank Charter Acts of 1833 and 1844; it was finally transferred to public ownership in 1946.

BANTU A large group of closely related languages, spoken by the majority of the black inhabitants in Africa south of the Equator. By association, the term is sometimes applied to the people themselves, especially in South Africa.

BAPTISTS Members of a Christian Protestant movement dating from the 16th century. They are now represented by many churches and groups of churches throughout the world, organized in independent congregations. Many follow the practise of baptism by total immersion, and insist that the rite should take place only when the initiate is old enough to appreciate its significance.

BARAKZAI Tribal group from which emerged Afghanistan's ruling dynasty, from 1837 to 1973. The brothers who founded the dynasty seized control of the country in 1826 and divided it between them; Dost Mohammed Khan consolidated and unified the family rule, c.1837, and his direct descendants held the throne until 1929 when, after the abdication of the reigning monarch, succession passed to a cousin's line; the military coup of 1973 overthrew the monarchy and a republic was declared.

BARBAROSSA Name of two Greek brothers, famous as Algerian Muslim pirates, Barbarossa I (c. 1473–1518) was killed by the Spaniards after a series of raids on the Spanish coast; Barbarossa II, also known as Khair ed-Din (c.1466–1546), took over command on his brother's death and in 1519 became a vassal of the Ottoman sultan, for whom he repulsed an invasion by the emperor **Charles V** in 1541.

BARDI Important Florentine family, established there in the 11th century, which flourished in trade and finance, especially from the mid-13th to the mid-14th century. It became the greatest merchant and banking company in Europe at that time, and exercised considerable political influence. Defaults on debt payment by **Edward III** of England and by Florence finally led to bankruptcy and collapse in 1345.

BARENTS, WILLEM (c. 1550–97) Dutch explorer of the Arctic, who in 1594 and 1595 rounded northern Europe to reach the Novaya Zemlya archipelago. He is remembered particularly for his charting of northern waters; the Barents Sea is named after him.

BARTH, HEINRICH (1821–65) German geographer and explorer. After travels in Tunisia and Libya (1845–7), he set off on a British-sponsored expedition across the Sahara. Returning after 16,000km (10,000 miles), he wrote *Travels and Discoveries in North and Central Africa* (1857–8), still one of the richest sources of information on the area. He became Professor of Geography at Berlin in 1863.

BASIL I (d.886) Byzantine emperor. Of peasant stock, he was the founder of the Macedonian dynasty, so called from his place of origin. He rose to be co-emperor with Michael III in 866, but murdered Michael in 867. He began formulating the legal code (completed by his son **Leo VI**) known as the Basilica.

BASIL II (958–1025) Most powerful of Byzantium's Macedonian emperors. He was crowned co-emperor with his brother Constantine in 960; claimed sole authority, 985; extended Byzantine rule to the Balkans, Mesopotamia, Georgia and Armenia. His conquest of the Bulgarian empire earned him the nickname "Bulgar Slayer".

BASTIDAS, RODRIGO (1460–1526) Spanish explorer who discovered the mouths of the Magdalena river in modern Columbia, and founded the Columbian city of Santa Marta.

BATLLE Y ORDO—EZ, JOSE (1856–1929) President of Uruguay. He founded a newspaper, *El Día*, 1886; elected president in 1903, by a narrow margin, he emerged victorious from the ensuing civil war (1904–5), and was re-elected, 1905–7, and again, after freely stepping down, 1911–15. He inaugurated a wide-ranging programme of social and economic reform. Defeated over constitutional reform in 1918, he went on to serve as president of the national executive council in 1920 and 1926.

BATU KHAN (d.1255) Leader of the **Golden Horde**. The grandson of **Genghis Khan**, in 1235 he was elected western commander-in-chief for the Mongol empire, and entrusted with the invasion of Europe. By 1240 he had conquered all Russia; by 1241, after defeating Henry II, Duke of Silesia, and the Hungarians, he was poised to advance further west. However, on hearing of the death of **Ogedei** (December 1241) he withdrew his forces to take part in the choice of successor. He later established the Kipchak khanate, or the Golden Horde, in southern Russia.

BAYEZID I, YILDIRIM (c. 1360–1403) Known as "the Thunderbolt". Ottoman ruler. Succeeding to the throne in 1389, he claimed the title of sultan and attempted to establish a strong centralized state based on Turkish and Muslim institutions. He conquered large areas of the Balkans and Anatolia; blockaded Constantinople, 1391–8; invaded Hungary, 1395, and crushed at Nicopolis in 1396 the crusaders sent to repel him. He was defeated by **Tamerlane**'s Mongol armies at Ankara in 1402, and died in captivity, with his empire partitioned between his sons and the restored Anatolian principalities.

BAYEZID II (c. 1447–1512) Ottoman sultan, succeeding to the throne in 1481. His reign marked a reaction from the policies of his father, **Mehmed II**. The conquest of Kilia and Akkerman (1484–5) gave the Ottomans control over the mouth of the Danube and the land route from Constantinople to the Crimea; the later years of Bayezid's reign were taken up by war with Venice (1496–1503), by growing social unrest in Anatolia connected with the rise of the **Safavids** under their leader Ismail, and by the struggle among the sons of Bayezid for the succession to the Ottoman throne.

BEAUMANOIR, PHILIPPE DE RÉMI, SIRE DE (c. 1246–96) French administrator and jurist; wrote *Coutumes de Beauvoisis* (c. 1280–3), one of the earliest codifications of French law.

BELGAE Ancient Germanic and Celtic people, inhabiting northern Gaul; some emigrated to southern Britain in the 1st century BC. Gallic Belgae were conquered by **Julius Caesar** in 57 BC and the British in 55–54 BC.

BELGRADE, TREATY OF Peace agreement of 1739 ending the Turkish–Austrian War of 1737–9. Austria surrendered most of its gains under the **Treaty of Passarowitz** (1718), and thus re-established the line of the rivers Danube and Save as the frontier between the two empires.

BELISARIUS (c. 494–565) Byzantine general. Under Emperor Justinian I he swept the **Vandals** out of North Africa and **Ostrogoths** out of Italy (533–40); repulsed Persian assaults (541–2).

BELL, JOHN (1797–1869) Nominee for president of the USA on the eve of the American Civil War. He entered Congress, 1827; became secretary for war, 1841, and a US senator, 1847–59. He opposed the extension of slave-holding, though a large owner himself; nominated on a Constitutional Union ticket, 1860, he at first opposed secession, then supported it.

BENEDICT OF NURSIA, ST (c. 480–c. 540) Founder of a Christian monastic order. He became a hermit, but *c.* 529 decided to form a monastic community, which he established at Monte Cassino in Italy, and for which, in the 530s, he composed the Benedictine Rule (a relatively short document of 73 chapters) which has served as the basis of Christian monastic organization.

BEN-GURION, DAVID (1886–1973) Israeli labour leader, politician and statesman; born in Poland. He became active in **Zionist** affairs, emigrated to Palestine in 1906 and became secretary-general of the labour movement in 1921. In the struggle to found an independent Jewish state, he cooperated with the British during the Second World War but led the political and military struggle against them, 1947–8. He was the first prime minister (and also minister of defence) of the new state of Israel, 1948–53, and again 1955–63. He continued to exert an influence as its founding father and elder statesman in retirement from the Negev Kibbutz of Sede Boker until his death.

BENTHAMITE Follower of the English utilitarian philosopher Jeremy Bentham (1748–1832). Benthamite thinking, summed up in the concept of the Pleasure Principle ("men seek pleasure and avoid pain") and the belief that institutions should be judged by their ability to promote "the greatest happiness of the greatest number", influenced many later legal and political reforms.

BERBERS Original peoples of north Africa, who were colonized by Rome. Invaded by the Arabs in the 7th century AD, they were converted to Islam after some resistance. Those in or near cities were gradually absorbed into Arabic culture, but Berber languages continue to be spoken, particularly in mountain and pastoral regions of Morocco and Algeria.

BERING, VITUS JONASSEN (1681–1741) Danish navigator and discoverer of Alaska. After a voyage to the East Indies, he joined the Russian navy of **Peter the Great**; in 1724 he was appointed by the tsar to establish whether Asia was joined to North America, and in 1728 sailed through the strait which now bears his name, into the Arctic Ocean. He died when his ship was wrecked on Bering Island, east of the Kamchatka peninsula.

BERLIN, CONGRESS OF Meeting of European statesmen in June–July 1878 under the presidency of **Bismarck** to revise the Treaty of **San Stefano** (1878), concluded by Russia and Turkey. Bulgaria, greatly reduced in extent, became an autonomous principality. The independence of Romania, Serbia and Montenegro was confirmed. Austria-Hungary was given the right to occupy Bosnia and Herzegovina, and Russia was confirmed in its possession of Ardahan, Kars and Batum.

BERLIN WALL Heavily fortified barrier built in 1961 by the East German government around the Western zones of Berlin. The Berlin Wall was the single most potent symbol of the **Cold War**. As levels of emigration from East to West Berlin increased in the 1950s and early 1960s, the East German government determined to construct what it called the Anti-Fascist Exclusion Wall. Though its stated purpose was to keep West Berliners out of East Berlin, in reality the Wall was a crude but effective means of preventing East Germans from escaping to the West. The opening of the Wall in late 1989 after the collapse of the communist government of East Germany was a vivid symbol of the end of the Cold War.

BERLUSCONI, SILVIO (1936–) Prime Minister of Italy (2001–2011) as leader of a centre-right coalition, and Italy's richest man. Born to a lower class family, Berlusconi graduated in Law before setting up his own business as a property developer. He also grew a media empire, which includes papers, radio and a television network, has interests in advertising and food, and owns the football club AC Milan. He first became Prime Minister in 1994, before his involvement in a tax fraud case destroyed the coalition government just over six months later. He again became embroiled in corruption charges in 2004 over claims that he tried to bribe a judge to favour a takeover battle his company was involved in. Politically, he is a staunch ally of the USA and the UK. He faced rising economic and social problems in Italy and was criticized for putting into place legislation to serve his own business interests.

BERNARD, ST (c. 1090–1153) He entered the Cistercian Order in 1113, only 15 years after the foundation of the monastery of Cîteaux, and soon became its leading light. Two years later, he founded the monastery of Clairvaux, also in southeast France, and remained its abbot for the rest of his life. Through personal influence, teaching and voluminous writings, he dominated the theological and to a large extent also the political life of his times, particularly by securing the recognition of Innocent II as Pope in 1130, by advice to his former pupil **Eugenius III** (Pope 1145–53), and by preaching the second **Crusade** in 1147.

BESANT, ANNIE (1847–1933) Theosophist, social reformer and Indian independence pioneer. She was a Fabian Socialist, with George Bernard Shaw, in the late 1880s, and was converted to the theosophic ideas of Helen Blavatsky, 1889–91. She spent much of her remaining life in India, jointly founding the Indian Home Rule League in 1916.

BESSEMER, SIR HENRY (1813–98) British inventor of the Bessemer steel-making process. He developed various mechanical devices, including a movable date stamp, and in the Crimean War the first rotary shell. In 1856 he announced a process for purifying molten iron with a blast of air; with contributions from other inventors, his work made possible the Bessemer converter and the mass production of cheap steel.

BETANCOURT, ROMULO (1908–81) Venezuelan political leader. Imprisoned while a student, and exiled to Colombia, he returned in 1936 to lead the anti-Communist left-wing underground movement; again exiled, 1939–41, in 1941 he organized Acción Democrática (AD), and became president of the revolutionary governing junta after the overthrow of President Medina Angarita, 1945. Forced yet again into exile by the Pérez Jiménez regime, 1948–58, he became president ofVenezuela, 1959–64.

BHONSLAS Dynasty of **Maratha** rulers in western India, founded by the family of King **Sivaji**. They were leaders in the 18th-century Maratha confederacy formed to resist the British; later they became British clients (1816–53).

BINDUSARA (d.272 BC) Early Indian emperor, succeeding his father, **Chandragupta Maurya**, in 279 BC. He campaigned in the Deccan, as far south as Mysore, and brought most of the subcontinent under Mauryan control.

BIN LADEN, OSAMA (1957–2011) Osama bin Laden was the leader of the fundamentalist Islamic network Al Qaeda, "the base". He claimed responsibility for the September 11 attacks on the USA, and he was also wanted for the 1998 bombings of the USA embassies in Kenya and Tanzania, and the attacks on US troops in Saudi Arabia and Somalia. Born to a wealthy Yemeni family in Saudi Arabia, his father was the owner of Saudi Arabia's biggest construction company. In 1979 he went to fight for the Islamic *jihad* against the Soviet invasion of Afghanistan, a successful mission that was supported and financed by Saudi Arabia and the USA. After the Soviets withdrew, bin Laden returned to Saudi Arabia, but his criticisms of the Royal Family and of the presence of American troops at holy sites there led to his expulsion in 1991. He then spent several years in the Sudan, but under US pressure he was expelled and returned to Afghanistan. After the September 11 attacks, the US administration under George W. Bush and their allies invaded Afghanistan as part of the "War on Terror", in an effort to capture or kill him and oust the Taliban from power. In the latter they were successful. Bin Laden was killed by an American special services unit in 2011.

BISMARCK, PRINCE OTTO VON (1815–98) German statesman, known as "the Iron Chancellor". He was appointed minister-president of Prussia, 1862; after wars against Denmark (1864) and Austria (1866), he formed the North German Confederation (1867), and after the **Franco-Prussian War** (1870–1) inaugurated the German empire (1871–1918). As German chancellor (1871–90) he instituted important social, economic and imperial policies and played a leading role in the European alliance systems of the 1870s and 1880s.

BLACK FLAGS Chinese bandits and mercenary groups active in Annam and Tongking, 1873–5, led by Liu Yung-fu, a former T'ai-p'ing rebel. Called on by the mandarins of Hanoi to oppose the French (1873), they were responsible for the defeat and death of several French commanders during a decade of bitter guerrilla war.

BLACKFOOT INDIANS A group of Indian tribes of Algonquin stock. They were one of the strongest Indian confederations in the early 19th century but were gradually defeated and subdued by the US settlers. Their name derived from the colour of their moccasins.

BLAIR, TONY (1953–) Labour Prime Minister of the UK (1997–2007). Blair became a barrister before winning the seat of Sedgefield for the Labour Party in 1983, rising swiftly through the ranks to be elected to the shadow Cabinet in 1988, to shadow Home Secretary in 1992 and to be the party's leader in 1994. As leader, Tony Blair revolutionized the Labour Party, creating what he termed "New Labour". This positioning put Labour nearer to the centre of the political spectrum, and to the dismay of many on the left, he drastically reduced the power of the trade unions, and opened the gates to the privatization of state-run services. The modernization of the party broadened its membership and led to its landslide victory over the Conservatives in the 1997 general election, with Blair becoming the youngest Prime Minister since Lord Liverpool in 1812. During his second term, he stood as a staunch ally to President George W. Bush of the USA following the September 11 terrorist attacks, which led to the invasion of Afghanistan and later the invasion of Iraq. He resigned the premiership in 2007 and from then until 2015 he was United Nations special envoy to the Middle East.

BLAKE, ROBERT (1599–1657) English admiral; he commanded **Cromwell**'s navy in the English Interregnum, and defeated the Dutch, the Spaniards, and the Barbary corsairs.

BLIGH, WILLIAM (1754–1817) British vice-admiral. He served on Captain **James Cook**'s last voyage; he was commanding the *Bounty* when the crew mutinied in 1789 in the South Seas and set him adrift in an open boat. On his voyage of exploration of 1791 he made discoveries in Tasmania, Fiji and the Torres Straits. He fought at Gibraltar (1782), Camperdown (1797) and Copenhagen (1801). He was governor-general of New South Wales, 1805–8, from which post he was deposed by force and imprisoned until 1810.

BLITZ Second World War term for a sudden attack, particularly from the air; derived from the German word *Blitzkrieg*, or lightning war.

BOETHIUS (c. 480–524) Late classical scholar and statesman, born in Rome. He was appointed consul under **Theodoric** the Ostrogoth in 510. He translated **Aristotle**'s *Organon* and helped to preserve many classical texts; he wrote on music, mathematics and astronomy. His **Christianity**, clear from some short treatises, is not mentioned in his larger works. After falling from favour with Theodoric, he wrote his *De consolatione philosophiae* in prison. He was executed on charges of treason.

BOGOMILS Balkan religious sect, flourishing from the 10th to the 15th century. It inherited **Ma-nichaean** doctrines from the **Paulicians**; believed the visible world was created by the devil; rejected baptism, the Eucharist, the cross, miracles, churches, priests and all orthodox Christianity. Its leader, Basil, was publicly burned in Constantinople *c.* 1100. Adopted by the ruling class in Bosnia, it also directly influenced the **Cathars** in Italy and **Albigensians** in France; it died out after the Ottoman conquest of southeast Europe because many of its adherents converted to Islam.

BOLESŁAW I CHROBRY, "THE BRAVE" (966–1025) First fully accepted king of Poland, son of **Mieszko I.** He inherited the principality of Greater Poland, 992; reached the Baltic, 996, and seized control of Cracow and Little Poland. Crowned by Emperor **Otto III**, 1000, he was embroiled in wars, 1002–18, with Emperor Henry II over lands seized in Lusatia, Meissen and Bohemia. He defeated Grand Prince Iaroslav I of Kiev (1018), and placed his son-in-law on the Kievan throne.

BOLIVAR, SIMON (1783–1830) Venezuelan soldier-statesman who freed six South American countries from Spanish rule. He participated in Venezuela's declaration of independence in 1811, fleeing to Haiti after the Spanish counter-revolution; liberated New Granada (Colombia) in 1819; Venezuela, 1821; Ecuador, 1822; Peru, 1824; and Upper Peru, renamed Bolivia, in 1825. A liberal political thinker but an autocratic ruler, he failed in his real ambition to establish a union of Spanish-American peoples; most of the nations he had helped to create were in turmoil or conflict when he died.

BOLSHEVIKS Named from Bolsheviki Russian for "those of the majority", the name adopted by **Lenin**'s supporters in the Russian Social-Democratic Workers' Party at the 1903 Congress when, advocating restriction of membership to professional revolutionaries, they won a temporary majority on the central committee. From 1912 they constituted a separate party. Seizing control of Russia in October 1917, in March 1918 they adopted the name "Communists".

BONAPARTE see **Napoleon I**

BONIFACE VIII (c. 1235–1303) Pope, 1294–1303. He reasserted papal claims to superiority over temporal powers; his Bull *Clericis laicos* (1296) led to conflict with **Edward I** of England, and particularly with **Philip IV** of France, over taxation of the clergy, but the dispute soon widened to cover the whole relationship of Church and state. He was briefly kidnapped at Anagni by the French, 1303, but soon released; to escape repetition of such treatment, the papacy took up residence at Avignon – the so-called "Avignon Captivity".

BONIFACE, ST (c. 675–754) Often called the Apostle of Germany; born in Nursling, Wessex. He was ordained priest *c.* 705 under his original name of Wynfrith. He left England in 716 to evangelize the Saxons. He was sent first into Hesse and Thuringia by Pope Gregory II (722–35), and then into Bavaria by Gregory III. He became Archbishop of Mainz, 751; organized German and reformed Frankish churches. He was martyred by pagan **Frisians**.

BOONE, DANIEL (1734–1820) American frontiersman, explorer and fighter in Kentucky and Missouri. He created the wilderness road, northwest of the Appalachians.

BOSE, SUBHAS CHANDRA (1897–1945) Indian nationalist leader; educated Calcutta and Cambridge, England. He was imprisoned (1924–7) for his part in **Gandhi**'s non-cooperation movement. On his release he was elected president of Bengal's provincial congress. He spent most of the next decade in prison or exile, until 1938 when he became president of the Indian National Congress; under house arrest (1940), he escaped to Germany. He formed an Indian volunteer force to attack the Western allies and in 1943, with Japanese support, invaded India from Rangoon. He died two years after his defeat, in an air crash in Taiwan.

BOURBONS European ruling family. Descended from Louis I, duke of Bourbon (1279–1341), grandson of King **Louis IX** of France (reigned 1226–70), the Bourbons held the thrones of France (1589–1791 and again 1814–48), Spain (more or less from 1700–1931), and Naples and Sicily (1735–1860). The Spanish line was restored after the death of **Franco** in 1975.

BOURGUIBA, HABIB (1903–2000) Tunisian politician. He became a journalist in 1930 on a paper which advocated self-government for Tunisia. He founded his own Neo-Déstour party in 1934 to achieve independence from France, but was imprisoned 1934–6, 1938–45 and 1952–4, and in exile 1945–9. He became first prime minister of independent Tunisia in 1956–7, its first president 1957–87, and "President for Life" 1975–87.

BOXER REBELLION Chinese popular uprising in 1900, aiming to drive out all foreign traders, diplomats and particularly missionaries. The name is derived from a secret society, the I-ho-ch'üan (Right and Harmonious Fists), which had earlier violently opposed the ruling **Ch'ing** (Manchu) dynasty, but in 1899 began to attack westerners. On 18 June 1900, as hostilities grew, the Empress Dowager ordered the execution of all foreigners; hundreds were besieged in the Peking legation quarter until relieved on 14 August by an international expeditionary force, which then looted the capital. Peace and reparations were finally agreed in September 1901.

BRACTON, HENRY DE (d. c. 1268) Medieval English jurist, judge of King's Court under Henry III (1247–57). Author of *De legibus et consuetudinibus Angliae* ("On the laws and customs of England"), one of the oldest and most influential treatises on common law.

BRADDOCK, EDWARD (1695–1755) English general who in 1754 was appointed to command all British land forces in North America; he was ambushed (with his army) and killed by mixed French and Indian forces while leading an expedition against Fort Duquesne.

BRAHMA Hindu creator of the universe who, with **Vishnu** and **Shiva**, form the leading trinity of Hindu gods.

BRAHMO SAMAJ Hindu theistic society, founded in 1828 by the religious reformer, **Rammohan Roy**. It split into two in 1865, when the philosopher Keshub Chunder Sen (author of *The Brahmo Samaj Vindicated*) founded a separate branch known as "Brahmo Samaj of India". It was the earliest modern reform movement in India.

BRASSEY, THOMAS (1805–70) English railway contractor, trained as a surveyor, in 1835 he built the Grand Junction line, and later helped to finish the London–Southampton link. Starting with the Paris–Rouen line (1841–3), he went on to build railway systems all over the world, including the 1770-km (1100-mile) Grand Trunk in Canada (1854–9).

BRAZZA, PIERRE SAVORGNAN DE (1852–1905) Piedmontese explorer and colonizer who made pioneering journeys through equatorial Africa, 1873–7. He negotiated treaties with African chiefs which were then taken up by the French, whose service Brazza subsequently entered, governing the region north of the Congo for France, 1887–97.

BRECKINRIDGE, JOHN CABELL (1821–75) Unsuccessful Southern Democrat candidate for the US presidency on the eve of the American Civil War (1861–5). Born in Kentucky, he entered the US Congress in 1851; vice-president to James Buchanan, 1857–61; US Senator, 1861; expelled after joining the Confederate army. He served as brigadier, major-general and later secretary for war in the Confederacy; fleeing to England at the end of hostilities, he returned in 1868.

BREDA, TREATY OF Inconclusive agreement, signed 31 July 1667, ending the Second Anglo-Dutch War (1665–7). France, which had supported the Dutch, gave up Antigua, Montserrat and St Kitts, in the West Indies, to Britain, but recovered Acadia (now Canada's Maritime Provinces); England acquired New York and New Jersey from the Dutch; Holland won valuable sea-trading concessions.

BREST-LIVOTSK, TREATY OF Peace agreement, signed March 1918, between Russia and the Central Powers. Russia recognized the independence of Poland, Finland, Georgia, the Baltic States and the Ukraine, and agreed to pay a large indemnity. The treaty was declared void under the general armistice of 1918.

BREZHNEV, LEONID ILICH (1906–82) Soviet leader. He joined the Communist Party, 1931; became Red Army political commissar, major-general, 1943; a member of the Communist Party Central Committee, 1952. He succeeded **Khrushchev** as first secretary of the Party, 1964; enunciated the Brezhnev Doctrine to justify invasion of Czechoslovakia, 1968, by Warsaw Pact forces; replaced Podgorny as president of the USSR, 1977–82.

BRIAN BORU (c. 941–1041) High king of Ireland. He succeeded as ruler of a small Irish kingdom, Dal Cais, in 972, and also of Munster. Brian defeated Ivar, the Norse king, in Inis, Cathaig in 977; attacked Osraige (982); was recognized as ruler of southern Ireland (997) and by 1005 claimed his position as king of all Ireland. He was killed after the battle of Clontarf.

BRITAIN, BATTLE OF Series of aerial encounters between the German Luftwaffe and the British Royal Air Force, mainly over southern England, fought between July and October 1940. As a result of her failure to win air mastery, Germany abandoned plans for a seaborne invasion of Britain.

BRONZE AGE In the Old World, the first period of metal-use, based on copper and its alloys. Beginning in the Near East in the 3rd millennium BC, and in Europe after 2000 BC, and independently in south-east Asia at the same time, this technology spread among both peasant and urban societies – Bronze Age civilizations included Sumer, Egypt, the Indus and Shang China.

BROOKE, SIR JAMES (1803–68) Founder of a dynasty of "white rajahs" in Sarawak, northwest Borneo. He served with the **English East India Company**'s army in the Burma War 1824–6; assisted the Rajah of Brunei in suppressing various rebellions, and in 1843 was made Rajah of Sarawak.

BRUCE see **Robert I of Scotland**

BRUNHILDE (c. 545–613) Twice regent of Austrasia and for a period the most powerful ruler in **Merovingian** France. The daughter of Athanagild, Visigothic king in Spain, she married Sigebert, son of Lothar, king of the Franks. The murder of her sister, Galswintha, precipitated a 40-year feud in Gaul. The deaths of her husband and her son, **Childebert II**, placed her at the head of affairs until 599 when palace officials drove her out. In 613 she was executed by being tied to a wild horse.

BRÜNING, HEINRICH (1885–1970) German statesman. He became leader of the Catholic Centre Party, 1929, and formed a conservative government in 1930 without a Reichstag majority. After parliamentary rejection of his major economic plans, he began to rule by presidential emergency decree. He resigned the chancellorship in May 1932 after the failure of both his foreign and his domestic policies.

BRUSATI Prominent family of medieval Novara, Italy. Supporters of the **Guelph** (anti-imperial) party, they enjoyed a brief supremacy in the city 1305–15, but were overcome by their Ghibeline (pro-imperial) rivals, supported by the **Visconti** family in neighbouring Milan.

BRUSILOV, ALEKSEY ALEKSEYEVICH (1853–1926) Russian general who led the Russian offensive against Austria-Hungary in June–August 1916; he became the supreme Russian commander in 1917. Under the **Bolsheviks** he directed the war against Poland, 1920; he retired in 1924 as inspector of cavalry.

BRUSSELS PACT Defensive alliance of 1948 providing for military, economic and social cooperation, signed by France, Great Britain and the Benelux countries.

BUDDHA, GAUTAMA (c. 486–c. 400 BC) Founder of the world religion known as **Buddhism**. Born on the northern border between India and Nepal, the son of a nobleman of the Hindu Kshatiya caste, traditionally he was inspired to change his life at the age of 29 by the sight of an old man, a sick man, a corpse and an itinerant ascetic. In the Great Renunciation he gave up his privileges and for six years practised extreme asceticism, then abandoned it in favour of deep meditation, receiving enlightenment as he sat under a tree. The remainder of his life was spent teaching and serving the order of beggars which he founded.

BUDDHISM Religious and philosophic system based on the teaching of Gautama, the **Buddha**, who rejected important features of his native **Hinduism** in the 6th century BC. In his first sermon at Benares he preached the Four Noble Truths and the abandonment of desire and sorrow by systematic pursuit of the Noble Eightfold Path, the ultimate end of which is Nirvana, the elimination of all desire and anguish. This remains the basis for the Dharma or Teaching, carried out through the Samgha or monastic Order. Since the Buddha's death the religion has developed along two distinct and sometimes conflicting lines: Theravada (or Hinayana), in southeast Asia, stressing monasticism and avoiding any taint of theism or belief in a god; and Mahayana, in China, Japan, Tibet and Korea, which embraces more personal cults.

BUGANDA Former kingdom and later administrative region, occupying 44,850 sq. km (17,311 square miles) of present-day Uganda, inhabited largely by the Baganda tribe. It was an important independent power from the 17th to the 19th century, becoming a British protectorate in 1894; limited self-government, under British rule, was granted in 1900.

BUKHARIN, NIKOLAI IVANOVICH (1888–1938) Bolshevik economist and theoretician. He lived in exile in New York until the revolution, when he returned to Russia (May 1917) and became leader of the Communist Party's Right faction, which advocated cautionary progress to full socialism through the continuation of the New Economic Policy (NEP). A member of the Politburo, 1918–29, and head of the Third International, 1926–9, he was expelled from the Politburo in 1929 because of his association with Trotskyist opposition to **Stalin**. Restored in 1834, when he became editor of *Izvestia*, he was again expelled in 1938 and was executed after the last of the Great Purge Trials.

BUNYORO One of the earliest East African kingdoms, founded in the 16th century and occupying territory now part of Uganda. It prospered until the 19th century, when it lost ground and power to neighbouring **Buganda**. Its last ruler, Kabarega, was deposed by the British in 1894, and his kingdom absorbed into the British protectorate in 1896.

BUONSIGNORI Italian banking house, founded in Siena in 1209, which became the foremost company in Europe. It began to collapse in 1298 and finally closed its doors in 1309.

BURGUNDIANS Germanic people, originally from the Baltic island of Bornholm (Burgundaholm), 1st century AD. In the 5th century they established a powerful kingdom in the Saône and Rhône valleys, extending to the Rhine. They were defeated and absorbed by the Franks in 534.

BURKE, EDMUND (1729–97) British statesman, orator and political theorist. He entered Parliament in 1765, and made a reputation with eloquent speeches and writings on the American question and on the arbitrary government of George III. He sought abolition of the slave trade; in his *Thoughts on the revolution in France* (1790) he bitterly condemned the outbreak of revolution and predicted increasing violence.

BURTON, SIR RICHARD FRANCIS (1821–90) Explorer and English translator of *The Thousand and One Nights*. He visited Mecca in 1853 and was the first European to reach Harar, Ethiopia, in 1854; with **Speke** he discovered Lake Tanganyika in 1858.

BUSH, GEORGE HERBERT WALKER (1924–) US political leader and 41st president. From a wealthy Connecticut family and active in the navy during World War II, he graduated from Yale (1948). After two terms in the House of Representatives from Texas (1967–71), he was ambassador to the UN, chairman of the republican National Committee and Director of the Central Intelligence Agency during the 1970s. He served as **Ronald Reagan**'s vice president (1981–9) and as president (1989–93).

BUSH, GEORGE W. (1946–) 43rd president of the USA and son of the 41st president (1989–1993), George Bush, he was sworn into office in 2001 after one of the most bitterly contested presidential races in history, which endured a recount and several legal challenges. The September 11 attacks on the World Trade Center in New York and the Pentagon in Washington D.C. came in his first year as President, in reaction to which he launched the "War on Terror", aimed at countries that sponsored terrorism and who were termed the "Axis of Evil". The Saudi born leader of Al-Qaeda who assumed responsibility for the attacks, Osama **bin Laden**, became his primary focus. In 2003, as part of the War on Terror, a US-led coalition (that sharply divided world opinion) invaded Iraq and toppled Saddam Hussein from power, ostensibly because of Iraq's production of weapons of mass destruction that contravened UN resolutions. No such weapons were found, and as a result, the war was heavily criticized, both by world governments and the public. Bush also received criticism for not implementing the 1997 Kyoto Protocol to cut greenhouse gas emissions, signed by his predecessor, Bill Clinton.

BUSHMEN see **San**

BUTTON, SIR THOMAS (d.1634) English navigator, and the first to reach the western shores of Hudson Bay (1612–13). He also discovered the Nelson River, which rises in Manitoba and runs into Hudson Bay.

BUWAYHIDS (Buyida) Dynasty originating in northern Persia. They occupied Baghdad, capital of the **Abbasid caliphate**, in 945; though **Shi'as**, they ruled the central lands of the caliphate in the name of the Abbasid caliph. Their power was ended by the occupation of Baghdad in 1055 by the **Seljuks**.

BYLOT, ROBERT English navigator and discoverer of Baffin Bay (1615); because he was suspected of disloyalty the bay was named after his lieutenant, **William Baffin**.

BYNG, JOHN (1704–57) English admiral, remembered mainly for an epigram by the French writer Voltaire who said that he was court-martialled and shot "*pour encourager les autres*" after failing to relieve Minorca.

CABANAGEM Revolutionary uprising, 1835–40, in the Paré region of Brazil. The term was coined from *cabana* or cabin, perhaps an allusion to the lowly origins of the insurgents.

CABOT, JOHN (c. 1450–c. 1499) Italian explorer (real name Giovanni Caboto). Precise details of his travels are much in dispute, but around 1484 he moved from Italy to London, and in 1496 was given authority by **Henry VII** to search for unknown lands; after one abortive attempt, he left Bristol in 1497 in a small vessel, the *Mathew*, and made landfall, probably in the region of Cape Breton, Nova Scotia. The fate of his second, larger expedition in 1498 remains unknown.

CABOT, SEBASTIAN (1476–1557) Explorer, cartographer and navigator. Before 1512 he worked for **Henry VIII** of England; seconded to assist Spain against the French, he was appointed in 1518 as pilot-major to the Spanish *Casa de la Contratación*; in 1526 he led an expedition intended for the Moluccas via the Magellan Straits, but diverted it to the Río de la Plata and spent three years exploring Paraná and Paraguay. He published a celebrated but unreliable world map 1544, and organized an expedition to seek the Northeast Passage.

CABRAL, PEDRO ALVARES (1467/8–1520) Reputed discoverer of Brazil, commissioned by the Portuguese king, Manuel I, to sail to India; he sighted and claimed Brazil for Portugal, 1500, before continuing the voyage in which he lost 9 out of his 13 ships in storms; he bombarded Calicut, established a Portuguese factory at Cochin and returned to Portugal with his four remaining ships loaded with pepper. He was not subsequently employed at sea.

CAINOZOIC Geological era, starting *c.* 65 million years ago, during which all surviving forms of mammal life (including Man) first evolved, and the earth's surface assumed its present form.

CALDERA RODRIGUEZ, DR RAFAEL (1916–2009) Venezuelan political leader. He was secretary of the Venezuelan Catholic youth organization 1932–4, and in 1936 founded the country's national union of students. In 1946 he founded the Committee of Independent Political Electoral Organizations (COPEI); an unsuccessful presidential candidate in 1947, 1958 and 1963, he finally became President, as the candidate of COPEI, in 1969, holding the post until 1974, in which year he was appointed senator for life.

CALIPHATE The office of caliph, regarded by **Sunnis** as successor to the Prophet **Mohammed** in his capacity as leader of the Islamic community. The first four caliphs ("patriarchal", "rightguided" or "orthodox" caliphs) ruled from Medina; they were succeeded first by **Umayyads** ruling from Damascus, 661–750; then by the **Abbasids** of Baghdad, whose dynasty continued until 1258, although effective power was held by various dynasties of sultans – **Buwayhids, Seljuks**. In the 10th century two other dynasties took the title of caliph; a branch of the Umayyads in Spain, and the **Fatimids** in Cairo. The last Abbasid caliph was killed by the Mongol conquerors of Baghdad in 1258, and the caliphate virtually came to an end. The title was revived by the Ottoman sultans in the 19th century, but abolished by the Turkish Republican government in 1924.

CALLIMACHUS (c. 305–c. 204 BC) Poet from Cyrene who worked in Alexandria, compiling a 120-volume critical catalogue of the great Library; only fragments of his 800 recorded works survive, but his Aetia (*"Origins"*) and his shorter poems had a profound influence on Roman authors, including Catallus and Propertius. He refused to write long epics, saying that "a large book is a great evil".

CALVIN, JOHN (1509–64) French theologian who established strict Presbyterian government in Geneva. He wrote *Institutes of the Christian Religion* (1536–59), setting out his teachings – that the state should support the Church, that biblical authority should override Church tradition, and that the sacraments, though valuable, are not essential to true religions. He strongly influenced the Huguenots in France, the Protestant churches in Scotland and the Netherlands, and the Puritan movement in England and North America.

CAMBYSES II (d.522 BC) Second Achaemenid Persian emperor, the eldest son of **Cyrus**, whom he represented in Babylon, 538–530 BC; he succeeded on Cyrus' death in 529. He invaded Egypt, taking Memphis in 525 and was returning home when he heard of the usurpation by his brother **Smerdis**, and died soon afterwards.

CAMINO, DA Medieval Italian family, prominent in the affairs of the city of Treviso. It first gained power through Gherado (*c.* 1240–1306), a noted soldier of fortune. His sons wavered between the rival **Guelph** and Ghibelline factions in Italian politics, resulting in the murder of one and the expulsion of the other from Treviso in 1312.

CANUTE see **Cnut the Great**

CAO, DIOGO 15th-century Portuguese navigator who explored much of the west coast of Africa. He was the first European to reach the mouth of the Congo (1482).

CAPETIANS Ruling dynasty of France, 987–1328. It was founded by Hugh Capet, elected king in 987 to replace the previous **Carolingian** line; gradually he and his successors extended their control, initially limited to the area around Paris, to cover the larger part of present-day France; they also began to develop many of the country's main political institutions, such as the *Parlements* (royal law courts) and the States General (representative assemblies). Notable Capetian kings included **Philip II Augustus** (reigned 1180–1223), (St) **Louis IX** (1226–70) and **Philip IV** the Fair (1285–1314).

CAPITALISM Economic system in which the principal means of production, distribution and exchange are in private hands, whether individual or corporate, and competitively operated for profit. A mixed economy combines the private enterprise of capitalism and a degree of state monopoly, as in nationalized industries.

CARACALLA (188–217) Roman emperor, born Marcus Aurelius Antoninus at Lugdunum (modern Lyons), son of Emperor Septimius Severus. He gained the imperial throne in 211 and in the following year extended Roman citizenship to virtually all inhabitants of the empire. He murdered his wife, Fulvia Plautilla, and younger brother, Geta. He was assassinated at Carrhae, Mesopotamia, while preparing his second campaign against Parthia.

CARDENAS, LAZARO (1895–1970) Mexican soldier and radical leader. Governor of home state of Michoacán, 1928–32; minister of the interior, 1931; president of Mexico, 1934–40. During his term of office he launched a Six-Year Plan, a land redistribution programme, the expropriation of foreign-owned oil companies (1938) and a renewed attack on the Catholic Church; he was minister of defence, 1942–5.

CARLOWITZ, TREATY OF A truce agreement, signed on 26 January 1699, ending hostilities (1683–99) between the Ottoman empire and the Holy League (Austria, Poland, Venice and Russia). Under its terms Transylvania and much of Hungary was transferred from Turkish control to Austrian, making Austria the dominant power in eastern Europe. In 1700 the armistice was confirmed by the Treaty of Constantinople.

CARNOT, LAZARE NICOLAS MARGUERITE (1753–1823) French military engineer and statesman who directed the early successes of the French revolutionary armies (1793–5); he was a member of the Directory, the five-man group ruling France, 1795–9. Although opposed to **Napoleon**'s rise to power Carnot later rallied to the emperor in resisting the invasion of France, 1814, and was minister of the interior during the **Hundred Days**, 1815. Carnot was also a mathematician and he held the prestigious post of Chair of Geometry at the Institute of Science. He died in exile.

CAROL II (1893–1953) King of Romania who supplanted his son Michael as legitimate ruler in 1930 and created a royal dictatorship. He was deposed in 1940.

CAROLINGIANS Royal dynasty descended from Pepin of Landen (d. AD 640), chief minister of the **Merovingian** king, Chlothar II. Pepin's illegitimate grandson was **Charles Martel**, after whom the dynasty was named. His great-great grandson was the emperor **Charlemagne**. The dynasty continued to rule in East Francia (Germany) until 911, and in West Francia (France) until 987.

CARRACK Large round sailing ship developed in the Middle Ages for both trade and naval warfare, particularly by the Genoese and Portuguese. Deep-keeled and high in the water, the vessel had two or three masts, castle fore and aft, and was usually well armed with cannon. Larger versions were used by the Portuguese in trade to the East Indies and Brazil in the 16th century.

CARRANZA, VENUSTIANO (1859–1920) President of Mexico. The son of a landowner, he was active in politics from 1877; as governor of Coahuila, in 1910, he supported **Madero**, and in 1913 led the opposition to Madero's successor, Victoriano Huerta. He set up a provisional government, defeated the armies of **Pancho Villa**, and was installed as first president of the Mexican Republic (1917). He fled during an armed uprising in 1920, and was betrayed and murdered in the mountains near Vera Cruz.

CARREIRA DA INDIA The round voyage between Portugal and India, inaugurated with **Vasco da Gama**'s pioneering expedition of 1497–8 and continuing until the age of steam. Under sail the journey averaged 18 months, including the stay at Goa.

CARRON Pioneer Scottish ironworks, established by John Roebuck. Founded with capital of £12,000 in 1760, it was first to use a cast-iron blowing-cylinder to increase airblast. Technicians trained there started iron-making in Russia and Silesia.

CARTIER, JACQUES (1492–1557) Explorer of Canada, commissioned by **Francis I** of France to sail in search of gold, spices and a new route to Asia; he entered the Gulf of St Lawrence in 1534, and on subsequent expeditions established a base at Quebec and reached Montreal.

CASIMIR I, THE RESTORER (1016–58) King of Poland. He ascended the throne in 1039. He recovered the former Polish province of Silesia, Masovia and Pomerania, lost by his father **Mieszko II**; he restored central government and revived the Catholic Church, but failed to throw off German suzerainty.

CASIMIR III, THE GREAT (1310–70) King of Poland. He succeeded to the throne in 1333. He concluded a favourable peace with the **Teutonic Order** in 1343, and annexed the province of Lwow from Lithuania during the 1340s. The last ruler of the **Piast** dynasty, he agreed in 1339 to the union of Poland and Hungary after his death. At home he unified the government, codified laws and founded new towns and the first university in eastern Europe at Cracow in 1364.

CASIMIR IV (1427–92) King of Poland. A member of the **Jagiellonian** dynasty, he succeeded to the Grand Duchy of Lithuania in 1440 and to the throne of Poland in 1447. He defeated the Teutonic Knights and recovered West Prussia for Poland by the Treaty of Thorn, 1466. Thereafter he sought to create a Polish empire stretching from the Baltic to the Black Sea but was checked by the Turks and, at the time of his death, by **Ivan III** of Russia.

CASTILLA, RAMON (1797–1867) President of Peru. Born in Chile, he fought for the Spaniards until captured by Chilean patriots; changing sides, he fought in Peru with **Bolívar** and **San Martín**. The first elected president, 1845–51 and again 1855–62, he built up Peru's economic strength by the exploitation of newly discovered guano and sodium nitrate deposits.

CASTRO, FIDEL (1926–) President of Cuba from 1976 to 2008. Law graduate, 1950; after failure to win power by a coup, 1953, he led the guerrilla group "26th of July Movement"; invaded Cuba in 1956 but failed to raise a revolt and fled to the mountains; regrouped, and finally displaced the Batista regime in 1959. He was boycotted by the USA after his **Marxist** aims became apparent; survived the Bay of Pigs invasion of 1961, and the Cuban missile crisis, 1962; with Soviet aid (to 1990) he promoted a programme of land and economic reform. In 1976 he sent troops to Angola (withdrawn 1991), and embarked on an increasingly active African and Central American policy. He retired as president in 2008 to be succeeded by his brother Raúl.

CATEAU-CAMBRÉSIS, TREATY OF Agreement signed in 1559 to end the war between France, Spain and England. Spain's claims in Italy were recognized by France, making the former the dominant power in southern Europe; France gained the bishoprics of Toul, Metz and Verdun; England finally surrendered Calais.

CATHARS (CATHARISM) A doctrinal heresy descended from the **Manichaeism** of the early Christian church but with some non-Christian roots, which from the mid-11th century spread rapidly in western Europe, throughout northern Italy and southern France (where the Cathars were known as **Albigensians**). Their chief tenet was the dualism of good and evil, which was contrary to Catholic belief although in some respects resembling it. They also devoted themselves to poverty and evangelism, in these respects resembling both the **Humiliati** and the monastic orders. **Innocent III** launched the Albigensian Crusade against them in 1208 and his successors combated them with the **Inquisition.**

CATHERINE II, THE GREAT (1729–96) Born a princess of the German principality of Anhalt-Zerbst, she married in 1744 Peter of Holstein-Gottorp who in 1762 became Tsar **Peter III.** Six months later she usurped his throne with the aid of her lover, G. Orlov. She advanced Russia's status as a great power, conquering the north shore of the Black Sea from Turkey, and with Prussia and Austria completed the partition of Poland in 1795. She carried out a number of domestic reforms, none of which improved the status of the serfs. She published her *Instruction for the drafting of a new code of laws* in 1767 and wrote many plays and historical works.

CATHOLIC LEAGUE Union of German Catholic princes, formed in 1609 in opposition to the Protestant Union of 1608, and headed by Maximilian I of Bavaria. Its armies, under Tilly (1559–1632), played an important part in the early stages of the Thirty Years' War (1618–48), in which they conquered Bohemia, 1619–22, and defeated Denmark, 1624–9.

CATHOLIC REFORMATION Movement initiated by the Catholic church at the Council of Trent (1545–63) to counter the spread of the **Reformation**. Extending into the 17th century, its dominant forces included the rise of the **Jesuits** as an educating and missionary group and the deployment of the Spanish **Inquisition** in other countries.

CAVALCABO Prominent family of medieval Cremona, Italy. Supporters of the **Guelph** (anti-imperial) party, they gained control of the city in the second half of the 13th century, retaining power until 1312 when they were driven out by Emperor Henry VII. In 1314 they returned, but were driven out permanently by the **Visconti** of Milan in 1344.

CAVOUR, COUNT CAMILLO BENSO (1810–61) Italian statesman. He abandoned court and an army career, visited England and then embarked on a career in finance, agriculture, industry and radical politics. In 1848 he founded the newspaper, *Il Risorgimento*, to champion monarchical and liberal aims, and promote democratic reforms. He entered the Piedmontese cabinet in 1850, and was given control of government, 1852, by the new king, **Victor Emmanuel II**. He was primarily responsible for creating the United Kingdom of Italy of 1861.

CEAUȘESCU, NICOLAE (1918–89) Roman-ian political leader. Active in the illegal Communist party, he was imprisoned for eight years, before and during World War II. Minister of agriculture (1950–4); deputy armed forces minister (1950–4); Politburo member and president of Romania (1967–89). He enforced rigid domestic policies, suppressed political opposition ruthlessly, and concentrated on economic development along strict **Marxist**-Leninist lines. He was executed in 1989 after the overthrow of his government in a bloody revolution.

CELTS Ancient people of western Europe called by the Greek *Keltoi* and by the Romans *Celtae*. Now more generally used of speakers of languages descended from these, notably Breton in France, Welsh, Cornish, Gaelic (Scots and Irish), and Manx in the British Isles. Archaeologically often used as synonymous with **La Tène** style.

CENOZOIC see **Cainozoic**

CENTRAL TREATY ORGANIZATION (CENTO) Defence alliance, originally known as the Baghdad Pact, between Iran, Iraq, Pakistan, Turkey and the UK, signed in 1955. The headquarters were moved from Baghdad to Ankara in 1958, and the name changed with the withdrawal of Iraq in 1959. The Pact was weakened from the first by the refusal of the USA, which had sponsored it, to become a full member. It aroused the hostility of **Nasser**, and an ill-judged attempt to recruit Jordan led to riots which nearly caused the fall of King Hussein. Dissolved in 1979.

CHALCEDON, COUNCIL OF Fourth ecumenical council of the Christian Church, called in 451 to pronounce on the nature of Christ; it condemned **Monophysitism** as a heresy.

CHALDEANS A group of Semitic tribes, related to the Aramaeans, who settled in the marsh areas of southern Babylonia *c.* 1000 BC. They eventually spread up the Euphrates, infiltrating into territories of many of the major cities of Babylonia, almost to Babylon. By the late 8th century BC, Chaldean chieftains, notably Ukin-zer and Marduk-apal-iddina (Merodach-baladan of the Bible), sought the kingship of Babylonia, producing endemic disturbance. A Chaldean dynasty, whose best-known ruler was Nebuchadnezzar succeeded to the kingship from 625 to 539 BC. In the Hellenistic and Roman period the term "Chaldeans" was used to describe Babylonian astrologers generally, without any ethnic basis.

CHAMBERLAIN, JOSEPH (1836–1914) British political leader. Mayor of Birmingham, 1873–6, and a pioneer of radical local government, he became a member of parliament in 1876. He was colonial secretary in the Conservative government, 1895–1903, during the last, and for Great Britain vital, stages of the partition of Africa; he was responsible for sending Kitchener to the Sudan, for declaring a protectorate over Uganda, and – most important – for the South African War of 1899–1902. He resigned to campaign for Imperial Preference (see **Ottawa Agreement**) and tariff protection for British industry.

CHAMORRO, VIOLETA BARRIOS DE (1929–) Nicaraguan politician and widow of the Nicaraguan journalist and writer Pedro Joaquin Chamorro, assassinated in 1978 because of his bit-ter opposition to the Somoza political regime. The National Opposition Union candidate for president in 1989–90, she was elected to the presidency in April 1990. She sought a balance between **Sandin-ista** and opposition forces in governmental programmes.

CHAMPA Ancient kingdom of Indo-China, originally occupying most of the central coastal region of modern Vietnam, and inhabited by the Chams, a people of Malay affinity. Founded *c.* AD 192, according to Chinese sources, it had close tributary relations with China down to the 16th century, but avoided a Chinese attempt at conquest in 1285. Frequent wars against the Vietnamese led to piecemeal loss of territory, and then to annexation of the main part of Champa by 1471; the kingdom disappeared completely *c.* 1700, apart from Cham communities surviving near Phan Thiet and Phan Rang. Its Hindu temples survive at various places, indicating Indian cultural influence.

CHANAK INCIDENT (1922) Landing of British troops at Çanakkale (Chanak) on the Dardanelles to oppose a Turkish takeover of the straits. **Lloyd George**, the British prime minister, was accused of recklessness and his government fell.

CHANCA Andean tribe occupying land in Andahuaylas, Peru. In 1440 they attacked but were heavily defeated by the neighbouring, previously insignificant, **Incas**.

CHANCELLOR, SIR RICHARD (d.1556) Navigator and pioneer of Anglo-Russian trade. In 1553 he was appointed pilot-general to Sir Humphrey Willoughby's expedition seeking a north-east passage to China. Separated from them by bad weather, he continued into the White Sea and overland to Moscow, where he was warmly received by Tsar **Ivan IV**. He returned to England in 1554 after he had negotiated the formation of the Muscovy Company.

CHANDELLAS Rajput warrior clan, ruling Bundelkhand, northern India, from the 9th to the 11th century. Defeated in 1001 by Muslim armies of **Mahmud of Ghazni** and expelled from their great fortress of Kalinjar (1023), they were reduced to vassalage by Prithviraja of Ajmer in 1082.

CHANDRAGUPTA II Indian king of the Gupta dynasty, reigning *c.* 375–415, son of Samadragupta. Traditionally renowned for his valour and chivalry, he fought a long campaign against the Shakas (388–409). He extended Gupta power, by war in northern India and by marriage in the Deccan, and took the title *Vikramaditya*, Sun of Prowess.

CHANDRAGUPTA MAURYA Founder of the first Indian empire, he usurped the throne of the Ganges Valley kingdom of Magadha, 321 BC. He exploited the power vacuum left by the retreat of **Alexander the Great** from northwest India, defeated the forces of **Seleucus I Nicator**, 305–303 BC and acquired Trans-Indus province (now part of Afghanistan). He is said to have been converted to **Jainism** at the end of his life, abdicating in 297 in favour of his son **Bindusara**, and dying, as a monk, by deliberate starvation.

CHANG CH'IEN (d. 114 BC) Chinese diplomat and explorer, sent in 138 BC by the Han emperor **Wu-ti** to establish contact with the **Yüeh-chih** tribes, and the first man to bring back to China reliable reports of central Asia. He was captured and held for 10 years by the **Hsiungnu** tribes but still completed his mission, returning after 13 years. He made many other journeys, his travels taking him as far as the Tarim Basin, Ferghana, Bactria, Sogdiana and the Hellenic outpost-states established by **Alexander the Great**. Besides information, his efforts gave China its first access to such valuable products as large, fast horses, grapes and alfalfa grass.

CHANG HSIEN-CHUNG (c. 1605–47) Chi-nese rebel leader in the last days of the **Ming** dynasty. Trained as a soldier, he was dismissed from the imperial army and started bandit raids in northern Shensi, 1628. He moved into Honan and Hupeh in 1635. Forced to surrender in 1638, he was nevertheless allowed to retain his forces, and rebelled again in 1639. In 1643 he failed to set up administrations in Wuchang and Changsha. He retreated into Szechwan, but captured Cheng-tu in 1644 and took the title of King of the Great Western Kingdom. His government disintegrated in a reign of terror in 1646, and he was killed the following year.

CHANG KUO-T'AO (1897–1979) A founder of the Chinese Communist Party (CCP). After playing a minor role in the May 4 Movement, he represented Peking Marxists at the first CCP Congress at Shanghai in 1921. He helped to found the CCP-sponsored Labour movement and developed close ties with the **Comintern**. From 1929 he played a major role in Communist base areas on the borders of Honan, Anhwei and Hupeh, and led his forces through Szechwan on an important leg of the Long March. From 1935 he engaged in bitter debates with **Mao Zedong**; attempting to set up an independent base in the far northwest, his troops were disastrously defeated in Kansu. After 1938 he defected to the Nationalists and lived in semi-retirement, moving to Hong Kong in 1949, and writing his autobiography.

CHAN TSO-LIN (1873–1928) Chinese warlord known as "the Old Marshal". Originally an officer in a Manchurian army, he built up control of southern Manchuria and much of northern China until 1928. After 1921 he controlled Inner Mongolia. Attempts to control the Peking government led to war with **Wu P'ei-fu** in 1922, in which Chang was initially defeated. In 1924 he concluded a pact with the Soviet Union, which recognized his regime in Manchuria as independent. Later that year he invaded northern China, seriously defeating Wu P'ei-fu and driving south almost to Shanghai. His power was backed by the tacit support of the Japanese, who supported him in Manchuria as a buffer against Soviet influence, and to whom he granted major concessions in Manchuria. Unable to counter the growing power of the **Kuomintang** (Nationalist Party) armies under **Chiang Kai-shek**, which invaded his territories in 1927, he abandoned Peking to them. He was killed when Japanese extremists blew up his private train.

CHARLEMAGNE (742–814) Emperor of the **Franks**, son of **Pippin III**. Succeeded as joint king, 768; sole ruler from 771. He conquered most of the Christian territory in western Europe, defeating the Lombards and converting the pagan Saxons, and he allied with the papacy to counter the dominance of Byzantium. On Christmas Day 800 in St Peter's, Rome, he was crowned and anointed by the Pope and became the first emperor of non-Roman origins and the first of the German emperors of the Middle Ages.

CHARLES I, OF ANJOU (1226–85) Angevin king of Naples and Sicily, younger brother of **Louis IX** of France. He acquired the country of Provence, 1246; defeated the last **Hohenstaufen** in 1266 and 1268 to conquer Naples and Sicily, and in 1277 became heir to the kingdom of Jerusalem. Transferring his capital from Palermo to Naples, he set off the revolt of the Sicilian Vespers, 1282, and was defeated by the alliance of the Sicilians and Peter III of Aragon in the Bay of Naples, 1284.

CHARLES I (1600–49) King of England, Scotland and Ireland, son of **James VI (and I)**. Succeeding in 1625, he came increasingly into conflict with his English parliament over religion, foreign policy and taxation. After being forced to sign the Petition of Right (1628), he ruled without Parliament until 1640; rebellion broke out in Scotland in 1638, in Ireland in 1641 and in England in 1642. Defeated in the civil wars that followed, he was captured in 1647 by the English army under **Cromwell**, tried and beheaded.

CHARLES IV (1316–78) King of Bohemia, 1346–78, and ruler of the German empire from 1355, son of John of Luxembourg and Elizabeth, sister of the last native Bohemian king. He reformed the finances and legal system, and built up the power of the monarchy in Bohemia, but left Germany largely to the princes; in 1356 he issued the **Golden Bull**, laying down a permanent constitution for the empire.

CHARLES V (1500–58) Holy Roman Emperor. He was the son of Philip I (died 1506), heir to the Burgundian states, and of Joanna (declared insane in 1506), heiress to Castile and Aragon, to which he succeeded in 1516. Elected Emperor in 1519, he annexed Lombardy (1535), and several Netherlands provinces, but was eventually defeated (1551–5) by an alliance of Turks, French and German Lutherans. He abdicated in 1556, leaving his German possessions to his brother Ferdinand (elected Emperor in 1558), and the rest to his son **Philip II**. He retired to a monastery in 1557.

CHARLES IX (1550–1611) Effective ruler of Sweden from 1599, and king 1604–11. The third son of **Gustavus I Vasa**; in 1568 he helped his brother, then crowned as **John III**, to depose their half-brother **Eric XIV**. A strong Lutheran, he first broke with John over religion and then, after the accession of John's Catholic son, **Sigismund III**, called the Convention of Uppsala, 1593, to demand the acceptance of **Lutheranism** as the state religion. Appointed regent in Sigismund's absence, he precipitated a civil war and deposed the king, 1599. He died after strengthening Sweden's metal-based economy and provoking the Kalmar War with Denmark, 1611–13.

CHARLES X GUSTAV (1622–60) King of Sweden, son of John Casimir, Count Palatine of Zweibrücken, and Catherine, eldest daughter of **Charles IX**. He fought with the Swedish armies in Germany, 1642–5. His cousin, Queen Christina of Sweden, appointed him commander of the Swedish forces in Germany and also her official successor. He was crowned in 1654, invaded Poland in 1655 and Denmark in 1657–8, and won an advantageous peace.

CHARLES XI (1655–97) King of Sweden, succeeding his father, **Charles X Gustav**, in 1660. He was kept in tutelage by aristocratic regents until Sweden's defeat by Brandenburg at Fehrbellin in 1675; he then established absolute rule, expanding the royal estates to cover 30 per cent of Sweden and Finland and rebuilding the armed forces to match those of Denmark. In 1693, the Swedish Diet granted him unrestricted powers to ensure his reforms.

CHARLES XII (1682–1718) Warrior king of Sweden, eldest son of **Charles XI**, succeeding to the throne in 1697. Brilliantly defeated the anti-Swedish coalition (formed in 1699 to crush Sweden's Baltic hegemony) of Denmark, Russia, Poland and Saxony, invading each in turn (1700–6). He invaded Russia again with Cossack help in 1708 but was routed at Poltava, 1709, taking refuge in Turkey which he succeeded in turning against Russia. Forced to leave Turkey in 1714, he was killed while fighting in Norway.

CHARLES ALBERT (1798–1849) King of Sardinia-Piedmont. Son of the Prince of Carignano, he was exiled from Italy and brought up in revolutionary Paris and Geneva, succeeding his father in 1800. He was involved in an abortive plot to displace his cousin as king of Piedmont in 1821. He ascended the throne on his cousin's death in 1831. He sought to lead the unification of Italy, granting representative government and declaring war on Austria in 1848. Defeats at Custoza, 1848, and Novara, 1849, forced his abdication. He died in Portugal.

CHARLES THE BOLD (1433–77) Duke of Burgundy, son of **Philip the Good**, inheriting the title in 1467. He attempted to conquer the lands dividing his territories of Luxembourg, Burgundy, the Low Countries and Franche-Comté; but was defeated and killed in battle. Soon after this, in the year 1483, Burgundy passed to the French crown, and Charles' other domains became part of the **Habsburg dominions**.

CHARLES MARTEL (c. 688–741) Reunifier of the **Franks**. The illegitimate son of Pippin of Herstal, Mayor of the Palace of Austrasia, he emerged, after a five-year struggle, as his father's successor and as effective ruler of all the Franks, 719. He defeated the Muslims, advancing north from Spain, near Tours, 733/4; subdued Burgundy, 733, the **Frisians**, 734, and the Aquitainians 735. He retired in 741, and died the same year.

CHÁVEZ, HUGO (1954–2013) Born into a poor Venezuelan family, Chávez served in the army until dissatisfaction with the existing political system encouraged him to found the Revolutionary Bolivarian Movement in the early 1980s. He was imprisoned after an attempted coup in 1992, founded the Fifth Republic Movement following his release and was elected president of Venezuela in 1998, a post he retained at subsequent elections until his death in 2013. His regime encouraged social, economic and political reform in Venezuela and Chávez was a key figure in re-orientating Latin America away from the influence of the United States.

CHEOPS (Khufu) Second king of Egypt's 4th Dynasty (early 26th century BC), succeeding his father, Snefru. He built the Great Pyramid of Giza and three subsidiary pyramids for his principal wives.

CHEPHREN (Khafre) Fourth king of Egypt's 4th Dynasty (late 26th century BC). The son of **Cheops**, he succeeded his brother, Djedefre. He built the second of the three pyramids of Giza and the granite valley temple linked to it by a causeway.

CH'I Large and powerful Chinese state in the period 771–221 BC, located on the eastern edge of the North China Plain (modern Shantung and Hopeh). In the 7th and 6th centuries BC Ch'i began to expand, absorbing its smaller neighbours; during this period it was also the most technologically advanced state in China. Under the semi-legendary Duke Huan it gained short-lived hegemony over all Chinese territories in 651. In the 3rd century BC a new ruling house again attempted to impose sole dominance on China, but it failed, and in 221 Ch'i was absorbed by Western **Ch'in**.

CHIANG KAI-SHEK (1887–1975) Chinese general and political leader. He took control of the **Kuomintang** in 1926 and established a stable republican government in Nanking, 1928–37. He fought warlords, Japanese invaders and the Chinese Communist Party (with occasional periods of alliance) until finally defeated in 1949. He withdrew to Taiwan (Formosa) to form the Chinese Nationalist government, of which he remained president until his death.

CHICHIMECS Barbarian and semi-civilized Indian groups who invaded central Mexico from the north in the 12th and 13th centuries and ended the rule of the **Toltecs**; the Aztecs originated as one of the Chichimec tribes.

CHILDEBERT II (570–95) King of Austrasia, son of Sigebert and **Brunhilde**. After the murder of his father he became the pawn of various aristocratic factions in Austrasia, which favoured alliance with one or other of his two uncles, Chilperic or Guntram. He led an expedition to Italy in 584; ousted the supporters of Chilperic in 585 and allied with Guntram; and after Guntram's death in 593 controlled almost all of Gaul.

CHILDERIC (d.481) Chieftain of the Salian Franks, occupying territory between the rivers Meuse and Somme. He helped the Romans to defeat the **Visigoths**, near Orléans in 463, and again in 469; and cleared the Saxon pirates from the area of Angers. He died in Tournai, where his richly equipped tomb was discovered in 1653, and was succeeded by his son **Clovis**.

CHILEMBWE, JOHN (1860–1915) Nyasaland missionary and rebel leader, now regarded as one of the spiritual forebears of modern Malawi. He worked closely with the European fundamentalist Joseph Booth, 1892–5. In 1897 he received a degree from the USA Negro theological college. On his return to Nyasaland in 1900 he founded the Providence Industrial Mission with Negro Baptist finance. He protested in 1914 against economic oppression and the use of Nyasa troops in the First World War. He was shot after leading a suicidal revolt against British rule.

CHIMU South American Indians, famous for their goldware and pottery, whose rule (1100–1400s AD) immediately preceded that of the **Inca** in Peru. Their comparable, though small-scale, civilization, centred at Chanchán in the Moche Valley about 480km (300 miles) north of Lima, was conquered by **Pachacuti** in 1465–70.

CH'IN First great Chinese imperial dynasty (221–206 BC): founded by **Shih Huang-ti**; *see* pp. 88–89.

CH'IN-CH'UAN RISINGS Series of risings of the aboriginal peoples of western and northwest Szechwan in 1745–9, flaring up intermittently again until 1776. The risings tied down large Manchu armies in difficult mountain terrain, and their suppression was extremely costly.

CHIN FU (1633–92) Chinese official responsible for major water improvements under the early **Ch'ing** dynasty. From 1677 he dredged and banked up the frequently flooding Yellow River, and made large-scale repairs to the Grand Canal.

CH'ING (or Manchu) Last imperial dynasty in China from 1644–1912. *See* pp. 192–3, 256–7.

CHOU Chinese dynasty, *c.* 1122–221 BC. The Western Chou (*c.* 1122–771 BC) were originally semi-nomadic barbarians from west of the North China Plain. They conquered the lands ruled by the previous Shang dynasty and extended them. Their territory was organized in a "feudal" system of virtually independent fiefs; in 771 central authority finally broke down. During the Eastern Chou (771–221 BC), China became one of the world's most advanced regions; its greatest philosophers, **Confucius** and **Lao-tzu**, lived at this time, and from this period date many of its most characteristic innovations.

CHREMONIDES' WAR The last flicker of Athenian aggression. In 267 BC a citizen called Chremonides called for a Greek league of liberation with the support of Egypt against the Macedonian king, Antigonus Gonatus; few others joined, and after an intermittent siege Gonatus captured the city in 262. Athens never again sought political leadership in classical times.

CHRISTIANITY Religion of those who have faith in **Jesus**. In the central traditions of Christianity the single God is nonetheless a trinity – the Father, the Son (incarnate in the human life of Jesus of Nazareth) and the Holy Spirit. Christianity spread despite persecution, and in the 4th century was adopted by the Roman ruling class. Despite divisions it has remained one of the great world religions, sending its missionaries all over the world.

CH'U One of the Chinese states which, with **Ch'i**, **Ch'in** and later, Chin, contended between 771–221 BC for the domination of China. Based on present-day Hupeh, in the fertile Yangtze valley of southern China, Ch'u had a completely distinctive culture of its own. It expanded very rapidly into Anhwei and Hunan, and eventually controlled all central China. In 223 BC it was finally absorbed by Ch'in, but 15 years later, when Ch'in collapsed, a Ch'u aristocrat, Hsiang Yü, briefly became emperor of China; but his reign only lasted a few months before the advent of the **Han** dynasty.

CHURCHILL, SIR WINSTON LEONARD SPENCER (1874–1965) British statesman and author. The son of Lord Randolph Churchill, he served as a soldier and journalist in Cuba, India, the Sudan and South Africa before becoming a Conservative member of parliament in 1900. He was a minister in both the Tory and Liberal governments between 1908 and 1929, serving as first lord of the admiralty, 1911 to 1915. During the 1930s he warned of the growing threat from **Nazi** Germany, and later directed Britain's war effort as first lord of the admiralty in 1939–40, then as prime minister and minister of defence, 1940–5. He was prime minister again in 1951–5. His works, written while out of office, include *The World Crisis, 1916–18* (1923–9), *The Second World War* (1948–53) and *A History of the English-speaking Peoples* (1956–8). He won the Nobel Prize for literature in 1953.

CHU TE (1886–1976) "Father" of the Chinese Red Army. Originally a military officer in Yunnan and Szechwan, he went to Shanghai in 1921 and joined the Chinese Communist Party in 1922. After studying in Germany (1922–6) he took part in the abortive rising in Nanch'ang in 1927. With **Mao Zedong** he built a famous fighting unit in the Kiangsi Soviet, took part in the Long March, commanded Communist forces in the Sino-Japanese War and became commander-in-chief during the civil war with the Nationalists. During the 1930s and 1940s he played a major role in developing Communist policies in rural areas, and in strategic planning. In 1949 he became vice-chairman of the central people's government and by 1958 was looked on as natural successor to Mao as head of state. However, in 1959 he was passed over in favour of Liu Shao-ch'i, and had little real power after that time.

CHU YÜAN-CHANG (1328–98) Chinese emperor, founder of the **Ming** dynasty. Born in Anhwei province, he joined a monastery, but between 1356 and 1364 led insurgent forces, gradually gaining control of the region north of the Yangtze, being proclaimed Prince of Wu in 1364. Driving out the Mongols in 1368, he established the Ming dynasty with its capital at Nanking and reigned for 30 years under the title Hung Wu.

CIMMERIANS Indo-European people driven from their homelands in southern Russia, north of the Caucasus and the Sea of Azov, by the closely-related **Scythians** in the 8th century BC. They were turned aside into Anatolia when they conquered Phrygia, 696–95. After their rout by Alyattes of Lydia, *c.* 626, they were absorbed by surrounding groups.

CISTERCIAN Religious order founded at Cîteaux, in southeast France, in 1098. It rose to great prominence under the influence of **St Bernard**; and by the end of the 12th century it had more than 500 monasteries all over Europe. The motive of the foundation was the re-establishment of the primitive rigour of the Rule of St Benedict, which had lately been neglected.

CLAPPERTON, HUGH (1788–1827) Scottish explorer of West Africa. He joined an expedition journeying south from Tripoli across the Sahara; in 1823 he reached Lake Chad, and travelled in what is now northern Nigeria. He made a second expedition to southern Nigeria; he died near Sokoto after crossing the Niger.

CLARK, WILLIAM (1770–1838) American explorer. With Meriwether Lewis he led a momentous expedition (1804–8) up the Missouri River and over the Rocky Mountains to the Pacific, opening vast territories to westward expansion.

CLAUDIUS I (10 BC–AD 54) Fourth Roman emperor, born Tiberius Claudius Drusus Nero Germanicus, nephew of the emperor **Tiberius**. He achieved power unexpectedly in AD 41, after the murder of his elder brother's son, **Caligula**; annexed Mauretania, north Africa, 41–2; invaded Britain, 43, and extended the empire in the east. He had his third wife, Messalina, killed on suspicion of conspiracy, and was almost certainly poisoned by his fourth, his niece Agrippina.

CLAUSEWITZ, CARL von (1780–1831) Prussian general and philosopher of war. He played a prominent part in the military reform movement after the disastrous defeat by **Napoleon** at Jena in 1806. He served as a staff officer with the Russian army, 1812–13, but returned to Prussian service in 1814–15. After the defeat of Napoleon he was appointed director of the War Academy, a purely administrative post which gave him ample time for historical and theoretical writings. His most famous and still influential book, *On War*, was published posthumously.

CLEMENT OF ALEXANDRIA (c. AD 150–c. 213) Saint, and principal reconciler of early Christian beliefs with the mainstream of Graeco-Roman cultural tradition. Born in Athens, he settled in Egypt, and became head of the Catechetical School, Alexandria. He taught many future theologians (e.g. Origen) and church leaders (Alexander, Bishop of Jerusalem), and wrote important ethical and theological works.

CLEMENT OF ROME (b.c. 100) Saint, first Apostolic Father of the Christian Church and Bishop of Rome at the end of the 1st century AD. Author of the *Letter to the Church of Corinth*, an important source for the Church history of the period.

CLEMENT IV (d.1268) Pope 1265–8. A Frenchman who had been in the service of **Louis IX**, his pontificate signified the growth of French influence in the Church which predominated during the next 100 years. He allied with **Charles of Anjou** to drive the **Hohenstaufen** out of Italy.

CLEOMENES III (c. 260–219 BC) King of Sparta, succeeding his father, Leonidas, in 235 BC. He successfully fought the Achaean League, 228–26; usurped the constitutionally jointly-held Spartan throne to establish virtual autocracy, 227; reintroduced many of the "communist" ideas of **Agis IV**. His predominance in the Peloponnese was challenged by the Macedonian, **Antigonus Doson**; defeated by Doson at Sellasia in 222, he escaped to Egypt and was interned by Ptolemy IV. He committed suicide after an abortive attempt at revolution in Alexandria.

CLEOPATRA (c. 70–31 BC) Last Ptolemaic ruler of Egypt, the daughter of King Ptolemy Auletes. Joint heir with her brother, she was made queen by **Julius Caesar** in 48 BC. She went to Rome as his mistress, but transferred her affections to **Antony**, who then left for four years, but returned after breaking with Octavian. She committed suicide after the Egyptian fleet was defeated at Actium and the troops of her ally, Antony, refused to fight.

CLINTON, BILL (1946–) US politician and 42nd president. He studied international affairs at Georgetown (1968) and as a Rhodes Scholar at Oxford (1968–70), then received his law degree from Yale (1973). He served as attorney general of Arkansas (1977–9); governor of Arkansas (1979–81; 1983–92) and, as the national Democratic candidate, in 1993 defeated George Bush to become US president. He was re-elected president in 1997 but his presidency was dogged by scandals.

CLINTON, HILLARY DIANE RODHAM (1947–) Democratic politician, lawyer, author, and wife of Bill Clinton, 42nd president of the United States. She became chair of the Task Force on National Health Care Reform in 1993 and represented the state of New York in the US Senate from 2001 to 2009. She lost the Democratic presidential primary to Barack Obama in 2008 and served as US Secretary of State in his first administration from 2009 to 2013. In 2015, she announced that she would run for the nomination of the Democratic Party for the 2016 presidential election.

CLIVE, ROBERT (1725–74) Conqueror of Bengal and founder of British power in India. He arrived in India in 1743 as a clerk in the **English East India Company**. He fought French, and later (1757) Indian, forces to establish British control in Bengal, where he was twice governor (1757–60) and 1765–7). His rule was marred by corruption scandals; despite successful Parliamentary defence in 1773, he committed suicide the following year.

CLOVIS I (c. 466–511) Founder of the kingdom of the **Franks**, succeeding his father, **Childeric**, as ruler of the Salian Franks in 481, and gradually uniting all other Frankish groups under his rule. He defeated the last Roman authority in northern Gaul in 486, defeated the **Burgundians** and the Aleman, and drove the **Visigoths** from Aquitaine in 507. Sometime before 508 he converted to Catholic Christianity, and was baptized at Rheims; he issued the Salic law for his people, and established his capital at Paris. His descendants, the **Merovingians**, ruled the Frankish kingdom until 751.

CLUNIAC The monastery of Cluny (near Mâcon, Burgundy) was founded in 910 by the Duke of Aquitaine, and wielded a tremendous influence on the life of the Church for the next two centuries. The respect in which the Cluniacs were held through their many foundations all over western Europe, the statesmanlike activity of their leaders and the hierarchical organization of the Order under the abbot of Cluny, combined to make it one of the foundation stones of the general reform of the Church led by Pope **Gregory VII**.

CNUT THE GREAT (c. 995–1035) King of England (where he is remembered as Canute), Denmark and Norway. The son of **Sven Forkbeard**, he went to England with his father in 1013; he divided the country with Edmund II in 1016, assuming rule over all the country on Edmund's death in the same year. He succeeded to the Danish throne in 1019 and invaded Scotland in 1027.

COELHO, DUARTE (c. 1485–1554) Portuguese soldier. He was granted the captaincy of Pernambuco in 1534, and developed it into the most flourishing colony in Brazil.

COKWE (Bajokwe) People occupying the southern region of Zaire, northeast Angola and northwest Zambia, formed by a mixture of aboriginal groups and **Lunda** invaders; they were famous ivory-hunters in the 19th century.

COLBERT, JEAN BAPTISTE (1619–83) Minister of Finance to **Louis XIV** of France. Personal assistant to Cardinal **Mazarin**, he became a dominant member of Louis' Council of Finance, and in 1665 was made Controller-General. He reformed taxes, founded state manufactures, created the French merchant fleet and laid the basis for France's economic dominance in late 17th-century Europe.

COLD WAR Global tension caused by superpower rivalry after the end of the Second World War. *See* pp. 302–3.

COLIJN, HENDRIKUS (1869–1944) Dutch statesman. Fought in Sumatra where he was later colonial administrator. He entered the Dutch parliament in 1909; became war minister, 1911–13; finance minister, 1923–5; prime minister, 1925–6 and 1933–9. In his second term as premier he instituted successful anti-Depression policies. He was forced to resign in 1939. Arrested by the Germans in 1941, he died three years later in a concentration camp.

COLLA People of the high Andes who in pre-Columbian times occupied the area south of Lake Titicaca. They were conquered by the **Incas** in the early 15th century.

COLLING BROTHERS English 18th-century stockbreeders, farming near Darlington, who developed the shorthorn cow, *c.* 1780, into an animal equally good for milk and meat.

COLTER, JOHN (c.1775–1813) US trapper and explorer, who in 1807 discovered the area now known as Yellowstone National Park. He was also a member of the Lewis and **Clark** expedition.

COLUMBA (521–79) Irish saint, famous as the missionary who carried Christianity to **Picts** in Caledonia (Scotland). He founded the monastery at Iona, 563, the mother house of numerous monasteries on the Scottish mainland.

COLUMBUS, CHRISTOPHER (1451–1506) Genoese navigator, discoverer of America and founder of the Spanish empire in the Americas. In 1492 he obtained finance from the Spanish court to seek the east by sailing west. His three ships, the *Pinta*, *Niña* and *Santa María*, sighted San Salvador on 12 October 1492. During his second voyage, in 1493, he founded Isabela, the first European city (now deserted) in the New World, in the Dominican Republic. His third journey, 1498–1500, revealed the mainland of South America. He was embittered when administrative disasters and lack of political sense made the king of Spain reluctant to trust his governorship. His last voyage, 1502–4, coasted Honduras, Nicaragua and the isthmus of Panama, and ended with his ships beached off Jamaica.

COMINTERN The Third Socialist International, set up in 1919 to replace the **Second International** by those who condemned it for its failure to prevent the First World War. Captured immediately by the leadership of Bolshevik Russia, it split the world socialist movement between evolutionary and revolutionary parties, fomenting a number of uprisings in Europe and in European colonies in southeast Asia in the 1920s. Extensively purged by **Stalin**'s secret police in the 1930s, it was formally dissolved in 1943.

COMMUNISM Revolutionary socialism based on the theories of the political philosophers Karl **Marx** and Friedrich Engels, emphasizing common ownership of means of production and a planned economy. The principle held is that each should work according to their needs. Politically, it seeks the overthrow of **capitalism** through a proletarian revolution. The first communist state was the USSR after the revolution of 1917. Revolutionary socialist parties and groups united to form communist parties in other countries. After the Second World War, communism was enforced in those countries that came under Soviet occupation. China emerged after 1961 as a rival to the USSR in world communist leadership and other countries attempted to adopt communism to their own needs. With the collapse of the USSR in 1990, communism disappeared from Europe. It survives in China and a small number of unreconstructed hardline states.

COMNENES Byzantine dynasty holding the imperial throne, 1081–1185. Isaac I, son of Manuel Comnenus, a Paphlagonian general, became emperor briefly from 1057 to 1059, but his nephew, **Alexius I** (reigned 1081–1118), consolidated the family's power. The elder line died out in 1185, but after the sack of Constantinople by crusaders (1204) relatives founded the empire of Trebizond, lasting until 1461, when David Comnenus was deposed.

CONFEDERATION OF THE RHINE Created by **Napoleon I** in 1806 after the dissolution of the **Holy Roman Empire**, to gather his client states into a federation of which he was "protector". Excluding Austria and Prussia, it formalized French domination over German territory, and lasted until Napoleon's defeat.

CONFLANS, TREATY OF Agreement concluded in 1465 between **Louis XI** of France and the League of the Public Weal, under which Louis agreed to return land captured on the Somme to the League's leader, **Charles the Bold**, duke of Burgundy, and promised him the hand of his daughter, Anne of France, with the territory of Champagne as dowry.

CONFUCIUS (c. 551–479 BC) Chinese philosopher. He served as a public administrator, *c.* 532–*c.* 517 BC, then spent the rest of his life teaching and editing the ancient Chinese classics. His sayings, collected after his death as *The Analects*, formed the basis for Chinese education and social organization until the 20th century. His philosophy was conservative: he advocated submission to one's parents and of wives to husbands, loyalty of subject to ruler, and conformity to established social forms. He advocated the supremacy of ethical standards and rule by "humanity" and moral persuasion rather than brute force, and laid great stress on ritual observance. Confucianism has been deeply influential in Japan, Korea and Vietnam as well as in China.

CONGREGATIONALIST Member of one of the independent Protestant churches established in the 16th and 17th centuries in the belief that each congregation should decide its own affairs. Among its famous followers were John Winthrop, founder of the Massachusetts Bay Colony in 1629, and **Oliver Cromwell**, Lord Protector of England, 1649–60. Congregationalism became the established religion in 17th-century New England; many such churches still survive in North America and in Great Britain.

CONSTANTINE I (c. 287–337) Roman emperor, known as "the Great". Born in Naissus, now Nis, Serbia, he was brought up at the court of **Diocletian**, and became Western emperor in 312 and sole emperor in 324. He was the first Roman emperor to endorse the Christian faith, and he issued the **Edict of Milan**, 313, extending toleration to all faiths; addressed the **Council of Nicaea**, 325, called to resolve some of its crucial theological disputes; founded many churches and was baptized shortly before his death. He built Constantinople as a new Rome on the site of Byzantium, 324, as his permanent capital, and was largely responsible for the evolution of the empire into a Christian state.

CONSTANTINOPLE, COUNCILS OF The first council, an ecumenical gathering of the Christian Church held in AD 381, reaffirmed the teaching of the **Council of Nicaea** and defined the doctrine of the Holy Trinity. The second, in 553, rejected the Nestorian version of Christianity and defined the unity of the person of Christ in his two natures, human and divine. This was reasserted in the third council in 680–1. The fourth, summoned in 869–70, excommunicated Photius, Patriarch of Constantinople (he was reinstated ten years later) and forbade lay interference in the election of bishops.

CONTRAS A counter-revolutionary insurgent force formed by the **Reagan** administration (1981–9) to fight against the **Sandanista** government in Nicaragua (1979–89). They included former supporters of the Somoza regime, members of the National Guard and disaffected opposition leaders. With substantial US military training and aid, they carried out military operations from Honduras, but proved unable to topple the Sandanistas and were demobilized in exchange for free elections in 1989.

COOK, JAMES (1728–79) Explorer of the Pacific Ocean. Appointed 1768 to take members of the British Royal Society to Tahiti and locate *Terra Australis Incognita*, or Unknown Southern Continent, he instead charted the coasts of New Zealand and established its insular character, explored the east coast of Australia, navigated the Great Barrier Reef (1770); on his second voyage of circumnavigation, 1772–5, he finally disposed of the notion of an inhabited southern continent; on the third voyage, 1776–80, he discovered the Sandwich (Hawaiian) Islands and proved that no navigable passage connected the north Pacific and north Atlantic. He was famous for his radical dietary methods, which protected all his men from the previously unavoidable scourge of scurvy. He was killed in Hawaii.

COPT Member of the Coptic Church, an ancient **Monophysite** branch of **Christianity**, founded in Egypt in the 5th century. Persecuted by Byzantines for theological reasons, but relatively secure after the Muslim conquest of Egypt, the Church, with its strong monastic tradition, survived. Its 3 to 4 million followers today still use the Coptic language, derived from ancient Egyptian, for their version of the Greek liturgy.

CORNISH REBELLION English uprising in 1497 against the heavy taxes levied by **Henry VII** to pay for his Scottish wars. The rebels killed a tax collector at Taunton (Somerset) and marched on London, but they were attacked and defeated in their camp at Blackheath by government troops; 2000 rebels died and the leaders were hanged.

CORREGIO, DA Italian family, prominent in the affairs of the Emilian city of Corregio from the 11th century until 1634, and of Parma in the 14th century. Its territories were sold to the house of **Este** in 1634. The dynasty finally died out in 1711.

CORSAIRS Pirates, particularly on the Maghreb ("Barbary") Coast of north Africa.

CORTE-REAL, GASPAR and MIGUEL Portuguese explorer brothers who made a series of voyages in the late 15th and early 16th centuries under royal commission to discover lands in the northwest Atlantic within the Portuguese domain. Gaspar travelled along the coast of southeast Greenland and crossed the Davis Strait to Labrador; Miguel visited Newfoundland and possibly the Gulf of St Lawrence in 1502. Both were lost at sea.

CORTÉS, HERNAN (1485–1547) Conqueror of Mexico. At the age of 19 he settle in Hispaniola and in 1511 sailed with Diego de Velásquez to conquer Cuba; from there, in 1518, he headed an expedition to colonize the Mexican mainland, and achieved a complete and remarkable victory over the Aztec empire. In 1542 he led an arduous and profitless expedition to Honduras. The rest of his life was spent fighting political enemies and intriguers both in New Spain and at home in Spain.

COSA, JUAN DE LA (c. 1460–1510) Spanish geographer and traveller. He owned **Columbus**' flagship, the *Santa Maria*, and served as his pilot. He compiled a celebrated map, dated 1500, showing Columbus' discoveries, **Cabral**'s landfall in Brazil, **Cabot**'s voyage to Canada, and **da Gama**'s journey to India. Sailed with **Bastidas** in 1500; explored Darien, 1504. He died during an expedition to central America and Columbia.

COSSACKS Bands of warlike adventurers recruited mainly from Ukrainian, Polish, Russian and Tatar fugitives and runaway serfs. Renowned for their horsemanship, courage and ruthlessness, they were active on the borders of the Ottoman empire with Poland and Russia from the 15th century. One of their bands in the service of the Stroganov family, under Yermak, conquered the Siberian Khanate for **Ivan IV**. The Cossacks' principal settlement was at Zaporzhye on the Dnieper, and from here they rebelled against Poland in 1648. The settlement was destroyed after the Peace of Kücük Kaynarca in 1774, but other Cossack hosts entered Russian service as cavalry regiments (e.g. Don Cossacks). They survived as semi-autonomous societies into the Soviet period, when they set up short-lived anti-Bolshevik governments.

COUGHLIN, FATHER CHARLES EDWARD (1891–1979) Populist and anti-semitic Catholic priest; born in Canada. From 1930 he broadcast weekly to large audiences in the USA, at first supporting President **F.D. Roosevelt**, but then dropping him in 1936. He edited an increasingly right-wing journal, *Social Justice*, until publication ceased in 1942 after the magazine was banned from the mails for infringing the Espionage Act.

COVENANTERS Those who signed the Scottish National Covenant in 1638, pledging to defend Presbyterianism against all comers. Covenanting armies entered England in 1640, 1644 and 1651; they were defeated by **Cromwell** at Dunbar (1650) and Worcester (1651). The Westminster Confession (1643), drawn up after agreeing the Solemn League and Covenant with the English Parliamentarians, defined the worship, doctrines and organization of the Church of Scotland. The movement faded away after 1690, when the official Scottish religion became Episcopalianism.

COVILHA, PERO DE 15th-century Portuguese explorer sent by the crown in 1487 to see whether the Indian Ocean connected with the Atlantic. His reports from Ethiopia, which he reached after travels in India and Arabia, were important in the Portuguese decision to send the fleet of **Vasco da Gama** to India in 1497–8. Covilha reached the court of the emperor of Ethiopia, whom he thought was a descendant of **Prester John**.

CRASSUS, MARCUS LICINIUS (c. 112–53 BC) Wealthy Roman, third member of the First Triumvirate with **Julius Caesar** and **Pompey**. He sought power and prestige to equal his political colleagues; invaded Mesopotamia. He was ignominiously defeated and killed by Parthian at the battle of Carrhae.

CRIPPS, SIR STAFFORD (1889–1952) British lawyer and politician. He became a member of the Labour Party in 1929, and served in the Cabinet 1930–1. A leading left-wing MP during the 1930s, he was ambassador to Moscow, 1940–2, and headed missions sent to India with plans for self-government in 1942–3 and 1946 (both plans were rejected by the Indian leaders). He held Cabinet office 1942–50, including the post of chancellor of the exchequer, 1947–50.

CROATS East European people who migrated in the 6th century from White Croatia, now in the Ukraine, to the Balkans. Their conversion to Roman Catholicism in the 7th century has continued to divide them from their Orthodox neighbours, the **Serbs**. The first Croatian kingdom, formed in the 10th century, was united by marriage with the crown of Hungary in 1091. In 1918 an independent Croatia was proclaimed, but it immediately entered the union of Slav states known as Yugoslavia; a Fascist-led independent state of Croatia, under Ante Pavelic, lasted from 1941 to 1945 before reunification with Yugoslavia under the Communist partisans. Independent again from 1991.

CROMPTON, SAMUEL (1753–1827) British inventor who pioneered the automatic spinning mule, 1779, so called because it combined the principles of the jenny and the water frame.

CROMWELL, OLIVER (1599–1658) Head of republican Britain. Elected to the English Parliament in 1640; he led the "New Model" army to victory in the Civil War, and supported the execution of **Charles I** in 1649. He crushed uprisings by the **Levellers**, 1649, and by opponents in Ireland and Scotland, 1649–51, unifying the British Isles for the first time in a single state. He was appointed Lord Protector (effectively dictator) by army council in 1653. He declined the offer of the monarchy in 1657.

CROQUANTS Peasants who rose in large-scale and well-organized revolts in the Saintonge, Angoumois and Périgord regions of France in 1593–5, 1636–7 and 1643–5. The colloquial meaning of the name is "clodhopper" or "nonentity".

CRUSADES The First Crusade, a holy war waged from 1096 until 1099 by Christian armies from western Europe against Islam in Palestine and Asia Minor, was inspired by a sermon of Pope **Urban II** in 1095. Its leaders included Robert of Normandy, Godfrey of

Bouillon, Baldwin and Robert II of Flanders. Nicaea and Antioch were successfully besieged, Jerusalem stormed in 1099, and the Christian kingdom of Jerusalem established by Godfrey of Bouillon.

The Second Crusade, 1147–9, was inspired by **St Bernard**. It was led by the emperor, Conrad III, and by **Louis VII** of France, but foundered on quarrels between its leaders and the barons of the kingdom of Jerusalem, who were in alliance with Muslim Damascus, which the newly-arrived crusaders wished to attack. The Crusade petered out fruitlessly, and the Latin kingdom was soon weaker then ever.

The Third Crusade, 1189–92, was led by Emperor **Frederick I Barbarossa** (who died before reaching Palestine), King Richard I of England and King **Philip II Augustus** of France. It aimed to regain Jerusalem, which had been captured by the Muslim leader **Saladin** in 1187. It failed to do so, but the coast between Tyre and Jaffa was ceded to Christians and pilgrimage to Jerusalem was allowed.

The Fourth Crusade (1202–4) was originally intended to attack Egypt, centre of Muslim power in the late 12th century. The crusading armies, heirs to a long hostility towards Byzantium, were diverted by Venice, which provided the transport first to Zara on the Adriatic, and then to Constantinople, which fell on 13 April 1204 and was subjected to three days of massacre and pillage. A horrified Pope **Innocent III**, who had called the crusade, was unable to re-establish control, and his legate absolved the crusaders from the vow to proceed to the Holy Land.

CULTURE SYSTEM A system of land cultivation introduced in the 19th century by the governor-general of the Dutch East Indies, van den Bosch. Under the system each cultivator set aside an agreed portion of his land for the cultivation of certain cash crops – primarily coffee, tea, sugar, indigo and cinnamon – to be delivered at fixed prices to the government in lieu of land rent. It was such a success that all the safeguards against exploitation of labour gradually broke down; Javanese agriculture benefited in various ways, but at the price of oppression and, in places, famine. The system was strongly attacked by the Dutch Liberals, who came to power in 1848, and abolition began in the 1860s. Coffee, the most profitable item in the system, was removed from it only in 1917.

CURZON LINE Ethnically defined frontier between the former USSR and Poland, proposed in 1919 by the British foreign secretary Lord Curzon (1859–1925). At the time it was not accepted by either party; after victory in the Russo-Polish war of 1919–20, Poland, as a result of the **Treaty of Riga**, 1921, retained over 129,500 sq. km (50,000 square miles) each side of the line. The Russo-Polish frontier as settled in 1945 in some respects conforms to the Curzon recommendations.

CUSHITIC Group of languages, related to Egyptian and Berber, spoken originally in the western highlands of Ethiopia; many elements are now partially absorbed into **Amharic**, the official national language. The most widely used Cushitic dialects today include Galla, Somali and the much-divided Sidamo group.

CYNICS Followers of the way of life of Diogenes of Sinope (c. 400–325 BC), nicknamed the Dog (hence Cynic, i.e. doglike), who pursued non-attachment or self-sufficiency by a drastic attack on convention, and by renouncing possessions, nation and social obligations, and choosing self-discipline and a simple life. Cynicism returned to prominence in the early Roman empire.

CYNOSCEPHALAE, BATTLE OF First decisive Roman victory over a major Greek army, fought in Thessaly in 197 BC against **Philip V of Macedon**, who commanded 25,000 troops.

CYPRIAN, ST (c. 200–58) Early Christian theologian. He practised law in Carthage, and was converted to **Christianity** c. 246. Elected Bishop of Carthage, c. 248, in 250 he fled from Roman persecution, but regained his authority on his return the following year. He was exiled in 257 in a new persecution under Emperor **Valerian**. After attempting to return, he was tried and executed.

CYRIL (826–69) and METHODIUS (816–85) Brother saints, known as "the apostles of the Slavs". They worked to convert the **Khazars**, northeast of the Black Sea; sent by Byzantine Emperor Michael III into Greater Moravia, 863. They translated the scriptures into the language later known as Old Church Slavonic, or Old Bulgarian. The "Cyrillic" alphabet, used today in most Slavonic countries, is named after St Cyril.

CYRUS II, THE GREAT (d.529 BC) Known as "the Elder" or "Cyrus the King" in the Old Testament. Founder of the Persian **Achaemenid** empire. Originally a vassal king to the **Medes** in Anshan (Fars province), 559 BC, he rebelled. After capturing the Median capital Ecbatana in 550, he conquered and in most cases liberated Babylonia, Assyria, Lydia, Syria and Palestine. He ordered the rebuilding of the Temple in Jerusalem.

DALHOUSIE, JAMES ANDREW BROUN-RAMSEY, 1st Marquis (1812–60) British colonial administrator. He was appointed the youngest-ever Governor-General of India in 1847; during his nine-year term he annexed vast territories, including the Punjab and Lower Burma, built railways, roads and bridges, installed a telegraph and postal system, opened the Ganges canal, acted against thuggee (murder and robbery), dacoity (armed robbery) and the slave trade, and opened the Indian Civil Service to native Indians.

DANEGELD Tax levied in Anglo-Saxon England by King **Æthelred II** (978–1016) to finance the buying-off of Danish invaders; it was preserved as a revenue-raising device by the Anglo-Norman kings who last made use of it in 1162. The name itself is Norman, replacing the earlier, Old English *gafol* (tribute).

DANELAW Region of eastern England, north and east of a line from the Dee to the Tees rivers, governed in the 9th and 10th centuries under the Danish legal code. Some of its legal and social elements survived the **Norman Conquest**, gradually dying out in the course of the 12th century.

DANTE ALIGHIERI (1265–1321) Italian poet, born in Florence. He was sentenced to death in 1301 on political charges, but escaped; the remainder of his life was spent in exile. His greatest work, the *Commedia* (written c. 1308–20, known since the 16th century as the *Divina Commedia*), is the earliest masterpiece written in Italian. It traces an imaginary journey through Hell, Purgatory and Heaven, and symbolically describes the progress of the soul from sin to purification.

DANTON, GEORGE-JACQUES (1759–94) French revolutionary who helped to found the Cordeliers Club, 1790; as Minister of Justice, 1792, he organized the defence of France against the Prussians. He was a member of the Committee of Public Safety 1793, but was overthrown by his rival, **Robespierre**, and guillotined.

DAOISM Ancient cult of China, tracing back philosophically to the legendary **Lao-tzu**, who held that there is a Way (*dao*), a sort of natural order of the universe, and that it is the duty of individuals to ensure that their life conforms to it. It developed as a mass religious movement in the 2nd century AD, with its own church and hierarchy; it emphasizes salvation, aided by magical practices based on the interaction of *yin* and *yang*, the powers of darkness (female) and light (male).

DAR AL-ISLAM House of Islam, the Muslim lands.

DARBY Family of English iron-masters whose enterprise helped to create the industrial revolution. Abraham Darby (c.1678–1717) was the first man to smelt iron ore successfully with coke instead of charcoal. His son, Abraham II, built over 100 cylinders for the **Newcomen** steam engine. His grandson Abraham III built the world's first iron bridge, over the Severn at Coalbrookedale, 1779, and the first railway locomotive with a high-pressure boiler (for Richard Trevithick, 1802). The new smelting process had a slow start, but in the second half of the 18th century developed rapidly, leading to a great increase in the output of pig-iron and of cast-iron goods.

DARIUS I (c. 550–486 BC) King of ancient Persia (reigned 522–486 BC). Son of Hystaspes, satrap of Parthia and Hyrcania; he extended Persian control in Egypt and western India; invaded Scythia across the Bosporus, 513. His attack on Greece was defeated at **Marathon**, 490; he died while preparing a second Greek expedition.

DAVID (d. c. 972 BC) King of the Israelites, son of Jesse. Reared as a shepherd boy, he slew the giant Goliath, champion of the Philistines. He was disaffected from Saul, king of Israel, but was accepted as king after Saul's death; he established his capital at Jerusalem. Traditionally believed to have composed many of the Biblical Psalms. Christian tradition claims that **Jesus** was among his descendants, as a member of the House of David, from which, according to Jewish belief, the Messiah must spring.

DAVIS, JOHN (c. 1550–1605) English explorer, who in 1585 made the first of three unsuccessful attempts to find a Northwest Passage through the Canadian Arctic; detailed in his later treatise, *The World's Hydrographical Description*, 1595. He fought against Spanish Armada, 1588; discovered the Falkland Islands, 1592; sailed with Walter Raleigh to Cádiz and the Azores, 1596–7. He was killed by Japanese pirates on the last of three voyages to the East Indies.

DELIAN LEAGUE Confederation of ancient Greek states, with its headquarters on the sacred island of Delos, originally created under the leadership of Athens in 478 BC to oppose **Achaemenid** Persia. Initially successful; however, freedom to secede was not permitted. In 454 BC the treasury was transferred to Athens, and the League became effectively an Athenian empire.

DEMOCRACY From the Greek *demos*, the community, and *kratos*, sovereign power. Government by

the people, usually through elected representatives. In the modern world, democracy has developed from the American and French revolutions.

DEMOSTHENES (384–322 BC) Ancient Greek statesman and orator. He led the democratic faction in Athens; engaged in bitter political rivalry with his fellow-orator Aeschines; roused the Athenians to oppose both **Philip of Macedon** and **Alexander the Great**. He died by self-administered poison.

DENG XIAOPING (1904–97) Chinese statesman. In 1924 he joined the Chinese Communist Party. Following the split between nationalists and communists (1927) he worked for the central committee in Shanghai. He participated in the "long march" led by **Mao Zedong** (1934–5), served in the Red Army against the Japanese and nationalists and was elected to the central committee after the establishment of the People's Republic of China (1949). Falling from power during the Cultural Revolution (1966–9), he was reinstated as vice-premier (1973), only to be removed again in 1976. In 1977 he returned as the dominant political figure, introducing free market policies in agricultural and industrial sectors and promoting cultural and scientific exchanges with Western powers.

DENIKIN, ANTON IVANOVICH (1872–1947) Russian general. After the revolution in 1917 he joined the anti-Bolshevik armies in south Russia. Promoted to commander in 1918, he led an unsuccessful advance on Moscow in 1919 and in 1920 resigned and went into exile.

DE THAM (c. 1860–1913) Vietnamese freedom fighter. He joined a local pirate band and started organizing formidable attacks on the French colonists. As "the tiger of Yen Tri" he built up a large guerrilla army; the great-uncle of Ho Chi Minh was a member. He attacked the French railway, 1894, and temporarily ran Yen Tri district as an autonomous empire. In 1906–7 he linked with the other main anti-French group under **Phan Boi Chau**. Implicated in the abortive "Hanoi Poison Plot" in 1908, he was later assassinated.

DIARMAT, MAC MAEL (1010–71) King of Leinster, Ireland, between 1040 and 1071. He extended his authority over much of the Scandinavian kingdom of Dublin (1071) and planned to make himself High King, but death intervened and Ireland disintegrated into warring sub-kingdoms until the Norman invasion of 1170.

DIAZ, PORFIRO (1830–1915) Dictatorial President of Mexico. He joined the army fighting against the USA (1846–8), in the War of the Reform (1857–60), and in opposition to the French (1862–7). Involved in unsuccessful revolts in 1871 and 1876, he returned later in 1876 from the USA and defeated the government at the battle of Tecoac. Elected president in 1877, he gradually consolidated power; he was re-elected in 1884 and effectively ruled the country until 1910, modernizing its economy at great social cost. The military supporters of **Madero** forced him to resign in 1911. He died in exile in Paris.

DIESEL, RUDOLF (1858–1913) Inventor of the heavy oil internal combustion engine bearing his name. Trained at Technische Hochschule, Munich; worked two years at the Swiss Sulzer Machine Works, and then in Paris at Linde Refrigeration Enterprises. He started work on his engine in 1885, making his first working model in 1893.

DENSHAWAI INCIDENT Anti-British incident in Egypt in 1906. British officers shooting pigeons near a village in the Delta became involved in a fight with peasants who owned the pigeons; one officer died of sunstroke. Savage punishment of villagers provoked strong demonstrations against the British.

DIOCLETIAN (245–316) Roman emperor, born Aurelius Valerius Diocletianus, in Dalmatia. Acclaimed by his soldiers as emperor in 284, at a time of deep economic, political and military trouble, he took sole control of affairs in 285 and forced through an immense programme of legal, fiscal and administrative reform, restoring much of Rome's former strength. He abdicated in 305.

DIODOTUS I Founder of the ancient Greek kingdom of Bactria, originally subject to the **Seleucid** kings, Antiochus I and II. He rebelled and made himself king (250–230 BC); he was succeeded by his son, Diodutus II Soter.

DISRAELI, BENJAMIN (1804–81) 1st Earl of Beaconsfield, statesman, novelist and twice British prime minister; born of a Jewish family but baptized as a Christian. He first stood for Parliament as a radical, but was elected as Conservative MP in 1837. Quarrelled with Sir Robert **Peel** over the repeal of the Corn Laws, 1846, and emerged as a leader of the rump of the Conservative Party. He succeeded Lord Derby as prime minister for a few months in 1868 and became prime minister again, 1874–80. He incorporated concern for the empire into the Conservative programme in his Crystal Palace speech of 1872 and saw a link between imperialism and social reform at home; his real concern was for

India and the route to India. Represented Britain at the **Congress of Berlin** in 1878; his ministry was associated with a forward policy in Afghanistan and South Africa.

DOENITZ, KARL (1891–1981) German naval commander and briefly head of state. In the First World War he served as a submarine officer. After the succession of **Hitler** he supervized the clandestine construction of a new U-boat fleet; he was appointed commander of submarine forces in 1936, head of the Germany navy in 1943 and head of the northern military and civil command in 1945. Named in Hitler's political testament as the next president of the Reich, he assumed control of the government for a few days after Hitler's suicide on 2 May 1945. Sentenced to ten years' imprisonment as a Nazi war criminal in 1946, he was released in 1956.

DOLLFUSS, ENGELBERT (1892–1934) Chancellor of Austria, 1932–4, who effectively made himself dictator until he was assassinated by Austrian Nazis.

DOMINICANS see **Friars**

DOMITIAN (AD 51–96) Roman emperor, born Titus Flavius Domitianus, son of Emperor **Vespasian**; succeeded his brother **Titus**, in AD 81. He is remembered for his financial rapacity and the reign of terror (particularly 93–6) waged against his critics in the Senate; he was murdered by conspirators, including his wife, Domitia Longina.

DONATUS (d. c. 355) Leader of the Donatists, a north African Christian group named after him, which broke with the Catholic Church in 312 after a controversy over the election of Caecilian as Bishop of Carthage; Donatus, appealing against the appointment, was over-ruled by a council of bishops, 313, by another at Arles, 314, and finally by Emperor **Constantine**, 316. The dissidents were persecuted, 317–21, then reluctantly tolerated; they continued to gain strength (perhaps through African nationalist feeling). In 347 Donatus was exiled to Gaul, where he died. The movement continued but, thanks to the teaching of St Augustine, and to state persecution, it had disappeared by c. 700.

DORIANS Last of the Hellenic invaders to press into Greece from the north, c. 1100 BC, perhaps from Epirus and southwest Macedonia, traditionally via Doria in central Greece. They recognized three "tribes", the Hylleis, perhaps coming down the east, the Dymanes down the west, and the Pamphyloi covering minor groupings. They spread through the Peloponnese and to the islands of Cythera, Melos, Thera, Crete, Rhodes, Cos and into southern Anatolia. Many unresolved questions about them continue to challenge archaeologists.

DOUGLAS, STEPHEN ARNOLD (1813–61) US Senator. He was elected to Congress in 1843 and to the Senate in 1846. He strongly supported "popular sovereignty" (local option) on the question of slavery. In 1858 he engaged in a series of highly publicized debates with **Abraham Lincoln**, to whom he lost in the presidential election. He condemned secession on the outbreak of the Civil War.

DRAKE, SIR FRANCIS (c. 1540–96) English seaman who led buccaneering expeditions to west Africa and the Spanish West Indies, 1566–75, 1585–6 and 1595–6. He circumnavigated the globe in his ship the *Golden Hind*, 1577–80; raided the Spanish fleet in Cádiz, 1587, and fought against the Spanish Armada, 1588.

DRAVIDIAN Group of seven major and many minor languages, including Tamil, Telugu, Kanarese, Malayalam, Gondi and Tulu, spoken mainly by some 110 million people in southern India (also known collectively as Dravidians); characteristically these are darker, stockier, longer-headed and flatter-faced than the Indic or Aryan races of northern India.

DRUID Member of a pre-Christian religious order in Celtic areas of Britain, Ireland and Gaul. It has been retained as a name for officers in the modern Welsh Gorsedd.

DUAL MONARCHY OF AUSTRIA-HUNGARY Political system, 1867–1918, established by the Compromise of 1867 which granted a large measure of autonomy to the Hungarian lands of the former Austrian empire.

DULLES, JOHN FOSTER (1888–1959) US lawyer and statesman. He began legal practice in 1911; became counsel to the US commission to negotiate peace after the First World War, 1918–19, and to other government bodies. He was special adviser to the secretary of state, 1945–51, and filled that post himself, 1953–9. He was associated with a vigorously anti-communist US foreign policy.

DUMA Lower house of the Russian parliament, established by Tsar **Nicholas II** in 1905; on the collapse of tsarism in February 1917 leading Duma politicians formed the Provisional Government.

DUPLEIX, JOSEPH FRANÇOIS (1697–1763) French administrator, Governor-general of Chandernagore 1731–41, and of Pondichery 1741–54. His expansionist ambitions in southern India were checked by **Robert Clive**, 1751–2; he was recalled in 1754.

DUTCH EAST INDIA COMPANY (Vereenigde Oostindische Compagnie, VOC). Powerful trading concern set up in 1602 to protect Dutch merchants in the Indian Ocean and to help finance the war of independence with Spain. Under able governors-general, such as Jan Pieterszoon Coen, 1618–23, and Anthony van Diemen, 1636–45, the company effectively drove both British and Portuguese out of the East Indies, and established Batavia (now Jakarta) as its base for conquering the islands. Growing corruption and debt led to the company's dissolution in 1799.

DUY TAN (1888–1945) Emperor of Annam, the son of Emperor Thanh Thai, whom he succeeded in 1907. His reign was a period of revolt against the French colonial power; after one revolt, which sought to make him a real emperor, he was deposed and exiled to Réunion in 1916. Later he served with the Free French forces in the Second World War; he died in an air crash.

DYILO, THOMAS LUBANGA (1960–) Congolese warlord who in 2012 became the first person convicted by the International Criminal Court, for the war crime of recruiting child soldiers. Founder of the Union of Congolese Patriots and a key player in the Ituri conflict (1999–2007).

EADGAR (c. 943–75) English king; younger son of Edmund I. He became king of Mercia and **Danelaw**, 957, on the deposition of his brother Eadwig, and in 959 succeeded to the throne of West Saxons and effectively all England. He reformed the Church in England.

EAM (Initials in Greek for National Liberation Front). One of the Greek resistance movements, formed in 1941 to fight the German and Italian armies of occupation. By 1944, when the Germans evacuated, it controlled two-thirds of the country. It rejected Allied orders to disarm in December 1944, but accepted the Varkiza Peace Agreement, 1945; it participated in large-scale civil war, 1946–9.

EAST INDIA COMPANY see **English East India Company** and **Dutch East India Company**

EC Founded in 1957 with the Treaty of Rome, which was signed by six nations and called originally the European Economic Community, the European Community was formed to promote economic and political cooperation as part of the process of post-war reconstruction. From 1986 it had 12 member nations. Despite undoubted benefits (between 1958 and 1962 trade between member states increased by 130 per cent) economic cooperation brought many problems – for example, the Common Agricultural Policy, developed to ensure a fair standard for farmers, led to massive over-production and higher prices. In 1992 Europe became in theory a single market, and the removal of physical, technical and financial barriers began. The **Maastricht Treaty** (1991) called for closer political union among EC member states and committed the EC to introduce a single currency, the Euro, by 1999. Though Britain and Denmark refused to join, the remaining states of the EC introduced the Euro in January 1999. In 1995 the EC became the EU, or European Union.

EDEN, ANTHONY, 1ST EARL OF AVON (1897–1977) British statesman and foreign secretary, 1935–8, 1940–5 and 1951–5. He supported the **League of Nations** in the 1930s and was **Churchill**'s deputy for a decade before succeeding him as prime minister (1955–7). Eden's determination to confront President **Nasser** of Egypt resulted in the **Suez** Crisis of 1956 which, added to poor health, led to his resignation.

EDEN TREATY Trade agreement between Britain and France, negotiated in 1786–7 by William Eden, 1st Baron Auckland (1744–1814), which gave the British free access to French markets. By encouraging the export of French corn to Britain, the treaty contributed to popular tension during the food crisis preceding the French revolution.

EDWARD THE CONFESSOR (c. 1003–65) King of England, son of **Æthelred II** the Unready. Exiled after Æthelred's death (1016) when the Danes again seized power in England, he returned from Normandy, 1041, and succeeded to the throne of his half-brother, Harthacnut, 1042; however, the main power in the kingdom remained first with Godwin, Earl of the West Saxons, then with his son, Harold, named as king on Edward's death. Claims that Edward had previously promised the throne to Duke William of Normandy led to the **Norman Conquest** (1066).

EDWARD I (1239–1307) King of England; the son of Henry III. He led the royal troops to victory in the Barons' War (1264–6); succeeded to the throne, 1272; conquered Wales (1277–83); established suzerainty over Scotland and defeated the Scottish revolt under **William Wallace**, 1298. His consistent utilization of Parliament in wide-ranging legislation consolidated its institutional position. He died on an expedition to suppress the revolt of **Robert Bruce** of Scotland.

EDWARD II (1284–1327) King of England, son of **Edward I**, whom he succeeded in 1307. He ruled, weakly and incompetently, through favourites such as Piers Gaveston (murdered 1312) and the Despensers (executed 1326). He was heavily defeated by the Scots at Bannockburn, 1314, and strongly opposed by the English barons, who in 1311 tried to subject him to control by a committee of "lords ordainers". He was deposed and put to death when his queen, Isabella, invaded from France with her ally, Roger Mortimer.

EDWARD III (1312–77) King of England, son of **Edward II**, succeeding in 1327. By 1330 he had freed himself from subjection to his mother, Isabella, and her ally, Roger Mortimer. Defeated the Scots, 1333 and 1346; at the start of the **Hundred Years' War** he defeated the French fleet at Sluys, 1340, and invaded France. His notable victories at Crécy, 1346, and Calais, 1347, with that of his son at Poitiers, 1356, were consolidated by the Peace of Brétigny in 1360. He resumed war in 1369, and by 1375 had lost all his previous gains except Calais, Bordeaux, Bayonne and Brest.

EIGHT TRIGRAMS Secret north Chinese sect, part-religious, part-political. It flourished, particularly in Chihli, Shantung and Honan, in the 19th century, and was involved in the palace revolution in Peking in 1814.

EISENHOWER, DWIGHT DAVID (1890–1969) 34th president of the USA, 1953–61. He was commander of the American forces in Europe, and of the Allies in north Africa, 1942; directed the invasions of Sicily and Italy, 1943; became Supreme Allied Commander, 1943–5, and Commander, NATO land forces, 1950–2. Under his presidency, the Korean War was ended (1953), **SEATO** formed, and federal troops were ordered (1957) to enforce racial desegregation of US schools at Little Rock, Arkansas.

EISNER, KURT (1867–1919) German socialist leader. In 1914 he opposed German aid to Austria-Hungary, and became leader of the pacifist Independent Social Democratic Party in 1917; he was arrested as a strike-leader the following year. After his release he organized the overthrow of the Bavarian monarchy and proclaimed an independent Bavarian republic. He was assassinated by a right-wing student.

ELCANO, JUAN SEBASTIAN DE (d.1526) First captain to make a complete circumnavigation of the earth. A Basque navigator, he sailed in 1519 as master of the *Concepción* under **Magellan**; after Magellan's death he took command of the three remaining ships and returned to Spain, 1522, with one ship, the *Victoria*, henceforth his family coat-of-arms carried a globe and the motto *Primus circumdedisti me* ("You were the first to circle me").

ELECTOR Historically, one of the small group of princes who, by right of heredity or office, were qualified to elect the Holy Roman Emperor. Originally, in the 13th century, there were six; from 1356 to 1623 there were seven – the archbishops of Mainz, Trier and Cologne, the king of Bohemia, the count palatine of the Rhine, the dukes of Saxony and the Margrave of Brandenburg. By 1806, when the Empire ended, there were ten.

ELIZABETH I (1533–1603) Queen of England. The daughter of **Henry VIII** and Anne Boleyn, she succeeded to the throne in 1558. Her re-establishment of a Church of England independent of Rome, 1559, led to her excommunication by Pope Pius V in 1571. She survived a Spanish attempt to put the sentence into effect (Spanish Armada, 1588). She made English authority effective in Ireland (1601).

ELLMAN, JOHN English 18th-century sheep-breeder, farming at Glynde, Surrey, who in about 1780 began developing short wool varieties, a process which eventually transformed the Southdown sheep from a light, long-legged animal into one solid, compact and equally good for mutton and for wool.

ENCYCLOPEDISTS Group of French writers, scientists and philosophers connected with the influential *Encyclopédie ou dictionnaire raisonné des sciences, des arts et des métiers*, edited 1751–72 by Denis Diderot (1713–84) assisted by d'Alembert (1717–83); the work and its contributors powerfully expressed the new spirit of 18th-century rationalism.

ENGLISH EAST INDIA COMPANY Founded in 1600 to trade with the East Indies, but excluded by the Dutch after the Amboina Massacre in 1623. The company negotiated concessions in Mughal India and won control of Bengal in 1757, but its political activities were curtailed by the Regulating Act of 1773 and the India Act of 1784. Its commercial monopoly with India was broken in 1813, and that with China in 1833. It ceased to be the British government's Indian agency after the Rebellion in 1857; its legal existence ended in 1873.

ENTREPOT Commercial centre, specializing in the handling, storage, transfer and dispatch of goods.

EON OF STEILA (d.1148) Christian heretic. He preached opposition to the wealth and organization of the Roman Catholic Church, gaining followers in Brittany and Gascony before being imprisoned by Pope **Eugenius III** at the Synod of Rheims. He died in prison; his followers, such as the **Henricians** and **Petrobrusians**, faded away.

EPICUREANS Followers of the Greek philosopher Epicurus (341–271 BC). To Epicurus happiness ("pleasure") was all; it consisted in freedom from disturbance. So the wise men free themselves from fear, through scientific understanding, and from desire by "doing without". The structure of the universe is atomic; death is annihilation; gods exist but do not intervene in human affairs. The Epicureans fostered friendship and discouraged ambition. The system was expounded by the Roman poet Lucretius (*c.* 94–55 BC).

EPIRUS, DESPOTATE OF Byzantine principality in southern Albania and northwest Greece, organized as a rival principality during the Western occupation of Constantinople after the Fourth Crusade. Founded in 1204 by Michael Angelus Ducas, it was continually attacked by Nicaea, Bulgaria and later, after the restoration of Michael VIII Palaeologus, by Byzantium itself. In the 13th century it was a pre-Renaissance centre for classical studies; it was re-annexed to Byzantium in 1337.

EPISCOPALIAN Member of the Protestant Episcopal Church of Scotland and the USA, a believer in the principle that supreme authority in the Church lies with the bishops assembled in council, rather than with a single head.

ERATOSTHENES (c. 276–c. 194 BC) The first systematic geographer. He directed the library at Alexandra, *c.*255 BC; wrote on astronomy, ethics and the theatre; compiled a calendar, showing leap years, and a chronology of events since the siege of Troy; calculated the earth's circumference with remarkable accuracy. He was known as Beta, because he was good without being supreme in so many fields. He is said to have starved himself to death after going blind.

ERIC XIV (1533–77) King of Sweden, 1560–8, the son of **Gustavus I Vasa**. He seized strategic territory in Estonia, prompting Denmark and Norway to initiate the Nordic Seven Years' War. He was accused of insanity and deposed by his half-brothers, 1568, after failing to win the war and after defying the Swedish nobility in order to make his commoner mistress, Karin Mansdotter, queen. He died in prison.

ERIK BLOODAXE (d. 954) King of Norway and of York in the 10th century, named to commemorate his murder of seven of his eight brothers. The son of **Harald Finehair**, he was expelled from Norway, 934; by 948 he was king of York and ruled there until expelled in 954. He was killed at Stainmore.

ESSENE Member of an ancient Jewish sect founded between the 2nd century BC and 2nd century AD. It was characterized by stern asceticism, withdrawal, communistic life, ceremonial purity, a rigorous novitiate lasting three years, identification of Yahweh with the Sun, and a mystic belief in immortality. The Dead Sea Scrolls, found in the Qumran (1947–1956), probably belonged to an Essene community; attempts to link **Jesus** to them are implausible.

ESTE Italian family which presided over an unusually brilliant court, ruling as princes in Ferrara from the 13th century until 1598, and as dukes in Reggio and Modena from 1288 until the mid-19th century. The dynasty was founded by the margrave Albert Azzo II (*c.* 1097); their connection with Ferrara ended when Clement VIII imposed direct papal rule.

ETRUSCANS A people in Italy inhabiting Etruria, the land between the rivers Tiber and Arno, west and south of the Apennine hills. Their origins are unknown, but they possibly came from Asia Minor. From 800 BC to their decline in the 5th century BC, they developed an elaborate urban civilization, particularly notable for its tombs; they were ultimately absorbed by Rome. The Etruscan language is still largely undeciphered.

EUGENIUS III (d.1153) The first Cistercian Pope (1145–53), a pupil of **St Bernard**, whose *De Consideratione* presented his views on how the pope should lead the Church. Forced to leave Rome because of conflict with the city and with **Arnold of Brescia**, he was finally re-established by the Treaty of Constance (1153) with **Frederick Barbarossa**.

EURIPIDES (480–406 BC) Last of the three great Athenian tragic dramatists; 19 of his 92 plays survive, distinguished by their concentration on real human problems expressed in contemporary language. He left Athens in 408, moved to Thessaly and then Macedon, where he wrote *The Bacchae*; he died at the court of King Archelaus.

EUROPEAN COMMUNITY see **EC**

EUSEBIUS (c. 265–340) Bishop of Caesarea. His *History of the Church* is the first scholarly work on the early institutions of Christianity.

EXARCHATE Under the Byzantine and the Holy Roman Empires, it referred to the governorship of a distant province; in the eastern Catholic Church, to the area of responsibility of certain high-ranking ecclesiastics known as exarchs (approximate equivalents of patriarchs or archbishops).

FAIRBAIRN, SIR WILLIAM (1789–1874) Victorian authority on factory design who wrote the classic treatise, *Mills and Millwork*. A builder of ships and bridges, he constructed many iron ships at Millwall, London, between 1835 and 1849, and also invented the rectangular tube used on **Robert Stephenson**'s Menai Bridge.

FANG CHIH-MIN (1900–35) Early leader of the Chinese Communist Party. He became prominent in Communist and **Kuomintang** affairs in Kiangsi during the 1920s; helped to found the Communist base in northeast Kiangsi, which developed into the Fukien-Chekiang-Kiangsi Soviet in the early 1930s. He led the 10th Army Corps when encircled by the Nationalist Army in mid-1934, and the following year was captured and executed by the Nationalists.

FAROUK I (1920–65) King of Egypt. The son of Fuad I, he succeeded to the throne in 1936. He was involved in the long struggle for power with the nationalist party, the **Wafd**; during the Second World War Britain, then in occupation of Egypt, forced him to appoint a Wafdist government. He was deposed and exiled after the military *coup d'état* organized by **Neguib** and **Nasser**.

FARROUPILHA REVOLUTION Provincial uprising in Rio Grande do Sul, southern Brazil; it flared intermittently, 1834–45, until finally suppressed by the armies of Pedro II under the Duque de Caxias. The name means "rags", alluding to the rebels' lack of uniforms.

FASCISM Originally the anti-democratic and anti-parliamentarian ideology adopted by the Italian counter-revolutionary movement led by **Mussolini**; characterized by advocacy of the corporate, one-party state, to which all aspects of life are subordinated. It was later extended to describe any extreme right-wing political creed that combines absolute obedience to the leader with a willingness to use force to gain power and suppress opposition.

FATIMA (c. 616–33) Mohammed's daughter, and first wife of **Ali**. The imams recognized by the **Shi'as** are her descendants, and Shi'as have a special reverence for her; her descendants led a moderate wing of the Shi'as, the second major division of Islam, and some of those claiming descent from her founded the **Fatimid** dynasty.

FATIMIDS North African dynasty claiming descent from **Fatima**, **Mohammed**'s daughter, founded in 908 in Tunisia by the imam, Ubaidallah. Muizz, the fourth Fatimid caliph, conquered Egypt and founded Cairo, 969. In the 11th century, they supplanted the **Abbasids** as the most powerful rulers in Islam, but were finally abolished by **Saladin** (1171).

FEDERALISTS Name, first used in 1787, to denote the supporters of the newly written US Constitution; and later for a conservative party which was hostile to the revolution in France, favourable to an alliance with Great Britain and generally supportive of central authority in America. From 1791 to 1801 Federalists controlled the national government, organized the new nation's administrative and tax machinery, and formulated a policy of neutrality in foreign affairs. In 1801 they were displaced by an opposition group led by **Thomas Jefferson**, and never again held national office.

FEITORIA Fortified factory or trading post, established by the Portuguese during their period of maritime dominance.

FENG YÜ-HSIANG (1882–1948) Chinese warlord, nicknamed "the Christian general". At first an officer in the Hwai army under **Yüan Shih-k'ai**, he served in the Peiyang army after the 1911 revolution. From 1918 he created a private army, controlling a large part of northwest China, 1912–20; he was involved in a series of *coups d'état* and civil wars, 1920–8, but never acquired a permanent territorial base. To relieve chronic financial pressures he sought the help of Russia, but in 1929 was forced to relinquish control of his troops to **Chiang Kai-shek**. His army, joined by **Yen Hsi-shan**, attempted to form a northern coalition against Chiang, and in 1929–30 they fought a bitter war. When it ended he joined the Nationalist government, but never again had any real power.

FENLAND REVOLT Prolonged local opposition, 1632–8, to government-sponsored measures to drain and enrich the fens of eastern England, thus depriving the local population of common rights. **Oliver Cromwell** was one of the leaders of the revolt.

FERDINAND III (c. 1199–1252) Saint and king of Castile (1217–52) and León (1230–52). He united the crowns of Castile and León, and completed the conquest of all Moorish dominions in Spain except **Granada**.

FERDINAND OF ARAGON (1452–1516) The son of John II of Aragon. His marriage in 1469 to Isabella of Castile united the two principal kingdoms in the Iberian peninsula. The kingdom of Granada was annexed by Castile in 1492, while in 1504 Ferdinand conquered Naples which remained under Spanish control until 1713. In 1512 he acquired Navarre. It was during the joint rule of Ferdinand and Isabella that the **Inquisition** was established in Castile in 1478, **Columbus**'s first voyage to the new world was supported, and the **Jews** were expelled from Castile in 1492.

FEUDALISM Political system of medieval Europe, based on the mutual obligations of vassal and superiors, linked by the granting of land (the feud, or fee) in return for certain services. The feudal lord normally had rights of jurisdiction over his tenants, and held a feudal court. Similar systems (sometimes also termed "feudal" by analogy) are found in other parts of the world (e.g. early China and Japan) at a similar stage of development.

FIANNA FÁIL Irish political party; founded in 1926 by **de Valera** to espouse republican nationalism and erase all English influence from Irish public life.

FIELDEN, JOSHUA (d.1811) Cotton industry pioneer. In 1780 he was still a peasant farmer, operating two or three weaving looms; by 1800 he owned a five-storey cotton mill in Todmorden, Yorkshire. After his death his sons developed the business – Fielden Brothers, Waterside Mills – into one of the largest cotton mills in Britain.

FIGUERES FERRIER, JOSÉ (1906–90) Costa Rican political leader. He worked as a coffee planter and rope-maker; exiled to Mexico 1942–4, he became Junta president of the Republic, 1948, but resigned in 1949; he was president of Costa Rica 1953–8 and 1970–4.

FISSIRAGA Prominent family of medieval Lodi, Italy. Supporters of the **Guelph** (anti-imperial) party, they rose to prominence in the 1280s; in 1311 their leader, Antonio Fissiraga, was captured by the **Visconti** of Milan and died in prison (1327).

FIUME INCIDENT Unsuccessful attempt to seize the Adriatic sea port in September 1919, by a private Italian army, led by the poet Gabriele d'Annunzio, to forestall its award to Yugoslavia at the Paris Peace Conference.

FIXED EXCHANGE RATES Regime under which the value of one currency bears a constant relationship to that of another: e.g. the pound sterling in the period 1949–67, when it was always worth US$ 2.80. Such relations linked most major currencies in the period 1947–71, under the so-called Bretton Woods System, but that then gave place to a period of mainly "floating" rates.

FLAMININUS (c. 227–174 BC) Principal Roman general and statesman during the period when Greece became a Roman protectorate. He defeated **Philip V of Macedon** at **Cynoscephalae** in 197 BC; declared that all Greeks should be free and governed by their own laws in 196; and supported Greek autonomy in Asia Minor during Rome's wars with the **Seleucids**.

FLAVIANS Dynasty ruling the Roman empire from AD 69 to 96. It was founded by **Vespasian** (69–79) and continued by his sons, **Titus** (79–81) and **Domitian** (81–96).

FLINDERS, MATTHEW (1774–1814) Mari-time explorer of Australia, born in Lincolnshire, England. He entered the Royal Navy in 1789, from 1795 to 1799 he charted much of Australia's east coast between Fraser Island and Bass Strait, and circumnavigated Tasmania; in 1801–2, as commander of the *Investigator*, he surveyed the whole southern coast, and in 1802–3 circled the entire continent. He was interned by the French in Mauritius, 1802–10; his *Voyage to Terra Australis* was finally published about the time of his death.

FOCH, FERDINAND (1851–1929) French soldier, marshal of France, a teacher of military history and author of many standard works. Appointed a general in 1907, he won distinction during the First World War in the first battle of the Marne, 1914, the first battle of Ypres, 1915, and the battle of the Somme, 1916. He was appointed as commander-in-chief of the French armies in 1917, and after the onset of the German offensive in spring 1918 was appointed to command all French, British and American forces.

FORREST, JOHN (1847–1918) 1st Baron Forrest, Australian explorer and statesman. He led several expeditions across Western Australia from 1869; became surveyor-general of Western Australia, 1883–90 and its first premier, 1890–1901. He held cabinet office in several ministries in the federal government of the new Commonwealth of Australia between 1901 and 1918.

FOURTEEN POINTS Programme put forward by US President **Woodrow Wilson** in 1918 for a peace settlement following the First World War. Several of the Points related to the right of self-determination of peoples; although statesmen at the Peace Conference were thinking of the rights of the successor states of the Austro-Hungarian and Ottoman empires, the principle was noted by colonial peoples in Asia and Africa. The final proposal for a "general association" to guarantee integrity of "great and small states alike" led to the setting up of the **League of Nations**.

FRANCIS I (1494–1547) King of France; he succeeded his cousin, **Louis XII**, in 1515. In 1520 he attempted unsuccessfully to win the support of the English king, **Henry VIII**, for his struggles with the **Habsburgs**; he pursued his rivalry alone in a series of Italian wars (1521–5, 1527–9, 1536–7, 1542–4), but finally abandoned Italian claims in 1544. He was a noted patron of Renaissance art.

FRANCIS II (1768–1835) The last Holy Roman Emperor. The son of Leopold II, he succeeded to the imperial title in 1792 and held it until dissolution of the empire by **Napoleon** in 1806. He continued to reign as the first emperor of Austria, under the title Francis I; through his chancellor, **Metternich**, he confirmed Austria's position as a leading European power.

FRANCISCANS *see* **Friars**

FRANCO, FRANCISCO (1892–1975) Spanish dictator. A general in the Spanish army, he organized the revolt in Morocco in 1936 which precipitated the Spanish Civil War of 1936–9, from which he emerged as head of state ("El Caudillo"). He was named regent for life in 1947. In 1969 he proposed that Prince Juan Carlos of Bourbon should ultimately take the throne, as indeed he did at Franco's death.

FRANCO-PRUSSIAN WAR Struggle provoked by rivalry between France and the growing power of Prussia, reaching a head over the candidacy of Leopold of Hohenzollern for the throne of Spain. Prussian armies under von Moltke invaded France and quickly won victories at Wörth, Gravelotte, Strasbourg, Sedan and Metz between August and October 1870. **Napoleon III** abdicated, and the Third French Republic was declared on 4 September 1870; Paris, under siege for four months, surrendered on 28 January 1871. Under the Treaty of Frankfurt (May 1871) France ceded Alsace and East Lorraine to the newly established German empire, and agreed to pay an indemnity of 5 billion francs.

FRANKS Germanic peoples who dominated the area of present-day France and western Germany after the collapse of the West Roman empire. Under **Clovis** (481–511) and his **Merovingian** and **Carolingian** successors they established the most powerful Christian kingdom in western Europe. Since the disintegration of their empire in the 9th century the name has survived in France and Franconia. In the Middle East, the crusaders were generally referred to as Franks, and the word came into several oriental languages to mean "European".

FRANZ FERDINAND (1863–1914) Archduke of Austria, nephew of, and from 1896 heir to, the Emperor Franz Joseph I (1830–1916). He was assassinated on 28 June 1914 at Sarajevo, an incident which provoked the Austrian ultimatum to Serbia that led directly to the outbreak of the First World War.

FREDERICK THE GREAT (1712–86) King of Prussia, son of **Frederick William I**, whom he succeeded in 1740. He entered the War of the Austrian Succession, won the battle of Mollwitz, 1741, and acquired the economically valuable province of Silesia, which he retained through the **Seven Years' War** (1756–63). He annexed West Prussia in the First Partition of Poland, 1772; formed the Fürstenbund (League of German Princes), 1785. He patronized writers and artists, including Voltaire; wrote *L'Antimachiavel*, 1740, and *History of the House of Brandenburg*, 1751.

FREDERICK I BARBAROSSA (c. 1123–90) King of Germany, 1152, emperor 1155; second of the **Hohenstaufen** dynasty. In 1154 he launched a campaign to restore royal rights in Italy; captured Milan, 1162, and Rome, 1166; supported the anti-pope against the powerful Pope **Alexander III**, but was defeated by the **Lombard League** (Legnano 1176); reached a *modus vivendi* with the papacy and Italian cities at the Peace of Venice (1177) and Peace of Constance (1183). He was drowned in Syria while leading the Third **Crusade**.

FREDERICK II (1194–1250) Last great **Hohenstaufen** ruler. He was elected German king in 1212, after civil war and disorder in Germany, Italy and Sicily following the early death of his father, **Henry VI**, in 1197. He left Germany for Italy in 1220 to concentrate his energies on restoring royal authority in Sicily (Constitution of Malfi, 1231); he was crowned emperor by Pope Honorius III in 1220, and led the Fifth Crusade, 1228–9, but his Italian ambitions brought him into conflict with Honorius' successors, Gregory IX and **Innocent IV**. He was excommunicated and deposed at the Council of Lyon (1245), and forced to make lasting concessions to German princes to win their support against the papacy and the Lombard cities. The conflict was continuing at the time of his death, and was only resolved when **Charles of Anjou** defeated Frederick's son and grandson at Benevento (1266) and Tagliacozzo (1286).

FREDERICK II OF PRUSSIA *see* **Frederick the Great**

FREDERICK AUGUSTUS I (1670–1733) Elector of Saxony (1694–1733) and, as Augustus II, king of Poland, 1697–1733. He succeeded as Elector of Lutheran Saxony in 1694, then became a Catholic in order to be elected king of Poland in 1697; elected by a minority of Polish nobles, he used his Saxon army to secure his coronation. He entered the **Great Northern War** and was defeated by **Charles XII** of Sweden (1702). Deposed in 1706 and his kingdom occupied until 1709 by Stanislaw Leszczynski, a rival Polish king, he was restored at the treaty of Stockholm, 1719. He was succeeded by **Frederick Augustus II**, his son (Augustus III of Poland).

FREDERICK AUGUSTUS II (1696–1763) Elector of Saxony (1733–63) and, as Augustus III, king of Poland (1735–63). The only legitimate son of **Frederick Augustus I** of Saxony. He married Maria Josepha, daughter of the Emperor Joseph I, in 1719. In 1733 he succeeded as elector of Saxony, and in the same year drove his rival Stanislaw I Leszczynski into exile and was elected King of Poland (as Augustus III) by a minority vote. He supported Austria against Prussia in the War of the Austrian Succession (1740–8) in 1742, and again in 1756 in the **Seven Years' War**. He failed to counter the growing influence of the Czartoryski and Poniatowski families.

FREDERICK WILLIAM (1620–88) Elector of Brandenburg, known as the Great Elector. He succeeded in 1640 and successfully reconstructed his domain after the ravages of the Thirty Years' War; created a standing army after agreement with the Estates; fought France and Sweden, 1674; defeated the Swedes at Fehrbellin, 1675, and concluded the **Peace of Nijmegen**.

FREDERICK WILLIAM I (1688–1740) King of Prussia, son of Frederick I, and father of **Frederick the Great**. After succeeding to the throne in 1713, he reorganized the administration and economy to sustain an army of 83,000 men, and won most of western Pomerania from Sweden under the Treaty of Stockholm, 1720.

FREI, EDUARDO (1911–82) Chilean political leader, and a founder member, in 1935, of the National Falange, later renamed the Christian Democrat Party. He edited a daily newspaper, *El Tarapacá*, 1935–7. He held office as minister of public works, and was president of Chile from 1964 until 1970, when the Christian Democrats were defeated by **Allende** in the presidential election.

FRÉMONT, JOHN CHARLES (1813–90) US explorer and mapmaker who headed expeditions to survey the Des Moines River (1841), the route west to Wyoming (1842), the mouth of the Columbia River (1843) and California (1845). He was the Republican Party's nominee for president of the USA, 1856; he was governor of Arizona, 1878–83.

FRIARS During the first decade of the 13th century St Francis (1181–1226) and St Dominic (1170–1221) were independently moved to raise the standard of religious life in Europe by instructing the populace (particularly in the towns) through preaching and example, in order to counteract the growing menace of heresy. The Franciscans (Order of Friars Minor, or Grey Friars) were informally recognized by Pope **Innocent III** in 1209 and formally established in 1223; the Dominicans (Order of Preachers, or Black Friars) were formally established in 1216. The Franciscan St Bonaventura (1221–74) and the Dominican St Thomas Aquinas (1226–74) were among their most prominent early members. Friars took the monastic vows of poverty, chastity and obedience, but differed from monks in two main respects; their convents were bases for preaching tours, not places of permanent residence like monasteries, and they sought education at the newly founded universities. Other 13th-century Orders of friars were the Austin Friars and the Carmelites.

FRISIANS Germanic people. They first entered the coastal provinces of western Germany and the Netherlands in prehistoric times, ousting the resident Celts; after the collapse of Rome, the territory was infiltrated by Angles and **Jutes** on their way to England. The Frisians were conquered and converted to Christianity by **Charlemagne**.

FROBISHER, SIR MARTIN (c.1535–94) Explorer of Canada's northeast coasts, who sailed in 1567 with three ships in search of a Northwest Passage to Asia; he reached Labrador and Baffin Island, but failed to find gold or establish a colony. He became vice-admiral to **Drake** in the West Indies, 1585, was prominent in fighting the Spanish Armada, and was mortally wounded fighting Spanish ships off the coast of France.

FRONDE Complex series of uprisings against the French government under **Mazarin** during the minority of **Louis XIV**. Leaders of the Paris *parlement* were imprisoned in 1648 after violent protests against taxation. They were freed by popular revolt in Paris, supported by a separate rebellion of the nobility in alliance with Spain, which escalated into open warfare. The Fronde disintegrated soon after the victory of the royal armies at Faubourg-St Antoine in 1652.

G

GADSDEN PURCHASE Sale to the USA of some 77,700 sq. km (30,000 square miles) of land along the Mexico-Arizona border, required by the US to provide a low pass through mountains for railway construction. The purchase was negotiated by US minister James Gadsden in 1853 at a cost of $10 million.

GAIKWARS Powerful **Maratha** family which made its headquarters in the Baroda district of Gujarat, west-central India, from 1734 to 1947. In 1802 the British established a residency on Baroda to conduct relations between the **East India Company** and the Gaikwar princes.

GAISERIC (d.477) King of the **Vandals**, also known as Genseric. He transported his whole people, said to number 80,000, from Spain to north Africa in 429; sacked Carthage, 439, after defeating the joint armies of Rome's Eastern and Western Empires, and declared independence. By sea he attacked, captured and looted Rome, 455; and fought off two major Roman expeditions (460 and 468).

GALLA Large ethnic group in Ethiopia. Cushitic-speaking camel nomads, in a series of invasions from their homelands in the southeast of the country they migrated north and east, and by the end of the 16th century had reached almost to Eritrea. Since then they have largely been assimilated into, and dominated by, the rival Amharic and Tigrean cultures.

GALLEON Powerful sailing ship developed in the 15th and 16th centuries for Mediterranean and ocean navigation. Larger than the galley, with a ratio of beam to length of 1 to 4 or 5, usually with two decks and four masts (two square-rigged and two lateen), it was heavily armed and used in particular by Spain in fleets across the Atlantic and in the annual voyage from Acapulco to Manila.

GALLIC WARS The military campaigns in which the Roman general **Julius Caesar** won control of Gaul. As described in his account, *De Bello Gallico*, the conquest took eight years, from 58 to 50 BC; in the first phase, 57–54 BC, Roman authority was fairly easily established, but suppression of a large-scale revolt in 53 BC, led by the Gallic chieftain, Vercingetorix, required all Caesar's skills.

GAMA, VASCO DA (1462–1524) First discoverer of a continuous sea route from Europe to India via the Cape of Good Hope. In 1497–9 he led a Portuguese expedition round Africa to India; a second voyage in 1502 established Portugal as controller of the Indian Ocean and a world power. He died shortly after his arrival to take up an appointment as the Portuguese viceroy in India.

GANDHI, INDIRA (1917–84) Indian prime minister and head of state, 1966–77 and 1980–6. The daughter of **Nehru**, she was elected to the premiership in 1966, and won national elections in 1967 and 1971; she led India in war against Pakistan, 1971. She declared a national emergency in 1975, after an adverse legal decision on her own election. Defeated in the elections of 1977, she was returned to office in 1980 as leader of the Congress I party. She was assassinated in 1984 by Sikh extremists.

GANDHI, MOHANDAS K (1869–1948) Indian independence leader. Born in a strict Hindu community, he studied law in England 1889–92, then worked in South Africa as a lawyer and subsequently as a leader of the civil rights movement of Indian settlers, 1893–1914. Entering politics in India in 1919, he turned the previously ineffectual Indian National Congress into a potent mass organization. He perfected the disruptive techniques of mass disobedience and non-violent non-cooperation; during protest against the Salt Tax (1930) 60,000 followers were imprisoned. Three major campaigns, in 1920–2, 1930–4 and 1940–2, played a major part in accelerating India's progress to Dominion status in 1947. He bitterly opposed partition, and worked incessantly to end the Hindu-Muslim riots and massacres accompanying the emergence of independent India and Pakistan. He was assassinated by a Hindu fanatic.

GARCIA MORENO, GABRIEL (1821–75) Theocratic president of Ecuador, 1860–75. He based his regime on ruthless personal rule and forcible encouragement of the Roman Catholic Church. All education, welfare and much state policy were turned over to clerics; political opposition and alternative religions were suppressed. He encouraged agricultural and economic reform, and Ecuadorian nationalism. He was assassinated.

GARIBALDI, GIUSEPPE (1807–82) Italian patriot and member of **Mazzini**'s Young Italy movement. He was a guerrilla leader in South America, and a founder of an independent Uruguay in her war against Argentina. He established himself as a national hero in 1849 as the defender of the Roman Republic against the French. In 1860 he led the expedition of "The Thousand" in Sicily, and occupied Naples, thus ensuring the unification of Italy. He had led a victorious force against the Austrians in 1859, and repeated the operation in 1866, but was defeated by the French in his attack on Rome in 1867.

GAUGAMELA Battlefield near the river Tigris, scene of **Alexander the Great**'s most notable victory, in 331 BC, when, greatly outnumbered, his Macedonian cavalry and Thracian javelin-throwers routed the Persian armies of Darius III by brilliant tactics, and opened the way to Babylon and Susa for him.

GAULLE, CHARLES DE (1890–1970) French soldier and statesman. He escaped to London after the French surrender to Germany, 1940; organized the Free French forces and led the French government-in-exile from Algiers, 1943–4. He was first head of the post-war provisional government, 1944–6. In 1953 he withdrew from public life, but returned in 1958 to resolve the political crisis created by the civil war in Algeria; hostilities ceased in 1962. He established the Fifth Republic, becoming its first President, 1959 and presided over France's spectacular economic and political recovery. Resigned in 1969 after an adverse referendum vote on constitutional reform.

GEDYMIN (c.1275–1341) (or Giedymin) Grand Duke of Lithuania, ancestor of the **Jagiello** dynasty. Came to power in 1316, ruling a vast pagan principality based on Vilna. He built the strongest army in eastern Europe to hold his empire in the east and south, while repelling the advances of the Knights of the **Teutonic Order** against the Prussians, who were one of his Lithuanian tribes.

GENERAL MOTORS America's largest industrial manufacturing corporation; in 1988 General Motors' worldwide sales of cars and trucks totalled 8.1 million units.

GENERAL PRIVILEGE Legal document, compiled in 1293, setting out limits of royal power in Aragon and Valencia. Approved, under protest, by King **Peter III** of Aragon, it was a source of acrimony between king and subjects until abolished in 1348 by Peter IV, the Ceremonious, after defeating his nobles at the battle of Epila.

GENGHIS KHAN (c. 1162–1227) Mongol conqueror. According to the anonymous *Secret History of the Mongols* Temujin (his personal name) first became leader of an impoverished central Asian clan. He overcame all rivals, gathering a fighting force of 20,000 men, and by 1206 was acknowledged as Genghis Khan by all the people of the Mongol and Tatar steppes. He invaded northern China, capturing Peking in 1215, and destroyed the Muslim empire of **Khwarizm**, which covered part of central Asia and Persia, between 1216 and 1223.

GEORGE II (1890–1947) King of Greece, 1922–3, but exiled on the formation of the republic in 1923. Restored in 1935, he was again exiled during the Second World War. He returned to Greece in 1947.

GERMAN CONFEDERATION A grouping of 38 independent German states under the presidency of Austria, set up at the **Congress of Vienna** (1815). Superseded by the Frankfurt Parliament in 1848, it was re-established in 1851, and then dissolved by Prussia after the Seven Weeks' War of 1866.

GHAZNAVIDS Afghan dynasty, founded by Sebuktigin, father of **Mahmud of Ghazni**, in 977. At its greatest extent the empire stretched from the Oxus river in central Asia to the Indus river and the Indian Ocean. Under Mahmud's son, Masud (reigned 1037–41), much northern territory was lost to the **Seljuks**; the last Indian possessions were conquered by **Muizzudin Muhammad** in 1186.

GHULAM Slave soldier, often recruited from lands outside the Islamic world.

GHURIDS Dynasty ruling northwest Afghanistan from the mid-12th to the early 13th century. Under **Muizzudin Muhammad** the empire was extended into northern India, helping the establishment of Muslim rule in the sub-continent.

GIRONDINS Members of a moderate republican party during the French revolution, so named because the leaders came from the Gironde area. Many were guillotined, 31 October 1793, after the group had been overthrown by the rival Jacobins the previous June.

GLADSTONE, WILLIAM EWART (1809–98) British prime minister. Entered Parliament in 1832 as a Tory; president of the Board of Trade, 1843–5, and colonial secretary, 1845–6. He resigned after the repeal of the Corn Laws; later became chancellor of the exchequer, 1853–5 and 1859–66. He led the newly-formed Liberal Party to victory, 1868, and was four times prime minister, 1868–74, 1880–5, 1886 and 1892–4. He was responsible for many military, educational and civil service reforms, and for the Reform Act of 1884; he was repeatedly defeated over attempts to bring about Irish home rule.

GODUNOV, BORIS FYODOROVICH (c.1551–1605) Tsar of Muscovy. He rose in power and favour at the court of **Ivan IV**, the Terrible, and was appointed guardian of Fyodor, the Tsar's retarded son, when Fyodor succeeded in 1584. Godunov banished his enemies and became effective ruler, and was himself elected tsar when Fyodor died without heirs in 1598. Plagued by war, pestilence, famine and constant opposition from the boyars (the old Russian nobility), he was unable to fulfil his desired programme of social, legal, diplomatic and military reforms. His sudden death during civil war with a pretender known as "the false Dmitri" precipitated Russia into a devastating "time of troubles".

GOEBBELS, PAUL JOSEPH (1897–1945) **Hitler**'s Minister of Propaganda. He entered journalism in 1921, and in 1926 was appointed by Hitler as district administrator of the National Socialist German Workers' Party (NSDAP), becoming its head of propaganda in 1928. On Hitler's accession to power (1933) he was appointed minister for public enlightenment and propaganda, controlling the press, radio, films, publishing, theatre, music and the visual arts. He committed suicide, with his wife and six children, in Hitler's besieged Berlin bunker.

GOETHE, JOHANN WOLFGANG VON (1749–1832) Most famous of all German poets, novelists and playwrights, Minister of State to the Duke of Saxe-Weimar, 1775, and one of the outstanding figures of European literature. His early novel, *The Sorrows of Young Werther*, 1774, expressed the reaction against the Enlightenment, the sensation of "emotion running riot" and the conflict between the artist and society. He returned to classicism after a visit to Italy, 1786–8, which affected his whole life and work; from this period onwards his work (*Faust*, part I and part II, 1808, 1832, *Wilhelm Meister*, 1791–1817, *Tasso*, 1789) has a philosophical content which lifts it out of time and place and gives it a universal quality.

GOKHALE, GOPAL KRISHNA (1866–1915) Indian independence leader. He resigned in 1902 from a professorship of history and political economy at Ferguson College, Poona, to enter politics; advocated moderate protest and constitutional reform. He was President of the Indian National Congress, 1905, and founder of the Servants of India Society, dedicated to the alleviation of poverty and service to the underprivileged.

GOLDEN BULL OF 1356 Constitution of the Holy Roman Empire, promulgated by the Emperor **Charles IV**; confirmed, *inter alia*, that succession to the German throne would continue to be determined by seven electors, convened by the Archbishop of Mainz, but that henceforth the electoral lands and powers would be indivisible, and inheritable only by the elder son, thus removing confusion over the right to vote; it sanctioned the primacy of the territorial princes under loose imperial suzerainty. It also rejected traditional papal claims to rule during periods when the throne was vacant.

GOLDEN HORDE Western portion of the Mongol empire, also known as the Kipchak khanate. Founded by **Batu** *c.* 1242, it dominated southern Russia to the end of the 14th century. It was finally broken up by **Tamerlane** to form three **Tatar** khanates: Kazan, Astrakhan and the Crimea.

GOLD STANDARD Monetary system in which the value of currency in issue is legally tied to a certain quantity of gold. During the last quarter of the 19th century virtually all major trading nations adopted this policy and most attempted to return to it after the break caused by the First World War; this attempt was abandoned in the slump of the 1930s. The US dollar finally came off gold in 1971.

GÖMBÖS, GYULA (1886–1936) Hungarian prime minister. In 1919 he set up a proto-fascist movement and helped organize the overthrow of the Communist government. At first he opposed the conservative premier, István Bethlen (1921–31), but joined his administration in 1929 and in 1932 was swept to power by the "radical right" movement. He advocated a reactionary, anti-Semitic programme and alliance with Germany and Italy, but was restrained by the head of state, Admiral Horthy.

GOMES, FERNÃO 15th-century Portuguese merchant who in 1469 was granted a monopoly to explore the West African coast and keep all trading profits. Gomes and his captains explored as far as the Congo River, and prepared the way for the voyages of **Vasco da Gama** to India in 1497–9.

GOMULKA, WLADYSLAW (1905–82) Polish Communist leader. A youth organizer for the banned Communist Party, 1926, and a wartime underground fighter, he was stripped of Party membership in 1949 after incurring the displeasure of Stalin, but re-admitted in 1956 to become First Secretary of the Central Committee. Resistance to his regime erupted in riots in 1968; he was deposed and retired in 1970.

GORBACHEV, MIKHAIL (1931–) Soviet statesman. After studying law at Moscow university (1953) he headed the Young Communist League in his native Stavropol. He became agriculture secretary of the central committee of the Soviet Communist Party (1978); a full member of the Politburo (1980); general secretary of the Soviet Communist Party (1985–91) and president of the Soviet Union (1988–91). He promoted economic and social reforms programs known as *glasnost* (openness) and *perestroika* (restructuring), and negotiated two arms limitation treaties (1987, 1990), effectively ending the Cold War. Opposed to the breakup of the Soviet Union, he met with growing opposition which brought about his resignation in 1991.

GORDON, CHARLES GEORGE (1833–85) British general, first distinguished for bravery in the Crimean War (1853–6). He volunteered for service in China, where his exploits in the "Arrow" war, the T'ai-p'ing Rebellion and the burning of the emperors' Summer Palace earned him the nickname "Chinese Gordon". In 1884 he was sent to the Sudan (where he had earlier been Governor-General) to evacuate British troops from Khartoum; he was besieged and killed by Sudanese followers of **Mohammed Ahmed al-Mahdi**.

GORGIAS OF LEONTINI (c. 483–c. 376 BC) Ancient Greek rhetorician, noted for his poetic language and carefully balanced clauses. In his treatise *On Nature* he argued the essential non-existence, unknowability and incommunicability of Being. He was portrayed with respect by **Plato** in *Gorgias*.

GORM King of Denmark, father of **Harald Bluetooth**; died after 935.

GOTHIC Relating to the art and language of the **Ostrogoths** and **Visigoths**. During the Renaissance, the word was used to typify the barbarism of the Middle Ages; it still refers to the style of church architecture, with characteristic pointed arches, predominant from the 12th to the 15th century, and to the painting and sculpture associated with it.

GOTT, BENJAMIN (1762–1840) English manufacturer of woollen cloth and philanthropist. In 1793 he established a woollen mill in Leeds, introducing an improved mechanical cloth-cutting device in spite of much hostility.

GOTTFRIED VON STRASSBURG German medieval poet, author of *Tristan*, the classic version of the story of Tristan and Isolde. He lived and worked in the late 12th and early 13th centuries.

GOULART, DR JOAO (1918–76) Brazilian political leader. He joined the Brazilian labour party, Partido Trabalhista, in 1945 and became national party director in 1951, minister of labour and commerce, 1953–4, vice–president of Brazil, 1956, was re-elected in 1961 and became president that year. He was deposed in a military *coup d'état*, 1964.

GOVERNMENT OF INDIA ACT British Act of Parliament of 1935 embodying a number of constitutional reforms, including "provincial autonomy" and a federal structure at the centre. Only the provisions relating to the provinces were implemented, the proposals for federation being rejected by the Indian political parties.

GRANADA, KINGDOM OF Last foothold of the Muslims in Spain. Ruled by the **Nasrid** dynasty, 1238–1492, it prospered by welcoming Moorish refugees from Seville, Valencia and Murcia; it built one of Islam's most famous architectural achievements, the Alhambra (Red Fortress). The kingdom was finally conquered by Christian forces in 1492.

GRANT, ULYSSES SIMPSON (1822–85) 18th president of the USA, 1869–77. He was commander-in-chief of the Union armies during the American Civil War. His administration (Republican) was marked by corruption and bitter partisanship between the political parties.

GREAT ELECTOR see **Frederick William, Elector of Brandenburg**

GREAT FEAR Series of rural panics, spreading through the French countryside between 20 July and 6 August 1789, at the onset of the French revolution. Following a series of peasant disorders, during which stores of grain were looted and châteaux burned, rumours of invasion by armed brigands spread in five main currents covering the greater part of the country, which stimulated further disorders that petered out as suddenly as they had begun.

GREAT NORTHERN WAR Struggle between Sweden and Russia, 1700–21, mainly for control of the Baltic. **Charles XII** of Sweden at first defeated an alliance of Russia, Denmark, Poland and Saxony (1700–6), but was heavily defeated at Poltava by **Peter the Great** of Russia in 1709. This advantage was lost when Turkey declared war on Russia in 1710, and fighting continued in Poland and Scandinavia until Charles' death in 1718. In the final settlement Sweden lost Livonia and Karelia to Russia (which gained permanent access to the Baltic Sea), and abandoned its claims to be a great power.

GREAT SCHISM A political split in the Catholic Church, lasting from 1378 to 1417, during which rival popes – one in Rome, the other in Avignon – attempted to exert authority. The result of a serious split among cardinals and high churchmen on ecclesiastical reform, and the political influence of the French monarchy, the Schism was resolved by the Council of Constance, 1414–17.

GREGORY I "THE GREAT" (c. 540–604) Pope, saint and one of the Fathers of the Christian Church. During his papacy (590–604), he strengthened and reorganized the Church administration, reformed the liturgy, promoted monasticism, asserted the temporal power of the papacy, extended Rome's influence in the West and sent St Augustine of Canterbury on his mission to convert the English.

GREGORY VII (c. 1020–85) Pope and saint, born in north Italy and given the name Hildebrand. He served under Pope Gregory VI during the Pope's exile in Germany after deposition by the Emperor **Henry III**. He was recalled to Rome by Pope **Leo IX**, and thereafter was often the power behind the papal throne. He was made a cardinal by **Alexander II** (1061–73) and elected by acclaim as his successor. From 1075 he was engaged in the contest over **lay investiture** with Emperor **Henry IV**, whom he excommunicated in 1076; after absolving him at Canossa in 1077, he re-excommunicated him after fresh attacks. Gregory was driven from Rome in 1084. He was canonized in 1606.

GRIJALVA, JUAN DE (c. 1489–1527) Spanish explorer. Sailing along the coast of Mexico, where he discovered the River Grijalva (named after him) in 1518, he was probably the first of the *conquistadores* to hear of the rich Aztec civilization of the interior.

GRUFFYDD AP LLEWELYN (b.c. 1063–d. 1000 BC) Briefly king of all Wales. He challenged the authority of existing dynasties holding power over Welsh kingdoms; seized control in Gwynedd in the northwest, Deheubarth in the southwest, and for a short period the whole country; he devastated the borderland with England.

GUELPH and GHIBELLINE The two great rival political factions of medieval Italy, reflecting the rivalry of Guelph dukes of Saxony and Bavaria and the **Hohenstaufen**. The names Guelph and Ghibelline came to designate support for the papal (Guelph) side against the imperial (Ghibelline) side in the struggle between the **Papacy** and the **Holy Roman Empire**.

GUEST, SIR JOSIAH (1785–1852) British industrialist. He created an improved smelting process at the family ironworks at Dowlais (near Merthyr Tydfil, Wales) and raised its annual iron production to 65,000 tons, mostly in the form of rails for the new railways.

GUEVARA, ERNESTO "CHE" (1928–67) South American revolutionary leader, born in Argentina. He qualified as a doctor of medicine, 1953; became chief aide to **Fidel Castro** in his successful Cuban revolution, 1959; wrote *Guerrilla Warfare*, 1960 and *Episodes of the Revolutionary War*, 1963. He was killed in Bolivia, trying to establish a guerrilla base there.

GUGGENHEIM, MEYER (1826–1905) Foun-der of modern American metal-mining industry; born in Switzerland, he emigrated to the USA in 1847. In the early 1880s he bought control of two Colorado copper mines, and quickly built up a worldwide network of mines, exploration companies, smelters and refineries. With his son Daniel (1856–1930) he merged all the family interests in 1901 into the American Smelting & Refining Company.

GUPTA Imperial dynasty, ruling in northern India from the 4th to the 6th centuries AD. It first rose to prominence under Chandragupta I, ruling over Magadha and parts of Uttar Pradesh (*c.* 319–35). Its power was extended and reinforced under **Samudragupta** (reigned *c.* 335–75), **Chandragupta II** (*c.* 375–45) and Kumaragupta (*c.* 415–54). The dynasty was later weakened by domestic unrest and **Hun** invasion, and effectively eliminated as a major political force by 510.

GURJARAS Central Asian tribe, reaching India with the **Hun** invasions of the 4th and 5th centuries AD. They settled in Rajasthan, in western India, and were reputed ancestors of the **Pratiharas**.

GUSTAVUS I VASA (c. 1496–1560) King of Sweden (1523–60), founder of the Vasa dynasty. He fought in Sweden's 1517–18 rebellion against Denmark, was interned but returned in 1520 to lead another rebellion against Denmark. He was elected king of Sweden in 1523, thus breaking up the **Union of Kalmar**. He introduced the **Lutheran** Reformation; and in 1544 persuaded the Diet to make the monarchy hereditary in his Vasa family line.

GUSTAVUS II ADOLPHUS (1594–1632) King of Sweden, grandson of **Gustavus I Vasa**. He succeeded to the throne in 1611 and made Sweden a major political and military power. He entered the Thirty Years' War on the side of the Protestants, 1630, and conquered most of Germany. He was killed at the battle of Lützen.

GUTIANS (Guti) Ancient mountain people from the Zagros range, east of Mesopotamia. They destroyed the empire of Akkad, *c.* 2230 BC, and exercised sporadic sovereignty over much of Babylonia for the next century. Traditionally they were eclipsed as a history force after the defeat of the last king, Tirigan, by Utu-Khegal of Uruk, *c.* 2130 BC. The Gutians were primarily remembered in later tradition as barbarians.

GUZMÁN BLANCO, ANTONIO (1829–99) President of Venezuela. He was appointed special finance commissioner to negotiate loans from Great Britain, seized control of the government in 1870; as head of the Regeneration party was elected constitutional president, 1873; ruled as absolute dictator until 1877, and again 1879–84 and 1886–8, laying the main foundations of modern Venezuela, and accumulating a vast personal fortune. Ousted by a *coup d'état* during one of his visits to Europe, he died in Paris.

H

HABSBURGS Major European royal and imperial dynasty from the 15th to the 20th century. The ascendancy of the family began in 13th century Austria. Frederick V Habsburg was crowned Holy Roman Emperor in 1452, as Frederick III; the title remained a family possession until the Empire was dissolved in 1806. At their peak, under Charles V (Charles I of Spain), Habsburg realms stretched from eastern Europe to the New World; after Charles' death, the house split into the Spanish line, which died out in 1700, and the Austrian line, which remained in power – after 1740 as the House of Habsburg-Lorraine – until 1918.

HADRIAN IV (c. 1100–59) Pope 1154–9. Born Nicholas Breakspear, and the only English Pope, he renewed the initiative of the papacy in the spirit of **Gregory VII**, notably in the incident of Besançon, when he claimed that the imperial crown was held from the Pope. He expelled the heretic **Arnold of Brescia** from Rome.

HADRIAN, PUBLIUS AELIUS (AD 76–138) Roman emperor. Adopted by **Trajan** as his son, whom he succeeded in 117. He abandoned the policy of eastern expansion in order to consolidate frontiers and initiated far-reaching military, legal and administrative reforms; his fortifications in Britain and Syria still stand. He travelled widely in the empire, encouraging the spread of Greco-Roman civilization and culture.

HAFSIDS Dynasty of **Berber** origin, ruling Tunisia and eastern Algeria *c.* 1229–1574. The most famous ruler, Mustansir (1249–77), used the title of caliph; his diplomacy averted danger from the Crusade of **Louis IX** and extended his influence into Morocco and Spain.

HAIDAR ALI (1722–82) Muslim ruler of Mysore, southern India. He created the first Indian army equipped with European firearms and artillery. He deposed the local rajah and seized the throne, *c.* 1761. He defeated the British several times between 1766 and 1780, but finally lost in the three battles of Porto Novo, Pollilu and Sholinghar. Before his death he implored his son **Tipu** to make peace with the invaders.

HAIG, DOUGLAS (1861–1928) 1st Earl Haig. British field marshal, commander-in-chief of the British forces in Flanders and France 1915–18, during the First World War. His strategy of attrition on the Somme (1916) and in Flanders (1917), especially at the third battle of Ypres (or Passchendaele), resulted in enormous British casualties.

HAILE SELASSIE I (1892–1975) Emperor of Ethiopia. A close relative of Emperor **Menelik II** (1889–1913), he was appointed to provincial governorships from 1908, became regent and heir apparent to Menelik's daughter Zauditu in 1916. He took Ethiopia into the **League of Nations** in 1923, and became emperor in 1930, introducing bicameral Parliament the following year. He was driven out by the Italian occupation of 1936–41 but he led the reconquest, with British aid, and began to modernize the country. He survived a coup threat in 1960, but in 1974 news of the famine in the Wollo district and an armed mutiny provoked a revolution which deposed him. He died under house arrest.

HAJJ UMAR, AL- (1794–1864) West African Tukolor warrior-mystic, founder of the Muslim empire based on Masina in the western Sudan (now in the republic of Mali). He became a member of the newly-founded militant religious order, the Tijaniyya. He made a pilgrimage to Mecca in 1826 and returned inspired to propagate Islam in the western Sudan. In 1852 he embarked upon a great and bloody *jihad* (holy war) which resulted in the conquest of much of the western Sudan. The campaign brought him into violent conflict with the French, who were expanding up the Senegal river. He was killed in battle. By the end of the 19th century his empire was finally conquered by the French.

HAKKA North Chinese people who migrated south under the Sung dynasty (1126–1279) to Kwangtung and Fukien where they remained a distinct social group, living in separate communities, usually in poor uplands. They were involved in many bitter communal feuds in the 18th and 19th centuries, culminating in the Hakka-Punti war in the 1850s. Many emigrated after the T'ai-p'ing rebellion, and they are now widely spread throughout East Asia.

HALLSTATT Early Celtic Iron Age culture, flourishing in central Europe *c.* 750–450 BC, named after an Austrian village in the Salzkammergut, where an archaeologically important cemetery was found in the 19th century. The culture was notable for elaborate burials, in which the dead person was placed in a four-wheeled chariot, of which examples have been found from the Upper Danube region to Vix in Burgundy.

HAMAGUCHI, OSACHI (1870–1931) Japanese statesman. Official of the finance ministry, 1895–1924, and finance minister 1924–6. In 1927 he was elected leader of the new Rikken Minseito (Constitutional Democratic) Party, and became Japanese prime minister in 1929. He decreed drastic deflationary policies, but was assassinated before they could take effect. The army forced his colleagues to resign, thus bringing democratic government to an end.

HAMDANIDS Bedouin dynasty controlling Mosul and Aleppo, 905–1004; renowned warriors and patrons of Arab art and learning.

HAMMADIDS North African Berber dynasty, a branch of the **Zirids**. In the reign of the Zirid leader Badis Ibn al-Mansur (995–1016) they gained control of part of Algeria; in 1067, under attack from the **Fatimids** and their Bedouin allies, they established themselves in the port of Bejaia (Bougia), and developed a successful trading empire until conquered by the **Almohads** in 1152.

HAMMARSKJÖLD, DAG (1905–61) Swedish and international statesman. Son of a Swedish prime minister, he entered politics in 1930 and became deputy foreign minister in 1951. Elected as secretary-general of the UN in 1953, he greatly extended the influence both of the UN and of its secretary-general striving to reduce the tensions caused by decolonization in Africa, particularly in the Congo (1960–1), where he was killed in an air crash.

HAMMURABI King of Babylon, reigning 1728–1686 BC. He succeeded his father, Sin-Mabullit, and extended his small kingdom (originally only 129km/80 miles long and 32km/20 miles wide) to unify all Mesopotamia under Babylonian rule. He published a collection of laws on a basalt stele, 2.4m (8ft) high, now in the Louvre museum.

HAM NGHI (1870–c. 1940) Emperor of Vietnam. He reached the throne in 1884 after intense intrigue following the death of his uncle, the emperor Tu Duc; at the instigation of his regents, Nguyen Van Tuong and Thou That Thuyet, he led a revolt against the French, 1885; he fled after its failure, was deposed in 1886, captured and exiled to Algeria.

HAN Chinese imperial dynasty, ruling from 206 BC to AD 9 (Former Han), and AD 25–220 (Later Han); *see* pp. 88–9.

HAN FU-CHÜ (1890–1938) Military officer who served under **Feng Yü-hsiang**, 1912–28. He was appointed governor of Honan in 1928; defecting from Feng in his confrontation with **Chiang Kai-shek**, in 1929, he controlled Shantung from 1930 to 1938 and brought it under the control of Nanking. In 1937 the Japanese invaded Shantung; he put up only token resistance and was executed for dereliction of duty the following year.

HANNIBAL (247–183 BC) Most famous Carthaginian general, son of another great soldier, Hamilcar Barca. He was commander-in-chief in Spain aged 26; after the outbreak of the Second **Punic War** against Rome (218–201) he led 40,000 troops, with elephants, over the Alps to smash the Roman armies at Lake Trasimene, 217, and Cannae, 216. Forced to abandon Italy in 203 as Rome had attacked Carthage itself, he was finally defeated at Zama in 202 and later driven into exile. He committed suicide.

HANSEATIC LEAGUE Association of medieval German cities and merchant groups which became a powerful economic and political force in northern Europe. With a centre for meetings in the city of Lübeck, the members established an important network of Baltic trade, and a string of commercial bases stretching from Novgorod to London and from Bergen to Bruges. In its heyday during the 14th century the Hansa included well over 100 towns; its influence gradually faded with the emergence of powerful competitor states, and the last meeting of the Diet was held in Lübeck in 1669.

HARALD BLUETOOTH (d.c. 985) King of Denmark from *c.* 940. He accepted the introduction of Christianity into his kingdom, and strengthened its central organization; he successfully defeated German and Norwegian attacks on Denmark, unifying its disparate elements.

HARALD I FINEHAIR (c. 860–c. 940) First king claiming sovereignty over all Norway, in the second half of the 9th century, the son of Halfdan the Black, ruler of a part of southeast Norway and a member of the ancient Swedish Yngling dynasty, whom he succeeded when very young. His conquests culminated in the battle of Hafrsfjord, *c.* 900; many defeated chiefs fled to Britain and possibly Iceland. The best account of his exploits is given in Snorri Sturlson's 13th-century saga, the *Heimskringla*.

HARALD II GREYCLOAK (d.c. 970) Norwegian king, son of **Erik Bloodaxe**. He overthrew his half-brother, Haakon the Good, *c.* 961, ruling oppressively, with his brothers, until *c.* 970. He is credited with establishing the first Christian missions in Norway. He was killed in battle against an alliance of local nobles and his former supporter, **Harald Bluetooth**.

HARA TAKASHI (1856–1921) First "commoner" (i.e. untitled) prime minister of modern Japan. Graduated from Tokyo university into journalism and then entered foreign service in 1882. He became ambassador to Korea in 1897, chief editor of the Osaka *Mainichi* newspaper in 1899. He helped to found the Rikken-Seiyukai (Friends of Constitutional Government) Party, 1900, and built it into an American-style party machine, meanwhile rising to ministerial and finally prime ministerial rank in 1918. He was assassinated by a right-wing fanatic after opposing the use of Japanese troops in Siberia.

HARKORT, FRIEDRICH (FRITZ) (1793–1880) Pioneer entrepreneur in the German engineering industry. In 1918 Harkort and Kamp, in partnership with Thomas (an English engineer), established works producing textile machinery and steam engines at Wetter in the Ruhr district. The plant was later expanded to include the puddling process. Harkort twice visited England to recruit skilled mechanics. He was a pioneer in the construction of steamships on the Weser and the Rhine, and was also a leading advocate of railway building in Germany.

HARSHA (c. 590–c. 647) Indian ruler, second son of a king in Punjab. He ultimately exercised loose imperial power over most of northern India. Converted from **Hinduism** to **Buddhism**, he was the first to open diplomatic relations between India and China (*c.* 641); his court, at Kanauj, his early years and his model administration are described in Bana's poem *The Deeds of Harsha*, and the writings of the Chinese pilgrim Hsüan Tsang.

HARUN AL-RASHID (c. 763–806) Fifth caliph of the **Abbasid** dynasty, immortalized in *The Thousand and One Nights*. He inherited the throne in 786, ruling territories from northwest India to the western Mediterranean; his reign saw the beginning of the disintegration of the **caliphate**.

HASHEMITES Direct or collateral descendants of the prophet **Mohammed**, who was himself a member of the house of Hashem, a division of the Quraysh tribe. In the 20th century, Hussein ibn Ali, descendant of a long line of Hashemite *sharifs* or local rulers of Mecca, and King of Hejaz, 1916–24, founded the modern Hashemite dynasty, carried on by his sons, King Feisal of Iraq and King Abdullah of Jordan.

HASSAN II (1929–1999) King of Morocco, 17th monarch of the Alaouite dynasty. The son of **Mohammed V**, he became commander-in-chief of the Royal Moroccan Army in 1957. Succeeding to the throne in 1961, he held the posts of prime minister, 1961–3 and 1965–7, minister of defence, 1972–3, and commander-in-chief of the army from 1972. He established strong monarchical government, and was the main force behind the abortive attempt to partition the former Spanish Sahara between Morocco and Mauritania.

HASTINGS, FRANCIS RAWDON-HASTINGS (1754–1826) 1st Marquis. Early governor-general of Bengal. He landed in India, 1813; defeated the Gurkhas, 1816; conquered the Maratha states and cemented British control east of the Sutlej river. He purchased Singapore, 1819, but resigned under a financial cloud, 1823; he was Governor of Malta 1824.

HASTINGS, WARREN (1732–1818) First governor-general of British India, 1774–85. He carried out important administrative and legal reforms, but was impeached on corruption charges, 1788; he was finally acquitted, after a long and famous trial, in 1795.

HAUSA West African people, organized from about the 11th century into a loose grouping of states centred to the west of Lake Chad. In the 16th century Kano became the greatest of the Hausa cities, but the Hausaland region only came under unified control after conquest by the Fulani in the early 19th century. They are now one of the largest ethnic groups in Nigeria.

HAVEL, VACLAV (1936–2011) Czech playwright and politician. Widely regarded as the leading Czech playwright of his generation, he commented on the struggles of contemporary intellectuals in his plays. His works were banned after the Soviet invasion (1968), but remained available abroad. In the 1970s he became spokesman for human rights groups and was imprisoned. After the resignation of the entire politburo, he formally entered politics to become the first president of an independent Czechoslovakia (1989) in the "Velvet Revolution". In January 1993 he was elected president of the new Czech Republic.

HAWLEY-SMOOT TARIFF US tariff, passed in 1930, which set the highest import duties in American history, attracted immediate retaliation from European governments, and is considered to be one of the factors responsible for deepening the Great Depression.

HAY, JOHN (1838–1905) US secretary of state (1898–1905). A skilful diplomat, he is best known for his Open Door Policy in China (1900). He also helped negotiate the end of the Spanish-American war (1898), was active in the decision to retain the Philippines, thus marking the USA as a major imperialist power, and completed the second **Hay-Pauncefote Treaty** (1901), granting the USA exclusive rights to build a canal across the Isthmus of Panama. He assisted in diplomatic efforts to assure Panamanian independence and the beginning of canal construction (1903).

HAY-PAUNCEFOTE TREATY Composite name for two Anglo-American agreements, signed in 1900 and 1901, freeing the USA from a previous commitment to international control of any projected Central American canal. It freed US hands for the building of the Panama canal, which was completed in 1914.

HAYES, RUTHERFORD B. (1822–93) 19th president of the USA, and the first chief executive to say openly that an isthmian canal must be American-owned. This pronouncement correlates with the beginning of a programme of naval expansion.

HEAVENLY PRINCIPLE SECT (T'ien-li chiao) Secret sectarian movement connected with the **White Lotus** society, with a large following during the late 18th century in northern China (Hopei, Honan, Shantung), led by Lin Ch'ing and Le wen-ch'eng, who began a rebellion in Honan in 1813. A small group infiltrated Peking and entered the palace.

HEGIRA (hijra) Arabic word for "emigration", and the starting date of Muslim era. By order of **Omar I**, the second caliph, in AD 639, Islamic letters, treaties, proclamations and events were to be dated by reference to the day, 16 July 622, on which the Prophet **Mohammed** migrated from Mecca to Medina.

HELLENISM Culture, philosophy and spirit of ancient Greece, spread across Asia and across Europe through the Roman adoption of Greek models; through thought and art, it touched Buddhism, Christianity, Hinduism and Islam. It was revived in the western world in the Renaissance and other renaissances. It is often associated with humanism, rationality and beauty of form.

HELLENISTIC The era from 323 to 30 BC when the eastern Mediterranean and the Near East were dominated by dynasties and state governments founded by the successors of **Alexander the Great**.

HENRICIANS Followers of Henry of Lausanne, an itinerant preacher of southern France in the 12th century, whose criticisms of the Church followed those of the **Petrobrusians** and were transmitted to the more numerous and better organized **Waldensians**.

HENRY II (1133–89) King of England. Grandson of Henry I, he became Duke of Normandy in 1150 and Count of Anjou in 1151. He married Eleanor of Aquitaine in 1152 after her repudiation by Louis VII of France. He succeeded to the English throne in 1154; in his own right and that of his wife, he ruled over domains extending from Ireland to the Pyrenees and Mediterranean. He was noted for his expansion of the judicial and administrative authority of the English crown; his generally successful reign was marred by quarrels with Thomas Becket, Archbishop of Canterbury, and with his own family.

HENRY II (1333–79) King of Castile, 1369–79. The natural son of Alfonso XI, Henry drove his brother Pedro (1356–69) from the throne with French aid and founded the Trastámara dynasty, which continued until 1504.

HENRY III (1017–56) German king 1039–56, and emperor 1046–56. He brought Church reform to Rome at the Synod of Sutri, 1046, and appointed a succession of Germans – notably **Leo IX** – to the papacy.

HENRY IV (1050–1106) German emperor, son of **Henry III** and Agnes of Poitou. He succeeded in 1056 under his mother's regency. He broke with Pope **Gregory VII** over the investiture issue in 1075, was excommunicated and declared deposed by him, but restored after performing penance to the Pope at Canossa in 1077; he was excommunicated again in 1080. He appointed Clement III as anti-Pope in 1084, but was outmanoeuvred by Pope **Urban II** and his position was weakened by the revolts of his sons Conrad and the future emperor, **Henry V**. He died after defeating Henry at Visé, near Liège.

HENRY IV (1533–1610) King of France, 1589–1610, son of Antoine, King of Navarre. He married Marguerite of Valois, daughter of the French king, **Henry II**, in 1572. He emerged as Protestant leader in the French wars of religion, and was excommunicated, 1585. Reconciled with King Henry III in 1589, he abjured the Protestant faith in 1593 and was crowned king in 1594. In 1598 he signed the **Edict of Nantes**, granting toleration to French Protestants. He married Marie de' Medici, 1600; authorized **Jesuits** to reopen colleges in Paris, 1603. He was assassinated.

HENRY V (1387–1442) King of England, son of **Henry IV**, whom he succeeded in 1413. In 1415 he reopened the **Hundred Years' War** in support of his claims to the French throne; won the battle of Agincourt, 1415, and conquered Normandy, 1419. Under the Treaty of Troyes he married Catherine of Valois and became heir to the French king, Charles VI. Renewed war, 1421, the year before his death.

HENRY VI (1165–97) Son of **Frederick I Barbarossa**, he was chosen as German king in 1190; married Constance, daughter of **Roger II** of Sicily in 1186, and inherited Roger's kingdom in 1189; crowned emperor in 1191, after Frederick's death on the Third **Crusade**. The ransom of Richard I, whom he held prisoner, 1193–4, enabled him to overcome internal opposition in the Lower Rhineland and Saxony led by **Duke Henry**, and then to finance his conquest of Sicily after the death of the rival claimant, King Tancred, in 1194. He died of malaria while preparing a crusade. Because his son **Frederick II** was then aged only two years, his death caused a succession dispute in the Empire.

HENRY VII (1457–1509) King of England. He became head of the royal House of Lancaster which challenged their cousins, the House of York, for the crown of England; exiled until 1485, when he defeated and killed the Yorkist, Richard III, he then became king and ended the civil war (**Wars of the Roses**). He founded the **Tudor** dynasty, which lasted until 1603, creating a strong central government in England after almost a century of disruption.

HENRY VIII (1491–1547) King of England, son of **Henry VII**, succeeding in 1509. His desire for a male heir caused his search for a means to declare his first marriage, to Catherine of Aragon, invalid; after papal refusal, and non-recognition of his second marriage in 1533 to Anne Boleyn, Parliament passed the Act of Supremacy, 1534, declaring Henry head of the English Church; monasteries were suppressed (1536, 1539). Wales was brought into legal union with England, 1534–6.

HENRY, DUKE OF SAXONY (c. 1130–95) Known as "the Lion". He spent his early years fighting for his father's duchies. He was granted Saxony in 1142 but had to wait until 1156 for Bavaria; founded Munich in 1157 and Lübeck in 1159. Stripped of his lands after breaking with **Frederick I Barbarossa**, 1179–80, he was twice exiled, 1181–5 and 1189–90, but was reconciled with Emperor **Henry VI** in 1194.

HENRY THE NAVIGATOR (1394–1460) Portuguese prince, third son of John I and Philippa of Lancaster. He helped in the capture of Ceuta, Morocco, in 1415, and at the age of 26, was made Grand Master of Portugal's crusading Order of Christ. Thereafter, he devoted much of his life to the encouragement of maritime trade and discovery, to the organization of voyages to west Africa and to occasional crusading operations in Morocco.

HERACLIAN DYNASTY Byzantine dynasty, ruling from AD 610 to 711, founded by emperor Heraclius (610–41) and ending with Justinian II (685–95, and again 705–11).

HERACLIUS (c. 575–641) Eastern Roman emperor. The son of a governor of Africa, in 610 he seized the crown from emperor Phocas; fought and defeated the Persians, 622–8; restored the True Cross to Jerusalem, 630; persecuted the **Jews**, 632. His armies were beaten by Muslim Arabs in 636, and Syria and Palestine (640) and Egypt (642) lost to Islam. In the meantime he restored the administration of the remaining provinces and laid the foundations for the medieval Byzantine state.

HERDER, JOHANN GOTTFRIED VON (1744–1803) German critic, linguist and philosopher who wrote on the origins of language, poetry and aesthetics. he was a leading figure in the literary movement known as *Sturm und Drang*. He made a famous collection of German songs (*Volkslieder*, 1778–9), wrote the *Essay on the Origin of Language* (1772), and at Weimar, where he became superintendent of schools in 1776, *Reflections on the Philosophy of the History of Mankind* (1778–91).

HEREDIA, PEDRO DE (c. 1500–54) Spanish soldier who founded Cartagena in modern Colombia in 1533, and several other New World cities. He amassed a vast fortune through his many expeditions to the interior.

HERERO Bantu-speaking peoples of southwest Africa, mostly in central Namibia and Botswana.

HERERO REVOLT A protest which broke out in 1904 against German colonial oppression of the Herero and other peoples of southwest Africa. In 1907, when the risings ended, over 65,000 Hereros out of an original 80,000 had been killed, starved in concentration camps or driven into the Kalahari Desert to die.

HERNANDEZ DE CORDOBA, FRANCISCO Name of two Spanish soldier-explorers active in the New World at the beginning of the 16th century. The first, born c. 1475, went in 1514 to the Isthmus of Panama with Pedro Arias de Avila, and in 1524 was sent to seize Nicaragua from its rightful discoverer, Gil González de Avila; after finding the towns of Granada and León and exploring Lake Nicaragua he defected to **Cortés**, and was executed by a rival in 1526. His namesake went to Cuba with Velázquez in 1511 and later commanded the expedition that coasted Yucatán and made the first recorded European contact with **Mayan** civilization; he died in 1517.

HEROD ANTIPAS (21 BC–AD 39) Tetrarch of Galilee during the lifetime of **Jesus**. The son of Herod the Great, he inherited part of his father's kingdom under the Roman suzerainty, c. 4 BC. He was goaded into beheading John the Baptist, but later refused to pass judgement on Jesus himself.

HERODOTUS (c. 484–c. 420 BC) Greek writer, known as "the father of history". He travelled widely in Asia, Egypt and eastern Europe; his *Histories*, a history of the Greco-Persian wars and the events preceding them, is one of the world's first major prose works, incorporating many vivid and, to contemporaries, almost incredible travellers' tales; modern research has sometimes shown even the wildest of them to contain an element of truth.

HIDEYOSHI see **Toyotomi**

HIMMLER, HEINRICH (1900–45) Head of the SS and responsible for the concentration camps during Hitler's Nazi regime (1933–45). As a young man, Himmler joined a nationalist paramilitary organization, participated in the "Beer Hall Putsch" in 1923, and was acting head of propaganda for the National Socialist German Worker's Party (NSDAP) in 1925. He rose from head of the Bavarian political police in 1933 to become head of the entire police and security apparatus of the Third Reich in 1936. He set up the first official concentration camp at Dachau in 1933 for political enemies, and in 1936 established a nationwide network of camps for political dissidents and so-called "asocials". In 1941 he authorized an additional system of extermination camps for the genocide of Europe's Jews, which he masterminded for the next three years. By the end of World War II, more than 6 million Jews and 5 million others had been exterminated in the "Final Solution". As the war came to an end, Himmler tried to negotiate an amnesty with the western powers for himself and top Nazi officials, by offering in return to release thousands of inmates from concentration camps. Hitler discovered the plan and aborted it. Himmler was caught by the British in 1945, but committed suicide by swallowing a cyanide capsule.

HINDENBURG, PAUL VON (1847–1934) German soldier, president of Germany 1925–34. Recalled from retirement in 1914 to take command in east Prussia after the Russian invasion, he won the victory of Tannenberg, and the first and second battles of the Masurian Lakes (1914–15). Appointed a field-marshal and supreme commander of all German armies, 1916, he became virtual dictator of German domestic policy, too, until the armistice. As President he was persuaded to appoint **Hitler** as Chancellor in 1933.

HINDENBURG LINE Fortified line on the Western Front in the First World War, taken up by German armies following the battle of the Somme in 1916. A formidable defence system, it was eventually pierced in September 1918 by the British and French forces.

HINDUISM Predominant religion of India; all-embracing in its forms, capable of including eternal observances and their rejection, animal sacrifice and refusal to take any form of life, extreme polytheism and high monotheism.

HIPPOCRATES (c. 460–c. 377 BC) Ancient Greek physician, traditionally regarded in the West as the father of medicine. He believed in the wholeness of the body as an organism, in the close observation and recording of case-histories, and in the importance of diet and climate. The works making up the Hippocratic Collection, forming the library of the medical school at Cos, where he taught, reflect the continuing effects of his work. The Hippocratic Oath is still used as a guide to conduct by the medical profession.

HIPPODAMUS OF MILETUS Ancient Greek architect who flourished in the 5th century BC. He is best known for the grid system of street planning, developed for the Athenian port of Piraeus, the pan-Hellenic settlement of Thurii and perhaps the new city of Rhodes.

HIROHITO (1901–89) Emperor of Japan, supposedly the 124th direct descendant of Jimmu, Japan's legendary first ruler. An authority on marine biology, and the first Japanese crown prince to travel abroad (1921), he succeeded his father in 1926. He tried, ineffectually, to avert war with the USA, and broke political deadlock in 1945 to sue for peace. He ended centuries of public imperial silence to broadcast Japan's announcement of surrender on 15 August 1945. He became a constitutional monarch, with greatly restricted powers and was succeeded, in 1989, by his son, Akihito.

HITLER, ADOLF (1889–1945) German dictator. Born in Austria, he moved to Munich in 1913, served in the German army, joined the National Socialist German Workers' Party and re-organized it as a quasi-military force. He tried unsuccessfully to seize power in Bavaria, 1923; wrote *Mein Kampf (My Struggle)* in prison, elaborating his theories of Jewish conspiracy and **Aryan** superiority. Appointed chancellor, 1933; in 1936 he remilitarized the Rhineland, in 1939 invaded Austria and Czechoslovakia and in 1939 Poland. His sweeping initial successes in the Second World War were followed by defeats in Russia and north Africa, 1942–3. He survived an assassination plot in 1944, but committed suicide in 1945 as the Russians entered Berlin.

HITTITES A people speaking an Indo-European language who occupied central Anatolia by the beginning of the 2nd millennium BC, quickly absorbing the older population. The Old Hittite kingdom, c. 1750–1500 BC, later expanded into the Hittite empire, c. 1500–1190, which at its greatest extent controlled all Syria and briefly much of northern Mesopotamia. After the collapse of the empire, various neo-Hittite kingdoms survived in the region for a further 500 years.

HOABINHIAN see **Bacsonian**

HOCHE, LOUIS-LAZARE (1768–97) French revolutionary general. He enlisted in the French Guards, 1784, was appointed corporal, 1789, as commander of the army of the Moselle (1793) he drove Austro-Prussian forces from Alsace. He suppressed the **Vendée** counter-revolution, 1794–6. He commanded an expedition to Ireland to help rebels against England which failed due to storms at sea.

HO CHIEN (1887–1956) Warlord who controlled Hunan province, 1923–37. He played a major role in the campaigns against the Communists, 1930–5, supported by Kwangsi and Kwangtung. On the outbreak of the Japanese war he became a minister in the National government. He resigned in 1945.

HO CHI MINH (1890–1969) President of the Democratic Republic of Vietnam (North Vietnam), 1945–69. He was a founding member of the French Communist Party, 1920, and founded the Indo-Chinese Communist Party, 1930. He escaped to Moscow, 1932, but returned to Vietnam, 1940. Imprisoned in China, 1942–3, he emerged as leader of the **Viet Minh** guerrillas; he declared Vietnam independent, 1945, and played a dominant role in both the first and the second Indo-China wars, 1946–52, and from 1959 until his death.

HOHENSTAUFEN German royal dynasty, ruling Germany and the **Holy Roman Empire**, 1138–1254, and Sicily, 1194–1268. It restored German power and prestige after the setbacks during the Investiture Contest (see **Lay Investiture**); it became increasingly embroiled with the papacy for control of Italy following the marriage of **Henry VI** to the Sicilian heiress in 1186. The extirpation of the dynasty by the French allies (**Charles of Anjou**) of Pope **Clement IV** in 1268 continued a period of disunity and territorial fragmentation in Germany and Italy. The Hohenstaufen period marked the high point of German courtly culture, exemplified by the works of Wolfram von Eschenbach, **Gottfried von Strassburg** and Walther von der Vogelweide.

HOHENZOLLERN German dynastic family, ruling in Brandenburg-Prussia, 1415–1918, and as German emperors 1871–1918. They were originally descended from Burchard I, Count of Zollern, in Swabia (d.1061); a subsidiary branch, the Hoh-enzollern-Sigmaringens, held the throne of Romania from 1866 to 1947.

HOLKARS Ruling dynasty of Indore, southern India, founded by Malhar Rao Holkar, a Maratha soldier who, at his death in 1766, had become virtual king in the region of Malwa. Power crystallized during the long reign of his son's widow, Ahalyabai (1767–95); family forces were defeated by the British in 1804, and princely power ended with Indian independence in 1947.

HOLY ROMAN EMPIRE Name first bestowed in 1254 to denote the European lands ruled by successive dynasties of German kings. It was used retro-spectively to include the empire of **Charlemagne**, on whom Pope Leo III conferred the title of Roman Emperor in 800; and also applied to the domains held by **Otto II** (d.983) and his successors. At its fullest extent the empire included modern Germany, Austria, Bohemia, Moravia, Switzerland, eastern France, the Netherlands and much of Italy. The title lapsed with the renunciation of imperial dignity by Francis II in 1806.

HOMER Putative author of the two great Greek national epic poems, *The Iliad* (or *The Wrath of Achilles*) and *The Odyssey*. The poems stand in a bardic tradition, using verse formulas, but each suggests composition by a single mind. Homer may have composed *The Iliad* in the 8th century BC in the eastern Aegean; the date of *The Odyssey* is less certain.

HOMFRAY family British industrialists. They built an ironworks at Penydarren, near Merthyr Tydfil, Wales, and built the first true railway from there to the sea; in 1804 Richard Trevithick made the first journey in a locomotive engine there, pulling truckloads of iron.

HOMININ Man, considered from the point of view of zoology; a member of the mammalian family **Hominidae**, which includes only one living species, **Homo sapiens**.

HOMINOID Animal resembling man, or with the form of a man.

HOMO SAPIENS Biological genus and species incorporating all modern human beings. It is characterized by a two-legged stance, high forehead, small teeth and jaw, and large cranial capacity; it dates back some 350,000 years.

HONECKER, ERICH (1912–94) German communist politician, in power 1973–89, elected chair of the council of state (head of state) 1976. He governed in an outwardly austere and efficient manner and, while favouring East-West detente, was a loyal ally of the USSR. He was replaced as head of state with the breaching of the Berlin Wall in 1989. He died in Moscow.

HONORIUS (384–423) Roman emperor, son of **Theodosius I**. He succeeded to the western half of the empire when it was divided after his father's death in 395.

HOOVER, HERBERT CLARK (1874–1964) 31st president of the USA. He organized American relief to Europe after the First World War; he was elected Republican president, 1929–33, but bitterly criticized for his failure to combat the depression. He opposed **Roosevelt's New Deal**; he sat as Chairman of the Hoover Commission, 1947–9 and 1953–5, on simplification of government administration.

HORROCKS, JOHN (1768–1804) Cotton manufacturer. In 1786 he erected a cotton mill at Preston, Lancashire. He was appointed by the **English East India Company** to be the sole supplier of cotton goods to India.

HOTTENTOTS see **Khoi**

HOUPHOUET-BOIGNY, FÉLIX (1905–93) President of the Ivory Coast. A planter and doctor, in 1945 he formed his own political party and was elected to represent the Ivory Coast in the French National Assembly, 1945–58. He entered the French Cabinet, 1956–9, working closely after 1958 with **General de Gaulle** to achieve peaceful decolonization. He became the first prime minister of the Ivory Coast in 1959, was elected its first president after independence in 1960, and was re-elected president in October 1990.

HOWE, WILLIAM (1729–1814) 5th Viscount Howe. British general who, after a distinguished career in the **Seven Years' War** (1756–63), commanded British forces during the American War of Independence (1775–8).

HOYSALAS Central Indian dynasty, ruling territory centred on Dorasamudra, near modern Mysore. It was founded by Vishnuvardhana in the first half of the 12th century, consolidated under his grandson, Ballala II, who won control of the southern Deccan, but overthrown in the 14th century by the Turkish sultans of Delhi.

HSIENPEI Group of tribes, probably of Turkic origin but according to some scholars of mixed Tungusic and Mongolian race. They first emerged as one of the Eastern Hue people in southern Manchuria, becoming vassals of the **Hsiungnu** after 206 BC. From the late 1st century AD they developed into a powerful tribal federation which dominated south Manchuria and Inner Mongolia. The final collapse of Chinese power in the early 4th century enabled them to invade north China repeatedly. Individual Hsienpei tribes established several short-lived dynasties during the 4th century, and from that time Hsienpei royal families ruled the dynasties Northern (Toba) Wei, Western Wei, Northern Chou, Eastern Wei and Northern Ch'i, which unified and controlled all of north China.

HSIUNGNU Chinese name for the vast alliance of nomad tribes that dominated much of central Asia from the late 3rd century BC to the 4th century

AD. They were first identified in the 5th century BC, when their constant raids prompted construction of the fortifications which later became the Great Wall of China. Their power was largely broken by the emperor **Wu-ti**; around 51 BC the tribes split into two great groups; the eastern horde, more or less submitting to Chinese control, and the western, which migrated to the steppes. Later, after the collapse of the **Han** dynasty, Hsiungnu generals, hired as mercenaries, founded the short-lived Earlier Chao and Later Chao dynasties in northern China, *c.* AD 316–30. No reference to them after the 5th century is extant; the theories linking then with the European **Huns** or the early Turkish empire of central Asia remain unsubstantiated.

HSÜAN-T'UNG (or Henry Pu-yi) (1906–67) Last emperor of China, succeeding at the age of three on the death of his uncle. He reigned under a regency for three years before being forced to abdicate in 1912 in response to the success of the 1911 revolution. He continued to live in the palace at Peking under the name of Henry Pu-yi until 1924, when he left secretly for a Japanese concession in Tientsin. He ruled as puppet emperor of Manchukuo, 1936–45, was tried as a war criminal in 1950 and pardoned in 1959, when he went to work as a gardener.

HSÜ HSIANG-CH'IEN (1902–91) Commander in Chinese Communist Army, a subordinate of **Chang Kuo-t'ao**, during the Long March, and commander of the Eighth Route Army troops in the early part of the Sino-Japanese War. He was a leading general in Shansi in the late 1940s during the civil war with the Nationalists, and a member of the Communist Party Central Committee in 1945. He re-emerged as a leading figure in the Cultural Revolution of 1966, and became a member of the CCP Politburo the following year.

HUARI Early Andean civilization (*c.* AD 600–1000), named after its most characteristic archaeological site, in the highlands of present-day Peru. Its distinctive motif, the "doorway god" with its rectangular face and rayed headdress, is also found among the vast ruins of Tiahuanaco, on the southern shore of Lake Titicaca, with which it appears to have been linked in its period of imperial expansion.

HUASCAR (d.1533) Son of **Huayna Capac**, on whose death (probably in 1525) he succeeded to the southern half of the Inca empire, based on Cuzco. He was soon involved in a succession war with his half-brother **Atahuallpa**, who had inherited the northern half of the empire and ruled from Quito. Huascar fled from Cuzco after a series of defeats, but he was captured and forced to watch his family and supporters being murdered. He was himself assassinated by Atahuallpa on the arrival of the Spanish invaders under **Pizarro**, for fear they would restore him to power.

HUAYNA CAPAC (d.c.1525) Inca emperor, young son of the principal wife (and sister) of the Inca **Topa**, whom he succeeded in 1493. He reigned most peacefully after an initial succession struggle. He conquered Chachapoyas, in northwest Peru, and later northern Ecuador, returning home on hearing that an epidemic (probably measles or smallpox, brought by Spanish settlers at La Plata) was sweeping his capital, Cuzco; he died after contracting the disease. (Scholars now suggest that his death may have occurred as late as 1530, but that the early date was given by the Cuzco Incas in an effort to "legitimize" **Huascar**'s rule.)

HUDSON, HENRY (c. 1550–1611) English seaman, after whom Hudson River, Hudson Strait and Hudson Bay are all named. He explored the islands north of Norway, 1607–8, in search of a Northeast Passage to Asia; in 1609, commissioned by the **Dutch East India Company** to find a Northwest Passage, he sailed up the Hudson river. In 1610, working again for the English, he passed through Hudson Strait and Hudson Bay, but died the following year after being abandoned by his mutinous crew.

HUDSON'S BAY COMPANY Incorporated in England, 1670, to seek a Northwest Passage to the Pacific, to occupy land around Hudson Bay and to engage in profitable activities. The company concentrated on fur-trading for two centuries; armed clashes with competitors led to a new charter, 1821. It lost its monopoly, 1869, as territories were transferred to the Canadian government but is still one of the world's major fur-dealing and general retailing organizations.

HUGUENOTS French followers of the Swiss religious reformer, **John Calvin**. Huguenot rivalry with the Catholics erupted in the French wars of religion, 1562–98; under the **Edict of Nantes**, 1598, the two creeds were able to co-exist, despite another religious war 1621–9, but when this edict was revoked by **Louis XIV** in 1685 many Huguenots preferred to flee the country; they settled, to the great benefit of the host states, in Great Britain, the United Provinces, north Germany and in those colonies overseas in which Protestants were tolerated.

HÜLEGU (c. 1217–65) Mongol leader, grandson of **Genghis Khan** and younger brother of **Möngke**, who led the epic campaign from east Asia to capture Baghdad in 1258; on the disruption of the Mongol empire after the death of Möngke, he remained to found the Il-Khan state, dominating Persia and the Middle East.

HUMILIATI A society of penitents in 12th-century Europe who followed a life of poverty and evangelism. This brought them into conflict with the hierarchy of the Church, and they were condemned as heretics by Pope Lucius III in 1184. They were in some respects similar to the **Cathars**, but unlike the latter did not originally hold doctrines at variance with the Catholic faith. They were finally suppressed in the late 16th century.

HUNDRED DAYS, WAR OF Napoleon's attempt, after being defeated and exiled in 1814, to re-establish his rule in France. It began with his return to Paris from Elba in 1815 and ended with his defeat by Great Britain and Prussia at the battle of Waterloo.

HUNDRED YEARS' WAR Prolonged struggle of England and France, beginning in 1337 and ending in 1453. English forces twice came close to gaining control of France: once under **Edward III** (victories at Crécy, 1346, and Poitiers, 1356; treaty of Brétigny, 1360), and again under **Henry V** (victory at Agincourt, 1415; Henry was recognized as heir to the French throne, 1420). England's resources were insufficient to consolidate these gains, however, and by 1453 the only remaining English possession in France was Calais, which was lost in 1558.

HUNS Mounted nomad archers who invaded southeast Europe across the Volga *c.* 370, and dominated lands north of the Roman frontier until the defeat of their most famous leader, **Attila**, in Gaul at the battle of the Catalaunian Fields in 451. Their empire broke up and disappeared from history, *c.* 455. The Huna who attacked Iran and India in the 5th and 6th centuries, and the **Hsiungnu** of central Asia, may have been related to the Huns, but this is unproven.

HUNTSMAN, BENJAMIN (1704–76) English steelmaker who invented the crucible process for making high-quality cast steel, *c.* 1750.

HURRIANS Near Eastern people, possibly from the region of Armenia, who briefly controlled most of northern Syria and northern Iraq in the 15th century BC. The principal Hurrian political unit was the kingdom called Mitanni, centred on the Khabur.

HUS, JAN (1372/3–1415) Czech religious reformer, born in Husinec, Bohemia. In 1409 he was appointed rector of the University of Prague; he was fatally involved in the struggles of the **Great Schism**; tricked by a promise of safe conduct into attending the Council of Constance, he was tried and burned for heresy. His death sparked off a Czech national revolt against the Catholic Church and its German supporters, particularly the Emperor Sigismund. *See also* **Hussites.**

HUSSEIN (d.1931) Hashemite sharif of the Hejaz, western Arabia. In 1915 he agreed to join the war of Great Britain against his Ottoman overlords. He proclaimed himself king of the Arabs in 1916 and began the war, aided by T.E. Lawrence, a British agent (Lawrence of Arabia), but his title was challenged by **Ibn Saud**, sultan of Nejd, after 1919. Hussein was forced to abdicate in 1924 and by 1926 Ibn Saud had conquered all of Arabia, although Hussein's sons ruled in Iraq and Transjordan.

HUSSEIN-McMAHON CORRESPONDENCE Letters exchanged in 1915 between Sir Henry McMahon, British High Commissioner in Cairo, and Hussein, sharif of Mecca and later king of Hejaz, setting out the area and terms in which Great Britain would recognize Arab independence after the First World War. Unpublished for decades, they remained a potent source of controversy and tension in the Middle East, especially in their ambiguous references to the future of Palestine.

HUSSEIN, SADDAM (1937–2006) Iraqi political leader. Active in the Ba'ath Socialist party since 1957, he brought his party to power through a bloodless *coup d'état* (1968). He served as deputy chairman of the Revolutionary Command Council (1969–79) and as President of Iraq (1979–2003). He declared war on Iran (1980) but the war ended in stalemate in 1988. After invading Kuwait in 1990, he faced war with the US-led forces in 1991. Despite overwhelming defeat, he maintained himself in power. Defeated in 1991, Iraq was subjected to harsh sanctions and a programme of forced disarmament. Suspicious that he was secretly arming with dangerous new weapons a combined US-UK force attacked Iraq in 2003 and overthrew the regime. Saddam was captured early in 2004, put on trial on human rights charges and executed 2006.

HUSSITES Followers of **Jan Hus**. They broke with the papacy, used the Czech liturgy, and made many converts in Bohemia. From 1420 they repelled numerous attacks by Catholic neighbours, retaining freedom of worship until the battle of the White Mountain in 1620 restored Roman Catholicism and forced the Hussites (and others) into exile.

HYKSOS Asiatic invaders, sometimes known as the Shepherd Kings, who overran northern Egypt *c.* 1648 BC, and established the 15th Dynasty. Their capital, Avaris, was located in the eastern delta of the Nile. They were said to have introduced the horse and chariot into Egypt. Their rule collapsed *c.* 1540 BC.

HYWEL DDA (d.950) Also known as Hywel the Good, and to chroniclers as "King of all Wales". On the death of his father, Cadell, *c.* 910, he succeeded as joint ruler of Seisyllwg (roughly, modern Cardiganshire and the Towy valley) and from 920 ruled alone following the death of his brother Clydog; he acquired Dyfed (southwest Wales) and Gwynedd (northwest Wales) by marriage and inheritance. His reign was noted for its peacefulness – internally and with England. Hywel's name is associated with the earliest written Welsh law-code.

I

IBALPIEL II An Amorite dynast, King of Eshnunna (modern Tell Asmar) in the Diyala region of ancient Iraq. He reigned from 1725 to 1696 BC, when he was overthrown by **Hammurabi** of Babylon.

IBO (now Igbo) People (and language) of southeast Nigeria; they were associated with the attempt to secede from Nigeria and set up the state of Biafra in the 1960s.

IBN BATTUTA (1304–c. 1368) A Moroccan and possibly the greatest of all travellers. On a pilgrimage to Mecca in 1325 he conceived an ambition to travel "through the Earth". Though he rarely ventured beyond the Muslim world he nonetheless reached the Niger in west Africa and Kilwa in east Africa. His Asian travels took him across Transoxi-ana, Afghanistan, India, the Maldives, Ceylon and Sumatra to China. He left a reputation as the most-travelled man on earth. Though received with stupefaction in Fez, his accounts of his journeys are almost entirely convincing.

IBN SAUD (c. 1880–1953) Founder of Saudi Arabia; born at Riyadh, now the Saudi Arabian capital. A member of an exiled ruling family, he recaptured Riyadh in 1902 and began the conquest of central Arabia. He established close relations with Britain in the First World War, occupied Hejaz in 1926 and formally established the kingdom of Saudi Arabia in 1932. He signed the first oil-exploration treaty in 1933.

ICONOCLASM The policy of banning, and often destroying, religious images, officially imposed in 8th- and 9th-century Byzantium. Veneration of icons, previously encouraged, was first prohibited by **Leo III** in 730; the resulting persecutions reached their peak in 741–75. The policy was reversed, 787–814, but then reimposed until the death of Emperor Theophilus, 842; the final restoration of icon veneration, promulgated in 843, is still celebrated as the Feast of Orthodoxy in the Eastern Church.

ICTINUS Ancient Greek architect working in the 5th century BC. He was largely responsible for the Parthenon at Athens, the Temple of the Mysteries at Eleusis and the Temple of Apollo Epicurius at Bassae; he was joint author of a lost treatise.

IDRIS (1890–1983) Former king of Libya. Leader of the Sanusi Order, 1916; he was proclaimed king of Libya at independence in 1950. He was deposed in a coup by the army in 1969, fled the county for exile in Egypt and in 1971 was sentenced to death *in absentia.*

IDRISI, ABU ABD ALLAH MUHAMMAD AL- (1100–c. 1166) Medieval geographer. After travel in Spain and north Africa, he entered the service of **Roger II** of Sicily in about 1145; he became a leading mapmaker and scientific consultant to the court of Palermo. He constructed a silver planisphere showing the world, a 70-part world map and a great descriptive work completed in 1154, *The Pleasure Excursion of One who is Eager to Traverse the Regions of the World.*

IDRISIDS Islamic dynasty, ruling a kingdom occupying the northern part of what is now Morocco from 789 to 926. It was founded by Idris I, a descendant of the Prophet **Mohammed**'s son-in-law, **Ali**; after his death in 791 his son, Idris II, reigned until 828, when the kingdom split into a number of principalities. The Idrisids founded the important city of Fez.

IEYASU *see* **Tokugawa**

IGNATIUS OF LOYALA, ST (1491–1556) Founder of the order of Jesuits. A page and soldier of **Ferdinand of Aragon**, he made a barefoot pilgrimage to Jerusalem, 1523–4; studied at Alcalá, Salamanca and Paris, where in 1534 he planned a new religious order, the Society (or Company) of Jesus, devoted to converting the infidel and counteracting the Protestant Reformation. His Society was approved by the Pope in 1540, and he was appointed its first Superior, or general, in 1541. He was canonized in 1622.

IGOR SVYATOSLAVICH (1151–1202) Russian warrior who succeeded to the title of Prince of Novgorod-Seversk in 1178, and that of Prince of Chernigov in 1198. He led an ambitious but unsuccessful campaign against the Kuman or **Polovtsy** nomads, ending in total defeat in 1185; escaping from captivity in 1186, he returned to resume his role.

ILIAD Ancient Greek epic poem in 24 books, better called *The Wrath of Achilles*, describing an episode in the Trojan War; attributed to **Homer**.

ILKHANIDS Mongol rulers of Iran, 1256–1353. The dynasty was founded by **Hülegü** after he seized Persia with an army of 13,000 men; captured Baghdad by 1258. They lost contact with the Chinese Mongols after the conversion of **Mahmud of Ghazni** (1255–1304) to Sunni Islam; the dynasty was later weakened by divisions between **Sunni** and **Shi'as**.

ILTUTMISH Founder of the Delhi sultanate, son-in-law successor of **Qutbuddin Aibak** as ruler of the Muslim conquests in India. During his reign, 1211–36, Delhi established itself as the largest, strongest state in northern India.

IMHOTEP Chief minister of **Zoser**, second king of Egypt's 3rd Dynasty (27th century BC); later worshipped as the god of medicine in Egypt. He was architect of the world's oldest hewn-stone monument, the step pyramid at Saqqara, the necropolis of Memphis.

IMPERIALISM The policy of extending the power and rule of a government beyond its own borders. A country may attempt to dominate others by direct rule or by less obvious means such as control of markets for goods or raw materials. Imperialism has been a constant feature of human history.

INCA Name for the Indian group which dominated the central Andes region in the 15th and 16th centuries; also for their emperor and any member of the royal dynasty. From the capital, Cuzco in Peru, they controlled in the 16th century a region extending from Ecuador to north Chile; although lacking either knowledge of the wheel or any form of writing, their society reached a high level of civilization before being destroyed by the Spaniards in 1533. Occasional Inca uprisings occurred until the 19th century.

INDULF King of Alba (Scotland), 954–62. He captured Edinburgh from the Angles of Northumbria before being killed in battle by the Danes.

INNOCENT III (1160–1216) Pope, 1198–1216. In conflicts with the empire, France and England he asserted superiority of spiritual over temporal power as **Gregory VII**, **Urban II** and **Alexander III** had done, but more widely and more successfully. With him the medieval papacy reached its highest points of influence over European life. He claimed to dispose of the imperial crown, and excommunicated **King John** of England. His methods were mainly but not entirely political; he reconciled some heretics as well as launching the Albigensian Crusade against them, showed favour to St Francis at the beginning of his mission, and in the Fourth **Lateran Council** (1215) imposed spiritual regulations on the whole Church. The Fourth **Crusade** was the major blemish on his career as Pope.

INNOCENT IV (c. 1190–1254) Pope, 1243–54. Continued the struggle of previous popes to establish the superiority of spiritual over temporal power in bitter conflicts with the Emperor **Frederick II.**

INÖNÜ, ISMET (1884–1973) Turkish soldier and statesman, succeeding **Atatürk** as president of the Turkish Republic (1938–50). He commanded the Fourth Army in Syria, 1916, became under-secretary for war in 1918, joined the independence movement and in 1921 led the Turks to victory in the two battles of Inönü (1921), from which he took his name. He successfully negotiated the **Treaty of Lausanne** and was the first Republican prime minister, 1923–38. He advocated one-party rule, 1939–46, but later, in opposition, ardently advocated democratic reform.

INQUISITION Established by Pope Gregory IX in 1233 as a supreme Church court to repress heresy following the Albigensian Crusade, it brought about a considerable reduction in the number of heretics. Torture was permitted in 1252, though used less in the 13th century than later. The Inquisition was reorganized as the "Sacred Congregation of the Roman and Universal Inquisition or Holy Office" in 1542, again as the "Congregation of the Holy Office" in 1908, and as the "Sacred Congregation for the Doctrine of the Faith', 1965. The Spanish Inquisition was established in 1478, abolished in 1820, and played an important part in imposing religious and civil obedience.

INUIT People of the western Arctic region, thinly spread in small settlements across the northern coasts of North America, from Alaska to Greenland. Of closely related physical type, language and culture, these groups, totalling some 50,000 people, share a common adaptation to the harsh living and hunting conditions of the Arctic tundra.

INVESTITURE CONTEST see **Lay Investiture**

IRAQ PETROLEUM COMPANY International consortium, set up to exploit oil concessions in Iraq under an agreement signed in 1925. In 1952 a 50-50 share agreement was reached with the government; in 1961, 99 per cent of the group's undeveloped concessions were nationalized, including the rich North Rumaila field. Under the arrangement finally agreed in 1975, IPC paid £141 million in a tax settlement, receiving 15 million tons of crude oil and the right to continue operating in South Rumaila.

IRON AGE The final period among archaeological periods of the prehistoric and early historic Old World, it takes in the barbarian tribes which were contemporaries of the classical civilizations of the Mediterranean, and much of Africa down to colonial times. Iron began increasingly to replace bronze after 100 BC, and can still be considered one of the world's most important materials.

IROQUOIS American Indians living round the lower Great Lakes. The Iroquois League, founded between 1570 and 1600, united five tribes – the Mohawk, Oneida, Onondaga, Cayuga and Seneca – as "the People of the Long House", playing a key part in early American history. After defeating their native enemies, they turned on the French; when joined by the Tuscarora in 1722, they became the "Six Nations"; split during the American revolution, the League disbanded under the Second Treaty of Fort Stanwix, 1784.

IQTA' Fief, government revenues granted to soldiers in lieu of salary.

ISAIAH Old Testament prophet, son of Amoz, who stood alongside the kings of Judah in the last part of the 8th century BC. The book that bears his name falls into two parts; there is glorious poetry and profound insight in all, and many passages are taken by Christians to presage the coming of Christ.

ISAURIAN emperors Dynasty of Byzantine (East Roman) emperors, 717–802.

ISLAMIC STATE A militant Sunni Islamist movement based in Syria and Iraq, rooted originally in the Al-Qaeda organization in the region following the overthrow of Saddam Hussein. In 2013, the movement declared the founding of the Islamic State of Syria and Iraq (ISIS), but changed the name to Islamic State in 2014, when it declared the movement at the centre of a world caliphate and embarked on a war of conquest across the region.

ISMAIL (1830–95) Khedive, or viceroy, of Egypt under Ottoman sovereignty, grandson of **Mo-hammed Ali**. He studied in Paris, and became viceroy in 1863; in 1867 he persuaded the Ottoman sultan to grant him the title of Khedive. He opened the Suez Canal in 1869 and expanded Egyptian rule in the Sudan. He carried further the process of economic and educational change begun by Mohammed Ali, but in doing so incurred a large foreign debt (£100 million by 1876) which ultimately led to British occupation in 1882. He was deposed in 1879 by the Ottoman sultan, in favour of his son.

ISMAIL I (c. 1487–1524) Shah of Persia (1501–24) and founder of the **Safavid** dynasty. In 1501 he established what some historians have regarded as the first truly Iranian dynasty since the Arab conquests, although the dynasty was Turkish-speaking and religious affiliation to **Shi'a** Islam provided the prime focus of loyalty to it. The strength of the state, resting on the Kizilbash (Turcoman tribes owing allegiance to the shah) enabled it to hold off serious threats from the Ottomans and the **Uzbeks** in 1510, and to stabilize its power on the Iranian plateau.

ISMAILIS Branch of the **Shi'a** division of Islam, which split from other branches over the question of succession to the sixth imam, and gradually developed theological doctrines of its own. Some Ismaili groups were politically active from the 9th to the 13th centuries establishing local rule in Bahrain and eastern Arabia then, on a larger scale, in Tunisia and Egypt (**Fatimid** caliphate); from there a further group, the "new preaching" led by Hasan-i Sabbah, established itself in northern Persia (see **Assassins**). Ismailis of different groups still exist in Syria, Iran, Yemen, Pakistan and India, where the Aga Khan is head of the most important group.

ISMET see **Inönü**

ISOCRATES (436–338 BC) Athenian orator and pamphleteer. Too nervous to speak, he nevertheless composed eloquently for others. He preached in favour of enlightened monarchy and Greek unity in face of the threat from Persia.

ITURBIDE, AUGUSTIN (1783–1824) First emperor of independent Mexico. An officer in the Spanish colonial army, 1797; in 1810 he rejected an invitation to join anti-Spanish revolutionaries, and successfully defended Valladolid for the royalists. After 1820, he led a conservative independence movement. He crowned himself Emperor Agustín I in 1822, but in 1823 abdicated in the face of mounting opposition. Returning from Europe, unaware of the death sentence passed in his absence, he was captured and shot.

IVAN III (1440–1505) Grand Duke of Moscow, succeeding his father, Vasily II, in 1462. By conquering Novgorod in 1478 he made Moscow supreme among the principalities of west Russia, known henceforth as Muscovy. He declared Muscovite independence of the Mongols and stopped tribute payments to the **Golden Horde**.

IVAN IV VASILIEVICH "THE TERRIBLE" (1530–84) Grand Duke of Moscow, 1533–84, and from 1547 Tsar of Russia. he conquered Kazan in 1552, Astrakhan in 1554, destroyed the free city of Novgorod in 1570, and annexed much of Siberia, to create a unified Russian state. Notoriously cruel, he killed his elder son in anger in 1581. His reign of terror was renowned for the establishment of the **oprichnina**, the forerunner of the political police.

JACKSON, ANDREW (1767–1845) Seventh president of the USA, 1829–37. A lawyer, planter and general, he defeated the British attack at New Orleans in 1815. He was elected as the champion of individual freedom and the common man in 1828. In 1832 he vetoed a bill for establishing a national bank, but otherwise supported strong federal government. He is credited – unjustly – with the introduction of the "spoils system", the dispensing of official jobs as rewards for political support, into American public life.

JACKSON, THOMAS JONATHAN "STONEWALL" (1824–63) Confederate general in the American Civil War, best known for his mobile tactics in the Virginia theatre, 1861–3.

JACOBINS Members of a French revolutionary club, founded in May 1789 among the deputies at Versailles. It was named from the former Dominican monastery where early meetings were held. Under the leadership of **Robespierre** the group became increasingly extreme, overthrowing the moderate **Girondins** in 1793 and instituting the Terror. The movement was eliminated after the *coup d'état* of July 1974.

JACQUARD, JOSEPH-MARIE (1752–1834) French textile-machinery inventor. He started work on the Jacquard loom in 1790, broke off to fight in the French revolution, and completed his designs in 1801. The machine, working on a punch-card system, was capable of duplicating all traditional weaving motions: it replaced all previous methods of figured silk-weaving. In 1806 his invention was declared public property, winning him a pension and a royalty on all sales. At first his looms were burned and he himself attacked by the handweavers of Lyons, fearing loss of employment, but by 1811, 11,000 looms were installed in France.

JACQUERIE Popular uprising in northeast France in 1358, named from the contemporary nobles' habit of referring to all members of the lower classes as "Jacques". Unrest began near Compiègne and quickly spread; peasant armies destroyed numerous castles and killed their inmates. Under their leader, Guillaume Cale (or Carle), the peasants joined forces with the Parisian rebels under **Étienne Marcel**. Cale's forces were crushingly defeated at Clermont-en-Beauvaisis on 10 June, and a general massacre followed.

JADWIGA (1371–99) Queen of Poland in her own right. Her marriage to **Władysław II Jagiełło** linked the thrones of Poland and Lithuania (1386).

JAGIEŁŁO, GRAND DUKE OF LITHUANIA see **Władysław II Jagiełło**

JAGIELLONIAN dynasty East European ruling family, prominent from the 14th to the 16th century. Founded by Jagiełło, Grand Duke of Lithuania, grandson of **Gedymin**, who married Queen **Jadwiga** of Poland in 1386, thus uniting the two crowns. It later also ruled Bohemia and Hungary.

JAINISM Early Indian religion, emphasizing nonviolence, frugality, and the purification of the soul; it regards the existence of God as irrelevant. Shaped and organized in the 6th century BC by the prophet Mahavira, its basic doctrines, at first transmitted orally, were finally codified in the 5th century AD. Much practised among merchants, traders and money lenders, it is followed today by several million people in western and northern India and around Mysore.

JAMES I OF ARAGON (1208–76) Known as "the Conqueror". Born in France, he was acknowledged as king of Aragon and Catalonia in 1214, taking full power in 1227. He conquered the Balearic Islands, and in 1233 began a successful campaign to recover Valencia from the Moors. He renounced his French territories in 1258. He formulated an important code of maritime law, and established the Cortes as a parliamentary assembly.

JAMES VI and I (1566–1625) King of Scotland, Ireland and England. The son of Mary Queen of Scots, he succeeded to the throne of Scotland, as James VI, on his mother's enforced abdication in 1567, and to that of England and Ireland, as James I, in 1603 on the death of **Elizabeth I.** In Scotland he created a strong government for the first time, but in England his absolutist policies, extravagant court spending and High Church and pro-Spanish attitudes made him unpopular.

JAMESON RAID Abortive attack launched from Bechuanaland into the South African Republic (Transvaal) in 1895–6, led by Dr (later Sir) Leander Starr Jameson, a colleague of **Cecil Rhodes**. It was intended to overthrow the Afrikaner government of Paul Kruger (1825–1904), but it resulted in the resignation of Rhodes, the worsening of Anglo-Boer relations and Jameson's imprisonment. Jameson, however, returned to public life as Prime Minister of Cape Colony 1904–8.

JANISSARIES "New Army", backbone of the Ottoman army, originally slave soldiers recruited from conquered peoples.

JARUZELSKI, WOJCIECH (1923–2014) Polish military and political leader. Working his way up the ranks of the military and the Communist Party he became chief of the general staff (1965–8), defence minister (1968–83), and party Politburo member (1970–90). As prime minister (1981–5) he proved unable either to reach a compromise agreement with the powerful independent union, Solidarity, or solve the country's economic problems. He became president in 1985 but resigned in 1990.

JASSY, TREATY OF Pact signed on 9 January 1792 to end the Russo-Ottoman war of 1787–92. It confirmed the **Treaty of Küçük Kaynarca** (or Kuchuk Kainarji), advanced the Russian frontier to the Dniester river, and reinforced Russian naval power in the Black Sea.

JATAKA A popular tale, relating one of the former lives of **Buddha**. The largest collection, the Sinhalese *Jatakatthavannana*, contains 547 stories; other versions are preserved in all branches of Buddhism, and some reappear in non-Buddhist literature, such as *Aesop's Fables*.

JEFFERSON, THOMAS (1743–1826) Third president of the USA, 1801–9. He trained as a lawyer; opposed British colonial rule; became a member of the committee which drafted the Declaration of Independence. He was minister to France, 1785–9; secretary of state in Washington's administration, 1790–3; vice-president, 1797–1801. As president he defended the rights of states and completed the **Louisiana Purchase**. In his old age he founded the University of Virginia.

JEM (d.1495) Claimant to the Ottoman sultanate, the younger son of **Mehmed II**. On his father's death in 1481 he attempted to seize the succession, but was pre-empted by his elder brother **Bayezid II**. He declared himself sultan but was defeated at Yenishehir (1481); after a further vain assault on Konya in 1482 he fled, first to Rhodes, then to France. In 1489 he came under the control of Pope Innocent VIII, who received a pension from Bayezid for keeping him safe. For 14 years he was the centre of European intrigues and schemes to invade the Ottoman realms. Charles VIII of France was making plans to use him in a **crusade** when he died.

JEROME, ST (c. 342–419/20) Born at Stridon, now in Yugoslavia, and educated at Tome, he was baptized *c.* 366. He retired for two years as a desert hermit in 375, was ordained priest in Syria in 378 and in 382 returned to Rome as secretary to Pope Damasus. In 385 he left for Palestine, and established a monastery at Bethlehem. He wrote voluminously, including his influential Latin translation of the Bible and numerous controversial polemics.

JESUIT Member of the Society of Jesus, a Roman Catholic order founded in 1534 by **St Ignatius of Loyola.** Organized to support the papacy, to fight heresy and to conduct overseas missionary activity, it quickly established a dominant influence in the Church. Though suppressed, 1773, by Pope Clement XIV and expelled by many European countries in the 18th century, it was restored by Pope Pius VII in 1814, and is now widely entrenched, particularly in education, with schools and universities all over the world.

JESUS OF NAZARETH (8/4 BC–c. AD 29) Jewish teacher whose preaching, personal example and sacrificial death provide the foundations for the religion of Christianity. The name is the Greek form of Joshua, Hebrew for "Jehovah is salvation"; to this is often added Christ, from the Greek *Christos*, the Hebrew *Messiah*, or "anointed one". Born near the end of the reign of Herod the Great, his ministry and Passion are recounted in the four Gospels of the New Testament. He was crucified, but is believed by his followers to have risen from the dead and ascended to heaven as the son of God.

JEW Originally a member of the tribe of Judah, the fourth son of Jacob, one of the 12 tribes of Israel which took possession of the Biblical Promised Land of Palestine; later a member of the kingdom of Judah, as opposed to the more northerly kingdom of Israel. After the Assyrian conquest in 721 BC, it applied to all surviving adherents of **Judaism**. In modern times it refers to an adherent of the Jewish religion whether by birth or by conversion, or to the child of a Jewish mother.

JEWISH UPRISING First of two major revolts, AD 66–73, against Roman rule in Judaea. The Romans were expelled from Jerusalem, 66, and the country rose in revolt; a revolutionary government was set up. Jewish forces finally succumbed to the Roman armies of **Vespasian** and **Titus**; Jerusalem was stormed, the temple burned and Jewish statehood ended in 70, and the Jews' last outpost, Masada, fell in 73. A second revolt, in 132–5, in the days of Emperor **Hadrian**, was suppressed with difficulty by the Romans after three years.

JINNAH, MOHAMMED ALI (1876–1948) Hailed as *Qaid-i-Azam*, "Great Leader", by Indian Muslims, he was founder and first Governor-General of Pakistan. Born in Karachi, he became a highly successful barrister, and in 1906 entered the Indian National Congress. He supported Hindu-Muslim unity until the rise of **Gandhi**. As president of the Muslim League, which he transformed into a mass movement, he adopted the demand for separate Muslim states in 1940, and headed the Muslims in their independence negotiations, 1946–7, securing the partition of India.

JOHANNES IV (d.1889) Christian emperor of Ethiopia. Originally a *ras*, or prince, of Tigre in northern Ethiopia, his strong, militaristic policies were largely thwarted by external threats – from Egypt, Italy and the Mahdist Sudan – and by the internal rivalry of Menelik, ruler of Shoa. Successful against Egypt, 1856–7, and Italy, 1887, Johannes was finally killed at the battle of Matama in a retaliatory invasion against the khalifa **Abd Allah** of the Sudan.

JOHN (1167–1216) King of England, youngest son of **Henry II**. He tried to seize the throne in 1193 while his brother Richard I was away on **crusade**. He succeeded in 1199 on Richard's death; lost Normandy and other English possessions to the French; was excommunicated, 1209, in a quarrel with Pope **Innocent III**. In 1215, after six years of strife with his barons, he was forced to accept **Magna Carta**, a charter confirming feudal rights and limited abuses of royal power. He died during renewed civil war.

JOHN II (1455–95) King of Portugal, nicknamed "the Perfect Prince"; succeeded his father, Alfonso V, in 1481. He broke the power of the richest family in Portugal, the Braganzas, and organized expeditions to explore west and central Africa.

JOHN II CASIMIR VASA (1609–72) King of Poland, son of **Sigismund III**. He fought with the **Habsburgs** in the Thirty Years' War and was imprisoned by the French 1638–40. Created a cardinal in 1647, he was elected King of Poland in 1648 on the death of his brother Władysław IV; he fled in the face of the Swedish invasion of 1655. He lost large areas of Polish territory to Sweden at the Peace of Oliva (1660) and to Russia at the Treaty of Andrusovo (1667). He abdicated in 1668, retiring to France as titular abbot of St-Germain-des-Prés.

JOHN II COMNENUS (1088–1143) Byzantine emperor, 1118–43. He fought unsuccessfully to end Venetian trading privileges, 1122; defeated **Pecheneg**, Hungarian, Serbian and Norman threats to the empire; attempted to confirm Byzantine suzerainty over the Norman kingdom of Antioch.

JOHN III (1537–92) King of Sweden, 1568–92. The elder son, by his second marriage, of **Gustavus I Vasa**, he overthrew his half- brother, **Eric XIV** in 1568 to seize the throne. A learned theologian, he hoped to reconcile the beliefs of **Lutheranism** and Roman Catholicism, and fought hard but unsuccessfully to impose his own liturgy, known as *The Red Book*, on the Protestant Swedes. He died bitter and frustrated, leaving an impoverished and divided kingdom to his son **Sigismund III**.

JOHN III SOBIESKI (1629–96) King of Poland and Grand Duke of Lithuania. In 1655–60 he fought in the Swedish war. He became commander-in-chief of the Polish army in 1668 and won victories over **Tatars**, Turks and **Cossacks**. He was elected king in 1674. In 1683 he led the army which drove the Turks back from the gates of Vienna, but failed in a long campaign (1684–91) to extend Poland's influence to the Black Sea.

JOHN XXII (1249–1334) Second Avignon Pope, elected 1316. A lawyer and administrator, he was accused of financial extortion and involvement in politics and lowering the reputation of the papacy as a religious force. He contested the election of Louis of Bavaria as German emperor (1324); declared a heretic by Louis and by the Spiritual Franciscans, whom he had criticized, in return he excommunicated and imprisoned Louis's candidate, the anti-Pope, Nicholas V (1328).

JOHN OF AUSTRIA (1545–78) Spanish military commander, often known as Don John, the illegitimate son of Emperor **Charles V**. He commanded a Christian fleet against the Turks in the Mediterranean, 1570–6, winning the Battle of Lepanto in 1571. He was commander of the Spanish army against the Dutch Revolt until his death.

JOHN CHRYSOSTOM, ST (c. 347–407) Father of the Christian Church. He became a hermit-monk, and was ordained priest in 386. A renowned preacher, he was appointed Archbishop of Constantinople in 398. In 403 he was indicted on 29 theological and political charges, was deposed and banished.

JOHNSON, LYNDON BAINES (1908–73) 36th president of the USA, 1963–9. Elected to Congress, 1937; senator for Texas, 1949; majority Senate leader, 1955–61. He was largely instrumental in passing civil rights bills of 1957 and 1960. He was elected vice-president in 1960, and succeeded after **John F. Kennedy**'s assassination in 1963. He inaugurated the Great Society programme, but came under increasing criticism over the US involvement in the Vietnam War; he refused renomination in 1968.

JOHNSTON, ALBERT SYDNEY (1803–62) Confederate general in the American Civil War. He was appointed a second-ranking Confederate commander in 1861, and in the following year was mortally wounded leading a surprise attack at the Battle of Shiloh.

JOINT-STOCK System of business finance in which the capital is contributed jointly by a number of individuals, who then become shareholders in the enterprise in proportion to their stake. It is usually, but not necessarily, combined with the principle of limited liability, under which the shareholders cannot be legally held responsible for any debts in excess of their share-capital.

JOLLIET, LOUIS (1645–1700) French Canadian explorer and cartographer. He led French parties of exploration from Lake Huron to Lake Erie, 1669, and down the Mississippi, 1672. This latter expedition reached the junction of the Mississippi and Arkansas rivers, but all Jolliet's maps and journals were lost when his canoe overturned; only the diary of the expedition's chaplain, **Jacques Marquette**, survived. He explored the coast of Labrador, 1694, and in 1697 was appointed Royal Hydrographer for New France.

JOSEPH II (1741–90) Holy Roman Emperor. Son of **Maria Theresa** and the Emperor Francis I, he succeeded to the empire in 1765, and to **Habsburg** lands in 1780. He continued his mother's attempts to reform and modernize the Habsburg dominions; introduced a new code of criminal law, 1787; suppressed the Catholic contemplative orders; agreed to the first partition of Poland. He was harassed by disaffection in Hungary and the Austrian Netherlands which compelled him to revoke some reforms.

JUAN-JUAN (also called Avars). Central Asian nomad people, controlling the northwest border areas of China from the early 5th to the mid-6th century and spreading to Europe, where they were finally destroyed by **Charlemagne** at the end of the 8th century.

JUÁREZ, BENITO (1806–72) National hero of Mexico. Of Indian parentage, he studied law and entered politics in 1831. Exiled to the USA in 1853, he returned in 1858 and fought in the civil war. After his election as Mexico's first Indian president in 1861, he instituted large-scale reforms, led opposition to the French-imposed **Emperor Maximilian** and defeated him in 1867. He was re-elected president in 1867 and again in 1871.

JUDAH Hebrew patriarch, fourth son of Jacob; also the Israelite tribe to which he was ancestor, and the kingdom established by this tribe in southern Palestine, *c.* 932–586 BC.

JUDAH HA-NASI (c. 135–c. 220) Jewish sage, known as "the rabbi" or "our saintly teacher", son of Simeon ben Gamaliel II. He succeeded his father as patriarch (head) of the Jewish community in Palestine. He codified the Jewish Oral Law (supplementing the Written Law, found in the Pentateuch of Moses), and set down his findings in the **Mishnah** (Teaching), which included regulations for all aspects of Jewish life.

JUDAH MACCABEE (d.160 BC) Third son of the priest Mattathias the Hasmonean, who initiated the revolt against the **Seleucid** king, Antiochus IV, and his decrees against **Judaism.** He succeeded his father and recaptured most of Jerusalem, re-dedicating the temple in 164 BC; he was killed in battle. Eventually, under his brother Simon, an independent Judaea emerged in 140 BC.

JUDAISM Religion of the Jewish people, distinguished by its pure monotheism, its ethical system and its ritual practices, based on the Pentateuch as interpreted by the rabbis of the Talmudic period (first five centuries AD) and their successors up to the present.

JULIAN (c. 331–63) Roman emperor, known as "the Apostate". He was educated as a Christian but reverted to paganism and tried to make the empire pagan again after his election as emperor in 360.

JULIUS CAESAR (c. 100–44 BC) Dictator of Rome. He was a patrician, general, statesman, orator, historian – one of the greatest leaders produced by the Roman republic. He wrote vivid accounts of his conquest of Gaul and his civil war with **Pompey**. He was murdered by Brutus and other conspirators.

JUPITER *see* **Zeus**

JUSTINIAN I (483–565) Byzantine emperor, born at Tauresium in the Balkans, Flavius Anicius Justinianus. He went to Constantinople, where his uncle was the Emperor Justin I, becoming co-emperor and then emperor in 527. He was most successful as a legal reformer (Codex Justinianus, 534) and a great builder (the Santa Sophia). His foreign policy, directed at defending and re-extending the imperial frontiers, achieved the reconquest of north Africa, Italy, southern Spain and western Yugoslavia, but the victories proved fragile.

JUTES Germanic people inhabiting Jutland; with the Angles and Saxons they invaded Britain in the 5th century AD, settling mainly in Kent, Hampshire and the Isle of Wight.

KABIR (1440–1518) Indian mystic, who attempted to combine what he regarded as the best elements in **Hinduism** and Islam, a project completed by his disciple **Nanak**. Kabir's thinking, much of it incorporated into the **Adi Granth**, the sacred book of the **Sikhs**, also contributed to the development of several Hindu cults, notably the Kabirpanth, with its total rejection of caste.

KACHINS Rice-farming tribesmen in northern Burma. They total some 500,000 people, with their own Kachin state, capital Myitkyina.

KADAR, JANOS (1912–89) Hungarian statesman. He became a member of the then illegal Communist Party in 1932, was elected to the Central Committee in 1942 and to the Politburo in 1945. Post-war minister of the interior; he was expelled in 1950. Rehabilitated in 1954 he joined Imre Nagy's government, forming a new administration after the suppression of the Hungarian revolution in 1956. Premier 1956–8 and 1961–5, and later first secretary of the Hungarian Socialist Workers Party.

KALMAR, UNION OF An agreement, concluded in 1397, under which Norway, Sweden and Denmark shared a single monarch. It broke down in 1523 with the rebellion of Sweden led by **Gustavus I Vasa.**

KALMYKS Buddhist Mongolian nomads, now mainly occupying the Kalmyk Autonomous Soviet Socialist Republic which is located in the steppes around the delta of the Volga.

KAMOSE Last king of Egypt's 17th Dynasty (c. 1648–1552 BC). He ruled the southern part of the country after the death of his father, Seqenenre II; he began the expulsion of the **Hyksos** from the northern part. He was succeeded by his brother, **Amose I**, founder of the 18th Dynasty.

KARA KHANIDS Turkic dynasty ruling the central Asian territory of Transoxania from 992 to 1211. In 992 they occupied Bukhara, capital of the then disintegrating Samanid dynasty. Split by internal rivalries, the land fell under the domination of the **Seljuks** in the late 11th century and then under the Kara Khitai. After a brief resurgence under Uthman (ruled 1204–11) the dynasty was extinguished in battle with the **Khwarizm**-shah.

KARA KOYUNLU (Black Sheep) Turcoman tribal confederation, ruling Azerbaijan and Iraq c. 1375–1467. They seized independent power in Tabriz under Kara Yusuf (ruled 1390–1400 and 1406–20); were routed by **Tamerlane** in 1400; captured Baghdad, 1410; annexed much of eastern Arabia and western Persia under Jihan Shah (ruled 1437–66). They were finally defeated in 1466 and absorbed by the rival **Ak Koyunlu** (ruler Uzun Hasan).

KARENS Agricultural tribesmen occupying a mountainous area in southeast Myanmar.

KASAVUBU, JOSEPH (c.1910–69) First president of independent Congo. He entered the Belgian Congo civil service, 1942; he became an early leader of the Congo independence movement, and in 1955 president of Abako (Alliance des Ba-Kongo). Joined with **Lumumba** in an uneasy alliance to share government power in 1960. He dismissed Lumumba in September 1960; he was deposed by **Mobutu** in 1965.

KAUNDA, KENNETH (1924–97) First president of independent Zambia. A school headmaster from 1944–7, he became in 1953 secretary-general of the North Rhodesia branch of the African National Congress, and in 1958 broke away to form the Zambia African National Congress. He became prime minister of Northern Rhodesia, and president of Zambia in 1964, but was defeated in the presidential election in October 1991.

KAZAKHS Traditionally pastoral nomads occupying a semi-arid steppe region in former Soviet central Asia to the east of the Ural river and extending into China. Their territory was incorporated into the Russian empire between 1830 and 1854. Russian colonization encroached on their best grazing lands before the revolution, and during the 1930s they were settled on collective farms. There are now over 5 million Kazakhs in the former USSR, most of whom live in Kazakhstan.

KEIR, JAMES (1735–1820) Scottish chemist. A retired army officer, he opened a glass factory in Stourbridge in 1775. Three years later he was placed in charge of the Boulton & Watt engineering works at Soho (Birmingham). In 1779 he patented an alloy capable of being forged or wrought when red hot or cold. In partnership with Alexander Blair he set up a chemical plant to make alkali products and soap.

KEMAL, MUSTAPHA *see* **Atatürk**

KENG, CHING-CHUNG (d.1682) Chinese general, son of Keng Chi-mao (d.1671) who became provincial governor of Fukien after 1660. On Chi-mao's death he succeeded him and in 1674 joined in the rebellion of the **Three Feudatories** to prevent losing control over the province. After initial success in southern Chekiang, he was attacked by superior forces and surrendered in 1676. For a time restored to his province, he was later taken to Peking and was executed.

KENNEDY, JOHN FITZGERALD (1917–63) 35th president of the USA, 1961–3. Member of the House of Representatives 1947–53, senator for Massachusetts 1953–61. He was the youngest candidate and the first Roman Catholic to be elected to the White House. He confronted the USSR in 1962 and successfully insisted that Russian missiles be withdrawn from Cuba. During his administration, the USA launched its first manned space flights. He was assassinated on 22 November 1963 in Dallas, Texas.

KENYATTA, JOMO (1891–1978) First president of independent Kenya. He returned from studying in London, 1946, and became president of the Kenya African Union the following year. Convicted and imprisoned for allegedly running the Mau Mau revolt in 1953, he was released in 1959 under restriction. He was leader of the Kenyan delegation to the London constitutional conference of 1962. He became prime minister, 1963–4, and president 1964.

KEPPEL, AUGUSTUS (1725–86) British admiral and politician. He served in the British navy from the age of ten. During the **Seven Years' War** (1756–63) he captured Belle Isle in 1761; he participated with **Pocock** and his brother Albemarle in the capture of Havana; he commanded the Channel fleet in 1776. He was court martialled after an indecisive battle with the French off Ushant, 1778, during the American War of Independence. A member of parliament from 1761, he became first lord of the Admiralty, 1782–3.

KETT'S REBELLION English uprising in protest against the enclosure of common land. It was named after Robert Kett, a Norfolk smallholder who led the revolt and stormed Norwich in 1549. He was soon defeated by government forces and executed.

KHALIFA *see* **Abd Allah**

KHANATE State, region or district governed by a khan; the title "khan" or "kaghan" was first assumed by the chiefs of a tribe – perhaps of Mongol speech and origin – inhabiting the pastures north of the Gobi desert in the 5th century AD, and known to the Chinese as **Juan-Juan.** The title was destined later to adorn half the thrones of Asia.

KHAZARS Turkic and Iranian tribes from the Caucasus, who founded a major trading empire in southern Russia in the 6th century AD. In 737 they moved the capital north to Itil, near the mouth of the Volga, adopted the Jewish religion, and started massive westward expansion. At their peak in the late 8th century they ruled a huge area, from Hungary and beyond Kiev almost to Moscow. Two Byzantine emperors, Justinian II (in 704) and Constantine V (in 732) took Khazar wives. The Khazars were crushed by **Svyatoslav** in 965.

KHITAN Nomadic tribes who, under the Liao dynasty (974–1125), controlled most of present-day Manchuria, Mongolia and part of northeast China. During the Five Dynasties, when China was weak and divided, they destroyed the Po-hai state in Manchuria and invaded northeast China before establishing a Chinese-style dynasty in 947 and adopting many Chinese administrative techniques. They carried on a border war with the Sung dynasty for control of northern China until 1004 when the Sung agreed to pay an annual tribute. The dynasty was destroyed in 1125 by one of its subsidiary peoples, the Jurchen (see **Ch'in**).

KHMER The predominant people of Cambodia; there are also communities of them in eastern Thailand and the Mekong Delta region of Vietnam. Their ancient civilization is exemplified by the remarkable, mainly Hindu temple complex of the Angkor area, dating from the 9th to the 13th century. After the 14th century most lowland Khmers became Theravada Buddhists; the conflicts with the neighbouring Thai and Vietnamese led to wars in the 17th and 19th centuries, and have re-emerged during and since the Cambodian war of 1970–5 (*see also* **Khmer Rouge**).

KHMER ROUGE Communist regime in Cambodia between 1975 and 1979. Originally organized to oppose the right-wing government of **Lon Nol**, President 1970–5. After defeating him and depopulating the capital, Phnom Penh, it subjected the country to a continuing reign of terror until its overthrow in 1979 by the Vietnamese. In 1991 the movement gained two of the 12 seats on the Cambodian Supreme National Council (composed of representatives of the country's warring factions).

KHOI (HOTTENTOTS) A nomadic pastoral people from Namibia, Botswana and the Northern Cape. Probably related to the **San**.

KHOISAN Relating to the Stone Age Bushmen (**San**) and Hottentot (**Khoi**) inhabitants of southern Africa.

KHOSRAU I ANOHSHIRVAN (d.579) Known as "the just", shahinshah of **Sasanid** Persia 531–79. He succeeded his father Kavadh, whom he helped to suppress the Mazdakite heretics. He also reorganized the bureaucracy and religious establishment, fought back against Byzantium, and restored the dynasty's flagging fortunes. He patronized both Greek and Sanskrit learning, and is reputed to have brought the game of chess to the West from India.

KHOSRAU II "THE VICTORIOUS" (d.628) (also known as Chosroes). The last great **Sasanid** king of Persia. He made a bid for power on the assassination of his father, Hormizd IV, in 590, but was expelled. He fled to Byzantine territory, and after being provided with forces by the Emperor Maurice (586–602) gained the Persian throne in the following year. When Maurice was murdered by the usurper Phocas in 601, Khosrau pledged vengeance against the whole Byzantine people, and invaded the empire with vast forces. Eventually he captured Antioch, Jerusalem and Alexandria, camping repeatedly along the Bosporus opposite Constantinople, but for lack of ships was never able to cross. **Heraclius**, a capable general, overthrew Phocas and, after numerous brilliant campaigns in Asia Minor, finally threatened the Sasanid capital at Ctesiphon. By this time both empires were exhausted, and social unrest at Ctesiphon forced Khosrau's son Shiruya (Siroes) to acquiesce in the killing of his father, and the ending of the war, in 628.

KHRUSHCHEV, NIKITA (1894–1971) Soviet statesman, first secretary of the Soviet Communist Party (1953–64) and prime minister (1958–64). A close associate of **Stalin**, he emerged as leader after his death. He promoted a policy of "peaceful coexistence" with other foreign powers, but the Cuban missile crisis with the USA (1962) and a dispute with China over borders and economic aid brought about his downfall in 1964.

KHWARIZM Ancient central Asian territory along the Amu Darya (River Oxus) in Turkestan; part of **Achaemenid** Persia, 6th to 4th centuries BC. Conquered for Islam in the 7th century AD; it was ruled by an independent dynasty, the Khwarizm-shahs, from the late 11th to the early 13th century; successively conquered by Mongols, Timurids and **Shaybanids**, in the early 16th century it became centre of the khanate of Khiva, under the **Uzbecks**. After repelling many invasions, it was absorbed as a Russian protectorate in 1873. As a result of the 1917 revolution it became the short-lived Khorezm Peoples' Soviet Rrepublic (1920–4). From 1924–91 the region was split into the Turkmen and Uzbeck SSRs, which became the independent states of Turkmenistan and Uzbeckistan respectively in 1991, following the collapse of the Soviet Union.

KIKUYU Bantu-speaking people of Kenya and their language; they were associated with the Mau Mau revolt against the British in the 1950s.

KILLIAN, ST (d.697) Irish bishop, known as the Apostle of Franconia; he was martyred at Würzburg.

KIM IL-SUNG (1912–94) North Korean leader. Involved in guerrilla resistance to Japanese occupation (1930s), he fought in World War II in the Soviet Red Army, returning to Korea in 1945. Head of the Democratic People's Republic of Korea (1948–94), he also became the nation's premier (1948–72) and president from 1972. His lengthy rule was characterized by rigid adherence to communist orthodoxy, economic backwardness and suppression of political opposition. He was succeeded by his son, Kim Jong Il.

KING, PHILIP PARKER (1791–1856) British naval officer, explorer of Australia and South America. He conducted surveys of Australia's tropical and western coasts from 1818 to 1822, and of the coasts of Peru, Chile and Patagonia from 1826 to 1830.

KING PHILIP'S WAR Savage conflict between Indians and English settlers in New England, 1675–6. King Philip (Indian name, Metacom) was chief of the Wampanoag tribe; during the fighting 600 white men died and entire Indian villages were destroyed.

KING WILLIAM'S WAR North American extension of the War of the Grand Alliance (1689–97) between William III of England, supported by the **League of Augsburg**, and **Louis XIV**'s France. The British captured parts of eastern Canada but failed to take Quebec; France penetrated into present-day New England but failed to seize Boston. the status quo was restored under the **Treaty of Ryswyck**. *See also* **Nine Years' War**.

KIPCHAKS *see* **Polovtsy**

KIPCHAK KHANATE *see* **Golden Horde**

KIRGHIZ Turkic-speaking people of central Asia. They were widely dispossessed of their traditional nomad grazing lands during Russia's 19th-century expansion. Their protest revolt in 1916 was bloodily suppressed, with more than a third of the Kirghiz survivors fleeing to China. The remainder now live mostly in Kirghizia.

KLONDIKE Tributary of the Yukon river, Canada. It became world-famous in 1896, when gold was found in Bonanza Creek; 30,000 prospectors swarmed in from all over the world. By 1911 the main deposits had been worked out and the population reduced to 1000; all mining ceased in 1966.

KNÄRED, PEACE OF Treaty concluding the Kalmar war of 1611–13, fought between Denmark and Sweden over the control of north Norway. It was provoked by Sweden's king, **Charles IX**, claiming sovereignty over the region. The Danes took the Swedish ports of Kalmar (1611) and Älvsborg's vital western harbour (1612). The ignominious peace, including the payment of a massive ransom for the return of Älvsborg was signed by Charles' son and successor, **Gustavus II Adolphus**.

KNIGHTS HOSPITALLERS OF ST JOHN Members of a military and religious order, the Hospital of St John of Jerusalem, founded in the 11th century to help poor and sick pilgrims to the Holy Land. The Order was recognized by the papacy in 1113; it became active in the **Crusades** but was driven from Palestine in 1291. It conquered Rhodes in 1310, and as the Knights of Rhodes grew in wealth and power until expelled by the Turks in 1522. The Order was moved by **Charles V** to Tripoli (to 1551), and thereafter to Malta until it was deposed by **Napoleon** in 1798, after which it took refuge in Russia. Reformed in 1879 as the charitable order of St John, its English branch is now widely known for its ambulance and first aid work.

KOHL, HELMUT (1930–) German statesman. He joined the Christian Democratic Union in his youth, becoming the party's deputy chairman in 1969. He was the party's candidate for the chancellorship in 1976 but was defeated. The collapse of Schmidt's centre-left coalition in 1982 enabled Kohl to recover and he led the CDU to victory in the elections which followed. As chancellor, Kohl adopted a cautious economic policy and reduced government spending. His foreign policy involved support for closer European integration. The CDU's disappointing showing in the 1987 elections forced him to rely increasingly on coalition partners. After the collapse of the **Berlin Wall** in November 1989, Kohl was able to bring about German re-unification during 1990. This success led to victory in "all-German" elections soon afterwards. Re-unification caused serious economic difficulties, however, and Kohl's austerity measures created discontent. He was defeated in the elctions for chancellor in 1998.

KOLCHAK, ALEXANDER VASILYEVICH (1874–1920) Russian counter-revolutionary admiral. He led a *coup d'état* within the **White** (Provisional) government in Siberia in 1918, and was recognized as ruler of Russia by the Western allies; but he was betrayed to the **Bolsheviks** and shot.

KONIEV, IVAN STEPANOVICH (1897–1973) Marshal of the Soviet Union. He was a front commander, 1941–3; senior commander in the liberation of the Ukraine, the Soviet drive into Poland (1944), and the attack on Berlin and liberation of Prague, 1945. Between 1956 and 1960 he was commander-in-chief of the **Warsaw Pact** forces.

KÖPRÜLÜ (also spelled Kuprili) Family of Pashas and generals of Albanian origin, who held high office in the Ottoman state in the second half of the 17th century. The founder of the family's fortunes, Köprülü Mehmed Pasha, was called to the grand vizierate in 1656 by **Mehmed IV** at the age of 80, being succeeded as grand vizier by his son Fazil Ahmed Pasha in 1661 and by his son-in-law Kara Mustafa Pasha (1676–83). The last significant member of the family was Köprülüzade Mustafa Pasha, grand vizier 1689–91. Their military and administrative reforms did much to arrest the decline of the Ottoman house (final reduction of Crete, 1669; conquest of Podolia, 1672), but the over-confident policies of Kara Mustafa Pasha, culminating in his failure before Vienna in 1683, severely damaged the fabric of the state and sowed the seeds of future defeat.

KORAN Holy book of Islam, believed by Muslims to be the word of God communicated to the Prophet, **Mohammed**. The text is said to have been definitely fixed by order of the third caliph, **Othman**; containing 114 chapters of different lengths and content, it serves as a basis of law and social morality as well as of doctrine and devotion.

KOREANA TRIPITAKA Korean collection of Chinese-language Buddhist scriptures from the 13th century; the most complete in the world.

KORNILOV, LAVR GEORGIYEVICH (1870–1918) Russian general. An intelligence officer during the Russo-Japanese war of 1904–5, and military attaché in Peking 1907–11, he was captured by the Austrians in 1915, escaping the following year. He was placed in charge of Petrograd military district after the February Revolution, 1917; he was appointed commander-in-chief by Kerensky. Accused of attempting a military *coup d'état* he was imprisoned, but escaped and took command of the anti-Bolshevik (White) army in the Don region. He was killed at the battle for Yekaterinodar.

KOŚCIUSZKO, TADEUSZ (1746–1817) Polish general and patriot. After military training in Warsaw, he went to America to join the "struggle for liberty" there (1777–80). He fought Russia and then Prussia in 1792–3 in an unsuccessful attempt to save Poland from a second partition. He led a national uprising against Russia and Prussia in 1794 which failed, and precipitated the final partition of Poland the following year. He spent much of the rest of his life in exile, attempting to enlist foreign support for the recreation of a Polish state.

KRUM (d.814) Khan of the Bulgars, 802–14. After **Charlemagne**'s defeat of the Avars in 796, he greatly extended the power and territory of the Pannonian Bulgars. His early forays against Byzantium were repulsed, but he decisively defeated Emperor Nicephorus I in 811, and besieged Constantinople in 813, though he died during a second siege the following year.

KRUPP, ALFRED (1812–87) German industrialist and arms manufacturer. He was the son of Friedrich Krupp (1787–1826), founder of the family's cast-steel factory at Essen in 1811. Alfred perfected techniques to produce first railway track and locomotive wheels, then armaments. The **Franco-Prussian War** (1870–1) was won largely with Krupp field-guns, and the firm became the largest weapon manufacturer in the world, at one time supplying the armies of 46 nations.

KUBLAI KHAN (1215–94) Mongol emperor of China, founder of the Yüan dynasty. Grandson of **Genghis Khan**, he was proclaimed Great Khan in 1260 in succession to his brother **Möngke**. He reunited China, which had been divided since the eclipse of the **T'ang** dynasty. His court was first described to the west by the Venetian, **Marco Polo**.

KÜÇÜK KAYNARCA, TREATY OF (also known as Kuchuk Kainarji) A pact signed on 21 July 1774 to end the Russo-Ottoman war of 1768–74. Under its terms the Ottomans renounced their previously undisputed control of the Black Sea and allowed Russia the privilege of representing the interests of the Orthodox Christians in Moldavia, Wallachia and the Aegean Islands. Much later, this provided the basis for Russian interference in the affairs of the Ottoman empire.

KU KLUX KLAN American anti-Negro secret society, founded in 1866 to assert white supremacy and oppose the rule of the "carpetbaggers" in the southern states. It was declared illegal in 1871, but was relaunched in 1915, and broadened to attack not only Negroes but also Jews, Roman Catholics and foreigners. Violently active during the early 1920s in the mid-West and South, and again in the South in the 1960s, it came under increasing attack as a result of Federal enforcement of the Civil Rights Acts of 1964 and 1965.

KUMANS *see* **Polovtsy**

KUN, BELA (1886–1937) Hungarian revolutionary leader. He led the Communist insurgents who overthrew the Karolyi regime in 1918. On becoming premier in 1919, he attempted to reorganize the country on Soviet principles but was forced into exile four months later.

KUO-MIN CHÜN (People's Army) Group of warlord armies led by **Feng Yü-hsiang, 1924–8.**

KUOMINTANG (also known as Chinese Nationalist Party) Political Party, ruling mainland China from 1928 to 1949, and since then (from Taiwan) claiming to be the only legitimate Chinese government. It evolved from a revolutionary group formed after the Chinese Republican Revolution of 1911 and was outlawed in 1913. Three short-lived governments were established under **Sun Yat-sen**, between 1917 and 1923 when the party allied with the Chinese Communists. Jointly they conquered most of the country, but split, 1927–8; cooperation was renegotiated in face of a Japanese invasion, 1937. Civil war was resumed in 1946, ending with Communist victory in 1949.

KURDS A Muslim people, speaking an Indo-European language, numbering up to 19 million, mostly in the mountains where Iran, Iraq and Turkey meet. Hopes of an autonomous Kurdistan emerging from a defeated **Ottoman** empire, raised by the 1920 **Treaty of Sèvres**, were still-born: Atatürk suppressed the Kurds. The Soviet Union, whose forces occupied part of Iran in the Second World War, encouraged the proclamation of a Kurdish republic but this collapsed after the Russians withdrew. In Iraq, fighting broke out with government troops in 1961. Nine years later, Baghdad offered the Kurds limited autonomy but the war restarted in 1974. Iranian support for the Kurds was withdrawn following an Iraqi-Iranian agreement in 1975. The Iraqis gassed Kurds at Halabja in 1988. The US-led coalition, which drove Iraq from Kuwait in 1991, encouraged an unsuccessful rising against Baghdad and created a safe haven for Kurds inside northern Iraq.

KUSHANAS Imperial dynasty, ruling in central Asia and northern India from the late 1st to the mid-3rd century AD, and traditionally founded by Kanishka, who succeeded to the throne of a kingdom extending from Benares in the east to Sanchi in the south, some time between AD 78 and 144. The Kushana empire lasted abut 150 years, until its kings in Taxila and Peshawar were reduced to vassals of the Persian **Sasanids**.

KYANZITTHA (1084–1112) One of the first great kings of Burma, responsible for the expansion of **Buddhism.**

KYOTO PROTOCOL (1997) An international agreement between the major industrialized nations to cut carbon emissions and reduce the threat of global warming. It came into force eight years later but the United States and Australia refused to ratify the agreement. By 2015, 192 nations participated by treaty or voluntarily in the programme and in a second agreement in Qatar in 2012 the goal of carbon emission reduction was extended from 2013 to 2020.

L

LA For all personal names prefixed by la, le, etc, see under following element.

LAIRD, MACGREGOR (1808–61) Scottish explorer, shipbuilder and trader. He designed the first ocean-going iron ship, the 55-ton paddle-steamer *Alburkah*, and in it in 1832 accompanied an expedition to the Niger delta. He ascended the river's principal tributary, the Benue, developed west African commerce in an attempt to undermine the slave trade and pioneered trans-Atlantic shipping routes. He promoted a second major expedition, penetrating 150 miles further up the Niger than any previous European, in 1854.

LAMAISM Form of **Buddhism**, established in Tibet *c.* 750. It is derived from Mahayana beliefs, combined with elements of erotic Tantrism and animistic Shamanism. In 1641 the Mongols inaugurated the appointment of the Dalai Lama, to rule Tibet from Lhasa, while the Panchen Lama from the Tashi Lhunpo monastery near Shigatse became spiritual head of the religion. The last Dalai Lama, 14th in a line claiming descent from Bodhisattva Avalokiteshvara, ancestor of the Tibetans, accepted exile in India in 1959. Lamaism temporarily lost its hold in Tibet, but again now has widespread support.

LANGOSCO Prominent family of medieval Pavia, Italy. Supporters of the **Guelph** (anti-imperial) party, they gained control of Pavia in 1300–15 and 1357–9, but lost it to their rivals, the **Visconti** of Milan.

LAO-TZU (c. 600 BC) Originator of the Chinese Daoist philosophy. Little definite is known of his life, though he is traditionally said to have met Confucius during the 6th century BC. His authorship of the *Dao te Ching*, one of the central Daoist texts, is unproven, and it certainly dates from a later period (probably 3rd century BC). Since his death he has been venerated as a philosopher by Confucians, as a saint or god by many Chinese, and as an imperial ancestor during the **T'ang** dynasty (AD 618–907).

LAPPS Inhabitants of northern Scandinavia and the Kola peninsula of Russia. The origin of these people is obscure, but their history goes back at least 2,000 years. The best known, but smallest, group are nomadic reindeer herders; their forest and coastal cousins rely on a semi-nomadic hunting and fishing economy.

LA TÈNE Celtic Iron Age culture, flourishing in central Europe from c. 500 BC until the arrival of the Romans, and in remote areas such as Ireland and northern Britain until the 1st century AD. It was named after an archaeological site excavated near Lake Neuchâtel, Switzerland. Most surviving near Celtic art – weapons, jewellery, tableware, horse and chariot decoration – is characteristically La Tène in motif and design.

LATERAN COUNCILS Four Church Councils were held at the Lateran Palace in Rome during the Middle Ages. The first (1123) confirmed the **Concordat of Worms** which ended the Investiture Contest; the second (1139) reformed the Church after the schism at Innocent II's election; the third (1179) marked the end of the conflict with **Frederick I Barbarossa** and introduced a two-thirds majority rule for papal elections; the fourth (1215), the high water mark of **Innocent III**'s pontificate, inaugurated large-scale reform to deal with the recent widespread dissatisfaction with the Church, and proclaimed a **Crusade**.

LATIN EMPIRE OF CONSTANTINOPLE From 1204 to 1261 the Byzantine capital, Constan-tinople, was ruled by a succession of western European crusaders after its capture by the Venetian-backed armies of the Fourth **Crusade**; its wealth was systematically pillaged before it was captured by Michael VIII Palaeologus, the Greek Emperor of Nicaea, in 1261.

LAUSANNE, TREATY OF Agreement signed on 24 July 1923 by First World War Allies with Turkish nationalists. It recognized the territory and independence of the New Turkish Republic which had replaced the Ottoman empire. Turkey abandoned claims to its former Arab provinces, recognized British and Italian right in Cyprus and the Dodecanese Islands, and opened the Turkish straits (Dardanelles) linking the Aegean and the Black Sea to all shipping.

LAY INVESTITURE The right claimed by many medieval rulers to appoint and install their own bishops. The denial of this right by the papacy gave rise to the Investiture Contest (1075–1122); a form of settlement was reached at the **Concordat of Worms.**

LEAGUE OF NATIONS Organization set up by the Allies for international cooperation at the Paris Peace Conference in 1919 following the end of the First World War. Weakened by the non-membership of the USA, it failed to halt German, Japanese and Italian aggression in the 1930s. Moribund by 1939, it was replaced in 1946 by the **United Nations**.

LEE, KWAN YEW (1923–2015) Political leader of the Republic of Singapore. An outstanding law student at Cambridge, he worked for labour unions before entering politics (1954). He founded the People's Action Party in 1955. When Singapore became a self-governing state he was elected prime minister, holding office for over 25 years (1965–90). He promoted economic development, regional cooperation and a policy of non-alignment. A conservative politician of authoritarian temperament, he was also a major spokesman of the Association of Southeast Asian Nations (ASEAN).

LEE, ROBERT E (1807–70) Commander-in-Chief of the Confederate (Southern) army in the American Civil War, 1861–5. He graduated top cadet from West Point military academy, 1829; fought in the Mexican War of 1846–8. In 1861 he resigned his commission to lead the Virginian forces; he was military adviser to Jefferson Davis, commander of the Army of Northern Virginia, and General-in-Chief of the Confederate Armies. He surrendered at Appomattox Court House on 9 April 1865. After the war he served as president of Washington College (later Washington and Lee University), Virginia.

LEGALISM Ancient school of Chinese thought, advocating institutional rather than ethical solutions in politics, and teaching that governments should rule by rigid and harshly enforced laws, irrespective of the views of their subjects. It was first adopted as a state ideology by the **Ch'in** dynasty (221–206 BC) and regularly revived since, particularly during periods of national crisis.

LE MAY, CURTIS (1906–1990) Leader of the US Strategic Air Command (1948–57) and Chief of Staff of the US Air Force (1961–5). He joined the Air Corps in 1928. By 1942 he was lieutenant colonel directing action in Europe, and in 1944 moved to the Pacific where his bombing campaign over Japan is estimated to have killed over 250,000 people. As Chief of Staff, he was known as a fierce anti-communist, pushing for greater military engagement in Vietnam and Cuba and argued for the use of nuclear weapons in battle; he was considered "trigger-happy" by many observers. He retired in 1965.

LENIN (1870–1924) Architect of the Russian revolution; born Vladimir Ilych Ulyanov. Converted to Marxism while training to be a lawyer, he was exiled to Siberia, 1897–1900. He led the Bolshevik wing of the Social Democratic Party from 1903. He returned from Switzerland in 1917 at the outbreak of revolution and in October overthrew Kerensky's government to become first head of the Soviet government, 1917–24. His influential writings include *What Is To Be Done?*, *Imperialism, the Highest Stage of Capitalism*, *The State and Revolution* and *The Development of Communism*.

LEO I, THE GREAT (d. 461) He succeeded to the papacy in 440, and was the founder of papal primacy.

As a theologian he defined Catholic doctrine, and secured the condemnation of the **Monophysites** at the **Council of Chalcedon** (451). He asserted the primacy of the Roman see against Constantinople. In 452 he saved Rome from the **Huns**.

LEO III (675–741) Byzantine emperor, founder of the Isaurian, or Syrian, dynasty. He seized the throne in 717, defeated the Arab attack on Constantinople, and went on to drive them from Anatolia. He launched the policy of **iconoclasm**, which opened deep religious conflict in the empire.

LEO VI (866–912) Byzantine emperor, known as "the Wise" or "the Philosopher". Son of Basil I the Macedonian, he became co-emperor in 870, and attained full power in 886. He issued a set of imperial laws, the **Basilica**, which became the accepted legal code of Byzantium.

LEO IX (Bruno of Egisheim) (1002–54) Pope and saint. He became Bishop of Toul in 1026, and in 1048 was appointed Pope by **Henry III** of Germany, a relation. He showed his reforming spirit by demanding also to be elected by the clergy of Rome; and also by condemning simony and clerical marriage, and by travelling widely in order to spread reforming ideas. He was defeated and briefly held captive by the Normans of southern Italy. His assertion of papal supremacy led to the great schism of 1054 between the Eastern and Western churches.

LEOPOLD II (1835–1909) King of the Belgians. The son of Leopold I, he succeeded in 1865. He was instrumental in founding the Congo Free State, 1879, over which he secured personal control in 1885. In the process of making a fortune out of harvesting rubber, he subjected its people to exploitation and human rights abuses on a massive scale. Under his guidance, Belgium became a significant industrial and colonial power. He handed over sovereignty in the Congo to his country in 1908.

LETTOW-VORBECK, PAUL VON (1870–1964) German general. He served in the Southwest Colonial Forces, helping to suppress the Herero and Hottentot rebellions; as commander of the (German) East African Colonial forces, he repelled a British landing in Tanganyika, in 1914, and with less than 17,000 troops pinned down British, Portuguese and Belgian forces of over 300,000 in East Africa, 1914–18. He led the right-wing occupation of Hamburg, 1919. He became a member of the Reichstag, 1929–30 and tried without success to organize conservative opposition to **Hitler**.

LEVELLERS Members of a radical movement both in the Parliamentary army and in London during the English Civil War. It advocated total religious and social equality among "freeborn Englishmen", and sought an extreme form of republican government based on the pamphlet *The Agreement of the People* (1648) written by its leader, John Lilburne (*c.* 1614–57). It was suppressed by **Oliver Cromwell** at Burford, Oxfordshire in 1649.

LEWIS, JOHN LLEWELLYN (1880–1969) US labour leader. In 1905 he became legal representative to the United Mine Workers of America, and its president from 1920 to 1960. With the American Federation of Labour (AFofL), he encouraged the organization of mass production workers into industrial unions. Expelled from the AFofL, these unions then set themselves up in 1935 as the Congress of Industrial Organizations (CIO), with Lewis as president. He himself resigned from CIO in 1940, and withdrew the mineworkers in 1942.

LEWIS, MERIWETHER (1774–1809) American explorer, *see under* **Clark, William**

LIBERATION FROM FRENCH RULE, WAR OF Penultimate struggle of the Napoleonic Wars, when the French armies, after their retreat from Russia in 1812, suffered a series of setbacks against a new coalition of Britain, Prussia, Sweden and Austria, culminating in defeat at the battle of the Nations (1813). The allies then advanced to Paris, Napoleon abdicated, peace was made with France and the **Congress of Vienna** was called (1814) to make a settlement for the rest of Europe.

LIGUE *see* **Catholic League**

LILIUOKALANI (1838–1917) Queen of Hawaii, 1891–5; born in Honolulu. She opposed the renewal of the Reciprocity Treaty, 1887, under which her brother, King Kalakaua, granted the USA commercial rights and Pearl Harbor; she supported Oni Pa's party, whose motto was "Hawaii for the Hawaiians". Deposed by the US-inspired provisional government in 1893, she abdicated in 1895 after a loyalist revolt. In 1893 she composed the famous Hawaiian song *Aloha Oe*.

LINCOLN, ABRAHAM (1809–65) Sixteenth president of the USA, 1861–5. Raised in the backwoods of Indiana, he was a self-taught lawyer. He entered Congress in 1847, eventually being elected president on an anti-slavery platform. He fought the Civil War (1861–5) to preserve national unity; proclaimed the emancipation of slaves in 1863, and was assassinated in 1865 by John Wilkes Booth, a fanatical southerner.

LI TZU-CH'ENG (c. 1605–45) Chinese rebel leader, born in Shensi. He was a bandit chieftain, 1631–45, during the final disturbed years of the **Ming** dynasty. After first operating in Shensi, he overran parts of Honan and Hupeh in 1639, and captured Kaifeng (1642) and all of Shensi (1642–4). In 1644 he also invaded Shansi, and in April seized Peking and proclaimed himself emperor. He was defeated by the combined tribes of General **Wu San-kuei** and the **Manchus**, and was driven from Peking, retreating first to Sian and then into Hupeh.

LIVINGSTONE, DAVID (1813–73) Scottish missionary and explorer. He started his mission career in the Botswana region in 1841. He crossed the Kalahari Desert; reached the Zambezi, 1851; and Luanda, 1853; discovered the Victoria Falls, 1855; and explored the basin of Lake Nyasa and the Upper Congo. He was feared lost in early 1870, but was found by **Stanley** near Lake Tanganyika in 1871.

LIVONIAN ORDER Society of German crusading knights, also known as Brothers of the Sword, or Knights of the Sword. They conquered and Christianized Livonia (covering most of modern Latvia and Estonia) between 1202 and 1237, but were reprimanded by both pope and emperor for their brutal approach to conversion. They were destroyed by pagan armies at the battle of Saule in 1236, and the following year were disbanded and reorganized as a branch of the **Teutonic Order**. After secularization (1525) the last Grand Master of the Order became Grand Duke of Courland, a fief of the Polish crown.

LLOYD GEORGE, DAVID (1863–1945) British statesman. Born into a poor Welsh family, he was elected a Liberal Member of Parliament in 1890, and entered the Cabinet as president of the Board of Trade (1905–08) and chancellor of the exchequer (1908–15), introducing an ambitious welfare and pension programme. When a coalition Cabinet was formed during the First World War, he became minister of munitions (1915–16), and minister of war (1916), replacing the Liberal Party leader, H.H. Asquith, as prime minister later the same year. In 1918 the coalition won a general election and Lloyd George represented Great Britain at the **Paris Peace Conference**, where he exercised a moderating influence on his allies. In 1922 the Conservative party withdrew its support from the coalition and the Liberals, divided between Asquith and Lloyd George, were heavily defeated in a new general election. Although Lloyd George became party leader, 1926–31, and remained in Parliament almost until his death, he became an increasingly isolated political figure, and the Liberal Party steadily declined as a political force.

LOCARNO PACT A treaty, signed 1 December 1925, between Great Britain, France, Germany, Italy and Belgium. Under its terms Britain and Italy agreed to guarantee the frontiers of Germany with Belgium and France and the continued demilitarization of the Rhineland. **Hitler** repudiated it on 7 March 1936, stationing troops on both sides of the Rhine and re-fortifying it.

LOCKE, JOHN (1632–1704) English philosopher. His most important political work, the second *Treatise of Civil Government* (1690) provided the theoretical justification for government with only limited and revocable powers; his main philosophical work, *An Essay concerning Human Understanding* (1690) was the basis for most 18th-century European thought on the function of reason and the importance of environment in life.

LOESS Fine, yellowish, often very fertile soil, carried by the wind; large deposits are found in Europe, Asia and North America.

LOLLARDS Members of a reforming religious movement, influential in the 14th and 15th centuries in Europe, especially in England under **John Wyclif**. It was widely popular for its attacks on Church corruption and its emphasis on individual interpretation of the Bible as the basis for a holy life, but was repressed under the English King Henry IV.

LOMBARDS German people ruling northern Italy, 568–774. Originally one of the tribes forming the **Suebi**, they migrated south from northwest Germany in the 4th century. By the end of the 5th century they occupied approximately the area of modern Austria north of the Danube, and in 568 crossed the Alps into Italy. The Lombard kingdom of Italy was conquered by the **Franks** in 774.

LOMBARD LEAGUE Association of north Italian cities, established in the 12th and 13th centuries to resist the authority of the **Holy Roman Empire**. The League was originally founded in 1167, with 16 members and the blessing of Pope **Alexander III** to defy **Frederick I Barbarossa**, hostilities ending in 1177 with the Peace of Venice and in 1183 with the Peace of Constance. In 1226 the League was revived and strengthened to avert new imperial ambitions by **Frederick II** but was dissolved after Frederick's death in 1250.

LONDON RIOT Popular demonstrations in 1641 by Londoners outside the House of Parliament and **Charles I**'s palace at Whitehall, demanding that the king's chief minister, Strafford, should be sentenced to death.

LONG, HUEY PIERCE (1893–1935) US senator and governor of Louisiana. He was elected governor in 1928 after a noisy demagogic campaign for the redistribution of wealth and became a senator in 1932. He was assassinated.

LON NOL (1914–85) President of Cambodia, 1970–5. He became a general in the army, then prime minister, 1966–7, and again in 1969. He seized power from Prince **Sihanouk** in a right-wing coup in 1970 but was ousted and fled to Bali in 1975 when the communist **Khmer Rouge** overran the country.

LOUIS I, THE GREAT (1326–82) King of Hungary, 1342–82. He succeeded his father, Charles Robert, a member of the Neapolitan dynasty of Anjou, who was invested with the kingdom after the extinction of the Arpád dynasty in 1301. Louis fought wars against Naples and Venice; in 1370 he acquired the Polish crown, but with little power, and won most of Dalmatia in 1381. One of his daughters, Maria, became Queen of Hungary; the other, **Jadwiga**, Queen of Poland.

LOUIS THE PIOUS (778–840) Emperor of the Franks, son of **Charlemagne**. He was crowned co-emperor in 813, was twice deposed by his four sons and twice restored (830 and 834); his death preceded the break-up of the empire.

LOUIS VI (1081–1137) King of France, also known as Louis the Fat. Son of Philip I, he was designated his successor in 1098, and crowned in 1108. He made substantial progress in extending French royal power and fought major wars against Henry I of England (1104–13 and 1106–20). He arranged an important dynastic marriage between his son, **Louis VII**, and Eleanor, heiress of Aquitaine.

LOUIS VII (c. 1120–80) Known as **Le Jeune** (the Young). King of France, succeeding his father, **Louis VI**, in 1137, after marrying Eleanor, heiress to the dukedom of Aquitaine, and thus effectively extending his lands to the Pyrenees. He repudiated Eleanor for misconduct in 1152, upon which she married his great rival, **Henry II** of England, who took over the claim to Aquitaine. The later years of his reign were marked by continual conflict with the English.

LOUIS IX (1214–70) Capetian king of France, canonized as St Louis. He was crowned at the age of 13. In 1228 he founded the Abbey of Royaumont, and in 1248 led the Sixth **Crusade** to the Holy Land. He sought peace with England by recognizing Henry III as Duke of Aquitaine. He died on a second Crusade, to Tunisia.

LOUIS XI (1423–83) King of France, son of Charles VII. He succeeded in 1461; in 1477 he defeated a rebellion of nobles, led by **Charles the Bold**, Duke of Burgundy. By 1483 he had united most of France with the exception of Brittany.

LOUIS XII (1426–1515) King of France. Son of Charles, Duke of Orléans, he succeeded his cousin, Charles VIII, in 1498. He embarked on fruitless Italian wars (1499–1504, 1508–13), and was finally driven out by the Holy League – an alliance of England, Spain, the Pope and the Holy Roman Empire – in 1513.

LOUIS XIV (1638–1715) The Sun King (*Le Roi Soleil*), ruler of France without a First Minister, 1661–1715, hence looked upon as the archetype of an absolute monarch. The son of Louis XIII and Anne of Austria, he succeeded in 1643 but remained under **Mazarin**'s tutelage until the cardinal's death. He extended and strengthened France's frontiers, built the palace of Versailles and set a European-wide pattern for courtly life. He founded or refashioned academies, supported artists and craftsmen, writers, musicians, playwrights and scholars, French and non-French. He was hated by Protestants for his revocation of the **Edict of Nantes**; and opposed by the maritime powers and the Austrian Habsburgs who feared that he aimed at European hegemony.

LOUIS XVI (1754–93) King of France, grandson of Louis XV. He married the Austrian Archduchess Marie-Antoinette in 1770, and succeeded to the throne, 1774. The early years of his reign saw France in a state of progressive financial and political collapse; with the outbreak of the French revolution in 1789 the royal family became virtual prisoners of the Paris mob. Their attempted flight in 1791 led to deposition, trial for treason and execution by guillotine in 1793.

LOUIS-PHILIPPE (1773–1850) King of France, son of Louis-Philippe Joseph, Duke of Orléans. Exiled, 1793–1815, during the French revolution and the Napoleonic period, he succeeded to the throne in 1830 after the reactionary regime of Charles X had been ended by the July revolution. His reign was characterized by financial speculation, the ostentatious affluence of the emerging middle class, and growing failure in foreign policy. He abdicated in 1848 after renewed revolutionary outbreaks, and fled to England.

LOUISIANA PURCHASE The western half of the Mississippi Basin, bought from Napoleon in 1803 by President **Thomas Jefferson** for under 3 cents an acre. It added 2,145,000 sq km (828,000 square miles) to the USA, at the time doubling its area, and opened up the West.

LUBA Also known as Baluba. Bantu-speaking peoples, widespread in southeast Zaire. The main present-day groups all trace their history back to the Luba empires which flourished, but finally broke down, in the 16th and 17th centuries. With the **Lunda** they established a series of satellite states, trading with and buying firearms from the Portuguese in Angola until colonized by the Belgians in the late 19th century.

LUDDITE Machine-smasher, originally a member of one of the bands of workers who systematically broke looms, textile plant and machine tools in Lancashire, Yorkshire and the east Midlands of England during the early industrial revolution (1811–16). Traditionally named after Ned Ludd, a possibly mythical leader of the rioters.

LUDENDORFF, ERICH VON (1865–1938) German soldier. Chief of staff to **Hindenburg** throughout the First World War, he was increasingly influential in German military and (after 1916) domestic policies. After the failure of the offensives on the Western Front of March 1918 he insisted upon an immediate armistice. He fled to Sweden at the end of the war, but returned in 1919 to take part in the Kapp Putsch (1920) and Munich Beer-Hall Putsch (1923). An early supporter of **Hitler**, he sat as a Nazi deputy in the Reichstag, 1924–8.

LUMUMBA, PATRICE (1925–61) First prime minister of Congo (later Zaire). He was educated at a Protestant mission school; became local president of the Congolese trade union, 1955; founded the Mouvement National Congolais, 1958, to work for independence from Belgium. Imprisoned in 1959, he was asked to form the first independent government in 1960. He was removed from office after opposing the Belgian-backed secession of Katanga province. He was murdered.

LUNDA Bantu people, originating in the Katanga-Shaba district of Congo (the central Lunda kingdom) and now spread widely over southeast Congo, eastern Angola, northwest Zambia and the Luapula valley. The Lunda of Kazembe were famous throughout central Africa as ivory and slave traders, especially with the Portuguese.

LUNG YÜN (1888–1962) Chinese warlord. A member of the Lolo minority peoples, he trained as a military officer and joined the staff of **T'ang Chih-yao** in Yunnan. In 1915 he joined the rebellion of Yunnan against **Yüan Shih-k'ai**, which left T'ang in control of the province. In 1927 Lung Yün ousted T'ang, and ruled the Yunnan region as an independent satrapy until 1945. He fostered the cultivation of the opium poppy and inflicted savage taxes on the population. He collaborated unwillingly with **Chiang Kai-shek** during the Japanese War 1937–45, but in 1944 joined a group opposed to the Nationalist government. In 1945 Chiang organized a coup which deposed him, but Lung was given a government post and Yunnan placed under his close relative Lu Han. In 1950 Lung went to Peking as a member of the Communist government, and served until he was purged in 1957.

LUPACA Andean people in the Lake Titicaca region of South America. In alliance with the Incas in the early 15th century they defeated their neighbouring rivals, the **Colla**, but were in turn overthrown and absorbed by the Incas in the 1470s.

LUTHER, MARTIN (1483–1546) German theologian and initiator of the Protestant Reformation. He was ordained priest in 1507, and taught at the University of Wittenberg, 1508–46. His attack on papal abuses provoked excommunication in 1520, but Luther advanced an alternative theology which was adopted by many states of northern Europe (the Lutheran Reformation).

LUTHERANISM A system of theology, originated by **Martin Luther** (1483–1546) and expressed in *The Book of Concord* (1580), which incorporated the three traditional Creeds, the Augsburg Confession, Luther's two Catechisms and the Formula of Concord (1577). The main tenets of Lutheranism are that justification is by faith alone and that the scriptures are the sole rule of faith. The Lutherans have traditionally made a sharp distinction between the kingdom of God and the kingdom of the world, so that the state has sometimes seemed autonomous in its own field.

LUVIANS (LUWIANS) A people established in southern Anatolia by the beginning of the 2nd millennium BC, speaking a language closely related to that of the **Hittites**. Many inscriptions are extant in the Luvian language, written in hieroglyphs commonly called "hieroglyphic Luvian".

LUXEMBOURGS European ruling dynasty. The initial line, founded by Count Conrad (d. 1086) held the lordship of Luxembourg but became extinct in

1136; a collateral descendant, Henry II, Count of Luxembourg, founded a second line including four emperors of the **Holy Roman Empire**: Henry VIII, **Charles IV**, Wenceslas and Sigismund. On the death of Sigismund in 1438 the family was replaced on the imperial throne by Albert II of Habsburg and his descendants.

LYNN RIOTS Popular revolt at King's Lynn, Norfolk, England in 1597 against the high price of food and the high taxes imposed by the government of **Elizabeth I** to pay for the war against Spain and for the conquest of Ireland.

M

MAASTRICHT, TREATY OF (1992) The agreement between the 12 European Community leaders to promote monetary and political union, thereby expanding the European Community's powers over matters previously controlled by national governments. The treaty also called for the introduction of a single currency for the **EC** by 1999 and laid the groundwork for a common defence policy.

MACARTHUR, DOUGLAS (1880–1964) American general who commanded the defence of the Philippines, 1941–2. From 1942–5 he was Commander, US Forces in the Pacific. He headed UN forces in the Korean War (1950–1) until dismissed by President **Truman** after a policy disagreement.

McCLELLAN, GEORGE BRINTON (1826–85) American general, commander-in-chief of the Union forces in 1861–2 during the American Civil War.

McCONNEL & KENNEDY Machinery manufacturers for the rapidly expanding English cotton industry in the late 18th and 19th centuries. For many years the firm was virtually the sole supplier of spinning mules to the industry. John Kennedy (1769–1855) made several improvements in the machines used to spin fine yarns.

McKINLEY, WILLIAM (1843–1901) 25th president of the USA. He served in the Civil War under Colonel (later president) **Rutherford Hayes**. He was a member of Congress, 1877–91, and governor of Ohio in 1891–5. He defeated the Populist candidate, **William Jennings Bryan**, in the presidential election in 1896 without ever leaving his front porch. He led the country into the Spanish-America war, 1896, and in the suppression of the subsequent Filipino revolt (1899–1902). Re-elected in 1900 with a huge majority, he was shot the following year by an anarchist at the Pan-American Exhibition in Buffalo.

MACEDONIAN DYNASTY Family of Byzantine emperors, founded by Basil I (867–86) and ruling, with some interruptions, until the death of Theodora (1056). Originally peasant marauders, murdering their way to power, they presided over almost two centuries of Byzantium's highest military, artistic and political achievements.

MACHIAVELLI, NICCOLO (1469–1527) Florentine statesman, historian and political theorist. In response to foreign invasions and the anarchic state of Italy in his time, he wrote his most famous work, *Il Principe* (*The Prince*) in 1513, advocating the establishment and maintenance of authority by any effective means.

MACMILLAN, HAROLD (1894–1986) British statesman. A Conservative MP 1924–9 and 1931–64, he was noted for progressive social views and for opposition to the policy of appeasement of the dictators, voting against his party on abandonment of sanctions against Italy in 1936. He was British minister resident at Allied headquarters in northwest Africa, 1942–5. He entered the Cabinet in 1951 and held various offices before becoming prime minister, 1957–63, and presiding over the peaceful decolonization of British Africa.

MADERO, FRANCISCO (1873–1913) President of Mexico 1910–13. He inspired, organized and eventually led the movement to displace the dictator **Porfirio Díaz**. His arrest in 1909 was soon followed by release and escape to Texas. In 1910 he declared himself the legitimate president, and was elected in 1911 after the military successes of his supporters, Pascual Orozco and **Pancho Villa**. He failed to implement **democracy** or stem corruption. He was arrested and assassinated in 1913 after betrayal by an army commander, Victoriano Huerta, in the course of a military revolt.

MADISON, JAMES (1751–1836) Fourth president of the USA, 1809–17. A member of the Continental Congress, 1780–3 and 1787–8, he played a leading role in framing the US Constitution (1787). He broke with the **Federalists** and helped to found the Democratic-Republican party; served **Thomas Jefferson** as secretary of state, 1801–9. During his presidency war broke out between America and Great Britain (1812–14).

MADRID, TREATY OF Agreement, also known as "Godolphin's Treaty", between England and Spain in 1670 to end piracy in American waters; Spain also

confirmed the English possession of Jamaica, captured in 1655.

MAGELLAN, FERDINAND (c. 1480–1521) (Portuguese name, Fernão de Magalhães) First European to navigate in the Pacific Ocean. He was prominent in Portuguese naval and military expeditions to Africa, India and the East, 1505–16. In 1518 he was commissioned by Spain to find a southwest route to the Spice Islands; after sailing through the strait later named after him between South America and Tierra del Fuego, he crossed the Pacific and reached Guam in 1521, with three of his five original ships, but their crews in a state of near-starvation. The round-the-world voyage (the first) was completed by **Elcano** with one ship and 18 survivors, of an original 270 men, after Magellan had been killed by local people near Mactan in the Philippines.

MAGGI Prominent family of Brescia, Italy, which gained control of the city in the later 13th century until the siege by Emperor Henry VII in 1311, after which other families replaced them.

MAGNA CARTA The Great Charter issued under duress by King **John** of England in 1215. Though its provisions, promptly repudiated by John, concerned primarily the relationships of a feudal ruler with vassals, subjects and the Church, revisions and reconfirmations in 1216, 1217, 1225 and most notably by **Edward I** in 1297 asserted the supremacy of the laws of England over the king. Thus it came to be regarded as a keystone of British liberties.

MAGNUS OLAFSSON "THE GOOD" (1024–47) King of Norway and Denmark, illegitimate son of Olaf Haraldsson (St Olaf). He was exiled to Russia with his father, at the age of four by **Cnut the Great**. Elected as king in 1039 by Norwegian chieftains, he gained sovereignty over Denmark by 1042. He was unsuccessfully challenged by Cnut's nephew, Sweyn. He agreed to share thrones with his uncle, Harald Hardrada, in 1045. He was killed in a Danish battle while planning to claim the English crown.

MAHABHARATA "The Great Epic of the Baharata Dynasty". This vast work of early Indian literature, running to 100,000 couplets (seven times as long as *The Odyssey* and *The Iliad* combined) related the struggle between two families, the Kauravas and the Pandavas, as well as incorporating a mass of other romantic, legendary, philosophic and religious material from the heroic days of early **Hinduism**. Traditionally ascribed to the sage Vyasa, it was more probably the result of 2000 years of constant accretion and reshaping before reaching its present form c. AD 400. Included in it is the *Bhagavadgita* (*The Lord's Song*), probably Hinduism's most important text.

MAHAVIRA Indian religious teacher of the 6th century BC, principal founder of **Jainism**. At the age of 30 he renounced his family and became an ascetic, wandering for 12 years in the Ganges valley seeking enlightenment. He shaped and organized the Jaina sect, named from his honorific title of *Jina*, the Conqueror.

MAHDI Islamic concept of the messianic deliverer, who will one day fill the earth with justice, faith and prosperity. The title has been frequently adopted by social revolutionaries since Islam's upheavals in the 7th and 8th centuries – notably by Ubaidallah, founder of the **Fatimid** dynasty in 908, Mohammed ibn Tumart, leader of the 12th century **Almohad** movement, and in 1881 by **Mohammed Ahmed al-Mahdi** on declaring rebellion against the Egyptian administration in the Sudan.

MAHDI, MOHAMMED AHMED AL- (d.1885) Mystic founder of a vast Muslim state in the Sudan. He gathered a growing band of supporters through his preaching and interpretation of Islam; in 1881 he proclaimed a divine mission to purify Islam under the title of al-Mahdi, the Right-Guided One. He swiftly mastered virtually all territory once occupied by Egypt; captured Khartoum in 1885, and created the theocratic state of the Sudan. He died in that year at his new capital, Omdurman; the theocratic state fell to forces under the British general Kitchener in 1898.

MAHMUD OF GHAZNI (971–1030) Muslim warrior and patron of the arts. He was the son of Sebuktigin, a Turkish slave who became ruler of Ghazni (comprising most of modern Afghanistan and northeast Iran). He succeeded to the throne in 998, and from 1001 to 1026 led 17 invading expeditions to India, amassing an empire including the Punjab and most of Persia. His capital, Ghazni, became an Islamic cultural centre rivalling Baghdad.

MAHMUD II (1785–1839) Reforming Ottoman sultan, nephew of Sultan Selim III. He was brought to the throne in 1808 in a coup led by Bayrakdar Mustafa Pasha, later his grand vizier. He was heavily defeated in wars with Russia, Greece, France and Britain, and by **Mohammed Ali**'s insurgents in Syria. He destroyed the moribund janissary corps in 1826, establishing a modern, European-style army in 1831 and a military academy in 1834. He introduced cabinet government, postal service, compulsory education and European dress.

MAIRE, JAKOB LE (1585–1616) Dutch navigator and South Sea explorer. With **Willem Schouten**, in 1615–16 he sailed through Le Maire Strait, rounded Cape Horn for the first time, and discovered some of the Tuamotus, the northernmost islands of the Tonga group, and the Hoorn islands.

MAJAPAHIT Last of the Javanese Hindu-Buddhist empires, founded after the defeat of the Mongol seaborne expedition against Java in 1292. It rose to greatness under Gaja Mada (d.1364), chief minister of King Hayam Wuruk, with whose death in 1389 its decline began. Its size is a matter for dispute; its effective sway was probably limited to east and central Java, Madura, Bali and Lombok, while its powerful fleets ensured the allegiance and tribute of the Spice Islands and the chief commercial ports of southern Sumatra and southern Borneo.

MAJI-MAJI East African revolt against German colonialism which broke out in 1905 and was suppressed in 1907.

MALAN, DANIEL FRANÇOIS (1874–1959) South African politician. Before entering politics, he studied for the Dutch Reformed Church, receiving a doctorate in divinity at the University of Utrecht, Holland (1905). In 1948 he led a "purified" National party faction to victory, serving as prime minister (1948–54) of the Republic of South Africa's first exclusively Afrikaner government. A right-wing nationalist, Malan is best known for introducing apartheid into South Africa. He retired from public office in 1954.

MALATESTA Italian family, ruling Rimini from the late 13th century until 1500. They first became lords of the city in 1295, when the **Guelph** leader, Malatesta di Verruchio (d.1312) expelled his Ghibelline rivals. Sigismondo Malatesta (1417–68) is often represented as the ideal Renaissance prince – a soldier who also cultivated the arts. In 1461 he was the subject of a **Crusade** launched by Pope Pius II which deprived the family of most of its powers. Sigismondo's son, Roberto il Magnifico (d.1482), recovered Rimini in 1469, but the dynasty was finally driven out by Cesara Borgia in 1500.

MALFANTE, ANTONIO 15th-century Genoese merchant, sometimes known, exaggeratedly, as "the first explorer of the Sahara".

MALINKE People of the ancient west African empire of Mali. As the Dyula, or travelling merchants, their traders have remained a potent factor in the economy of the region since the 13th century.

MAMLUKS Generically, military slaves or freedmen, mainly from the Caucasus or central Asia, and employed by many medieval Muslim states. A group of them established a sultanate which ruled Egypt and Syria 1250–1517, until defeated by the **Ottomans**.

MANBY, AARON (1776–1850) English engineer. In 1821 he patented his design for an oscillating steam engine, widely used for marine propulsion, and in 1822 launched the first practical iron ship, the **Aaron Manby**, sailing from London to Paris. He also founded an iron works at Charenton (1810) which made France largely independent of English engine-builders, and in 1822 formed the first company to supply gas to Paris. He returned to England in 1840.

MANCHESTER SCHOOL Group of 19th-century British political economists advocating free trade and *laissez-faire*, led by Richard Cobden (1804–65) and John Bright (1811–89).

MANCHUS People of Manchuria (northeast China) who in 1644 founded the imperial dynasty known as the **Ch'ing**.

MANDATE Former colonial territory, assigned by the **League of Nations** to a victorious Allied power after the First World War under supervision of the League, and in some cases with the duty of preparing it for independence. Great Britain thus assumed responsibility for Iraq, Palestine (from the Ottoman empire) and Tanganyika (from Germany); France for Syria and Lebanon and Belgium for Ruanda-Urundi. The arrangement was replaced by the **United Nations**' Trusteeship System in 1946, except for Southwest Africa (Namibia), where South Africa retained its mandate until 1990.

MANDE A west African language group, the Mande-speaking people, found primarily in the savannah plateaux of the western Sudan, where they developed such complex civilizations as the Solinke state of Ghana, around 900 to 1100, and the empire of Mali which flourished in 14th and early 15th centuries. Today the most typical Mande groups are the Bambara, the Malinke and the Solinke, speaking characteristic Mande versions of the Niger-Congo group of languages.

MANDELA, NELSON (1918–2013) Born in Umtata in the Transkei, Mandela moved to Johannesburg and qualified as a lawyer. In 1944 he joined the African National Congress, becoming its deputy national president in 1952. In 1956 he was arrested and charged with treason but was discharged after a five-year trial. After the Sharpeville massacre and the banning of the ANC in 1960,

Mandela went underground but was captured and condemned to life imprisonment in 1964. He was released in February 1990, an event marking the real beginning of political change in South Africa, and resumed leadership of the ANC in the search for a negotiated political settlement. In 1994 he was elected the first president of a multi-racial South Africa.

MANDINGO West African people, related to the larger **Mande** language group, occupying parts of Guinea, Guinea-Bissau, Ivory Coast, Mali, Gambia and Senegal. The many independent tribes are dominated by a hereditary nobility which in one case, the Kangaba, has ruled uninterruptedly for 13 centuries: starting as a small state in the 7th century, Kangaba (on the Mali-Senegal boundary) became the focus for the great Malinke empire of Mali, reaching its peak around 1450.

MANICHAEISM Dualist religion founded in Persia in the 3rd century AD by Mani, "the Apostle of Light", who tried to integrate the messages of **Zoroaster**, **Buddha** and **Jesus** into one universal creed. It is often regarded, wrongly, as a Christian heresy: properly it is a religion in its own right, and has influenced many other sects, Christian and otherwise, in both East and West. It became extinct in the Middle Ages, but some scriptures have been recovered in this century in Egypt and Chinese Turkestan.

MANSA MUSA Most famous of the emperors of ancient Mali, he reigned 1312–37. He pushed the frontiers of the empire out to the edges of the Sahara, the tropical rainforest, the Atlantic and the borders of modern Nigeria. He made a lavish pilgrimage to Mecca and actively promoted Islam among his subjects; he also developed Saharan trade, introduced brick buildings and founded Timbuktu and Jenne as world centres of Muslim learning.

MANSUR, ABU AMIR AL- (c. 938–1002) ("Almanzor" in medieval Spanish and Latin texts) Chief minister and effective ruler of the **Umayyad** caliphate in Córdoba, 978–1002. He overthrew and succeeded his vizier in 978, and fought 50 campaigns against the Christians of northern Spain, including an expedition against the great shrine of Santiago de Compostela in 997.

MANSUR, ABU JAFAR AL- (c. 710–75) Second caliph of the **Abbasid** dynasty, great-grandson of **Abbas, Mohammed**'s uncle; he succeeded to the caliphate in 754 on the death of his brother as-Saffah. He completed the elimination of the deposed **Umayyad** dynasty, and founded the city of Baghdad, begun in 762.

MANUEL I COMNENUS (1122–80) Emperor of Byzantium, son of **John II Comnenus**, he succeeded in 1143. He tried but ultimately failed to build alliances in the West; was defeated in 1156 at Brindisi and expelled from Italy. He forced Jerusalem to recognize Byzantine sovereignty in 1159. In 1167 he added Dalmatia, Bosnia and Croatia to his empire. He broke ties with Venice in 1171. His armies were destroyed by the **Seljuk** Turks at Myriokephalon in 1176.

MANZIKERT, BATTLE OF Fought near the town in Turkish-held Armenia (today Malazgirt, Turkey) in 1071; the **Seljuks**, under Sultan Alp-Arslan (1063–72) decisively defeated the Byzantine armies under Emperor Romanus IV Diogenes (1068–71). The victory led to Seljuk conquest of almost all Anatolia, and fatal weakening of Byzantine power.

MAORI Member of the aboriginal Polynesian people inhabiting New Zealand at the time of its European discovery.

MAO ZEDONG (1893–1976) First chairman of the People's Republic of China (1949–77). He helped to found the Chinese Communist Party in 1921, and until 1926 organized peasant and industrial unions. After the Communist split with the **Kuomintang** in 1927 he set up Communist bases in Hunan, and later in Kiangsi. In 1934–5 he led the Long March of the Red Army from Kiangsi to Yenan. He became the dominant figure in the Party after 1935, establishing it as a peasant-based party. During the second Sino-Japanese War (1937–45) he worked for national unity, and after a bitter civil war in 1949 expelled Nationalist forces from mainland China. In 1966 he launched the Cultural Revolution.

MARATHAS Hindu people of western India, famous in the 17th and 18th centuries for their warlike resistance to the **Mughal** emperors. Now the term covers the 10 million or so members of the Maratha and Kunbi castes in the region bounded by Bombay, Goa and Nagpur, or more loosely the 40 million speakers of the Marathi language.

MARATHON, BATTLE OF A famous victory in 490 BC won on the coastal plain northeast of Athens by the Greeks, under the Athenian general Miltiades, over an invading army of Persians. It is remembered *inter alia* for the feat of the runner Phidippides, who raced 150 miles in two days to warn the Spartans and to return with the news that their forces would be delayed by a religious festival.

MARCEL, ÉTIENNE (c. 1316–58) Provost of merchants of Paris, deputy to the Estates General (the French national assembly). He proposed in 1355–6 that the Estates should control royal revenues and purge crown officials. He led Paris in a revolt against the crown in 1357–8, and supported the **Jacquerie**. He was assassinated in 1358 after the revolt collapsed.

MARCHAND, JEAN-BAPTISTE (1863–1934) French explorer and general who in 1897 led a remarkable 18-month march from Libreville, in Gabon, to the Upper Nile, occupying Fashoda in 1898. He withdrew after a prolonged confrontation with Kitchener which provoked an international diplomatic crisis.

MARCH FIRST MOVEMENT Non-violent movement following Korean Declaration of Independence on 1 March 1919, which sparked national and international movement to free Korea from Japanese imperial rule.

MARCION (c. 100–160) Originator of a religious sect challenging Christianity throughout Europe, north Africa and western Asia from the 2nd to the 5th century. Possibly the son of a bishop of Sinope, he went to Rome *c.* 140, formed separate communities and was excommunicated in 144. He preached the existence of two gods: the Old Testament Creator or Demiurge, i.e. the God of Law, and the God of Love revealed by Jesus, who would overthrow the first. He compiled his own version of the New Testament (the *Instrumentum*), largely based on St Luke and St Paul's Epistles. After his death the Marcionite sect survived many persecutions and remained significant, particularly in Syria, until the 10th century.

MARGARET (1353–1412) Queen of Norway. The daughter of Valdemer III of Denmark, she married Haakon VI of Norway (1343–80), and became effective ruler of Norway and Denmark, *c.* 1387, and of Sweden, 1389. She was regent on behalf of her great-nephew, Eric of Pomerania, who was crowned ruler of Sweden, Denmark and Norway at the **Union of Kalmar** in 1397.

MARI (Cheremiss) Finno-Ugrian speaking peoples now living mainly in the Autonomous Republics of Mari, on the middle Volga, and Bashkir.

MARIA THERESA (1717–80) Elder daughter of the Emperor Charles VI, and one of the most capable **Habsburg** rulers. She was Archduchess of Austria and Queen of Hungary and Bohemia in her own right, and always overshadowed her husband, the elected Emperor Francis I (1745–65). She died after 15 years of widowhood and a troublesome co-regency with her son, **Joseph II**.

MARINIDS Berber dynasty, ruling in Morocco and elsewhere in north Africa from the 13th to the 15th centuries, replacing the **Almohads** on the capture of Fez (1248) and Marrakesh (1269). They launched a holy war in Spain which lasted until the mid-14th century. Despite many attempts, they failed to re-establish the old Almohad empire; after a period of internal anarchy, the related Wattasids assumed control of Morocco in 1465, but were finally expelled, by the **Saadi** sharifs, in 1549.

MARQUETTE, JACQUES (1637–75) French Jesuit missionary and explorer, the first Frenchman to sail on the Mississippi (1673); he explored much of its length with **Jolliet**.

MARRANO Insulting Spanish term for a **Jew** who converted to **Christianity** in Spain or Portugal to avoid persecution but secretly continued to practise **Judaism**; also used to designate the descendants of such a person.

MARSHALL PLAN Popular name given to the European recovery programme, proposed in 1947 by US Secretary of State General George C. Marshall (1880–1959), to supply US financial and material aid to war-devastated Europe. Rejected by Eastern European countries under Soviet pressure, it came into force in Western Europe in 1948 and was completed in 1952.

MARSHALL, WILLIAM (1745–1818) Agriculturalist and leading improver, famous for his 12-volume *General Survey, from personal experience, observation and enquiry, of the Rural Economy of England* (1787–93). He proposed setting up a governmental Board of Agriculture, put into effect by Parliament in 1793.

MARTIN IV (c. 1210–85) Pope from 1281 to 1285. He supported **Charles I** of Naples and Sicily, and opposed the Aragonese claims after the **War of the Sicilian Vespers.**

MARX, KARL HEINRICH (1818–1883) German philosopher, economist and social theorist whose account of change through conflict is known as historical, or dialectical, materialism. His *Das Kapital* is the fundamental text of **Marxist** economics and his systematic theses on class struggle, history and the importance of economic factors in politics have exercised an enormous influence on later thinkers and political activists.

MARXIST Follower of the social, political and economic theories developed by Karl **Marx**. Characteristic beliefs include dialectical materialism, the collapse of **capitalism** through its internal contradictions, the dictatorship of the proletariat and a withering away of the state after the achievement of a classless society.

MASON-DIXON LINE Originally a boundary line between the American states of Pennsylvania and Maryland named after the English surveyors, Charles Mason and Jeremiah Dixon, who first delineated it, 1763–7. It later became a symbolic frontier between slave and free states in the American Union.

MATABELE (also known as Ndebele) Southern African people, who broke away from the **Nguni** of Natal in the early 19th century. Under **Mzilikazi** they migrated to the High Veld area of modern Transvaal, and later the Marico valley. In 1837, after confrontation with Dutch settlers in the Transvaal, they crossed the river Limpopo into Matabeleland (southern Rhodesia). The resulting state grew powerful under the leadership of Mzilikazi's successor, Lobengula. They were finally defeated by settlers of the British South Africa Company in 1893.

MATACOS South American Indians, forming the largest and most important group of the Chaco Indians in the Gran Chaco region of northwest Argentine. They were first encountered by Europeans in 1628, and resisted Christianity and colonization, suffering large-scale massacre, before being placed on reservations and in Spanish government colonies. They are now gradually being incorporated into the *mestizo* (mixed blood) population of the Chaco.

MATILDA (1046–1115) Countess of Tuscany. She was a strong supporter of Pope Gregory VII. Having acknowledged (*c.* 1080) papal overlordship of her lands, strategically placed across the route of German invasions of Italy, she eventually made Emperor Henry V her heir, thus giving rise to much conflict between the Empire and the Papacy.

MATTHIAS CORVINUS (1440–90) Elected King of Hungary (1458) and claimant to the throne of Bohemia from 1469. He acquired Moravia, Silesia and Lusatia in 1478, Vienna in 1485, and built up the most powerful kingdom in central Europe. He was also a patron of science and of literature.

MAURYAS First Indian dynasty to establish rule over the whole sub-continent. The dynasty was founded in 321 BC by **Chandragupta Maurya**, and steadily extended under his son Bindusara and Grandson **Ashoka**. Power was gradually eroded under **Ashoka**'s successors, finally dying out *c.* 180 BC.

MAXIMILIAN I (1459–1519) Holy Roman Emperor, son of Frederick III. He married Mary of Burgundy in 1477; was crowned king of Germany in 1486 and emperor in 1493. He achieved a partial reform of the imperial administration, but failed in 1499 to subjugate the Swiss cantons. He was succeeded by his grandson **Charles V**.

MAXIMILIAN (1832–67) Emperor of Mexico. Younger brother of the Austrian emperor, Francis Joseph I, in 1863 he accepted the offer of the Mexican throne as an unwitting pawn in the plot by Mexican opponents of **Juárez** and the French emperor, **Napoleon III**. He was installed by French troops and crowned, 1864. His attempts at liberal reform were nullified by local opposition and lack of funds. He was deserted by the French in 1867, surrounded, starved and tricked into surrender by the armies of Juárez and shot in June that year.

MAYA Indian people of the Yucatán peninsula and the adjoining areas of southern Mexico, Guatemala and Honduras. The Classic period of Maya civilization (marked by fine buildings, magnificent art and an advanced knowledge of mathematics and astronomy) falls between the 3rd and 9th centuries AD. Archaeologically it is best represented at the southern cities of Tikal, Copán, Uaxactún, Quiriguá and Piedras Negras. In the 9th century, for reasons still poorly understood, Classic Maya civilization declined. Mexican (see **Toltec**) influence became important, and the main centres of power shifted to Chichén Itzá and Mayapán in northern Yucatán. Although the Spanish conquest destroyed much of the political and religious life, the Maya still exist as a linguistic and cultural unit in their original homelands.

MAYFLOWER Famous ship that carried the 102 pilgrims of the later USA from England to found the first permanent New England colony at Plymouth, Massachusetts, in 1620. Her precise size is not recorded, but she was probably about 180 tons and some 27m (90ft) long. Originally she set out for Virginia, but was blown north first to Cape Cod and then to Plymouth.

MAZARIN, JULES (1602–61) Italian-born French statesman. He pursued a career in papal service, 1625–36, was brought into the service of Louis XIII by **Richelieu** in 1639 and, on French nomination, was made a cardinal in 1641. He inherited Richelieu's position as Louis XIII's first minister. The king made him godfather to the future **Louis XIV**, over whose training for kingship he had a good deal of influence. He showed skill both in handling the civil wars of the **Fronde** and in negotiating gains for France under the treaties of **Westphalia** (1648) and the Pyrenees (1659).

MAZZINI, GIUSEPPE (1805–72) Italian revolutionary and patriot. He founded the highly influential Young Italy movement and a journal of that name in 1831. Following the failure of the invasion of Savoy in 1834, and banished from Switzerland, he arrived in London in 1837. In 1849 he was First Triumvir, in effect executive ruler, of the Roman Republic, an office filled with tolerance and enlightenment. As a republican, he refused to acknowledge the Italian Kingdom of 1861.

MEADE, GEORGE GORDON (1815–72) Union general in the American Civil War, best remembered for his victory in the battle of Gettysburg (1863).

MEDES The branch of the Iranian invaders settled in the northwest of present-day Iran. Under Cyaxares (*c.* 625 BC) the Medes became a major military power which, once it had settled accounts with the Scythian invaders of northern Iran, made an alliance with Babylon to destroy the hated Assyrian empire. Under the last king, Astyages, the Medes were defeated by the Persian **Cyrus II the Great** in 550 BC, in whose empire the "Medes and Persians" were held in equal honour. Thereafter, especially under the Sasanids, the Medes became effectively merged with the other groupings which came to constitute the Iranian nation-state.

MEDICI Most important of the great families of Florence. Their origins are obscure, but they were established in the 13th century in the cloth trade and in finance, and soon exercised considerable political influence. The family developed three lines: that of Chiarissimo II, who failed to gain power in Florence in the 14th century; that of Cosimo the Elder (1389–1464) who became the hereditary, although uncrowned, monarch of Florence; and that of Cosimo, who became Grand Duke of Tuscany in 1569. The line ended with the death of Gian Gastone, 1737. The family provided many rulers and patrons, and three Popes.

MEGALITH (meaning "great stone") Monument constructed of large undressed stones or boulders, usually as a ritual centre (e.g. a stone circle) or burial monument (e.g. chambered cairn). Of many different kinds, megaliths were erected by simple agricultural communities in many parts of the world, most notably in **Neolithic** Europe during the 3rd millennium BC.

MEHMED I, ÇELIBI (d.1421) Younger son of **Bayezid I** and reunifier of the Ottoman state after the defeat of Ankara (1402), the death of his father and the civil war (1403–13) with his brothers. Mehmed, from a territorial base at Amasya, moved to defeat successively Isa in Brusa, Süleyman in Edirne (1403–11), and Musa in Rumeli (1411–13), while maintaining nominal allegiance to the Timurids, and later overcoming both dangerous social revolts and Byzantine-inspired attempts to place his brother Mustafa on the throne (1415–16). By his death the prestige, if not the full authority, of the sultanate was restored, enabling it to survive the further shocks of the first years of **Murad II**'s reign.

MEHMED II, FATIH ("the Conqueror") (1432–81) Ottoman Sultan succeeding in 1451. By the conquest of Constantinople in 1453 Mehmed II obtained for the Ottoman state a fit site for the capital of a would-be universal world empire. His reign is a record of unceasing warfare: against Hungary, Venice, the **Ak Koyunlu** and the Knights of St John. The last vestiges of Greek rule disappeared (in the Morea 1460, in Trebizond 1461); Serbia (1459), Bosnia (1463) and Karaman (1466) were annexed; Moldavia (1455) and the khanate of the Crimea (1475–8) rendered tributary.

MEHMED IV AVCI ("the Hunter") (1642–93) Ottoman sultan, succeeding in 1648. His reign was most notable for the emergence in 1656 of the grand vizierate as the dominating institution of the state under the ministerial family of **Köprülü**. He fought incessant and not altogether unsuccessful wars in the Mediterranean (reduction of Crete, 1644–69, ended by the 13-year siege of Candia); and on the northern frontiers of the empire (invasion of Translyvania 1654, conquest of Podolia 1672). Against the **Habsburgs** he was less successful (St Gotthard campaign 1663, second unsuccessful siege of Vienna 1683). The subsequent loss of Hungary (1684–7) fuelling popular resentment, and exacerbated by the Sultan's withdrawal from matters of state and notorious obsession with hunting, precipitated his deposition in 1687 and detention until his death.

MEIJI Name meaning "enlightened rule" by which the Japanese emperor, Mutsuhito, was known during his long reign. Mutsuhito (1852–1912) came to the throne in 1867; within a year the "Meiji Restoration" ended two and a half centuries of semi-isolation in Japan under the **Tokugawa** shogunate. Under his rule, industrialization and modernization began, and a Western democratic constitution was adopted (1889). By the time of his death, Japan was widely accepted as a world power; his role was largely symbolic, new political leaders being more directly responsible for the reshaping of the nation.

MELGAREJO, MARIANO (1818–71) Bolivian dictator. A general in the Bolivian army, he deposed José Maria Achá in 1864 to become president. He conceded to Chile some of Bolivia's claim to the rich nitrate deposits of the Atacama Desert. He was deposed and assassinated in the same year.

MENELIK II (1844–1913) Emperor of Ethiopia. He was enthroned in 1889, and in 1896 defeated an Italian invasion at Adowa to ensure his country's independence and consolidate its power. He greatly expanded the boundaries of Ethiopia by conquering Galla lands in the southwest and Ogaden in the east.

MENES Traditionally, the first king to unite Upper and Lower Egypt, *c.* 3100 BC; he may also have founded the royal capital of Memphis. He is said by the historian Manetho to have ruled for 62 years and to have been killed by a hippopotamus.

MENSHEVIKS Named from **Mensheviki**, Russian for "the minority". Moderate faction in the Russian Social Democratic Party, which generally supported the **Bolshevik** regime during the civil war, after which most Mensheviks were either liquidated or absorbed into the Russian Communist Party, or emigrated.

MENTUHOTEP I Governor of the Theban province who, according to tradition, in *c.* 2120 became the first king of the 11th Dynasty and "ancestor" of the Middle Kingdom, *c.* 2040 BC.

MENTUHOTEP II (d.c. 2010 BC) King of Egypt's 11th Dynasty. He acceded *c.* 2060 to the throne of Upper Egypt. In 2046 he launched a campaign against the Herakleopolitan kingdom of Lower and Middle Egypt and by *c.* 2040 had reunited the country.

MERCANTILISM Economic theory much favoured in the 16th and 17th centuries, under which a country's prosperity was held to depend on its success in accumulating gold and silver reserves. It favoured a strict limitation of imports and the aggressive promotion of export trade.

MEROVINGIANS Frankish dynasty, ruling much of Gaul from the time of **Clovis** to their replacement by the **Carolingians** in 751.

MESOLITHIC The middle part of the **Stone Age** in Europe, representing hunting and collecting groups in the period of present-day climatic conditions after the end of the last glaciation, 10,000 years ago. It succeeded the reindeer-hunting groups of the **Palaeolithic**, and was gradually displaced by the incoming farmers of the **Neolithic**.

METAXAS, IOANNIS (1871–1941) Greek military leader. After reaching the rank of general he emerged as dictator of Greece in 1936; he defeated the Italians when they invaded the country in 1940.

METHODIST Member of one of the several Protestant denominations which developed after 1730 from the Church of England revival movement led by John and Charles Wesley. it emerged as a separate church in 1791 with supporters in both North America and Great Britain.

METHODIUS, ST *see* **Cyril**

METHUEN TREATY Commercial agreement signed in 1703 between England and Portugal. It was named after John Methuen (*c.* 1650–1706), at that time British ambassador to Lisbon. The treaty gave a preferential tariff on Portuguese wine in exchange for freer import of English woollens, and helped to promote the drinking of port in England.

METTERNICH, PRINCE KLEMENS WENZEL LOTHAR VON (1773–1859) Austrian statesman. He was ambassador to various nations, and minister of foreign affairs, 1809; following a period of collaboration with France, he then joined the victorious alliance against **Napoleon**. He was a leading figure at the **Congress of Vienna**, 1814–15, during which he restored the Habsburg empire to a leading place in Europe. He continued to be dominant in the Austrian government until the revolution of 1848.

MEWAR Independent state in northern India, first prominent in the 8th century under the Rajput clan of the Guhilas. Under Hamir in the 14th century it defied the Muslim armies of **Alauddin**; enriched by the discovery of silver and lead, it continued to battle with the Delhi sultanate and their **Mughal** successors. The state was in decline after Rana Sanga's defeat by Babur in 1527; **Akbar**'s long war against Rana Pratap was inconclusive, but Pratap's son accepted Mughal suzerainty.

MEZZOGIORNO Name for the region of Italy south of Rome, covering roughly the area of the former kingdom of Naples. Its longstanding backwardness, unemployment and low standard of living (half the per capita income of the north) have made it a perpetual preoccupation of Italian governments and planners.

MIAO Mountain-dwelling people of China, Vietnam, Laos and Thailand. Divided into more than a hundred groups distinguished by dress, dialect and customs, its members all share a heritage of Sino-Tibetan languages. In China they are concentrated in the provinces of Kweichow, Hunan, Szechwan, Kwangsi and Yunnan and Hainan island.

MIDLAND RISING Peasant rebellion in 1607 in several shires of the English east Midlands, caused mainly by the enclosure of common land by landlords which deprived the local population of grazing rights.

MIESZKO I (d.992) First ruler of united Poland, a member of the **Piast** dynasty. He succeeded as Duke of Poland *c.* 963; he expanded his territories into Galicia and Pomerania. In 966 he accepted (Roman) **Christianity** from Bohemia, and placed his country under the protection of the Holy See (mainly in the hope of securing papal protection against the "crusade" of the Germans against the Slavs).

MIESZKO II (930–1034) King of Poland, succeeding to the throne in 1025. He lost much territory to Bohemia and the **Holy Roman Empire**.

MILAN, EDICT OF Proclamation issued in AD 313, granting permanent religious toleration for people of all faiths throughout the Roman empire. It was jointly promulgated by the emperors Licinius in the Eastern and **Constantine I** in the Western empire.

MILNER, ALFRED (1854–1925) 1st Viscount Milner, British statesman and imperialist. As High Commissioner for South Africa, 1897–1905, he was responsible for the reconstruction of the Transvaal and Orange River Colony after the South African War. He was a member of the War Cabinet, 1916–18, War Secretary, 1918, and Colonial Secretary, 1919–21.

MILITARY FRONTIER At the end of the 16th century the Habsburg frontier (*Militärgrenze*) consisted of a long strip of southern Croatia in which immigrants, holding land in return for military service, manned a line of forts. The system was later extended to Slavonia and subsequently to the Banat of Temesvár and Transylvania, thus covering the whole frontier with the Ottoman empire. Highly unpopular among the Croats and Hungarians, it was finally abolished in 1872.

MILOŠEVIĆ, SLOBODAN (1941–2006) Serbian leader of Yugoslavia (1989–2000) and, from 2001, in the custody of the International War Crimes Tribunal at the Hague for war crimes and genocide in Kosovo, Bosnia and Croatia. Graduating with a law degree, Milosevic was a part of the communist movement from an early age. He became prominent in Serbian politics in the early 1980s, becoming head of the Serbian Communist League, and then President of Serbia by 1989. As communism was crumbling down around Eastern Europe, Croatia, Slovenia, Bosnia Herzegovina and later Macedonia were rumbling with nationalist aspirations, and their movement to form republics led to the Croatian (1991) and Bosnian (1992) wars. It is from this period and the later Kosovan War (1999) that the charges of genocide and war crimes have arisen and led to Milosevic being termed "The Balkan Butcher". In 2000, with severe economic difficulties as a result of sanctions, and Montenegro threatening to leave Yugoslavia, Milosevic was voted out of office. A year later he was arrested, and became the first head of state to be tried for war crimes.

MING Chinese imperial dynasty ruling 1368 to 1644; *see* pp. 184–5.

MINISTERIALES Originally of servile status, from the 11th century onwards they served as stewards, chamberlains and butlers to kings and other lords in Germany. Gradually, as they assumed military, administrative and political functions, their social status improved until, in the 14th century, their estates and offices became hereditary, and they were accepted as members of the nobility.

MINOS Early king of Crete, referred to by **Homer** and Thucydides. According to legend he was the son of Zeus and Europa, and husband of Pasiphae. Knossos was said to have been his capital and the focus of his vast seapower. The "Minoan" civilization of Crete (*c.* 3000–1500 BC) was named after him by Sir Arthur Evans, excavator of Knossos.

MISHNAH Compilation of the oral interpretations of legal portions of the Bible by the **Pharisees** and Rabbis; codified by **Judah ha-Nasi**, in Palestine around AD 200, it served as the basis for the **Talmud**.

MITCHELL, SIR THOMAS LIVINGSTONE (1792–1855) Australian explorer. Born in Scotland, he joined the British Army in 1811 and served in the Peninsular War. As surveyor-general of New South Wales (from 1828) he surveyed the province, constructed roads and (1831–47) led four major expeditions to explore and chart the Australian interior. He produced *Australian Geography* (1850) for use in schools – the first work to place Australia at the centre of the world – and published his expedition journals.

MITHRAISM Worship of Mithra or Mithras, ancient Indian and Persian god of justice and law; in pre-Zoroastrian Persia a supporter of Ahura Mazda, the great god of order and light. In the Roman empire Mithraism spread as a mystery-cult with Mithras as a divine saviour, underground chapels, initiation rites, a common meal, and the promise of a blessed immortality. The adherents were men only, mostly soldiers, traders and civil servants. In the 4th century it was ousted by **Christianity**.

MITHRIDATES (120–63 BC) King of Pontus, in Asia Minor. He assumed the throne as Mithridates VI, known as "the Great". He fought three wars with Rome, finally being defeated by **Pompey**.

MITTERAND, FRANÇOIS (1916–96) French president. He was active in the resistance in the Second World War and became a deputy in 1946, holding various offices in the Fourth Republic. He was critical of **de Gaulle**'s Fifth Republic, set up in 1958, and unsuccessfully challenged the general in the 1965 presidential elections. He tried to unify the French left, achieving success with the setting-up of the Parti Socialiste in 1971. He displaced Giscard d'Estaing as president in 1981 and introduced a policy of nationalization. Economic problems soon forced him to adopt austerity measures and abandon many socialist principles. He was obliged to cooperate with a Gaulist prime minister, Jacques Chirac, after 1986. Mitterand defeated Chirac in the 1988 presidential elections, restoring socialist pre-eminence. Despite ill-health and troubles with his party, he managed to remain in office until 1995, when he retired and was replaced by Chirac.

MOBUTU SESE SEKO (1930–97) President of Zaire (formerly Congo). He enrolled as a clerk in the Belgian Congolese army in 1949. In the mid-1950s he edited a weekly newspaper *Actualités Africaines*. He joined **Lumumba** in 1958 as a member of *Mouvement National Congolais*; and became chief of staff of the Force Publique after Congo gained independence in 1960. He supported **Kasavabu** and then ousted him in a coup in 1965, put down a white mercenary uprising in 1967 and nationalized the Katanga copper mines. In 1977 he defeated an invasion of Shaba province (Katanga) from Angola. By 1992 he found himself challenged by a growing pro-**democracy** movement, which criticized the harshness of his rule and laid accusations of human rights abuses. In May 1997 Mobutu was forced to give up the presidency. His successor, Laurent Kabila, renamed the country the Democratic Republic of Congo.

MOHAMMED (Muhammad) (c. 570–632) Prophet and founder of Islam, born in Mecca in western Arabia (now part of Saudi Arabia). When aged about 25 he married Khadija, widow of a wealthy merchant (later he made several other marriages, some for political reasons). In about 610 he received a religious call, regarded by himself and his followers as revelations from God, later written down in the **Koran**. He was forced by opposition in Mecca to emigrate to Medina in 622 at the invitation of some Arab groups there; this emigration, or **Hegira**, is the starting point of the Muslim calendar. In Medina he became first arbitrator, then ruler of a new kind of religious and political community, the Umma. He conquered Mecca in 630 and then unified much of Arabia under his leadership. After his death he was succeeded as leader of the Umma, but not as prophet, by **Abu Bakr**, first of the line of caliphs.

MOHAMMED ABDUH (1849–1905) Islamic religious reformer, born in Egypt. In 1882 he was exiled for his political activity after the British occupation of Egypt. Returning, he was appointed appellate judge in 1891. He suggested many modernizing liberal reforms in Islamic law, education, ritual and social thought.

MOHAMMED ALI (1769–1849) Founder of modern Egypt; born in Macedonia. He was appointed Ottoman viceroy in Egypt, 1805. He took Syria from the Turks in 1831 but was forced to give it up in 1840 after European intervention. In the following year he was compensated by recognition as hereditary ruler of Egypt and the Sudan.

MOHAMMED V (1906–61) King of Morocco. He succeeded his father as sultan of Morocco in 1927, then under French tutelage which he worked to remove. Deposed and exiled by the French, 1953–5, he was first reinstated as sultan and then recognized as sovereign (1956) and first king of Morocco (1957).

MÖNGKE (d.1259) Mongol leader, grandson of Genghis Khan. He played a prominent part in the great Mongol drive into western Asia and Europe. Elected Great Khan in 1251, he planned a world conquest, from China to Egypt.

MONISM Philosophic doctrine that asserts the single nature of phenomena and denies duality or pluralism (i.e. the separateness of mind and matter). Religiously, it is also the doctrine that there is only one Being, not an opposition of good and evil, or a distinction of God from the world.

MONOPHYSITES Those who followed Eutyches and Dioscorus, Patriarch of Alexandria (d.454), who taught that there was only one nature, not two, in the person of **Jesus** Christ. This doctrine was condemned by the **Council of Chalcedon** (451). Modern churches which grew out of Monophysitism are orthodox in belief though they retain some Monophysite terminology, notably the Coptic, Syrian and Armenian variations.

MONROE, JAMES (1758–1831) Fifth president of the USA. He negotiated the **Louisiana Purchase** (1803). During his presidency, 1817–25, he drew up with his secretary of state, **John Quincy Adams**, the Monroe Doctrine, which has aimed at excluding foreign influence from the Western Hemisphere ever since.

MONTAGNARDS Hill-dwellers in Indo-China. In Vietnam they cultivate rice on burned-out forest land, live in longhouses or huts raised on piles, trace their descent through the female line, and speak a variety of Mon-Khmer and Malayo-Polynesian languages.

MONTANIST Follower of the heretical Christian sect founded in Phrygia by Montanus and by two women, Prisca and Maximilla, in the 2nd century AD. The group was ecstatic and prophetic, restoring belief in the present power of the spirit; there was mystical identification with the divine and ascetic practice. **Tertullian** was a notable convert, but by the 3rd century the sect was under condemnation; it persisted in Phrygia until the 5th century.

MONTCALM, LOUIS, MARQUIS DE (1712–59) French general who as commander-in-chief of the French Canadian forces defended Canada against the British in the French and Indian War (1756–60). He was killed during the battle for Quebec on the Heights of Abraham.

MONTESQUIEU, BARON DE (1689–1755) French political philosopher. His main works included *Lettres Persanes* (1721), satirizing French life and politics, and *L'Esprit des Lois* (1748), his masterpiece, which first set out many of the key ideas in modern democratic and constitutional thought, characteristic of the Enlightenment and of rationalism.

MONTEZUMA II (MOCTEZUMA II) Montezuma II (1502–1519) tried to consolidate the Aztec empire, reducing the opportunities for social advancement by warriors and merchants and concentrating power in the hands of the top nobility. However, Montezuma was also a notable warrior who extended the Aztec domain so that in Central Mexico only the Tarascans and Tlaxcalans remained undefeated. At the time Cortés arrived in 1519 the Aztecs were fighting a bitter war with the Tlaxcalans, which the Spanish were able to exploit.

MONTFORT, SIMON DE (c. 1160–1218) Baron of Montfort (near Paris). He became a leader of the Albigensian Crusade and Count of Toulouse after the battle of Muret, 1213; he extended north French and Catholic influence in the south of France. He was the father of Simon de Montfort, Earl of Leicester, the opponent of Henry III of England.

MORDAUNT, SIR JOHN (1698–1780) British general. In 1756 he commanded the army assembled in Dorset to repel an expected French invasion; in 1757 he led an unsuccessful expedition (with Admiral Hawke) to attack the French naval base at Rochefort, and was court-martialled for his failure.

MORELOS, JOSÉ MARIA (1765–1815) Mexican priest and revolutionary. He joined Hidalgo's insurrection against the Spanish colonial government, 1811, and took command in southern Mexico after Hidalgo's death, leading a successful guerrilla army but with too few men to consolidate his victories. In 1813 he called the Congress of Chilpancingo, which declared Mexican independence, but two years later was captured, defrocked and shot as a traitor after directing a heroic rearguard action against the Spaniards.

MORENO, MARIANO GARCIA (1778–1811) Argentine independence leader. He practised as a lawyer in Buenos Aires; in 1809 published his "Landowners' petition" (*Representación de los hacendados*) attacking restrictive Spanish trade laws, and in 1810 joined the revolutionary junta which replaced the Spanish administration. He became secretary for military and political affairs; founded Argentina's national library and official newspaper, *La Gaceta de Buenos Aires*. He was forced to resign after prematurely advocating complete separation on a diplomatic mission to London.

MORGAN, JOHN PIERPONT (1837–1913) US financier. In 1871 he joined the New York firm of Drexel, Morgan & Co. (renamed J.P. Morgan & Co. in 1895); under his guidance this became one of the world's greatest financial institutions, deeply involved in US government borrowing, reorganization of the US railways and the formation of such massive industrial groups as US Steel, International Harvester and the General Electric Company. By the time of his death his name was accepted everywhere as a symbol of "money power"; he had also formed a great art collection.

MORSI, MOHAMED (1951–) The first democratically elected head of state in Egyptian history, he served as fifth president of Egypt from June 2012 to July 2013 representing the Muslim Brotherhood, a Pan-Islamic religious and social movement founded in Egypt. He was removed from the presidency by a military coup following massive demonstrations against his rule. On 16 May 2015, he was sentenced to death by an Egyptian court for his alleged role in the Wadi el-Natrun prison break during the 2011 revolution.

MOSES Israelite leader, prophet and lawgiver who flourished some time between the 15th and 13th centuries BC. According to the Old Testament, he was born in Egypt; he led the Israelites out of slavery, and travelled 40 years in the Sinai desert seeking Canaan, the land promised to the descendants of **Abraham**. He received the Ten Commandments, the basis of Jewish law; he died within sight of the promised land.

MOSLEY, SIR OSWALD (1896–1980) Leader of the British Union of Fascists. He served as a member of parliament, successively as a Conservative, Independent and Labour representative. He left the Labour Party in 1930 to found the right-wing "New Party" and, later, the BUF or Blackshirts. He was imprisoned by the British government during the Second World War, and subsequently lived in France.

MOSSADEQ, MOHAMMED (?1880–1967) Iranian politician. As prime minister, 1951–3, he nationalized the Anglo-Iranian oil company. After a struggle for power with the Shah and his supporters, and with Western oil interests, he was overturned by a *coup d'état* in 1953 and imprisoned until 1956.

MOUNTBATTEN, LOUIS, EARL (1900–79) British military commander. A grandson of Queen Victoria, he entered the Royal Navy in 1913 and was personal aide-de-camp to the British sovereign from 1936. He was allied chief of combined operations, 1942–3; supreme commander Southeast Asia, 1943–6; last viceroy (1947) and first governor-general (1947–8) of India; commanded the Mediterranean fleet (1948–9 and 1952–4); and became first sea lord (1955–9), chief of UK defence staff and chairman of chiefs of staff committee (1959–65). He was killed by Irish terrorists in 1979.

MSIRI (d.1891) African king, also known as Ngetengwa and Mwendo. Born near Tabora, now in Tanzania, in 1856 he settled in southern Katanga (Shaba). With a handful of Nyamwezi supporters, he seized large parts of this valuable copper-producing region, and by 1870 had largely displaced the previous Lunda rulers. His rejection of overtures from the British South Africa Company in the 1880s resulted in the Copper Belt being divided between Great Britain (Zambia) and Belgium (Zaire). He was shot while negotiating with emissaries from **Leopold II** of Belgium's Congo Free State.

MUBARAK, HOSNI (1928–) Egyptian military officer and politician who served as president of Egypt from October 1981 (after the assassination of Anwar Sadat by Islamic militants) until February 2011, when popular unrest forced him to step down. In late May 2011, judicial officials announced that Mubarak, along with his two sons – Alaa and Gamal – would stand trial over the deaths of anti-government protesters. In November 2014, he was finally acquitted in a retrial.

MUGABE, ROBERT (1924–) Leader of Zimbabwe (1987–). Graduating from Fort Hare University in South Africa, Mugabe returned to what was then Rhodesia in 1960, joining the Zimbabwe African People's Union (Zapu) but left within three years to form the rival Zimbabwe African National Union (Zanu). He was jailed without trial for 10 years and, following his release, fought against Ian Smith's Rhodesian Front government from Mozambique. After the Lancaster agreement in 1979, he became Prime Minister of a coalition government with Zapu's leader Nkomo in 1980, and further consolidated his power when a large arms cache discovery at Zapu's properties led to Nkomo's removal from government. Mugabe became President in 1987 and his increasingly nationalist policies of removing land from white farmers and redistributing amongst black farmers, his role in the war in the Congo, his stifling and oppression of political opposition, and his heavy handed control of the media, have all contributed to Zimbabwe's degenerating economy and tarnished his reputation.

MUGHALS Dynasty of Muslim emperors in India.

MUHAMMAD IBN TUGHLUQ (c. 1290–1351) Indian empire-builder, who succeeded his father in 1325 as ruler of the Delhi sultanate. He extended the frontiers far into southern India, fighting many campaigns to consolidate his gains; he failed, however, to impose coherent control, and saw his domains begin to crumble before he died.

MUIZZUDIN MUHAMMAD (d.1206) Greatest of the **Ghurids**. He helped his brother to seize power in Ghur, northwest Afghanistan, *c.* 1162, expelled Turkish nomads from Ghazni, 1173; invaded northern India, 1175; annexed the **Ghaznavid** principality of Lahore, 1186. He was defeated by a **Rajput** coalition at Tara, 1191, but returned to rout them in 1192. He was assassinated in 1206.

MUJIBUR RAHMAN (1920–75) Bengali political leader. He worked for Bengali rights until independence from British rule (1947), founded the Awami League (1949) opposed to the domination of West Pakistan, of which he became general secretary (1953) and president (1966). Tensions resulting from his party's majority victory and demand for autonomy from West Pakistan (1970) resulted in an India-Pakistan war, and an independent Bangladesh (1971). In 1975 he became president with dictatorial powers, but was killed in a coup the same year.

MUKDEN, BATTLE OF Main land engagement of the Russo-Japanese War (1904–05). Mukden (Shenyang), the industrial centre of Manchuria, became a tsarist stronghold after Russia obtained extensive railway building rights in the region (1896). The battle lasted over two weeks, starting in late February 1905 and ending with Japanese occupation of the city on 10 March.

MULVANY, WILLIAM THOMAS (1806–85) Irish industrialist. An engineer and civil servant 1833–49, he went to the German Ruhr district in 1854 and directed the opening of coalmines and ironworks there. In 1858 he organized an association of Ruhr industrialists (the *Bergbauverein*) which transformed the Ruhr into the largest coalfield and industrial complex on the European continent.

MÜNSTER, TREATY OF An agreement signed in January 1648 as part of the arrangements known collectively as the Peace of Westphalia, which ended the Thirty Years' War. It brought Spanish recognition of the independence of the Dutch Republic and brought to an end the Dutch Revolt.

MURAD I (*c.* 1326–89) Third ruler of the Ottoman state, succeeding **Orkhan** in 1362. He controlled (or profited from) the continuing Turkish expansion in the Balkans which brought Thrace and later Thessaly, the south Serbian principalities and much of Bulgaria under Ottoman control. Byzantium, Bulgaria and Serbia were successively reduced to vassalage after the defeat of hostile coalition forces at Chirmen (Chermanon) in 1371 and Kossovo in 1389; Murad was killed during the latter battle. Ottoman territory was also expanded in Anatolia (acquisition of Ankara, 1354; hostilities with the Karaman in the 1380s).

MURAD II (1404–51) Ottoman sultan, son of **Mehmed I**. Succeeding to the throne in 1421, he spent the early years of his reign overcoming rival claimants backed by Byzantium or Karaman. After a seven-year war with Venice, Murad took Salonika in 1430. The later years of his reign were dominated by the struggle with Hungary for the lands of the lower Danube, Serbia and Wallachia. Murad gained control over Serbia in 1439 but in 1440 failed to take Belgrade; by 1443 the Ottomans were forced on to the defensive at Izladi, and in the following year, having made an unfavourable peace with Hungary and Karaman, Murad abdicated in favour of his 12-year-old son **Mehmed II**. Following the penetration of the Balkans by a Christian army, Murad led the Ottoman forces to a crushing victory at Varna in 1444. Two years later he reassumed the throne; in 1448 he defeated the Hungarians once more at Kosovo.

MUSSOLINI, BENITO (1883–1945) Italian dictator. He practised as a schoolteacher and journalist; having been expelled in 1914 from the Socialist party for advocating support of the Allied powers, in 1919 he organized the Fascist party, advocating nationalism, syndicalism and violent anti-**communism**, backed up by a para-military organization, the Blackshirts. He organized a march on Rome in 1922. He was appointed prime minister and then, as Il Duce (the Leader), established himself as totalitarian dictator. He invaded Ethiopia in 1935, formed the Rome-Berlin Axis with **Hitler** the following year, and in 1940 declared war on the Allies. He was defeated in 1943, installed by Hitler as head of a puppet state (Republic of Salo) in northern Italy and shot by Italian partisans in 1945.

MWENEMUTAPA (later Mashonaland) Kingdom of southeast Africa between the 14th and 18th centuries, with its capital probably at Zimbabwe; famous for its gold deposits, which attracted Portuguese traders, based in Mozambique, from 1505 onwards.

MYCENAEAN Ancient Greek civilization flourishing c. 1600–1100 BC, culturally influenced by **Minoan** Crete. It was centred on the city of Mycenae, in Argolis, where the most famous surviving monuments include the citadel walls with the Lion gate, and the treasury of Atreus.

MZILIKAZI (d.1870) Matabele (Ndebele) chief. He fled from Zululand to set up a new kingdom north of the Vaal river, but was defeated by the Boers, 1836; he withdrew across the Limpopo river and established the Matabele kingdom.

N

NABOPOLASSAR (d.605 BC) King of Babylon and destroyer of Assyria, a notable of one of the Kaldu (Chaldaean) tribes of southern Babylonia. While governor of the Sea-land province, he assumed leadership of an insurrection against the Assyrians in 627 BC. He founded the last native Babylonian dynasty, the Chaldaean, in 626, quickly gaining control of much of Babylonia. He unsuccessfully besieged Ashur, 616, formed an alliance with the **Medes**, 614, and made a joint assault on Nineveh which was completed in 612. He was succeeded by his son, Nebuchadnezzar.

NANAK (1469–1539) Founding guru of the Sikh faith, combing Hindu and Muslim beliefs into a single doctrine. The son of a merchant, he made an extended pilgrimage to Muslim and Hindu shrines throughout India, returning to the Punjab in 1520 and settling in Kartarpur. His teaching, spread by a large following of disciples, advocated intensive meditation on the divine name; many of his hymns still survive.

NANKING TREATY *see* **Opium War**

NANTES, EDICT OF Order, issued in 1598 by **Henry IV** of France, guaranteeing freedom of worship to French Protestants. Its revocation in 1685 by **Louis XIV** forced many non-Catholics to flee the country, weakening the French economy and creating much international friction.

NAPIER, SIR CHARLES JAMES (1782–1853) British general and prolific author. He served under **Wellington** in the Peninsular War, and led the British conquest of Sind, 1841–3.

NAPOLEON I (NAPOLEON BONAPARTE) (1769–1821) Emperor of the French; *see* pp. 224–5, 228–9.

NAPOLEON III (CHARLES LOUIS NAPOLEON BONAPARTE) (1808–73) Emperor of the French, son of Louis Bonaparte and nephew of **Napoleon I**. He was exiled, like his uncle, after 1815. He wrote *Les Idées Napoléoniennes* in 1839, was involved in two unsuccessful insurrections, in 1836 and 1840, and returned to France after the 1848 revolution, to be elected president by a huge majority, and to become emperor in 1852. During his highly prosperous reign, central Paris was rebuilt, Cochin China was acquired and the Suez canal opened. He was defeated by **Bismarck** in the **Franco-Prussian War** (1870–1), and after the collapse of his regime in 1871 went into exile in England.

NARAI (d.1688) (also Narayana) King of Siam from 1657 until his death. In his struggle to free his country's foreign trade from Dutch control he sought the help of the **English East Indian Company**'s factors at Ayutthaya. Their inability to help caused him to turn to the French, whose cause was espoused by his Greek adviser, **Constant Phaulkoni**, a convert to Catholicism. After an exchange of missions between Versailles and Lopburi, Narai's up-country residence, **Louis XIV** sent a naval expedition which seized the then village of Bangkok and the port of Mergui (now in Myanmar) with the declared aim of converting Siam to **Christianity**. The resulting national uprising, led by Pra Phetraja, forced the French to withdraw; Pra Phetraja became regent, and on Narai's death a few months later his successor.

NARAM-SIN The last great ruler of Sumer and Akkad, in ancient Mesopotamia, and grandson of **Sargon**. He reigned *c.* 2213–2176 BC, and was a famous warrior whose victories are commemorated in several extant carvings and monuments, including the impressive stele found at Susa, now in the Louvre museum.

NASRIDS The last Muslim dynasty in Spain, which rose to power under Muhammad I al-Ghalib (died 1272) and ruled Granada from 1238 until its conquest by the Christians in 1492.

NASSER, GAMAL ABDEL- (1918–70) Egyptian politician. As an army officer he became the leading member of the group which overthrew King **Farouk** in 1952, under the nominal leadership of General **Neguib**. In 1954, after a power struggle with Neguib, he became prime minister, and in 1956 president until his death. His regime was marked by socio-economic changes – reform of land-tenure, building of the Aswan High Dam – and initially by a foreign policy of neutralism between the great powers and leadership of the Arab nationalist movement, which led to the short-lived union with Syria in the United Arab Republic (1958–61), two wars (with Israel, Great Britain and France, 1956, with Israel, 1967), and increasing dependence on the USSR.

NATIONALISM A movement that consciously aims to unify a nation, create a state or liberate it from foreign or imperialist rule. Nationalist movements became a potent factor in European politics in the 19th century. Since 1900, nationalism has been a strong force in anti-imperialist movements in Asia and Africa.

NATO *see* **North Atlantic Treaty Organization**

NAVAJO North American Indian tribe which probably emigrated from Canada to the region of the southwest USA between 900 and 1200. After a long history of raids against white settlers in New Mexico, 8000 Navajo were captured by a force under Colonel Kit Carson (1863–4) and interned for four years in New Mexico; in 1868 they were released and sent to a reservation. Today some 100,000 Navajo survive, many still occupying the 62,180 sq km (24,000 square miles) reservation in New Mexico, Arizona and Utah. They form the largest Indian tribe in the USA.

NAZISM Term formed from the abbreviation for the National Socialist Germany Workers' Party – leader **Adolf Hitler**. Its creed covered many of the features of **Fascism**. Its special characteristics were a belief in the racial superiority of the "**Aryan** race" and of the German people who, as the purest carriers of Aryan blood, constituted a master race destined to dominate the sub-human Slav peoples of eastern Europe and Russia; virulent anti-semitism expressed in the systematic extermination of the Jewish population throughout Europe, the Jews being accused of an insatiable desire to corrupt and destroy Aryan purity and culture; anti-urbanism and anti-intellectualism, the peasant being held to be purified by his contact with the land; the personality and ruthless political leadership of Hitler, who believed himself destined to risk all to lead the German people to the empire which would last for 1000 years.

NAZI-SOVIET PACT (also known as Molotov-Ribbentrop Pact) Mutual non-aggression pact signed on 23 August 1939 between Germany and Soviet Russia, containing secret protocols which divided eastern Europe between the signatories: eastern Poland, Latvia, Estonia, Finland and Bessarabia to Russia; western Poland and Lithuania (later transferred to the Russian sphere) to Germany. The Russians invaded Poland 17 days after the Germans, on 17 September 1939.

NDEBELE *see* **Matabele**

NEGUIB, MOHAMMED (1901–84) Egyptian soldier and president. He was second in command of Egyptian troops in Palestine in the first Arab-Israeli war in 1948. Adopted as their titular head by the Egyptian officers who made the revolution of 1952, after the revolution he became prime minister and president of the republic, 1953–4. He was deprived of office after a struggle for power with the real leader of the officers, **Nasser**.

NEHRU, JAWAHARLAL (1889–1964) The first prime minister of independent India, 1947–64. Educated in England, in 1920 he joined the nationalist movement led by **Gandhi**, and was imprisoned eight times between 1920 and 1927. He was four times president of the Indian National Congress Party: 1929–30, 1936–7, 1946 and 1951–4.

NELSON, HORATIO (1758–1805) First Viscount Nelson. British naval hero, who rose to the rank of admiral in 1797 during the French Revolutionary Wars, winning decisive victories at the Nile (1798) and at Copenhagen (1801). He was killed in 1805 during his most famous battle, Trafalgar, which effectively ended the threat of a French invasion of England.

NEOLITHIC The last part of the **Stone Age**, originally defined by the occurrence of polished stone tools, but now seen as more importantly characterized by the practice of agriculture, for which sharp stone axes were essential forest-clearing equipment. Such cultures emerged in the Near East by 8000 BC, and appeared in Europe from 6000 to 3000 BC.

NERCHINSK, TREATY OF Peace agreement signed in 1689 between Russia and China, as a result of which Russia withdrew from lands east of the Stanovoy mountains and north of the Amur river. The settlement lasted until the treaties of **Aigun** (1858) and **Peking** (1860) brought Russia to its present boundary with China in the Far East.

NERO (AD 37–68) Roman emperor, succeeding to the imperial title in AD 54. He murdered his mother, Agrippina, in 59. After the fire of Rome in 64 he began a systematic persecution of Christians, and in the following year executed many opponents after the discovery of a plot to depose him. He committed suicide when the governors of Gaul, Spain and Africa united in revolt.

NESTORIANS Followers of Nestorius whose Christian teachings, condemned by the councils of Ephesus (431) and Chalcedon (451), stressed the independence of the divine and human natures of Christ. They are represented in modern times by the Syrian Orthodox Church (approximately 100,000 members in Iran, Syria and Iraq) which first accepted this version of **Christianity** in 486.

NETANYAHU, BENJAMIN (1949–) Israeli politician and leader of the centre-right Likud party, who twice served as his country's prime minister (1996–99 and 2009 onwards). In March 2015, he was elected to his fourth term as prime minister and is currently the second longest-serving prime minister in Israel's history after David Ben-Gurion. Over the course of his premierships, he moved Israel further away from the achievements of the peace process in 2000 and widened the gap between Israeli and Palestinian communities.

NEVSKY, ALEXANDER (c. 1220–63) Prince of Novgorod. He defeated the Swedes on the river Neva (hence his name) in 1240; and the Teutonic Knights on frozen Lake Peipus, 1242. He thought resistance to the Mongols hopeless and cooperated with them; in return the Khan made him Grand Prince of Vladimir (i.e. ruler of Russia) in 1252.

NEWCOMEN, THOMAS (1663–1729) English inventor of the atmospheric engine. As an ironmonger, he saw the high cost and inefficiency of using horses to drain the Cornish tin mines, and after ten years of experiment produced a steam machine for this purpose. The first known engine was erected near Dudley Castle, Staffordshire, in 1712. He also invented an internal-condensing jet to produced a vacuum in the engine cylinder, and an automatic valve gear.

NEW DEAL Social and economic programme, instituted 1933–9 by President **F.D. Roosevelt** to combat the effects of world depression in the USA. He used the Federal government to promote agricultural and industrial recovery, to provide relief to the unemployed, and to institute moderate economic and social reform.

NE WIN (1911–2002) Military dictator of Burma. He joined the nationalistic "We-Burmans Association" in 1936, and in 1941 went to Taiwan (Formosa) for military training with the Japanese. He was chief of staff, Burma National Army, 1943–5, commander-in-chief of the Burmese army after independence in 1948, and served as prime minister in the 1958 "caretaker" government. He stepped down in 1960 on the restoration of parliamentary administration, but in 1962 led a *coup d'état*, establishing a Revolutionary Council of the Union of Burma and declaring the Burmese Road to Socialism. He broke Chinese and Indian control of the economy and expelled 300,000 foreigners. He resigned in 1988 under pressure from pro-**democracy**, communist and nationalist forces.

NGO DINH DIEM (1901–63) President of the Republic of Vietnam. Born into one of Vietnam's royal families, he was interior minister of the emperor Bao Dai's government in the 1930s. In 1945 he was captured by **Ho Chi Minh**'s communists, and fled after refusing Ho's invitation to join his independence movement. Returned in 1954 to head the US-backed government in South Vietnam, but took dictatorial powers, and as a Roman Catholic imprisoned and killed hundreds of Buddhists. He was abandoned by the USA, and was assassinated during a military *coup d'état*.

NGUNI One of the two main Bantu-speaking groups of southern African peoples, including the Swazi, Pondo, Thembu, **Xhosa**, **Zulu** and **Matabele** (Ndebele) nations, mainly occupying land east of the Drakensburg mountains, from Natal to Cape Province.

NICAEA, COUNCILS OF The first council, which was also the first ecumenical gathering of the Christian Church, was called in 325 by the Emperor **Constantine**; it condemned the heresy of Arianism and promulgated the Nicene Creed, which affirms the consubstantiality of Christ the Son and God the Father. The second Nicaean (or seventh ecumenical) council took place in 787 as an attempt to resolve the controversy over **iconoclasm**; it agreed that icons deserved reverence and veneration but not adoration, which was reserved for God.

NICAEA, EMPIRE OF Founded in 1204 by the Byzantine leader Theodore I Lascaris after the Western occupation of Constantinople during the fourth **Crusade**. Crowned emperor in 1208, Theodore gradually extended his territory to include most of western Anatolia. His successors, while fighting off the despots of Epirus and the Mongols, also attempted to retake Constantinople; success came in 1261 when the Nicaean general, Michael Palaeologus, was able to establish himself as Michael VIII and found the last dynasty of Byzantine emperors.

NICEPHORUS II PHOCAS (c. 913–69) Byzantine emperor, who fought as a general under Constantine VII and Romanus II and usurped the throne in 963. He defeated Arab, Bulgarian, Italian and Western imperial enemies. He was murdered in 969 by his own general John Tzimisces, who in turn usurped the throne as John I.

NICHOLAS II (1869–1918) Last tsar of Russia, son of Alexander III. He succeeded in 1894; granted, but then largely withdrew liberal reforms after the revolution of 1905. He was forced to abdicate in March 1917, and was shot at Yekaterinburg (Sverdlovsk, now again Yekaterinburg) by the **Bolsheviks** in July 1918.

NIEN REBELLION Insurrection led by peasant bandit confederations in Anhwei, Honan and Shantung, areas which had suffered from the disastrous flooding of the Yellow River in the 1850s.

NIJMEGEN, TREATIES OF Agreements signed 1678–9 to end the Dutch War (1672–8) between France, Spain and the Dutch Republic. France returned Maastricht to the United Provinces and suspended her anti-Dutch tariff of 1667; Spain gave up Franche-Compté, Artois and 16 Flemish garrison towns to France, thus losing its "corridor" from Milan to the Spanish Netherlands (the Spanish Road). In 1679 the German emperor, Leopold I, accepted the terms, slightly strengthening French rights in Alsace, Lorraine and on the Rhine.

NIMITZ, CHESTER WILLIAM (1885–1965) American admiral, commander-in-chief of the Pacific Ocean Area, 1942–5.

NINE YEARS' WAR Conflict between **Louis XIV** of France and his neighbours, 1689–97, led by William II of England and the Netherlands, allied in the **League of Augsburg**. Their aim was to restrain French territorial expansion, mainly at the expense of the Spanish empire, and in this they eventually succeeded. *See also* **King William's War**.

NIVELLE, ROBERT-GEORGES (1856–1924) French general. After two brilliant victories at Verdun, he was appointed commander-in-chief of the French armies on the Western Front in 1916, but was replaced by Pétain in 1917 after the disastrous failure of the spring offensive and widespread mutiny.

NIXON, RICHARD MILHOUS (1913–94) 37th president of the USA. Trained as a lawyer he was elected to the House of Representatives in 1946 and 1948; elected Republican senator for California, 1950. He was vice-president to **Dwight D. Eisenhower** (1953–61); defeated for the presidency by **John F. Kennedy**, 1960, and in the contest for California governorship, 1962. He re-entered politics to defeat Humphrey in the presidential election, 1969, and was re-elected in a landslide victory, 1972. He resigned office in 1974 at the climax of the investigation into the Watergate scandal arising out of an attempt to burgle the Democratic election headquarters during the 1972 campaign.

NIZAM Hereditary title of the rulers of the Indian state of Hyderabad; members of the dynasty founded by Asaf Jah, Subadhar of the Deccan, 1713–48.

NKRUMAH, KWAME (1909–72) The first prime minister of independent Ghana (formerly the Gold Coast colony). He graduated from Achimota College in 1930. He wrote *Towards Colonial Freedom* in 1947 in opposition to British rule, and in 1949 formed the Convention People's Party, instituting a programme of non-cooperation. After independence (1957) he became first president of the Ghana republic, 1960; in 1964 he declared a one-party state, but was deposed two years later by the army while on a visit to China.

NOBEL, ALFRED BERNHARD (1833–96) Swedish industrialist, chemist and inventor of dynamite. He began the manufacture of nitro-glycerine in Sweden in 1860; his first factory blew up, killing his younger brother Emil. He perfected a much safer dynamite, and patented it in 1867–8. He made an immense fortune from this and from his share of the Russian Baku oilfield. When he died he left the bulk of his money in trust to establish the Nobel prizes for peace, literature, physics, chemistry, medicine and, more recently, economics.

NOK One of the Iron Age cultures in west Africa, flourishing on the Benue plateau of Nigeria between 500 BC and AD 200. It is characterized by its distinctive clay figurines depicting both animals and men.

NORIEGA, MANUAL ANTONIO (1938–) Panamanian military and political leader. Educated at the Military Academy in Peru before becoming a lieutenant in the Panamanian National Guard in 1962. In 1970 he became head of Intelligence Services and in 1983 dictator and president of the republic of Panama. Courted by the CIA during the 1960s, he was eventually charged with drug trafficking and forcibly deposed and removed by US troops in 1989 to be indicted. He was jailed for 40 years, later commuted to 30.

NORMANS Name derived from Nordmanni, or Northmen, to describe the Viking invaders who in the late 9th century established themselves on the lower Seine, in France. In 911, under their leader Hrolfr (Rollo), they obtained from the French king, Charles the Simple, rights to territory in northern Normandy; in 924 and 933 their control was extended, particularly westward, to include the whole area now known as Normandy. In the 11th century, under Robert and Roger Guiscard, and Duke William (**William I, the Conqueror**) respectively, their descendants conquered both Sicily and England.

NORMAN CONQUEST Name given to the successful invasion of England in 1066 by Duke William of Normandy, crowned king as **William I, the Conqueror**. English resistance was broken and the whole country overrun by 1071. Stabilization was achieved by expelling the **Anglo-Saxon** landowners and parcelling out the conquered territory among Williams' followers, as tenants-in-chief and vassals of the king.

NORTH ATLANTIC TREATY ORGANIZATION (NATO) Defensive alliance signed in 1949 between Belgium, Canada, Denmark, France, Iceland, Italy, Luxembourg, Netherlands, Norway, Portugal, United Kingdom and USA. Greece and Turkey joined in 1951; West Germany in 1954. France ceased to participate fully in 1966. NATO's headquarters are in Brussels; it deployed some 800,000 land troops in Europe.

NORTHERN RISING Attempted rebellion in northern England against **Elizabeth I** in 1569–70. Led by the Catholic earls of Northumberland and Westmorland, its object was to restore Catholicism by placing the imprisoned (Catholic) Mary Queen of Scots on the English throne. Faced by royal armies, the rebels melted away, although 800 of them died in the only direct clash; the leaders fled abroad.

NORTH GERMAN CONFEDERATION Political union of north German states set up under Prussian leadership after the Seven Weeks' War in 1866. It was enlarged in 1871 after the Franco-Prussian War to become the new German empire.

NOVATIAN (c. 200–c. 258) Roman theologian, author of *De Trinitate* (*On the Trinity*). He at first supported those Christians whose faith lapsed under persecution, but later strongly condemned all apostasy. After 251, when Cornelius became Pope, this led him to break with the Church and set himself up as a rigorist anti-Pope, at the head of the Novatianist Schism. He was excommunicated in 251, and probably martyred *c.* 258 under the Emperor **Valerian**, but the sect continued to spread in East and West and lasted until the 6th century.

NU-PIEDS Peasants who rebelled in protest against high taxes in Normandy, France, in 1639; named after the salt-gatherers of Avranches, who walked barefoot on the sands. They feared that the introduction of a salt tax (*gabelle*) would reduce sales of their product, and took a leading part in the uprising, which was crushed after four months in a pitched battle with government forces outside Rouen.

NURI ES-SAID (1888–1958) Iraqi statesman. An officer in the Ottoman army, in 1916 he joined the revolt of Sharif **Hussein** against the Ottomans, and in 1921 joined Hussein's son Faysal when he became king of Iraq. He held various ministerial posts, including that of prime minister. In 1941 he fled Iraq with the regent, Abdullah, during the period of rule by **Rashid Ali**, returned after the British military reoccupation, and dominated Iraqi politics, with intervals, until he was killed during an army coup. He was associated with the strongly pro-Western policy which led to the formation of the Baghdad Pact (**Central Treaty Organization**) in 1955.

NYAMWEZI A Bantu-speaking people of east Africa, occupying a large area between Lake Victoria and Lake Rukwa. In the 19th century they played a major part in the opening up of the east African interior to European trade from the coast.

NYERERE, JULIUS (1922–1999) President of Tanzania. Founder president of the Tanganyika African National Union in 1954, he was elected to the Tanganyika legislative council in 1958, and became chief minister, 1960–1, and prime minister, 1961–2. He was president, first of Tanganyika, 1962–4, and then of Tanzania from 1964–85. He remained in power after 1985 as leader of the only legal party, but in 1992 promised to end the one-party system. The author of *Freedom and Unity* (1967) and Swahili translations of Shakespeare, he developed theories of African socialism, and put these and other economic self-sufficiency policies into practice. He resigned in October 1995.

NYSTAD, TREATY OF Agreement in 1721 between Russia and Sweden to end the **Great Northern War**. Russia gained Sweden's Baltic provinces (Estonia and Livonia) and thus a "window on the west", but restored Finland to Sweden.

O

OBAMA, BARACK HUSSEIN (1961–) 44th president of the United States and the first African-American president. After studying law in Harvard, Obama was elected to the Illinois State Senate in 1996 and the US Senate in 2004 before winning the presidential election for the Democratic Party in 2008. He received the Nobel Peace Prize in 2009 and was re-elected in 2012. The passing of the Affordable Care Act in 2010 and the end of combat operations in Iraq and Afghanistan were among the landmarks of his presidency, which was marked by conflicts with the conservative opposition.

OCTAVIAN see **Augustus**

OFFA (d.796) King of Mercia, central England, in the 8th century. He constructed an earthwork which still survives (Offa's Dyke) between his kingdom and Wales. He claimed the title "King of the English" after establishing control over most of the country south of the river Humber.

OGEDEI (d.1241) Mongol ruler, third son of **Genghis Khan**. He was given chief command, in preference to his brothers, Jochi and Chagatai, during the latter part of the Khwarizian campaign, 1220–2; elected Great Khan in 1229, in 1235 he completed the conquest of the **Ch'in** in northern China and declared war on China's Sung dynasty, and in 1236 conquered Korea. He planned the western campaign that finally carried the Mongols from Siberia to the Adriatic.

O'HIGGINS, BERNARDO (1778–1842) Liberator of Chile, and its first head of state. The son of a Spanish officer of Irish origin; he became a member of the Chilean national congress in 1811; and then led Chilean forces in **San Martín**'s Army of the Andes, triumphing over the royalists at the battle of Chacabuco in February 1817. In 1823 he was exiled to Peru, where he died.

OJEDA, ALONSO DE (1465–1515) Spanish adventurer, who sailed under, and later quarrelled with, **Columbus**. In 1499, with **Vespucci**, he explored the coasts of Venezuela and Guiana, landing in the area later claimed by Spain (1593) under the name Surinam. He commanded the first mainland settlement in South America, on the Gulf of Urabá, 1509 – a disastrous failure.

OLDENBURGS Danish royal family, of German origin. Christian, Count of Oldenburg, was elected king of Denmark and Norway in 1448; his direct descendants ruled until 1863, when the succession passed to the present Glücksburg branch.

OLGIERD (d.1377) Grand Duke of Lithuania, reigning 1345–77, son of **Gedymin**, father of **Wladyslaw II Jagiello**. He invaded Mongol-dominated Russia in 1362–3, seizing the principality of Kiev, but failed to take Moscow in 1368–72. He died fighting the **Tatars**.

OLOF SKÖTKONUNG (d.1022) "The Tax King". Christian king of the Swedes and the Gantat; son of Erik the Victorious. He joined the Danish king, **Sven Forkbeard**, to defeat Norway in 1000; though he became a Christian he failed to impose the new religion on his subjects.

OMAR IBN AL-KHATTAB (c. 591–644) Second Muslim caliph, and the first to assume the title "Commander of the Faithful". At first he opposed Islam, but was converted *c.* 617; his daughter Hafsa became **Mohammed**'s third wife. He aided the first caliph, **Abu Bakr**, in his campaigns, succeeding him without opposition in 634, and carried further the conquests he had begun in Palestine, Syria, Iraq, Persia and Egypt. He was assassinated by a slave of Persian origin.

OPEC see **Organization of Petroleum Exporting Countries**

OPIUM WAR Fought between Britain and China, 1839–42, over Chinese attempts to prevent the import of opium from British India in payment for British imports of Chinese tea and silk which had previously been paid in silver, the only exchange acceptable to the Chinese. After a series of defeats, under the terms of the Nanking Treaty China ceded Hong Kong Island to Britain, opened five Treaty Ports to British trade, and relaxed many economic restrictions on foreign merchants.

ORGANIZATION OF PETROLEUM EXPORTING COUNTRIES (OPEC) Multinational organization established by Iran, Iraq, Kuwait, Saudi Arabia and Venezuela (1961) to coordinate petroleum policies and provide members with technical and economic aid. In 1973, in support of the Arab war against Israel, OPEC first halted oil production and then increased prices by 250 per cent, triggering a major worldwide economic recession, but increasing both the revenues and the political influence of the member states. By 1982, however, many nations had reduced their consumption of OPEC oil, forcing a decrease in production and a fall in prices.

ORIGEN (c. 185–254) Scholar and theologian, deeply influential in the emergence of the early Greek Christian Church. He wrote many important commentaries, treatises and polemics, culminating *c.* 232 in his *Hexapla* which reconciles six different versions of the Old Testament.

ORKHAN (1274/88–1362) Second ruler (*beg*) of the Muslim principality founded by his father, **Osman I**, whom he succeeded in *c.* 1324. He captured Bursa in 1326, Nicaea (Iznik) in 1331 and Nicomedia (Izmit) in 1337 from Byzantium; by annexing the neighbouring emirate of Karasi in 1345 he was able to involve the Ottomans in the civil wars in Byzantium, and secured a bridgehead in Europe (Rumeli). Orkhan's sons seized Tzympe in 1352, Gallipoli in 1354 and Adrianpole (Edirne) in 1361, thus opening the Balkans to Turkish conquest and Ottoman expansion.

ORMEE REVOLT Part of the **Fronde** rebellion against **Louis XIV** of France, 1648–53. Bordeaux defied authority until reduced by siege; the rebellion took its name from the *ormes* (elm trees) under which the rebels met to discuss policy.

ORTELIUS, ABRAHAM (1527–1606) Publisher of the first modern atlas, *Theatrum orbis terrarum* (Antwerp, 1570). He worked as a cartographer, antiquary and book dealer.

OSMAN (c. 1258–c. 1324) Founder of the Ottoman dynasty, a leader active among the Turks settled in the northwest Anatolian borderlands with Byzantium in the latter part of the 13th century. He emerges into history *c.*1301; after a constant struggle he had by his death conquered most of Bithynia from Byzantium.

OSTROGOTHS Germanic people who occupied the Ukraine in the 4th century AD. During the reign of their great hero King Ermanaric (d.372), they extended their empire from the Black Sea to the Baltic, but were dispossessed *c.* 370 by the advancing Huns. The tribe then wandered and fought in eastern and central Europe until the end of Hunnish domination, *c.* 455. Under their king, **Theodoric** (ruled 493–526), they moved into Italy and established themselves as rulers, with their capital at Verona, until finally dispersed by the armies of **Justinian I** in the mid-6th century.

OTHMAN (d.656) Third Muslim caliph after the death of **Mohammed**. Born into the rich and powerful **Umayyad** clan of Mecca, *c.* 615 he became Mohammed's first influential convert, and was elected caliph in 644 after the death of **Omar**. He promulgated the first official version of the **Koran**, and continued the policy of conquest.

OTTAWA AGREEMENTS A series of arrangements, concluded at the Imperial Economics Conference in 1932, under which Great Britain, having reversed its traditional Free Trade policies and imposed tariffs on most foreign food and raw material imports, allowed free or preferential entry to goods from the British empire. In return, the colonies and dominions agreed to use tariffs against British goods only to protect their own domestic industries. The underlying doctrine, known as Imperial Preference, was substantially modified by the General Agreement on Tariffs and Trade (GATT) in 1947, and finally evaporated on Britain's entry to the European Economic Community (EC) in 1973.

OTTO I, THE GREAT (912–73) German emperor. As king of East Francia he crushed rebellions involving his brothers Thankmar and Henry (938–9) and his son Liudolf (953–4). He defeated the Magyars at the battle of the Lechfeld (955). He received the imperial crown in 962. By marrying his son **Otto II** to the Byzantine Princess Theophano, 972, he achieved recognition of his Western Empire in Constantinople.

OTTO II (955–83) Son of **Otto I**, and German king from 961, he held the imperial throne jointly with his father from 967 and alone from 973. He tried without success to drive the Greeks and Arabs from southern Italy, 982.

OTTO III (980–1002) German emperor, son of **Otto II**. He was German king from 983 under the regency of his mother (until 991) and grandmother (until 994), being crowned emperor in 996.

OTTO OF FREISING (c. 1111–58) German bishop, historian and philosopher, half-brother to King Conrad III. He entered the Cistercian monastery at Morimond, Champagne, *c.*1132, and became bishop of Freising in 1138. He wrote a world history from the beginning to 1146, and also the *Gesta Friderici*, celebrating the deeds of the **Hohenstaufen** dynasty, particularly of his nephew, **Frederick I Barbarossa**.

OTTOCAR II (1230–1278) King of Bohemia, son of Wenceslaus I, reigning 1253–78. He made his kingdom briefly the strongest state in the **Holy Roman Empire**. He led crusades against the heathen Prussians and Lithuanians, and annexed lands from Styria to the Adriatic. Eclipsed after the election of Rudolf of Habsburg as emperor in 1273, he was forced to renounce all territory save Bohemia, and Moravia. He was killed at the battle of Dürnkrut, attempting to reconquer Austria.

OTTOMANS Turkish Muslims; *see* pp. 156–7, 186–7, 208–9, 236–7, 252–3.

OWEN THE BALD (d.1015) Last king of the Britons of Strathclyde, a state between Scotland and England, centred on Glasgow, which was annexed by Scotland after Owen's death.

OWEN, ROBERT (1771–1858) Early British socialist and social reformer. He was manager of a model cotton mill at New Lanark, 1799, and pioneered shorter working hours, employee housing, education and co-operative stores. He was partly responsible for the Factory Act of 1819, and formed the Grand National Consolidated Trades Union in 1843.

OXFORDSHIRE RISING Popular revolt in 1596 in the English Midlands against the enclosure of common land by landlords, depriving the local population of grazing rights.

PACHACUTI (d.1471) The ninth **Inca** emperor, reigning from 1438 until his death. He led his people's victorious expansion out of the Cuzco valley towards Lake Titicaca; with his son, **Topa** Inca, he conquered the **Chimú;** he founded the great fortress of Sacsahuaman. His mummified body was found by Juan Polo de Ondegardo, Spanish *Corregidor* of Cuzco, in 1539.

PÁEZ, JOSÉ ANTONIO (1790–1873) First President of Venezuela. Part-Indian, he joined the revolution against Spain in 1810 and became one of the chief Venezuelan commanders to **Simon Bolívar**. He participated in the defeat of the Spaniards at Carabobo, 1821, and Puerto Cabello, 1823; in 1829 he led the movement to separate Venezuela from the larger state of Gran Colombia, and effectively controlled the country from his election as president in 1831 until 1846, when he was forced into exile, returning as dictator in 1861. Driven out again in 1863, he retired to New York.

PAHLEVIS Dynasty in Iran, founded by **Reza Shah Pahlevi** in 1925. Overthrown 1979.

PAINE, THOMAS (1737–1809) Writer and radical. Born in England, Paine spent time in America and France where he wrote the highly popular pamphlets *Common Sense* and *The Age of Reason*. Through his talents as a writer he advocated democracy, republicanism, American independence from Britain and the abolition of slavery. After returning to England, he then fled to France in 1792 to avoid arrest for treason, but refused to be a party to the execution of Louis XVI and was himself imprisoned during the Terror. While in prison in France, conservative opinion regained the upper hand in British politics and the radical movement began to unravel. As a result of the backlash against his republican ideas, he spent his last years depressed and drunk in America. Other thinkers and scholars were to rebuild his reputation in the public memory, however, and his bones were exhumed by William Cobbett ten years later and brought back to his homeland.

PAL, BIPIN CHANDRA (1851–1932) Indian schoolmaster, journalist and propagandist. After a brief visit to the USA in 1900, he became involved in the movement for Indian self-government (*swaraj*), editing newspapers and giving lectures which advocated non-cooperation with the British. In 1908 he was arrested; he lost his influence to **Tilak** and later to **Gandhi**.

PALAEOLITHIC The first part of the **Stone Age**, from the first recognizable stone tools in Africa over 2 million years ago, to the advanced reindeer-hunters who decorated their caves with wall-paintings in France and Spain around 20,000 years ago. It is divided into the Lower Palaeolithic, associated with early types of man, and the Middle and Upper Palaeolithic, associated with anatomically modern man.

PALAS Warrior dynasty of northern India, controlling most of Bengal and Bihar from the 8th to the 10th century. Founded by Gopala, under his son, Dharmapala, it became a dominant power in east India, with alliances from Tibet to Sumatra. It reached Benares in the 10th century but was blocked by the **Chola** king, Rajendra, and was forced back to defend Bengal, under King Mahipala, after whose death the dynasty declined, giving way to the Sena line.

PAN CH'AO Chinese general, explorer and administrator. Born into a famous scholarly family, he preferred a military life, and was dispatched with a small expedition in 73 to repacify the **Hsiungnu** tribes. He quickly established a highly effective technique for fomenting inter-tribal tensions. Appointed Protector-General of the Western Regions in 91, during the next ten years he briefly conquered virtually the whole area from the Tarim basin and the Pamirs almost to the shores of the Caspian – the greatest westward expansion China has ever known.

PANTAENUS (d.c. 190) Christian teacher, convert from Stoicism. He made a missionary journey to India. The first head of the Christian Catechetical School in Alexandria, he influenced his associate and successor, **Clement of Alexandria**.

PAOLI, PASQUALE (1725–1807) Corsican patriot, elected president by the islanders during the struggle against Genoese rule. He was forced to submit after Genoa sold the island to France in 1768 and went into exile in Britain 1769–90. He returned in 1793 to lead the revolt against the French revolutionary government. He persuaded the British to take control of Corsica, 1794–6.

PAPACY The office or position of the Pope, as head of the Roman Catholic church. Also the papal system of government, both ecclesiastical and political, particularly during the centuries in which the papacy counted among the major states of Europe.

PAPANDREOU, ANDREAS (1919–96) Greek socialist politican, founder of the Pan-Hellenic Socialist Movement (PASOK), prime minister 1981–9 and 1993–6. In 1989 he became implicated in the alleged embezzlement and diversion of funds to the Greek government of $200 million from the Bank of Crete. The subsequent scandal lead to his loss of the Greek prime ministership. In 1992 Papandreou was cleared of all corruption charges. He was re-elected prime minister the following year.

PAPEN, FRANZ VON (1879–1969) German politician, elected chancellor in 1932. He played a substantial part in **Hitler**'s rise to power, and helped to prepare the German annexation of Austria in 1938. He was found not guilty of war crimes at the Nuremberg Trials in 1945, but was sentenced to eight years' imprisonment; he was released in 1949.

PARAMARAS Rajput clan, prominent in northern India from the 9th to the 12th century. Mainly based in Malwa, with their capital at Dhar, near Indore, they were defeated by Turks from Afghanistan in 1192.

PARIS COMMUNE Name assumed on 26 March 1871, in emulation of the Jacobin Assembly of 1793, by a Central Committee established by rioters who had refused on 18 March to recognize the Assembly of Bordeaux which had accepted Prussian peace terms; the revolutionary socialist movement was crushed, with thousands of casualties, by government troops between 21 and 28 May.

PARIS, FIRST PEACE OF Signed on 30 May 1814, it consisted of seven separate treaties negotiated between the restored Louis XVIII of France and the principal European allies. The limits of France were fixed at approximately those of 1 January 1792; Britain restored certain colonies to France and acquired Malta. (*See also* **Congress of Vienna**.)

PARIS PEACE CONFERENCE see **Versailles, Treaty of**

PARIS, SECOND PEACE OF Signed on 20 November 1815, following the "**Hundred Days**". It deprived **Napoleon** of Elba, reduced France to the limits of 1790, provided for an army of occupation and imposed an indemnity of 700 million francs. (*See also* **Congress of Vienna**.)

PARIS, TREATY OF (1763) Treaty which ended the **Seven Years' War** (known in North America as the French and Indian War). France ceded to Great Britain all her territory east of the Mississippi, including Canada; Spain similarly gave up Florida to Great Britain, but received the Louisiana Territory and New Orleans from France.

PARK CHUNG HEE (1917–1979) South Korean leader. He graduated from Taegu Teacher's College in 1937 and from the Japanese Manchurian military academy at the top of his class in 1944, and went for further training at the Imperial Military Academy in Tokyo. He fought in the Korean War for the south and rose to the rank of Major General by April 1961, when he led a bloodless coup to overthrow Prime Minister Chang Myŏn's government that followed the ouster of President Syngman Rhee in 1960. Park was elected President three times in fair elections (1963, 1967, and 1971) and twice in rigged elections (1972 and 1978). He normalised relations with Japan (1965), sent troops to support South Vietnam (1970s), and laid the industrial foundations for South Korean world leadership in steel, shipbuilding, chemicals, and consumer electronics. His authoritarianism led to his assassination in 1979 at the hands of the Director of the KCIA.

PARK, MUNGO (1771–1806) Scottish explorer of Africa, who sought the true course of the river Niger; his account *Travels in the Interior of Africa* (1797) made him famous. He returned in 1805 to head a second expedition, but was drowned during a skirmish.

PARSEES Modern followers of the Iranian prophet **Zoroaster**. The majority of the sect is descended from the Persian Zoroastrians who fled to India in the 7th century to escape Muslim persecution.

PARSONS, SIR CHARLES ALGERNON (1854–1931) Inventor of the steam turbine. He entered Armstrong engineering works, Newcastle upon Tyne, in 1877 and in 1884 patented the steam turbine, at the same time thus producing the first turbo-generator. In 1897 his powered experimental ship, the *Turbinia*, attained the then record speed of 34 knots.

PARTHIAN EMPIRE Founded in 247 BC when Arsaces, a governor under **Diodotus**, king of the Bactrian Greeks, rebelled and fled west to found his own kingdom south of the Caspian Sea. Under **Mithridates** (171–138 BC) Parthia extended its control over the whole Iranian plateau and into the Tigris-Euphrates region. After the famous Parthian victory over the Romans at Carrhae (53 BC) Parthia was almost continuously at war with Rome, and prevented any permanent Roman expansion beyond the Euphrates. The empire was finally eclipsed in AD 224 by the rise of the **Sasanids**.

PASSAROWITZ, TREATY OF Signed on 21 July 1718, it ended the Austro-Turkish and Venetian-Turkish wars of 1716–18, and marked the end of Ottoman expansion into Europe. Under its terms, the Ottoman empire lost substantial Balkan territories to Austria.

PATHET LAO Left-wing nationalist movement in Laos, founded in 1950. It joined with the **Viet Minh** to oppose French colonial rule in Indo-China. The first Congress of Neo Lao Hak Sat (Lao Patriotic Front) was held in 1956; throughout the 1960s and early 1970s it fought a civil war against the US-supported government in Vientiane. Its control of the northeast provinces of Sam Neua and Phong Saly was recognized in 1954, when Laos gained independence; it won control of the entire country in 1975.

PATRICK, ST (5th century) British cleric who brought Christianity to Ireland in the mid-5th century. Patron saint of Ireland; associated particularly with Armagh. He wrote *Letter to the Soldiers of Coroticus* and *Confessions*, an account of his work.

PÄTS, KONSTANTIN (1874–1956) President of independent Estonia. He founded the nationalist newspaper, *Teataja* (*The Announcer*) in 1901, and entered politics in 1904. He was sentenced to death by the Russian authorities in 1905 after an abortive rising. Returning from exile in 1910, in 1918 he became head of the provisional government despite his arrest by German occupation forces. He was prime minister 1921–2, 1923–4, 1931–2, 1932–3 and 1933–4, and became dictator after an attempted Fascist coup in 1934. He was deported to the USSR after the Soviet invasion in 1940 and was believed to have died some 16 years later.

PAUL, ST Jewish convert to **Christianity**, who became the leading missionary and theologian of the early Church. He was born a Roman citizen in Tarsus, now in Turkey. Brought up a **Pharisee**, he persecuted the followers of **Jesus** until his conversion by a vision on the road to Damascus. He became the Apostle to the Gentiles, undertaking three great journeys to the cities of Asia Minor and Greece. His letters, maintaining contact with the communities established there, remain fundamental documents of the Christian faith. Paul was arrested in Jerusalem, *c.* 57, taken to Rome in 60, and probably martyred during the reign of the Emperor **Nero**, between 62 and 68.

PAULICIANS Sect of militant Armenian Christians, founded in the mid-7th century. Influenced by earlier dualist thought, notably **Manichaeism**, its members believed that there were two gods: an evil one, who created the world, and a good one responsible for the world to come. It was suppressed by Byzantine military expeditions in the late 7th and early 9th centuries; many followers then moved to Thrace as frontier soldiers, where they helped to form the ideas of the **Bogomils**.

PEASANTS' REVOLT 14th-century uprising in the English countryside and towns of villeins, free labourers, small farmers and artisans. Initially in protest against the Poll Tax of 1381 and stringent labour regulations imposed after the Black Death, it was concentrated mainly in East Anglia and the southeast. Under the leadership of Wat Tyler, a vast mob invaded London, executing royal ministers and destroying the property of supposed enemies of the common people, extracting promises of redress from the young king, Richard II. However, the insurgents were dispersed, Tyler slain, and insurgent action in other areas vigorously suppressed; the reforms and royal pardons were then revoked.

PEASANTS' WAR A series of rural uprisings in 1524–5 in Austria and central Germany, mainly directed against heavy manorial duties and exactions. Despite the accusations of Catholics that the rebellion was provoked by Lutheran theology, there is little evidence for this. **Luther** himself condemned the peasants, and the rebels were cut down, in several bloody battles, by the combined forces of Lutheran and Catholic landlords.

PECHENEGS Turkic nomads, ruling the steppes north of the Black Sea from the 6th to the 12th century. In the 10th century they controlled the land between the rivers Don and Danube; held back with difficulty by Russians and Hungarians, they then attacked Thrace and increasingly threatened the Byzantine empire until they were finally annihilated, at the gates of Constantinople, by Emperor **Alexius I Comnenus** in 1091.

PEEL FAMILY The first Robert Peel introduced the calico printing industry to Lancashire, England, when he took the initiative in founding the firm of Haworth, Peel & Yates in Blackburn in 1764. His son Robert (1750–1830) greatly expanded the business and by the end of the 18th century employed some 15,000 workers in various mills. He was an enlightened employer, and when he became a member of parliament introduced the first Factory Act (1802). He had been created a baronet in 1800. His son Sir Robert Peel (1788–1850) was prime minister from 1841 to 1846.

PEKING CONVENTION Series of agreements made in 1860, reaffirming and extending the Tientsin treaties of 1858. Tientsin was opened as a Treaty Port; Britain obtained control of Kowloon, the city on the mainland opposite Hong Kong island; French missionaries were given a free hand to buy and develop land; war vessels and merchant ships were allowed to navigate in the interior; and Russia obtained the Maritime Provinces east of the Ussuri river.

PELAGIUS Christian teacher and monk, whose belief in man's responsibility for his own good and evil deeds led him into bitter controversy with the 4th-century Church fathers. In Rome *c.* 380 he attacked the lax morality he attributed to the doctrines of Augustine. Cleared of heresy charges at Jerusalem in 415, he responded to further attacks from **Augustine** and **Jerome** by writing *De libero arbitrio* (*On Free Will*). He was excommunicated by Pope Innocent I in 417, and condemned at Carthage in 418; the date of his death is unknown.

PENINSULAR WAR Struggle, fought in the Iberian peninsula, 1808–14, between France and an alliance of Britain, Spain and Portugal, in the course of the Napoleonic Wars. Initially forced to evacuate from Corunna (1809), the British, under the future **Duke of Wellington**, returned to fight first a defensive engagement at Torres Vedras, then a successful offensive (1812–14) which drove all French troops from the region.

PEQUOT WAR Massacre of the Pequot tribe of North American Indians by British colonists in 1636–8, precipitated by the murder of a Boston trader. By the early 20th century hardly any of the tribe remained in their ancestral lands in Connecticut.

PERICLES (*c.* 495–429 BC) Athenian statesman. As a radical democrat he dominated the city-state from *c.* 460 BC until his death. He converted the League of Delos from an equal alliance into an Athenian empire, and led Athens in the Peloponnesian War against Sparta. His famous *Funeral Speech*, setting out his vision of an ideal Athens, is reported by **Thucydides**.

PERKIN, SIR WILLIAM HENRY (1838–1907) Discoverer of aniline dyes. In 1853 he entered the Royal College of Chemistry, London, and while working as a laboratory assistant attempted the synthesis of quinine, but instead obtained a substance later named aniline purple, or mauve. In 1856 he produced tyrian purple, the first dyestuff to be produced from coal tar. He was knighted in 1896.

PERMIANS Finno-Ugrian-speaking peoples, including the Votyaks and the **Zyrians**, living in the northwest region of Russia.

PERON, JUAN DOMINGO (1895–1974) Argentine head of state. He entered the army, 1911, became minister of war and secretary for labour, 1944; vice-president, 1944–5, and president, with strong backing from the trade union movement, 1946. Removed from office during the 1955 revolution and exiled to Spain, he returned and was elected to the presidency, 1973.

PERRY, MATTHEW (1794–1858) US naval commander who headed the expedition to Japan of 1853–4 which forced that country to end its 200-year-old isolation and open trade and diplomatic relations with the world. Perry had earlier captained the first US steamship, the *Fulton* (1837–40); his Japanese exploit, taking four warships into the fortified harbour of Uraga, made him world-famous. Later he strongly urged US expansion in the Pacific.

PERSEUS (*c.* 212–165 BC) Last king of classical Macedonia, son of **Philip V**. He succeeded to the throne in 179 after plotting his brother's execution. He tried to dominate Greece, but by his success precipitated the Third Macedonian War (171–168) with Rome; he was finally defeated at Pydna, southern Macedonia, by the armies of Lucius Aemilius Paullus, and died after three years in captivity.

PERUZZI Important family of Florence, prominent in trade and finance in Europe in the late 13th century, and second only to the **Bardi**. During the **Hundred Years' War** the firm made large loans to **Edward III** of England; these were cancelled in 1342. The king of Naples also defaulted and the king of France exiled them and confiscated their goods; bankruptcy and collapse, both financial and political, followed.

PETER, ST (d.c. AD 64) Foremost of **Jesus**' disciples and recognized by the Roman Catholic Church as its first pope. Originally a fisherman called Simon, or Simeon, from Bethsaida, he was named by Jesus "Cephas", meaning rock (in Greek, *petros*). After Jesus' death he emerged as the first leader of the early Church, preaching and healing. His later career is obscure, but his residence, martyrdom and burial in Rome can be taken as certain.

PETER I, THE GREAT (1672–1725) Tsar of Russia. He succeeded to the throne in 1682, and took full control in 1689. War with the Ottoman empire, 1695–6, gave Russia access to the Sea of Azov. He made an extensive tour of western Europe, 1697–8, introduced western technology to Russia, and drastically reformed the system of government. With the **Great Northern War** (1700–21) he won through to the Baltic, and founded the city of St Petersburg which he made his capital.

PETER III (1728–62) Tsar of Russia. He succeeded his aunt, the Empress Elizabeth, in 1762, and immediately ordered Russia's withdrawal from the **Seven Years' War**, thereby causing discontent among his army officers, who deposed and killed him after a reign of only six months. He was succeeded by his wife, **Catherine the Great**.

PETROBRUSIANS Followers of Peter de Bruys, leader (1104–25) of a radical opposition in France to the doctrine and organization of the Roman Church. He rejected infant baptism, transubstantiation, the sacrifice of the Mass, and the organization of worship. He claimed scriptural authority for all his teachings, but he was burned in 1125 as a heretic. His ideas were also taken up by the **Henricians**.

PHAN BOI CHAU (1867–1940) First 20th-century Vietnamese resistance leader. He trained for the mandarin examinations; in 1903 he wrote *Cau huyet thu le than* (*Letters Written in Blood*) urging expulsion of the French colonial rulers. He directed, from Japan, the Duy Tan Hoi (Reformation Society) aiming to put Prince Cuong De on the throne. After exile from Japan in 1908 he reorganized in China and planned the assassination of the French governor, Albert Sarraut, in 1912. He was imprisoned until 1917; converted to Marxism; seized in 1925 and taken to Hanoi, but released after immense public protest.

PHARISEES (and Sadducees) Leading, and antagonistic, Jewish religious sects during the second temple period (to AD 70). Emphasizing the interpretation of the Bible, the development of the oral law and adaptation to new conditions, the Pharisees evolved eventually into the Rabbis of the **Mishnah** and the **Talmud**. The Sadducees believed in the literal truth of the Bible and excluded all subsequent interpretations as well as beliefs in immortality, or devils and angels. The Pharisees, with their dislike of violence, survived the destruction of the temple by the Romans (AD 70); the Sadducees did not.

PHAULKON, CONSTANT (1647–88) An innkeeper's son from Cephalonia who ran away to serve as cabin boy on an English trading vessel and was later taken to Siam by a merchant of the **English East Indian Company**. Entering the service of King **Narai**, he was promoted to superintend foreign trade. After a quarrel with the chief of the English factory at the capital, Ayutthaya, he supported the French cause at court, but his support for **Louis XIV**'s intervention in Siam in 1687 brought about his downfall in the following year when his patron died. Narai's successor had him publicly executed.

PHIDIAS (c. 500–c. 432) Ancient Athenian sculptor. Appointed by **Pericles** to oversee all the city's artistic undertakings, he was responsible for the design and composition of the marble sculptures of the Parthenon. None of his most famous works – three monuments to Athena on the Acropolis and a colossal seated Zeus at Olympia – survive in the original. Exiled on political charges some time after 432 BC he went to Elis; his date of death is unknown.

PHILIP "THE BOLD" (1342–1404) Duke of Burgundy, son of the French king John II. As a boy he distinguished himself at the battle of Poitiers in 1356; succeeding to his title in 1363, he was co-regent (1382–8) to Charles VI and effective ruler of France during much of the rest of his life.

PHILIP "THE GOOD" (1396–1467) Duke of Burgundy, son of John the Fearless, he succeeded in 1419. He supported the claims of the English king **Henry V** to the French throne but made peace with the rival monarch, Charles VII, in 1435. He also acquired extensive territories in the Netherlands, and founded the Order of the Golden Fleece in 1429.

PHILIP II AUGUSTUS (1165–1223) First great Capetian king of France, son of Louis VII. He succeeded to the throne in 1179; fought a long, mainly successful campaign to win control of English possessions in France; took part in the Third **Crusade**, 1190–1; acquired major territories in the west and north of France, and began the Capetian conquest of the territory of Languedoc.

PHILIP IV (1268–1314) Known as "the Fair". Capetian king of France, the second son of Philip III, he became heir on the death of his brother Louis in 1276, and succeeded in 1285. He fought major wars against England, 1294–1303, and Flanders, 1302–5. Continually in conflict with the papacy from 1296, he transferred the papal Curia to Avignon during the Pontificate of Pope Clement V (1305–14).

PHILIP II OF MACEDON (c. 380–336 BC) Ruler of Macedon from 359 to 336 BC; father of **Alexander the Great**. He made Macedon a major power. He penetrated Greece by war and diplomacy, defeating Athens and Thebes at the battle of Chaeronea, 338, and bringing the warring city-states of Greece into a forced unity through a federal constitution with himself as leader. He was assassinated while planning an invasion of Persia.

PHILIP V (238–179 BC) King of Macedon, succeeding his cousin, **Antigonus Doson**, in 221. He allied with Carthage against Rome in the Second **Punic War**, and ended the resulting First Macedonian War (215–205) on favourable terms, but suffered a decisive defeat in the Second War at **Cynoscephalae** in 197. The resulting peace treaty confined him to Macedonia and imposed severe indemnities. Seven years of cooperation with Rome relaxed these conditions and his last decade was spent in trying to re-establish control in the Balkans.

PHILIP II (1527–98) King of Spain, Spanish America and the Two Sicilies (1556–98), also ruler of the Netherlands and Lombardy (1555–98) and, as Philip I, King of Portugal (1580–98). Son of Emperor **Charles V**, he became King of England, 1554–8, through his marriage to Mary Tudor. Sought unsuccessfully to suppress the revolt of the Netherlands from 1566 onwards; conquered Portugal in 1580; failed to invade England with his Armada in 1588.

PHRYGIANS Ancient Anatolian people, dominating central Asia Minor from the 13th to the 7th centuries BC. Traditionally of Thracian origin, they settled in northwest Anatolia in the 2nd millennium BC, and after the collapse of the **Hittites** founded a new capital, Gordium, in the central highlands. In about 730 BC the eastern territories fell to Assyria; c. 700 BC the legendary king Midas was defeated by the Cimmerians, who burned Gordium and transferred the land to the Lydians.

PIAST First ruling dynasty in Poland, traditionally named after the wheelwright whose son, Ziemowit, inherited the estates of the Prince of Gniezno in the late 9th century. The dynastic territories were consolidated under **Mieszko I**; his son **Bolesław I** was the first king of Poland, and established the Polish frontiers in east and west. The last Piast in the main line, **Casimir III the Great**, died in 1370.

PICTS A group of tribes occupying Scotland north of the river Forth in early Christian times. The name, signifying "painted people", was first mentioned in Latin texts in AD 297. Known for their fierce raiding and their characteristic towers ("brochs") and symbol stones, they successfully blocked Anglian attempts to control them at the battle of Nechtansmere in 685. The connections between the kings of the Picts and the Scots (Irish immigrants in southwest Scotland) grew closer in the 9th century, leading to the creation of the medieval kingdom of Scotland.

PIKE, ZEBULON MONTGOMERY (1779–1813) American explorer. Commissioned in the US army in 1799, he led parties to the headwaters of the Mississippi, 1805–6, and Arkansas and Red rivers, 1806–7. He was promoted to the rank of brigadier-general in 1813, but was killed in the same year in the assault on York (now Toronto, Canada).

PILGRIMAGE OF GRACE Popular uprising in 1536 in the English counties of Yorkshire and Lincolnshire. The participants were mainly protesting against the religious policies of **Henry VIII**, especially the closure of the monasteries. Its leaders were executed in 1537.

PILGRIM FATHERS Group of English puritan refugees, mostly of the Brownist sect, who sailed in the **Mayflower** in 1620 to found Plymouth Colony, New England.

PILSUDSZKI, JOSEF (1867–1935) Polish general and statesman who struggled to liberate Poland from Russian control from 1887. He was imprisoned in Siberia, 1887–92. After the outbreak of the First World War, he commanded Polish legions under Austro-Hungarian sponsorship, 1914–16. After the Russian revolution he assumed command of all Polish armies and proclaimed himself head of a new independent Polish state. He defeated the Soviet Union in the war of 1919–21 (*see* **Treaty of Riga**). He resigned in 1922, but a right-wing military *coup d'état* in 1926 brought him back to supreme power until his death.

PINEDA, ALVAREZ 16th-century Spanish explorer. In 1519 he led an expedition which followed the Caribbean coast from Florida to the Pánuco river, already reached from the south by **Grijalva** in 1517. Pineda's voyage ended all hope of finding a direct sea contact between the Caribbean and the Pacific.

PINOCHET UGARTE, GENERAL AUGUSTO (1915–2006) Former Chilean head of state. He rose to prominence when appointed commander of the Santiago zone by Chile's Marxist President **Allende** in 1972. He succeeded General Carlo Prats as commander of the army, and emerged after a violent coup (supported by the US administration) as head of the ruling military junta, 1973; he assumed sole leadership in 1974. He was responsible for the purge of left-wing supporters, and is estimated to have killed more than 3,000 people. He stood down as head of state in 1989 following a plebiscite in favour of democratic elections. He remained army commander. During his rule, Chile's economy was transformed and the country emerged as one of the most stable and successful in Latin America. In 1998, he was arrested in the UK on a warrant from the Spanish Government. The UK refused his extradition on the grounds that he was unfit to stand trial. Chile subsequently stripped him of immunity, but in legal proceedings there, again pronounced him unfit to stand trial.

PINZÓN, MARTÍN ALONSO (c. 1411–93) Part-owner of **Columbus**'s two ships, the *Pinta* and the *Niña*, which took part in the discovery of the Americas. Pinzón commanded the *Pinta* under **Columbus**, but left the expedition after reaching the Bahamas to search independently for gold. After rejoining the main body he broke away again on the homeward voyage, hoping – but failing – to be first with the news.

PINZÓN, VICENTE YA—EZ (c. 1460–1523) Spanish explorer, younger brother of **Martin Alonso Pinzón**. Commanded the caravel *Niña* in **Columbus**'s fleet throughout the 1492–3 voyage to the Americas. Later he probably sighted the Amazon estuary and sailed with **Juan Díaz de Solís** along the coast of central America.

PIPPIN III ("the Short") (d.768) First **Carolingian** king, son of **Charles Martel** and father of **Charlemagne**. He became effective ruler of the **Franks** in 747. In 751 he deposed the last Merovingian king and was crowned king himself.

PITT, WILLIAM (1759–1806) Known as "the Younger". English statesman, second son of the 1st Earl of Chatham (the elder Pitt). He entered Parliament in 1781, became chancellor of the exchequer 1782–3, and prime minister 1783–1801 and again 1804–6. He played a leading part in organizing coalitions against France on the outbreak of the Revolutionary Wars (1793–1802); passed the Act of Union with Ireland, 1800; resigned after George III refused to grant Catholic emancipation in 1801 but was recalled to organize new opposition to the French.

PIZARRO, FRANCISCO (c. 1478–1541) Conqueror of Peru, illegitimate son of a Spanish soldier. He went to the Caribbean in 1502, and in 1513 was deputy to Vasco Balboa when he discovered the Pacific Ocean. He led a small force of Spanish adventurers to conquer (and, in fact, to destroy) the **Inca** empire in Peru, 1531–3, and founded the city of Lima in 1535.

PIZARRO, HERNANDO (c. 1501–78) Spanish conquistador, the younger half-brother of **Francisco Pizarro**. He accompanied Francisco to Peru in 1531, and in 1534 returned to Spain with the royal share of the Inca **Atahuallpa**'s ransom. He returned to Peru, and in 1537 was seized at Cuzco by the Pizarros' rival, Diego de Almagro. After his release he led an army to defeat and execute his captor, 1538. He was imprisoned in Spain, 1540–60.

PLANTAGENETS *see* **Angevins**

PLATO (c. 427–347 BC) Athenian philosopher, an associate of **Socrates** and the teacher of **Aristotle**. He is best known through his 25 surviving *Dialogues*, his letters, and his *Apology*, in defence of Socrates. The ten books of *The Republic*, later modified by *The Laws*, outline a complete system for the ideal society. His Academy, outside Athens, was founded to train statesmen; it lasted nearly 900 years after his death, being closed finally by Emperor **Justinian** in 529.

PLEISTOCENE Geological era, characterized by a series of major ice advances, starting approximately 2.5 million years ago and ending in about 8000 BC. During this period Man evolved from pre-human origins to his present appearance and bodily form.

PLINY THE ELDER (AD 23–79) Roman encyclopedist, accepted as the foremost Western authority on scientific matters until medieval times. After a short army career he settled down to accumulate knowledge and to write. His only surviving work (out of seven known titles) is the vast *Historia Naturalis*; its information, though fascinating and far-ranging, varies considerably in accuracy when checked with other sources.

PLO (Palestine Liberation Organization) Formed in 1964 as an umbrella organization to represent the world's estimated 4.5 million Palestinians, dedicated to the creation of a "democratic and secular" Palestinian state. Its charter also called for the elimination of Israel. In 1969, Yasir Arafat, moderate leader of the major faction al-Fatah, became chairman. The PLO formed the effective government over the Palestinian enclaves in Gaza and the West Bank after the 1993 peace agreement.

POCOCK, SIR GEORGE (1706–92) British admiral. He commanded a squadron in the Indian Ocean, 1757–9, and in 1762–3 commanded the fleet which carried an expeditionary force under the Earl of Albemarle to Cuba.

POL POT (1925–98) Original name Saloth Sar. The leader of the Khmer Rouge since its early days as the Communist Party of Kampuchea in the 1960s. Under his premiership between 1975 and 1979, Cambodia was subjected to widespread terror, in which millions of Cambodians died. The Vietnamese invasion of Cambodia in 1979 led to his removal and flight. He conducted a guerrilla resistance to the new Cambodian government from isolated border regions until shortly before his death. See also Khmer Rouge.

POLENTA, DA Italian family dominating the city state of Ravenna from the end of the 13th to the middle of the 15th century. It first rose to power under Guidoe da Polenta, a leader of the **Guelph**, or pro-papal faction in the city; from 1322 it was rent by violent intra-family rivalries, and in 1441 the city fell under Venetian control.

POLO, MARCO (1254–1324) Medieval traveller from Venice. He went to Asia in 1271 as a merchant and jeweller with his father and uncle, who had already visited the court of the Mongol khan at Karakorum. He stayed for almost 17 years in China and neighbouring territories in the service of **Kublai Khan**. He escorted a Chinese princess to Persia in 1292 and returned to Venice in 1295. Captured at sea by the Genoese, while in prison he began to dictate an account of his travels: the book has been a bestseller ever since, and subsequent investigation has confirmed almost all its observations, although at the time Polo was thought to have invented most of them.

POLOVTSY Russian name for the Kipchak (Turkish) or (Kuman) Byzantine tribes who dominated the Eurasian steppes in the mid-11th century. They controlled a vast area between the Aral and Black Seas; fought Russians, **Pechénegs**, Byzantines and Hungarians. Dispersed in 1237, when the Mongols killed Bachman, the eastern Kipchak leader, some were absorbed into the **Golden Horde**, others (the Kumans) fled to Hungary.

POLYGNOTUS Ancient Greek painter from Thasos, at work in Athens and elsewhere, 475–447 BC, and famous for works such as the Fall of Troy in the Stoa Poikile at Athens and the vast murals in the Hall of the Cnidians at Delphi, now known only from contemporary descriptions. He was noted for his realism (e.g. transparent drapery) and for moralism.

POMPEY THE GREAT (103–48 BC) Roman statesman and general. He campaigned in Spain and Italy against pirates in the Mediterranean, and against **Mithridates** of Pontus. Consul in 70 BC, in 61 he formed the First Triumvirate with **Crassus** and **Julius Caesar**. He raised an army to defend the state when civil war broke out in 49, but was defeated by Caesar at Pharsalus (Greece) in 48 and fled to Egypt, where he was murdered.

PONCE DE LÉON, JUAN (1460–1521) Discoverer of Florida, in search of the mythical Fountain of Youth. He sailed with **Columbus** in 1493; in 1508–9, as deputy to the governor of Hispaniola, he helped to settle Puerto Rico. In 1513 he reached Florida, without realizing it was part of the North American mainland; he probably sighted the north coast of Yucatán on his return passage to Puerto Rico. He was mortally wounded in 1521 by **Seminole** Indians when on a second expedition to explore his discovery.

PORTSMOUTH, TREATY OF Agreement signed in New Hampshire, USA, to end the Russo-Japanese War of 1904–5. Russia recognized Japan as the dominant power in Korea, and ceded the lease of Port Arthur, railway concessions in the south Manchurian peninsula, and the southern half of Sakhalin Island. Both powers agreed to recognize Chinese sovereignty in Manchuria.

POTASSIUM-ARGON METHOD Technique for dating the original formation of rocks of igneous origin. It involves measuring the ratio of radioactive argon to radioactive potassium in the sample, and depends for its validity on several crucial assumptions about initial purity, steadiness of decay rates, absence of other factors affecting the radioactive decay process, etc.; but in modern, improved forms it has been used to establish geological age as remote as 4500 million years and as recent as 20,000 years.

POTSDAM CONFERENCE Last inter-Allied conference of the Second World War, held from 17 July to 2 August 1945. The main participants were **Truman**, **Churchill** (with **Clement Attlee**, who became prime minister during the conference) and **Stalin**; they discussed the continuation of war with Japan and the form of the forthcoming European peace settlement.

POWELL, JOHN W. (1834–1902) US Professor of Geology who led four expeditions to explore 1450km (900 miles) of the Green and Colorado rivers, 1869–75; director of the geological survey of the Rocky Mountains, 1875–80, and of the US Geological Survey, 1880–94.

PRAIEIRA Last significant revolutionary uprising in imperial Brazil. The anti-conservative, anti-Portuguese rebellion broke out in Pernambuco in 1848 and was suppressed by 1850. "Praieira" was the nickname given to liberals whose newspaper was printed in the Rua da Praia in Recife.

PRATIHARAS Warlike people of northern India, reputedly descended from the **Gurjaras**. By the end of the 8th century they ruled a large part of Rajasthan and Ujjain, and controlled the strategic city of Kanauj. Under King Bhoja they successfully held back the Arab advance into northern India, but were eclipsed by various enemies when a Turkish army sacked Kanauj in 1018.

PRAXITELES Ancient Athenian sculptor, working between 370 and 330 BC. Only one of his works survives in the original, the marble *Hermes carrying the infant Dionysus*, but by transforming the aloof, majestic style of his archaic and classical predecessors into more graceful and sensuous forms he changed the whole culture of Greek art. A few Roman copies of his works exist, including two of the masterpiece *The Aphrodite of Cnidus*, now in the Vatican and the Louvre.

PREMYSLIDS First Czech ruling family, founded by Premysl, a ploughman, who married the Princess Libuse. They held the throne of Bohemia from *c.* 800 to 1306. In 1198 Premysl Ottocar I raised the country from a principality to a hereditary kingdom within the **Holy Roman Empire**.

PRESTER JOHN Legendary Christian king, variously believed to rule in central Asia and east Africa. His fabled kingdom, and its riches, captured the medieval imagination between the first **Crusades** and the early 16th century. His story, probably based on garbled reports of the Negus of Abyssinia, played a part in the motivation of many well-financed expeditions, including the final successful efforts of Portugal to reach Asia by sea.

PRODICUS Greek Sophist from the island of Ceos (Kea), active in the 5th century BC and renowned for his precise distinctions between words.

PROTAGORAS (c. 485–c. 412 BC) Most famous of the Greek Sophists, author of the constitution for the pan-hellenic settlement of Thurii, and best known for his assertion that "man is the measure of all things". He taught in Athens and other cities for 40 years. He expressed agnosticism in his text *Concerning the Gods*, but the story of his trial for impiety may be a later invention.

PROTESTANTISM One of the three main branches of **Christianity** since the Reformation of the 16th century. It was originally characterized by belief in justification by grace through faith, the priesthood of all believers and the over-riding authority of the Bible. The main early groups were **Lutherans**, **Calvinists** and **Zwinglians**, with the Church of England including both Catholic and Protestant elements. Other groups from the Anabaptist and Independent traditions, as well as those emerging later such as the Society of Friends (**Quakers**) and the **Methodists**, are also included within the term.

PRUTH, TREATY OF THE A pact signed on 23 July 1711, after the Ottomans had defeated the armies of **Peter I the Great** of Russia on the river Pruth (now the frontier between Romania and Moldavia). Russia agreed to relinquish the fortress of Azov, to demilitarize Taganrog and the Dnieper forts, cease interfering in Poland and the affairs of the Crimean Tatars, and allow safe conduct to **Charles XII** of Sweden. His delay in complying with these terms led to a renewed declaration of war in 1712 and the conclusion of a new, though similar, peace agreement at Adrianople (Edirne) in 1713.

PTOLEMAIC DYNASTY Line of Macedonian kings, founded by **Ptolemy I Soter**. They ruled Egypt from 323 to 30 BC, the last of the line being **Cleopatra**.

PTOLEMY Greek astronomer and geographer of the 2nd century AD. He worked in Alexandria, and wrote a *Geography*, with maps, which became the standard medieval work on this subject; an *Optics*, and a mathematical and astronomical treatise, popularly known as *Great Collection or Almagest*, which pronounced that the Earth was the centre of the Universe. He worked out a close approximation to the value of ϖ in sexagesimal fractions, and he divided the degree of angle into minutes and seconds.

PTOLEMY I SOTER (c. 367–c. 282 BC) Founder of the Ptolemaic dynasty, rulers of Egypt from 323 to 30 BC. He was born in Macedonia, rose to become a general of **Alexander the Great**, and after Alexander's death became satrap of Egypt, Libya and Arabia. He fought off Macedonian attacks (322–1 and 305–4) and in 304 assumed the titles of King and Soter (Saviour). An outstanding administrator, he was also author of a history of Alexander (since lost), and founder of a library and museum.

PUGACHEV, YEMELYAN IVANOVICH (1726–75) Pretending to be Peter III, the murdered husband of **Catherine II**, he led a revolt, in September 1773, among a group of **Cossacks** in the Urals, and was joined by factory serfs, Bashkirs, state peasants and serfs. In August 1774 he sacked the city of Kazan, but then turned south down the Volga, where he was defeated by Russian troops in August 1774. He was executed the following year.

PUNIC WARS Three wars in which Rome and Carthage, hitherto friendly, contested supremacy in the western Mediterranean in the 3rd and 2nd centuries BC.

First Punic War (264–41 BC): the clash came when Carthage threatened to gain control of the Straits of Messina. Carthage was a sea-power, Rome a land-power: to defeat their enemy the Romans had to build a large fleet, which gained a series of brilliant victories. The war, which was also fought by land in Sicily, resulted in the ejection of the Carthaginians from Sicily; Rome made the island its first overseas province.

Second Punic War (218–201 BC): caused by **Hannibal**'s advance from Spain into Italy, where after a series of great victories (especially Cannae in 216) he was gradually forced on to the defensive. In 204 Publius Scipio led an expeditionary force to Africa, thus compelling the return of Hannibal, and defeated him at Zama. Scipio had also driven the Carthaginians from Spain, which became a Roman province. Carthage survived but was no longer a great Mediterranean power.

Third Punic War (149–146 BC): Roman suspicions led to the outbreak of a final war. The Romans invaded north Africa; after a desperate siege the city of Carthage was totally destroyed and its territory made into the Roman province of Africa.

PUTIN, VLADIMIR (1952–) Russian president 2000–08, 2012–. After graduating from Leningrad State University, Putin joined the KGB in 1975, working for the service until 1991. During the early 1990s, he was deeply involved in St Petersburg politics before moving to Moscow, where he quickly rose through the ranks, becoming head of the Russian FSB security organization in 1998. Appointed as deputy prime minister in 1999, Putin's political career was bolstered by a successful military offensive in Chechnya, culminating in his election to the presidency later that year, following Yeltsin's surprise resignation. Upon completing his second term, in 2008 he became president Dimitri Medvedev's prime minister, before being elected president again in 2012. Putin's third term in office was marked by his support for Russian separatism in Ukraine and the annexation of the Crimea.

PUTTING-OUT SYSTEMS Method of industrial production, widely practised in 17th-century Europe. Raw materials were supplied by manufacturers to workers in their own homes or small workshops, and the finished output was then collected and sold, after payment on a piecework or wage basis; it was gradually superseded by the development of the factory system.

PYRRHUS (319–272 BC) King of Epirus, northwest Greece. He fought Macedon, and was then called to help Greek cities in Sicily and southern Italy against the expanding power of Rome. He defeated the Romans, but with crippling losses, at Asculum in 279 BC (hence a "Pyrrhic victory"), and was forced out of Italy in 275 BC. He died in a street fight in Argos three years later.

PYTHAGORAS (c. 580–497 BC) Greek philosopher and mathematician. He emigrated from Samos to southern Italy; founded a school based on the belief that the soul could be purified by study and self-examination; taught transmigration of souls; discovered the numerical basis of the musical scale; taught that numbers form the basis of the universe. Pythagoras' Theorem, which states that the square on the hypotenuse of a right-angled triangle is equal to the sum of the squares on the other two sides, is probably attributable to his school.

Q

AL-QAEDA ("the Base") A militant Islamist group which had its roots among Arab fighters who joined the *jihad* against Soviet forces in Afghanistan in the late 1980s. Its founder and first leader Osama bin Laden transformed the movement into a global network. Al-Qaeda's radical interpretation of Islam labelled many more moderate Muslims as "apostates" whom it was legitimate to attack. Bin Laden directed the movement in attacks on the United States, culminating in the hijacking and flying of airplanes into targets in New York and Washington on 11 September 2001. The resultant United States attack on Afghanistan, whose Taliban Islamist government had sheltered al-Qaeda, led the movement's leadership to scatter and go underground. The long US campaigns in Afghanistan, and subsequently Iraq from 2003, rallied support for al-Qaeda amongst Sunni communities who feared political marginalization, while al-Qaeda trained jihadists who fled from Afghanistan established sister movements in North Africa, the Arabian peninsula and Central Asia. Al-Qaeda's difficulties mounted after the assassination of bin Laden in a US special forces operation in 2011 and under his successor, the Egyptian cleric Ayman al-Zawahiri, it became more a flag under which diverse jihadist movements operated than a centrally directed movement. While the outbreak of the Syrian Civil War in 2012 initially seemed to offer al-Qaeda a chance to regain momentum, it was by 2015 sidelined by the Islamic State movement, which had conquered a substantial area of Syria and Iraq and declared a "caliphate", both achievements which, for radical jihadists, eclipsed those of al-Qaeda.

QADISIYYA, AL- Battle, 637, in which the armies of Islam defeated the **Sasanid** Persians, and completed the conquest of Iraq.

QAJARS Iranian dynasty, ruling a unified Persia, 1779–1925. The reign of Fath Ali Shah (1797–1834) saw the beginning of intense European rivalry for control of the country; Nasir ud-Din Shah (1848–96) exploited Anglo-Russian suspicions to preserve its independence, but the Anglo-Russian division of Persia into spheres of influence in 1907, followed by Russian and British occupation of parts of the country in the First World War, led to a *coup d'état* (1921) and the emergence of the **Pahlevi**. Ahmed Shah, the last Qajar, was formally deposed in 1925.

QIZILBASH Literally "red heads". Türkmen supporters of the Safavids named after their red hats.

QUAKERS (also known as the Society of Friends). Radical religious movement without clergy or creed, originating in mid-17th-century England and rapidly developing in North America from the colony of Pennsylvania, founded by Quaker William Penn under royal charter in 1681. Today Quakers in the world number around 200,000.

QUEBEC ACT One of the Intolerable Acts or Coercive Acts which led up to the American War of Independence. This measure (1774) established a new administration for the Northwest Territory, ceded to Great Britain by France after the **Seven Years' War** (1756–63), and extended its frontiers to the Ohio and Mississippi rivers; the trans-Appalachian claims of the other (largely Protestant) American colonies were thus jeopardized in favour of French Catholics.

QUTBUDDIN AIBAK (d.1210) Muslim ruler in India. Born in Turkestan and sold as a child slave, he entered the service of **Muizzudin Muhammad** where he rose from the position of stableman to that of general. He led many mounted campaigns between 1193 and 1203, and was freed after Muhammad's death in 1206. He laid the foundations for the emergence of the Delhi sultanate under **Iltutmish**.

R

RABIH ZOBEIR (d.1900) Leader of native opposition to the French in Equatorial Africa from 1878 until his death at the battle of Lakhta.

RADCLIFFE, WILLIAM (1760–1841) An improver of cotton machinery in England. With the aid of Thomas Johnson he invented a cotton dressing machine which enabled the fabric to be starched before the warp was put on to the loom; he went bankrupt in 1807. He started another mill, but this was destroyed by **Luddite** rioters in 1812. He was the author of *Origin of the New System of Manufacture, commonly called Power Loom Weaving* (1828).

RAFFLES, SIR THOMAS STAMFORD (1781–1826) Founder of Singapore. He was appointed assistant secretary to the newly formed government of Penang in 1804, and lieutenant-governor of Java in 1811. He was recalled to England in 1816, but returned to the East as lieutenant-governor of Benkulen, 1818–24, and in 1819 established a British port at Singapore, henceforth the centre of British colonial activity in southeast Asia.

RAHMAN, MAJIBUR (1920–75) Usually known as Sheikh Majib, first president of Bangladesh. He founded the East Pakistan Students' League, and during the 1950s was secretary and organizer of the Awami League, seeking autonomy for East Pakistan. He was imprisoned in 1958, and the resulting mob violence led to the breakaway of the province in 1971 as the new state of Bangladesh. Rahman was elected as its first head of state in January 1972. He was assassinated in 1975.

RAJARAJA (d.1014) King of the **Cholas** in southern India, reigning 985–1014. He attacked the alliance between Kerala, Ceylon and the Pandyas, seized the Arab trading centre of Malabar, launched a naval attack on the Arab-held Maldive Islands, devastated Ceylon and its capital Anuradhapura. He was succeeded by his son Rajendra after two years of joint rule.

RAJPUTS Literally "Sons of Kings"; members of landowning and military castes, according to one view descendants of central Asian invaders, who dominated large parts of north and western India, especially Rajasthan, from about the 8th to the 18th century.

RAMAYANA Shorter of India's two great epic poems, composed by the poet Valmiki. Its surviving text runs to 24,000 couplets celebrating the birth, education and adventures of Rama, the ideal man and king, and his ideal wife, Sita.

RAMSES II, THE GREAT (d.1224 BC) Third king of Egypt's 19th Dynasty; son of **Seti I**. He succeeded *c.* 1304 BC; fought the Hittites in an indecisive battle at Qadesh on the Orontes in the fifth year of his reign; 16 years later he signed a lasting peace treaty with the Hittite king, Khattushilish. He is remembered for his military prowess and vast building activities; he constructed the famous rock-temples of Abu Simbel.

RAMSES III The last great pharaoh of Egypt, reigning 1184–1152 BC as the second pharaoh of the 20th Dynasty. He fought two major wars against the Libyans and one against a confederation of northerners, who included Philistines, and two minor campaigns in Palestine and Syria. His greatest monument was his funerary temple at Medinet Habu (western Thebes), in which his wars are represented; he also built a small temple at Karnak, which he dedicated to Amun. Late in his reign he survived a palace conspiracy to murder him.

RAMMOHAN ROY (1774–1833) Hindu religious reformer. He published a tract against idolatry in 1790; in 1816 he founded the Spiritual Society in Calcutta, which in 1828 developed into the **Brahmo Samaj** movement. He was active in the campaign to abolish suttee, the ritual burning of Hindu widows; he was granted the title of rajah by the Delhi emperor.

RANJIT SINGH (1780–1839) Known as the Lion of the Punjab, he was the son of a **Sikh** chieftain. In 1799 he seized Lahore, capital of the Punjab, and proclaimed himself maharajah in 1801. His aim to unite all Sikh territories in India was thwarted by the British in 1809. With a modernized army, he inflicted many defeats on Afghans and Pathans in the 1820s and 1830s, and, jointly with the British, planned to invade Afghanistan in 1838.

RAPALLO, TREATY OF Agreement signed in 1922 between Germany and Soviet Russia, which established trade relations and cancelled pre-1914 debts and war claims.

RASHID ALI AL-GAILANI (1892–1965) Iraqi prime minister. He supported German war aims in 1939; resigned his post, January 1941, and then seized power in April; he refused the British permission to move troops through Iraq (agreed under a 1930 treaty), but lost out in a sharp, 30-day war when promised German help failed to arrive, and went into exile in Iran as a pro-British government was formed.

RASHTRAKUTAS South Indian dynasty, founded in the 8th century AD by Dantidurga, a feudatory of the Chalukyas. From their central territory in the north Deccan, they fought wars and formed alliances throughout India. The best-known king, Amoghavarsha (reigned 814–80), patronized **Jainism**. They were eclipsed in the late 10th century by the later Chalukyas.

RASULIDS Muslim dynasty, ruling Yemen and the Hadhramaut from 1229 to 1454, named after Rasul, a Turkish officer of the **Abbasid** caliph. His grandson Umar I ibn Ali controlled Yemen and Mecca 1229–50; later Rasulid rule was confined to the Yemeni highlands.

RATANA, T W (1870–1939) Maori religious and political leader in New Zealand. In 1920 he founded the Ratana Church, which had widespread popular appeal among Maoris and helped create for them a stronger supra-tribal identity in society and politics, notably through the Ratana-Labour Party Alliance.

RATHENAU, EMIL (1838–1915) German industrialist and electrical pioneer. In 1883 he founded Deutsche Edison-Gesellschaft to exploit German rights in the patents of Thomas Edison; the company was renamed Allgemeine-Elektrizitäts-Gesellschaft (AEG) in 1887. With **Werner von Siemens** he founded the Telefunken company in 1903.

RATHENAU, WALTHER (1867–1922) German statesman. He succeeded his father, Emil, as head of the vast electrical engineering firm, AEG. In 1914 he set up the War Raw Materials Department to organize the conservation and distribution of raw materials essential to Germany's war economy. He founded the Deutsche Demokratische Partei (DDP) and advocated industrial **democracy** and state intervention in industry. He was minister of reconstruction, 1921, and as foreign minister in 1922 he negotiated the **Treaty of Rapallo** which normalized relations with the Soviet Union. He was assassinated after accusations that he favoured "creeping **communism**".

RAZIYYA Briefly sultana of Delhi, she succeeded to the throne during the period of anarchy following the death of her father, Iltutmish, in 1236. She provided both political stability and military leadership, but her sex and her unwillingness to share power created growing resentment, and ultimately she was murdered.

REAGAN, RONALD (1911–2004) US actor, Republican politician and 40th president (1981–9). After acting in over 50 Hollywood films and becoming leader of the actors' union he joined the Republican Party in 1962 and secured the governorship of California for two terms (1967–75). He defeated Democratic incumbent Jimmy Carter in the presidential election of 1980 and served two consecutive terms. As president he supported deflationary policies aimed at reducing taxes and government spending, popularly called "Reaganomics". In foreign policy he increased military spending, maintained a tough anti-Soviet posture, authorized US intervention in Grenada (1983), CIA operations in Nicaragua and the bombing of Libya (1986). Reagan died in 2004.

REFORMATION Religious and political movement in 16th-century Europe to reform the Roman Catholic church which led to the establishment of Prostestant churches. Anticipated from the 12th century by the Waldenses, Lollards and Hussites, it was set off by the German priest Martin **Luther** in 1517 and became effective when the absolute monarchies gave it support by challenging the political power of the papacy and confiscating church wealth.

RENÉ OF ANJOU (1409–80) Duke of Lorraine, 1431–52, of Anjou, 1434–80, and Count of Provence, 1434–80. He made an unsuccessful bid to become king of Naples, 1435–42; in 1442 he retired to Anjou and later (1473) to Provence, where he patronized poets and artists. In 1481 his lands (except for Lorraine) passed to the French crown.

RESTITUTION, EDICT OF (1629) Decree of the Holy Roman Emperor Ferdinand II (1619–37) that all imperial Church lands taken by secular princes since 1552 should be restored. The measure was brutally enforced by a large imperial army and provoked an alliance of German Protestant rulers against the Emperor. With Swedish aid provided by **Gustavus Adolphus**, the alliance defeated the imperial forces at the battle of Breitenfeld, 1631.

REULEAU, FRANZ (1829–1905) French engineer, best known for his geometric studies on the underlying principles of machine design, set out in his *Theoretische Kinematic*, published in Germany in 1875 and translated into English as *the Kinematics of Machinery* in 1876.

REZA SHAH PAHLEVI (1878–1944) Ruler of Iran, 1925–41. An army officer, he organized a successful revolution in 1921 and deposed the **Qajar** dynasty to become shah in 1925. He instituted a reform and modernization programme; he abdicated in 1941, when British and Russian armies occupied Iran.

RHEE, SYNGMAN (1875–1965) South Korean political leader. Jailed and tortured in his early twenties for his nationalist views, he then studied for six years at American universities until 1910 and lived in exile, working for the Korean Methodist Church in the USA (1912–45). A leader of the independence movement, he returned to the newly established Republic of Korea to become its president (1948–60). Known for his dictatorial and militant anti-communist stance, he was forced to resign amid accusations of election fraud and corruption.

RHODES, CECIL JOHN (1853–1902) Financier and imperialist. He emigrated from Great Britain to South Africa in 1870, and made a fortune from Kimberley diamond mines and Transvaal gold. In 1881 he entered the Cape Colony parliament and strongly advocated British expansion in Africa: he negotiated the annexation of Bechuanaland in 1884, and having sent white settlers into Mashonaland "founded" Rhodesia. He became prime minister of Cape Colony, 1890–6, but resigned after the **Jameson Raid** into the Transvaal.

RICHARD II (1367–1400) King of England, 1377–99. Son of Edward the Black Prince, he succeeded his grandfather, **Edward III**; he was in conflict with a baronial group, the Lords Appellant, to 1397, and was deposed in 1399 by a cousin, Henry of Lancaster, later crowned **Henry IV**; he died in prison, possibly murdered.

RICHELIEU, ARMAND-JEAN DU PLESSIS, DUC DE (1585–1642) French cardinal and statesman. As secretary of state (1616–17) and chief minister (1624–42) to Louis XIII, he destroyed French Protestant power (the siege of La Rochelle, 1628), undermined Spanish power in Italy (war of Mantua, 1627–31), declared war on Spain and intervened in the Thirty Years' War against the **Habsburgs** from 1635, although he died before much success had been gained (*see also* **Mazarin**)

RIENZO, COLA DI (c. 1313–54) Popular leader in medieval Rome. In 1343 he was sent to Avignon to plead the cause of Rome's new popular party before Pope Clement VI. In 1347 he assumed dictatorial powers with popular acclaim and reformed taxes, courts and political structure, attempting to re-establish Rome as the capital of a "Sacred Italy". He successfully suppressed an uprising by the nobles, but was forced to resign before the end of the year; reinstated in 1354 (but for only two months), he was seized and killed trying to quell a riot.

RIGA, TREATY OF (1920) Agreement by which Soviet Russia recognized the independence of Latvia (formerly a Russian province).

RIGA, TREATY OF (1921) Agreement between Poland and Soviet Russia following a war (1919–21) provoked largely by the claim of the new Polish state (created in 1918) that its eastern frontier of 1772 (prior to the first partition) should be restored. The treaty gave Poland large parts of Belorussia and the Ukraine. It lasted until the **Nazi-Soviet Pact** of 1939.

RIM-SIN Last ruler of Larsa, in ancient Mesopotamia, who reigned *c.* 1747–1688 BC. Son of Kudur-Mabuk, probably an **Amorite** chieftain from the borders of Elam, in 1719 he overthrew Isin, the old rival of Larsa, for control of southern Babylonia. He fought frequently with **Hammurabi** of Babylon, who finally defeated him in 1688.

RIPON, GEORGE FREDERICK SAMUEL ROBINSON (1827–1909) 1st marquis and 2nd earl of Ripon, viceroy of India. He was appointed viceroy in 1880, and attempted many reforms but generated much opposition, resigning in 1884 after the forced withdrawal of his proposal to give Indian judges power over European defendants. He became secretary for the colonies, 1892–5, and Lord Privy Seal, 1905–8.

RIZAL, JOSÉ (1861–96) Filipino novelist, poet and patriot, born in Manila. At the University of Madrid he led a movement for reform of Spanish rule in the colony; he returned to the Philippines in 1892, and founded the non-violent Reform society, *Liga Filipina*. Exiled to Mindanao, he was arrested after an insurrection by a secret nationalist group, the Katipunan; although he had no connection with it, he was shot. His martyrdom and his masterly verse-farewell, *Ultimo Adiós*, inspired the fight for Filipino independence.

ROBERT I "THE BRUCE" (1274–1329) King of Scotland, crowned in 1306 in defiance of the English king, **Edward I**. He consolidated his power during the weak reign of **Edward II**, and inflicted a heavy defeat on the English at Bannockburn in 1314. The title and Scotland's independence were recognized by the English in 1328, the year before his death.

ROBERT OF ANJOU (1278–1343) King of Naples 1309–43; he was the grandson of Charles I, conqueror of Sicily from the **Hohenstaufen** (1286). He unsuccessfully attempted to secure a dominant position in Italy, in alliance with France and the papacy. The kingdom rapidly declined after his death.

ROBESPIERRE, MAXIMILIEN FRANÇOIS MARIE-ISIDORE DE (1758–94) French revolutionary leader. He practised as a provincial lawyer; led the radical **Jacobin** faction, and played a leading part in the 1793 overthrow of the **Girondins** by the extremist Mountain group. As a member of the Committee of Public Safety, 1793–4, he became virtual dictator, establishing the Terror and eliminating his rivals Hébert and **Danton**; he introduced the cult of the Supreme Being. He was overthrown and executed after the *coup d'état* of July 1794.

RODNEY, GEORGE BRYDGES (1718–92) British admiral who commanded in the West Indies in the **Seven Years' War** and again in the American War of Independence. He captured Martinique (from the French) and the neutral islands of St Lucia, Grenada and St Vincent in 1762; and defeated the Spanish fleet to relieve Gibraltar in 1780. His subsequent failures were redeemed by his victory over the French fleet at the battle of the Saints (Dominica) in 1782, for which he was created Baron Rodney.

ROGER II (1095–1154) Founder of the Norman kingdom of Sicily. He succeeded his brother as Count of Sicily in 1105; made Palermo his capital, 1130; acquired Calabria, 1112, and Apulia, 1127; was crowned King of Sicily, 1130. He made Sicily a major meeting place for Christian and Arab scholars.

ROGGEVEEN, JACOB (1659–1729) Dutch explorer. After retirement from law practice in Batavia, he fitted out a private fleet to search for the reputed southern continent in the South Pacific, 1721–2. Though he circumnavigated the globe, his only significant discovery was Easter Island.

ROMANCE The group of languages derived from the spoken Latin of the Roman empire. Influenced by local languages in the successor states of Rome, the romance group comprised French, Spanish, Italian, Portuguese, Romanian, Catalan and Romansch.

ROMANOVS Ruling dynasty in Russia from 1613 until the Revolution of 1917. The family came to prominence when Anastasia Romanova married **Ivan IV the Terrible**. In 1613 the grandson of Anastasia's brother, **Michael Romanov**, was elected tsar; the succession thereafter, though remaining within the family, was frequently disorderly. In 1917 **Nicholas II** abdicated in favour of his brother Michael, who refused the throne, thus ending the royal line.

ROMANOV, MICHAEL (1596–1645) First of the Romanov tsars in Russia, reigning 1613–45. Distantly related to Fyodor I (reigned 1584–98), last tsar of the previous Rurik dynasty, he reluctantly accepted popular election to the throne at the end of Russia's 15-year "Time of Troubles". The 16-year-old tsar at first shared power with relatives of his mother, who had been forced to become a nun by **Boris Godunov**, and later with his father, who had been forced to become a monk, the Patriarch Filaret.

ROOSEVELT, FRANKLIN DELANO (1882–1945) 32nd president of the USA, first elected 1932. He formulated the **New Deal** policy to combat world depression; inaugurated the Good Neighbour Policy in Latin America; in 1933 he recognized the USSR. He was re-elected in 1936 and again in 1940, when he provided lend-lease support for Great Britain. With **Churchill**, he issued the Atlantic Charter; after the Japanese attack at Pearl Harbor he led the USA into the Second World War, and with **Chiang Kai-shek** at Cairo in November 1943 resolved to continue the war until Japan's unconditional surrender. Re-elected for a fourth term, he died after the 1945 **Yalta** conference of Allied leaders.

ROOSEVELT, THEODORE (1858–1919) 26th president of the USA. He worked as a writer, explorer and soldier before entering politics in 1881. He became assistant navy secretary, then led the US **Rough Riders** in Cuba during the Spanish-American War (1898). He was governor of New York, becoming vice-president in 1900 and succeeding to the presidency in 1901 after the assassination of **McKinley**. He acquired the Panama Canal Zone in 1903. He left office in 1909, and failed to win back the presidency in 1912.

ROSAS, JUAN MANUEL DE (1793–1877) Dictatorial governor of Beunos Aires, 1829–52. Born into a landowning and military family, he acquired large ranches and controlled a force of *gauchos* (cowboys); in 1827 he was appointed head of the provincial militia, and distinguished himself fighting insurgents (1828–9) and Indians (1833). He accepted the governorship, 1829–32 and from 1835, and ran a ruthless police state. He was overthrown in 1852 by a coalition of Brazilians, Uruguayans and Argentine opponents at the battle of Caseros. He fled to England and died in exile.

ROSES, WARS OF THE Civil war between rival claimants to the English throne: the dynasty of York (whose emblem was a white rose) and that of Lancaster (a red rose). The Yorkists rose against the Lancastrian king, Henry VI, in 1455, and deposed him in 1461. After a series of struggles involving Edward IV, Edward V and Richard III, the conflict was finally resolved in 1485, when Richard was defeated at Bosworth Field by the Lancastrian claimant, Henry Tudor, who was enthroned as **Henry VII** and married the Yorkist princess, Elizabeth, daughter of Edward IV, thus uniting the warring factions.

ROSKILDE, PEACE OF Treaty ending the war between Sweden and Denmark (1655–8) for control of the Baltic; it gave Sweden permanent possession of the strategically important region of Scania, Blekinge and Bohuslän.

ROUGH RIDERS Popular name for the First Volunteer Cavalry, recruited by **Theodore Roosevelt** from cowboys, police, miners and athletes to fight in the Spanish-American War, 1898.

ROUSSEAU, JEAN-JACQUES (1712–78) Swiss-French writer, born in Geneva. He quarrelled with most of the accepted conventions and established authorities of his time, and explored many of the themes later to form the basis of 19th-century Romanticism and modern **democracy**. His main works include *Du Contrat Social* (1762), setting out a new theory of the relationship between the individual and the state; his autobiographical *Confessions* (published posthumously); and his novels *La Nouvelle Héloïse* (1761) and *Emile, ou l'éducation* (1762).

ROYAL NIGER COMPANY British trading company in west Africa. In 1886 Sir George Goldie's National African Company received a royal charter, changed its name, and was authorized to administer the delta and territories adjoining the course of the rivers Niger and Benue. It engaged in complex struggles with the French, the Germans and local rulers, conquering several emirates; in 1899, after many complaints and disputes, the charter was transferred to the British government.

RUDOLF IV (d.1365) Habsburg Duke of Austria, reigning 1358–65. He forged a charter, the *privilegium majus*, claiming vast lands, privileges and the hereditary title of archduke from his brother-in-law, Emperor **Charles IV**. The document was declared fraudulent by Italian scholar-poet Petrarch; the resulting war ended with the granting of Austria's claim to the Tyrol. He founded the University of Vienna (1365).

RYSWYCK, TREATY OF Agreement, signed September–October 1697, ending the War of the Grand Alliance (1689–97). **Louis XIV** (for France) accepted William III's right to the English throne, restoration of the *status quo* in the French and British colonies, the return of Catalonia, Luxembourg and parts of the Spanish Netherlands to Spain, and a favourable trade treaty with the Dutch. The German emperor recovered many French-fortified places along the Rhine, while Lorraine was restored to Duke Leopold.

SAAD ZAGHUL *see* **Zaghul, Saad**

SAADIS Muslim dynasty, claiming to be descendants of the Prophet ("sharifs") and ruling Morocco from the mid-16th to the mid-17th century.

SAAVEDRA, BALTAZAR DE LA CUEVA HENRÌQUEZ ARIAS DE (1626–86) Spanish colonial administrator. In 1674 he was appointed Viceroy of Peru, Chile and Tierra Firme (a territory which included the Isthmus of Panama); his prosperous rule ended in outcry in 1678, when he tried to relax commercial monopolies. He was held captive for two years while charges were heard, and was exonerated in 1680. He returned to Spain, and held a seat on the Council of the Indies.

SABINES Ancient Apennine people of central Italy, northeast of Rome. According to legend the Sabine women were abducted by the Romans under Romulus; by the 3rd century the Sabines had become fully Romanized.

SADAT, MOHAMMED ANWAR EL- (1918–81) Egyptian President. Commissioned in the Egyptian army in 1938, he was one of the group of officers, headed by **Nasser**, who planned the 1952 revolution. He was vice-president, 1964–6 and 1969–70, and became president after Nasser's death in 1970. In alliance with Syria he launched war against Israel in October 1973. In 1977 he opened a new round of discussions on peace between Israel and Egypt with his visit to Jerusalem. He was assassinated in 1981 by Muslim fundamentalists.

SAFFARIDS Muslim dynasty ruling much of eastern Persia in the 9th century. By 873 the empire stretched from northeast India to Khurasan; after failing to annex Transoxania in 900 its wider empire collapsed, but Saffarids retained local power in eastern Persia until the 15th century.

SAID, AL BU Muslim dynasty ruling in Oman, *c.* 1749 to the present, and Zanzibar, *c.* 1749–1964. It was founded by Ahmed ibn Said, who displaced the Yarubid imams of Oman to seize power there and in east Africa. In the 18th century they held Bahrain and parts of Persia; at the peak of their power under Said ibn Sultan (1806–56) they established commercial relations with the USA, France and Great Britain. The dominions were divided by Great Britain on the death of Said. The Zanzibar line was overthrown in 1964 when the island became part of Tanzania.

ST BARTHOLOMEW'S DAY MASSACRE Massacre of **Huguenots** (French Protestants) by French Catholics, which began on St Bartholomew's Day, 24 August 1572, and quickly spread from Paris to other French towns.

SALADIN (c. 1137–93) Western name of the founder of the **Ayyubid** dynasty, and the crusaders' most successful foe. He became sole ruler of Egypt and Islamic Syria, 1186; destroyed the crusaders' army at Hattin, northern Palestine and re-entered Jerusalem, 1187. He also neutralized the gains of the Third **Crusade**.

SALAZAR, ANTONIO DE OLIVEIRA (1889–1970) Dictator of Portugal. He was finance minister during the Depression, 1928–32, and became prime minister in 1932 after restoring economic order. He established authoritarian rule on Fascist lines in 1933 and maintained personal control until his death.

SALIANS One of many Frankish tribes which moved from central Europe (3rd century AD) and settled in the area north of the Rhine, near the modern Ijsselmeer. Thence, in the 5th century, they expanded south approximately to the river Loire. From them sprang the **Merovingian** dynasty, later superseded by the **Carolingians**, which conquered Aquitaine and Burgundy and reunited most of Gaul. The term is also used of the dynasty which came to power in Germany with Conrad II in 1024; the line died out with his great-grandson in 1125.

SALISBURY, ROBERT CECIL, 3rd MARQUESS OF (1830–1903) British statesman. He entered politics as a Conservative, and became foreign secretary 1878–80, a post which he also held through most of his three periods as prime minister, 1885–6, 1886–92, 1895–1902. On the whole he inclined towards cooperation with the **Triple Alliance** against Great Britain's imperial rivals, France and Russia, but was reluctant to conclude "binding alliances" in Europe and was therefore often associated with the so-called policy of splendid isolation.

SALLE, ROBERT CAVELIER SIEUR DE LA (1643–87) French explorer. He emigrated to Montreal in 1666; traded and surveyed along the

Illinois and Mississippi rivers from the Great Lakes region to the gulf of Mexico. He founded Louisiana in 1682.

SAMANIDS Iran's first native dynasty after the Muslim conquests, ruling 819–999. It developed Samarkand and Bukhara as centres of art and culture and assumed the economic leadership of northern Persia, but weakened after the mid-10th century.

SAMGUK SAGI 12th-century history of ancient Korea up to 918; it defined the Korean identity.

SAMNITES Ancient Italian peoples occupying the territory of Samnium, in the southern Apennines in Italy, who were subjugated by Rome in the 4th to the 3rd century BC.

SAMORY (c. 1830–1904) Islamic hero and defender of the western Sudan against French colonial expansion in the late 19th century. Between 1865 and 1870 he built up a powerful chiefdom, and by early 1880 ruled an empire stretching from the Upper Volta and Upper Niger to Futa Jallon. In 1890 he set up his own firearms industry. He was finally defeated in 1898 on the Cavalla River, and died in exile.

SAMOYEDS People of the northern coasts of the former Soviet Union, from the White Sea to the Taymyr peninsula. Speaking a Uralic language, they are noted reindeer herders, fishermen and hunters.

SAMUDRAGUPTA (d.c. 375) Indian king, succeeding his father Chandragupta I, founder of the **Gupta** dynasty, *c.* 355. From his capital, Pataliputra, in the Ganges valley, he extended control or exacted tribute throughout the greater part of the sub-continent.

SAMURAI Japanese warrior caste. Originally restricted to landed military houses, it became more open to able warriors of all kinds, especially during periods of civil war, such as that which lasted from *c.* 1450 to 1600. After 1603, when the rule of the **Tokugawa** *shoguns* initiated 250 years of peace, the Samurai became a closed hereditary class, often turning from military to administrative and artistic pursuits. Its feudal privileges were quickly abolished after the **Meiji** restoration of 1868.

SAN (Bushmen) Nomadic people, speaking a distinctive click language, living in the Kalahari Desert area of Namibia and Botswana.

SANDINISTAS Members of Sandinist National Liberation Front (Frente Sandinista de Liberación Nacional: FSLN), named for César Augusto Sandio (1893–1934), assassinated guerrilla leader of the Nicaraguan resistance against US military occupation (1927–33). The FSLN, founded in 1962, began as a guerrilla campaign and ended in a full-scale civil war, resulting in the overthrow of the Somoza regime (1979). They pursued a course of social **democracy**, with Daniel Ortega as president of the National Assembly (1985–90), in spite of pressure from the US-supplied counter-revolutionary forces through the 1980s. In free elections (1989), **Violeta Chamorro**, the opposition candidate was elected president.

SAN-FAN REBELLION *see* **Wu San-kuei**

SAN MARTÍN, JOSÉ DE (1778–1850) Argentine liberator; with **Simon Bolívar**, he led an army of liberation in the epic crossing of the Andes; with **Bernardo O'Higgins** he freed Chile in 1818, and in 1821 invaded Peru from the sea and took the Spanish stronghold of Lima. After a quarrel with Bolívar, he retired to France.

SANSKRIT Classical language of ancient India, in use mainly from *c.* 500 BC to *c.* AD 1000, but kept alive to the present day as the sacred language of the Hindu scriptures as well as of much secular literature. Also used in early inscriptions in south and southeast Asia, notably in ancient Cambodia. It is an Indo-European language, and hence ultimately related to Greek and Latin.

SAN STEFANO, TREATY OF Agreement ending the Russo-Turkish War, 1877–8. It created a large tributary state of Bulgaria, stretching from the Danube to the Aegean and covering all Macedonia except Salonika, granted independence to and enlarged Serbia, Montenegro and Romania, and gave Russia acquisitions in the Caucasus and a large indemnity. Fiercely opposed by Britain and Austria, the treaty was largely overturned at the **Congress of Berlin** in 1878.

SANTA ANNA, ANTONIO LÓPEZ DE (1794–1876) Mexican *caudillo*. He fought off the Spanish reconquest attempt in 1829, and became president of Mexico in 1834. He quelled Texan resistance at the Alamo, 1836, but was later defeated and captured; seizing power again in 1839 he ruled until 1845, but was routed by US troops in the Mexican War of 1864–8. His services were refused by both Emperor **Maximilian** and his enemies, and Santa Anna died poor and blind.

SANUSI WAR Resistance between 1912 and 1931 to Italian attempts to annex Libya, led by a brotherhood formed among the desert tribes (the "Sanusis", founded in 1837). While the European powers were involved in the First World War, the Sanusis drove the Italians back to the coast and directed opposition to the French in Tunisia. In the 1920s they were defeated, but after the Second World War their leader became King of Libya.

SAPPHO (b.c. 612 BC) Greek poetess, who lived at Mytilene in Lesbos. Her affection for a group of young women and girls associated with her in celebrating the cult of Aphrodite is ecstatically described among the surviving fragments from her seven books of poems in the Aeolic dialect. She looks at her emotions honestly and expresses them with a rare gift of verbal music.

SARGON Semitic king of Akkad, reigning *c.* 2296–2240 BC. One of the world's earliest empire-builders, he defeated the Sumerian ruler Lugalzagges of Uruk, seized all southern Mesopotamia, and achieved conquests as far afield as northern Syria, southern Anatolia and Elam in western Persia.

SASANIDS Iranian dynasty, named after Sasan, an ancestor of **Ardashir I**, who founded the family fortunes in AD 224. Under his leadership, Persis defeated the **Parthians** and created a major but frequently fluctuating empire extending from the Roman and Byzantine frontier in the west to central Asia where it absorbed most of the territories of the **Kushanas**. They were finally eclipsed by the Islamic invasions of 637–51.

SATAVAHANAS Indian dynasty, controlling the Andhra region in the delta of the Krishna and Godavari rivers. First mentioned in the 1st century AD, when King Satakarni made many conquests, it revived under Gautamiputra and his son Vasishthiputra in the early 2nd century, under whom lands were acquired from Kathiawar on the west coast to northern Madras on the east. They were displaced by the **Vakataka** dynasty.

SATNAMIS Members of one of a group of Hindu sects in India. The oldest, founded by Birbham in the 16th century, was part of an attempt to bring together **Hinduism** and Islam. Another was launched at the end of the 17th century by the Rajput religious leader, Jagji-van Das. Modern Satnamis are found mainly among the Chamars, northern India's hereditary caste of leather-tanners; they follow the teachings of the 19th-century Chamar saint, Rai Das.

SAUDI (as-Saud) dynasty Founders and rulers of Saudi Arabia. Originally small rulers in central Arabia, they created their first – but short-lived – large state in the 18th century. The present state was created by Ibn Saud, who was followed after his death (1953) by four sons in succession: Saud (deposed 1964), Faisal (assassinated 1975), Khaled (d.1982) and Fahd.

SAUNDERS, SIR CHARLES (1713–75) British admiral. He commanded the fleet which carried General **James Wolfe**'s army to conquer French Canada in 1759. He was appointed First Lord of the Admiralty in 1766.

SAXONS German people originating in Schleswig-Holstein and along the Baltic. They responded to the decline of the Roman empire with a policy of active piracy in the North Sea, developing in the 5th century AD into substantial settlements along the coasts of Britain and Gaul. The Saxon wars, initiated by **Charlemagne**, lasted 32 years and ended with the absorption of the continental Saxons into the Frankish empire.

SAYYID MUHAMMAD BEN ABDULLAH (d.1920) Known as the "Mad Mullah", a Somali chief who proclaimed himself **Mahdi** (religious leader) in the 1890s and began systematic raids against British and Italian positions around the Red Sea. He won territorial recognition in 1905 but resumed raids after 1908, keeping the Europeans confined to the coast until his death.

SCALA, della Italian dynastic family, also known as Scaligeri, hereditary rulers of Verona, founded by Mastino I (d.1277). Power was built up by his descendants, notably Cangrande I (1291–1329), the patron of **Dante**, but then frittered away in family quarrels. Their power was terminated by the **Visconti** of Milan, who conquered Verona in 1387.

SCANIAN WAR Fought between Sweden and Denmark, 1674–9, over the rich and strategically important province of Scania, or Skåne (at the southern tip of modern Sweden), which had been captured from the Danes in 1658. The Danish army reconquered Scania, but **Louis XIV** vetoed the return of the territory.

SCHLEICHER, KURT VON (1882–1934) Last chancellor of Germany's Weimar Republic, nicknamed "the Hunger Chancellor". He joined the German army in 1900, and in 1919 entered the newly-formed Reichswehr, becoming a major-general in the ministry of war in 1929. He helped bring down **Brüning**, and succeeded **Papen** as chancellor in 1932. He offered to aid **Hitler** if he could retain control of the Reichswehr, but was dismissed by **Hindenburg** in January 1933 after Hitler's refusal, and was murdered by the SS during the "Night of the Long Knives" the following year.

SCHLIEFFEN, ALFRED GRAF VON (1833–1913) German field-marshal, and chief of the German general staff, 1891–1906. In 1905 he devised the Schlieffen Plan, which, in the event of war, would involve the defeat of France by a vast outflanking movement through the Low Countries; in a revised form this provided the basis of German strategy at the outbreak of the First World War.

SCHOUTEN, WILLEM (1567–1625) Flemish navigator, discoverer of Le Maire Strait, between Tierra del Fuego and Staten island, and of Cape Horn. He was the first captain to traverse the Drake Passage, linking the Atlantic and Pacific south of Tierra del Fuego; Drake himself followed the Magellan Passage, further north.

SCHWARZKOPF, NORMAN (1934–2012) US Army General. Served in two tours of duty in Vietnam, but is best known as the Commander of Operation Desert Storm during the 1991 Iraq war. Desert Storm was an allied US-led invasion of Iraq authorized by several UN resolutions following Saddam Hussein's invasion of Kuwait in 1990, and is often described as the world's first televised war. He became a very popular general and his success as leader earned him the title "Stormin' Norman". Schwarzkopf retired after the war, but came to prominence again as a critic of the war on Iraq in 2003.

SCOTTSBORO BOYS Nine Negro youths of Alabama, USA, charged in 1931 with the rape of two white girls in a railway freight car. The death sentences pronounced by the Alabama courts provoked accusations of racial prejudice from Northern liberals and radicals, and the US Supreme Court twice reversed the Alabama court decisions. In 1937 four were finally sentenced to life imprisonment, and the others released.

SCYTHIANS Nomadic Indo-European people, settling in Scythia, north of the Black Sea, on the lower Don and Dnieper rivers, before the 7th century BC. They were famous for the skill of their mounted archers and their rich gold jewellery; they were displaced by the closely-related Sarmatians in the 3rd century BC.

SEATO *see* **Southeast Asia Treaty Organization**

SECOND COALITION, WAR OF THE Struggle between France and a combination of Austria, Britain and Russia in support of Turkey, 1799–1802. After initial success in Italy and Switzerland, the alliance was crippled by France's victories over Austria at Marengo and Hohenlinden in 1800. Peace was signed with Austria at Lunéville (1801) and with Britain at Amiens (1802).

SECOND INTERNATIONAL Socialist organization founded in 1889 after the collapse of the First International. One of its main objects was to reconcile the working classes of Germany and France and to prevent war, possibly by means of a general strike, but it broke up when the main socialist parties of Europe decided to support their governments on the outbreak of war in 1914.

SÉGUIN, MARC (1786–1875) Distinguished French engineer who constructed railways, locomotives and suspension bridges. In 1828 he invented a multi-tubular locomotive boiler at almost exactly the same time as – but independently of – a similar invention in England by **Robert Stephenson** and Henry Booth. In 1831 a Séguin locomotive ran on the St Étienne-Lyons line, the first railway in France.

SEJŎNG, KING Sage king of the Chosŏn dynasty; designer of the Korean script. Reigned 1418–50.

SELEUCIDS Near-Eastern dynasty dominating Syria and Asia Minor from 312 to 63 BC. It was founded by **Seleucus I Nicator** (reigned 312–280 BC), a close associate of **Alexander the Great**. Its capital established at Antioch-on-the-Orontes, the dynasty sought to Hellenize Asia through Greek settlements; it was constantly at war with the Ptolemies. Power in the east was lost in the 3rd century, in Asia Minor in 198; after 129 it became a local dynasty in northern Syria, and it was finally eclipsed during the Roman invasion of Syria and Cilicia, 65–63.

SELEUCUS I NICATOR (c. 358–280 BC) Founder of the Seleucid dynasty, rulers of Asia Minor until the reign was largely absorbed into the Roman empire. He fought alongside **Alexander the Great** in Persia and married a Bactrian princess, 324. After Alexander's death he became governor of Babylon, and allied with **Ptolemy I** to prevent Antigonus Monophthalmus of Macedonia from inheriting Alexander's imperial throne; he helped to defeat Antigonus at Ipsus, 301; moved his capital to Antioch-on-the-Orontes. A ruler of high integrity, he was murdered by Ptolemy Ceraunus, son of Ptolemy I.

SELIM I YAVUZ (the Inexorable) (1470–1520) Ottoman sultan, 1512–20. The youngest son of **Bayezid II**, he rebelled against his father in 1511, engineering his deposition and overcoming his own brothers Ahmed and Korkut, 1512–13. He proscribed and massacred the Anatolian Turcoman adherents of the **Safavid** shah, **Ismail**, defeating him at Chaldiran and occupying Tabriz, his capital. This radical shift in the Middle Eastern balance of power brought **Selim** into conflict with the **Mamluks** of Egypt: in 1516–17 he successively conquered Syria and Egypt, abolished the Mamluk sultanate and annexed its territories to the Ottoman state. By the time of his death the Ottomans ruled in Jerusalem, in Cairo and in Mecca and Medina: a vast increase in the size, prestige and wealth of the empire.

SELJUKS Ruling family of the Oghuz branch of the Turkish peoples who began settling in lands of the **Abbasid** caliphate, becoming Muslims, in the 10th century. They established a local power, quickly expanded it and occupied Baghdad, capital of the caliphate, in 1055. They ruled most of the lands of the caliphate, under Abbasid suzerainty, with the title of sultan. The empire split after the death of Nizam al-Mulk, but a branch remained as rulers of part of Anatolia (incorporated in the Muslim world by Seljuk conquest from the Byzantines) from the early 12th century until the Mongol conquest in the 13th century.

SEMINOLE North American Indian tribe. In the early 18th century they separated from the Creek Indians ("seminole" means separate) and moved from Georgia into northern Florida. They fought two wars against the USA to avoid deportation and repel white encroachment (1817–18, while still under Spanish rule, and 1835–42); after the final surrender most of the tribe settled in Indian territory, which in 1907 became the state of Oklahoma.

SEMITES Speakers of the Semitic group of languages, of which Arabic, Hebrew and **Amharic** are the main languages still current. Akkadian, the language of Babylon and Assyria, was superseded by Aramaic during the 1st millennium BC, though still written for certain purposes down to the first century AD; Aramaic, once widespread, survives in small enclaves and in the liturgy of the **Jews** and some Eastern churches.

SENDERO LUMINOSO *see* **Shining Path**

SENGHOR, LEOPOLD SEDAR (1906–2001) President of Senegal 1960–90. He studied in France (the first black African to obtain his *agrégation*), served in the French army (1939–40) and in the Resistance. He helped to draft the constitution of the Fourth French Republic in 1946 and sat in its Assembly between 1946 and 1958. He formed his own political party in Senegal in 1948, which won power in 1951, and worked in both Paris and Dakar for a federation of independent French west African states; when this failed he ran for office as resident of Senegal, and was elected (1960). He resigned in 1980 and became the first African to be accepted by the French Academy (1984).

SENNACHERIB King of Assyria, 704–681 BC. He gained experience as a senior commander during the reign of his father, Sargon II, and on his accession devoted himself energetically to the defence of the empire. The rising strength of **Chaldean** and Aramaean tribes in Babylonia, backed by Elam, produced a dangerous instability, which Sennacherib made repeated attempts to resolve by both political and military means, finally sacking the capital, Babylon, in 689 BC. A rebellion in the west, politically linked to the disaffection in Babylonia, led to a campaign in 701 BC, which included the attack on Jerusalem mentioned in the Bible. Sennacherib had a keen interest in technological innovation; his most enduring work was the replanning of Nineveh as the Assyrian capital. He was murdered by a son or sons.

SEPHARDIM From the Hebrew word *Sepharad* for Spain, it refers to the **Jews** of Spain, and after the expulsion of 1492–7 their descendants down to the present day. It is used in distinction to **Ashkenazim** who have slightly different customs and rites.

SERBS Slav people. Serbia, the largest and most populous republic of Yugoslavia, emerged as a separate principality in the 9th century and an independent kingdom in 1217. It was conquered by the Turks (1389) and incorporated into the **Ottoman** empire (1459); it regained its independence in 1829. Blamed for the assassination of Archduke **Franz Ferdinand**, which precipitated the First World War, it became part of Yugoslavia in 1918. Serbia backed Croatian and Bosnian Serb separatists in civil war from 1991, after Croatia, Slovenia and Bosnia-Herzegovina declared independence. Formed new Yugoslav state in 1992 comprising Serbia and Montenegro.

SESTERCE A small silver coin, originally worth one-quarter of a Roman denarius. It was the most common unit of Roman currency.

SETI I King of Egypt's 19th Dynasty, he reigned 1318–1304 BC. He campaigned in Syria, continued work on the Temple of Amun at Karnak, and built his own splendid temple at Abydus.

SEVEN YEARS' WAR Complex struggle, fought 1756–63, between Prussia, supported by Britain, and a coalition of Austria, Russia and France. It arose from Austrian attempts to regain Silesia, lost to Prussia in 1748 (War of the Austrian Succession) and extended by colonial rivalries between Britain and France. The untimely death of Elizabeth of Russia saved Prussia from annihilation while, overseas, Britain destroyed French power in North America, the Caribbean and India.

SÈVRES, TREATY OF Agreement between First World War allies and the Ottoman empire providing for dismemberment of the empire and Greek occupation of part of its Turkish heartland (Izmir and its surrounding region). It was signed reluctantly by the sultan's government on 10 August 1920, but was totally rejected by Turkish nationalists under Mustafa Kemal (**Atatürk**); it was replaced in 1923 by the **Treaty of Lausanne**.

SEWARD, WILLIAM (1801–72) US secretary of state, 1861–9, best remembered for negotiating the purchase of Alaska in 1867 from Russia, called at the time "Seward's Folly", He was a leading anti-slavery agitator; he became governor of New York, 1839–43, and helped to found the Republican Party, 1855. A close adviser to **Lincoln**, he was stabbed by a co-conspirator of Lincoln's assassin, John Wilkes Booth, but survived.

AL-SHABAAB ("the Youth") A Wahhabist terrorist group in Somalia, fighting a jihadi campaign against Somalia's government, AMISOM (the African Union peacekeeping mission) and Kenya. It emerged from the defeated Islamic Court Union after 2006, and pledged allegiance to al-Qaeda in 2012. In 2014, it had 7,000–9,000 militants, but military defeats and the killing of many of its leaders have led to losses in strength and territory.

SHAHJAHAN (1592–1658) Mughal emperor of India and builder of the Taj Mahal. Third son of the emperor Jehangir, and grandson of **Akbar**, he rebelled in 1622 in an ineffectual bid to win the succession, was reconciled with his father in 1625, and in 1628 proclaimed himself ruler after his father's death. He created the city of Shahjahanabad, and the Taj Mahal (1623–49), in memory of his favourite wife, Mumtaz Mahal. He was imprisoned in 1657 during a power struggle between his four sons, and died in captivity.

SHAILENDRA DYNASTY Rulers from *c.* 700 to 1293 of the Sri Vijaya kingdom. Their ardent support of **Buddhism** is reflected in such architectural masterpieces as the great Borobudur complex in Java.

SHAKA (c. 1787–1828) Zulu king. He was appointed in 1810 by the **Nguni** leader, Dingiswayo, to train and command the fighting men of northeast Natal; he pioneered the highly disciplined use of the short, stabbing assegai. He established himself as ruler on Dingiswayo's death in 1818 and crushed all rivals in Natal-Zululand before being assassinated by his half-brothers.

SHALMANESER III King of Assyria, 858–824 BC. He was the son and successor of Ashurnasirpal II, whose imperialist policies he continued, although stability and not expansion was his primary objective, as shown in Babylonia where he provided massive military aid to support the ruling dynasty without seeking personal kingship. In a long series of campaigns he broke the power of the Aramaean and neo-Hittite state of Syria and Cilicia, consolidating control of the routes from the Mediterranean and Asia Minor. In the north he acted to defend Assyria against the growing power of Urartu (Armenia). He defended the eastern borders by sorties into the Zagros mountains to secure recognition of Assyrian suzerainty.

SHAMIL (c. 1830–71) Caucasian resistance leader. In 1830 he joined the Muridis, a Sufi sect engaged in a holy war against the Russians who had seized the former Persian province of Daghestan. He succeeded as imam in 1834, establishing Daghestan as an independent state; surviving the capture of his main stronghold, Ahulgo, in 1838, he was finally defeated by massive Russian forces in 1859, and was exiled to the Moscow district. He died on a pilgrimage to Mecca.

SHAMSHI-ADAD I A major king in northern Mesopotamia, 1749–1717 BC, and older contemporary and possibly former suzerain of **Hammurabi**. The son of a minor ruler of nomad **Amorite** stock, he first gained control of Assyria, and from that base annexed the kingdom of Mari on the middle Euphrates. This gave him an empire controlling important trade routes, stretching from the Zagros mountains to the Euphrates and at times beyond, and northwards to the borders of the Anatolian plateau. Much of his correspondence, and that of his two sons appointed as sub-kings, has been found on clay tablets which have been excavated at Mari, and shows his skill and attention to detail in diplomatic, military and administrative matters.

SHANS A Thai people now forming the Shan state of the Union of Burma. The word is a variant of "Siam", but the Siamese came to call themselves **Thai**, "free", and their country Thailand. The Shans infiltrated Upper Burma in the 13th century, and when Pagan fell, *c.* 1300, strove for nearly three centuries with the Burmans for dominance; they sacked Ava, the capital, in 1527. In the 1550s the rulers of the Sittang state of Toungoo finally forced the Shan states to accept Burman overlordship. After the British annexation of Upper Burma in 1886, their *sawbwas* (chieftains) accepted British overlordship; later they were joined into the Shan States Federation. After independence in 1948 the Union government abolished the powers of the *sawbwas*.

SHANG CHIH-HSIN (1636–80) Son of Shang K'o-hsi (d.1676), governor of Kwangtung 1650–71, who succeeded his father. In 1673 his father's retirement provoked the rebellion of **Wu San-kuei**; in 1676 he joined the rebels, but the following year submitted to the **Manchus**. In 1680 he was accused of plotting a fresh rebellion, was arrested and ordered to commit suicide.

SHANKARACHARYA (c. 788–820) Brahmin philosopher. He was a famous interpreter of *Vedanta* and originator of the Monist (*Advaita*) system of Hindu thought. He established influential religious centres (*mathas*) at Badrinath in the Himalayas, Puri in Orissa, Dwarka on the west Indian coast, and Sringeri in the south; he argued that the visible world is an illusion (*maya*) and that reality lies beyond the senses.

SHARIFIAN DYNASTY Saadi rulers of south Morocco from 1511. They secured Ottoman aid and managed to extend their control over the rest of Morocco in the 1550s and to expel the Portuguese in 1578. In 1591 they sent an expedition of Ottoman-trained troops across the Sahara and destroyed the Songhay empire. Disputed successions after 1610 weakened their authority, and the last Saadi was assassinated in 1660.

SHARON, ARIEL (1928–2014) Born in Palestine while it was a British mandate, Sharon joined the Haganah, the Jewish underground military organization, at the age of 14, and later fought in the first Arab-Israeli War in 1948–9. He rose to the rank of Brigadier General and fought in the 1967 Arab-Israeli War and the 1973 Yom Kippur War. He was first elected to the Knesset in 1974, but resigned a year later to work as Security Adviser to Yitzak Rabin. He was again elected in 1977, and in 1982, as defence minister, his invasion of Lebanon resulted in the deaths of thousands of people. In 1983, an Israeli tribunal found him indirectly responsible for the massacres at the Sabra and Shatila refugee camps during that invasion, and he was removed from office. Despite this, he remained a key political figure and took several ministerial posts, including construction and housing minister, where he was responsible for the biggest drive in settlement activity since 1967. Under Netanyahu's leadership, he became foreign minister of the Likud party in 1998 and took over leadership of that party in 1999 when Netanyahu lost the general election. He won the 2001 general election from Ehud Barak, and his policies have included the building of the West Bank Barrier and the assassination of key resistance leaders.

SHAYBANIDS Central Asian dynasty, controlling Transoxania in the late 15th and early 16th centuries after defeating the descendants of **Tamerlane**; it was replaced at Bukhara by the Astrakhanids in 1599.

SHENG SHI-TS'AI (1895–1970) Warlord from Manchuria, sent to Sinkiang in 1929. He established control there, 1933–43, with strong support from the USSR, giving extensive concessions to the Soviet Union in return. In 1942 he went over to the Nationalists and demanded Soviet withdrawal, which was completed in 1943. In 1944 he tried to renew Russian links; he was removed from the province.

SHERIDAN, PHILIP HENRY (1831–88) Union general in the American Civil War. He cut off the Confederate retreat at Appomattox in 1865, forcing the surrender of the Southern commander, General **Robert E. Lee** to General **Ulysses S. Grant**. He was army commander-in-chief from 1883 until his death.

SHERMAN, WILLIAM TECUMSEH (1820–91) Union general in the American Civil War. He entered the army but resigned his commission in 1853; reappointed a colonel in 1861, he was promoted to general after the first Battle of Bull Run. He destroyed the Confederate forces on his famous march through Georgia, 1864; he was appointed commanding general of the army in 1869.

SHER SHAH (c. 1486–1545) Afghan emperor of northern India. A soldier under the **Mughal** king of Bihar, he became ruler of Bihar, and conquered Bengal in 1539. He defeated the Mughal emperor, Humayan, in 1539 and again in 1540, and took the royal title of Fariduddin Sher Shah. He effected notable fiscal, social and administrative reforms.

SHIH HUANG TI (c. 259–210 BC) Creator of the first unified Chinese empire. He attained the throne of Ch'in, northwest China, in 246 BC. By 221 he had annexed the territories of his six major rivals and proclaimed empire over them. He expanded Chinese control into southern China, establishing centralized administration and a network of roads, extending and consolidating the Great Wall, and unified the Chinese writing system. He entered into bitter controversy with Confucian scholars at his court, culminating in the Burning of the Books in 213.

SHI'ISM One of two main divisions of Islam, which split from the other, the **Sunni**, over the question of succession to the Prophet **Mohammed**, which Shi'as believe to have gone to his son-in-law **Ali** and then to a line of imams (hence their name, *Shi'at Ali*, party of Ali). They later split into a number of groups recognizing different lines of imams: Zaidis in Yemen, **Ismailis**, and the main or Twelver group recognizing a line of twelve imams, the last of whom is believed to have gone into hiding. This kind of Shi'ism is widespread today in Lebanon, Iraq, India, Pakistan and Iran, where it is the state religion.

SHIMONOSEKI Treaty of agreement ending the first Sino-Japanese War (1894–5). China recognized the independence of Korea, ceded Taiwan, the Pescadores Islands and the Liaotung peninsula (including Port Arthur) to Japan, paid a large indemnity, and opened four new ports to foreign trade. Later in 1895 Russia, France and Germany forced Japan to return south Liaotung to China in return for a larger indemnity.

SHINING PATH (Sendero Luminoso) Peruvian revolutionary movement employing guerrilla tactics and extreme violence in the name of Maoism, founded as the Communist Party of Peru in Ayacucho (1970) as an offshoot of other parties. The leader, philosophy professor Abimael Guzmán, and his followers envision revolution as a long-term military offensive aimed at the destruction of all traces of "bourgeois" influence, including political and military figures, and municipal targets. Expanding their activities from the highlands to the capital city of Lima, they remain a force in Peru despite the capture of Guzmán in September 1992.

SHINTŌ Ancient religion of Japan. It lacks both an acknowledged founder and an organized body of teaching. It is characterized by worship of ancestors and heroes, a wide variety of local cults, and belief in the divinity of the emperor. It was largely superseded in the 6th century by **Buddhism**, but revived in the 17th century and was the official state religion from 1867 to 1946.

SHIVA Hindu god, combining within himself many apparently contradictory qualities: destruction and restoration, asceticism and sensuality, benevolence and revenge. In Sanskrit the name means "suspicious one"; he is worshipped as the supreme deity by various Shiva sects in India.

SICILIAN VESPERS Revolt against the French conqueror of Sicily, **Charles I of Anjou**, during the hour of vespers on Easter Monday, 30 March 1282. Encouraged by Peter III of Aragon, the Sicilians massacred 2000 French officials; after long wars between France and Aragon, Peter III's son, Frederick III, won recognition as king under the Peace of Caltabellotta, 1302.

SIEMENS, ERNST WERNER VON (1816–92) German engineer and inventor who discovered a process for galvanic gilding and plating, 1841. He supervised the construction of the first long telegraph line in Europe (Berlin to Frankfurt-am-Main, 1848–9). With Halske he set up a telegraph factory which constructed many telegraph lines in Russia; his brother Carl ran a subsidiary company in Russia while another brother, William, was in charge of the London branch. A new company (Siemens Brothers) manufactured and laid underwater cables. He invented the electric dynamo in 1866 and was actively concerned with the application of electric power to locomotives, trams, lifts and street lighting.

SIENIAWSKI, MIKOLAJ HIERONIM (1645–83) Polish general *Voivode* (Army leader) of Volhynia (1680) and *Hetman* of the crown (1682), he fought successfully against **Tatars** and **Cossacks**. In 1683 he led the advance guard of the army led by King **John III Sobieski** to relieve Vienna.

SIGISMUND III (1555–1632) King of both Sweden and Poland, son of John III of Sweden and Catherine of Poland. Sigismund thus belonged to both the Vasa and the **Jagiełło** dynasties, but his efforts to unite the two lines and the two countries ended in disaster. Elected to the throne of Poland, 1587, he also inherited the Swedish crown in 1592, and tried to restore Catholicism to Sweden. When he left Sweden for Poland, the regent, his uncle (later **Charles IX**), rebelled, defeating him at Stängebrö, 1598, and deposing him, 1599. The two countries remained intermittently at war until 1660.

SIHANOUK, PRINCE NORODOM (1922–2012) Cambodian statesman, King of Cambodia from 1941–55, he then became its prime minister 1955–60, and head of state, 1960–70. In 1970 he was deposed by the National Assembly and Council of the Kingdom, and in Peking set up a Government of National Union. He returned as nominal head of state after the Communist (**Khmer Rouge**) victory in 1975, but was removed from office the following year. He became Cambodian head of state again in 1991.

SIKHS Members of an Indian religious community founded by the 16th-century teacher **Nanak**. Outwardly distinguished by carrying the five K Symbols: Kesha (uncut hair), Kanga (a small comb), Kara (an iron bangle), Kirpan (a small dagger) and Kacha (a type of underwear), in the 18th and early 19th centuries they emerged as a militant warrior brotherhood, particularly under the leadership of **Ranjit Singh**.

SIMON THE HASMONEAN (d.135 BC) Younger brother of **Judah Maccabee** who in 142 established a new Jewish state independent of the **Seleucid** rulers of the Near East; the state survived until quarrels among the descendants of Simon led to the establishment of Roman control in 63 BC.

SINCLAIR, UPTON (1875–1963) American novelist. His first major success, *The Jungle* (1906), embodied his personal, bitterly controversial investigation into working conditions in the Chicago stockyards; a series of similar works established him as a leading Socialist critic of US **capitalism**. He ran for governor of California as the Democratic candidate in 1934.

SINDHIAS Ruling dynasty of Gwalior, western India, founded by Ranoji, a **Maratha** official, in the 18th century. Under Sindhia Mahaduji (reigned 1761–94) the family established a virtually independent empire in northwest India, holding off the troops of the **English East India Company**, 1775–82, defeating the **Rajputs** and the **Marathas**, 1793, and taking the **Mughal** emperors, Shah Alam, under their protection. Later Sindhias, however, accepted British pre-eminence (from 1818); their kingdom survived as a native princedom under the British, and was later absorbed into the Indian union.

SIOUX (also called Dakota). North American Indian tribes once occupying vast areas of Minnesota, Montana, the Dakotas and the Western plains. From 1851 to 1876 they organized a resolute and often successful resistance to the advance of white settlers; discovery of gold in the Black Hills of Dakota brought a vast new influx of white fortune-hunters. Despite victory at the Little Big Horn (1876), the Sioux were finally crushed in the Tongue River valley.

SIVAJI (c. 1627–80) Founder of the 17th-century **Maratha** kingdom in west India. He carved out his kingdom from **Mughal** and Bijapur territory and carried on a protracted war against the former. He was enthroned as an independent sovereign in 1674 and devoted his later life to social reform and the advancement of religious toleration.

SLOVENES South Slav people inhabiting the former Yugoslav province of Slovenia; they number about two million. Gained independence in 1991, after brief opposition from the Yugoslav army.

SMERDIS Short-lived Persian emperor in 522 BC, son of **Cyrus II the Great** and younger brother of **Cambyses II**, on whose order he was secretly put to death by the king's officer Prexaspes. Subsequently imperial powers were usurped by Gaumata, the majordomo, who put his brother in the place of the vanished prince ("Pseudo-Smerdis") while Cambyses was campaigning in Egypt. After Cambyses' death, "Smerdis" was recognized as king for eight months before being killed by **Darius I**.

SMETONA, ANTANAS (1874–1944) Lithuanian statesman who signed the Lithuanian declaration of independence, 1918; he became first president, 1919–20, and again after a *coup d'état* from 1926–40. After the Soviet invasion, he fled to western Europe in 1940, and then to the USA.

SMITH, ADAM (1723–90) Scottish economist and philosopher. Professor of Logic, Glasgow University, 1751, and of Moral Philosophy, 1752–64. His *Inquiry into the Nature and Causes of the Wealth of Nations*, 1776, laid the foundations for the new science of political economy.

SMITH, IAN DOUGLAS (1919–2007) Rhodesian political leader. Served in the British Royal Air Force, 1941–6. He became a member of the South Rhodesia legislative assembly, 1948–53; of the parliament of the federation of Rhodesia and Nyasaland, 1953–61, and of the right-wing Rhodesia Front Party. As prime minister of Rhodesia (1964–79) he declared unilateral independence (UDI) in 1965. In 1979 a peaceful transfer to black majority rule was engineered. Smith remained a member of parliament in the renamed Zimbabwe until 1987, when he was suspended. He susequently resigned as leader of the opposition party.

SOCIALISM Belief in communal or collective ownership of the means of economic production and distribution, and the right of all to share equally in the benefits and opportunities created by society. In Europe it reached back to the Middle Ages ("when Adam delft and Eva span, who was then the gentilman?") and was influential in the 16th and

17th centuries (e.g. the **Levellers** in England); in the 19th century it broke up into various sub-divisions – Utopian (or Saint-Simonian) socialism, Marxian socialism, Christian socialism, democratic socialism – each differing in the emphasis placed on particular parts of the programme, and the political methods considered acceptable to achieve them.

SOCRATES (469–399 BC) Athenian thinker. None of his own work survives; he is best known through **Xenophon**'s memoirs and the early *Dialogues* of his pupil **Plato**. He was independent but critical of **democracy**, and was condemned to death by a popular jury. Plato's *Apology* and *Phaedo* purport to be accounts of his defence and last days.

SOLIDUS Byzantine gold coin, first issued by the Emperor **Constantine** in the 4th century AD. One of the most stable units of currency in economic history, it remained important in international trade for over 700 years.

SOLÍS, JUAN DÍAZ DE (c.1470–1516) Spanish explorer. He first visited central America in 1508 with **Vicente Yáñez Pinzón**. In 1515 he left Spain with three vessels and a commission to explore the lands 1700 leagues (8000 km/5000 miles) south of Panama. He reached the Plate River in 1516, sailed up the Uruguay River and was killed and eaten by Charrua Indians in sight of his crew; the survivors gave valuable information to **Sebastian Cabot.**

SOLOMONIDS Ruling dynasty in Ethiopia from 1770 to 1975. It was founded by Yekuno Amlak, prince of the inland province of Shoa, who claimed direct descent from the biblical King Solomon. Under Amda Sion (1314–44) and Zara Yaqob (1434–68) it consolidated power at home and repelled the Muslims to the north. It was finally eclipsed with the deposition of **Haile Selassie**.

SOPHIST Name applied to itinerant purveyors of higher education for fees in 5th- and 4th-century Greece. Their leading figures, such as **Protagoras**, were spoken of with much respect, but conservative opinion found their influence disturbing.

SOPHOCLES (c. 496–406 BC) Athenian dramatist. Also a statesman, general and priest. He won first prize at Athenian festivals with 24 tetralogies, i.e. 96 of his 123 plays. Seven plays survive: *Ajax*, *The Women of Trachis*, *Antigone*, *King Oedipus*, *Electra*, *Philoctetes*, *Oedipus at Colonus*, and a fragment of *The Trackers*. He said that he created men as they ought to be, whereas **Euripides** wrote about men as they are.

SOTHO/TSWANA One of two main Bantu-speaking groups of southern African peoples, occupying the areas of Botswana, Lesotho, Orange Free State, and the north and east Transvaal since *c.* 1000.

SOTO, HERNANDO DE (c. 1500–42) Spanish explorer. He first sailed to Central America, c. 1519, and in 1532 took part in the conquest of Peru. He was appointed governor of Cuba in 1537 by **Charles V**, and given a contract to conquer Florida: landing near Charlotte Bay in 1539, he fought his way through today's southern USA as far west as Oklahoma, discovering the Mississippi river in 1541. He died on the return journey.

SOUTHEAST ASIA TREATY ORGANIZATION (SEATO) Set up in 1954 between Australia, France, New Zealand, Pakistan, the Philippines, Thailand, the United Kingdom and the USA to resist possible aggression by Communist China after the Korean War. Pakistan withdrew in 1972; at the 1975 Council meeting it was agreed that the organization should be phased out.

SOVIETS Originally revolutionary councils elected by workers during the Russian revolution of 1905. They were revived in 1917 to include bodies elected by workers, peasants and soldiers; it signified the primary units of government in the former USSR.

SPARTAKISTS Members of the *Spartakusbund*, a German revolutionary socialist group in the First World War, led by Rosa Luxembourg and Karl Liebknecht, and named after the Roman slave-rebel, Spartacus. It later became the nucleus of the German Communist Party.

SPEER, ALBERT (1905–81) German architect and **Nazi** leader. A member from 1931 of the German Nazi party; as minister of armaments between 1942 and 1945 he made widespread use of slave labour from concentration camps for which, at the end of the Second World War, he was sentenced to 20 years' imprisonment. His brilliant and efficient organization of industry contributed greatly to German strength. His memoirs, *Inside the Third Reich*, present an intimate picture of life in the entourage of **Adolf Hitler**.

SPEKE, JOHN HANNING (1827–64) British explorer who with Richard **Burton** reached Lake Tanganyika in 1858, and then journeyed alone, becoming the first European to see Lake Victoria and identify it as a source of the Nile.

SPUTNIK First artificial space satellite put into orbit, in 1957, by the USSR. Meaning "companion", "fellow traveller", it signalled the Soviet Union's growing technical capability and helped to precipitate a new phase in the USA-USSR arms race.

SRI VIJAYA Maritime empire, controlling the Strait of Malacca and much of the Malay Archipelago from the 7th to the 11th century.

STALIN (1879–1953) Born Joseph Vissarionovich Dzhugashvili. Son of a Georgian shoemaker, he trained for the priesthood but was expelled in 1899 after becoming a **Marxist**. In 1917 he became Peoples' Commissar for Nationalities in the Soviet government, and general secretary of the Communist Party of the Soviet Union from 1922 until his death. He eliminated all rivals after the death of **Lenin** in 1924; promoted an intensive industrialization, the forced collectivization of agriculture, and the development of a police state. He signed a non-aggression pact with Nazi Germany in 1939, resulting in the Russian occupation of eastern Poland and Finland; and led resistance to German invasion, 1941–5. Three years after his death his regime was denounced by **Khruschev** and a "destalinization" programme instituted.

STANDARD OIL US company formed in 1870 by John D. Rockefeller to refine and distribute petroleum. By 1879 it controlled almost 95 per cent of all oil refined in the USA and became the first industrial "trust", provoking the Sherman Anti-Trust Law of 1890. It was dissolved by the Supreme Court in 1911 and forced to operate as separate corporations charters in different states. Its principal component, the Exxon Corporation, became the company with the highest turnover in the world in 1975, with annual sales of nearly $50,000 million.

STANISŁAW II PONIATOWSKI (1732–98) Last king of independent Poland, being elected king with the support of **Catherine the Great** after the death of Augustus III in 1763. He failed to counter successive partitions of Poland by Russia, Austria and Prussia, despite the short-lived revival of 1788–94, and abdicated in 1795 as the three countries finally absorbed all Polish territory.

STANLEY, SIR HENRY MORTON (1847–1904) British explorer. As a young war-correspondent, he was sent by a New York newspaper to find the Scottish missionary traveller **David Living-stone**; he met him near Lake Tanganyika in 1871, to secure the "scoop of the century". He crossed Africa from Zanzibar to the mouth of the Congo, 1874–7, and founded the Congo Free State in 1879 on behalf of **Leopold II** of the Belgians, after Great Britain had turned down his offer to acquire the territory. He was a member of parliament, 1859–1900.

STAUFEN *see* **Hohenstaufen**

STAVISKY, SERGE ALEXANDRE (1886–1934) French financier who founded a credit organization in Bayonne and issued bonds later found to be fraudulent. The scandal that followed his death – said by police to be suicide but widely believed to be murder – precipitated a major political crisis, culminating in the resignation of two prime minsters and a riot outside the Chamber of Deputies in which 15 died.

STEFAN DUSHAN (1308–55) Most famous king of medieval Serbia. He deposed his father and seized the throne in 1331; annexed Macedonia, Albania and large areas of Greece from Byzantium; took the title "Tsar of the Serbs and Greeks"; granted a major new code of laws.

STEIN, BARON HEINRICH VON (1757–1831) Prussian statesman. As chief minister, 1807, he instituted a programme of reform including the emancipation of serfs and municipal self-government; exiled by **Napoleon**, 1808, he became counsellor to Tsar Alexander I, 1812–13, and played a leading part in forming the anti-Napoleonic alliance between Russia and Prussia.

STEPHEN (c.1097–1154) King of England, third son of Stephen, Count of Blois and Chartres, and Adela, daughter of **William I**. Raised by Henry I and given large estates in England and Normandy, he pledged his support to Henry's daughter Matilda, but instead usurped the crown in 1135. Most of his reign was spent in civil war with Matilda (finally defeated 1148); after the death of his son, Eustace, he reluctantly designated Matilda's son, later **Henry II**, as his successor.

STEPHEN I (977–1038) First king of Hungary, a member of the Arpád dynasty, and son of the leading Magyar chief, Geisa (Geza). He decisively defeated a pagan uprising after the death of his father in 997, and was anointed king in 1000. He founded bishoprics, abbeys and encouraged church-building; and fought off an invasion by Emperor Conrad I in 1030. He was canonized in 1083.

STEPHEN OF PERM, ST (1335–96) Russian Orthodox bishop who led a mission to the **Zyrians**.

STEPHENSON, GEORGE (1781–1848) English railway pioneer. He built the first successful steam locomotive, 1814; constructed the Stockton and Darlington line, 1825; his *Rocket* won the first open speed contest for railway engines, 1829. With his son, Robert, he built many early track systems both in Great Britain and overseas.

STEPHENSON, ROBERT (1803–59) Civil engineer. He was a partner with his father, George Stephenson, and others in the firm of Robert Stephenson & Co. which built locomotives for British and many Continental railways.

STIMSON, HENRY LEWIS (1867–1950) American statesman. He was secretary for war, 1911–13, in the Cabinet of William Howard Taft, and went on to serve in the administration of five presidents, of both parties, up to 1945. He was secretary for war to **F.D. Roosevelt**, 1940–5, and chief advisor to both Roosevelt and **Truman** on atomic policy: he justified the bombing of Hiroshima and Nagasaki on the grounds that it saved more lives than it cost.

STINNES, HUGO (1870–1924) German industrialist, grandson of **Matthias Stinnes**. He trained as a mining engineer, and founded the Stinnes Combine. Head of German industrial production in the First World War, he took advantages of the post-war hyper-inflation to extend interests in coal, iron, power and transport into timber, insurance, paper manufacture and newspapers. At his death he was probably the most powerful financier in Europe; the company is known now as Stinneskonzern.

STINNES, MATTHIAS (1790–1845) German industrialist who built up large coal mining and river transport interests in the Ruhr; the sinking of a deep shaft in his colliery Graf Beust (near Essen) in 1839–41 began the northward expansion of mining in the Ruhr.

STOICS School of philosophers, founded by Zeno (*c.* 332–264 BC), who taught in Athens at the Stoa. To the Stoics, "God is all and in all. Call him Zeus, Nature, Universe, Reason – all is in his hands. Virtue is the only good, moral weakness the only evil; to all else – health, wealth, position, pain – man should be indifferent." Notable Stoics were Zeno's successors, Cleanthes and Chrysippus; Panaetius and Posidonius, who transplanted the philosophy to Rome; and, under the Roman empire, the statesman Seneca, the ex-slave Epictetus, and the half-agnostic Emperor Marcus Aurelius.

STOLBOVO, PEACE OF Settlement ending the Russo-Swedish war, 1610–17. The Swedes invaded northern Russia and captured Novgorod in 1611; expelled from there, they besieged Pskov. Anglo-Dutch mediation produced an agreement that Sweden would withdraw its troops, but retain Karelia and Ingria, between Finland and Estonia, thus effectively denying Russia any "window to the Baltic" for the next century.

STOLYPIN, PIOTR ARKADEVICH (1863–1911) Russian statesman. Minister of the interior and prime minister, 1906–11, he tried to save imperial Russia by agrarian reform and the forcible suppression of the revolutionary movement. He was assassinated.

STONE AGE The earliest stage in the development of human culture, characterized by the use of stone, as opposed to metal tools. It is normally sub-divided into an Old Stone Age (**Palaeolithic**), Middle Stone Age (**Mesolithic**) and New Stone Age (**Neolithic**). The Old Stone Age covers the whole of human development during the **Pleistocene** Ice Age; the other two occupy the earlier part of the post-glacial period from 8000 BC onwards.

STROESSNER, ALFREDO (1912–2006) President of Paraguay; son of a Bavarian immigrant father and Paraguayan mother. He fought in the Chaco War (1932–5); rose to be general in the Paraguayan army in 1951, associated with the Colorado party and became president in 1954 after a palace revolution. He steadily accumulated dictatorial powers, and was voted president for life in 1977. He was deposed by Andrés Rodríguez in a military takeover in 1989.

STRUTT, JEDEDIAH (1726–97) A pioneer in the development of the early English cotton industry. In 1758–9, he patented an improved stocking frame and set up a mill in Derby, England, to manufacture the "Derby Patent Rib". In 1768 he entered into partnership with **Arkwright** to exploit Arkwright's new spinning frame.

STUART, JOHN McDOUALL (1815–66) Explorer of South Australia. Born in Scotland, he served as draughtsman in **Sturt**'s expeditions of 1844–6 before making six expeditions (1856–62) to the Australian interior, reaching Van Dieman Gulf.

STURT, CHARLES (1795–1869) Explorer of Australia. Born in Bengal, he was educated in England. Military secretary to the governor of New South Wales in 1827, in 1828–9 he traced the Macquarie, Bogan and Castlereagh rivers, then traversed the Murrumbidgee and Murray rivers, 1829–30, and in 1844–6 penetrated north from Adelaide to the Simpson Desert.

SUCRE, ANTONIO JOSÉ DE (1795–1830) Liberator of Ecuador. Born in Venezuela, at the age of 26 he was appointed by **Bolívar** to free the southern part of Gran Colombia, now Ecuador, from Spanish control. He defeated the royalists at Quito, May 1822, and routed 9000 Spaniards at Ayacucho, forcing withdrawal. He dislodged the last Spanish survivors from Upper Peru, now Bolivia, whose legal capital carries his name.

SUEBI (SUEVES) Germanic peoples, including the Marcomanni, Quadi, Hermunduri, Semnones and Langobardi (**Lombards**). In the 1st century AD they mostly lived along the river Elbe, apart from the Lombards, who established long-lasting control in northern Italy, their best-known group, dislodged by the **Huns**, entered Spain in 409 and consolidated a quasi-independent kingdom in the northwest (Galicia, Lusitania, Baetica). Their Christian king, Rechiar, was defeated by the **Visigoths** in 456, but the Visigoths finally absorbed the last Suebian territory in 585.

SUEZ WAR Joint military intervention by Great Britain, France and Israel after Egypt nationalized the Suez Canal Company in 1956. After some early success, the action was condemned and halted by the intervention of the **United Nations**, and especially the USA. The Canal, blocked by Egypt during the fighting, was reopened in 1957.

SUHARTO, RADEN (1921–2008) Indonesian political leader. During World War II he served with the Japanese defence forces and then fought in the anti-Dutch guerrilla movement. After independence (1949) he led the army which in 1965 slaughtered more than 300,000 communists and leftists after an attempted coup. Suharto took control of the government in 1967 and was elected president seven times. He maintained close ties with Japan and the west and was chair of the Non-Aligned movement. He resigned from the presidency in 1998 amid accusations of nepotism and corruption and against a background of nationwide protest sparked by economic collapse.

SUI Short-lived but important Chinese dynasty, ruling from AD 581. It reunited China in 589, after three centuries of disorder following the collapse of the Han dynasty. The Sui built a great network of canals linking Lo-yang with Yangchow, Hangchow and the northern territories near Peking. It fell in 618, to be replaced by the T'ang dynasty the following year.

SUKARNO (1901–70) Indonesian statesman; he helped to found the Indonesian Nationalist party in 1928. Imprisoned by the Dutch colonial authorities, 1933–42, he was released by, and cooperated with, the Japanese, 1942–5. At the end of the Second World War he proclaimed himself president of an independent Indonesia, and spent the next four years trying to force the Dutch to relinquish their hold on the country. In 1959, after ten years of democratic rule, he assumed dictatorial powers (he declared himself president for life in 1963), and increased contacts with the Chinese Communists. Following a military coup in 1965 Sukarno was deposed (1967) and kept under house arrest until his death.

SULEIMAN I (c. 1496–1566) Ottoman Sultan known as "the Lawgiver", and to the West as "the Magnificent". He succeeded his father **Selim I** in 1520; expanded and reinforced the Ottoman empire and encouraged the development of art, architecture, literature and law. He conquered Belgrade (1521) and Rhodes (1522); defeated the Hungarians at Mohács (1526); seized large parts of Persia and Iraq. He deveoped a formidable navy to dominate the Mediterranean, and brought the Ottoman empire to the practical limits of its power and expansion (unsuccessful siege of Vienna 1529, and of Malta 1565).

SULLA (138–78 BC) Roman general, led the aristocratic party in civil war with the popular leader Marius, and made himself dictator after Marius' defeat. He initiated sweeping constitutional and legal reforms, giving more power to the Senate, but was notorious for cruelty to political and military opponents.

SULTAN Authority, the holder of secular power in a Muslim state and protector of the caliph.

SUMERIANS The predominant people in southern Mesopotamia from the beginning of the 3rd millennium. Immigration of Semites (*see* **Akkadians, Amorites**) changed the balance by the end of the millennium, the last Sumerian dynasty collapsing in 1940 BC. Their cultural achievements included the invention of writing and the creation of the first cities. Their language, of agglutinative type, has not been positively related to any other.

SUN CH'UAN-FANG (1884–1935) Warlord who controlled Kiangsu, Chekiang, Anhwei, Fukien and Kiangsi in 1925–7 at the time of the Northern Expedition. He lost control of his provinces in 1927, allowing the Nationalists to capture the lower Yangtze valley. With the aid of **Chang Tso-lin** he attempted to recapture Nanking in August of that year but was routed; he retired from public life. He was assassinated.

SUNNI One of the main two division of Islam, and the majority in most Muslim countries. It split from the other main group, the **Shi'as**, over the question of succession to the Prophet **Mohammed**, which

Sunnis believe to have passed to the caliphs. The name is derived from *Sunna*, or words and deeds of the Prophet as recorded in the Hadith or Traditions; Sunnis thus claim to be following the example of the Prophet.

SUNNI ALI Emperor of Songhay in west Africa, who reigned *c.* 1464–92. From his home territories on the Middle Niger he reduced many former Mali provinces to Songhay dependencies; he created a professional army and river-navy; seized Timbuktu, controlled the commerce of the western Sudan, and introduced many advanced administrative reforms.

SUN YAT-SEN (1866–1925) First (provisional) president of the Republic of China (1912). He studied medicine in Hong Kong and Canton; entered politics with the formation of the Revive China Society, 1884, and was exiled in 1896 after instigating an abortive uprising, but attempted to organize a series of further uprisings in south China. He returned from the USA in 1911 during the anti-**Ch'ing** (Manchu) revolution, and was elected provisional head of state but resigned after a few months. In 1923 he gained control of the country, with Russian support; reorganized the **Kuomintang** to resemble the Soviet Communist Party. His Three Principles of the People inspired both Nationalists and Communists.

SUN YEN-LING (d.1677) Chinese general. His wife was the daughter of a commander in Kwangsi, and in 1660 she was given command of his former army. In 1666 Sun was sent to Kwangsi as its military governor; in 1673 he joined **Wu San-kuei**'s rebellion; wavering in his allegiance after 1676, he was killed on Wu San-kuei's orders.

SUPPILULIUMA (d.c. 1322 BC) King of the **Hittites**, who won the throne *c.* 1344 BC. He successfully invaded northern Syria, driving back Egyptians and Mitannians to add territory as far as Damascus to his empire.

SUTRI, SYNOD OF Council of the Roman Church held in 1046, convoked at a diocesan seat north of Rome by Pope Gregory VI at the insistence of Henry III, king of Germany. The synod deposed Gregory, who had purchased his post, and two other rival pontiffs; it elected a German as Pope Clement II (1046–7), who inaugurated a thorough reform of the Church culminating in the pontificate of **Gregory VII**.

SVEN ESTRIDSSON (c. 1020–74) King of Denmark, nephew of the English and Danish king, **Cnut the Great**. He was chosen as ruler by the Danish nobles in 1047 after the death of **Magnus**; his title was vigorously disputed by Harald Hardrada, but the struggle ended early in 1066, when Harald was killed during an invasion of England (battle of Stamford Bridge). Sven himself sponsored a serious Danish attack on England in 1069, withdrawing after an agreement with **William I** in 1070. His dynasty ruled Denmark for 300 years.

SVEN FORKBEARD (d.1014) King of Denmark, son of the Danish king, **Harald Bluetooth**. After a rebellion against his father, he seized the throne *c.* 986. He unsuccessfully invaded Norway, and in 994 attacked England, being expensively bought off by **Æthelred II**. He was virtual ruler of Norway after 1000. He led a series of expeditions against England, and became king in 1013 after forcing Æthelred into exile.

SVYATOSLAV (d.972) Early Russian hero, grand Prince of Kiev. He attempted to establish a Russian commercial empire over the steppes from Bulgaria to the Volga, 962–972; crushed the **Khazars**, **Volga Bulgars** and Danubian Bulgars, but was defeated by Byzantine Emperor John Tzimisces in 971. He was ambushed and killed by the **Pecheneg**.

SWAZI Bantu-speaking herdsmen and cultivators, living mainly in the independent African kingdom of Swaziland and in the adjacent South African territory of the eastern Transvaal.

SYAGRIUS Last Roman ruler of Gaul, overthrown by **Clovis** near Soissons in 486.

SYKES-PICOT AGREEMENT Secret pact between the First World War allies for the dismemberment of the Ottoman empire. it was signed on 7 May 1916, with the assent of imperial Russia, by Sir Mark Sykes for Great Britain and François Georges-Picot for France.

TACITUS, CORNELIUS (c. AD 55–c. 120) Roman historian. His works include *Dialogue on Orators* (*c.* 79–81), *Agricola* (*c.* 98), *Germania* (*c.* 98) and fragments of two longer works, the *Histories*, covering the period 68–70 (the original probably went down to 96), and the *Annals*, covering 14–68.

TAJIKS (Tadzhiks) Ancient Iranian people within Tajikistan, a mountainous country adjoining Afghanistan, Pakistan and India. They are mainly livestock keepers by occupation and Muslims by religion.

TALAS, BATTLE OF (751) The prince of Tashkent called upon the Muslims to oust the Chinese after their invasion (747). In this battle the Arabs decisively defeated general Kao Hsien-chih, transferring control of the area west of the Pamirs and Tien Shan mountains (Transoxania) from China to Islam and establishing the boundary between the two civilizations.

TALLEYRAND, CHARLES-MAURICE DE (1754–1838) French statesman and diplomat. Destined for the army but crippled by an accident in childhood, he entered the Church in 1775; became Bishop of Autun in 1788, but was excommunicated for his radical Church reorganization during the French revolution. Foreign minister under the Directory, 1797–9, and to **Napoleon I** until resigning in 1807. He intrigued with Tsar Alexander I for Napoleon's defeat, and in 1814 became foreign minister to Louis XVIII. At the **Congress of Vienna** (1814–51) he secured favourable terms for France. He was made Duc de Talleyrand-Périgord in 1817, and French ambassador to England, 1830–4.

TALMUD Principal repository of Jewish law and lore. It consists of the **Mishnah** and the Gemarra, an explanation of the Mishnah and a general presentation of the traditions taught and transmitted in the Rabbinical academies and preserved in two versions: the Palestinian, edited around AD 400, and the Babylonian, around 500.

TAMERLANE (1336–1405) Known as Timur Lang, from his lame leg, hence Tamerlane. Born near Samarkand, later his capital, he concluded the Mongol age of conquest, although his background was Turkish rather than Mongol, and he was no nomad but a product of the sophisticated Islamic society of Transoxania. He conquered, with legendary barbarity, a vast Asian empire stretching from southern Russia to Mongolia and southwards into northern India, Persia and Mesopotamia. He adorned his capital with splendid buildings, many of which still stand today. He died on an expedition against **Ming** China; after his death the empire soon fell apart.

TAMIL Dravidian language spoken by some 30 million southern Indians, one-third of the population of Sri Lanka (Ceylon), and scattered communities in South and east Africa, Mauritius, Malaysia and Fiji. Tamil literature dates back to the 3rd century BC; it remains the official language in the Indian state of Tamil Nadu (Madras).

TANCHELM (d.1115) Religious radical who criticized the Roman Church, especially its hierarchical organization. He preached to large congregations in the Low Countries (mainly Utrecht and Antwerp) but was eventually murdered by a priest.

T'ANG Imperial Chinese dynasty ruling AD 618 to 907; see pp. 138–90.

T'ANG CHI-YAO (1881–1927) Chinese military leader. Appointed military governor of Kweichow, 1912, and of Yunnan Province, 1915 until his death, he gave crucial support to rebels opposing **Yüan Shih-k'ai** in his bid to re-establish the empire. After the death of **Sun Yat-sen** in 1925, he made an abortive bid to lead a new national government.

TANGUTS Tibetan-speaking peoples of northwest China, who established the 11th-century kingdom of Hsi-hsia in the area of present-day Kansu and northern Shensi. The Tangut tribes, straddling the main trade route from China to the West, remained tributaries to the Sung dynasty from 960 to 1038; from 1038 to 1044 they attempted, under their emperor, Li Yüan-hao, to conquer the whole of China, but withdrew on payment of an annual tribute. The kingdom then survived until 1227, when it was overrun by the Mongols.

TANTRIC BUDDHISM This form of belief, evolved chiefly between the 6th and the 11th centuries AD, aimed at recreating in the individual the original spiritual experience of Guatama the **Buddha**, and emphasized sexo-yogic practices. Tantric art and sculpture made much use of male and female images to symbolize the process of spiritual growth and fulfilment; *Vajra-Yana* or the "adamantine path" was its largest school.

TASMAN, ABEL JANSZOON (c. 1603–c.1659) Dutch explorer, discoverer of New Zealand, Tasmania, Tonga and the Fiji Islands. He served with the **Dutch East India Company**, 1633–53, carrying out two major voyages in the Indian Ocean and the South Pacific, reaching Tasmania (named after him) in 1642; he circumnavigated Australia without seeing it.

TATAR (also spelled Tartar) First found in an inscription of 731, the name came to be applied to the forces of **Genghis Khan** and his successors, and in Europe was confused with Tartarus, the classical hell, which seemed an appropriate place of origin for these dreadful hordes. The name was later loosely and inaccurately applied to some of the Turkic peoples of the Russian empire for example, Volga Tatars, Crimean Tatars. At the present time there is a Tatar Autonomous Republic within the Russian Federation with its capital at Kazan on the Volga.

TEHERAN CONFERENCE Meeting held from 18 November 1943 to 12 January 1944 at which the Allied leaders – **Churchill**, **Roosevelt** and **Stalin** – concerted plans for an Anglo-American invasion of France and a Russian offensive against eastern Germany.

TE KOOTI (c. 1830–93) New Zealand Maori resistance leader. While imprisoned, he founded the Ringatu cult, which is still extant. After escaping, he conducted skilful guerrilla campaigns (1868–72).

TENNANT, CHARLES (1768–1858) Scottish pioneer industrial chemist. He set up a bleachworks and in 1798 patented a new liquid for bleaching textile fabrics, which was soon widely used by Lancashire bleachers. In 1780 with three partners he set up a chemical plant near Glasgow to manufacture bleaching powder and other alkali products. When he died the firm was operating one of the largest chemical plants in the world.

TENNESSEE VALLEY AUTHORITY (TVA) US federal agency, formed in 1933 to develop natural resources (particularly hydro-electric power) in the states drained by the Tennessee River system – Tennessee itself, Kentucky, Mississippi, Alabama, North Carolina, Georgia and Virginia.

TEN YEARS' WAR (1868–78) Cuba's first war for independence from Spain. It ended inconclusively with promises of political and economic reform, set out in the Convention of Zanjon, 1878. The nationalist leader, Antonio Maceo, refused to accept the accompanying conditions and fled the island to prepare for renewed struggle.

TERTULLIAN (c. 170–c. 220) Early Christian theologian. Born in Carthage and trained as a lawyer, he was converted to **Christianity** *c.* 195. Writing in Latin rather than Greek, he provided the Western Church with much of its basic terminology; his *De Praescriptions Haereticorum* (197–8) championed orthodoxy; in *De Testimonio Animae* he claimed that the soul is naturally Christian; in his great *Apology* he praised the martyrs: "the blood of Christians is seed".

TEUTONIC ORDER (also called Knights of the Cross). Organization of German crusaders, founded in 1190 at Acre, Palestine. It moved to central Europe in 1211, and in 1226, at the invitation of the Polish duke, Conrad of Masovia, began the conquest of pagan Prussia. Under its Grand Masters, with its headquarters at Marienburg, it controlled the eastern Baltic, conquering Pomerania and other areas of Poland. It absorbed the **Livonian Order** (Knights of the Sword) in 1237. It was defeated by the alliance of Poland and Lithuania at Tannenberg (Grünwald) in 1410, and broken by the Treaty of Thorn (Torun) in 1466. It was secularized as the duchy of Prussia (1525) becoming a fief of Polish kings.

TEWFIK PASHA (1852–92) First khedive of Egypt under the British occupation. He was appointed Khedive in 1879 by the Ottoman sultan in succession to **Ismail** Pasha. The growth of tension between England and France, representing the interests of foreign creditors of Egypt, and nationalist sentiment with **Arabi Pasha** as its chief spokesman, led to the weakening of Tewfik's power in favour of Arabi, but British military intervention and occupation in 1882 restored him as a figurehead under British control.

TE WHITI, ORONGOMAI (1831–1907) New Zealand Maori leader. He claimed to be a prophet and refused to take part in the Maori rebellions of the 1860s, preaching instead passive resistance and complete segregation from the Europeans. Imprisoned by the British 1881–3 and 1886, he still exercised great influence over the Maoris.

THATCHER, MARGARET (1925–2013) British Conservative politician and first woman prime minister (1979–90). With degrees in chemistry from Oxford (1947) and law, she entered parliament in 1959 and served as secretary of state for education and science (1970–4), establishing a reputation for toughness. Following Conservative election defeat (1974), she won the party leadership (1975), and became prime minister in 1979. Her programme, which beame know as "Thatcherism". combined a restraint on public spending, privatization of major industries, and fiscal caution. In 1990 she was succeeded as prime minister by her chancellor of the exchequer, John Major.

THEOCRITUS (c. 300–250 BC) Pastoral poet from Syracuse, who worked in Cos and Alexandria. His *Idylls* and his lyrical descriptions of country life seem a form of escape from urban Alexandria; he strongly influenced Virgil and, through him, all pastoral poetry.

THEODORET (c. 393–c. 455 AD) Christian theologian. Born in Antioch, he was appointed Bishop of Cyrrhus in Mesopotamia, and played a prominent part in the **Nestorian** controversy (for long defending Nestorians against **Cyril**), culminating with his appearance at the **Council of Chalcedon** in 451, where he finally agreed to condemn Nestorian beliefs. His works include a *Church History* and a brilliant defence of **Christianity** against paganism.

THEODORIC THE GREAT (c. 454–526) Ostrogothic king of Italy, son of a chieftain. He succeeded his father in 471, led migrations of his people into the Balkans and (in 489, on orders of the Emperor Zeno) Italy. He murdered Odoacer, the previous Italian ruler, in 493, to gain control of the country, though acknowledging imperial supremacy; he issued an edict imposing Roman law on his followers, tolerated Catholicism and sought friendship between Goths and Romans.

THEODORUS Known as Theodorus the Lector, an early Greek Church historian of the 6th century. Though only fragments of his work have survived, it is an essential source for events between the time of **Constantine I** (313) and Justin I (518).

THEODOSIUS I, THE GREAT (c. 346–95) Roman emperor, 379–95. Appointed by Gratian to rule the Eastern empire after the death of **Valens**, he also administered the Western empire after the death of Maximus in 388. He established Catholicism as the official Roman religion, 380; condemned Arianism and paganism; after the massacre of Thessalonica he submitted in penance to **Ambrose**. After his death the empire was finally divided into two halves.

THEOPHRASTUS (c. 372–c. 287 BC) Ancient Greek philosopher taught by **Aristotle** whom he succeeded as head of the Lyceum. Theophrastus was a great teacher, with classes attended by as many as 2000; he influenced the foundation of the Museum at Alexandria. Of his works, the *Enquiry into Plants* and the *Etiology of Plants* survive intact, and his *Doctrines of Natural Philosophers*, reconstructed by 19th-century scholars, provide the main foundation for the history of early thought. His entertaining *Characters* has been much enjoyed and imitated.

THIRD COALITION, WAR OF THE Struggle between Napoleonic France and an alliance of Britain, Austria, Russia and Sweden, formed in April 1805. Britain's naval victory at Trafalgar established Allied supremacy at sea, but on land there were only defeats: Austria at Ulm (1805), Austria and Russia at Austerlitz (1805), and Prussia, joining late, at Jena (1806). Further Russian defeats, at Eylau and Friedland (1807) and the elimination of Sweden brought hostilities to an end with the treaty of Tilsit (1807).

THIRTY TYRANTS Vituperative name given to the men who ruled Athens on behalf of Sparta for eight months after its defeat (404 BC) in the Peloponnesian War. The group included **Socrates**' former associate, Critias, who died in May 403 when a democratic army under Thrasybulus defeated the tyrants at Piraeus; the survivors were massacred two years later in Eleusis, where they had taken refuge.

THOMAS, ST One of the twelve Apostles. He doubted the Resurrection until he saw and touched the wounds of **Jesus**; he is traditionally believed to have gone to India as a missionary.

THOMAS, SIDNEY GILCHRIST (1850–85) English metallurgist and inventor, who discovered a new process for making steel which eliminated phosphorus from pig iron. It was applied both to the Bessemer converter (1875) and to the Siemens open-hearth process, perfected by Percy Carlyle Gilchrist.

THREE FEUDATORIES REBELLION see **Wu San-kuei**

THUCYDIDES (c. 460–c. 400 BC) Athenian historian. He served as a general in the Peloponnesian War but was exiled after failing to defend an important strongpoint in Thrace. He had already begun his classic history of the war and completed eight books, breaking off at 411, seven years before the end of hostilities.

THURINGIANS Germanic people, first documented *c.* AD 350. They were conquered by the **Huns** in the mid-5th century; by 500 their revived kingdom stretched from the Harz Mountains to the Danube, but they were defeated by the **Franks** in 531 and were subsequently ruled by them.

TIBERIUS (42 BC–AD 37) (Tiberius Claudius Nero Caesar Augustus). Second Roman emperor, stepson of the Emperor **Augustus**, he succeeded in AD 14 at the age of 56. In his first years he greatly strengthened Rome's finances and institutions; after his son's death in 23 he gradually withdrew from affairs, retiring to Capri in 27 where he gained the reputation of an arbitrary, cruel and merciless tyrant. In 31 he arranged the execution of Sejanus, to whom he had delegated his authority and who plotted against him.

TIENTSIN TREATIES Agreements forced on the Chinese government in 1858 by Britain and France to allow free access, the posting of resident officials in Peking, and the opening of the new trade ports. Similar agreements were then made by Russia and the USA.

TILAK, BAL GANGADHAR (1856–1920) Militant Indian nationalist. He taught mathematics, owned and edited two weekly newspapers, was twice imprisoned by the British; in 1914 he founded the Indian Home Rule League; he signed the Lucknow Pact in 1916 as the basis for a Hindu-Muslim political alliance. His books include *Secret of the Bhagavad-gita*, written in prison between 1908 and 1914.

TIMES, THE London newspaper, founded in 1785 by John Walter under the title *Daily Universal Register*, its present name was adopted in 1788. Known as "The Thunderer" under the editorship of Delane (1840–79) for its incorruptibility and independence of government.

TIMUR see **Tamerlane**

TIPU (c. 1749–99) Indian sultan, known as "the Tiger of Mysore"; son of **Hader Ali**. He fought frequently against the **Marathas**, 1769–79, despite being publicly caned by his father for cowardice in 1771. He defeated the British on the Coleroon river in 1782 and succeeded to the Mysore throne in the same year. He signed the Treaty of Bangalore with the British in 1784, though he fought several further aggressive and partially successful campaigns against them. He was killed during the final British assault on his capital, Seringapatam; he is remembered in the Mysore saying: "Haidar was born to create an empire, Tipu to lose one".

TITO, MARSHAL (1892–1980) Born Josip Broz. Yugoslav head of state. He led Communist resistance to German occupation of Yugoslavia, 1941–5 and in 1945 became head of the Federal People's Republic with Soviet support; he broke with the USSR in 1948 to pursue a neutralist foreign policy and an independent version of **communism**. He served as president from 1953 until his death.

TITUS (AD 39–81) Roman emperor, son of Vespasian. He served in Britain, Germany and under his father in Judaea; on Vespasian's accession as emperor he took charge of the Jewish War, killed many (reputedly one million) Jews and sacked Jerusalem in 70; he was made commander of the Praetorian Guard in 71. He was much criticized for taking Berenice, sister of the Jewish king, Herod Agrippa II, as his mistress. He succeeded his father as emperor in 79, helped to rebuild Rome after the fire of 80, and completed the Colosseum.

TLAXCALANS Indians of the central Mexican plateau. Relations between the Tlaxcalans and the Aztec confederation were always uneasy, and at the time of the Spanish conquest they joined **Hernán Cortés** as his principal local ally; continued loyalty to Spain brought many privileges.

TOCHARIANS Central Asian peoples, occupying the basin of the upper Oxus river in the 2nd century BC. They were joint founders, with the **Kushanas**, of the Kushana empire. They are not necessarily identical to the speakers of the "Tocharian" language, one of the Indo-European group, whose main surviving manuscripts, found in Chinese Turkestan (Tarim Basin) date from the period AD 500–1000.

TŌJŌ, HIDEKI (1884–1984) Japanese general and statesman, he was prime minister at the time of the Japanese attack on Pearl Harbor. After a military career he became vice-minister (1938–9), then minister (1940–4) of war, and also prime minister, 1941–4. He resigned after the fall of Saipan; tried, after the war, by the Tokyo War Crimes Court, he was found guilty and hanged.

TOKUGAWA Dynasty of hereditary *shoguns* or military dictators, effectively ruling Japan from 1603–1868. It was founded by Ieyasu (1542–1616), who mastered the country after the death of **Toyotomi Hideyoshi** and established his capital at the fishing village of Edo (now Tokyo). He organized a new pattern of fiefs and administration which lasted unchallenged until the 19th century. Under his son, Hidetada (1579–1632), and grandson, Iemitsu (1603–51), Japan eliminated Christianity and virtually closed itself to foreign trade and influence. These three rulers consolidated the family's control, which lasted until the 19th century, when Tokugawa Keika accepted the near-peaceful handing over of power to the emperor, **Meiji**.

TOKUGAWA IEYASU (1542–1616) Founder of the **Tokugawa** shogunate.

TOLTECS Ruling people in Mexico from the 10th to the 12th century. The name is associated with their capital, Tula, or "place of the reeds", located 80km (50 miles) north of Tenochtitlán, present-day Mexico City. They captured and sacked the great city of Teotihuacán *c.* 900; under their leader Quetzalcoatl and his successors they established a wide-ranging empire, introducing to it metal-work and ambitious architectural and sculptural techniques. They were overwhelmed by nomad **Chichimec** invaders, including the **Aztecs,** who destroyed Tula in the mid-12th century.

TOPA (d.1493) Inca emperor, who succeeded to the title in 1471 after the abdication of his father, **Pachacuti**. After an early setback, invading the rain forests near the Tono River, he established a reputation as a great conqueror: he defeated the revolt led by the **Colla** and **Lupaca**, extended the boundaries of his empire to highland Bolivia, northern Chile and most of northwest Argentina; and finally succeeded in incorporating the previously unconquered southern coast of Peru. He devoted the rest of his reign to administration.

TORAH Hebrew name for the Law of Moses, or Pentateuch, the first five books of the Old Testament of the Bible: *Genesis*, *Exodus*, *Leviticus*, *Numbers* and *Deuteronomy*; also the scroll containing these books, used ceremonially in the synagogue.

TORDESILLAS, TREATY OF Treaty between Spain and Portugal, 1494, to determine ownership of lands discovered or to be discovered in the west. It granted Spain exclusive rights west of a north-south line 370 leagues west of the Cape Verde islands – a 1493 Bull of the Spanish Pope Alexander VI had put the line 270 leagues further east – with Portugal taking lands east of the line. Portugal thus established claim to the so far undiscovered Brazil; but the treaty was never accepted by the other Atlantic powers.

TOTONAC Central American Indians, farming both the highlands and the hot coastal lowlands of eastern Mexico, mainly in the states of Vera Cruz, Puebla and Hidalgo. The two Totonac languages, Totanac and Tepehuan, are believed to be related to ancient **Mayan**.

TOURÉ, AHMED SEJOU (1922–84) President of the Republic of Guinea. A trade union organizer, in 1952 he started a political party, the Guinea Democratic Party; he became vice-president of the government council in 1957, and first president of Guinea on independence in 1958.

TOUSSAINT-L'OUVERTURE (1743–1803) Haitian independence leader, born into a family of African slaves in the part of Haiti which formed the French colony of St Domingue. He joined the slave rebellion and declared in favour of the French Revolutionary government; recognized by the French Directory as lieutenant-governor in 1797, he expelled British and Spanish forces and gained control of the whole island in 1801. The French government, now under Napoleon, sent invasion forces in 1802, and he was defeated and taken to France where he died in prison. The French restored slavery to Haiti.

TOWNSEND, FRANCIS (1867–1960) US doctor who helped lay the foundations for the modern American social security programme. He devised the Old Age Revolving Pension Plan which mobilized support for federal action in this area.

TOYOTOMI HIDEYOSHI (1536–98) Unifier of 16th-century Japan. He served as a chief lieutenant to the feudal general, Oda Nobunaga (1534–82), and after his death became the emperor's chief minister (1585). In 1590 he conquered the islands of Shikoku and Kyushu to unify the country; he energetically promoted internal peace, economic development and overseas expansion. He died after an unsuccessful invasion of Korea.

TRAJAN (AD 53–117) (Marcus Ulpius Trajanus). First Roman emperor to be born in the provinces – in Italica, near Santiponce, Seville. He served in the army in Syria, Spain and Germany, was named consul in 91 and chosen as emperor in 98. He is famous as a builder, social reformer and extender of the empire in the East and in Dacia, modern Romania (celebrated by Trajan's Column, still standing in Rome). He died in Cilicia after invading Mesopotamia and taking Ctesiphon, the Parthian capital.

TRASTÁMARA see **Henry II, King of Castile**

TRIPARTITE PACT Agreement signed on 27 September 1940 between Germany, Italy and Japan, setting up a full military and political alliance (the Rome-Berlin-Tokyo Axis) to support one another in the event of a spread of the Second World War to the Far East.

TRIPLE ALLIANCE (1882–1915) Defensive treaty signed on 20 May 1882 pledging Germany and Italy to mutual support in the event of a French attack, and obliging Austria-Hungary to support Italy in such an event in return for a promise of Italian neutrality in the event of a Russian attack on Austria–Hungary. It was extended between 1887 and 1909 by supplementary agreements providing for diplomatic support in the Near East and north Africa.

TROTSKY, LEON (1879–1940) Russian revolutionary leader and theorist. Born Lev Davidovich Bronstein, he spent long periods in prison and in exile before returning to Russia in 1917 to play a major part in bringing the **Bolsheviks** to power. He was commissar for foreign affairs, 1917–18, and commissar for war, 1918–25. The most prominent revolutionary after **Lenin**, he was an effective organizer of the Red Army during the civil war. After Lenin's death in 1924 he was increasingly in conflict with **Stalin**, and was exiled in 1929. He founded the Fourth International in 1938, and published the *History of the Russian Revolution*. He was murdered by a Soviet agent in Mexico.

TRUMAN, HARRY S. (1884–1972) 33rd president of the USA, 1945–53. The son of a Missouri mule trader, he entered politics as country judge, 1922–4; US senator, 1935 and re-elected 1940; vice-president in 1944, succeeding as president in 1945 on the death of **F.D. Roosevelt**. He ordered the atomic bombing of Hiroshima and Nagasaki in 1945; in 1947 enunciated the Truman Doctrine on the "containment" of the Soviet Union, and established the Central Intelligence Agency (CIA). He inaugurated the **Marshall Plan** and was re-elected, 1948, and supported in 1949 the formation of the **North Atlantic Treaty Organisation** (NATO); he ordered the US engagement in Korea in 1950.

TSHOMBE, MOÏSE (1919–69) Congo (Zaire) political leader. He became a member of the Katanga Provincial Council, 1951–3, and president of Conakat (*Confédération des Associations Tribales du Katanga*) in 1959. His plans for a federated Congo after independence were rejected in favour of a central state. He declared Katangan independence in 1960, but was defeated by UN forces in 1963. Appointed by **Kasavubu** as premier of the Congo in 1964, he was dismissed in 1965 and was sentenced to death *in absentia* in 1967. Hijacked to Algeria in 1967, he died in captivity.

TUAREG Berber nomads from the central and western Sahara; Hamitic-speaking Muslims.

TUDORS English ruling dynasty from 1485 until 1603, founded by **Henry VII** and continued through his descendants **Henry VIII**, Edward VI, Mary I and **Elizabeth I**.

TULUNIDS Muslim dynasty ruling in Egypt and Syria from 868 to 905. It was founded by Ahmed ibn Tulun, a Turk who arrived in Egypt as vice-governor under the **Abbasids**.

TUNG-MENG-HUI Chinese political party, originally founded as a secret society by **Sun Yat-sen** in 1905.

TUNGUSY People of the sub-arctic forest in eastern Siberia. Originally nomadic hunters, fishers and reindeer breeders, they moved from the Ob and Yenisey river basins east to the Pacific, and north from the Amur basin to the Arctic Ocean. Since the Russian revolution (1917) most were settled on collective farms.

TUPAMAROS Members of a Uruguayan urban guerrilla movement. It first came to prominence in 1968, preaching socialist revolution on the Cuban pattern. Its violent campaign of bombing, assassination, robbery, kidnapping – and a spectacular prison break in 1971 when 106 leading Tupamaros escaped from the Uruguayan national penitentiary – brought increasingly severe retaliation; by 1974 over 2000 members were held in a new maximum-security prison and the movement had apparently been crushed.

TUTANKHAMUN King of Egypt's 18th Dynasty. Of uncertain parentage, as a child he succeeded his brother Smenkhkare, who had been co-regent and successor to **Akhenaten**. During his reign (1345–1335 BC) the worship of the old gods, suppressed by Akhenaten, was restored. In 1922 his long-lost tomb was discovered almost intact by the British archaeologist Howard Carter.

TUTHMOSIS III (d.1436 BC) Greatest of Egypt's warrior kings of the 18th Dynasty. Son of Tuthmosis II and a minor wife named Isis, he ascended the throne as a young boy but was overshadowed for nearly 20 years by his stepmother, Queen Hatshepsut, until her death in 1482 BC. He conducted 17 campaigns in Palestine and Syria, extending Egypt's empire to the banks of the Euphrates; his campaigns in Nubia gave Egypt control over all the gold mines and territory as far as the Fourth Cataract of the Nile.

TWENTY-ONE DEMANDS Claims pressed by Japan on China during the First World War, asking for privileges similar to, but more extensive than, those enjoyed by the Western powers, including railway and mining concessions, coastal access and power to intervene in financial, political and police affairs. An ultimatum, presented on 5 May 1915, forced capitulation on most points by the Chinese president on 25 May and greatly increased anti-Japanese feeling in China.

UIGHURS Nomadic Turkic-speaking peoples of central Asia, who ruled a substantial area north and northwest of China in the 8th and 9th centuries and later settled in Kansu and the Tarim Basin, establishing a distinct way of life and a literary language. The modern Uighurs live mainly in Sinkiang and the former Soviet central Asia.

ULFILAS (c. 311–c. 382) Converter of the Goths to Christianity. In 341 he was consecrated Bishop of the Gothic Christians by Eusebius, the Arian patriarch of Constantinople. After initial persecution, the **Visigothic** leaders accepted the **Arianist** doctrine, while Ulfilas created a Gothic alphabet and made the first Germanic translation of the Bible, some of which still survives.

ULMANIS, KARLIS (1877–post 1942) Latvian independence leader. Trained in agronomy, he worked to free Latvia from the century-old Russian control during the 1905 revolution. He fled to the USA, was amnestied in 1913 and founded the Latvian Farmers' Union, 1917. Appointed head of the provisional government by the national independence council, 1918, he held power from 1918–21 and then in 1925–6, 1931–2 and 1934–40. He resigned in 1940 in the face of a Russian military ultimatum; was arrested in July by the Soviet authorities and deported. His fate is unknown.

UMAYYADS Dynasty of caliphs, founded by Muawiya in 661, in opposition to **Ali**, **Mohammed**'s son-in-law and fourth caliph. They were deposed by the **Abbasids** in 750 although a branch continued to rule Muslim Spain from 756 to 1031.

UNION, ACT OF Treaty signed in 1707 under which Scotland and England (which had shared the same rulers since 1603) became jointly the Kingdom of Great Britain. The agreement stipulated a single government, but separate churches and legal systems; Scotland recognized the Hanoverian succession.

UNITARIANS Members of a Protestant Christian denomination, characterized by belief in one God, as opposed to the more orthodox doctrine of the Trinity. It first emerged as a distinct church in Poland and Transylvania in the late 16th and 17th centuries, and was widely followed in England and North America in the 18th and 19th centuries.

UNITED FRUIT COMPANY US-based multinational company, specializing in the shipment of tropical produce. Founded in 1899 in a merger of Central American shipping, railroad and banana-planting interests, it was merged into the United Brands Company in 1968.

UNITED NATIONS (UN) International organization, founded in 1945 as a successor to the **League of Nations**. Its aims are to maintain world peace and security, and to promote economic, social and cultural cooperation among nations. The original membership of 50 had risen to 193 in 2015. Its main divisions are the Security Council and the General Assembly; special agencies include the World Health Organization (WHO), Food and Agriculture Organization (FAO), UN Educational, Scientific and Cultural Organization (UNESCO), etc.

U NU (1907–1995) Burmese independence leader. He was expelled from Rangoon university in 1936, and in 1940 was imprisoned by the British for sedition. He became foreign minister in 1943 in the pro-Japanese government, and was first prime minister of independent Burma in 1948–58 and 1960–2, when he was ousted by General **Ne Win** in a *coup d'état*. Released from prison in 1969, he began to organize a resistance movement from abroad. From 1989–92 he was placed under house arrest.

UPANISHADS Prose and verse reflections on the **Vedas** and forming with them the central corpus of Hindu sacred literature. Numbering 108 in their surviving form, the oldest were composed probably *c.* 900 BC; teaching based on their mystical and philosophic speculations is known as the *Vedanta* – the conclusion of the *Vedas*.

URBAN II (c. 1042–99) Pope, 1088–99. He inherited many of **Gregory VII**'s ideas about the freedom of the Church from state interference, and in addition established at Rome the administrative organizations to operate it. He preached the First **Crusade** in 1095.

URNFIELD Late Bronze Age culture in central Europe, flourishing from the late 2nd to the early 1st millennium BC. It is characterized by the practice of burying the cremated ashes of the dead in ceramic urns. It was a direct predecessor of the Celtic **Hallstatt** period.

USUMAN DAN FODIO (1754–1817) Muslim Fulani mystic and revolutionary reformer, and founder of a militant Islamic state in what later became northern Nigeria. He began teaching Sufi doctrines in 1775, and was hailed as deliverer by oppressed Hausa and fellow Fulani peoples. He launched a *jihad* (holy war) from Gabir in 1804, conquering most of northern Nigeria and beyond, establishing the Fulani-ruled Sokoto caliphate before retiring in 1815, disillusioned by the corruption of his supporters.

UTRECHT, PEACE OF Treaties concluded in 1713 which, with those of Rastadt and Baden (1714), ended the War of the Spanish Succession. **Louis XIV**'s grandson Philip was recognized as king of Spain on condition that the kingdoms of France and Spain would never be united and with the cession of the Spanish Netherlands and Spain's Italian territories to Austria and Savoy. Gibraltar and Minorca were ceded to Great Britain, with a 30-year monopoly on supplying slaves to the Spanish colonies. Portugal obtained frontier rectifications in South America at Spain's expense. Louis XIV recognized the Protestant succession in Great Britain (thus abandoning the Stuart cause) and the title of king for the ruler of Brandenburg-Prussia. He also ceded Nova Scotia, Hudson's Bay, Newfoundland and St Kitts to the British, against incorporation of the principality of Orange and the Barcelonette valley into France. The Dutch Republic secured the right to garrison, at Austrian expense, fortresses in the southern Netherlands. At the 1714 treaties between the Emperor Charles VI and Louis XIV, Landau was ceded to France and the electorros of Bavaria and Cologne, Louis XIV's allies, were restored to their lands and dignities. Formal peace between Austria and Spain was not made until 1720.

UZBEKS A people of Turkish origin who arrived in the area around Samarkand and Tashkent in the 6th century AD. In the 14th century they became the core of the empire of **Tamerlane**, and in the 16th century the basis for the conquests of **Babur**. Later the area disintegrated into small city-states. Russia annexed the region in the 1860s, although incorporation was not complete until the 1920s; now mostly concentrated in Uzbekistan.

UZKOKS Balkan Christians who fled from the Ottoman conquest in the late 15th century and settled around the Adriatic port of Fiume, whence they attacked both Turkish and Christian (especially Venetian) shipping.

VACA, ALVARO NU—EZ CABEZA DE (c. 1490–1560) One of two Spanish survivors of a voyage of exploration from Florida to New Mexico, 1528–36, who wrote a description of the fabulous riches he claimed to have seen. Many others were thereby encouraged to go to their deaths prospecting there.

VAKATAKAS South Indian dynasty, dominating the western Deccan from the mid-3rd to the later 4th century AD. It achieved its greatest power under King Pravaresena I in the early 4th century; Rudrasena II married the daughter of **Chandragupta II**, and after his death, c. 390, the Vakataka territory was absorbed into the **Gupta** empire.

VALENS (c. 328–378) Eastern Roman emperor, who on the death of the Emperor Jovian was appointed co-emperor by his brother, Valentinian I, in 364. He twice devastated the Visigothic lands north of the Danube (in 367 and 369); fought an inconclusive war with Persia 376; was defeated and killed by the **Visigoths** at the battle of Adrianople.

VALERA, EAMON DE (1882–1975) Irish statesman. He was elected president of the Irish Nationalist Party, Sinn Fein, in 1917, and president of the Irish Parliament, the Dáil, while imprisoned in England in 1918–19. He refused to accept the Irish independence treaty in 1921; in 1926 he formed a republican opposition party, Fianna Fáil. He was prime minister of the Irish Free State, 1937–48, and again – following full independence – in 1951–4 and 1957–9; and president of the Irish Republic 1959–73.

VALERIAN (c. 190–c. 260) (Publius Licinius Valerianus) Roman emperor. He gained the throne in 253, but left government to his son Gallienus while he led campaigns against the Goths and the Persians. He was captured by the Persians in 260 and died in captivity.

VALIDE SULTAN Queen Mother, a leading figure in the sultanate in the 17th century.

VANDALS Germanic people, displaced from central Europe by the 4th-century incursion of the Huns. They reached north Africa, via Spain, and established their kingdom there in AD 429. At first federated with Rome, they seized their independence in 439 and captured Rome itself briefly in 455. Attacked in 533 by the Byzantine armies under **Belisarius**; they were obliterated in 534.

VARGAS, GETULIO DORNELLES (1883–1954) President and dictator of Brazil. He became state president of Rio Grande do Sul in 1928, and Liberal candidate for national president in 1929, seizing the presidency by force in 1930 after his defeat. Under a new constitution he was re-elected in 1934, and in 1937 he introduced the corporate-style dictatorship of Estado Nôvo (New State). He laid the foundations for the modern nation, and linked Brazil to the Western alliance in the Second World War. He was ousted in 1945, re-elected constitutional president in 1951, and committed suicide during the 1954 political crisis.

VARUS, PUBLIUS QUINTILIUS (d.AD 9) Roman general. He became consul in 13 BC, governor of Syria, 6–4 BC, and commander in Germany, AD 6–9. He committed suicide after the destruction of his army by the Germans in the Teutoburg forest.

VASVAR, TREATY OF Agreement signed on 10 August 1664, ending an Austro-Turkish war (1663–4) after Austria had been called in to help the independent principality of Transylvania repel a Turkish invasion. Under its terms Hungary, which had not been consulted, lost numerous fortresses to the Turks, and the resulting fury generated several later anti-Habsburg rebellions.

VAUBAN, SEBASTIEN LE PRESTRE DE (1633–1707) French engineer, military architect and town planner. He revolutionized defensive fortification, building a ring of fortresses on France's frontiers; he planned port fortifications and also towns connected with the many forts. He was made a marshal of France in 1703.

VEDANTA Most influential among the Six Systems of Hindu philosophy. Decisive in refuting non-Brahminical schools of Hindu thought, it argues the existence of Absolute Soul in all things, and the union of the individual and his Absolute Soul as salvation. It was forcefully promoted by the Brahmin **Shankaracharya**.

VEDAS Collection of ancient Sanskrit hymns, sacred verses and devotional formulae (*mantras*), preserved by Hindu tradition – first oral, then written – since the first appearance of Aryan-speaking peoples in north India, *c.* mid-2nd millennium BC. The three major compilations – *Rig*, *Yajur* and *Sama* – form the *Trayividya* or "threefold knowledge"; a fourth, the *Artharvaveda*, is made up of more homely chants, spells and incantations, of lesser religious significance.

VENDÉE UPRISING Largest and most successful royalist counter-attack against the first French Republic. In 1793 peasant troops, under their own and various aristocratic leaders, scored a number of victories, but were unable to hold the region's coastal ports and establish contact with Britain. Defeat came in October 1793, but the trouble continued sporadically until finally put down by **Napoleon**.

VERONA, LEAGUE OF Alliance of Italian city states (1164), including Vicenza, Verona and Padua, formed to oppose the Emperor **Frederick I Barbarossa**; it was absorbed into the larger **Lombard League** in 1167. Verona was ruled by the da Romano and **della Scala** families from the mid-13th century until conquered by the **Visconti** family of Milan in 1387; it was then subject to Venice from 1404 until 1797.

VERRAZZANO, GIOVANNI DA (c. 1485–c. 1528) Florentine who in 1524 explored the North American coast from Cape Fear, North Carolina, probably as far north as Cape Breton, Nova Scotia. During his voyage he became the first European to sight New York Bay and Narragansett Bay, and he proved North America to be a continuous landmass. His name is commemorated in New York's Verrazzano-Narrows Bridge, linking Brooklyn and Staten Island.

VERSAILLES, TREATY OF (1783) Also known as the Treaty of Paris. Treaty which ended the American War of Independence. Great Britain recognized US sovereignty to the Mississippi River and ceded Florida to Spain. The agreement also called for payment of debts, US access to Newfoundland fishing-grounds and fair treatment for Americans who had stayed loyal to Great Britain.

VERSAILLES, TREATY OF (1919) Agreement signed on 28 June 1919 between Germany and the Allies after the First World War. Germany was made to accept responsibility for paying heavy war reparations, to give up Alsace-Lorraine to France, yield much territory to Poland, Belgium, Denmark and Japan, and to lose all its overseas colonies. Danzig became a Free City under a **League of Nations** High Commission; the Saar was also placed under League control until 1935, when by plebiscite its citizens voted to be reunited with Germany. The Rhineland was to be permanently demilitarized and occupied by the Allies for 15 years. The Treaty embodied the Covenant of the League of Nations; failing to secure a two-thirds majority in the US Senate, it was not ratified by the USA. The Versailles Treaty with Germany was paralleled by the treaties of Trianon with Hungary, of Neuilly with Bulgaria, of St Germain with Austria and of Sèvres with the Ottoman empire.

VESPASIAN (AD 9–79) Roman emperor. Of humble parentage, he became proconsul in Africa, 63–66, led victorious armies in Palestine, 67–68; was proclaimed emperor by troops during the civil wars following the death of Nero, and was recognized by the senate in 69. He reorganized provinces in the Eastern empire; secured the pacification of Wales and much of north Britain; and used tax reform, tolerance and a vast building programme to restore political stability.

VESPUCCI, AMERIGO (1454–1512) Explorer, cosmographer and propagandist. Born in Florence, he moved in 1492 to Seville as the **Medici** representative. He participated in several voyages of exploration, including one along the north coast of Brazil and Venezuela in 1499, and down the east coast of Brazil, possibly as far as Rio de la Plata, in 1501–02. He is credited, on slender evidence, with the first suggestion that America was a continent separate from Asia; even, by some contemporaries, with being its discoverer – hence the name "America", first used on the world map of Martin Waldseemüller in 1507. From 1508 to 1512 Vespucci was pilot-major of the House of Trade of the Indies.

VICTOR EMMANUEL II (1820–78) First king of united Italy, son of **Charles Albert**, king of Sardinia-Piedmont, whom he succeeded on his father's abdication in 1849. He entrusted government in 1852 to Count **Cavour**, and led Italian troops in the Franco-Piedmontese victories over the Austrians at Magenta and Solferino, 1859. Rather against the wishes of his ministers, he secretly encouraged **Garibaldi** to conquer Sicily and Naples. Proclaimed king of Italy in 1861, he acquired Venetia in 1866 and Rome in 1870.

VICTORIA (1819–1901) Queen of Great Britain and Ireland, 1837–1901, and Empress of India, 1876–1901. She succeeded her uncle, William IV; married in 1840 Prince Albert of Saxe-Coburg-Gotha (1819–61) later styled the Prince Consort. She attached particular significance to her right to be consulted about foreign affairs and, in the latter part of her reign, identified herself with her people's imperial aspirations. She went through a period of intense unpopularity when she shut herself away from the public after the Prince Consort's death, but re-emerged as the symbol of both national and imperial unity. Her diamond jubilee in 1897 was an ostentatious celebration of the apogee of Great Britain's world power.

VIENNA, CONGRESS OF Convened in fulfilment of Article XXXII of the **First Peace of Paris** and formally opened at the end of October 1814. The principal powers reconstructed Europe following the many territorial changes of the previous two decades, their decisions being embodied in the final Act of Vienna of 9 June 1815. Legitimate dynasties were restored in Spain, Naples, Piedmont, Tuscany and Modena; the Marches, Legations and other territories were restored to the Holy See; the Swiss Confederation was restored and guaranteed; 39 German states were formed into a confederation; Belgium, Holland and part of Luxembourg were united under the kingdom of the Netherlands; the kingdom of Lombardy-Venetia was placed under the Emperor of Austria; the Congress Kingdom of Poland was created and placed under the Tsar of Russia, the rest of Poland going to Austria and Prussia; Prussia in addition acquired nearly half of Saxony, Swedish Pomerania and certain territories on both banks of the Rhine; Dalmatia, Carniola and Salzburg went to Austria.

VIET MINH League for the independence of Vietnam, founded in 1941 by **Ho Chi Minh**. It emerged as a coalition of nationalist and Communist groups, and between 1946 and 1954 successfully fought to expel the French colonial administration. The dominant element of the party in North Vietnam, and since the military victory of 1975 throughout the country, is Lao Dong (Workers Party or Communist Party).

VIJAYANAGAR Powerful Hindu kingdom of southern India, founded in 1336 by a local prince, Harihara, who in 1343 built his new capital of Vijayanagara (City of Victory) to give the state its name. In 1485 a change of dynasty brought the Saluva family to the throne. Its greatest influence was achieved under Krishna Deva Raya (1509–30); the continued struggles with the Muslim Deccan culminated in a crushing defeat at the battle of Talikota in 1565 from which the kingdom never recovered.

VILLA, PANCHO (1877–1923) Mexican revolutionary leader, son of a farm worker. He joined **Madero** in 1909 and led a north Mexican troop in his successful revolution. Imprisoned in 1912, Villa escaped to the USA, returning in 1913 to form his famous División del Norte. He was joint leader of the successful revolt against Madero's successor, the dictator Victoriano Huerta, in 1914, but broke with his co-revolutionary **Carranza**, and fled to the mountains. He was pursued by a US expedition in 1916 after executing 16 Americans and attacking New Mexico, but was pardoned in 1920. He was assassinated three years later.

VILLAFRANCA, PEACE OF (1859) Preli-minary peace between **Napoleon III**, **Victor Emmanuel II** and Francis Joseph I of Austria which brought to an end the Franco-Piedmontese hostilities against Austria. A definitive peace, which provided for the cession of Lombardy to Sardinia-Piedmont, was signed at **Zürich** on 10 November 1859.

VILLARET-JOYEUSE, LOUIS THOMAS (1750–1812) French vice-admiral. He led the French fleet during the Revolutionary Wars; ordered to protect a grain convoy by the Committee of Public Safety in 1794, he suffered severe losses at the hands of the British at the battle of the "Glorious" First of June, but succeeded in getting the convoy safely home to Brest; recalled by **Napoleon I** to lead the abortive expedition to recover St Domingue. In 1802 he was made governor of Martinique, which he was forced to yield to the British in 1809. In 1811 he became governor of Venice, where he died.

VILLENEUVE, PIERRE-CHARLES-JEAN-BAPTISE-SILVESTRE DE (1763–1806) French vice-admiral. He commanded the French fleet at the battle of Trafalgar in 1805; disgraced in the eyes of **Napoleon I** by his failure, he committed suicide.

VIRACOCHA (d.c. 1438) Inca emperor who took his name from the ancient Inca god of creation. He began in the early 15th century to substitute permanent conquest for his predecessors' pattern of intermittent raiding, successfully extending Inca influence into the Titicaca basin. He became em-broiled in a civil war with his son, later **Pachacuti** Inca.

VISCONTI Milanese family dominating northern Italy in the 14th and 15th centuries. The family probably became hereditary viscounts of Milan in the 11th century, adopting the title as their surname; by war, diplomacy and marriage they extended their control over large territories between 1300 and 1447. The name died out with Filippo Maria (1392–1447) when he was succeeded by his son-in-law, the *condottiere* Francesco Sforza, who founded his own dynasty, ruling the Visconti domains until the 16th century. Through the female line, Visconti blood was transmitted to almost all the great European ruling houses: Valois in France, Habsburg in Austria and Spain, and Tudor in England.

VISCONTI, GIANGALEAZZO (1351–1402) Lombard ruler. He succeeded his father in 1378 as joint ruler of Pavia and Lombardy with his uncle, Bernabo, whom he put to death in 1385. Recognized as Duke of Milan in 1395, he became master of northern Italy, including Verona, Bologna and Perugia; in 1399 he bought Pisa and seized Siena; he founded Milan cathedral. He died of plague, with the conquest of Florence and his project for a great unified state in northern Italy incomplete.

VISHNU Hindu deity: God the Preserver in the Hindu trinity; the object of special or exclusive worship to Vaishnavas, a major sect of Hindu belief. Traditionally, Vishnu manifested himself in nine incarnations (most recently as the **Buddha**) to save men from evil; his tenth and final incarnation is still to come.

VISIGOTHS Germanic people, closely linked with the **Ostrogoths**, who occupied the former Roman province of Dacia (modern Romania) in the 3rd century AD. Forced by the **Huns** to take refuge in the Roman empire in 376, they revolted and defeated the Romans at Adrianople in 378 and began the wars and wanderings that included the Sack of Rome in 410 and the establishment of the Visigothic kingdom which, from 418 to 507, covered most of Spain and Gaul. They were defeated by the **Franks** at Vouillé in 511 and retreated to Spain, where their Christian state (first Arian, but Catholic from 589) was finally destroyed in 711 by Muslims invading from north Africa.

VLADIMIR (c. 956–1015) Grand prince of Kiev, saint and first Christian ruler of Russia. Son of **Svyatoslav** of Kiev, he became Prince of Novgorod in 970, and by 980 had linked Kiev and Novgorod, and consolidated Russia from the Ukraine to the Baltic. He signed a pact *c.* 987 with the Byzantine emperor **Basil II** to give military aid and accept Christianity. He agreed to the appointment of a Greek Metropolitan, or archbishop, in Kiev, thus checking Roman influence on Russian religion. During his reign he expanded education, legal institutions and poor relief.

V.O.C. *see* **Dutch East India Company**

VOLGA BULGARS A Turanian people, emigrating northwards from the Black Sea in the 9th century to the junction of the Volga and Kama rivers. They adopted Islam, founded an independent state, and built up a rich fur trade based on the cities of Bulgar and Suvar (early 11th century). They were conquered by the Mongols, 1237; their territory was won by Muscovy after the capture of Kazan (1552) but they themselves seem to have vanished long before.

VOLSCI Ancient Italian People, mainly known for their opposition to Roman expansion in the 5th century BC. Originally related to the Osco-Sabellian tribes of the upper Liris valley, they later moved into the fertile area of southern Latium where for 200 years they fought against Rome and the Latins. Defeated during the Latin revolt in 338 BC, they finally submitted in 304, and were quickly Romanized.

WAFD Egyptian nationalist party during the generation after the First World War. The name refers to the delegation, led by **Saad Zaghlul** which asked the British High Commissioner in Cairo for permission to put the Egyptian case for independence to the British government. Exile of leaders by the British in 1919 led to violence, martial law, and a long crisis which ended in the British declaration of limited Egyptian independence in 1922, the grant of a constitution, 1923, and the assumption of power by the Wafd, now organized as a party, in 1924. It soon lost office, but its leaders, Zaghlul and then Nahas, played an important part in later activities and negotiations which led ultimately to the Anglo-Egyptian treaty of 1936. Subsequently Nahas was prime minister on several occasions, including during much of the Second World War, and the Wafd continued to play the leading role as spokesmen of Egyptian aspirations for complete independence until dissolved after the military revolution of 1925. Reformed in 1978, the party soon dissolved itself. The New Wafd party boycotted the elections in 1990.

WAHHABI Member of the Muslim puritan movement founded by Mohammed ibn Abd al-Wahab in the 18th century. Originating in the Nejd district of central Arabia, it was adopted by a local dynasty, the **Saudis**, who created the first Wahhabi empire, crushed by **Muhammad Ali** of Egypt acting on behalf of the Ottomans in 1818; revived in the mid-19th century, it was again destroyed, this time by the Rashidis of northern Arabia. The state was reformed, and expanded by Ibn Saud to become the modern kingdom of Saudi Arabia in 1932, with the Wahhabi version of Islam as its official faith.

WALDENSIANS (Waldenses) Christian movement founded around 1170 by Peter Waldo (or Valdez) (*c.* 1140–1217), characterized by its poverty, simplicity and evangelism. The Waldensians (also known as the Poor Men of Lyons) exalted personal conduct and the setting of a good example above priestly ordination. Waldo preached no doctrinal heterodoxy (which distinguished his movement from that of the **Cathars** with their dualistic **Manichaeism**), but he was nevertheless critical of the manners of the clerical hierarchy of his time. He was condemned at the Council of Verona (1184) for preaching without licence. As they operated in much the same areas as the Cathars, the Waldensians were also attacked in the Albigensian Crusade of 1208. Although the victim of continual persecution, the Waldensian church still survives in some districts of northern Italy.

WALESA, LECH (1943–) President of Poland. The son of a carpenter, he became an electrician at the **Lenin** Shipyard in Gdansk (1967–76), the scene of violent anti-government protest in 1970. Although dismissed for unauthorized labour agitation, he remained active in the underground labour movement, founding Solidarity, a free trade union in 1979. Solidarity was crushed in 1981, by the Communist government, but survived under Walesa's leadership to win recognition again in 1989, in the wake of mass strikes and demonstrations. In 1990, Walesa was elected president of the Polish Republic.

WALLACE, SIR WILLIAM (*c.* 1270–1305) Scottish national hero, son of Sir Matthew Wallace, a landowner near Renfrew. He organized resistance to the claims of the English king, **Edward I**, to rule Scotland, and annihilated a large English army near Stirling in 1297. He ravaged Northumberland and Durham, was badly defeated and discredited at Falkirk in the following year, and was arrested in Glasgow and executed in London in 1305.

WALLIS, SAMUEL (1728–95) Circumnavigator, discoverer of Tahiti, the Wallis Islands and some of the Tuamotu and Society Islands; in 1767 the British Admiralty sent him to survey the extent of Oceania.

WANG FU-CH'EN (d.1681) Chinese general. He was a subordinate of Wu San-kuei in the campaigns against the remnants of Ming forces in southwest China in the 1650s. In 1670 he became governor of Shensi. Wu San-kuei asked him to rebel in 1673 – he refused, and offered to lead his army against Wu. In 1674 he quarrelled with the Manchu commander sent against Wu and murdered him, joining the rebellion. In 1675–6 he controlled much of Shensi and Kansu, but surrendered to the Manchus in 1676 and committed suicide after the final failure of the rebellion.

WANG MANG (d.AD 23) Chinese emperor, known as "the Usurper", founder of the short-lived Hsin dynasty, AD 9–23, which separated the two halves of the long Han period. He became regent to the imperial throne in 8 BC, at a time when the Han succession was confused; dismissed in 5 BC and reinstated four years later, he finally manoeuvred his way to supreme power in AD 9. By the time of his death a series of natural disasters and widespread rebellion, known as the Revolt of the Red Eyebrows, had precipitated his overthrow. This brought about the restoration of the Han line in AD 25. He instituted many reforms of administration and the economy, for which he claimed Confucian scriptural precedents. These sweeping reforms raised much discontent: for example, he attempted to nationalize land and free all slaves.

WARSAW PACT (Treaty of Friendship, Co-operation and Mutual Aid) Agreement signed in 1955 which formed the basis for mutual defence cooperation within the former Soviet bloc. The original participants were Albania, Bulgaria, Czechoslovakia, East Germany, Hungary, Poland, Romania and the Soviet Union, but Albania withdrew after the Soviet-led invasion of Czechoslovakia in 1968. East Germany withdrew after unification (1990). The Pact was formally wound up in March 1992.

WASHINGTON, GEORGE (1732–99) American soldier and statesman. A farmer and country gentleman of Virginia, as a lieutenant-colonel in the Virginia militia he fought against the French, 1754–8; married "the prettiest and richest widow in Virginia" in 1759, and became one of the largest landowners in the state. He was a member of the Virginia House of Burgesses, 1759–74, and delegate to the first Continental Congress. Appointed commander of the colonial armies in 1775 on the suggestion of **John Adams**, despite several military defeats in 1777–8 he retained the confidence of Congress, and forced the British surrender at Yorktown in 1781. After the peace of 1783 he resigned his command and returned to farming. He was elected chairman of the Constitutional Convention, 1787, and first president of the USA, 1788 (inaugurated 30 April 1789); he was re-elected in 1792. Declining to serve a third term, he gave his "Farewell Address" in September 1796.

WATERLOO, BATTLE OF Final defeat in 1815 of **Napoleon I**, emperor of the French, by the armies of his enemies: Dutch and British forces led by the **Duke of Wellington**, Prussian led by Marshal von Blücher.

WATT, JAMES (1736–1819) Scottish inventor. At the age of 17 he started making mathematical instruments. In 1764, while repairing a model Newcomen pump, he started a series of improvements which transformed the steam engine into the major power unit of the industrial revolution: separate condenser (1765), sun-and-planet gear (1781), double-acting engine (1782), centrifugal governor (1788), pressure gauge (1790). He was elected a Fellow of the Royal Society in 1786.

WEDGWOOD, JOSIAH (1730–95) Leading English potter in the 18th century. He introduced great improvements in the manufacturing process, and in 1769 he opened his new Etruria factory, and in 1774 he made two dinner services for **Catherine II** of Russia. Wedgwood played an active part in securing the construction of the Trent and Mersey Canal in 1777, which greatly improved the transport facilities of the pottery industry.

WEICHSEL GLACIAL STAGE see **Würm Glacial Stage**

WELLESLEY, RICHARD COLLEY (1760–1842) Marquis of Norragh, Anglo-Irish statesman and administrator, brother of the Duke of Wellington. Governor-general of Madras and of Bengal, 1797–1805, he defeated **Tipu**, Sultan of Mysore, but was recalled and threatened with impeachment over the cost and scale of his military annexations. As lord lieutenant of Ireland, 1821–8, and 1833–4, he tried to reconcile Protestants and Catholics.

WELLINGTON, DUKE OF (1769–1852) Victor of Waterloo and later prime minister of Great Britain. Born Arthur Wellesley, he gained an early military reputation in India, and was raised to the peerage after victories in the Peninsular War (1808–14). With the Prussian Marshal von Blücher he defeated **Napoleon I** in 1815 at Waterloo. A member of various Conservative Cabinets between 1818 and 1827, he became prime minister 1828–30, and opposition leader after the passing of the 1832 Reform Act.

WENCESLAS (1361–1419) King of Germany and Bohemia; son of Emperor Charles IV. His drunken and ineffective rule reduced Germany to anarchy between 1378 and 1389; deposed there in 1400, he clung on in Bohemia as a pawn of the aristocracy. He supported **Jan Hus** but failed to protect him from execution.

WESTERN RISINGS A popular English rebellion in 1549 in Cornwall and Devon against the introduction of a Protestant liturgy by Edward VI, which was defeated by government troops; also, in 1628–31, riots in southwest England against the efforts of **Charles I**'s government to enclose and cut down royal forests and thus deprive the local population of common rights.

WESTMINSTER, STATUTE OF (1931) Act of the Parliament of the United Kingdom declaring that the self-governing dominions of Canada, Australia, New Zealand, South Africa, Ireland and Newfoundland were to be regarded equally as "autonomous communities" within the British empire, though united by a common allegiance to the Crown. It recognized their sovereign right to control domestic and foreign affairs and to establish their own diplomatic corps.

WESTPHALIA, PEACE OF Name given to 11 separate treaties signed in 1648, after five years of negotiation, to end the Thirty Years' War. The **Habsburg** emperors lost most of their authority over the German princes, promised full toleration for Calvinist princes, promised full toleration for Calvinist states, accepted the secularization of all Church land (carried out 1555–1624), and formally recognized the independence of the Swiss Confederation. Sweden and Brandenburg made substantial territorial gains in north Germany; France gained extensive rights and territories in Alsace and Lorraine.

WETTIN Ancient Germany ruling dynasty, named after the castle of Wettin on Saale below Halle, which played a major role in German eastern expansion. Conrad (d.1156) received the March of Meissen. The dynasty split into two branches in 1485: the Ernestines in Thuringia, the Albertines in Saxony. The latter was a leading territorial state in Germany from 1555 to 1815.

WHITE LOTUS REBELLION The White Lotus was a Buddhist millenarian sect founded before the 13th century. Under the Manchu (**Ch'ing**) dynasty (1644–1911) it became an anti-dynastic movement, aiming to restore the **Ming**. Between 1796 and 1805 White Lotus leaders led a series of large-scale risings in the mountainous regions of central China, using guerrilla tactics; however, there was no coordination of the rebels, who were eventually contained and put down by the organization of local militias at vast expense.

WHITE RUSSIANS Traditional name for the people of Belarus (White Russia).

WHITES, THE Name used during the Russian Civil War (1918–20) to describe the anti-Bolshevik forces which fought against the Communist Red Army, and after that to describe Russian emigrés.

WILFRID, ST (*c.* 634–*c.*709) Born in Northumbria, he entered the monastery of Lindisfarne and, after the Synod of Whitby, became bishop of York. He fought to establish Roman customs; helped to convert the **Frisians** and the South Saxons; established monasteries at Ripon and Hexham; and encouraged **Willibrord** and Suidbert to evangelize the Saxons of Germany. His forceful personality and strong principles led to him twice being deposed from his see.

WILKINSON, JOHN (1728–1803) A pioneer English ironmaster who developed a greatly improved method of boring cylinders. The new technique was first used to bore cannon, and was then adapted to the production of boilers for steam engines. In 1779 Wilkinson cast the components for the first iron bridge, over the Severn at Coalbrookedale, and in 1787 built a small iron ship on the Severn.

WILLIAM I, THE CONQUEROR (*c.* 1028–87) First Norman king of England, son of Robert I of Normandy whose dukedom he inherited in 1035, becoming effective ruler in 1042. In 1063 he annexed Maine, and in 1066 successfully invaded England, where he introduced major legal and religious reforms. From 1072 he spent most of his time in Normandy; in 1085 he ordered the compilation of the Domesday Book, a unique survey of England's landholdings.

WIILIBALD, ST (*c.* 700–86) Anglo-Saxon missionary in the eastern Mediterranean and Germany, a nephew and associate of **St Boniface**. He was made bishop of Eichstätt in 741.

WILLIBRORD, ST (658–739) Anglo-Saxon bishop and missionary, disciple of St Egbert in Ireland, 678–90. He was sent to convert the **Frisians**, and became their archbishop in 695. He worked with the **Merovingian** kings, Pippin II and **Charles Martel**, to extend Christianity in northern Europe. He died at his monastery of Echternach, and was adopted as the patron saint of Holland.

WILLOUGHBY, FRANCIS (*c.* 1613–66) Founder of the British colony of Surinam. He first supported Parliament in the English Civil War, then joined the Royalists. As Lord Willoughby of Parham he was appointed governor of Barbados in 1650, and the following year successfully implanted settlers in Surinam.

WILSON, WOODROW (1856–1924) 28th president of the USA, an outstanding chief executive whose two terms in office (1913–21) covered the First World War and the Paris Peace conference. A controversial figure during the first years, Wilson won temporary fame as the world's greatest leader after the war, but his power and influence later declined. The US Senate repudiated the **League of Nations**, which he had ardently advocated, and ill-health sapped his capacity to govern.

WISCONSIN GLACIAL STAGE see **Würm**

WITOLD (1350–1430) Grandson of **Gedymin**, Lithuanian grand duke and national leader, also known in Lithuania as Vytautas the Great. He fought a long struggle with his cousin **Władysław II Jagiełło**, king of Poland, which ended in 1401 when Władysław recognized him as Grand Duke of Lithuania, while remaining his suzerain. In alliance, the cousins broke the power of the **Teutonic Order** at the battle of Tannenberg (Grünwald) in 1410.

WITTELSBACH Bavarian dynasty enfeoffed with the duchy of Bavaria after the fall of **Henry, Duke of Saxony** in 1180. A collateral line held the Palatinate from 1214 to 1777. The Bavarian Wittelsbachs, imperial supporters in the **Thirty Years' War**, were rewarded with the Upper Palatinate in 1684. Raised to the rank of king by Napoleon in 1806, they continued to rule until 1918.

WITTE, SERGEI YULYEVISH (1849–1915) Russian politician. Promoted the building of the Trans-Siberian railroad (begun 1891), known as the "Witte system", linking European and Asiatic Russia. Russian minister of communication (1892) and finance (1892–1903) and first constitutional prime minister of the Russian empire (1905–6). He sought to combine authoritarian rule with modernization along Western lines and persuaded Tsar Nicholas II to issue the "October Manifesto" (1905) supporting a measure of representative government but fell from favour in 1906. He opposed Russia's entry into World War I and died dispirited, foreseeing disaster for the tsarist empire.

WŁADYSŁAW II JAGIEŁŁO (1351–1434) Grandson of Gedymin, son of **Olgierd**, grand duke of Lithuania (from 1377). On his marriage to Queen **Jadwiga** of Poland in 1386, he united the two crowns and styled himself Władysław II, King of Poland. At the head of Polish and Lithuanian armies he defeated the knights of the **Teutonic Order** at the battle of Tannenberg (Grünwald) in 1410. He gave his name to the **Jagiełłonian** dynasty.

WOLFE, JAMES (1727–59) British general. He served in the Low Countries, Scotland and Cape Breton Islands before commanding the British army at the capture of Quebec in 1759; after defeat at Beauport, he climbed the heights of Abraham to surprise and rout the French army. He thus gained Canada for Britain, but died of wounds during the battle.

WORMS, CONCORDAT OF Agreement concluded in 1122 between Pope Calixtus II and Emperor Henry V, which ended the Investiture Contest in compromise. The Emperor conceded full freedom of election to episcopal office, surrendering the claim to bestow spiritual authority by investiture; but bishops were to be elected in his presence so that he might nevertheless influence the elector's choice. Thus neither side gained all that **Gregory VII** and **Henry IV** had demanded, but each secured valuable concessions from the other; papal headship of the Church was recognized, but the emperor retained some control over its leaders in Germany.

WRIGHT BROTHERS American aviation pioneers. Together Orville Wright (1871–1948) and his brother Wilbur (1867–1912) built the first stable, controllable, heavier-than-air flying machine, which made its first successful flights (the longest of 259.6m/825ft) at Kitty Hawk, North Carolina, in 1903.

WU P'EI-FU (1874–1939) Chinese warlord. He served with the Pei-yang armies under **Yüan Shih-k'ai**, and with the Japanese army during the Russo-Japanese War of 1904–5. After Yüan's death in 1916, Wu became the most powerful general of the Pei-yang armies, and in 1922 drove back the Manchurian armies of **Chang Tso-lin**. This made him China's most powerful military figure, and he dominated the shaky Peking government from 1922–4. His ruthless suppression of a workers' strike on the Hankow-Peking railway in 1923 cost him much of his popularity and the support of his main ally **Feng Yu-hsiang**. Decisively defeated by Chang near Tientsin in 1924, he retreated to Hupeh; in 1925–6 allied himself with Chang in a war against Feng Yu-hsiang and invaded Honan. In 1926–7 he was defeated by **Chiang Kai-shek**'s Northern Expedition and took refuge in Szechwan; he took no further major part in affairs.

WÜRM GLACIAL STAGE The latest phase of major ice advance in Alpine Europe, starting *c.* 70,000 years ago and ending around 10,000 years ago; it is equivalent to the Wisconsin period in North American and Weichsel in Scandinavia.

WU SAN-KUEI (1612–78) Chinese general. He served in the **Ming** armies, defending the northeast frontier against the **Manchus**, but he appealed to the Manchus for aid when Peking was attacked in 1644 by the rebel **Li Tzu-ch'eng** (*c.* 1605–45), and with their aid drove Li from Peking, where the Manchus set up the **Ch'ing** dynasty. He refused appeals to aid a restoration of the **Ming** emperors, and commanded the southwest province of Yunnan on behalf of the Manchus, growing increasingly powerful and eventually controlling much of southwest and west China. In 1673 he led the Rebellion of the Three Feudatories and attempted to set up his own Chou dynasty, invading central China in 1674. He died of dysentery three years before the rebellion was finally crushed in 1681.

WU-TI (156–87 BC) Powerful Chinese emperor of the former **Han** period, 11th son of Emperor Ching Ti. He succeeded to the throne in 140 BC; aggressively extended China's frontiers to include much of south and southwest China; north Vietnam, northern Korea and much of central Asia, and established effective defences against the **Hsiun-gnu** in the north. He finally established the sup-remacy of the emperor, created a tightly knit bureaucracy, levied unprecedented taxes and made Confucianism the state religion.

WYATT'S REBELLION English uprising in 1554 against the marriage of Mary Tudor (reigned 1553–8) to Philip II of Spain. Three thousand men from Kent marched on London and reached Fleet Street before surrendering; their leader, Sir Thomas Wyatt (son of the poet of the same name), was executed, and Princess Elizabeth, later Queen **Elizabeth I** (whom Wyatt had wished to place on the throne) was imprisoned in the Tower of London.

WYCLIF, JOHN (c. 1330–84) Religious reformer and translator of the Bible into English. As a vigorous anti-clerical he was patronized by John of Gaunt, who continued to support him, but not his views, when he denied the miracle of transubstantiation in the Mass; he was condemned as a heretic in 1381. His followers are known as **Lollards**.

WYNFRITH *see* **Boniface, St**

WYNTER, JAN WILLEM DE (1761–1812) Dutch admiral and politician. In 1785 he led the "patriot party" which deposed the Stadholder William V, but fled to France when William was restored in 1787. In 1795 he accompanied the French army which conquered the Netherlands, and the French placed him in charge of the Dutch navy; in 1797 he led it to its defeat by the British at the battle of Camperdown.

XENOPHON (c. 430–c. 355 BC) Greek soldier and author. He studied with Socrates, about whom he wrote the *Memorabilia*, *Symposium* and *Apology*. His *Anabasis* describes the epic retreat of 10,000 mercenaries from Persia after the failure of Cyrus the Younger's expedition against Artaxerxes II. In exile he wrote the *Hellenica*, a history of Greece, and other works on sport and politics.

XERXES I (c. 520–465 BC) King of Persia (reigned 486–465 BC). Son of **Darius I** by his second marriage; chosen to succeed over his elder brother. He reconquered Egypt, which had rebelled at the end of Darius's reign; invaded Greece in 480 after digging a canal through the Mount Athos peninsula, forced the pass at Thermopylae and occupied Athens before meeting a crushing defeat at Salamis (480) by sea and at Plataea (479) by land. He was responsible for the finest work at the Persian capital of Persepolis. He was assassinated by conspirators headed by his chief guard, Artabanus.

XHOSA A people, and their Bantu language, in Cape Province, South Africa; now the inhabitants of the Transkei, the first so-called "independent homeland" inside South Africa.

YAHYA KHAN, AGHA MOHAMMED (1917–82) Pakistan soldier and politician. Commander in East Pakistan (now Bangladesh), 1962–4; commander-in-chief of the Pakistan army, 1966–9, and president of Pakistan and chief administrator of martial law, 1969–71. He was forced to resign after his failure to suppress the revolt in East Pakistan which led to the setting up of the state of Bangladesh.

YALTA CONFERENCE Meeting of Allied war leaders (led by **Roosevelt**, **Churchill** and **Stalin**) at Yalta in the Crimea, 4–11 February, 1945. It reaffirmed the decision to demand unconditional Axis surrender, planned a four-power occupation of Germany, and agreed a further meeting to finalize plans for the **United Nations**. It was also agreed that the British and Americans would repatriate all Russians in Allied hands. Stalin, for his part, was prompted to declare war on Japan.

YAO Mountain-dwelling people of south and southwest China and of Southeast Asia, related to the Miao who share a similar heritage of Sino-Tibetan languages. in Kwangtung some have turned to wet-rice cultivation, but most remain in the highlands practising primitive slash-and-burn agriculture.

YASSIN, SHEIKH (1938–2004) Founder and spiritual leader of Hamas, the Palestinian militant organization fighting against the Israeli occupation. A quadriplegic from an accident in childhood, Yassin was a devoted Islamic scholar, studying at al Azhar university in Cairo where the Muslim Brotherhood organization was founded. He became a member of the Palestinian branch of the Brotherhood, but it was after the first *Intifada* in 1987 that the Palestinian Islamic movement called itself Hamas, meaning "zeal". The Israeli government sentenced Yassin to life imprisonment in 1989, but he was released in 1997 as part of a trade-off with Jordan. Following the Aqaba summit in 2003, at which Mohammed Abbas, the then Palestinian Prime Minister, pledged an end to violence, Hamas called a ceasefire. However, this was short lived, and violent activity from both sides ensued. In March 2004, the Israeli government assassinated him. His successor, Abdel Aziz al Rantissi was assassinated 26 days later.

YELTSIN, BORIS (1931–2007) Russian president. He joined the Soviet Communist Party in 1961 and its central committee in 1981. After **Gorbachev**'s takeover in 1985, he became party leader in Moscow, where he introduced a programme of rapid reform. However, his outspoken attacks on communist hardliners led to his demotion. In May 1990 he became president of the Russian Republic and his criticism of Gorbachev became more open. In August 1991 he played a key role in defeating the hardline coup mounted against Gorbachev. The prominence he gained led swiftly to his elevation to the leadership of the new Russian Federation after the collapse of the USSR at the end of 1991. He survived another coup attempt in 1994, but growing lawlessness and economic hardship weakened his leadership. Though re-elected in 1996, by 1998 the rapid decline of the Russian economy and of his health had left him an isolated figure. Yeltsin resigned in 1991, naming **Vladimir Putin** as his successor.

YEN HSI-SHAN (1883–1960) Chinese general and military governor. A Japanese-trained army officer, he emerged as a warlord in Shansi after the overthrow of the **Ch'ing** (Manchu) dynasty in 1911, and ruled as absolute dictator of the whole region from 1917 until the end of the Second World War. In 1930 he joined **Feng Yu-hsiang** in an abortive northern alliance against **Chiang Kai-shek**, but was afterwards confirmed in command of Shansi, where he instituted a sweeping programme of provincial reforms in 1934. In 1937 he lost most of Shansi to the Japanese, and from 1939 was in constant conflict with the Chinese communists. He was driven from the province in early 1949; he went to Taiwan and became premier until 1950.

YEZHOV, NIKOLAI IVANOVICH (1894–1939?) Soviet political leader who joined the Communist party in 1917 and served as a political commissar in the Red Army. He was a member of the central Committee of the Soviet Communist party from 1934 and headed the people's commissariat of internal affairs (NKVD) (1936–8), which under his direction carried out **Stalin**'s purges. As a result, his name became inextricably linked with the great Terror (Yezhovshchina). He was probably assassinated in 1939, but the circumstances surrounding his death remain unknown.

YORKSHIRE RISING Major revolt in 1489 against the attempts of the English King **Henry VII** to collect a parliamentary grant of £75,000. The king's lieutenant, the earl of Northumberland, was killed before the rebels were suppressed.

YOUNG TURKS Popular name for the Committee of Union and Progress, an association of army officers and others who compelled sultan **Abdül Hamid II** to restore the 1876 constitution in 1908 and deposed him in 1909. Subsequently it became the Ottoman empire's dominant political party, in 1914 bringing Turkey into the First World War. It was disbanded after the Central Powers' defeat in 1918.

YÜAN SHIH-K'AI (1859–1916) First President of the Republic of China. He was sent to Korea with the Anhwei army, 1882, and became Chinese commissioner in Seoul, 1885–94; he helped to create a new model army after defeat by Japan in 1895. In 1901 he became viceroy of China's metropolitan province, Chihli, and commander of China's most powerful army, the Pei-yang chün. He was removed from his post in 1907 but exercised power through his former military subordinates, and was recalled by the **Ch'ing** (Manchus) after the outbreak of the 1911 revolution as supreme commander. In 1912 he was recommended by the emperor to be president, replaced the provisional president, **Sun Yat-sen**; increasingly dictatorial, he precipitated civil war in 1913 by murdering the revolutionary party chairman, and in 1916 tried to create a new imperial dynasty.

YUDENICH, NIKOLAI NIKOLAYEVICH (1862–1933) Russian general. After service in the Russo-Japanese war and the First World War, he took command of the anti-Bolshevik forces in the Baltic after the Russian revolution. In 1919, with some British support he led an unsuccessful advance on Leningrad (then called Petrograd, now reverted to St Petersburg), and went into exile.

YÜEH-CHIH Central Asian peoples, first identified in Chinese sources in the 2nd century BC, living as nomads in Kansu, northwest China. Under attack by the **Hsiungnu**, they moved west into Sogdiana and Bactria, displacing the Greek rulers there, *c.*150 BC. Their descendants, with the **Tocharians**, founded the Kushana empire, ruling northern India and central Asia until about AD 300. Yüeh-chih and Kushana missionaries helped spread **Buddhism** and Indian culture in China.

YUNG-LO (CHU TI) (1360–1424) Chinese emperor, the third of the **Ming** dynasty, and fourth son of Hung-we. He rebelled against his nephew in 1399, and seized the throne in 1402 after two years of destructive civil war. He invaded Annam, 1406–7, and began a series of major maritime expeditions into the Indian Ocean. He personally conducted campaigns to crush the Mongols in 1410, 1414 and 1422–4, and expanded Chinese power in Manchuria and the Amur valley. He rebuilt the Grand Canal, and transferred the capital from Nanking to Peking in 1421.

ZAGHLUL, SAAD (1857–1927) Leader of Egyptian **nationalism** during that period when it first became a mass movement. He became prominent as a minister and politician before 1914; from 1918 he was leader of the **Wafd**, and in 1924 was appointed prime minister shortly after the British declaration of limited independence for Egypt; he was, however, forced to resign soon afterwards.

ZAGWE Ethiopian dynasty of Semitic origin which displaced the Aksumite kings in the 12th and 13th centuries. It did much to expand and centralize the Christian empire of Ethiopia.

ZAIBATSU Large-scale Japanese business groups, normally organized around the commercial, industrial and financial interests of a single family. The biggest and best known were the Mitsui, Mitsubishi, Yasuda and Sumitomo empires, all of which grew up and flourished in the period from 1868 to 1945. In 1946, after Japan's defeat, the Zaibatsu were ordered to dissolve into their component companies, but most are now, for practical purposes, reassembled.

ZAIDI Dynasty of rulers in Yemen, southern Arabia. Founded by imam al-Hadi in northern Yemen in the 9th century, they expanded their power in the 12th century, and again after 1635, when they expelled the Ottoman Turks. Driven back to northern Yemen in the 1710s, they were forced to recognize Ottoman suzerainty in 1849. After the Ottoman collapse in 1918 they became rulers of all Yemen until a military coup in 1962 deposed the last Zaidi imam.

ZANGI (1084–1146) Iraqi warrior who inflicted the first serious defeat on Christian crusaders, recapturing Edessa in 1144. He founded the Zangid dynasty, which ruled northern Iraq and Syria, 1127–1222.

ZANGIDS Muslim Turkish dynasty, ruling northern Iraq and part of Syria from 1127 to 1222. It was founded by Zangi (1127–46), who mounted the first Islamic counterattack against the Christian **Crusades**. **Saladin**, founder of the **Ayyubid** dynasty in Egypt, was a Zangid general, and ultimately brought the family territories under his rule.

ZAPATA, EMILIANO (1879–1919) Mexican revolutionary leader. He supported **Madero** in the 1911 overthrow of **Díaz**; forbidden to redistribute land to the peasants, he issued the Plan of Ayala and renewed revolution under the slogan "Land Liberty". He fought constantly, first against the dictator Huerta in 1913, and then with **Pancho Villa** against the moderate government of **Carranza**. He was ambushed and assassinated.

ZARATHUSTRA *see* **Zoroaster**

ZEALOTS Extreme Jewish resistance party against the Roman domination of Judaea. It played a major part in the **Jewish uprising** of AD 66–73.

ZENO OF CITIUM (c. 334–c. 262 BC) Ancient Greek philosopher, best known for his paradoxes demonstrating the unreality of motion.

ZEUS Supreme god of Greek mythology, also identified with the Roman Jupiter; born in Crete (Mount Ida), son of Rhea and Cronus, whom he overthrew.

ZHIVKOV, TODOR (1911–98) Bulgarian political leader. He worked as a printer in Bulgarian communist circles in the 1920s. Some claim he led the coup overthrowing the pro-German regime in 1944. He served as secretary of the Bulgarian communist party in 1954, premier in 1962 and president in 1971 but resigned in November 1989 when communist power in eastern Europe collapsed. He was convicted of embezzlement in 1992 and sentenced to seven years' imprisonment.

ZHUKOV, GEORGIY KONSTANTINOVICH (1896–1976) Marshal of the Soviet Union and leading Russian hero of the Second World War. He served in the Imperial Russian Army, 1915–17, joining the Red Army in 1918; he was cavalry commander in the Civil War. In command of the Mongolian-Manchurian frontier in 1939, he became general officer commanding the Kiev Military district in 1940, and in 1941 chief of the general staff. He directed the defence of Leningrad and then Moscow after the German invasion; was appointed marshal in 1943; and led the final assault on Berlin in 1945. He was briefly commander-in-chief of the Soviet forces in Germany, GOC of Odessa military district 1948–52; minister of defence 1955, after supporting **Khrushchev** against Malenkov. He was dismissed in 1957 and retired into private life.

ZIONISM Jewish national movement. It emerged in the latter part of the 19th century, and was placed on a firm and permanent organizational basis by Theodor Herzl, author of *The Jewish State*, who convened the first Zionist Congress at Basle in 1897. It sought the creation of a Jewish national homeland in Palestine which most Jews regarded as their ancestral land; this aim was achieved in 1948 when the UN voted to create the state of Israel.

ZIRID Muslim Berber dynasty ruling, under various branches, Tunisia, eastern Algeria and Granada from 972 to 1152. They were given a free hand in northwest Africa when their suzerain, the **Fatimid** caliph al-Muizz, moved his capital to Cairo. They were finally conquered by the **Almohads**.

ZOLLVEREIN German customs union established in 1834 when 18 states, some of which had formerly belonged to the Prussian, central German and southern German customs unions, formed, under Prussian auspices, a free trade area. By 1841 most German states had joined; Hanover and Oldenburg joined in 1854; Austria remained outside; Schleswig-Holstein, Lauenburg, Lübeck and the Mecklenburgs joined after the defeat of Austria in 1866 by Prussia, whose power in Germany had been much enhanced by the Zollverein. Hamburg and Bremen joined in 1888.

ZOROASTER (Zarathustra) Prophet and religious reformer of ancient Iran, the founder of Zoroastrianism. His personal writings were the Old Iranian texts known as the *Gathas*, in which he emphasized the ethical aspects of religion against mere conformity with ritual requirements. Theologically, these ideas were expressed in the cult of Ahura Mazda, "the Wise Lord", as the highest god, in opposition to beliefs never defined but which some have thought included forms of Mithraism. Thus arose the "dualistic" theology of later Zoroastrianism, which depicts creation not as the immediate rule of an omnipotent just god, but as a long contest between the divine forces of good and evil. This theology provides a simple solution for the problem of suffering, and may have influenced theories concerning the role of Satan in developing Christianity.

ZOSER (Djoser) Second king of Egypt's 3rd Dynasty; he is traditionally said to have reigned for 19 years during the 27th century BC. With his chief minister and architect, **Imhotep**, he built the first of the great stone pyramids at Saqqara, near his capital, Memphis.

ZULU Nguni-speaking group in Natal, southern Africa. In the early 19th century they joined with related peoples under Shaka, their leader, to form the Zulu empire. They engaged in sporadic warfare with other African peoples and with the advancing European settlers, and were finally defeated in 1879 at Ulundi.

ZÜRICH, PEACE OF Agreement in 1859 between **Napoleon III** of France and Franz Joseph of Austria to settle the Italian problem after a general rebellion against Austrian rule. Lombardy was ceded to Piedmont, Venetia remained Austrian (to 1866); the central states of Italy voted to join Piedmont, and Nice and Savoy voted to become French (1860).

ZWINGLI, HULDREICH (1484–1531) Swiss religious reformer. He was pastor in Glarus, 1506, and rector and teacher of religion at the Great Minster, Zürich, 1519. He established the Protestant **Reformation** in Zürich, 1520–3, although failing to agree about doctrine with **Luther** and other German reformers, 1529. He was killed at the battle of Kappel while serving as chaplain in Zürich's army during its campaign against the Swiss Catholics.

ZYRIANS Finno-Ugrian speaking Arctic people, mostly inhabiting the Komikomi area of northwest Russia.

Index

U

Wiluna – Zwickau

Wiluna W Australia goldfield 260/1
Wiman Korean founder 70/4
Winchester S England bishopric 115/3; Viking raid 121/1
Windau (*Latv.* Ventspils) S Baltic occupied by Teutonic Knights 160/2
Windmiller Mounds W USA early site 45/1
Windmill Hill S England early farming 41/1
Windward Coast W Africa 182/1
Windward Islands W Indies disputed by British and French 174/3 (inset)
Winslow North American explorer 179/3
Winton E Australia railway 260/1
Wisbech E England Industrial Revolution 223/1
Wisconsin state of N USA federal state in 291/3; Depression 293/1; income and population 337/2, 3; civil unrest 344/1; poverty and working poor 345/2, 3; religion in 345/4
Wismar N Germany WW1 279/1
Withlacoochee SE USA ⚔241/3
Witkrams stone tools 96/3
Witte, Sergei 255
Wittenberg E Germany Reformation 205/1
Wittstock N Germany ⚔213/3
Władysław IV Vasa king of Poland 176
Włodzimierz (Vladimir)
Wochkirch E Germany ⚔204/4
Wood Lake N USA ⚔241/3
wool Black Death and wool trade 158; Spanish 200
Woodward, Edward North American explorer 179/3
Worcester W England ⚔207/1; Industrial Revolution 223/1
World War I Turkey 252; Russia 255, 282; and restriction on US immigration 246, causes of 275; history 278; world economy and 292; writing, history of 365
World War II Canadian immigration increases 249; and European colonialism 285; events leading to 294; Africa and the Pacific 296/1; racism and deportations 300/1; cost to USSR 341; escalation since 348
Worms SW Germany Concordat of 130; bishopric 131/1
Wounded Knee C USA ⚔241/3
Wreocensaete Anglo-Saxon tribe of C England 109/4
writing hieroglyphic 44, 74; ancient Eurasia 55; Indus civilization 70; Linear A and B 75; cuneiform 86; Indian scripts 148
Wrocław (*Ger.* Breslau) SW Poland founded 122/3
Wroxeter (Viroconium)
WTO (World Trade Organization) 315/1, 354, 355/3
Wu early state of C China 139/3
Wu E China Late Chou domain 69/4; trading centre 93/5
Wu-an (*n/s* Wu'an) N China late Chou city site 69/4
Wu-ch'ang (*n/s* Wuchang) C China Ming provincial capital 184/1; mutiny and revolution 257/3; captured by Kuomintang 286/1; industry 311/1
Wu-ch'eng (*n/s* Wucheng) C China Shang city 68/2
Wu-ch'ieh (*n/s* Wuqie) N Vietnam Han prefecture 88/2
Wuci (Wu-tz'u)
Wudu (Wu-tu)
Wu-han (*n/s* Wuhan) C China taken by Kuomintang 286/1; industry 287/3; student unrest 355/2
Wu-hsi (*n/s* Wuxi) N China attacked by Ti 91/2
Wuhu E China captured by Communists 287/4
Wu-lei (*n/s* Wulei) Sinkiang centre of former Han protectorate 89/3
Wu-ling (*n/s* Wuling) C China Han commanderie 88/2
Wu-lu (*n/s* Wulu) NE China Han prefecture 88/2
Wu-lu-mo-ssu (Ormuz)
Wuppertal (Barmen-Elberfeld)
Wuqie (Wu-ch'ieh)
Württemberg region of S Germany Reformation 205/1; Thirty Years' War 213/3; unification of Germany 239/3
Würzburg S Germany massacre of Jews 117/3; bishopric 115/3; university founded 158/2; industrial development 235/1
Wusung (*n/s* Wusong) E China treaty port 256/2
Wu-ti emperor of China 89
Wu-tu (*n/s* Wudu) NW China Han commanderie 88/2
Wu-tz'u (*n/s* Wuci) NE China Han prefecture 88/2
Wu-wei (*n/s* Wuwei) NW China conquered by Han 89/3; Han commanderie 88/2
Wuxi (Wu-hsi)
Wu-yüan (*n/s* Wuyuan) N China Han prefecture 88/2
Wu-yüeh (*n/s* Wuyue) early state of E China 139/3
Wyclif, John movement of protest 115; critical of papacy 160
Wymondham E England 16C revolt 207/1
Wyoming state of NW USA federal state in 291/3; Depression 293/1; income and population 337/2, 3; poverty and working poor 345/2, 3; religion in 345/4

X
Xanthus (*mod.* Günük) W Anatolia Greek colony 85/1; Alexander's route 86/1
Xerxes I king of Persia expedition into Europe 82; invasion of Greece 84
Xhosa people of SE Africa 265/3, 286/2; African ethnic group 318/2
Xi (Hsi)
Xia (Hsia)
Xian (Hsien)
Xi'an (Hsi-an)
Xianbi (Hsien-pi)
Xiangfen (Hsiang-fen)
Xiangyang (Hsiang-yang)
Xiangzhou (Hsiang-chou)
Xianrendong (Hsien-jen-tung)
Xianyang (Hsien-yang)
Xiapi (Hsia-p'i)
Xiaxiang (Hsia-hsiang)
Xoconusco Aztec province 165/2
Xing (Hsing)
Xingan (Hsin-kan)
Xingtai (Hsing-t'ai)
Xingyuan (Hsing-yüan)
Xining (Sining)
Xinjiang (*W/G* Hsin-chiang, *a/s* Sinkiang) province of NW China GDP per capita 354/1; minority unrest 354, 355/2
Xiongnu (Hsiung-nu)
Xisha Qundao (Paracel Islands)
Xiutu (Hsiu-t'u)
Xixia (Hsi-hsia)
Xizang (Tibet)
Xoconusco Aztec province 165/2
Xu (Hsü)
Xuanfu (Hsüan-fu)
Xuantu (Hsüan-t'u)
Xun (Hsün)
Xuyi (Hsü-i)
Xuzhou (Hsü-chou)

Y
Yadavas dynasty of W India 143/1, 147/1
Yadz Seljuq rule 152/2
Yafa, Yafo (Jaffa)
Yakuts people of C Siberia 176/2, 254/2
Yakutsk C Siberia founded 176/2; fur trade 221/2
Yalta Conference and future of Europe 299; frontiers of Germany 302
Yamagata N Japan city and prefecture 268/1; industry 268/1
Yamaguchi city and prefecture of W Japan 268/1
Yamana Shugo family of C Japan 137/3
Yamalo-Nenets AD W Siberia Russian Federation 357/1
Yamamoto, Isoruku 296
Yamanashi prefecture of C Japan 268/1
Yamasees SE USA ⚔ 241/3
Yamkhad (*mod.* Aleppo) Syria Amorite kingdom 57/2
Yampi Sound W Australia early settlement 261
Yan (Yen)
Yan'an (Yenan)
Yanaon (*mod.* Yanam) E India French settlement 216/2 (inset), 259/3
Yang Chien (*later* Sui Wen Ti, emperor of China) 90
Yang-chou (*n/s* Yangzhou) E China early bishopric 114/1; T'ang prefecture 138/1; Sung provincial capital 139/5
Yangtsun (*n/s* Yangcun) N China Boxer Rebellion 273/3
Yangtze River Three Gorges Dam 354, 355/2
Yang-yüeh (*n/s* Yangyue) C China Western Chou domain 69/3
Yanling (Yen-ling)
Yannina N Greece Ottoman Empire 237/2
Yanqi (Yench'i)
Yanukovych, Viktor Ukrainian president 357/3
Yao people of E Africa 265/1
Yao people of S China, uprising 193/1
Yao-yang (*n/s* Yaoyang) NE China Han prefecture 88/2
Yarim Tepe N Mesopotamia early site 39/1
Yarkand (*n/s* Yarkant *Chin.* Sha-ch'e) W China Han expansion 89/3
Yarmouth (*a/c* Great Yarmouth) E England WW1 279/1
Yarmuk *river* Israel battle of the 112; ⚔ 113/1
Yaroslavl W Russia acquired by Muscovy 177/1; industry 255/1; Russian Revolution 283/1; urban growth 341/2
Yaş (*Rom.* Iaşi *Eng.* Jassy) Moldavia Ottoman Empire 157/1
Yasi tribe of Caucasus 129/1
Yatenga early state of W Africa 155/1
Yathrib (Medina) Jewish community 111
Yatvagi E Slav tribe of W Russia 129/1
Yaxchilán Mayan hieroglyph 64
Yazdigird III Persian emperor 112
Yazgard III death of 140
Yeh-lang (*n/s* Yelang) SW China Han prefecture 88/2
Yekaterinburg (*f/c from 1924* Sverdlovsk) W Siberia founded 177/1; industrialization 213/1; railway to east 254/2; Tsar shot 283/1
Yekaterinodar (*since 1920* Krasnodar) Caucasus founded 177/1; industry 255/1; urban growth 255/1
Yekaterinoslav (*since 1926* Dnepropetrovsk) C Russia founded 177/1; industry and urban growth 255/1; Bolshevik seizure 283/1
Yelang (Yeh-lang)
Yelets W Russia founded 177/1
Yelizavetgrad (*since 1935* Kirovograd) W Russia industry 255/1
Yellow Ford NE Ireland ⚔ 207/1
Yellow River (*Chin.* Huang Ho) N China Shang sites 68/2; change of course 257/1
Yellowstone N USA ⚔ 241/3
'Yellow Turbans' revolt 89
Yeltsin, Boris Russian leader 341, 356, 357
Yemen (*a/c* Yemen Arab Republic, North Yemen) pre-Islamic culture 110; trade 111; spread of Islam 113/1; introduction of Christianity 114/1; Civil War 331/3, 359/1; UN peacekeeping 349/2; terrorist casualties 351/3; in Gulf War 353/3; population growth 361/3; Arab Spring 358, 359/1. See also South Yemen
Yen (*n/s* Yan) NE China Chou domain 69/3, 69/4, warring state 89/1; 139/3; trading centre 93/5
Yen (*n/s* Yan) C China Western Chou domain 69/3
Yenan (*n/s* Yan'an) N China destination of Long March 287/3; captured by Communists 287/4
Yen-ch'i (*n/s* Yanqi *a/c* Karashahr) Sinkiang Han expansion 89/3
Yenije-i-Vardar (*Gr.* Yiannitsa) E Greece Balkan Wars 274/2
Yeniseysk C Siberia founded 176/2; fur trade 221/2
Yen-ling (*n/s* Yanling) N China Late Chou city site 69/4
Yerevan Armenia Ottoman conquest 186; urban growth 341/2
Yergöğü (*Rom.* Giurgiu) Wallachia Ottoman Empire 157/1
Yerushalayim (Jerusalem)
Yevpatoriya town of Khanate of Crimea 177/1
Yew, Lee Kuan PM of Singapore 314
Yezo (Hokkaido)
Yi N China Chou city site 69/4
Yiannitsa (Yenije-i-Vardar)
Yicheng (I-ch'eng)
Yihsien (*n/s* Yixian) N China attacked by Hsienpei 91/2
Yiling (I-ling)
Ying C China Western Chou domain 69/3
Yingkow (*n/s* Yingkou *W/G* Ying-k'ou *a/c* Newchwang) Manchuria industry 287/3
Ying-t'ien-fu (*n/s* Yingtianfu) NE China Sung province capital 139/5
Yin-p'ing-tao (*n/s* Yinpingdao) W China Han prefecture 88/2
Yixian (Yihsien)
Yixun (I-hsün)
Yiyang (I-yang)
Yizhou (I-chou)
Yochow (*now.* Yueyang *W/G* Yüeh-yang) C China treaty town 256/2
Yogyakarta (Jogjakarta)
Yokohama C Japan treaty port 197/4; industrialization 197/1, 268/1
Yola W Africa Barth's travels 264/2
Yom Kippur War 331
Yong (Yung)
Yongshi (Yung-shih)
Yongxing Jun (Yung-hsing Chün)
Yongzhou (Yung-chou)
York (*anc.* Eburacum) N England Christian centre 104/1; bishopric 115/3; Danish Viking base 121/1; revolt against Henry VIII 207/1; Industrial Revolution 223/1
York River NE USA ⚔ 241/3
Yorktown E USA ⚔ 224/3
Yoruba city states 155/3; people of W Africa 267/1
Yoruba Kingdoms (*a/c* Yorubaland) W Africa 155/1, 265/1
Yoshinori shogun 137
You Bet W USA mining site 240/1
'Young Turks' revolution 273
Ypres (*Dut.* Ieper) S Belgium medieval fair 134/1; centre of urban revolt 159/1; WW1 279/1 (inset)
Yüan-mou (*n/s* Yuanmou) W China site of early man 31/1
Yuan dynasty 142
Yucatán region of E Mexico early Indian states 44/2; Mayan civilization 64/1; Mayapán dominant city 164; European discovery 173/2; modern province 255/1
Yüan Shih-k'ai 286
Yüeh (*n/s* Yue) E China warring state 89/1
Yüeh (*n/s* Yue) border people of SE China 69/4
Yüeh-sui (*n/s* Yuesui) W China Han commanderie 88/2
Yüeh-yang (Yochow)
Yü-fu (*n/s* Yufu) C China Han prefecture 88/2
Yugoslav Federation formed 347
Yugoslavia (*f/c* Kingdom of Serbs, Croats and Slovenes) created after WW1 288/2; socio-political change 292/2; WW2 295/4, 299/2; Cold War 305/1; collapse and Civil War 347/3; UN peacekeeping 349/2. See also Serbia, Croatia, Montenegro, Herzegovina, Dalmatia, Slovenia, Bosnia, Macedonia
Yukon Territory NW Canada development 248/1
Yü-lin (*n/s* Yulin) N China Ming frontier defence area 184/1
Yü-lin (*n/s* Yulin) S China Han commanderie 88/2
Yü-men Kuan *n/s* Yumen Guan) *pass* NW China 89/3
Yün (*n/s* Yun) C China Western Chou domain 69/3
Yung-cheng emperor of China 192
Yün-chung (*n/s* Yunzhong) N China Han prefecture 88/2
Yung (*n/s* Yong) W China Western Chou domain 69/3
Yung-chou (*n/s* Yongzhou) SW China T'ang prefecture 138/1
Yung-hsing Chün (*n/s* Yongxing Jun) N China Sung province 139/5
Yung-lo emperor of China 185
Yung-shih (*n/s* Yongshi) NW China Han prefecture 88/2
Yunnan (*W/G* Yün-nan) province of SW China under the Ming 184/1; rebellion against Ch'ing 193/2; Manchu expansion 193/1; Muslim rebellion 257/1; Hsin-hai revolution 257/3; warlord control 286/1, 2; famine 311/2; GDP per capita 354/1; student protests 355/2
Yün-nan-fu (*n/s* Yunnanfu *n/c* K'un-ming) W China Ming provincial capital 184/1; 257/1
Yunzhong (Yün-chung)
Yuriev (Dorpat)
Yü-yang (*n/s* Yuyang) NE China Han prefecture 88/2
Yuzhsiblag Siberia labour camp zone 341/3

Z
Zabah W Syria Aramaean city 61/2, 3
Zacatecas N Mexico modern state 251/1
Zacynthus (Zante)
Zadar (Iadera)
Zadracarta N Persia Achaemenid Empire 82/1; Alexander's route 87/1
Zagreb (*Ger.* Agram *Hung.* Zágráb) Croatia WW1 279/1; WW2 299/2
Zagwe dynasty 154
Zaidi imams extent of 151/1
Zaïre (Democratic Republic of Congo) becomes DR Congo 321/1, 324
Zakinthos (Zante)
Zakro E Crete city and palace site 75/2
Zama Tunisia Roman Empire 98/3
Zambia (*form.* Northern Rhodesia) independence 306/2; South Africa attacks 318/2; politics 319/1; democratization 321/1; population growth 361/3
Zamora NW Spain Santa Junta 206/2
Zancle (*mod.* Messina) Sicily Greek colony 85/1; Roman Empire 98/2
Zangke (Tsang-k'o)
Zante (*anc.* Zacynthus *mod. Gr.* Zakinthos) SW Greece Venetian territory 209/1
ZANU terror campaign 318/2, 350/1
Zanzibar *island* E Africa Muslim colony 155/1; Portuguese settlement 174/2; Omani control 265/1; British naval base 270/2; occupied by British 267/1; British protectorate 307/1; union with Tanganyika 319/1
Zapata, Emilio Mexican revolution 334
Zapatistas Mexican terror campaign 350/1
Zapolya, John Sigismund Prince of Transylvania 186
Zaporozhye tribe of SW Russia 177/1
Zaporozhye E Ukraine urban growth 255/1, 341/2
Zapotec early civilization of C America 44/2; Mesoamerican people 64
ZAPU terror campaign 318/2, 350/1
Zara (*anc.* Iadera *S. Cr.* Zadar) Croatia Venetian expansion 135/2
Zaragoza (Saragossa)
Zaranj Afghanistan
Zaria Nigeria Hausa city state 155/1, 183/1, 265/1, 267/1
Zariaspa (Bactra, Balkh)
Zashiversk E Siberia founded 176/2
Zawilah Libya early trade 154/2
Zawi Chemi N Mesopotamia early village 39/1
Zealand (*Dan.* Sjaelland) island of E Denmark lost to Sweden 210/1
Zeeland district of W Netherlands Burgundian possession 167/2; province of Dutch Republic 207/1
Zeelandia Formosa Dutch settlement 174/2
Zeila (*Som.* Saylac *early Chin.* Sa-la) Somalia Muslim colony 155/1
Zeitz C Germany bishopric 130/2
Zenawi, Meles prime minister of Ethiopia 322
Zengi, al-Din ruler of Aleppo 124
Zenica C Bosnia Civil War 347/3
Zenta (*mod.* Senta) Serbia ⚔ 219/1
Žepa E Bosnia Civil War 347/3
Žepce C Bosnia Civil War 347/3
Zeugma E Anatolia founded 86/1
Zhangjiakou (Kalgan)
Zhangye (Chang-yeh)
Zhao (Chao)
Zhaoming (Chao-ming)
Zhawar Campaign Afghan war 351/1
Zhejiang (*W/G* Che-jiang, *a/s* Chekiang) province of SE China GDP per capita 354/1; protests 355/2
Zhelezinsk W Siberia founded 176/2
Zhendingfu (Chen-ting-fu)
Zheng (Cheng)
Zhengzhou (Cheng-chou)
Zhigansk C Siberia founded 176/2
Zhitomir Ukraine Bolshevik seizure 283/1
Zhmud tribe of S Baltic 129/1
Zhou (Chou)
Zhoukoudian (*W/G* Chou-k'ou-tien) N China site 31/1, 33/3, 35/1
Zhuya (Chu-ya)
Zimbabwe S Africa early kingdom 155/1; building Great 155/3; modern state (formerly Rhodesia) 287/1; South African attacks 286/2; Mugabe's presidency of 318, 319/1, 321/1
Zionism 326–7
Zionist Congress 237
Zomba E Africa British occupation 267/1
Zorndorf (*Pol.* Sarbinowo) Poland ⚔ 218/2
Zou (Tsou)
Zou E Crete Minoan palace 75/2
Zufar (Dhofar)
Zulu people of SE Africa 265/1, 318/2; African ethnic group 318/2
Zululand territory of SE Africa annexed by Britain 265/3
Zunyi (Tsunyi)
Zurich (*Ger.* Zürich) Switzerland Reformation 205/1; ⚔ 229/1
Zuttiyeh C Israel site of early man 31/1
Zweibrücken W Germany principality 212/1
Zwenkau Germany early site 41/1
Zwickau E Germany industrial development 235/1

Picture credits